MW00861433

The Morphophonological Development
of the Classical Aramaic Verb

Linguistic Studies in Ancient West Semitic

edited by

Cynthia L. Miller-Naudé and Jacobus A. Naudé

The series Linguistic Studies in Ancient West Semitic is devoted to the ancient West Semitic languages, including Hebrew, Aramaic, Ugaritic, and their near congeners. It includes monographs, collections of essays, and text editions informed by the approaches of linguistic science. The material studied will span from the earliest texts to the rise of Islam.

The Morphophonological Development of the Classical Aramaic Verb

by

JOSEPH L. MALONE

EISENBRAUNS | University Park, PA

This book's seeing the publicational light of day owes much to the excellent work of publisher and editor Jim Eisenbraun, for which the author is profoundly grateful.

Warm thanks also for subventional assistance are proffered to Barnard College, Columbia University, in particular to Provost Linda Bell and Dean Bobby O'Rourke.

Library of Congress Cataloging-in-Publication Data

Names: Malone, Joseph L., author.
Title: The morphophonological development of the classical Aramaic verb / by Joseph L. Malone.
Other titles: Linguistic studies in ancient West Semitic ; 13.
Description: University Park, Pennsylvania : Eisenbrauns [2019] | Series: Linguistic studies in ancient West Semitic ; 13 | Includes bibliographical references and index.
Summary: "A diachronic and synchronic account of the verb morphology and phonology of Aramaic, a subfamily of Semitic, from its appearance in history early in the first millennium BCE until approximately the second millennium CE"— Provided by publisher.
Identifiers: LCCN 2019021298 | ISBN 9781575069753 (cloth)
Subjects: LCSH: Aramaic language—Verb. | Aramaic language—Morphology. | Aramaic language—Phonology.
Classification: LCC PJ5207.M35 2019 | DDC 492/.2—dc23
LC record available at https://lccn.loc.gov/2019021298

Eisenbrauns is an imprint of The Pennsylvania State University Press.

The Pennsylvania State University Press is a member of the Association of University Presses.

It is the policy of The Pennsylvania State University Press to use acid-free paper. Publications on uncoated stock satisfy the minimum requirements of American National Standard for Information Sciences—Permanence of Paper for Printed Library Material, ANSI Z39.48–1992.

to the spirit of Michael Patrick O'Connor

OLLAMH ÁRD I bhFOGHLAIM
CARA CAOINTE I mBÁS

Scholar lofty in learning
Friend mourned in death

Contents

Part Two
Genealogy and Dialectology

Part Three
Appendixes and
Supplemental Matters

Part Four
Indexes

0. Introduction

0.1. Goals of the Book; Dialects Covered

This book offers a diachronic and to some extent synchronic account of the verb morphology and phonology of Aramaic (A) from its appearance in history, early in the first millennium BCE, until approximately the second millennium CE—a 2000-year period for convenience to be dubbed "Classical." Aramaic is a subfamily of Semitic closely related to Hebrew and other Canaanite languages, the two subfamilies constituting together the Northwest branch of the Semitic phylum.

Though the number of processes and patterns to be covered is substantial, the study makes no claim to exhaustiveness, a reservation that holds all the more so with respect to the "dialects" focused by the study: thirteen chosen from a total nearly twice that number. And yet the varieties selected do make for a good chronological and geographical spread, thus facilitating reasonably adequate extrapolation for Classical A as a whole. The reservation on exhaustiveness also holds, explicitly in the book's title, on the internal-linguistic domain of the study: The Morphophonological Development of the Classical Aramaic *Verb*. The feeling was that the operation of A morphophonology should be largely demonstrable through its manifestation in the verb—specifically, the finite verb—and that extension of the purview to other parts of speech, though desirable in principle, would entail inordinate inflation of an already extremely long volume.

It may be noted toward the beginning of the preceding paragraph that reference to the language-variety objects of study appeared in scare-quotes: the "dialects" focused. Though in the sequel the quotation marks will for expository convenience be dropped, the reservation on the bona fide dialectal nature of several of the targeted varieties will hold. This is because the varieties are approached via, and hence tend to be identified with, the orthographic texts where they are manifested. Since, moreover, the texts in question appertain to language forms no longer spoken for a millennium or more, and there can be no firm warrants on textual homogeneity or linguistic consistency, we necessarily work with multiple analytic handicaps, and in the process run multiple analytic risks. However, as historical linguists we have no choice but to proceed despite at times severe and unavoidable limitations.[1] The ins and outs of

1

all these factors will be picked up again in specific settings at many junctures throughout.

Thumbnail characterizations of the thirteen dialects follow immediately. These sketches are pooled composites from various sources, principally Garbini 1960, Moscati et al. 1964, Kutscher 1972, as well as the individual dialect sources listed under each heading. (Some of these sketches may be too simple to capture the full reality of A dialect relations, an issue that will be returned to in §19—in particular under consideration of the detailed portrayal in Beyer 1986.)

Yaʔudic (Y), the language of the state of Šamʔal Yaʔudi, 10th–8th centuries BCE. Attested in two inscriptions, those of Panamuwa I and Bar-Rakib (Panamuwa II), sometimes referred to as the Żincirli inscriptions. Primary source for this book: Donner and Röllig 1966–69 (= DR) I 38–40 (with translation and discussion in DR II 214–32), whence citations will be given as "214:n" or "215:n," 214/215 being Donner and Röllig's numerical tags for Panamuwa I/II respectively, and n. = pertinent line(s). (Yaʔudic is sometimes considered non-Aramaic, an independent Northwest Semitic dialect. Though the evidence for non-Aramaic status is weightier in the nominal system than in that of the verb, a few points concerning the verb will be noted throughout which do appear to set Y apart from (the rest of) Aramaic; see, e.g., §7.1 w n. 2 (= with note 2), §7.2(α), §9.1.2, §11.2. In this book, Y is in any event included as one of the thirteen prime types of Aramaic studied, if only to see where the chips may fall. Readers may determine to their own satisfaction whether the evidence adduced seems compelling enough to merit admitting Yaʔudic to the ranks of the Aramaic dialects.)

Old Aramaic (O), roughly contemporaneous with Yaʔudic (10th–8th centuries BCE), known from a variety of inscriptions found mainly in northern Syria. Primary source for this book: Degen 1969 (De).

Imperial Aramaic (I), the lingua franca of the Assyrian, Babylonian, and Persian empires, 7th to 4th centuries BCE. Primary source for this book is the Jewish-Egyptian variety presented and analyzed in Leander 1928 (L) as well as Muraoka and Porten 2003 (MP).

Biblical Aramaic (B), the type of A codified in the Bible, primarily in the books of Ezra and Daniel (Ezra, Dan), and held to manifest a form of language of approximate vintage 5th–2nd centuries BCE. Biblical Aramaic will be considered in two registers[2] correlating with rather significant phonological differences, or appearing to: that corresponding to redactions in Tiberian (Tib, tbB) orthography on the one hand, and that corresponding to redactions in Babylonian (Bab, bbB) on the other. The Tiberian register will be taken as the usual object of study in this book, and accordingly forms marked simply "B" will, context allowing, implicitly refer to Tiberian items. The primary source for this book is Bauer and Leander 1927 (BL)—though occasionally forms will be referenced directly to their biblical source in the format "book chapter: verse" (e.g., [hɔhɔrväθ], Ezra 4:15). (Though Biblical Aramaic is widely considered to be a late form of Imperial Aramaic, it will be seen to manifest a number of morphophonological properties setting it apart. Additionally, the richness of detail represented in vocalized texts—especially the Tiberian—also sets it off as a unitary object of study.)

Palmyrene (P) is the language of the oasis city-state of Palmyra, flourishing between the 1st century BCE and the 3rd century CE. Primary source for this book: Hillers and Cussini 1996 (HC).

Nabatean (N) is the language of the kingdom of Nabatea, centered in the city of Petra (present-day southern Jordan), 1st century BCE – 3rd century CE. Primary sources for this book: Cantineau 1932a, 1932b (Cg, Cl).

Targumic (TR), referring specifically to the language investing the Onkelos Targum (of the Pentateuch) and the Jonathan Targum (of the Prophets), itself a manifestation of that sort of Jewish Palestinian Aramaic once called "Judean," roughly 2nd century – 5th century CE. Redactions include both Babylonian and Tiberian vocalizations, the Bab manifestation making for the usual object of study in this book; hence, conversely to the treatment of Biblical Aramaic (above), an unprefixed citation of a TR form should, in want of a statement to the contrary, be understood as bbTR. Among Tib redactions, the version of the Onkelos Targum published at Sabbioneta in 1557 appears to sport a type of TR with a number of special characteristics and will accordingly be granted subregisterial status of its own: Sab (sbTR), to be taken as a subregister of Tib (tbTR). Primary TR source for this book: Dalman 1905, 1927 (Da). (TR is frequently taken to be a split language type, having a Western (W) A consonantal text overlaid by a vocalization of Eastern (E) A vintage. It is unclear whether the findings of this book can support such a view, which tend rather to peg TR as a moderately conservative dialect of vintage predating the W–E split, and in point of morphophonological features—at least in the verb—relatively homogeneous to boot; for some discussion, see §19(γ).)

Christian Palestinian (CP) is the language used by the Melkites, 5th – 8th centuries CE. Primary sources for this book: Schulthess 1903, 1924 (Sl, Sg).

Samaritan (SM), the Aramaic dialect of the Samaritans, its prime codification being the Samaritan Targum to the Pentateuch though there are later embodiments as well; roughly 4th – 10th centuries CE. Primary source for this book: Macuch 1982 (Macs). (SM is one of three dialects for which traditional pronuniciation (trad pron) is taken as part of the evidence, relevant forms being tagged with "t"; e.g., <qBl> t[qǽbbəl] 'nimm an', Macs 81. See §22.1.)

Galilean (G), the dialect of Galilee, especially as codified in the Jerusalem Talmud but also in the aggadic Midrashim and various other documents; roughly 3rd – 10th centuries CE. Primary sources for this book: Dalman 1905, 1927 (Da); and as supplementary and amendatory to Da, Kutscher 1972, 1976.[3]

Syriac (SR), pristinely the language of Edessa, later, on the basis of theological disputes, split into two opposed registers, a (linguistically more conservative) Eastern branch, Nestorian (Nes, nsSR), maintaining its see in Edessa, and a Western branch, Jacobite (Jac, jcSR), centered in Nisibis. The usual register taken as object of study in this book is Nestorian, whose forms accordingly will, context ensuring clarity, be tagged simply "SR" rather than "nsSR." SR, of the classical type focused in this book, may be dated roughly from the 3rd to 10th centuries CE (though reference will occasionally be made to a precedent language type, Old Syriac). Primary sources for this book: Nöldeke 1898 (Ns), Brockelmann 1965 (B).

Talmudic (TL), par excellence the language of the Babylonian Talmud, also extends to later texts such as the writings of the Gĕʾonim, and may be dated roughly 3rd – 10th centuries CE. TL will be considered per se in accordance with the consonantal text (normally of the Babylonian Talmud), but usually more fully on the supplementary basis of two traditional pronunciations: Yemeni (Yem, yTL) and Ashkenazic (Ash, aTL). Primary sources for this book: Morag 1988 (Mor) for Yemeni, and Margolis 1910 (Mar) for Ashkenazic. (It will not be disguised that Margolis's Ashkenazic renditions often fall under suspicion of being more like scholarly interpretations than oral transmissions uncontrivedly passed down through the generations; and worse yet, evidence will be seen here and there that his renditions may have been distorted by undue influence from Tiberian orthography (*Schematisierung*). And yet the very presentation of such evidence may have the value of whetting our acumen at separating out the chaff from the grain in the pursuit of linguistic reconstruction. And on the other side, we will occasionally see evidence {§0.1, §0.2, §0.2.1} that Margolis's renditions actually preserve some features of the original TL dialect more faithfully than do the justly prized renditions of Morag's Yemeni informants. Both brands of TL trad pron are treated in §22.2.)

Mandaic (M), more specifically Classical Mandaic, is the liturgical language of the Gnostic Mandeans, flourishing in Mesopotamia and Persia roughly from the 3rd to 8th centuries CE. Primary sources for this book: Macuch 1965 (Macm), Nöldeke 1875 (Nm), Malone 1967 (Mal). (Mandaic is the third dialect in this book whose reconstruction is based in part on traditional pronunciation; see §22.3. Moreover, the testimony of Modern Mandaic is also strongly evidential.)

0.2. Preliminary Set-Up

0.2.1. The Core Structure of Aramaic Morphology

Aramaic, being a Semitic language, is possessed of the kind of morphology sometimes called *internal-flective*. In a Semitic internal-flective system, core stems, most perspicuously of the major morphological categories verb and nominal (subsuming nouns and adjectives), are decomposable into two discontinuously organized constituents: a (typically) consonantal *root* "interdigitated" with a (typically vocalic) *scheme*.[4]

In turn, roots and schemes are made up of *radicals* ($\sqrt{}$) and *schematics* ($\int$). Since a Semitic root typically consists of three radicals, it will be symbologically convenient to adopt a "type root" as a variable notation for root-at-large. For reasons adduced in Malone 1993 (THP), traditional candidates like *pʕl* and *qtl* are eschewed in favor of *qsm*, in this book set off in capitals to make unambiguous its role as type root (as opposed to actual, concrete root). Hence *QSM* is equivalent to the more cumbersome *1* $\sqrt{2}$ $\sqrt{}$ *3*$\sqrt{}$ {§0.2.1} (equivalently 1$\sqrt{}$C 2$\sqrt{}$C 3$\sqrt{}$C).

Interdigitation with the scheme for the *dynamic* (as opposed to *neuter*) *active* (as opposed to *passive*) simple perfect (sim pf), *1ʃa 2ʃa*, thus produces an internal-flective stem (henceforth *miʃkal*, plural *miʃkalim*)[5] *1*$\sqrt{}$*C 1ʃa 2*$\sqrt{}$*C 2ʃa 3*$\sqrt{}$*C,* more tersely *1*$\sqrt{}$*Cʃa 2*$\sqrt{}$*Cʃa 3*$\sqrt{}$*C,* and more tersely yet *QaSaM.*

Roots are typically *lexical* morphemes, and schemes *grammatical* morphemes. Semitic *miʃkalim* are most frequently supplemented by affixes (suffixes, prefixes, sometimes infixes) of a run-of-the-mill sort attached to the hosting *miʃkal* by "-" (indicating attachment generically) or by "+" (indicating specifically morphemic attachment). Thus, when *QaSaM* is joined by the second masculine singular (2ms) suffix *tā*, we have *QaSaM-tā* or *QaSaM+tā*. A more condensed (and less informative) representation will be given as *QaSaMtā*, attachment boundary suppressed. (Context will dictate which sort of representation is best deployed, all three referring to the identical linguistic object.)

More on internal-flection will be presented as the occasion arises, next in §1 n. 1. Also, as soon will be seen, a third sort of internal-flective representation is appealed to in *autosegmental* applications, the so-called *skeleton*. An autosegmental version of *QaSaM* is given in (0A) without comment. Autosegmentalism is per se discussed in §23.4 and frequently appealed to throughout the book (next in §1.3.2 n. 14). {§0.2.1, §0.2.2}

(0A)	root	Q		S		M
		|		|		|
	skeleton	C	V	C	V	C
			|		|	
	scheme		a		a	

0.2.2. Some Basic Symbological Conventions

Several sorts of linguistic and paralinguistic representation types (or levels) are used throughout. Some of the most frequently appearing instances are briefly introduced here; all are comprehensively listed and defined in §25.

Linguistic forms are large, with no further commitment to type/level, appear in *italics*, transcribed in accordance with the general symbological system detailed in §20. Thus *QaSaM*.

Specifically *phonetic* forms appear in square brackets ([QaSaM]), while specifically *phonological* forms are adorned with solidi (/QaSaM/). Intermediate representations—those derivationally "between" / / and [ ]—appear bounded by verticals (|QaSaM|). (Details on these Generative-Phonological distinctions, and more, are laid out in §23.)

The prime paralinguistic symbol in the book is a pair of angle brackets, indicating transliteration, i.e., orthographic as opposed to phonetic or other linguistic representation. Thus <QSM> might stand for an unpointed (ḥaser) spelling of SR [Q˛SáM], while <QSaM> represents the pointed spelling of the same linguistic item. For transliteration, see §21.

Even as italics signal neutrality (noncommitment) with respect to form type/level, the single-shafted arrow (→) is neutral with respect to whether a *process* is functioning {§0.2.2} diachronically (as a *change*) or synchronically (as a *rule*). Thus X → Y = "X is replaced by Y," irrespective of whether X has diachronically (historically) changed into Y (X > Y), or rather X is being (re)represented as Y by a synchronic rule (X Ø Y).

Accident aside, an item X may be *unattested* for any of three reasons: (*) Its earlier (diachronic) existence is inferred; i.e., it is *reconstructed*: *X. (*) It is ruled out as ill-formed (e.g., ungrammatical, or flying in the face of prevailing phonological canons): @X. (*) The specific form itself fails to show up in extant (or available) texts but is believed to constitute a linguistic legitimate object at the same time as (synchronically with) the other linguistic objects being discussed; i.e., it is *constructed*: cX.

Notes to §0

[1] Just one frequent handicap encountered in working in historical linguistics may be mentioned here: the necessity of dealing with statistically impoverished samples. Several years ago, a paper by the author focusing on Classical Mandaic was rejected by a distinguished linguistics journal on the advice of an anonymous referee who, reacting to the fact that the author had supported his argument on the basis of a solitary linguistic form, stated in the report to the editor that "Spring is not of one lark made." Ah, good sir or madam, but sometimes it *must* be. Historical linguists have no choice but to proceed on whatever corpus remains from the wear and tear of the centuries, be it ever so paltry. (Nor of course does the moral hold for Semitic linguistics alone; see, e.g., Klar and Jones 2005.)

[2] The locution "register" is pressed into service as a technical term for subtypes of what is meant by "dialect," a term explained above to be used in an unconventional way. In short, neither "dialect" nor "register" are used in this book in their fully conventional senses.

[3] Kutscher considers the forms cited by Dalman to be frequently suspect of bowdlerization by European transmitters, a danger he attempts to avert by adhering to texts devoid of unwarranted interference, texts which came to light subsequent to Dalman's work. Kutscher's cautions will be sounded and illustrated at pertinent spots throughout (e.g., §7.4.1, §17.9.2 n. 26a, §17.19 n. 102).

[4] In the conventional literature, schematics are often called "vowel patterns."

[5] Quite a few Hebrew (especially), Aramaic, and Arabic technical terms will be employed in this book, each to be defined upon first appearance and all listed alphabetically and redefined in §25. All metalinguistically functioning Hebrew/Aramaic forms, including technical terms, will be presented in Israeli Levantine Hebrew transcription, making use of a Romanization adapted from Rosén 1962.

Part One

Patterns and Processes

1. System of Verb Stems[1]

1.1. Strong Verb Stems

1.1.1. Simple (sim)

perfective (pf)

plain[2]:	QaSaM, QaSiM, QaSuM
labial passive (pas)[3]:	QuSaM
palatal passive (pas)[3]:	QaSīM *or* QuSīM
reflexive-mediopassive (rmp):	h-it+QaSiM,
	(*occasionally* h-it+QaSaM)[4]

imperfective (impf)[5]

plain[6]:	aSQuM, iQSaM, aQSiM
labial pas:	uQSaM
palatal pas:	aQSīM
rmp:	it+QaSiM (*occasionally* it+QaSaM)[4]

imperative (impa)[7]

plain:	QǎSuM (~QĭSuM?), QĭSaM, QǎSiM
labial pas:	QŭSaM
palatal pas:	QǎSīM
rmp:	h-it+QaSiM (*occasionally* h-it+QaSaM)[4]

1.1.2. Intensive (int)[8]

pf, impa

plain:	QaSSim (*occasionally* QaSSaM)[4]
passive:	QuSSaM
rmp:	h-it+QaSSaM

imperfective

plain:	i+QaSSiM
passive:	i+QuSSaM
rmp:	it+QaSSaM

1.1.3. Causative (cau)[9]

pf, impa

plain:	h+aQSiM (*occasionally* h+aQSaM)[4]
passive:	h+uQSaM
rmp:	h-it+h+aQSaM

     imperfective[10]
        plain: (i+h+)aQSiM
        passive: (i+h+)uQSaM
        rmp: it+h+aQSaM

1.2. Geminate (gem) Verb Stems[11]

1.2.1. Simple

     perfective
        plain: QaM(M); QaMaM, QaMiM, QaMuM
        labial pas: QuM(M); QuMaM
        palatal pas: QaMīM *or* QuMīM
        rmp: h-it+QaMiM; h-it+QiM(M)
     imperfective
        plain: aQQuM, iQQaM, aQQiM; aQMuM, iQMaM,
                     aQMiM
        labial pas: uQQaM; uQMaM
        palatal pas: aQMīM
        rmp: it+QaMiM; it+QiM(M)
     imperative
        plain: QuM(M), QaM(M), QiM(M); QăMuM, QĭMaM,
                     QăMiM
        labial pas: QuM(M); QŭMaM
        palatal pas: QăMīM
        rmp: h-it+QaMiM; h-it+QiM(M)

1.2.2. Intensive

     pf, impa
        plain: QaMMiM
        passive: QuMMaM
        rmp: h-it+QaMMaM
     imperfective
        plain: i+QaMMiM
        passive: i+QuMMaM
        rmp: it+QaMMaM

1.2.3. Causative

     pf, impa
        plain: h+aQQiM; h-aQMiM
        passive: h+uQQaM; h-uQMaM
        rmp: h-it+h+aQQaM; h-it+h+aQMaM

imperfective
   plain: (i+h+)aQQiM; (i+h+)aQMiM
   passive: (i+h+)uQQaM; (i+h+)uQMaM
   rmp: it+h+aQQaM; it+h+aQMaM

1.3. Hollow (hol) Verb Stems[12]

1.3.1. Simple

pf, impa
   plain: QåM, QïM, QůM
   labial pas[13]:   QůM
   palatal pas[13]: QïM
   rmp: h-it+QïM
imperfective
   plain: aQůM, iQåM, aQïM
   labial pas: uQåM
   palatal passive: aQïM
   rmp: it+QïM

1.3.2. [14] Intensive

pf, impa
   plain: QayyiM, QawwiM, QawMiM
   passive: QuyyaM, QuwwaM, QuwMaM = QūMaM
   rmp: h-it+QayyaM, h-it+QawwaM, h-itQawMaM
imperfective
   plain: i+QayyiM, i+QawwiM, i+QawMiM
   passive: i+QuyyaM, i+QuwwaM, i+QuwMaM =
                   i+QūMaM
   rmp: it+QayyaM, it+QawwaM, it+QawMaM

1.3.2. Causative

pf, impa
   plain: h+aQïM
   passive[13]:   h+uQïM (*and* h+iQïM?)
   rmp: h+it+h+aQåM
imperfective
   plain: (i+h+)aQïM
   passive[13]:   (i+h+)uQïM
   rmp: it+h+aQåM

1.4. Defective (def) Verb Stems[15]

1.4.1. Simple

> *perfect*
>> plain: QaSay, QaSiy
>> labial pas: QuSay, QuSiy
>> palatal pas: QaSiy *or* QuSiy
>> rmp: h-it+QaSay, h-it+QaSiy
>
> *imperfective*
>> plain: aQSay, aQSiy, iQSay, iQSiy
>> labial pas: uQSay, uQSiy
>> palatal pas: aQSiy
>> rmp: it+QaSay, it+QaSiy
>
> *imperative*
>> plain: QăSay, QăSiy, QĭSay, QĭSiy
>> labial pas: QŭSay, QŭSiy
>> palatal pas: QăSīy
>> rmp: h-it+QaSay, h-it+QaSiy

1.5. 1 √w Verb Stems[16]

1.5.1. Simple

> *imperfective*
>> plain: aSuM, iSaM, aSiM
>> labial pas: uSaM
>> palatal pas: aSīM
>> rmp: it+waSiM
>
> *imperative*
>> plain: SuM, SaM, SiM
>> labial pas: SuM?
>> palatal pas: SīM?
>> rmp: h-it+waSiM

1.6. 1 √n Verb Stems[17]

1.6.1. Simple

> *imperative*
>> plain: (nă)SuM (~(nĭ)SuM?), (nĭ)SaM, (nă)SiM
>> labial pas: nŭSaM, SuM?
>> palatal pas: (nă)SīM?
>> rmp: h-it+naSiM

Notes to §1

[1] Miškalim are indicated by *QSM* (for the standard three radicals) interdigitated with (schematic) vowels. Miškalim with more than three radicals (n. 8 below) are indicated in one and/or two ways, illustrable on the basis of the SR quadriradical (quad) *9Awdɛð* (for the hedge *A*, see §20.2 n. 7b) 'enslave' (built on √9bdd): "representation-ally," whereby this miškal instantiates *QASS'ɛM,* bringing out the fact that the cluster *wd* functions as a complex 2 √ (*SS'*); or "derivationally," whereby the same miškal instantiates *QaSMɛM,* bringing out the fact that the last two radicals stand/stood in a derivational relation (one being a copy—reduplicate—of the other). "+" marks standard (linear) morpheme boundaries, in §1 exclusively setting off prefixes from stems (miškalim) or from other prefixes. "–" hedges on the presence/nature of a boundary at the indicated juncture (e.g., whether in the rmp-prefixed alternation *hit~it* the *h* should be segmented out as a (sub)morphemic entity sui generis, a hedge indicated by *h-it*).

[2] The plain simple stem evidences at least residual distinctions in *event type* absent from the passive, reflexive-mediopassive (rmp), and all other categories of the derived verb. Exponence of this event type is via the second schematic, whereby there are at least loose, statistical ablaut relations between the perfective system on the one hand and the imp system (that of the imperfective-imperative) on the other. Thus while 2ʃ*a in the pf tends to mark *dynamic* lexemes (sometimes called "active," a term to be eschewed for possible ambiguity vis-à-vis the antonym of passive)—i.e., verbs proto-typically denoting volitional physical action on the part of the denotatum of the subject—the corresponding imp encodation of dynamism is usually via 2ʃ*u, sometimes 2ʃ*i. And where *neuter* lexemes tend to be marked in the pf by 2*ʃi or 2*ʃu, corresponding imp marking is usually via 2 *a and *u, respectively (cf. Brockelmann 1908: 544)—"neuter" being antonymous to "dynamic," in reference to verbs prototypically of involuntary nonaction (in the literature frequently called "stative"). Also, from the earliest days, phonological factors appear to have interacted with semantic (event type) in favoring 2ʃselection; e.g., 2ʃ*a tends to correlate with 2~H or 3~H (as in Hebrew, cf. THP 56)—an effect typologically but not genetically akin to the historically subsequent process of *lowering* (§17.10).

[3] (a) The labels "labial" and "palatal" reflect invariance of schematic /u/ and /ī/, respectively, plausibly even when schematic assignment varies under certain phonological conditions (see note 13). This much said, it should be observed that there is some evidence for *hybrid* passives, housing both *u* and *ī*; thus *QuSīM* posited here as a variant to *QaSīM* for at least the perfective of the simple passive—cf. the B Bab variant [gŭlī̇́] < *gulī́y* with labial color of 1ʃ preserved via schwa coloring by inheritance, §17.23; as well as evidence for occasional *u-ī* hybridism in other binyanim, note 13b below. Such hybrids will provisionally be classified as palatal, inasmuch as they appear to occur as variants to forms lacking *u* but always containing *ī*. (b) The assumption is made that the simple verb originally inflected freely for both types of passive, while the derived verb was by and large restricted to the labial type, though *u-ī* hybrids occasionally appear as well. This assumed tendency for simple-derived cleavage may, however, be too sweeping (Bauer and Leander assume that the palatal sort was exclusive to the simple verb and the labial to the derived, BL §28o) but extant data are just too meager to be sure.

In any event, though the passive is to be found in the earliest dialects—at least Y, O, I, and B—it has with one possible exception been replaced by the reflexive-mediopassive (rmp) in the later dialects. The one possible exception is SM, though it is uncertain whether forms such as <D²nṣyryn> t[dɑanṣírən] 'die sich unterworfen haben' (Macs 145) are genuine residua of the palatal passive (here < *ðī=naṣīrū) or rather might be morphologically participial forms functioning syntactically as perfectives (< *ði=naṣīrīn). The latter is suggested by the suffix <-yn> t[- n] but not clinched, since participial suffixes sometimes migrate into the finite verb of the later dialects independently of the question of the passive (pin, §17.17).

[4] At times, the simple rmp shows reflexes of 2ʃ*a, at least in TR and TL, and perhaps in G as well (Da 256, 267, 274f; Mar §5g). Does this occur frequently enough to pass as retention of an ancient pattern? In the case of the pf, one thinks immediately of Arabic conjugation VIII, *ifta9ala*; but there are also occurrences in the imp system, where Arabic shows 2ʃi. While Margolis surmises subtle phonetic conditioning, Dalman leans toward erroneous scribal practice as an explanation. (Dalman also lists for TR various appearances of unexpected 2ʃ*a in other binyanim, Da 256.) Similar instances of 2ʃa are occasionally found in at least the perfective of the intensive and causative. See also §6.3 n. 42.

[5] Should the vowel immediately preceding Q in the impf be considered morphologically *schematic* or *prefixal*? Pretheoretically, the easiest case would seem to be the intensive (§1.1.2), where the first *i* of, e.g., *iQaSSiM* may uncontroversially be taken as prefixal. But in the simple and causative (§1.1.3) verbs, one might defend either a prefixal analysis along the lines of *a+QSʃuM, (i+h-)a+QSʃiM* or a schematic analysis like *1ʃaQS2ʃuM, (i+h+)1ʃaQSaʃiM*—and it will immediately be apparent that for the cau the quandary extends beyond the impf to the other paradigms as well, e.g., pf/impa prefixal *h-a+QSʃiM* vs. schematic *h+1ʃaQS2ʃiM*. In favor of the schematic analysis might be the distribution of the passive vocalism *u . . . a*, where the *u* not only invests the position of controversy in the sim and cau (the controversy being, e.g., whether we are dealing with *u+QSʃaM* or *1ʃu QS2ʃaM*), but also occupies what is almost certainly a schematic position in the int: e.g., *QuSSaM* qua *Q1ʃuSS2ʃaM* ("almost certainly," but the role of mp "infixed *u*" gives pause—i-lap, §17.9); see also note 6, next. On the other hand, it is unclear that signal distribution, like *u . . . a*, must needs be morphologically homogeneous. Pending evidence deciding the issue one way or the other, the vowel occurring /__Q in the sim and cau will be considered to be 1ʃ, but in deference to tradition will freely be referred to as a "prefixal vowel." And the corresponding vowel in the int will be taken to be purely prefixal.

[6] Notice the ablaut between 2ʃ (independent variable) and 1ʃ (dependent variable), specifically 2ʃa dictating 1ʃi, while otherwise the prefix vowel is 1ʃa—"Barth's Law," Kurylowicz 1962: 30f. The same color distribution holds in the sim impa, with the differences that there (*) the corresponding vowels are reduced—see note 7, next—and (*) ablaut *ă . . . u* may have alternated with *ĭ . . . u* (evidence for which is forthcoming from B, TR, SM, TL, and M (in part); but see §17.23.3 w (17.23Bi)). Incidentally, the color identity of the impf-impa vowels in question may provide another argument for the schematic componency of the impf segments; see note 5, preceding.

[7] The underlying sim impa system is the only spot in the pA verb to be reconstructed with reduced vowels, by hypothesis unstable both in pA and in the antecedent

pSemitic system, an instability that might partially explain (a) the variety of sim impa resolutions evolved across the Semitic languages (cf. Moscati et al. 1964: 145), as well as (b) the color lability of 1ʃ across the descendant dialects of A (sip, §17.25) ("*underlying* reduced vowels," because it will be assumed that [ə] could be inserted by excrescence to forfend against syllabic-canonic violations; note 8b, next, and §2.3.2.1(α), §4.3).

[8] (a) Analogous in formation to the intensives are the so-called *quadriradicals* (or *quadriliterals*), lexemes consisting of four radicals rather than the usual three. Quadriradicals typically show a heterophonous cluster as value of the second radical (in this book to be notated 2 $\sqrt{}$ 2′ $\sqrt{}$ or SS'); for instance, TR $\sqrt{gndr}$ 'rollen', G $\sqrt{bl9s}$ 'ekeln' (Da 252). Quadriradicals may inflect for analogs of plain and rmp; e.g., for the roots just cited, pf pf 3ms [gænd態r], 3mp <?TBl9swn> respectively (lc). In origin, quadriradicals are quite motley; Nöldeke (Ns 125s) provides an instructive sampling—explicitly for SR, but other dialects show kindred formations—including obsolete causatives (cf. note 9, next), various sorts of denominals, and assorted reduplicative patterns. These latter, in turn, may bear diverse functions, including occasional service qua hollow intensives (note 14). Reduplications (denominalizing, in this case) of miškal $QaSS'VM$ where S' = M, e.g., (SR) $9Awdeð$ 'zum Sklaven machen', are of particular interest in view of the autosegmental assumptions adopted in this book (§23.4) since, though of marked status in A at large, $QaSMVM$ appears to instantiate a less-marked association pattern than do run-of-the-mill intensives of miškal $QaSSVM$; see note 14 below and §23 n. 10a,b.

(b) The A dialects also at times sport *quinquiradical* formations, typically by clustering 1$\sqrt{}$ in addition to 2$\sqrt{}$ ($QQ'aSS'VM$); e.g., SR $ššraɣrɛɣ$ 'Phantasien erregen' (Ns 126) (ə by repair-strategic excrescence, §4.3, to dispel canonically illicit onset @CC′), denominalizing reduplication from $šr5ɣ5$ 'Lämpchen' where $QQ'aSS'VM = QSaMSVM$, M $\sqrt{zrmby}$ 'shake' which is used in rmp, $nezdšrambí$ 'will be shaken' (Macm 251, DM 171) ($zd ← tz$ by rmt, §10).

(c) For all their importance, quadriradicals and quinquiradicals will at best be cursorily treated at various spots in this book. A thorough study of their formation and derivation would certainly constitute a worthy contribution to Semitic and general linguistics. (For some pioneering work in the general area, see Bat-El 1989.)

[9] In addition to *h, the causative prefix may also have assumed the form *ʔ; see §9.1.2 for discussion. There are also residual appearances of prefixes current elsewhere in Semitic, e.g., *š (general in Akkadian); see §6 n. 33, §10 n. 1.

[10] For discussion of *i+h+*, see §9 n. 3.

[11] For discussion of the structure of the geminates, see §3. In the following display, unmarked form types precede marked types on a given line and are separated from these by a semicolon: e.g., $QaM(M)$ is the normal structure of the plain simple pf, while $QaM\overset{\circ}{V}M$ is a marked choice. Note also that the geminable radical is labeled as 3$\sqrt{}$ *(M)* rather than as 2$\sqrt{}$ *(S)*. Since by definition geminates show identity of the two post-1$\sqrt{}$ radicals whenever they surface, the choice between 2$\sqrt{}$ and 3$\sqrt{}$ as the positional value of these consonants may be nothing more than terminological. Yet something of substance may be involved after all, and what evidence there is weighs in favor of identifying the value of the radical in contention as 3$\sqrt{}$: For one thing, hollow verbs (§1.3) commonly launch WW as 2$\sqrt{}$ in the intensive binyan, which virtually forces identification of the terminal radical as 3$\sqrt{}$ for the hollow gizra (n. 12, next); but this formation has made

some inroads into the geminate gizra as well, e.g., TL *9ayyel*, M *ayyel* as int of *√9l 'enter' (§6.2.1), suggesting that the value of *l* is 3√.

[12] (a) Note that the radical following the first is identified as 3√ (*M*), just as in the case of the geminates (n. 11, preceding). This identification in the case of the hollow verb is rather compelling: appearance of *yy, ww* is the intensive, which looks in every way like an overt 2 / somehow submerged in the other categories; and if it is 2√, the radical following it is virtually forced to be 3√. (The question of how counterparts of intensive *yy, ww* manage to be "submerged" in most categories will be largely side-stepped in this book, though in a few spots (e.g., §6.1.1.2, §6.1.2 n. 7, §6.3 with n. 37) it will be suggested that the hollow-characteristic [QV̂M] ⇐ strong-like /QaWV̊M/ (pf), /Q(V̆)WV̂M/ (imp). (Hollow 2√W surfaces elsewhere in A as well; e.g., in strong-style formations of the Yem TL sim pf like [Qš̆yéM], [QɑyMā̆], etc.—§6.2.2 TL.)

(b) The intensive aside, the hollow verb normally shows one phonetic stem vowel. It is not entirely clear whether the quest for the schematic value of this single vowel constitutes a substantive issue. Offhand, it seems likeliest that at least the historical origin of this vowel may vary with the processes that created it, or with the varying conditions attending those processes; cf. n. 13a, next. Generally in this book, the single phonetic stem vowel of the hollow gizra will be tagged simply as "ʃ" without further differentiation, though the considerations presented in §6.1 n. 3a suggest 2ʃ.

(c) It will be noted that the ʃ is in all cases but the int reconstructed as V̊, i.e., as long or short. This reflects the assumption, spelled out in §6, that pA evinced *closed-syllabic shortening* (css, §17.4), which in certain contexts would make for a short ʃV̊ (in alterna⁻ tion with ʃV̄ elsewhere).

[13] Three observations on the passive: (a) The B sim pf passives of √š̆Wm 'put', 3ms [š̆ím], 3fs [š̆ūmá̆θ] (BL 173f) might gingerly be interpreted as ⇐ /š̆ayim/ and /š̆uyam+at/ respectively, by a rule (say, s-e-cnd, §8.1) preserving the color of the *chromatic* schematic, 2ʃī in in the first case, 1ʃu in the second. Alternatively, color-preservation might be *functionally* guided on the hypothesis that: multi-schematic miškalim generally have *one* distinctive vowel; the distinctive vowel is *u* in the labial passive and *ī* in the palatal passive; the color of that distinctive vowel is preserved by the rule (perhaps s-e-cnd, differently formulated) in the hollow gizra funneling two underlying schematics into one surface schematic; cf. n. 16b below. Observe also that the Bab variant [š̆ɔmǽ̆θ] may reflect the opposite schematic distribution of color, /š̆ayum+at/, by straightforward s-e-cnd^s-coa (§11). (b) postulation of *uQīM* as the hol cau passive, smacking of a labial-palatal hybrid, is motivated by B pf 3fs [hɔ̆qīmá̆θ] at Dan 7:4 (and as varia lectio at Dan 7:5)—[ɔ̆] via *schwa coloring by inheritance* (§17.23). Either the hollow causative variant miškal < *uQīM* (as in Arabic conjugation IV) or ⇐ /uQuyaM/ by rules assimilating *u* to *y* (cf. §8.1.1) and then condensing |iyal| to [ī] (at odds, admittedly, with the mechanism suggested for sim [š̆ūmá̆θ] under point (a) above). (c) for the possibility of a variant *h+QīM*, see §17.23.3 bbB.

[14] The quadriradical miškal (n. 1) *QawMVM* appears as (what seems to be a lexically determined) alternative to usual *QaWWVM* in at least B, CP, and SM (BL 146f, Sg 70f, Macm 193e). It is noteworthy that marked *QawMVM* and less marked *QaWWVM* are both derivable autosegmentally from underlying √QwM by tagging (*QawwVM*) / failing to tag (*QawMVM*) the two skeletal positions of 2√ for identity and then letting association apply left-to-right (§23 n. 10):

(a)

$$Q \quad w \quad M$$
$$C\,V\,C'\,C'\,V\,C \quad \Rightarrow$$
$$a$$

$$Q \quad w \quad M$$
$$C\,V\,C'\,C'\,V\,C \quad \Rightarrow$$
$$a$$

$$Q \quad w \quad M$$
$$C\,V\,C'\,C'\,V\,C$$
$$a$$

$$\Rightarrow \quad Q \quad w \quad M$$
$$C\,V\,C'\,C'\,V\,C \quad \Rightarrow$$
$$a$$

$$Q \quad w \quad M$$
$$C\,V\,C'\,C'\,V\,C$$
$$a$$

(b)

$$Q \quad w \quad M$$
$$C\,V\,C\,C\,V\,C \quad \Rightarrow$$
$$a$$

$$Q \quad w \quad M$$
$$C\,V\,C\,C\,V\,C \quad \Rightarrow$$
$$a$$

$$Q \quad w \quad M$$
$$C\,V\,C\,C\,V\,C$$
$$a$$

$$\Rightarrow \quad Q \quad w \quad M$$
$$C\,V\,C\,C\,V\,C \quad \Rightarrow$$
$$a$$

$$Q \quad w \quad M$$
$$C\,V\,C\,C\,V\,C$$
$$a$$

[15] Defective stems differ from strongs essentially in collapsing all 2ʃ distinctions to *a ~ i*, though the resulting alternations are distributed unevenly across the various subparadigms; see din in §8 n. 1. (Only the simple stem is sketched here, but int and cau may readily be filled in along the same lines.)

[16] (a) The 1 √w verbs function essentially like strongs except in the simple imp system other than rmp, where they lack phonetic expression of 1 √w (V̆)—a deficiency in part filled in by various mechanisms in the individual dialects, especially in the impf subsystem; see frf, §17.7, and wic, §17.33. (b) The hunch that the labial passive of the sim impa may have been *SuM* rather than *SaM* rests on the fact that plain =/= labial distinctivity in the sim resides in 1ʃ (cf. §1.1.1), so that in the circumstance of systemic nonappearance of 1ʃ its distinctive color may have been transferred to 2; cf. in the opposite direction, in the gem verb, §3.2 (3L).

[17} (a) The 1 √n verbs function as strongs except in the simple impa system other than rmp, where at least some lexemes lack phonetic expression of 1 √n V̆. This deficiency was at least to some degree later filled in by the action of wic, §17.33. (b) Cf. note 16b, preceding.

2. System of Verb Affixes

2.1. Prefixes (Imperfective)

y-   3ms when unaccompanied by a number-gender suffix (§2.2.2), 3 alone when so accompanied. (Corollary: m is unnmarked vis-à-vis f marked, s is unmarked vis-à-vis p marked)

t-   3fs or 2ms when unaccompanied by a number-gender suffix, usually or always 2 when so accompanied. (The hedge alludes to the possibility of residual 3fp usage; see ftg, §16.2 <u>SM</u> (z′) w n. 24)

ʔ-   1s

n-   1p

There is also evidence of a precative/jussive prefix $l(V')$-, perhaps in complementary distribution with y- (in the shape l-) or perhaps preceding y- and eclipsing it by e-cond (§8.1) $lV'+y+V- \rightarrow lV''$-. See §17.19 for discussion, where also is treated later replacement of y- by l- (or n-), especially in the E dialects.

(The frequent appearance in Galilean of n- in lieu of ʔ- for 1s is taken by Dalman to instantiate a conventionalized mannerism rather than an out-and-out linguistic change ["Selbstermunterung," Da 265], while Beyer interprets it as a genuine syncretism [§16], a hallmark of the dialect [1986: 25, 76]. Food for thought is the categorical systematization of just this syncretism in modern Ma9lula Aramaic; Spitaler 1938:147.)

2.2. Suffixes[1]

2.2.1. Before Bridge Formation (§2.3.2)

2.2.1.1. Mood Suffixes

(-ā#)   impa, short impf
-i   long impf
-inni   energic impf

2.2.1.2. Number-Gender Suffixes

-ū; -ī; -ā(na)	mp; fs; fp :	impa, short impf
-ūna; -īna; -āna	mp; fs; fp :	long impf
-ůnna; -ı̊nna; -ånna	mp; fs; fp :	energic impf

20

2.2.1.3. Subject Suffixes (pf)

-a	3ms	-ū (*or* -ŭ^E ?)		3mp
-(ă^E)t	3fs	-ă^E		3fp
-tă^E	2ms	-tūm#, -tū-		2mp
-tĭ^E	2fs	-tinna (*or* -tinnă^E ?)		2fp
-t	1s	-nā, -n-, -nū		1p

2.2.1.4. Object Suffixes

-hĭ^E, -hŭ^E	3ms	-hŭm	3mp
-hă^E	3fs	-hĭ^En	3fp
-kă^E (*or* -ka?)	2ms	-kum	2mp
-kĭ^E	2fs	-kin	2fp
-nī	1s	-nā (*or* -nă^E ?)	1p

2.2.2. After Bridge Formation (§2.3.2)[2]

2.2.2.1. Mood Suffixes

(-ā #)	impa, short impf
-∅	short or long impf
-in#, -inn-	energic impf

2.2.2.2. Number-Gender Suffixes

-ŭ^L; -ī; -ā(n)	mp; fs; fp : impa, short impf
-ŭ^Ln; -īn; -ān	mp; fs; fp : long impf
-ŭ^Ln #, -ŭ^Lnn-;-ĭ^Ln #,-ĭ^Lnn-; -ă^Ln #, -ă^Lnn-	mp; fs; fp : energic impf

2.2.2.3. Subject Suffixes (pf)

-∅	3ms	-ŭ^L (*and* -∅?)		3mp
-(ă^E)t	3fs	-ā, -∅		3fp
-t(ā)	2ms	-tŭ^Lm#, -tŭ^L-		2mp
-t(ī)	2fs	-tĭ^Ln# (*and* -tĭ^Lnnā# ?), -tĭ^Lnn-		2fp
-ĭ^Lt#, -t-	1s	-nā, -n-, -nū		1p

2.2.2.4. Object Suffixes

-(ĭ^{EL})h(ī), -(ĭ^{EL})h(ū), -(ā^{EL})hī	3ms	-(ă^E)hŭm^{EL}	3mp
-(ă^E)h(ā)	3fs	-(ă^E)hĭn^{EL}	3fp
-(ă^E)k(ā) (*or* -(ā)k?)	2ms	-(ă^E)kŭm^L	2mp
-(ĭ^E)k(ī)	2fs	-(ă^E)kĭn^L	2fp
-(ă^E)nī (*and* -(ĭ^E)nī?)	1s	-(ă^E)na (*or* -(a)nā ?)	1p
		(*and* -(ī)na, -(ă^E)na ?)	

2.3. Analysis of Suffixes

2.3.1. Ancipitality

By *ancipitality* is meant the ambivalence in quantity of certain vowels, originally, in particular, those occurring in auslaut of certain prosodically prominent constituents, e.g., the intonational phrase (§23.5 (23Z′))—an ambivalence subsequently generalized to specific medial vowels bearing certain relations of symmetry or functional similarity to the original ancipitals. Notice, for instance, that auslaut ancipitality seems to be the rule for all but the 1st persons in the object suffixes of §2.2.1.4 ("V̠" representing an (early-)ancipital vowel, as will be picked up below). And that in this light it is plausible to assume that the same kind of length-ambivalence was then passed on by analogy to the 3p suffixes, though the vowels of these do not stand in auslaut (and that, incidentally, the paradigmatic spreading apparently did not catch up with the 2p forms—petering out short of completion being in fact commonplace for analogical processes).

Two sorts of ancipitality will be recognized: *early ancipitality* (e-anc), marked by superposed "E," dating from pA or even proto-Semitic (cf. Brockelmann 1908: 74), though persistent or reprising in the post-pA period as well; and *late ancipitality* (l-anc), marked by superposed "L," which by hypothesis arose later in the history of Aramaic, manifesting somewhat different distributional patterns from dialect to dialect.

The litmus for distinguishing between e-anc and l-anc, a distinction by no means always clearly drawable, is sensitivity to the midding (§17.11) of *i,u* to *E,o*: if, e.g., lengthened *i* results in [ī] despite mid-favoring conditions, e-anc is involved because diachronically e-anc^mid and hence mid is bled by the e-anc-induced length; whereas if [ē] results, l-anc is at play because mid^l-anc. Thus while the TR 2fs suffix [-íx] reflects e-anc ([rə̆ḥemtíx] 'ich liebte dich(fs)' Da 366), 3ms [-ě́h] shows l-anc ([šə̆ʔiltě́h] 'ich fragte ihn' lc).[3]

2.3.2. Bridge Formation (brf)

2.3.2.1. The Mechanics of brf

An early chain of events triggered the semantic and morphological realignment of several instances of *i* and *a* in the impf and pf systems, a nexus of mutations that caused these vowels to switch allegiance from a variety of roles in/as subject or number-gender suffixes to the role as string-initial elements in object suffixes. In allusion to their being de facto sandwiched between the stem(+ subject) complex to the left (fore) and the (original) object complex to the right (aft), these vowels in their new role will be called *bridges*—and the nexus of events leading to this new role will be called *bridge formation* (brf).[4]

It will be suggested that bridges evolved in two or three superstages. (α) First, with the development of *minor vowel harmony* (mvh) from (some) object-suffix vowels regressively onto vowels bearing little or no functional load.[5] (β) Then, in the wake of *short apocope* (sap, §17.22) and the ensuing loss of short subject, mood, or number-gender vowels in auslaut, with the metanalysis of inlaut (partial) allomorphs of these lost vowels at the behest of neater paradigmatic unity. This metanalysis was then followed by generalization of the newly emergent pattern, including spread to homoparadigmatic forms not originally affected.

In addition to and maybe partially overlapping with these two sequenced process complexes (α, β), (γ) the newly emerging bridges became targets of (generalized) ancipital lengthening (§2.3.1); and, in some dialects, new long-vocalic bridges may also have been created as a byproduct of *long apocope* (lap, §17.9).

(α) The pre-object vowels a priori most susceptible to minor vowel harmony would be those with zero functional load and inherently impoverished chroma—i.e., ə repair-strategically inserted by *excrescence* (exc, §4.3) /CC__C to forfend against an impermissible three-member cluster (§20.1) such as would arise in appending a *C*-initial object suffix to a monoconsonantal subject desinence on a strong-3√ stem; e.g., pf 1s^3fs or 1p^3fs, *QaSáM+t+hă̧*^{E} → *QaSáM+tə̧hă̧*, *QaSáM+n+hă̧*^{E} → *QaSáM+nə̧hă̧*.[6] If next mvh imparted the color of the suffix vowel to ə (qua species of sco, §17.23) and the resulting *V̌′* promoted (§14.1) to *V̊′*, bridge formation would have de facto commenced; not only from 3fs, but from other object suffixes as well, plausibly those later possessing the harmonic canon *V′CV′*—thus, illustrating the process on 1s as subject, 3ms *QaSaMtíhi̧*^{E}, 3fs *QaSaMtáhă̧*^{E}, 2ms *QaSaMtákă̧*^{E}, 2fs *QaSaMtíki̧*^{E} (assuming adjustment of accentuation upon promotion in avoidance of contracanonical antepenultimate stress, §4.1).[7]

Next in line after excrescent ə for vulnerability to mvh should be short full vowels with low functional load: in the pf, *a* of 2fp *-tinna* both because 2fp encodation is infrequent and because the shape *-tinn* is sufficiently distinctive even without an extra vowel, let alone its color; also probably 3ms/3fp *a* despite the mutual opposition because short ancipitality of 3fp is rare (§2.3.4.3) as is 3fp encodation of any sort; in the impf, mood suffix *i* on energic *inni*, and *a* on long/energic number-gender suffixes *-ūna, -īna, -āna* / *-ůnna, i̊nna, ånna*.

It is likely enough that these early manifestations of mvh at the service of (emergent) bridge formation overlapped with incipient short apocope ((β), next), de facto shoring up and ultimately preserving distinctivity between at least 3ms and 3fs—originally *-hi* ≠ *-ha*, in the middle period (by mvh) *-ihi* ≠ *-aha*, then following sap *–ih* ≠ *-ah* (putting aside the question of length for the moment; (γ) below)—that is, from *–hi* ≠ *-ha* to *–ih* ≠ *-ah*, the distinctive vowel opposition of 3ms ≠ 3fs has de facto metathesized.

Adding to the sketch examples above, we would now have such as: *QaSaMtinnihî, QaSaMtinnahä́; QaSaMaká, QaSaMikî; yaQSuMinnihî, yaQSu-Minnahä́; yaQSuMūnaká, yaQSuMūnikî*, etc.

Let us also provisionally assume that the reshapings just discussed were variable, at least in the early stage.

(β) When short apocope (§17.22) emerged, an immediate consequence was to skew the distribution of suffix shapes by deleting $\overset{\circ}{V}$ in auslaut while leaving homomorphemic inlaut tokens untouched. This skewing may be assumed to have made direct functional impact on the light-suffixed (note 1b) long and energic impf, since auslaut loss of declarative **-i* effectively neutralized the mood opposition with the short impf, which by hypothesis had never shown an opposing suffix (except for optionally occurring, low-frequency **-ā*); §2.2.1.1, §2.3.4.1.[8] And in those slots of the suffixal paradigm at large where the targeted $\overset{\circ}{V}$ had played no modal role, its preservation inlaut vs. its loss auslaut set up an ambiguity in morphemic allegiance. This is so because, while the pre-sap opposition of intransitive (= lacking object suffixes, abbreviated "intr") $X\overset{\circ}{V}\# \neq$ transitive (= object-suffixed, "tr") $X\overset{\circ}{V}Y\#$ made it manifest that $\overset{\circ}{V}$ grouped with *X*, post-sap $X\# \neq X\overset{\circ}{V}Y$ rather made it appear that $\overset{\circ}{V}$ grouped with *Y*. And in default of evidence to the contrary, new generations of speakers would in fact metanalyze $\overset{\circ}{V}$ so that it actually *did* come to group with *Y*.

The steps for these developments are spelled out for the (strong $3\sqrt{}$) pf in (2A). Stage I represents the pre-sap state of affairs, where *C* in the inlaut column represents the initial consonant of the object suffix and *V′* stands for results of precedent vowel-harmonic metanalysis as discussed under (α) above.[9] Thus on the first row (3ms) *a+C* ~ *V′C* means that original 3ms-marking *a* (*a+C*) has variably been metanalyzed (and possibly reshaped) to *V′* as part of the object suffix of which *C* is (was) initial; so 3ms^3ms may at this stage be expressed either by *QaSaM+á+hî*, where *a* signals 3ms subject, or as *QaSaM+íhî* where *í* (< *á*) functions as part of the 3ms object suffix, an early manifestation of bridge formation. On the fifth row (1s), we have excrescence-bearing *tə̆C*, excrescence being evoked /3√Ct__C to forfend against a triconsonantal cluster *3√CtC*; similarly on the last line (1p).

Stage II represents the first, pre-metanalytic impact of sap (auslaut *-tinn* > *-tin* by degemination, §3.1 (3F)(vii)), while at III rebracketing has taken place. By stage IV all instances of $\overset{\circ}{V}$ have been assimilated (and where appropriate reshaped) to bridge status. And lastly, at V, bridge formation has spread to all slots of the paradigm except those where the object suffix is immediately preceded by a long vowel (and hence there never was a sap-susceptible *V* to begin with), viz. 2s ancipitally long *tā* or *tī*, 3mp *ū*, 2mp *tū*, 3fp ancipitally long *ā*, 1p *nā*. (Note also that the alternate string *t-V'C* for 3fs inlaut at stage V is due to the redistribution of **-at ~ *-t* discussed in §2.3.4.3 **3fs**).

(2A)

	I	sap >
	auslaut	*inlaut*
3ms	a	a+C~V'C
3fs	at~āt	at+C~āt+C
2ms	ta~tā	ta+C~tā+C
2fs	ti~tī	ti+C~tī+C
1s	t	tăC~tV'C
3mp	ū	ū+C
3fp	ā~a	ā+C~a+C~V'C
2mp	tūm	tū+C
2fp	tinna	tinna+C~tinnV'C
1p	nā	nā+C~năC~nV'C

	II	>
	auslaut	*inlaut*
3ms	∅	a+C~∅+V'C
3fs		
2ms	t~tā	ta+C~tā+C
2fs	t~tī	ti+C~tī+C
1s		
3mp		
3fp	ā~∅	ā+C~a+C~∅+V'C
2mp		
2fp	tin	tinna+C~tinnV'C
1p		

	III	>
	auslaut	*inlaut*
3ms	∅	∅+aC~∅+V'C
3fs		
2ms	t~tā	t+aC~tā+C
2fs	t~tī	t+iC~tī+C
1s	t	t+ăC~t+V'C
3mp		
3fp	ā~∅	ā+C~∅+aC~∅+V'C
2mp		
2fp	tin	tinn+aC~tinn+V'C
1p	nā	nā+C~n+ăC~n+V'C

	IV	**>**
	anlaut	*inlaut*
3ms	Ø	Ø+V'C
3fs		
2ms	t~tā	t+V'C~tā+C
2fs	t~tī	t+V'C+tī+C
1s	t	t+V'C
3mp		
3fp	ā~Ø	ā+C~Ø+V'C
2mp		
2fp	tin	tinn+V'C
1p	nā	nā+C~n+V'C

	V	
	auslaut	*inlaut*
3ms	(Ø	Ø+V'C)
3fs	at~āt	t+V'C~at+V'C~āt+V'C
2ms	(t~tā	t+V'C~tā+C)
2fs	(t~tī	t+V'C~tī+C)
1s	(t	t+V'C)
3mp	(ū	ū+C)
3fp	(ā~Ø	ā+C~Ø+V'C)
2mp	(tūm	tū+C
2fp	(tin	tinn+V'C)
1p	(nā	nā+C~n+V'C)

(γ) Because of the prominence of sap as a catalyst for brf, discussion and illustration has hitherto been limited to short vowels. However, long vowels also play a role, and the development of $\bar{V}$-bridges may be considered a third superstage in the overall brf complex. This is in the first instance so because ancipitally induced length variation (§2.3.1) came to be transferable from the original suffix vowels to the newly developing/developed bridges; and in the second instance, for the dialects affected by *long apocope* (lap, §17.19), because the resulting auslaut-inlaut imbalance between Ø and $\bar{V}$ set up a relation much like the earlier relation triggered by sap between Ø and $\overset{\circ}{V}$. These factors thus led to the emergence of long-vocalic bridges, which then might be generalized to slots in the overall paradigm other than those where they were formed.

In dialects subject to lap, it is difficult to be sure whether a given $\bar{V}$-bridge has developed on the basis of generalized ancipitality or, rather, as a consequence of lap—or indeed as a result of synergy by both factors.

In either event, the dialect all hands down showing the highest incidence of $\bar{V}$-bridge development is SR. By way of illustration, the spread of an $\bar{A}$-bridge into originally bridgeless impa ms^3ms is sketched in (2B), in (i) assuming ancipital origin, in (ii) as a byproduct of lap.

In (i), we assume that on its first (pA) run, ancipitality has licensed *-a, -ta(-),* and *-hī.* Then sap triggers a first run of brf, primarily regrouping *ta+hī* to *t+ahī* and secondarily extending the formation into the previously bridgeless impa (with attendant stress adjustment).[10] Then, ancipitality stirs again, generalizing length from *ī of -hī* onto coconstituent bridge *a.* Finally, at ". . ." various per se irrelevant processes take place (red, e-cnd, mid, l-cnd).[11]

In (ii), we start with a slightly different ancipital distribution, with 2ms *-tā(-),* a difference that accordingly in default of sap immunizes *QaSaMtá̄+hī* from brf—but not *QǒSúM+hī,* which may still pick up a new bridge *a* in the backwash of sap's acting on forms like *QaSáMa* (as in (i)). Next, though r-e-anc could apply to *QǒSuM+áhī,* we assume it does not, and that rather in the wake of the perfunctory processes at ". . ." lap of *tɔ̄ > t* triggers r-brf *tɔ̄+y > t+ɔ̄y* with results spread to the impa.

(2B) (i)

	pf 3ms	pf 2ms	pf 2ms^3ms	impa ms^3ms
e-anc	QaSáMa	QaSáMta	QaSaMtá+hī	QǒSúM+hī
sap	QaSáM	QaSáMt	—	—
brf	—	—	QaSaMt+áhī	QǒSuM+áhī
r-e-anc	—	—	QaSaMt+ā́hī	QǒSuM+ā́hī
. . .	QǒSáM	QǒSáMt	QǒSaMt+ɔ̄y	QǒSoM+ɔ̄y
lap	—	—	—	—
r-brf	—	—	—	—
	[QǒSáM]	[QǒSáMt]	[QǒSaMtɔ̄y]	[QǒSoMɔ̄y]

(ii)

	pf 3ms	pf 2ms	pf 2ms^3ms	impa ms^3ms
e-anc	QaSáMa	QaSáMtā	QaSaMtá̄+hī	QǒSúM+hī
sap	QaSáM	—	—	—
brf	—	—	—	QǒSuM+áhī
r-e-anc	—	—	—	—
. . .	QǒSáM	QǒSáMtɔ̄	QǒSaMtɔ̄+y	QǒSoM+áy
lap	—	QǒSáMt	—	—
r-brf	—	—	QǒSaMt+ɔ̄y	QǒSoM+ɔ̄y
	[QǒSáM]	[QǒSáMt]	[QǒSaMtɔ̄y]	[QǒSoMɔ̄y]

The results of bridge formation prior to lap but subsequent to mvh and sap (as well as various other early processes thereby triggered, like epn (§17.6) and deg (§3.1 (3F)(vii)) are displayed in §2.2.2. The bridges themselves are underscored in §2.2.2.4, where they appear as the initial element of an object suffix complex.

2.3.2.2. brf and Ancipitality

A few observations might be made about suffixal ancipitality in the wake of bridge formation. (α) Perhaps all bridges are early-ancipital, a pattern likely inherited from originally ancipital suffixes (§2.2.1.4) and then generalized.[12] (β) Auslaut early ancipitality following bridge formation takes the form of $-\emptyset$ ~ $-\bar{V}$, rather than $-\overset{\circ}{V}$ ~ $-\bar{V}$ as in the period prior to bridge formation—a transformation not specific to the object suffixes, but holding for the subject suffixes as well; compare 2fs $-t\overset{E}{\imath}$ $(= -ti$ ~ $-t\bar{\imath})$ of §2.2.1.3 with $-t(\bar{\imath})$ $(= -t$ ~ $-t\bar{\imath})$ of §2.2.2.3. This effect is due to the action of sap (§2.3.2.1 (β)).[13] (γ) Late ancipitality developed subsequently to bridge formation—as in fact follows from l-anc's necessarily post-mid date of appearance in the A dialects (§2.3.1). Note that l-anc shows up in subject suffixes no less than in object suffixes and makes a cameo showing among the number-gender suffixes as well (§2.2.2.2).

2.3.2.3. *a* as the Unmarked Bridge

Observe that in most or all of its fully clear occurrences, *i* qua bridge is limited to slots where the auslaut vowel is or was *i* (in objects, 2fs and allos of 3ms, 1s), whereas *a* qua bridge is unrestricted. This suggests that in cases where mvh (§2.3.2.1(α)) is not involved, *a* is selected as the default bridge.

2.3.2.4. Spreading of Bridges

Bridges may be symptomized as such by their spreading to paradigmatic slots other than those where they originated. SR, charactertized by especially heavy usage of bridges in any event, provides a nice illustration. Consider eight forms in sketch: impf (intr) 2ms [tɛQSóM], 2ms^3ms [tɛQSoMə́y], (intr) 2mp [tɛQSə́Mún], 2mp^3ms [tɛQSə́Múnə́y]; and impa (intr) ms [Qə́SóM], ms^3ms [Qə́SoMə́y], mp (intr) [Qə́SoMún], mp^3ms [QuSMúnə́y]. On the transitive forms, notice the 3ms suffix complex [-ə́y] <l-cnd $-\overset{\backsim}{a}$-hī, with long bridge $-\bar{a}$- (§2.3.2.1(γ)).

We may assume a sequence of events something like the following: (α) *-a* is lost from the etymon of [tɛQSə́Mún] by sap, but remains caught medially in the etymon of [tɛQSə́Múnə́y] where it is lengthened either as a generalization (decontextualization) of the type of ancipitality seen in (2B)(i) or qua bridge formation as in (2B)(ii); (β) mp *ūn* is imported from the impf to the impa (hii, hti, §7.2(δ, ζ)), in the transitive forms dragging its object-marking dependencies along for the ride (-*ūn*ə́*y*); (γ) by this time, the element ɔ̄, having lost its original function and been reinterpreted as an asemantic bridge, is fobbed off onto corresponding singulars, [tɛQSoMə́y], {Qə́SoMə́y}, where it is etymologically unjustified.[14]

2.3.3. Composition of Suffix Complexes

For both pre-bridge and post-bridge stages (§2.2.1 and §2.2.2, respectively), the templates for composition are those given in the flow charts of (2C)—the only difference being the shift of certain instantiations of *i, a* from constituent-final status within mood, number-gender, or subject suffixes to bridge duty with the object suffixes.

(2C)

imp system: (prefix -) stem - $\left\{ \begin{array}{l} \text{mood suffix} \\ \text{number-gender suffix} \end{array} \right\}$ (- object suffix)

pf system: stem - subject suffix (- object suffix)

This established, nothing more can be said with confidence concerning composition in the pre-bridge stage; by hypothesis, the suffixes of §2.2.1 should compose freely subject only to the templates of (2C)—though admittedly this may be too bold a conjecture (aggravated by the fact that the listings of §2.2.1 and §2.2.2 are intentionally designed to be liberal combinatorily, with little attention to context sensitivity. Restrictions will to some extent be brought out in the discussion of actual forms from the dialects (§2.3.4)); cf. point (ε) below.

Coming to the post-bridge stage, the main difference centers on free deployment of the now bridge-bearing object suffixes (§2.2.2.4), concerning which the following points should be noted:

(α) A bridge never immediately follows a vowel; thus, while pf 3ms^3fs may in principle be realized as any of *QaSaM-áhā, QaSaM-áhā, QaSaM-áh,* or *QaSam-áh,* 3mp^3fs may only be realized as *QaSaMű-hā* or *QaSaMű-h.*

(β) Immediately following a consonant, a bridge is preferentially but not consistently deployed. And in some cases where a bridge fails to appear postconsonantally, the resulting *CC* cluster dates from the pre-bridge period (i.e., is given in terms of §2.2.1); e.g., immediately following 3√ of the ms imperative, which by hypothesis never ended in a mood vowel. Examples will be reviewed among the ensuing dialect-specific illustrations (§2.3.4), notably from TR.[15]

(γ) As a supplement to (α, β), -*CCV̄#* appears to be consistently realized as -*CCV̄#*. The reason for this may be therapeutic, in that -*CC#* <sap -*CCV̊#* would be repaired by epn (§17.6), but *V̊* of the resulting -*CV̊C#* would bid fair to lose the distinctiveness borne by the original *V̄* of -*CCV̄#*—contrast the therapeutic mvh discussed under §2.3.2.1(α).

(δ) In a very general way, one of the four potential expansions of -*V̊CV̄#* seems to be disfavored in most dialects, perhaps in all dialects but I. This marked expansion is -*V̊CV̄*. (I examples will be given in §2.3.4.3.)

(ε) As alluded to earlier, the displays of §2.2 to the tune of the compositional rules and tendencies detailed in this section will overgenerate, if overgeneration is judged against actually attested suffixes across the dialects. But any attempt to curtail such overgeneration would entail displays so bogged down with restrictions and special cases that any semblance of generalization and pattern-capture would be buried under the details; and then there is the problem of distinguishing between principled absence of a given complex and accidental lacunation in the available data. So deviations from the larger patterns have been entered in the displays only when licensed by a relatively high level of confidence (e.g., *-ka* in §2.2.1.4, *-(ā)k* in §2.2.2.4). Something more like the actual state of the data bases will be glimpsed next in §2.3.4, along with discussion of concrete examples from the dialects.

2.3.4. Discussion of the Suffixes Class by Class

2.3.4.1. Mood Suffixes

For discussion of the subtypes of the impf, see §7.2.

To judge by SM (especially) and M, pA made at least some use of an impa-short impf suffix *-ā*, doubtless cognate to Hebrew [-ɔ̄] of similar function (Waltke and O'Connor 1990: 568). This suffix is parenthesized in §2.2.1.1 and §2.2.2.1 to indicate its optionality (probably rarity). Cf. SM <wʾmllḫ 9mK> 'und ich will mit dir reden' (~ suffixless <wʾmll lwTK>), <qwmḫ> t[qǔmα] 'steh auf!' (~ <qwm>) (Macs 116), and probably (despite Macuch's silence) <nšm9ḫ> t[nišmǽ] 'lass uns hören' vs. <nšm9> t[nîšmæ] 'wir hören' (Macs 175);[16] in M this formative is apparently limited to /__pp with *√whb 'give', e.g., <(a)hbalia> 'gib mir!' (Nm 246) [həβālî] ~ (prothesized, §17.18) [ahBālî] (< *habā =lî; for the absence of *√w, §1.5; for suffixation of lî, §17.15.2).[17]

The choice of *i* (§2.2.1.1) as value of the original long/energic impf suffix (roughly indicative, declarative) is at best the least of several evils—see §7.2—and is gingerly adopted only because it provides a relatively mechanical accounting for *i* qua bridge (§2.3.2.1).

Though the energic in the transitive verb, manifested by auslaut *-in#* (§2.2.2.1) < deg (§3.1 (3Fvii)) *-inni#* (§2.2.1.1) is apparently rare, a few traces are attested in at least I (§7 n. 1).

The hypothesis that the light slots of the short impf were originally suffixless differs from the analogous case of the light impa (= ms) in the apparent absence of evidence for bridgeless object-suffixation (§2.3.3(β)); e.g., while TR ms^1s may take the form of [QǎSóM-nī] (cf. §2.3.4.3 1s), analogous 3ms^1s like @[yiQSóM-nī] are never found, only bridgeful [yiQSǎM-ǽnī] and the like. The dearth of bridgeless forms may of course simply be reflecting thorough leveling of the long-short impf distinction (§7.2(γ)) but may alternatively be witnessing to the erstwhile presence of a short-impf mood vowel, whatever that may have been (*-a, like the Arabic subjunctive? See note 8).

2.3.4.2. Number-Gender Suffixes

For the subsequent spread of the *n(n)*-bearing suffixes (long/energic impf) into hitherto *n(n)*-less areas (impa and short impf, but also pf), see #7.2(δ, ζ) (hii, hti); see also §7.7 for reciprocal confusion of *n* and *nn*.

Evidence for auslaut **a* on the heavy *n(n)*-bearing suffixes, as in Arabic, comes from bridge behavior in SR (especially) and M (sporadically): e.g., SR [nə̆šabbə̆ḥūnə̆y] 'sie preisen ihn' (Ns 134) <l-cnd(§8.2), prp(§17.19), red(§4.2) *yi-šabbiḥ-ūn-áḥī* <brf(§2.3.2), e-anc(§2.3.1) *yi-šabbiḥ-ūná-hi*; M <nišailunakin> 'they'll ask you(fp)' (Mal 59), qua [nīšeylonnāxén], if the bridge should be ancipitally long a la SR, or qua [nīšeylonnăxén], if the bridge should reflect unlengthened **a* subject to red (§4.2). In either event, the variant <nišailunkin> (lc) bespeaks reduced **a* either qua homonymous but heterographic [nīšeylonnăxén] since [V̆] in M is frequently represented by <V> ~ <∅> (§2.1.8), or qua smp-processed (§17.26) [nīšeylonxén]. (Note the transparentively restored prefix vowel [ī] of [nī], typical of M (§15.3.1.1).)

Observe that late ancipitality may have developed on mp **ů*-bearing suffixes, or, more accurately, on descendants of such suffixes, in various dialects; e.g., M impa <-iun> interpretable qua [-yón] as per <ahribiun> 'destroy(mp)!' in Modern M pronounced [ahréβyōn] (Macm 275) hence Classical [ahreβyón]. (For more on the developmental nexus leading from **-ů* to *yon*, see §7.2(δ) n. 8, as well as n. 18a below.)

The uncertainty as to vowel length in the eneregic (*ů̊, ĭ̊, ă̊*) bespeaks uncertainty as to whether /__nn induced closed syllabic shortening at this early stage. The testimony of later dialects is sparse and conflictual; see css (§17.4).[18]

Evidence for the usual fp **-ā* having an *n*-bearing variant, **-āna*, at least in the light impf, comes from I (e.g., <TD9n̄> 'you(fp) should know', MP 105; note that Muraoka and Porten interpret this allosuffix, following Arabic, as **-na*) and possibly Y (Beyer 1986:12 no 6).

2.3.4.3. Subject Suffixes (pf)

3ms. As was the case with impf **-i* (§2.3.4.1), postulation of **-a* as desinence of the pf 3ms provides a source for a bridge. Also like **-i*, **-a* finds less merely circumstantial evidence for its onetime existence through the behavior of the defective verb. However, while such evidence for **-i* is weak and ambiguous at best (§7.2, §11.1 w n. 2), the classical argument for **-a* (e.g., BL 63) is straightforward and strong: original **QaSáy-a* (for example) will by e-cnd (§8.1.1) explain later cA [Qə̆SÁ], while suffixless **QaSáy* would predict incorrect @[Qə̆SÁy]/@[Qə̆SÉ], and similarly **-i* (also @[Qə̆SÁy]/@[Qə̆SÉ]) or **-u* (@[Qə̆SÁw]/@[Qə̆SÚ]).

3fs. (α) In the intransitive verb, **-at* is pervasively the unmarked manifestation, **-t* quite rare (e.g., B [hiθgə̆zérɛθ] (BL 174) < mvh(note 5), epn(§17.6), low(§17.10) **hitgazir-t*). In the transitive verb, however, the situation is less clearcut, inasmuch as a number of factors obscure our view of the pristine **-at* ~ **-t* distribution, factors including: (*) accordion confusion of [-t] qua ≤ **-t* with [-t] qua < reoccluded (§5.1) -θ < reduced -aθ < spirantized **-at*; and (*)

transparently motivated replacement of *t* by [θ] or of θ by [t] (cf. §15.3.1.3). Despite these blurring factors, overall consideration suggests the prominence, though not absolute dominance, of a distribution like -*at/__C*, -*t/__V* *after bridge formation* (§2.3.2) *but before spirantiziation* (§5.1), whereby the pA (and indeed pSemitic) allomorphs *-*at* and *-*t* were tendentially redistributed in preconsonantal and prevocalic position, respectively. Thus, a pre-bridge from like sim pf 3fs^3fs *QaSaM-at-ha* would favor replacement by *QaSam-t-ha*. This view makes it possible to explain various otherwise unaccounted for factors, e.g., syncretism (e) in §16.2; see also §15.3.1.3 n. 29b. (β) Note that *a* of *-*at* may occasionally appear as long, presumably by ancipitality (§2.3.1); e.g., B [silqɔ̄θ] (~ usual [silqáθ])—BL 137.[19]

    2ms. For the ancipitality, cf. B [śámtɔ̄] (BL 173) < *-*tā* ~ [śámt] (lc) <sap (§17.22) *-*ta*.[20]

    2fs. Cf. SM <ʾTyTy> t[ātī́ti] 'kommst du?' (Macs 206) < *-*tī* ~ <ʾTyT> t[ã́tət] (lc) < *-*ti*.[21]

    1s. Postulation of *-*t* which then epenthesizes (§17.6) to -*it*, whose *i* subsequently undergoes l-anc in SR and M. This differs from the traditional position (e.g., BL 101) of reconstructing *-*tu* (like Arabic), whose *u* is apocopated before epenthesis, and of having no analog of l-anc. The reason for dispensing with *u is that no trace of this vowel is internal-reconstructable for 1s within nA, neither as a bridge vowel (§2.3.2) nor otherwise.[22] Note also that occasional instances of long-vocalic -*Tī* will be taken as deriving from -*I̊T* by a process of "mitotic" vowel copy rather than as instatiating ancipitally induced length of an original *i, an analysis presumably motivated for Hebrew. For discussion and examples, cf. vco (§13) for the latter point; for the former points, epn and uap (§17.6, §17.31). For discussion of transparentive spread of -*I̊T* (< *it*) to medial position, see §15.2.2.[23]

    3p. m *-*ū*, f *-*ā*, overtly in auslaut in dialects not (usually) affected by lap or i-lap (§17.9), e.g., TR [(ů̃)šmǽ9ū] '(und) sie(m) hörten', [(ů̃)vlǽ9ã] '(und) sie(f) verschlangen' (Da 262f),[24] while in dialects undergoing (i-)lap, only untrammeled inlaut in transitive verbs when the subject suffix gets caught between the stem and the object suffix, e.g., TL <qDm<u>w</u>K> a[qaddŏmúx] 'they(m) anticipated you' (Mar 58, 158*), SR [aθmŏhɔ̃́n] 'sie(f) überraschten uns' (Ns 139).[25] Also in inlaut, at least TR and SR give evidence of ancipitally *short* 3fp *-*a*- in certain transitive slots; §16.2 <u>SR</u> (ε), <u>TR</u> (β). Several dialects replace their reflexes of *-*ū*/*-*ā* (which are often ∅ by lap) with -*Ůn(n)/-Ån(n)* imported from the impf ()hii, hiti—§7.2(δ, ζ); and in one of these, M, late ancipitality is manifested in its special hii-affected reflex 3mp [-yōn], the derivation of which is essentially identical to that of the homophonous mp impa suffix discussed in §2.3.4.2; e.g., <akaliun> 'they(m) ate' (Macm 263) [axalyón] ~ [axalyɔ́n]. The similarly patterned 3fp pf [-yān] (e.g., <rgazian>

'iratae fuerunt'(lc) [r̆ɣazyắn]) might also involve l-anc, but unprovably since *a* is not subject to mid.[26]

2p.[27] A crosscurrent of reciprocal assimilations rendered the m and f suffixes identical in all but vocalism by the time of B, possibly to m /-tūn(-) ~ /-tŭnn(-)/, f /-tīn(-)/ ~ /-tĭnn(-)/, with distributional details varying from dialect to dialect but with frequent retention of original /-tū-/ /__object suffix (§2.2.2.3); see §7, especially §7.3. The crisscross of assimilations was interwoven with a few independent sound changes (notably sap(§17.22)^deg(§3.1 (3Fvii))^*final m assimilation* (fma) whereby suffixal *m#* > *n#* [28]) but in any event ended up generalizing the f dentoalveolarity of the nasal and homogenizing the quantity of the vowel in both directions. O and I still maintain mp *m,#* (<-Tm>), though I already shows alternation with generalized *n#* (~ <-T(w) n>). The clearest (and thoroughest) manifestation of l-anc is in SR, which pervasively fields mp [-tōn(n)], fp [-tēn(n)] (spelt <-town>, <-teyn>), though B shows the Bab variant [ẖǎzē̄θǒn] 'ihr(mp) habt gesehen' (~ tb[ẖǎzē̄θū́n]) (BL 161, who consider the Bab form "abnorm")—alternatively accountable as an incidence of *ē. . .ū > ē. . .ō* mvh (n. 5 above; see also §7.7). It is also likely in SR that *-ēn(n)* of *-tēn(n)* spread by hii to the pf/impa qua renewed 3fp/fp suffix, thus accounting for the otherwise puzzling palatal vocalism in slots originally sporting *a—pfr, §7.2(δ) with n. 13.)[29]

For more on reflexes of 2fp *-tinnắ, see §7.3.

1p. For inlaut + *n(ā)-, cf. ^3ms TR [ʔɔ̆θev-nắhī] (Da 368) (cau of hollow *√θwb; accordion *θ > t > θ* via occ^spr (§17.14, §5.1), for shortening of ʃ*ī to [e], see §6.1.1.1), TL [ʔɔ̄θev-nḗh] (Mar 123*) (cau of *√wθb). For auslaut *-nā, cf. TR [bɔ̆héθ-nā̱] (Da 263), and note that such as TL a[ʔǎmár-ṉ] (Mar 86*) bespeaks < *-nā via lap (§17.9) rather than original < *-n, which should have triggered epn (§17.6) to something like @[ʔǎmárin] (cf. 1s a[ʔǎmárī] (Mar 88*) < *ʔamár-t via epn^mtr(§17.12)). Evidence for an allomorph *-nū, like Hebrew, is afforded by TL (cau ^3ms y[ʔæqrī-nū̱-hū] ~ y[ʔæqrī-nū̱-æh] (Mor 328), -nū́æh bespeaking uap^ptg (§17.31, §17.16) on ancipitally short *-nūhu), and sporadically by SM (intransitive <-nw> t[-nu]).[30]

2.3.4.4. Object Suffixes [31]

3ms. Four points might be observed about the alloshapes of this suffix complex: (α) It shows either palatal or labial auslaut (-hĭ̃ ~ -hŭ̃) under circumstances not (any longer) fully transparent (see §8.2.2). (β) of four possible expansions of -V̊hV̊# (§2.3.3(δ)), two are generally favored, -V̄hV̄# and -V̊hV̊#; note, e.g., the likely alternation of both in P <yPThyhy> ~ <yPThh> 'he'll open it' (HC 402). Moreover, the generalization appears to extend beyond this case where the lead-off vowel is a bridge, inasmuch as -V̄hV̄ is favored whether the lead-off is a bridge (SR [tɔ̆zaddɔ̆qīn-ī́w] 'du(fs) berechtigest ihn' (Ns 139) < l-cnd(§8.2) -ī́hu), a suffix (B int impa mp^3ms [ẖabbɔ̆l-ū̱́-hī] (BL 177)), or a

stem-suffix portmanteau (B sim pf 3ms^3ms [bǎnɔ̄́-hī] (lc) < e-cnd (§8.1) -2ʃa
3√y-a-, 3mp^3ms [šǎnɔ̄́-hī] (lc) < -2ʃa 3√y-ū-); contrast B sim pf 3ms^3ms
[šaθr-ḗh] < -íhi or -íhu via sap/uap^mid^l-anc (§17.22/31, §17.11, §2.3.1).
[32] Judging by the prevalence of auslaut strings of certain shapes reckoned
against their developmental history, we may conclude that the preference for
-V̄hV̊# and -V̊hV̊# set in later than e-cnd but earlier than l-anc.[33] However,
exceptions to this preference exist; e.g., I appears to favor -hV̄# irrespective of
the length of the preceding vowel, thus <yTq̇l-nhy> 'er wird es wagen' (L51)
is plausibly [-innÍhī] (on energic -inn-, §7.1). (γ) As per (β), the 3ms may
evince lengthening by either early or late ancipitality, though the early type
may be limited to P (see above) as well as to SR, where in fact in the impf they
sometimes constitute options for one and the same φ-complex, e.g., 2ms^3ms
[tɛQSǝMíw] (early) ~[tɛQSǝMḗh] (late). (δ) SR apparently alone among the
dialects shows a third alternant in the impf 2ms^3ms, [tɛQSoMɔ̄́y] < l-cnd
-ā́hī, with anc-lengthened bridge [-ɔ̄-]. That extension into the impf may be a
relatively late development is clued by transparentized 2ʃ[o] (vs. reduced 2ʃ[ǝ]
with the two *-i- bridges). (ε) Note finally for the 3ms complex an instantiation of the mandated -CV̄# /C__ (§2.3.3(γ)): TR int impa ms^3ms [tæqqéfhī]
(Da 375).

3fs, 2ms, 2fs. These three slots will be considered together on the basis of
their canonic similarity -(V̄')CV̊'—*with* the reservation that 2ms perhaps shows
its options frozen at -(V̄')CV̊', whence it would be unclear whether any options
had existed to be frozen in the first place. It will be recalled that the color identity of the two vowels, indicated by the prime tick, is at least in upshot com-
municationally serviceable, abetting successful conveyance of φ-information
even when the auslaut vowel has been lost by apocope (§2.3.2.1(α)). Note
that the generally dispreferred canon -V̊CV̄# (§2.3.3(δ)) appears to be favored
in I, as was the case with its 3ms manifestation; e.g., pf 1s^2fs <BrKTKy>
(Kutscher 1970:111) plausibly interpreted as [-Íxī]. Some examples of diverse
realizations of various slots: TR sim pf 3mp^3fs [kævšûhā̱](Da 367), int impa
ms^3fs [pælléγhā̱], B sim pf 3ms^3fs [ḥaθmáh] ~ [ḥaθmɔ̄́h] (BL 177); TR sim
pf 1s^2fs [rǎḥemtíx] (Da 366), TL int pf 1s^2fs y[sækkæntíx] a[gɔ̄raštéx] (Mor
299, Mar 101*); TL int pf 3ms^2ms [næššǝqɔ̄́x] (Mor §15.21, sim pf 3ms^2ms
a[našqɔ̄́x] (Mar 139*).[34]

1s. When bridge-bearing, normally *-ā́nī, though perhaps occasionally
vowel-harmonic *-íní (mvh, §2.3.2.1); e.g., M <subqin> 'leave me!' (~ normal <subqan>) (Mal 643), TL <Pr9yn> y[pær9ín] 'ʃallem ʔoti!' (~ <Pr9n>
y[pær9ǽn]) (Mor 296). However, the ending <-in>, <-yn> might be subject to
a different interpretation, as reflecting importation into the impa of the impf
energic *-inn- as an object bridge (§7.1) (an importation otherwise unattested
in either dialect); cf. TR tb[pǎroqínnī] (~ normal bb[pǎróqnī]) (Da 375), SM
<smqny> {sic} t[šēmǣʔinni] 'höre mich!' (Macs 229).[35] Observe the con-

stancy of auslaut -*ī* in dialects not undergoing lap (§17.9)—and the cue that lap rather than sap (§17.22) was at work in the consistent SR spelling of the suffix as <-ny> rather than as @<-n> (B 144, 146).[36]

3p, 2p. The gender pairs of the 3p and 2p object suffixes are mutually more similar than the gender pairs of the 2p subject suffixes (§2.3.4.3) with which they otherwise manifest canonical and segmental similarity.[37] This aside, there are at least three points of difference, especially in the case of the 3p: (ε) The 3p object items came to be rivaled, and ultimately at least in part replaced, by *in(n)*-bearing elements whose *in(n)*, in turn, came to be confused with the energic *inn* frequently appearing as an object bridge; all this is extensively treated in §7.4. (ζ) The 3p suffixes either started life as independent pronouns (as still the case in I and B, and partially in SR, where they function as enclitics), or at the very least were to some extent rivaled by isofunctional independent pronouns (§7.4, §17.15). (η) Unlike the 2p subjects, the 3p and 2p objects evince both early and late anc of the pronominal vowel—the diachronic appearance (and possible synchronic reality) of early anc thinkably but uncertainly arising by virtue of the *in(n)*-elements ((ε) above) originally having long pronominal vowels while the other elements had short pronominal vowels; some of this possibility is visible in the independent 3p pronouns ((ζ), preceding) of B, where 3mp [himmố(n)] derives by hypothesis < l-anc -*ón* < mid -*ún*, whereas competing [ʾinnún] is an *nn*-bearing element with original *ū* (and ditto the corresponding 3fp [ʾinnín] (BL 69).[38] Two final remarks on 3p, 2p: (θ) In addition to the overt evidence for an *a*-colored bridge /__2p from M (§2.3.4.2) and SR ([nappǝqūnǝxón] 'sie bringen euch hinaus' (Ns 134)), evidence for a vocalic bridge having been in that slot is given by spirantization (§5.1) of postconsonantal *k*, e.g., B [yǝšēzǝvinx̲ón] (BL 177), by hypothesis < *-inn-ak̲úm* via fma (§2.3.4.3 2p), p-red^spr^smp (§4.2, §5.1, §17.26), and mid^l-anc (§17.11, §2.3.1). (ι) Unlike the 2mp subject suffix *-tūm* (§2.2.2.3), the mp object-suffixal *-m* fails to give way to -*n* (fma) in I, though I does begin to show cases of -*m* > -*n* in the structurally similar nominal-prepositional system (in the so-called possessive suffixes in the mp slots); see MP 153. In all later dialects, on the other hand, fma -*m* > -*n* goes on to become a fait accompli throughout the entire morphology.

1p. Even as the bridge of 2ms may be invariably long, the unmarked *a*-color bridge of 1p is, to judge by those orthographies and traditional pronunciations capable of capturing the distinction, invariably short; e.g., TR sim pf 3ms^1p [ræṭšǽnā] (Da 363), SR int pf 3ms^1p [qabbǝlán] (Ns 132), TL sim impf 3ms^1p a[lifrŭqinnán] (Mar 13), auslaut *-ā̲* in the two E dialects being lost by lap. [39] It is also possible that the 1p at times supported long *i*-colored bridges, as per TL sim impf 3ms^1p y[limṭǝyín] (~ normal y[limṭǝyǽn]) (Mor 323); if so, it perhaps spread by analogy from 1s where it would be justified by minor vowel harmony (§2.3.2.1 n. 5). And SM t[-an] (§16.2 SM, syncretism (x)) suggests a variant with ancipitally short auslaut, *-na (likewise possibly G, though in that case lap of *-na may be responsible; §17.9.2, §24.2 under *√²1p).

Notes to §2

[1] (a) In the displays of §2.2.1 and §2.2.2, "-X#" indicates that suffix X is restricted to auslaut (word-final) position; "-X-" that X is an inlaut (medial) suffix, i.e., that it is necessarily followed by another suffix; "-X" conveys that X occurs either in auslaut or in inlaut (though elsewhere in this book, in default of a statement to the contrary, "-X" = "X in auslaut position"). Other symbols used in the displays of §2.2 will be explained in due course. (b) Occasionally, forms of the imp system ending in (reflexes of) *-∅ or *-i will be referred to as *light* or *light-suffixed*, the balance as *heavy* or *heavy-suffixed*. And in the pf system, similar terminology will be deployed a bit differently, *light suffix* referring to subject desinences of canon $-\overset{\circ}{V}C\#$, whether that canon is original (e.g., 3fs $-a\theta$) or developed (e.g., 1s $-i\theta$ after epenthesis, §17.6).

[2] The occlusive symbols "t, k" rather than the archiphonemic symbols "T, K" are used for the pA stops *t, *k with no prejudice to the possibility that spirantization (§5.1) may already have begun to change these stops to fricatives (θ, x) postvocalically by the time bridge formation took place. This license is taken with an eye to enhancing item-by-item comparability of §2.2.1 and §2.2.2 in the absence of extraneous differences. (A similar license may have to be assumed for a few additional processes as well.)

[3] (a) The difference in 2ʃ, [e] vs. [i], reflects transparentation (§15.2.1.1) or its absence respectively. (b) Too great a store should not be set by the term "ancipitality" per se with respect to either e-anc or l-anc; and especially the latter is unlikely to have been a bona fide, prosodically motivated anciptital process at any time. But since both processes target the same general class of suffixes, and in the case of most of the 3rd person object suffixes even the selfsame vowel, it seems on balance heuristically useful to provide some common nomenclature. And "ancipitality" bespeaks a plausible surmise for at least the first origins of the pattern.

[4] Much of this characterization of bridges holds of at least one other element widespread in the A dialects: reflexes of the onetime energic suffix *-inn(i) (§7.1).

[5] By *minor vowel harmony* (mvh) is meant any of a family of (semi)vowel-to-vowel assimilation processes, whereby either of the Vs in a string $V(C)V$ imparts some or all of its features to the other V, or, in the semivocalic case, W imparts features to V in VW (§20.2(δ)). mvh arises again and again in the A dialects, individual instances being probably not genetically but rather topologically related, reflecting a structural tendency common to the A idiom at large. In addition to (α) below, see §2.3.4.3 2p, §2.3.4.4 1p w n. 39, §4.3, §4.4.3, §7.7 w n. 33, §8.1.1 nn 4+5, §8.1.3 n. 18, §9.1.4, §9.2.3.1, §11.2 TR, §12.1 n. 1, §12.2 B (δ) w n. 7, §12.2 M (β) n. 19, §13 TL (β, γ) w n. 5, §17.9.1, §17.23.3 M, §20.2 (δ).

[6] Though it will be suggested shortly ((2A), stage III) that -tɔ̆hăl/-n+ɔ̆hắ became morphologically organized as -t+ɔ̆hăl/-n+ɔ̆hắ in the course of bridge formation, it is not certain whether excrescence at first rendered the like of -t+ɔ̆hắ or -tɔ̆+hắ, or perhaps even -t+ɔ̆+ha. (In THP 65 it is suggested, in part following a principle introduced by Watkins [1962] and evidence from Bolozky 1977—more in §15.3.1.3 n. 28—that phonetically motivated V-insertion processes interrupting C+C′, where C = staminal and

C' = suffixal, render $C+VC'$ rather than $CV+C'$. But here both flanking consonants are suffixal.)

[7] Some discomfort with this account of excrescence at the service of bridge formation lurks behind the need for the resulting schwa to promote (and subsequently for the containing word to undergo) stress adjustment. Consider that such a stipulation is not required under the traditional view that pf 1s was *-tu* (§2.3.4.3).

[8] Alternatively, it is possible that the short impf was marked by *-a*, like the Arabic subjunctive. Subtle circumstantial evidence in favor of the short impf having had suffixal encodation of *some* sort might be the fact that the later dialects consistently show bridges in the impf—unlike the impa, whose assumed original suffixlessness arguably resonates in a certain amount of later bridgelessness (especially in TR); see §2.3.4.1. In any event, should the short impf have been encoded by *-a* in pA, we will have another source for latter bridge *-A-* (possibly the unmarked bridge color; §2.3.2.3).

[9] Various simplifications are utilized in displaying (2A) with an eye to sharper exposition; e.g., a few allomorphs of subject suffixes are omitted (3fp, 2fp, 1p—§2.2.1.3). Also, unchanged entries are omitted from stages II, III, IV, but are parenthesized at stage V.

[10] pf 3ms and pf 2ms are chosen as representative trigger-slots, with no claim to exhaustiveness.

[11] Transparentation may also have taken place, as per the preservation of open-syllabic short-vocalic 2ʃ as well as its mid coloring, [o] rather than [u]; In fact, a special favoring condition for transparentation in cases like this may be afforded by bridge formation itself, since at the stage antecedent to $Q\breve{o}SuM+\acute{a}h\bar{\imath}$ was $Q\breve{o}S\acute{u}M+h\bar{\imath}$, with 2ʃ preserved on a phonetic basis.

[12] "Perhaps. . . ." The hedge involves 2ms and 1p, whose bridges may be invariantly long and short, respectively (§2.3.4.3). But even so, at least 2ms would then probably involve "frozen ancipitality"—frozen at long $\bar{a}$—rather than ancipitality never having arisen at all, because otherwise there would be an unexplained discrepancy between the length of the bridge (long) and the length of the likely sap-triggered origin of the bridge (§2.3.2.1(β)), short *-a*.

[13] Even putting aside dialects affected by lap-induced brf (§2.3.2.1(γ)), there are a number of stages with distinct surface dispositions of bridge length (abstracting away from specific morphological quirks). It might be useful to consider a developmental profile for some of this, supplementing the discussion in §2.3.2.1. Let us assume that: (a) sap started as a variable process, so that the chain $-\mathring{V} > -\emptyset$ should be expanded to $-\mathring{V} > -\mathring{V} \sim -\emptyset > -\emptyset$; (b) the variable disappearance of pre-bridge $-\mathring{V}$ was sufficient to begin the semantic bleaching necessary for metanalytic bridge formation; (c) as a corollary to (a), $[-\mathring{V}] \sim [-\emptyset]$ is phonologized as $/-\mathring{V}/$ plus s-sap. These developments would interact over several stages as follows in (d), derivation tracked on a hypothetical sim pf hollow verb $Q\bar{a}M$ inflected as intr 3ms and tr 3ms^3fs. (Stress and ancipitality are assumed in / / for simplicity; also, there is some compression of stages for the same reason, as well as an expository distinction drawn between stages and transitions. Since (d) is designed to bring out somewhat different aspects of brf from those detailed in §2.3.2.1, there is incomplete overlap between (d) and (2A, B); e.g., (d) omits any analog of stage II in (2A), and on the other hand initial variability of sap is not registered in (2A):

(d)

Stage I.   /{{QáM}a}/   /{{{QāM}á}hā}/   ~ /{{{QāM}á}ha}/
           (no rules)
                        [QáMa]   [QāMáhā]   ~ [QāMáha]

Transition I.   Emergence of variable d-sap, which impacts on pf 3ms -*a* by
                 desemanticizing it, so that it lingers on as a mere diacritic desinence
                 in the intr but rebrackets as part of the object in the tr, creating a
                 bridge.
                 This ushers in:

Stage II.   /{{QáM}a}/   /{QáM}{á{hā}}/   ~ /{QáM}{á{ha}}/
           Variable s-sap
                        [QáM] ~ [QáMa]   [QāMáhā] ~ [QāMáh] ~ [QāMáha]

Transition II: Phonological-level ancipitality is inherited onto the bridge from the
                 auslaut; sap becomes categorical, resulting in irretrievable loss of
                 diacritic /-a/ in the intr and restructuring to /-a{h(ā)}/ (or simply
                 /-ah(ā)/) in the tr.
                 This ushers in:

Stage III.   /{QáM}/   /{QāM{á{h(ā)}}}/ ~ /{QāM{á{h(ā)}}}/
           (no rules)
                        [QáM]   [QāMáhā] ~ [QāMáh] ~ [QāMáhā] ~ [QāMáh]

[14] (a) That this fobbing off onto the singulars may have occurred relatively late
is possibly clued by transparentized 2ʃ[o] (§15.5.1)—a transparentation absent in the
impf allos with bridge *i, whether affected by e-anc ([tɛQSə̆Mʃ́w] ← -íhū) or by l-anc
([tɛQSə̆Mɛ́h] ← -íhŭ). Discussion of the SR impf leads to a few points on the composition of A bridges: (b) We have seen that bridges are molded from *i and *a. There
is also evidence for a rare bridge *ay, origin unknown, most clearly from the SR imp
system where it appears as an allo /__1s (e.g., [tɛQSoMáyn], note trp of 2ʃ), but also
possibly from TL as the usual alternant of the 1s^2ms suffix complex spelt <-TyK>
and interpreted into Tiberian vocalization by Margolis (e.g., Mar 58, 153*, 169*) as
<-tɔ̄yx> which is thinkably supposed to convey a[-tɔ̄yx] but probably represents a[-tɔ̄x],
in agreement with Morag's Yemeni renditions (e.g., <šDrTyK> y[šæddærtɔ́x], Mor 299
+ n. 47). Since *i and *a are two thirds of the pA short vowel system (§20 (20D)), the
question arises as to whether bridges are ever made of the missing vowel, *u. Three
possible instances might be mentioned, two from SM and one from G, only the G case
plausibly involving a true bridge: (c) Macuch is probably correct in his assumption that
SM variably shored up the pf 3ms intr of the defective verb by incorporating the 3ms
independent pronoun hū qua subject suffix: e.g., <mḥw> ~ <m9w> t[mǽʔu] 'er schlug'
(Macs 203), ← smc(§22.1 (22B)) mă9áw ← r-l-cnd (§8.2) incorporated mă9áhū ←
mahā́ hū́. (Macuch is also right in surmising that such incorporation sets up syncretism
(§16) with 3mp (lc), homonymous t[mǽʔu] being derived along the lines of ←smc
mă9áw ← mă̆háw ← e-cnd(§8.1) mă̆háyū.) In light of such incorporation, bridge-

smacking <wm9w̲nwn> ~ <wm9w̲Twn> 'und er schlug sie' is best analyzed as instantiating *either* (incipient) generalization of incorporation to medial position *or*, possibly, incorporation chronologically preceding suffixation of the 3mp object pronoun in SM (i-pat, §17.15.1; for <T>, tom, §17.30). (d) G at times shows an unexpected <w> in the sim impa s^3ms, sandwiched between stem and obj suffix: ms^3ms <PTh̲wnh>, ms/fs^3ms <ŝBqw̲Th> (Da 375f) (genderwise plausibly a case of syncretism (fgm, §16.1), though the orthography may disguise phonetic differences; for the shapes of the suffixes apart from <w>, see §7.2(ζ), §17.30). (e) SM <wˀPqw̲Ty> 'und ich habe ausgeführt' (Macs 188). The similarity (graphemic identity) of <-wTy> to Hebrew [-ôθî] characteristic of simple geminate and hollow verbs (THP 45f) was noticed by Macuch, who explains the SM form as a Hebrew-induced distortion. Note that normally with a verb like this we expect unremarkable <-T> t[-ət], which in fact is attested as a variant: <ˀPqT> t[æbbɛ́qət] (lc).

[15] (a) There are cases where determination of bridges and their segmental environment is not foregone: e.g., should the suffix complex of TR hol cau pf 1p^3ms [ˀǒθevnɑ̃hī] (Da 368; for 2ʃ[e], see §6.1.1.1) be analyzed as bridgeless [-nɑ̃-hī] or as bridgeful [-n-ɑ̃hī]? (b) When the miškal ends in *-2ʃi 3√y*, TR consistently shows bridge -æ- in pf (e.g., cau 3ms^1p [ˀæḥzǒyɛ́nɑ̃], and so all examples listed in Da 384f) except /__3mp, which then shows the bridgeless truncated allosuffix *-n(n)ūn* via the i-pat convention discussed in §17.15.1 (β) (e.g., [ˀæḥzīnṹn], Da 385). At the very least, this distribution strongly suggests that in the early stages of bridge formation *-2ʃi 3√y* was reacted to as *-iy* as opposed to *-ī*, an option enabled by *diphthong-monophthong equivalence* (dme, §8.1.1), and that the *y* was treated as a consonant along the grain of (β) in the text. (Whether the reaction was later reversed, at the time of i-pat, seems less foregone, however. Suffixation of *(ˀ)innūn* may have simply proceeded with a dispreference for bridges; note in particular forms like 3fs^3mp [nǒsevæθnṹn], where allomorph *-nūn* is inserted /C__, C an unambiguously true consonant (θ) as opposed to an ambivalent semivowel like *y*, quite against the grain of (β); see (17.15A) and attendant discussion in §17.15.1.) The bridgeful vs. bridgeless pattern discussed here was at least partially noted by MP 140 n. 658. (The TR pattern in the impa differs from that of the pf just discussed, in that bridgelessness is likely to be the norm—also in consonance with (β). Thus we find int ms^1s [ˀæssī́nī], not @[ˀæssǒyɛ́nī] (Da 391). The Bab int ms^3fs form <šæwyǒhɑ?> (lc), prima facie [šæwyǒhɑ̃], is suspicious independently of the bridge question for its ultimate stress; contrast the Tib (Sab) variant <šæẘiyhɑh>, expectedly and straightforwardly interpretable as bridgeless and baritone [šæwẘíyhɑ̃].)

[16] Derivation of the subminimal pair by the smc (§22.1) might proceed as follows:

(a)		nišmá9
	c-prm	—
	c-pen	níšma9
	c-pra	—
	c-dgt	níšmā
	c-vcr	—
	r-c-pra	níšma
		t[níšmæ]

(b)   nišmá9ā or nišmǎ9ā́
     c-prm   —   nišma9á́
     c-pen   —   nišmá9ā
     c-pra   nišmǎ9a
     c-dgt   nišmǎa
     c-vcr   nišmǎ
     r-c-pra   —
                     t[nišmǽ]

[17] It is unclear whether the stress was originally penultimate (*hábā) or ultimate (*habā́), an uncertainty registered for SM as well (n. 16, preceding). If ultimate, input to mediate pronoun attachment (§17.15.2) would be reduced hǎβá́ or reduced-then-prothesized ahBá̌, remaining only to be destressed under the domination of suffix lí. If, however, the input to m-pat was penultimately stressed, the steps would presumably be háβā=lí → haβālí r-red→ hǎβālí (r-pro → ahBālí).

[18] (a) When late ancipitality is indicated in §2.2.2 as involving the masculine plural suffixes -ū, -ūn, -ů̄n (number-gender, §2.2.2.2) and -ū (subject, §2.2.2.3), the sense is that *reflexes* of one or more of these formatives give evidence of developing l-anc, not least of all reflexes of nasal-bearing number-gender suffixes imported by hii/hti (§7.2(δ/ζ)), from the imperfective into the pf (thus in a sense becoming reflexes of subjectival -ū) or impa. A path frequently followed in this development might start with the short value of -ů̄n, which first undergoes midding (§17.11) and, finally, late ancipitality; i.e., -un mid> -on l-anc> -ōn—a sequence of mutations plausibly followed by M [ahreβyőn] (shy of the insertion of [y], for which see §7.2(δ) n. 18) attendant upon hii-importation of the suffix from the impf. (b) Other processes affecting the number-gender suffixes include: pin, whereby finite verb desinences are reshaped under the influence of (roughly) corresponding participial desinences (the primary manifestation is replacement of mp Ů̄ by Ī̊), §17.17; vco, whereby suffixes of canon V'C' are expanded to (V')C'V'(C'), §13, and in the opposite direction mtr, whereby they are truncated to V', §17.12; lap deletes stressless -ū, -ī, -ā, while i-lap compensates for this in the case of -ū by de facto infixing replacement of 2ʃ (e.g., QǝSáMū → QǝSů́M), §17.9.

[19] Other processes affecting reflexes of *-at(-) include: mtr, rendering -Ā, §17.12; vco, expanding -Aθ- to -(A)TA(T)-, §13, ayd, replacing -Aθ by -Ay, §17.2.

[20] Both allosuffixes may then be neutralized to T by the action of lap (§17.9); see also n. 21, next.

[21] Then neutralization to T may come about by the agency of lap, as was true with the 2ms counterpart, n. 20 (preceding). In dialects where this takes place, moreover, the result is loss of the gender distinction (at least on the surface)—syncretism of the type called *formal gender merger* (fgm), §16.1. The qualification "at least on the surface" is necessary because the distinction thus lost in *auslaut* may be retained in *inlaut*, as is true of SR; and in such an event, the distinction is best considered maintained *phonologically*, though lost phonetically by rule (in this case, s-lap). The dialects actually show interesting diversity with general regard to 2s encodation; for instance, while SR shows gender neutralization in the *intransitive* (= auslaut, by d-sap^d-lap) but maintenance in the *transitive* (inlaut, by generalization of the [tɔ̄] ≠ [tī] distinction rescued from d-lap by dint of being medial), SM shows the opposite pattern, partially maintaining 2ms ≠

2fs distinctivity in the *intransitive* (putting certain SM-specific quirks aside, by 2ms <-Th> t[-tα] ~ ,<-T> t[-t], 2fs <-Ty> t[-ti] ~ <-T> t[-t]) but totally neutralizing the distinction in the *transitive* (by generalizing reflexes of originally 2ms *tå̊, not through sound change but apparently through primary syncretism; §16 with chart (16J)—syncretism (f)). Two additional observations: (*) SR also maintains 2ms ≠ 2fs *orthographically*, via morphophonemic-historical spelling: <-T> ≠ <-Ty> disambiguating [-t] by directly representing /-ta/ ≠ /-ti/ (<-T> ≠ <-Ty>, respectively—the morphophonemic function) as well as *-tā ≠ /-tī/ (<-T> ≠ <-Ty>, respectively—the historical function). (*) The generalized reflexes of originally 2ms *tå̊ medially in SM may bespeak synchronic restructuring of (the reflexes of) *a* as a bridge vowel. For more varieties of 2ms ≠ 2fs disposition across several other dialects, see discussion and charting of syncretism (f) in §16.

[22] (a) A point arguably in favor of *-tu* as preferable to the *-t* of this book is that only the latter would appear to engender canonical difficulties in the pre-bridge period for transitive verbs containing strong 3√ + 1s + obj by creating an impermissible CCC sequence—e.g., 1s^2fs *QaSáMtkī*—while the traditional reconstruction entails no such discomfort—*QaSaMtúkī*. Notwithstanding, the position of this book is that the like of *QaSáMtkī* was automatically ameliorated by repair-strategic excrescence, which furthermore triggered early bridge formation: *QaSáMtkī* → *QaSáMtə̆kī* → *QaSaMtíkī* (§2.3.2.1(α)). (b) For arguments against interpreting Akkadian-spelled <-tu> in the Aramaic Erech incantation as [-tu], see Gordon 1940: 33f.

[23] Other processes affecting reflexes of 1s *t* include: ayd, creating allomorph *-Ay*, §17.2; and mtr, creating allomorph *-ī* from epenthesized *-IT*, *§17.12*.

[24] For proclitic *wa > å̊* by lco, see §12.2 TR (δ).

[25] "only untrammedly in inlaut"; traces of at least *-ū* may remain in auslaut in defective verbs, but ordinarily in more or less disguised form: e.g., *QaSáyū* e-cnd^coa > TR [Qš̆Ső], e-cnd^mvh > SR [Qš̆Sów], where erstwhile *-ū* betrays itself by auslaut labiality differing from the original *-ū* in the specifics of its manifestation. (On the other hand, transparentized shapes like [Qš̆Sű] do occasionally occur (§15.3.2).)

[26] Other processes affecting 3p reflexes include: mtr, accordionwise lopping off nasal auslaut earlier imported by hii, e.g., 3mp *-ū* hii> *-Ůn* mtr> *-ū*,§17.12; pin, replacing finite suffixal vowels with participial analogs, e.g., *Ů > Ĭ*, §17.17; i-lap, de facto infixing original suffixal *ū*, §17.9.

[27] There is some faint evidence from SM that at least the original auslaut vowel of 2fp was ancipital, *-tinna* ~ *-tinnā*; see §7.2(δ) SM.

[28] At least G occasionally extends fma to stems, including 3√ of a few verbs, e.g., <?yPrsn> 'it was divulged' (if built on √prsm, Kutscher 1976:59), <ṭ9n> 'to taste' (ib 102).

[29] Another process affecting 2p reflexes is mtr, whereby *-tV̊n > -tV̄*; §17.12.

[30] (a) Pace Margolis, who interprets <-nw> as a[-nō], e.g., a[?iš̆tə̆mōða9nő̆hī] 'we identified him' (Mar 120*), a[ḥaxarnóah] 'we gave her in rent' (Mar113*) ([oa] ←ptg *ō* /__h# (<sap *-ha)). (b) Other processes affecting 1p reflexes include: nae, whereby *-nā* is replaced by *-nan*, §7.2(δ) n. 11, and arp, introducing palatal allomorphs (e.g., M *-nīn*), §17.1.

[31] In several dialects, object suffixes at large develop *T*-bearing allos (by tom, §17.30).

[32] Observe that ptg (§17.16) stalls /__H# in all and only instances of the suffix complex [-ě̂h] <l-anc <mid <uap/sap *-íhV̊, i.e., @[-éah] is never forthcoming, neither in B nor in the other dialects generally undergoing ptg; note, e.g., TL a[qaṭlě̂h] (Mar 159*), impf y[tiqṭə̌rě̂h] (Mor 381). Contrast with cases like these the like of B [réaḥ] 'Duft' (BL 39) and, with the selfsame morphemic instantiation as /__h in manqué [-ě̂h], TL a[ḫǎxarnóah] (n. 30 above), y[ʔæqrīnúæh] (§2.3.4.3 1p). Especially forms like the latter are telling, closing the door as they do on the possibility that ptg requires /__ √H#, a stratagem that works (but how realistically?) for Hebrew; THP 67. In fact, the notable failure of this specific morphological object to participate in guttural-on-vowel assimilation is probably of even longer-standing vintage if l-anc postdates *lowering* (§17.10), whereby we should expect -íh > -áh l-anc> -ǎ́h > [-ɔ̌h], a result as little forthcoming as [-éah]. No matter how ingeniously brainstormed over more than a century of scientific Semitics, A [-ě̂h] retains mysteries.

[33] Derivations showing this are set forth in (a). (Observe that, in light of (a), it would appear the V̊hV̊# / V̄hV̄# preference came into force at a time when at least the surface (phonetic-level) realization of this pair of strings was [V̊h#]/[V̄hV̄#].)

(a)

	-a 3√ y-a-hi	(-3√ C-)i-hi
e-anc	-ayahi ~ -ayahī	-ihi ~ -ihī
e-cnd	-āhi ~ -āhī	
sap	-āh ~ -āhī	-ih ~ -ihī
PREFERENCE		
ACTIVATED	-āhī	-ih
mid		-ēh
l-anc		-ēh
	[-ɔ̌hī]	[-ēh]

[34] (a) Margolis interprets [gɔ̄raštéx] as Hebrew, which would explain 2ʃ [a] (THP 69f). Morag is silent here on the analogous 2ʃ [æ] in [sækkæntî́x], and concerning another instance in the same lexeme ([sækkæntû̃n]) limits himself to mentioning that this is the only case he's aware of in TL of miškal *QaSSaM* with *M* ≠ [+low] (Mor 147 n. 124). Since int √skn also occurs in (post-Biblical) Hebrew, it is possible Margolis's surmise might apply here as well. However, since the other particulars of both forms are decidedly Aramaic (Hebrew would show c[gḗrɔštî́x], c[sikkantî́x], c[sikkantém]), a more plausible explanation might be (lexical) retention of pre-Aramaic *2ʃa (cf. Arabic *QaSSaM*). (b) Observe that hap variably drops auslaut 3s *h* in some dialects (categorically in M); §9.2.2.

[35] However, weighing against the energic interpretation for at least TL is the vowel length in y[pær9î́n] rather than expected @[pær9ě̃n] (mid, §17.ll.3). (While Morag's transcription does not directly indicate vowel length (§22.2), in this specific context the color clinches the interpretation as long (failure of mid).)

[36] Three dialects, CP, SM, and G, at times show a 1s object suffix of shape -í; see ndr, §17.13.

[37] In fact, the canonical similarity may have been actually once greater than that of the forms as reconstructed in §2.2; e.g., 2fp *-kin could have been *-kinna (cf. subject *-tinna). However, lack of alternations makes postulation of such extra convergence risky.

[38] The *n*-less B variant [himmṓ], found in the book of Ezra, is problematic. What made for loss of *-*n*, given that mtr (§17.12) is otherwise unattested in B?

[39] (a) The shortness of the *a*-color bridge is also supported by B <howða9:tɛnɔʔ>'du hast uns kund getan' (Dan 2:23), pace Brockelmann's interpretation as long [ɛ̄] (1908: 256). Bauer and Leander correctly take the vowel to be short [ɛ] on the basis of the Bab variant <howDæ9tænɑ>; moreover, interpretation as [ɛ] is typologically and perhaps genetically supported by the similar case of Hebrew $aC\overset{\circ}{\jmath} \rightarrow \varepsilon C\overset{\circ}{\jmath}$, formulable as Midding Umlaut (THP 81f). This would make the B case another instance of minor vowel harmony (§2.3.2.1(α) n. 5). (b) The fact that Margolis represents the 2ʃ of the TL forms as [ŭ] in (his rarely used) Roman transcription rather than as Tiberian <ɔ̆> (in accord with his general practice) supports the call for caution against too narrow a phonetic interpretation of his transcriptions (§22.2).

3. Geminate Formation (gmf)

3.1. The Autosegmental Framework to Be Assumed

The fundamental idea to be developed here is a theoretically updated version of a hypothesis of some venerability within Semitics: that the peculiarities in the formation of geminate verbs derives from the misfit between biconsonantal roots and the triconsonantal templates into which those roots are inserted during the formation of stems (miškalim)—a misfit likely to have arisen from lagging overlap of the ancient Afroasiatic biradical pattern onto the innovative Semitic mold of triradical size.

In terms of the branch of phonology called *autosegmentalism* (§23.4), it has become customary since the pioneering work of John McCarthy(1979) to explicate the formal interweaving of the Semitic root and scheme into three partially independent components: the so-called *melodic* tiers, one for consonantal roots and the other for vocalic schemes, associated to a so-called *skeletal* tier consisting of an ordered sequence of consonantal and vocalic positions normally devoid of other content. Prefixes and suffixes differ from these *internal-flective* staminal arrays in that they comprise only one melodic tier rather than two. Thus, at the earliest level prior to final synthesis, pA impf sim 3mp **yaQSuMūna* might look something like (3A):

(3A) y   Q S M   u   n   a

    C   + V C C V C   +   V V C V

             a   u

Synthesis is then completed with *association* (3B), and possibly *tier conflation* (3C). (Note the one-to-two melody-to-skeleton explication of long segments, here suffixal *ū.*)

(3B) y   Q S M   u   n a

    C   + V C C V C   +   V V C V

             a   u

(3C) y a Q S u M ū n a

44

Since the autosegmental derivation of prefixes and suffixes is usually perfunctory, perhaps always so in Aramaic, in what follows and passim arrays like those in (3A) and (3B) will be presented as in (3D):[1]

(3D)

```
        Q S M                          Q S M
        | |  \                         | |  \
y + V C C V C + ū n a     y + V C C V C + ū n a
            |                         \   |
          a u                          a u
```

Preliminary to discussion of the geminates, composite associated representations of the plain and rmp pA binyanim for the strong verb will be given in (3E). For simplicity, passives are omitted and no suffixes are included:

(3E) (i) **sim** pf

```
          Q  S  M
         /   |   \
        C V C V C     (⇒  ⎛QaSaM⎞ )
          \   /            ⎨QaSiM⎬
          a ⎛a⎫            ⎝QaSuM⎠
            ⎨i⎬
            ⎩u⎭
```

impa[2]

```
          Q  S  M
         /   |   \
        C V̌ C V C     (⇒  QǎSuM)
          \   |            QǎSiM
        ⎧a⎫⎛u⎞            QǐSaM
        ⎨ ⎬⎜i⎟
        ⎩i⎭⎝a⎠
```

impf[2]

```
           Q  S  M
           |  |   \
 ⎛y⎞- V C C V C     (⇒  ⎛CaQSuM⎞ )
 ⎜t⎟      |  /            ⎨CaQSiM⎬
 ⎨?⎬    ⎛a⎫⎛u⎞            ⎝CiQSaM⎠
 ⎝n⎠    ⎨i⎬⎜i⎟
        ⎩ ⎭⎝a⎠
```

(ii) sim rmp <u>pf, impa</u>

$$
\begin{array}{c}
\text{Q S M} \\
\diagup\ |\ \diagdown
\end{array}
$$

h-it　+　C V C V C　　　($\Rightarrow$ hitQaSiM)

　　　　　| |

　　　　　a i

<u>impf</u>

$$
\begin{array}{c}
\text{Q S M} \\
\diagup\ |\ \diagdown
\end{array}
$$

$\left\{\begin{array}{c} y \\ t \\ ? \\ n \end{array}\right\}$ -it +　C V C V C　　　($\Rightarrow$ CitQaSiM)

　　　　　　　| |

　　　　　　　a i

(iii) int <u>pf, impa</u>

$$
\begin{array}{c}
\text{Q S M} \\
\diagup\ \wedge\ \diagdown
\end{array}
$$

C V C′ C′ V C　($\Rightarrow$ QaSSiM)

　　 |　　 |

　　 a　　 i

<u>impf</u>

$$
\begin{array}{c}
\text{Q S M} \\
\diagup\ \wedge\ \diagdown
\end{array}
$$

$\left\{\begin{array}{c} y \\ t \\ ? \\ n \end{array}\right\}$ -i +　C V C′ C′ V C　($\Rightarrow$ CiQaSSiM)

　　　　　　 |　　 |

　　　　　　 a　　 i

(iv) int rmp <u>pf, impa</u>

$$
\begin{array}{c}
\text{Q S M} \\
\diagup\ \wedge\ \diagdown
\end{array}
$$

h-it +　　C V C′ C′ V C ($\Rightarrow$ hitQaSSaM)

　　　　　　　　　\diagdown_____\diagup

　　　　　　　　　　　 a

impf

$$\left\{\begin{array}{c} y \\ t \\ ? \\ n \end{array}\right\}\text{-it} + \overset{\displaystyle \text{Q S M}}{\text{C V C' C' V C}} \quad (\Rightarrow \ \text{CitQaSSiM})$$

a

(v) cau pf, impa

$$\text{h} + \overset{\displaystyle \text{Q S M}}{\text{V C C V C}} \quad (\Rightarrow \ \text{haQSiM})$$

a   i

impf

$$\left\{\begin{array}{c} y \\ t \\ ? \\ n \end{array}\right\} + \overset{\displaystyle \text{Q S M}}{\text{V C C V C}} \quad (\Rightarrow \ \text{CiQaSSiM})$$

a   i

(v) cau rmp pf, impa

$$\text{h -it} + \text{h} + \overset{\displaystyle \text{Q S M}}{\text{V C C V C}} \quad (\Rightarrow \ \text{hithaQSaM})$$

a

impf

$$\left\{\begin{array}{c} y \\ t \\ ? \\ n \end{array}\right\} \text{- it - h} + \overset{\displaystyle \text{Q S M}}{\text{V C C V C}} \quad (\Rightarrow \ \text{CithaQSaM})$$

a

Hitherto, association between the elements of the melodic and skeletal tiers has gone unexplained. It is conventional to assume some sort of simple algorithm to do the job; and in the case of Aramaic this might in the normal (unmarked) case be assumed to be front-to-back association, one melody to one skeletal position unless one-to-many association is forced in order to complete an exhaustive coupling or in order to fulfill some other requirement. Thus, in the sim rmp pf, Q, S, and M associate to the first, second, and third Cs in that order, while a and i lock onto the first and second Vs, respectively; but in the int rmp pf, S must associate to both Cs in order to fulfill the requirement that $C' = C'$, and a must join to both Vs for the sake of exhaustive coupling.

Now to the geminate verb, for which the same skeletal and melodic tiers are assumed as for the strong verb but which differ from the latter in fielding biconsonantal roots. This difference in turn evokes various subsidiary principles and constraints, some of them needed independently. These include:

(3F)(i)   *Direction of association:* though front-to-back is preferred (unmarked), back-to-front is permissible if forced by various circumstances (marked).[3]

(ii)   *Antiwedging* (Malone 1999): when one radical associates to two Cs flanking a V, either the V may be *extruded* (unmarked option) or the radical may undergo *meiosis* (marked option).

(iii) *Constraint:* the sequence $1 \sqrt{C} V 1 \sqrt{C}$ is prohibited.

(iv)   *Constraint:* the sequence $3 \sqrt{C} V 3 \sqrt{C}$ is preferred (or perhaps mandatory) in the sim rmp but elsewhere dispreferred (marked).

(v)   *Constraint:* extrusion ((ii) above) is disallowed if a sequence CCC would result.

(vi)   *Special color copy* (scc): an extruded $2ʃ$ in the rmp or sim impa imparts its color to $1ʃ$.

(vii) *Degemination* (deg): $C'C'$ reduces to C' immediately preceding a consonant (/__C) or in auslaut (/__#) (also, irrelevantly to geminate verbs, perhaps occasionally /V̄__; see §7.7 n. 33, §17.15.1(α)).

Procedures (i)–(iv) are inextricably involved in word-building and, hence, in a standard generative-phonological model (§23.1) are taken to precede (and inform) the phonological level of representation (/   /); cf. the morphological rules of THP (chapter 7). In a Lexical-Phonological model (§23.3), (i)–(iv) would form part of the word-building operations (wrb) of the initial stratum. Procedure (vii), degemination (deg), being the only operation to require context exterior to the constituents being built (/__#, /__(suffixal) C), operates posterior to the phonological level. One other postphonological operation will be seen to play an intimate role in geminate formation: *promotion* (prm) of closed-syllabic $V̆$ to $V̊$ (§14.1).

3.2. The Autosegmental Structure of Geminates

Consider now how the unmarked geminate sim pf is formed:

(3G) **gmf-lu**   (α)   Q   M

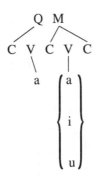

(β) front-to-back association (with spreading for the sake of exhaustive coupling) (3Fi):

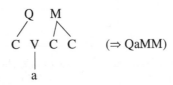

(γ) extrusion of wedged-in *V* (3Fii):

$$
\begin{array}{c}
\text{Q} \quad \text{M} \\
\diagup \quad \wedge \\
\text{C} \;\; \text{V} \;\; \text{C} \;\; \text{C} \quad\quad (\Rightarrow \text{QaMM}) \\
| \\
\text{a}
\end{array}
$$

A marked geminate of the sim pf replaces extrusion with meiosis (3Fii), making for results canonically similar to the strong verb (3Ei):

(3H) **gmf-lm**

$$\text{Q M} \quad\quad\quad \text{Q M M}$$

C V C V C $\Rightarrow$ C V C V C $(\Rightarrow$ $\left\{\begin{array}{l}\text{QaMaM}\\\text{QaMiM}\\\text{QaMuM}\end{array}\right\})$

with associations: first structure has Q linked over C V, M over C V C; melody a under second V, and set $\{a, i, u\}$; second structure Q over C V, M M over C V C.

Derivation of the sim impa proceeds in parallel fashion, with the special twist that the extruded *V* imparts its color to the *V̆* (3Fvi) and the closed-syllabic *V̆* promotes to *V̊* (§14.1):

(3I) **gmf-2u**

$$\text{Q M} \quad\quad\quad \text{Q M}$$

C V̆ C V C $\Rightarrow$ C V C C $(\Rightarrow$ $\left\{\begin{array}{l}\text{QuMM}\\\text{QiMM}\\\text{QuMM}\end{array}\right\})$

melody: $\left\{\begin{array}{l}a\\i\end{array}\right\}$ and $\left\{\begin{array}{l}u\\i\\a\end{array}\right\}$; second: $\left\{\begin{array}{l}u\\i\\\alpha\end{array}\right\}$

(3J) **gmf-2m**

$$\text{Q M}$$

C V̊ C V C $(\Rightarrow$ $\left\{\begin{array}{l}\text{QăMuM}\\\text{QăMiM}\\\text{QĭMaM}\end{array}\right\})$

melody: $\left\{\begin{array}{l}a\\i\end{array}\right\}$ and $\left\{\begin{array}{l}u\\i\\a\end{array}\right\}$

Notice that marked-unmarked status of the choices in (3G-J) coinvolves constraint (3Fiv), in that *3 √C V 3 √C* = MVM is generally dispreferred. However, the marking status is reversed in the sim rmp, so that there extrusion is a rare option—and when it is allowed, it may be preceded by ssc (3Fvi) copying the color of 2ʃ onto 1ʃ:[4]

(3K) **gmf-3u**

```
        Q   M                           Q   M   M
       ╱   ╱‾                          ╱   │   ╲
 - it + C  V  C  V  C  meiosis ⇒  - it  C  V  C  V  C  (⇒ itQaMiM)
          │     │                          │     │
          a     i                          a     i
```

(3L) **gmf-3m**

```
        Q   M                           Q   M   M
       ╱   ╱‾                          ╱   │   ╲
 - it + C  V  C  V  C  scc    ⇒  - it  C  V  C  V  C  extrusion ⇒
          │     │                          │     │
          a     i                          a     i
```

```
              Q   M
             ╱   ╱╲
 - it + C  V  C  C   ( ⇒ itQiMM)
          │
          i
```

The type-wise most widespread geminate resolution, affecting not only the sim impf but the entire cau system as well, preferentially avoids violation of constraint (3Fiv) by reversing the direction of association from front-to-back to back-to-front:[5]

(3M) **gmf-4u**

```
              Q     M
             ╱╲     ╲
```

$$\begin{Bmatrix} y \\ t \\ ? \\ n \end{Bmatrix} - V\ C\ C\ V\ C\ (\Rightarrow \begin{Bmatrix} \text{CaQQuM} \\ \text{CaQQiM} \\ \text{CiQQaM} \end{Bmatrix} \text{; and for the cau plain, -aQQiM,)}$$

with middle columns $\begin{Bmatrix} a \\ i \end{Bmatrix}$ $\begin{Bmatrix} u \\ i \\ a \end{Bmatrix}$ and for the cau rmp, -ithaQQaM

The corresponding marked pattern assumes the usual front-to-back mapping but incurs violation of constraint (3Fiv)—though in this case mitigated by the fact that such violation is in effect mandated to avoid violating absolute constraint (3Fv). This formation, like (3H), results in canonical similarity to the strong verb:

(3N) **gmf-4m**   Q   M

$$\begin{Bmatrix} y \\ t \\ ? \\ n \end{Bmatrix} - V \quad C \quad C \quad V \quad C \; (\Rightarrow \begin{Bmatrix} CaQMuM \\ CaQMiM \\ CiQMaM \end{Bmatrix}$$

with $\begin{Bmatrix} a \\ i \end{Bmatrix}$ under the first V, $\begin{Bmatrix} u \\ i \\ a \end{Bmatrix}$ under the second V

; and for the cau plain)

-aQMiM, for the cau rmp,

-ithasQMiM

The int system evinces one common resolution: front-to-back association with extrusion prohibited by constraint (3Fv):

(3P) **gmf-5**   Q   M

$$C \quad V \quad C' \quad C' \quad V \quad C \; (\Rightarrow \quad \text{plain QaMMiM, rmp -itQaMMaM,})$$

with a under the first V, $\begin{Bmatrix} i\ (\text{plain}) \\ a\ (\text{rmp}) \end{Bmatrix}$ under the second V

addition of impf prefixes not affecting

the disposition of the miškalim

There is one more set of rather different possibilities for mapping geminates, gmf-6, to be considered (in §3.4) after first looking at examples of gmf-1-5 across the dialects. But preliminary to this, we should briefly consider gmf-1-5 in phonetic context at the time they emerged. Since by hypothesis most of the Aramaic changes studied in this book had not yet arisen, the bare-stem type examples used in the exposition throughout the preceding pages would in most cases be unaffected by the specific trappings of concrete morphophonological settings. Two systematic exceptions to this generally correct prediction involve forms of the simple geminate verb falling prey to degemination (3Fvii), to wit: pf forms with suffixes beginning in a consonant, e.g., 2ms *-ta* or 1s *-t* added to gmf-1u-built (3G) *QaMM, QaMMt(a)* → *QaMt(a)*; and suffixless (hence ms) impa forms built by gmf-2u (3I), *QuMM* → *QuM*.[6]

3.3. The Individual Dialects

Y̲. <wPŝŝ> 'und er abrogierte' (DR I 215:8): *either* (unmarked) int [wapaššíša] *or* marked sim [wapašáša] (gmf-1m); <Tḥq> 'du sollst schreiben' (DR I 214:34): unmarked sim [taḥúqqi] (gmf-4u).

Q̲. <ysB> 'er umringt' (De 72): unmarked sim [yassúbi] (gmf-4u); <ymll> 'er redet' (De 73): int [yimallíli] (gmf-5).

I. <9lw>, <9l>, <9lT> 'sie sind, er ist, ich bin eingetreten' (L 66): unmarked sim's [9állū], [9ál] (< *9álla* by sap^deg, §17.22, (3Fvii)), [9allIθ] (< *9ált*, note 6) (all three forms by gmf-1u)[7], <Gzh> 'schere sie!' (lc) [gUzzǎh] ← *gǎzuz-ǎh* (gmf-2u), <Tmr> 'du magst bitter sein' (lc) [timmár]; cau <hn9lT> 'ich habe hereingebracht' (lc) [han9ǎléθ] <gds(§17.8) *ha99ǎlíθ* (gmf-4u), cau <hGŝŝ> 'er hat ausspioniert' (L 67) [haγšéš] (gmf-4m); int <TrGG> 'du magst begehren' (L66) [tǎraggéγ] (gmf-5).

B. sim pf 3fs [9alláθ] (gmf-1u), but the kětiv form to this kěrey shape is spelled <9llT> suggesting gmf-1m-derived [9alǎláθ] (or perhaps transparentized [9ǎlaláθ]—cf. [bǎṭeláθ] (§15.2.1.1)—or barytone [9ǎlálaθ]) (BL 167), sim impa mp [góddu] (lc) (gmf-2u) with [ó] ← *ú* by mid (§17.11); cau pf 3mp [haddíqu] (gmf-4u) (BL 168), cau pf 3ms [han9él] (lc) (gmf-4u, [n9] <gds(§17.8) *99*), [taṭlél] (gmf-4m) (lc); int impf 3ms [yǎmallíl] (gmf-5) (BL 167). See also note 5.

P. int pf 3ms <ṭll> (HC 368) [ṭallél] (gmf-5); cau pf 3ms^3ms <ʔBrh> (HC 350) [ʔabbǎréh] (gmf-4u).

N. Poorly and questionably attested (Cg 81), but perhaps sim rmp impf 3ms <yTPṣ> (gmf-3m); int rmp impf 3ms <yTPṣṣ> (gmf-5).

TR. [9ǽlliθ] 'ich trat ein' (Da 330—cf. §6 n. 1) (gmf-1u), [9ól] 'komm herein!' (Da 331) (gmf-2u), [tibbóz] 'du wirst berauben' (Da 330) (gmf-4u); sim rmp pf 3ms [ʔiθnǎsés] (Da 333) (gmf-3u); int [ḥælléliθ] 'ich bohrte' (Da 332) (gmf-5).

CP. <9lTwn> ~ <9llTwn> ~ later form <9lḷTwn> 'ihr tratet ein' (Sg 68) [9altÚn] (gmf-1u) ~ [9ǎlaltÚn] ~ [9ǎlIItÚn] (2 [I] by att, §12) (gmf-1m), <9wlw> 'tretet ein!' (Sg 69) [9Úllū] (gmf-2u), <Tqwṣ> 'du versprichst' (Sg 68) [tIqqÚṣ] (gmf-4u); sim rmp <ʔTBzz> 'wurde geplundert' (Sg 69) [Iθbǎzéz] (gmf-3u); cau <ʔṭl> ~ later <ʔṭll> 'beschattete' (lc) [aṭṭél] (gmf-4u) ~ [aṭlél] (gmf-4m); <ml(y)l> 'locutus est' (Sl 111) [mallél] (gmf-5).

Both by Schulthess's explicit notations ("später") and in the observation that, e.g., the variant [9ǎlIItÚn] by its 2ʃ [I] manifests CP's growing penchant for palatal vocalism, we may conclude that CP gradually came to prefer the strong-like pattern of geminate formation (gmf-m) over the original sui generis shapes (gmf-u).

SM. <9(ʔ)l> t[9ál] ~ <9ll> t[9å̤lal] 'kam herein' (Macs 197) (gmf-1u ~ 1m), <9lw> T[9ǽllu] ~ <9llw> t[9ē̤lå̤lu] 'kommet!'(Macs 199) (gmf-2u ~ 2m),

<Tqṣ> t[tíqqɑṣ] 'wirst abschneiden', <yrTT> t[yírtɑt] 'wird zittern' (Macs 197) (gmf-4u ~ 4m); int <Gšš> t[gǽššəš] 'rang' (Macs 200) (gmf-5).

Macuch (Macs 197) explicitly recognizes the SM penchant for the strong-like pattern (gmf-m).

G. <9lyT> ~ <9llyT> 'ich ging herein' (Da 330) (gmf-1u ~ 1m), sim impa fs <rwqy> ~ <rwqqyn> (Da 331) (gmf-2u ~ 2m), <Ty9wl> 'sie geht hinein' (Da gmf-4u), <Tṣnn> 'sie wird kalt' (lc) (gmf-4m); sim rmp <ʾyTšys> 'wurde schwach' (Da 333) (gmf-3u); int <qlyl> 'er erleichterte' (Da 332) (gmf-5).

To judge by the relative frequency of Dalman's examples, gmf-u is the pattern of preference in G.

SR. [pɛkkḗθ] 'ich zerschlug' (Ns 123) (gmf-1u), [bóz] 'beraube!' (lc) (gmf-2u); sim rmp [ɛθbǎzɛ́z] 'wurde beraubt' (lc) (gmf-3u); int [mallɛ́l] 'spoke' (Payne Smith 1903: 273) (gmf-5).

TL. <rqh> ~ <rqqh> 'she spit' (Mar 49) (gmf-1u ~ 1m), <Dwq> 'grind!' (lc) (gmf-2u), <lG(w)zw> ~ <lGzzw> 'they'll cut' (lc) (gmf-4u ~ 4m); int <ḥDD> 'whet!' (Mar 48) (gmf-5).

M. <pasat> t[pássat] 'she destroyed' (Macm 145) (gmf-1u), <hup> 'lava!' (Macm 318) (gmf-2u), <nimuk> 'graditur' (Macm 316) (gmf-4u); sim rmp <et(i)psis> ~ <etpis> t[étpes] 'he was destroyed' (Macm 145) (gmf-3u ~ 3m); int <malil> 'he spoke' (Macm 461) (gmf-5).

3.4. Some Special Cases

Though metaplasm back and forth across the various weak gĕzarot is endemic to Aramaic (and more generally Semitic at large), at times especially salient concentrations might suggest the agency of a specific mechanism. A case in point may be the frequent assumption of defective-like shapes by originally geminate roots in TL (Mor 233, Mar 49). This phenomenon might be accounted for by a rather natural extension of the apparatus already adopted for the garden varieties of geminate verb in A (gmf-1 – gmf-5).

One aspect of that account, an aspect shared by much contemporary generative theorizing, is its *parametric* nature: that is, formulation of the relevant processes at least in part in terms of binary choices (*settings*) along certain dimensions of variation (*parameters*). Specifically, the system adopted involves hierarchical interaction between the parameters of spreading and extrusion, where the latter is subject to either a positive setting (extrusion takes place: gmf-1u, -2u, -3m, -4u) or a negative setting (extrusion fails to take place: gmf-1m, -2m, -3u, -4m). But what now if the other parameter, spreading, should also be subject to binary setting? To see this, let us return to the initial auto-segmental complex presented under gmf-1u, (3G(α)):

(3Q) [= (3G(α))]   Q   M

$$\text{C V C V C}$$

$$a \quad \begin{Bmatrix} a \\ i \\ u \end{Bmatrix}$$

If we follow the usual procedure—e.g., front-to-back association—but fail to spread (negative setting on the spreading parameter), we will derive this result:

(3R)

$$\begin{array}{c} Q \quad M \\ \diagup \quad \diagup \\ \text{C V C V C} \\ \mid \quad\quad \mid \\ a \quad\quad \begin{Bmatrix} a \\ i \\ u \end{Bmatrix} \end{array}$$

If we assume, as we probably must, that the Aramaic verb demands full as-sociation, and yet the negative setting for spreading has left the job undone, we might explore the possibility that the job is completed by some *designated filler* chosen on the positive setting of a *filling* parameter. Since we will have occasion to observe that /ay/ may function as inert material elsewhere in A verb morphophonology (notably as a *quasi-inert string*, §15.3.2), let us desig-nate the filler as /y/, which then, in guise of a sort of 3√y ersatz, proceeds to trigger neutralization of any 2ʃ i or 2ʃ u to 2ʃ a, as commonly throughout the A verb (§8.1.1 with n. 1):

(3Q) [= (3G(α))]

$$\begin{array}{c} Q \quad M \quad y \\ \diagup \quad \mid \quad \diagdown \\ \text{C V C V C} \quad (\Rightarrow \text{QaMay}) \\ \mid \quad\quad \mid \\ a \quad\quad a \end{array}$$

—an operation that effectively metaplasticizes a geminate verb to a defective.

A case in point, given by Margolis orthographically (Mar 49) and fleshed out by Morag in Yemeni trad pron (Mor 370), is *√mṣ <mṣyT> y[mə̆ṣé̄θ] 'you sucked', structurally indistinguishable from an original defective like *√ḥzy <ḥzyT> y[ḥə̆zé̄θ] 'you saw' (Mor 253).

This sort of association-cum-filling may accordingly be formulated as a sixth way of reconciling the pristine clash of biconsonantal root and triconsonantal skeleton, de facto metaplasm to the defective gizra:[8]

(3Q–S) = gmf-6

Notes to §3

[1] The status of tier conflation is questionable (Malone 1989a). It is possible that phonological reality is accurately enough modeled by associated tiers alone (3B)—if amplified by various constructs suppressed here (prosodic scaffolding, feature geometry, etc.; §23.5, §23.3)—and that presumed conflated representations (3C) take too seriously the conventions of linear alphabetic orthography. Should tier conflation, however, correspond to a genuine linguistic operation, it must occur late enough in a derivation to accommodate processes and constraints whose proper operation or registration presuppose *non*conflated tiers: e.g., epenthesis vis-à-vis Geminate Integrity (§5.1 n. 1). It will in any event be the expository practice of this book to represent cenematic (= phonetic/phonological) strings *as if* tier conflation has taken place, unless specific aspects of interaction between tiers are focal to the discussion.

[2] Recall that in the imp system selection of 1ʃ ({a, i}) is constrained by ablaut in terms of 2 ({u, i, a}); see §1 n. 5.

[3] Recent work (on African tone languages) suggests that stipulated directional mapping of this sort may be epiphenomenal; see Zoll 2003. However, study of the proposal relative to issues other than tonal mapping remains for the future.

[4] For an instance of the marked option in a dialect not treated in this book, cf. <yTBz> 'wird geraucht' from the Palestinian Targum (Da 334); but see also entries under N and M below.

[5] The corresponding Hebrew pattern gives *CaQuMM, CaQiMM, CiQaMM*, which at first glance appears to involve a simple reversal of associational direction, back-to-front, so that *M* spreads to the last two *C*s of *CCVC*. But, unlike front-to-back results under (3G, I, K), the expected pattern cannot be derived, because *CCVC* lacks a vowel between the first two *C*s. Hence, despite intriguing similarity between A *QQVM* and Hebrew *QVMM*, the two do not easily lend themselves to parallel autosegmental formulation. In THP, the Hebrew pattern is explicated by metathesis (50f). (Occasionally one finds a Hebrew-like formation in Aramaic: e.g., B cau labial passive <huʷ9aluw>, which Bauer and Leander consider to be an instance of Hebrew-based Schematisierung (BL 167). If solely (3M) were at work, we should expect [hů9álū], with degemination of 9 (by mls, §9.3.1).

[6] The Aramaic dialects tend to shun consonant clusters under a variety of circumstances (§20.1, §23.5): biconsonantal groups initially and finally, and sometimes immediately preceding a reduced vowel—perhaps because V̆, qua "inert element" (Malone 1995), is too weak to prevent the *CC* from bonding over V̆ with the next following *C*, making for the equivalent of *CCC*; and triconsonantal groups are categorically avoided.

Various mechanisms have developed as repair strategies to preempt or undo the formation of such groups in the course of morphological building (e.g., affixation) as incidental byproducts of phonetic-phonological processes. We have already encountered a few of these mechanisms and will have occasion to see others in the course of the book: for instance, *prothesis* and *epenthesis* in reaction to initial and final CC, respectively (§17.8, §17.6); *simplification* in response to $C'C'$ in $C'C'\check{\partial}C$ (§17.26); *excrescence* to break up CCC—and occasionally CC as well (§2.3.2.1(α), §4.3). It may immediately be seen that (v) and (vii) of (3F) also fit in here. Both constraints deal with CCC, though under different conditions: while (v) *prevents* $C'C'VC'$ from becoming $C'C'C'$ (by extrusion), (vii) *dispels* an already formed $C'C'C$ by degemination to $C'C$. Then (vii) also deals with auslaut $C'C'$, degeminationg it to C'.

This in turn brings up the issue of possible mechanism overlap. For instance, if $C'C'C$ may be dispelled either by degemination ($\rightarrow C'C$) or by excrescence ($\rightarrow C'C'\check{\partial}C$), what decides which is to operate in a given case? Since the procedures and constraints of (3F) are posited as foundational to the formation of geminate verbs, all else being equal they should be assumed to operate at or adjacent to the deepest (earliest) levels of the phonology synchronically, subject only to the considerations discussed at the end of §3.1, and diachronically to remain in place unscathed in default of any mutation, such as rule reordering, disturbing that state. Thus, on this basis, constraints (v) and (vii) should be expected to enjoy applicational priority over other, more general operations like excrescence. This much said, however, it appears we do have to deal with one order-disrupting mutation of the type indicated. To see this in perspective, let us first consider a likely hypothesis on the origins of sim forms like impa ms *QuM, pf 2ms *$QaMta$, pf 1s *$QaMt$—and on why the latter should then have epenthesized (§17.6) to $QaMMit$ rather than to phonetically expected @$QaMit$.

As we have seen, it is the position of this book that the traditionally labeled geminate roots were originally *bi*radical; and that gemination of either the initial of these two radicals (as by gmf-4u, (3M)) or the final (as by gmf-1u, (3G)) is part of a diachronic-typological strategy to assimilate the biradicals to the innovative Semitic canon of *tri*radicality. However, as we have also seen, not *all* Aramaic "geminate" forms are triradical on the surface. For instance, in the simple verb impa ms *[QuM], pf 2ms *[QaMta], and pf 1s *[QaMt] are phonetically biradical—and have presumably *remained* phonetically biradical right along, having resisted the forces that reshaped most of their homoparadigmatic congeners into triradical canons (e.g., impa *[QuMMū]). What accounts for the resistance of such as *[QuM], *[QaMta], *[QaMt] to conform to the new phonetic norm? Presumably it is the countervailing pressure of the specific phonetic context involved in forms like these—in particular, the auditory-perceptual difficulty of lengthening (geminating) consonants other than prevocalically. And the resistance of such formations to phonetic gemination is codified in degemination (3Fvii).

The overall developmental nexus is synoptized in the trajectories of (a) below, which are moreover designed to provide an answer to the question raised earlier: when epenthesis (§17.6) came along, why did it reshape *$QaMt$ to *$QaMMit$, rather than to *$QaMit$, as would be expected on a straightforward phonetic basis?

At pre-Aramaic (and possibly pre-Semitic) stage I, it is speculated that biradical roots were mapped to biconsonantal templates (skeletons). Other aspects of the three formations dealt with are intentionally modeled as close to later Aramaic as possible, in default of any clear evidence to the contrary (from comparative Afroasiatic). Observe that the sim impa was presumably structured at this time like a handful of proto-Semitic nouns sometimes assumed to have been biradical with reduced schematic, like *bə̆n* 'son', *šə̆m* 'name'.

Next, a *skeletal mutation*, from biconsonantal to triconsonantal, ushers in the Semitic, specifically here Aramaic, era at stage II. (A related mutation in the scheme tier should also be assumed, at least in the case of the impa, but will not be further pursued here.) Since the roots remain biradical despite change of the template from bi- to triconsonantal, subsidiary mechanisms are required to implement the two-to-three association transforming { }-structure to / /-structure; this is the task of most of the procedures in (3F). A rule of degemination (s-deg, (3Fvii)) is added to the grammar to alleviate the phonetic (perceptual) difficulties in other than prevocalic position.

When *epenthesis* (epn, §17.6) arose, dissolving word-final clusters by inserting a vowel between the constituents (-*CC#* > -*CV̊C#*), we would expect stage III, where 1s *QaMt* > *QaMit*. This is expected on the assumption that new sound changes are usually added, qua rules, at the shallowest (latest) derivational level (layer) (§23.2). However, by the unanimous testimony of the later dialects, *QaMt* epenthesizes to *QaMMit*, becoming canonically identical to homoparadigmatic 3fs *QaMMat*. In fact, the proposal might be reasonably made that though the first-blush result of epenthesis was in fact phonetically expected *QaMit*, this subsequently succumbed to reshaping to *QaMMit* exactly on the analogy of *QaMMat*. Nor would this constitute ad hoc piecemeal appeal, in that replacement of *QaMit* by *QaMMit* would fully streamline the paradigm of the intransitive simple pf along the contours of one, surface-phonetic (and phonetically natural) generalization: allostem *QaMM* occurs prevocalically, allostem *QaM* elsewhere (= preconsonantally and in auslaut).

As was demonstrated in Malone 1971a, analogical reshaping (transparentation, §15) sometimes "settles in" for the grammar of the generations following that of the livewire reshaping itself as a mutation of *rule reordering* in the synchronic grammar.

This is proposed here, in stage IV of (a), where s-epn has moved from its latest-level order at stage III over s-deg deeper (earlier) into the phonology. (In this vein, it may not be a coincidence that epenthesized 1s allomorph *it*, or its reflexes, ultimately ends up in some dialects *restructuring* from derived allomorph (|it|) to underlying/lexical shape of the morpheme in question (/it/); see §15.2.2.2. Structurally speaking, this might be a consequence of dynamic mutation, which started with the reordering just discussed. Once s-epn leaped over s-deg deeper into the phonology, it may in some dialects have kept moving closer and closer to the phonological level itself; and once this initial level was reached, restructuring of |it| to /it/ would eo ipso have been realized, to the tune of annihilation (rule deletion) of s-epn itself.)

(a)   I
　　{ / QM x CV̌C xʃu }   { / QM x CVC xʃa + ta }   { / QM x CVC xʃa + t }
　　　　　　/QŭM/   /QaMta/   /QaMt/
　s-prm　　|QuM|
　　　　　　[QuM]   [QaMta]   [QaMt]

　　　　　　tier mutation (skeleton, scheme) >

II

	{ / QM x CV̆CVC xʃa u }	{/ QM x CVCVC xʃa +ta}	{ / QM x CVCVC xʃa +}
	/QŭMM/	/QaMMta/	/QaMMt/
s-prm	|QuMM|		
s-deg	|QuM|	|QaMta|	|QaMt|
	[QuM]	[QaMta]	[QaMt]

d-epn >

III
{same as at II}

	/QŭMM/	/QaMMta/	/QaMMt/
s-prm	|QuMM|		
s-deg	|QuM|	|QaMta|	|QaMt|
s-epn			|QaMit|
	[QuM]	[QaMta]	[QaMit]

rule reordering >

IV
{same as at III}

	/QŭMM/	/QaMMta/	/QaMMt/
s-prm	|QuMM|		
s-epn			|QaMMit|
s-deg	|QuM|	|QaMta|	
	[QuM]	[QaMta]	[QaMMit]

[7] Note in the derivation of [9ál] from *9álla (< **Rálla by ufb, §9.1.3) the order sap^deg, rather than deg^sap as might be expected on the basis of sap's arising chronologically posterior to deg. However, for a certain class of processes there is in fact no contradiction between orders x^y and y^x. This is so when either or both operations are *rerun* processes. A rerun process is one that either *reprises* (recurs) over time—not the "same" event as the original process, in the strict ontological sense, but one similar enough to the original to be arguably a typologically or analogically induced recurrence thereof—or *persists* over time, making itself felt whenever the circumstances (conditions) originally triggering it themselves recur—and hence *is* ontologically the "same" as the original process, being merely the continuation of a protracted event (even if that event seemed for a time to be dormant). It is in fact often difficult or impossible to distinguish between reprise and persistent processes, in which case the generic term, rerun process, may and will be used—with little damage done by the vagueness, since reprise and persistent processes have much in common. In any event, degemination is in all likelihood a long-lived rerun process, probably of the persistent sort, within Aramaic, so that when sap dropped the final -*a* from *9álla*, the -*ll* thus now exposed in auslaut fell victim to degemination, which had so to speak been lurking in the wings. It will sometimes be useful to mark a process as a rerun; and this will be done by prefixing "r-" to the basic process abbreviation—in this case "r-deg." In fact, however, degemination will normally be indicated, as here, by "deg" alone. In the course of the book, we

will have many occasions to consider specific reruns again, and to consider possible varieties (for instance, analogically induced reruns, e.g., §8.1.2(α), §9.2.3.2, §10 n. 10, §15.3.1.2, §17.21.1). (Occasionally, pairs of primary and rerun processes will be designated "early" ("e-") and "late" ("l-"), respectively. Processes so treated will normally involve salient differences between early and late manifestations and will accordingly be treated as distinct processes.)

[8] The question as to whether the setting for negative spreading could be followed by a negative setting for negative filling was pursued in Malone 1998c, where the answer returned was "no." However, it is possible that answer was too strong. A pure application of -spreading^-filling to the sim pf could give the results in (a), where it will be noted that, despite a certain heterogeneity, no slot is clearly impossible:

(a)   3ms [QáM]   (also given by gmf-1u)
      3fs [Qə́Máθ]   (see §15.3.2 (15P,Q))
      2s [QáMt]   (also given by gmf-1u)
      1s [Qə́Meθ]   (not per se attested, but questionably recoverable as
                       distinct from gmf-6-formed [Qə́Mə́θ])
      3mp [Qə́Mű]   (see §15.3.2)
      3fp [Qə́Mán]   (also given by gmf-6)
      2p [QaMtón]   (also given by gmf-1u)
      1p [QáMn]   (also given by gmf-1u)

By the way, corresponding to the full-blown metaplastic forms represented by Morag in Yem trad pron, Margolis gives Ash hybrids, e.g., a[maşşə́θ] 'you sucked' (Mar 132*). If such are considered genuine, their accounting poses a worthy challenge. One possibility is *overlapping derivation*, wherein (b) the partes communes are unproblematically shaped (*Qa*), (c) the instruction to spread *M* to the tune of extrusion (gmf-1u) as well as the instruction to fail to spread, to the tune of filling with *y* (gmf-6) are accomplished in parallel plains, and finally (d) the results are amalgamated in a relatively natural way since (e) *MM* and *M* have the same ordinal positional value for consonantism reckoned from front to back on the skeletal tier, qua $2\sqrt{}$ (pace §1 n. 11), and (f) *ay* positions last, i.e., qua $2ʃa\ 3\sqrt{}y$. These results are portrayed in (g):

(g)

$$Q \quad M \quad\quad Q \quad M$$
$$\mathrm{C\ V\ C\ V\ C} \Rightarrow \mathrm{C\ V\ C\ C}$$
$$a \quad \begin{Bmatrix} a \\ i \\ u \end{Bmatrix} \quad\quad a$$

$$\Rightarrow \quad Q \quad M$$
$$\mathrm{C\ V\ C\ C\ V\ C}$$
$$a \quad\quad a \quad y$$

$$Q \quad M \quad\quad Q \quad M$$
$$\mathrm{C\ V\ C\ V\ C} \Rightarrow \mathrm{C\ V\ C\ V\ C}$$
$$a \quad \begin{Bmatrix} a \\ i \\ u \end{Bmatrix} \quad\quad a \quad a \quad y$$

It remains for future research whether other apparent Ash hybrids, like hollow defective a[dōṣɔ̌yě́h] 'he thrust it in' (Mar 102*), can be derivationally accommodated—assuming they are genuine enough to warrant it.

For a survey of metaplasms among hol, gem, and def in M, see Macm 253–55.

4. Stress and Processes
of Syllabic Mutation

4.1. Stress (str)

4.1.1. The Pattern

The edge of the evidence favors the view that the fundamental Common Aramaic stress pattern is *end stress*, where "end" refers either: to (α) the ultima (*oxytone stress*, o-str) or; to the penult (*barytone stress*, b-str) when the ultima is taken to be extrametrical (metrically inert) as might be the case when the rime of the actual ultima is (β) a short vowel, (γ) a long suffix vowel, (δ) a suffixal V̊C sequence.[1] These extrametricalities are moreover hierarchical, such that: (β) always extrametrical ≫ (γ) usually extrametrical ≫ (δ) occasionally extrametrical. Type examples from the verb: (α) int rmp impa ms *hitQaSSáM*, (β) sim pf 3ms *QaSáMa*, (γ) sim pf 3mp *QaSáMū* (a long suffixal vowel is almost always extrametrical in the verb system, less thoroughly in the nominal system where, e.g., nominal-derivational *-ú̄* is never extrametrical (= always stressed), (δ) sim pf 3fs *QaSáMat* (~ non-extrametrical *QaSaMát*; extrametricality of V̊C is normally limited to subject suffixes).

A reconstructed system along these lines is witnessed in the reactions of several processes widespread in Aramaic, most notably *reduction* (§4.2). The essential correctness of the reconstruction is more directly witnessed in the orthographic accentual system (*tĕ9amim*) of Tib B.

It is possible that this cluster of stress patterns was anteceded by an earlier system along the lines of that commonly assumed for Classical Arabic. But the evidence from Aramaic itself for such an earlier system is dubious at best, the broader issue of comparative Semitics aside. It will consequently be the general policy of this book to exclusively assume the typical Aramaic system sketched above, only occasionally alluding to the possibility of an antecedent Arabic-like system.[2]

4.1.2. The Individual Dialects

Especially extrametricality condition (δ) shows variation across those dialects providing adequate evidence to decide such matters. A positive setting for this condition is the norm for TR and TL, and possibly for Bab B, CP, SM, and G. M restricts (δ) to forms with pp object suffixes (§17.15.2), and there is no trace of (δ) in SR. The disposition of Y, O, I, P, and N is moot. As will be pointed out as we now go through the individual dialects, (δ)-type extrametricality is inextricably tied up with *transparentation* (§15), in that atonicity of the subject suffix has as at least a de facto consequence that the form will include, tonosyllabically if not always segmentally, the shape of the 3ms, the least-marked member of the pf paradigm.[3] As is discussed in §15.2.1, it is at times impossible to know whether a given case of suffix atonicity has a purely tonogenetic origin, as treated in this section, or a purely transparentive source, or indeed involvement of both factors.[4] The special case of the general stress pattern/process (str) where extrametricality is *not* taken will occasionally be labeled "o-str" (*oxytone*, i.e., ultimate stress), while in parallel fashion a positive option of extrametricality will be said to involve "b-str" (*barytone*, i.e., penultimate).

B. Since prime examples and discussion are provided in §15, just a few additional points will be made here. Though both registers show V̆C atonicity, as Morag (1964: 126–27) correctly observes, it is more frequent in Bab B than in Tib B; e.g., where Tib B shows oxytone [nɛfqáθ], Bab B shows barytone [nɔ̆fǽqæθ] 'sie ist augegangen' (BL 136).[5] B also shows a few cases of rhythmically induced *stress retraction* (str); e.g., normally oxytone [wīhīváθ] 'und sie wird gegeben', but [yɔ̆hī́vaθ lɔ̆hốn] (BL 174) when the pp [lɔ̆hốn] immediately follows (quasi)enclitically (see §17.15 n. 75).

Nonrhythmically induced Tib B barytones, the minority pattern for the register, show some interesting properties. With but few exceptions ([sɔ̆́faθ], [hēēɪ́yaθ]), 3fs cases appear to be derived from *-t rather than from *-at (§2.3.4.3), with the consequence that their extrametrical vowel is epenthetic (§17.6), making for suffixal homonymy with 1s (also < *-t): e.g., 3fs [haddéqɛθ] like 1s [hăqémɛθ], 3fs [hištɔ̆xáhaθ] like 1s [haškáhaθ]. However, the striking aspect of this is that the color of the epenthetic vowel appears as if it were dictated by the Tiberian Hebrew pattern (THP 93f.), rather than by that of Aramaic at large (contrast 1s TR [ʔæškǽhiθ] (Da 261), TL y[9ɔ̆vǽði̯θ] (Mor 125).

In this book, the Hebrew-like nature of B epenthesis is interpreted as reflecting, not Schematisierung on the basis of Hebrew, but rather linguistically genuine epenthesis at a *later* stage than for Aramaic at large—a rerun process (r-epn) having somewhat different properties from the general A version (primary epn, or epn tout court). Though it may seem the reverse of intuitive that a *later* process (r-epn) should share characteristics with a related language (Hebrew) while the *earlier* process (epn) goes its own (Aramaic) way, the idea was developed largely in independence from the verb in Malone 1971 that general A epenthesis developed *earlier* than the Hebrew version, and that the two languages, qua Northwest Semitic dialects in contact, evinced *reciprocal wave influence*—an idea of which the present conception of epn, r-epn bids fair to be a special case. There are, moreover, additional facets of the overall complex pointing toward a late date for the epenthesis of Tib B barytones, as is discussed in detail in §17.6, where epenthesis at large is treated. While it is uncertain whether coeval or earlier dialects may also have been affected (to some extent) by r-epn, B itself is in fact heterogeneous in manifesting both r-epn and primary epn—a state of affairs historically suggesting that both forms of the process came ultimately to be present simultaneously over the same general region (though plausibly prevalent in distinct geographical subsections, reflecting lag in the wave spreading through the entire speech area; cf. §18.2). In the Tiberian register, moreover, epn and r-epn may be complementarily distributed with respect to stress, primary forms always reshaping to oxytone (not demonstrable on 3fs, but 1s [šim9éθ], yið9éθ], [šabbŏhéθ], never the like of @ [šắmé9iθ], @[yšðá9iθ], @[šabbáhiθ]); and possibly the other way around as well, r-epn forms always remaining barytone (but inconclusively, in view of the small number of attested items as well as the presence of ambiguous forms; note however 1s [hăqémεθ], [šắmεθ], no oxytone variants like @[šōméθ]). The whole complex skein is plausibly unraveled in §17.6.

In unambiguous forms, the Babylonian register shows a preponderance of primary epn forms, with no demonstrable stress correlation (note 1s [9ắvǽðIθ]).[6]

TR. While only about 30% of the relevant 3fs and 1s forms listed in BL 173f for B are barytone, the balance oxytone, 100% of the TR examples listed in Da 259–61 are barytone; see also §15. However, on Da 78 Dalman claims that [QiSMV̆θ] is the norm for the Tib register(s), citing without source [tiqfáθ], [šim9áθ]. (On the other hand, on Da 261, the only Tib form cited is barytone sb[tšxóliθ].)

CP. Barytones as per sim rmp <yDByqT> 'sie erreichte', sim plain <yqyDT> 'sie brannte' ~ oxytones per <šBqT> 'sie liess', <šlqT> 'ich stieg hinauf' (Sg 2), interpretable as [IddšvÍqaT], [yšqÍðaT] (ml <y>) ~ [šavqáT], [salqéT] (lack of ml and, crucially, <C̊> [Ca] bespeaking nonreduced 1ʃ (as well as failure to attenuate, §12)).[7]

SM. Though the ravages of the Samaritan circuit (§22.1) make it impossible to be certain, the most straightforward hypothesis is that SM was originally barytone on a regular basis, showing, e.g., t[bā̊ṭā̊nɑt] 'wurde schwanger' (Macs 145), with only rare traces of the oxytone pattern, e.g., t[nǽttɑt] 'sie stieg herab' (Macs 174) < ná˹Taθ < naḥTáθ < *naḥatát.[8]

G. Predominantly barytone, inasmuch as the majority of 3fs and 1s sim pfs with *2ʃ i or *2ʃ u listed by Dalman (Da 260f) are spelled with <y>, <w>;

e.g., <z9y̲rT> '(sie) wurde weniger', <ŝqw̲9T> '(sie) versank', <ḥsy̲lyT> '(ich) hörte auf'.

SR. SR verb stress is exclusively oxytone; e.g., light-suffixed pf intransitive 3fs 3fs [QɛSMáθ], 1s [QɛSMéθ].

TL. The orthography betrays a good deal of barytonicity, as do both Yem and Ash trad pron. There is moreover much agreement across the three types of evidence concerning specific instances, though Morag explicitly cites what may be certain patterned discrepancies between orthography and Yem trad pron. Some examples: <ŝkyb⁷> 'she lay' (Mar 37) prima facie interpretable as [šɔ̆xÍvā] < *sakíbat (with apocope of *t by mtr, §17.12, as is usual for TL); contrastr oxytone [šæxbá̆] in Yem trad pron (Mor 124)—and though there is no reason to believe in this case that the two forms are textually indentical, Morag tells us (Mor 125) that while one subtradition of Yem trad pron always responds to 1s <QSy̲My> with barytone [Qɔ̆SÍMī], yet another subtradition responds with oxytone [QæSMí].[9] Note also, like TR, forms with 2ʃ [e], seemingly bespeaking transparentation (§15.2.1.1); e.g., y + a [šɔ̆fé̜liθ] 'I looked down' (Mor 125, Mar 174*).[10]

M, as discussed in §15.2.1.1, shows traces of barytone accent only in pp object forms. Otherwise it deploys solely oxytones, like SR.

Unlike the extrametricality of type (δ) just multiply illustrated, to which A overall shows heavy incidence of both positive and negative reaction, type (γ) extrametricality is virtually categorical across all dialects; that is, long suffixal vowels in auslaut are virtually always extrametrical, making for a barytone stress pattern. Apparent cases to the contrary—i.e., incidence of accented (long) vowels in auslaut—are best taken as reflecting apocope of -*n* (mtr, §17.12) from suffixes earlier of shape *-V̌n, a phenomenon frequent in SM and TL. M shows cases of this apocope as well, but not in the 3mp, so that the form <birku> 'they blessed' (Mal 345f) might indeed be a genuine though hapax case of (γ)-negative [-ű] ≤ *-ű́, the whole form being interpretable as [berkű].[11]

4.2. Reduction (red)

4.2.1. The Mechanics

Looked at comprehensively over the dialects that patently manifest it, which is to say all as of B at the latest, *reduction* (red) is a prosodic process either *deleting* or *weakening* the nucleus of light pretonic open syllables, cases to be labeled *full* (f-red) and *partial* (p-red), respectively. The simplest cases might be illustrated with type examples of the 3ms (after sap, §17.22) and 3fs sim pf: 3ms **QaSáM* reduced to [Qə̌SáM, where *1ʃ a is weakened to schwa or other reduced (ḥatuf) vowel because light (short, monomoraic) nucleus of the pretonic open syllable *Qa*; and 3fs **QaSaMát* full-reduced to [QISMaT] ([I] and [T] hedging on the incidence and chronology of frequent correlatives attenuation and spirantization, §12, §5.1), where *2ʃ a is targeted as nucleus of *Sa*.

While the red-targeted syllable of [Qə̌SáM] is uniquely determined, given the above formulation of the overall process, the same cannot be said of [QISMáT], because **QaSaMát* contains *two* candidate target syllables, *Qa* and *Sa*. Had the former been targeted, the result would be @[Qə̌SaMáT]. And though we do find shapes like this, notably B [bə̌ṭeláθ], it seems most likely that such is a result of transparentation (§15.2.1.1), at least historically, because in stress-induced reduction systems, as that of Aramaic clearly is (along with those of Hebrew, Old Irish, English, Russian, and many other languages), it is characteristic for the process to move outward (backward, forward) from the stressed syllable in domino-fashion, reducing the first syllable encountered— in this case *Sa*.

It will be worth dwelling on this aspect of reduction for a moment. The A reduction algorithm is also typical in showing two characteristics of *iterativity*: (α) if reduction of a target still leaves one or more additional targets in the path, it or they may also be reduced, e.g., int impf 2mp (after sap) *tiQaSSiMún* → *tiQaSSV̆Mún* → [tV̆V̆QaSSV̆Mún]; (β) the results of an earlier application may have impact on possible subsequent applications, e.g., *QaSaMát* (above) on its way to [QISMáT] first reduces to *QaSMáT*, whereby deletional loss of 2ʃ a changes the syllabic structure of 1ʃ a from nucleus of an open syllable to that of a closed syllable, thereby rendering it immune to further reduction.[12]

In addition to being an iterative process, reduction in some dialects functions as a *rerun* process. Thus after the independent 3mp pronoun *(ʔ)innún* is suffixed (§17.15) to TR tb *yə̌šælláḥ* 'er wird senden', the result is either tb[yə̌šællæḥinnún], or tb[yə̌šællə̌ḥinnún] (Da 371), where ʃ2 æ is reduction-weakened though reduction as a primary sound change had already long since taken place. This secondary occurrence of reduction may be attributable either to the original change's having lingered in the dialect, perhaps latently, since the days of its first emergence (*persistent* process); or to its having rearisen de novo in the dialect, whether as a manifestation of the same structural-phonetic forces that originally evoked it or as an analogically based copycat change of the original (*reprise* change). It is often difficult to distinguish the two modalities. Is there, for instance, a statute of limitations for a persistent change's latency, so that if too much time passes before reemergence it must be (re)interpreted as a reprise change? Or is the distinction between persistence and reprise even legitimate to begin with?

Hitherto, weakening (p-red) and deletion (f-red) have been mentioned as manifestations of reduction without defining the conditions for either. The commonest pattern is: (γ) deletion when the target syllable immediately follows a light syllable (e.g., **QaSaMát* > [QISMáT]); (δ) weakening immediately following a closed syllable (e.g., int pf 3fs **QaSSiMát* > [QaSSV̌MáT] or (ε) when the target syllable is initial (**QaSáM* > [QV̌SáM];[13] (ζ) variation (transdialectal, intradialectal) between both resolutions immediately following a syllable with rimal *V̄* (B weakening [yǎšēzǎvinnɔ́x] 'he'll free you' (Dan 6:17), SR deleting [tēzpín] 'du(f) wirst leihen' (B137) < *tēzafín).*[14]

Finally, there are what would seem to be anomalous or at least unusual cases of unexpected (η) weakening in lieu of deletion (e.g., B [tiqǎfáθ] ~ [tiqǎfáθ] 'sie würde übermütig' (Dan 5:20), or (θ) deletion in lieu of weakening (e.g., possibly B bb[t9iðḗ] ~ bb[t9æðḗ] 'sie vergeht' (~ normal tb[tɛ9dḗ] (BL 45). Such a possible instantiation of (θ) might be implemented via modification of case (e) of (4F,G) below, but it seems more likely that Bauer and Leander are correct in suggesting that an original sequence **V9* could amalgamate to a fully pharyngealized vowel ("ein mit Kehlkopfpressung gesprochener Vokal" (13)), which the scribes heard as [9V]; cf. also Blevins and Garrett 1998. (In this book, such will be transcribed [ti̱ðḗ] ~ [tæ̱ðḗ], [V̱] symbolizing a pharyngealized vowel.)

4.2.2. The Individual Dialects

In general, the earlier unvocalized dialects afford little if any evidence for reduction.

B. (γ) [silqáθ] 'sie ist augestiegen' (BL174) (contrast unusual (η) [tiqV̌fáθ] in §4.2.1 above); (δ) [šabbǎhḗθ] 'ich lobte' (BL 173); (ε) [kǎθáv] 'er schrieb' (lc); (ζ) weakening [yǎšēzǎvinnɔ́x], §4.2.1.

P. Possibly (ε) the second variant of <9nh> ~ <9ynh> 'he answered him' (HC 398), with <y> as ml for reduced [I].

TR. (γ) [mæn9ǽnī] 'er hielt mich zuruck' (Da 362) < *mana9ání;* (δ, ε) [pæqqǎðǽx] 'er befahl dich' (Da 363), [rǎγéz] 'war zornig' (Da 258); (ζ) weakening [šēṣǎyúhī] 'sie ertilgten ihn' (Da 387).

CP. Not much to go by, but the first ml in <šyDyT> 'warf' (Sg 27) suggests (ε) [šI̱ðéT], and participles spelt like <9myryn> 'wohnende' (Sg 18) suggest (ζ) weakening [9āmI̱rín].[15]

SM. (γ) t[nǽttɑt] (§4.1.2 SM); (δ) t[titqɑddǎson] 'werdet geheiligt' (Macs 158) < (reconstructed) living SM [tiθqaddǎsÚn] (see smc, §22.1); (ε) t[kǎtɑb] 'schrieb' < living SM [kă̰θáβ] (smc); (ζ) perhaps deletion ~ weakening as per <TylDy> earlier t[tildi] ~ modern t[tḭ̄ā̰di] 'du(f) wirst gebären' (Macs 180).[16]

S̲R̲. (γ) [yahbɔ́h] 'er gab sie' (Ns 132) < *yahₐB̆ắh*; (δ, ε) [qabbɜ̆lɛ́h] 'habe ich empfangen' (Ns 193), [šɜ̰θέq] 'schwieg' (Ns 103); (ζ) [tēzpín] (§4.2.1).

T̲L̲. (γ) y[gænvä̰] 'hu ganav ʾotah' (Mor 124), a [naqtán] 'he seized me' (Mar 138*), both < *QaSₐMV́* . . . ; (δ) y[tæbbɜ̆rä̰] 'hi šibra' (Mor 146), a[ʾaškɜ̰hɛ́h] 'he found him' (Mar 171*); (ε) y+a[šɜ̰xév] 'he lay down' (Mor 123, Mar 138*); (ζ) in the verb, apparently weakening in both traditions, y+a[tēxɜ̰lǘn] 'you(mp) will eat' (Mor 165, Mar 87*).[17]

M̲. (γ) <ligtat> [leγtä̰θ] 'she seized' (Macm 263), cf. m[gétlat] 'she killed' (Macm 24), both < *QaSaMắT*; (δ) <anhirat> [anh̰rä̰θ] 'she illumined' (Macm 265), cf. m[ahrέβat] 'she destroyed'' (Macm 266); (ε) <lgat> [lɔ̆γát] 'he seized' (Macm 263), cf. m[gɜ̰tál] 'he killed' (lc); (ζ) no unambiguous verb examples encountered, but probably deleting as per such as participial <napqin> [nāfqén] 'ei exeunt' (Macm 278), cf. m[qagä̰tlen] 'they are killing' (Macm 280), both < *QāSiMín*.

4.3. Excrescence (exc)

Several dialects give evidence of a process whereby a consonant cluster is loosened through the *excrescence* (exc) of a vowel, usually reduced, between its members. Such excrescence is especially prevalent when one of the consonants, normally the first one, is a guttural.

B̲. Excrescence in B is especially prominent in the Tiberian register: tb[lɛhɜ̆wón] 'sie werden sein' (BL 153), where as usual the reduced vowel assumes chameleonwise the color of the nearest preceding vowel through the porous guttural (by mvh, §17.23.3); similarly tb[yɔ̆hahă̰wḛ́] 'er zeigt an' (Bl 158). It will be noticed that the clusters in both these examples contain not only the characteristic guttural, but a semivowel as well. This is in fact the majority pattern for Tib B. Though exc is not totally absent from the Babylonian register, it is there much less frequently; e.g., the counterparts of the preceding cases lack it: bb[lihwón], bb[{yɔ̆}hæḥwḛ́] (llcc). In B and other dialects, too, it is at times impossible to know whether a given reduced vowel is to be accounted for by exc or rather by partial reduction; thus, though the [ɔ̆] in [tiqɔ̆fáθ] was earlier (§4.2.1) attributed to p-red, it might actually reflect insertion by exc—an accordion-like event, involving as it would a predeletional and a postdeletional vowel appearing in the same slot: *taqipát* full reduction and other processes > *tiqfáθ* exc > [tiqɔ̆fáθ].

<u>TR</u>. [yæ9ǯvḗð] 'macht' (Da 269).

<u>CP</u>. Excrescence may be bespoken in ml usages like <yBylˀ> 'er veraltet'(Sg 291), interpretable along the lines of [IvI̲lé] (with loss of *y*- by ymn, §14.2), or <yBw9w̲n> 'sie suchen' (Sg 73) as [IvŪ̲9Ůn] (note the expected guttural catalyst in the latter, 9, and the expected porosity of the same as concerns the color of the excrescence, in this case mvh-copying (§2 n. 5) the vowel of the suffix -Ůn).

<u>SM</u>. While it is commonplace for the loss of a guttural consonant in the coda of a syllable to trigger compensatory lengthening of the nucleus of that syllable, it is rare for such compensatory lengthening to attend upon the loss of a guttural consonant in the onset. And yet SM trad pron appears to give evidence of just this: e.g., (reconstructed) living SM *nið9ál* 'we fear' <nDhl> > t[nēdā́l] (Macs 123), where loss of 9 (< *ḥ, by gtl) has apparently brought about lengthening of the 2ſ nucleus to [ā́]. However, this typological quirk receives a rather natural explanation—at least for forms of this shape—in the hypothesis that before the loss of the guttural (§22.1 (22Bv)) the dialect underwent excrescence to *nið̆ǎ9ál*, whereupon with dropping of the guttural the resulting hiatus is resolved by running together the two vowels, excrescent and 2ſ, to form a long vowel.[18] In the event the hiatus is not resolved, and the resulting vowel sequence is instead maintained into trad pron, the prediction is that there should be no compensatory lengthening because, as noted above, the loss of guttural onsets is expected at large to remain uncompensated. This prediction appears to be born out in <ym9y> t[yæmǽˀi] 'he strikes' (Macs 207) < living SM *yamǎ9í* (where the length disposition of *ǽ..i* follows from the action of the smc; in which vein, note also that [ˀ] is hiatus-breaking; §22.1 (22Bvi(ε))). If despite typological rarity the lossd of 9 (< ḥ) had triggered (re) lengthening of the auslaut vowel, the trad pron would have been @[yæmǽˀí].

<u>SR</u>, <u>TL</u>, <u>M</u>. Of the E dialects, only TL gives any hint of excrescence— <Ty9y̲rwq> (~ <Ty9rwq>) 'she'll flee' (Mar 38)—and only Margolis's Ashkenazic trad pron provides any phonetic investiture ([tε9ǧróq] ~ ([tε9róq]), or plausibly [ti9i̲róq] (~ [ti9róq]), §17.23.3).[19]

4.4. Aufsprengung (auf)

4.4.1. Excrescent Aufsprengung

We may propose that languages with stress-induced vowel reduction systems, like the later Aramaic dialects and Hebrew, frequently have what might be called anti-pyrrhic prosodic constraints prohibiting excessively long sequences of reduced syllables. Observing that absolutely no sequencing of such syllables occurs in Aramaic of the classical period, we may hypothesize

a corresponding constraint with repair strategy power dictating that whenever
a tandem of reduced syllables arises in the course of morphophonological operations, it is immediately dispelled by elisional denucleation of the second
such syllable—a process to be called *schwa haplology* (swh). Thus, in outline,
. . .*CV̆CV̆CV*. . . → . . .*CV̆CCV*. . . . But in consequence of this repair, another
violation is incurred by allowing the first reduced vowel to become nucleus of
a closed syllable, a violation immediately corrected by *promoting* (prm) the offending segment to full-vowel status (§14.): . . .*CV̆CCV*. . . → . . .*CV̊CCV*. . . .
Because it tends to function in a unitary manner, this complex swh^prm will
be given the unitary label *Aufsprengung* (auf)—more narrowly *excrescent Aufsprengung*, inasmuch as in it the lead-off *V̊* in . . .*CV̆CV̆CV*. . . is a product of
excrescence (§4.3).

The individual dialects:

<u>B</u>. Corresponding to excresced tb[lɛhĕwṓn] (§4.3), fp [lɛhɛwyṓn] (BL
161) has undergone Aufsprengung: ← prm *lɛhɛwyṓn* ← swh *lɛhĕw̆y̆ṓn* ←
exc *lɛhw̆ăy̆ṓn* (the color of the resulting [ɛ. . .ɛ] is primarily determined by
mid^aop, §17.11.3, and secondarily by sco, §4.4.3 below). (Observe that these
are Tiberian forms. Even as the Babylonian variant of [lɛhĕwṓn] fails to ex-
cresce, [lihwṓn], so the Bab variant of Tib fp [lɛhɛwṓn] fails to undergo auf,
[lihwĭyắn].)

<u>TR</u>. Corresponding to ms bb[yæ9̆ŏvéð] (§4.3), there is aufgesprengt
Sb[yæ9æbDū́n] (Da 272). TR auf will receive further attention in §4.5 (For the
{§4.4.1, difference between Bab 3 √[v] and Sab 3 √[b], see §5.2.)

<u>CP</u>. <yTḥyrmwn> 'anathematizati sunt' (Sg 70) is plausibly interpreted by
Schulthess as (cau rmp pf 3mp) [ettaḥermṓn] (Sg 28), i.e., ← prm *IttaḥŏrmŪ́n*
← IttaḥŏrŏmŪ́n.[20]

<u>SR</u>. With low-colored auf, [tɛðaḥlī́n] 'du(f) fürchtest', [tɛšabqū́n] 'ihr las-
set' (Ns 37); with palatal color, [nɛzɛbnū́n] 'sie kaufen' (lc). (For the variation
in color, §4.4.3.)

<u>TL</u>. Ashkenazic trad pron only, pattern identical to that of Tib B (Tiberian-
based Schematisierung?): [tɛhɛwyī́n] 'you(fs) will be', [ʾaḥarvḗh] 'I'll destroy
him' (Mar 106*, 115*).

<u>M</u>. A few systematic exceptions apart, Aufsprengung has become the M
resolution par excellence of /CCV̆C/ irrespective of feature disposition (generalized Aufsprengung): [nīseGDắ] 'they(f) will worship' ← *nesgŏðắ*, [tiseBqan]

'you(s) will forgive me', [īθeGBéβ] 'he was bent' ← *eθgə̆βéβ* (gmf-3u, §3.2 (3K)) (Mal 543, 526, 454).[21]

4.4.2. Sonorant Aufsprengung

We have just seen how Aufsprengung can be triggered as byproduct of a tandem of repair strategies to remove canon-offensiuve . . . *CV̆CV̆*. . . . It can also be triggered by a string . . . *CΛV̆*. . . , Λ a sonorant (semivowel, liquid, nasal), when—as frequently in languages at large—*ΛV̆* first amalgamates to Λ̦ (vocalic Λ), then breaks to *V̆Λ*, which finally closed-syllabically promotes to [V̊Λ]. This nexus of processes, to be called *sonorant Aufsprengung*, is also represented in Aramaic—ambiguously with excrescent auf in the case of strings of pre-excrescent shape . . . *HΛə̆*. . . (some examples were tacitly presented in §4.4.1 and will be picked up directly below).

B. bb[hæšilṭắx] 'er hat dich zu Herrn gesetzt' (Dan 2:38) ← *hæšə̆lṭắx* ← *hæšlṭắx* ← *hæšlɔ̆ṭắx* (for this input form to auf, cf. the Tiberian variant, unaufgesprengt [hæšlə̆ṭɔ́x]); bb[yiθirmḗ] 'er wird geworfen' (Dan 6:13) (~ unaufgesprengt tb[yiθrə̆mḗ]). Observe that both these clear cases of sonorant auf are Babylonian while the Tiberian variants remain unaufgesprengt. Is this reason enough to disambiguate tb[lɛhɛwyɔ́n] (§4.4.1) as instantiating excrescent auf rather than sonorant auf (which would bespeak ← *lɛhw̦yɔ́n*)?

TR. bb[yisimqū́n] 'werden rot' (Da 272) ← *yisəmqū́n* ← *yism̦qū́n* ← *yismə̆qū́n*; similarly sb[yizirqū́n] (Da 94) ← *yizr̦qū́n*.

SM. <wʾⁿsBT> t[wētænsébɑt] 'und sie wurde genommen' (Macs 154) ← smc (§22.1) *wə̆ʾIθǎnsíβaθ* ← *wə̆ʾIθn̦síβaθ*.

CP, TL. The forms cited under excresecent auf (§4.4.1) ambiguously manifest sonorant auf as well.

M. As mentioned under excrescent auf (§4.4.1), M has generalized Aufsprengung as the unmarked phonological response to /CCV̆C/. There are any number of cases that might pass muster as sonorantly aufgesprengt: e.g., the sim rmp sequence [ūīθelGét īθerGél] 'and held and fettered' (DM 231).

4.4.3. Some General Observations

(γ) The color of the aufgesprengt vowel (i.e., the [V̊] promoted from a *V̆* whether ← *V̆C* ←*V̆CV̆*—excresecent auf—or ← *V̆Λ* ← Λ̦—sonorant auf) is either palatal or low.

(β) In dialects where schwa coloring (§17.23) is progressive-assimilatory through a guttural (mvh), *V′Hə̆* → *V′HV̆*—i.e., in B, TR, and aTL, the color of the aufsprengt [V] is determined by this pattern of sco whether auf is unambiguously excrescent (e.g., TR *yæ9ə̃Bə̃đứn* → *yæ9æ̆Bə̃đứn* . . . → [yæ9æBə̃ứn]) or ambiguously excrescent/sonorant (e.g., B *lɛhə̆wə̆yə̃n* → *lɛhɛ̆wə̆yə̃n* . . . → [lɛhɛwə̆yə̃n], alternatively *lɛhw̥yə̃n* → *lɛhə̆wyə̃n* → *lɛhɛ̆wyə̃n* → [lɛhɛwyə̃n]).

(γ) Nexus (β) aside and with reservations registered due to paltry data in some dialects (e.g., CP, SM), the color of an aufsprengt *V*, whether excrescent or sonorant, is determined through *sco by stipulation*: *palatal* in B, TR, CP, *low* in SM, *low* ≫ *palatal* in SR, and *palatal* ≫ *low* in M (for the low cases, see §6 nn 25, 27).

4.5. Interactions

Consider again the role of schwa haplology in the derivation of TR sb[yæ9æbDứn] (§4.4.1): ← prm *yæ9æbđứn* ←swh *yæ9æ̆bə̃đứn* ← exc *yæ9bə̃đứn*. Repair strategies like swh may differ from run-of-the-mill sound changes in being, in a manner of speaking, *reactive* rather than *teleological*, and as such may sometimes represent but one of a number of alternative reactions adequate to correct the pattern violation at stake. In the case in point, the violation is the sequence of reduced vowels *ə̆bə̆*, which might however alternatively have been rectified by deletion of the first *V̆* rather than the second, or by promotion of either. In fact, at least one of these alternatives is actually at times manifested in TR: promotion of the first *V*, as per bb[ti9ibə̆rứn] 'ihr gehet vorüber' (Da 273) ← *ti9ĭbə̆rứn* (← exc *ti9bə̆rứn*). So when faced with a violatory string such as *V̆CV̆*, TR at large may choose either of two corrective paths: swh^prm (sb[yæ9æbDứn]) or prm alone (bb[ti9ibə̆rứn]). This pair of alternatives we might systematically relate by assuming either that swh is optional (4A) or that swh and prm are in a (chronological/synchronic) *loop* (§23.3) with one another (4B), in which case the order prm^swh involves swh lying fallow because bled (preempted) by prm upon removal of the offensive *V̆CV̆*:

(4A) excrescence (^ schwa haplology) ^ promotion

(4B) $\qquad$ ⎧ ^ schwa haplology ^ promotion

excrescence ⎨

$\qquad$ ⎩ ^ promotion ^ schwa haplology

Let us provisionally adopt the optional haplology model, noting that the results of both construals are indeed attested as variants of the same form: bb[ti9ibə̆rứn] from prm alone, as we have just seen, and also bb[ti9ibrứn] (Da 273) from swh followed by prm.

Recall now that reduction has been shown at times to be a rerun process (§4.2.1), and note that rerunning on a string such as *ti9ib(ʒ)rūn* would give [tʒ9ib(ʒ)rūn]—also in fact attested in the Sabbionetan subregister (lc), where the Tiberian orthography allows the symbol < : > to be interpreted as either sounded (*na9*) [ʒ] or silent (*naḥ*) [Ø] (§21.5). Hence, enrichment of (4A) to (4C), with optional rerun reduction:

(4C) excrescence (^ schwa haplology) ^ promotion (^ rerun-reduction)

If promotion is generalized from a strict repair strategy to a transparentively motivated optional process at large (§15), we have an explanation for various forms homoparadigmatic to sb[yæ 9æbDũn] such as 1s [ˀæ9æbéð] (Da 272), where promotion from *ˀæ9ǽbéð* is not coerced by the exigencies of TR canons but is favored at the behest of paradigmatic unity in that what is effectively a first schematic becomes phonetically manifested as a uniform short vowel throughout the 1 √H imperfective. The marked (◊), suffixless slots in (4D) represent forms reshaped by extension of promotion, to conform to the homo-paradigmatic suufixed forms:

(4D)   ◊   c[yæ9æbéð]   [yæ9æbDũn]
       ◊   c[tæ9æbéð]   c[yæ9æbDãn]
       ◊   c[æ9æbéð]   c[tæ9æbDũn]
          [tæ9æbDĩn]   c[tæ9æbDãn]
       ◊   [ˀæ9æbéð]   ◊ c[næ9æbéð]

Taking it finally that excrescence too is an optional process allows an account of forms like sb[tæ9béð], and permits us to consolidate the pooled resources of TR potential for variation as per (4E)-(4F), with attested examples in (4G):

(4E) (excrescence) (^ schwa haplology) (^ promotion) (^ rerun-reduction)

(4F)

(a)			+prm	+red
(b)				-red
(c)		+swh	-prm	+red
(d)				-red
(e)	+exc		+prm	+red
(f)				-red
(g)		-swh	-prm	+red
(h)				-red
(i)			+prm	+red
(j)		+swh		-red
(k)			-prm	+red
(l)	-exc			-red
(m)			+prm	+red
(n)		-swh		-red
(o)			-prm	+red
(p)				-red

(4G) (a) sb[tɜ̆9ibrű̃n] [22]

(b) sb[[yæ9æbDű̃n][23], sb[tāfiršű̃n] (Da 273) [24], bb[yi9ibrű̃n]
(Da 272)

(c, d) — ruled out by prohibition against [V̆CC]

(e) sb[tɜ̆9ibɜ̆rű̃n][22], sb[yɜ̆9ibǽr](Da 269), bb[tɜ̆9iróq](Da 270)

(f) sb[ˀæ9æbéð], sb[ˀæ9æðí̆](Da 257), sb[yæ9æbéð](Da 269),
sb[tæ9æbɜ̆ðí̆n][23], sb[tiddæhɜ̆lű̃n][25]

(g) —ruled out by prohibition against [V̆CV̆]

(h) tb[ˀæ9ǽvǽr](Da 257), bb[tæ9š̆Bǽr](Da 271)

(i, j, k, l) —ruled out since +swh requires +exc

(m, n) —derivation impossible to the extent that +prm presupposes
+exc [26]

(o) —derivation impossible since +r-red requires +exc

(p) sb[tæ9béð], bb[yi9róq](da 269), sb[ti9bɜ̆rű̃n](Da 273),
bb[yi9bɜ̆rű̃n](da 272)

As may readily be seen in (4G), postulation of of the simple optional process chain in (4E) accounts for what sometimes has been taken as a suspiciously bewildering congeries of variants. It will be noted that all possible combinations licensed by the chain are attested—primarily in Tiberian registers and, within these, most prominently apud Sabbioneta.

It might finally be mentioned that this nexus of process interactions seems to be effectively limited to TR. Other dialects by and large stick to the straight and narrow of (4F(b, h, p)), though SR shows some (nonverb) instantiation of (a) (for examples, see B 99).[27]

Notes to §4

[1] It might be possible to drop the restriction "suffixed" from case (γ) if all instances of nonsuffixed auslaut [-V̄] should derive from *[-V̄ 3 √Γ(V̊)], or perhaps for that matter even from purely abstract */-V̄ 3 √(V̊)Γ as long as stress is reckoned before one of the condensing or coalescing processes (§8, §11). This is so because under either of these conditions there would be no instances of -V̄ at the time/level extrametricality is reckoned, -V̊ 3√Γ (V̊) stressing to -V̊ 3√Γ (V̊) either by clause (α) (for -V̊ 3√Γ) or (β) (for -V̊ 3√Γ V̊), and then condensing/coalescing to [-V̂] too late for extrametricality to make a ruling one way or the other. For instance, in the high-frequency sim pf 3ms of the defective verb, *QaSáya* e-cnd → *QaSá* . . . → [QǎSÁ].

[2] If posited, an earlier Arabic-like system may be assumed to have had a stress that (a) recedes from the end of a (prosodic) word toward the beginning no farther than the antepenult, but stops on (b) an ultima which is both closed-syllabic and long-vocalic, or (c) a medial syllable which is either closed-syllabic or long-vocalic. If the examples just preceding in the text are assumed to have had antecedents subject to such a rule, three of them will have antepenultimate stress under clause (a): **QáSaMa, **QáSaMū (*Mū* is long-vocalic but not closed-syllabic), **QáSaMat (closed-syllabic but short-vocalic). The remaining example would fall to clause (c)—**hitQáSSaM—as would hol sim short-impf 2mp **taQúMū. Clause (b) would apply to the corresponding singular: **taQúM.

Though the typical Aramaic system described in the text and the Arabic-like system just sketched appear very different, there is at least one vantage—building on one version of so-called *metrical stress theory* (cf. Kenstowicz 1994: ch. 10)—according to which they differ primarily in what might be called *metrical orientation*, and secondarily in extrametricality (for more on the framework assumed in what follows, see §23.5 in this book). To address the secondary facet first, the Arabic-like system would have the same extrametricalities as the typical Aramaic system, but all these would be categorical rather than hierarchically variable. Then, as concerns metrical orientation, the Arabic-like system would be *trochaic* while the typical Aramaic system would be *iambic*. In both cases, the dynamic would be: proceeding from the extrametricality-reckoned end of the prosodic word, lay down a trochaically/iambically defined *stress foot* (§23.5 (23Z′)) as soon as a matching structure is encountered. An *unresolved* trochaic stress foot would consist of a tandem of two light syllables, with the first stressed, where "light syllable" means one bearing one *mora* (weight measure, μ), i.e., a short-vocalic open syllable: hence S̆S̆; thus **QáSaMa, **QáSaMū, **QáSaMat, all with

Qá Sa as the foot and *Ma, Mū, Mat* extrametrical. An unresolved iambic foot would be the mirror image: hence S̆S̆; thus **QaSáMa, *QaSáMū, *QaSáMat*, with *Qa Sá* the foot and *Ma, Mū, Mat* extrametrical. In a *resolved* foot, trochaic and iamic patterns are neutralized to one stressed heavy syllable, i.e., a stressed syllable bearing two or more morae, S̆$^{µµ(...)}$—which is to say, a closed-syllabic or long-vocalic syllable. The prediction from this neutralization is that in cases when extrametricality works out the same for the two systems, a form bearing a metrically heavy syllable will be stressed identically in both: thus *taQŭ́Mū*, with *Qŭ́* as the heavy and *Mū* extrametrical; and *taQŭ́M*, with *Qŭ́M* heavy and no extrametrical. However, *hitQaSSaM* diverges: ***hitQáSSaM* in the Arabic-like system with *QáS* heavy and *(S)aM* extrametrical, but **hitQaSSáM* in the typical Aramaic system, which restricts *VC* extrametricality to subject suffixes and hence treats *SáM* as the heavy. Similarly *QaSaMat* may diverge when the option of V̊C extrametricality is not taken for the iambic system and hence *Mat* counts as resolved ^{µ}S̆$^{µ(...)}$, giving **QaSaMát*, while in the trochaic system with obligatory extrametricality the result, as we have seen, is ***QáSaMat*.

[3] E.g., for **2ʃi Yem trad pron of TL in 1s shows both [Q̌ǒSéMiθ] and [Q̌ǒSíMī], the former including the full 3ms shape [Q̌ǒSéM] while the latter defaults segmentally on schematic vowel height, presumably because analogical reshaping is partially overridden by synchronic phonology which, we will assume, preferred [í] as realization of stressed /I/ /__Cī (a synchronic spinoff of mid, §17.11). Such overriding of transparentive processes is a common enough phenomenon, and we will see other A examples here and there (e.g., suppression of anticanonical stress, §15.2.1.1, epenthesis, §15.3.1.3, vowel-lengthening ips, §15.3.1.1). Contrast either of these barytone (penultimate) form types with the considerable deviation from 3ms in oxytone (ultimate) variants of shape [QaSMí]. (For all these shapes, see Mor 123, 125.) It seems difficult to distinguish overriding of the sort discussed here from repair-strategic tweaking. Indeed, the two reactions bid fair to be one and the same essential phenomenon.

[4] It is indeed possible that *all* instantiation of apparent extrametricality of type (δ) is transparentive in origin, in which case A extrametricality would be limited, at least originally, to types (α) and (β), i.e., -V̊ and -V̄, with no C-final type permissible. Note, incidentally, that a third source of barytonicity is rhythmically based stress retraction, as occasionally in B (§4.1.2, just below) and structuralized in a special way in M (§4.1.2 below, also §15.2.1.1 with n. 5).

[5] Stress is not orthographically represented in Bab B, but barytonicity is clued in the case of 1s by [e] in a stressed closed syllable ~ [i] elsewhere (via mid, §17.11); e.g., bb<9æBDe̱T> ~ <9æBæDi̱T> interpretable as oxytone [9ævð̌éθ] ~ barytone [9ævǽð̌iθ] (Tib shows solely oxytone [9ævð̌éθ]) (BL 129). The same criterion is applicable to TR and TL, with, however, the interfering factor that in these dialects the clearcutness of [e] ~ [i] is frequently blurred by transparentation (§17.11.3). (Note incidentally the unexpected [ɛ] in tb[nɛfqáθ], by aop; §17.11.3.)

[6] (a) Stress and epenthesis are both rerun processes, but in distinct ways. The cA stress pattern (§4.1.1) is *persistent*, reasserting itself in essentially the same way over the generations each time a feeding sound change arises (e.g., one providing a new stressable syllable). Epenthesis, on the other hand, presents an *early* form ((primary) epn) and a *late* form (r-epn), differing from one another in color of the epenthetic vowel. While str affects all dialects in largely the same way except in parametric preference (e.g., in

specifics of extrametricality where options allow), epenthesis is dialect-conditioned (to the extent that the evidence is rich enough to provide testimony): r-epn may affect only B (both registers, but especially Tib) while primary epn plausibly affects all A dialects (including B, especially the Bab register). The unmarked insert in r-epn is *e* (which may → ε by atonic opening), while postgutturally *a* is inserted, and *i* following *y*. In primary epn, the insert is uniformly *i* (subject to → *E* by midding, which in turn may → *ē* by late anticipality and even further → *ī* by heightening). For detail, see §17.6.

(b) While the barytone forms cited in the text clearly illustrate the operation of r-epn in *Tiberian* B, unambiguous testimony of the same process in *Babylonian* B is only forthcoming in one form: the cau pf 1s variant <hăqeymæT> at Dan 3:14, interpretable as [hăqémæθ], with æ ← ε (§20.2(γ)), cf. Tib [hăqémɛθ], and contrast the primary-epn-derived covariant bb[hăqémi̲θ] (BL 149). Various Babylonian 3fs forms are ambiguous between derivation < *-*t* to the tune of r-epn and < *-at* with epenthesis irrelevant: e.g., <hiTGŏzæræT> (lc) univocally spelling [hiθgŏzǽræθ] but this in turn derivationally ambiguous—either < hiθgŏzɛ́rɛθ <r-epn *hitgazír-t (the detail of the relevant vocalism would be . . . *ír*. . . r-epn,low(§17.10)> . . . *áre*. . . aop > . . . *áre*. . . mvh (§2.3.2.1) > . . . *ére*. . . (§20.2(γ)) > [. . . ǽræ . . .] or < barytone *hitgazír-at (. . . *íra*. . . low > . . . *ára*. . . (§20.2(γ)) > [. . . ǽræ . . .]).

[7] Admittedly, the evidential value of sim rmp's like <yDByqT> is open to question, since ml <y> might represent 2ʃ [ī] lengthened by ssl (§17.28), in which case the form could just as likely represent oxytone [IddŏvīqáT]. (For auslaut [-aT] rather than [-aθ], §12.2 n. 12.)

[8] Though the accentual and length properties of trad pron vowels are dictated almost wholly by smc and so lend minimal testimony for earlier states, the very presence of 2ʃ [V] is a probable witness to original barytonicity, inasmuch as the oxytone pattern in the sim verb would normally have led to the deletional reduction of 2ʃ—but only "normally," because SM also shows sporadic evidence of *both* (a) weakening rather than expected full reduction—see, e.g., the case of <9BDh> in §12.2 w n. 13 and §24.2 under *√9bd (so that t[bātắnɑt] might conceivably derive from living SM [baṭănáθ], [ă] subsequently promoted, stressed, and lengthened by smc), *and* (b) even analogical restoration of expectedly deleted vowels (so that t[ắ] might, again conceivably, be the reflex of a postdeletional vowel reinserted into earlier oxytone *baṭnáθ* on the analogy of the undeleted 3ms 2ʃ; and while such a transparentive origin of 2ʃ [V] has been suggested for the A dialects at large (§15.2.1.1), SM shows at least a modicum of evidence for reinsertion independent of the pf paradigm focal to the account in §15.2.1.1—see n. 16 below.

[9] As discussed in §22.2, the forms in Yem trad pron are being *interpreted* for stress in the corresponding reconstructed TL forms, inasmuch as the stress pattern of Yem trad pron per se is given by rules based solely on syllable structure and hence incapable of reflecting the original TL barytone-oxytone distinction in most cases.

[10] As per the examples presented to date for the various dialects, the light suffixes par excellence enabling barytone stress are 3fs [-AT] and 1s [-IT]. TL may be alone in possibly extending extrametricality to the impa fp suffix spelt <-n> in <qtwln> 'kill!' (Mar 8). But since according to both Yem and Ash trad pron, this suffix was pronounced [-Ān], with long [Ā] (y[ā], a[ɔ]), it seems dubious that this form was actually barytone, positioning of an extraheavy (trimoraic) syllable of shape [V̄C] posttonically being

against the grain of A tonosyllabic canons. It appears more likely that the form was actually oxytone [qŏṭUlÁn], of purely transparentive origin. (True, such a formation would also seem to violate another tonosyllabic canon, that disfavoring open short-vocalic syllables in pretonic position. But there are already several exemptions from this canon, which therefore may have been rather shortlived; see, e.g., §4.2.1, §7.4.1, §13 n. 3, §15.2.1–3.)

[11] Before leaving the treatment of stress, it might bear mentioning that all three E dialects—SR, TL, and M—give evidence in the later stages of at least some systemic backward shifting of the accentual pattern, though not precisely in the same way or to the same degree across the dialects (B 46, Mor 117–19, Macm 137). Since the trad pron of SM also shows this tendency (§22.1), it is quite likely that backward accent shift formed part of the wave of changes sweeping over later Aramaic across the E–W divide (§19 with (19H))—a possibility enhanced by the fact that there are modern descendants on both branches showing such patterns (W Ma9lula, E M, and some varieties of SR). In this book, we will normally assume the earlier stress systems described in this section (§4.1).

[12] The qualification "at least historically" registered in the preceding paragraph with regard to the like of B [bŏṭeláθ] anticipates the possibility that a diachronic iterative process might mutate synchronically to some noniterative modality; e.g., a case might be made for reinterpreting *QaSaMát* d-red > *QaSMáT* d-att > [QISMáT] as /QaSaMát/ s-red ⇒ |QŏSMáT| s-prm(§14) ⇒ [QISMáT], where s-red is a *noniterative* reduction rule simultaneously reducing both open syllables /Qa/ and /Sa/ (cf. Chomsky and Halle's "*-convention" (1968); an early approach to M in this manner is Malone 1972c).

[13] Deletion in lieu of weakening applies in the event *prothesis* takes place: [(ʔ)V̊QSáM]. Of course, once the prothetic vowel appears, we are dealing with a special case of pattern (γ). See §17.18 for discussion.

[14] (a) Which ultimately < **tizapína* (with *i* replaced by *ay* (via frf, §17.7) which coalesces to *ē*). If weakening as opposed to deletion holds universally in A /CC__, as proposed above, and if *y* counts as *C*, then either f-red was the norm /V̌C__ and coales‐ cence (*ay* > *ē*, §11) predated red in SR, or p-red was the norm /V̄C__ and *V̌* > Ø/V̄C__ is a later codicil of SR reduction—likely a reprise thereof, since it is commonplace for reprise changes to differ (usually modestly) in conditions from their primary originals (as it is also common for persistent changes to shift in conditions, frequently by widen-ing, as time goes on). In either event, the final step in the accordion *p* > *f* > [p] is mootly given by either reo or as a systemic merger in Nes SR (§5.2).

(b) The most probable interpretation of (γ–ζ) is that reduction aims to delete but stops short at weakening when full loss would incur a canonic violation; thus, both (δ) and (ε) might reflect a constraint disfavoring complex syllable onsets, while (ζ) might reflect a dispreference for extraheavy (trimoraic) syllables—unsurprisingly vari-able, since the A dialects normally tolerate such in auslaut position (e.g., sm impa ms [QuM]).

(c) The conception just expressed under (b) that "reduction aims to delete but stops short at weakening" should be integrable with Kaufman's view (1984), buttressed by several types of evidence, that, diachronically, reduction started out as pure weakening only to reach the deletional stage several centuries later.

[15] (a) Schulthess does not specify the person of <šyDyT>; (b) he (Sg 10) interprets the <T> of such as <ḥsyTʔ> 'beata' as < *3 √D + T (i.e., by dca, §10 n. 3) bespeaking deletional (ζ) of original *ḥasīdatā̃—but the origin might just as well have been *ḥasīdtā̃, given the general allomorphic pattern of fs *-at ~ *-t in pSemitic.

[16] The qualification "perhaps" in view of Macuch's judgment that earlier t[tildi] ist "zwar ursprünglicher" (lc), consideration of which takes us down a tangled garden path of issues central to SM's behavior vis-à-vis reduction. If earlier t[tildi] (stress omitted because of uncertainty as to the chronology of c-pen in the development of the Samaritan circuit) should indeed be "ursprünglicher" than modern t[tīl̥ádi] in the sense that the latter was derived from the former, we apparently must have recourse to an analogical insertion process (with forms like t[tīl̥ɑd] 'ich werde gebären', (Macs 180f) as model for the inserted 2ʃ, subsequently tonically lengthened by c-pra). There are, however, escape-hatches from that conclusion. We might assume that (the forerunner of) t[tīl̥ádi] did in fact coexist in earlier trad pron with t[tildi], but that only the latter happened to get recorded (by Petermann 1873), and that the actual alternation between the two forms at that time stemmed *either* from the reason given in the text, (ζ)-variation between deletion and weakening, *or* from inheritance of short ~ long impf forms (§7.2) t[tīl̥ádi] < short *tiládī ~ t[tildi] < long *tiladína, in which case we need only assume deletion as the SM value of (ζ). Of these two possibilities, the former seems more likely, because far from deletion ruling the roost in modern trad pron, earlier t[tildi] may be one of the rare traces of deletion left, weakening being the decidedly favorite resolution— e.g., from the same paradigm (1 √w) t[wyīl̥ɑ́dən] 'u. sie gebären', t[wyīrɑ́ton] 'u. sie werden erben' (Macs 181). More radically, SM trad pron gives evidence of pervasive pattern (η), whereby generally expected deletional reduction is replaced by weakening: e.g., <ḥšBh> t[9āšɑ́bɑ] 'er hielt sie' (macs 226), apparently < living SM [9ašɑ́βɑ̆h] in lieu of general A-expected [ḥašBɑ̆h]—and so far (virtually) all object-suffixed forms. (Alternatively, it may be that SM extended subject suffix extrametricality to include object suffixes, or simply refashioned such forms transparentively, so that we are dealing with [9ašɑ́βah] or [9ašaβɑ̆h]. In any event, SM shows a strong preference for maintaining generally reducible 2ʃ. Note, incidentally, in these forms 9 < *ḥ by gtl, §9.3.2.)

[17] The qualifications "in the verb, apparently . . ." are prompted by the fact that Morag documents both deletion and weakening in (e.g.) the participle (91f).

[18] (a) By the theory of "inert elements" proposed in Malone 1995, the result should have been a *short* vowel if the input was ăa. However, the long vowel result is duly predicted if the input was aa.

(b) Though (apparent) V-lengthening-compensated guttural onset loss may perhaps thus be explicated with the help of excrescence in strings *VC | HV′* where *V′* → *V̄′* (| marks the syllable break), such an explanation is not available for strings of shape *V | HV′*, in default of any consonant cluster for excrescence to interrupt. By hypothesis of this book, however, *V′* in *VHV′ may* compensatorily lengthen as per trad pron. This said, the evidence for this position is rather tenuous, since the end product of the *H*-deletion process (dgt) almost always consists of a single long vowel t[V̄″] via fusion of *VV̄′*—and in that event the necessity of positing lengthened *V̄′* as part of an unattested intermediate stage is eminently contestable; cf. several derivations in §22.1 (22C), viz. (η, θ, ι). The closest thing to palpable evidence for intermediate *V̄′* is derivation (λ), where in lieu of fusion, *gliding* (qua hiatus-breaking) takes place, the end product being t[yiyyǽ̯t] with duly lengthened [æ].

(c) Note also that an alternative, non-excrescent hypothesis is proposed for the like of t[nēdā́l] in §22.1 n. 3.

[19] Examination of Morag's index of forms (*Miftaḥ curot hapo9al*, Mor 352–88) under the headings 1 √h, 1 √ḥ, 1 √9—including entry √9rq—reveals no trace of the phenomenon.

[20] Schulthess also lists [i̯əza9ez9ōn] 'sie erschüttern' (lc), but without providing the orthographic form (and none appears in Sl either).

[21] (a) Note that in association with Aufsprengung, M regularly lengthens the nucleus of the now open immediately preceding syllable (and in the process heightens $ē →$ *ī*, §11.2); cf. also note 24 below. (b) Systematic exceptions to Aufsprengung include: (*) forms with plural object suffixes (§15.5.1), with [tīšeBqón] contrast [ešbə̆qenxón] 'I'll forgive you (mp)' (DM 447); (*) metathesized (rmt, §10) sim rmp forms (Malone 1985), with [īθeGBéβ] contrast [eštə̆βéq] 'was expelled' (DM 448); (*) causatives and (quadriradical) intensives, [albə̆sáx] 'he clothed you' (Mal 379) (contrast B bb[hæsilṭǽx], §4.4.2 B), [hambə̆láθ] 'she labored' (DM 129).

[22], [23] Orthography-induced ambiguous pairs between < : > [ə̆] and < : > [∅] (§21.5). (Admittedly, there is no guarantee that any given actual form must be interpretable both ways; so the risk is real for exaggeration in the possibilities bespoken by (4E, F, G).)

[24] Wherein either (a) *a* of *tafiršŭ́n* undergoes lengthening as a further repair strategy (targeting an atonic open-syllabic *V̆*), or (b) interpretation of <α> as [ā] is spurious, the matter rather being Schematisierung based on Tiberian orthography, as frequently suspected of the Sabbionetan subregister (Malone 1974b). If (a), we face the sticky question of when maintenance of atonic open-syllabic *V̆* constitutes an occasion for repair strategy visitation and when it does not. Cf. also note 10 above.

[25] (a) While the preceding note ([24]) documents a Sabbionetan strategy to remove (the orthographic appearance of) an atonic short-vocalic open syllable by (orthographically) rendering it long-vocalic, this case shows the alternative strategy of (orthographically) turning it into a closed syllable via (orthographic) gemination of the 1√. (In this connection, note that this is a *simple plain* form, not a *rmp* form, in which case the gemination would be expected by assimilation of 1√d to the rmp prefix *T* (§10).) The fact that the result is (orthographically represented as) *dd* rather than (as) ðð will be taken to be manifestation of *geminate spirant reocclusion* (gsr). (Incidentally, it cannot be ruled out that forms like sb<ʔæ9æbeD> stand for "virtually" geminated *ʔæ99æbéð* in view of the Tiberian orthographic restriction against <9̄>, so that even here a(n orthographic) repair strategy may be intended. There are, however, forms where the absence of any strategy is rather clear: e.g., sb<mæšiyr:yɑn> [mæširyɑ́n] 'Lager' (~ bb[mæširyɑ́n ~ mæšrə̆yɑ́n) (Da 94, 169). Remarks parallel to those offered in this note vis-à-vis [tiddæḥə̆lū́n] are in order for forms ambiguous as to prefix-vowel length, e.g., impf 3mp sb<yiziyr:quwn> (Da 94), as either unrepaired [yi̱zirqū́n] or repaired [yī̱zirqū́n].)

(b) In fact, the orthographic ambiguity in this general area reaches even farther, in that in Babylonian orthographies, and to some extent in Tiberian versions like Sabbioneta, absence of symbols for ḥataf vowels may have led to their representation by the vowel point used for corresponding shorts (or for the color irrespective of length); §21.5. To the extent that this may be so, forms spelled in certain systems may be ambiguous between (f) and (h) of (4F, G), to cite one important set of cases.)

[26] (a) "to the extent that. . ."; i.e., inasmuch as in the pattern type under consideration here it is always the excrescent syllable that is targeted by promotion and (m – n) fail to excresce. However, it might be viable to synchronically explicate various instances of transparentation by applying s-prm to $2\int \breve{V}$ of nonexcrescent origin; e.g., TR [ʾōnẹqī́hī] (§15.5.1) ⇐ |ʾōnǎqī́hī|—see also the nonexcrescent yet promotable $\breve{V}$ of the simple impa; §17.25. (b) Observe that the prohibitions listed here are not necessarily mutually exclusive; thus, this prohibition (on (m, n)) equally applies to (i, j).

[27] The topic of §4.5 was the concern of Malone 2004.

5. Spirantization (spr) and Reocclusion (reo)

5.1. The Fundamental Nature of Spirantization

All dialects as of B at the latest were subject in one fashion or another to a process of *spirantization* (spr), whereby traditionally labeled nonemphatic (nonphranyngealized, nonuvularized (Malone 1976)) singleton stops—i.e., *p, t, k, b, d, g*—weakened to homorganic slit fricatives, f (or φ), θ, x, v (or β), δ, γ, in immediate postvocalic (or sometimes postsemivocalic) position. Since consonant weakening involves change of manner of articulation in the direction of vowel (and semivowel) space, the process is understandable as one of progressive assimilation (spreading of (semi)vocalic features forward onto an adjacent stop). The exclusion of emphatic stops, whatever its phonetic motivation, exempts *ṭ* and *q*. Also geminate clusters (*pp*, etc.) are universally exempt.[1]

Unpointed A orthographies usually make no distinction between stops and corresponding spirants[2] (henceforth the term "spirant" will be specialized in reference to slit fricatives, while *rilled* fricatives—*š, s, z, ṣ*—will be called "sibilants," the term "fricative" serving as a generic over both). Since this graphemic neutralization makes it difficult or impossible to ascertain the precise disposition of spr in most dialects, our focus will essentially be limited to B, TR, and SR.[3]

5.2. Spirantization and Reocclusion; The Individual Dialects (in Particular B, TR, SR)

In the conception of this book, an aufgesprengt form like sim impf 2mp [ta9avðū́n] shows spirantization to be *persistent* around reduction: *ta9budū́n* s̲p̲r̲ → *ta9buðū́n* red→ *ta9bǝðū́n* exc → *ta9ǎbǝðū́n* spr → *ta9ǎvǝðū́n* swh → *ta9ǎvðū́n* prm → [ta9avðū́n]. On the other hand, if as also in accord with the conception of this book, reduction necessarily feeds *prothesis* (pro, §17.18), the occlusive [t] in prothesized [ʔištíw] 'they drank' is counterpredicted: *šatíyū* e-cnd → *šatíw* spr → *šaθíw* red → *šǝθíw* pro→ @[ʔišθíw]. This problem can be solved, or at least patched up, by appealing to an accordion-like process of *reocclusion* (reo) whereby a postconsonantal spirant (*f, θ, x, v, ð, γ*) reverts to its corresponding stop value (*p, t, k, b, d, g*); thus *šatíyū* → *šatíw* → *šaθíw* → *šǝθíw* → *ʔišθíw* reo → [ʔištíw]. A formulational challenge for reocclusion is

82

specification of precise conditions in addition to *C+spirant*. Note in particular the maintenance of the postconsonantal spirant in the light-suffixed oxytone sim pf: 1s [qirᵥéθ], [9avₔéθ]; and in the anlaut of the 2mp object suffix [-xōn] in such as [yᵅšēzᵅvinx̱ōn]. Hence, the extra condition might provisionally be taken to stipulate that the reoccluding spirant be 2√.[4]

Note, finally, that semivowels also act as conditioners to spr: [hayθí] 'er brachte' (BL 169).

So, anticipating comparison with TR and SR, we may take the hub of spr-reo in B to consist of:

(α) the ordering spr^red^reo^exc^spr^swh^prm;

(β) the condition on reo that the postconsonantal reoccluded *C* be 2√;

(γ) the condition on spr that the spirantized *C* immediately follow either a vowel or a semivowel.

(Beyond this hub, there is more that might be said about stop-spirant relations in B, much of it beyond the purview of this book. For occlusion in pf 2s [hištᵅxáhat̲], see §15.3.1.3. For spirantization across clitic boundaries, as well as a congeries of lexical exceptions, see BL 42–44; see also §2.1.1 n. 4 and §21.6 in this book.)

TR. The hub stop-spirant nexus of TR differs from that of B in all three parameters (the second (β) requiring certain straightforward but by no means conclusive assumptions about the orthography):

(α) Spirantization is only variably persistent: spr^red^reo^exc^(spr)^swh ^prm;

(β) The restrictive coindition on reocclusion is generalized from "second radical" to "any radical";

(γ) The semivocalic condition on spr is optional (i.e., an otherwise spirantizable *C* in the environment /W__ may or may not spirantize, whereas /V__ it must).

The evidence for (α) was presented in (4G), where forms such as sb[tᵅ9ib(ᵅ)rū́n], sb[yæ9æb̲Dū́n], sb[yæ9æb̲éð], bb[yi9ib̲rū́n] show spr failing to affect 2√, while forms like sb[ˀæ9æ̇ð̲í] and tb[ˀæ9æ̇ᵥǽr] do show such spr.

The evidence for (β) lies in forms like bb[ů̱rk̲ívá] 'und sie(f) ritten' (Da 263) < *warakíbā and tb[tibbæht̲ín] 'du schamst dich' (Da 271) < *titbahiθína[5], where stop status is explicitly indicated by the grapheme dageš—and it will be assumed that forms not explicitly marked for stop-fricative status (especially those couched in Babylonian orthography), like <ræDP̲uwK> (Da 366), <næsBuwhiy> (Da 367), may be interpreted as having undergone reo as well (hence [ræðp̲ú̱x] 'sie verfolgten dich', [næsb̲ú̱hī] 'sie nahmen ihn', Da 367), interpretations which would beg the question were it not for unambiguous cases like [ůrkívā], [tibbæhtín]. For nonreocclusion of nonradicals (affixes), cf. [9æddî(ʾ)æθxṓn] 'sie hat euch(mp) erbeutet' (Da 364).[6]

SR. Spirantization in SR (α) differs from its counterparts in B and TR primarily in ordering, in that its rerun occurs spr^exc while in B and TR the order is exc^spr. Reocclusion (β) works the same as in TR (without the complication of syncretism mentioned in note 6; [qabbɛlθḗh] 'she received him'), while in (γ) the trigger for spr must be vocalic, not also semivocalic as in B and TR. SR may also give evidence of a fourth clause to the hub (δ), vis-à-vis which the disposition of B and TR is inconclusive.

(α) spr^red^reo^spr^exc^swh^prm

Evidence for this ordering comes on the one hand from the constancy of the stop value of 2√ in aufgesprengt forms like [nɛzɛbnṹn] (§4.4.1), and on the other hand from the systematic respirantization of 3√ in 2√ʾ-deleted forms like [kēwáθ] 'sie litt Pein'(Ns 108)—as per the following derivation (5A), wherein also Nöldeke's interpretation is accepted of the stopped variant <kɛʾbáθ> as geminate [kɛbbáθ].[7]

(5A)	*kaʾibát	*yazbinúna
. . .		
spr	kaʾiváθ	—
red	kaʾváθ	nazbǎnún
reo, att(§12)	kiʾbáθ	nizbǎnún
mid(§17.11)	keʾbáθ	nezbǎnún
rga~aga(§9 n. 14)	kebbáθ ~ kēbáθ	—
spr	kēwáθ	—
exc	—	nezǒbǎnún
swh	—	nezǒbnún
prm	—	nezebnún
svs(§20.2(ζ))	[kɛbbáθ] ~ [kēwáθ]	[nɛzɛbnún]

(β) The restrictive condition on reocclusion is "spirant must be √", as in TR. For instance: [kɛθbáθ] 'elle a écrit', [kaθbḗh] 'il l'a écrit' (Du 115), sim rmp impf 2fs [tɛθyazpín] (B 137)—all vs. sim pf 3fs^3ms [QǒSaMθḗh], sim pf 3fs^2ms [QǒSMaθxṓn] (B 145).

(γ) Spirantization is blocked /W__; e.g., [aytí] 'brachte' (B 92).

(δ) This component of the hub involves the relation of spr to *degemination* (deg, §3.1 (3Fvii)), a persistent process—not only for SR, but likely for all of A—dictating as an especially important case that word-final geminate clusters be rendered singleton as soon as they arise, i.e., C'C'# → C'#.[8] While in the noun at least the synchronic ordering of deg and spr is spr^deg (e.g., |lɛ́bb|

'Herz'—spr (stalled by Geminate Integrity, note 1 above)^+deg ⇒ [lέb], Ns 66), in the verb the order is rather deg^spr: e.g., |pákk| 'zerschlug' deg ⇒ |pák| spr ⇒ [páx] (Ns 123).[9]

Though geminate phonetic reflexes of 3√ C'C' are usually retained /__V (e.g. [pɛkkế̃θ] 'ich zerschlug', lc), note that the transparentively renewed (§15.2.1.3 n. 9) variants of sim pf 3mp and 3fp, built as they are diachronically on the least-marked 3ms *QaS*, show singletons open to spirantization: [pax̲ûn], [pax̲ế̃n].[10], [11]

Specific to SR appear to be: in the Nes register, nonspirantization of *p* and spirantization of *b* as [w] (B 12)[12]; in SR at large, a characteristically Greek rendition of Greek <π> in borrowings as an *un*aspirated voiceless stop, never spirantizable (Ns §25), in this book to be transcribed π.

(For more of SR stop-spirant relations, including spr across clitic boundaries, see Ns §23–§25.)

5.3. Diachronic Origins of spr-reo Patterning

A few retrospective thoughts on the diachronics behind the patterns seen in §5.2:

(α) The persistence of spirantization around reduction and the give-and-take between spirantization and reocclusion are likely to have had the same etiology: *chronological and geographical overlap of spirantization and reduction in the period directly following their emergence.* This is so in that spr^red^spr may effectively recapitulate some of the original overlap: spr both precedes and follows red exactly as a byproduct of their original chronological overlap. The interplay between spr and reo lends itself to a different sort of interpretation: reocclusion would not per se have existed at the earlier stages, being rather an epiphenomenon of spirantization being bled by reduction in the order red^spr; while positive application of spr would have the opposite interpretation, spr^red. And of course the coexistence of red^spr and spr^red within one and the same dialect would point again to overlap: one process sometimes preceding and at other times following the other process, precisely because originally both processes (largely) shared the same time and space. It might finally be surmised that the historical sense of the restrictive conditions on reocclusion (2√, √) reflects the upshot of the dialects' attempting to impose a structural orderliness on the processes affecting them. At the inchoative stage, on the other hand, it would not be surprising if the conditions for red^spr vs. spr^red were considerably more chaotic—perhaps altogether nonexistent in that rampant free variation might have been the rule of the day (cf. Malone 1992). (For a distinguished attempt at more precise dating of red and spr, see Kaufman 1984.)[13]

(β) Reocclusion and spirantization both show cline-like behavior diachronically with respect to their conditions. In reo, generalization of the $2\sqrt{}$ condition in the earlier dialect (B) to $\sqrt{}$ in the later dialects (TR, SR) follows a commonplace developmental path: widening of conditions over time. In the case of spr, on the other hand, progressive *retrenching* of conditions seems to be the case: first both vowels and semivowels (B), then shrinking of the semivowel condition (TR), and finally loss of the semivowel condition altogether (SR). (This apparent retrenching of conditions in B might however point to B's being an "anachronic" dialect; see §19(δ).)

Notes to §5

[1] An explanation for the exemption of geminates from the vantage of Autosegmental Phonology (§23.5) resides in so-called *Geminate Integrity* (cf. Kenstowicz 1994: 410–12). To see how this works, consider that standard autosegmental modeling of gemination has it that the characteristic length/doubling stems from the geminate occupying two successive *C*-positions on the skeletal tier, while the segmental value of the geminate results from the duo *C-positions* being linked to a single-rooted bundle (or geometry) of features on the melodic tier. Thus, allowing "t" to stand for the bundle of features defining the nonemphatic voiceless dentoalveolar stop *t*, geminate *tt* will be modeled like this:

(a)   melodic tier   t

       skeletal tier   C   C

Now what happens if spr attempts to apply to say, M *attí* 'he brought' (cf. §9.2.1.1)? If the result were @[aθθí], the *second* [θ] would by hypothesis be illegitimate because only the *first* [θ] corresponds to a *C*-position, which is properly postvocalic; and if the result were @[aθtí], the problem would be, again by hypothesis, illegitimate splitting of the singleton melody *t*. So Geminate Integrity claims that in such an impasse *nothing* happens; spirantization simply stalls.

That said, however, it is noteworthy that Geminate Integrity de facto leaks, and the literature is replete with real or apparent countercases, some but not all with conventionally theorized escape-hatches. Two may be mentioned here from Aramaic.

(b) Though Classical M <atia> is interpreted in this book as [attí], well behaved with respect to Geminate Integrity, Modern M shows [áθθí]. How come? Because, as will be picked up in note 3, Modern M has largely *lexicalized* the old spirant-stop alternation, and in the case of the reflex of *√ʔty 'come(sim), bring(cau,int)', the Modern descendant of *2√t is θ. Hence *tt > θθ* in *attí > áθθí* is not via spr, but via analogical leveling.

(c) Again in Modern M, but this time possibly in Classical M as well, [θt] arises, now plausibly by spr, when suffixal *t* is added to postvocalic radical *t*: e.g., m&t[méθton] 'you(mp) died' (Macm 12, 325), the morphemic independence of the two morphemes, radical and suffixal, in this instance being supported by the spelling <mittun> (cf.§15.3.1.2). In situations like this, apparent violation of Geminate Integrity has at times been attributed to the cluster in question constituting a so-called "fake geminate," whereby *two* melodic *t*s would a priori be involved rather than one; hence (d), unlike (a), would not comprise an Integrity-relevant configuration. (In this specific instance, however, it may be that [θt] emerged under transparentation rather than in response to fake gemination; cf. note 8 below and §15.3.1.2.)

(s) melodic tier   t   t
                       | |
     skeletal tier   C   C

[2] An occasional exception is the use of <w> for the spirantized counterpart of *b*, notably in SM and G; for the rationale, see note 13c below.

[3] The four traditional pronunciations appealed to in this book tend to leave us for several reasons more or less in the lurch. SM trad pron has evolved in an interesting way per se, but for the most part keeps us in the dark as the nature of spr in the days of the dialect's florescence (though a partial exception involves the labial obstruents, briefly discussed in note 13 below). Yem trad pron of TL has for the most part lexicalized the values of stop vs. spirant per root in a way unrevealing of the original situation, while Ash trad pron seems to ape Tiberian B a bit too closely for comfort (and yet both traditions here and there provide food for thought—see again note 13 below). M trad pron follows the Modern language, which in turn has heavily lexicalized (there is weak evidence only for: the spirantal value /V__, when V remained phonetic; for the stop value of original geminate stops $C'C'$ upon simplification of $C'C'$ə̆ to C' (§17.28); and for the spirantal value immediately following a prothetic vowel (pro, §17.18)—all together suggesting a partial ordering red^spr^pro^spr^smp, with spr persisting at least around pro (see Malone 1997.)

[4] Since the bridge [-in-] in [yə̆šēzə̆vinxṓn] derives from *-inn-* (§7.1), we might be able to exclude reocclusion of [-xōn] by reordering reo^smp(§17.26). However, such a tack will not work for TR and SR [-xōn], as we will soon see.

[5] The derivation of this form involves a double accordion on 3√:

θ occ(§17.14) > *t* spr > θ reo> [t].

[6] (a) Forms like sb[ʾæškæḫt͛æ̃nã] 'sie hat uns gefunden' (Da 364) are provisionally taken to reflect *syncretic replacement* of θ (< *t*) by *t* (§2.3.4.3, §16.2(e)) rather than reocclusion. (Admittedly, there appears to be significant overlap between reo and syn, and it is quite possible that deeper scrutiny might entail reducing much of one process to the other.) (b) Observe that forms like sb<yæ9æbDuwn> are cautiously interpreted as [yæ9æbDū́n] (above in the text), not as [yæ9æbdū́n] despite first-blush satisfaction of (β), because by hypothesis of the ordering in (α) contact between 2√ and 3√ is achieved (by swh) too late for reo to apply.

[7] The dotted line (. . .) on the first derivational line of (5A) represents possible assumed processes (e.g., sap, §17.22), even if properly orderable among or following the processes explicitly listed in the derivation. Note that if <kɛʾb̊aθ> is, contra Nöldeke, interpreted as [kɛbáθ] with adr (§9.2.1.1) deleting ʾ without compensatory lengthening, we would have to engage in some fancy stipulative footwork to ensure nonderivation of @[kɛwáθ] in light of the variant [kēwáθ] ≠ @[kēbáθ]. This consideration suggests the correctness of the interpretation of the like of impf jc<neʾxul> as [nēxúl] rather than

as [nềxúl] in the disquisition of §9.2.1.2. Hence, in this book [kɛbbáθ] ~ [kēwáθ] will be adopted, incidentally following the lead of an analysis for a different cross-section of morphology in a closely related dialect, M (Malone 1991). Observe finally that acceptance of the like of [kēwáθ] (and [nềxúl]) requires morphologically conditioned inhibiting of hei (§11.2) in the Jacobite register, to forfend against @[kīwáθ] (@[nīxúl]).

[8] A touchstone for taking deg to be a pan-Aramaic persistent rule undoing word-final geminates "as soon as they arise" may be M [méθt] 'you died', <mitt> m+t[méθt] (Macm 12, 325), if this form is derived from *mítta (short *ʃi* by css enforced in pA, see §6 n. 6), with ancipitally short-vocalic *-ta (§2.3.1). In that case, as soon as *-a is dropped by sap (§17.22), the resulting *mítt* should by deg whittle to *mít*, thus subverting any development by purely phonetic mechanisms of eventual [-θt]. If such a derivation should be granted, either (a) deg would have to be formulated without the clause "as soon as they arise" so as to allow *mitt* to linger long enough for spirantization to break up the fake geminate to *-θt* thus preempting further relevance of deg, or (b) a nonphonetic, analogical process would have to be appealed to, call it "x," deriving accordion-like *mítta* sap > *mítt* deg > *mít* . . . x > [méθt], x thus assimilating the morphologically anomalous auslaut *-t* to strong-patterning *-3√θt*. (c) However, if derivation from *mítta* is given up in favor of derivation from ancipitally long-vocalic *míttā*, deg can be kept intact with its clause "as soon as they arise" because the relevant apocope process is now lap (§17.9), and lap arose diachronically later than spirantization (§19 (19F, G)) so that the occasion for deg never arises: *míttā* spr (of the fake geminate) > *míθtā* lap (plus css, mid) > [méθt]. The working assumption in this book is that M [me t] bespeaks either (b) or (c), so that "as soon as they arise" is not jeopardized for deg; cf. note 1 above and more discussion in §15.3.1.2.

[9] (a) As will be discussed below (§5.3), such apparently bizarre, contrastive ordering is characteristic of SR spirantization, a disposition with a rather straightforward diachronic explanation. Also, differential phonological behavior for noun vs. verb is not alien to the Northwest Semitic languages; for Hebrew, cf., e.g., the behavior of tonic lengthening (THP 95–97). (b) The sense of the qualification "at least . . . synchronic ordering" may be demonstrated on the attempt to derive [léb] diachronically from its pA etymon *líbbu* on the assumption that d-deg is a pan-Aramaic persistent change rendering auslaut geminate clusters singleton as soon as they arise. Once the case vowel *-u* is lost by uap (§17.31), we are left with *líbb* which will, by hypothesis, immediately be whittled by d-deg to *líb*. But then, what is to prevent the later change of spr from converting this to *lív*, ultimately giving SR @[léw]? In default of an answer to this question, we are left to assume that SR only later engaged in a bit of phonological reorganization, including replacement of *lív* (or *líw*) by *líb*, as part of a system-wide "solution" to spirantization's apparent surface ambivalence as to whether to apply or not (§5.3). Thus, the *synchronic* account of [léb] via s-spr^s-deg would be given *diachronically* by rule reordering (§23.2 (23J)) targeting an antecedent stage *lív*, the trajectory being the accordion chain *líbbu* > *líbb* > *líb* . . . > *lív* . . . > [léb]. (c) For justification of synchronic retention of 3√C'C' in such as |lébb|, |pákk|, cf. homoparadigmatic forms like emphatic state [lɛbbɔ́], 1s [pɛkkḗθ] (Ns 66, 123).

[10] As pointed out in note 9, preceding, [pɛkkḗθ] and the like incidentally provide justification for positing the synchronic reality of /kk/ (appealed to in |pákk| above), and ditto such as emphatic [lɛbbɔ́] for the nominal system (cf. |lébb| above). But then how

are the like of [paxū̃n], [paxḗn] to be accounted for synchronically? A nice way to ac-complish this is via *Lexical Phonology* (§23.3), whereby (a) rules are ordered within *strata* (b) which in turn are ordered among themselves, and (c) individual rules may either be assigned to specific strata or (d) recur in the same order on each stratum. This apparatus is brought to bear in (1) on the problem of [paxū̃n], whose derivation is con-trasted with that of the subminimal pair member [pakkū̃n] 'sie zerschlugen mich'. The following assumptions are adopted: (e) phonologically, 3mp intransitive /ūn/ (< long impf *-ūna* via hii, §7.2( )) contrasts with transitive /ū/ (< pf *-ū*); (f) the object suffix /n/ is first person irrespective of number (< 1s *-nī*, 1p *-nā* by lap, §17.9; see also §16.2 <u>SR</u> (δ)); (g) the order of the rules (wrb = *word building*) is fixed (for the recurrence of spr, cf. (α) above in the text), (h) except for red which is confined to Stratum I. The as-sumed odd qualities of [paxū̃n] (and in parallel, feminine [paxḗn]) are now accounted for as follows: (i) /ūn/ is lexically marked to defer wrb till Stratum II; (j) |a| escapes reduction because in Stratum I where red is lodged a is stressed, contra the conditions of red; (k) [x] of [paxū̃n] is a singleton spirant rather than a geminate stop (as [kk] of [pakkū̃n]) because in Stratum I the bare stem (*pakk*) still constitutes a "word" indepen-dently of its suffix-to-be (*ūn*), and hence *kk* still so-to-say occurs in auslaut, subject to the chain deg^spr. Results like this can pretty much be generalized into a (relatively) unitary account of diachronic-synchronic dystony arising from transparentation: to cap-ture the *diachronic* effect of analogical leveling (notably here the restoration of ʃa from ʃǎ), the morphological parts are sewn together (by wrb) on a later than original stratum, when it is "too late" for pertinent rules (here notably red) to skew the morphological pattern cenematically. (For treatment of similar issues in the TR verb, see Malone 1988.)

(1) Stratum I	/pakk/, /ū/, /n/	/pakk/, /ūn/
wrb	|pakkūn|	—
str	|pakkū̃n|	|pákk|, |ū̃n|
deg	—	|pák|, —
spr	—	|páx|, —
red	—	—, —
spr	—	—, —
Stratum II		
wrb	—	|páxū̃n|
str	—	|paxū̃n|
deg	—	—
spr	—	—
	[pakkū̃n]	[paxū̃n]

[11] Concerning "the disposition of B and TR {being} inconclusive" vis-a-vis (δ): No relevant B forms are attested, and none from TR have come to light. (At least B shows deg^spr in the nominal system—e.g., [ráv] 'gross' (BL 181)—while interest-ingly SR shows spr^deg (cf. note 9 above and [ráb], Ns 65). For discussion, see §5.3.)

[12} There are various ways that this semivocalization might be implemented. In this book it will be achieved on the rerun of spr. (If it were also allowed to modify the primary run, there would be no way for the process reo to distinguish between *w*

< *b and *w ≤ w, with the consequence that forms containing [w] ≤ *w, like [ḥaðwɔ̄]
'Freude' (B 58), would be distorted to @[ḥaðbɔ̄].)

[13] The traditional pronunciations of SM and TL were left out of the text account
for the reasons adduced in note 3. And yet there are perhaps a few things about each to
be said with respect to spr and reo:

(a) In SM trad pron, ±spr is fully neutralized to stop values except in the case of the
labials. These show an interesting complex of developments treated in §21.1 SM. Since
these developments in part influence the consonantal orthography, it may be correct to
surmise that massive SM reocclusion (plus the special twists evidenced by the labials)
impacted the dialect during the period of its florescence.

(b) Though the overall reflex of Yem trad pron is to freeze stop-spirant values lexically (Mor 77–81), there are a few roots that seem either wholly (e.g., √ytb) or in part
(e.g., √yhb) to show living alternations. In addition to unsurprisingly revealing postvocalic spr following an original undeleted vowel as well as maintenance of the stop value
in undisturbed original complementary positions (#__, C__), there is some evidence
of reocclusion of √C /C__: e.g., pf 3fs [yæhḇɔ̌] (~ barytone [yɔ̌hǽvæθ]) (Mor 203f),
3ms^2ms [yæhḇɔ̌x] (219). Ash trad pron, on the other hand, follows Tib B in maintaining the spirant value: [ʔaharv̠ḗh] (§4.4.1 TL). But despite this seeming propensity of
Ash trad pron to follow Tib B anent stop-spirant distribution a bit too closely to fully
avoid a charge of Schematisierung, in the matter of 2 *t occlusion (§15.3.1.3 the tradition may have gone its own way in fielding a (subtly) unique distribution of stop and
spirant reflexes, viz. [θ] /V̄__, [t] /V̊__ (close but, crucially, not identical to the Tiberian
Hebrew pattern (THP 65(a))., e.g., [qɔ̌nḗθ] 'you purchased' (Mar 160*), [hōōð49at] 'you
declared' (Mar 120*)—and while the environing [a] in the latter might be a later insert
by (rerun) exc^prm (cf. §8 n. 13), notice these -exc participial forms: [bɔ̄lɔ̌9át] 'you(m)
swallow' (Mar 94*), [bɔ̄9ḗθ] 'you(m) require' (Mar 95*), [gɔ̄v(ɔ̌)yɔ̌θ] ~ [gɔ̄vḗθ] 'you(f)
collect' (Mar 96*).

(c) Although the evidence is for the most part weak at best, it will be useful to make
summary decisions on the likely disposition of spirantization in the ten dialects omitted
from focal discussion in this chapter. These specifications sidestep many thorny questions (e.g., largely, the disposition of reocclusion), and appeal implicitly to complementary or supplementary points adduced elsewhere in the book. Some of the rationale for
the groupings adopted is laid out in §24.1:

- spr is assumed to have emerged later than Y and O.
- I, P, and n. are assumed to spirantize along the lines of B.
- The W dialects—CP, SM, G—are taken to spirantize along the lines of TR except that CP may have reoccluded θ to t (§12.2 n. 12) and the labials in minimally SM and G show various special properties, notably: At least the voiced
  bilabial stop b spirantizes to homorganic bilabial β (rather than to labiodental
  v). At the same time, the bilabial semivowel w fortifies β to (except in anlaut
  where it remains semivocalic, so that in particular reflexes of the conjunctive
  proclitic *wa= are pronounced with initial [w-]). That is, the fricative β becomes
  something of {notes to §5: note [13] concluded} a phonetic magnet, triggering
  neutralization both from above (stop space) and below (semivowel space): b >
  $β$ < w. (The evidence for this special behavior of the labials is given for SM

in §21.1. For G, see the panoply of spelling interchanges adduced by Kutscher 1976:16f. Note also that spirantization of the *voiceless* bilabial p will be taken to be labiodental f, despite the suggestions made for early or pre-SM in §21.1.)

- The L dialects of the E group, TL and M, are also assumed to spirantize along the rough lines of TR, except that M is like SM and G in showing $b >$ (though not also w) $> \beta$).

- Though SR is treated above in the body of the chapter, it might be apposite to remark here again that at least the Nestorian register of this dialect also shows a few special labial quirks: b "spirantizes" to w, and p fails to spirantize.

6. Hollow-Geminate Rapprochement (hgr) and Hollow-Geminate Neutralization (hgn)

6.1. Hollow-Geminate Rapprochement

Though hollow-geminate forms that have *systemically* merged under phonological or morphosyntactic conditions perhaps appear in only three dialects (TR and the two L dialects, TL[1] and M),[2] forms attesting to at least *sporadic* merger, or to incomplete rapprochement between these two gĕzarot, show up at least as early as B. In what follows, any instance of formal *similarity* developed between hollows and geminates will be tagged *hollow-geminate rapprochement* (hgr), while limiting cases of such development—those leading to out-and-out phonetic *identity* of whole hollow and geminate forms—will be referred to as *hollow-geminate neutralization* (hgn). Like the complete neutralizations, the incomplete rapprochements are usually of the hollow verb being reshaped in the direction of the geminate. Moreover, the incomplete rapprochements normally appear in the causative, and assume either one or sometimes both of two principal guises: (α) *short schematic generalization* (ssg), whereby a 2ʃ in the hollow, unmarkedly long, appears as short, thus manifesting conformity to the unmarked geminate pattern (a gem 2ʃ is always short unless affected by either of the marked processes ssl, §17.28, or tln, §17.29);[3] (β) *causative initial strengthening* (cis), whereby the reduced (§4.2) syllable housing the cau prefix in the hollow verb is rendered full-vocalic in any of three ways (thus approaching the corresponding syllables in the geminate verb which is full-vocalic a priori, being closed by either geminate 1√ 1√ (gmf-4u, (3M)) or heterophonous 1√ 3√ (gmf-4m, (3N)).

6.1.1. Short Schematic Generalization (ssg)

6.1.1.1. ssg in the Causative

Observe that while the cursory description of cis offered above (§6.1) is couched in dynamic terms—"the reduced ... syllable ... is rendered full-vocalic"—ssg is introduced neutrally: "2ʃ ... appears as short." The reason for this terminological difference is that the hollow-toward-geminate bias labeled "ssg" is accomplished by reshaping within Aramaic only in a minority of cases, the bulk of it rather being inherited from pA, and possibly earlier, in terms of the pattern reconstructed in (6A), a pattern similar to that evinced by Hebrew and Arabic:

(6A) In the pA hollow causative, 2ʃ /V̄/ was realized as [V̊] in a closed syllable (that is, closed syllabic shortening (css, §17.4), was already in force).

Evidence for (6A) may be seen in several causative forms of B √qWm, 'raise' (BL 149,151): pf 2ms [hăqḗmtɔ̄], contrast 3mp [hăqī́mū]; 1s [hăqḗmɛθ], because the syllable was not yet opened in pA (by epn, §17.6); contrast canonically similar 3fs (labial passive) [hɔ̆qīmáθ] where the corresponding syllable always had been open, < *huqīmát; impf 3ms [yᵊ̆hɔ̆qḗm], bb[yᵊ̆hāqḗm] ~ bb[yᵊ̆hāqī́m], reflecting <u>either</u> the possibility of (α) residual (formal though not functional) short impf ~ long impf alternation (*yihaqím ~ *yihaqī́mi, §7.2),[4] <u>or</u> (β) persistence of css in the wake of sap (§17.22), but on its rerun with simple syllable closure (/__C#) working out as a variable conditioner, lacking the clout of double closure (/__CC). Assuming (β) over (α) for the sake of compact demonstration, these results are compositely presented in (6B):

(6B)
possibly
but not
necessarily

pre-pA	**haqī́mtā	* *haqī́mū	**haqī́mt	**huqīmát	**yihaqī́mi
css					
applies					
deriving					
pA	*haqī́mtā	*haqī́mū	*haqī́mt	*huqīmát	*yihaqī́mi
epn			haqī́mit		
sap					yihaqī́m
±r-css					yihaqím ~ yihaqī́m

. . .

[hăqḗmtɔ̄]   [hăqī́mū]   [hăqḗmɛθ]   [hɔ̆qīmáθ]   [yᵊ̆hāqḗm]~[yᵊ̆hāqī́m]

Patterning similar to that in B is found for TR; cf.: [ʔᵊ̆θḗvnā̆], contrast [ʔᵊ̆9ī́qū]; epenthetic [ʔᵊ̆rḗmiθ], contrast [ʔᵊ̆ðī́qæθ]; /__C# variability with [ʔᵊ̆qḗm] vs. [ʔᵊ̆γíæḥ]([íæ] ← ī́ by pgn, §17.16). TR also shows extension of ssg beyond its inherited distribution, e.g., 3fs [ʔᵊ̆θḗ̆væθ]—contrast conservative [ʔᵊ̆ðī́qæθ]. (Examples from Da 323.)

Additional instances are to be found in at least SM (Macs 195f) and the Yem trad pron of TL (Mor 227f). SM: epenthetic 1s t[āqḗmət] vs. non-epenthetic 3ms^3ms t[āqī́me] (note that though length of the focal vowel is neutralized by the smc, the cue to the original disposition lingers in the color difference;

c-pra, §22.1 (22Biv)). TL: y[ʾæḥéxt] vs. y[ʾæḥíxū] ([æḥ] ← mls, §9.3.1, *aḥḥ*
with geminate √ḥḥ by g-cis, §6.1.2).

In view of the effects of ssg so far demonstrated, what is to be made of
instances of the opposite disposition, whereby ssg-expected [Ĭ] rather shows
up as [ī]? While sporadically found in such as SM epenthetic t[ābĭsət] (Macs
195f), such anti-ssg [ī] constitutes the pervasive and regular reflex in Ashkenazic TL (contrast Yem [ʾæḥéxt], above, with Ash [ʾaḥíxt] (Mar 111*) as well
as in SR.

A plausible explanation is that the original disposition of the pA hollow
causative, with its ssg-induced alternation *2ʃ ī ~ *2ʃi, set up the potential for
two diametric trajectories: rapprochement to the geminate verb, on the basis of
the short alternant 2ʃi; or generalization of the long alternant 2ʃī as hallmark
of the hollow paradigm. This latter resolution, later fully achieved in at Ash TL
and SR, might be called *long schematic generalization* (lsg).[5]

6.1.1.2. ssg in the Simple Verb

Only two cases of hollow-to-geminate rapprochement manifested by shortness of 2ʃ in the hollow simple verb have come to light, a hapax from B and an
apparently general pattern from SM.

The B case, via ssg, is [wīháx] 'and let it{them} be brought back', analytically 'and let it go' (Ezra 6:5), plausibly a retention of the short impf *wayihák*
⇐ */wa=y-i 1√h a 3√k /) via spr^red^att (§5.1, §4.2, §12)). In addition to
[wīháx], there is the unmarkedly structured procliticless variant [yə̄hɔ́x] (Ezra
5:5, 7:13) with [ɔ̄] ⇐ /ā/ via lsg (BL 148).[6]

The SM case does not strictly speaking involve ssg but will be included
here anyhow because of its convergence with ssg in shortening hollow 2ʃī; the
analysis will be picked up again in §6.3 (ghr). The linear descendant of hollow
sim rmp *-itQĭM* in SM trad pron is the improbable seeming [-iwwAQAM] ~
[-uwwAQAM]. But the improbability may be dispelled with the adoption of
three linked assumptions: (α) that in the sim rmp SM metathesized 1√C with
2√w; (β) that this metathesis took place on the phonological level; and (γ) that
on that level hollow verbs were structured like strong verbs—this latter an
assumption provisionally to be adopted for pA and, in fact, for all A dialects.
Against this backdrop, then, pA *[-itQĭM] corresponded to */-itQawiM/ (the
process or processes deriving [ī] ⇐ /awi/—a special case of cnd (§8)?—not
further to be pondered in this book); while in SM trad pron [-iwwAQAM]
~ {-uwwAQAM] ⇐ /-ItwaQIM/ via processes independently needed, notably /Tw/ ⇒ [ww] by rrf (§10), /I/ ⇒ [A] by ssn (§12.2 <u>SM</u> (α)) and the smc
(§22.1). The metathetic process at the heart of this nexus will be called *metathetic simple initial strengthening* (m-sis), for its similarity to metathetic causative initial strengthening (m-cis), this latter process shared by at least three
dialects (including SM) and to be treated in §6.1.2. In fact, the similarity of the

two processes, including assumptions (α, β, γ), may provide a kind of support for the bona fides of both.

6.1.2. Causative Initial Strengthening (cis)

Consider the following four cau forms: B [tɔ̄séf] 'it will terminate' (Dan 2:44), TR [yāθív] 'er wird zurückgeben' (Da 316f), SR [ak̲k̲ín] 'machte fertig' (Ns 121), TL y+a[ʔɔ̄qém] 'raised' (Mor 227, Mar 159*).

Each of these de facto deviate from canonical hollow cau [-ɔ̆QĪM] in the direction of canonical geminate cau [-AQQIM] by showing a strengthened "dereduced" anlaut syllable, whether this strengthening is achieved by *gemination* of 1√ (g-cis), exactly as in the case of the geminates (SR [ak̲k̲ín]), or by *increasing* (lengthening) instead of reducing the nucleus of the anlaut syllable (i-cis) (B [tɔ̄séf], TR [yāθív]), or finally by diphthongization and coalescence of the anlaut syllable (TL [ʔɔ̄qém]) ← *ʔawqém*), which can perhaps be interpreted as essentially radical *metathesis* (m-cis) (√wqm ← √qwm).[7] Also, the B and TL forms manifest additional rapprochement to the geminate verb by having short ʃ[e] rather than long ʃ[ī], via ssg (§6.1.1).

As was noted, forms like B [tɔ̄séf] evince double rapprochement to the geminate verb: short 2√ (ssg), and strengthened anlaut syllable (cis). Forms like TR [yāθív] differ in evincing only cis, while the like of TR [ʔɔ̆rémiθ] (§6.1.1.1) manifest just ssg. Forms strengthened by diphthongization, like TL [ʔɔ̄qém], have to date revealed no ssg-less congeners like (@)[ʔɔ̄qím]—a state of affairs that follows from the analysis proposed in note 7. And though the like of SR [ak̲k̲ín] do show ssg-ful congeners, e.g., M [akkén] 'calmed' (DM 208), a moment's reflection will reveal that cases like this—hollows marked by both ssg and cis by gemination (g-cis)—instantiate not *partial* rapprochement to the geminate gizra but rather *full* metaplasm to this gizra. Verbs like this have effectively changed allegiance from hollow to geminate, and as such will be discussed in the next section (§6.2).

Examples follow of cis in the hollow cau (including cau rmp) for the dialects where this is clearly attested.[8] Discussion is given as notes to the table:

(6C) Partial reshaping of the cau (and cau rmp) hollow verb in the direction of the geminate verb by strengthening the anlaut syllable through. . .

	g-cis	*i-cis*	*m-cis*
B	[yaḥīṭū][9] ~ [yōḥīṭū] 'they are repairing' (Ezra 4:12)		
TR	[10]	[ʾānǽḥ] 'lass!' (Da 316)	
SM		[11]	t[w(y)ittúwwi]{?}[12] 'und er lebt' (Macs 189
G			<ʾyTwqm> 'wurde aufgerichtet' Da 326)
SR	[akkíl] [13] 'maass' (Ns 121		
TL	a[ʾaḥíxt][9] 'you laughed' (Mar 111*)		y[ʾittōθǽv], a[ʾittōθáv] 'hušav' (Mor 230, Mar 177*)

6.2. Hollow-Geminate Neutralization (hgn)

As was mentioned in the preceding section concerning partial merger of the cau hollow with the geminate verb, in the event two primary marks of partial merger coincide—ssg and g-cis—we de facto have complete merger, at least on the surface. Cases in point include: possibly but improbably the B variant <yaḥiyṭuw>, depending as it does on interpretation of <iy> as mid-defaulting short [i] rather than as long [ī] (note 9, whither also for the [ḥ]); TR [ʾæṣṣéθ] 'horte' (Da 316); TL y[ʾæḥéxt] 'caḥaxta' (Mor 229) (note 9 again for [ḥ])— contrast the partially merged Ash [ʾaḥíxt]; M <aqim> 'he raised' (DM 407) qua [aqqém] (cf. Modern [áqqem], Macm 328).

Of the cau forms like those just illustrated, only those of M clearly represent *integrally full* mergers; cf. homoparadigmatic <aqmat> 'she raised' (Macm 320) qua [aqmáθ] (cf. Modern [áqmat], Macm 328), unambiguously manifesting deletion of *short* 2ʃ red^smp (§4.2, §17.26): [aqmáθ] ⇐ s-smp |aqqŏmáθ| ⇐ s-red |aqqImáθ|.[14] The B case is unlikely to represent a full merger in any event, as was discussed in note 9, and paucity of attested forms makes it uncertain whether the relevant tokens of TR and TL [e] ⇐ short /I/, in an integrally metaplastic geminate formation, as in M, rather than ⇐ long /ī/ affected by s-css^s-mid (§6.1.1.1, §15.6, §17.11) in a *fractionally* metaplastic formation continuing to be marked by hollow-characteristic 2ʃ /ī/ at the phonological level, despite having developed a geminate-like initial syllable.[15] But though the evidence is thus inconclusive for the fullness of the metaplasm to geminate in the case of the B, TR, and TL *plain* causative, the evidence is strong for such total metaplasm in the *rmp* causative of TR and TL. This will be picked up shortly in the discussion of the sometimes complex interfluences among four subsystems: hollow and geminate gĕzarot, plain rmp, and causative rmp binyanim (§6.3). But first, brief consideration of full hollow-geminate merger in the remaining verb types. For expository purposes, the intensive will be presented prior to the simple.

6.2.1. Intensives

With one likely spurious exception, merger of the hollow and geminate intensives in the narrow sense—i.e., reshaping of forms of one of the gĕzarot to those of the other—is restricted to the two L dialects, TL and M,[16] and in both is limited to the int of √9l 'enter' assuming the shape √9yl either variably (TL) or categorically (M): TL y&a[9Ayyél] ~ a[9allél] 'he caused to enter' (Mar 48, 147*; Mor 243); M <aiil> 'he made enter' (Macm 320). This aside, the two L dialects appear to consistently field √QM for geminates and √QWM for hollows in the case of intensives.[17]

6.2.2. Simples

Full neutralization between hollow and geminate gĕzarot in the plain simple verb assumes two general forms: hollow > geminate, by far the majority direction; and geminate > hollow. The process ssg is always at least de facto involved in hol > gem, though other processes may be afoot as well.

B. Only two cases, both from the pf and in antithetical directions—

hol > gem: *√śWm pf 2ms [śámt(ɔ̄)], variants of the 1sg-derived [śɔ́mtɔ̄]. By hypothesis, the former variant isomorphically continues ssg-derived pA *śámtā̊, while [śɔ́mtɔ̄] bespeaks B's trend to deploy constant 2ʃ [V̄] in the hollow simple plain verb with the help of 1sg; cf. the forms listed in BL 148f, all of which shows 2ʃ [V̄] except for [śámt(ɔ̄)], [wīháx] (§6.1.1.2), and possibly but not necessarily impf 3fs <t:nuð> (all other similarly structured forms being spelled with <uw> for clearly long 2ʃ [ū], e.g., <t:ðuwr> [tɔ̄ðúr]).

gem > hol: *√dq 3mp [dɔ́qū] (BL 167, Da 330 n. 2).

TR. A network of reciprocal analogical levelings has neutralized the entire intr pf system—all slots of both gĕzarot manifest 2ʃ [V̊] except for 3ms and 3mp, where 3ms always shows 2ʃ [V̄] and 3mp 2ʃ [V̄] ~ 2√ [V̊]. Examples (from Da 319f, 330): 3ms *hol [qɔ̊́m], *gem [9ɔ́l]; 3fs *hol [qɛ́mmæθ], [méttæθ], *gem [9ǽllæθ]; 2ms *hol [ḥǽstā̊]; 2fs *hol [tǽvt]; 1s *hol [ḥǽbbiθ], [sébbiθ], *gem [9ǽlliθ]; 3mp *[bɔ̊́θū], [qǽssū], *gem [9ɔ́lū], [bǽzzū]; 3fp *hol [qɛ́mmā], *gem [9ǽllā]; 2mp *hol [tævtū́n]; 1p *hol [tévnā], *gem [bǽznā].[18]

In the impa, there is evidence of gem > hol merger with a statistical bias, in that while *hol ms forms appear invariantly as [QV̄M] (e.g., [qū́m] 'steh auf!', Da 320), *gem forms appear [QV̊M] ~ [QV̄M] (e.g., [9ól] ~ [9ū́l] 'tret ein!', Da 331). As concerns the impf, the Sabbionetan subregister shows frequent hol > gem merger; e.g., *√ðWb [yiddóv] 'wird fliessen' (Da 315f) (with [d] < *ð by occ (§17.14).

SM. In the impa, SM gives evidence of statistically biased hol > gem merger in the ms, i.e., merger in the opposite direction from that shown by TR; e.g., *gem t[gǽd] 'führe!' (Macs 198), but *hol t[dǽr] ~ [dǽr] 'wohne!' (Macs 191).

TL. At least in the singular, Yem trad pron shows variable neutralization in the less frequent direction geminate > hollow: 3ms [QǎM] (*gem [kǎṣ] 'kava9' like *hol [bǎθ] 'lan'), with *2ʃ i [QǒyéM] (*gem [9ǒyél] 'nixnas' like *hol [nǒyém] 'nam'—note the strong treatment of 2√/y/, §1.3 n. 12a); similarly, 3fs [QæyMǎ], 2ms [QǒyéMt], 1s [QǒyéMīθ] ~ [QæyMí]. Such formations alternate, at least in part lexically, with geminate-specific shapes like (3ms) [QǽM] (gmf-1u) and [QǒMéM] (gmf-1m), §3.2 (3G, H), as well as metaplasms to 3√y as frequent in Yem trad pron (cf. §3.4 with n. 8). On the *hollow side there appear in 3fs what seem to be hol-gem hybrids of shape [QǽMæθ] ~ [QæMǎ]; cf. geminate [QǽMMαθ] and hollow c[QǎMæθ]. (All forms Mor 210–12, 233–34). (Margolis's Ash trad pron largely shows standardly predicted shapes in the hol and gem sim pf—with the possible exception of hol formations like 2ms [qǒmt], Mar 158*, betraying long schematic generalization, as in SR, while Yem trad pron sports the assumedly more conservative [qǽmt], Mor 211, betraying the original effect of closed-syllabic shortening of 2ʃ; §6.1.1.1. In this vein note systematic neutralization with geminates like [mǽṣt], Mor 234,< gmf-1u *máṣṣtǎ via (3Fvii). For striking "concurrent" sim gem hybrids like Ash [maṣṣḗθ], see §3.4 n. 8.)

In the impa, Yem trad pron gives evidence of the same sort of variation as TR: invariant y[qǔm] vs. variable y[9ól] ~ [9úl] (Mor 215, 257). Contrast invariant Ash a[qǔm], a[9ól] (Mar 129*, 147*).[19]

As concerns the impf, the Ash trad pron reveals some hol > gem (*√qWm [liqqǒmǔ] (~ [lēqūmū]) 'they'll stand' (Mar 158*), *√mWt [limmǒθǔn] (~ [yǒmūθū(n)] ~ [lēmūθū]) 'they'll die' (Mar 129*)), while conversely Yem trad pron reveals some gem > hol (*√ḥṣ [tēḥúṣ] 'taḥacoC' (Mor 235)).[20]

6.2.2.1. The Case of Mandaic

Though M has apparently enhanced the hol-gem distinction in the sim pf via 1sg—e.g., *√qWm m[qǎmt] 'you stood' (Macm 325) vs. *√ps t[pást] 'you destroyed' (Macm 145)—there appears to be pervasive hollow > geminate neutralization in the imp system. While the impa is straightforward in this respect—e.g., *√qWm m[qóm] 'stand!' (Macm 326), hence gem-like [qóm] also in the Classical language—the impf shows some interesting developments. To start with the orthography, both historical hollows and geminates show representation of 2ʃ by <i> ~ <∅>, with <∅> more frequent in the *geminates (50% of the sim-plus-cau sample tokens (individual forms), 57% of the types (roots)) than in the *hollows (tokens 40%, types 22%).[21]

In both simples and causatives, the <i> – <∅> distribution tends to break down into three sorts: uinvariant <i>, variable <i> ~ <∅>, invariant <∅>. Though in the cau <i> might represent 2ʃ [e] transparentively unreduced (§15.2.1), <∅> is most unlikely to—M orthography using defective (ḥaser) writing most sparingly (§21.8). Moreover, <i> in the simple impf should only very rarely signal transparentively unreduced 2ʃ [e], since the overwhelming majority of the sim verbs in the sample show 2ʃ /o/, not /e/; e.g., <timu̱t> 'you(ms) will die' vs. <timi̱tun> 'you(mp) will die' (DM 263).

On balance, the prima facie most likely interpretation of the three sorts of <i>, <∅> distribution might run along lines like these:

(α) invariant <i>— in both sim impf and cau, [ɔ̆], but alternatively in the cau [ī] reflecting *hollow 2ʃ ī whether original or via gem > hol;

(β) <i> ~ <∅>— either [ɔ̆] ~ [∅] or [ɔ̆] ~ ([ɔ̆] ~ [∅]) (M orthography signaling medial [ɔ̆] roughly according to the hierarchy <∅>/<i> ≫ <a> ≫ <u>, §21.8 with n. 29),[22] realization as [∅] depending upon enabling phonological circumstances, notably *1 √C 1 √C ɔ̆ → 1 √C* via smp (§17.26);

(γ) invariant <∅>— [∅], notably via smp, as under (β).

All of these possibilities, as now will be seen, are in the running, with the qualification that (α) must likely be modified for the sim impf. For smoothness of expository flow, we will review the cases in the reverse order (γ, β, α):

(γ′) invariant <∅>. The cau of the *hollow root *√qWm, with invariant <∅>, must reflect a case of hol > gem neutralization followed by (probably lexically dictated) smp; an example was incidentally provided earlier: <aqmat> 'she raised', m[ăqmat] (§6.2), qua originally hollow *haqīmát subject to neutralization to gem (to the tune of other changes) > (ʔ)aqqə̆máθ smp > [aqmáθ].

(β′) variable <i> ~ <∅>. We would have such instances of hol > gem as: sim <tih(i)qun> 'ihr fürchtet' (Nm 249) as either [teh(h)ɔ̆qón] ~ [tehqón] or [teh(h)ɔ̆qón] alone;[23] cau <an(i)dH> 'erschütterte sie' (Nm275) as either [annɔ̆ðá̆] ~ [anDá̆] or [annɔ̆ðá̆] alone or unreshaped hollow [anīðá̆] (prefixal [a] < ă by prm, §9.3.1) ~ reshaped [annɔ̆ðá̆] (~ [anDá̆]).

(α′) invariant <i>. Such hol > gem neutralizations as sim <tiṣitun> 'ihr höret' (Nm 249) if interpreted as [teṣṣɔ̆θón], cau <arimat> ';sie erhob' (Nm 251) qua either reshaped [arrɔ̆máθ] or unreshaped [arīmáθ].

As it happens, there is an alternative interpretation for the presumed [ɔ̆]-bearing form types just considered under (α′, β′, γ′), at least those of the heavy-suffixed sim impf like [teṣṣɔ̆θón]. When we turn to the trad pron of M, t[néqmon] (Mal 537) for sim impf <niqmun> 'they'll stand' (Nm 249) supports the hol > gem analysis of *√qWm proffered under (γ′), even as m[ăqmat] does so for <aqmat>. At first glance, t[arímat] (Macm 321) for <arimat> under (α′) would seem to support interpretation as unreshaped [arīmáθ], but it actually likewise supports reshaped [arrə̆máθ], once it is recognized that [ə̆] is often rendered as t[ī] (and m[ī]) (Macm 320)[24] and that pretonic geminates are likewise often rendered as simplices (Malone 1997).

However, now trad pron appears to throw a curved ball when it renders both *gem <tirigun> 'ihr begehret' and *hol <tigirun> 'ihr treibt Ehebruch' (Nm 249) as t[tīréggon] and t[tīgérron] respectively (Mal 545f). These traditional pronunciations are hardly compatible with the interpretation so far prescribable as [terrə̆yón] and [teggə̆rón], but rather are canonically quite similar to homoparadigmatic *strong* impf's like <tišiplun> 'you(mp) will sink' t[tīšáflon] (Mal 546).[25]

If such trad pron's are taken seriously, as they should be, [26] the likeliest interpretation is that at least some cases of original sim *geminates like [terrə̆yón] and reshaped *hollows like [teggə̆rón] were (*again*) reshaped to the like of [tīreGGón] and [tīyerrón] on the analogy of strongs like [teQSə̆Món] being changed to [tīQeSMón] by Aufsprengung (§4.4).[27] In the causative, on the other hand, no such Aufsprengung-mimicking should be expected, since this process, which in large part is morphologically conditioned, does not occur in the (strong) cau.[28]

The results of this excursus on the M hol⊹gem cau and sim impf are summarized in chart (6D):

(6D)	spelling	hypothesized pronunciation	key processes	trad or mod pronunciation	strong model
sim *hol	<tigirun>	[tīyerrón]	hgn(§6.1), gmf-4m (§3.2 (3N))	t[tīgérron]	[tīšeflón]
	<tih(i)qun>	[tehqón]	hgn, gmf-4u (§3.2 (3M)), +smp (§17.26)		
		~ either [teh(h)ə̆qón]	hgn, gmf-4u, -smp		[tezmə̆rón][29]
		or [tīheqqón]	hgn, gmf-4m		[tīšeflón]
sim *gem	<tirigun>	[tīreGGón]	gmf-4m	t[tīréggon]	[tīšeflón]
	<ninzun>[30]	[nenzón]	gmf-4u, smp		
cau *hol	<arimat>	either		t[arímat]	
		[arrə̆máθ]	+hgn, gmf-4u, -smp		[anhə̆ráθ][31]
		or [arīmáθ]	-hgn		
	<aqmat>	[aqmáθ]	+hgn, gmf-4u, +smp	m[áqmat]	
cau *gem	<aṭmun>[32]	either [aṭmún]	gmf-4u, +smp		
		or [aṭṭə̆mún]	gmf-4u, -smp		[šargə̆zū́n][33]

6.3. The Geminate-Hollow-rmp Nexus (ghr)

We have now seen that, minimally, seven of the thirteen dialects taken as focal to this book (B, TR, SM, G, SR, TL, M) give evidence of at least a modicum of hollow-geminate interfluence. These seven again, joined by CP and possibly by P, also show interfluence of the sim and cau rmps in the hollow verb. Then, when these two interfluences intersect, as they do in TR, TL, and quite likely M, we are faced with neutralization across two binyanim (sim rmp, cau rmp) and two gĕzarot (hol, gem), a situation potentially making for merger —anticipating the diagrams to be used—across as many as three quadrants of formal-functional space (TL) or two pairs of two quadrants (M resolution (a)), as well as distinct couplings of single quadrants (e.g., B vs. TR).

Several dialects moreover show interaction, often rococo, with other processes, on balance making for one of the most intricate developmental nexuses in Aramaic morphophonology. The overall phenomenon will be referred to as the *geminate-hollow-rmp nexus* (ghr).

The following grid (6E) provides likely beginner miškalim, assuming assimilation of rmp-cau **th > *tt (rca, §9.2.2); cf. also §1.2, §1.3. Note that the 2ʃ is long in the hollow (with abstraction away, for the sake of sharper exposition, from the long/short alternation induced by ancient css, §1.3 n. 12a), short in the geminate, $\overset{\circ}{i}$ in the sim rmp, $\overset{\circ}{a}$ in the cau rmp. In the geminate, marked options (built by gmf-3m and gmf-4m, §3.2 (3L, N)) are given in parentheses. Note that a biradical sequence . . . $Q\overset{\circ}{V}M$ . . . may presuppose the action of deg (§3.1 (3Fvii)), whereby $M \leftarrow MM$.

(6E)

	simple rmp	causative rmp
hollow	*-itQīM-	*-ittaQāM
geminate	*-itQaMiM- (*-itQiM-)	*-ittaQQaM- (*-ittaQMaM-)

Central to the ghr nexus is a family of processes blurring or altogether neutralizing the formal distinction in the hollow verb between the simple and causative rmp. These processes will be called generically *hollow-rmp blur* (hrb), and are specifically manifested in any of four forms:

(6F) <u>hrb-1</u>. Plausibly subsequent to spr and red (§5.1, §4.2), hol sim rmp prefixal *iθ* and hol cau rmp prefixal *ittə̆* are neutralized to *ittə̆*; sim-characteristic 2ʃī and cau-characteristic 2ʃā neutralize to 2ʃī ~ 2ʃā.

<u>hrb-1a</u>. *iθ > ittə̆* (like hrb-1); 2ʃī > 2ʃā.

<u>hrb-1i</u>. *iθ > ittə̆* (like hrb-1); 2ʃā > 2ʃī.

<u>hrb-2</u>. *iθ ~ ittə̆*; 2ʃī ~ 2ʃā.

In addition to hrb, we will be dealing with the processes enumerated in (6G).

(6G) <u>geminate formation</u> (§3.2), specifically gmf-3u, gmf-3m, gmf-4u,
gmf-4m (3K–M).
<u>hollow-geminate neutralization</u> (hgn, §6.2).
<u>hollow rmp metaplasm</u> (hrm, to be described below, under <u>SM</u>).
<u>increasing (lengthening) causative initial strengthening</u> (i-cis,
§6.1.2).
<u>metathetic causative initial strengthening</u> (m-cis, §6.1.2).
<u>metathetic simple initial strengthening</u> (m-sis, §6.1.2).
<u>simplification</u> (smp, §17.26).
<u>short schematic generalization</u> (ssg, §6.1).

<u>B.</u>
(6H)   I   >   II   =   II′

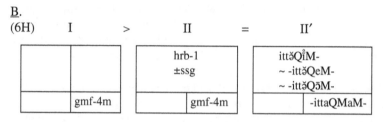

B undergoes what will be taken to be the original form of hrb, hrb-1,
whereby (α) cau rmp prefixal *ittə̆* replaces sim rmp *iθ* and (β) there is reciprocal and variable spread of 2ʃ color. B also undergoes partial rapprochement
of the hollow to the geminate in variably replacing hollow-proper 2ʃ V̊ with
geminate-proper 2ʃ V̊ (ssg).

These effects are attested to by one pair of variant forms, [yittə̆ɕə́m] ~
[yittə̆ɕém] 'wird gemacht', forms classified by BL (§46o) as sim rmp. The first
of these has picked up both prefix shape and low schematic color of the cau
rmp, effectively thereby becoming *formally* a cau rmp, though by hypothesis
of BL remaining *functionally* a sim rmp.[34] The alternant [yittə̆ɕém], on the
other hand, albeit likewise picking up the cau rmp prefixal shape, has retained
sim rmp palatal schematic coloring though shortening same via ssg. (A third
variant <yĭt:ɕim> might be ambiguously interpreted as either +ssg [yittə̆ɕím] or
-ssg [yittə̆ɕím].)

Note finally in passing that the sole attested geminate form, cau rmp
[yiʃtaxlə̆lṹn] 'they are completed' (Brown 1979: 1097), is built on the marked
pattern gmf-4m and sports a residual shape of the cau prefix anlaut, [s] (§1
n. 9), metathesized with rmp [t] by rmt (§10).

<u>P.</u>
(6I)   I   >   II   =   II′

				hrb? ssg?			-ittə̆QV̊M-?	

The hypothesis that P may have undergone hrb is based on <ʔT̂ŝm> 'was placed' (HC 413). However, there are two grounds for being skeptical about this hypothesis: (γ) Hillers and Cussini mark the gloss as questionable. (δ) The participial form <mTzBnʔ>, 'she is sold' (HC 361), presumably [miθzabbŏná], suggests that P either optionally or obligatorily foregoes rmt (§10), since otherwise we should expect metathesized @<mzDBnʔ> @[mizdabbŏná]—and if P truly evades rmt, then <ʔT̂ŝm> could very well represent sim rmp [ʔiθsí̃m] (or even [ʔiθsím], §17.27), untouched by hrb. (Note that interpretation of <ʔš̌{T}Kḥ> 'was found' (HC 415) as support for rmt is rendered dubious by the fact that Hillers and Cussini are marking the crucial <T> as restored.)

TR.

(6J)

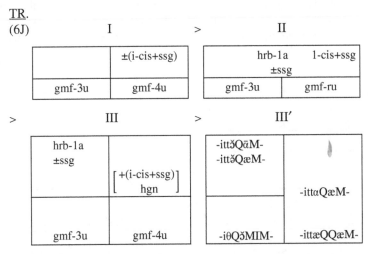

The complex development in TR contrasts with the simplicity of the situation in B and P.

Let's assume that at stage I the hollow cau rmp forms begin to partially assimilate to geminates by shortening 2ʃ (ssg) and by strengthening the prefix syllable through lengthening of the cau vowel (i-cis). However, this complex process is at first variable (±(i-cis+ssg)), so that nonreshaped hol cau rmp forms remain, which then, at stage II, serve as comodels for merger with the hol sim rmp via a form of hrb, hrb-1a, which generalizes the low vowel alternants of 2ʃ, as opposed to B's fielding both low and palatal vowels via hrb-1. (It is plausible to speculate that hrb-1a may have been a subsequent modification of hrb-1, rather than a variant version of hrb.) TR, like B, also undergoes variable 2ʃ shortening (ssg) of the forms affected by hrb-1a.

The interaction of these processes leads in the first place to unambiguously cau rmp forms like [ʔittāqǽm] 'wurde aufgestellt' (Da 326), formed by i-cis+ssg, unambiguous because ex hypothesi bypassed by hrb-1a which rather took the remaining cau rmp forms of shape -ittŏQāM- as models for merger with thec sim rmp. This led to forms like [ʔittŏš̌á9] 'wurde angestrichen' (Da

324), at first formally ambiguous between cau rmp and sim rmp, but ultimately confined altogether to sim rmp inasmuch as cau rmp was now fully served by i-cis+ssg-molded forms of shape *-ittŏQæM-*.[35] The formally renewed sim rmp was also served by ssg-affected forms like [ʾittŏ9ǽr] 'erwachte' (lc).

Then, at stage III, the boundary between cau rmp hollow and cau rmp geminate gives partially way (hgn) in the direction gem > hol, when forms like *geminate [ʾittā9ǽl] 'wurde hereingebracht' (Da 334) become formally indistinguishable from *hollows like [ʾittāqǽm] 'wurde aufgestellt'. But this boundary collapse is merely partial, because some original cau rmp geminates of shape *-ittæQQæM-* remain unaffected; e.g. [ʾittæḥ(ḥ)ǽl] 'wurde entweiht' (lc).

These processes will have affected formal relations across three of the four quadrants of the sim rmp – cau rmp interaction, all in fact but gem sim rmp, which continued to be unambiguously served by *-iθQŏMIM-*; e.g., [ʾiθbŏzéz] 'wurde geplündert' (lc).

CP.

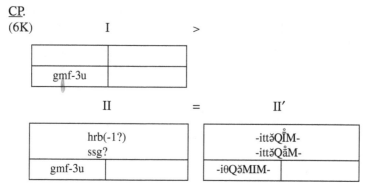

That is, CP may be best interpretable as similar to B, except that the orthography leaves undecidable the question of 2ʃ vowel quantity. Evidential for hrb is *√ṣyd <ʾTṣyD> 'wurde gefasst' (Sg 70), qua [Ittŏṣĭð]; and for the 2ʃ å variation required by hrb-1, *√gwb <ʾyTGBwn> 'sie antworteten' (Sg 24), if representing [Ittŏɣåʊ̊n] (though other interpretations will come easily to mind).

For gem sim rmp, cf. <ʾTBzz> 'wurde plündert' (Sg 69), [Iθbŏzéz].

SM.

(6L)

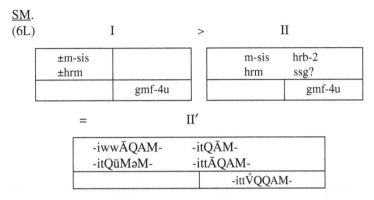

The SM developments, unusual enough to begin with, are further disguised by a network of sound changes peculiar to the traditional pronunciation of this dialect (smc, §22.1). But the *type* of evolution involved here, abstracting away from its specific manifestations, is much like that of TR at stage II (6J): a hrb merger (hrb-1a in the case of TR, hrb-2 in the case of SM) remains less than complete because of competition or preemption by other changes (i-cis+ssg in TR, m-sis and hrm in SM). (Note that the sketch shapes represented in (6LII′) are those of SM trad pron, rather than (antecedent) shapes reconstructed for living SM.)

By m-sis, peculiarly shaped hol sim rmp's like <hw'q'm> ~ <ʔwqm> t[iwwä́qɑm] ~ [uwwä́qɑm] 'wurde aufgestellt' (Macs 192f) are formed from (the like of) *|ʔitqV̌wím| *[ʔiqqím] by metathesis to |ʔitwV̌qim| [ʔiwwV̌qím], which subsequently by the smc and a lowering process[36] abuts upon t[iwwä́qɑm] ~ [uwwä́qɑm][37] by hrm, hol sim rmp's may reinvest to t[-itQūMəM-] probably realizing /-itQawMiM-/ (differing essentially only in 2ʃ from the /-itQawMaM-/ at times encoding hol int rmp in B (n. 16), e.g., *√rWm t[itrúməm] 'wurde erhoht' (Macs 192).

Though some hol sim rmp's were thus reshaped away from hol cau rmp by m-sis or hrm, a sufficient number remained to interact with hol cau rmp by a form of hrb specific to SM, hrb-2. Though this process appears to follow hrb-1 with respect to 2 I ~ 2 A (e.g., <ʔTryhyT> 'sie ist zufrieden' (Macs 196),[38] <ʔTrm> t[iträ́m] 'wurde gehoben' (Macs 192)), hrb-2 may be unique in generalizing not the reflex of cau rmp prefixal *-itt–alone, but this in variation with the sim rmp prefix shape. Thus <ʔTrm> t[itr m] is prefixally sim rmp while homorizous <wDʔTrm> t[wdittä́rɑm]'und das gehoben wird' (Macs 196) is probably cau rmp.[39]

Finally under SM, note that the gem cau rmp [40] appears to be formed in the usual A way, gmf-4u, but the results may possibly be slightly disguised by some process raising the prefixal vowel in the only root adduced by Macuch, *√9l, following the loss of 9 and resolution of the resulting hiatus by insertion of t[yy]; e.g., <ˀTy9l> ~ <ˀT9yl> t[ittíyyæl] 'wurde hereingebracht' (Macs 202).[41]

<u>G</u>.
(6M)

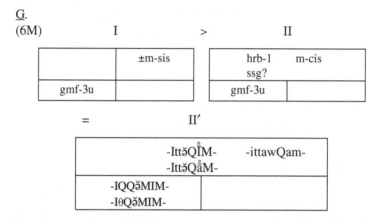

That is, G falls out much like CP, including the indeterminacies induced by the ḥaser orthography, except that some original hollow cau rmp are immunized from merger with sim rmp by m-cis. Examples: of hrb-1-neutralized forms, <ˀyTṣyDwn> 'sie wurden ergriffen' (Da 325) with 2ʃ Ī and homoparadig-matic <ˀyTṣD> 'er wurde ergriffen' (lc) with 2ʃ å̊; of immunization by m-cis, <ˀyTwqm> 'er wurde aufgestellt' (Da 326); of gmf-3u-formed gem sim rmp, <ˀy9ll> 'er wurde eingebracht' (Da 373).

<u>SR</u>.
(6N)

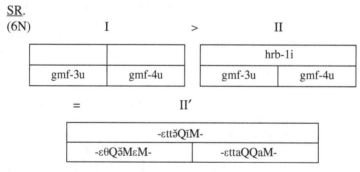

Full neutralization of hol sim rmp and hol cau rmp with generalization of 2ʃ ī; maintenance of the strong form of gem sim rmp (gmf-3u), and the unmarked A form pf gem cau rmp (gmf-4u): e.g., [ɛttɔ̌ŋī́s] 'überredete sich' (Ns 120); [ɛθqɔ̌ṣéṣ] 'wurde angerechnet', [ɛttabbáz] 'wurde geplündert' (Ns 123).

TL.

(6P)

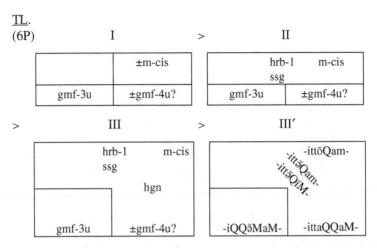

I > II

	±m-cis
gmf-3u	±gmf-4u?

hrb-1 ssg	m-cis
gmf-3u	±gmf-4u?

> III > III′

hrb-1 ssg	m-cis
hgn	
gmf-3u	±gmf-4u?

-ittōQam- -ittōQam- -ittōQīM-	
-iQQŏMaM-	-ittaQQaM-

In TL, at least three of the four quadrants of the space end up with shared forms when sim rmp – cau rmp merger brought about by hrb-1 is followed by hgn, which ushers in hol-gem merger. Thus, originally geminate cau rmp y[nittŏḥíl], a[littŏḥíl] 'will be desecrated' (Mor 241, Mar 113*) ends up with hollow 2ʃ ī (by hgn), which in turn has sim rmp chroma (by hrb-1). The color alternation in 2ʃ typical of hrb-1 is shown by a comparison of the forms just considered with y[ʔittŏxǽn] 'huxna' (Mor 219).

Immunization from hrb and hgn applies to some hol cau rmp forms via m-cis, as with G, e.g., y&a[ʔittōθÁv] 'was refuted' (Mor 219, Mar 177*). Some gem cau rmp forms may also resist hrb and hgn to judge by a[nittaḥál] ~ [littaḥál] (Mar 113*), variants of the forms cited above, and a[ʔittōrá9] 'grew worse' (Mar 166*), < *ʔittaḥḥál and *ʔittarrá9 via mls (§9.3.1), respectively without and with compensatory lengthening of the prefix V (= spreading of the deleted component of the geminate to the prefix V). However, gmf-4u is marked as questionable in the diagram because the forms are adduced by Margolis alone, Morag only offering Yem variants consonant with hrb + hgn, as per examples in the preceding paragraph and y[ʔittŏrǽ9] 'nišbar' (Mor 241; see lc note 41 for the probable irrelevance of the gloss difference between the Ash and Yem variants).

Finally, the entire gem sim rmp quadrant may escape merger via gmf-3u, as in several other dialects: a[ʔizdaq(ŏ)qīnán] 'we obligated ourselves' (Mar 110*), y[ʔiθqŏṣṣǽṣū] 'nikcĕcu' (Mor 241).[42],[43]

<u>M.</u>
(6Q)

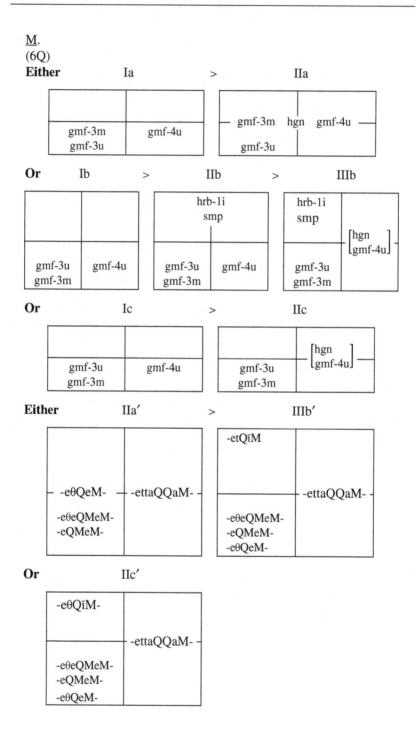

The preceding trio of alternative solutions for M—and this is just a sample—reflect the indeterminacy engendered by ambiguities in both orthography and traditional pronunciation.

To start with something relatively clear, all three solutions agree on hol-gem neutralization (hgn) enabling originally gem cau rmp -*ettaQQaM*- to migrate into the hollow verb; thus *√rWm <etaram> [ettarrám] 'he raised himself', *√šWm <etasimat> [ettassə̆máθ] 'she was placed' (Macm 322f). All three solutions also recognize that strong formation (gmf-3u) has immunized at least some gem sim rmp forms from merger; e.g., -rrf (§10) <etigbib> [īθeGBéβ] 'gibbosus fuit', <etgibat> [eθgebbá̆θ] 'gibbosa fruit'; +rrf ˄smp <emrar> [emrár] 'became bitter' (lc).

Here transalternative unity ends. Most focally at stake are forms like *hollow <etqis> 'he drew himself together' (DM 40f) and *geminate <etpis> t[étpes] 'he was destroyed' (Macm 145). To take the latter first, though 2ʃ <i> is ambiguous as to quantity, 2ʃ t[e] makes it possible that the form should be interpreted as gmf-3m-shaped [eθpés] < *hitpíssa, from root *√ps with gmf followed by sap (§17.22), ˄deg (§3.1 (3Fvii)), hlr (§9.2.2), ˄adr (§9.1.1), spr (§5.1), mid (§17.11). If then <etqis> is interpreted as [eθqî́s] < *hitqî́sa (ṣ > [s] via eds, §9.1.3 n. 8), we abut upon solution IIC′: the sim rmp remains free of merger, while the cau rmp merges hol > gem.

Suppose, however, that <etqis> and <etpis> represent the same phonetic type. In that case, t[étpes] dictates ct[étqes], which suggests that hol > gem has applied in the sim rmp no less than in the cau rmp, most straightforwardly interpretable as taking hgn to have generalized from cau to sim. This is the essence of solution IIa′.

The two preceding solutions involve two and four of the quadrants respectively across the stages of development involved. If however *three* were involved, all but that of the gem sim rmp as in the case of TL, <etpis> might continue to be interpreted as [eθpés] while <etqis> gets reinterpreted as [etqî́s] < (ʔ)Ittə̆qî́s, reflecting a hrb-engendered hybrid with the prefixal shape of the hol cau rmp and the schematic vocalism of the hol sim rmp, à la SR (thus hrb-1i). The mechanics of such a solution, IIIb′, suggest that perhaps first hrb-1i neutralized hol sim rmp and hol cau rmp (stage IIb), whereupon hgn neutralized hol cau rmp and gem cau rmp, in the process pushing the results of the hrb-1i neutralization into the hol sim rmp space (*chaîne de propulsion* à la Martinet 1964) as of stage IIIb. The net result is minimally different from IIC′—prefixal [t] rather than [θ]—but arrived at through a distinct interaction of processes.

The preceding competition among M solutions IIa′, IIIb′, and IIC′ suggests some of the analytic hijinks attendant upon indeterminacy, a factor so often at work in the diachronic mode. And as mentioned earlier, additional solutions will easily come to mind—e.g., modifications of IIIb′ and IIC′ with ssg-engendered 2ʃ [e] in lieu of 2ʃ [ī], compounding the number of plausible resolutions.

Is it possible to see any developmental unity across the dialects with respect to the geminate-hollow-rmp nexus? One possibility is diagrammed in (6R), which covers the core movements of all hypotheses sketched in (6H–Q) with the exception of M hypothesis (6Qc). In accordance with (6R), all dialects but TR and the L dialects TL, M limit themselves to collapsing the hollow sim rmp and hollow cau rmp via hrb, indicated by X at stage I, though these dialects differ among themselves in the specific form of hrb utilized—and also on whether or not the work of hrb is helped along by the synergy of ssg.[44] They likewise vary on whether or not they partially disambiguate the effects of hrb in deploying cooccurrent, specialized forms of either hol sim rmp (SM; *-iwwāQaM-, -itQūMəM-* (6L II′)) or hol cau rmp (G; *ittawQaM-* (6M II′)). Such specialized forms are omitted from (6R) as are similar forms deployed in the geminate (lower) quadrants.

Next, at the second stage, the picture engendered by hrb is complicated by the emergence of hgn (and sometimes ancillary processes), indicated by Y, whereby the hollow and geminate cau rmps are neutralized. And Y then interacts with X in one of two distinct ways: (*) by pushing the form-types affected by X into distinct hollow sim rmp space (a Martinesque *chaîne de propulsion*), as with TR and M hypothesis (b) (the stage marked "II"); (*) or by pooling the effects of X and Y and thus effectively making for homonyny across three quadrants, as with TL ("II′").

Finally, M hypothesis (a) at stage III can be viewed as a development from II by the redeployment of hgn across the sim quadrants (X).

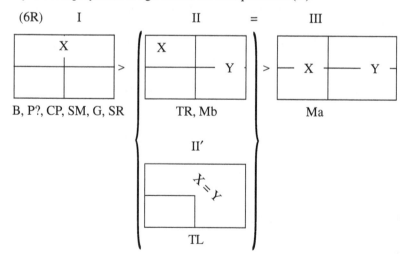

6.4. Summary; Developmental Profiles of the Individual Dialects for hgr and hgn

A summary of the major hollow-geminate interfluences covered in this chapter appears in (6S). The direction of the neutralizations, hol > gem or gem > hol, is not indicated—though hol > gem is generally more frequent. It will be noted that of the sixteen interfluences listed, at most two are categorical ("+"), both in M (categorical status clear in the cau rmp, possible in the cau plain), the balance being variable ("v"). Interfluences are indicated as full ("f") or partial ("p"), by (congeries of) processes dubbed in the text hollow-geminate neutralization (hgn) and hollow-geminate rapprochement (hgr), respectively), the latter covered in §6.1, the former in §6.2.

Also included is a figure (between 4 and 1) approximating the degree of *morphophonological integration* of the interfluence in question, this in turn being considered in each case a function of (α) the properties of the processes responsible for the neutralization as well as of (β) the approximate quantity and category of forms so affected. The highest score under (α), 4, is awarded to *restructurings* (§23.2), i.e., cases where the processes in question have themselves vanished (*rule deletion*) to the tune of corresponding mutations in the phonological/lexical representations. Restructuring, in turn, is assumed in all cases of full neutralization (hgn), but is not limited to such cases; notably, the partial restructuring process m-cis is assumed to have triggered restructuring. Score component (α) in non-restructuring instances is determined by the degree to which the rule in question operates in terms of *intrinsic phonetic factors* (as opposed to morphological, lexical, or "diacritic" factors —or to prima facie phonetic factors, which, however, fail to cohere phonetically: e.g., when short schematic generalization shortens a vowel in an *open* syllable, as opposed to a closed one as would bespeak phonetic naturalness). Impressionistic assessment of such factors leads to (α)-score components in the range of 3–1, with a maximally intrinsic-phonetic process scoring lowest. High scoring under (β) bespeaks a rough assessment of the relative number of forms affected (relative to the conditions of the pertinent rule(s)) as well as the nature of any category restrictions placed on affected forms (positive morphological conditions being higher-valued than lexical conditions); range 4–1.

The raw scores so obtained are summed up and averaged out to yield the final score plotted in the cells of (6S): raw (α)-scores divided by the number of processes (including restructuring, rst), this dividend being then added to the raw (β)-score, and this sum finally being divided by two.

Relevant (groups of) processes are also listed, usually by label, sometimes by citation of section for discussion.

(6S)

	B	TR	SM
sim plain	v	v	v
	p,f	f	f
	2	3	2.5
	hgn,ssg	hgn	hgn
cau plain	v	v	v
	p	p(,f?)	p
	1.6	1.75	2
	ssg,g-cis,i-cis	ssg,i-cis	ssg
int plain			
cau rmp		v	
		f	
		3.5	
		ghr	

	SR	TL	M
sim plain		v	v
		p,f	f
		3.25	3.5
		hgn,§6.2.2	hgn
cau plain	v	v	v(or +?)
	p	p,f	f
	2	3	4
	g-cis	hgn?,ssg,lsg, g-cis,m-cis	hgn
int plain		v	v
		f	f
		2.5	2.5
		hgn	hgn
cau rmp		v	+
		f	f
		3.5	4
		ghr	ghr,§6.3

Notes to §6

[1] Primarily but not exclusively as per the Yemeni tradition documented by Morag (in Mor).

[2] "Systemically merged under phonological or morphological conditions," i.e., cases of a hollow assuming a geminate shape or vice versa in a sufficient number of forms to constitute a structurally conditioned class. The sense of this excludes what are

(hypothesized to be) (a) stray lexically conditioned instances of merger, (b) phonologically conditioned hapax legomena (e.g., B [šámtō] as a closed-syllable short-vowel variant to patently hollow [šɔ́mtō], §6.2.2), (c) cases of hollow-geminate collapse via merger with a formation not per se identifiable as either hollow or geminate (e.g., the occasional appearance in SR of reduplicative *QaMQɛM* in such a function (note 16 below)).

[3] (a) The $\overset{\circ}{V}$ in the gem cau flanked by the two radicals is 2ʃ, as per the mechanics of gmf (§3); and the $\bar{V}$ in the hol cau flanked by the two radicals is assumed to be 2ʃ, having the same color distribution as does the so-flanked $\overset{\circ}{V}$ in the geminate.

(b) Though in many paradigmatic slots of the hollow and geminate only two radical positions appear, whether short (both gĕzarot) or long (geminate only), these will be identified as 1√–3√, as discussed in §1 note 8. Since identification of the lead-off radical as 1√ is just about foregone for both gĕzarot, and pegging of the final radical in the hollow verb as 3√ is largely uncontroversial, any arbitrariness will devolve upon identification of the follow-up radical in the geminate verb as 3√. In fact, the overall disposition of hollow-geminate rapprochement suggests the correctness of this identification. Thus when by short schematic generalization (§6.1.1) hollow cau -ŏ*QiC*- is partially assimilated to the geminate as -ŏ*QiC*-, or indeed with the addition of causative initial strengthening (1c) fully assimilated thereto as -a*QQiC*-, identification of *C* as *M* (= 3√) makes for a stronger (because fuller) model to the process than would identification as *S* (2√).

[4] Lengthening of the causative-prefixal vowel in [yɔhɔ̄qem] and variants is attributable to i-cis (§6.1.2).

[5] "Fully achieved in . . . the two L dialects," except for stray lexical hollow-to-geminate metaplasms, that is; e.g., the causative of *√nWḥ in Ash TL, thoroughly metaplasticized to √nḥ (Mar 135*). For 1sg in the *simple* pf (most clearly in SR and M), see §15.2.1.4.

[6] The assumption is that closed-syllabic shortening was in effect for the simple as well as the causative hollow verb in pA, remaining perhaps as a variable rule in the impf in the wake of short apocope (cf. (6B)); but that the resulting pattern subsequently remained more intact in the causative, even tending toward generalization of 2ʃ V̥ (ssg), while in the simple verb the proclivity was toward generalization of 2ʃ V̄ (lsg). The B hapax [wīháx] goes against the grain of these paired tendencies, either retaining original css-engendered short *2ʃ a or shortening *ʃ2 ā (for the ambiguity, cf. *yihaqīm* ~ *yihaqī̆mi* in (6B))—in any event manifesting simple-verb-exceptional ssg. The variant [yɔhɔ́x], on the other hand, is consonant with the tendencies, in particular with the tendency to maintain/generalize 2ʃ V̄ in the simple hollow verb. (Note that the jussive force of [yɔhɔ́x] at Ezra 7:13 suggests that the etymon was short-imperfective, hence by hypothesis containing pA *2ʃ a, *yihák, in which case the B form would reflect the *positive* action of lsg.)

[7] Thoroughgoing formulation of m-cis as a metathetic process would require assuming (a) that the hollow verbs are characterized by /w/ explicitly appearing in 2√ position, and (b) that s-m-cis operates at a rather deep level of the phonology. A sketch derivation of [ʔōqém] might look roughly as in (d), with s-m-cis formulated as in (c):

(c) sd: a   1√C   2√w,   where a = +causative
          1   2   3
     sc: 1   3   2   (food for theoretical thought: is the result *a 1√w 2√C*
                            or *a 2√w 1√C* ? If standard autosegmental modeling
                            is assumed, the answer must apparently be *a 1√w*
                            2√C; for the argument, see Malone 1985)

(d)   /ʔ a 1√q 2√w i 3√m/
     s-m-cis |ʔ a w   q   i m |
     s-str |ʔ a w   q   í m |
     s-coa |ʔ   ō   q   í m |
     s-mid   [ʔ   ō   q   é m]

The origins of this pattern are obscure; Hebrew has a similar nexus, limited to the labial passive (THP 51f). (Observe that for the process to work straightforwardly the assumption is being made, at least in this case, that the synchronic phonological value of 2√ is specifically *w*, though in general hollow verbs are interpreted cautiously in this book (e.g., in §24) as having archiphonemic 2√W. This caution is prompted by a number of unsettled issues attending identification of hollow 2√, not to be resolved in this work.)

[8] In dialects lacking vocalization or trad pron, g-cis and i-cis are likely to go undetected.

[9] [ḥ] rather than [ḥḥ], by mls (§9.3.1). Moreover, the B form might actually be fully metaplastic to geminate in the unlikely event that <iy>, the spelling appearing here at Ezra 4:12, represents not [í], but [í], with open-syllabic default of mid; cf. note 10. However B, unlike TR, shows no hint of metaplasm to geminate anywhere else. Also unlike TR, <iy> in B orthography is unlikely to represent short [i] (except perhaps /__w, §8.1.1 under *ĭy*ŭ̊), for which ml-less <i> almost always appears; contrast the spelling of several clear [i]-cases in BL 174 vs. Da 262.

[10] <ʔæṣiyTuw> 'höret!' (Da 316) belongs here if interpreted as [ʔæssíθū], but not if interpreted as [ʔæṣṣíθū], in which case it would represent full metaplasm to geminate (§6.2) with open-syllabic default of mid; cf. note 9, preceding.

[11] Perhaps <hBˁšT> t[ābíšət] 'ich habe Leid getan' and <hqmT> t[əqémət] 'ich habe aufgestellt (Macs 196), but mootly, because the prefix vocalism would become t[ā] (< ă) anyway, by c-pra (§22.1 (22Biv)). However, the latter form does reflect shortening of 2ʃ by ssg (§6.1.1.1)—notwithstanding the length (t[ē]), due again to c-pra.

[12] While the form is indeed probably cau rmp on the root *√ḥy(y) and t[uww] most likely does derive from the string *awḥ*, where *a* = prefixal, *w* = original 2√ metathesized by m-cis and *ḥ* = displaced 1√, the technical problem is whether *√ḥy(y) qualifies as a hollow root as pertinent to the present rubric; cf. §8.1.1 n. 7.

[13] Note that forms like [akkíl] and [akkín] (above in the text) differ minimally from morphologically identical forms like [aðíq] 'schaute', a run-of-the-mill hollow causative which owes its full prefix vowel to promotion (§9.3.1, §14.1).

[14] The question of the M hol-gem causative will be returned to in discussion of the simple verb of that dialect (§6.2.2).

[15] However the terminology is tooled, we are dealing with four distinct kinds of potential result here: *full vs. partial merger* X *integral vs. fractional merger*. In *full*

merger, a given form will become phonetically identical to a form of another class; say, as here, a(n originally) hollow form will become indistinguishable from a corresponding geminate form. In *partial* merger, the forms will become phonetically *similar* but fall short of identity. *Integral* merger, on the other hand, targets not only given forms but all homoparadigmatic forms as well; while in *fractional* merger, the neutralization falls short of targeting all homoparadigmatic forms. Suppose H1, H2, H3 stands for a paradigm of hollow verbs; G1, G2, G3 for a corresponding paradigm of geminate verbs; and HG1, HG2, HG3 for a corresponding paradigm of *hybrids*—forms intermediate in shape between hollows and geminates. Suppose finally that H1, H2, H3 is subject to various merger operations of the types just proffered; then, we might have the results in (a):

(a)	G1, G2, G3:	full integral merger
	G1, H2, H3:	full fractional merger
	HG1, HG2, HG3:	partial integral merger
	HG1, H2, H3:	partial fractional merger

Harking back to the terminology introduced at the outset of the chapter (§6.1), *hollow-geminate neutralization* (hgn) involves *full merger*, while *hollow-geminate rapprochement* (hgr) in the narrow sense involves *partial merger*. Moreover, this typology lends itself to explication in generative-phonological terms (§23), a portion of which will be undertaken here on the relatively concrete basis of two sketch forms from the hollow-causative in a dialect of roughly the vintage of B. Following the discussion in the text, let's take a case of *full* merger by virtue of g-cis plus either ssg or css. Since both g-cis and ssg are by hypothesis *unconditional* processes, applying irrespective of syntagmatic frame, the decided diachronic tendency is for them to trigger *restructuring* pursuant to their dictates—i.e., to affect the lexical-phonological forms which are input to the phonology; this is portrayed in (b) for the pf 3ms, where the phonetic output, [ʔaQQíM], is indistinguishable from a cradle geminate. But what if the processes responsible for the merger are rather g-cis and css, a *conditional* process requiring the focal vowel to be in a closed syllable? Since conditional processes characteristically fail to trigger restructuring, they rather tend to enter the synchronic phonology as *rule additions* (§23 with (23D, E, F)), as portrayed again for the pf 3ms in (c) (for simplicity of exposition g-cis in this demonstration will be subjected to the same mutations as ssg/css, restructuring in (b) but rule addition in (c)). Observe now that the phonetic result of (c) is identical to that of (b), [ʔaQQíM]; so that both (b) and(c) involve *full merger*. Consider now what happens when a homoparadigmatic form, pf 3mp, is treated in parallel: while the restructuring triggered by unconditional ssg likewise leads to a form indistinuyishable from a corresponding geminate, [ʔaQQíMū] in (d), the rule addition involving conditional css rather abuts upon a hybrid form, [ʔaQQíMū] in (e), identical neither to a canonical hollow ([ʔɔ́QíMū]) nor to a canonical geminate ([ʔaQQíMū]). In sum, the results of (b) and (d) reflect *full integral merger*; that of (c) *full fractional merger*; and that of (e) *partial fractional merger*.

(b) /ʾ+aQīM/   d-(g-cis,ssg) <u>by restructuring</u> > /ʾ+aQQiM/
                ((lexical form targeted))

    s-str |ʾaQíM| s-str |ʾaQQiM|
    s-red |ʾƷQíM| s-red   —
        [ʾƷQîM]   [ʾaQQíM] (= (c))

(c) /ʾ+aQīM/   d(g-cis, css) <u>by rule addition</u> > /ʾ+aQīM/
                ((intermediate form targeted))

    s-str |ʾaQíM| s-str |ʾaQíM|
    s-red |ʾƷQíM| s-red |ʾƷQíM|
                        s-g-cis, s-css |ʾaQQíM|
        [ʾƷQíM]   [ʾaQQíM] (= (b))

(d) /ʾ+aQiM+ū / d-(g-cis,ssg) <u>by restructuring</u> > /ʾ+aQQiM+ū/

    s-str |ʾaQīMū| s-str |ʾaQQíMū|
    s-red |ʾƷQíMū| s-red   —
        [ʾƷQíMū]   [ʾaQQíMū] (≠ (e))

(e) /ʾ+aQiM+ū / d-(g-cis, css) <u>by rule addition</u> > /ʾ+aQiM+ū/

    s-str |ʾaQíMū| s-str |ʾaQíMū|
    s-red |ʾƷQíMū| s-red |ʾƷQíMū|
                        s-g-cis,s-css |ʾaQQíMū|
        [ʾƷQíMū]   [ʾaQQíMū] (≠ (d))

It might be useful to illustrate one more generally important result. Since it is charac-teristic of *all* changes to start out their synchronic phase as rule additions (§23.2), even unconditional changes, what will things look like if we so treat unconditional ssg? The result is displayed in (f), where it will be seen to be identical in upshot to that given by restructuring in (d). This is as it should be, however. A development like (f) should in fact be understood as constituting the stage immediately preceding (d)—such that likely in the very next generation a system hosting an unconditional rule mutates into a suc-cessor system where the impact of that rule targets the lexical-phonological level itself.

Unconditional phonological rules are extremely unstable because by definition they destroy the very alternations that, by dint of counterfoiling, justify their continued ex-istence as rules.

(f) /ʾ+aQiM+ū/   d-(g-cis, ssg) <u>by rule addition</u> > /ʾ+aQīM+ū/
    s-str |ʾaQíMū| s-str |ʾaQíMū|
    s-red |ʾƷQíMū| s-red |ʾ QíMū|
                                s-g-cis, s-ssg |ʾaQQíMū|
        [ʾƷQíMū]   [ʾaQQíMū] (=(d))

[16] The qualification "merger . . . in the narrow sense" is meant to exclude merger of forms from both gĕzarot to some third shape type, which happens sporadically in B (to *(iθ)QōMV̊M*) and Sr (to *QaMQɛM*): e.g., B *geminate [ʾɛštōmám] 'was appalled' (Dan 4:16; *Tʃ* > [ʃt] by rmt, §10), *hollow [hiθrōmámtɔ̄] 'you rose up' (Dan 5:23); SR *geminate [balbɛl] 'verwirren' (B 99) and *hollow [ramrɛm] 'erheben' (B 97f). TL in Yem trad pron also shows one case apiece of third-party merge, to *QāMeM*: *geminate

[(dæhwą̃) ḥą̄ṭéṭ] (Mor 243)—unless [ḥą̄ṭéṭ] is participial, in which case *QāMeM* is expected for geminates, a possibility suggested both by the syntax and by Morag's gloss 'mĕḥatet'; and *hollow [līną̄fə́féh] 'yašiv 9alav ʔavir bimnifa' (Mor 222). (A possible *hollow case for Y is <wPšš> 'und er abrogierte' (DR I 215:8) if the root is cA *√pWš 'remain'—but it may not be; cf. Donner and Röllig's different suggestion (II 227).)

[17] With the twist that the Yem trad pron sports a number of schematic variations and at least one case of a geminate assuming a defective shape; see Mor 243, 245, 221f., 224.

[18] The possibility cannot be discounted that the items here interpreted as formally full geminates of shape [QǽMMV-] actually represent gen-hol hybrids of shape [QǽMV-], as in TL via Yem trad pron (below). None of the examples provided by Dalman are pointed with the dages which would clinch the interpretation as [QǽMMV-]; e.g., [qǽmmæθ], so interpreted here in the text, is spelled <qæmæT>, not <qæm̆æT>.

[19] Perhaps also I, where we find in the sim impa *hol mp <qmw> but *gem fs <9w̄ry> 'führe!' (L 611, 66)—though the overscore on <w̄> may mark the reading as dubious.

[20] For prefixal ē] (both trad prons), see §15.3.1.1 (ips).

[21] The sample contained considerably more *hollows (55 tokens, 22 types) than *geminates (8 tokens, 7 types).

[22] A form illustrating all four of these possibilities will be provided in (6D) with n. 31.

[23] [h(h)] since it is unclear to what extent mls (§9.3.1) applied in M.

[24] [ɔ] may alternatively be rendered by t[V̊], as will, e.g., be seen in (6D) n. 31.

[25] The discrepancy in vowel coloring between t[tīréggon], t[tīgérron], and t[tīšáflon] may well be due to the fact that the latter form, and other similar forms as well, stem from the same informant (Sheikh Abdullah).

[26] The main caution to be sounded concerning M trad pron is that it tends toward what Macuch calls "ābāgādical"—that is, reading pronunciation (Macm 126). But the trad prons involved here deal with features that are patently not ābāgādical, notably the distinction between simplex 1√ t[r], t[g] and geminate 3√ t[gg], t[rr] (both simplices and geminates of this sort being spelled as singletons.

[27] Support for this analysis may be afforded by sporadic, prima facie anomalous forms like impf 1s^3ms <egababH> 'I bend him' (DM 79), at first blush seeming to constitute some sort of dittographical error. Under the proposal adopted here, this spelling would represent [īγaβ̆æβ̆í], differing from expected c[īγaBBí] by the presence of an [ă] inserted between 2√ and 3√ for reasons now to be explained. In terms of the so-called *Obligatory Contour Principle*, or OCP, a sequence of two identical autosegmental melodies is prohibited (Kenstowicz 1994: 323ff.). With relevance to A verb structure, this implies that, while a one-to-two radical(melody)-to-skeleton configuration is permitted as a model of a geminate radical cluster, as, e.g., is found in the intensive binyan (§1.1.2) or geminate gizra (§1.2) and is portrayed below in (a), on the other hand a two-to-two mapping of the same configuration is prohibited, as in (b) (m = arbitrary radical melody):

(a)   m   (b)   @   m   m

With this in mind, McCarthy (1986) proposes that when a configuration like (b) is about to be formed as a byproduct of morphological or phonological operations, the illicit formation may be thwarted by *antigeminational* disruption of the potential geminate via either insertion of a vowel or, if circumstances allow, by maintenance of a vowel which normally would be lost.

In light of this, assume the likelihood that synchronic systematization of the geminate > strong reshaping proposed in the text takes the form of unmarked geminate formation gmf-4u (§3.2 (3M)) being replaced by marked gmf-4m (3N); then, with antigemination in mind, let (c) and (d) be derivations of {e + √gb X ʃa X CCVC + ī} *1s + bend X impf + 3ms* 'I bend him', where (c) is the constructed, nonreshaped counterpart of (d), the reshaped item [ī͜γaβăβí] in focus. (For the rules and their ordering, see especially §3 n. 5 and §4.4; spirantization (spr), whose conditions for M are not fully clear, is simply assumed up to the point of probability but not beyond (§5 n. 3); bear also in mind that the synchronic interpretation of Aufsprengung as isomorphic to diachronic exc^swh^prm (§4.4) is assumed for lack of concrete evidence to the contrary, though a simplification like d-(exc^swh^prm) > s-auf is plausible; from the first to the second line of gmf, tier conflation is tacitly assumed, the operation whereby autosegmental tiers are amalgamated into a unitary, temporally oreganized string—but see §3 n. 1 for a qualification.)

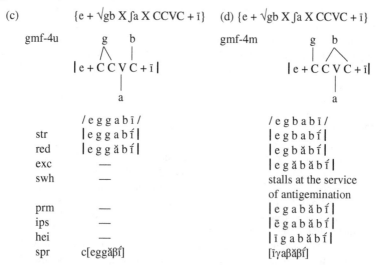

Note too that the rarity of forms like [ī͜γaβăβí] likely stems from M regularly resisting antigemination, and rather allowing the momentary OCP violation to be repaired by the default process *fusion*, whereby a configuration like (b) automatically rewires to the like of (a); see McCarthy 1994 and Malone 1989a for evidence of optional antigemination in another Semitic language. Fusion would dictate the commonplaceness of forms like [tīyerrón], vis-à-vis the rarity of antigeminational resolutions like c[tīyerə̆rón].

(One possible catch to this analysis involves spirantization (spr), assumed here to (synchronically) apply late in the derivation primarily for the expository purpose of enhancing the clout of the demonstration by allowing antigeminational failure of swh between *fully identical* melodic segments, |b| and |b|, rather than between *near* identical melodies, |b| and |β|, had spr applied before red. In fact, however, though not enough evidence remains to be fully sure (§5.1 n. 3), the chances are good that in Classical M spr was in fact ordered before red, and may have been persistent to boot—as is suggested by the overall warp and woof of findings for the dialects; cf. §5.2, §5.3. Be that as it may, antigemination (and other OCP effects) have frequently been found to apply between *non*identical melodic segments as long as they are sufficiently similar as reckoned in terms of critical number of feature agreements; cf. the phenomenon of *antiwedging* as developed in Malone 1999. So the argument set forth in this note is actually likely to hold for |bă̆β| just as cogently as for |bă̆b|.)

(Incidentally, there is a synchronic price to pay by the sim impf geminates for ap-ing the strongs along the lines of (3ms and 3mp for illustration) *neQSóM : neQQóM = nīQeSMón : *neQQə̆Món > nīQeMMón*. This is so in that the reshaping entails giving up a synchronically unmarked mechanism (gmf-4u (§3.2 (3M))) for a synchronically marked mechanism (gmf-4m (§3.2 (3N)))—and that only in part of the paradigm (here 3mp) while another part (here 3ms) continues being formed unmarkedly. The reason for this discrepancy is the coincidence that while strong *nīQeSMón* is shaped by synchron-ically unmarked processes, geminate *nīQeMMón* requires at least one marked process, gmf-4m. The moral of this brief excursus is that, contrary to one widely held traditional view, the simplification achieved by analogical reshaping may trigger complication elsewhere in the system.)

[28] One more observation might be made about the reshaping of gem sim impfs to the strong canon. This is the occasional fielding of apparent defective forms as expo-nents of *geminate (original or < **hollow) roots in the sim impf, but most frequently in slots where the defective normally assumes a strong shape: e.g., <nimitiun> 'sie wedren sterben' (Nm 249) interpreted as [nīmeθyón], cf. "true" defective <nizikiun> 'they'll be justified' (Mal 537) [nīzexyón], both manifesting the strong canon [nīQeSMón]—and note the (relative? complete?) absence of homoparadigmatic gem > def forms in slots where the strong canon is absent in the defective; e.g., <nimut> 'he'll die' (DM 263), not @<nimtia> like <nizkia> 'he'll win' (DM 168) [nezkī́]. How should this lopsided distribution be interpreted? Might one legitimately appeal to a so-called "peeking rule," whereby gem → def may go through only when the phonetic result will look strong?

[29] 'ihr spielt' <tizmrun> (M=Nm 227); strong verbs usually undergo Aufspren-gung, but a minority fail to.

[30] 'sie spritzen weg' (Nm 249).

[31] 'she illumined' <anhirat> ~ <anhrat> ~ <anharat> ~ <anhurat> t[anhárat] (Mal 385).

[32] 'they closed me in' (DM 180).

[33] 'they enraged me' <šargzun> (Mal 405); [š-] is a residual causative prefix (§1 n. 9).

[34] An important issue will be left unaddressed in this book: does *formal* neutralization always correlate with *functional* neutralization? Only a thorough syntactic-semantic text analysis could provide the answer. In the specific case of Aramaic *√šWm, intimation that something like functional collapse of the sim-cau opposition might ultimately have been favored by formal mergers like hrb may be implicit in a mutation like ptc (§17.20). See also Malone 1974a for the case of SR √škḥ.

[35] This much of the nexus provides a nice illustration of a Martinesque *chaîne* (Martinet 1964: 59), one which might be called a *chaîne d'affortissement*: first step, variable strengthening of cau *ittə̆* to *ittā;* next step, strengthening of sim *iθ* to *ittə̆* borrowed from cau; final step (if not a facet of the preceding), loss of the option for cau *ittə̆*.

[36] Specifically, *second schematic neutralization* (§12.2 <u>SM</u> (α)).

[37] (a) For the abstract-phonological nature of m-sis, cf. §1 n. 9. (b) It is possible that in addition to m-sis, SM also had some showing of m-cis, but with uncertain relevance to the present context; see note 12.

[38] The linguistic import of the second <y> is unclear. It may conceivably reflect a type of syncretism; see §16.2 <u>SM</u> for discussion.

[39] "May be unique" because in unvocalized texts across the dialects <T> can be ambiguous between [tta] or [ttə̆] and [t] or [θ]. Note also t[ǽ] as the reflex of *ə̆(ă)*, and the mootness of whether ssg has occurred or not given neutralization of vowel length— both effects of the smc (§22.1).

[40] No clear cases of gem sim rmp have come to light; it is possible they may have mereged with cau rmp or int rmp—see Macuch's discussion (Macs 199f).

[41] "May possibly be disguised . . . by some process": because there may be some other explanation for the <y>; cf. the morphologically identical P variant <yTʾy9l> (~ <{y}Tʾ9l>), HC 396.

[42] 2ʃ [A], likely because retention of pSemitic *2ʃ a seems rather common, at least in TL, in sim rmp forms (cf. Arabic conjugation VIII [ifta9ala]), perhaps especially following emphatics (here [ṣ]) and sonorants (note y[ʾikkə̆lǽl] 'nixnas lə̆ḥupa', Mor 240) as hinted at by Margolis (Mar §5g); see §1.1.1 n. 4. However, if such 2ʃ [A] should be due to influence from the cau rmp, perhaps the gem sim rmp quadrant hasn't fully escaped merger after all.

[43] Morag reports a number of other formations relevant to the hol – gem sim rmp – cau rmp intersection. But though all are of interest to the history and structure of TL per se—notably presumed geminate forms like y[ʾiṭṭŭs] ~ [ʾēṭŭs] 'nitkasa' (Mor 241 w n. 40)—they will be omitted here as lacking sufficient comparative Aramaic clout.

[44] The varieties of hrb might also be developmentally ranked on the assumption that earlier forms were formally more representative of of the binyanim which were being functionally merged, while as time went on the resulting (syncretically) merged category (hollow sim/cau rmp) assumed more uniformity. If a developmental sequence like this is strictly adhered to, SM would sport the most conservative form of hrb, hrb-2, where both prefix shape and schematic vocalism represent the pooled resources of the original components (sim *iθ* ~ cau *ittə̆*, sim 2ʃ ī ~ cau 2ʃ ā). Next would come hrb-1, where the prefix shape is ironed out to *ittə̆* but ī and ā continue to alternate in 2ʃ (B, G, TL, and perhaps CP). And finally 2ʃ ī ~ 2ʃ ā would join the prefix shape in ironing out to uniformity: to 2ʃ ī via hrb-1i (SR, M) or to 2ʃ ā via hrb-1a (TR). Should this sequencing be diachronically faithful to chronology, we presumably must assume dialect pocket-

ing (§18.2 with (18I, J)) to account for various deviations from the rule-of-thumb that chronological precedence correlates with developmental priority; e.g., SM, a late dialect, shows a more conservative form of hrb than early B (see §19 with (19F)). (It must of course be borne in mind that exceptions to the stated rule-of-thumb are demonstrably legion in any number of thoroughly studied areas of historical linguistic inquiry; witness the notable conservatism of Modern Icelandic over against the other contemporary Scandinavian dialects.)

7. Suffixal *n(n)*

An important aspect in the development of the Aramaic verb is the evolution of its suffixes, and one strong facet of this in turn is the spread of the dento-alveolar nasals, whether singleton (*n*) or geminate (*nn*). There appear to be several sources of this spread, to be considered in the ensuing sections of the chapter: the energic suffix of the imperfective, shaped **inn* (postconsonantally) or **nn* (postvocalically) (§7.1); the long-imperfective gender-number suffixes of shape **V̄na* (§7.2); the 2fp perfective suffix of shape **tinnǎ* (§7.3); the originally independent 3p pronouns containing **n(n)* (§7.4); the 1s object suffix **nī* (§7.5); mitosis of etymologically justified **n* (§7.6).

Before embarking on this survey, it will be convenient to draw a terminological distinction between *light* and *heavy* paradigmatic slots. A *light* slot in the first instance is an impf slot originally ending in modal **-i* (long or energic impf) or devoid of any desinence at all following the stem (short impf), while a *heavy* slot in the first instance is an impf slot (originally) ending in a number-gender suffix, whether long (**-ūna, *-īna, *-āna*), energic (**-ůnna, *-ĭnna, *-ånna*), or short (**-ū, *-ī, *-ā*). (For these distinctions, see §2.2.1, §2.2.2, §2.3.4, §7.2.)

The characterizations of the preceding paragraph are qualified as being made "in the first instance," because secondarily the light–heavy distinction may be extended to homologous slots of the impa and pf. Such extension is straightforward in the case of **-ū, *-ī, *-ā* since these slots in the impa and pf are both homophonous with the corresponding light impfs, and archimorphemically isofunctional (e.g., 3mp pf **-ū* is in archimorphemic correspondence with mp short impf **-ū*, "mp" because common to both 3mp **yaQSuMū* and 2mp **taQSuMū*). The notion of *heavy suffix* may also be used in cases of weaker homology; e.g., 2mp pf **-tū(m)* vis-à-vis impf **-ū(na), *-ůnna*, inasmuch as the latter suffixes, despite their shape discrepancy with **-tū(m)*, are archimorphemically related to it qua mp (and indeed commonality of the labial vocalism abets).

7.1. Energic **(i)nn*

If the presumed original emphasis-connoting power of energic **(i)nn* lasted into pA, no clear trace of it remains even in the earliest attested dialects (De 80 with n. 87, L 40, BL 88). But it did not simply lose its emphatic function without compensation, at least not in the early dialects O, I, and B. In these varieties, the **(i)nn* suffixes bearing an object pronoun tend to replace the long-impf forms (§7.2) in their lingering semantic opposition to the short impf, an opposition that might loosely be characterized as indicative vs. subjunctive. Thus O **inn*-ful <y9Br̲n̲h̲> 'er zürnt ihn' vs. **inn*-less <ʔ{1} Tŝryh̲> 'du mögest ihn nicht losbinden' (De 109, 114); I <ʔsBl̲n̲K̲> 'ich werde dich ernähren' (L 51) vs. <ʔrḥ9h̲> 'ani roce lirḥoc ʔoto' (Kutscher 1970: 82);[1] B [yǎšēzǎvi̲n̲n̲ɔ̲̄x̲] 'he will deliver thee' (Dan 6:17) vs. {ʔal=yǎvahǎl̲ɔ̲̄x̲] 'let it not trouble thee' (Dan 4:16), [yǎvahǎl̲u̲n̲n̲ánī] 'they troubled me' (Dan 4:2) vs. [yǎvahǎl̲ū̲x̲] 'let them (not) trouble thee' (Dan 5:10).[2]

In the later non-Eastern dialects, where a sufficient number of forms are attested to be certain,[3] singular object suffixes built on originally energic **(i)nn* become the shape of choice in the impf, reaching a peak in G, where probably all variant **(i)nn*-less suffixes become obsolete.[4] In the other non-E dialects, **(i)nn*-ful and **(i)nn*-less suffixes continue to alternate, but with a preference toward the former. In the Eastern dialects, finally, the preference falls to the opposite side, ascendancy redounding to the **(i)nn*-less forms. And even as G represents the extreme non-E position of total **(i)nn* generalization, among the E dialects, SR reaches the extreme of total **(i)nn* expungence.[5]

Examples (suffixes underscored—for non-E dialects **(i)nn*-bearing forms preceding **(i)nn*-less forms, for E dialects the other way around—and forms separated by "vs." when both suffix types are cited): **non-E—** TR: [yæḥšǎni̲n̲n̲éh] 'er wird ihn ergreifen' (Da 370) vs. [yæḥnǎx̲é̲h] 'er wird ihn weihheben' (Da 268); CP: <yškḥ̲n̲h̲> vs. <yškḥh̲> both 'er findet ihn' (Sg 78f); SM: <yqym̲n̲h̲> t[yāqīmí̲n̲ne] 'er wird ihn befestigen' (Macs 196) and <ylBš̲n̲h̲> 'er bekleidet ihn' vs. <ylBšh̲> same gloss (both Macs 228); G: <y9BD̲y̲n̲y̲h̲> 'er diehnt ihm' (Da 370). **E—** SR: 3ms^3ms [nɛQSǎMé̲h] ~ [nɛQSǎMí̲w] (Ns 131; on [-éh] ~ [-íw], see §2.3.4.4); TL: <lyŝwyyK̲> 'he'll set you' vs. <yDKr̲y̲n̲K̲> 'he'll remember you' (both Mar 60); M: <nigiṭlH̲> [nīɣeṭl̲í̲] 'we'll kill him' (Mal 516).

*(i)nn also makes a modest incursion into the impa and pf of SM and G, e.g.: SM impa <ʔqm̲n̲h̲> 'dirigiere ihn!' (Macs 196), <Kwn̲n̲h̲> t[kūnén̲n̲ē̲][6] 'bereite es!' (Macs 194), pf ˌwʔ9my̲n̲h̲> 'zeigte ihm' (Macs 233), <smKT̲h̲h̲> t[sāmɑktí̲n̲ne] (~ **(i)nn*-less <smKTh̲> t[sāmɑktē̲] 'ich habe ihn versehen' (Macs 227); G impa <qP̲h̲n̲y̲h̲> 'schlage ihn!' (Da 375), pf <ʔwTB̲y̲n̲y̲h̲> 'siedelte ihn an' (Da 363). There is no trace of exenergic *(i)nn* encroachment in the other dialects except for what may be one incipient showing in TR, tb[hǎvi̲n̲n̲ǎ̲] 'gib sie!' (Da 374).

(It should be mentioned that distribution of exenergic *(i)nn* as a bridge-like formative is difficult to distinguish from that of the homonymous element of pronominal origin discussed in §7.4, especially §7.4.3.)

7.2. Long-Imperfective *$\bar{V}n(a)$ (Including Energic *$\overset{\circ}{V}n(n(a))$)

Although the most salient feature of the long-short opposition are the re-
flexes of long 2fs *$\bar{\imath}n(a)$, mp *$-\bar{u}n(a)$, fp *$-\bar{a}n(a)$ vs. those of the corresponding short suffixes *$-\bar{\imath}$, *$-\bar{u}$, *$-\bar{a}$, the other φ-slots were in all likelihood also
differentially marked, assumedly in this book by *$-i$ for the long impf and
*$-\emptyset$ (no suffix) for the short impf (§2.2.1, §2.2.2, §2.3.4). However though
the long ≠ short syntactic opposition lingered at least as late as B, and possibly even later, the original *$-i$ ≠ *$-\emptyset$ signal may very well have been lost for
most verbs by apocope (§17.22), a change likely antedating I. The qualification
"for most verbs" is warranted by the fact that at least one gizra, the defective
(*3 √y, which by adn (§9.1.4) also largely subsumes *3 √$^{\gamma}$ as of I), may well
preserve a trace of the old *$-i$ ≠ *$-\emptyset$ opposition for a considerably longer time.
Whatever the precise phonetic disposition of the opposition may turn out to
be, in O corresponding φ-slots are spelled long <-h> vs. short <-y> (Deg 76,
where Degen plausibly if not compellingly interprets these as spelling [-ē] vs.
[-ay] respectively). Does any equivalent trace extend later than the O period?
The matter remains to be settled. Here, suffice the suggestive observation for I
that to judge by the forms identified in L 63–66 as long ("Voll-Aor.") or short
("Kurz-Aor."), the longs are written <-h> while the shorts show <-h> ~ <-y>.
The working assumption of this book is that no trace of the original *$-i$ ≠ *$-\emptyset$
opposition remains as of approximately B, which regularly fields [-ē] as reflex
of either (§11.2).

For the matter of longf/short impf in the light defective impf, see especially
condensatory coalescence (k-coa) in §11.

When it comes to long-impf *$-Vna$ vs. short-impf *$-V$:

(α) Y at first blush seems to show exclusively short-impf <-w>, but upon
closer examination it seems more likely that this dialect simply lacks the long–
short opposition to begin with and that <-w> is just its unique encodation of
mp. If correct, this may tie in with the fact that, alone among the ancient dialects, Y shows no opposition between *$(i)nn$-ful and *$(i)nn$-less object suffixes
(see n. 2). Example: <y9BDw> 'sie arbeiten' (DR I 214:7).

(β) In O, I, and B, the distribution of impf *$-\bar{V}n(a)$ vs. *$-\bar{V}$ continues to be to
at least some extent semantically motivated. Examples (for B) from the same
biblical verse 'Thus then *shall you say* {long impf [tēmə̄rū́n]} ... *let them per-
ish* from the earth {short impf [yēvā́ðū]})'.[7]

(γ) The later dialects have lost the semantic basis for the opposition, which
they by and large neutralized in favor of the long and/or energic (cf. n. 7);
and while there are occasional retentions of short impf *$-\bar{V}$, most apparent
instances, notably in SM, TL, and M, actually derive from *$-\bar{V}na$ or *$-\overset{\circ}{V}nna$:

sap(§17.22) > -*V̄n*, -*V̊nn* deg (§3.1 (3Fvii)) > -*V̄n*, -*V̊n* mtr (§17.12) > [-*V̄*].
Examples: P <yˀmrwn> 'they(m) say' (HC 340), <TBrKn> 'they(f) bless (HC
350) (<T-> by ftg, §16.2 SM (z′) w n. 24); n. <yqBrwn> 'ils ensevelissent' (Cl
141); TR [tæ9bə̆ðín] 'du(f) tust' (Da 271), [tæ9bə̆rún] ~ [ti9bə̆rún] ~ [ti9ibrún]
'ihr geht hinüber' (Da 268, 273), [yæ9bə̆ðá̃n] ~ tb[yæ9æbDá̃n] 'sie(f) dienen'
(Da 273) (variants depending upon ±att, ±auf—§12, §4.4); CP <yThrmwn>
'sie(m) werden gebannt' (Sg 21), <yhKmn> 'sie(f) machen weise' (Sg 63),
<yzBnyn> 'sie(f) kaufen' (Sg 20—<yn> either thanks to the palatal factor to
be discussed under (δ) below and §7.4, or by *stressed closed-syllabic raising*, scr, a CP-specific process whereby *á* in a closed syllable frequently →
Í—§12.2 n. 11); SM <yqBrwn> t[yæqríbon] 'sie(m) werden darbringen' (Macs
161) ~ <yqrBw> t[yæqríbu] (lc, <-w> t[-u] by mtr), <ysGyˀn> t[yæsgiyyá̃n]
'sie(f) werden vermehrt' (Macs 215), <wyylDn> t[wyīl̥á̃dən] 'und sie(f) ge-
bahren' (Macs 161, with t[-ən] by the palatal factor, (δ) below and §7.4); G
<yhtlwn> 'sie(m) verfallen' (Da 272), <yhm9n> 'sie(f) säuern' (Da 273); SR
[nεQS̆ə̆Mún] 'they(m). . .', [nεQSə̆M̃ə́n] 'they(f). . .'; TL <ysPDwn> 'they(m)
will lament' (Mar 38), <l(y)sGrw> ~ <n(y)sGrw> 'they(m) will study' (lc, <-w>
by mtr), <lylPn> 'they(f) will learn' (lc); M <niligtun> t[nīláɣton] 'they(m)
will hold' (Macm 125), interpretable as [nīleGtón]—in the corresponding fp,
M shows <-an> ~ <-a>: <nirimza(n)> qua [nīremzán] ~ [nīremzá̃] 'they(f) will
wink' (Mal 543).[8]

(δ) Importation of reflexes of long/energic impf *-*V̄na*/*-*V̊nna* to the intransitive pf or impa (*heavy intransitive importation*, hii) is most prevalent
in the later dialects CP, SM, G, SR, TL, M,[9] but may be seen incipiently in
TR[10] and perhaps even as early as I (Coxon 1977). CP, SM, G, SR, TL, M
again also show some palatal vocalization in the fp slots of these tenses and the
impf as well, though apparently only CP and M unconstrainedly: G (pf only),
SR (pf and impa only), TL (impa only), M (if at all, pf only). Though much
of this palatal vocalization may originate from generalizing *-inna* of pf 2fp
-tinna qua signal of fp (§7.3), there is some evidence of a different, perhaps
even pA origin.[11] Palatal fp cases will be adduced here along with nonpalatal
instances (< *-āna*, *-ắnna*), with further discussion of palatality itself—the
phenomenon to be called *the palatal factor*, pfr—deferred till §7.3.

Now to specific examples:

CP. Pf 3mp <ˀTm̊ṅ̊wn> 'wurden gezählt' (Sg 72) (normally <-w>, occasionally <-∅> (lap, §17.9)); pf 3fp <ˀTmlˀyn> 'completae sunt' (Sl 73) (normally <-y>); impa mp <DmwKwn> 'schlafet!' (Sg 62) (normally <-w>); impa
fp normally like <zBnyn> 'kaufet!' (lc) (note that occasional <-ˀn> might be
interpreted as either palatal or [-ắn] (Sg 7, 9; §21.2 w (21G)). (CP also shows

palatality in the impf fp, e.g., <yzBny̱n̲> 'sie kaufen' (Sg 20), though forms like <yʔḫKmn̲> are ambiguous between [-Ĭn] and [-ån̥].)

SM. Pf 3mp <w9Brn̲> t[wɑbbằron̲] 'und sie kamen durch' (Macs 156), <ʔmrw̲n̲> 'dixerunt' (Macs 99) (usually <-w>, as ~ <ʔmrw> (lc)); pf 3fp <w(ʔ)rKBy̱n̲> t[wærkằbə̱n̲] (Macs 146) (usually <-y> t[-i], as ~ <w(ʔ)rKBy> t[wærkắbi] (lc)); impa mp <hȚqDšw̲n̲> t[itqɑddắšon̲] 'heiliget euch!' (Macs 151) (usually <-w>, as ~ <hȚqDšw> t[itqɑddắšu] (lc)); impa fp usually like <DBqn̲> t[dēbắqɑn̲] (Vilsker 1981:62), though Macuch cites unexemplified also palatal <-nh> t[-innæ] (Macs 148) (whose t[inn] suggests an origin in the pf 2fp, §7.4 below).

G. Pf 3mp usually like <slqw̲n̲> (Da 262); pf 3fp <ʔKḥsy̱n̲> 'wurden schlecht' (Da 263) (usually <-n>); impa mp usually like <PwTḥw̲n̲> 'öffnet!' (Da 277).[12]

SR. Pf 3mp [QšSaM̍ún] (with preservation of 2ʃ [a] suggesting later addition of [-ūn], ~ older [QšSáM] spelled <QSaMw̲> reflecting < *QaSáMū apocopated by lap); pf 3fp [QšSaMé̍n] (~ older [QšSáM] spelled phonetically by the Jacobites <QSaM>, but <QSaMy> by the Nestorians with silent <-y> bespeaking an apparent originally palatal suffix but more likely instantiating purely morphemic spelling, with <-y> signaling "feminine"); impa mp [QšSoM̍ún] (with later addition of [-ūn] as with the pf, cued by preservation of 2ʃ, ~ [QšSóM] <QSoMw̲>); impa fp [QšSoMé̍n] (~ <QSoMy̲>).[13]

TL. Pf 3fp <-n> probably [-ān] (as per <nTrn̲> 'they fell off' a[nǎθaron̲] (Mar 139*) y[næθrɑ̱n̲] (Mor 127)[14]) possibly ~ <-ʔ> [-ā] via mtr (e.g., <yqrʔ̲> y[yǎqærā] (Mor 127)); impa fp <-n> ~ <-yn>, probably [-ān] ~ [-īn] (e.g., <qtwl(y̲)n̲> a[qǎṭulɔn̲] (Mar 159*) y[qǎṭulīn̲] (Mor 131)).[15] Margolis also reports one case of hii in the 3rd *masculine* plural: <ʔTw̲n̲> a[ʔǎθó̍n̲] 'they(m) came' (Mar 52, 9*).[16]

M. Pf 3mp <-un> rarely appears on strong 3√ (<piršun̲> [peršón]'they understood', <apun̲> [appón] (*√ʔp) 'they enfolded' (Mal 350)) where we usually find <-Ø> < *-ū by lap, but is common on 3√y (e.g., <ṣbun̲> m[ṣóβon̲] 'they baptized' (Mal 351)) where with equal frequency a trace of n-less *-ū is captured by coa^hei leading to such as <ṣbu> [ṣǎβú̍] (lc). However <-iun> is not rare on strong 3√ (<gtaliun̲> m[gǎṭályo̍n̲] 'they killed' (Mal 352)) while only occasionally appearing on 3 √y—in fact, only on such as < *3 √H by r-adn, §9.2.3.2 [17] (<šumaian̲> 'they heard' (Mal 353)).[18] The pf 3fp usually shows up as <-Ø> whether < *-ā by lap or through neutralization with 3mp by fgm (§16.1), but <-ian> sometimes appears under conditions like those for <-iun> (<prašian̲> [pǎrašyắn̲] 'they discerned', <sbaian̲> 3 √y < *3 √9 'they were satisfied' (Mal 363)),[19] while palatal suffixation (usually *n*-less) may residually be seen in <(e)qnia> t[éqnī] 'they acquired' and <ehzia> t[éhzī] 'they saw' (<e-> t[e-] by pro, §17.18) (Mal 362).[20] In impa mp <-un> and <-iun> distribute pretty much under the same conditions as the pf 3mp suffixes of the same shape. The one attested case of impa fp <atian> 'come!' (Mal 656) is best interpreted as [aθyą́n], with 3 √[y] + allosuffix [-ą́n].

(ε) In the heavy slots of the transitive impf, most dialects deploy *either* reflexes of the long impf (SM <Dy9m<u>wnh</u>> t[æd-yēmmū́ne] 'damit sie ihn sehen' (Macs 229), SR [nə̆šabbə̆<u>hū</u>nḗ<u>h</u>]'sie preisen ihn hoch' (Ns 134)) *or* of the energic impf (TR tb[yiqtə̆<u>lunnǽnā</u>] 'sie töten uns' (Da 373), M [nīnesB<u>onnī́</u>] 'they take him' (Mal 540f)), while TL evinces reflexes of both but for the most part those of the energic (a[yiqbə̆<u>runnḗh</u>] 'they'll bury him' (Mar 157*), y[tiqrə̆9<u>unnḗh</u>] 'taḥtĕxu ʔoto' (Mor 296)).[21] However, the tendency documented in §7.1, whereby in the light transitive the non-Eastern dialects preferentially use energic *inn as a bridge to the object suffixes, whereas the Eastern types of A prefer bridgeless formation, may be partially reflected in the fact that two of the three E dialects—specifically, the L ones (TL and M)—more frequently use reflexes of the *n*-less short impf in the heavy transitive impf; e.g., TL y[lifsə̆<u>lū́hū</u>] 'yifsĕlu ʔoto' (Mor 295), M [nīneGD<u>ū́y</u>] 'they'll draw him out' (Mal 540f). This preference arguably reflects the light impf tendency in that the short-impf suffixes are nasalless, hence bridgeless, as favored for the light impf transitive by the E dialects (including the two L ones). (Is a corollary of this that nasal-bearing heavy suffixes are felt to be bridgeful whether the nasal is singleton (long impf) or geminate (energic impf)? It may very well be, given the tendency of suffixal *n* and *nn* toward phonological equivalence; §7.7.)

(ζ) The patterns discussed under (ε) for the heavy transitive impf by and large also hold for propagation to the impa and pf, a phenomenon to be called *heavy transitive importation* (hti). This is so in that: -*Vnn*-bearing impfs tend to correlate with -*Vnn*-bearing impas/pfs (thus M pf [də̆h<u>onnán</u>] 'they pushed us', Macm 370—cf. Modern [hez<u>ónna</u>] 'they saw her', Macm 372—like impf [naṣt<u>onnán</u>] 'they will seduce us', Macm 373, cf. [nīnesB<u>onnī́</u>] under (ε)) and likewise -*V̄n*-bearing impfs vis-à-vis -*V̄n*-bearing impas/pfs (thus SR [də̆wo<u>hū́nɔ̄́y</u>] 'opferet ihn!', Ns 136, like [nə̆šabbə̆<u>hū</u>nḗ<u>h</u>] (ε)); short-impf preferences preferences tend to correlate with nasalless formations in the impa/pf (thus TL <ʔmt<u>whw</u>> 'carry(mp) him!' (Mar 61) like y[lifsə̆<u>lū́hū</u>] (ε), M [leɣṭ<u>ū́y</u>] 'they held him', Macm 163, like [nīneGD<u>ū́y</u>] (ε)). However, these preferences are subtlized by the fact that nasalless formations, original in the impa and pf, are not rare even in dialects that fail to use the short impf in the heavy transitives: thus CP <ẙḥB<u>wy</u>> 'legten ihn', Sg 79 (in fact, CP shows exclusively nasalless forms in the pf/impa heavy transitive); SM <hPqwh> 'bringet sie heraus!' (also +hti, as <hy9Twnh> 'bringet ihn herab!' ,[22] Macs 230); G <ʔPqwh> 'bringet ihn heraus!' (also +hti, as <ŝBqwnyh> 'verlasset ihn!', Da 376). (Observe that, to the extent TL and M preference for *n*-less heavy transitives in pf/impa truly correlates with their equal preference for the short impf in heavy transitives, and to the extent that nasalful or nasalless preferences across the tenses (impf, impa, pf) constitute an approximately unitary system in the dialects—to the extent these regularities hold, hti is complemented, notably in TL and M, by a sort of "anti-hti" dictating that the short impf (e.g., M [nīneGDúy]) exert its influence on the pf/impa by *blocking* hti via maintaining the A-original, nasalless formations (e.g., M [leγtúy]). That is, we are faced with what might be called a *pattern conspiracy* making for the functional equivalence of the underlined terms in the following proportion:

(7A) long impf : <u>short impf</u>   =   +hti : <u>-hti</u>

  ⎵⎵⎵⎵⎵⎵⎵⎵⎵⎵⎵⎵⎵⎵⎵⎵   ⎵⎵⎵⎵⎵⎵⎵⎵⎵⎵⎵⎵⎵⎵⎵⎵

        impf system   pf/impa systems

(η) It might finally be noted that both hii and hti evidence some variation in the tightness of bonding between staminal host and suffixal import, variation redolent of that noted in connection with other sorts of supervenient attachment (see especially §7.4 below and §17.15). To cite just two antithetical cases from TL: while in the Yemeni tradition pf 3fp attachment is intimate (synchronically effected at a deeper phonological level or on the phonological level itself), [næθr-ān], in the Ashkenazic tradition attachment is loose (synchronically shallow-level, too late for certain crucial rules to bind the constituents tighter together), [nə̄θar-ɔ̄n]; see §7.2 (δ) with n. 15. Patterns manifested through such variation remain to be uncovered and codified.

7.3. 2fp pf **tinnā̃́*

As a result of the reciprocal assimilations sketched in §2.3.4.3, the m ≠ f opposition in the post-I reflexes of pf 2mp **-tūm*, 2fp **-tinnā̃́* came to be borne exclusively by vowel quality, m U ≠ f I, while vowel length and the consonantal frame fell out identically for both genders in either of two sets, /-tV̄n/ (B, TR, TL) or /-tV̊nn/ (SR, M), in most other post-I dialects relevant forms being either unattested (P, N) or ambiguous as to disposition (CP, G). SM may be unique in maintaining a flex of ancipitally lengthened (§2.3.1) **-tinnā* (see below).

Note that, morphemically, the /t/ is segmentable as the signal of the 2nd person, leaving the residua of the suffix pairs de facto in the role of signaling the number-gender features: /-ūn/, /-Ůnn/ as mp, /-īn/, /-I̊nn/ as fp. And even as nasal-bearing heavy suffixes have migrated from the impf to the impa/pf, as we have seen in §7.2, so fp /-in/, /-Inn/ has migrated from the pf to the impf/ impa, accounting for at least some, probably most, of the fp palatal endings we saw in §7.2 (δ)—the incidence of the so-called *palatal factor* (pfr). In this connection, note also that one SM allo of the fp impa, -nh. T[-innæ], plausibly reflects 2fp pf *-*tinnā*, with auslaut lengthened by ancipitality (though ultimately shortened in trad pron to [-æ] by c-pra of the Samaritan circuit, §22.1 (22B)).

7.4. Independent 3p Pronouns Containing *n(n)*

7.4.1. Description

Though there is some disagreement on their origins (cf. Brockelmann 1908: 305f.), most dialects as of B show independent 3p pronouns containing *n(n)*: [23] thus B mp [ʾinnún] (~ [himmṓ(n)]), fp [ʾinnín]; P mp <hn(w)n> (HC 360); TR mp [ʾinnún], fp [ʾinnín] (Da 107); CP mp <h(y)nwn> ~ <ḥnŵn> ~ <ʾnwn>, fp <h(y)nyn> ~ <ʾnyn> (Sg 32); SM mp <hnwn> ~ <ʾnwn> t[ínnon], fp <hnyn> ~ <ʾnyn> t[ínnən] (Macs 131); G mp <ʾynwn>, fp <hynyn> ~ <ʾynyn> ~ <ʾynwn> (by fgm, §16) (Da 106); SR mp [hɛnnṓn], fp [hɛnnḗn] (B 48); TL mp <ʾynwn> (Mar 16); M mp <hinun> t[hén(n)on], fp <hinin> ~ <hinen> t[hén(n)en] (Macm 154).

Most of these dialects in turn—likely at least P, TR, SM, G, TL, M—show evidence of then having attached (a possible reduction of) the pronoun to the verb as an object suffix (§17.15.1): P <9Drn̲w̲n̲> ~ <9Drn̲n̲> 'he aided them' (HC 395); TR [dǝværinnún] 'er leitete sie' (Da 363); SM <wmt̲n̲w̲n̲> 'und er kam zu ihnen' (Macs 233); G <qByl̲y̲n̲w̲n̲> 'he received them' (according to Kutscher (1976: 143) more genuine than the variant <qBylynhw>, which he considers to be TL intrusion—cf. also §17.19 n. 102); TL a[t̲ǝ9emin̲n̲ún] (Mar 118*), y[šǝ́ʾelin̲n̲ǝ́hú] (Mor 291—the [h] appearing here, as well as in other dialects below, will be discussed in §7.4.2); M <lgat̲in̲(h̲)un̲> 'he grasped them' (Macm 356) interpretable as [lǝ́yat̲ennón] ~ [lǝ́yat̲enhón] (for this cf. in part Macm 163). Note how the unreduced 2ʃ in TR, G, TL, M betrays the late addition of the suffix, specifically later than reduction (§4.2). Especially TR and TL also show forms where 2ʃ is in fact reduced, betraying integration of the new suffix into the morphophonology: e.g., TR [bæddǝrin̲n̲ún] (~ unreduced [24] sb[bæddārin̲n̲ún]) 'er schickte sie weg' (Da 363); TL a[davrin̲hǭ] 'he led them' (Mar 101*), y[hænqin̲n̲ún] 'ḥanak ʾotam' (Mor 291).[25]

Though SR appears to achieve 3p object pronominalization syntactically, as does B, the form of the pronoun used is not independent [hɛnnṓn, [hɛnnḗn], but rather *h*-less [ɛnnṓn], [ɛnnḗn], a difference usually interpreted as betraying *enclisis* (B 48, Ns 44)—which suggests that SR is at an earlier stage of the way toward full suffixation.[26]

Once these suffixes have become part of the pronominal object marking system, there is no way for naïve native speakers to distinguish the nasal component, especially the geminate *nn*, from that originally serving to mark the energic. And so the way is even further cleared for metanalyzing the *nn*, as also its alternative shape *n* (by smp, §17.26), as an object marker, and then propagating the results across the tenses beyond the pale of the third person plural. See §7.4.3.

7.4.2. Formatives Containing *n(nə̆)-h*

Though the fact that 3p object suffixes containing the sequence *n(nə̆)-h* may be found exclusively in TL and M[27] might suggest an L innovation, an explicitly articulated hypothesis as to how this sequence may have arisen in L remains elusive. One promising idea would be that insertion of *h* constitutes a metanalytic reshaping delimiting *n(nə̆)* fore as (part of) a bridge and *h* aft, together with the string following it, as the 3p pronoun proper—*h* being the morpheme at large for 3rd person in the independent pronouns. However, while this hypothesis can be made to work pretty well for M, in TL it runs smack into the problem that the independent 3p pronouns themselves contain the presumably inserted *h* in question, where the preceding *n(nə̆)* can hardly be taken as (part of) a bridge. Moreover, the TL independent 3p pronouns contain no other *h* that might have served as a model for the insertion in the first place; contrast, e.g., TL mp <ʔynh̠w>, fp <ʔynh̠y>, containing apparently modelless "inserted" *h*, with M mp <h̠inun>, fp <h̠inin> containing initial, uninserted *h* which may easily have served as model for suffixal <-inh̠un>, <-inh̠in> with <h> inserted between bridge <in-> and pronominal <-un>, <-in>.

The alternative hypothesis would take *h* not as an innovation but rather as a retention, reflecting original independent pronouns (and subsequent suffixes) shaped along the lines of **hin-hŭm^{EL}* / **hin-hĭn^{EL}*, **ʔin-hŭm^{EL}* / **ʔin-hĭn^{EL}*, **hinnV̊-hŭm^{EL}* / **hinnV̊-hĭn^{EL}*, **ʔinnV-hŭm^{EL}* / **ʔinnV̊-hĭn^{EL}*. The core pronouns in these forms, mp **hŭm*, fp **hĭn*, are identical to the object suffixes posited in §2.2.2.4, while the lead-off constituents represent perhaps originally presentative morphemes akin to Hebrew *hen, hinnē*, Arabic *ʔinna*. The *h ~ ʔ* variation is plausibly related to that seen in the causative and rmp prefixes (§9.1.2, §9.2.2) and in fact bids fair to be of ancient Semitic vintage—cf. right here Hebrew *h̠innē* vs. Arabic *ʔinna* (and for the larger picture, Brockelmann 1908: 520–22). In accordance with this general view, the TL independent pronouns spelt <ʔynhw>, <ʔynhy> would following Yem trad pron (y[ʔinnə̆hŭ́], [ʔinnə̆hí́]) reflect **ʔinnV̊hŭm*, **ʔinnV̊hĭn*, while Ash trad pron (a[ʔinhó́], [ʔinhé́]) would bespeak either **ʔinhŭm*, **ʔinhĭn* or the same etyma as reflected in Yem trad pron but with the option taken for smp (§17.26): **ʔinnV̊. . .* red > **ʔinnV̊. . .* smp > **ʔin. . . .* Both traditions register loss of auslaut nasal by mtr, with resulting vowel quality differences (to the extent they reflect genuine TL registerial realities) bespeaking differing ancipitality dispositions: e.g., y[. . .hŭ́] bespeaking < **. . .hŭm*, a[. . .hó́] bespeaking *either <. . .hóm <* mid(§17.11) **. . .hŭm or <. . .hóm <* l-anc(§2.3.1) *. . .hóm <*

mid *. . .húm* (the +l-anc differences being indistinguishable inasmuch as mtr lengthens the vowel rendred final upon truncation in any event, i.e., . . .V̊C# mtr > . . .V̆#).

Finally, *h*-less pronouns and suffixes (e.g., TL <ʔynwn>, M [-ennón], [-ennén]) would reflect progressive assimilation of *h* by *n*, i.e., . . .*nh*. . . > . . .*nn*. . . , variably in the L dialects and categorically in the others (§7.4.1).

This hypothesis of *h* as retention may rest a bit uneasy with some inasmuch as the assimilation . . .*nh*. . . > . . .*nn*. . . , hypothesized to be the general case in A, is variably bypassed by TL and M in a way unstatable within family tree theory (§18.1), given the assumptions made in this book as to A dialect branching (§19 (19F)). To see this, consider with the simplified genealogical tree in (7B) that only the boxed dialects TL and M show retention of *h*, while the circled dialects, SR and all those of the West (W), have totally eradicated *h* by assimilation.[28] As may readily be seen, there is no branch in (7B) where categorical assimilation may be plotted so as to be inherited downward (= forward in time) to the exclusion of just the boxed dialects. In accordance with the family tree all-or-none way of assessing changes, if *categorical assimilation* (cta) took place on branch 1—that is, during the period before W–E differentiation—the prediction would be that cta should also have affected TL and M. Plotting cta on branch 2 would erroneously exclude SR from the pale of the change, while occurrence along branch 3 would not only incorrectly *ex*clude the W dialects but would also incorrectly *in*clude TL and M. Attempts to plot cta along branches 4, 5, 6, 7 will likewise result in erroneous distributions.

(7B)

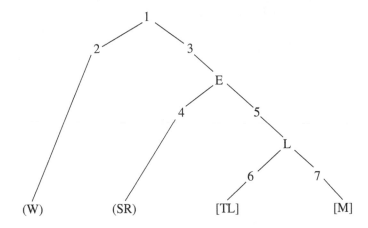

On the other hand, the wave model of dialect development (§18.2) makes it possible to capture cta as excluding just TL and M while by and large respecting the genealogical relations portrayed in (7B). The wave explication is displayed in (7C). At stage I, there exists a relatively undifferentiated Aramaic space set off via the isoglosses represented by (1) from, say, related Northwest Semitic speech varieties. By convention, the linguistic changes constituting (1) are spread, with relative homogeneity throughout the A dialect space—with the exception of the *dialect pocket* symbolized by (2), a space into which, for whatever reason, *nh > nn* assimilation fails to extend in categorical form (for short, cta). At stage II, further isogloss bands have developed setting off the W dialects (3W) from the E (3E), but within the latter region dialect pocket (2) remains (relatively) stationary in continuing to resist cta. Finally, at stage III, the E space has split into an approximately northern subspace—that is, (pre-) Syriac (4SR), and a roughly southern or lower subspace, (4L), which moreover is approximately coterminous with (2). That is, the dialect pocket of cta resistance has by now, through the agency of subsequent linguistic changes, come to be defined as the L dialect area—subsequently to further differentiate into TL and M.

As mentioned, *nh > nn* assimilation is variable in the L dialects; specifically, it is the majority option in M[29] but the minority option in TL. In the latter dialect, at least the mp formative alternates with *h*-less allos, both in the independent pronoun (<ʾynwn>) and in the pronominal suffix (<-ynwn>). (And in this vein, a disturbing note for the *h*-as-retention hypothesis just formulated is that Margolis marks (by "†") both <ʾynwn> and <-ynwn> as *archaic* vis-à-vis <ʾynhw>, <-ynhw> (Mar 16, 59). Perhaps sociolinguistic *evaluation* as "archaic" is out of kilter with actual historical development for some reason. But perhaps rehabilitation of the *h*-as-innovation hypothesis is somehow in order. (For a somewhat different view on the development of (some of) these pronominal formatives, see §8.1.4.))

(7C)   I

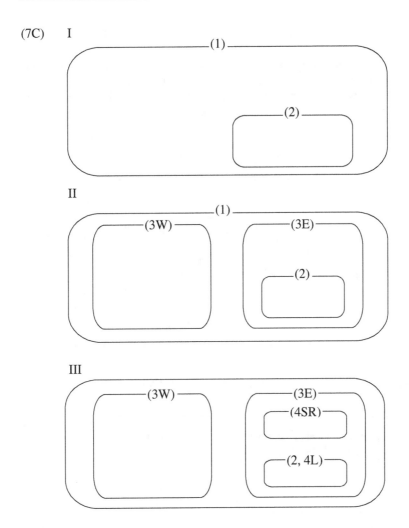

II

III

7.4.3. Generalization of the Function of *n(n)*

Once *n(n)*-bearing 3p pronouns have been incorporated as object suffixes, little will stand in the way of confusing the function of these pronominal *n(n)*s with that of the *n(n)*-bearing formatives deriving from the energic suffix and now serving as bridge-like stem-to-suffix markers (§7.1). Hence, incorporation of pronominal *n(n)* will de facto introduce bridge-like *n(n)* immediately preceding 3p object suffixes, inviting the generalization that /__3p is a favored environment for the appearance of object-marking *(V)n(n)*. It is thus not surprising that a corresponding pattern developed in some dialects. Notably, TL and M have generalized the pattern from /__3p to /__p, TL tendentially and M absolutely.

A summary of object-marking *(V)n(n)* distribution appears in (7D). (The qualification "at least" in the heavy-suffixed quadrants reflects uncertainty for several dialects due to orthographic indeterminacy. Note that here "-*(V)n(n)*" = "do(es) not accompany obj suffixation with *(V)n(n)*".)

(7D)

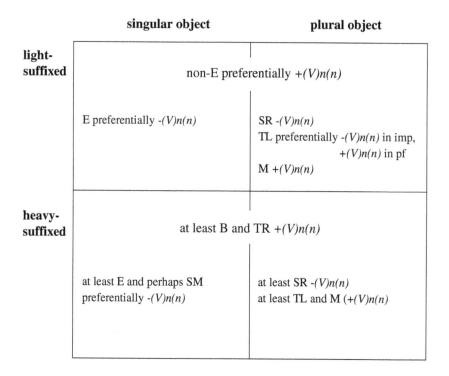

	singular object	**plural object**
light-suffixed	non-E preferentially +*(V)n(n)*	
	E preferentially -*(V)n(n)*	SR -*(V)n(n)* TL preferentially -*(V)n(n)* in imp, +*(V)n(n)* in pf M +*(V)n(n)*
heavy-suffixed	at least B and TR +*(V)n(n)*	
	at least E and perhaps SM preferentially -*(V)n(n)*	at least SR -*(V)n(n)* at least TL and M (+*(V)n(n)*

7.5. The 1s Suffix *nī*

After a certain point, the convergence of several factors as just detailed (§7.1–§7.4) will take its toll and establish something like a weak spot, or special receptivity, for Aramaic to deploy dentoalveolar nasals as suffixal components in the verb system. One such nasal that was there all along is that contained in the 1st person singular object suffix *-ni*. And at least one dialect, SM, appears to have deployed a local pattern derived from this *n*. The evidence for this comes most clearly from the traditional pronunciation, while the writing system, which makes no distinction between simplex [n] and geminate [nn], representing both as <n>, may well disguise an actually wider distribution of this pattern. In any event, the pattern has taken root in the 2ms^obj space of the pf system, as per these illustrations: <DKrThy> t[dākɑrtắni] 'errinere dich an mich!'[30] an example of the bellwether t[-ni] straightforwardly continuing pSemitic *-nī; then <9BDThy> t[9ābɑdtắne] 'du hast ihn gemacht', <ˤBDThwn> t[ˤābɑdtắnan] <DˀwqrThn> t[dūqɑrtắnæn] 'dass du uns geehrt . . . hast' (all from Macs 227).

7.6. Mitosis of Etymologically Justified *n*

Both TR and G show what analytically and etymologically appears to be an excess of *n*-bearing componency in the mp^3mp suffix complex: e.g., TR pf <ˀælep̊uwnuwnuwn> 'sie lehrten sie' ~ expected <ˀælePuwnuwn> (without graphemic representation of 2ʃ [ll]) (Da 367)—the latter likely [-ŭn(n)ŭn] with 3mp subjective -ū̊(n)- + 3mp objective -(n)ūn, the former [-ŭn(n)ŭn(n)ŭn] with supernumerary -ū̊n(n)-. For such reduplication-like florescence of inflectional morphology, we might use the term *mitosis* (mit) (earlier labeled "metastasis" in Malone 1998a).[31] TR also shows such forms in the impf: <yə̊šæB̊ɧuwnuwnuwn> 'sie werden sie loben', <yiqtə̊linuwn̊uwn> 'sie werden sie toten' (<-i-> instead of <-u(w)-> by pin, §17.17) (Da 373). Despite Dalman's belief that all such mitotic forms are scribal errors (Da 369), they are multiply attested, especially in the impf where [-ŭn(n)ŭn(n)ŭn] is the decided statistical choice for 3mp^3mp. As for G, Dalman cites only one instance, the impa <ˀt̊9wnwnwn> 'verführet sie!' (Da 376), over against one example each of nonmitotic <-wnwn> and (by pin) <-ynwn> (Da 392). (For further discussion, see §13, §17.15.1.)

7.7. Generalization and Spread of *n(n)*-Bearing Patterns

The interaction and interfluence of factors documented in this chapter may well have led to perception of a certain general phonological equivalence relation among the four instantiations of $\bar{V}n(n)$. Especially prominent in making for this tendency is the breakdown of fundamental distinctness between reflexes of the heavy long impf *-$\bar{V}na$ and energic *-$\bar{V}nna$, with the ambivalence of vowel length in the latter (induced by css, §17.4) and further mutual rapprochement of both suffix types upon sap^deg (&17.22, §3.1 (3Fvii)) whittling to to -$\mathring{V}n$. Moreover, when midding (§17.11) is implicated, vowel quality enters the equation making for -ū̊n(n) ~ -ő̊n(n) ~ -ĭn(n) ~ -ĕ̊n(n). It is also conceivable that the phenomenon of early ancipitality (§2.3.1) acted as a contributing factor to the $\bar{V}n(n)$ equivalence, supplying as it does a precedent for $\mathring{V}$ ~ $\bar{V}$ in suffixes; and that subsequently, after the emergence of midding, in badminton fashion the $\bar{V}n(n)$ equivalence contributed to the development of late ancipitality (§2.3.1). Then, too, the mid-born *ĭ* ~ *ĕ̊* and *ŭ̊* ~ *ő̊* facet of $\bar{V}n(n)$ equivalence was likely to be reinforced by the *ī* ~ *ē* variation independently spawned by the originally dissimilation-triggered variation *iy ~ *ay (§8.1.1 with n. 1).

And the selfsame high ~ mid vowel equivalence received further support from some transparentively motivated variations, e.g., 3mp pf def [Qɜ̌Sű] ~ [Qɜ̌Ső] (§15.3.2), and 2ʃ [i] ~ [e] (§15.2.1, §15.5.1).

It is characteristic of languages to systematize variation by specializing one or another alternant in diverse and often arbitrary morphophonological nooks and crannies.[32]

One possible case in point for V̊n(n) might be the tendency to distribute V̊ qualitatively pursuant to *vowel harmony*, so that certain morphophonologically defined sequences of vowel nuclei are homogeneous with respect to height; e.g., in the sim pf 2mp, vowel-harmonic B bb[ḥɜ̌zē̱ē̱θ̱ó̱n] versus otherwise expected tb[ḥɜ̌zē̱θ̱ṷ̈n] (Dan 2:8). Since cases like this are sporadic, they will be said to instantiate *minor vowel harmony* (§2.3.2.1 with n. 5).[33]

Notes to §7

[1] (a) I also seems to show a few cases of **inn* bare of object suffixes, e.g., the second verb in <ʾnThnh wʾslmn lKy> 'ich will es geben und (es) dir bezahlen' (lc, L40). See llcc for additional examples, not all of which are plausibly indicative; perhaps the long ≠ short impf opposition was beginning to wane, as it ultimately disappeared altogether in later Aramaic (see below). Note, however, that Kutscher (1970: 68) disputes Leander's and Porten and Muraoka's claim that the forms in question are energic to begin with. (b) The tendency for I to replace long-impf transitive forms with exenergic *nn*-bearing forms is partially obscured by the haplographic practice of using only one <n> in spelling 1s object forms instead of the expected tandem <nn> (exenergic + 1s -*ni*); Kutscher 1970: 110.

[2] Note the absence of Y from this grouping of earlier dialects. The little bit there is to go on suggests that Y patterned with the later dialects (below) in showing asemantic alternation between **(i)nn*-ful and **(i)nn*-less object forms: e.g., from the same line of the same text, <PlKTŝh . . . PlKTŝnh> 'und er soll ihn . . . zerschmettern . . . und er soll sie . . . zerschmettern' (DR I 214:31).

[3] "later non-Eastern dialects," i.e., TR and the Western dialects CP, SM, and G; see §19 with (19F). (No pertinent forms are attested in P or N.)

[4] An apparent exception is **inn*-less <ysʾBTyh> 'er soll es unrein machen' (Da 370), with *T*-bearing <-Tyh> [-Tĕ̊h] 'it(m)'. But since the process creating the [-Tĕ̊h] (tom, §17.30) is almost certainly posterior to the **(i)nn*-leveling phenomenon under discussion, we cannot say whether the introduction of *T*-bearing suffixes displaced **(i) nn*-ful forms, **(i)nn*-less forms, or both.

[5] While M shows no trace of **(i)nn* in stems with a singular object, it shows such reflexes robustly in stems with a plural object; §7.4.3.

[6] By the normal rules governing SM traditional pronunciation, we should expect t[kūnnéne], with short auslaut (§22.1 (22B(ivβ))). The pronunciation is also noteworthy in appearing to have blended the expected shape of the suffix, t[-ínne] (as in t[sāmɑktínne], next in the text), into the bare stem constituent t[kūnen].

[7] The writing system will usually make it impossible to know whether a presumed instance of long-impf **-Vna* in O might not rather be a case of energic **-Vnna*; and while in principle the difference should be conveyable in I via presence (long) or ab-

sence (energic) of ml's <w>, <y>, contrasting forms are apparently not attested (cf. the paradigms in L between pp. 50 and 51). In the later dialects, as we will see, reflexes of the heavy long-impf and heavy energic suffixes became confused. For these reasons, the two varieties of heavy inflection will often be treated together.

[8] While loss of final consonants by mtr is frequent in both the SM and (especially) the TL verb, it is quite restricted in M, the impf fp suffix *-an* being one of its few systematic targets. Note that the likelihood in later Aramaic of [-V̄#] stemming from mtr-truncation of -V̊n#, rather than from continuation of the ancient short impf, is enhanced by: (a) reduction (§4.2) of (penultimate) 2ʃ, suggesting suffixal (ultimate) stress at the time reduction arose, the pattern expected if the suffix was originally long-impf *-V̄na* or energic *-V̊nna* (see conditions of str, §4.1); (b) in the E L dialects TL and M (§19 (19F)) the fact that the [-V̄#] in question was not apocopated by lap or i-lap (§17.9), a fate it should have succumbed to if a true descendant of original short-impf *-V̊#* and hence unstressed (see again conditions of str; in this vein, TL forms like <lyhDw̱r̲> 'they return', Mar 38, might reflect genuine residua of the old short impf if < *yahdúrū* with infixing apocope by i-lap, §17.9). As concerns point (a) in TL, note the convergent testimony of the Yemeni and Ashkenazic trad prons of forms like 'they will study', y[ligrɔ́sǘ] (Mor 130), a[niɣrɔ́sǘ] (Mar 100*). As for M, <nirimza> clearly betrays the process chain called Aufsprengung (§4.4): [nīremzá] ← *nIrɔ̆mɔ̆zá̄* < *nIrmɔ̆zá̄*.

[9] It might not be a coincidence that the same dialects, with the possible exception of M, show replacement of pf 1p *-nā* by *-nan* (*-nā* extension, nae), a connection that Dalman also seems to recognize (Da 95), though he conceives of the change a bit differently. Two points on this. (a) The reservation about M stems from the fact that the only circumstance under which M might deploy a reflex of *-nan* is /__pp, where, moreover, its appearance is obligatory; e.g., <traṣnalun> 'we raised for them' Macm 269). If a reflex of *-nan* is truly involved /__pp, the auslaut *n.* will have been lost by regressive assimilation—i.e., <traṣnalun> will be interpreted as [tɔ̆raṣn̲allón]. However, the possibility cannot be excluded that the <na> in question represents pA *-nā,* hence [tɔ̆raṣn̲alón]. For further discussion, see m-pat, §17.15.2. (b) Though instances of 1p *-nā* may still be found in TL (considered by Wajsberg 2006 to largely stem from Palestinian importation), e.g., <sBrn'> a[sɔ̆várnɔ̄] (Mar 37, 140*), a homophonous [-nĀ] occasionally appears for the 1s; e.g., y[pæyésnā] 'rikaxti' (Mor 221). This [-nĀ] has obviously migrated from the participle (pin, §17.17), but does its doing so mean that 1p [-nAn] (along with departicipial [-ı̊nnAn], pin) has gained sufficient ascendancy to allow 1s [-nĀ] into the same paradigmatic space? If so, a prediction would be that the pair 1s [-nĀ] : 1p [-nAn] will cooccur in relatively late texts, while 1p [-nĀ] will bespeak older texts (and in fact Margolis does mark off such forms with "†" as archaic). We may perhaps view this as implicating a Martinesque *chaîne* (Martinet 1964:§2.28, §2.29), whereby for whatever reason the pf begins to renew its subject suffixes. However, renewal does not proceed en bloc: the conservative system in (c) stage I is first disrupted in the 1p, stage II, where expulsion of [-nĀ] then enables the selfsame shape, of a different (participial) origin, to expel (or at least compete with) the old suffix at stage III.

(c)	I	II		III	
1s	-iθ	-iθ	——>	-nĀ ——>	-iθ
1p	-nĀ	——> -(ı̊n)nAn ——> -nĀ		-(ı̊n)nAn	

(d) It is tempting to speculate that hii arose as a therapeutic response to lap (§17.9), inasmuch as the latter effectively neutralized 3ms, 3mp, 3fp of the intr pf (e.g., sim [Qɔ̌SáM < *Qɔ̌SáM, Qɔ̌SáMū, Qɔ̌SáMā*) and all four slots of the intr impa ([Qɔ̌SÚM] < *Qɔ̌SÚM, Qɔ̌SÚMī, Qɔ̌SÚMū, Qɔ̌SÚMā*). However, of the hii-manifesting dialects, at least SM shows no trace of lap, and M but rarely deploys hii in verbs with strong 3√, despite the fact that such verbs are exactly the province of lap.

[10] Note sim impa fp [qɔ̌rǽn] (Da 349), whatever its precise derivation. ([æ] is plausibly a condensation, §8.1.1, of 2ʃ a 3√y + I̥n where 3√y < *3√ ? by adn (§9.1.4) and the suffix of shape I̥n, rather than expected *ān*, instantiates the fp palatal factor to be discussed next in the text.)

[11] Suggestive here might be the suffixes discussed in Brockelmann 1908: 412–15. Incidentally, the possibility of a pA origin for at least some of the fp manifestations need not be in conflict with a late origin for hii. It is possible that hii, spreading wave-like across dialect boundaries which had long since crystallized, may have functioned as a vehicle for the spread of pA fp palatality, itself lain dormant for centuries in a local dialect pocket. See §18.2 for general discussion of this sort of phenomenon.

[12] Also, G seems to be the only dialect to show extension from impf 2fs: specifi-cally, in the pf 2fs form <9BDTyn> 'du dientest' (Da 261), and as the normal pattern in the impa fs, e.g., <zwBnyn> 'kaufe!' (Da 276).

[13] (a) The display in (c) reveals something of the function of "feminine <-y>" which, when silent (= spelling [-Ø]), is the sole spelling if *historical* (impa fs, < *-ī) but alternates with <-Ø> if purely *morphemic* (impf 3fs, < *-Ø and pf 3fp, < *-ā—in the latter case the Nestorians use <-y> and the Jacobites <-Ø>). Plural instances, moreover, are often accompanied by an additional morphogram, the plural-denoting diacritic *sɔ̌yɔ̌mē*, <°°> ((§21.7). (b) Observe also from (c) that in the hii-slots (impa fp, pf 3fp) the super-venient suffix ,[-ēn], differs in shape from impf [-ɔn], although the impf formative is generally assumed to constitute the model for hii in the Aramaic dialects at large. One might speculate that [-ēn] reflects the palatal factor acting upon a reflex of *-āna during/following hii; or that [-ēn] is imported not from the impf but from the pf, in particular from a segmentation of the SR reflex of 2fp *-tinnã̇ (§7.3); (or in fact that both these factors are involved, the palatal factor which acted upon *-āna being exactly *-(t)innã̇).

(c) **impf**

3fs	[-Ø] <-Ø>~<-y>	*-Ø	**pf**		
3fp	[-ɔn] <-ɔn>	*-āna	3fp [-Ø] (ns<-y>~jc<-Ø>)~[-ēn]<-eyn>by hii		*-ā
			impa		
2fs	[-īn] <-iyn>	*-ina	fs [-Ø] <-y>		*-ī
2fp	[-ɔn] <-ɔn>	*-āna	fp [-Ø] (<-y>~<-Ø>)~[-ēn] <-eyn> by hii		*-ā

[14] However, the register of Halaxot Pɛ̌sukot (Morag 1967–68:74) shows <-æn>, suggesting [-Ån] (<ʔiydriysæn> 'nidrɛ̌su').

[15] "possibly ~<-ʔ> [-Å] via mtr . . .": Because an alternative is that [-ā] in [yɔ̌qærā] reflects unapocopated *-ā, as suggested in §17.9.2 TL—a preferable hypothesis to the extent that the resulting barytone stress pattern [yɔ̌qærā], predictable /__CV# (§4.1.1 (γ)), explains the retention of 2ʃ [æ] without further ado, while [-ā] < mtr *-ān would lead us to expect @[yæqrã́] (like [næθrã́n]) < mtr *yaqrã́n* < red *yaqarã́n* unless 2ʃ a has

been restored by transparentation (§15.5.1). (Recall that both Morag's and Margolis's transcriptions are largely moot with respect to stress placement (§22.2). And while a string $VC\overset{\circ}{V}C\#$ is facilely stressable $\acute{V}C\overset{\circ}{V}C\#$ (by generalization of type (δ) extrametricality, §4.1.1), the same does not hold of penultimate stress for $VC\bar{V}C\#$, as in a[nə̄θarə̄n], a[q tul n]. Would accordingly a minimax resolution between the competing demands of transparentation and phonotactic canonicity predict oxytone [nə̄θarə̄n], [qə̄ṭulə́n] over barytone [nə̄θárə̄n], [qə̄ṭúlə̄n]?)

[16] Wajsberg (2005) considers (*all* instances of?) +hii to be symptomatic of context-identified Galilean passages within the Babylonian Talmud.

[17] The value of $*\sqrt{\text{H}}$ is usually 9, as will be assumed in subsequent discussion. However, occasionally $*\sqrt{\text{h}}$ or $*\sqrt{\text{ḥ}}$ (possibly < ufb $**\sqrt{\text{X}}$) may follow suit.

[18] This seemingly jumbled distribution merits closer attention. Comprehensive scrutiny of the attested types, displayed sketchwise in chart (a), suggests an explanation along the following lines. All -hii forms (1, 4, 7) developed to the tune of pure phonetic changes (with the exception of the ancient merger of $*3\ \sqrt{\text{y}}$ and $*3\ \sqrt{\text{ʔ}}$, where for the most part $*3\ \sqrt{[ʔ]}$ restructured as $3\ \sqrt{\text{/y/}}$ (adn, §9.1.4), and hence in what follows will be treated as $3\ \sqrt{\text{y}}$). Thus $*QaSáy\bar{u}$ (cell 4) e-condenses (§8.1.1) to $QaSáw$ before lap has a chance to remove the suffix following reduction, contrary to what happens in the other two cases, $*QaSáM\bar{u} > Q\check{s}SáM$, $*QaSá9\bar{u} > Q\check{s}Sá9$; and finally $QaSáw$ red^coa^hei > [Qə̌Sǔ] while $Q\check{s}Sá9$ > [Qə̌Sǎ] by degutturalization (§9.1.3 n. 6). This much said, the strongs and original defectives (< $*3\ \sqrt{\text{y,ʔ}}$) react uniformly to hii when it comes along, adding n-bearing suffixes from the impf on the *phonological* level, so that (approximately) /Qə̌SaM+onn/ s-str^s-red^s-prm $\Rightarrow$ [QeSmón] (cell 2) and /Qə̌Say+onn/ s-str^s-cnd,s-coa $\Rightarrow$ [Qə̌Sõn] (cell 5). How then explain the fact that only the $*3\ \sqrt{9}$-derived +hii forms evince not merely phonological accommodation (cell 8) but phonetic accommodation as well (cell 9)? A plausible account would have it that [Qə̌Sõn] in cell 8 is only an *apparent* case of phonological accommodation, the actual situation being that both [Qə̌Sõn] and [Qə̌Sāyõn] are alternative instances of *phonetic* accommodation. Pursuing this line of thought, when hii attached -ŏn to $Q\check{s}Sǎ$ (< $Q\check{s}Sá9$), the resulting vowel cluster -aŏ̄- violated prevailing canons and was alternatively resolved *either* by hiatus-breaking y-insertion (cell 9) *or* by a coalescence-like process of monophthongization (cell 8)—the latter resolution coincidentally merging with the e-cnd^coa result of cell 5 and so inviting the erroneous assumption that [Qə̌Sõn] of cell 8 was a case of *phonological* accommodation. In summary, at an earlier stage, strongs and original defectives (1 – 6) accommodated hii phonologically. At a later stage, however, when $*\sqrt{9}$ left the ranks of the strongs and realigned with the defectives, the aftermath of hii with its impermissible vowel cluster -aŏ̄- was repaired by either of two sorts of *phonetic* accommodation, monophthongization (8) or hiatus-breaking insertion (9); thus [Qə̌Sõn] should be dropped from cell 8 down to cell 9. (Note finally that if hiatus-breaking y, as in cell 9, is morphologically bracketed to the right (forward) with the suffix rather than to the left (backward) with the stem, as may follow on principle (§2.3.2.1 n. 6), we have an explanation of forms like <gṭaliun> [gə̌ṭalyŏn], where the distribution of [-yŏn] has been extended to the strongs.)

(a)   **strong**   **defective** (< *3 √y, ʔ)   **defective**(< *3 √9)

	1	4	7
-hii	Qə̃SáM	Qə̃Sū́	Qə̃Sá̃
	2	5	8
+hii (/ /-level)	QeSMón	Qə̃Són	Qə̃Són
	3	6	9
+hii ([ ]-level)			Qə̃Sāyő̃n

[19] The account of <sbaian> qua [sə̃β̃āyő̃n] should be parallel to that given for the corresponding 3mp in n. 18, preceding. Ditto for strongs like [pə̃rašyő̃n].

[20] That the <-ia> in question is [-ī] and not perhaps [-yā] < mtr -yő̃n is supported by pp-bearing (m-pat, §17.15.2) forms like <audibun> 'sie(fp) bekannten sie(mp)'(Nm 261), plausibly [oddi̦β̃ón] but hardly @[od(də̃)yā̦β̃ón] (or @[od(də̃)yā̦bbón]) (for awd > owD > odd, see §11.2 with n. 17). Note also the pf 3fp of *√hwy 'be' spelled <huen> ~ <he(n)> (Nm 267), qua [hə̃wī́n] ~ [hī́(n)] (2 /[w] ~ [Ø] by wdr, §17.32).

[21] When using an n-bearing heavy transitive impf, the Yem tradition deploys exclusively energic -V̊nn-, while the Ash tradition vacillates between energic -V̊nn- and long -V̊n-, deploying the latter at least in the case of defective verbs: e.g., [yə̃lawwōnḗh] < *yilawwayūnáhi.

[22] <hy9Twnh>, cau of *√nḫt; assuming hti, roughly coeval general Aramaic would show [haḥḥə̃θūnḗh] < *hanḥitū́hV̊—but SM shows attenuation of the cau vowel (§12.2), spelled <y>, while <9> either directly represents [9] < ḥ (gtl, §9.3.2) or instantiates historical spelling of such a 9 subsequent to degutturalization (c-dgt, §22.1 (22B)): in sum, <hy9Twnh> spells either [he99ə̃Tūnḗh] or [hittūnḗh].

[23] N shows only n-less 3mp <hm> (Cg 51).

[24] In fact lengthened, as frequently in Sabbioneta—either as a repair strategy to better integrate the form into the phonology, or as a graphophonological calque (Schematisierung) on Hebrew (as surmised in Malone 1974b).

[25] Another symptom of the 3p object pronouns in TL tending to be less integrally attached to their hosts (despite the appearance of items like [ḥænqinnū́n]) is their occasional appearance as independent words (Mar 57)—as altogether generally in the case of SR (below).

[26] As concerns the two dialects within the same time span but unrepresented here: N shows no attested 3p object forms; CP shows n-less 3mp <hwn>, 3fp <hyn> ~ <hʔn> (Sg 33), but see n. 27, next. As for the spelling of <hʔn>, note that in CP <ʔ> as ml occasionally represents [Ī̊] (Sg 9).

[27] CP impf <yDBrynhwn> 'er leitet sie' (Sg 79) is best taken as containing energic <yn> + pronominal <hwn>, rather than pronominal <ynhwn>; cf. n. 26, preceding. For possible G <qBlynhw>, recall Kutscher's skepticism (§7.4.1).

[28] The diagrams in (17B–C) are simplified so as to sharpen the discussion, the simplification consisting in omission of pre-W dialects (Y, O, I, B, P, N, TR) from consideration. Had these earlier dialects been included, at least B, P, and TR would behave like the W varieties and SR.

[29] In addition to the usual M 1p forms ending in <-inan> [-ennan], Nöldeke cites (Nm 279) the apparent hapax <asar<u>inhan</u>> 'fesselte uns', interpretable as [asar<u>enhán</u>]. Though Nöldeke considers this form an error, it might rather bespeak incipient gener- alization of *h* from mark of 3p object to p object marker tout court. (Alternatively or additionally, it might reflect influence from the *h* in <anhin>, a rare allolex of the Run- of-the-mill 1p independent pronoun <anin> (Macm 84).)

[30] The imperative translation apparently reflects using the SM pf as a calque of the Hebrew conversive [wăzɔ̄xartánī] (Gen 40:14).

[31] Ben-Asher (1970: 285 n. 21) documents a case of the TL participle, which he calls *haxpala muta9it* ('false reduplication').

[32] For the case of pretonic lengthening of *e* in Hebrew, see Garr 1987 (also THP 86).

[33] For the bare-bones length ambivalence in reflexes of the heavy energic, con- sider TR sb[yæðbăq<u>ā</u>nnɔ̃x] 'sie(f) werden dich erreichen' vs. sb[yɔ̃šæbbɔ̃ḥænnǽnī] 'sie(f) werden mich preisen' (Da 373). (Dearth of examples makes it impossible to be sure, but the ambivalence may have crystallized here in an instance of mini vowel harmony, §2.3.2.1 with n. 5, ā̃ . . . ã̃, æ . . . ǽ) Some interesting relevant alternations are found in the impf defective verb of Yem TL and, especially, Tib TR. While TL shows two of the possibilities in (a), TR shows all four (forms from Mor 324, Da 389f.).

(a)   **realization of 2ʃ V 3 √y (+i)**

	[e̊̄]	[i̊]
realization [nn]	TR sb[yæyTĕnnã́h] 'er wird sie bringen'	TR tb[yæssĭnnǽnā] 'er wird uns heillen' [ʔæmḥĭnnḗh] 'ʔake ʔoto'
of		
bridging [n]	TR tb[ʔæyTēnḗh] 'ich werde ihn bringen' TL y[ʔæḥmēnḗh]	TR tb[ʔæqnīnún] 'ich werde sie erwerben'
nasal	'ʔarʔe ʔoto'	

Though a variety of diverse mechanisms lie behind these alternations, they in any event de facto contribute to the perception of equivalence among *V̄n, V̊n, V̄nn, V̊nn*. One possibility is that the focal vocalism ([e̊̄], [i̊]) in all quadrants but the lower right derives from e-cnd^(k-)coa (§8.1, §11.1) of 2ʃ a 3 √y (+i), the simplest outcome being [ē] (lower left clearly, upper left possibly), [e] (upper left) resulting from $\bar{e}$ by css (§17.4), and [i] (upper right) resulting from e by *rule reversal*, a not uncommon phenomenon whereby a process $x \Rightarrow y \,/\, z$ (here, simplifying, mid; $i \Rightarrow e \,/\, stressed$) expands to include its own reverse $y \Rightarrow x \,/\, -z$ (here, $e \Rightarrow i \,/\, unstressed$). Another possibility is that [ɪ̊] in the two right quadrants results from 2ʃ i 3 √y (+i), which in the first instance $\rightarrow \bar{\imath}$ (as clearly in the lower right) and subsequently may $\rightarrow i$ by css (upper right). For the *ay ~ iy* relation lying behind this possibility, widespread in Aramaic, see din, §8.1.1 n. 1. Consider finally that [n] (lower quadrants) derives from *nn* as one way of dispelling an uncomfortably heavy sequence $\bar{V}C'C'$ (geminates appear to exert greater resistance to an immediately preceding long vowel than do heterophonous clusters), the alternative being to maintain $C'C'$ while shortening $\bar{V}$; see css.

8. Condensation (cnd) of Vowel-Glide-Vowel Sequences (*VΓV*)

By *condensation* (cnd) of *VΓV* is meant any of various processes that shorten a vowel-glide-vowel group either to a vowel-vowel sequence by deletion of the intervening glide (*partial condensation*, p-cnd) or, more thoroughly, to a long vowel or offgliding diphthong by amalgamating the vowel-vowel sequence resulting from p-cnd (*full condensation*, f-cnd). Condensation apparently occurred at two stages, largely depending on the identity of the intervening glide: *early condensation* (e-cnd) or *late condensation* (l-cnd). Partial condensation seems to be a mode of solely e-cnd.

Early condensation primarily targets *VyV*, as does partial condensation, the latter best taken as a version of e-cnd falling short of completion (§8.1.1). Also, some instances of *VhV* may possibly fall within the purview of e-cnd (§8.1.4), though most cases of *VhV* pertain to late condensation (§8.2).

Where no ambiguity is likely to arise, "e-cnd" will be understood to refer to the same process as "f-cnd."

8.1. Early Condensation (e-cnd), Including Partial Condensation (p-cnd)

8.1.1. Description and Examples

In the verb, the *VyV* targeted by e-cnd or p-cnd is always 2ʃ V 3√y followed by a suffixal *V*, whether 3√y is original, derives from *3√w (§17.34), or from *3√ʔ (by adn, §9.1.4; see also §8.1.2). Moreover, 2ʃ V̄ is rare, only *ī* being attested (see below); and since *uy early *either* advance-assimilated to *iy* (= *ī* by virtue of what might be called *diphthong-monophthong equivalence*, dme, whereby homosyllabic *V'W'* = *V̄'* for [+high] sequences, hence *iy* = *ī*, *uw* = *ū*) *or* height-dissimilated to *ay*,[1] ʃ2 is at the time of e-cnd/p-cnd always *a* or *ĩ*. Summarizing, the inputs to e-cnd/p-cnd are compositely displayed in (8A):

(8A) i̊yi̊   i̊yŭ̊   ayi̊   ayŭ̊
       i̊yå̊   ayå̊

Letting *Vx y Vz* stand for any of the groups of (8A), p-cond results in *Vx (ʔ) Vz*, where *(ʔ)* represents a possible hiatus-breaking [ʔ] ("possible" because it cannot be excluded that the grapheme <ʔ> involved here is a purely orthographic representation of hiatus). Borrowing from the lexicon of the Arabic grammarians, hiatus-breaking [ʔ] might be called *hamzatu 'l-waṣl*.

Coming to full condensation, if *Vz* is glidable—that is, *ĭ* or *ŭ*, the result is an offgliding diphthong *VxWz*: hence *ĭyĭ* → [ĭy] (= [ī]), *ĭyŭ* → [ĭw], *ayĭ* → [ay], *ayŭ* → [aw]. If *Vx* = *Vz* in quality, the result is a long vowel: hence *ĭyĭ* → [ī] (as above), *ayå* → [ā]. This leaves solely *ĭyå* unaccounted for; and indeed, this group is only subject to p-cnd, [ĭ(ʔ)å].

The groups of (8A) are not all equally prone to e-cnd. In particular, *ĭyĭ, ĭyŭ,* and *ayā* (unlike *aya*) frequently stall at [ĭ(ʔ)ĭ], [ĭ(ʔ)ŭ], [a(ʔ)ā] by p-cnd; and a group may fail to condense at all, remaining [VyV] (or, as we shall see at least for TR *ayā*, the group may undergo some other modification not involving cnd)—a tendency especially strong for *iyV̊* with unstressed *i,* as we shall see below.

Examples:

ĭyĭ̊. No instances of *īyĭ* uncovered. Clear cases of *iyĭ̊* rare, probably because of the proclivity of this group to dissimilate to *ayĭ̊* (above and n. 1); observe, however, I <ʔTyh> 'bring(fs) him!' (MP 148), plausibly [ʔattị̄h] < **haʔtiyị̄hi*, TR copulative sim impa fs [wæḥzị̄] (Da 348) < *-*iyī*, and TL int impf 2fs y[tǝɣællị̄] (Mor 268) < *-*iyī́n* (with apocope of -*n* by mtr, §17.12).

ĭyŭ̊. One case of *īyŭ̊* has come to light, B sim palatal passive pf 3mp [rǝmī́w] (BL 174) < **ramị̄yŭ*. As concerns *iyŭ̊*, note three B instances of int active pf 3mp spelled the same as the passive <-iyw> but by hypothesis with short 2ʃ [i]: [šawwī́w], [šannī́w], [šǝ̄rī́w] (lc) (for [-ɔ̄r-] < -*arr*-, mls, §9.3.1).[2] TR shows three reactions to pf 3mp *-*íyū*: -cnd (copulative) [ŭštíyū] ~ +p-cnd [ŭští(ʔ)ū], +e-cnd (rmp) [ʔittǝlī́w] (Da 343f). SR shows pf 3mp [-íw] for all derived binyanim of the defective gizra (B 139). TL shows cau pf 3mp +e-cnd a[ʔayθī́w], impa mp +p-cnd a[ʔayθí(ʔ)ū] (Mar 92*).

ĭyå. TR provides int pf 3fs^2mp tb[9æddí(ʔ)æθxṓn] (§5.2 TR) as a partial condensation of *-*iya*.

It is noteworthy that when *iyV̊* has unstressed *i,* notably and perhaps exclusively in object-suffixed forms, the group normally fails to undergo cnd with the result that *i* is later reduced (§4.2). Thus we find, most regularly in the pf of the int and cau which tend to select *i 3√y, such as 3ms^2ms [QaSSǝyyáx], 3ms^2fs [Qassǝyéx], 3mp^1s [QaSSǝyū́nī], etc.

ayĭ̊. TR sim impa fs (copulative) e-cnd [ŭrmǽ], and sim impf 2fs e-cnd [tiv9ǽn] (§11 TR), cau impa fs e-cnd [ʔōḥǽ] ~ p-cnd [ʔōḥǽ(ʔ)ī] (Da 348); SM int impa fs <ḥwy> t[ǽbbi] (Macs 212) < *ḥawwáy* < e-cnd *ḥawwáyī (t[i] < *ay* by smc, §22.1 (22B); note also the SM-specific occlusion t[bb] < *ww*, §21.1 w (21D)); SR impf 2fs [-en] for all binyanim of the defective gizra (B 139).[3]

ayŭ̊. O sim impa mp <ŝlw> (De 77) interpretable as [šǝláw] or (if coa, §111.1, has taken place) [šǝlō̄] < **siláyū*. I sim impf 3mp <yBnwn> (L §40f). B sim pf 3mp [rǝmṓ] (BL 174). P sim pf 3mp <Bnw> (HC 347). TR sim impa mp [qǝrṓ] (Da 348) ultimately < **qĭráʔū* but directly ⇐ /qǝrayū/ (see §8.1.2). CP sim impa mp <ʔṮ̥w̰> (Sl 20). SM sim pf 3mp <ʔTw> t[ä́tu] (Macs 207). G sim pf 3mp <mtw̰n> (Da 343) (suffixal -n by hii, §7.2(δ)). SR [-ɔw] e-cnd in sim pf 3mp intransitives [QšSɔ́w], but p-cnd [-ɔ(ʔ)ū] in corresponding transitives (e.g., ^2ms [QšSɔ(ʔ)ṹx], ^2mp [QšSɔ(ʔ)ūxón] (B 139, 146).[4] TL sim pf 3mp <ʔTw̰n> a[ʔäθṍn] (§7.2(δ)), y[tšnṍ](Mor 254). M sim impa mp^3fp <hzu̱nin> (<Macm 374) = [hšzo̱nnén] < staminal *ḥĭzáyū + suffixal [-nnén] (§7.4.1).

ayā̱. For ayā̱, +e-cnd (infrequent) TL sim pf 3fp y[ʔštā̱n] (Mor 276); TR sim pf 3fp + p-cnd (copulative) [u̥qræ̱(ʔ)ā] (Da 344) (unless this is unabashed 3√ʔ [u̥qræ̱ʔā] either as historical residue escaping adn, §9.1.4, or as conditioned synchronic redployment of 3√/ʔ/ ~ 3√/y/ qua manifestation of adn; see §8.1.2), -cnd tb[kšhā̱yā̱] ~ tb[kšhǽyyā̱] (lc).[5]

For aya, e-cnd is overwhelmingly the rule; all the following examples are osim pf 3fs (Y, O, I, P, G) or 3ms (B, N, TR, CP, SM, SR, TL, M): Y <hwT> (DR I 215:2) qua [hawat] < *hawayát/*hawáyat;[6] [O <{h}wt (De 76); I <hwT> (L 64); P <hwT> (HC 359); G <hw(w)T> (Da 353); B [bšθ́] (BL 177) <* ba9áya; N <Bnʔ> ~ <Bnh> (Cg 83); TR [9šθ́ä] (Da 341); CP <ʔTʔ> (Sg 9); SM <ʔTʔ> ~ <ʔTh> t[ä́tɑ] (< living SM [ʔä́θä́] or perhaps +adr [aθä́] by smc, §22.1 (22B)); SR [QšSǒ́] (B 139); TL <hwh> (Mar 52); M <hua> t[éhwā] ~ [hówā] (Mal 310).[7]

8.1.2. Competition from Alef-Defective Neutralization or Transparentation

Two issues interacting or interfering with e-cnd and p-cnd require special comment: alef-defective neutralization (adn, §9.1.4) and transparentation (§15).

(α) In principle, almost all of the forms treated in §8.1.1 as partially condensational might be reinterpreted as 3√ʔ-forms, whether as part and parcel of adn or as original *3√ʔ-forms which have incidentally escaped adn.[8] In either event, the groups considered in §8.1.1 to be [Vw (ʔ) Vz], with antihiatic "(ʔ),'' would be reanalyzed as [Vw ʔ Vz], with fullblown phonetic [ʔ] as 3√. If [Vw ʔ Vz] should be part and parcel of adn, synchronic systematization of adn—that is, s-adn (< d-adn)—would dictate that as a result of the neutralization 3√[y] is deployed in some (structural, lexical) slots—the majority—while 3√[ʔ] is used in others. Thus, TR [u̥qræ̱(ʔ)ā] (§8.1.1 ayā̱) would be reanalyzed as [u̥qræ(ʔ)ā], with [ʔ] dictated not by descendance from *3√ʔ but rather by redeployment of ʔ ~ y as manifestation of adn, as in (8Bi). If on the other hand 3√[ʔ] should have escaped adn, the situation would be as portrayed in (8Bii).[9]

(8B)

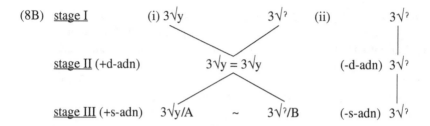

Another subissue of adn vis-à-vis cnd, specifically e-cnd, is the fact that although e-cnd preceded adn chronologically, yet when adn finally emerged, affected forms subsequently appeared to condense (§see §9.1.4 for further specifics). Two possible accounts of this are suggested, (8Ci) and (8Cii):

(8C) (i)
stage I	QaSáyū	QaSá²ū
stage II (e-cnd)	QaSáw	—
stage III (adn)	—	QaSáyū
stage IV (r-e-cnd)	—	QaSáw
[QaSáw]	=	[QáSaw]

(ii)
stage I	QaSáyū	QaSá²ū
stage II (e-cnd)	QaSáw	—
stage III (adn)	—	QaSáw
[QaSáw]	=	[QaSáw]

The difference between (8Ci) and (8Cii) is that, while in (i) the neutralization in final form is achieved by a rerun of e-cnd,[10] in (ii) it is achieved by adn "copying" the relevant 3√y phonetic forms rather than by deriving them through the agency of r-e-cnd. But the comparison between the two models is not complete until corresponding phonological forms are added, as in (8D):

(8D) (i)
stage I	[QaSáyū]	⇐ /QaSayū/	[QaSá²ū]	⇐ /QaSa²ū/
stage II (e-cnd)	[QaSáw]	⇐ /QaSayū/	—	
stage III (adn)	—		[QaSáyū]	⇐ /QaSayū/
stage IV (r-e-cnd)	—		[QaSáw]	⇐ /QaSayū/
	[QaSáw] =		[QaSáw]	

(ii)
stage I	[QaSáyū]	⇐ /QaSáyū/	[QaSá²ū]	⇐ /QaSa²ū/
stageII (e-cnd)	[QaSáw]	⇐ /QaSayū/	—	
stage III (adn)	—		[QaSáw]	⇐ /QaSayū/
	[QaSáw] =		[QaSáw]	

Assuming that sufficient dialect-internal motivation (relative to each dialect) continued subsequent to stage II for /QaSayū/ to be posited as the phonological representation for [QaSáw] on the left (*3√y) side derivations of (8D),[11] the hypothesis of (ii) is superior because simpler than that of (i), and because [QaSáw] ⇐ /QaSayū/ on the right (*√ʔ) side of (8Dii) is virtually predicted in the wake of the restructuring /QaSaʔū/ > /QaSayū/. Or looked at from another perspective, [QaSáyū] ⇐ /QaSayū/ at stage III in (i) must be reckoned extraneous until and unless independent evidence is forthcoming for a phonetic form like [QaSáyū], as opposed to [QaSáw], ever deriving from *QaSáʔū.

(β) Even as many of the forms analyzed as p-condensive [V̄ (ʔ) V̄] in §8.1.1 could, in terms just explained under (α), be alternatively viewed as [V̄ʔV̄], with ʔ bona fide 3√ʔ, so some of the same forms might be analyzed as *transparentized* (§15.2.1), in particular as taking the least marked 3ms shape as base and adding the suffix complex to that. Thus the verb that was considered p-condensed in §8.1.1 i̯ẙå, tb[9æddi(ʔ)æθxõn], might be reanalyzed as [9æddī(ʔ)æθxõn], with long 2ʃ, the result of taking 3ms [9æddí], adding the suffix complex [-æθxõn] to the tune of anti-hiatic "(ʔ)," and normalizing the stress to that of a unitary word.

8.1.3. Auslaut of the Defective Imperative

At times, e-cnd may be obscured by interfering factors. In one such case, a diphthong resulting from e-cnd of *ayī* shows an unexpected long nucleus.[12] The most prominent manifestation of this is the fs of the defective imperative in SR, irrespective of binyan. Thus [ɛstóy] 'trinke!' (B 96) < *šĭtáyī (the anlaut [ɛ-] by pro, §17.18), where normally we should expect @[ɛstáy].

Looked at by itself, this unforeseen lengthening seems quite puzzling. However, comprehensive scrutiny of the entire 3√y impa paradigm across the Aramaic dialects reveals that several of these show unexpected and disparate means of *differentiating the fs from the ms*. But before considering individual mechanisms, a general hypothesis as to the motive for such differentiation.

As we have seen (§1.4, §8.1.1 with n. 1), the auslaut of the bare 3√y verb stem in almost all conjugations for A at large is, abstracting away from possible coa (§11.1), *-ay ~ -iy (= -ī)*, where moreover the choice between *-ay* and *-iy* is erratic and idiosyncratic. Consider then that the ms impa, being suffixless, should end in *-ay ~ -iy* in the 3√y verb, while the corresponding fs, ending in suffix *-ī*, should e-condense to identity with the ms: *-ayī > -ay, -iyī > -ī (= -iy)*. So it is understandable that the individual dialects may have sought to restore the ms ≠ fs opposition each in their own particular ways.

SR, to begin with the dialect on whose note this section was introduced, appears to have selected as mechanism a pattern that shows up elsewhere in A as well: *tonic lengthening* of the fs impa, to be called *impa tonic lengthening* (itl).[13] Thus [ɛštóy], while the ms remains unlengthened [ɛštáy].

Farther afield, though itl of *-ay* is necessary and sufficient for the fs, elaboration of the ms is more rococo in SR than in any other dialect. In the simple

plain conjugation, while some verbs lexically select -*ay*, others select -*iy* ([ḥɔ̌ðị́]
'freue dich!'), and yet others alternate -*ay* ~ -*iy* ([imáy̱] ~ [imí̱] 'schwöre!'),
and at least one, *√ʔty 'come', follows a general Aramaic pattern (n. 15 below)
in encoding 3√ as /ʔ/ (via adn, §8.1.2(α)): thus [tɔ̌] 'komme(ms)!' with [-ɔ̌] ⇐
aap (§9.1.4) |-aʔ| ⇐ s-low (§17.10) /-V̊ 3√ʔ/ (with apheresis of 1√/ʔ 1ʃ V̊ by
wic, §17.33). This latter mechanism also appears as a lexically marked option
in the simple rmp ([ɛttɔ̌wɔ̱̌] 'bereue!'), while in this conjugation at large the Jacobite register of SR normally shows unadorned -*ay* (jc[eθQɔ̌Sáy̱]) and Nestorian rather shows stress retraction with bobbing of -*V* 3√y—that is, *retraction
with bobbing* (rwb)—though 3√y lives on in the orthography as a silent <y>
(ns[ɛθQáS] spelled < ʔɛθQaSy>); and the other derived conjugations all show
[-ɔ̌] ⇐ /-V̊ 3√ʔ/ by aap.

Though none of the dialects evidently dovetails with any other in most particulars, two of SR's patterns appear in TR: deployment of *-*ay* ~ *-*iy* in the
ms of the simple impa (e.g., [bɔ̌né̄], [-é̄] < coa *-*ay*, ~ [bɔ̌ní̄] 'baue!' (Da 348));
and, alternatively for the ms, rwb, which appears in the int and cau as well as
in the sim (e.g., [ʔé̄ʃt] 'trinke!' < *šɔ̌tV́y, [šǽw] 'setze!' < *šawwV́y (with [w]
from *ww* by deg, §3.1 (3Fvii)), bb[ʔǽ9d] ~ sb[ʔǽ9æd] 'entferne!' < *ʔa9dV́y
(lc)).[14]

TR is also like SR with respect to two singleton Tiberian variant forms:
sb[ʔiθɑ̌̄] 'komme(ms)!' (Da 357) ⇐ /-V̊ 3√ʔ/ (§8.1.2 (α))[15]; and sb[ʔōḥǎy]
'beeile dich(fs)!' (Da 348) by itl. Normally, however, TR differentiates fs
from ms not by itl but by specializing coalescence of *-*ay* to [-ǣ] rather than
to [-ē] (cf. Garr 1991): thus, as Bab variant to tb[ʔōḥǎy], bb[ʔōḥǽ] (~ p-cnd
[ʔōḥǽʔ].([16]

The other general respect in which TR differs from SR is in showing [-ī]
in the derived-stem ms impa when rwb is not employed: e.g., [ṣællí̄] 'bete!',
[ʔiθgɔ̌lí̄] 'erscheine!', [ʔiθnæbbí̄] 'sage weise!' (Da 348). (An exception, in addition to the syncretic instances of √ʔty shown in n. 16, is [mænné̄] 'bestimme!'
(lc).)

Aside from slight complications with two roots in TL, the other two Eastern
dialects, the Low varieties TL and M, are relatively straightforward by comparison, the generalization being that, whether simple or derived, ms shows
[-ī] (TL <B9y> a&y[bɔ̌9í̄] 'seek!' (Mar 95*, Mor 251),[17] M <hzia> m[hézī]
'see!' Macm 336, 352)) and fs shows reflexes of -*ay* (TL [-ay], M [-ey]) (TL
<Tʔy> 'come!' a[táy], y[tǽy] (Mar 91*, Mor 277), M <hzai> 'see!' (Macm
336) m[héze] (Macm 352) with coalesced (§11.2) atonically shortened auslaut
(Malone 1997) interpretable as Classial [hɔzɛ̌̄]).

The remaining dialects reveal either paucity of forms and/or orthographic
(and for SM, t-phonetic) indeterminacy making for uncertainty as to the full
pattern.

Y and P show nothing.

O shows only <hwy> 'sei(ms)!' (De 77); B [šé] 'nimm(ms)!', [ḥéyī] 'lebe(ms)!' and [ménnī] 'bestelle(ms)!' (BL 172);[18] and N solely the questionable <qry> 'lis(ms)!' (Cl 144).

I shows <-y> as exclusive for fs, and as usual for ms (ms exceptions: <ʾTh> (note 15), <rTʾ>, <ŝʾ> (L §40 d,o; §42a)).

CP generally shows <-y> for both genders, but also a good number of <-ʾ> forms (e.g., <rm̊ʾ> 'wirf(ms)!' (Sg 73)) suggesting [-ē] (§21.4), and at least one variant in <-ʾy> for fs (<ʾ̊Tʾy> 'bringe!' (lc)) suggesting either [-ay] or [-āy]. If the interpretation ms [-ē] ≠ fs [-ay] should be what is represented, we may be faced with yet another special way of differentiating the genders: coalescing (§11.2) the ms, failing to coalesce the fs. But if <-ʾy> should represent [-āy], CP would show at least a smattering of itl, the pattern for SR.

SM shows <-y> t[-i] for both genders (<šry> t[íšri] 'wohne(ms)!' (Macs 209), <hwy> T[ǽbbi] 'benachrichtige(fs)!' (Macs 12)), with the exception of sim *√ʾty (n. 15). Since both <-y> and t[-i] are moot with respect to monophthongal or diphthongal origin (in traditional pronunciation, *ī and *ay normally merge to the former by coa^hei (§11.2), and then shorten in unstressed auslaut by the smc (§22.1 (22B)), we just can't know whether the genders were differentiated in the heyday of living Samaritan.

In G, we generally find <-y> ~ <-yy> for both genders, though there is ms <B9ʾ> 'suche!' (Da 348) (and, unsurprisingly, √ʾty is special (n. 15)). Gingerly, the major pattern suggests either undifferentiated <-y> [-ī] ~ <-yy> [-ay] for both genders, or differentiation solely of the diphthong with ms [-ay] but fs [-āy] by itl.

8.1.4. Possible Early Condensation of *ayhu*

Though early condensation most perspicuously involves the glide *y* while *h* falls to the pale of late condensation (§8.2), there is a bit of evidence that at least some tokens of *h* may have been subject to e-cnd along with *y*. In verb morphology, the clearest instance of e-cnd targeting *h* is the TR sim impa ms^3ms variant [rŏmő̄hī] 'wirf ihn!', alongside more run-of-the-mill variants [rŏmḗhī] and sb[rŏmíhī] straightforwardly analyzable as < *rĭmáy-hī (via coa, §11.2) and < *rĭmíy-hī respectively. The apparently anomalous [ō] of the first variant will fall into place if: (α) the string exclusive of -hī < *rĭmáy-hū by e-cnd of *ayhū* to *aw* (note that both glides, *y* and *h*, are elided in the process) which then coalesced to ō;[19] and (β) the supernumerary suffix -hī is added to rŏmő̄, presumably as a measure to restore transparency. To be sure, such an analysis might seem farfetched were it not for the support of the nominal system, where a similar analysis has been traditionally offered for the mp^3ms possessive suffix not only in TR [-ő̄hī], but also of the same shape in B, as well as for SR [-ɔ́w] still spelled <-ɔwh̄y> with a trace of the apocopated *-hī (B 49; the superposed grapheme *linea occultans* indicates silence of <h>, and the

<y> following it is silent by virtue of lacking vocalization (being ḥaṣer)). Bauer and Leander also propose that SR 3p object suffixes [-ɛnnṓn], [-ɛnnḗn] derive by *h*-targeting e-cnd from *-innahumu, *-innahinna (BL §38q). This seems plausible and might provide a partial alternative to (or step toward a partial explication of) what in this book is taken to be late ancipitality (§2.3.1)—and with minimal modification to the hypotheses on 3p pronominal structure proffered in §7.4.2.

8.2. Late Condensation (l-cnd)

8.2.1. Description and Examples

Excepting whatever cases may have been subject to e-cnd (§8.1.4), the group $\bar{V}x$ *h* $\bar{V}z$ (and possibly $a_x yh\bar{\imath}_z$), with 3s pronominal *h*, is subject to condensation to $VxWz$ in the E dialects (categorically in SR and M, but rarely in TL)—and because of the relatively advanced chronology of the dialects so affected, the process will be called *late condensation* (l-cnd). Unlike e-cnd, l-cnd requires that $Vx \neq \bar{V}z$ and that $\bar{V}z$ be high.

Examples:

*āhī *and/or* *ayhī, *with bridge* *ā/*ay. SR impa ms^3ms, e.g., sim jc[QǯSuMṓy], ns[QǯSoMǎy]. The interpretation would be straightforwardly *QǯSUM-á-hī, with ancipitally lengthened bridge *ā (§2.3.4.4 3ms) and ns[ǎy] understandable by regressive palatalization (§20.2(δ), Ns 35), if it weren't for the facts that: (α) the suffix complex is spelt jc<-oyh̄y>, ns<-ayh̄y> (indicating silence of auslaut <-h̄y>), where the first <y> suggests a reflex of *ay; and (β) reflexes of *ay clearly do show up in homoparadigmatic ms^1, in both registers [QǯSUMáyn]. Point (α) loses a bit of its edge with the observation that the spelling <-Ayh̄y> also appears in pf 2ms^3ms, e.g., jc<QSaMtoyh̄y>, though here a reflex of *-tāhī is strongly expected. Nevertheless, a clear resolution of *āhī vs. *ayhī is yet to be found.

*ūhī, with 3mp *ū. SR jc[eštawdǯ9ū́y] 'sie erkannten ihn' (Ns 141); M <ligtuiH> 'they took him' (Macm 163), interpretable as [leɣtū́y].

*ōhī, with *ō < e-cnd^coa **a 3√yū. TL <ʔmtwy> 'heviʔuʔoto!' (Mor 238 with n. 76), interpretable as living TL [ʔamtṓy], though Morag reports it to be realized in Yem trad pron as y[ʔæmṭǯyū́h], as if non-condensed < *ʔamṭiyū́hV̄ (see §8.1.1 for the propensity of *iyV̄ with unstressed *i to forego cnd), -V̄ lost by sap or lap (§17.22, §17.9).[20]

*ūhū, with 3mp *ū. Escapes l-cnd because of the countervailing identity of vowels; cf. TL –lap y[qæṭlū́hū] 'harguʔoto' (Mor 293).

*īhū, with 2fs *ī. SR pf 2fs^3ms, e.g., sim [QǯSaMtī́w].

8.2.2. 3ms suffix *-*hī* ~ *-*hū*

Of these two allomorphs, *-*hī* is clearly the unmarked in Aramaic at large. The alternant *-*hū* is restricted to immediately following a (long) high vowel, where, however, *-hī* may also occur subject to dialect-specific restrictions. Thus /ī__, TR shows *-hī ~ *-hū (sb[ʔōneqî́hī] ~ bb[ʔōniqî́hū] 'stille(fs) ihn!', Da 376), while I shows *-hī (<hByhy> 'gib(fs) es!', L 60) and SR shows *-hū ([Qə̆SaMtî́w]), §8.2.1). In the environment /ū__, TL shows *-hī ~ *-hū (<ʔDḥwhy> a[ʔaddə̆ḥû́hī] 'they thrust him out' (Mar 59, 135*), y[qæṭlû́hū] (§8.2.1)), while other dialects show exclusively *-hi (I <ŝBqwhy> 'verlasset ihn!' (L 52); B [ḥabbə̆lû́hī] 'destroy(mp) it!' (Brown 1979: 1091); TR [næsbû́hī] 'sie nahmen ihn' (Da 367); SR and M examples in §8.2.1).

When other than following a (long) high vowel, only *-hī occurs. Thus: / Ā__. B [bə̆nốhī] 'he built it' (Brown 1979: 1084); TR [hə̆fấhī] 'er bedeckte ihn' (Da 385), [bă̆hæntấhī] 'du prüftest ihn' (Dalman 1938: 51), [ʔæθqə̆nấhī] 'wir bereiteten es' (Da 361); SR examples in §8.2.1.

/ō__. B [šə̆nốhī] 'they changed it' (Brown 1979:1116); TL [ʔamṭóy] (§8.2.1). Other than following a *V̄*. O <wymhʔhy> 'vĕyakehu' (Steiner 2000–2001: 240); TR [tæqqéfhī] 'stärke ihn!' (Da 375).

Notes to §8

[1] Similarly, *iw* earlier developed into either *uw* (= *ū* by dme) or *aw*. Together, these mutations of *uy* and *iw* appear to have created a weak spot in Aramaic morphophonology, propagating widespread instances of *iy ~ ay* and *uw ~ aw*—a state of affairs to be called *diphthong interchange* (din) even when, as particularly holds of *uw ~ aw*, the interchange holds mediately through coalescence (§11.1), under the guise of *ū ~ ō* and *ī ~ ē*. In the verb system, din makes for rampant 2ʃi 3√y ~ 2ʃa 3√y in the defective verb (§1.4); and, significantly though to a lesser degree, *uw ~ aw* contributes to *ū ~ ō* in the suffixal system ("contributes"; for other factors leading to *ū ~ ō*; see §7.7). A few examples follow:

iy ~ ay. TR int pf 1s [šæwwî́θī], [millḗθι] (Da 343); quadriradical rmp impf 3ms [yištælhî́], [yištēsḗ] (Da 346); sim impa ms^3ms [rə̆mî́hī] ~ [rə̆mḗhī](Da 391). TL sim rmp pf 1p y[ʔištə̆lî́n] ~ [ʔištə̆lḗláyn] (Mor 264); int impf 3ms y[līmællî́] ~ [līmællḗ]; sim pf 2mp^3fs y[šə̆rī̆θû́hā] ~ [šə̆rē̆θû́hā] (Mor 323). M sim pf 1p <huinin> ~ <huainin> (Nm 264); int pf 1s^2mp <kasitinkun> ~ <kasaitinkun> (Nm 288) (M forms interpretable as [hə̆wīnî́n] ~ [hə̆weynín], [kassī̆θenxón] ~ [kasseyTenxón]).

uw ~ aw. B sim pf 2mp tb[ḥăzē̆θû́n] ~ bb[ḥə̆zē̆θṓn] (§7.7). TR sim pf 3mp^2fs [kə̆rû́hā] ~ [kə̆rṓhā] (Da 387); int rmp impf 3mp [yištæ9(9)û́n], 2mp [tiθgārṓn] (Da 347). TL sim pf 3mp y[bə̆xû́], [9ə̆ḏṓ]; sim impf 3fp (gender by fgm, §16.1) y[tištû́n] ~ [tištṓn] (Mor 256 w n. 45); sim impa mp y[mə̆nû́] ~ [mə̆nṓ].

[2] (a) To judge by Bauer and Leander's transcription, e-cnd of the Bab variant of of [rə̆mî́w] fails to take place: [u̯i]*rmí̆u̯* (BL 164), equivalent in the system of this book to *wirmiyu*. Similarly int active bb[šænnî́yū] corresponding to tb[šanní̆w]. (b) Observe that e-cnd of *-iyū* renders [-iw], never mid-processed (§17.11) @[-ew], by hypothesis because /__w provides a mid-resistant environment, the high *w* tending to preserve the high *i*. (Bauer and Leander interpret e-condensed *-í̆yū* as [-î́w] (BL 64), whose long [î́] provides a cost-free explanation for resistance to mid. Food for thought.)

[3] (a) The string *a 3√y + i#, with declarative suffix *-i* characteristic of the long impf (§2.3.4.1), is preempted from cnd by *condensatory coalescence* (§11.1). (b) The

Sabbionetan variant [ʾōḥ̊ɐ́y]may show e-cnd followed by a minor version of the fs impa tonic lengthening characteristic of SR (itl, §8.1.3).

[4] (a) The partially-condensed forms are noteworthy in failing to feed reduction (§4.2) of ɔ, i.e., [Qɔ̌Sɔ(ʾ)ú̈x] ≠ @[QaS(ʾ)ú̈x] (a phenomenon likely also attested in TR; n. 8 below). As a conjecture, perhaps the vowel cluster resulting from p-cnd, here [-ɔ(ʾ)ū-], shares with the corresponding e-condensed diphthong, here [-ɔw-], the phonological property of one bimoraic syllable rather than a sequence of two monomoraic syllables (for "mora," §23.5). If so, it is an intriguing question how this equivalence should be captured. (While failure of reduction here would follow automatically from reinterpreting [-ɔ(ʾ)ū-] as [-ɔ̄(ʾ)ū-], per se legitimate on the basis of the spelling <-ɔʾuw->, the fact that the Jacobite spelling is <-aʾuw-> clinches interpretation of the lead-off vowel as short. Nestorian [ɔ] is by labial assimilation (mvh, §2.3.2.1 with n. 5) of a to the following ū; see §20.2 (δ).)

(b) The conditions for p-condensed forms in [-ɔ(ʾ)ū-] could likely be restated in terms of stress, as is the case with the $iy\overset{\circ}{V}$ strings discussed above. The generalization will probably be that $\overset{\circ}{V}y\overset{\circ}{V}$ tends to resist full cnd when the first $\overset{\circ}{V}$ is atonic.

[5] We should expect tb[kɘ̆hɐ́ɛyā]. Do the actual forms represent Schematisierung on the basis of assumed patterns of Tiberian orthography? Alternatively for the first variant, perhaps we are witnessing an instance of minor vowel harmony (§2.3.2.1 with n. 5): tb[kɘ̆hɔ́yɔ̄], or [kɘ̆hɔ́y] if length should be implicated along with quality.

[6] Cf. also §15.3.2.

[7] It appears that the verb "live" is best taken to reconstruct as geminate *√hy in pA, with the lexical peculiarity that while the sim impf assumes the unmarked formation, via gmf-4u (§3.2 (3M)), e.g., TR 2ms [tēḥḗ] (Da 354) < *tiḥḥáyi (§11.1; mls, §9.3.1), the sim pf is formed by the marked process gmf-1m (§3.3 (3H)); thus, e.g., TR 3ms [ḥɘ̆yɐ́] (Da 353) < *ḥayáya via e-cnd of a 3√y a followed by reduction. Note, however, that the immediate outcome of e-cnd, ḥayɐ́, does not further undergo e-cnd iteratively to produce @ḥɐ́. While various possible accountings of this result will come easily to mind, we already have one in place: the resistance of the string ayā to e-cnd.

[8] "almost all"; for instance, the TR form tb[9æddi(ʾ)æθxṍn] presents two points against being reinterpreted as containing 3√ʾ: most cogently, the nonreduction of i; and secondarily, the failure of low (§17.10) to ʾ-assimilate i to a (whereas under the hiatus interpretation, most clearly where "(ʾ)" is taken as purely orthographic, non-lowering of [9æddiæθxṍn] follows immediately from the absence of any guttural to trigger the lowering in the first place). However, this latter factor is tempered by the fact that low is not a categorical process.

[9] Should (8Bi) be the case, [ůqrǽʾā], deriving as it does from *√qrʾ, would involve a species of accordion: *ʾ (neutralization with y by adn) > y (synchronic redeployment) > ʾ, lending the impression that there had been no change at all—that is, that *ʾ ≥ ʾ (as in fact would be the case in (8Bii)).

[10] "in final form" relative to the curtailed derivations being used, that is; thus, in several later dialects, [QaSáw] > [Qɔ̌Sṍ] by red and coa (§4.2, §11.1).

[11] "for /QaSayū/"; or for whatever phonological derivation turns out to be synchronically motivated from stage to stage. In point of fact, /QaSayū/ is plausibly motivated, at least in dialects where ay maintains its transparency /__C, comprising 6 of the 10 slots of the pf paradigm; e.g., 1p [QaSáynā]. By extrapolation, the like of /QaSayū/

is reasonably posited as "solution" to [QaSáw] by a proportion like [QaSáM-nā] ⇐ /QaSaM-nā/ : [QaSámū] ⇐ /QaSaM-ū/ == [QaSáynā] ⇐ /QaSay-nā/ : [QaSáw] ⇐ X solved as /QaSay-ū/, with a rule, s-e-cnd, formulated to bridge the phonetic-phonological discrepancy.

[12] There may also be a case of an unexpectedly short monophthong in lieu of an expected long vowel; see §15.3.2.

[13] This is the usual pattern in the sim strong verb of Modern Mandaic (e.g., [šóxoβ] 'lie down(ms)!' ≠ fs [šúxūβ] (Macm 275), with the accent moved to the penult as characteristic of the Modern language. It is also a pattern available to both genders in (modern) Ma9lula Aramaic (e.g., ms [šqṓl], fs [šqū̃l], Spitaler 1938:153).

[14] The distributional interactions of rwb make for an intriguing skein: (a) rwb targets the defective impa in SR, TR, and at least sporadically TL (n. 17 below), but not identical binyanim across the three dialects—sim rmp in SR; sim, int, and cau in TR; sim or int in TL. The lack of cohesion in either dialect grouping or targeted binyanim suggests that rwb may have been an early Aramaic phenomenon that lingered in only a few dialect pockets that subsequently developed along individual lines. (b) In the vein of (a), in SR rwb also affects the sim rmp of the *strong* verb: [εθkáθb] (Ns 103) < *hitkatíb, with 3√[b] rather than spirantized [w] (the manifestation of spirantized *b* in nsSR, §5.2 n. 12), not by reo (§5.2) upon extrusion of *2ʃ i (the strong verb analog of defective 2ʃ V̌ 3√y—bobbing in the defective) but, by hypothesis, because *2ʃ i was extruded prior to the emergence of spr. Moreover, unlike the defective verb, where rwb affects only ms, in the strong sim rmp all φ-slots may be affected (and when they are, all four are rendered homophonous by lap (§17.9) though graphemically distinguished by traces of the apocopated -suffix, mp <-w>, fs and fp <-y> in turn distinguished by use of the grapheme *sə̄yə̄mē*, <°°>, over the fp form). It is likely that extension of rwb from ms to the remaining φ-slots was triggered by lap, since in the wake of lap other impa paradigms with strong 3√, as the hollow and geminate, also showed full homonymy of all four slots. So extension of rwb in the strong verb (and possibly other gə̄zarot like 1√y) would then make such φ-slot neutralization a regularity of all verbs with strong 3√. (c) SR also shows partial extension from strong sim rmp to strong int rmp, partial in that it is confined to the later period of the Jacobite register: for instance, jc[eθbárrə̃x] (Ns 103) < *hitbarrák. (d) Since prothesis (§17.18) at large in Aramaic is crucially fed by reduction, and red does not affect the earliest dialects, the fact that a demonstrably prothetic vowel may be created by rwb as a landing site for the retraction (e.g., TR [ʔéšt] in the text) appears to be in conflict with taking rwb to be an early A process. An escape-hatch from this conflict is suggested by the fact that rwb is an *impa* process, and that the sim impa contains a [V̌] (1ʃ) *not* generated by red; so that what comes to mind is the possibility that the group #CV̌C is unstable in A irrespective of chronology, and when favorable conditions arise—like rwb—#CV̌C may mutate to #V̊CC. So there is an early prothesis (e-pro) intimately associated with rwb and the sim impa, and a later prothesis (l-pro—in most connections in this book labeled simply "pro"; §17.18) intimately bound up with red. (e) Similarly in a roughshod way, failure of 2√ to spirantize in TR tb[ʔǽ9æd] (text) may be identified with *excrescence* in forms like [tæ9ə̃bǽr] (§4.5 (4Gh)), the immediately resulting ǽ being then promoted (§14.1) by virtue of occurring in a closed syllable. But an important implication of this analysis is that rwb, so far hypothesized to have occurred in early Aramaic without narrower qualification, must

have taken place following epn (§17.6) because in the contrary case we would expect @[ˀǽ9æ͓ð̣], in view of epn^spr.

All this suggests that the emergence of rwb "early in A."
(For some further interesting angles on sim rmp – int rmp rapprochement in SR, see Fassberg 2000–2004.)

[15] In fact, all dialects in which sim impa ms of *√ˀty is attested show at least one variant interpretable as ending in [-Ā] ⇐ /-V̊ 3√ˀ/: I <ˀTh> (L 67, MP 142) (other verbs usually <-y>); TR bb[ˀeθǽ] ~ tb[ˀi̭θɑ̄́] (Da 357); CP <ˀyTˀ> (Sg 65, 73) (~ <ˀTˀ>, lc, probably [Iθέ]; see §21.4 for <ˀ̭> [Ī̭]); SM <ˀTh> (Macs 209) (other verbs usually <-y> t[-i] as also variant <ˀTy> t[éti], lc); G <(ˀy)Tˀ> (Da 357) (~ <ˀTy>, lc); SR [tɔ̌́] (§8.1.3); TL <Tˀ> a[tɔ̌́] (Mar 91*) y[tǽ] (Mor 277); M <ata> (Macm 33). (There is no attestation for Y, O, B, P, N.)

[16] Note that the sim impa fs of √hwy 'be' shows two e-condensational variants: -coa bb[hi̭wǽy] ~ tb+sb[hŏwǽy] (alternatively, the Sab variant perhaps interpretable as [hĕwǽy], §17.23.3) ~ +coa bb[hi̭wǽ] (Da 354). There are also a few fs impas with auslaut [-ɑ̄́], perhaps best understandable as ⇐ /-V̊ 3√ˀ/ (§8.1.3(α)): [ˀiθrӡ̌δɑ̄́] 'werde gezuchtigt!' (Da 348), tb[ˀi̭θɑ̄́] 'komme!' (Da 357). This latter form, however, is homonymous with the homoparadigmatic ms (n. 4 above), a fact that extends to the Bab vasriant [ˀeθǽ]. The resulting syncretism may indeed even extend across binyanim to the causative, at least in the ms, to judge by the homography of impa cau ms bb<ˀeyTæˀ>, tb<ˀiyθɑˀ> (Da 358). For such sim-cau syncretism to be complete we would require length homogenization of [ˀV-], either to [ˀV̄-] (< prm (§14.1) 1√ˀV̄-) or to [ˀV̄-] (< coa (§11.2) ˀa 1√y-)—in which vein, be it noted, tb[ˀī-] as a reflex of ˀa 1√y- is anomalous for TR, where coa of *ay* normally stops at low [æ] (less frequently) or mid [ē] (more frequently) rather than going all the way (by hei) to high [ī]. In any event, hedging on the resolution of vowel quantity in ˀV-, the results of this possible cross-gender cross-binyan syncretism (§16) are tabulated here:

(a)

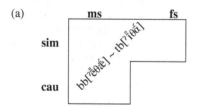

	ms	**fs**
sim		
cau	bb[ˀeθǽ] ~ tb[ˀi̭θɑ̄́]	

[17] The "slight complications with two roots in TL": (a) √ˀty—in the causative, [-ī] for both genders in the Yem tradition, <ˀyyTy> 'hevi(ˀi)' y[ˀæytī̭] (Mor 280), but in Ash only for ms, a[ˀayθī̭] (Mar 92*), fs being a[ˀēθɔ̌́] (lc)—all this bringing to mind the syncretisms seen in TR (n. 16, preceding). (b) √dly—one case of rwb in impa ms <Dl> 'herim!' ~ unmarked <Dly>, y[dǽl], y[dŏlī̭] respectively (Mor 257). If y[dǽl] is taken to be sim, as suggested by Morag's listing, we are apparently faced with a different codicil of rwb from the prothesis seen in TR (n. 14). This codicil in the TL case would be *simple impa promotion* (sip, §17.25), in particular, promotion to A as frequent for the dialect under other conditions in the sim impa (e.g., a[šavqúah] 'leave(mp) him!', Mar 168*): thus *dǎlī̭ rwb+sip > y[dǽl]. Alternatively, however, y[dǽl] might be an

intensive impa, < *dallī̂*, with *ll* whittled down by deg (§3.1 (3Fvii)). This latter interpretation is in fact adopted by Margolis (Mar 103*).

[18] Penultimate accent rather than expected [mɛnnī̂] perhaps due to a partial sort of rwb, lacking the bobbing; 1ʃ [ɛ] rather than expected [a] perhaps due to minor vowel harmony, *a . . . ī > ɛ . . . ī (§2.3.2.1 w n. 5)*.

[19] The issue of *-hī ~ -hū* allomorphy will be addressed in §8.2.2.

[20] Morag (lc) also reports an unapocopated variant y[ˀæmṭɔ̌yū̲ḥī̲] in a different Talmudic passage (no spelling provided). (Recall that l-cnd is variable in TL, applying less frequently than not.)

9. Gutturals

This chapter breaks down into three broad subsections: what might be called special processes (§9.1); the history of the major Aramaic gutturals, *ʾ, h, 9, ḥ* (§9.2);[1] and, finally, two special topics, the proclivity of gutturals toward vowels and profiles of degutturalization (§9.3).

9.1. Special Processes
9.1.1. Alef Dissimilation (ads)

The proto-Semitic process (Brockelmann 1908: 239) of *alef dissimilation* (ads), *ʾV 1√ʾC > ʾVC* in the sim impf, is inherited into pA and duly shows up in Y, O, and I.[2] No relevant forms happen to be attested in B, P, or N, and in the later dialects (TR, CP, SM, G, SR, TL, M), any traces of ads are neutralized by *1√ʾ > 1√W* (*simple alef replacement* (sar), §9.2.1.2) and/or possibly other paradigmatic levelings (e.g., there is some evidence that M bypassed sar by assimilating *V 1√ʾC' > VC'C'*; §9.2.1.1 below).

9.1.2. Causative Prefix *h* vs. *ʾ*

It is possible that pA had a lopsided way of marking the causative: by the prefix **h* initially (i.e., in the pf and impa), as in Hebrew, but medially (i.e., in the impf) either by **h*, again as in Hebrew, or by schematic ablaut alone, as in Arabic.

Alternatively, it is possible that pA had only **h*, medially as well as initially; but that a tendency developed to lose this *h* (perhaps to the tune of canonical repair-strategic replacement by *ʾ* as a perfunctory onset, at least in anlaut—another function of *hamzatu 'l-waṣl*, §8.1.1)—and that resulting medial groups . . . *V(ʾ)a* . . . ultimately shortened to . . . *a* . . . .

In either event, with the possible exception of Y, the earlier A dialects—O, I, B—show a distinct preference for the presence of *h* medially.

As of P, the dialects begin to forfeit the medial *h* bearing forms in favor of equivalents lacking *h*—a phenomenon to be invested in a process called *medial h-less causative* (m-hlc). As a consequence, it becomes a regularity of subsequent dialects to mark the causative by ablaut alone. (There are a few exceptions to this, the verb *hymn* 'believe' prime among them—if indeed its *h* should be taken as (formally) causative rather than as 1√ of a quadriradical root.)

At the same time or a bit earlier, starting with I and B, it is likely that Aramaic begins also to drop initial causative *h* or replace it by *ʾ*—a change to be called *initial h-less causative* (i-hlc). Consequently, by the time of P or N, *h*-less ablaut becomes the decidedly majority pattern in all A dialects. This change is qualified as "likely" because there exists the possibility that causatives prefixed with an initial *ʔ*, as in Arabic, also date back to proto-Semitic. And if so, we should properly be talking about the preference for *h* vs. *ʔ* changing over time, rather than one shape being lost or replaced by the other.[3]

9.1.3. Pharyngeal Dissimilation (phd); The Uvular Fricatives *X, R*

Various alleged *pharyngeal dissimilations* (phd)[4] are intricated with the question of what may have happened to the proto-Semitic voiced emphatic dentoalveolar spirant *ð̣ before it fully merged with *9*. In the interim period, it is spelled <q>: invariably at first (Y, O), then in variation with <9> (I, less in B), before finally being asymptotically replaced by <9> ("asymptotically" because there are sporadic holdouts with <q>, notably in M).

This book will adopt the frequent assumption that this <q> was pressed into service to spell the voiced uvular spirant [R] into which proto-Semitic *ð̣ had mutated. It will also be assumed that this mutation took the form of jumping positions of articulation from front (dentoalveolar) to back (uvular), leaving the features of continuance (fricative status) and voice untouched—actually, a kind of deletional simplification if the so-called traditional feature of "emphasis" is manifested by uvularization, as suggested in Malone 1976, since by those lights [ð̣] qua uvularizaed dentoalveolar would contain features of both positions of articulation while [R] contains the uvular feature alone. This mutation will be called *spirant hopping* (shp), spelled out in a bit more detail in §17.24.

The reason for assuming that <q> was pressed into service to spell [R] in addition to its original role of representing [q] is that the (originally Canaanite) orthography had no dedicated letter for [R] (because Canaanite has no [R]), and so <q> was appealed to as the only available grapheme already spelling a uvular consonant ([q]). That is, <q> [q,R] became a sort of "archispelling" or generic spelling; <q> was used to spell "uvular consonant," of which at the time there were exactly two, [q] (≤ *q) and [R] (< * ð̣ by shp).

Of course, the comparative method (§18.4) demonstrates that Aramaic had another uvular in its ancestry, *X*, the voiceless counterpart of *R*. But this *X* very early—prior to Old Aramaic—merged backward with pharyngeal *ḥ*, as in fact also its voiced companion *R* merged backward with *9 prior to the emergence of spirant hopping*. And Aramaic orthography is from the earliest days quite consistent in spelling reflexes of original *X* and *R* with the letters for the segments with which they merged, <ḥ> and <9>, respectively. This ancient-vintage backward merger will be called *uvular fricative backing* (ufb).

Since ufb ridded the A system of the uvular fricatives (*X, R*) and shp subsequently reintroduced *R*, we are dealing with a Martinesque front-to-back-moving *chaîne de traction* (Martinet 1955: 59–62): first, the uvular fricative space is vacated by backward merger into pharyngeal space (ufb), and then the vacated uvular space is partially refilled by movement from the dentoalveolar region (shp).

The resulting system is best viewed as marked and lopsided, the singleton *R* lacking the support of a homorganic *X* and, to boot, the category uvular fricative instantiates a less than commonplace articulation—one in fact that the language earlier got rid of by ufb. So we may assume that shp, whatever its precise impetus, resulted in an unstable arrangement, one that the language soon ironed out by a *reprise of ufb* (r-ufb). Looking back from this point, we are dealing with a chain of events along these lines:

(stage I) *ʠ; *X, *R; *ḥ, *9   ufb >   (stage II) ʠ; ḥ, 9   shp >
(stage III) R; ḥ, 9   spelling introduced >   (stage IV) R <q>; ḥ <ḥ>, 9 <9>
r-ufb >   (stage V) ḥ <ḥ>, 9 <9>.[5]

Against this backdrop, at least two nexuses of *pharyngeal dissimilations* (phd) take place: one whereby *9* under the same-word copresence of another pharyngeal *(ḥ, 9)* mutates in both position and manner of articulation to merge with the nearest *back*ward-lying stop, *ʔ*; and the other whereby *9* under similar environing conditions merges with the nearest *forward*-lying stop, *g*.

(α) Backwards dissimilation *9 > ʔ*, to be labeled b-phd, the more widespread of the two nexuses, varies in scope from dialect to dialect. There are three relevant verb roots (target segment (dissimilandum) boldfaced, catalyst (dissimilans) italicized): *√9rʠ 'encounter' shp > √9rR r-ufb √**9r9** b-phd > √**ʔr9** (at least TR, CP, G, SR, M, and probably SM—moreover, dialects inflecting the root for causative show car, §9.2.1.2; for more on b-phd of *√9rʠ, see §9.2.3.1 with n. 27); *√ʠ9p 'duplicate' shp > √R9p r-ufb > √**99p** b-phd > √**ʔ9p** (SR [ɛ9áp] (Brockelmann 1928: 38), with loss of 1√ʔ by adr, §9.3.2; see also note 9(c) below); and *√ʠhk 'laugh' shp > √Rḥk r-ufb > √**9ḥk** b-phd > √**ʔ**ḥk (only M, where the dissimilated *ʔ* is lost by M-typical adr, §9.3.2—[ehkáθ] 'she laughed', [ehkíθ] ~ [ahkíθ] 'I laughed', [īhexīBón] 'I laughed at them', DM 9, and for the other processes shaping these forms §5.1.8, §5.2, §9.2.1.1, §17.15). Observe that, at least for the verb, b-phd is *regressive*, the dissimilans occurring later in the word than the dissimilandum. (In the nominal system, on the other hand, we find at least one case of regressive ~ progressive variation variation for one and the same root: *√ʠl9 'rib' shp > √Rl9 r-ufb > √**9l9** in SR ([ɛl9ʃ], B23, with *ʔ > ∅ by adr) but √**9l9** in G ([9illāʔá], Jastrow 1903: 1085).[6]

(β) Frontward dissimilation (f-phd) *9 > g* is attested in largely the same dialects as is the backward pattern seen in (α), only adding TL and subtracting TR. As concerns the mechanics of f-phd, observe that while there are *two* consonants forwardly closest to *R* from the pure vantage of p.o.a., *g* and its voiceless partner *k*, the actual dissimilation *R > g* unsurprisingly preserves voice (sacrificed in (α) *9* > *ʔ*, but necessarily so in that no voiced counterpart of *ʔ* exists; observe also that *h* is not targeted, though like *ʔ* it is a voiceless laryngeal—plausibly because, qua glides, *9* and *ʔ* are both lax, to the exclusion of tense *h*; §20.1. A somewhat different idea about the essence of b-phd is presented in §9.2.3.1 n. 27.) Examples of f-phd forms (though not all points of their analysis) are from B 23; Brockelmann 1928: 113, 127; Macm 95f.; DM 9, 81: *√ð̣Rt (as in Arabic) ufb > √ð̣9ṭ shp > √R9ṭ r-ufb √99ṭ f-phd > √g9ṭ (SR [gə̆9áṭ] 'evomuit', M with further *9* > *ʔ* > *y*, §9.2.1.2, §9.2.3.1 below, in the noun [gə̆yūṭá] 'poena';[7] *√ð̣ħk (again as in Arabic) 'laugh' shp > √Rħk r-ufb > √9ħk f-phd > √ghk (SR [gə̆héx], M with *ħ* > *h*, §9.2.4, [gə̆héx]. Also, it will be recalled from (α) that M *√ð̣ħk is variably subject to *both* dissimilatory patterns;[8] thus alongside *9* > *g* in pf 3ms [gə̆héx], we have 3fs [ehkáθ] derived from *9* > *ʔ*. For CP, SM, G, and TL all showing √ghk < √ð̣ħk, see Sl 36, Kutscher 1976: 34 with n. 80, Sokoloff 2002b: 126, Sokoloff 2002a: 276 (the TL manifestation appears to be limited to the nominal <GhKnʔ> 'jester').[9]

9.1.4. The Merger of 3√y and 3√ʔ Verbs

There seems to be a long-rooted assumption that the A-characteristic merger of *3√ʔ and *3√y verbs, to be called *alef-defective neutralization* (adn), was at least in part catalyzed by the coincidence that in the 3ms (hence least marked) slot of the pf verb (and most particularly the dynamic simple (§1 n. 2)—hence, again, least marked paradigm) the auslaut string *-a 3√y a first condensed to -*ā* (§8), whereupon *-a 3√ʔa apocopated to -*aʔ* (§17.22), which in turn vocalized to -*ā* by *alef apocope* (aap), an early manifestation of the widespread drift in later Aramaic to lose gutturals (§9.3.2).

But though this hypothesis on the genesis of adn stands a fair chance of being correct, it behooves the investigator to be on guard, because there is simply not a lot of independent evidence for aap in the earlier, unvocalized dialects. What there is a lot of, starting with I, is evidence for adn. But it is not cricket to construe evidence for adn as support for aap simply because one's theory of adn assumes aap as a cardinal trigger. It may even turn out, when we know more, that the genesis of adn had nothing to do with aap, and that we will just have to shop around for a new explanation of what kicked off adn in the first place.

This said, it is also a tricky matter to find independent evidence for aap in an unvocalized dialect impacted by adn, especially in the finite verb. To see why, consider that for aap to take place at all, we need to have instances of *Vʔ#*. We would thus need to rummage around for i 3√ʔ#, u 3√ʔ#, a 3√ʔ#, ī 3√ʔ#, ū 3√ʔ#, or ā 3√ʔ#, there being no verbs ending in an *ʔ* other than one that is third radical. We can pretty confidently set aside the last three cases; a long vowel would probably only show up in three frames: various forms of the hollow verb (§1.3), or in the palatal passive of the simple verb (§1.1.1), or in forms affected by second schematic lengthening (§17.28)—but to my knowledge there is no attestation of early Aramaic verbs of these types ending in $3\sqrt{?}$. As concerns the first three strings, with short vowels, it is likely enough that most of them would have been neutralized to a $3\sqrt{?}\#$ by low (§17.10). But assuming that at least some forms escaped low, aap would then give us *ī#*, *ū#*, *ā#*, which in the prevailing orthographies would likely be spelled <y#>, <w#>, <?#> ~ <h#>. However, all but <w#> could equally represent reflexes of *i $3\sqrt{y}(+i)\#$ and *a $3\sqrt{y}(+i)\#$ (any antecedent *u $3\sqrt{y}(+i)\#$ having been absorbed by the other two; §8.1.1 w n. 1)—that is, *ī#* and ay# (or *ē#* if a coalescent process, §11.1, has applied). (The grouping of the long impf with that of the short impf in the case of the defective gizra, *V̊ $3\sqrt{y}+i\#$ with *V̊ $3\sqrt{y}\#$, reflects the fact that auslaut *a $3\sqrt{y}+i\#$ of the long impf early undergoes condensatory coalescence, k-coa, to *ē#*). To date, no relevant (suffixless) verbs in <w#> having shown up, the provisional conclusion must be that no convincing evidence has emerged for (verb-affecting) aap in nonvocalized dialects where adn has occurred.

Coming finally to a profile of the dialects, adn shows up clearly in I as a variable process, thereafter becoming ever more robust though residua of the original $*3\sqrt{?} \neq * 3\sqrt{y}$ distinction may stubbornly linger.[10] Whether adn emerged earlier than I is questionable; there appears to be no evidence for it in O,[11] but Y shows one otherwise puzzling form that adn could explain: <qrny> 'er rief mich an' (DR I : 214.13), difficult as adn-less [qara?ánī] but fine as adn-affected [qarā́nī] (⇐ s-e-cnd /qarayanī/ < d-adn /qara?anī/; cf. §8 (8Dii)).

Any conclusive report on aap is, as per the preceding discussion, altogether elusive. We might guess that aap is clearly manifest as of the first vocalized dialect—B. But doubts linger even so. Thus SR has a handful of $3\sqrt{?}$ verbs that are quite different in appearance from the run-of-the-mill, which have duly undergone adn. One such maverick is int <baya?> 'trosten' (Ns 109). How is this to be interpreted phonetically? If [bayya] (stress?), we are left with a short vowel implausibly in final position. If [bayyā́], we are forced to extend the distribution of the long low vowel, of tightly constrained occurrence to begin with, to the only position where it is not evoked by palatal assimilation (mvh) /__y (§20.2(δ)). If, however, aap should play no role in SR, <baya?> might be straightforwardly interpreted as [bayyá?].[12]

9.2. The Major Aramaic Gutturals: *?, h, 9, ḥ*

9.2.1. The Laryngeal Stop / Lax Laryngeal Glide (alef) *?*

9.2.1.1. Loss of *?* by Contact Assimilation

? is clearly the most labile of Aramaic gutturals and has shown a tendency to lose its segmental identity since the earliest days. We will first consider the fate of adconsonantal *?*, keeping in mind that in the Aramaic verb any adconsonantal *?* will normally also be advocalic (i.e., we find no strings in the verb such

as *C$^?$C*, *#$^?$C*, or *C$^?$#*; the former two are phonotactically prohibited, and though *C$^?$#* is imaginable if only at a phonologically intermediate stage—e.g., as a result of rwb (§8.1.3) on the sim impa of √Q$^?$y—no such forms are attested.

Specific quasi-morphological processes aside, such as the replacement of the causative prefix or first radical by semivowels (§9.2.1.2), the earliest manifestation of the lability of $^?$ is probably its tendency to totally assimilate to an adjacent consonant or vowel.

The very first appearance of this weakness seems to be advocalic assimilation dissimilatorily (haplologically) triggered by the presence of another, preceding $^?$, as as we have seen in the process of ads (§9.1.1). Thereafter, as of B at the latest, come various at first sporadic manifestations of $^?$ contact assimilation by assumption without a dissimilatory trigger. Note, e.g.: in O, <$^?$hBD> ~ conservative <$^?$h$^?$BD> [$^?$iha$^?$bídi] 'ich werde zerstören' (De 71f. with n. 64); in I, <nm{r}> 'wir sagen', contrast conservative <y$^?$mr> [yI$^?$már] 'er sagt' (L 21); in P, <yhDnh> 'he'll take it' with assimilation of 1√$^?$, contrast its maintenance in such as <y$^?$mr> 'he'll say' (HC 336, 340); in TR, <$^?$iTæhæD> 'er wurde gefangen', vs. <$^?$iT$^?$æBæl> 'er klagte' (Da 303), the former [$^?$ittæh(h)ǽð], the latter [$^?$iθ$^?$æbbǽl]; in CP, <$^?$Tmr> ~ conservative <$^?$T$^?$mr> (Sg 65) 'es wurde gesagt' [Ittǎmár] and [Iθ($^?$)ǒmár], respectively, also cau pf 3fs <$^?$BDT> (Sg 66) (though 1√$^?$ is usually replaced by *w*, §9.2.1.2); similarly in G, <$^?$yTmr> ~ <$^?$yT$^?$mr> (Da 303); and TL <$^?$yTmr> (Mar 41), also <$^?$TyK> a[$^?$ǒθǒyǒx] 'he brought you'—contrast a[$^?$ayθīθáh] 'you brought her' (Mar 92*), with replacement of 1√$^?$ by *y* (§9.2.1.2); in M< <nimar> t[nímmar] 'he'll say' (Macm 113), interpretable as [nimmár].[13]

In adducing these examples, it has been hypothesized that the lability of $^?$ is manifested through contact assimilation, which basically means that a group *V$^?$C'V* may assimilate either to *V̄C'V* (advocalic assimilation) or to *VC'C'V* (adconsonantal), while *VC'$^?$V* may plausibly assimilate only to *VC'C'V*. (Assuming syllabification *V$^?$ | CV* and *VC | $^?$V*, assimilation of a coda to an adjacent nucleus, *V$^?$ > V̄*, is common as grass in languages at large, while similar assimilation of an onset, *$^?$V > V̄*, is rare though not unprecedented (within Aramaic, at least SM to judge by trad pron; §4.3 with n. 18).)[14]

Since in most of these cases the prevocalized orthographies are moot, expected <$^?$C> and <C$^?$> both being simply replaced by <C> (unless retained as historical spelling), another possibility arises: that *V$^?$CV* and *VC$^?$V* might have been simplified to *VCV* by uncompensated loss of $^?$. However, contact assimilation is rather being posited in such cases for the admittedly challengeable reason that assuming a relation of ancestry between at least some of the earlier dialects and later vocalized ones, an early uncompensated loss of $^?$ would often have opened a syllable to later reduction in a way that the later dialects never seem to show. Take for instance I <n̄m{r}> 'wir sagen' (above). If reduction was either still a living process at the time of I (more probable) or had not yet arisen (less probable), then deletional loss of $^{?}$ to *nimár* should have ultimately led to something like @[nə̆már]. But such forms seem to be uniformly alien to the later dialects, which always agree on showing something with a full vowel in the first syllable (e.g., M [nimmár] (above), B [nēmár] (BL 139); see §9.2.1.2, next).

On the other hand, uncompensated deletion of $^{?}$ in the later, post-reductional period is certainly a possibility to be reckoned with. Various cases in point will be presented at appropriate junctures, the process(es) responsible to be called *alef drop* (adr).

Sound changes frequently catch on and even expand in specific structural nooks and crannies, and the contact assimilation of $^{?}$ is no exception. One favorite niche for $^{?}$ to disappear in this way is as 1√ in the causative verb, and most particularly in the root √$^{?}$ty 'come', causative 'bring'. In this role, contact assimilation of $^{?}$ competes as a minor contender with the widespread replacement of √$^{?}$ by a semivowel, in the case of √$^{?}$ty always *y* (§9.2.1.2). Thus, though causative /$^{?}$ty appears not to be attested in O, we saw above <$^{?}$hBD> as an alternative to <$^{?}$h$^{?}$BD> in the causative of √$^{?}$bd; I shows a few forms like <$^{?}$>-less <yTw> 'sie mögen bringen', as opposed to normal semi-vowel replaced (car, §9.2.1.2) <hyTy> [hayTī] or [hēθī] 'er brachte' < *ha$^{?}$tíya*, etc.; P shows <$^{?}$Ty> ~ <$^{?}$yTy> 'he brought'; CP likewise <$^{?}$̊Ty> ~ <$^{?}$ẙTy> (and on balance Schulthess's Lexicon (Sl) lists about even numbers of <$^{?}$>-less and <y>-ful forms in the causative of √$^{?}$ty); TL shows a[$^{?}$ɔyɔ̃x] (above); M, like CP, shows about equal numbers of <$^{?}$>-less and <y>-ful (= <i>-ful) forms, e.g., <atiun> ~ <aitiun> 'they brought me' (and note that Modern M has fully generalized the <$^{?}$>-less conjugation, [áθθī] 'he brought', etc.)[15]

9.2.1.2. Other Losses of $^{?}$; Semivocalization of 1√$^{?}$ in the Simple Imperfective and the Causative at Large

Mention was made of the quasi-morphological replacement of 1√$^{?}$ by a semivowel, *y* or *w*, in the causative and in the impf of the simple verb—processes to be named *causative alef replacement* (car) and *simple alef replacement* (sar), respectively.

Both car and sar are clearly in evidence by the time of B, where in fact both semivowels play a lexically or registerially determined role: thus by car both Tib B and Bab B show √$^{?}$bd > √wbd in the causative (tb[tə̆hōvéθ], Bab B[tə̆hōvǽθ] 'you shall destroy' with [ō] < coa (§11.2) a 1√w < a 1√$^{?}$) but √$^{?}$mn > √ymn in the at least formally causative root for 'believe' (Tib B [hēmín], bb[hēmén] 'he believed' with [ē] < coa a 1√y < a 1√$^{?}$)[16], whereas with sar Tib B selects 1√y (e.g., [yēxúl] 'he'll eat') and Bab B 1√w ([yōxúl]).

After B, all dialects (P, N, TR, CP, SM, G, SR, TL, M) consistently show car (when not preempted by assimilatory loss of 1√$^{?}$, §9.2.1.1), in each one 1√w probably appearing more frequently than but never to the total exclusion of 1√y. Indeed, 1√y is always the choice in the causative of √ʔty 'bring' and of √ʔmn 'believe' (n. 16). (It might be revealing to study the lexeme-by-lexeme incidence of 1√w vs. 1√y within and across the individual dialects.)

The post-B situation with *simple*(-binyan) alef replacement (sar) is less even. P and N maintain their simple impfs in <ʔ>, while TR regularly shows a 1√y by sar (which normally > [ē] by coa, but perhaps occasionally we find i 1√y > [ī]; Da 300 n. 1);[17] CP and SM usually show sar, and when they do, the replacement is 1√y (as generally holds for sar across all dialects), but both show some lexical retentions of 1√ʔ (which then contact-assimilates at least in SM); G, TL, and SR faithfully show 1√y by sar,[18] whereby the Jacobite register of SR lexically cleaves its verbs into two groups, one in which the coalesced ē < a 1√y is raised by hei (e.g., jc[nīmár] 'he'll say') and the other in which hei fails to apply (e.g., jc[nēxúl] 'he'll eat')—and the Nestorian register is uniformly –hei (ns[nēmár], [nēxól]);[19] M appears to avoid sar altogether for assimilation (§9.2.1.1) of 1√ʔ to 2√, with which it clusters (with the SR forms just adduced, cf. M <nimar> t[nímmar], <nikul> t[níxxol]).

As concerns ʔ in #ʔV̆, there is some evidence it may in some dialects drop (by adr, §9.2.1.1), which is almost certainly its fate in SM, SR, and M—these three dialects being moreover those having the highest likelihood for ʔ ultimately disappearing unconditionally. It will also be assumed that CP ended up losing ʔ (for reasons laid out in §9.3.2 n. 42).

Though the change by reduction of VCʔV to VCʔV̆ does not per se alter the way a dialect resolves ʔ (§9.2.1.1), in environments other than /C__ reduction of V̄ to V̆ does seem by and large to have a bearing on an immediately preceding ʔ (and sometimes other gutturals). That is, ʔ in #ʔV̄ may react differently from ʔ in #ʔV̆; and ʔ in V̄ʔV certainly reacts differently from ʔ in V̆ʔV.

To take the second case first, though there may be earlier intimations in the nonverb (I, B), the verb gets clearly involved as of TR in a process whereby both ʔ and V̆ are (variably) elided in V̆ʔV—*schwa-alef drop* (sad). sad shows up variably in at least TR, CP, SM, and TL; and categorically in SR and M. On the other hand, intervocalic ʔ immediately preceded by a *full* vowel begins to change, variably at first (CP) and subsequently categorically (SM, G, TL, M), to y—a process to be called *alef palatalization* (apl). Giving prevailing canons for the structure of verbs and the conditions of various changes, notably reduction, apl almost always assumes the form ʔʔ > yy, notably in the intensive.[20]

In anlaut position, there is a growing tendency of even earlier vintage (as of B) for #ʔV̆ to promote to #ʔV̄, a tendency which subsequently becomes categorical in the dialects where ʔ ends up totally lost (by adr; SM, SR, M).

However, this tendency toward promotion of V̆ in #ʔV̆ is in one structural niche competed with by the polar strategy of apheretic loss of the entire string. This niche is the simple impa verb, where apheresis is incipient as early as TR, then becomes and remains variable through CP, SM, G, SR, TL (though not

M, whose testimony for this process is sporadic and questionable at best). See wic (§17.33) for details.

9.2.2. The Laryngeal Fricative / Tense Laryngeal Glide *h*

After *ʔ*, the most labile guttural in Aramaic is probably *h*, though in certain cases (to be discussed below) this segment shows great tenacity.

Possibly as early as B but clearly as of P, *h* shows a tendency toward apocope *(h apocope,* hap), though there seems to be considerable unevenness attending the progress of this change through the later dialects. It appears to be absent in N, incipient in TR, CP, and G, while in SM it is categorical to judge by trad pron but spotty to judge by the orthography. Coming to the Eastern dialects, hap appears to be nonexistent in SR, while it is variable in TL and fully categorical in M.[21]

A yet earlier manifestation of *h*-lability may be the assimilation or loss of 3p *h* under adjacency to an immediately preceding *n.* in the object suffixes and independent pronouns; a process which, if genuine, is categorical in all dialects but the L ones, TL, and M, where it is variable (and possibly CP, where there may be sporadic retentions of unassimilated *h*; see §7 n. 27). Detailed discussion will be found in §7.4.2, where also an alternative is considered which effectively reverses the hypothesis: *-n(nə̆)-* > *-n(nə̆)-h-* with inserted *h*, rather than *-n(nə̆)-h-* > *-nn-* with deleted/assimilated *h*.

Another early loss of *h* may be in the rmp prefix **hit-*, which by this hypothesis changes to *(ʔ)IT-* as early as I, a loss or replacement (by *ʔ*) thenceforth manifested, essentially categorically, in all subsequent dialects with the striking exception of B (there are no relevant forms attested in N). This change will go by the name *h-less rmp* (hlr). Once again, as with the similar causative processes m-hlc and i-hlc (§9.1.2), there is the possibility that the *h*-less rmp forms themselves date back to pSemitic (they constitute, be it noted, the regular pattern in Arabic conjugation VIII, even as do *h*-less causatives in conjugation IV).

(Another issue involving *h*, *ʔ*, the rmp, and the causative is whether the geminate cluster *tt*, which forms part of the prefix complex marking the rmp causative in TR and all subsequent dialects, should be analyzed as formed by contact assimilation to rmp **t* of causative **h* (i.e., **th* > *tt*) and/or of causative **ʔ* (**tʔ* > *tt*).[22] There is mighty little direct evidence for either **th* or **tʔ*: the I-vintage Aśoka bilingual shows <ʔThhsynn> 'they were made strong' (Coxon 1977: 297) (for 2ʃ <y> qua possible [ī], see §17.28; for <-n> as auslaut of the 3mp suffix, §7.2(δ)); and G shows <ʔTʔPq> 'er wurde herausgebracht' (Da 297). The relevant assimilatory process, *T+ʔ/h* > *tt*, will be called *rmp-causative assimilation* (rca).)[23]

The incidence of adsegmental assimilation of *h* in *VhCV* and *VChV* is considerably weaker than that of *ʔ* (§9.2.1.1). A few stray nonverb instances apart (e.g., in TR (Da 98), CP (Sg 19)), only three dialects show any evidence of *h*-assimilation in the verb: SM, G, and SR.[24]

The situation with SM is tricky, because trad pron can often give the impression of assimilation to *C* or *V* while other factors may actually be responsible. For instance <yhBT> t[yḗbɑt] 'she gave' looks as if it may < *yehBáθ* by aga (*VhCV* > *V̄CV*), whereas there is a likelier alternative derivation from *yĕháβaθ* (via the smc and allied processes, §22.1 (22B), §20.2(ζ)): c-prm → *yeháβaθ* c-pra → *yēháβaθ* c-dgt → *yēáβaθ* c-vcr → *yḗβaθ* oba,svs → [yḗbɑt]. This derivation is likelier in that light-suffixed perfectives normally reconstruct as barytone for SM (hence *yĕháβaθ*) rather than as oxytone (*yehBáθ*); see §4.1. A genuine case of adsegmental assimilation of *h* may be <ylK> 'er wird gehen', ~ <yhlK> (Macs 366). Retained *h* is quite tenacious in such circumstances to judge by the frequency of orthographic <VhCV>/<VChV>, though by the testimony of trad pron (§22.1) *h* has been totally eliminated. We may assume that the orthography by and large captures an earlier stage than does the trad pron, both representing genuine linguistic stages, though both again being to some extent possibly imperfectly reflected: in the first case, by such as historical or inverse spelling (§17.14 n. 21, §21.1 <u>SM</u>); in the latter case, by interference notably from Arabic—these cautions holding not merely (or even especially) for *h*, but for all gutturals.[25] Note that *h*-less impf forms of √hwy 'be' are best taken not as reflecting assimilation in the frame *VhCV* (V √h 2√w V), but rather elision in the frame *ə̆* 1√h V upon lexically conditioned loss of 2√w followed by prefixal *V* r-red > *ə̆*; see §17.32.[26]

G and SR show rga assimilation in the frame *VhCV* incipiently. For instance, G <yBwn> 'gebet!' [yĬbbŬn] ← *yĬhBŬn*; and similarly for the same root √yhb in SR anytime the string *VhBV* arises (Ns 26), while the Nestorian register for √bht also shows <bɛhlaT>, <ʔɛTBaḥlaT> with understroke for non-pronunciation (Du 101).

9.2.3. The Voiced Pharyngeal Fricative / Lax Pharyngeal Glide 9

9.2.3.1. Loss and Retention of 9

The voiced pharyngeal glide *9 ultimately disappears in M, in part disappears and in part widens its distribution in SM, but shows at best a weak tendency toward change in the other post-TR dialects. Perhaps the most widespread symptom across these post-TR dialects for the tendency of 9 to weaken is its *dissimilation* to ʔ when a second 9 appears in the same word, notably in *√9r9 'happen', by b-phd as discussed above in §9.1.3(α).[27] The shape √ʔr9 clearly occurs in CP, G, SR, TL, and possibly in SM (<D9r9> ~ <D9rh> ~ <Dhr9> t[dǽræ] 'was passiert ist' (Macs 12)—despite 1√ being represented by <9> in two of these variants, by hypothesis attributable to historical spelling or general dgt-attendant orthographic helter-skelter (§21.2(ζ)) and M (Drower

and Macuch (DM) show only participial <aria> [ārī́] (with <ia> [ī] /I 3√y/ by
ʔ < *9 being pulled into the orbit of adn, §9.1.4), actually moot as to whether
*1√9 was lost by dissimilation as opposed to by the general M loss of all gut-
turals but *h* (< *ħ, *ḥ (≤ **ḥ or < ufb **X)) (§9.3.2)). For more on √ʔr9, and
3√9 > 3√ʔ > 3√/y/, see §9.2.3.2.

In both M and SM, the lability of 9 is manifest in spelling as well as in
pronunciation (trad pron in both dialects, but also testimony of the modern
language for M).

Consider some examples of *1√9, *2√9, and *3√9 for M: <abad> m[éβad]
'he did' < *9abáda like <amar> m[émar] 'he said' < *ʔamára (Macm 296,
500, 518) (for the discrepancy between anlaut <a> and m[e], see §17.23.3 with
(17.23D)); <tan> 'he carried' < *ṭa9ána like <šal> 'he asked' < *šaʔála (Macm
329); <šma> 'he heard' < *šamí9a (*i* > *a* by low, §17.10) like <qra> 'he read'
< *qaráʔa (Macm 638, 333).

Similar examples for SM: <9rq> ~ <ʔrq> t[ǻraq] 'er floh' < *9aráqa like
<ʔmr> T[ǻmar] 'er sagte' < *ʔamára (Macs 11, 171); <z9q> t[zǽq] 'er rief' <
*za9áqa like <sʔB> t[sǽb] 'er wurde alt' < *saʔába (Macs 173; the [æ] – [ɑ]
difference weakly correlates with the *9, *ʔ difference, in that *9 shows a tendency to cooccur with a preceding low vowel realized as t[æ], whereas *ʔ or
*y under similar circumstances selects t[æ ~ ɑ̄]); <šm9> t[šǽmæ] 'er hörte'
< *šamí9a like <qrʔ> t[qɑ́ra] 'er rief' < *qaráʔa (Macs 175, 205; once again,
the 2ʃ [æ] – [ɑ] difference correlating with /__*9,*ʔ respectively, 1ʃ [æ] – [ɑ̄]
likely following suit by minor vowel harmony, §2.3.2.1 with n. 5). (It will have
been observed that, with the exception of <9rq> ~ <ʔrq>, SM orthographically
reflects the original *9, *ʔ distinction, whereas in M, writing the difference is
neutralized.)

On balance, the most likely interpretation of the foregoing M and SM data
for *9 is that this guttural ultimately disappeared in both dialects, unconditionally in M and conditionally in SM,[28] the disappearance itself plausibly
being of ʔ with which 9 had merged (by gtl, §9.3.2) as the first symptom of its
weakening: 9 > ʔ > ∅.

Though 9 > ʔ > ∅ (gtl^adr) may have held for both M and SM, this chain
of processes did not work out identically in the two dialects. Thus, take the
sim rmp pf's *hitʔamíra 'was said' and *hit9abída 'was done'. While both
dialects agree in showing no trace in trad pron of either *ʔ or *9, and both
forms end up canonically identical *within* each dialect, the pairs end up anything but identical *across* the two dialects: M <etmar> t[étmar] and <etbid>
t[étβed] (Macm 90), but SM <(w)ʔTʔmr> t[(w)ētǻmɑr] and <ʔT9BD> t[ētǽbəd]
~ [ētǽbɑd] (Macs 173).[29] While M has undergone adconsonantal assimilation, pga (§9.2.1.1 n. 4b), t 1√ʔV (< *tʔa, *t9a) shifting to *ttV̆*, which subsequently shrinks to *t* by M-favored smp (§17.26), SM has *either* undergone
advocalic assimilation (c-dgt, n. 25) of t √ʔǎ to *tā/tǣ* (see §4.1.3 with n. 18 for

such SM-specific compensatory lengthening of a nucleus by the onset) *or* has followed up simple, uncompensated loss (e-dgt, n. 25) of *ʔ* (< *ʔ, *9) with open-syllabic tonic lengthening in the wake of c-prm^c-pen (by c-pra, §22.1 (22F)).

Turning now to other post-TR dialects, CP shows some evidence for at least incipient loss of *9, but not much. There is at least one and possibly two sim rmp pf's: <ʔT(ʔ)rsT> 'sie wurde verlobt' (Sg 65), comparable to the M and SM forms just considered if correctly derived < *hit9arísat (for reservations, see Kutscher 1976: 81); and possibly <ʔyl9wn> 'they got tired' (Kutscher 1976: 81) where 2√<9> in lieu of expected 2√<ʔ> (*√lʔy) may constitute inverse spelling in the wake of *9 > *ʔ* ([IllǯʔÛn]) or even total loss [IllÛn]), with silent but etymologically unjustified <9>, like <gh> in English <delight> (Hoenig-swald 1960: 9f.).[30]

Like CP, G also shows <ʔrs> for expected <9rs> (assuming *√9rs), <ʔrsTh> 'you betrothed her', as well as perhaps a few other similar *9-weakened forms (see Kutscher 1976: 81).

In the Eastern dialects, the evidence for *9 > ʔ/Ø runs the gamut from (virtu-ally) nonexistent in SR to fully consummated in M, with TL in the middle, showing at least a modicum of such weakening. In addition to several ex-amples of this to be presented in §9.2.3.2, a linguistically TL bowl incanta-tion (Müller-Kessler and Kwasman 2000) shows apparently inversely spelled <wyK9wB> 'and he'll have pain', with <9> in lieu of expected <ʔ>, presum-ably [wǎyixʔóv] or possibly assimilated [wǎyikkóv], as well as <ʔBDnyKw> 'your practitioners' (not a verb, but patently derived from *√9bd 'do').

9.2.3.2. Excursus on Analogically Induced Reprises; Some Aramaic Cases in Point Involving *9 > ʔ*

When convergent sound change affects a heavily structured grammatical system, as opposed to a random congeries of lexical items, the issue often arises as to whether so affected portions of the system will be in addition af-fected by analogical reshapings aiming at further integration into preexisting morphophonological patterns. That is, using [a, b, . . .] as variables for pho-netic segments, if [a] > [b] after preexisting cases of [b] already vary with (~) [c] within some grammatical system, it is always possible that the sound change [a] > [b] may be followed up by an analogical change ([a] >) [b] ≫ [b] ~ [c] so that the "new" [b] will be better integrated into the system where the "old" [b] is already in an organic alternational relation with [c].

However, though such nexuses are common, they are notoriously suscepti-ble to reconstructional ambiguity. Assume that the actual sequence of changes is: <u>stage I</u>, [b] > [b] ~ [c]; <u>stage II</u>, [a] > [b]; <u>stage III</u>, ([a] >) [b] ≫ [b] ~ [c]. How do we know that the actual sequence of changes was not rather: <u>stage I</u>, [a] > [b]; <u>stage II</u>, [b] > [b] ~ [c]? That is, how do we know that there are actually "new" vs. "old" [b]s, rather than only "middle-aged" [b]s? Though sometimes investigators get lucky enough to find independent factors helping to answer such questions, as often as not they do not get so lucky—in which case, the best they can do is rely on rules-of-thumb and hope for the best.

One such rule-of-thumb is sometimes available when multiple dialects are being compared, if one adopts a family-tree interpretation (§18.1). Say that evidence for [b] > [b] ~ [c] appears in dialects δ, ε, ζ, while only dialect δ gives evidence of [a] > [b]. This distribution suggests that [b] > [b] ~ [c] took place earlier than [a] > [b], because the former is shared by all three dialects while the latter is confined to just one; see figure (9A).

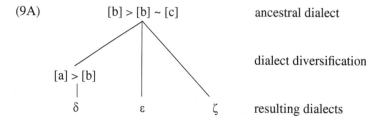

Given these assumptions, if δ then shows traces of [b] ~ [c] developing in the [b]s which derived from [a]s, we might feel justified in interpreting such instances of [b] ~ [c] in terms of secondary analogy along the lines of figure (9B) rather than in terms of primary sound change as in figure (9C)—this latter quite clearly conflicting with our initial family-tree based assumption, as expressed in figure (9A), that [b] > [b] ~ [c] preceded [a] > [b] in history.

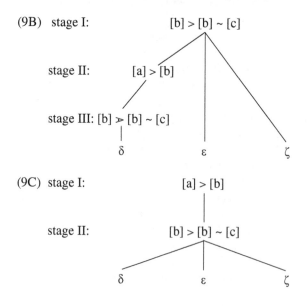

However, as useful as such a family-tree based interpretation can be under favoring special circumstances, there may in the absence of such special circumstances be competing wave-theoretic interpretations (§18.2), which return us to square one concerning the competition between the hypothesis of secondary analogy and that of primary sound change. One such wave-theoretic interpretation is that the change [a] > [b] may have been confined to a *dialect pocket* in a speech form ancestral to δ, ε, ζ—that is, to a subarea whose speech was ancestral only to δ. In the terminology of this book, a pocketed mutation like [a] > [b] vis-à-vis δ will be said to constitute a *shafted* change and will be represented as in figure (9D). This diagram conveys that although the change [b] > [b] ~ [c] is general to the entirety of ancentral dialect γ, including the dotted-lined area, yet the change [a] > [b] is confined to only the dotted-lined area, which in this diagram demarcates a dialect pocket within γ ultimately developing into daughter dialect δ. This is portrayed by the dotted-lined *shaft* extending from γ to δ. Moreover, change [a] > [b] chronologically precedes change [b] > [b] ~ [c], as per the hoop (⌢) connecting the two changes.

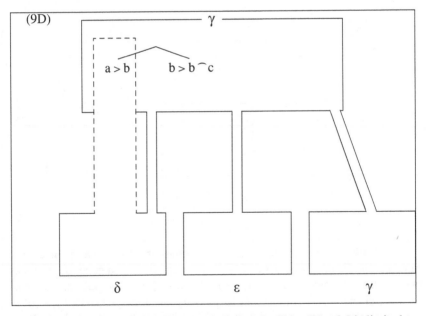

(9D) γ

a > b   b > b⌢c

δ   ε   γ

The upshot of this is that the change chain [a] > [b] > [b] ~ [c] is limited to the pre-δ area of γ, while the rest of γ—which will develop into ε and ζ—is affected by [b] > [b] ~ [c] alone.

The situation is wave-theoretically explicated in figure (9E), where first γ contains only the isogloss [a] > [b] in one specific pocket (top diagram); next, γ develops isogloss [b] > [b] ~ [c], which spreads to include the [a] > [b] pocket

(middle diagram), and finally γ splits into three daughter dialects δ, ε, ζ (bottom
diagram).

(9E)

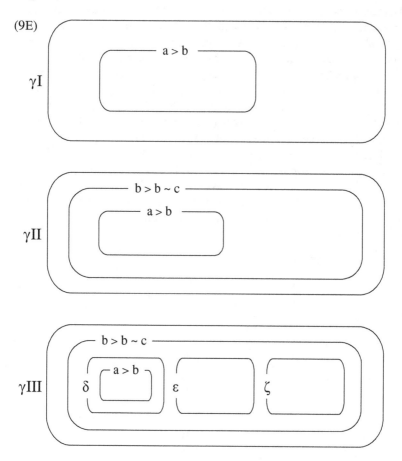

The moral of this excursus is that, in the throes of reconstruction, the investigator will often be faced with a nexus that might be solved either by positing
a secondary, analogical change (([a] >) [b] ≻ [b] ~ [c]) in the wake of a similar
primary change ([b] > [b] ~ [c]) or by positing one unitary change ([a] > [b] >
[b] ~ [c]) to the tune of a special shafting hypothesis; and it is not clear which
solution (if either) is the correct one.

Pretty much exactly this quandary arises for Aramaic, in association with
the weakening of 9 to ʔ, at least for CP and the Low Eastern dialects TL and
M. Take the case of b-phd dissimilation 9 . . . 9 > ʔ . . . 9 discussed earlier
(§9.1.3). When the change targets the 1√9 of a causative verb, the question
arises whether the resulting 1√ʔ should be further changed to a semivowel by

car (§9.2.1.2). But the inventory of dialects clearly affected by the dissimilation (TR, CP, G, SR, M) is properly included in the inventory of those clearly
affected by car (B, P, N, TR, CP, SM, G, SR, TL, M), which suggests that the
dissimilation was chronologically posterior to, and therefore would have come
along too late to feed, car, with the consequence that the semblance of such
feeding might rather mean that a secondary, analogical reprise was actually
involved. However, if the dissimilation can be shafted back to an early enough
stage, feeding of the actual car might be possible after all.

For the sake of orderliness, it will be the policy of this book to "decide"
such matters, all else being equal, in favor of the secondary, analogical alternative. However, the fact must never be lost sight of that this may turn out in any
given case to be a bogus solution.

With these qualifications in mind on the confidence level of the solution, let
us consider some secondary, analogical reprises in the wake of *9* weakening to
?, beginning with the pair of changes just mentioned, the dissimilation *9 . . . 9*
> *? . . . 9* and car.

When CP dissimilated √9r9 to √?r9 the resulting causative of the verb,
?a?rá9, was changed to [ōrá9] / [ōré9] (§12.2 n. 11 for the possible [e]) (<?wr9>
'occurrit', Sl 19) on the analogy of such primary-derived verbs as [ōvéð]
(<?wBD> 'perdidit', Sl 1), with original root *√?bd. (Observe that various other
9-weakening dialects with √?r9 < √9r9 fail to show this effect because they fail
to field their √?r9 in the cau, notably the E varieties SR and M.)

It may be noteworthy that the two dialects that have most thoroughly degutturalized, SM and M, do not reprise car in the wake of *9 > ?*. Contrast original
*√? <aukil> 'he fed' (Macm 299) and its car-derived *? > w [okkél] (← *owkél*,
§11.2 with n. 17) over against original *9 <adia> 'he brought over' (lc) [addí]
or [āðí]; similarly, SM *? <yyKl> 'er wird zu essen geben' and its car-derived
*? > y t[yíkɑl] (Macs 178) over against earlier *9 (< **h*, §9.2.4, no **9* examples having come to light) <y9Km> ~ <yḥKm> 'er belehrt' t[yákkəm][31]
(Macs 173).

Results similar to that with CP vis-à-vis car might be seen with TL vis-à-
vis sar (§9.2.1.2): *√9md (< **√Rmd via ufb, §9.1.3) <lymwD> 'he'll dive'
(Mar 88*) [lēmÚð] with *9 > ? > y* on the analogy of such original *√? verbs
as <TyKwl> 'you'll eat' (Mar 38) [tēxÚl] with sar-derived *? > y*. Once again,
SM fails to level the relevant *√9 and *√? paradigms—contrast the near minimal pairs *9 <y9BD> t[yébbǎd] ~ [yébbɑd] 'er tut' (Macs 172) and *? <y?BD>
t[yíbɑd] 'geht verloren' (Macs 176).[32] In M *9 <nibad> 'he does' and *?
<nimar>. 'he says', t[níββad] and t[nímmar] (M 91) ergo [nibbáð] and [nim-
már], the dialect shows its failure to deploy sar with the result that *?C', *9C'
> ?C' rga > [C'C'].

When *9 > ? affects 3√, we might wonder whether the results are further leveled to the wide-spread Aramaic merger of * 3√? And * 3√y inflections, dating
back as early as I (adn, §9.1.4)—an effect recognizable as *r-adn*.

Though 3√9 > ʔ in TL is sporadic at best, there are attested forms showing that the results may be analogically reshaped as if adn had applied: e.g.,
<PD9wh> ~ <PDywh> 'they wounded him' (Mar 150*), the former variant
bespeaking either conservative [paddə̆9ṹh] or etymologically spelt [paddə̆ʔṹh],
and the latter variant spelling clearly bespeaking analogically reshaped
[paddə̆yṹh].

The two pervasively degutturalizing dialects react differently, M showing
variable reshaping and SM showing none. In M, for instance, <šmatun> 'ye
heard' (Macm 286) looks like a *√9 form whose 9 has contact-assimilated
either to the suffix ([šə̆mattón]) or to the 2 ([šə̆māTón]), while the variant
<š(a)maitun> (lc) rather clearly has been reshaped to 3√y by a reprise of adn to
[šə̆meyTón]; cf. <qraitun> 'ye called' (*√ʔ) or <huaitun> 'ye were' (*√y). SM
on the other hand shows no overlapping: <šm9twn> t[šǽmǽtton] 'habt gehört'
(Macs 135) vs., e.g., <hwyTwn> t[ābíton] 'ihr waret' (Macs 203).

9.2.4. The Voiceless Pharyngeal Fricative / Tense Pharyngeal Glide ḥ

*ḥ, the most change-resistant guttural, nevertheless shows some propensity
to weaken in either of two ways: by laxing to 9, to be called *voiceless pharyngeal laxing* (vpl) (spottily in CP, perhaps more frequently in G, robustly in
SM); or by depharyngealizing to h, *voiceless pharyngeal glottalization* (vpg),
(at least incipiently in TL, full throttle in M).[33]

Turning first to vpl, CP shows <šB9> 'mehrte sich' (Sg 19), while in G
we find <rT9> 'boil', <9zm> 'trim' (Kutscher 1976: 3f.), <nD9wK> 'we will
mock' (ib 73). Apart from the massive degutturalization characteristic of SM,
a phenomenon in which vpl may have been a contributing subprocess, more
direct evidence for vpl may be seen, orthographically, in the preponderance of
<9> for expected <ḥ> (e.g., <G9nT> ~ <GhnT> 'sie beugte sich' (Macs 173),
<w9rBw> ~ <wḥrBw> 'und vernichteten' (Macs 146)) and, phonetically, in
the frequent trad pron of *ḥ as [9] initially preceding a low vowel (n. 28): e.g.,
<9mh> ~ <ḥmh> t[9ā́mɑ] 'sah', <ḥsK> t[9ā́sɑk] 'verweigerte' (Macs 171).

Weakening of ḥ by depharyngealization to h (vpg) rather than by laxation
to 9 is the path taken by TL, at least inchoatively (e.g., <lhDr> ~ <nhDr> 'he'll
restore' (Mar 106*), root *√hðr), and fully in M: e.g., <hza> m[hézā] 'he saw'
(Macm 87, 571), <tigihkun> 'ye'll laugh' (DM 81) and m[géhex] 'he laughed'
(Macm 562), <ptahnin> t[pə̆táhnīn] 'we opened' (Macm 86).

At times SM and M assimilate ḥ rather than, or more likely subsequent to,
weakening it. As in both dialects such assimilation is probably best viewed as
part and parcel of a larger, general degutturalization pattern not limited to *ḥ,
and as such will be discussed in its own section below (§9.3.2), only a handful
of examples will be presented here. For M, contrast weakened but unassimilated <ptahnun> t[pə̆táhnun] 'we opened them' with (rga-)assimilated <ptanH>
t[pə̆tánnī] 'we opened it' (Macm 86) < *pataḥníh where orthography and trad

pron agree; and <plah> t[pɔ̌lä̃]'served' (Macm 87; loss in this case by apo-copating advocalic assimilation, hap, §9.2.2), where only trad pron manifests the assimilation. (M may also variably merge this 3√H-depharyngealized lex-eme to 3√/y/ status via r-adn, §9.1.4; see §17.18.1 M.) For SM, <yḥKmwn> t[yēkkä̃mon] 'sie wissen' (Macs 172). Note that, for this dialect, evidence for assimilation resides solely in the traditional pronunciation.

It was earlier seen (§9.2.1.2 n. 26) how groups composed of *ʔ/h* and *V̆* some-times act in a special way. As it turns out, M also shows a few comparable cases of *ḥ* and *V̆*, though it is likely that *ḥ* had already weakened to *h* when these changes took place. Apheresis: <ṣub> (cf. also §17.33 n. 159) alternating with non-apherized <ḥṣub> ~ <ḥṣab> 'they shrank' (DM 151) < *ḥɔ̌ṣávū (to the tune of general or infixing apocope, §17.9); hypheresis: <ašlan> t[äšlan] 'he drew me out' ~ intact <ašlhan> t[äšlɔ̌han] (Macm 83) < *hašliḥánī (again to the tune of apocope and various other processes).

9.3. Special Topics

9.3.1. Proclivity of Gutturals Toward Vowels

As we have seen several times in the foregoing pages, the relative lability of gutturals frequently leads to their deletion, and this in turn is often accompa-nied by compensatory lengthening of an immediately preceding vowel—and in the case of SM trad pron, even of an immediately following vowel (see §4.3 with n. 18). This phenomenon arguably instantiates a special proclivity toward vowels; and we have incidentally witnessed other manifestations of such a proclivity as well, notably the tendency of onset *ʔ* to catalyze promotion of nucleic *V̆* to *V̊* (§9.2.1.2). Elsewhere in the book, also, this general tendency is manifested—for instance, in various epenthetic processes where gutturals play a prime catalytic role in inducing vowel insertion (especially excresecence, §4.3).

There is a tendency for *ʔ, and to a lesser extent *9, in anlaut position, es-pecially in the sim impa, to catalyze promotion of an immediately following *V̆* to *V̊*. Evidence may be found for this process as early as B, again for TR (with some reservations to be aired below), and then for all subsequent dialects save CP and SM—these two being to date moot because the nature of CP and SM orthography leaves us in the lurch, in addition to which what might be testimony for the process in SM trad pron is overlaid by the later, SM-specific process-tandem c-prm^c-pra turning all instances of pretonic *V̆* into *V̄* (§22.1 (22B)).

In B, the process seems at first blush to be rampant in the Babylonian reg-ister and triggered not only by *ʔ and *9 but by *h as well. However, closer examination makes it likely that this pattern merely reflects the fact that the supralinear pointing system had (with one possible exception) no symbols for chromatic (ḥatuf) [V̆] and accordingly borrowed the <V> points to represent them:[34] thus, e.g., bb<ˀæzǽl> 'ging' (Dan 2:17) corresponding to tb<ˀǎzal> (BL 139) need not represent [ˀæzǽl] but might just as well be a way of writing [ˀǽzǽl]—and will in fact be so interpreted (§17.23.3). However, sublinear forms like the homoparadigmatic impa <ˀezel> 'geh!' (BL §18p, §44k) suggest that B did in fact occasionally promote V̊, at least following ˀ. (This does not preclude the possibility that Bab B really did evince postguttural promotion under circumstances wider than those obtaining for Tib B; it rather renders the question largely moot. See §17.23.3 for specific interpretations in this regard.)

The first-blush situation in TR is similar to that in B, the supralinear vocalization again making it largely uncertain whether a given token of <V̊> should be interpreted as [V̊] (or even [V̄]) postgutturally promoted from V̆, or whether as [V̆] itself, not promoted but merely colored (sco, §17.23) in a way not captured by the all-purpose schwa point (transliterated <ə̆>) afforded by the prevailing orthography. However, since Sabbionetan TR is written in sublinear, Tiberian orthography, a form like <ˀeyhey> (Da 354; 1s impf of √hwy, 2√w dropped by wdr, §17.32) suggests unambiguously promoted [ˀehḗ], while a form like sb<9iyBeD> 'tue!' (Da 93) might likewise seem to suggest an unambiguously promoted 1ʃ interpretation like [9ivéð] or [9īvéð] but for the fact that not even the sublinear orthography has a point for [ĭ], for which rather the basic vowel point <i> was likely pressed into service (§17.23.3). In fact, overall patterning suggests that sublinearly written TR may have occasionally deployed the basic vowel point <æ> even for [ǎ] (in addition to its use for [ǽ]) despite availability and reasonably frequent use of <ǎ> (hataf patah). [35] Though the evidence is thus anything but conclusive, it will be assumed that TR does in fact undergo anlaut-guttural induced promotion, specifically /#(ˀ,9)__; see §17.23.3.

Scrutiny of the G examples presented in Da 276–78, 300 reveals that in pertinent sim impas 4 out of 7 ms forms show ml <y> /#<ˀ>__ (e.g., <ˀyz(y)l> 'geh!' vs. <ˀmwr> 'sag!'), as do 2 out of 7 /#<9>__ (e.g., <9yBD> 'tu!' vs. its alternant <9BD>), while the lone instance /#<h>__ shows no ml for 1ʃ (<hryB> 'zerstöre!'). On this basis, it will be surmised that G underwent promotion under conditions similar to those assumed for TR (and subject to the same reservations). Likewise for TL, on the basis of the little evidence gleanable from Mar 38f, 54 (e.g., <9yByD> 'do!', perhaps best interpretable as promoted [9i̊véð] despite the fact that both Morag and Margolis provide solely unpromoted realizations: [9ǎ̆véð] Mor 131, [9ǎvéð] Mar 145*—Morag notes the fact 44) that 1ʃ <y> appears in printed editions of the Talmud (bidfusim)).

The cases of SR and M are special, in that both these dialects end up losing ˀ completely, M in addition losing 9. Both dialects show evidence of prm /#*ˀ__, while only M promotes /#*9__ as well.[36] This might be interpreted as: either SR promoting exclusively /#*ˀ__, like B, and M more widely /#(*ˀ,*9)__, like TR, G, and TL; or both dialects exclusively /#ˀ__, but M only after *9 > ˀ. In either event, a simple family-tree account of prm /#H__ will be excluded, the neat assumption of early /#ʔ__ (B) expanding to later /#(ʔ,9)__ (TR, G, TL) being discomfited at least by SR retaining conservative /#ʔ__.[37] (For the color of the promoted vowel, which in the sim impa reflects the original 1ʃ–2ʃ ablaut—unconditionally in SR, conditionally in M—, see §17.23.3.)

There is one puzzling feature of prm /#H__. Of two a priori prime candidates, peninitially stressed sim pf and sim impa forms with 1√*ʔ or √*9, why is the actual process overwhelmingly limited to the impa in all the dialects?[38]

Another manifestation of guttural proclivity toward vowels in Aramaic is the tendency, registered since B but likely to have present earlier though disguised by unrevealing orthography, for a postvocalic geminate $\mathring{V}H'H'$ to shorten to the tune of compensatory lengthening of the vowel—that is, > $\bar{V}H'$. The process is actually partially independent of vowels in that some gutturals—especially tense ḥ, h—often shorten without compensation—that is, > $\mathring{V}H'$. The focus of the process is also frequently wider than gutturals, subsuming the liquid r. The resulting natural class may be characterized as *low consonant*, symbolized "L," which also constitutes the set of conditioners for the process of *lowering* (§17.10). Comprehensively, then, $\mathring{V}L'L' > \mathring{V}L'$, to be called *medial low shortening* (mls). Some examples: B [bōríx] 'er lobte' (BL 58) < *barríka ($\mathring{V}L'L'$ > $\bar{V}L'$), [yǝvahǎhalunnánī] 'sie schrecken mich' (BL 59) < *yibahhalunnánī ($\mathring{V}L'L'$ > $\mathring{V}L'$); TR [bāréx] 'er lobte' (Da 92) ($\mathring{V}L'L'$ > $\bar{V}L'$), [ʔittæḥǽl] 'er wurde entweiht' < *hittaḥḥála ($\mathring{V}$ 2√L'L' > $\mathring{V}$ 2√L'; for the formation, see §3.2 (3M)— however, in cases like this where $\mathring{V}$ does not lengthen and where the prevailing orthography resists marking <H> for gemination, a -mls interpretation cannot be ruled out, and such dubious cases in the book at large will be transcribed along the lines of [ʔittæh(ḥ)ǽl]); in CP and G, orthography disguises likely effects of mls; in SM, the wholesale loss of gutturals and prosodic revamping via smc (§22.1 (22B)) make it impossible to say concerning $\mathring{V}H'H'$, but according to trad pron $\mathring{V}rr$ remains unscathed, e.g., <BrK> t[bǽrrǝk] 'segnete' (Macs 156); while SR appears in general to limit the process to $\mathring{V}H'H' > \mathring{V}H'$ (though the orthography by itself has no way of indicating the $H'H' > H'$ part), the Nestorian register occasionally shows $\mathring{V}rr > \bar{V}r$ (Ns 14);[39] as for TL, though its (unvocalized) orthography makes it per se impossible to know, the trad pron of the Yemenis (Mor 145) appears to converge enough with the Ashkenazic trad pron tacitly informing Margolis's representations (in Mar) to suggest that TL did in fact undergo some form of mls (cf. Malone 1998b), e.g., y&a [qĀréviθ] (Mor 118, Mar 161*) 'I offered', without compensation y&a [niṣtA9Ár] (§10 TL), -mls y[ʔi99ǒṣívū] 'hit9acvu' (mor 376) (Yem trad pron only, Ash invariantly showing +mls, [ʔi9ǎṣívū] (Mar 149*)); in M, though $\mathring{V}rr$ remains unaltered in both the Modern vernacular and trad pron (e.g., [bárrex] 'he blessed', Macm 264), trad pron shows vacillation in $\mathring{V}hh$ (< *$\mathring{V}hh$ or *$\mathring{V}ḥḥ$, §9.2.4, both *$\mathring{V}ʔʔ$ and *$\mathring{V}99$ showing apl > *$\mathring{V}yy$, §9.1.2) between uncompensated shortening (e.g., [néhoθ] (Macm 106) < *neḥḥóθ 'he'll descend') and no change at all (e.g., [áhheθ] < ʔaḥḥéθ 'he brought down').[40]

9.3.2. Profiles of Degutturalization

Following the deuvularizations $X > ḥ$, $R > 9$ of the I period and earlier ((r-) ufb, §9.1.3), Aramaic was left with four gutturals: ḥ, 9, h, ʔ. In the preceding pages of this chapter, various subsequent weakenings and losses of these four segments have been documented for the ensuing dialects, and it was at several spots mentioned that two of these varieties, SM and M, come close to losing the gutturals altogether. In effect, each had effectively reduced the original sextet of gutturals to one: 9 in SM and h in M. Moreover, even these two segments were in jeopardy. This was especially so in SM, where 9 only lingered in anlaut position under restricted conditions (n. 28); and while h was securer in M, it was nevertheless subject to loss by contact assimilation (§9.2.2), notably by spreading either from an immediately preceding vowel ($V̊h\# > V̊\#$ (hap), $V̊hC > V̊C$ (aga)) or from an immediately following consonant ($V̊hC' > V̊C'C'$ (rga)).

As it turns out, though degutturalization (dgt) in SM and M is unquestionable, all other post-TR dialects also participate in varying degrees, as portrayed in the six developmental displays in (9F).[41] Note that displays (i) and (iii) present conservative-radical pairs of what might be called primarily *(guttural) laxing* dialects (gtl) (i) and primarily *depharyngealizing* dialects (dpr) (iii). Observe that SM follows up its primary laxing strategy (step (γ)) with depharyngealization as secondary (step (δ)); and that at least four dialects, cutting across the (i)–(iii) divide and including the otherwise wholly conservative SR (ii), lose ʔ (by adr, step (β)).[42]

These degutturalization strategies appear to fall out rather neatly in sync with the dialect groupings assumed in this book (§19 (19F)). The laxing varieties (i) are the Western dialects, while the depharyngealizing pair (iii) comprises the Low subdivision of the Eastern group.[43]

(9F) (i) **laxing (gtl) dialects**

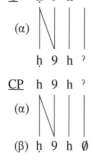

(ii) <u>SR</u>   ḥ h 9 ʔ

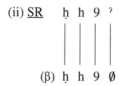

(β) ḥ̊ h 9 Ø

(iii) **depharyngealizing (dpr) dialects**

TL   ḥ h 9 ʔ

(δ)

ḥ̊ h 9 ʔ

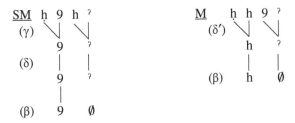

(α) Variable pharyngeal laxing ([+tense, +RTR] > [-tense, +RTR])
(β) Loss of ⁷ (adr)
(γ) Categorical laxing ([+tense] > [-tense])
(δ) Variable depharyengealization ([+RTR] > [-RTR])
(δ′) Categorical depharyngealization ([+RTR] > [-RTR])

Notes to §9

[1] "Major," i.e., excluding the uvular fricatives *X and *R, which are treated briefly in §9.1.3.

[2] The structural description of ads might also fit the √⁷ *⁷-causative pf and imp, predicting, e.g., pf 3ms *⁷a- 1√⁷SáMa > [⁷áSáMa]. However, no relevant forms are attested. (As we will see in §9.1.2, the early dialects preferred the *h-causative in anlaut position.)

[3] M cau impf forms like <neiasbrak> 'wir belehren dich', as opposed to such as <nalb(i)šak> 'er bekleidet dich' (Nm 273), are taken in this book to reflect transparentation (§15.3.1.1) by extension of the simple-conjugational prefixes with shape *(C)Ǐ-* —*impf prefix strengthening* (ips)—into the derived conjugations, even prevocalically as here: hence [nī(y)asbə̆ráx] with prefixal vowel lengthening and where [y] if present is a hiatus breaker (what might be called *yā⁷u 'l-waṣl*), or possibly [niyyasbə̆ráx] with gemination of the post-prefixal consonant. On the other hand, forms like <nalb(i)šak> [nalbə̆̄šáx] are viewed as conservative by virtue of escaping transparentation. However, it is conceivable that the judgment of conservatism should be reversed, <neiasbrak> instantiating retention of an earlier impf prefix vowel in something (after bridge formation, §2.3.2) like *ni-ha-sbir-ák* 1p-sub-cau-LEARN-2ms.obj—while more frequently the prefix vowel was lost along with the h, possibly after this had shifted to ⁷, leading ultimately to the like of [nalbə̆̄šáx] (plausibly by ə̆⁷V′ > V′ via sad, §9.2.1.2, upon prior reduction of the prefix vowel to schwa). And whichever the correct view might turn out to be, it is interesting to observe that there appear to be statistical biases in the distribution of [-ī(y)a-]/[-iyya-] vs. [-a-] prefixes. The former is overwhelmingly favored in 1s (qua [ī(y)a-/[iyya-] with ⁷ unconditionally lost by adr, §9.2.1.1), makes a rather impressive appearance in 3m/1p [nī(y)a-]/[niyya-] (for 3m *n-*, see §17.19), and shows at least three instances in 2 or 3fs [tī(y)a-]/[tiyya-]—corpus count from Mal 550–74.

[4] For an insightful generativer perspective on several of these dissimilations, notably for SR, see Boas 1993.

[5] For more detail on this chain, see n. 7 below. This chain simplifies out at least two complications: (a) that r-ufb starts as a *variable* process, most clearly in I, and (b) that the demise of [R] must coexist with the survival of <q> as variable historical

spelling for [9] < R, most perspicuously in M where <arqa> 'earth' is always tradition-ally pronounced [ara] (Macm 54) betraying degutturalization < ˀar9ắ or ˀarRắ (it is a regularity of Classical spelling – to – traditional pronunciation relation in M that when-ever the result of any *x > y is spelled <x ~ y>, traditional and Modern pronunciations both yield exclusively [y'], where [y'] = [y] or patent development thereof). <q> also once spells what is taken to be [R] qua reflex of *ð̣ in B, <ˀar:qɔˀ> (Jer 10:11); the fact that the Masoretes failed to flag this form as kĕtiv for kĕrey [ˀar9ɔ̃́]/[ˀarRɔ̃́] admittedly weakens the hypothesis, accepted in this book, of historical spelling.

[6] (a) Brockelmann also lists Jacobite [eháð] 'gedachte' for expected @[9šháð] (as in Nestorian), but this would seem to be a case of assimilation, *9. . .h > ˀ. . . =h (> ∅. . .h*, §9.2.1.1), *h* and *ˀ* both being laryngeal (glottal).

(b) A third p-phd verb is often assumed, *√mXð̣, qua etymon of /mḥˀ/ 'strike': √mXð̣ > √mḥð̣ > √mḥR > √mḥ9 > √mḥˀ. However, since the root is attested with 3√ˀ As early as O, and O shows no trace of the crucial step *R > 9*, consistently spelling as it does *R* (< ð̣) with <q>, the complex of events assumed in this book forces agreement with Degen, who rejects the derivation of √mḥ from *√mXð̣ (De 42; see also De 36f (<q> spelling reflexes of ð̣) and 72 (sim pf 3mp <mḥˀw> ≠ @<mḥqw>)).

(c) There exist various possibilities as to why b-phd fails to apply in a given dia-lect: (*) b-phd simply does not target that dialect; (*) some subtle structural condition is wanting; (*) b-phd is lexically (variably) codetermined. A case in point where this question arises is I sim impf 1s^3ms <ˀrḥ9h> (≠ @<ˀrḥˀh>) (§7.1, assuming the root √rḥ9 < *√rḥð̣).

[7] (a) While there is no M verb based on this root, M reflexes of *√QˀM and *√Q9M (including < **√QRM) might in general be interpreted as *either* straightforward pho-netic developments in the wake of *degutturalization* (dgt) *or* as realignments with the hollow-geminate gizra (§6.2.2.1) doubtless catalyzed by a critical amount of phonetic convergence with this gizra. In either case, there is to judge by Modern M cognates a special twist to developments in the simple pf. (Relevant forms for all are adduced on Macm 329–31.) To start with the general pattern, note simple impf 3ms <nišul> 'he asks' interpretable as [neššól] *whether* straightforwardly ← neš ˀól by degutturalization to the tune of adconsonantal assimilation (spreading from š; pga, §9.2.1.1 n. 14b) *or* ⇐ /ne-ššol/ built by gmf-4u (§3.2 (3M))—or indeed plausibly by both, the convergent result of degutturalization catalyzing restructuring to geminate. The case of 3mp^3ms <nišilunH> 'they ask him' involves distinct phonetic interpretations: *on the one hand* [neššɔ̃lonnĩ] *whether* ← neš ˀɔ̃lonnĩ by dgt or ⇐ /ne-ššol-onn-ī / by gmf-4u, but *on the other hand* alternatively [nīšellonnĩ] qua geminate by gmf-4m (§3.2 (3N)) ⇐ /ne-šlol-onn-ī / via s-red^s-auf (§4.2, §4.4). Simple impa <šul> 'roga!' as [šól] either by sad, §9.2.1.2, ← šɔ̃ˀól or ⇐ /šoll/ via gmf-2u with degemination (§3.1 (3Fvii), §3.2 (3I)). In the case of the intensive, <šaiil> 'he asked' as [šeyyél] either by dgt via apl, §9.2.1.2, and vowel assimilation from ša ˀˀél, or qua hollow-pattern realization of the gem-hol gizra.

(b) While in the gem-hol gizra verbs of the sim pf largely maintain their original gem or hol shapes, thus 3fs *gem [QaMMáθ] but *hol [QāMáθ], to judge by the pronun-ciation of the Modern cognates (Macm 331) superposed on the Classical orthographic forms (Macm 329), the M sim pf reflexes of *√QˀM, *√Q9M turn out to be effective gem-hol portmanteaus, thus 3fs [QāMMáθ]. Following Malone 1989c, such a result follows from four assumptions based on autosegmental representation of the forms: (*) that degutturalization removes a segment (e.g., $^{?}$) but not the skeletal position of that segment; (*) that, following Levin 1985, skeletal positions are devoid of any segmental bias, thus undifferentiated X rather than C vs. V; (*) that the dangling skeletal position may then be refitted with a new segment by spreading to an adjacent segment; and (*) that in fact, under phonotactically enabling conditions, the spreading may be to both adjacent segments simultaneously. Thus (using representations simplified by the omission of syllabic nodes above the skeleton):

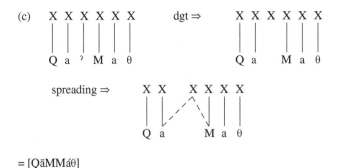

(c) X X X X X X   dgt ⇒   X X X X X X

        Q a ? M a θ   Q a   M a θ

    spreading ⇒   X X   X X X X

                    Q a   M a θ

= [QāMMáθ]

The result in (c) is not, it might be noted, general for M, there being other lexemes/ paradigms calling for spreading either leftward alone or rightward alone; e.g., to judge by trad pron of orthographic forms, <šimat> t[šímat] 'she heard', <šmanin> t[ššmánnīn] 'we heard' (Macm 92), respectively [šímáθ] ⇐ |šiØmáθ|, with rightward spreading from |i|, and |ššmaØnĭn|, with leftward spreading from |n|. (Here, "Ø" stands for the position of the deleted guttural as determined by the skeletal X. In the case of |šiØmáθ|, the guttural 3√ has metathesized prior to deletion; for details, Malone 1985 and n. 14b below.)

[8] (a) One more note on $R > g$. Since at least M gives evidence of another sort of dissimilation involving target g, viz. dissimilation of the emphatic sequences $q. . .t̞$, $t̞. . .q$ to $g. . .t̞$, $t̞. . .g$—call it *emphatic dissimilation* (eds)—(√gt̞l 'kill', √gt̞r 'tie', √lgt̞ 'grasp'), the fact that <g> spells the changeling segment in both $R > g$ and eds may have some unrecognized significance. (eds may also target some other sequences; e.g., $q. . .s̞ \rightarrow q. . .s$, §6.3.) (b) It is traditionally held that eds was preceded in the history of Aramaic by an antipodal process, which might be called *emphatic assimilation* (eas), by dint of which, e.g., proto-Semitic √qtl > later A √qt̞l (only Y and O maintain the unassimilated root shape √qt̞l; Kutscher 1970: 59).

[9] (a) The stage changes portrayed in (b) provide a more systemic view of the major shifts described in this section, plus a few others (e.g., occlusion, §17.14) to better sharpen the profiles of the developing system. A change symbolized as $X ⫸ Y$ means that some Xs remain in the system, while $(X) ⫸ Y$ conveys that all Xs have shifted to Y. Note the persistent effect of adn on stages VI^VII; it seems likely that r-ufb and adn overlapped in I, where both appear as variable processes, becoming (asymptotically) categorical only in the later dialects. (For the topology of the cross-sections, cf. §20.1 (20A).)

(b)

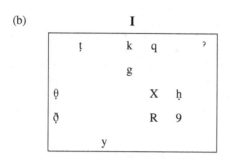

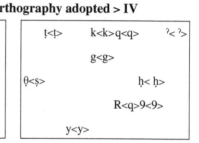

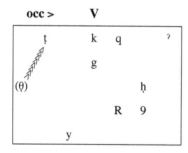

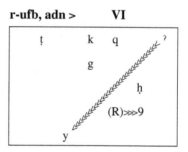

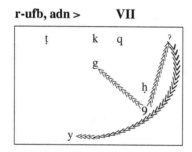

(c) It is striking, and at first pass unsettling, that in apparently all instances of phd, b-phd, and f-phd alike, one of the two 9s involved in the dissimilation derives through *R (by r-ufb) from **ð̱ (by shp), usually as dissimilandum but in two cases as dissimilans ($\sqrt{}$ʾr9 < *$\sqrt{}$9r in several dialects, and $\sqrt{}$9lʾ < *$\sqrt{}$ð̣l9 in G though SR shows the usual flow with $\sqrt{}$ʾl9 < *$\sqrt{}$ð̣l9). Why are there seemingly no instances of an 9 deriving from original **9 (vacuously) or from original **R (by primary ufb)? The knee-jerk response to this uneasy situation is to essay reformulation of the dissimilations in terms of either ð̣ itself of its shp-derivative R. Several such attempts, however, have either turned out to be untenable or at best entailed implausible and unduly complex conditions. I suspect that the seemingly invariant involvement of **ð̣ is, au fond, coincidental—a judgment offhand supported by reexamination of the corpus presented above plus perusal of all the 1$\sqrt{}$ʾ And 1$\sqrt{}$9 entrees in Brockelmann 1928. Defense of this position goes along the following lines: A dissimilating root disconfirming the **ð̣ -factor as sketched would have to assume of the original shapes listed in (d):

(d)   (i)   **$\sqrt{}$RRM   (ii)   **$\sqrt{}$99M
        (iʹ)   **$\sqrt{}$QRR   (iiʹ)   **$\sqrt{}$Q99
        (iʺ)   **$\sqrt{}$RSR   (iiʺ)   **$\sqrt{}$9S9

        (iii)   **$\sqrt{}$R9M, **$\sqrt{}$RXM, **$\sqrt{}$RḥM, **$\sqrt{}$9RM, **$\sqrt{}$9XM, **$\sqrt{}$9ḥM
        (iiiʹ)   **$\sqrt{}$QR9, **$\sqrt{}$QRX, **$\sqrt{}$QRḥ, **$\sqrt{}$Q9R, **$\sqrt{}$Q9X, **$\sqrt{}$Q9ḥ
        (iiiʺ)   **$\sqrt{}$RS9, **$\sqrt{}$RSX, **$\sqrt{}$RSḥ, **$\sqrt{}$9SR, **$\sqrt{}$9SX, **$\sqrt{}$9Sḥ

However, *none* of these shapes appear to be attested in extant Aramaic corpora. This result is immediately predictable for (i, ii) inasmuch as roots with identical 1$\sqrt{}$ and 2$\sqrt{}$ are alien to ancient Semitic or extremely rare at best. And while the shapes of (iʹ, iiʹ) at first blush seem to be unexceptionable, it will be recalled from §3 that roots with identical 2$\sqrt{}$ and 3$\sqrt{}$ are fundamentally *biradical*, so that $\sqrt{}$QRR and $\sqrt{}$Q99 are more accurately represented as $\sqrt{}$QR and $\sqrt{}$Q9, in which case dissimilation is preempted by default of one crucial radical. As concerns (iii, iiiʹ), shapes like this are predicted to be rare on the basis of Semitic's general dispreference for excessively similar adjacent radicals (Greenberg 1950), similarity being reckoned in terms of shared features, in which case (iii, iiiʹ) default by presenting adjacent pairs of articulatorily close uvulars (R, X) and pharyngeals (9, ḥ). And coming finally to the shapes in (iʺ, iiʺ, iiiʺ), none of these seem to be attested either, whether due to scantiness of available corpus or for violation of some subtler restriction targeting cooccurrent uvular/pharyngeal radicals even when separated by another consonant (2$\sqrt{}$). In sum and on balance, the primary reason for the apparent constant involvement of **ð̣ in phd would stem from the fact that ð̣, qua dentoalveolar, is featurewise sufficiently distant from its uvular/pharyngeal partner. (None of the preceding should, incidentally, be viewed as incompatible with the fact that shp and ufb subsequently create some of the shapes ruled here as marginal or marked. On the other hand, however, phd then proceeds in many cases to reduce the tension by lessening the offensive similarity induced by shp/ufb—such reduction being arguably the prime driving force behind dissimilation at large.)

(e) The cited perusal of Brockelmann 1928 produced some interesting results as byproducts: (*) Consider that at one stage in its derivation, SR [ɛ9ap] (above in the text, under (α)) would have triggered one of the shape configurations considered above to be Semitic-alien, specifically (dii) $\sqrt{}$99M: $\sqrt{}$ð̣9p shp > $\sqrt{}$R9p ufb > $\sqrt{}$99p, subsequently dissimilated (b-phd) to $\sqrt{}$ʾ9p. Since $\sqrt{}$99p instantiates an unstable configuration for Aramaic above and beyond providing a structural description for b-phd, it is perhaps not surprising that the language (SR, in this case) has provided alternative repair strategies for the investment of this uneasy configuration in the sim pf: reshaping to the *geminate* gizra ([9ap] 'duplicare', Brockelmann 1928: 537) and, alternatively, to the *hollow* gizra ([9ɔ̌p] 'duplicare', ibid., 517). The geminate solution is also adopted in the case of **⁹aðada 'pampinare', which ends up in SR as [9að] (ibid., 511). (*) Though it is hard to be sure because of the variability of phd (n. 6 above), prima facie when dissimilans and dissimilandum reside in different conjuncts of reduplicated *QaMQɛM* quadriradicals (§1 n. 8), phd stalls: [9al9ɛl] 'flatu dissipare', [9aw9ī] 'vagire' (ibid., 525, 514, 516).

[10] In all dialects, the influence of *3√y is dominant over that of *3√ʔ, though again many (perhaps all) dialects show evidence of *3√ʔ-effects as well; e.g., TR sim impa ms^3fs tb[qɔ̌rɑ́hɑ̄](Da 391), plausibly < *qirɑ́ʔha. See also n. 14b below and §8.1.2 (α).

[11] Note, e.g., the preservation of 3√ʔ In <wymḥʔhy> 'vĕyakehu' in the 8th century B.C.E. Bukān inscription (Steiner 2000–2001: 240).

[12] On balance, the most likely (or least unlikely) hypothesis on <bayaʔ> and kindred runs along the lines of (a), where two homoparadigmatic forms are included (and concerning which the reader may easily verify that the *entire* paradigm cited at Ns 109 also falls into line):

(a)		*bayyíʔa (*3ms*)	*bayyiʔát (*3fs*)	*bayyíʔū (*3mp*)
I:	*sap,low,red,spr*	bayyá ʔ	bayyɔ̌ʔɑ́θ	bayyɑ́ʔū
II:	*adn dissimilatorily resisted in roots of shape √Qyʔ*	bayyá ʔ	bayyɔ̌ʔɑ́θ	bayyɑ́ʔū
III:	*sad, r-adr (the latter too late to feed the systemic rounding (a > ɔ̌,§20.2(δ)) following up (primary) adr)*	bayyɑ́	bayyɑ́θ	bayyɑ́ū
IV:	*r-e-cnd*	bayyɑ́	bayyɑ́θ	bayyɑ́w
V:	*lap (too late!)*	[bayyɑ́]	[bayyɑ́θ]	[bayyɑ́w]

The <ʔ> in the orthographic representation of such forms is courtesy of historical spelling.

[13] (c) Though SM gives the appearance of advocalic assimilation in forms like <ʔT(ʔ)mr> t[ētɑ́mɑr] 'wurde gesagt' (Macs 153) < *hitʔamíra, the same result is given by the likelier derivation from intermediate (and possibly living SM) (ʔ)iθ(ʔ)ămár via smc (§22.1 (22B)) involving inter alia promotion of ă to a (c-prm) followed by stress shift (c-pen) and tonic lengthening (c-pra); and in that event, the loss of ʔ might have been by uncompensated deletion antedating smc—as is assumed in the derivation of this form offered in §22.2 (22C( )).

(b) While Ash TL shows advocalic assimilation (aga; see n. 14b below) of 1√ʔ in the causative of √ʔty (a[ʔɔ̌θyɔ́x]), Yem TL appears to show adconsonantal assimilation (rga, n. 14b) if forms like cau pf 3fs <ʔæTæy> of the Halaxot Pĕsukot (Mor 116 n. 121) should be interpreted as [ʔættǽy]. Morag also cites participial [mætyã̌] (Mor 280), plausibly interpretable as deriving from *mættə̌yã̌* by simplification (§17.26). In any event, replacement of √ʔ by *y* in the cau is by far the most frequent result in both traditions (car, §9.2.1.2).

(a) "ʔ contact-assimilation by assumption without a dissimilatory trigger." Sometimes another ʔ is de facto involved, and in such instances the possibility of dissimilatory triggering will remain open in default of disconfirming evidence. In the case of TL <ʔTyK> a[ʔɔθ̌ɔyɔ̌x], for example, we would need to examine the behavior of forms with other subject prefixes like 1p c<n̪TyK>—but Margolis adduces none. Note also in the case of the O hapax <ʔhBD> that the conceivable trigger ʔ would differ from that of ads (§9.1.1) in not being *local*, since in <ʔhBD> *h* intervenes (clear in the variant <ʔh̪ʔBD>).

[14] (a) "*VCʔʔV* may plausible assimilate only to *VC′C′V*." M gives the prima facie impression of *VCʔʔC > V̄C′V*, e.g., <šimat> t[šĭmat] 'she heard' (Macm 92), hence [šĭmaθ] < *šIm²áθ* < (§9.3.2) *šim9áθ*. However, M shows evidence of metathesizing a third radical guttural around the second radical in contact, *VC′ 3√H V > VHC′V*—a process to be called *radical metathesis* (rdm). In light of this, [šĭmáθ] derives immediately from *sIʔmáθ*, an unproblematic instance of advocalic assimilation. For details on rdm, see Malone 1985; cf also n. 7 above.

(b) It will be convenient to dispense some labels to distinguish among these modes of contact assimilation—with no claim, however, that two distinct labels necessarily mark two distinct processes diachronically or synchronically (e.g., *VHC′V → V̄C′V* and *VHC′V → VC′C′V* are best taken as disjuncts of one and the same synchronic rule in M; see Malone 1991). Moreover, since other gutturals sometimes assimilate in the same or similar patterns to ʔ (as we will see in later sections), most of the labels will be generalized with *H* as assimilandum. Thus, generalizing *VʔC′V* to *VHC′V*: *VHC′V → V̄C′V* will be called *advocalic guttural assimilation* (aga) (except in reference to ads, §9.1.1); *VHC′V → VC′C′V regressive guttural assimilation* (rga); *VC′HV → VC′C′V progressive guttural assimilation* (pga) (except when identified with prf, §10, which will be the case when *C′H* = rmp *T+ʔ* (or occasionally *h*)). Sometimes all three process types (or any two) will be referred to without further differentiation as *guttural assimilation* tout court (gta).

(c) Though discussion of concurrently adconsonantal and advocalic *H* has been on the frames *VHC′C, VC′HV* in order to simultaneously illustrate the involvement of either vowel, at least *VHC′#* is also an attested frame with the value *V 3√H+t#*, *t* = 1s or in the wake of apocope (sap/lap, §17.22/9) 2s. The phonetic result depends both upon the identity of 3√H (notably 3√ʔ invites → 3√y by adn, §9.1.4) and upon what sort of follow-up operation, if any, dispels the auslaut cluster *Ht* (epn in the case of 1s *t*, §17.6, exc^prm when *t* = 2s, §15.3.1.3). As concerns the possible frame *VC′H#*, no relevant forms appear to be attested in the verb, as indeed none are for the specific case *VCʔʔ#*

[15] (a) Note that [áθθī] betrays adconsonantal assimilation, hence reconstructively for the Classical language as well. ([θθ] represents root-specific lexicalization of the spirantal value, as frequently in the Modern language; Malone 1997.) On the other hand, at least Ash TL shows advocalic assimilation (a[ʔɔθ̌ɔyɔ̌x], n. 13b above).

(b) However, forms like M <atiun> might with equal right be interpreted as *intensive*. In fact, in dialects like M and also SM, the causative and intensive binyanim have the potential to become *totally* neutralized in 1√H verbs—not merely formally, but functionally as well, since the causative and intensive systematically manifest a great deal of semantic overlap, in particular in encoding causative/factitive force (frequent in int, almost universal in cau). The realization of this potential for M is dramatically underscored by Drower and Macuch, who simply conflate all int and cau forms of √ʔty into one undifferentiated listing (DM 42). The mechanics of this convergence are sketched in (c), displaying all permutations of the active verb (the passives work out in parallel fashion), adapted from §1.1.2, §1.1.3 for the √H verb. (For SM, cf., e.g., Macuch's conflated int/cau items for *√ḫðr 'zurückgehen' on Macs 173.)

(c)   **intensive**   **causative**

pf,impa *plain* HaSSiM   rga,   h+aHSiM
                              dgt→ <u>aSSIM</u>   ← dgt

            rmp h-it+HaSSaM   rga,   h-it+h+aHSaM
                              prf,   rca,
                              dgt→ <u>IttaSSaM</u> ← dgt

impf   *plain* i+HaSSiM   rga,   i+h+aHSiM
                              red+   red+
                              apl→ <u>š̌yaSSIM</u> ← apl

            i+HaSSiM   red+   aHSiM
                              dgt+
                              sad→ <u>aSSIM</u> ←rga

            rmp it+HaSSaM   rga,   it+h+aHSaM
                              prf→ <u>IttaSSaM</u> ← rca

[16] "At least formally causative," since this lexeme may (pan-Aramaically) have been metanalyzed to quadriradical √hymn.

[17] "Regularly" but perhaps not categorically; cf. the possible hapax tbᵂ<ʔæḥæ̌Diyn̈aK> 'ich fange dich' (Da 372), understandable as a sporadic instance of contact assimilation (rga, §9.2.1.1) in lieu of the usual sar. The form is interpretable as [ʔæḥ(ḥ)æ̌ðinnắx] (< ʔaʔhudinnắk).

[18] However, Müller-Kessler and Kwasman 2000 adduce for what is alleged to be TL (on an incantation bowl) <DTy̱ʔKwl> 'that you will eat' (162f.) in the same text as <DnyKwl> 'so that he will eat'; and from Standard Literary Babylonian <Dy̱ʔKl> 'so that he will eat' as well as <wy̱ʔzlwn> 'and they will go' (p. 163). They consider this to be historical spelling, but their statement that Nöldeke (Nm) adduces such from the Talmud proper is erroneous.

[19] Brockelmann (B 90) correlates jc[nēxúl]-like vs. jc[nīmár]-like behavior with what he calls (original) "transitif" vs. "intransitive status" (= "dynamic" vs. "neuter" in terms of this book, §1 n. 2) and bypasses anything like sar entirely to derive jc[ē] < ē̄ < aʔ vs. jc[ī] < ē̄ < iʔ, thus appealing to an ancient difference in prefix vowel ablaut. To the extent that he should be able to establish dynamic-neuter correlations independently, his position may be in essence correct.

[20] (a) There are two possible ways of understanding the mechanics of apl: *either* ʔ > *y*—that is, ʔ palatalizes to *y* intervocalically; *or* ʔ > ∅ > *y*—that is, ʔ is dropped intervocalically and the resulting hiatus is filled by epenthetic *y* (yāʔu 'l-waṣl). In the intensive,

the crucible par excellence for apl, change by the first hypothesis is unproblematic: for instance, bipositional alef of *QaᵖᵖIM* is simply infused with palatality so that > *QayyIM*. However, epenthetic *QaᵖᵖIM* > *QaIM* > *QayyIM* poses the interesting problem of how the epenthesized palatal emerges as geminate. Obviously it has everything to do with the canonical structure of the intensive miškal, with its hallmark geminate 2√. But if the fundamental job of apl is to break up the hiatus in *QaIM*, singleton *y* should suffice. One approach to this, modeled autosegmentally (§23.4), would take it that the ᵖᵖ-deletion making for *QaIM* targets only the melodies (segments), leaving the corresponding skeletal positions in place; and the inserted palatal consonantism automatically spreads to said skeletal positions—along these lines:

(b)

(If apl should be typologically related to the palatal instances (1√ᵖ > *y*) of car/sar (§9.2.1.2), the *first*-listed hypothesis above bids fair to be closer to the mark of what actually happened.)

(c) Looking back, it is noteworthy that there are so many instances of ᵖ > *y* in Aramaic: adn (§9.1.4), and in this section car, sar, and apl. What makes for this convergence of what at least offhand seems to be a none-too-natural process type? (It might be noted in this connection that Aramaic may likewise host instances of the reverse process, *y* > ᵖ: in the verb, partial condensation (p-cnd, §8.1) under one interpretation (whereby *VyV* loses *y* and the hiatus is resolved by ᵖ-insertion, → *VᵖV*); and in the nominal system, the widespread replacement of the adjectival + emphatic suffix complex of shape *-āy+ā* by *-ĀᵖĀ* (plausibly a special case of p-cnd).)

[21] M trad pron, despite its disposition toward phonetically realizing forms as they are spelled (Macuch's "ābāgādical pronunciation," Macm 60), consistently suppresses auslaut <h> to the tune of compensatory lengthening of the preceding vowel; e.g., <plah> t[pɔ̄lā̇] (Macm 87). Such instances of historical spelling of final <h> are rather rare to begin with.

[22] "TR and all subsequent dialects." (a) The cau rmp is not attested in Y or O, and though B evidences one form, it is built on neither *h nor *ᵖ but on the residual *š-prefix (§1.1.3 n. 9—and hence subject to metathesis with rmp *t, §10): [yištaxlɔ̄lūn] (§6.3 B). (b) SM might be a partial exception to manifesting cau rmp [tt], to judge by the trad pron of the presumed cau rmp of *√ḥzy, e.g., <yTḥzy> t[yēt̯ǟzi] 'wird erscheinen' (Macs 216), which suggests that the *th or *tᵖ cluster escaped assimilation to fall victim to SM-specific degutturalization without compensatory gemination (whether earlier e-dgt, n. 25 below, or later c-dgt, §22.1 (22Bvγ)); contrast expected cases of resolution as [tt] in <yTnDy> t[yittǽndi] 'soll gebracht werden' and <wyTwDy> t[wyittū́di] (lc). If however t[yētǟzi] and the like are actually *simple* rmps, as per a tacit, competing list given on Macs 210, derivation of the singleton t[t] would proceed unproblematically from *yiθḥāzī́* (or *yiθθǟzī́*, gtl §9.3.2) upon loss of 1√ḥ (or 1√9) (again, via (22Bvγ)).

[23] Though his wording is a bit too ambiguous to be fully certain, Duval (Du 106 n. 1 continued from p. 105) seems to say that some native SR grammarians treated the

TT resulting from rmp+cau *$t^{?}$* or *th* as what modern phonologists would call a "fake" geminate, so that it evades the principle of Geminate Integrity (§5 n. 1) in applying spr (§5.1) just to the first (rmp) *T*: *$hit^{?}aQSáM$* or *$hithaQSáM$* > [εθtaQSáM]. If this tradition should be genuine, and not merely a puristic orthoepic conceit, it poses some food-for-thought to phonological theory. Consider the following derivation fragments, for standard [εttaQSáM] (i), vs. the [εθtaQSáM] prescribed by some (ii):

	(i)		(ii)
(a)	hit+ha. . .		hit+ha. . .
(α) "+" *ignored*	hitha. . .	(α) "+" *respected*	hit+ha. . .
(β) *assimilation*	hitta. . .	(β) *assimilation* —	hit+ha
(γ) *spr*	—	(γ) *spr*	hiθ+ta. . .
	ε tta. . .]		[εθta. . .]

While in (i) at step (α) the simple morpheme boundary (+) is invisible to (ignored by) phonological rules, as is the unmarked case in languages at large, in (ii) it is respected—and as a consequence Geminate Integrity in (i) frustrates spr at step (γ) because the absence of + forces *tt* to be taken as a unit, while in (ii) the continued organicity of + marks off just the first *t* as within the pale of spr, which therefore successfully effects *t → θ*.

The problem with this is that in (ii) the organicity of + might be expected, pari passu, to inhibit assimilation at step (β). And while ways of evading this seemingly paradoxical consequence might no doubt be worked out, it is at least possible that the paradox is real, and points to the speciousness of forms like [εθtaQSáM] under the given morphophonological circumstances. If so, this case might just provide an additional example of how linguistics may serve as a tool to its sister discipline philology (Malone 1974b). (In a somewhat similar vein, linguists in recent years have been exploring the possibility of isolating so-called "linguistic viruses," patterns licensing a variety of what are strictly speaking malformations, (pseudo-)patterns often instigated (or invented) by puristic legislation (see, e.g., Sobin 1997).)

[23] Four, if CP is added on the basis of cau <?PKT> 'ea subvertit' (Sl 52) qua [applíxaT]/[appɔ̌xáT] if taken to be assimilated from *$^{?}ahpikat$*, and five, if M is added for the like of [messî̄θ] 'I anointed' (Malone 1985: 97), when interpreted as directly ← *mehsî̄θ*. (a) However, it is likely enough that [applíxaT]/[appɔ̌xáT] represents assimilation from *$^{?}a^{?}pikat$*, CP at least incipiently (Sg 19) joining with SM, G, TL, and M in fielding *√?pk *either* instead of *√hpk (probably SM and M except for residua of *√hpk) *or* as an allo-root to *√hpk (G, TL). Note in this vein that at least in SM and TL √?pk > √ypk by sar/car, e.g., SM sim impf 2ms/3fs <TyPK> t[tî̄fɑk] (Macs 177), TL cau participial <myPK> (Jastrow 190:105). (For evidence of √?pk (~ √hpk) in SM, G, TL, M, see respectively: Macs 12, 367; Jastrow 1903: 105, 367; llcc; DM 31, 151.)

(b) As regards the ilk of M [messî̄θ], all cases in point involve *h* < *$^{*}h$* and so will be considered under the rubric of *ḥ* (§9.2.4). (To be sure, the laryngeal *h* is weaker than the pharyngeal *ḥ*, so it is likely enough that the M assimilations targeted *h* (< *ḥ*) after all. However, there seems to be no additional evidence to that effect. (For discussion of the assimilation in [messî̄θ] and related forms, see Malone 1985).)

[25] Certain *2√h and *2√ʾ causative forms are ambiguous as to whether they have undergone degutturalization or rather have metanalyzed to hollow; ambiguities, moreover, may be found involving either early degutturalization (e-dgt), typified by uncompensated loss of the guttural, or late degutturalization on the Samaritan Circuit (c-dgt, §22.1 (22B)) characteristically showing both positionally conditioned lengthening of adjacent segments and variable adjacent-vowel coloring. Thus on *√shd (< **√śhd by §17.27), <ʾsyD> ~ <ʾsD> t[ä́səd] 'legte Zeugnis ab' (Macs 140) may either < e-dgt ʾashíð (or ssl-affected ʾashíð, §17.28) by uncompensated *h* > ∅ or < metanalyzed ʾäsíð, the differences in *V* length being neutralized by smc; and on *√šʾr, <ʾsyrw> t[āsíru] 'sie liessen übrig' (Macs 174f) either < c-dgt ʾašʾíru by uncompensated e-dgt plus ssl ʾī > ī, or < metanalyzed ʾäšíru. In both cases, the spelling with ml <y> may but need not favor the metanalytic interpretation; contrast the unmetanalyzed ml-less participles built on *√shn 'besitzen', <mshn> t[mä́sən] < e-dgt mashín, and *√dhl 'fürchten', <mDhl> t[mädḗl] < c-dgt maðhíl, the latter with compensatory and vowel-coloring *hī* > *ē*. (Note that, apart from SM, at least *√shd metanalyzes to √syd in CP, as pointed out by Macuch (Macs 140); see entries in Sl 132f., where <h> lingers only in the participial form <mshD> 'testatus est', itself varying with hollow <m̊syD>.)

[26] √hwy aside, there is at least a tendency in most of the post-TR dialects to simplify ə̌hV to V (by generalization of sad, §9.2.1.2); e.g., SR yə̌háv > [yáw] 'il a donné' (Du 101). SR also shrinks the pf copular hə̌wə̌ to wə̌ when functioning enclitically (perhaps by a mechanism at least typologically akin to similar apheresis of 1√Hə̌ in the sim impa; §17.33).

[27] The dissimilation *9. . .9* > *ʔ. . .9* possibly involves deletion of the pharyngeal feature (whatever it may be, likely [RTR] "retracted tongue root") from *9*, leaving *ʔ* as the unadorned rock-bottom segmental manifestation of gutturality, call the feature [GUT]. In such terms, assuming a privative rather than binary modeling of features, the dissimilation would boil down to the deletion portrayed in (a). (The hypothesis that dissimilation is a special case of deletion was proposed by David Odden in a source I have been unable to recover.)

(a) $$\begin{bmatrix} \text{GUT} \\ \text{RTR} \end{bmatrix} \quad \ldots \quad \begin{bmatrix} \text{GUT} \\ \text{RTR} \end{bmatrix} \quad > \quad [\text{GUT}] \quad \ldots \quad \begin{bmatrix} \text{GUT} \\ \text{RTR} \end{bmatrix}$$

(To capture this suggestion, a somewhat different feature system would have to be appealed to from that used in this book. In particular, while the monolithic feature [RTR] corresponds to the binary [+RTR] displayed in §20.1 (20C), and [GUT] corresponds to [-stomatic], a mechanism is wanting whereby [-stomatic, +RTR] > [-stomatic, -RTR] would automatically trigger subsidiary changes of [+back, +continuant, +voiced] to [-back, -continuant, -voiced]; cf. the Redundancy Conditions of chapter 6 in THP.)

[28] *9* is variably retained in SM, according to trad pron, in initial position when onset to a low vowel as nucleus—that is, /#__ǣ or /#__å̄. An intriguing related phe‗ nomenon involving *9A* and revealed in trad pron is occasional gemination of an immediately following *C*, whether the *9* itself is retained (t[9ɑ́bbɑr] 'er kam durch') or not (t[wɑbbä́ron] 'und sie kamen durch') (Macs §52). A case might perhaps be made for viewing the *9* as a trigger to consonantal pretonic lengthening in the period prior to trad-pron-registered shift of the accent to the penult (c-pen, §22.1 (22B)), but subsequent to

1ʃ V̆ promotion (c-prm): *9ASAM* c-prm → *9ẮSÁM pretonic lengthening* → *9ASSÁM* c-pen t[9ÁSSAM]. For further discussion, see §22.1 n. 2a.

[29] "Canonically identical," though not segmentally. Note in M 2ʃ t[a] ~ t[e] due to low (§17.10); and in SM 1ʃ t[ã] ~ t[æ], due to (apparently) free alternation (§22.1), as well as 2ʃ t[ə] ~ t[α] due to *second schematic neutralization* (ssn, §12.2(α)) or possibly to retention of *a* from proto-Semitic (as in Arabic conjugation VIII; see §1.1.1 n. 4). However, intricated with these vowel alternations SM does evidence a pair of canonically *dissimilar* alternants, keying on singleton ~ geminate 2√ due to the pretonic lengthening discussed in n. 28, preceding: t[ētǽb(b)əd] ~ t[ētǽb(b)ād].

[30] The hedge ("possibly") on <ʔyl9wn> is prompted by the eventuality that not *√lʔy, but *√l9y, might be involved; cf. Y <wTl9y> 'und sie wird schwach werden' (DR I 214: 32).

[31] t[yǎ́kkəm]; it is characteristic of SM c-dgt to compensatorily lengthen both an immediately following consonant (*9k → kk*) and any adjacent vowel (*a9 → ã*); see §22.1 (22B).

[32] t[yě́bbəd] ~ t[yě́bbɑd] via both ad-*C* and ad-*V* compensatory lengthening (n. 31, preceding), with mid-coloring of the prefix vowel either as part and parcel of c-dgt (§22.1 (2B)) or earlier via partial attenuation of *a* /__HC (§12.1); t[yî̊bɑd] via <hei *ē* < coa *ay* (§11.2).

[33] For general discussion of both changes, see Kutscher 1976: 67–96. These processes should be considered as specific strategies in the overarching degutturalization nexuses to be discussed in §9.3.2: vpl as a tool for guttural laxing and vpg as a tool for depharyngealization.

[34] (a) The one possible exception is <ӟ>, which according to Morag (1964: 120 n. 13) appears in some Bab manuscripts. (b) Note that in examination of Bab B forms, discussion is based on Bauer and Leander's transcription of actual supralinear textual forms. (Many of the latter are given in Kahle 1913.)

[35] Though Dalman liberally cites <ӑ> in passageless—and hence possibly constructed—illustrations (e.g., Da 72), TR forms provided with a textual source rarely contain <ӑ>; one example is cau pf 3ms <ʔæ9ǎ̆vær> (Da 259). A more tortured issue is the question of Sabbionetan <ӗ>; see §17.23.3.

[36] SR cases like jc<9ehað>(B §35) are best taken as historical spelling of depharyngealized [eháð], reflecting ∅ < ʔ assimilated from 9; see n. 6.

[37] In view of jc[eháð] (n. 36, preceding), if the conservatism of SR in retaining the restrictive environment /#ʔ__ should bespeak an early pre-SR dialect pocket never penetrated by the expanded environment /#(ʔ,9)__, there must have been a reprise of prm in post-SR, specifically in the Jacobite register. Otherwise the Jac assimilation 9...h > ʔ...h (n. 6) would have been too late to feed (primary) prm.

[38] Excepting possibly a few Sabbionetan TR pf forms with 1ʃ <ɔ> accounted for in Malone 1974b as "schematisiert" on the model of Tiberian Hebrew.

[39] According to Duval (Du 109), the native grammarian Barhebraeus claims (a) that V̆rr is maintained unscathed in only three intensive forms of √šr (e.g., [nǒšarré̌]) and (b) that V̆ḥḥ never changes.

[40] When V̊ of V̊L'L' is *i* (and maybe *u*, evidence is inconclusive), *iL'L'* may assimilate to *ēL'* (and perhaps *uL'L'* to *ōL'*). This effect is forthcoming in at least B, TR, and TL (and probably other dialects as well, the matter being obscured by orthography or

other factors). While at least typologically akin to other mid vowel, resulting assimilatory processes like partial attenuation (§12.1) and adguttural midding (§17.11.2), *iL'L'* → *ēL'* seems not to be out-and-out identifiable with these, since in default of the vowel lengthening, the assimilatory effect often fails under otherwise morphophonologically comparable conditions: e.g., sim impf, Yem TL geminate (§3.2 (3M)) [lē9úl] ← *li99úl*, [nēhél] ← *nihhíl* but -mls [lirróq], also nongeminate [ni9bǽr], [lihléf], [nirmḗ] (Mor 377, 362, 384, 376, 363, 383); B [tēröa9] but [tir̄šúm] (BL 167, 171); TR [yē9ól] but [yi9róq] (Da 328, 269). Though there are prima facie instances of *iL'L'* → *iL'*—that is, mls without assimilation, none seem altogether beyond the pale of alternative interpretation. Thus Dalman offers <yirowq> (Da 328) as evidence for nonassimilatory mls /__r, but the scarcity of pointing with dageš in supralinear texts makes it plausible that this form is –mls [yirróq] (cf. TL y[lirróq], above), in which case the failure of assimilation is expected. Somewhat differently, Ash TL +rrf (§10) rmp forms like pf 1s <ʾi9aṯariy> (Mar 150*), whereas the Yem counterpart [ʾi99ættǣrī] (Mor 377)— along with some 15 similar forms (Mor 352–84)—makes it probable that the TL norm is to forego mls in +rrf rmp forms; it seems likely that Margolis's interpretation has been swayed by the presumed Tiberian spelling rule that gutturals cannot be marked by dageš (because presumably, unlike *r* (Malone 1998b), nongeminable). (On the other hand, Margolis cites one case of what is apparently a genuine, exceptionally +mls rmp form—and here the assimilatory effect is indeed present: [ʾēr̄ɔxás], Mar 165*. Morag's informants unsurprisingly render this -mls, [ʾirr̄ɔxǽs] (Mor 383). See also §12.2 n. 4.)

[41] Since the goal of the displays is to present the guttural system of each dialect and how it arrived at that state from the earlier common 4-segment system, changes listed are limited to those either removing segments from the system entirely (e.g., CP, SM, SR, M ʾ > ∅) or merging them with other guttural segments (e.g., CP, SM *ḥ* > 9).

[42] (a) "At least four dialects," leaving open the possibility that ʾ might also have been lost in one or more others. (The evidence that CP undergoes adr derives primarily from the pattern of inverse spelling examined in §14.2 CP (α), bolstered by the analysis of <yʾšwl> as [ēšÚl] in (β), implying that 2√ʾ > ∅. The possibility of adr for G should also be further studied; cf. §17.33 n. 159. (b) Tentatively, one environment is surmised as at least possible for appearance of phonetic [ʾ] in adr-dialects: by insertion as an antihiatic buffer intervocalically, an eventuality to be notasted [V(ʾ)V]. (Note that at least in SM trad pron such an [ʾ] is explicitly mentioned by Macuch (Macs 76).)

[43] While the strategies other than the primary ones may not fall out as neatly à la family tree, this should cause no consternation. They may have spread wavelike across the W – E(L) boundary after the dialects were (in the process of being) differentiated; or they might represent independent mutations evoked as natural moves in an overall drifty toward degutturalization.

Finally it should be noted that the general position adopted in this book concerning Aramaic guttural weakening and loss is fairly conservative, in particular via the disposition to interpret guttural letters at face value in the absence of evidence to the contrary. There is, however, a very good chance that deterioration of the gutturals in the later dialects was massive indeed. This thesis is developed with special acumen and detail by Kutscher in 1976: 67–96; and while the focus of his treatment is G, much of importance is set forth for other dialects as well, especially CP, SM, and TL. (For TL see also Nm §7 with footnotes).

10. Reflexive Mediopassive (rmp) *T*

Three things may happen when (a reflex of) the rmp prefix **t* (*T*) comes in contact with 1√C': (α) the prefix may totally assimilate to the radical, *TC'* → *C'C'* (*regressive rmp fusion*, rrf); (β) the prefix may metathesize with the radical, always a sibilant (Σ'), usually but perhaps not always picking up the sibilant's features of voice and retraction, *TΣ'* → *Σ'T'* (*rmp metathesis*, rmt);[1] (γ) the radical may totally assimilate to the prefix, *TC'* → *TT* (*progressive rmp fusion*, prf).[2] A fourth process, *snap* (snp), is peculiar to Mandaic, and discussion will be deferred until that rubric.

Roughly speaking, we have something like the following general scenario. Both rrf and rmt are rather spottily (if at all) attested in the earliest dialects, which in the case of rrf probably bespeaks incipience but for rmt merely the happenstance of textual limitations. Though rmt may predate Aramaic, while rrf arose within it, the two processes compete in the case of 1√Σ forms, rmt ultimately settling in as the all-hands-down unmarked choice. In the earliest stages, 1√Σ forms at times appear to escape both processes, an exemption that in later dialects becomes vanishingly rare or altogether disappears. While rmt is probably pan-Aramaic with a steady-state condition (rmp *T* + 1√Σ), rrf shows a somewhat lopsided distribution toward the end of its trajectory (coming into full bloom only in G and the Low dialects TL and M) and widens its conditions through time (from dentoalveolar stop 1√ through stomatic (non-guttural) 1√ irrespective of dentoalveolarity to 1√ at large).[3]

The process prf is common for *T 1*√*ʔ* in at least TR, CP, G, TL, SR (earlier period), and M, but for *T 1*√*Ŧ* a minor option manifested only in CP and SR.

Now to the individual dialects:

O. No evidence of rrf. Two forms relevant to rmt are <{yŝ}Tḫṭ> 'es möge verwüstet werden' and <yTŝm9> 'es möge ertönen' (De 42), the first apparently witnessing +rmt, the second –rmt. However, the interpretation of <{yŝ} Tḫṭ> as +rmt suffers from the uncertainty that the first two letters are either restored, or at least questionably identified on the inscription—as per Degen's marking them off; and <yTŝm9> has been interpreted by at least one scholar (Zeev Ben-Ḥayyim apud Kutscher 1970: 30) as *causative* rmp, in which case rmt would be fustrated by intervention of the cau prefix between rmp *t* and 1√ś. So any judgment on the status of rmt in O must remain tentative.

I̲. No trace of rrf, but rmt is in full force: e.g., <ʔšTKhw> 'sie würden ge-funden', <ʔzDhrw> 'nehmt euch in acht!' (L 20)—note in the latter via <D> the voice assimilation of rmp *t to 1√z.

B̲. rmt fully developed, as per, e.g., the following three forms, the last two of which also evince retraction (uvularization, "emphasis") and voice assimila-tion, respectively: int rmp impf 3ms [yištawwḗ] (Dan 3:29), int rmp impf 3ms [yiṣtabbá9] (Dan 4:12), sim rmp pf 2mp [hizd̊mintū́n] (Dan 2:9, kĕrey). A first whiff of rrf may perhaps be seen in the kĕtiv form of the latter, interpretable as [hizz̊mintū́n] (BL 111).

P̲. rmt: As per <ʔš{T}Kh> 'was found' (HC 415), with the same caveat on the restored/blurred {T} as was sounded above for O {yŝ}.[4] At the same time, int rmp <yzBn> 'is sold' (HC 362), suggesting [yizzabbán] < *yitzab-báni, bespeaks rrf—as do the sim rmp participles <mqrʔ> ~ <mqrh> 'called' (HC 407).[5] So, very tentatively, it seems as if *t 1√C might be resolved by either rmt or rrf.

N̲. No evidence for rrf, but rmt appears in <yzTry> 'il se méprisera', with-out voice assimilation of rmt *t to d; and rmt appears to remain fallow in <yTzBn> 'il sera vendu', <yTŝnʔ> 'il sera changé' (Cg 73).

TR. rmt: sim rmp pf 3ms [ʔištˢʔǽr] 'blieb übrig' (Da 306), int rmp pf 3fs [ʔištāʔǽvæθ] (Da 307) (with [āʔ] ← a?? by mls, §9.3.1), sim rmp pf 3ms [ʔiṣtˢlī̊v] 'wurde gehenkt' (Da 259) (with long 2ʃ [ī] by ssl, §17.28), int rmp pf 3ms [ʔizdæbbǽn] (lc).

rrf: Consistently when 1√ is a dentoalveolar stop (sim pf 3ms [ʔidd̊xǽr] 'gedachte' (lc)); sporadically when 1√ is a stomatic other than dntlv stop (sim rmp impf 3mp [yibbæhtū́n] 'sie werden beschämt', 2fs [tibbæhtī́n] (Da 253); int rmp 2ms or 3fs bb+tb[tinnættǽl], but 3m3 -rrf bb[yiθnættǽl]

prf: Variably /__1√ʔ, at least in int rmp; e.g., pf 3ms [ʔiθʔæbbǽl], but [ʔittæh(h)ǽð] (Da 303).

CP. rmt: <ʔštBq> 'wurde verlassen' (Sg §54.1), <ʔzDlP> 'emporte sich' (Sg §35a), <ʔṣtlB> 'wurde gekreuzigt' (lc).

rrf: Only when 1√ is a dntlv obstruent—<ʔTBrT> 'sie zerschellte' (Sg 22), <ʔtmr> 'verbarg sich' (lc), <TDKrwn> 'ihr gedenkt' (Sg 21); when the obstru-ent is 1√Σ, there is competition with rmt, thus for √ṣlb there is rmt <ʔṣtlB> as above, or rrf <ʔṣlBw> 'wurden gekreuzigt' (Sg 22).

prf: Regularly but variably /__ʔ, "vereinzelt" /__dntalv C; e.g., <ʔT̲rsT> ~ <ʔTrsT> 'sie wurde verlobt' (Sg 65).

SM. rmt: Unmarkedly applies (<ʔsTlq> t[istã̊ləq] 'stieg hinauf', <ʔzD9q> t[izdḗq] 'wurde gerufen', <TṣTDy> t[tiṣt̃ãdi] 'wirst furchten'), but may al-ternatively give way to rrf (<ʔšTm9> t[ištǽmæ] ~ <ʔšm9> t[iššǽmæ] 'wurde gehört') and in one instance possibly stalls without giving way to rrf and is subsequently subject to Aufsprengung (§4.4), separating the resulting cluster (<ʔT̲sKmw> t[ētǽskḗmu] 'kam(en) zu Ende') (Macs 153f).

rrf: Unmarledly applies /__dntalv stop (<ʔD̲BqT> t[idd̲ābḗqət] 'ich halte mich fest', <Dṭmrw> t[diṭṭāmā́ru] 'die verborgen wurden' (Macs 154), variably—and not merely sporadically—/__stomatic(nonguttural) C (<ʔTPrq> t[iṭf̲ā́rɑq] ~ <ʔPrq> t[iff̲ā́rɑq] 'wurde gelöst' (Macs 152). The stomatic condition will also be assumed to extend to *Tw* → *ww*, whether w̲ = 1√ (§17.34) or metasthesized 2√ (§6.1.1.2); and perhaps also occasionally to *Ty* → *yy* (if <yy̲B>, Macs 180, ← *yiθy̲ə̌hḗβ*, with *h* → Ø, §9.3.2) though normally *Ty* escapes rrf. There is one possible exception in the way of rendering the condition "/__dntalv stop" categorical, one where the preserved cluster is then subject to Aufsprengung: <TT̲DKrwn> t[tētidkā́ron] 'werdet erwähnt' (Macs 154).[6]

G. rmt: sim rmp pf 3fs <ʔyŝT̲ʔlT> [7] (Da 396) and <ʔystrKT> (Da 260), 3mp <ʔyzDr9wn> (Da 262).

rrf: Not only /__stomatic C (<ʔyPsyq> 'wurde geteilt', etc.) but /__guttural C as well, excepting ʔ (<ʔy9Tr> 'wurde reich', etc.); -rrf forms are also found (<ʔyTB̲l9> 'wurde verschlungen', <ʔyT9ByD> (~ +rrf <ʔy9ByD>) 'wurde gemacht', etc.) (Da 259).

prf: /__ʔ, e.g., sim rmp pf 3ms <ʔyT̲mr> (Da 303); see also <ʔyTŝlT> (n. 7, above).

SR. rmt: [ɛṣt̲ə̌mɛ́x] 'stützte sich', [ɛṣt̲ə̌lɛ́w] 'ward gekreuzigt' (B 24), [ɛzd̲akkí̲] 'ward gerechtfertigt' (B 16).

rrf: Only /dntalv stop (sim rmp 3ms [ɛdd̲ə̌ní̲], int rmp 3ms [ɛṭṭabbár], [ɛṭṭayyÁw], but a minority of native grammarians prescribe -rrf in such cases ([ɛθ̲d̲ə̌ní̲], [ɛθ̲ṭayyÁw], [ɛθ̲ṭabbár]) (Du 105f. with n. 1). Of the latter, the like of [ɛθtabbár] is especially interesting, attesting as it does to a reaction to what are sometimes called "fake geminates." That is to say, while true geminates—those *C′C′*s whose members belong to the same morpheme, e.g., 2√bb of [ɛθtabbár]—adhere to Geminate Integrity (§5 n. 1) and so forgo spirantization—conversely, fake geminates—those *C′C′*s whose members are heteromorphemic, that is, *C′+C′* (in our case rmp *T′* + *1√T′*)—are subject to spr, presumably because the morpheme boundary interrupts the cluster so as to structurally confine the domain of the rule to the rmp prefix. As we see elsewhere (§5 n. 1), such a reaction of fake geminates to spr shows up in other dialects of Aramaic as well.[8]

prf: Duval (Du 106) lists sim rmp impf 3ms [nɛṭt̲ə̌hɛ́] (√dhy), [nɛṭt̲ə̌hɛ́q] (√dhq), 2ms or 3fs [tɛṭt̲ə̌xár] (√dkr), all judged as "vulgaire."[9] In the case of *T* √*1ʔ*, prf is largely preempted by adr+prm (§9.3.1)—[ɛθ̲ɛmár] 'wurde gesagt' (B 90) ← *ʔθ̲ʔə̌már*—except for √ʔhd and various other verbs "einer älteren Sprachperiode" that do show prf—[ɛṭt̲ə̌hɛ́ð] 'wurde genommen' (lc). (We may assume that the nexus adr+prm has spread from its original locus /#__ (§9.3.1), replacing prf medially in the sim 1$\sqrt{}$' rmp. And, in fact, this nexus has apparently become the strategy of preference in dealing with 'ǯ elsewhere as well; thus, 2$\sqrt{}$'ǯ → [ɛ] in heavy forms of the sim impf such as 3mp [nɛšɛlũn], B 87.)

TL. rmt: Unmarkedly applies (y[lištæm9ǽn] (Mor 386) a[lištam9ə́n] (Mar 173*), 'they(f) will be heard', y+a[ʾizdAbbÁn] (Mor 360, Mar 108*) 'it was sold', y+a[nistA9Ár] (Mor 154, Mar 156*) 'we'll be grieved'), though with some competition from rrf (y[ʾizzə̌ríq] (Mor 142, 2ʃ [ī] by ssl, §17.28) a[ʾizzə̌réq] ~ rmt [ʾizdə̌réq] 'was sprinkled').

rrf: Variably /__C at large, including guitturals except ʾ, unmarkedly at least in the case of nonsibilant stomatics, and categorically in the case of dntalv stops; y+a[ʾippə̌líγū] (Mor 141, Mar 151*) 'they differed in opinion' (long 2ʃ by ssl), <ʾyT9qrw> ~ <ʾy9qrw> (Mar 41) y[ʾi99ə̌qū́r] 'ne9ekru' (mor 141) (2ʃ [ū] by i-lap, §17.9), y[ʾittə̌qī́l] 'netkal' (Mor 142) a[ʾittə̌qī́lə] 'she stumbled' (ssl) (Mar 179*).

prf: Categorically /__ʾ, e.g., <ʾyThyD> a[ʾittə̌héð] (Mar 41, 86*) y[ʾittə̌hī́ð] (Mor 352) 'it was closed' (see also n. 7, above).

M. (Because of special interconnections among the M developments, it will be useful to lay out the discussion in a different order from that followed for the other dialects.)

rrf: Obligatorily /__dntalv stop, in which case if *C'C'ǯ* results smp takes this to [C'] (<etriṣ> 'he was consecrated' (Macm 267) [etré̦ṣ] ← (ʾ)*Ittə̌ré̦ṣ*, cf. t[é̦treṣ] (lc), similarly <edgar> 'they were heaped' (DM 103) [edGár], cf. t[édgar] (Macm 125) (ultimately < *hitdagírū*, with apocope by lap, §17.9), <niṭaršun> '(they)shall be dispersed' (?) (DM 183) [neṭṭaršón] (without smp because 2ʃ a is full, not reduced); variable /__other C (except ʾ whether < *ʾ or *9, §9.3.2), smp once again applying if *C'C'ǯ* should result (<etparaqt> 'thou wast saved' but <eparqit> 'I was saved', <ethasab> 'he cogitated' but <ehaial> 'he became strong' (Macm 266f), even /__Σ as a minority option to rmt, <nisihpun> 'they shall be overturned' but via rmt <esthip> 'he was overturned' (Malone 1999: 251).)

prf: Consistently /__ʾ, whether < *ʾ or *9 (<etbid> 'factus est' (Macm 301) spelling [etBéð] < *hit9abída, <etkil> 'was eaten' (lc) [etKél] < *hitʾakíla).[10]

rmt: [11] <estadar> 'was set in order' (251) [estaddár], <ezdaqar> 'he rejoiced' (lc) [ezdaqqár], <estamar> 'is suppressed' (252) [estammár].

A seemingly peculiar sequel of rmt is that otherwise expected Aufsprengung is bled; <eštqil> 'was removed' (254), [eštə̌qél] ≠ @[īšeTqél]. (In Malone 1999, it is speculated that this resistance to auf was phonetic-prosodic in origin, but later became morphophonological.)

We have seen that although several dialects undergo prf /__ʾ, only M simplifies a resulting *ttə̌* to *t* ([. . .etSVM. . .], the other dialects all leaving the result at [. . .IttǯSVM. . .]. But observe then that when $2\sqrt{}$ is sibilant, we are de facto faced with a recurrence of the string conditions once conducive to rmt, in . . .*ItꞭ̲VM.* . . ; and only in M do we encounter these string conditions, through the agency of smp. Of several $1\sqrt{}^{\,?}\,2\sqrt{}\Sigma$ roots listed in DM, only two, $\sqrt{}^{\,?}$sr 'fetter' and $\sqrt{}^{\,?}$šd 'pour', additionally meet the morphological and canonical conditions required to actually trigger rmt; and triggered indeed it is: <estar> 'he was fettered' (DM 30), [esTár] (cf. t[éstar], Macm 90); <estid> 'was poured' (DM 40), [esTéð] (cf. t[ésted], Macm 90).[12]

    snap (snp): In M, and seemingly only in M, sim rmp forms with $1\sqrt{}\Sigma\ 2\sqrt{}T,\underline{t}$ which undergo weakening reduction of 1ʃ—that is, verb forms of canonical shape. . .*ITΣǯꞭVM.* . . with Ɐ = T,t, appear to select rrf rather than the expected rmt. There are apparently no exceptions attested; e.g., <estar> 'were cast down' (252), [esTár] (where [T] = $2\sqrt{}$, not the rmp prefix) rather than rmt-expected @[estəθár].

    As is discussed in Malone 1999, it is mighty peculiar and in fact implausible that such forms should systematically select rrf over rmt, so peculiar and implausible that it seemed worth the while to search about for an alternative account. What is finally proposed is that such forms are products of a process dubbed *snap* (snp), whereby a string. . .*ITΣǯꞭVM.* . . (Ɐ = T,t) does in fact undergo rmt to. . .*IΣTǯꞭVM.* . . . But this result causes prosodic tension by virtue of T and Ɐ being both feature-compositionally and string-positionally (across weak ǯ) too close for comfort, a tension then relieved by T being reassociated to (and hence spread from) Σ—whereupon the resulting. . .*IΣΣǯꞭVM.* . . duly undergoes smp and comes out [. . .IΣꞭVM. . .] (e.g., [esTár] 'were cat down' cited above).

Notes to §10

    [1] At least rmt may also effect metathesis of the residual causative-prefixal *ǯ (§1.1.3 n. 9), e.g., B impf 3mp [yištaxlǯlṹn] (BL 172)

    [2] (a) A situation quite similar to that of prf obtains when ʔ in $T'+^{\,?}$ is not radical but *prefixal*, specifically, causative-prefixal. Since the resulting assimilation to *tt* fails to overlap perfectly across the dialects with that attendant upon prf, the two processes will be treated separately. For the causative-prefixal case, including that of $T'+h$ with variant prefixal *h*, see §9.2.2 where the process is called *rmp-causative assimilation* (rca).

    (b) A number of special symbols are used in this chapter, defined in §20.1(α) and §26 but usefully recapitulated here: T = archiphoneme for {t, θ} (i.e., *t±spr, §5.1); Ɐ = dentoalveolar stop, {t, ṭ, d (,ḍ)}; C' = C identical to one or more others marked C' in the same expression/derivation, special case here C'C' = geminate C (as opposed to CC as C-cluster irrespective of composition)—and by extension, C'T' = a cluster whose initial segment (C') agrees maximally featurewise with the final segment which is a dntalv stop (T'); Σ = sibilant, {s, ś, š, ṣ, z} (not to be confused with S = $2\sqrt{}$).

    [3] (a) "dentoalveolar stop." It is possible that dentoalveolarity per se is a favoring condition, stoppage (occlusion) being merely the limiting (virtually categorical) case;

note for instance that in dialects showing rrf in a relatively early stage (B, P, TR, CP) at least one instance of dentoalveolar nonstop assimilation may be found. (At the same time, lexical assimilation involving nondentoalveolars also makes a rather early appearance (*q* in P, *b* in TR; see below).

(b) It will be apposite to mention here that the Aramaic dialects have a tendency to contact-assimilate sequences of dntalv consonants even when rmp *T* is not involved, a congeries of variable sporadic processes collectively to be called *dentoalveolar contact assimilation* (dca)—spreading usually being regressive but at times progressive. Thus Nöldeke's interpretation of SR conjunctive int impf 2ms <wattaše²> as [wat̲t̲aššé] ← *waθtaššé* (with conjunctive *wa* procliticized to prefixal θ + √t) (Ns §26, §36); CP <ḥsyT²> 'beata' [ḥəsi̭t̲t̲á] ← ...*Dt*... (§4.2.2 n. 17); M <ašiṭinun> 'ich verschmähte sie' [aššeṭṭennón] ← ...*ṭT*... (§15.3.1.2 n. 27); I <ylTy> (~ <ylDTy>) 'you(fs) bore', presumably [yəli̭t̲t̲i̱] (~ unassimilated [yəli̭ðti̱]) (Kraehling 1953: 180 (V, lines 5, 6), Kutscher 1970: 72).

[4] Though in this book "{ }" translates any pair of flanking marks used by the various authors to indicate missing or unclear letters, Hillers and Cussini use two distinct such marks, nowhere explaining the difference between them: "< >," as here, and "[ ]", e.g., HC 415. (Degen, lc and elsewhere in De, uses "[ ]".)

[5] For the rationale of citing nonverb forms, see n. 3 above. Other verb forms attesting -rrf may be found in Hillers and Cussini's glossary (HC 333ff) under √²gr, √b9², √gb² (perhaps), √ḥzy, √9ll.

[6] It is perhaps suspicious that the marked exceptions from both rmt (t[ētæskému]) and rrf (t[tētidkắron]) are followed up by the relatively rare (for SM) process complex Aufsprengung. Moreover, [tētidkắron] is additionally anomalous in prosodically behaving, in all ways except for the suffix itself, as if it were a reflex of the ancient *short* impf, rather than of the *long* or *energic* impf bespoken by the actual shape of the suffix t[-on]. See the simplified and stylized (mainly in the order of processes) derivations (a, b, c), noting in particular that t[tētidkắron] appears to be a blend of (b) and (c). (For the processes appealed to in these derivations, see §3.1 (3Fvii), §4.2, §4.4, §5.1, §5.3 n. 13a, §9.2.2, §17.10, §17.11, §17.14, §17.22, §22.1.)

	(a)	(b)	(c)
	hitsakímu	titðakirű̃n(n)a	titðakírū
hlr,low,occ,sap,spr	²iθsaxímū	tiθdaxarű̃n	tiθdaxárū
deg,mid,red	²iθsɔ̃xémū	tiθdaxrŰ̃n	tiθdɔ̃xárū
auf	²iθasxému	—	tiθiDxárū
oba,smc,svs	[ētæskému]	@[titdákron]	@[tētidkắru]

[7] In light of the fact that TL shows lexical metaplasm of √š²l > √²šl in the cau (<²wŝlh> a[²ŏšílɔ̄] 'she loaned' (Mar 46, 168*) ←coa,mtr (§11.2, §17.12) *²a²šílaT* ← car (§9.2.1.2) *²a²silaT*) and, relevant here, in the sim rmp (3ms <²yTŝyl>, 1s <²yTŝly> 'asked for the dissolution of a vow' (Mar 41)), the G variant to <²yŝT²lT> in the text, <²yTŝlT>, is better taken to derive ← *²Iθ²ə̃šílaθ* via prf (below in the text), than ← *²Iθš²ílaθ* via sad (§9.2.1.2) and failure of rmt.

[8] Caution is warranted, however, in accepting the SR grammarians' orthoepic pronouncements; cf. §9.2.2 n. 23, where a very similar nexus invites at least some suspicion of "linguistic virus."

[9] Brockelmann (B 17) restricts SR prf to the environment /__ǯ, but the noun [mɛttīnǯnūθǯ] 'judicium' (Brockelmann 1928: 146, Du 106), built on √dWn, shows that the process is not so restricted, at least not in the nominal system. (Nor does the restriction itself hold for the CP verb, to judge by forms like <TTKrwn> (above), most straightforwardly interpretable as [tIttaxrŮn], with [. . .tta. . .] ← . . .Tda. . . .).

[10] The processes prf and rrf split the labor of the gutturals down the middle, ʔ< *ʔ, *9 conditioning prf and h < *h, *ḥ conditioning rrf. And while this might seem to constitute evidence that the two processes visited M only after the dialect had thus funneled the earlier four gutturals down to the two, alternative hypotheses exist. For instance, prf and rrf may have visited pre-M earlier than the double merger of *ʔ, *9, *h, *ḥ, rrf being sensitive to [+tense] *h, *ḥ, prf to [-tense] *ʔ, *9 (THP 28). Or, say, rrf was originally conditioned solely by *h and prf by *ʔ, the later h < *ḥ and ʔ < *9 subsequently following suit by analogy in the wake of the merger (via reprise of depharyngealization, §9.3.2).

[11] Ensuing discussion of rmt and snp is largely based on Malone 1999, whither also all unidentified page citations refer.

[12] The technical point arises that if rmt should be morphologically conditioned, in particular by requiring that the metathesizand T to be [+rmp] (as is defended for Semitic at large in Malone 1971b), then the morphologic feature [+rmp] must survive both prf and smp in order to properly condition r-rmt. In fact, this result seems to follow (almost) automatically from the conventional autosegmental view. First of all, when prf totally assimilates 1√ʔ to rmp T, autosegmentally it does so by having the content of T replace that of 1√ʔ—specifically by spreading the mother feature-geometric node of T, along with its full congeries of dependents, to that of 1√ʔ and "snipping off" the original dependent complex of the latter. Thus, unless one adheres to a brand of phonology that restricts such operations to intrinsic phonetic material, the [+rmp] will spread along with everything else. And finally, when smp takes place it will assume the autosegmental form of deleting one of two identical melodic nodes with no damage to the joint dependents of both, in sketch (letting M = melody, D = dependents):

(a)

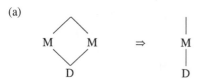

So [+rmp] survives smp as well, and will be there to condition r-rmt. (Incidentally, the autosegmental view should also correctly predict maintenance of the morphologic feature [+II] ("second person") inherent in the Tiberian Hebrew suffix -t throughout a derivation like -nt# → -tt# → [-t#], a phenomenon discussed under the aegis of a more old-fashioned approach in THP (65 note a). This is important for Aramaic as well, as per §15.3.1.3.)

11. Coalescent Processes

11.1. Description

By "coalescent processes" are meant mutations whereby falling diphthongs become long monophthongs through the amalgamation of their nuclei and offglides. In general for the Aramaic dialects, two such processes may be distinguished: a purely coalescent process whereby *ay, *aw fuse respectively to some long palatal monophthong (usually $\bar{e}$, but in certain types of systems sometimes $\bar{æ}$) and to $\bar{o}$—a process to be called *coalescence* (proper) (coa); and a hybrid condensation (§8)—coalescence mutation changing *ayi, or perhaps more narrowly *ayi#, to $\bar{e}(\#)$ (or, again, in certain types of systems, to $\bar{æ}\#$ or $\bar{æ}(\#)$)—this to be called *condensatory coalescence* (k-coa), which is, or appears to be, limited to operating on auslaut *a 3√y+i of the impf verb.[1] While coa first makes its appearance in I, k-coa dates froim O.[2]

The balance of this section will deal with aspects of coa, further consideration of k-coa being deferred until the individual dialects are discussed in §11.2.

Under certain conditions, in some types of Aramaic, coa may so to speak undershoot or overshoot. Undershooting coa, or *partial coalescence* (p-coa), refers to a stage of the fusion process where the nucleus has been colored (palatal, labial) and raised to mid but the glide still lives on as an imdependent segment: M *ey, ow*, SR *ɔw*. A few dialects also show what appears to be *over*shooting, in that *ay, *aw end up fused not to mid-level $\bar{e}$, $\bar{o}$, but all the way up to high-level $\bar{\imath}$, $\bar{u}$. In fact, such *heightening* (hei) is best taken not as an immediate manifestation of coalescence, but as an independent process taking $\bar{e}$, $\bar{o} \rightarrow \bar{\imath}$, $\bar{u}$, conditions allowing, even when the mid vowel may not itself be a product of coa; thus, in M the 3ms object suffix *-$\bar{e}h$ (< **$ih\overset{\circ}{V}$ by sap^mid^lanc^hap, §17.22, §17.11, §2.3.1, §9.2.2) always > [-$\bar{\imath}$]. Heightening may evince either phonetic motivation, as with M 3ms [-$\bar{\imath}$], or be transparentively evoked; e.g., when *-$\bar{o}$ as portmanteau reflex of **-a 3√y-$\bar{u}$ (b e-cnd, §8.1.1) with mp **-$\bar{u}$ heightens to [-$\bar{u}$] in mimicry of the strong verb suffix (§15.3.2).

A necessary condition for coa is homosyllabicity of nucleus and offglide, presumably because the syllable provides a structural proximity requisite for the fusion to take place. In the event the glide rather functions as onset (or onglide, §23.5) to the following syllable, the process lies fallow: for B cau pf 3mp, contrast successful coa of homosyllabic *ay with failure of the same sequence heterosyllabically in the two respective underscores of [hē̱θáy̱ū] (BL

197

169), < *hayǀtáǀyū*. Similar lapses are TR [ʔištænnǽyū]and TL a[hǎwa̰yɔ́n] (§15.4). (The *a√V* of many such instances is transparentively motivated.)

A mixed case is presented by the sequences **ayy, *aww*. In these, **ay, *aw* appear to be homosyllabic by virtue of the first mora of the geminate being structurally part of the same syllable as **a*, but the second mora's role as onset (or onglide) to the following syllable tends to undermine holistic first syllable allegiance by dint of Geminate Integrity (§5 n. 1), which dictates that either all of **yy, *ww* participate in coalescence, or none so participate. Since the second mora cannot be rationalized as belonging to the first syllable, the prediction is that **ayy, *aww* should not coalesce [3]—a prediction vindicated by such as B int impf 3ms^1s [yɔ̄ḥawwinnánī] (BL 164), TR int 2ms [(di)Thǽwwǽr] (Da 318), SR int pf 3ms [qayyɛ́m] (Ns 121), TL int pf 3ms [9Ayyɛ́l] (Mor 243, Mar 147*), y[9ǽwwɛ́θ] (Mor 221), a[kawwɛ́n] (Mar 123*).

There are also a few cases (SR, M) of *partial coalescence* (p-coa) by regressive color assimilation from the offglide, not violative of Geminate Integrity because leaving the geminate (*ww*) per se unchanged. Thus, SR [ɔww] is the usual reflex of **aww* (e.g., int pf 3ms [tɔwwéš], Ns 121), certainly of one cloth with nongeminate [ɔw] adduced above (see also §20.2( )).[4] Similarly, M int pf 3ms [šẹyyɛ́l], < **ayy* itself derived from ***a⁇* by apl (§9.1.3 n. 7). (A maximally assimilated case of this type is afforded by the Modern M reflex, [šíyyel]; Macm 331.)

Two additional points before moving on to the individual dialects:

(α) It seems likely that coa remained to one extent or another a variable process in all the dialects it affected. Though a few intrinsically phonetic conditions may here and there be glimpsed (e.g., perhaps closed syllabicity favoring), this change rather tends by and large to ignore such conditions and sweep over a dialect by general variability tempered with lexical conditions (e.g., the proclivity of *√ʔty in the causative ('bring') to be exempt) or morphological differentiation (e.g., TR's tendency to coalesce *ay* to mid *ē* when *y* = 3√, but to low *ǣ* when *y* is derived from suffixal **ī* through e-cnd (§11.2)).

(β) The homogeneity of (α) in conspiracy with the fact that monophthongization of diphthongs is an extremely common type of change among the world's languages renders coa a poor metric for gauging genetic or diffusional relations among the Aramaic dialects. At a hazard, we may judge that the Eastern dialects (especially SR) and G are more resistant to coa than are the other dialects from B onward.

11.2. The Individual Dialects

Y, O. No evidence for coa proper, but O arguably attests to k-coa in that its long- impf sim defective light verbs end in <-h>, bespeaking [-ē] < **-ay+i*, while its short-impf counterparts show final <-y>, interpretable as [-ay] < **-ay* (for **-ay+i, *-ay*, see §1.4, §2.3.4.1, §7.2). Y shows <-y> **-ay* uniformly, irrespective of the long-short distinction, likely betraying the nonexistence of the opposition within the dialect (§7.2(α)). A few examples:

(11A)   *verbs with syntax-semantics compatible with*

	long impf	**short impf**
Y	<yrqy̲>	<{y}rqy̲>
	'es wird ihm gefallen'	'möge es ihm gefallen'
	(DR I 214:22)	(DR I 214:18)
O	<yhwẖ>	<Thwy̲>
	'er wird sein'	'sie möge sein'
	(De 76)	(De 77)

I. <-h> in the def light long impf, <-y> ~ <-h> in the short; e.g., long <ʔhwẖ> 'ich bin' but short <TGly̲> 'du magst enthüllen', <TB9ẖ> 'du sollts suchen' (L 63). Taking <-h> as [-ē] and <-y> as [-ay], this pattern is interpretable *either* to the effect that the long-short opposition is breaking down via spread of long [-ē] <k-coa *-ayi *and/or* to the effect that coa is beginning to fuse short-impf *-ay to [-ē]. Independent evidence for the appearance of coa may be seen in ml-less <ŝzBK> 'er rettete dich' (L 61), [śē̲zə̌vǎx] < *šay̲zibǎka. (That coa was not categorical may be seen in <yhy̲Th> 'er wird bringen' (L 67) if [yǎhay̲Té]—cf. §11.1(α) for the proclivity of cau *√ʔty to resist coa—though +coa [yǎhē̲θé̲] might be intended on the basis of either historical spelling or use of <y> as medial ml for [ē].)

B. **k-coa.** The long-short opposition seems to have disappeared from the def light impf, fused [ē] being the regular signal of both; e.g., (ex-)long [tɛhě̲wé̲] 'wird entstehen' (BL 279), (ex-)short [tiqné̲] 'du sollst kaufen' (BL 284)—"regular signal" because there is at least one case of [-ē] ~ [-ɛ̄] variation attested, [ʔǎhaww ̲é̲] ~ [ʔǎhaww ̲ɛ̲] 'ich werde behaupten' (Dan 2:24).[5] There is no clear relation between this instance of variation and the long-short opposition.[6]

coa. In the case of *ay variability is the rule, at times under virtually identical intrinsically phonetic conditions. Thus cau pf +coa 3mp passive [hē̲θó̲yū] (BL 175) but -coa 3ms active [hay̲θí̲] (BL 173); +coa sim pf 1s active [hǎwē̲θ] (lc) but -coa cau pf 3fs passive [hē̲θáyiθ] (BL 174) ([i] by epn, §17.6) though both < *-a 3√y+t (§2.3.4.3);[7] sim pf 2nd person +coa plural [hǎzē̲θó̲n] (lc) but -coa singular [hǎzáy̲θɔ̄] (lc)—differing in stress properties, it's true, note however +coa [hǎzē̲θó̲n] 'stressed like -coa [hay̲θí̲] (above).

*aw normally undergoes coa to [ō]—sim pf 3mp [bǎnó̲] (BL 161) < -áw <e-cnd(§8.1) *-áyū, sim impf 3ms bb[y̲ɔ̄xól] (BL 139) < yaw- <sar (§9.2.1.2) *yaʔ-. In rmp impf 2mp [tiθrǎmú̲n] ō is jacked up one more notch by hei, possibly for transparentive reasons (§15.3.2); the Bab variant foregoes this modification, bb[tiθrǎmó̲n].

P̲. **k-coa.** [ē], as per [-h] ~ [-ʔ]; e.g., <Dy yB9h̲> 'who will inquire', <Dy yTB9ʔ̲> 'when it is requested' (HC 348).

coa. *ay > [ē] may be bespoken by <ʔTy> 'he brought' (HC 344) qua [ʔēθí], though contact-assimilated [ʔāθí] or [ʔattí] cannot be excluded (§9.2.1.1). In either event, there is a variant <ʔyTy>, whether for uncoalesced [ʔayTí] or as historical spelling for [ʔēθí].

*aw > [ō] is attested in the variant <yhn> to sim impf 3mp <yhwn> (HC 359), either [yihwṓn] with haplographical <w> for [wō] or [yə̆hṓn] via wdr (§17.32).

N̲. **k-coa.** [-ē], spelled <-ʔ>; e.g., <yhwʔ> 'il sera' (Cg 84, 108).[8]
coa. Uncertain.

TR̲. **k-coa.** Unmarkedly [-ē], e.g., sim impf 3ms def [yi9dḗ] (Da 345) (~ [yə̆9iDḗ] ~ sb[yi9ĭ̊Dḗ], §4 (4Ge,f) for the syllabic structure of the variants), though [-æ] is favored in various slots, e.g., rmp impf, as int 3ms [yiθkæssǽ] (Da 91).[9]

coa. *ay > [ē] or [æ], depending on morphophonological conditions; e.g., [ē] ← a *1√y* (whether original * 1√y, sim impf 3ms sb[yē̲tǽv], inserted by frf (§17.7), sim impf 3ms [yē̲rǽθ], or < 1√ʔ By car (§9.2.1.2), cau pf 3ms tb[ʔēθí][10] (Da 309, 358)) *or* < *3√y /__{C,#} (sim impa ms^1s [mə̆hḗnī], Da 391, int impa ms [mænnḗ], Da 348) though there are inroads from [æ] (cau impa ms^1s [ʔæšqǽnī], Da 391). [æ] ← a *3√y* <e-cnd *a 3√yī with fs *-ī (sim imp fs [ŭrmǽ], sim impf 2fs [tiv9ǽn] (§8.1.1)).[11]

*aw > normally [ō] though with occasional heightening to [ū]; e.g., def sim pf 3mp^3mp [ŭmhōnū́n] but also [ŭmhūnū́n] (Da 387), the latter either transparentively motivated (§15.3.2) and/or through a process of minor vowel harmony: *ō. . .ū → ū. . .ū* (cf. §2.3.2.1 with n. 5).

CP̲. **k-coa.** <-y> ~ <-ʔ> at least the latter [-ē], especially when bearing a superposed dot (Sg 9f); <yyTʔ> ~ <yʔTy> ~ <yʔ̊Tʔ̊> 'kommt' (Sg 73). The variant spelling with <-y> is more likely to be allographic for [ē] or even to represent [ī] < *-i 3√yi (by e-cnd§8.1.1) than to bespeak retention (and redistribution) of the ancient short impf *-ay; note, e.g., that the 1s possessor of a plural noun, a priori likely to be [-ay], is spelled <-y> ~ <-yy> ~ <-ʔy> (Sg 50), whereas the latter two graphies seem never to appear as reflexes of def impf *-a 3√yi.

coa. Likewise probably [ē] when < *ay; note, e.g., the initials of the three variants for 'kommt' above, plausibly all spelling [ēθḗ], fore by coa (and ymn, §14.2) aft by k-coa.

Reflexes of *aw are almost always spelled <w>, probably usually for [ō]; e.g., <ʔTw> 'sie kamen' (Sg 72) (While pointing with the subposed dot, <w̥>, might point to heightened [ū], e.g., <ʔTmlw̥> 'impleti sunt' (Sl 111) qua [Iθmə̆lū́], there is the caution that the upper dot and lower dot often distribute helter-skelter (Sg 10).)

SM. The ravages of the Samaritan Circuit (§22.1 (22B)) leave us quite in the dark as to the specifics of both k-coa and coa, neutralizing as they do fused and nonfused diphthongs alike and reapportioning both quantity and quality pursuant to later conditions having no direct bearing on the coalescent processes themselves. Thus, e.g., any of *ay(i)*, *ē*, or *ī* emerge as t[ī] in open syllables other than atonic auslaut (<yymr> t[yímær] 'er sagt', <ʔymnwn> ~ <y(y)hymnwn> t[(y)īménon] 'sie glauben', Macs 176f.), t[i] in atonic auslaut (<ʔTy> t[ăti] 'sie(f) kamen', Macs 207), and t[ə] in posttonic closed syllabic position (<ʔTT> t[ătət] 'ich kam', Macs 206). A parallel distribution holds for *aw*, *ō*, *ū*: t[ū], t[u], t[o].

G. **k-coa.** The light def impf uniformly ends in <-y>, irrespective of binyan: e.g. 3ms sim <ylqy>, rmp <yTBry>, int <yṣly>, int rmp <yTPny>, cau <yḥmy> (Da 345). Since likely [-ay] is spelled <-yy>, cf. the 1s^pl possessed nouns <ḥBryy>, <Īmhyy> (Da 204), <-y> probably represents either [-ē] < k-coa *-ayi* or even [-ī] <e-cnd *-iyi* (cf. CP above).

coa. *ay* variably > [ē] (assumed value) ~ unchanged [ay], partially by structural specialization of conditions (e.g., for *a 1√y* perhaps +coa in the sim, <TyKwl> (Da 300), -coa in the cau, <ʔyyKl> (Da 302)) and partially by free alternation (e.g., sim pf 2ms +coa <hwyyT> ~ -coa <hwyyT>—unless the alternation is rather between *2ʃ i* and *2ʃ a*, in the latter case –coa). Reflexes of *aw* are uncertain of interpretation always being spelt <w>; e.g., <hww> 'sie waren' (Da 354).

TL. (The following statements are subject to the qualifications of n. 13b below.)

k-coa. Uniformly [-ē], y&a[niv9é] 'we'll seek' (Mor 356, Mar 95*).

coa. *ay* > [Ay] ~ [Ā] ~ [ē], distributed largely under structural-lexical conditions, with free alternation in certain slots. Uncoalesced [Ay] appears to be categorical /__# irrespective of origin; thus <e-cnd *-ayī* y[tǽy], a[táy] 'come(fs)!', loss of -T by mtr (§17.12) in *-ayT* y[ḫăzǽy] 'raʔiti' (Mor 253) a[ʔayθáy] ~ [ʔēθáy] 'I brought' (Mar 92*).[12] In the environment /__C, [ē] is the usual result, though [Ay] and [Ā] prevail in certain nooks—[Ay] realizing the car-processed result of *√ʔty in the causative (categorically in Yem trad pron, see Mor 354f.), varying with [ē] in Ash trad pron (e.g., a[ʔayθáy] ~ [ʔēθáy] above); in alternation with [ē] ~ [Ā] in defective sim pf 1p verbs (where only Ash avails itself of [Ay]) (a[tănáynō] but a[hăwḗnŏ] ~ [hăwáyin] ([i] by epn, §17.6) (Mar 178*, 106*) ~ y[hăwḗn] (Mor 255), a[bŏ9ǻn] (for coa-produced a[ā], see n. 1 above) ~ y[bŏ9ǽn] (Mar11, 95*; Mor 255).[13]

aw > [ō] /__C in both traditions and /__# in the Ash tradition, Yem there showing [ō] ~ (coa^hei >) [ū]; y&a [ʔ ō̠θév] 'he seated' (Mor 367, Mar 122*), y[9ŏð ō̠] '9avru', y[bŏ9ū̠] ~ [bŏ9ó̠] 'they sought' (Mor 253f, Mar 95*). However, the Halaxot Pĕsukot register apparently maintains -coa [æw] (~ [ɑw], §20.2(δ) ← *a 1√w* in the causative; Morag 1967–68: 85.

SR. **k-coa.** Uniformly, [-ē], in both registers (e.g., sim impf 3ms ns[nɛQSế], jc[neQSế]) although Jacobite under most other circumstances, heightens *ē* at large to *ī*. (Rather than attribute the k-coa exemption to something special in the interaction of processes, a tricky matter to formulate in any event, the position will be taken that the unmarked Jac heightening *ē* → *ī* is subject to morphological-lexical exceptions, among them impf *-ē* (the case of k-coa under discussion) and the 3ms object suffix *-ēh* (< l-anc (§2.3.1) *-eh* < mid (§17.11) *-ih* < sap (§17.22) *-ihi/*-ihu* (§2.3.4.4).)[14]

coa. SR **ay* seems to warrant this descriptive generalization (a few complications or murky spots aside): **ay* coalesces in a closed syllable subsequent to the action of sap (§17.22) but prior to the action of lap (§17.9); in a syllable open within the same derivational stretch, coalescence of **ay* is governed by morphological conditions.

Thus sim pf 1s [QǎSếθ] ← **QaSáyt,* but 2ms [QǎSáyT] ← **QaSáytā* because at the time or level of coalescence the syllable containing *ay* is still open and in forms with these morphological specifications coa lies fallow.

An interesting facet of this regularity may be seen in corresponding object-suffixed forms: 1s^2ms [QǎSēθố x] vs. 2ms^1s [QǎSaytốn]. Despite the likelihood that these form types were once systematically homonymous save for the object suffixes, along the lines of **QaSayták* vs. **QaSaytánī,* coalescence reacts to the forms differentially, as if the syllable were closed in 1s^2ms but open in 2ms^1s—as if, that is, the choice of coa were guided *transderivationally* by the primary conditioning of coa on the corresponding intransitive forms, coalesced 1s [QǎSếθ] vs. uncoalesced 2ms [QǎSáyt]. Was this transderivational sensitivity built into coa when it first arose diachronically? Or did it only arise later, as a brand of transparentation (§15) designed to coalesce the reflex of only 1s^2ms **QaSayták* to match (an ancestor of) 1s [QǎSếθ], all the while failing to coalesce the reflex of 2ms^1s **QaSaytánī* so that it might retain its similarity to (an ancestor of) [QǎSáyt]? In either event, an independent question is what form the *synchronic* mechanism ended up assuming. One possibility is afforded by a Lexical Phonological framework (§23.3), where forms corresponding to intransitives like [QǎSếθ] and [QǎSáyt] are taken to be building blocks—by suffixation—to corresponding transitives like [QǎSēθốx] and [QǎSaytốn]. That way, the syllable closure (or any other structural difference synchronically replacing syllable closure in the wake of the diachronic event d-lap) conditioning *ay* → *ē* would already have taken place by the time (lexical stratum) for suffixation to be realized:

(11B)

	⋮	⋮	
stratum n:	|Qš̌Sáyt|	|Qš̌Sáytə|	
stratum n+1:	|Qš̌Sét|		*s-coa*
	|Qš̌Séθ|		*s-spr*
		|Qš̌Sáyt|	*s-lap*
stratum n+2:	|Qš̌Séθ+ɔ́x|	|Qš̌Sáyt+ɔ́n|	*s-suffixation (wrb)*
	[Qš̌Sēθ+ɔ́x]	[Qš̌Sayt+ɔ́n]	*s-destressing*

A similar account, at least historically, might be given for the differential reaction of *ay* qua object-suffixal bridge in such as sim impa ms^1s [QɔSoMáyn] (< *-áy+nī) vs. ms^3fs [QɔSoMḗh] (assuming < *-áy+ha). Coalescence fails to apply in the case of [-ayn] because during coa's diachronic tenure the syllable was open (*ay / nī) and morphological conditions fail to call for the process; while in the case of [-ēh] coa does apply because the syllable was closed in the wake of sap (*-ayh <sap **-ayha).

Rather different is sim pf 3fp [QɔSáy] < *QaSáyā, in that prior to apocope of *-ā by lap, coalescence of *ay was not actually an option left fallow for morphological reasons but was rather out-and-out prohibited by the fact that the constituents of the diphthong were split over distinct syllables (cf. §11.1): *Qa / Sa / yā. And though homosyllabicity was finally achieved in the wake of lap, it was too late, coalescence having already run its course.[15]

In the balance of *ay* cases, ±coa is structurally conditioned; e.g., *ay* resulting from sar (§9.2.1.2) coalesces (sim impf 3ms [nēmár]) while that resulting from car (lc) fails to (cau pf 3ms ['aytí], [haymén], Ns 112f.—though the latter form may have been metanalyzed as quadriradical int built on √hymn, §9.2.1.2 n. 16). (This account of [ē] ~ [ay] < *ay* holds, incidentally, for the *Nestorian* register. In Jacobite, the corresponding reflexes are ([ī] ~ [ē]) ~ [ay], with *ē* unmarkedly heightening to [ī].)

Coming finally to *aw in SR: This diphthong fully coalesces in closed syllables (def sim impf 3mp [nɛQSṓn]) but stops at *partial* coalescence in open syllables (Nestorian only: sim pf 3mp [QɔSɔ́w], cau pf 3ms [ɔwsép] 'mutuum accepit' (Brockelmann 1928: 300)—Jacobite uncoalesced [QɔSáw], [awséf]; see §20.2(δ)). (Fully coalesced *ō* goes on to [ū] by hei in the Jacobite register but, unlike the parallel case of front *ē*, has no exceptions; thus ns[nɛQSṓn] corresponds to jc[neQSū́n].)

M̲. **k-coa.** -*ē* heightened to [-ī]; [nehyī́] 'he'll live' ([h] <dpr ḥ, §9.3.2), cf. t[néhyī] (Mal 284).

coa. *ay*. By and large, fully coalesced in closed syllables (<qrit> 'you(s) called' (Macm 334) [qš̌rḗT]), though there is at least one exception, the partially coalesced <hzait> 'you(s) saw' (Macm 119) [hš̌zéyT]; regularly partially coalesced in medial open syllables (<qraitun> 'you(p) called' (Macm

335) [qə̆re̲y̲Tón], <a̲i̲tia> t[é̲y̲θī] 'he brought' (Mal 282), [e̲y̲Tí̲]), though there may be some generalization of full coalescence into open syllables to judge by such (rare) forms as <qri̲tun>, a variant to <qraitun> (Macm 335). In auslaut syllables, *ay fully coalesces, to judge by Modern pronunciation: <hza̲i̲> 'see(fs)!' m[héz̲e̲], hence Classical [hə̆z̲é̲] (< *hĭ̆záyī, §8.1.1).

It is also possible that ±hei plays an oppositional role in the def pf 2s (-hei), <qrit> [qə̆ré̲T] (above) ≠ 1s (+hei) homographic <qrit> (Macm 334) interpreted as [qə̆rī̆θ] —cf. Modern 2s [hézet] ≠ 1s [hézīt] (Macm 350)—but the possibility cannot be excluded that some or all of the <i>-forms realizing *2ʃ V 3√y instantiate *2ʃ i rather than *2ʃ a (cf. §8 n. 1).

*aw. As reflex (by e-cnd) of **a 3√yū, coalesced [ō] /__C (<hzun> 'they saw' (Macm 334) [hə̆zṓn]), in auslaut /__# coalesced and by assumption also heightened (<rmu> 'they threw' (lc) [rə̆mū̆]).[16] As reflex of car-derived **a 1√w, partially coalesced ow disguised by adconsonantal assimilation ([ott̆ə̆βúy] 'they seated him' (Mal 283) ← owtͻ̆βúy) at times even further disguised by subsequent smp (§17.26) (~ [ot̲Búy], lc).[17], [18]

Notes to §11

[1] (k-)coalescence to ε̄ and æ is limited to 7-color and 6-color vowel systems, respectively (§20.2 (20G, H)), ε̄ in fact occurring only in one Tib B variant (§11.2 below). Also, to judge by Margolis's transcription, Ash TL shows coa to ā under restricted circumstances (§11.2). If this is genuine, it might mean that the chevron shape often assumed for 7-color vowel systems, wherein a figures as a low mid vowel as in (a) below, should be revised—at least for Ash TL—to a front-heavy array sporting more front vowels than back, as in (b). This is typologically plausible in that the actual acoustic-articulatory vowel space is anatomically lopsided, the front space being longer than the back, and the high space wider than the low—both properties registered in system (b). In any event, if (b) should be a more faithful portrayal of the Ash TL vowel space than (a), coa ay → ā would involve palatalization, like → ε̄ and → ē. If system (a) should be more like it, ay → ā would properly not be coalescence at all but rather a special case of loss (y) to the tune of compensatory lengthening (a → ā).

(a)	i	u	(b)	i	u
	e	o		e	o
	ε	ɔ		ε	ɔ
	a			a	
	chevron			**front-heavy**	

Finally, it might be that the apparent Ash TL ay → ā in fact distorts a nonproblematic instance of ay → æ (as in Yem TL, §11.2), the actual TL vowel system being 6-color (c) by virtue of lacking ε̥̄, whose presence in Margolis's Ash tradition would rather reflect Tiberian-based Schematisierung.

(c) i u
    e o
    æ α

Though evidence for this position is not overwhelming, it is suggestive that the three conditions for the appearance of [ɛ̊] in Margolis's interpretations of the verb (no [ɛ] being found)—/H__ by sco (§17.23), /__H or /1s ʾ__ by a-mid^aop (§17.11)—on the one hand do *not* hold for Yem trad pron of TL but on the other hand *do* hold for B (d), a situation suspicious by virtue of the chronological and dialectal distance between TL and B; cf. also §17.23.1.2.

(d) | Ash TL | Yem TL | Tib B |
|---|---|---|
| ʾɛ̊θố (Mar 91*) | ʾə̆tű (Mor 354) | ʾɛ̊mar (BL 139) |
| tɛhɛ̆wố (Mar 106*) | tịhwɛ́ (Mor 360) | tɛhɛ̆wɛ́ (BL 161) |
| tɛhɛwyín (Mar 106*) | tịhwə̆yín (Mor 360) | lɛhɛwyṍn (BL 161) |
| lɛhšóv (Mar 116*) | lịhšǽv (Mor 363) | tɛ9dɛ́ (BL 161) |
| ʾɛ̊šqól (Mar 175*) | ʾǽšqól (Mor 129) | ʾɛqrɛ́ (BL 161) |

(One might object to this charge appealing to the fact that the Ash TL – B concord with respect to ɛ̊ holds exclusively of *Tiberian* B, the Babylonian register rather aligning with Yem TL, as per (e); so that a charge of Schematisierung might just as rightly or wrongly be made against *Yemeni* TL. However, while in the Ash TL – Tib B nexus we are faced with special processes appeariung to be *shared*, whether absolutely (aop) or conditionally (sco, mid), in the Yem Tl – Bab B case any impression of sharing merely reflects the *absence* of special processes, and by dint of this constitutes a sort of dual null case. Moreover, observe that Yem TL and Bab B *disagree* on two accounts in the frame /ʾ__: for 1√ʾ In the sim impa, where only Bab B promotes ə̆ to e, [ʾemǽr] (§17.23.3 (17.23B)); and for 1s prefixal ʾ in the sim impf, with Yem TL showing [æ], [ʾǽšqól], by failure of attenuation (§12), and Bab B rather showing [i], [ʾiqrɛ́], either by attenuating or by preserving the ancient *i. . .a* ablaut pattern (§1 n. 1) assuming < *ʾiqráʾi.)

(3) Bab B

ʾemǽr (BL 139)
tịhwɛ́ (BL 161)
lịhwĭyắn (BL 161)
tị9dɛ́ (BL 161)
ʾiqrɛ́ (BL 161)

[2] The implication is that at the time k-coa fused *ayi* to *ē*, *ayC* and *ay#* remained unchanged. A priori, one might think that *ayC*, *ay#* would be more prone to coalescence than *ayi*, since in the former cases *a* and *y* are homosyllabic while in *ayi* *a* ends one syllable and *y* is onset to the following syllable, with *i* as nucleus (*a / yi*). One may only conjecture. Perhaps *i* imploded (devocalized) into *y*, making for *ayy*, now a syllable with a heavy coda (offglide) whose palatal quality then pressed back onto the nucleus. The stage would then be set for facile coalescence.

[3] The discussion is in terms of *morae* (weight units; in most cases—as here—equivalent to skeletal positions) rather than in terms of *segments* (autosegmentally, melodies), since a representation such as "*yy*" is properly speaking no more than a conventional portrayal for a configuration like (a). In this vein, conventional representations of geminates employing the colon, as "*y:*" are less misleading than the "*yy*" type. But the latter is used in this book in deference to Semitist tradition.

(a)   melodic tier

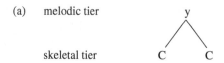

       skeletal tier   C   C

[4] M [šeyláθ] 'she asked' will also be a case in point (<šailat> ~ <šiilat> t[šéylat], Macm 17), derived by smp (§17.26) from *šayyǝláθ* (< **ša²²ilát* by apl, §9.2.1.2), if the p-coa [ey] ← *ay* took place earlier than the smp *ay* ← *ayyǝ*. Perhaps relevantly, the order coa^smp rather clearly occurs in TR int pf 3ms^1s [šæ̰wyǽnī] (Da 69) ← *šæwwǝ̆yǽnī*—because TR normally coalesces **aw* to [ō]; and if the order were smp^coa, the form should be @[šōyǽnī]. (By the way, though smp disrupts a geminate, it does not violate Geminate Integrity. This is because, unlike the case vis-à-vis coalescence just discussed in the text, the structural description (sd) of simplification involves the skeletal tier alone, whereas that of coa involves both skeletal and melodic tiers in a discrepant way. The comparison is portrayed in (a) vs. (b), where targeted melodic and skeletal portions of the sds are boxed off. Observe that in (b) the melody *w* is within the box while the second linked skeletal *C* is outside the box. This discrepancy stalls the process, and the geminate remains integral, hence untargeted by coalescence. (What at first blush might seem an exception to Geminate Integrity as applied here, SM t[wæ̰̆yu] 'und sie lebten' (Macs 220) if < **wǝ̆hǽyyū* after loss of *ḥ*, §9.2.4, is actually more likely derived unproblematically < **waḥ(ǎ)yṓ* since in Aramaic √*ḥyy* (√*ḥy*) tends to act like a defective verb in the sim pf, via gmf-1m, §3.2 (3H), the characteristic geminate behavior, via gmf-4u, §3.2 (3M), being reserved for the impf, cf. §8. n. 7. the result (twæ̰̆yu] from **waḥ(ǎ)yṓ* (or * *wa9(ǎ)yṓ*) follows smoothly from the Samaritan Circuit, §22.1 (22B) (or, more faithfully to the spelling <wḥw>, from r-e-cnd processed **waḥṓ* / **wa9ṓ*).)

(a) **(partial) sd of smp:** *delete the second mora of C'C'*

(b) **(partial) sd of coa:** *amalgamate homosyllabic nucleus and offglide by pooling the features of their melodies*

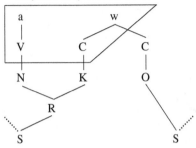

[5] Or '(dass) ich behaupten möchte', hence ambiguous between (original) long or short function.

[6] Might the variation be somehow connected to the fact that the accent is pausal V̋ (siluk), as opposed to contextual V̌? (For the general distinction, see §20.3, §21.6, §17.29.)

[7] There are variants [hēθɔ́yiθ] (with unexpected tonic lengthening, §17.29—the Masoretic accent pašta should not trigger tln, §21.6) and [hēθíyiθ] (possibly transparentized, §15.2.1, §15.4).

[8] I have been unable to track down a variant <yhwh̲>, which appears in my notes.

[9] Dalman plausibly suggests (Da 338) that the penchant toward [æ] in the rmp impf is transparentive in origin, at first in mimicry of strong 2ʃ [æ̊] as unmarked encodation in cau and int (waiving length) and then by extension into sim.

[10] Alternating with -coa [ʾayθí], unsurprisingly (§11.1(α)).

[11] Since e-cnd^coa, the differentiation between such as [mə̌h̲ḗnī] adn [tv9ǽn] vis-à-vis tongue height of coa was presumably dependent on morphological conditions. Assuming the synchronic survival of the fs suffix /-ī/ in the [æ] cases, and a formulation of the rule s-e-cnd along the lines of /a 3√y+ī/ ⇒ |aØ+y|, where /-ī/ lives on as |-y| for input to p-coa, the latter could be conditioned to ⇒ [æ] (as opposed to [ē]) by perseverance of the feature complex [+f, +s].

[12] Something more must be said about the latter result, since when mtr fails to apply, coa goes through: y[h̲ə̌zḗθī], a[h̲ǎzḗθī] ([-ī] by vco, §13), a[h̲ǎzḗθ] (Mor 253, Mar 112*). There are two broad possibilities:

(a) mtr^coa, so that prior occurrence of mtr bleeds coa/__#. This order is diachronically striking, since coa is (in one form of the other) pan-Aramaic, while regular mtr of 1s *-t is exclusive to TL, which suggests the order d-coa^d-mtr. Or there may have been a rule reordering making for s-mtr^s-coa, though the systemic pressure for such a mutation remains to be sought out.

(b) Perhaps alternatively, d-coa was variable, at least in the environment /__1s T, and when later d-mtr arose, the members of *h̲ə̌záyT ~ *h̲ə̌zḗT ~ *h̲ə̌záy ~ *h̲ə̌zḗ were pared down to conform to ay/__#, ē /__C. More on this below in the text.

[13] (a) The fact that [Ā] appears /__1p n is plausibly related to its frequent occurrence in the def absolute mp participle, also /__n; e.g., y[sāɣén], a[soɣǽn] 'going' (Mor 259, Mar 140*).

(b) The preceding statements on yTL k-coa and coa fail to cover the special behavior of the 3√r-less simple verb for 'say' if this verb should be built on *√ymy, as has been sometimes suggested—or, perhaps more accurately, on √ʾmy, itself a blend of *√ymy X √ʾmr (cf. §17.3 n. 3). Under these circumstances, this lexeme shows the normal behavior for a TL 3√y simple verb except that in auslaut *-a 3√y(+i) undergoes *open* (k-)coa to [-ǽ] (rather than close (k-)coa to [-ē] or forgoing amalgamation altogether and remaining by p-coa at [-æy]): 2ms impf [tēmǽ], impa [ʾemǽ] (for 1ʃ [e], §17.23.3 with n. 120a); contrast pf 3ms [ʾɔ̌mā́] < e-cnd *ʾamáya. (For the forms, Mor 353.) If, on the other hand, the [-ǽ] forms derive from [-ǽr] by mtr (§17.12), we are faced with the problem of why mtr should yield front [-ǽ] in the imp system but back [-ā́] in the pf. Perhaps the forms result from a melding of both influences, √ʾmy and mtr. (Note that Margolis's Ash trad pron shows uniform [ɔ́]: impf 3ms [lēmɔ́], impa ms [ʾɛ̌mɔ́]—Mar 88*. Taken at face value, a[lēmɔ́] favors the hypothesis < mtr *lēmár*, because derivation from *√ʾmy should normally render @[lēmā́] by open l-coa from *-áyi (see also n. 1 above).

[14] Of course, fobbing off exceptionality onto morphological-lexical conditions falls short of explanation. Also, the behavior of at least [-ēh] is problematic in other ways, in SR and A at large; prominently, why is this formative (in its pre-l-anc state) exempt from low (§17.10)? See §2.3.4.4 n. 32.

[15] Recall also from §8.1.1 that e-cnd of *ayā* is rare, explaining why 3fp [Qɔ̌Sáy] is not rather @[Qɔ̌Sɔ́].

[16] "by assumption"; no trad pron or Modern pronunciations happen to be available for the reflex of *aw in full auslaut, but the pp-encliticized form <arhubH> 'they smell at it' is traditionally pronounced [arhu̱bī] (Macm 483f.). Clitic hosts in languages at large tend to resemble free forms more than do affixed hosts—and in the specific case of this form, moreover, the pp *b* binds more loosely with the host than does its congener *l*; see §17.15 for details. Enclitic aside, <arhubH> is relevant in being a cau pf 3mp likely built on the synchronic root √rhy (though diachronically probably < *√rWḥ, DM 425), hence its stem ending in coalsceable |aw| ⇐ s-e-cnd /a 3√y+ū/ (or similarly). Finally, the two auslaut-coalesceable nonverbs adduced by Macuch show high-vocalic trad pron: t[gu] (why short [u]?) 'within' < *gaw, t[ū] 'or' < *ʾaw (Macm 120). (Concerning the metaplasm *√rWḥ > √rhy, it is apposite to mention that M appears to have a penchant for developing new 2√h roots; see Malone 1985: 113 with n. 13.)

[17] Unearthing and analyzing M spelling patterns is a delicate matter, and the procedure to be employed here is by no means unchallengeable.

(a) Certain spellings are interpretable as normally diphthongal or monophthongal, though the degree of normality is subject to tempering by historical or inverse spelling, phenomena not always detectable. <ai> normally spells [ay] or [ey]; <ii> usually gives [ey] (unless the first <i> is, as but rarely, used for [y], e.g., <iidlat> [yeðláθ] 'she brought forth' (Macm 13); <au> [aw] or [ow] (though occasionally in anlaut <a> seems rather to be historical flotsam of vanished *ʾ < **9 (§9.3.2.), e.g., <autrana> 'wealth' (DM 11), best interpreted as [oθrānā́] (< **9uθrānā́) with monophthangal [o]); <i>, <e>, auslaut <ia>, and <H> when representing the 3ms object suffix, spell any palatal monophthong, in our present focus on dediphthongal coalescences, normally [ī] or [ē] (though <ia> may also spell [yā̊], e.g., <hia> [hɔ̌yā́] 'he lived' (DM 140)); <u> and in anlaut <eu>, normally [ū] or [ō].

(b) When available, Modern or traditional pronunciations are taken to disambiguate (a); e.g., <ligṭu̱> 'they held her' as [leɣṭṹ] in light of t[léɣṭṹ] (Macm 282) but <hzun> 'they saw' as [hə̆zǫ̆n] in light of m[hézǫ̆n] (Macm 334, 350).

(c) Instance of < > -t,m [ ] disagreement are to be decided case by case.

(d) If only < > is available, all else being equal, the interpretation is: <ai> as [ey], <au> as [ow]; when interpretation as a monophthong by coalescence seems warranted, <i>, <e>, <H>, auslaut <ia> as [ī]; <u>, anlaut <eu> as [ū].(This last strategy is one way of optimizing reconstructed vowel spacing, the assumption being that unmarked interpretation of <ai> as [ay] and of <i> (< *ay) as [ī] (< hei < coa), or of <ai> as [ey] (by p-coa) and of <i> as [ē] (by full coa), would be diachronic-typologically less likely that either [ey] – [ī]—the interpretation chosen here—or [ay] – [ē]; the intuition (with credit at least in spirit to Martinet 1964) being that either arrangement (e–i) or (e–ii) would be systematically more natural than (e–iii) or (e–iv), assuming in each column that the boxed units are diachronically related:

(e)

	i	ii	iii	iv
	ī	ī	ī	ī
	ē	ē	ē	ē
	ey	ey	ey	ey
	ay	ay	ay	ay

(The displays in in (e–i) – (e–iv) are not meant to suggest that the unboxed units are diachronically unrelated to those boxed. On the contrary, all four segments are by hypothesis related, each of the upper three deriving from *ay* by successively incremental change: *ey* by p-coa, *ē* by p-coa then full coa, *ī* by p-coa then full coa then hei. The point is rather that the boxed values prepresent the *unmarked* cases. In the inrepretation chosen in this book, (e–i), this is tantamount to a claim that usually *ay* either raises one notch to *ey* or three notches to *ī*, though there are circumstances where it failes to raise at all or raises only two notches, to *ē*. Interpretation (e–i) was chosen over (e–ii) on the impression that trad and Mod pron show [ey] and [ī] more frequently than [ay] and [ē] as reflexes of *ay* ([ay] in fact being quite rare or even unattested in the verb (the only instance, m[háymen] 'believe' (Macm 251)appearing to be a tacit reconstruction rather than an actually attested form—a conclusion cued by its absence from Macuch's Vocabularyof the Vernacular (Macm 493) as well as his general discussion of diphthongs (119–23).)

At times, the effects of coa and hei are disguised by secondary changes: *owC′* > [oC′C′] (*owTéβ* > [ottéβ] 'he seated'), a process that also feeds smp (*ottə̆βán* > [otBán] 'he seared me'); in Mod and trad pron, Macuch almost always represents the mid front vowel as short, [e], whether genuinely so or as a transcriptional quirk, but in either event, this will be assumed *not* to involve any actual shortening within Classical M per se—thus, m[hézeṭ], t[éhzeṭ] 'you saw' (Macm 350, Mal 281) will be taken to reflect Classical [hə̆zḛ́T] (~ ehzḛ́T] by pro, §17.18).

[18] It may be noted that, despite the variability of *ay coalescence across the dialects, this diphthong is never preserved as a reflext of sar-derived sim impf *a 1√y; contrast car-derived cau *a 1√y, which does at times surface as [Ay]. this invariance may be a point in favor of Brockelmann's derivation of sim impf [Ī] directly from *a 1√y (§9.2.1.2 n. 19).

12. Attenuation

11.1. Description

Aramaic, like Hebrew, shows a propensity to raise unstressed closed-syllabic *a* to, or at least toward, *i*, a process whose original etiology may have been to damp sonorancy under prosodic circumstances (atonicity, closed-syllabic position) inherently antithetical to sonorancy (see Malone 1972b for details). Such an etiology well fits the label traditionally given to this process, first in German as "Verdünnung," and then calqued into various other languages of Semitic scholarship, including English, as *attenuation*—the term to be adopted in this book, abbreviated "att."

Due to prevailing morphological canons, the usual environment for attenuation in A is /__CCV, with the focal *a* immediately pretonic—though antepretonic foci also often occur.

While the prototypic focal-syllable closing structure is /__CC, as indicated, sometimes /__CV̌C appears to be required; more in n. 2 below.

Historically, att seems to have arisen posterior to reduction (§4.2), which feeds it—notably in the robust category of conditions below dubbed "β." It is likely enough, again historically, that the ordering red^att was at close quarters, there being no clear evidence of any other process ever intervening.

Though *full* attenuation aims at whichever level of front vowel is unmarkedly highest in a given dialect, *i* if possible, *partial attenuation* (p-att) stops short of this goal—at *E* in a system where full att would reach *i*. Partial att is normally, though not always, evoked by adjacencyof a guttural.[1] (A similar result is often evoked in the frame /__rr but apparently to be accounted for by a separate mechanism; see n. 4 below.)

Att and p-att will be presented together for the various dialects under four descriptive categories (α, β, γ, δ) of structural conditions. Common to all of these is the tendency for an adjacent guttural to stall att at midstream, via p-att, or to frustrate the process altogether. The categories are presented in terms of their focal vowel.

(α) The prefix vowel of the simple impf *aQSúm-, *-aQSím-. Attenuation of this *a may have been predisposed by the third ablaut pattern of this set, *-iQSám-, whose *i, of apophonic origin (§1.1.1 n. 6), antedates attenuation proper. Though details and subpatterns differ from dialect to dialect, a guttural adjacent to *a (especially following it as 1√H) tends to inhibit attenuation—a tendency likewise operative in most of the other categories below.

211

(β) 1ʃ*a/__S(V̆)M in the simple pf. Att is most robust in nongeminate intransitive light-suffixed forms (*QaSMV̊T); less so in corresponding geminate forms (*QaMMV̊T) or in 3ms^obj forms (*QaSMX́, X́ an object suffix with vocalic (bridge) anlaut).

(Extension to 2ʃ *a will be catalogued under (β').)

(γ) *a/__C(V̆)C in derived forms. Under this general category, there is a special proclivity toward att of prefixal *a in the causative of *√škḥ 'find'—possibly because with this lexeme the causative frame has lost its functional basis, with the consequence that the verb is drifting toward simple status, a status in certain slots reinforced by attenuated [I] < *a lending itself to metanalysis as *either* prothetic in the pf and impa, a role often played by [I] (§17.18) *or* as attenuated simple-prefixed in the impf ((α) above), where att is especially robust; see Malone 1974a. (However, dialects undergoing att of *a in √škḥ and yet retaining causative *h (§9.1.2) caution against accepting this hypothesis too fully, h-bearing forms not lending themselves to formal metanalysis as simples; see §12.2 B for discussion.)

(δ) The vowel of the conjunctive proclitic *wa/__C(V̆)C.[2]

12.2. The Individual Dialects

Y.O.I. Since mls are never used for short vowels in these three dialects, their disposition for attenuation is moot.

B. (α) 2ms [tiršúm], [tintén]; while *2ʃ a forms such as [tilbáš] may either likewise be cases in point, or, rather, instantiate repetition of original apophonic *i (§12.1 (α)). There are alternations likely to be explicable via ±att/__1√H, suggesting moreover a strength hierarchy for H as conditioner, to wit, ʔ ≫ 9, ḥ ≫ h such that ʔ always inhibits the process (3fs [tēxúl] < *taʔkúli mediated by [ē] < coa (§11.2) ay < sar (§9.2.1.2) aʔ); 9 and ḥ sometimes either inhibit att out-and-out or stall it at p-att (-att 2mp tb[ta9bǎðǔn], 3mp tb[yaḥlǒfún], p-att 3fs tb[tɛ9dḗ], contrast bb[tiḥlǒfún], bb[ti9dḗ]; h either allows +att altogether or at worst stops it a p-att (3fs bb[tiḥwḗ], tb[tɛḥɛ̌wḗ]).[3] It will be noted that the Tiberian rergister is more prone to stall attenuation completely or partially than the Babylonian register, which favors full att despite the guttural—a tendency we will see more of below. It will also be noted that the alternations just illustrated were qualified as "*likely* to be explicable via ±att." This reservation is warranted by the possibility that at least some of the presumed +att and +p-att cases may be retentions of original apophonic *i (or an a-mid changeling thereof; see n. 1), a caution sounded for [tilbáš] above. In this case, the caution holds most clearly for the defective instances, as tb[tɛ9dḗ], bb[ti9dḗ], whose [-ē] derives by k-coa from -ay+i, the *2ʃ a of which (§8 n. 1) may have arisen early enough to apophonically select prefixal *i before attenuation ever emerged (§12.1(α)). And whether it did or not, the midding of the prefixal V to [ɛ] (or, more accurately, to e aop > [ɛ]) is certainly evoked by the guttural;

see n. 1. While the cases just reviewed involve the regressive att-inhibiting frame /__H, the progressive frame /H__ under category (α) is limited to the 1s prefix *ʔ. This stalls attenuation at p-att (or triggers adguttural midding if apophonic *i is involved) in two cases *[ʔɛqré], [ʔɛv9é]) and allows it full range (or leaves apophonic *i untouched) in one ([ʔindá9])—all in the Tiberian register, whereas, as with /__H above, the Babylonian register is less responsive to influence from the guttural (bb[ʔiqré]) (BL 161).[4]

(β) [qirvéθ] (observe the ineffectiveness of the r to stall att; n. 4 above), [tiqɔ̌fáθ] (observe the inorganicity of ɔ̌; n. 2).[5] 2√H systematically stalls at [9avðéθ], [ʔamréθ]) as does transitivity ([haθmáh] ~ [haθmɔ̌h]. att is also stalled in geminate intransitives; [naddáθ]. Observe unexpected p-att in [nɛfqáθ], as well as unexpected stalling of att in bb[nǽtléθ] (but +att tb[nitléθ])—derivations in whichi Bauer and Leander plausibly attribute to the influence of n (BL §10t).

(γ) Nothing in the finite verb, but one Bab variant of the cau infinitive tb[haškɔ̌hɔ̌] is +att, bb[hiškāhá̌] (~ -att [hæškāhá̌]) (BL 135). For the special propensity of cau √škh to attenuate, see §12.1(γ). The fact that application of att in the infinitive does not make for formal metanalysis from cau to sim, the hypothesis there expressed, might or might not prove confounding for that hypothesis. It need not be confounding if bb[hiškāhá̌] bespeaks incipient lexicalization, and hence defunctionalization, of a trait, +attenuation, that started out with the functional commitment to turn the verb formally from causative into simple. On the other hand, it might be disturbing if the extant corpus of B is taken as faithfully representative of the dialect's actual paradigm of the verb √škh for the following reason. In order for +att to successfully trigger metanalysis of √škh from cau to sim by making it appear that prothesis §17.18) has taken place, the target vowel must occur in the environment /#(ʔ)__—that is, in anlaut (#__) or separated from anlaut by at most a glottal catch (#ʔ__), the choice depending on whether prothesis was bare (#__) or bolstered by a virtually empty consonant with the canonical function of providing a nonnull onset (#ʔ__, *hamzatu 'l-waṣl*). But to judge by the extant corpus of B neither of these prerequisite frames for the metanalyzed vowel would ever be met because the verb √škh in the relevant paradigm (pf)[6] always occurs /#h__ (B does show h- ~ ʔ- variation of the causative-prefixal anlaut at large but not for √škh). A similar pattern holds in the impf, where the constancy of prefixal h would disable att, if it applied, from making a token of cau √škh formally identical to simple; e.g., 2ms [tɔ̌haškáh] would not pass as simple even if it were attenuated to @[tɔ̌hiškáh]. (For discussion of cau ʔ ~ h, see §9.1.2.)

(δ) Bab B is much clearer than the Tib register in showing attenuation thwartable by a following guttural: +att [wiv9á̌] (Dan 2:16; BL 161), -att [wæhwɔ̌] (Dan 2:35, BL 263). In Tib B, the only circumstance where att clearly occurs is /__y ([wīhax] = *wi-yháx*). Preguttural att appears to fail (tb[wahăwɔ̌], corresponding to bb[wæhwó] at Dan 2:35, but since Tib B is like Tib Hebrew in the frame $w\overset{\circ}{V} = h\overset{\circ}{V}$, with the color of $h\overset{\vee}{V}$ (sco, §17.23) rubbing off onto proclitic $w\overset{\vee}{V}$ by a species of minor vowel harmony (§2.3.2.1 n. 5), we cannot be fully sure here that *wa did not priorly undergo att or p-att, only to be returned à l'accordion to identical wa by color harmony from ă.[7] Likewise, as in Tib Hebrew (THP 78), any possible action of att preceding a true consonant in the frame /__C(V̌)C is preempted by *labial coalescence* (lco), dictating that conjunctive $w\overset{\circ}{V}$ fuse to [ů] ([ův9ó] (Dan 2:16), [ůsăɣáð] (Dan 6:23)).[8]

P. N. The orthography leaves us in the lurch.

TR. (α) [yiɣnón] 'stiehlt', [yiθqǽf], [tismóx] 'stützest' (Da 269f.). In the environment /__H, -att bb[yæ9ǒBéð] ~ sb[yæ9ǎbéð] but +att bb+sb[yi9ǐróq] (lc)—where, be it noted, possible promotion of the excrescent ĭ to i must follow att if the condition /__CV̆C is to be maintained for cases like this (see §4.5 for prm of exc-generated V post-1 √9 in these forms). In the environment /H__, -att bb[ʔæfrǔq] ~ +att sb[ʔifrǔq] 'ich löse ein' (Da 272); see also n. 15 below.

(β) tb[šim9éθ] 'ich hörte' (Da 78)—att in intransitive light-suffixed verbs not testable for Bab texts, the frame apparently always being barytone: [QǒSV̊MV̊θ] in strong verbs (§4.1.2.), where 1ʃ has been reduced; and [QÁSSV̊θ] in geminates, where att is foiled by stress ([qǽlliθ] 'ich war gering' (Da 330)). Transitives generally resist att ([šælḥǽnī] 'er sandte mich' (Da 362)); but Dalman does cite one apparent +att case: [riḥǒmǽh] 'er liebte sie' (Da 363)—unless this form is intensive ← mls riḥḥǒmǽh[9] (in which case it would fit under (γ), next).[10]

(γ) **cau-** sb[niškǽḥ] (~ næškǽḥ) (Da 274), also impf 2mp [ti9dón] (Da 347), impf 3ms^1s [yiḥzě̃n(n)ǽnī] (Da 388); **int-** [nissīθī] 'ich versuchte' (Da 343), plus an additional form of √nsy, Da 88), pf 1s [milléθī] (Da 343), see also √rḥm under (β), preceding; **int rmp-** 2ʃ in [ʔizdæbbentún] (§17.17.1).

(δ) +att /__y (int impf 3ms [wīšælláḥ] = wi-yšælláḥ (Da 269)), variably /__H (sim impa ms [wiḥwī́] but pf 3ms [wæḥzǎ́]) where possible effects may also be disguised by lco (cf. under B above) (sim impa ms [ůhzī́]), which also occurs preceding a strong C (sim pf 3fp or impa fp [ůrkívǎ́]) (all Da 240); cf. n. 8.

CP. Since this dialect shows a predilection for vowel palatalization on a variety of fronts, it is not always clear whether attenuation is responsible for a given instance of $A \to I$ as opposed to one of the other palatalization processes. The following profile of CP att is presented with this caution in mind.[11]

(α) Few probative forms encountered in default of mls or pointing. The like of sim impf <yḥm?> (Sl 65), whether 3ms or 1s interpretable as [Iḥmé], suggests att of *ya-, despite the following guttural, as a precondition to ymn (§14.2 CP (α) with (14A): ya- att → yl- ymn → [I-]. (Unless the prefixal vowel is always palatal, by i. . .a ablaut (§1.1.1 n. 6), < yiḥmáyi.)

(β) Surprisingly, CP seems to forego att in light-suffixed intransitives, generally one of the most att-friendly environments: <šBqT> 'sie liess' (Sg 62) [šavqáT], <ẙD9̥T̂> 'ich wusste' (Sg 76) [yað9éT], in addition to other forms (llcc) with the dot superposed on the anlaut grapheme. CP also fails to show att in geminates: <9̥lyT> 'ich trat ein' (Sg 62) [9alléT] (unless this is barytone [9állIT]).[12]

(β′) Attenuation "später" caught up with 2ʃa in sim pf gem 2mp ţo judge by forms like <9llTwn> 'ihr tratet ein' (Sg 68), interpretable as [9ə̥lIltŬn].

(γ) **cau-** various forms of √škḥ (Sl 205), <ʔBDT> 'sie vernichtete' (Sg 66) [Ibbə̆ðáT] (note (§21.4) that the superposed dot on <ʔ> in older texts indicates [Ĩ], even though on strong <C>s it normally conveys [å]), plus additional forms at Sg 63; **int-** <ysʔ> 'ich heile' (Sg §34.1, §53.2a2) [Issé] (with apheresis of prefixal ʔV̆- by såd, §9.2.2.2, or generalized wic, §17.33).

(δ) Schulthess assumes generalization of lco (**B** above) without argument or examples (Sg 56) and later (93) cites what he interpretts as *ūfᵉqað* (= [ũfə̆qáð] in this book) but provides neither source nor spelling; nor does any such form appear in his lexicon (Sl). If he is correct, the issue of +att or -att is effectively mooted. (In this book it will be assumed that at least in the special case of [wI-] ← wə̆ = yə̆- attenuation is *not* involved, but rather ymn^vdc; see §14.2 CP n. 11, with special reference to derivation (aiv).)

<u>SM.</u> Since the SM circuit (§22.1 (22B)) may rather formidably veil the work of reconstruction, some of the following conjectures must be taken with circumspection.

(α) <yGnB> t[yígnæb] 'stiehlt' (Macs 147), <Tqs> t[tíqqɑṣ] 'wirst abschneiden' (Macs 198); /__H <yḥKm> t[yékkæm] 'er weiss' (Macs 172). Two exceptions to att under (α) have been noted: <ym9y> t[yæmǽʔi] 'schlägt' (Macs 207), <nšwy> t[nǽšbi] 'bereiten wir uns' (Macs 208f.). (A couple of observations: (*) 2ʃt[æ] in the +att cases need not be a reflext of *a and hence the ablaut frame *-iQSaM, in view of the SM tendency to neutralize 2ʃ to t[A] (cf. Macs 104, 147f.). (Though conditions are not fully clear, this neutralization may be opposed in the environment /__CC by a complementary neutralization to [I]: together, 2ʃ V̆ → [I] /__CC, → [A] elsewhere (i.e., -/__CC), the overall process to be called *second schematic neutralization* (ssn).) (*) Though the two -att instances cited (t[yæmǽʔi], t[nǽšbi]) are defective verbs, there are +att defectives as well—e.g., <yBny> ~ <yBnh> t[yíbni] 'baut' (Macs 207).)

(β) Attenuation is largely preempted by synergy of predilection for barytone light sim pf forms and the penchant to retain or restore 2ʃ to full vowel status, in any event (§4.2.2 with n. 16); e.g., <BţnT> t[bāţắnɑt] 'wurde schwanger' (Macs 145), <9BDh> t[9āb(b)áde] 'machte ihn' (Macs 226).[13] However, one form that seems to have escaped full-2ʃ status appears *not* to have undergone att: <nḥTT> ~ <n9TT> t[nǽttæt] 'sie stieg herab' (Macs 194), plausibly ← *na9Táθ* < *naḥitát*.

(γ) A few cau forms: <wTy̲9Twn> (~ <wT9T̲wn> ~ <wThTwn>) 'ihr werdet herunterbringen' (Macs 188) < *wə̆Taḥhə̆θŮn*, *√nḥt, and unsurprisingly (§12.1 (γ)) <nšKḫ> t[ni̲škæ] 'wir finden' (Macs 175). (There are hints of other manifestions of att in other binyamin, none conclusive: sim rmp pf <ˀTrḥṣnn> t[itre̲ṣṣínnɑn] 'wir hoffen' (Macs 154), if ← *(ˀ)iθre̲ḥṣinnán* upon renewal of the 1p suffix by pin (§17.17) and ensuant opening of the 2ʃ syllable triggering a reprise (at least synchronically) of red^att, ultimately < *hitra̲ḥísnā*; int <wqi̲yyậmɑn> 'und schlug einen Bund mit uns' (Macs 193), though Macuch may be correct in claiming that this is a denominal form built on <qyˀm> 'Bund'.

(δ) No att in the one (nonverb) form encountered, which has escaped otherwise widespread generalization of the conjunctive allomorph t[w-] (or [wə̆-], §22.1 SM): <wBymh> t[wæbyámmɑ] 'und im Meer' (Macs 71) (see also n. 8 above).

G. (α, β) The ml <y> seems never to appear in Dalman's listings for either prefixal V̌ or 1ʃ in -V̲Q̲S̲V̌M-, QV̌SMV̌T despite its use under (γ), next—and, it might be added, in segolate or dissyllabic nominals of similar morphophonemic structure to (α, β) verbs: for instance, <my̲lḫˀ> 'Salz' (Da 88) [mI̲lḥậ]. While at least in the case of (α), nonappearance of <y> may be attributable to mere conservative orthography becoming conventionalized in a high frequency structure type (as, e.g., the M regularity of leaving [V̌] unspelled in sim pf and impa [QV̌SV̌M], §21.8), it would be rash to commit oneself to a stance on att here one way or the other.

(γ) **cau-** <ny̲ŝKḫ> (unsurprisingly), <ny̲Glynwn> 'wir lassen sie auswandern' (Da 390); **int-** <ˀy̲lPn> 'er lehrte uns' (Da 88).

SR. (α) Uniformly +att(^mid): [tɛxtowín] 'tu(f) écriras' (Du 173), and this despite possible adjacency of one or more gutturals: [ɛxtów] 'werde ich . . . schriftlich darlegen' (Ns 198) < *ˀa-*, att presumably occurring prior to the loss of ˀ (§9.3.2); [ɛ9béð] '(hätte) ich thun (sollen)' (Ns 201) < *ˀa̲9bíd(i)*.[14]

(β) +att in the intransitive, whether geminate ([bɛzzáθ] 'sie hat geplundert', Ns 123) or not ([yɛð9éθ] 'weiss ich', Ns 194); -att in the transitive ([yahbóˀh] 'gab sie', Ns 132).

(γ) +att only, and consistently, in (ex-)causative √škḥ 'find', [ɛškáḥ], etc. (Brockelmann 1928: 775)—see Malone 1974a.

(δ) -att ([wa̲šbów] 'ils . . . capturèrent', Du 375).

TL. (α) Though Morag's Yem and Margolis's Ash traditions agree on the cardinal point that the sim impf prefix unmarkedly attentuates—e.g., y[li̲t9úm], a[li̲t96m] 'he'll taste' (Mor 129, Mar 118*)—they fail to agree on the guttural conditions: while 1s *ˀa- simply fails to attenuate in Yem (y[ˀæzbón] 'ekne', Mor 129), in Ash it undergoes p-att (^aop, ¶17.11) even /__H (a[ˀɛšqól] 'I'll take (Mar 175*), [ˀɛ9béð] 'I'll do' (Mar 145*));[15] and in the environment

/__H at large, Yem consistently shows full att while Ash vacillates between p-att (favored) and no att (y[ni̯9véð], y[li̯9bŏðǘ] (Mar 145*)). Which of the traditions ismore faithful to the original pronunciation, in the case of disagreement? At least in the 1s condition, whether a guttural follows or not, the frequent spelling with ml <y> is in sync with Ash p-att, but perhaps not with Yem failure to attenuate at all: e.g., the relevant forms above are spelled <ʔy̲ŝqwl> (~ < ʔŝqwl>), <ʔy̲zBwn>, <ʔy̲9ByD> (Mar 38, Mor 129).[16]

(β) Possibly without exception, TL lacks att of 1ʃa in the sim pf: *either* preempting occurrence with a barytone stress pattern (y[y̲léðæθ] 'yalda' (Mor 124), a[šŏqáliθ] 'I took' (Mar 175*)) *or*, when showing an oxytone pattern on a light-suffixed verb—Yem only—leaving 1 a unattenuated (y[šæxbã̄] 'saxva' Mor 124). In the other subcategories of (β), att also remains fallow: e.g., transitive y[šævqǽnī] '9azav ʔoti' (Mor §15.11), a[šaqléh] 'he took him' (Mar 175*).[17]

(γ) **cau-** According to Morag (Mor 102f.), att is not found in the pf but is widespread in the impf (except 1s), a phenomenon that he attributes to the prevalence of [i] as the prefixal vowel in the other binyamin, e.g., y[ni̯hdǽr] (~ -att [næhdǽr] 'yahzir', y[li̯qdŏmǘ] 'yakdimu';[18] ±att variation in the causative also shows up for Margolis's Ash tradition—including counterparts of the two forms just cited, a[nɛhdár] (p-attenuated /__h) (Mar 106*), a[li̯qdŏmǘ] (Mar 158*)—though apparently not subject to the same paradigmatic distribution as in Yem, e.g., pf a[ʔi̯tlá9] (~ -att [ʔaṭlá9]) 'he turned sideways' (Mar 118*); **int-** Morag reports a few transitive forms, e.g., 3ms^3mp [li̯qqŏṭinnŏhǘ] (Mor 298, 369).

(δ) lco, at least immediately preceding a nonglide: y[ůnfǽl] (§16.2 TL (a′)).

M. (α) Consistent +att, not impeded by flanking gutturals: <ȩbad> ~ <ȩbid> 'I'll do', <ȩhdar> 'I'll turn', <ȩhuia> 'I'll be', <ȩkul> 'I'll eat' (DM 2, 131, 133; Macm 297), [ȩbbáð] ~ [ȩbbéð], [ȩhdár], [ȩhwî́], [ȩkkól] < *9, *ḥ, *h, *ʔ, respectively. (For the *HC′* → *C′C′* instances, via rga, see §9.2.1.1 n. 14b; some but not all such cases may reflect original ablaut *i. . .a*, §1.1.1 n. 6, whereby att accordingly applies vacuously.)

(β) M shows +att in the nongeminate light formations with strong 1√, intransitive and transitive[19] alike (<ligtat>, <ligtan> 'she took, he took me' (DM 230) [lɛɣṭáθ], [lɛɣtán]), but not in the geminate (<pasat>, <pasH> 'she destroyed, he destroyed it(m)' (DM 375), [passáθ], [passî́]. With glide 1√, not only guttural but semivowel as well, att is variable (<abdat> ~ <ebdat> 'she did' (DM 2) [aβDáθ] ~ [eβDáθ], <iahbit> ~ [ehbit] 'I gave' (DM 189) [yahBî́θ] ~ [ehBî́θ]—for *9 > ∅ and *yI > e, see §9.3.2, §14.2 M—<Dlahamlat> 'which(f) did not bear', <hiblat> 'she writhed' (DM 129, 149) [dŏ=lā=hamláθ], [heβláθ].

(β′) See (γ3) below.

(γ) There are from one to three manifestations, depending on one's interpretation:

(γ1) M attenuates *2ʃa in the sim rmp, not merely in the strong verb (<etgiblat> 'she was formed' (Macm 266) [eθgeβláθ]) but equally in the geminate verb, even /__H (<etnihat> 'she was appeased' (Macm 322) [eθneh(h)áθ]);

(γ2) If M show any trace of 1ʃa att in the causative, it is likely to be found in what Drower and Macuch take to be the "rigid form <leška> = <liška> and <laniška> only in the idiomatic {sense} 'to be (un)able'" (DM 464). In that eventuality, a form like <laniška> 'we are unable' would be felt to function synchronically as sim [lā=neškā́], but in fact diachronically would ultimately derive from the causative, < *lā=nihaškíhi after a chain of changes—att probably the latest—had neutralized the two binyamin in many paradigmatic slots.[20]

(γ3) There is a tendency for [e] to appear, instead of low (§17.10) expected [a], in the intersection of circumstances 2ʃ in closed-syllabic pretonic position within an int or cau verb; e.g., <šadi̱rtH> (~ expected <šadartH>) 'thou sendest him' (DM 450) <šadde̱rtí>, <abi̱rtunH> 'ye have ferried her over' (DM 4) [abbe̱rtonnā́] < *ʔa9b... (via rga, §9.2.1.1 n. 14b), <šabi̱htH> 'I praised him' (DM 447) [šabbe̱htí]. Cases with apparently assimilated 3√H may well belong here, too, like <aški̱nin> (~ <aškanin>) 'we found' (DM 465), *√škh, but it is impossible to be sure, because verbs with lost *3√H tend to follow the leadof their ancient *3√ʔ congeners and neutralize with *3√y (adn, §9.1.4)— thus <aškinin> might not be [aškennín] but rather [aškī̱nín] ⇐ /a+ 1√š 2√k i 3√y + nīn/. (In the same vein, it is possible that the phenomenon at times extends to *3√H sim verbs with original *2ʃi, like <šmi̱tinan> (~ <šmatinan>) 'thou didst hear us' (DM 469), but the matter remains moot for the same reason.) The question here is: are the cases of [e] for [a] of the sort under discussion a manifestation of att? And if so, are we dealing with an accordion-like chain wehre ʃi low > a att e? Or did the power guiding att rather stall low from applying? Or, indeed, did low fail to apply for some independent reason? Or, finally, is the apparent involvement of low merely a mirage induced by scanty data, with M showing a tendency to deploy att on 2ʃa of *any* origin, not merely that assimilated by low? These questions must await decisive data not yet forthcoming. (It is also possible that at least some of these manifestations, notably of low-deviant [e] in such as [šadde̱rtí], are transparentive in origin; see §15.5.1.)

(δ) We are led by stray examples encountered as well as by Macuch's statement (Macm 245) to believe that the reflex of the conjunctive proclitic *wa was unconditionally generalized as <u> [ů] by lco (see B (δ) above), a verb case in point being <uhpakt> 'and thou hast turned' (Macm 451) [ůh(š̌)Páxt].

Notes to §12

[1] Though treated as an independent process in most contexts in this book, the work of p-att is at least sometimes achieved as a special case of *midding* (mid), normally the assimilatory type *adguttural midding* (a-mid); §17.11. That is, what in this

chapter will be taken as *a* p-att → *E* may at times actually bespeak the accordion-like chain *a* att → *i* (a-)mid → *E*—"accordion-like," in that the focal vowel starts off and ends up at a lower position than it occupies midstream; compare the trajectories in (a):

(a)

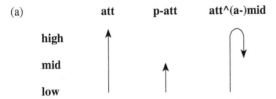

Though evidence for att^(a-)mid of this sort (there are other sorts, too—irrelevant here) is perhaps not available in the verb system, the behavior of the noun for 'dream' in B provides a clear demonstration. The 1s possessive form of this noun, [ḥɛlmî] 'my dream (Dan 4:6), is on the surface segmentally, syllabically, and stresswise identical to the verb [nɛfqáθ] '(a decree) went forth' (Dan 2:13) with respect to focal [ɛ], sve for the guttural trigger, but with the crucial difference that while the latter might be derived *either* with p-att (**napaqát . . . nafqâθ*, p-att *nefqáθ* aop (§17.11) > [nɛfqáθ]) *or* with (att^)mid (**napaqát . . . > nafqâθ*, att > *nifqâθ* mid *nefqáθ* aop > [nɛfqáθ]), the former can only be derived with a-mid (*ḥilmî* a-mid > *ḥelmî* aop > [ḥɛlmî]) for the simple reason that no **a* was ever present to begin with, so that p-att is preempted (the free form of this noun is [ḥḗlɛm], Dan 4:2, < **ḥílmu* via uap^epn+mid^aop, §17.22, §17.6; contrast [mḗlɛx] 'king', Dan 2:10, < **málku* via uap^epn^aop^mvh (whereby the sequence *á* ... *ɛ* harmonizes to *ɛ́* ... *ɛ*, §2.3.2.1 with n. 5).)

However, while a *synchronic* account might thus be forced to posit s-att^s-(a-)mid over s-p-att, all else being equal, on the basis of relative simplicity and attendant psycholinguistic considerations of computational ease and the like, *diachronically both* d-att^d-(a-)mid *and* d-p-att might be genuine in the event mid of the subtype (potentially) relevant to the verb either antedated att or chronologically overlapped it. Let us suppose, for instance, the same general phonetic forces to be at work in motivating the actual midding of *ḥilmî* to *ḥelmî* (> [ḥɛlmî]) and the potential mutation of *nafqáθ* to *nefqáθ* (> [nɛfqáθ]). Imagine now that attenuation commences to raise *a* to *i*. In such a system, with a predisposition to lower *i* to *e* (as per *ḥelmî*), it seems reasonable to assume that the full trip upward *a* → *i* would be stopped by *e* by virtue of the same pressures that made/make for *i* → *e*. And if so, we have a natural case of two distinct processes—p-att and (a-)mid—converging on the same target (see (b)) diachronically, cost free, whatever the ultimate synchronic resolution might turn out to be.

(b)

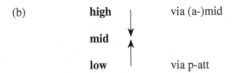

[2] In specific cases, the process might be simplified—and rendered more natural—by omitting "(V̆)" from the conditions in (β, γ, δ). However, at large in Aramaic (and Hebrew) it does not seem possible to curtail various processes from "ignoring" V̆. In

Malone 1995, it is proposed that this is symptomatic of reduced vowels being "inert elements" in the Northwest Semitic languages; note also that at least five Tiberian Hebrew processes similarly contain "(V̌)" in THP: AO (60), CM (70), CS (71), LC (78), and SA (94). For more on inert V̌ in Aramaic, see §6 n. 27, §14.1 nn. 1 and 6. See also Nancy Hall's theory of "intrusive vowels" (2006).

[3] For something about the descriptive nuts and bolts of such hierarchies, see THP 79.

[4] Since *r*, qua low sonarant, forms a natural class with the gutturals—as in fact per their function as common conditioners to lowering (§17.10)—the question arises as to whether the mid palatal coloring in [wəðθə̄rŏa9] 'and it shall destroy' (Dan 2:40) < *watạrrŭ9i (conjunctive sim impf on √r9, root X scheme interdigitated by gmf-4u, §3 ((3m)) bespeaks p-att, along the lines of . . . *arr* . . . p-att > . . . *err* . . . mls (§9.3.1) > . . . *ēr* . . . . Though the net process complex works out like p-att, doubtlessly bespeaking typological convergence, neither p-att nor its isofunctional partner att^a-mid (n. 1 above) are plausibly involved per se. This is because *singleton r* never inhibits att or triggers p-att: cf.]tịršúm] (above in the text) ≠ @[taršúm], @[tɛršúm]. And while one, on the sole basis of B, with its limited corpus, might get away with positing *geminate rr* as the conditioner, this ploy won't work for Ash TL, whose disposition is otherwise very much like that of B, becuase there the mid palatal coloring appears only attendant upon degemination by mls; e.g., sim rmp pf of 3ms a[ʔə̄rŏxás] (Mar 165*) < *hitrakása (for *2ʃa, see §1.1.1 n. 4), where . . . *itr* . . . rrf (§10 TL) > . . . *irr* . . . > [. . .ēr. . .]. When (rarely) degemination fails to apply, no mid vowel appears; e.g., [gịrrő] 'arrow' (Malone 1998b)—likewise in the Yemeni tradition, y[ʔirrŏxǽs] (which apparently never shows mls of *irr*, §9.3.1 TL, though it may withi *arr*). On balance, we must seemingly build the midding feature directly into mls, not only for *rr* (*irr* → *ēr*) but for gutturals as well (*iH'H'* → *ēH'*), hence, compositely, *Il'L'* → *ēL'*; and, consequently, the undeniable similarity to p-att/(att^)(a-)mid must be chalked up to typological convergence. See also §9.3.1 n. 40.

[5] In this case, it seems possible that the ŏ was inserted (by exc, §4.3) into the frame /q__f posterior to att, in which case a species of accordion effect is involved, since *2i would have been priorly lost from that selfsame slot by red: *taqipát spr > taqifáθ att > tiqfáθ exc > [tiqŏfáθ]. Alternatively, the ŏ may indeed have been part of the frame, there by courtesy of the *partial* (weakening) reduction (p-red) in lieu of the expected *full* sort (f-red) (§4.2.1): *taqipát spr > taqifáθ p-red > taqŏfáθ att > [tiqŏfáθ]. In either event, the presence of ŏ seems marked. (*2ʃi is motivated, by the way; see homoparadigmatic forms at Dan 4:8, 9, 17.)

[6] The other potentially relevant paradigm is the impa, which, however, is unattested for √škḥ in extant B texts.

[7] For the vowel harmony effect elsewhere in B, f. [wɛʔə̆nŏ́š] 'und ein Mensch' (BL 263).

[8] Labial coalescence also occurs in TR and M (see below in the text), under increasingly wider conditions than in B—specifically, while lco in B is limited to /__true consonant (i.e., excluding semivowels and gutturals), in TR it is beginning to invade /__H, while in M it is fully generalized irrespective of environment. The trad pron of SM may similarly have been fully generalized [w-]; that is, where lco *vocalizes* (re-

flexes of) the proclitic conjunction **wa-*, SM trad pron may *consonantize* (semivocal-ize). (For the reservation conveyed by "may," §22.1 SM.)

[9] Note that the p-att-like midding effect of mls discussed in n. 4 above is not forthcoming here, by hypothesis, because the reflex is short-vocalic ([ṛiḥə̆mæh]), compensatory lengthening being foregone as frequently when the geminate guttural is ḥḥ (§9.3.1).

[10] Dalman cryptically alludes to the 1ʃ[i] of this form as being tied up with the fact that its 2ʃ is phonlogically palatal. Though unclearly and incompletely articulated, this suggestion provides food for thought in that modern Ma9lula Aramaic shows a similar color symbiosis between 2ʃ and att of 1ʃ in the sim pf—e.g., 3fs+att [ðị̆mxaθ], cf. 3ms [iðmex̱]; but 3fs -att [za̱bnaθ], cf. 3ms [izba̱n] (Spitaler 1938: 152; forms retranscribed to the phonetic system used in this book).

[11] The most salient of these processes variably dictates *á → é* / __C where *C* is a coda, process that might be called *stressed closed syllable raising* (scr). Since attenuation is likewise conditioned in closed syllables (or quasi-closed in the special case of / __CV̆C, see n. 2), it is possible that *á → é* represents an extension of att into stressed syllable position. Examples include the cau mp pf <ʔTwsP̱> 'wurde hinzugefügt' (Sg 60) [Ittōsé̱f] < **ʔittawsá̱f* ([é] cued by the dot under <P̱>, §21.4), the sim pf <9yl> 'trat ein' (Sg 68) [9él] < **9ál*; perhaps the cau pf <ʔškyḥT> 'du fandest' (Sg 62) [aškéḥt] < **aškáḥt*—unless [é] here bespeaks failure of expected low (§17.10) since *ʔaškáḥt* itself would derive ultimately from ***haškị̆hta* (and in the event low *did* apply, note the semi-accordion ***í > á > é*, palatal > low > palatal). Another defacto *a → I* process is the tendency to analogically extend 2ʃ from the imp system into the pf (Sg 60); e.g., <9ByD> 'machte' [9ðvé̱ð]; cf. impa <9BḎ> ~ <9ByD> 'fac!' (Sl 140) likewise [9ðvé̱ð]. (This case of course might alternatively be accounted for by the closed-syllablic *á → é* process. A test case might involve an *open* syllable, but none yet have been incidentally encountered. Note, too, that the analogical process might also involve *á → U* when the imp 2ʃ is labial, e.g., likely <B9wT̊hẘn> 'misit eos' (Sl 29) [bə̆9U̱ThÚn] (for [T], see n. 12, next) homoparadigmatic imp forms of which are, however, not attested. Observe that a possible case in point like <šmw9> 'hörte' (Sg 60) [šə̆mÚ9] (for prefixal [I-], §14.2) implies *either* (a) that low (§17.10) had bypassed the latter—because otherwise we'd have (@)[Išmá̱9], failing to serve as a model for 2ʃ labialization—*or* (b) that, less plausibly, reshaping was based on phonological 2ʃ /U/ and that, accordingly, labialization of 2ʃ was still motivated despite the effects of low. Hypothesis (a) seems more likely, low being rather weakly represented in CP to begin with. But Schulthess opens a third possibility (Sg §42): that 2ʃa has been assimilated to adjacent labial 2√m. Slipper business.)

[12] It seems perilous to assume spirant value for auslaut <T>, in particular <T̊>, though postvocalic. Schulthess's discussion (Sg §6.1), especially with cross-reference to §45) suggests, despite his silence on the matter, that CP may have undergone despirantization of θ, at least in verb-suffixal position (as incidentally in Modern Mandaic).

[13] For the variable gemination of 2√ in the like of t[9ā̆b(b)ā̆de], see §9 n. 28.

[14] In SR and M (below), mid is systematically fed by att (though marked instances of [i] remain in both dialects); see §17.11 for details. The point to bear in mind in the context of att is that the [E] in question is not evoked by p-att or the like; or, if it

might have been, the effect is neutralized by the systemic occurrence of mid. In what follows, "att^(mid)" will often be abbreviated to "att" alone.

[15] Consider the fact that Yem TL and Bab TR show [ʔæ-] as the 1s anlaut of the rmp impf—TL y[ʔæmmŏlíx] (vs. a[ʔimmŏlíx]) 'I'll take command' (Mor 154, mar 131*); TR sim bb[ʔæθqŏṭíl] (~ sb[ʔi̭θqŏṭíl]) 'ich soll getötet werden', cau (with š as prefixal, §1.1.3 n. 9) or int (with š metanalyzed as 1√) [ʔæštēzǽv] 'ich werde gerettet' (Da 272)—while [I] appears as the vocalism of the remaining rmp φ-slots, as well as of 1s in the non-rmp derived conjugations. A possible explanation for this at first glance puzzling distribution is in-progress generalization of æ as realization of 1s impf vocalism (portmanteau with [+rmp])—in the first instance from the simple plain conjugation, where attenuation has bypassed this φ-slot because of /ʔ__; and then from the plan causative, likewise normally bypassed as morphologically (diacritically) exempt (but see below). Once æ has invested 1s in the rmp conjugations, the sole holdout is the plain intensive—the only slot typically hosting *reduced* vocalism, hence not lending itself to fully stable color opposition ("typically" in view of the possibility of promotion to V̊, whether by transparentation, ips §15.3.1.1, or under guttural influence /#H__, §9.2.2.2, §9.3.1; e.g., TR [ʔe̥šællém], Da 272). And in counterpoint, the vocalism typical of the non-1s φ-slots is *i* in all but the plain intensive whenever preempted by V̆ (again modulo possible promotion) and the plain causative—where, in fact, *i* may also be licensed to spread by (γ)-category att, which in fact at least in Yem TL it does tend to do, *except in 1s* (see below in the text). So all this boils down to a tendential vocalism pattern like (a) for the impf prefix in Bab TR and Yem TL, regardless of binyan:

(a)	**singuler**	**plural**
3m	i	i
3f	i	i
2m	i	i
2f	i	i
1	æ	i

[16] A somewhat different possibility is cued by the fact that, in borrowings from Tiberian Hebrew into Tiberian-transcribed texts in the Yemeni tradition, ε is spelled with pataḥ (Breuer 2003: 125); that is, Hebrew ε merges downward to æ. On that basis, we might assume that TL itself had ε, as in fact does Margolis's transcription, and that spellings like <ʔyzBwn> duly reflect the like of [ʔεzbón], subsequently merged to y[ʔæzbón]. Finally, the analogical extension ʔi- > ʔæ- discussed in n. 15, preceding, would take place (y[æ] being a reflex not only of ε, but equally of *a* as relevant to the role of causative *ʔa- in that extension). (In this book, it will be assumed that living TL did *not* have [ε] but rather a 6-color system like that of Yem trad pron [i, e, æ, u, o, α]. Needless to say, this assumption fails to automatically explain the translinguistic ε → æ noted above, and the issue must ultimately be revisited and resolved.)

[17] (a) "Possibly without exception. . . ; Yem only": Margolis presumes (Mar *87) to document one case of an attenuated oxytone light-suffixed pf, 3fs (impersonal) a[ʔixfáθ] 'es kümmert . . . um'. In this book, however, Jastrow (1903: 65) will be followed, according to whom this item is rather a fs noun of miškal *QiSMatu in the (syn-

tactically frozen) construct state. (b) There may be a subtle subregularity to the Yem patterns: failure of the light suffix to drop its -*T* (via mtr, §17.12) always correlates with oxytone stress, while apocope of same may cooccur with either oxytone or barytone, perhaps subject to idiolectal or subregisterial dictates; see Mor 124f. for details (especially the paragraph headed *Curot šesiyuman těnu9ati*).

[18] Cf. n. 15 above.

[19] Nöldeke lists (Nm 280) <ru̱dpunan> as a sim variant of int <radpunan> 'verfolgten uns', which might suggest a sporadic vowel-harmonic instance of labialization of attenuated 1ʃe under the influence of the 3mp suffixal vowel *o*, [roðPonnán] (cf. §2.3.2.1 with n. 5). However, since sim pf verbs with plural object suffixes normally preserve 2ʃ from reduction (§7.4.1), if this were a garden variety form, we should rather expect something like c[rɜ̆ðafonnán]. Hence, <rudpunan> should be treated with skepticism.

[20] There is no hint of 1ʃa att in the finite verb of the intensive, but one possible though questionable case has come to light in an infinitive: <lbi̱šqirH> 'to gaze intently upon him' (DM 71). Drower and Macuch pronounce this form "irreg.," a verdict justified independently of ±att. We should expect something like c<lbašqurH> [lɜ̆βašqūrí].

13. Vowel Copy

Various dialects (TR, SM, TL, M) show evidence of a subject suffix (partially) of shape $V'C'$ assuming an extended shape $V'C'V'$. Though other hypotheses have sometimes been offered for this phenomenon (or these phenomena)—two ideas, which might possibly be collapsed to one—will be pursued in this book: *vowel harmony* (vha), notably where the additional V' results from total progressive assimilation of a preexisting vowel by virtue of the V' of the original $V'C'$ sequence spreading its color rightward—that is, $V'C'V \rightarrow V'C'V'$;[1] and *mitosis* (mit), notablyl where the derived V' is inserted rather than color-assimilating to a preexisting vowel—that is, $V'C' \rightarrow V'C'V'$, perhaps but necessarily as the outcome of $V'C' \rightarrow V'C'V'C' \rightarrow V'C'V'$, where the initial step is the mitosis proper and the final step involves loss of the mitotically copied C' (whether by deletion—e.g., mtr, §17.12—or by regressive assimilation to a following C). Generically, vha and mit together will be referred to as *vowel copy* (vco)—because $V'C' \rightarrow V'C'V'$ is common to both hypothesized processes, and it is not always possible to be sure which of the two subprocesses is actually at work in a given case (let alone some altogether extraneous process, as will be mentioned at appropriate spots).

At times, the results of vco are partially obscured by the action of subsequent processes; e.g., *reduction*, whereby $V'C' \rightarrow V'C'V'$ may further $\rightarrow C'V'$, giving the impression of metathesis. There may also just possibly be nonassimilative extensions of vco, whereby, for instance, $V'C' \rightarrow V'C'V' \rightarrow C'V'$ sets up a "copy-cat" $C'' \rightarrow C''V''$ because of a special preexisting bond betwewen C' and C'' as exponents of homoparadigmatic φ-morphemes. Detail will be presented case by case.

The workings of vco will be presented dialect by dialect, for convenience grouped in descending order of frequency by morphological category of the suffix(es) affected. (α) <u>1s</u>: a mit process common to all of TR, SM, TL, M; (β) <u>3fs</u>: similar to (α), appearing in TR, SM, M, likely also a mit process but possibly an instance of vha in TR; (γ) <u>3mp^3mp</u>: a mit and/or vha process probably exclusive to TR (robustly), though just possibly making a sporadic appearence in SM as well in the somewhat different frame 3ms^3mp; (δ) <u>2(m)s</u>: a possible "copy-cat" extension of (α, β) appearing sporadically in M and, just maybe, in SM.

<u>TR.</u> (α) The unmarked exponent of pf 1s in the defective verb, irrespective of binyan, is clearly [-θī]: e.g., sim [ḥɔ̌zḗθī], int [šæwwī́θī], cau tb[ʔæsgī́θī], sim

rmp [ˀiθrʒ9íθī] (Da 343). Nöldeke appears to assign this suffix shape the same origin as its Hebrew counterpart (Nm 257), while in this book it will be taken to derive via mit from |-ITI|, a partial (nucleic reduplication of /-IT/—that is, /-IT/ ⇒ |-IT-I|, with subsequent lengthening of the reduplicate to conform to the phonotactic requirement that all auslaut vowels surface as long. In turn, /-IT/ would reflect a restructuring of epenthesized *-t; see §17.6 for this.[2] Nöldeke's idea, while appealing (and by no means out of the running), runs into the problem that positing a 1s allosuffix *-tī for Aramaic strongly invites copositing an ancipitally short counterpart *-ti, and we have seen that 1s *-ti encounters the difficulty that it unexpectedly reacts differently from homonymous 2fs *-ti (most notably, whle 2fs *-ti fails to trigger epn, §17.6, its i being subsequently apocopated by sap, §17.22, e.g., sim *QaSáMti > Qə̆SáMt, the 1s suffix *does* trigger epn, resulting in Qə̆SáMiθ (or alternatives with oxytone stress, or late ancipitality, etc.)—inexplicably, if homonymous 1s *-ti is assumed). It is unclear why 1s mit has latched onto the defective verb. In TR, the syllabic-prosodic considerations appealed to in the TL and M cases (below) do not hold.

(β) TR shows vco of pf 3fs *aT* at least superficially similar to the case of 1s under (α), but there are two differences as well: vco of *aT* appears in the strong verb rather than the defective; and while 1s vco is, in TR, limited to the intransitive verb, that of *aT* is restricted to the transitive, specifically the frame /__^3mp. This latter discrepancy renders analysis of the 3fs phenomenon analytically ambiguous in a few ways. Take the case of sb[bə̆læ9ə̆θænnű̃n] (~ -vco bb[bə̆læ9æθnű̃n]) (Da 364). If derived in a fashion maximally comparable to (α), /-aT/ would undergo partial mit to |-aT-a|, upon whichi the reduplicate |-a| would be phonotactically induced to geminate the anlaut of the 3mp allosuffix |nūn| (for this surfacing unadulterated, cf. the variant just cited, bb[bə̆læ9æθnű̃n]) for the sake of avoiding an unstressed open-syllabic short vowel.[3] However, alternatively, sb[bə̆læ9ə̆θænnű̃n] might bespeak mit of /-aT/ to fully reduplicative |aT-aT| followed by regressive assimilation of |Tn| to [nn]. And, finally, the type of vco responsible for sb[bə̆læ9ə̆θænnű̃n] might not be mit at all but rather vha, [-ə̆θænnű̃n] deriving not from |-aT-a(T)-nūn| but from |-aT-innūn| by vowel harmony of a. . .i to a. . .a, the ^3mp allosuffix having the less truncated (and closer to original) shape innūn (§7.4, §15.15.1).

(γ) Like the 3fs^3mp case under (β),but much more extensively,[4] TR shows mit or vha of 3mp^3mp, typified by int pf [ˀællefūnű̃n(n)ű̃n] (~ -vco [ˀællefű̃n(n)ű̃n]) (Da 367). Here, prima facie, *either* the subject suffix ūn (n courtesy of hti, §7.2(ζ)) has undergone mit to ūnű̃n(n) immediately preceding (n)nūn serving as object suffix, *or* the i of the object suffix in shape innūn has undergone vha shift to u immediately following subject-suffixal ūn.[5] However, these implementations have been qualified as "prima facie" because *if* the unreduced 2ʃ[e] should be a specific byproduct of 3mp object suffixation, as was taken to be the case with 2ʃ[æ] of [bɔ̆læ9æθnű̃n] under (β), as opposed to a general reflex of transparentation (§15.2.1.2), *then* the following picture emerges. First, intransitive c-ʔælléfū̃ is suffixed by the foreshortened shape of the 3mp object formative (-nű̃n), and the stress is adjusted (ʔælléfūnű̃n). Then full mit applies *either* to the rime of the (now) object suffix (-ű̃n), again to the tune of stress adjustment ([ʔælléfūnūnű̃n]) *or* to the whole of said suffix (-nű̃n) adjusted for stress and ±css ([ʔælléfūnű̊nnű̃n]). While it is uncertain which of this rather staggering congeries of possibilities is closest to the truth, let alone some combination, it might be noted that the *midness* of 2ʃ[e] suggests transparentation in any event, since normally in TR stressed, open-syllabic 2ʃÍ surfaces as [i] (see §17.11); e.g., [qæbbị́lū] (Da 262). Note, finally, cases where the role of vco has been obscured by the subsequent action of pin (§17.17), whereby subject-suffixal ū̃ is replaced by participial ī̃; e.g., sb[yiqṭɔ̆lị̄nű̊nnű̃n] 'sie werden sie töten' (Da 373).[6] (See also §17.15.1 with n. 72, where possibilities grow even more rococo—not least of wll when the *impf* is considered to the tune of analytic ambiguities following from uncertainty as to whether the 3p object is added to the *short* impf (*-ū̃), to the *long* (*-ū̃n(a)), or to the *energic* (*-ū̊n(n(na)).)

SM. (α) The 1s shape [-Tī] appears "gelegentlich" in the defective verb, e.g., <ḥzˀTy> (~ -vco <ḥz(y)T>) (Macs 206), and at least once in a verb with strong 3√: <ˀmrTy> (~ -vco <ˀmrT>) 'ich sagte' (Macs 146).

(β) Likely only <qrˀTh> 'es(sie) wird zufallen' at Deut 31:29 of the Samaritan Targum (Macs 206) corresponding to Hebrew conversive [qɔ̄rɔ̄θ]—probable interpretation of the SM form, [qặrā́θā] or [qặrā́θā] (for ā̄θ or aθ as possible resolutions of *a 3√y-at, see §15.3.2 (15P, Q)); contrast -vco cases such as <BKT> t[bắkɑt] 'sie weinte' (Macs 205), interpretable as [bặxā́θ] or [bặxā́θ].

(γ) Just possibly, 3ms^3mp <wm9wnwn> ~ <wm9wTwn> 'und schlug sie' (Macs 233), with the <T> of the second variant courtesy of tom (§17.10). However, it seems equally or more likely that rather the *second* <w> spelling a duplicate 3mp object marker (<-wn>), it is the *first* <w> reflecting the SM-specific process of suffixing the 3ms pronoun *hū̃ to a defective pf 3ms (hence unmarked) base (§2.3.2.4 n. 14c) prior to suffixation of the 3mp object (by i-pat, §17.15.1).

(δ) Since <-Ty> in the pf < šqrTy By> (~ normal <šqrT By>) 'du hast mich betrogen' and <-T< > (see §21.4 (21J) for "<" and the other SM vowel points) in the pf <rʾB<yT̊ wˀˇGʾmʾlTL<> 'du bist hergewaschen und erzogen worden' (Macs 90) lend themselves to interpretation as [-Tī], and since <šqrTy> is explicitly 2ms and <wˀˇGʾmʾlTL<> possibly (Macush doesn't tell us), we might be faced with a "copy-cat" extension of pattern (α) such that normal 2ms -T (as in rʾB<yT̊>) expands to -Tī in mimicry of homoparadigmatic 1s -Tī. However, SM, unlike M, where such an interpretation seems more cogent (below), already fields [-TV̄] allomorphs of 2ms [-T] in the shape of [-tā], reflexes of the ancient long-ancipital *-tā* not being subsequently apocopated by lap (§17.9)—in contradistinction to M, where lap is normal. So deployment of copy-cat vco smacks as unmotivated. Alternatively, we may be dealing with inchoative *syncretism* (fgm, §16.1) of the 2ms ≠ 2fs opposition, [-Tī] being a normal (albeit rare) exponent of 2fs into which the 2ms would then be collapsing. Of course, in that case, the *direction* of the presumed neutralization would be striking, 2fs > 2ms usually being expected qua marked > unmarked. The puzzle remains.[7]

TL. (α) In the defective verb, +mit pf 1s forms might (for the hedge, see below) occupy mid frequency between -mit, -mtr (§17.12) variants as the least frequent and -mit, +mtr variants as the most frequent (simple sketch stems used in illustration): -mit -mtr [QǯSḗθ] ← -a 3√y+t ≪ +mtr [QǯSḗθī] ← -a 3√y+t-it (by mtr if full mit) or ← -a 3√y+t-ī (if partial mit) ≪ -mit, +mtr [QǯSáy] ← -a 3√y (the [ē] ~ [Ay] difference via ±coa, §11.2). Examples on √ḥzy, 'see' (Mar 112*, Mor 253): a[ḥăzḗθ] ≪ a[ḥăzḗθī], y[ḥăzḗθī] ≪ a[ḥăzáy], y[ḥăzǽy]. While it might be possible to claim a therapeutic motivation for mit in TL—syllabic-prosodic and disambiguative—all such claims turn out, at the most charitable, to require qualificiation.[8] (It should be noted finally that the presumed mid position of [QǯSḗθī] as TL encodation of pf 1s ultimately requires reconciliation with the evidence presented by Morag (Mor 253) and Wajsberg (2006: 36 with n. 18) to the effect that the distribution of +vco forms like this in TL is quite circumscribed. Wajsberg, moreover, considers +vco in TL to be largely a Palestinian import.

M. (α, β, δ) are in evidence, 1s /-eT/ (§17.6.2) and 3fs /-aT/ behaving in an altogether parallel fashion (α, β, respectively) except for a few possible extensions from 1s to 2s (δ)—as well as possible comlication by late ancipitality (§2.3.1) in the case of 1s, which yields -īT, clearly when mit does not apply and perhaps but unclearly when mit does apply as well (mit^l-anc); see §17.15.2. It is peculiar to M that mit, primarily operative in the defective verb but with some instantiations in the strong verb as well, is limited to forms auslaut-suffixed withi a prepositional pronoun (pp), a morphological construction much affected by this dialect (m-pat, §17.15.2). Since it is characteristic of M m-pat in the absence of of mit that the auslaut *T* of the 1s or 3fs suffix is eclipsed, by *C*-spreading in the case of dative-accusative *l* ([nǝfallắ] 'she fell' ⇐ | nǝfal+aT+l+ắl, analytically, 'fell-she-to-her(self)') and by *V*-spreading with locative-instrumental *b* ([gǝṭarīBí] 'I tied on him' ⇐ |gǝṭar+īT+B+í| 'tied-I-on-him', with spreading vacuous because the input vowel is already long), it is simplest to take M mit to be of the full-copying sort: e.g., [hǝnå̄θå̄llí] [she pleased me' ⇐ |hǝnay+aTaT+l+í| 'pleased-she(-to)-me',[9] [qǝrīθĪllí] 'I called him' ⇐ |qǝrey+eTeT+l+í| 'called-I(-to)-him'.[10] M mit is extensively treated in Malone 1988a, where it is hypothesized that the process counteracts canonical subparity, as well as opacity qua deviation from the strong verb as model. In this vein, note how application of the process in the forms just cited recanonizes them in the mold of the strong verb—perhaps even overshooting in vowel length (see n. 8 above). Thus, [hə̆nåθå̄llí] like [nə̆fallá̄].

Notes to §13

[1] vha is at least typologically related to the congeries of vowel-harmonic processes dubbed *minor vowel harmony* (mvh) in §2.3.2.1 with n. 5. With more knowledge than at present available, it might well turn out that vha is a special case of (one or more manifestations of) mvh.

[2] We must apparently assume that mit operates, or at least ended up operating, on the phonological level, since on the phonetic level epenthesized I, necessary for the mit account, has condensed in the defective verb with the tail end of the stem base. A synchronic derivation for, e.g., tb[ʔæsgíθī] might run along the lines of |ʔa+sgIy+IT-I| s-str, s-e-cnd, s-spr (§4.1, §8.1.12, §5.1), s-auslaut lengthening ⇒ [ʔæsgíθī]— ~ -mit bb[ʔæsgíθ] (Da 343) ⇐ |ʔa+sgIy+IT|.

[3] (a) Despite the fact that, perhaps especially in the frame /__^3p (§7.4.1, §17.15.1), such vowels are not always expunged: cf., in fact, 2ʃ in [bə̆læ9æθnű̄n]. Are affixal vowels (as here the reduplicate in -aT-a) perhaps more prone to repair-strategic reinforcement than staminal vowels (as here 2ʃæ)? Clearly, appeal to phonotactic repair strategies must be tempered with skepticism until and unless the matter is better understood.

(b) One might propose that mit to |-aT-a| is also manifested in the variant [bə̆læ9æθnű̄n], where, however, the reduplicate is then deleted by s-r-red as an alternative phonotactic ploy to gemination of *n*. However, such a process would effectively obliterate the work of mit, setting up an accordion making it impossible (or at least extremely tricky) to be aware mit had ever taken place. I would propose that, while such a nexus might take place *diachronically*, it should be universally prohibited *synchronically*—for default of cues to the language aquirer (the child) that any such process had ever existed; so that, to the extent /-aT/ ⇒ |-aT-a| is taken to be a genuine synchronic process, a vco account of [bə̆læ9æθnű̄n] is ruled out.

[4] In fact, 3fs^3mp vco is limited to the Sabbionetan register, while with 3mp^3mp the process is widespread throughout all varieties of TR.

[5] Note the unsettling number of uncertainties centering on the shape of the object suffix, e.g.: full *innūn* if vha applies (*ūn-innūn*); apheretic *nnūn* if partial mit applies, in which case closed-syllable shortening (css, §17.4) may or may not be triggered (*ūnu-nnūn* or *ūnūn-nnūn*; foreshortened *nūn* either as an alternative to css under partial mit (*ūnū-nūn*), or in combination with full mit, in which case the question of css emerges again (*ūnun-ūn* or *ūnūn-ūn*). All three allomorphs of the object suffix are independently attested in other venues.

[6] Why might vco of patterns (β, γ) have arisen in just the slots where they are attested? In matters of morphophonological change not essentially guided by primary semantic or phonetic (= articulatory, auditory) factors, including most matters of transparentive, analogical change, it seems likely that something like *artistic whimsicality* typically plays a leading role, and that the results often constitute what might be

called *mini-patterns* rather than far-reaching system-wide configurational mutations. In the case in point, note the congruity of examples we have seen, [ʔællefūnŭn(n)ū́n] and sb[bǝlæ9ǽθǽθænnŭ́n], with, e.g., tb[wīhāvįttįnnŭ́n] 'und du(fs) hast sie gegeben' (Da 365), where the apparent anomaly of the subject-suffix shape derives not from vco but from pin (§17.17). Together, these forms constitute a mini-pattern occupying a modest but real subregion of the pf paradigm, sub^3mp, the mini-pattern specifically being -*V'C(C)V'n(n)ū̃n*, where subject-suffixed consonantism *C(C)* is flanked by color-identical vocalism *V'*, the whole running into a constant *n(n)ū̃n* containing the value 3mp object. (An objection may be raised that postulation of such weakly evidenced phenomena as mini-patterns violates analytic guidelines of simplicity and generality. However, deployment of such guidelines must always be tailored to the domain of inquiry, and what characterizes this specific domain is freedom from internal constraints, notably those of meaning or sound-structure in the narrow sense—a domain, that is, where esthetic capriciousness can, and by hypothesis does, come into its creative own. Contrast this palping area of the linguistic elephant with another where simplicity and generality cannot afford to be subtilized: language acquisition, and the overriding imperative to formulate a reasonable theory of how the child can internalize within an astonishing short time a structured system with virtually transfinite innovative potential.) ("Artistic whimsicality" of linguistic patterning was seminally probed within the narratival intonational system of modern Ma9lula Aramaic in Malone 1992b.)

[7] Perhaps compounded by <nsBTyT> 'du(f) hast genommen', a 2fs form that Macuch maybe correctly judges to be erroneous (Macs 146) but that may just constitute a species of partial mit where the *consonant* is copied, instead of the vowel as normally: i.e., -*C'V'* → *C'V'C'* rather than the usual -*V'C'* → -*V'C'V'*. (An unproblematic variant of this form is also attested: <nsBTy> t[nāsǽbti] (lc), hence [nǎsáβtī].)

[8] (a) Not all dialects manifesting similar type-(α) mit show such motivation; notably, TR does not. (b) A claim that (such as) [QǯSḗθī] both restores canonical syllabic weight to underpar -mit, +mtr [QǯSÁy] and counters pathological homonymy of the latter with 3fs [QǯSÁy] (← mtr *QǯSÁy+t*) encounters the objections: that (c) [QǯSḗθī] whose [-ḗθī] weighs 4 μ overshoots strong model [QǯSV̄Mī] ~ [QǯSV̄Mīθ] where [-V̄Mī] ~ [V̄Mīθ] weighs only 3 μ; that (d) presumed undercanonical [QǯSÁy], with 2 μ-weighing [-Áy], is in fact the unrivaled encoding of the def fs impa (§8.1.3); and that (e) putatively rescuing [QǯSḗθī] is tagged by Margolis with "†" indicating archaic/conservative status (vs. [QǯSÁy], e silentio innovative, and in any event most frequent qua encodation of 1s). Though it would be possible to frame at least imaginable ripostes to these objections—e.g., to (c), the general-linguistic prosodic-syllabic literature over the past decade or so appears to show *under*weight as problematic, not *over*weight—the issue will be left in this uneasy state. (For prosodic-syllabic canons and moraic weight in general, see §23.5.)

[9] What is here taken to be 3fs extension by mit, Nöldeke relates to 3fs Hebrew defectives in pause; his example, [gǝlōθō] (Nm 257).

[10] Note the homonymy of 1s and 3ms suffixes on the pp, the former < *-*í̆*, the latter < hap, hei (§9.2.2, §11.1) -*éh* < 1-anc (§2.3.1) -*éh* < mid (§17.11) *-*íh* < sap (§17.22) (-*íhV̊*. Note also the hedging on *V*-length: [V̊ll] because of uncertainty as ro css (§17.4), and in the case of 1s because of uncertainty concerning 1-anc as well; [å̄θ] due to the dubious outcome of *a* 3√y+at (SM (β), above).

14. Promotion (prm) and y-Monophthongization (ymn)

14.1. Description

Promotion (prm) refers to $\check{V} \rightarrow \overset{\circ}{V}$—that is, the enrichment (promotion) of a reduced vowel to full vowel status. While prm-like effects may be evoked by a variety of factors (notably transparentation, §15), prm in the narrow sense will be taken to be induced in one environment categorically and in another occasionally or usually (depending on dialect): the categorical condition is *closed-syllablic position* (pan-Aramaically as of the emergence of reduction, §4.2, throughout the Classical period);[1] while the occasional/usual condition is as nucleus to a guttural onset, especially though not exclusively in anlaut, sometimes with concomitant or correlative deletion of the guttural.[2] Promotion will be taken generally to involve advancement to *short*-vowel status ($\check{V}$), though prm to *long* ($\bar{V}$) cannot be ruled out; e.g., perhaps at times /#H__CV (§9.3.1). This possibility will be picked up again below in association with *u*-monophthongization.

In one form or another—and to some extent another—prm makes its appearance as of B at latest, most likely showing up in all subsequent dialects (though uncertainly in a few because of unrevealing orthography: P, N, CP). Since prm is treated extensively elsewhere in the book (notably §4.4.1, §9.3.1, §15, §17.23.3, §17.25), it will be discussed only incidentally in the balance of this chapter except where, as immediately below, further consideration is prompted by its similarities to or differences from *y*-monophthongization.

The process to be called *y-monophthongization* (ymn) is in large part similar to the *H*-deletional case of promotion (above, with n. 2), substituting *y* for *H*,[3] both of which may implicate concomitant loss of the glide (variably—across dialects—for *H*, categorically for *y*), occur most frequently in anlaut and may involve advancement of $\check{V}$ either to short $\check{V}$ or to long $\bar{V}$ (a tad more confidently in the case of ymn, $\check{V} \sim \bar{V}$ there receiving support from M trad pron; see §14.2). The processes differ, beyond what has just been said, in that: while the $\check{V}$ in $H\check{V}$ is unrestricted as to color, the focal vowel of ymn is (with some possible deviations, as, e.g., in n. 16 below) palatal; and only ymn, in some dialects, may clearly operate upon a full-vocalic focus in addition to a reduced-

230

vocalic one—that is, $y\overset{\circ}{\breve{V}} \to \overset{\circ}{\breve{V}}$. (To the extent this process is confined to focal $y\overset{\circ}{\breve{I}}$, it may be motivated, (partially) independently of the $y\breve{V}$ brand of ymn, to break up homophonous onglide-nucleus diphthongs, which tend to be universally unstable; cf. §14.2 SM.)[4]

The issue of vowel length in the outcome of ymn and prm is perhaps best approached separately for two central cases: closed-syllabic prm, on the one hand (notably $\breve{V}CC \to \overset{\circ}{\breve{V}}CC$ in association with excrescent Aufsprengung, §4.4.1);[5] and, on the other hand, prm plus ymn together in open-syllablic cases withi a concomitant guttural or y, in which case loss of same guttural or semivowel is often (H) or always (y) involved. Impressionistically, in $\breve{V}CC \to \overset{\circ}{\breve{V}}CC$, syllable closure reacts antagonistically to the impoverished and speeded-up articulation defining a reduced vowel; perhaps there is a universal tendency for closed syllables to require more expansiveness for their nuclei, at least in non-allegro speech. In open-syllabic cases with concomitant Γ (H or y), on the other hand, the issue becomes the role of Γ as possible catalyst to the advancement of the vowel, whether to short or long status. Does the advancement bespeak Γ somehow "rubbing off" onto the vowel and so increasing its bulk, whether the "rubbing off" ispartial (Γ remains) or complete (Γ deletes)? At least for the Γ-deletional cases, two hypotheses seem worth exploring: (α) The glide *vocalizes* ($\Gamma \to \overset{\circ}{\Gamma}$) setting up a vowel cluster with the nucleus, a cluster then resolved by amalgamation into the nucleus, creating a new vowel, short ($\overset{\circ}{\Gamma}\breve{V} \to \overset{\circ}{\breve{V}}$) or long ($\overset{\circ}{\Gamma}\breve{V} \to \bar{V}$), the choice being either parametric or dependent on (presently unclear) properties of glide vocalization. This general hypothesis may receive support from the special case of SM c-dgt (§22.1 (22Bvi)), where $H\overset{\circ}{V}$, H an onset, $\to \bar{V}$ in apparent violation of the general-linguistic expectation that loss of an onset, in contradistinction to a coda, remain uncompensated by lengthening of the nucleus, a lengthening there (§22.1 n. 3) gingerly explained in terms of autosegmental spreading theory. (β) Plausibly only for resoultion as a long vowel, $\Gamma V \to \bar{V}$ is taken as a special cse of *prothesis* (§17.18), such that $\Gamma\breve{V}C \to \overset{\circ}{V}\Gamma C \to \bar{V}C$, or even $\Gamma\breve{V}C \to \breve{V}\Gamma C \to \overset{\circ}{V}\Gamma C \to \bar{V}C$, where the step $\breve{V}\Gamma C \to \overset{\circ}{V}\Gamma C$ would constitute an instance of closed-syllabic prm/ymn as discussed above ($\breve{V}CC \to \overset{\circ}{\breve{V}}CC$). This general approach is advocated, for ymn, by Margolis (Mar §5r).[6]

14.2. The Individual Dialects

B. The process of y-monophthongization is limited to the Babylonian register, where it is variable. Thus, corresponding to Tiberian pf[yšháv] 'er hat gegeben', [yšðá9] 'er erkannte', and impf [yšqím] 'er errichtete', we find +ymn bb[(ʔ)īhǽv], bb[(ʔ)īðǽ9],[7], and -ymn bb[yšqím] (BL 142). The corpus of attested relevant forms is too small to decide whether exemption of bb[yšqím] has anything to do with [y] being prefixal, whereas in the +ymn cases it is radical.

TR. It is striking that while in B ymn appears confined to the Babylonian register, in TR is is largely though not fully limited to the Tiberian register, perhaps especially the Sabbionetan. Though variable, +ymn is probably the unmarked response, at least apud Sabbioneta. Unlike B, ymn in TR may affect prefixal *y* (though of course, as mentioned, apparent absence of such ymn in B may simply bespeak limitations of the extant corpus); it also shows up in anlaut, in the sim rmp (a binyan-gizra intersection not attested in B). Examples (from Da 309 with n. 1): pf[īðǽ9] 'wusste' (~ bb[yǎðǽ9]); sb[īhǽv] 'gab' (~ bb[yǎhǽv]); impf sb[īḥűv] 'wird schuldig sein' (~ bb[yǎḥűv]; sim rmp pf sb&bb[ʔiθīl̥íð] (2ʃ[ī] by ssl, §17.28) (~ bb[ʔiθyǎléð]]).[8]

CP. Though the writing system makes it less than foregone, this dialect will be taken to apportion ymn, in the verb, to full-vocalic *yl-* → *l-* in anlaut and reduced-vocalic *-yV̆-* → *-l-* in inlaut; e.g., respectively: [Ittél] 'gibt' (Sg 24)[9], [Ibéð] 'tut' (Sg 61), on the one hand, and [θIðV̥9t] 'innotuisti' (Sl 79), [θIl̥éð] 'wurde geboren' (Sg 76), on the other. Anlaut *yV̆-* in the verb will be interpreted as remaining,[10] at least when *y-* is radical ([yǎxél] ~ [yǎxél] 'konnte', Sg 24, 76); for prefixal *y-*, see excursus (β) below.

The orthographic usages investing these interpretations show some interesting facets, to be discussed during the following presentation of the spellings themselves: <ˀTl>, <y9BD> (for <y> here spelling [I-], see excursus (α) below); <ˀyTD9T>, <ˀTylD> (notice how inlaut <-∅-> ~ ml <-y-> for the reflex of *1√yǎ cues short [I] rather than long [ī]);[11] <yKl> ~ <yˀKl> or <ỹKyl> (for the superposed dot on <ˀ> in <ˀTl> above qua signal of a palatal vs. on <ỹ> here qua signal of [ǎ], Sg 9 and Sg 11, respectively), <yqwm>.

Two excurses on aspects of these interpretations and the orthographic usages investing them—

(α) <y9BD> qua [I9béð] because in this case and generally the spelling is not only the norm for 3ms, but one of two norms for 1s as well.[12] In default of any uncontrived way of deriving [y-] from *ˀ- (§2.1), this suggests a pattern of *inverse spelling*, which in turn would attest not only to ymn having applied to *yi- (possibly < **ya- via att, in CP not inhibited /__H, §12.2 CP (α)) but equally to loss of ˀ- (adr, §9.2.1.1), whether original in 1s (hamzatu 'l-qaṭ9) or secondary in 3ms as a reflex of ymn, assuming there was such a reflex to begin with (hamzatu 'l-waṣl). The rationale for such inverse spelling is actually quite straightforward, the present case being laid out in the display of (14A). Once two signals (here *[yi-], *[ˀi-], spelled distinctly (here <y->, <ˀ->), have merged (here by ymn, adr), subsequent generations of scribes (and other writers) will normally be deprived of motivated criteria for deciding when to use which spelling. If, for whatever reason, a decision is made that entails matching signal and spelling in a way turning out to be etymologically congruent, one speaks of *historical spelling*, while the results of the anti-etymological choice are called *inverse spelling*. And in this light, the analytic benefit of discovering inverse spelling may be readily seen: it provides evidence that one or more suspected sound changes (in this case, ymn and adr) have in fact taken place, inasmuch as had they *not* taken place, the spelling in question (in this case, <y-> for the reflex of *[ʔi-]) would remain a puzzle.

(14A)   ([yi-]   <y->   ymn

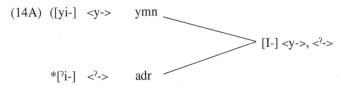

[I-] <y->, <ʔ->

*[ʔi-]   <ʔ->   adr

(β) At first blush, verbs with prefixal *$y\check{V}$- would indeed appear to undergo ymn as per highly frequent inverse spellings with <y-> for 1s, as we have just seen. In the case of *$y\check{V}$-, however, this <y-> is normally followed by an unexpected <ʔ>—a letter that likewise normally appears in the case of homoparadigmatic 3ms; e.g., <yʔqwm> 'steht auf' (Sg 25,70), presumably < *$y\ddot{\partial}q\acute{u}m$. Upon further examination, it turns out that this spelling, in variation with less frequent unaccompanied <y->, is the overwhelming representation of choice for any form containing at most one true consonant between the prefix and 2ʃ: e.g., not merely hollow verbs (<yʔqwm>, just cited), but also 1√y verbs, however derived (<y(ʔ)Kwl> 'ich esse', Sg 65, <yʔrwT> 'erbt', Sg 75), and verbs with adr-lost 2√ʔ (<yʔšwl> 'ich frage', Sg 66). Since of this group at least the 1√y forms (whether being such by sar, §9.2.1.2, or of other provenience) will be expected always to have had full vocalism /__2√, usually [ē] < coa (§11.2) *a 1√y*, it seems likely that the <ʔ> in such forms is in fact a ml for [ē] (cf. Sg 9) in *all* such forms, not the 1√y alone, but notably also the hollows, which presumably will have promoted their ŏ to *e* or *ē* (probably *ē*) transparentively via ips (§15.3.1.1). And if so, it is likely enough that the CP failure of ymn to apply to anlaut *y$\check{V}$-*, with radical *y* ([yŏxél] above) can be analytically extended to prefixal *y$\check{V}$-* as well, the prefix <yʔ-> cases being derived by full-vocalic ymn; e.g., *yŏqúm* ipr → *yēqúm* ymn → [ēqúm].[13]

SM. Spellings like <9DʔᵉBDwTK> 'bis sie dich vernichten' (~ 9dʏʔBDwnK>) (Macs 229) and <ʔymnwn> 'sie glauben' (~ <ʏ(h)ymnwn>) (Macs 177) suggest ymn as [(ʔ)Ĭ], especially when supported by the testimony of trad pron, as in the latter case t[īménon] ((~ t[yīménon)(lc). Was the resulting vowel long or short? That it was long is suggested by the trad pron of the like of <ʔTʏlD>, t[ētᵢləd] 'wurde geboren' (Macs 182)—not because t[ĭ] is long, which is true of all nonfinal open-syllabic *V*s in trad pron but because its height normally bespeaks an input long vowel, a mid vowel in complementary fashion usually attesting to a short input (as, e.g., in the rmp prefix of the same form, t[ēt-] < *ʔIθ-). The fact that forms like <yhBwn> ~ <yḥBwn> t[iyyǽbbon] 'sie werden erzählen' (Macs 212), with antihiatic [yy] in the wake of the lost guttural (c-vcr case (γ), §22.1 (22B)), seem not to alternate with -ymn forms like

@t[yiyyǽbbon]—contrast such as <wyTwḥy> 'und er lebt' +ymn [wi̥ttúwwi] ~ -ymn t[wy̥ittúwwi] (Macs 184)—appear to point to dissimilation of yiyy to iyy, possibly a special case of the tendency to dissimilate yǐ to ǐ discussed in §14.1.[14] Observe that while ymn of the sort attested in t[ị̄ménon] may be reflected in the orthography, <ʾymnwn>, the type of process describable as yiyy → iyy apparently never is, the anlaut of the like of t[iyyǽbbon] always being spelled historically, <yḥBwn>. This difference at least hints support for yiyy → iyy constituting a dissimilatory reaction independent from and subsequent to ymn proper, a conclusion strengthened by the fact that the yy, by hypothesis enhancing the propensity to dissimilate, itself arose after the degutturalization ḥ → ∅ led to the vowel cluster ǒIʃa then dissolved by antihiatic glide insertion (c-vcr) case (γ)).[15]

It is possible that SM is like CP was hypothesized to be, fielding full-vocalic ymn initially and reduced-vocalic ymn medially, though differing from CP in rendering the focal vowel as long rather than short: #yĪ- → #ī-, -yǒ- → -ī-. For the first case, a few subsidiary assumptions would be in order: t[i̥menon] more facilely <y̱aymǒŰn> (<ʾymnwn>) than <y̱ǒẖaymǎnŰn> (<y(h)ymnwn>) (see §9.1.2); if t[iyyǽbbon] is taken as ymn-derived (rather than via an independent, dissimilatory process), it is either equivalent to t[īyǽbbon] (the iyy = īy equivalence by dme, §8.1.1) or ← īyyǽbbon via css (§17.4); and t[wi̥ttúwwi] ← ītt by css. The prediction that #yǒ- should remain unaffected by ymn may be supported by the invariance of sim pf <y-> t[yā-] < yV̆-, the length of t[ā] via changes of the smc (c-prm^c-pra, §22.1 (ααβ)). However, it is possible that the failure of ymn here derives not from any restriction against mutating initial yV̆, but from nonsatisfaction of a requirement that the focal vowel be palatal (§14.1,with n. 14a) while the SM realization of sim pf yV̆- prior to the smc was plausibly [yǎ-] (see §17.23 for discussion.[16]

G. Consistent spelling with <y-> in anlaut, <-y-> ~ <-yy-> in inlaut, under all conditions but possibly one, suggests that G for the most part dispenses with ymn: <y̱mwT> 'stirbt' (Da 320) [y̱ǒmű̱θ], <y̱Tqn> 'ordnet' (Da 269) [y̱ǒθaqqén], <y̱TB> 'setze sich' (Da 308) [y̱ǒθéβ], <ʾTy̱lD> 'ward geboren' (Da 313) [ʾIθy̱ǒléð], <TTy̱ylD> 'sie wird geboren' (lc) [tIθy̱ǒléð].

The one possible exception apparently favoring ymn, specifically, -yǒ- → -I- under mechanics like those suggested in n. 11 (aiv, biv), is postproclitic position, to judge by sim pf forms on √yhb 'give' cited in Kutscher 1976: 16. These forms are ms <whB>, <DhB>, and mp <DhBwn>, plausibly interpretable as [wIháβ], [dIháβ], and [dIhaβŰn]. (Observe that if the suffix -Űn of the latter, imported from impf to pf by hii (§7.2(δ)), were more deeply integrated into the morphology, so as synchronically to be introduced on the phonological level, we should expect @[dǒyahBŰn], which would presumably be spelled <DyhBwn> or <DyyhBwn>.)[17]

SR. In SR and the other two Eastern dialects, there is little occasion to track ymn vis-à-vis the impf prefix *y-, since this has for the most part been replaced by *n-* or *l-* (prp, §17.19). But for the retentions that do exist in Old SR and conservative texts of TL, reflexes of *y- are consistently spelled <y->, which either leaves the issue of prefix-targeting ymn moot or suggests that in fact it did not take place. (For representative Old SR instances, see Drijvers 1972: xii, 78, 92, 93, 97, 111, 112.)

To judge by its usual spelling <yi-> and occasional unvocalized spelling <ʔy->, SR manifests ymn of 1√yǯ as [ī] (e.g., sim pf 3mp [īrɛ́θ] 'erbten' spelled <yirɛθw> ~ <ʔyrTw> (Ns 115)); and the process extends to inlaut position in the sim rmp, where it is spelled <-iy-> (e.g., impf 3ms of √yd9 'know' [nɛθīðá9] <nɛTiyDa9> (lc)).

It might also be observed that Old SR, despite its mootness on prefixal *y-, apparently occasionally generalized ymn to 1√yI (<ʔyTrT> 'ich gabe genommen', <ʔyD9T> 'sie wusste'—both found following the negative proclitic <lʔ>, for whatever that might be worth; lc n. 1, also Sg 76).

TL. To judge by spelling, TL variably shows ymn of #1√yǯ: <ʔyTyB> (~ <yTyB> 'he sat', <ʔyTyBT> (~ <yTyBT> 'you(ms) sat' (Mar 37); <ʔyTyBw> (~ <TyBw> 'sit(mp)!' (Mar 39).[18] While Margolis's Ash trad pron treats such as unabashadly +ymn, probably > [(ʔ)ī] (represented by Margolis in Tiberian transcription as <ʔiy>)—a[(ʔ)īθévt] (~ [yǯθévt]), [(ʔ)īθívū] (Mar 122*)—the Yem trad pron documented by Morag shows only one case, and that post-proclitic—<wʔyTyB> rendered as y[wīθév] 'věyašav',[19] where in fact an alternative Yem reading tradition gives apparently sim rmp y[wǯʔiyyǯθév] (Mor 200 n. 4) (with *Ty > yy* by rrf, §10 TL). Neither tradition extends ymn to inlaut: typical is a&y[ʔiθyǯlīðA] 'she was born' (Mar 121*, Mor 205).

M. M ymn is manifested by [ē] ~ [ī] of both *1√yǯ and *√yI, [e] ~ [ī] being cued by trad pron though there are too few forms in the available corpus to be sure whether the alternation is lexically or otherwise based. Examples of *1√yǯ: <ehab> t[éhaβ] (Mal 308) [éhaβ], <eda> t[ída] 'he knew] (Mal 310) [īðá], <etib> t[íteβ] ~ [íteβ] 'he sat' (Mal 308) [īθéβ]; note also <ehabilH> t[ehaβíllī] 'I gave to him' (Mal 341), <edanin> t[īdánnīn] 'we knew' (Mal 370). Examples of *√yI: <etbit> t[étβīt] ~ [ítβīt] 'I sat' (Mal 339) [eθBíθ] ~ [īθBíθ]. In M, ymn under the stated conditions is almost exceptionless.[20]

14.3. Summary Profiles of the Dialects on ymn

A few of the parameters of ymn are laid out in table (14B) for their gross disposition in the eight dialects surveyed—"gross" rather than fine-tuned, so that only broadest developmental patterns will be suggested by the display. The columns are organized into four quasi-oppositional sets (i–iv), opposing columns are organized into of each set separated by dotted lines. Set (iii) does not indicated presence/absence of ḥamzatu 'l-waṣl, and "inlaut" under set (iv) subsumes variability in addition to categorical status, and a blank cell signals mootness/preemption. Scores are given beneath each column, the majority result preceding that of the minority in each set. The figure appearing in the left column, summing up the "+"s for the dialect in question for columns (i, ii, iv), provides a rough score of ymn robustness (the higher the figure the more robust the process).

(14B)

	(i)		(ii)		(iii)		(iv)	
	$I\sqrt{y}$	*prefixal y*	$y\breve{\partial} \rightarrow$	$yl \rightarrow$	$\rightarrow \bar{\imath}$	$\rightarrow I$	*anlaut*	*inlaut*
B 3	+	–	+	–	+	–	+	?
TR 5	+	+	+	–	+	–	+	+
CP 6	+	+	+	+	–	+	+	+
SM 6	+	+	+	+?	+	–	+	+
G 3	+	–	+	–	–	+	–	+
SR 5	+	–	+	+	+	–	+	+
TL 3	+	–	+	–	+	–	+	–
M 4	+		+	+	+	+	+	
	8	3	8	4	6	3	7	5

Notes to §14

[1] (a) At least Modern M tolerates closed-syllablic $\breve{V}$, though promotion is decidedly more frequent; see Malone 1997: 145. (b) /__CV̌C may also at times count as a closed-syllabic environment for promotion, as illustrated, e.g., in § n. 27; see also §12.1 with n. 2. This is no doubt a manifestation of the frequent phonological inorganicity of $\breve{V}$ in Northwest Semitic, as observed elsewhere (e.g., lc).

[2] That is, it is possible a causal link may obtain between prm and degutturalization (dgt, §9.3.1) under certain conditions—though at large the processes are independent. The brunt of the evidence is from SR and M, where, when the gutturals that are lost unconditionally (*ʔ in SR, *ʔ and *9 in M) occur as onset to $\breve{V}$ as a nucleus, the $\breve{V}$

always promotes—with the qualification that loss of the guttural by adconsonantal assimilation preempts the prm; thus, e.g., with SR *1√ʾ we find two patterns in sim rmp stems that have undergone reduction of 1ʃ: -rrf(§10)^dgt(twice), +prm [εθεSέM] ← *ʾiTʾɔ́SίM* (unmarked) and +rrf^+dgt(only once), -smp [εttɜ̠SέM] ← *ʾiTʾɔ́SίM* (marked). The possibility that anlaut position is favorable to promotion may incidentally find support in similar behavior in some other languages; cf. Odden 2006: 440 (especially constraint *pwl̠V), as well as the case of Kera as discussed by Pearce 2006: 268. (It might be noted that both Kera and Aramaic are Afroasiatic languages.)

[3] Which suggests that the two processes might be at least partially conflated, subsuming /H__ and /y__ both under /Γ__ (Γ =glide). It might be observed that H and y function similarly as conditioners elsewhere in A as well, e.g., in licensing variable resistance to attenuation in M (§12.2 M̲ (β)—in which case we arguably are dealing with assimilatory bonding, Ha = [-high, +low] [-high, +low] and dissimilatory polarization, ya = [+high, -low] [-high, +low], respectively), which in turn suggests affiliation to the widespread assimilation–dissimilation nexus $iy \sim ay$, din, treated in §8.1.1 n. 1.

[4] (a) Concerning the (tendential) requirement that the focal vowel of ymn be palatal, in the case of $\v{V}$ this will usually accord with the assumption ɜ̆, the unmarked reduced vowel, is in the default case palatal (§17.23.1.1).

(b) Possible independent motivation aside, $y\mathring{\v{V}} \to \v{V}$ might constitute an instance of *rule modification* via generalization (simplification) of conditions from $\v{V}$ (reduced vowel) to V (vowel irrespective of length properties) but for the uneasiness that in one dialect, CP, anlaut ymn may be confined to focal $y\mathring{V}$-, $y\mathring{\v{V}}$- remaining unaltered; see §14.2.

(c) The qualification "*only* ymn . . . may *clearly* operate upon a full-vocalic focus" is prompted by the fact that when $H\mathring{\v{V}} \to \v{V}$, the loss of H may be independent of prm; see n. 2.

[5] It is possible that a complementary circumstance for closed-syllabic prm is $\v{V}C\# \to \mathring{V}C\#$ as part of epn, §17.6, disguised by total lack of alternations with [V̌]. That is, formulation of epn as $CC\# \to C\mathring{V}C\#$ may be, at least diachronically, a kind of unawares foreshortening for actual $CC\# \to C\v{V}C\#$ prm $\to C\mathring{V}C\#$.

[6] It might be observed that the various hypotheses adduced in this subsection may entail among themselves affronts to the principle of so-called *Moraic Preservation*, according to which processes are prohibited from increasing the number of *morae* (quanta of weight measurement) in a representation (though their disposition/arrangement may be affected). This will always be so when $\v{V}$ promotes to $\bar{V}$, since whatever the moraic weight of $\v{V}$ (for conventionally assumed properties of morae, see §23.5), that weight will not exceed the one mora normally awarded to $\mathring{V}$ (at least in the default case), and $\bar{V}$ will necessarily be heavier than $\v{V}$ (long vowels bearing two morae in the unmarked situation). If, moreover, Northwest Semitic (and hence, Aramaic) $\v{V}$ should be *weightless* qua "inert element," as proposed in Malone 1995, then *any* instance of prm or ymn would entail violation of Moraic Preservation to at least one degree. Of course, neither Moraic Preservation nor the theory of inert elements is cast in gold; see in the former vein Malone 1989c.

[7] "(ʾ)" indicating, as elsewhere (§17.18), uncertainty as to whether [ʾ] appears as a canonical requirement to forfend against an onsetless syllable (hamzatu 'l-waṣl).

[8] Note the absence of hamzatu 'l-waṣl in the forms with anlaut ymn, as [īðǽ9]; contrast B bb[(ˀ)īðǽ9]. This is cued by the spelling <yi(y)-> —which, were it not for the support of inlaut [ˀiθīl͎íð], might be taken to spell -ymn [yi-] (cf. §21.5).

[9] The root is √ntl, restructing from *√ntn being facilitated by assimilation of frequently collocated *lV̊ 'to' onto *3√n, a development shared by at least SR (B 87); see §17.3 n. 3c. Also [tt] ← *nt* by rna (§17.21).

[10] The qualification "in the verb," because anlaut ymn does occur "in isolierten Nomm" (Sg 24).

[11] Inlaut ymn to [I] also extends to conjunctive forms such as <wTB> 'und er setze sich' (Sg 76), qua [wIθév] ← *wǎ̆=yǎ̆θév*, with elision of the conjunctive ǎ̆ in the wake of creation of the vowel cluster ǎ̆I by ymn. Observe that in *wǎ̆=yǎ̆θév*, the assumed origin of [wIθév], **wa= > wǎ̆=* must have occurred through the agency of some process other than reduction qua strictly phonetic change. This is so because, had **wa=waθíba* come into CP via strictly phonetic changes alone, plausibly wpl^occ, sap, mid, spr, red (§17.34, §17.14, §17.22, §17.11, §5.1, §4.2) and possibly att (§12), the result would be *wa=y(ǎ̆)θév* without att, or *wI=y(ǎ̆)θév* (*wIyθév = wīθév* via dme, §8.1.1) with att applying—would-be results in CP spellable <wyTB> had either actually occurred. Moreover, conjunctive forms canonically like these are clearly attested elsewhere in Aramaic; see type (δ) att for several dialects in §12.2. These opposing developments may be reconciled in the view that clitics, like **wa=*, in languages at large tend to be ambivalent between (re)acting phonologically as proper parts of the words co-constituted with their hosts (**waθíba* in this case), resulting in the like of *wIyǎ̆θév* or *wīθév*, and behaving as if they were phonologically independent units, leading to the ilk of *wIθév*. Furthermore, something similar is true of the clitic's host: in the case of **=waθíba*, reflexes visible in *=yθév* on the one hand bespeaking part-of-word cohesion with the clitic, and *=yǎ̆θév* on the other attesting to the **=waθíba* reflext (re)acting phonologically as an independent word despite its clitic co-constituent. Since the issue of clitic-cum-host phonological reactance is of significant import throughout A beyond the parochial question of CP [wIθév], it will be worth looking at a general explication. To this end, see the synchronic derivations in (a–b), mock-ups based on CP [wIθév] but designed for suggestiveness vis-à-vis A at large. The models in (a) explicate clitic phonological dependence vs. independence via synchronic retention of **wa* as /wa/ vs. restructuring as /wǎ̆/, respectively ((ai, ii) vs. (aiii, iv)), in interaction with host dependence vs. independence via full (deletional) vs. partial (weakening) reduction ((ai, iii) vs. (aii, iv)). Rules and similar mechanisms employed are stress (str, §4.1), spirantization (spr, §5.1), full/partial reduction (f-red/p-red, §4.2.1), attenuation (assumed for simplicity of exposition to apply) (att, §12), y-monophthongization (ymn, this chapter), promotion (prm, this chapter), *vowel declustering* (vdc, whereby ǎ̆V̊ ⇒ V̊ but V̊V̊′ ⇒ V̄′), and diphthong-monophthong equivalence (dme, §8.1.1). An alternative synchronic model might be explored in terms of Lexical Phonology (§23.3), most perspicuously in the play-off between antithetical derivations (bi) (doubly dependent; cf. (ai)) and (biv) (doubly dependent; cf. (aiv)). Critical here is the view that morphophonological dependence be synchronically explicated via having the morpholexical building blocks of words amalgamated via a *word building* mechanism (wrb) on an early lexical stratum (stratum 1 of (bi)), while the phonological rules proper (str, spr, etc.) then apply on a later stratum (stratum 2 of (bi)). Morphophonological *in*dependence, on the other hand, has it that the

rules first apply to each morpholexical part of the word, each part as a self-contained unit, (stratum 1 of (biv), whereupon word building takes place (stratum 2 of (biv)), after which the rules reapply to the newly constituted whole (stratum 3 of (biv)).

(a) **/wa/ retained**

	deleting reduction			**weakening reduction**	
(i)	/wa=yatIb/		(ii)	/wa=yatIb/	
str	|wa=yatÍb|		str	|wa=yatÍb|
spr	|wa=yaθÍv|		spr	|wa=yaθÍv|
f-red	|wa=yθÍv|		p-red	|wa=yǯθÍv|
att	|wI=yθÍv|		att	|wI-yǯθÍv|
mid	|wI=yθév|		mid	|wI=yθév|
ymn	—		ymn	|wI=Iθév|
prm	—		prm	—
vdc	—		vdc	|wīθév|
dme	|wīθév|		dme	|wīθév|

restructuring to /wǎ/

	deleting reduction			**weakening reduction**	
(iii)	/wǎ-yatIb/		(iv)	/wǎ-yatIb/	
str	|wǎ=yatÍb|		str	|wǎ=yatÍb|
spr	|wǎ=yaθÍv|		spr	|wǎ=yaθÍv|
f-red	|wǎ=yθÍv|		p-red	|wǎ=yǯθÍv|
att	—		att	—
mid	[wǎ=yθév|		mid	|wǎ=yǯθév|
ymn	—		ymn	|wǎ=Iθév|
prm	[wI=yθév|		prm	—
vdc	—		vdc	|w=Iθév|
dme	|wīθév|		(-dme)	|wIθév|

(b)

(i)		/wa/, /yatIb/
stratum 1:	wrb	|wa=yatIb|
stratum 2:	rules	[wīθév]

(iv)		/wa/, /yatIb/
stratum 1:	rules	|wǎ|, |yǯθév|
stratum 2:	wrb	|wǎ=yǯθév|
stratum 3:	rules	[wIθév]

[12] The other norm for 1s is <ʾy->, a pretty straightforward instance of historical spelling (with <y> as ml for short [I], as frequent in CP; Sg 8).

[13] There is no conflict between taking <ʾ> as ml for [a] in (the like of) 1√y <yʔKl> 'konnte' but as [ē] in instances of prefixal-*y* forms like those just discussed, supported as both are by distinct paradigmatic distributions, notably the clustering of weak pre-2√ verbs in the latter case (a sample of 85-odd items with prefixal *y*- were examined, weaks and strongs alike), as well as supporting alternations like <y̌Ky̌l> in the former case (cf. also Sg 11 (his §14d)).

[14] These items have been multiply deformed by a congeries of processes (partially) independent of the issues focuses on here, the former deriving ultimately from int *yihawwayúna (*√ḥwy), the latter from cau rmp *wa=yithaḥyíyi (*√ḥyy (*√ḥy)). In the former case, observe especially the SM-specific occlusion w → [b] (§21.1 SM); in the latter case, the metathesis (with position of articulation switch) √ḥyy → √why (best taken as an instance of m-cis, §6.1.2 with n. 7, followed by case (δ) of cys, §17.5).

[15] Note that lateness of the guttural loss (and hence a fortiori of yiyy → iyy) is likewise reflected in failing to be registered orthographically, <yhBwn> ~ <yh̲Bwn> —though the <h>-variant may bespeak a blurring of guttural distinctions heralding the loss. (Does <h> spelling a reflex of *ḥ suggest that SM ḥ > Ø was mediated by depharyngealization, ḥ > h > Ø, as in TL and M? If so, how do we reconcile this with the hypothesis that loss of SM ḥ proceeded not by depharyngealization but by laxing, ḥ > 9 > Ø, as developed in §3.2? Perhaps <ḥ> ~ <h> reflects no more than a global, jumbled deployment of guttural letters in the wake of guttural weakening and loss, as proposed by Macuch (Macs 14–22).)

[16] A possible challenge to both these hypotheses, that SM fails to undergo ymn of #yV̄- and requires the focal point to be palatal, may be seenin a pair of sim impa variants built on √yhb (< *√whb, §17.34) 'give': ms t[ấʔəb], mp t[ā̆ʔébu]; Macs 174), shapes that follow without snag from the smc on the assumption < yắhíβ, yắhíβū as long as ymn applies to yă-. There is, however, an uneasy complication to be worked out before taking t[ấʔəb], [ā̆ʔébu] as manifestly evidential for ymn of #yă-: that such a #yă-, if correctly so interpreted, is not original, since 1√y < *1√w sim impas are inherited into Aramaic as 1√-less SV̄M, such variants being in fact attested for this root in SM (e.g., mp t[ébu] < *híbū, t[ắbu] < *hábū); hence, weak imperative change (§17.33) must be invoked to have restored the 1√yă- subsequently apherized by ymn; but no other 1√y verbs evince such behavior in SM.

[17] There is food for thought in the fact that the interpretation actually proffered here, [dIhaŬn], follows nearly but not quite automatically from model (biv) in n. 11, while model 11 (aiv)—equivalent to 11 (biv) for the unadorned matter of procliticcum-host—would not be up to the task. Thus, adding -Ŭn to 11 (aiv) would give the results in (a) below, while adding it to 11 (biv) would work out as in (b) below (sta = stress adjustment: word-internal . . . / . . . / . . . is reduced to either oxytone . . . Ø . . . / . . . or barytone . . . / . . . Ø . . . depending on prevailing tonological/lexical allowances (equivalently, . . . / . . . / . . . is destressed to . . . Ø . . . Ø . . . and the prevailing stress rule reapplies: r-str)):

(a)	/wə=yahab+Ůn/
str	|wə=yahab+Ů́n|
spr	|wə=yahaβ+Ů́n|
f-red	|wə=yahβ+Ů́n|
att, mid, ymn, prm, ver, dme	—
	@[wə̆yahβŮ́n]

(b)   /wa/, /yahab/, /Ůn/

     stratum 1: rules |wɔ̌|, |yɔ̌háβ|, |Ůn|

     stratum 2: wrb |wɔ̌=yɔ̌haβ+Ůn|

     stratum 3: rules |wIháβŮn|

     stratum 4: sta   [wIhaβŮn] or [wIháβŮn]

[18] While <yTyBw> ~ <TyBw> suggests wic(§17.33)^ymn, the opposite order ymn^wic is actually just as plausible—in whichi cse the analogical restoration of 1√ 1ʃ would conform to whatever phonetic realization d-ymn had set up. In turn, the consequences of such d-ymn^d-wic might settle in synchronically in any number of ways, depending on the overall economy of the morphology obtaining at the time. For example, if the original inheritance from proto-Semitic of 1√ 1ʃ-less impa *phonetically* should hsve been accompanied by the presence of 1√ 1ʃ *phonologically*, the discrepancy being mediated by a rule of 1√ 1ʃ apheresis—call it "kwatz"—then it is likely enough that d-wic would be manifested by a mutation of *rule deletion* (§23.2 with (23G)) targeting kwatz, so that the 1√y 1ʃɔ̌ from the phonological level would then be subject to s-ymn. That is, if d-ymn^d-wic should be the case, it would bid fair to involve the transformation of stage I to II to III as in (a):

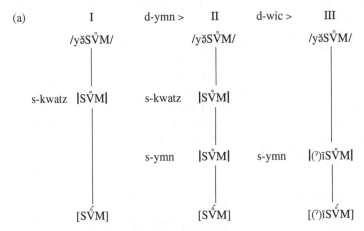

(a)   I   d-ymn >   II   d-wic >   III

Though s-ymn is fallow at stage II,it is active in forms not subject to s-kwatz—e.g., homoparadigmatic pf forms. If, on the other hand, the order of events should have been d-wic^d-ymn, we would hve something like the scenario in (b):

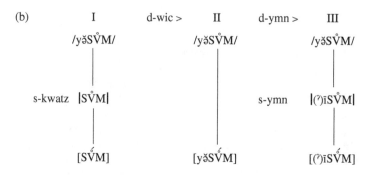

As far as I can tell, the ordering hypotheses expressed in (a) and (b) are pretty much of equal simplicity or complexity. (True, (a) contains two more symbols than does (b), "s-kwatz" and "s-ymn" in stage II. However, the facet of the nexus that leads to this is merely the *continuance* from one stage to the next of a given rule unless something has happened (in diachrony) to change matters; and the fact that this continuance is represented by *repeating* the symbols from one stage to the next reflects no more than expository convention. The moral is that we must always be leary of automatizing simplicity metrics by merely "counting symbols," as was subscribed to in the heady early days of the generative revolution.)

An alternative synchronic explication of essentially the same nexus, in terms of *restructuring*, is developed in §17.13 n. 156.

[19] The view espoused here is that <wʔyTyB> y[wīθév] *either* represents a clitic-host resolution like (aiv) in n. 11 except that TL ymn renders a long vowel while CP ymn gave a short vowel—TL /wə̆=yatIb/ ⇒ y[wīθév]—*or* it represents a resolution like (aii), where the long–short vowel difference between the two dialects is immaterial, the result being long [ī] in either event—TL /wa=yatIb/ ⇒ y[wīθév]. To be sure, y[wīθév] might rather reflect (ai) or (aiii), in which case ymn would not be involved. However, the presence of <ʔ> in the spelling favors +ymn (aii) or (aiv), where <ʔ> would be interpretable as hamzatu 'l-waṣl, while its presence in the forms corresponding to -ymn (ai, aiii) wuld be mysterious.

[20] (a) "almost" in light of <iidlat> m[yédlat] 'sie hat geboren' (Macm 13); but there is a real possibility that the distribution of [ye] with 1√[y] is wider in *Modern* M than it was in the Classical language. Note that [yédlat] is a Modern form; cf. Macuch's discussion (Macm 110), and note that <iidlat> may be an archaizing spelling of the Modern form rather than a representation of a genuine Classical form. Also: (*) The bearing of t[yétβat] 'she sat', t[yéhβīt] 'I gave' on the question of [ye-] in the Classical language is uncertain in view of the spelling <iatbat>, <iahbit>, suggesting -ymn. In fact, along with these forms, <iahbat> t[yéhβat] 'she gave' suggests that we are rather dealing with a tendency in trad pron to palatalize *a* /y__, and not with a genuine retention of Classical phonetic norms. (Forms all from Macm 97. For the scarcity of t[æ] as a rendition of the low short vowel, see §23.3.) (*) If <yama> 'he swore' (~ +ymn <ema>), DM 192, invites interpretation [yămā́], ymn in this variant may be foiled by the likely requirement that the reduced vowel be palatal (see sco, §17.23).

(b) "under the stated conditions": internally in the sim rmp, ymn is preempted in M by prf^smp (§10 <u>M</u>, §17.26), e.g., <ethib> t[étheβ] 'he was given' (Mal 97), [ethéβ] ← smp *(ʔ)Ittə̆hÍβ* ← prf *(ʔ)Iθyə̆hÍβ,*

(c) The pronunciation t[íddun] 'they knew' of <edun> (Macm 135) in lieu of expected [ídun] (cf. t[ída], above in the text) is redolent of the repair-strategic *iC′* → *iC′C′* ~ *īC′* attendant upon M ips discussed in §15.3.1.1.

15. Transparentation

15.1. Introduction

This chapter deals with some of the major Aramaic manifestations of *transparentation* (trp)—that is, analogical change impacting on, or instrumental through, morphophonology. There will be a twofold focus: (α) the replacement of morphological units of a (relatively) marked shape by functionally equivalent units of a (relatively) unmarked shape, stems by stems (§15.2) or affixes by affixes (§15.3); and (β) the achievement of transparentive effect by manipulating processes (rules), usually by suppression (§15.4). The chapter closes with a potpourri of special issues (§15.5).

Though the bent of this chapter is indebted to at least the spirit of the thinking of some grand luminaries in the area of analogical change, notably Jerzy Kuryłowicz (e.g., 1945), it must be stated at the outset that nothing like a full-blown theory of transparentation will be essayed here. At best, ideas will be gingerly proferred as orderly and plausible points of departure toward an ultimate theory. One consequence of this exploratory approach is excess of competing possible accounts of one and the same transparentive pattern—risky in that as alternative solutions multiply, the eventuality looms ever closer that nothing is really being explained, all possibilities being countenanced by the framework adopted. But the hope of course is that hypotheses prompted by the framework will ultimately be found to narrow the options asymptotically toward a truly viable theory.[1]

In examining Aramaic transparentation, attention will be primarily focused on those dialects whose orthographies and/or oral traditions most easily lend themselves to phonetic interpretation: B; TR; and the E dialects SR, TL, and M.

15.2. Stem-Based Transparentation

15.2.1. Least-Marked Homoparadigmatic Stem Base

15.2.1.1. General Introduction; Strong Stem Bases with Light Subject Suffixes

In a stem-affix morphology, such as that of Aramaic,[2] it is often the privatively, least-marked member of a paradigm that will be found to work as model. In the A verb system, this criterion most clearly picks out the ms of the intransitive impa and, following apocope of suffixal *-a* (sap, §17.22), the 3ms of the intransitive pf. In the impf, the complication of an equipollent prefix system makes the issue less straightforward. Presumably, the one slot best suited to function as model would again be 3ms, being formally suffixless following sap-neutralization of the long–short opposition (§7.2) as well as functionally least marked by virtue of traditional criteria such as text frequency. Or, perhaps the model need not be a unique slot but a composite of all the suffixless (light) forms: 3ms, 2fs, 2ms, 1s, 1p.[3]

In any event, in the wake of reduction (§4.2), this would predict as models $Q\check{s}S\mathring{V}M$ for the sim impa and pf, as well as $y\mathring{V}QS\mathring{V}M$ (3ms) or $C\mathring{V}QS\mathring{V}M$ (composite) for the sim impf. And, indeed, it seems that whether teleologically or incidentally or by some amalgam of both, these form types have played a prominent role in A transparentation.

Revisiting the sim pf for starters, in addition to the post-reductional light-suffixed forms—that is, 3fs and 1s of shape $Q\mathring{V}SM\mathring{V}T$—where -$\mathring{V}T$ is the light suffix, 3fs -$\acute{A}T$ or 1s $\acute{I}T$—four of the five dialects selected for scrutiny show at least traces of an alternate shape $Q\check{s}S\mathring{V}M\mathring{V}T$. This is immediately suggestive of transparentation in that $Q\check{s}S\mathring{V}M\mathring{V}T$ contains the segmental shell of unmarked 3ms $Q\check{s}S\mathring{V}M$. Thus, up front, B [bǎṭelaθ] 'sie hörte auf' (BL 102), TR [tǎxéliθ] ~ [tǎxóliθ] 'ich war kinderlos' (Da 261), TL y[ššféliθ] 'hibati lěmata' (Mor 125); and, disguised a bit by pronoun attachment (§17.15.2), M [nǎfalallá] 'sie fiel nieder' (Nm 226), analytically 'she fell to/for herself' (ethical dative; cf. Modern Hebrew *nafla lah*) < **nǎfálaθ lǎ́h*.

To be sure, the barytone stress pattern $Q\check{s}S\mathring{V}M\mathring{V}T$ manifested by most such forms may very well have resulted from a natural tonological algorithm as opposed to an active transparentively motivated reshaping process; cf. the discussion in §4.1. However, aspects of these barytone forms hint that even though the stress pattern itself may have developed under strictly syllabic-tonological conditions, yet active transparentation came finally to play a role. The most pervasive of such hints is the *mid vocalism* of forms like TR [tǎxéliθ] ~ [tǎxóliθ], TL y[ššféliθ], in lieu of the high [í], [ú] expected on a purely phonetic basis, since midding (§17.11) by and large requires that the vowel affected be in a *closed* syllable. But when it is recognized that the homoparadigmatic 3ms forms do meet the conditions of midding, the 2ʃ being in a closed syllable in default of a *V*-anlaut suffix that might open it, transparentive reshaping emerges as most likely. Stated proportionally with *2ʃ a and *2ʃ i for illustration, $Q\check{s}S\acute{A}M : Q\check{s}S\acute{A}M\text{-}\mathring{V}T = Q\check{s}S\acute{E}M : *Q\check{s}S\acute{I}M\text{-}\mathring{V}T > Q\check{s}S\acute{E}M\text{-}\mathring{V}T$.

The case of final-stressed B [bǎṭeláθ] is more blatantly transparentive, defaulting as it does on *two* conditions favoring midding, closed syllabicity and stress of the vowel to be midded, as well as violating the conditions of reduction (§4.2) vis-à-vis the same vowel. All in all, what is suggested is an *oxytone* target for the transparentation, such that a form along the lines of c-*biṭl-áθ* (cf. [silqáθ], [tiqfáθ] BL 174) is replaced by *bǎṭel-áθ* on the model of the least-marked homoparadigmatic member, 3ms c-*bǎṭél*.[4]

The situation in M has a few special facets. Suppose we assume that the barytone (penultimate) stress pattern was originally favored whenever the immediately following word was stressed on the first syllable and the verb, immediately preceding this initially stressed word, was separated from that word by a syntactic boundary weak enough for the power of the adjacent stresses to come into contact. Under such circumstances, an *ultimately* stressed verb like [nefláθ] (or any of its predecessors back to *napalát*) would be dispreferred in a syntactic grouping like *nefláθlá* (< *napalát láhå̌*) because of the *stress clash* resulting from two virtually adjacent stresses, while the penultimate alternative, *nə̆fálaθ lá* (< *napála láhå̌*) would be favored due to the buffer syllable *laθ* (< *lat*) between the two stresses. Finally, when m-pat (§17.15.2) arose, the preference would likely get built into the resulting synchronic process as a structural condition, leading univocally to M verb-enclitic complexes like [nə̆falallá],[5] never @[neflallá].[6]

15.2.1.2. Strong Stem Bases with 3p Object Suffixes

Another factor contributing to the emergence of the least-marked stem shape as a new base for inflection is the attachment of originally independent 3p pronouns as object markers—a process that took place in at least P, TR, SM, G, TL, and M, and seems to have been incipient in SR (§7.4.1, §17.15.1). While this process is similar in effect to that just considered in §15.2.1.1, it differs in that the transparentation follows automatically upon suffixation of the 3p pronoun without the need to posit special mechanisms like 2ʃ i > e in absence of the conditions of mid. To see why, take TL a[ṭə̆9eminnún] 'he tasted them' (Mar 118*) and y[šə̆ˀelinnə̆hú] 'šaˀal ˀotam' (Mor 291). Prior to the change, these forms would have been phrasal, along the lines of *ṭə̆9ém ˀinnún* and *šə̆ˀél ˀinnə̆hú*, so that upon demotion of the independent pronoun to suffix status, the only subsidiary changes would have been part and parcel of the demotion itself, or well nigh: suppression of the staminal accent to conform with the prevailing stress pattern (sta, §14.2 n. 17); and loss of pronoun-anlaut ˀ (§17.15.1 n. 64).[7]

15.2.1.3. Strong Stem Bases with Heavy Subject Suffixes

As has been seen (§7.2(δ)), several dialects import nasal-bearing subject suffixes from the (originally long or energic) impf into the impa and pf: CP, SM, G, and the E dialects SR, TL, and M. The phonetic results of this importation are sufficiently interpretable in the E dialects to see that SR and TL add the new suffixes to the bare phonetic stem, which is tantamount to transparentizing on the base of the least-marked member of the paradigm: e.g., SR cau impa fp [abbɛzén] (Ns 123) (on √bz, formation via gmf-4u, §3.2 (3M)), cf. ms c[abbéz], mp^3ms [dŏwoḥūnə̆́y], cf. ms [dŏwóḥ] (~ [dŏwáḥ], Payne Smith 1903: 81); TL sim impa fs y[qŏ̆ṭulín], a[qŏ̆ṭulón] (Mor 131, Mar 159*), cf. ms [qŏ̆ṭúl].[8] The situation here is similar to that of §15.2.1.2, except that,

while there the suffix importation was *syntagmatic*, the cooccurrent 3p changing morphosyntactic allegiance from independent word to suffix, in this case
importation is *paradigmatic*, the nasal-bearing suffix originating in a parallel
subsystem.[9] (A case might be made for at least SR and TL nasal importation (hii) playing a therapeutic role, since the E dialects largely lose the *-V̄
subject suffixes of the impa and pf by lap (§17.9) making for extensive neutralization—possibly total in the intr impa, where all of ms *-∅, fs *-ī , mp *-ū,
fp *-ā may converge on [-∅]—and importation of isofunctional nasal-bearing
formatives from the impf either restores the oppositions (if lap^hii) or allows
lap to go through with communicational impunity (if hii^lap). Observe in this
vein that, in TL, hii-importation to the pf is limited to 3fp—e.g., a[nə̄θarǫn]
'they fell off' (Mar 139*)—food for thought in light of the fact that in the 3mp
pf TL undergoes not neutralizing lap but opposition-maintaining i-lap, so that
hii-importation to 3mp pf would be functionally pointless.)[10]

15.2.1.4. Hollow Stem Bases

The E dialects, with the possible exception of TL, show uniform [1 √C Ā
3 √C] in the hollow sim pf with low schematic (§1.3.1). On the assumption
that the original Aramaic situation rather involved this stem shape in alternation with [1 √C Å 3 √C] in the environment /__CC, as in Arabic and Hebrew (e.g., 3mp [Qā́Mū], [Qǒ́Mū] vs. 1s [Qā́Mtu], [Qā́Mtī]), we are dealing
with a transparentive generalization of the least-marked 3ms, which is long-
vocalic, throughout the paradigm. There may also be evidence of this process,
inchoatively, in B; thus [śǒ́mtǒ] ~ [śā́mtǒ] 'du hast gesetzt' (Dan 3:10 (BL
148f.)).[11] SR [qǒ́mt] and M [qā́mt] 'you stood' (B 141; §6.2.2.1 above) are
pervasively representative for both dialects. TL in Margolis's Ashkenazic tradition falls out like SR and M, while the Yemeni tradition shows short-vocalic
[QǽM] /__CC.[12]

The process leading to uniform ∫V̄ is *long schematic generalization* (lsg);
see §6.1.1.1.

15.2.1.5. Defective Stem Bases

Consider the following doublets of defective verbs in B and TR, inflected
for sim pf 3fs: B [mə̆tǒ́θ] ~ [mə̆tǒyáθ] 'sie reichte' (BL 161, 164), TR 3fs
bb[kə̆hā́θ] but 3fp tb[kə̆hā́yā] or perhaps [kə̆hāyā́] (accent is not indicated orthographically) 'sie wurden trübe' (Da 342, 344). While the first member of
both sets rather straightforwardly reflects *QaSay-at* with *aya* e-condensed
(§8.1) to [Ā],[13] the second member is interpretable as transparentized on the
basis of 3ms *QǒSÁ* with the [y] primarily an antihiatic insertion (ya'u 'l-waṣl)
forfending against the vowel cluster that would result from the auslaut of *QǒSÁ*
being contiguous to the anlaut of suffixal *-Aθ, -Ā*.[14] A similar analysis holds
for TR [hǒzā́'ǽh] 'er sah sie' (Da 385), with the difference that this form shows
antihiatic ['] (hamzatu 'l-waṣl), the favored device for this function in Aramaic.
We will return to the question of defective verb transparentation in §15.4.

15.2.2. Less-Marked Homoparadigmatic Stem Base

15.2.2.1. General Introduction; 3fs Stem Bases with Object Suffixes

Consider the following comparative TR – SR cross-section of the int pf defective verb (Da 341f., 386; B 139, 147):

(15A)		TR	SR
	3ms	[næssí]	[QaSSí]
	3fs	[hæwwíʔæθ]	[QaSSə̌yáθ]
	3fs^3fs	[9ænnīθǽh]	[QaSSə̌yaθǒh]

It is possible to interpret the TR forms either as processed by sound changes / phonological rules alone or as transparentized along the lines of §15.2.1. In the former event, the 3fs item might be either barytone [hæwwí(ʔ)æθ] or oxytone [hæwwi(ʔ)ǽθ]; in any case, the group *-iya being p-condensed (§8.1) to [-í(ʔ)æ-]; and 3fs^3fs [9ænnīθǽh] would derive either < *9anniyatáha or < *9anniytáha (for *-at ~ *-t, §2.3.4.3). In the transparentized interpretation, 3fs would be [hæwwí(ʔ)æθ] or [hæwwi(ʔ)ǽθ], in either case reflewcting addition of -æθ to the least-marked homoparadigmatic stem base, hæwwí; and in parallel fashion [9ænnīθǽh] would reflect 9ænní + -θǽh, with no phonetic difference from the nontransparentive account.[15]

On the SR side, however, the 3fs^3fs form follows from neither of these two analysis types: the transparentive account is foiled by the absence of the would-be staminal base, QaSSí; and the nontransparentive analysis is ruled out by failure of the vowel of the subject suffix -aθ- to delete by reduction (§4.2). Note, however, that even as TR [9ænnīθǽh] under the transparentized analysis contains homoparadigmatic 9ænní, so [QaSSə̌yaθǒh] de facto contains homoparadigmatic [QaSSə̌yáθ]. The difference is that while 9ænní is, according to the the proposal developed in §15.2.1, the least-marked homoparadigmatic stem, in [QaSSə̌yaθǒh] QaSSə̌yáθ is a less-marked homoparadigmatic stem— intransitive 3fs^′ being patently less marked than transitive 3fs^3fs.

So the proposal being fielded here is that there are at least two possible modalities of stem-based transparentation:[16]

(15B*) *modalities of stem-based transparentation:*
    (i)   least-marked homoparadigmatic stem
    (ii) less-marked homoparadigmatic stem

Now this question arises. QaSSə̌yáθ is not merely less marked than QaSSə̌yaθǒh; it is also feature-wise contained in QaSSə̌yaθǒh. That is, a verb syntactically functioning as 3fs^3fs (sub^obj) contains within it a (virtual) verb functioning as 3fs (sub). Do all instances of stem-based transparentation possibly involve featural base containment? At first blush, the answer would seem to be glaringly negative in the case of least-marked stem base, as considered in §15.2.1. Take the situation of B 3fs [bə̆ṭeláθ], §15.2.1.1. Not only would this form fail to contain the features of its base, [bə̆ṭél], but in fact containment would entail feature clash, [bə̆ṭél] being 3m̲s̲. However, this clash can be obviated if we assume a *privative* rather than equipollent disposition of (at least relevant) features (n. 3 above) and define [bə̆ṭél] not as 3ms but either as 3s, "masculine" being the default gender interpretation qua unmarked (vs. "feminine" as marked), or as 3, "singular" also being the default number interpretation qua unmarked (vs. "plural" as marked), or even as ∅—that is, featureless, if in addition "third" can be taken as the default person interpretation qua unmarked (vs. "first" and "second" as marked).

In fact, independent evidence for a privative solution along these lines—specifically, for the like of [bə̆ṭél] being featurewise either 3 or ∅—is forthcoming from SR, where the fp impa of the defective verb is, irrespective of binyan, formed by suffixing fp [-ēn] (§7.2(δ)) to the fs form ending in the portmanteau [-ɔ̄y] (§8.1.3); e.g., in the simple verb, the plural of fs [Qə̆Sɔ́y] is fp [Qə̆Sɔ̄yén]. Observe first that the transparentation at work here is of the type *less*-marked stem base, since *Qə̆Sɔ́y* is explicitly (though phonologically a bit disguised) fs, the *least*-marked (ms) homoparadigmatic form being rather *Qə̆Sí* (§8.1.3 for all this). Consider next that if *equipollent* feature registration were involved, [*Qə̆Sɔ̄yén*] would contain the clashing specifications f̲s̲ (by virtue of [Qə̆Sɔ́y-]) and f̲p̲ (by virtue of [-ēn]). Privative interpretation, however, saves the day: [Qə̆Sɔ́y-] is structurally registered not as fs but as f alone (the "singular" value being supplied by default), while [-ēn] may indeed be registered as fp. But then fp manifestly includes f free of clash.

In light if all the preceding, the following principle is at least provisionally offered:[17]

(15C*)   i. In stem-based transparentation, whether the base is least or merely less marked, the resulting form contains the features of the base;

         ii. whereby relevant features may be privatively registered.

15.2.2.2. 1s Stem Bases with Object Suffixes

Even as SR shows a case of less-marked stem transparentation with miškal + 3fs, so TR, TL, and M (for this latter cf. §17.6.2) manifest an incipient case with miškal + 1s as base—unsurprisingly in that 3fs and 1s frequently evince parallel behavior (e.g., with respect to stress, §4.1). Examples:

TR: sb[yə̆hævittɑ̃h] 'ich gab ihr' (Da 366), where the base is underscored, cf. bb[yə̆hæviθ] 'ich gab' (Da 309), and [tt] rather than [θ] may represent an (optional) repair strategy to bring the transparentized form nearer to the dialect's canon by closing at least one of the short open-syllabic unstressed syllables;[18]

note that an untransparentized variant is also attested, bb[yə̆hævtǽh], where
the suffix *t* remains unepenthesized (§17.6) because /__VC.[19]

TL: a[ˀamriθáh], or [ˀamrīθáh] if vowel lengthening has taken place as a
repair strategy—the spelling as pointed by Margolis is <ˀam:riyθah̭ᵂI said it(f)'
(Mar 88*); similarly y[ˀæ̆škə̆hiθǽh] or [ˀæ̆škə̆hīθǽh] 'macati ˀotah' (Mor 303
n. 67). While at first blush these forms, possible repair lengthening aside, appear to contain the segmental shells of impeccably constructed 1s intransitive
forms—*ˀamrÍθ* and *ˀæškə̆hÍθ*—this impression is spurious, because TL does not
evidence 1s pf forms in oxytone [-Íθ] (cf. §4.1.2): simple-conjugation forms
ending in [-I] are invariably barytone [Qə̆SV̊Miθ], while sim oxytones always
appear with the suffix bobbed by mtr (§17.12), in shape y[QæSMÍ]; and causative forms are always barytone, e.g., a[ˀargéšiθ] 'ich rauschte' (Mar 164*).
However, things fall rather nicely into place if we appeal once again to the
notion of repair strategy, assuming a third mechanism to normalize short unstressed open syllables in addition to the closure and vowel lengthening called
upon earlier: *reduction*. Thus, for example, taking *ˀAškÁhiθ* as (less marked)
base and adding -*Áh*, stress adjustment (along with possible suffixal vowel
lengthening) would be followed by reprised reduction of 2ʃ A: *ˀAškÁhiθ* +*Áh*
sta (plus possible *V*-lengthening) → *ˀAškAhi̊θÁh* r-red → [ˀæ̆škə̆hi̊θǽh].[20]

15.2.2.3. 1s Stem Bases with Object Suffixes, Cont.:
Permissibly Alternative Analyses

Consider, finally, the variant pairs in (15D), the TR forms given above in
§15.2.2.2, one of the TL forms being from n. 20 and the other from Mar 171*:

(15D)	1s -*t*-		1s -*IT*-
TR	bb[yə̆hævtǽh]	~	sb[yə̆hævittáh]
TL	a[ˀaškahtinhó]	~	a[ˀaškə̆hi̊θinhó]

The striking thing about these forms is that the more conservative members
of the pairs, tagged as such by underscore, are diametric from one pair to the
other: *t* is the conservative suffix shape in the TR set, 1s^3fs, while conversely
IT represents the conservative shape in TL 1s^3mp. The reason for this cat's-
cradle discrepancy follows from the fact that 1s^3fs in Aramaic has always
been morphological, so that the phonetic conditions for epenthesis (§17.6) to *IT*
never arose; while, conversely, 1s^3mp in A was at first syntactically encoded
(n. 20c), whereupon emergence of *IT* on phonetic grounds is legitimately expected. This much granted, and the -*IT*- in [yə̆hævittáh] having been accounted
for transparentively (§15.2.2.2), how shall we account for -*t*- in [ˀaškahtinhó]?
One possibility is via a reductional repair strategy from *ˀaškahiθinhó* (as proposed in §15.2.2.2). But another possibility is transparentation, though diametric to [yə̆hævittáh] in direction. The idea is that [ˀaškahtinhó] assimilates the
treatment of 3p suffixes to the overarching morphological system where object

suffixes constitute word-internal items capable of conditioning, positively or negatively, run-of-the-mill phonological rules—in this case, s-epn, negatively. Of course, this view of things appears to conflict directly with the hypothesis expressed in n. 20a, where the like of [yɜ̌hævittǎ̃h] would rather assimilate the treatment of *non*-3p suffixes to the canons of a new, emergent system structured on the model of 3p inherited forms.

Observe now that in terms of trp on the basis of less-marked homoparadigmatic stem (15Bii), *both* such results can be accommodated, the slack notion being that of "homoparadigmatic." In the case of [yɜ̌hævittǎ̃h], this would be taken to refer to *the conjoined set of transitive and intransitive slots*, whereby intransitive 1s emerges as the less-marked feature-sharing (15C) stem. But in the case of [ʔaškaḥtinhő], "homoparadigmatic" would be identified in reference to just *the subset of transitive slots*, whereby transitive 1s^obj, or perhaps 1s^3ms (cf. y[ʔæškæḥtḗh], Mor 386), would function as the model. Thus, provisionally, this codification:

(15E*) The notion "homoparadigmatic" with respect to a transparentive model may refer to any including set or subset of systematically related φ-inflected forms (choices possibly constrained by conditions yet to be determined).

(If the developmental slack countenanced by this analysis seems analytically disturbing, we must remind ourselves that analytic reductions must not exceed the bounds of attested variation in the domain of inquiry. And in this light, each member of each of the pairs in (15D) is actually attested. The analytic slack at play here corresponds to legitimate linguistic slack in the data itself.)

15.3. Affix-Based Transparentation

15.3.1. Prefix- and Suffix-Based Transparentation

Letting S = stem, A = affix, and Xt = transparentivized X, we have seen (§15.2) that in stem-based transparentation either $A\ S \rightarrow A\ St$ or $S\ A \rightarrow St\ A$. This prompts the question of whether there might be complementary or competing species of trp whereby $A\ S \rightarrow At\ S$, $S\ A \rightarrow S\ At$. The answer seems to be affirmative, though it is not always easy or even possible to distinguish such cases, to be called *affix-based transparentation*, from the stem-based type—and perhaps in particular from the less-marked subtype (§15.2.2).

One difference between stem-based trp and affix-based trp involves the model: while in the stem-based type, the model appears to belong to the *same* binyan and gizra as the transparizand—this is the implication of "homoparadigmatic" in the formulation of (15B)—in the case of affix-based trp the model rather belongs to a *different* binyan/gizra intersection, one that is adjudged to be less marked with specific respect to the base, even if in other respects the model form type might be more marked than the transparizand. That is, markedness is reckoned *parochially* rather than globally. Moreover, consideration of especially the first instance of affix-based trp (§15.3.1.1) will make it clear that the linguistic level of the transparentive process is *phonetic*, or at any rate low-level phonological—likely a property of stem-based trp as well. Succinctly:

(15F*)   While stem-based transparentation seeks its base in the same binyan and gizra as the transparizand, affix-based trp seeks its base in a binyan/gizra parochially and phonetically determined to be less marked.

While comparison of (15F*) with (15B*, C*, E*) offhand makes stem- and affix-based transparentation seem widely discrepant, at least some of this impression is due to the relative paucity of cases considered. In what follows, we will see patterns bidding fair to narrow the gap a bit. For instance, in §5.4 we will be looking at possible instances of stem-based trp where the base is *not* homoparadigmatic. And in any event, a more integral synthesis of transparentation is essayed at the end of the chapter, in §5.6.

15.3.1.1. Impf Prefix Strengthening (ips)

The most prominent instance of affix-based trp so far to emerge is restoration of impf prefix vowels in those binyan/gizra intersections where said vowels are normally reduced to $\breve{V}$, most notably in the simple hollow verb, post-reductionally of the canon -$\underline{\breve{V}Q\bar{V}M}$-, and in the intensive of most gĕzarot, canonically -$\underline{\breve{V}QASSVM}$-. Transparentive restoration of impf prefixal -$\breve{V}$- to full-vowel status will be called *impf prefix strengthening* (ips).

Impressionistically, the model for ips might most straightforwardly be assumed to be the prefix vocalism of the simple strong verb, this instantiating the least-marked categories of binyan and gizra, an assumption which on the face of it would predict strengthening to short vowel status, -$\underline{\breve{V}Q\bar{V}M}$- → -$\underline{\mathring{V}Q\bar{V}M}$-, -$\underline{\breve{V}QASSVM}$- → -$\underline{\mathring{V}QASSVM}$-. However, the edge of the evidence is that we actually find either of two sorts of overshoot: $\breve{V}$ → $\mathring{V}$ fortified by $1\sqrt{}$ gemination (-$\underline{\breve{V}Q\bar{V}M}$- → -$\underline{\mathring{V}QQ\bar{V}M}$-, -$\underline{\mathring{V}QASSVM}$- → -$\underline{\mathring{V}QQASSVM}$-), or strengthening to *long*-vowel status (→ -$\underline{\bar{V}Q\bar{V}M}$-, -$\underline{\bar{V}QASSVM}$-). Two possible explanations come to mind: (*) repair-strategic prevention of unadorned -$\underline{\mathring{V}Q\bar{V}M}$-, -$\underline{\mathring{V}QASSVM}$- from violating the Aramaic-wide (preferential but not absolute, §4.1.2 n. 10) stricture against short vowels in open unstressed syllables; (*) or probably in the case of $1\sqrt{}$ gemination only, closer conformity to the model, since -$\underline{\mathring{V}QQ\bar{V}M}$-, -$\underline{\mathring{V}QQASSVM}$- makes for a tighter segmental-syllabic match to simple-strong –$\underline{\mathring{V}QS\bar{V}M}$- than would unadorned $\breve{V}$ → $\mathring{V}$ without concomitant gemination.

ips in the intensive binyan shows up in the three Eastern dialects; in descending order of thoroughness: M (unrestricted) ≫ Yem TL (3m always but with occasional extension to 1p, homonymous with 3ms by virtue of prp, §17.19) ≫ SR (1s only). While ips in Yem TL appears to exclusively assume the lengthening form *i* → *ī* ([līθǽqqǎnū] 'yexinu', [niɣārǎšéh] 'yidḥe ʔotah', [nīqæbbǎléh] 'někabel ʔoto', [lī9æyyǎnǽn] 'nivdok', Mor 148, 222, 300f.)[21] and only the geminated manifestation in SR ([ɛkkannǎšéx] 'ich sammlə dich', Ns 134), in M the two modes are apparently in variation (<nibaṭil> t[nībáṭṭel] ~ [nibbáṭṭel] 'he frustrates', Macm 128, hence Classical [nīβaṭṭél] ~ [nibbaṭṭél]).

Also, M is unique in frequently showing *prevocalic* extension of the impf-prefixal vocalism immediately preceding causative *a* (< adr *ʔa, §9.2.1.1), especially in 1s: <eiapriš> 'ich erklare' (Nm 227) whether interpretable as [iyafréš] (equivalent to [īafréš]by dme, §8.1.1, with [y] on double duty as anti-hiatic) or [īyafréš] = [iyyafréš] (prefixal *ī* + antihiatic *y*, dme-engendered *yy* on double duty as mock-up for 1√-gemination), <leiaprišinkun> 'er unterrichtet euch' (Nm 280) liy(y)afrǎšenxón]. (Alternatively, but less likely, this pattern might bespeak retention rather than innovation, reflecting the original vocalism of -*i̱*+*h*+*a̱* . . . (- impf prefix + cau prefix + cau 1ʃ . . .), §1.1.3, §9 n. 3.)

When it comes to ips in the simple hollow verb, its effect might seem at first blush difficult to distinguish from those of processes at the service of hollow-geminate rapprochement (§6), especially inasmuch as the geminational manifestation of ips (-V̌QV̄M- → -V̊QQV̄M-) would differ from full-blown hollow-geminate metaplasm (-V̌QV̄M- → -V̊QQV̊M-) only in the quantity of 2ʃ. When this factor is disentangled (assuming it should be disentangled in the first place; note in particular the similarity of ips to g-cis and i-cis, §6.1.2), the most orderly resolution might be this: There is no geminational ips in the simple verb; in fact, there is—with one apparent exception (n. 22)—no straightforward vowel-lengthening ips in the sim verb either. Rather, in the sim verb ips assumes the striking form of pressing into service as strengthened impf prefix vowel the portmanteau *ē* from the 1√y verb, itself reflex (via coa, §11.1) of prefixal *a + *1√y (including (< *1√ʔ via car, §9.2.1.2). Thus, to use 2ms in sketch illustration, transparizand *tǎQǔM* undergoes ips to *tēQǔM* on the model of *tēSóM* (← *taySúM*), despite the morphological discrepancies of the frames, and in particular despite the fact that *ē* qua ips-replacement functions as a prefix-radical portmanteau (the like of /A + 1√y/). But as strained as such a development may at first blush seem, its ilk is not unprecedented in Aramaic developmental morphophonology; we will soon see the case of an original schematic-radical-suffix string pressed into transparentive service as pure suffix (§15.3.2). Moreover, the mechanics of sim ips follow almost automatically from a few tentative principles. These in part have been codified in (15F*)—the organicity of (at least affixal) transparentive bases as *phonetic* entities; thus [ē] as a model, not its derivational correlative /Ay/ or the like. In addition, it is at least implicit in (15B*, C*, E*) that transparentive bases may be *formatives*—that is, cenematic strings realizing plerematic constituents or phonological derivatives of such. In this case, [ē] passes muster as a phonological derivative of prefixal /A/ (or motivated analog) inasmuch as [ē], although a portmanteau because ⇐ /A+ 1√y /, by virtue of coalescence cannot be dispersed into proper string-organized cenematic parts discretely encoding the prefix (/A/) and the radical (/y/).

Continuing, we may assume that the motivation for ips replacement of prefixal $\check{\partial}$ by $\bar{e}$ (← Ay) in the simple verb is fundamentally the same as that driving replacement of by $\bar{\imath}$ (or by i plus gemination) in the intensive (and perhaps M causative): analogical rapprochement to the unmarked norm of the strong simple verb (short I) repair-strategically fortified by lengthening or gemination to forfend against a canonically undesirable short unstressed vowel in an open syllable. But why, in the simple verb, achieve this goal by the seemingly out-of-phase means of portmanteau $\bar{e}$, rather than (as would appear) more straightforwardly by importing strong i and subjecting it to lengthening or gemination? Tentatively, through adherence to the principle gingerly formulated in (15G*). In accordance with this principle, "ready-made" formatives may be selected over formatives subject to distortion (as by repair strategies), even if the ready-made strings should be less than ideal in other respects (e.g., $\bar{e}$ by virtue of its portmanteau status, and for at least one of the dialects to be considered, TL, by virtue of its color as well—unmarked sim impf prefix vowels in TL being high rather than mid).[22] So in the sim impf e is expropriated from the 1√y gizra *just because it is ready-made* (and, by hypothesis, passes muster on certain similarity conditions); while in default of such a ready-made model for the intensive verb, i from the strong gizra is employed but then subject to repait-strategic manipulation (lengthening, gemination).

> (15G*)   A transparentive process may select as base an unadulterated
> formative F from paradigm P in preference to an adulterated
> form G from paradigm Q as long as certain enabling conditions
> of transparizand-to-base similarity are respected.

Simple-verb ips appears in both traditions of TL, most probably in CP, and possibly in M as well.

For TL, consider the like of y[lēnū́m] ~ [lēnī́m] 'yišan', y[lēmūθū́] 'yamutu' (Mor 213f.; accent omitted on the latter form because of uncertainty as to whether < mtr (§17.12) *yamū́tū́n, or rather < residual short-impf *yamū́tū (§7.2(γ)), a[nēnū́m] 'we'll sleep', a[nēmūθū́] 'they'll die' (Mar 129*, 136*; same reason for accent omission). (The judgment that the vowel point cerey used by both Morag and Margolis (§21.4) represents long [ē] is reinforced by the frequent copresence of ml <y> (§21.2).)[23]

For CP, see §14.2 with n. 13.

For M, the fact that $\bar{e}$ typically heightens to $\bar{\imath}$ (§11.2) makes it impossible to know whether the trad pron [nī́qum] of <niqum> 'he'll stand' (Macm 824) respresents lengthening ips, as in the intensive (above), or rather 1√y-borrowing ips where prefixal [ī] < ē by heightening; in either event we may interpret the Classical pronunciation as [nīqū́m]. There is also an alternate trad pron [níqqom] (lc), representing full-blown hollow-to-geminate merger, [niqqóm] (note the telltale short 2ʃ; see above). It might also be noted that M is wont by one mechanism or another to retain or restore the full-vowel value of other, non-impf prefixes—and, moreover, to subject them to repair-strategic lengthening. Thus, attendant upon Aufsprengung, [nīleGṭón] (← *nileGṭón* ← *nilə̆Gṭón* ← *nilə̆Gə̆ṭón* ← *nilgə̆ṭón*, cf. §4.4; cf. <niligṭun> t[nīláɣṭon], Macm 125) where the full-vocalic prefix has ostensibly failed to reprise reduction upon auf-induced opening of the syllable (contrast TR forms such as sb[tə̆ʒ9ibrū́n], §4.5 (4Ga)); similarly in the rmp prefix [īθ-] (< *hit-) upon Aufsprengung, except that here full vocalicity is independently mandated for anlaut vowels, §9.3.1—[īθenséβ] 'he was taken', cf. <etinsib> t[ītánseβ] (Macm 125). In view of the (partially) distinct origins of these restored/retained full vowels, are we perhaps dealing with what is sometimes called a "rule conspiracy" teleologically geared to maximizing $\overset{\circ}{V}$ / minimizing $\overset{\smile}{V}$? In any event, it seems likely enough that a synchronic systematization might treat many or all such cases the same way (as in fact in Mal, and notably in Malone 1972c).

15.3.1.2. Geminate Integrity at Stem-Affix Seams

There may be a few manifestations of Aramaic affix-based transparentation that turn crucially on the maxim of *Geminate Integrity* (§5.1 n. 1), a tendential principle of universal phonology that dictates that the internal components of geminate clusters may not be process-altered in ways discrepant to their structure as modeled autosegmentally. To see how this works, consider the representation in (15H), where *X X* on the skeletal tier portrays a succession of two timing slots—two, because it is characteristic of geminates to be (approximately) twice as long as corresponding singleton segments—and *t* on the melodic tier is shorthand for a configuration of features defining the intrinsic phonetic properties of *t*—that is, those of a voiceless dentoalveolar stop. Now consider the process of *epenthesis* (§17.6), whereby a consonant cluster is interrupted via an intrusive vowel, unmarkedly short *I* as modeled in (15I). How is this representation to be slotted into that of (15H) without distortion? The difficulty posed by a task like this leads many to conclude that the goal is unaccomplishable without violating Geminate Integrity, and that therefore geminate stops are immune to epenthesis without special dispensation. The same holds somewhat differently but to the same general effect vis-à-vis spirantization (§5.1 n. 1), since the instruction to spirantize a stop postvocalically might work out for the melody *t* per se, or for the first *X* per se but fails for the *second X*, which occurs not /V__ (postvocalically), but rather /X__; and so once again, geminate stops are taken to be immune to spirantization without special dispensation.

(15H)   skeletal tier   X   X

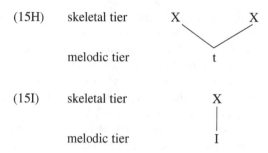

          melodic tier   t

(15I)   skeletal tier   X

          melodic tier   I

As it turns out, there are possible escape hatches from the preceding conclusions as concerns the cased of presumed transparentation to be considered
here. But first the cases themselves will be presented, formulated as instances
of affix-based trp; and only then, at the end of the subsection, will reservations
be adduced.

Geminate Integrity would lead us to expect that an auslaut sequence of two
identical consonants should not be subject to epenthesis. And, indeed, epenthesis normally stalls under those circumstances; cf., e.g., the fate of geminate
$3\sqrt{}$ $3\sqrt{}$ # in sim pf 3ms (after loss of *-a by sap, §17.22): B [9ál] 'er trat ein'
(BL 167) < deg (§3.1 (3Fvii)) 9áll < sap *9álla, SR [páx] 'er zerschlug' (§5.2
SR (δ)), etc., rather than such as @[9ălél], @[pɔ̌xéx] had epn treated the final
geminate on a par with other instances of CC#.[24]

Consider now, however, that when the word-final geminate is tt# composed
of $3\sqrt{}$t + 1s t, epenthesis does apply: Y <mTT> 'ich starb' (DR I #226:4); I
<9ŝTT> 'hašavti' (Kutscher 1970: 79), <myTT> ~ <mʔTT> 'ich starb' (L 61);
CP <n̊ḥṪṪ̊> 'descendi', <ʔḥṪ̊Ṫ> 'deduxi' (Sl 122), these latter interpretable
as [naḥTéT], [ʔaḥ(ḥ)ŝTéT]; SR [mīθ́éθ] 'ich starb' (B 141); M <anh(i)tit> 'I
lowered' (Macm 294).

These formations may be interpreted as affixed-based transparentive, in that
the unmarked shape of the 1s suffix—that used in the simple strong verb—
appears on the stem despite the phonetically rooted strictures of Geminate
Integrity.[25]

Given the evidence for 1s trp from Y, the process is likely to date from
Proto-Aramaic.

A similar explanation may lie behind M <mitt>, <mittun> 'thou didst die,
ye died', to judge by trad pron t[méθt], [méθton] (Macm 12) interpretable as
reflecting Classical [méθt], [méθton] where Geminate Integrity would dictate
that the cluster $3\sqrt{}$t + suffixal t should remain unscathed in 2p as [-tt-] and in
the singular degeminate to [-t] (and perhaps also spirantize to [-θ]). Similarly,
TR tb[ʔăheθ̱téh] 'sie führte ihn nieder' (Da 364) where $3\sqrt{}$T + 3fs t remain
ungeminated (the root of this causative appears to be a hgr-affected derivative
of √ḥt, itself a metaplasm of √nḥt with 2ʃ shortened to [e] by ssg, §6.1.1).[26]

There is, as alluded to, an escape hatch from concluding that the formations reviewed in this subsection are transparentively engendered. This turns on the fact that the cases considered are all what is sometimes called "fake geminates" (§5.1 n. 1)—that is, geminates built up from singletons belonging to distinct morphemes. Autosegmentally, fake geminates—or heteromorphemic geminates, as they are properly called—fall out differently from tautomorphemic cases, as structured in (15H), at least in early derivational stages. Early-derivational heteromorphemics rather model as in (15J), where the separate melodies correspond to the separate morphemic allegiances definitional of this type of geminate. And given this difference, it will immediately be seen how the factors may be defused that led to the Geminate Integrity effect in the case of (15H). As concerns epenthesis, the structure (15I) is unproblematically slotted into (15J) as portrayed in (15K); and postvocalic spirantization is equally facile, in that the first $X - t$ pairing in (15J) may occur postvocalically without incurring any untoward overlap with the second pairing, which itself occurs wholly and discretely in postconsonantal position (i.e., after the first $X - t$).

Of course, these differences between tautomorphemic and heteromorphemic geminates hold only for *early*-derivational stages, *later* stages rather being neutralized to the like of (15H) by a presumably universal operation sometimes called *fusion*. And so much of the disagreement on Geminate Integrity vis-à-vis heteromorphemic geminates boils down to disagreement on the stage where (when) fusion takes place.[27]

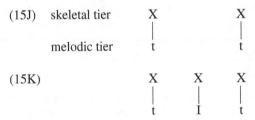

(15J)   skeletal tier   X   X
                            | |
         melodic tier   t   t

(15K)   X   X   X
                            | | |
                            t   I   t

15.3.1.3. Spirantization and Suffixal *T*

At least in SR the simple strong allomorph of the 2nd person suffix, [t], replaces marked allomorph [θ] in postvocalic slots of the defective gizra in all binyanim: thus, 2s sim [QǎSít] (replacing *QǎSíθ) like strong [QǎSV̊Mt], int [QaSSít] like [QaSSéMt]; also in transitive slots, like 2s^1s int [QaSSītín]; 2mp [QaSSītón], 2mp^3ms [QaSSīt̥ǒnnǒy] (B 126, 139, 144, 146, 148). Either incidentally or teleologically, this instance of affix-based trp introduces disambiguation between 2s ans 1s in defective slots built on *2ʃi: thus in the int, 2s [QaSSít] ≠ 1s [QaSSíθ]—whereas, in default of trp, the two slots would be neutralized in *QaSSíθ. It is unclear whether other A dialects show anything analogous (or homologous) in the finite verb, though at least TR and and perhaps TL give evidence of a partially similar pattern in the independent 2s pronoun and, built on that pronoun, the subject-suffixed participle. In the finite verb, B shows sim rmp 2ms [hištə̆xáḥaṯ] in surface minimal parity with 3fs [hištə̆xáḥaθ̱]; similarly, TL cau 2ms a[hōðá9aṯ] (Mar 120*) (corresponding to Yem [hōð̆ǽ9t] (Mor 208), where *t* remains postconsonantal so that the question of trp does not arise). However, when the overall clockwork of the relevant historical phonology is taken into account, [hištə̆xáḥat] and [hōðá9at] need not instantiate trp but may rather show *excrescence* in the environment /H__C# followed by closed-syllabic *promotion* after spirantization has petered out as a phonetic force; see (15L) and compare the similar result in rwb-affected TR tb[ʔǽ9æd] discussed in §8.1.3 with n. 14.

(15L)		**3fs**	*hitšakíḥ-t	**2ms**	*hitšakíḥ-ta
	rmt (§10)		hištakíḥt		hištakíḥta
	epn (§17.6)		hištakíḥat		—
	sap (§17.22)		—		hištakíḥt
	spr (§5.1)		hištaxíḥaθ		hištaxíḥt
	red (§4.2)		hištə̆xíḥaθ		hištə̆xíḥt
	low (§17.10)		hištə̆xáḥaθ		hištə̆xáḥt
	exc (§8.1.3 n. 14f.)		—		hištə̆xáḥă̆t
	prm		—		hištə̆xáḥat
			[hištə̆xáḥaθ]		[hištə̆xáḥat]

If trp should nevertheless be responsible for B [hištə̆xáḥat] and TL a[hōðá9at], observe that we must apparently assume that replacement of the marked suffix allomorph, *-aθ*, was not by strong model *-t* per se but rather by an epenthetic modification of this, *-at*—presumably in conformity with the principle formulated in (15M), for which we will here and there see further evidence (e.g, §4.1.1 n. 3, §15.2.1.1 (sta)).[28]

> (15M*)   Replacement of an allomorph by a transparentive model may be accompanied by phonetic modification of that model at the behest of prevailing phonetic canons.

Though the focus of this book is the finite verb, the following fact cannot be divorced from the matter of this subsection: that both the Sabbionetan register of TR and the Ashkenazic trad pron of TL give evidence of 2s suffix transparentation in the participle, as well as in the 2s independent pronoun where this sort of trp probably originated. Thus TR sb[ʔǽt], and likewise TL a[ʔát] (Mar 89*); then TR sb[mǽšqḗt] 'du tränkst' (Da 352), TL a[bɔ̄lə̆9át] 'you swallow' (Mar 94*). If this patterning is transparentive in origin, we must presumably assume that as a first step the *T* in auslaut of *ʔáT* was identified with (strong) verb-suffixal *-t* and on the basis of that identification replaced by *-t* despite the category discrepancy between the host of the model (verb) and that of the target (pronoun) and that the results of this reshaping were then fobbed off onto the suffixal participle.[29]

15.3.2. Quasi-Inert Strings (q.i.s.s)

A tentative subtype of affixal trp with special ramifications for the theory of analogical reshaping may be seen in such defective verb forms as B [tiθrə̆mū́n] 'ihr werdet geworfen' (BL 164); TR [mə̆ḫū̆nū́n] 'sie schlugen sie' (Da 387), [yištæ9(9)ū́n] 'sie werden erzählen' (Da 347); TL y[pænnū́] 'radfu' (Mor 268). The transparentive clout of such forms seems intuitively clear: *ū(n)* from the strong verb is replacing *ō(n)* of the marked defective gizra (*-n* courtesy of hii/ hti, §7.2). But for all its intuitive appeal, this hypothesis raises a tough question: how is it transparentive, and not in fact obscurative, for a suffix shape to replace a nonsuffix shape? For indeed, *ō(n)* is not precisely the defective counterpart of strong *ū(n)*. Yes, *ō(n)* <u>includes</u> the function of *ū(n)* but it also includes the function of the 2ſ 3√ string, because, at least historically, *ō(n)* arose through condensation (§8.1) of the *2ſa 3√y ū(n)* tail end of the stem. Consequently, *ō(n)* is actually a stem-suffix *portmanteau* rather than a pure suffix sui generis.

However, *ō(n)* is not the only squishy facet of defective verb morphophonology. There is a general tendency, perhaps starting with e-cnd (§8.1) and growing stronger to the tune of subsequent sound changes like coa and k-coa (§11.1), for the tail end of def verbs to exhibit a species of opacity in the form of sporting a homogeneous *V̄* where strong verbs have a *V̊C* sequence sharply articulated into the discrete morphophonological functions of 2ſ and 3√. Thus, corresponding to the *2ſA 3√M* of strong sim pf *QŏSÁM*, defective *QŏSÁ̆* shows a portmanteau *Ā̆*; and similarly in the impf, the *2ſ U 3√M* of strong *-IQSÚM* is at least in the later dialects answered by def *-ē̆* (< *-ay+i*) in *-IQSĔ́*. And even when *2ſA 3√y* fails to coalesce, the tendency to neutralize *ay*, *uy*, *iy* (= *ī*) all to *ay* (§8.1.1 n. 1) still leans in the direction of rendering the tail end of defective stems plerematically inert. These considerations lead to this hypothesis:

(15N)   *-Ā̆, -Ay, -Ē̆* at the end of defective stems have partially lost their morphosyntactic organicity, becoming bridge-like or empty-suffix-like elements to be called *quasi-inert strings* (q.i.s.s).[30]

In view of (15N), we may predict what might be called the *major plerematic divide* to fall out differently between the strong and the defective verb, falling immediately after 3√ in the strong verb but immediately after 2√ in the defective; see (15P) (where 3fs is omitted from (b) as recipient of special attention at the end of the subsection; and where the option *-ay ~ -ɔ̄* in 3fp under (b) bespeaks the tendency of e-cnd to stall on input *-AyĀ̆* (§8.1.1), the result *-ɔ̄* of +e-cnd being immediately reinterpreted as suffixal on the model of clearly suffixal *-ɔ̄* in the strong verb (a)).

Observe now that the only slot in (15P(b)) containing an element straddling the q.i.s. – suffix frontier is 3mp $\bar{o}$, a string whose value as distinctive φ-signal disqualifies it as a q.i.s. and whose full-blown suffix status is compromised *either* by its derivation ⇐ / ayū /, should that retain its validity synchronically, *or* in any event by its lack of motivated identifiability with the strong suffix $\bar{u}$. However, this anomaly can be expunged by a slight realignment of slot and filler: replace defective 3mp $\bar{o}$ by strong-modeled $\bar{u}$ and shunt it rightward to full-blown suffix position, whereupon the overall structure of the defective paradigm will be smoothed out to *stem (q.i.s.) (suffix)*—with the possible exception of 3fs, to which we now turn.

(15P)   (a)   s t r o n g   s i m p l e   p e r f e c t i v e

	stem	-	suffix	stem	-	suffix
3m	QǎSaM			QǎSaM		ū
3f	QiSM		aθ	QǎSaM		ō
2m	QǎSaM		tō	QǎSaM		tūn
2f	QǎSaM		tī	QǎSaM		tīn
1	QiSM		eθ	QǎSaM		nō
	singular			**plural**		

(b)   d e f e c t i v e   s i m p l e   p e r f e c t i v e

	stem	- q.i.s. -	suffix	stem	- q.i.s. -	suffix
3m	QǎS		ō	QǎS		ō
3f				QǎS	(ay)	ō
2m	QǎS	ay	θō	QǎS	ay	θūn
2f	QǎS	ay	θī	QǎS	ay	θīn
1	QǎS	ē	θ	QǎS	ay	nō
	singular			**plural**		

Across the Aramaic dialects, the 3fs suffix of the intransitive defective pf shows either of two forms, to judge by those traditions and/or orthographies affording sufficiently clear testimony: -$A\theta$ (the predominant shape in B, possibly also in M)[31] or -$\bar{A}\theta$ (TR, SR, TL). It seems that either of these can be defended as reflecting the original pA shape with just about equal plausibility—and the other member of the pair derived from that on an equally plausible analogical basis. The traditional view, espoused, e.g., by Bauer and Leander (BL 154), has it that -$A\theta$ was a purely phonetic reflex of -*ayat* by approximately the process chain in (15Qa), adjusted to the framework of this book, and subsequently in some dialects transparentized along the lines of (15Qb)—again adjusted to the framework of this book. However, the alternative laid out in (15R) seems equally likely. And in consequence, no commitment will be made in this book one way or the other.

(15Q) (a) *-*ayat* e-cnd(§8.1.1) > -*āt* css(§17.4) > -*at* spr(§5.1) > -*aθ*
       (b) stem   q.i.s.   suffix   >   stem   q.i.s.   suffix
           Qə̆S   *aθ*   *Qə̆S*   *ā*   *θ*

(15R) (a) *-*ayat* e-cnd > *-*āt* spr > -*āθ*
       (b) stem   q.i.s.   suffix   >   stem   q.i.s.   suffix
           Qə̆S   *ā*   *θ*   *Qə̆S*   *aθ*

In closing this discussion of q.i.s.s, observe that the proposal envisages the emergence of defective verb shapes where a suffix is attached directly to 2√, with no phonetic trace of the (presumably original) 2ʃ 3√. With this in mind, consider the second of two Yem TL variants, 3fs^3fs in the sim pf built on √qly, 'sarfa ʔotah' (Mor 322 w n. 52): [qə̆lā̃θǽh] (straightforwardly < *qalay-at-āh(a)) ~ [qælták]. Similarly TR [ůsnǽh] 'und er hasste sie' (Da 385), where the exponent of the miškal is 1√s 2√n immediately followed by the 3fs object suffix -*æh*.

15.4. Stem-Based Transparentation, Cont.; (Anti)Process-Implemented Transparentation

If defective forms from §15.2.1.5 like B [mə̆tɔ̆yǽθ] or TR sb[kə̆hǽyā] comprise transparentations on the basis of least-marked stem, e.g., *mə̆tɔ̆-y-aθ* (with antihiatic *y*), what are we to make of the like of (15S)? These do not constitute run-of-the-mill 3√y forms; e.g., in lieu of TR [ʔištænnǽyū], we should expect c[ʔištænnɔ̆]—or, with 2ʃi , [ʔištænníw], actually attested as a variant (lc). And while the items in (15S) are canonically similar to the forms in §15.2.1.4, they are patently not subject to the same analysis as these; e.g., TL a[hăwáyɔ̆] cannot be analyzed as *hăwa-y-ɔ̆*, stem – antihiatic – suffix, because *hawa* is not a well-formed stem, transparentive or otherwise. However, if the *y* is interpreted as third radical rather than as antihiatic anaptyxis—*hăway-ɔ̆*—forms like these easily pass muster as *transparentized defectives*—specifically, ones wherein 3√y surfaces as strong rather than being eclipsed by the action of e-cnd. So it seems it may be in order to posit (15T) as a supplement to (15Bi–ii).

(15S)   TR [ʔištænnǽyū] 'sie veränderten sich' (Dalman 1938: 429)
        TL a[hăwáyɔ̆] 'she was' (Mar 106*)
        a[hăwayɔ̆́n] 'they(f) were' (lc)

(15T*) *modalities of stem-based trp, continued:*
        {(15B*) (iii)} least-marked strong stem

Of course, if (15T) is a principle of general scope, it should give evidence of application beyond the confines of the defective verb; and so it does—note examples in (15U) of strong-like geminates (with TL a[qə̆šéšn] contrast the variant a[qaššēnán], lc),[32] 3√Ls reacting like strong 3√Cs (contrast the variant [bašqartī], lc), as well as 1√ns reacting like strong 1√Cs (contrast [neppošbón] 'will increase to them', DM 304). Moreover, since (15T) implies transparadigmatic application—from the strong gizra to various marked gĕzarot—we ought to expect cases of the least-marked form of the target gizra being reshaped on the model of the least-marked form of the strong gizra, an impossibility in the homoparadigmatic operations of (15Bi–ii) where the least-marked form of the target would itself be the model. And, indeed, this expectation is met; see (15V), where (3)ms forms have themselves been transparentized.

(15U)   TL a[qăšéšn] 'we grew old' (Mar 163*)
        M [bašqertī] 'I recognized him' (DM 71)
        M [băhorennón] 'erwahle sie(p)!' (Nm 269)
        M [nenpolbón] 'it will come upon them' (DM 303)

(15V)   TL a[gărár] 'he dragged' (Mar 101*)
        TL a[liθmăsér] 'he will be handed over' (Mar 132*)
        M [băhór] 'choose!' (DM 53)
        M [nenpóš] 'may it increase' (DM 304)

Now there is this: all the cases of strong-based trp presented in (15S, U, V) are at least de facto reshaped, or appear to be, by virtue of a primarily expected process failing to apply: e-cnd (§8.1.1) in the case of the defectives (15S), gmf-1u (§3 (3G)) with the geminates, low (§17.10) with the 3√Ls, and rna (§17.21) with the 1√ns. If these processes had applied, we would have c[ʔištænnő], c[QăSŚy], c[hăwő], c[hăwŝn], c[qášn], c[bašqartī], c[băharennón], c[neppolbón], c[gár], c[liθmăsár], c[băhár], c[neppóš]—some of which do in fact occur as variants.[33]

    The correlation between strong-stem-based trp and trp implemented by process stalling—or *antiprocess*-implemented trp, as it might be called—is in fact but a special case of something quite a bit wider. Most of the instantiations of trp based on a homoparadigmatic model, as considered in §15.2, likewise show such correlations: notably with reduction as antiprocess, though in the case of §15.2.1.4 the omitted process is closed-syllabic shortening (§17.4); e.g., B -css [ŝ̆mtɔ̄] in variation with untransparentized, +css [ŝ̆mtɔ̄]. Moreover, antiprocesses may also be implicated with affix-based trp (§15.3); e.g., -red again, for instance in ips (§15.3.1.1), M [nībattél] in lieu of @[năbattél]. And then, while the antiprocess correlation is certainly the most frequent, there may also be *positive*-process correlations—that is, cases where a process applies beyond the pale of its normal conditions; e.g., +epenthesis in the like of SR [mīθḗθ], or +spirantization in M [meθtón] (§15.3.1.2).

    These considerations lead to (15W), where "formative" subsumes at least stem and affix:[34]

(15W*) Formative-based trp may be implemented by (re)activating, deactivating, or otherwise manipulating one or more processes.

If this is granted, the question arises as to whether (15W) might not be strengthened such that formative-based trp *must* be implemented by process manipulation. Provisionally, the answer is negative. Take the case of B [mə̌ṭɔyá̱θ] discussed at the outset of this subsection. As far as I can see, this shape cannot be derived by manipulation of any independently motivated process, though it can be straightforwardly derived by *formative replacement*: specifically, by replacing the stem shape with that of the least-marked homoparadigmatic member, 3ms *mə̌tɔ̌*, and then smoothing out the combination through insertion of antihiatic *y* and adjustment of the stress.

I propose that the relation between formative replacement and process manipulation vis-à-vis transparentation runs along lines like these (cf. Malone 1992a):

(15X*) Transparentation is usually first implemented by formative replacement, and then often integrated into the overall morphophonology by process manipulation.

15.5. Extensions and Additions
15.5.1. Extended Patterns

In §15.2.1–§15.2.3, some patterns of stem-based transparentation were considered where 2ʃ surfaced in the shape appropriate to the least-marked homoparadigmatic member (cf. (15Bi)); and where, moreover, the reshaping had in the first instance been catalyzed by nontransparentive factors (a barytone stress pattern with incidental transparentive effect (§15.2.1), attachment of suffixes to an already independent verb (§15.2.2,3)). In this section, some extensions of those patterns will be discussed.

Extension of transparentized 2ʃ is spotty in B, being perhaps limited to bb[šæbbíhū] 'sie preisen' (~ untransparentized tb[šabbá̱hū]) (BL 134), cf. least-marked strong [šakkín] (BL 173), and Christian Ginzburg's reading of a few homorizous forms showing unexpectedly midded *e*, e.g., [hizdə̌me̱ntū́n] 'ihr habt verabredet' (BL 109, 114).

Extension of transparentized 2ʃ is quite robust in TR, where especially in the strong verb it has invaded many slots of the pf and at least several in the impa system; e.g., [dīle̱ǽθnī] 'dass sie mich gebar' (Da 364), tb[ʔōθe̱vinnáx] 'ich werde dich ansiedeln' (Da 372), [ʔōni̱qíhī] ~ sb[ʔōne̱qíhī] 'säuge(f) ihn!' (Da 376)—for *-hū* ~ *-hī*, see §8.2.2; [ʔōni̱qíhū] is *either* based on less-marked fs *ʔōníqī* (15Bii) *or*, though based on least-marked ms *ʔōnéq*, accommodated to the prevailing phonology by *e* → *i* /__*Cī*, reflecting the conditions of mid (§17.11), cf. (15M).[35]

The main turf for expansion of 2ʃ trp in SR is the transitive impa, where, most clearly in verbs with strong 3√, all slots have been affected except mp^obj: see examples in Ns 134f., including [sǎma9áyn] 'höre mich!', [raḥ(h)ɛmḗh] 'liebe sie(s)!' (< *-áy-ha, §8 n. 8 for bridge -ay-), [ašlɛmɔ́y] 'übergieb ihn!'[36] Transparentation, then, apparently spread variably from the impa to the impf, but only to the 2ms—that is, to that cross-section of the paradigm identical in φ-features to the least-marked impa, 2ms (2 by implication, person features being redundantly limited to 2 in the imperative system):[37] thus, e.g., sim 2ms^1s/1p [tɛQSo̲Máyn] like ms^1s/1p [Qɔ̌So̲Máyn].[38]

TL, in both traditions but especially in Yemeni, is very much like TR in the pf: thus, e.g., 1s^2ms y[hæsse̲rtǎx] (where also note with 2ʃ failure of low, §17.10, despite /__r), cf. TR [pæqqe̲ðtǎx]—though almost totally lacking in open-syllabic manifestations (only 1p y[bæšše̲lînnǽn][39] (Mor 147) to date, as opposed to TR's robust showing). TL shows less deployment than TR in the imp system: in the impf, to date, only 3ms^1p y[lifro̲qinnǽn], Mor 295,[40] and y[lĭ9æyye̲nǽn] discussed in n. 21; in the impa, only a cluster of Ash intransitives, e.g., mp [ʔaɣmírū] (note again the failure of low—though in cases like this interpretation as [ʔaɣmírū], with low-immune long [ī] via ssl, §17.28, cannot be excluded), fs [baššél̲ī] (Mar 96*, 99*).

In M, nonreduction of 2ʃ in pf and impa conditioned by 3p object suffixation (§15.2.1.2) has spread to the remaining plural object persons: e.g., ^2mp [bǎraxenxón] 'er hat euch gesegnet' (Nm 269), [pǎsaqennán] 'schnitt uns ab!' (Nm 279).[41] It is also possible that low-defiant instances of 2ʃ[e] /__L, like [sadde̲rtî], treated in §12.2 M (γ3) as extensions of attenuation, might alternatively (or additionally) belong here under this rubric, comparable (and plausibly cognate) to the ilk of TL [hæssertǎx] (above). (Since midding *i* → *e* in M is virtually unconditional, the appearance of of [e] rather than [i] in closed unstressed position fails to clue the analyst as to possible transparentive interference.)

15.5.2. Partial Transparentation

Up to this point, it has been assumed that transparentation is a wholecloth phenomenon, in that complete morphosyntactic units—stems (15B, T) or affixes (15F), generically referred to as "formatives" in (15W)—are integrally replaced by others of identical function but differing shape, whether the replacement itself is accomplished directly or by the intermediation of processes (15X). Occasionally, however, we run across instances of what is intuitively transparentation but where the target appears to be *part* of a formative rather than the whole string. Thus, though the usual miškal for the A sim rmp *(h)itQaSiM (§1.1.1) for the most part remains invariant across the tenses, 1ʃ [a] is in SR and G occasionally replaced by 1ʃ [U] in the impa on the model of the sim plain verb; e.g., SR [ɛθku̲rkǘy] 'umgebet ihn!'—untransparentized [εθka̱rkúy] (Ns 142), G <ˀyT9w̲qryn> (Da 277). Observe that cases like these apparently instantiate stem trp *across binyanim*, a phenomenon hitherto limited to affix trp (15F).

Thus (15T) should be more fully specified as (15Y):

(15Y*) *modalities of stem-based trp, continued:*
{(15B*) (iii)} least-marked strong stem, where "least marked" may refer to either gizra or binyan

In default of a sufficient number of clear instantiations, it is impossible to be sure what the limitations might be on partial transparentation. Provisionally, the SR and G cases involve a *schematic* serving as model. Perhaps something like (15Z) is in order:[42]

(15Z*) A transparentive model must be a *formative*, i.e. a morphological constituent; and since formatives may be built of smaller formatives, transparentive models may at times occur in a whole-to-part relation. To date, the following model-types have emerged with sufficient clarity to posit them: affixes, stems of varying sizes, and schematics—the last two in a whole-to-part relation.

Patterns of partial trp that cannot be accommodated under (15Z) are also imaginable. One possibility involves stem-based trp, where a reduced vowel duly receives the color of its model but not also the full-vowel status; thus perhaps TL a[lifru̯qinnán] (or [lifra̯qinnán]), discussed in n. 40. However, there is another way of looking at this form whereby *full* transparentation is afoot, the semblance of partial trp being due to the supervenience of a repair strategy in the guise of r-red with the goal of better adjusting the transparentive replacement to the canonical norms of the phonology. Involved would be an accordion chain along these lines: *lifra̯qinnán* trp > *lifro̱qinnán* r-red > [lifru̯qinnán] (with possible [ŭ] rather than [ŏ] making for systemic accommodation to a 3-member subsystem of reduced vowels, [ĭ, ŭ, ă]; cf. §17.23.3).

15.6. Summary and Consolidation

(The proposals in the section generalize—perhaps with less than due constraint—on hypotheses framed earlier in the chapter, notably encapsulated in statements tagged with an asterisk: B*, C*, E*, F*, G*, M*, T*, W*, X*, Y*, Z*.)

In the preceding sections, several parameters of transparentation have been considered. A transparentive process has been taken to consist, in the primary instance, of *replacement* of a morphological constituent, or *formative*, by a functionally equivalent formative as *base* or *model*. The suggestion was also made that, secondarily, most prominently as a tool of integrating the results of "raw" transparentation into the overarching morphophonology, diachronic replacement may be synchronically explicated as *rule manipulation*.

What determines a base? In all instances, a base formative is *less marked* than the formative it replaces (the *transparizand*), in the limiting case the *least-marked* of the *paradigm*.

What constitutes the paradigm? A paradigm relative to transparentation may be *either* a systematic set of φ-forms of which both the base and the transparizand are members *or* a pair of systematic sets of φ-forms, one containing the base and the other the transparizand. In the former case, the base is less marked than the transparizand in φ-features—limiting case, least marked in φ-features. In the case of the paired sets, the set containing the base is less marked than that containing the transparizand with respect to the stem's binyan and/or gizra (even when the transparizand is itself affixal rather than staminal)—limiting case, least marked in binyan and/or gizra—and additionally the base may be less/least marked in φ-features, as in the one-set mode of transparentation.

At least φ-function and perhaps binyan can be represented by *features* as components of a form. To the extent that this can be formulated privatively, relative markedness can be captured in terms of feature inclusion: e.g., a 3mp may serve as a model for (and hence transparentively replace) a 3fp form in that the φ-features of the latter ([f, p], assuming 3 as the unmarked person value) properly include the former ([p], m being the unmarked gender value); similarly perhaps a cau rmp or int rmp might be featurally coded ([cau, rmp], [int, tmp]) as more marked than sim rmp ([rmp]) which in turn would be more marked than the least-marked (unmarked) sim plain ([ ], equivalently in notation [∅]).

Markedness among gĕzarot might be registered in terms of the processes applicable to a form's root, a simple metric (perhaps too simple) being: the more processes, the more marked the root. Thus √ʾty, with say +car, +spr, +e-cnd (§9.2.1.2, §5.1, §8.1.1) would be more marked than √qṣ9 with merely +low (§17.10).

In conjunction with potential bases of transparentation being formatives, it will be recalled that the layered, part–whole relation characteristically holding between formatives may lead to competing transparentive models for one and the same transparizand, as illustrated in §15.2.2.3.

Posttransparentively, a form may be susceptible to various operations with an eye to better integration into the prevailing morphophonology. This may proceed along either or both of two paths, themselves not always clearly distinguishable.

(α) On the one hand, a form may be subjected to reprises of various processes that have been integrated into the phonology as synchronic rules. Since the reprise processes will in the nature of things be vacuously duplicated by the established rules they mimic, these rules being ordered earlier than the nonce rule introducing the transparentized form (a special case of "A-rule" in the sense of Malone 1969), there will be a tendency for the system to simplify by pushing the transparentized form deep enough into the phonology to precede the original rules to the tune of the reprise's self-destructing. Moreover, the pushing-in may go all the way, so that the upstart form, or more frequently a phonological retooling thereof, usurps the phonological representation itself of the form it is replacing—a phenomenon known in the GP literature as *restructuring*. A concrete though somewhat simplified example of such a process is given in (15Z′), turning on the M form [peršón] 'they understood' (§7.2 (δ), §15.2.1.3) competing with its own original variant [pŏráš] (also attested, in the conjunctive form <upraš> 'and they understood', DM 381). In (15Z′), at the first (unstable) stage, I, the rule *heavy intransitive importation* (hii) has "renewed" the derivation of 3mp pf by effectively tacking impf-imported -*ón* onto the old phonetic form *pŏráš* (rendered three ways ambiguous, 3ms, 3mp, 3fp, by suffix-destroying lap). At this stage, the only reprise rule activated would be r-str (also known as "stress adjustment," sta), but at the next stage, II, phonological integration proceeds further by reprising reduction (and following that up with promotion, prm, of closed-syllabic *ŏ*, canonically forbidden). At III, finally, we see the phonology pruned of redundant processes, str and r-str, red and r-red, by the strategy of placing a retooled version of *pŏráš-ón* in a position to *feed* str and red—this position being in fact at the phonological-lexical level itself. At this point, the derivation of [peršón] has been *restructured*, and is now comparable to, say, that of 3fs [peršáθ] 'she understood' (<piršat>, lc) ⇐ /peraš-at/.[43]

(15Z′)	**I**	>	**II**	>	**III**
	/peraš-u /		/peraš-ū/		/peraš-on/
str	|peráš-u |	**str**	|peráš-ū|	**str**	|perašón|
lap	|peráš|	**lap**	|peráš|	**lap**	—
red	|pŏráš|	**red**	|pŏráš|	**red**	[peršón]
hii	|pŏráš-ón|	**hii**	|pŏráš-ón|		
r-str(=sta)	[pŏrašón]	**r-str**	|pŏrašón|		
		r-red	|pŏršón|		
		(r-)prm	[peršón]		

(β) Then, apart from systemic integration via the established phonology, as discussed under (α), a transparentized form may be subject to apparently adventitious *repair strategies* to ensure a better fit into the system. Examples are the cases of TR syllable strengthening reported in §15.2.2.2 (with n. 17) to forfend against a short unstressed open syllable in the wake of trp, whether the strengthening takes the form of *C*-gemination [yŏhævittắh]) or *V*-lengthening ([wīhạvittinnún], which also shows *C*-gemination in [tt]). Despite its importance, no systematic study of repair strategies has been undertaken in this book.

Relatedly, and indeed perhaps identically, adequate attention has not been paid to the question of how the shape of a transparentized formative's co-constituents are selected or modified as a result of the transparentation. Take the case of TR def sim pf 3ms^3fs [hə̆zā'ǽh] (§15.2.1.5), and note that the transparentized stem *hə̆zā* is fitted out with the suffix complex -*æ-h*, -*æ-* a bridge (§2.3.2), though postvocalically (recall that ' is antihiatic) it might be supposed that bridgeless allosuffix -*hā* would be selected, as, e.g., in the impa (Da 391). Is the selection of -*æ-h* causally connected to the transparentation in some way? Or does it rather simply reflect a quirky selectional restriction of the def pf (as opposed to the impa)?[44] This possibility is suggested by the array of Dalman's examples at Da 385, but the matter should be studied more thoroughly before any definite conclusion is reached.

(Given the tentative codification of the ways and means of transparentation as essayed in this chapter, it is quite improbable that every instance of an intuitively transparentive phernomenon in Aramaic will be reducible to the conditions formulated in the preceding pages without modification of those conditions. Take the CP case of generalizing the 2ʃ of the imp system into that of the pf, e.g., [ššmŮ9] on the model of [IšmŮ9] (§12.2 n. 11). This presumably constitutes an instance of schematic substitution (§15.5.2), but since the 2ʃ of the imp system is functioning as model for that of the pf, does it follow that the imp system is *unmarked* over against the pf? It might also be noted that, while we have seen cases of transparentation across distinct binyanim or gĕzarot, this CP nexus involves influence across distinct *tenses*.)

Notes to §15

[1] Apparent flaccidity of analytic possibilities may, however, at times answer to a real flaccidity in the data, in which situation it is a virtue rather than a vice; see §15.2.2.3 for a likely case in point. Note also two modalities of flaccidity, whether real or apparent: the analysis may predict two or more forms of differing shape (as in the case of §15.2.2.3 just referenced)—pernicious just in case one or more of the shapes is never attested; or a form of one shape may be accounted for by two or more differing analyses.

[2] With no prejudice to its Semitic, internal-flective fundament (§0.2.1).

[3] As just preluded, crucial to the matters at hand are the concepts of *privative* and *equipollent* opposition. Let *A,B,C* stand for arbitrary meanings (or syntactic functions) and *a,b,c* for forms conveying meanings or functions. Moreover, let *A,B,C* be a *paradigm*—that is, a systematically related set of meanings/functions. Then the pairings *Aa, Bb, Cc* constitute an *equipollent* system, wherein each meaning/function is conveyed by a specific form; while *Aa,Bb,C*—equivalently in notation *Aa,Bb,C∅*—involves a *privative* opposition, wherein one meaning/function, here *C*, is conveyed by the *absence* of a corresponding form. Thus, by way of illustration, the 3ms of the sim intr impf, *yIQSÚM*, is equipollently signaled inasmuch as the prefix *yI-* marks this form specifically as 3ms as opposed to the other slots in the paradigm which are likewise oppositionally marked (by *'I-*, *tI-*, etc.); whereas in the corresponding pf paradigm, 3ms is privatively signaled, inasmuch as *Qə̆SÁM* qua 3ms follows from the absence of any suf-

fix (in opposition to explicitly suffixed 2ms *QšSÁM-tĀ*, etc.). (This sketch illustration assumes prior occurrence of various processes, such as sap, red, att.)

[4] (a) Note that the result is not @[bə̌ṭél-áθ], presumably because certain patterns tend to be off limits to disruption as fallout from analogical reshaping, the immutable regularity being in this case that B words contain at most one primary stress; cf. the mechanism *stress adjustment* (sta) introduced in §14.2 G̲ (see also (c, d) below).

(b) An interesting issue is synchronic accommodation of [bə̌ṭeláθ], a marked formation in a system hosting primarily isofunctional untransparentized forms of shape *QiSMáθ*. Lexical Phonology (§23.3) provides a framework whereby markedness of formation would correlate with later-stratal word building (wrb), versus earlier-stratal wrb as hallmark of corresponding unmarked structrures. (Concerning instrumentation, the choice between earlier and later wrb could be effected via lexical marking, e.g., √bṭl would be tagged in the lexicon as requiring a later wrb derivation, at least when combining with 3fs sim pf.) The gist of the idea is sketched in (c, d). (For simplicity, tier conflation—§23.4 (23T, U) (iii)—is assumed; for attenuation, see §12.)

(c)	**unmarked**		(d)	**marked**	
	/QaSiM/, /at/			/QaSiM/, /at/	
stratum I			**stratum I**		
wrb	|QaSiMat|		*str*	|QaSíM |,	|át|
			spr	— ,	|áθ|
			red	|QšSíM |,	—
			att	— ,	—
			mid	|QšSéM|,	—
stratum II			**stratum II**		
str	|QaSiMát|		*wrb*	|QšSéMáθ|	
spr	|QaSiMáθ|		*sta*	|QšSéMáθ|	
red	|QaSMáθ|				
att	|QiSMáθ|				
mid	—				
	[QiSMáθ]			[QšSeMáθ]	

(e) Another possible B transparentation similar to [bə̌ṭeláθ] is [ʔiθkə̌riyyáθ] 'sie erschak', BL 164, if built on 3ms *ʔiθkə̌rí* + *áθ* and if in addition to stress adjustment we assume insertion of antihiatic -*y*- at the stem-suffix seam and appeal to dme (§8.1.1) in explanation of *ī* = *iy*: comprehensively, *ʔiθkə̌rí* + *áθ* → *ʔiθkə̌rí* – *y* – *áθ* = *ʔiθkə̌ríy* -*y*- *áθ* sta → [ʔiθkə̌riyyáθ].

(f) Observe that the Babylonian register sports several *QšSV̊MV̊T* forms, but lack of a system of tĕ9amim leaves it moot whether they are oxytone like [bə̌ṭeláθ] or barytone like TR [tə̌xéliθ], above in the text—which, though itself unadorned by tĕ9amim is cued as barytone by nonmidded [-iθ]; see also n. 6 below.

(g) Note finally that there is a variant to [bə̌ṭeláθ] spelled <b:ṭiláθ>, which might represent: *either* [bə̌ṭiláθ] wherein transparentation is purely syllabic, midding having been omitted (an apparent option for B in any event) or resisted/undone due to the inhospitable unstressed open-syllabic condition; *or* [bə̌ṭīláθ] with 2ʃ lengthened in analogical mime of the palatal passive (§1.1.1 with n. 3), appropriately in view of the semantic affinity between passive and neuter (which latter this lexeme is, as marked by *2ʃi, §1.1.1 n. 2).

[5] The process may also have been generalized to cover homoparadigmatic forms like [amarellə̆xón] 'ich sagte euch' (Nm 241) < **ʔămárIθ lə̆xón*, though the two pre-pat stresses of the corresponding oxytone group, **ʔămrÍθ lə̆xón*) (or *ʔImrÍθ lə̆xón*), are not strictly adjacent, being separated by the syllable *lə̆*. Alternately, the *ə̆* of such syllables, being an *inert vowel* (Malone 1994), may not be strong enough to make for a buffer, as sometimes is the case in Tiberian Hebrew (Malone 1989d). (A note on the presumed 1s suffix **-Iθ*: When in auslaut, this suffix always appears long-vocalic, via l-anc (§2.3.1), as *-īθ*. But if [amarellə̆xón] is assumed to be derived from **ʔămárIθ lə̆xón*, we would need to assume the viability of a stressed syllable immediately preceding a superheavy (trimoraic) auslaut *-V̄C#*, an uncomfortable assumption at best. Perhaps d-m-pat^d-l-anc.)

[6] To conclude discussion of transparentized *Qə̆SV̂MV̂T*, observe that barytone forms like TR [tə̆xéliθ] and TL y[nə̆féliθ] would require a different LP synchronicization than that illustrated for B in n. 4, even apart from the perfunctory differences required to account for the resulting stress discrepancy ([bə̆ṭeláθ] oxytone, [tə̆xéliθ] barytone). One possibility is that TR and TL suffixes are not stressable as units independent of their host stems, so that the equivalent of B

     "**stratum I** *str* |QaSíM|, |át|" in n. 4 (d) would be TR/TL
     "**stratum I** *str* |QaSíM|, |at|", and similarly for 1s "|it|".

[7] Data is provisionally absent for B and SR in that the orthographies of both dialects isolate the 3p object markers as if they are independent words. However, the possibility cannot be excluded that, despite this orthographic convention, the linguistic factors might in relevant respects be identical to those of TR, TL, and M, where the 3p object markers are written as attached to their hosting verbs at close quarters. This might be the case in that all the dialects involved employ a type of orthography that, in unadorned form, provides just a *duo* of choices—write a unit attached or unattached— for a *triplet* of linguistic possibilities: word (conventionally unattached), affix (conventionally attached), or, relevant here, clitic (no firm convention). (The stipulation "in unadorned form" recognizes the possibility of elaborating an orthography with special devices, including devices intentionally or incidentally designed to capture clitic status. In fact, B shows exactly this with the stroke *makef*, though it is not clear that clitic status—specifically, enclitic status—is always signaled by this device; see §21.7). The eventuality of enclitic status being involved here is most likely for SR, which spells the 3p pronouns without initial <h> when functioning as object markers. Textual samples of both dialects should be examined for additional possible hints toward clitic function.

[8] Assuming transparentation, note how [də̆woḥūnə̆́y] may accordingly manifest *two* marks of trp, 2ʃ[o] rather than expected [a] (via low, §17.10) and *Cə̆CV̊C-* in lieu of expected *CV̊CC-*. Such clustering of transparentive properties can provide a species of reciprocal check on the bona fides of the analysis; if, e.g., there should be doubt as to whether *Cə̆CV̊C-* is in this case transparentively motivated, the cooccurrence of 2ʃ[o] despite low-inviting /__ḥ may provide at least circumstantial evidence that transparentation is in fact involved. (However, while the general moral holds—cooccurrence of *X* and *Y* in the same form stands to reinforce the interpretation of both singly as witnessing *Z*—in this particular case, the at-large variability of the process low renders applicabil-

ity of the rule-of-thumb questionable. Hence [o] in [dǎwoḥūnɔ́y] (as well as in [dǎwóḥ]) might be due either to transparentation or to the negative option of low (or to synergy of both). (If transparentive, [dǎwóḥ] requires a somewhat different account from that developed in this subsection; see §15.4 below.)

[9] SR provides an especially motivated case for synchronic Lexical-Phonological (LP, §23.3) modeling of least-marked stem transparentation in terms of later-stratum word-building, assuming the correctness of Nöldeke's interpretation of sim impa fp <Bowzeyn> as [bozə́n] (Ns 123). Since the root is geminate √bz, gmf-1u (§3.2 (3G)) would predict @[bozzə́n] if this were a run-of-the-mill case of stem + suffix combination with no transparentive interference. The lack of phonetic gemination in √z suggests that degemination (§3.1 (3Fvii)) has taken place despite the fact that the suffix *-ēn* ostensibly renders the √z medial rather than final—an effect that would hold, however, if *-en* has been added subsequent to *bóz* (← deg *bózz*) being constituted as an independent word. Thus, this LP explication of the synchronic upshot (for concision assuming miškalim as basic lexical units, if necessary (as here) composed in part by gmf):

(a)   /bozz/, /en/
    stratum I   *str* |bózz|, |én|
                  deg |bóz|, —

    stratum II *wrb* |bózə́n|
                  sta   [bozə́n]

[10] While SR and TL evidence late-stratum systematization of hii (cf. n. 9, preceding), M, the third E dialect, shows early-stratum integration. Thus sim pf 3mp <piršun> (DM 381) [peršón], rather than would-be early-stratum @[pǎrašón] (cf. 3ms <praš> (lc) [pǎráš]); see §15.6 (α) for an alternative non-LP derivation of this form. M [peršón] is, however, a rare form, the dialect normally limiting hii to defective verbs; e.g., <bnun> 'they offered up' (analytically, 'built') (DM 66) [bǎnón]. (M usually allows the lap-affected strong verb to remain uncompensated, such that, e.g., sim pf [QǎSáM] serves indiscriminately for 3ms, 3mp, 3fp; but occasionally disambiguation is achieved via *-yV̊n* for the 3p, thus for the sim pf m [QǎSaMyón], f [QǎSaMyán]—see §7.2 (δ) with n. 19. In all these respects, the M impa behaves similarly to the pf.

[11] Pace Bauer and Leander, who rather consider an original uniform *CāC* to have developed a short-vocalic allostem *CaC* "nach der gew. Form des Noml. Qal {= pf sim}" (BL 149).

[12] Margolis (Mar 127*) lists Ash <lɔt:θeh̊> for 'I cursed him'. Since his normal rendering of 1s^3ms is <-teh̊> [-tə́h] (e.g., [qǎṭaltə́h], 159*), the spelling of this form suggests [lɔ̊ṭǎθə́h], presumably with excrescent [ǎ] (§4.3) to forfend against creation of a superheavy syllable [lɔ̊ṭ] medially (though no categorical restriction is involved, in light of tolerated superheavies like [qɔ́mt], Mar 158*). Note that spirantization of 1s suffixal θ by excrescent ǎ implies for Ash TL recursion of spr around red, as for B and and TR; see §5.2. Morag cites no forms for Yem trad pron susceptible of direct comparison.

[13] "rather straightforwardly": for the qualification, see §15.3.2.

[14] "primarily an antihiatic insertion": in view of the possibility that the *y* might be metanalyzed as 3√—a possibility equally holding for ʾ in the like of [ḥǎzāʾǽh], directly below (see §9.1.4 for 3√y ~ 3√ʾ in the def verb). (Such metanalysis would, to be sure, partially warp the prevailing morphophonology, notably here in fielding a long 2ʃ for

the sim pf. But such may be a path along which morphophonological systems at times mutate. All this is admittedly speculative.)

[15] Both the ambiguity of vowel length ([i] or [ī]) in the 3fs form and the indeterminacy of stress are implicit in the corresponding orthographic form: <ḥæwiyˀæT> (Da 342).

[16] The items tagged with an asterisk, like (15B*), are subject to (consolidated and summary) revision in the concluding section of this chapter, §15.6.

[17] In the foregoing discussion, and elsewhere as well, the notation "3," "f," "m," "s," "p," etc., is informally used in lieu of more rigorous feature notation. And while there are a plethora of such notations in currency, it may be useful to mention here two widespread conventions: (a) when an equipollent opposition is (or can be rendered) binary, one core feature is employed to the tune of opposing signs ("coefficients")—thus, the opposition "fs" ≠ "fp" may be modeled as "[+f, -p]" ≠ "[+f, +p]"; (b) when a feature system is stated in privative terms, coefficient-less features are used—thus, "fs" ≠ "fp" modeled as "[f]" ≠ "[f, p]".

[18] The suffixal syllable of the base is targeted, while the equally uncanonical staminal syllable *ha* is left untouched; contrast tb[wīhā̲vittū́n] 'und ihr gabet ihnen' (Da 365), where the identical staminal string is in fact repaired, not by closure but by nucleic lengthening (considered to be Hebrew-modeled Schematisierung in Malone 1974b, a hypothesis that can still by no means be excluded, as cannot the similar but more general hypothesis of *orthography*-modeled Schematisierung, whereby the endeavor would be made to stick to the (implicitly sensed) "rules" of Tiberian pointing even at some cost of phonetic infidelity). Note that [wīhā̲vittinū́n], with 2s subject, is despite its segmental and syllabic likeness to [yɘ̆hævittä́h] not in fact a product of the sort of transparentation being considered here. Rather, it plausibly represents an extension of *participial intrusion* (§17.17), itself a species of trp.

[19] Note the ancipitally induced difference in vowel length in the suffix shapes of the two variants: sb[yɘ̆hævittä̲h], bb[yɘ̆hævtä̲h]; see §2.3.4.4.

[20] (a) Synchronic systematization of this nexus likely abuts upon restructuring of 1s /t/ to /īt/. Let's assume *vowel lengthening* (vlg) tout court; with some expository compression:

(b)

	I		**II**
	/ˀaškiḥ+t+ah/ *d-trp^repair strategies >*		/ˀaškiḥ+t+ah/
s-str	ǀˀaškiḥtä́hǀ	*s-str*	ǀˀaškiḥtä́hǀ
s-low	[ˀaškaḥtä́h]	*s-low*	ǀˀaškaḥtä́hǀ
		s-trp	ǀˀaškáḥiθ+ä́hǀ
		s-sta	ǀˀaškaḥiθä́hǀ
		s-vlg	ǀˀaškaḥīθä́hǀ
		s-r-red	[ˀaškɘ̆ḥīθä́h]

	d-restructuring (and concomitant **III**			
	simplification of rule interaction) >		/ˀaškiḥ+īt+ah/	
		s-str	ǀˀaškiḥītä́hǀ	
		s-spr	ǀˀaškiḥīθä́hǀ	
		s-low	ǀˀaškaḥīθä́hǀ	
		s-red	[ˀæškɘ̆ḥīθǽh]	

Note how the system at stage II lends itself to simplification at stage III, after speaker awareness of the original transparentive strategy has died out (*rule deletion* of s-trp plus its entailed repair strategies). The case of [ʔamrīθáh] would be even more complex, but explication will be foregone here.

(c) Observe the possible bellwether role of ^3p forms like TL a[ʔaškə̆hi̭θinhő] 'I found them(m)' (Mar 171*) in this sort of trp. This form being reflex of originally periphrastic *ʔaškáhiθ ʔinhő* or the like via i-pat (§17.15.1), [-i̭θ-] does not here represent in the first instance a transparentation of *-t-* but rather reflects the legitimate, epn-processed shape of the suffix from the days when *ʔaškáhiθ* was an independent word. We may speculate that forms like [ʔaškə̆hi̭θáh] represent generalization of *i̭θ* from /__3p to /__any object pronoun, whereupon full-blown trp is achieved.

(d) M <anhiritilun> 'ich leuchtete ihnen' (Nm 226), qua [anhə̆rī̭θellón], might just instantiate a sporadic instance of trp of the type considered in this section, but there are other possible analyses; see m-pat (§17.15.2).

[21] For the sporadic use of *l-* in 1p, see prp (§17.19). Attachment of *-An* disambiguates this form as 1p (rather than 3ms), a therapeutic measure rarely used. CP manifests a similar disambiguation of 1s̲ from 3ms of the otherwise homonymous [I-] (§14.2 CP̲ (α)); e.g., <y9BDʔn̲ʔ> 'ich tue', <yhyn̲ʔ> 'ich bin' (Sg §16 Anm 1). The attached forms in both dialects plausibly represent (contracted) forms of the independent pronouns (TL 1p <ʔnn>, CP 1s <ʔn̲ʔ>), as proposed by both Margolis (Mar 146* under <9aynɔʔ>) and Schulthess (Sg, lc). Observe that Margolis's Ash counterpart of Morag's Yem [lī9æyyenǽ̲n] shows the pronominal attachment in a fuller form, *-nan*: [lə̆9ayyennán] (Mar, lc)—where, be it noted, ips is absent, as consistently in Margolian versions of the intensive. Observe also that ʃ2 [e] must be transparentively accounted for in both traditions, in Ash no less than in Yem by virtue of the color (despite default of phonetic conditions of mid, §17.11), but in Yem alone by virtue of its status as a full vowel (rather than reduced). The phenomenon witnessed in TL and CP will be generically called *disambiguative impf attachment* (dia)—"generically" in that discrepancy of dia-triggering homonymies renders the two manifestations of the process more likely to be typologically than genetically unitary, though stimulus diffusion from one to the other dialect cannot be ruled out.

[22] The Yem trad pron of TL shows one instance of long-vocalic ips in the simple verb, [tī̆qű] in the specialized sense '(the matter) stands (unresolved)"; when used in the literal sense, 'stands (up)', normal [ē] is used (Mor 213 with n. 12)—and Margolis reports uniform [ē] for either sense in his Ash trad pron (Mar 158*). Absence of 3√m is courtesy of mtr, §17.12.2 TL̲ (γ).

[23] It is noteworthy that though +ips and –ips forms alternate in both traditions, in the *third person* +ips always and only occurs in forms with prefixal *l-* or *n-* (as in the examples just cited) while –ips is always and only the mark of forms with *y-* (e.g., y&a[yə̆mūθū] 'they'll die', Mor 214, Mar 129*). The implied clustered process pairs, +ips and +prp (§17.19) on the one hand, -ips and -prp on the other, are likely to respectively mark innovative (*lē-, nē-*) and conservative (*yə̆-*) forms—the idea being that the conservative forms date from a time before ips and prp arose (and were trapped in arachaic or archaizing text sections).

[24] (a)The nonforthcoming epenthesized forms should not be confused with strong-like geminate formations of canon *Qə̆SAM* (*Qə̆MAM*), to be treated in §15.4. (b) It will

be observed that, while epn is stalled by Geminate Integrity, deg is not. This is because the operation of deg can be autosegmentally formulated in a straightforward way: delete one of the two X-positions; see (c). ("Delete one of two": intuitively the second, since that one abuts the "silence" of #; however, in Tiberian Hebrew, rule interaction apparently forces the (presumably homologous) process, Final Shortening, to delete the *first* X-position—see THP 74 n. (a).)

(c)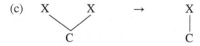

[25] To judge by forms like SR [mīθḗθ], the process could just as likely be formulated as *stem*-based trp, in light of least-marked homoparadigmatic 3ms [mī̊θ]. However, M <anh(i)tit>, whose <i> ~ <∅> suggests [ŏ], supports the affix-based view: [anhŏθī̊θ] contains a *reduced* allostem, anhŏθ-, whereas a stem-based account would require @[anheθī̊θ] (spellable <anhitit>, with constant 2ʃ <i>). (There is also testimony from Modern M, where 'I died' is [méxtīt] while 'he died' is [mḛ̊θ] (Macm 325, 499); so that stem-based trp would predict @[mḛ̊θīt]. (2√ [x] oddly appears in 1s and 3fs of the pf in Modern M, as well as in the related noun [móxta] 'death'; Macm 499).)

[26] A parallel account may be in order for SR <miyTt>, <miyTtown> (Ns 121), to the extent that the spelling <Tt> can represent [θt]. Analysis of the material in Ns §26, §137 suggests on balance the option of transparentized [mī̊θt], [mī̊θtón] or Geminate-Integrity-respecting [mī́t] (← deg mī́tt; for [-t] ≠ [-θ], §15.3.1.3), [mī́ttón]); apparently, such cases may also be spelled <tt>, e.g., <ʔAvhɛtt>, <ʔAvhɛttɔn> 'beschämtest, beschämtest uns' (Ns 20). In turn, spellings like <tt> can be interpreted as *morphophonemic orthography*, a species of paralinguistic transparentation, whereby in this case /C′C′/—or more accurately |C′C′|—is written <C′C′> even though the prevailing orthographic canons (for Northwest Semitic consonantal spelling at large) dictate that geminate clusters be represented <C′> as for singletons. The morphophonemic essence of such spelling is revealed especially sharply in auslaut, where deg would render the phonetic results a singleton: thus <ʔAvhɛtt> in agreement (for relevant points) with phonological /a-bhet+t/, or, more accurately, with intermediate-level |a-Bhet+t|, rather than with phonetic [Awhét] (for [-t], cf. §15.3.1.3); contrast, e.g., I <nhT> 'du bist abgestiegen' (L 57), where /-t+t/ is indeed represented by the singleton letter <-T> (for the hedge A = a/ɔ, see §20.2 n. 7b). In SR, morphophonemic orthography is the general practice whenever each /C′/ represents (part of) a separate morpheme, e.g., root and affix; for discussion and examples, Ns §26, §36. (SR morphophonemic orthography was said to correlate "more accurately" with intermediate |C′C′| than with underlying /C′C′/ in view of the fact that <TT> can represent |TT| ⇐ /TØ/ (Ø a "ghost consonant," §21.3) *either* < rmp + cau *t+h or *t+ʔ (§9.2.2 w n. 23) *or* < rmp + 1√ *t+ʔ via prf (§10 SR). Nöldeke notes that "in älterer Zeit" such cases were often spelled with singleton <T>, Ns 25.)

M is perhaps best interpreted as not generally deploying morphophonemic orthography—note <etriṣt> 'du wurdest aufgerichtet' (Nm 223) [etreṣt] where [t] ← rmp T + 1√t + 1ʃŏ via smp (§17.26), and <taqinH> 'wir richteten ihn ein' (Nm 277) [taqqennī́] where [nn] ← 3√n + 1p n—cases to the apparent contrary actually encoding transparentively derived heterophonous clusters of a cloth with those adduced in the text (<mitt>)

[méθt] etc.): e.g., <abhiṭṭinun> 'ich beschämte sie(mp)' (Nm 282) if [aβheθtennón] (in which vein <asiṭṭinun> ~ <asitinun> 'ich verschmähte sie(mp)' (Nm 283) is interesting, representing a causative (originally) hollow stem on *√šWṭ (DM 454) merged formally with geminate (§6.2.2.1), the first spelling showing phonetically straightforward [asettennon], the second progressively assimilated (by dca, §10 n. 3b) [ašettennón]).

For G, note non-morphophonemic <myTw(n)> 'ihr seid gestorben' (Da 319). For SM ditto, <yThy> t[yiṭṭǽni] 'wird uberliefert' (Macs 213) (rmp *T* + 1√t, rmp int impf). CP shows non-morphophonemic spelling of the finite verb, though some instances of <TT> for rmp *T* + 1√t apprear in the participle, e.g., /tmh <ʔT̥mḫ> 'abstupuit' (Sl 221) [Ittǎméh] (§12 n. 11) but mp participle <mTTmhyn> (lc); similarly with √tqn 'constitui' and perhaps √tql 'pedem offendere' ("perhaps" because it is unclear whether <mT-Tql>, which Schulthess tags as "corr{ectior}" than variant <m̥T̥ql̥>, is attested or not). For TR, note morphophonemic <wuTtæn̊eynuwn> 'und du wirst sie(mp) erzahlen' (Da 389), conjunctive int impf with 2s *T* + 1√t, if [ŭttænněn(n)un]. (TR shows some exceptional incidence of <C'C'> apparently spelling intensive 2√[C'C'], but the peculiar way that <ǎ> positions relative to this suggests that the originally intended pronunciation was misunderstood by the vocalizers; see bb<Diyqæyǎ̊ymæh> under *√qWm in §24.2.)

[27] The story is actually even more complicated, but this is not an apposite venue for protracted discussion. There are also other perspectives on the matter of geminates over against disruptive processes. Lowenstam and Prunet 1987, for instance, hold that failure of Geminate Integrity for fake geminates may bespeak the members of such clusters belonging to separate phonological domains; and in Malone 1989a, a theory is developed wherein Geminate Integrity may be violated even by tautomorphemics.

[28] (a) ". . .suffixal allomorph, -*aθ*": the excrescent vowel, *a*, brackets rightward with the suffix rather than leftward with the stem. This follows the bracketing convention adduced in THP 65 Notes. (Northwest Semitic evidence for this convention may be seen in Malone 1976b; and also implicitly in Bolozky 1977, where allegro deletion of originally epenthetic *e* in Modern Hebrew depends upon its inclusion in a suffix, specifically feminine nominal -*et*.) See also §2.3.2.1 n. 6.

(b) Is the fact that the anomalous kĕrey form at Dan 4:19 for 'thou art grown great' is [rǎváθ] rather than @[rǎvát] evidential against the trp hypothesis for such as [hištǎxáhat]?

[29] (a) The TL reshaping appears to be restricted to /V̊__; contrast maintenance of /V̄__, as in [bǝ9éθ] 'you require' (Mar 95*), similarly with √gby, √9ṣb (Mar 96*, 149*). (The TL situation bears comparison with the similar but more complex case of Tiberian Hebrew treated in THP 65 n. (a)—and indeed Hebrew-based Schematisierung cannot be excluded.)

(b) On the assumption that in the pf transitive verb the preferential ancient Aramaic shape of the 3fs suffix after bridge formation was *t prevocalically (§2.3.4.3 3fs (β)), as preserved in TR and yTL (e.g., [ʔǎheθtéh], §15.3.1.2, y[ššqælṭéh] 'hi lakha ʔoto', Mor 292), the fact that SR (variably for the Jacobite register, Ns 129) shows (e.g., sim 3fs^3ms [QǎSaMθéh], B 145) might be interpreted as trp-replacement of *t* (< *t*) by *θ* on the model of the intransitive -*aθ* modified by r-reductive deletion of *a* for the sake of tighter canonicity; cf. (15M). Evidence from SR itself that *t might have been originally available under these circumstances is perhaps forthcoming in [bǎtɛnθǎxón] 'sie war mit euch schwanger' (Ns 132); because if [θ] here should stem from *at, derivation from predicted *baṭinatakúm should yield [bɛṭnæθxón]—itself an attested variant (lc). On the other hand, [bə̆ṭɛnθə̆xón] is straightforwardly derivable from *baṭintakúm as long as trp of *t to θ is assumed. However, the very fact that *at may apparently alternate with *t for one and the same form, as per these two examples, makes it possible that at least some tokens of 3fs [Cθ] may derive from *Cat under subsidiary conditions to be determined. Consequently on balance assumption of unique original *t for cases like [Qə̄SaMθ ḗh] is open to question. (The phonetic facts in most of the other dialects are unclear. Ash TL preponderantly agrees with Yem in showing [t]—see, e.g., the Glossary in Mar 84*ff. under √ʔsr, √kbš, √lbš, √qrṣ, √šbq—but also shows a few forms with θ: at least [ʔappeqθ ḗh] 'she brought him out' (Mar 138*), [ʔištə̆metθán] 'she escaped from me' (Mar 173*).)

[30] (a) There may be some other factors either contributing to, or contributed from, the morphological feebleness of q.i.s.s: for instance, the fact that at least in Ash TL ē may function as an inert buffer (bridge) between stem and suffix in reshaped geminate verbs (see discussion of [maṣṣē ̆θ] 'you sucked' in §3 n. 6); and the role of y as a hiatus-breaker-become-suffix element in M 3p [-yŏn], [-yǎn] (§7 n. 19).

(b) The theory of q.i.s.s was in part prefigured more than a century ago by Jacob Barth, who recognized that the tail-ends of defective verbs in Semitic constitute a frequent mine for fielding innovative suffix material ("Die {semitische Mutter}Sprache sah in {3√y, 3√w} nicht mehr Radicale, sondern hinter dem Stamm angefügte Zusatzelemente" (1894: 372, more generally 369–74)).

(c) Observe in the general vein of defective verbs as hosts for q.i.s.s the appropriateness of the term "defective" ((Arabic nāqiṣ).

[31] "possibly alone in M": on the face of it, the Modern language shows [-at] ~ [-āt], the former preferred (e.g., [hə̆zát] ~ [hézāt] 'she saw', Macuch 1989: 303, 310, 62); however, since Modern M shows widespread vowel length exchanges under poorly understood circumstances (Malone 1997: 150), it is not foregone that m[-at] ~ [-āt] faithfully reflects Classical M [-aθ] ~ [-āθ].

[32] TL appears not to evince any fully unmarked geminates in sim pf 1p, which would be predicted by gmf-1u (3G) ^ constraint (3Fv′) to be QaSn(an). While the form a[qaššēnán] is in part constructed by gmf-1u, it is simultaneously built up with the "filler" [ē]; see the suggestion in §3 n. 6 for a hybrid derivation in parallel plains. For 1p -n ~ -nan, §7 n. 11. (To complete the picture for TL sim pf 1p, Margolis lists variants with the archaic/archaizing suffix [-nə̄] (lc and Mar 49) whose auslaut V̄ has escaped lap, §17.9. Morag lists no examples for sim pf 1p at all (Mor 234).)

[33] "a *primarily* expected process failing to apply": because in the wake of such failure, various other processes either fail to apply (e.g., red, §4.2, in the case of 2ʃ of [hă w̲a̲y̲ón]) or apply when they otherwise would not (e.g., red again, of 1ʃ of the same form [hă w̲ay̲ón]); on a purely phonetic basis, we would expect failure of e-cnd to lead to @[hawyón]—or @[hōyón], +coa (§11.2).

[34] (a) "at least stem and affix"; other possibilities will be considered in §15.6. (b) "or otherwise manipulating"(in (15W): e.g., in Malone 1971a, it is proposed that analogical replacement in Aramaic of segolate nominals of shape QV́SV̆M by counterparts of shape Qə̄SV́M (on the model of the dissyllabic miškal) may have been implemented by *process reordering* (cf. §23.2 (23J)).

[35] "reflecting the conditions of mid": specifically, by a kind of *rule reversal*, mid effecting $i \rightarrow e$ under conditions which exclude /__Cī. This sort of relation, between a process $A \rightarrow B/C$ and a reverse thereof $B \rightarrow A/\text{-}C$, may obtain when, as here, a constitutent (*ʾōneq*) is removed (here by trp) from an environment favoring some aspect of the constituent's shape (here, /__C# favoring *e*) to another environment disfavoring the same aspect (here, /__Cī). Such rule reversals are among the tools implementing modifications dictated by (15M).

[36] "most clearly in verbs with strong 3√": in contrast, the question of 2 trp in the defective transitive impa is quite ambiguous, though, gingerly, it will be assumed that the defective gizra follows the strong in transparentizing all slots of the tr impa but mp; that is, plotting "+" for positive application of trp and "-" for negative into the cells of Brockelmann's displays (B 144–49), that the pattern is as portrayed in (a):

(a)

strong	transitive	imperative	
object=	=1s/1p	=3ms	=3fs
subject			
=ms	+	+	+
=fs	+	+	+
=mp	–	–	–
=fp	+	+	+

The display in (b) gives representations of Brockelmann's def sim impa entries, to be commented upon in the sequel:

(b)

object=	1s/1p	3ms	3fs
subject			
=ms	Qə̆Sín	Qə̆Síw	Qə̆Síh
=fs	Qə̆Sɔ́yn	Qə̆Sɔ(ʾ)íw	Qə̆Sɔ(ʾ)íh
=mp	Qə̆Sɔ(ʾ)ún	Qə̆Sɔ(ʾ)úy	Qə̆Sɔ(ʾ)úh
=fp	Qə̆Sɔ̄yēnɔ́n	Qə̆Sɔ̄yēnɔ́y	Qə̆Sɔ̄yēnɔ́h

The ms forms are taken to be vacuously transparentized, in the sense of the word that attaching the object suffixes (in their phonetic shape) to the least marked stem of the larger impa paradigm, i.e. intransitive ms *Qə̆Sí* (for the auslauts of the def impa, §8.1.3), gives the same results as diachronic derivation with no transparentive interference; e.g., [Qə̆Síw] < *Qə̆Sí* + *w* or < l-cnd *Qə̆Síhū*.

The fs forms are more clearly transparentized: the appropriate less marked stem, fs *Qə̆Sɔ́y*, is either immediately suffixed (*Qə̆Sɔ́y* + *n*), or filled out with a bridge + suffix combination (-*íw, -íh*), stress-adjusted, and then subjected to a rerun of partial condensation (e.g., *Qə̆Sɔ́y – íw* sta → *Qə̆Sɔ́yíw* r-p-cnd → [Qə̆Sɔ(ʾ)íw]).

The mp forms, despite canonic similarity to homoparadigmatic items taken to have undergone trp, are best conceived of as simple partial condensations with no transparentive intereference; e.g., [Qə̆Sɔ(ʾ)úy] < *Qə̆Sayúhī* (note that the substring *-úhī* also undergoes l-cnd; *a* > [ɔ] by mvh, §20.2 (δ)).

In the fp forms, finally, trp may be taken as primary rather than extended, being triggered by importation of nasal-bearing -*ēn*- (§7.2 (ζ), §15.2.1.3, §15.2.2.1).

The issue of the 2ʃ-transparentive appearance of the results of partial condensation also arises in the defective transitive pf, specifically concerning sim 3fp^obj, e.g.,

3fp^3ms [QšSayɔ́y] (B 149) < *QaSayā́hī. This sketch form looks distinctly transparentive, not because e-cnd has apparently failed to operate on *-ayā-, unsurprisingly given the resistance of this string to condensation (§8.1.1), but because on top of that 2ʃa has failed to reduce; that is, we don't get @[QaSyɔ́y]. In this book, however, [QšSayɔ́y] is not taken to reflect full escape of ayā from condensation. Rather, the position adopted is that ayā has undergone *partial* condensation, where, however, the elided 3√y is then replaced by antihiatic y; see also §8.1.1 n. 4. Such an accordion-like analysis is admittedly uncomfortable, but on balance the evidence of pattern congruity seems to warrant it. In particular, the strong transitive pf (imported nasal-bearing forms aside, §7.2 (ζ)) is uniformly *non*transparentive vis-à-vis 2ʃ; and the intensive counterparts of defective simple 3fp^obj likewise fail to transparentize (e.g., [QaSSšyɔ́y] ≠ @[QaSSīyɔ́y], B 148f.), important in that 2ʃ trp is normally homogeneous across binyanim.

[37] This sort of implication can be formally captured by a redundancy condition along the lines of [imperative] → [imperative, 2]; cf. chapter 6 of THP.

[38] The fact that in verbs with strong 3√, 2ʃ trp is restricted to 2ms reflects the fact that, in the case of strong 3√ impas, trp is based on the *least*-marked homoparadigmatic stem—that is, 2ms, as opposed to *less*-marked stem as in the case of the defectives (n. 36). And while parallel considerations might lead us to expect that, in the *defective* impf we should see evidence of impa-extended trp occurring in other φ-slots, there appear to be only rare forms showing anything of the sort—notably 2fs^3ms [lɔ̄ tɛšrēyɔ́y] 'ne le libère pas' ("une forme poétique . . . usitée dans le sens d'un impératif," Du 203), where, however, trp seems to be based on the 2ms stem: tɛšrḗ - y (antihiatic) -ɔ́y. Is gender neutralization perhaps involved (fgm, §16.1)? Note that formally 2fs variants are seemingly attested, e.g., ^1s [tɛqrēnɔ́n] ~ [tɛqrēnī́n] (lc). (Alternatively, however, the stem base of [tɛšrēyɔ́y] might derive from a residual 2fs *short* impf *tišráyī, ē unproblematically < ayī by e-cnd (§8.1.1).

[39] *-in-* by pin (§17.17).

[40] Margolis represents this form as <lif:rɔ̆qiw̃nán> (Mar 153*), at face value interpretable as [lifrɔ̆qinnán], but then speculates that it really was probably pronounced [lifrŭqinnán] ("man wird aber wohl *lifrŭkinnan* . . . gesprochen haben"); Mar 13. He also provides the original, uninterpreted spelling: <lyPrwQynn> (lc). All this conspires to hint, though not prove, that Margolis's reading of TL was at least in part interpretive rather than simply handed down from generation to generation—and hence not unadulterated (Ashkenazic) traditional pronunciation. The discrepancy between <ɔ̆> and [ŭ] should also caution us that Margolis's Tiberian representations—and such is the overwhelmingly majority vehicle of his phonetic interpretation—may at times, as here, be warped in the direction of orthodox Tiberian spelling conventions, in particular as concerns pointing in the broad sense (including nikud, dageš, mapik, meteg, etc.). With these caveats in mind, see also §15.5.2 for more on this form.

[41] As spelled out in §17.15.1, in the light-subject impf M normally reduces—or, more strictly, reprise-reduces—2ʃ in the wake of plural object suffixation, e.g., [elgă̆tenxón] 'ich werde euch greifen' (Nm 280); the failure of the dialect to (re)reduce in pf/impa, as in the examples cited in the text or [lɔ̆γaṭennón] 'he grasped them' (DM 230), plausibly reflects the phonotactic malaise of such an operation in the environment /#CɔC__. Now it happens that corresponding light-subject impf forms with *singular* objects are normally subject to Aufsprengung (§4.4.1); e.g., *elgă̆ṭáx* → [īleGṭáx] 'I'll seize

you(ms)' (lc). Since Aufsprengung is by and large the unmarked M response to *CCə̆*, why doesn't this process likewise normally affect *plural*-object forms; that is, why do we systematically get -auf results like [elgə̆ṭenxón] rather than the like of [īleGṭenxón]? There are three credible hypotheses. (a) Because auf imposes a phonetic condition met by *elgə̆ṭắx* but not by *elgə̆ṭenxón*—that the syllable immediately following the auf-deleted *V̆* preferentially be stressed. (b) Because *ə̆* in *elgə̆ṭắx* is by *primary* reduction (red) while *ə̆* in *elgə̆ṭenxón* is by *reprise* reduction (r-red), and red^auf^r-red'; so that it was too late for *elgə̆ṭenxón* to become [īleGṭenxón]. (See §15.5.1 for M's restoration /__plural object suffix of full-vocalic 2ʃ, in this example = *o* r-red → *ə̆* in *elgə̆ṭenxón*.) (c) Because the differential outcome was the result of a Martinesque *chaîne de traction* (Martinet 1964: 59ff.), in that when (such as) *elgə̆ṭắx : elgoṭenxón* changed by auf to *īleGṭắx : elgoṭenxón*, 2ʃo was now "free" to (reprise-)reduce without disturbing the diacritic opposition between singular-object correlative stem shapes (earlier characterized by *QSə̆M*, now by *QeSM*) and plural-object correlative stem shapes (earlier *QSV̊M*, now *QSə̆M*); that is, proportionally (earlier) *QSV̊M : QSə̆M* = (later) *QSə̆M : QeSM*, where the substantively overlapping member *QSə̆M* has changed its role functionally. This might be called the *proportional deployment hypothesis* and presupposes for its viability that the dialect would, so to say, have vested interest in preserving singular-object correlative shaping vs. plural-object correlative shaping as a desirable morphophonological embellishment—and also that the canons of the dialect continued to treat short open-syllabic unstressed *V̊* as subpar and therefore replaceable by *V̆*. Whatever the relative merits of these competing hypotheses, they all must cope with a modest number of exceptions in both directions (as clued by hedged wording above, "normally," "preferentially"); e.g., on the one hand -auf [tešbə̆qán] 'du hast mich verelassen' (~ normal +auf [tīšeBqán]) (Nm 271), and on the other hand +auf [nīβerKennán] 'er wird uns segnen' (~ normal -auf [neβrə̆xennán]) (Nm 279). Hypothesis (a) could be maintained in the face of such exceptional forms by making the stress condition on auf variable rather than categorical. In the case of (b), unexpected forms like [tešbə̆qán] might appeal to auf itself being variable, while the like like of [nīβerKennán] might bespeak some modest reprise activity for auf. For (c), finally, the rationale might be that diacritically-based morphophonological sets tend to leak. It is imaginable that all three hypotheses may be to some extent valid—and synergistically so at that.

[42] (a) Technically, schematics, like radicals, are not full-blown morphological constituents—unlike their immediately including formatives, schemes, and roots, which are. Schematics and radicals are best taken as Semitic-specific (or Afroasiatic-specific) stem-building elements sharing properties of both morphemes (plerematic) and phonemes (cenematic); in which capacity at least the schematics function quite similarly to the *vowel grades* (Vokalstufen) of Indo-European, to which they may be genetically related. (For discussion of some of the attributes of schematics and radicals, see Malone 1985.)

(b) Might *radicals*, like their complement schematics, count as formatives for purposes of transparentation? They are clearly manipulable in the type of lexical root amalgamation known as *blending* (cf. §17.3 n. 3), but it is not clear that blending constitutes transparentation in the sense of this book.

[43] The decision was made to model the derivations in (15Z′) "monostratally" in order to graphically underscore the tension between rules (str, red) and their reprises

(r-str, r-red). If the derivations were to be revamped à la Lexical Phonology, at dia-chronic stages I and II hii would be part of *word building* (wrb) on the first line of the *second stratum*, while / peraš-ū/ would occur on the first, word-building line of the *first stratum*. At III, finally, there would be only one stratum active, the first. [pǎrašón] at stage I would be generated by *early* wrb, and [peršón] at III by *late* wrb.

[44] Historically, in the strong verb, pf 3ms^3fs and impa ms^3fs differed in the presence of a subject suffix in the former but not in the latter; e.g., sim **QaSaM-a̠-hǎ̃́* vs. **QĭSuM-hǎ̃́*. In the wake of sap (§17.22), ex-suffixal *a* was reinterpreted medially as a bridge and ultimately ancipital *-hǎ̃́*, originally manifested as *-hā ~ -ha* but post-sap as *-hā ~ -h*, settled into a preferential distribution *-hā /C__, -h* /bridge__; details on all this in §2. The point is that, if uninterrupted, these developments would lead to TR-vintage pf 3ms^3fs [QæSMǽh] but impa ms^3fs [QǒSóMhā̠], whence the now morphologically dictated suffix-shape preferences might easily be generalized to other gĕzarot where other, earlier changes (like e-cnd, §8.1) might have rendered stem-suffix boundaries less transparent. Review of Dalman's entries at Da 363, 375 provides some support for this view, albeit weakly.

16. Syncretism (syn)

16.1. Description

Syncretism (syn) is the phenomenon whereby the members of an inflectional paradigm are formally reduced in number by merger in the face of functional continuation at the original cardinality—that is, when a system becomes (to some extent) syncretic, a balance of say n functional categories coded by p formal categories changes to n coded by $p - q$.[1] Considered statically, syncretism is symptomized by formal homonymy in the face of function distinctivity. For example, in the first declension of Latin, the form *amicae* 'friend(f)' is by virtue of the homonymous ending *-ae* three ways syncretic between genitive singular, dative singular, and nominative plural—syntactic categories that retain their functional distinctivity in the system at large as evidenced by maintenance of differential signals in other declensions: e.g., third declensional genitive singular *-is* ≠ dative singular *-ī* ≠ nominative plural *-ēs*.

Syncretism, like many linguistic concepts, may be analytically plagued by shades of gray, a state of affairs exacerbated in turn by the fact that the term "syncretism" is not defined identically by all scholars. Some, for instance, take it that genuine syncretism requires that the manifesting homonymy not constitute the formal manifestation of a functionally valid linguistic category for the system in question. Such a restrictive condition might, for example, disqualify one of the most prominent manifestations of syncretism to be proposed in the following pages for Aramaic: *formal gender merger*—fgm—of masculine and feminine, the objection being that the result makes for a linguistically natural *epicene (common)* gender category. However, in the usage of this book, syncretism will be construed quite broadly and liberally—so that processes resulting in m – f homonymy are considered no less syncretic than, say, collapse of the formal distinction between 3fs and 2ms in the impf, an ancient warp of common Semitic.

In tabulating and discussing syncretic patterns, it will be useful to field certain dimensions of classification.

primary / secondary. A syncretic pattern will be considered *primary* to the extent that the formal collapse of the two (or more) categories giving rise to the pattern is direct and unmediated, not a byproduct of some other essentially nonsyncretic process or processes. A syncretic pattern will be construed as *secondary* to the extent that it does in fact result as a consequence of one or more nonsyncretic processes, typically but not necessarily sound changes. (There will be chiaroscuro cases in both directions. Thus, an apparently primary syncretism may anciently have been secondary, the originally engendering changes no longer reconstructible; a possible case in point is syncretism (j) (§16.2 TL below). And it may be unclear, or unknowable, whether a given process has a syncretic or nonosyncretic teleology; see, e.g., discussion of syncretism (d) in n. 13.)

pure / conflative. The syncretic neutralization of two or more category contrasts is *pure* to the extent that the resulting grouping fails to constitute a linguistically (as a rule semantically or syntactically) natural class, and *conflative* to the extent that it does constitute such a natural class. (Shades of gray may abound here too. How do we determine whether a grouping is linguistically natural? Is it possible for a given grouping to be natural in one language but unnatural in another? See, e.g., discussion of possible 2s – 1s syncretism (u) in n. 24.)[2]

phonologic / phonetic. A syncretism will be adjudged *phonologic* to the extent that the synchronic representations of its component categories, or ex-categories, are phonologically/lexically identical; but *phonetic* to the extent that the underlying representations of the categories are (still) distinct, the syncretism itself being synchronically manifested through the agency of one or more linguistic rules, normally phonological rules. Thus TL [-tǔn], 2mp or 2mp^1s, is phonologic because both instances ⇐ /-tūn/ even though historically 1s [-tǔn] < d-lap *-tǔnī; whereas TL [-úah], (3)mp^3ms or (3)mp^3fs, is phonetic because ⇐ s-ptg, s-lap /-ūhū/ (^3ms) vs. /-ūhā/ (^3fs); see §16.2 TL (ε) for discussion. (Lack of precision in applying the phonologic/phonetic distinction notably turns on uncertainty in determining what the phonological/lexical representation should be in given cases.)

categorical / variable. A syncretic neutralization is *categorical* if it always takes place, *variable* if the original distinctions continue to be found in variant forms. (Determination of this dimension is precariously at the mercy of the (usually unstated) sampling techniques employed in the secondary sources so heavily drawn upon by this book.)

Next, in §16.2, five dialects will be profiled for the quantity and quality of their syncretic disposition: TL, M, SR, TR, SM,[3] discussion of each dialect commencing with a tripartite (pf, impf, impa) plotting of its individual syncretisms (designated by lowercase roman letters)[4] and closing with a tabulation of values along the four dimensions just explained. The chapter ends with a brief synopsis and conclusion (§16.3).

16.2. The Individual Dialects

<u>TL.</u> (16Ai)　　　　　　　　TL perfective

sub= obj	=3ms	=3fs	=2ms	=2fs	=1s	=3mp	=3fp	=2mp	=2fp	=1p
=∅	a′	a′	f1	f1				e′16		
=3ms		e2	e2 f2	e2 f2	e2	g′2	g′2	e′23 h2	h2	
=3fs		e3	e3 f3	e3 f3	e3	g′3	g′3	e′23 h3	h3	
=2ms	a1?		f4	f4	a4? g4?	g′4	g′4	h4	h4	
=2fs	a1?		f5	f5	a5? g5?	g′5	g′5	h5	h5	
=1s	b	e6	e6 f6	e6 f6		g′6	g′6	e′16 h6	h6	
=3mp	c d s7	e7	e7 f7 f′	e7 f7	d e7	d e7 g′7 s7	e7 g′7	h7	h7	d
=3fp	c s8		f8 f′	f8		g′8 s8	g′8	h8	h8	
=2m,fp			f9,10	g′9,10		g′9,10	g′9,10	h9,10	h9,10	
=1p	b		f11	f11		g′11	g′11	h11	h11	

　(16Aii)　　　　　　　　　TL imperfective

sub= obj	=3ms	=3fs	=2ms	=2fs	=1s	=3mp	=3fp	=2mp	=2fp	=1p
=∅	i1	j1	j1 k1	k1		m1	m1	n1	n1	i1
=3ms	i2	j2	j2 k2	k2	1?	m2	m2	n2	n2	i2
=3fs	i3	j3	j3 k3	k3	1?	m3	m3	n3	n3	i3
=2m,fs	i4,5	j4,5	j4,5 k4,5	k4,5		e′4,5 m4,5	m4,5	n4,5	n4,5	i4,5
=1s	i6	j6	j6 k6	k6		m6	m6	n6	n6	i6
=3mp	d i7 i′ s7	d′ j7	d′ j7 k7	d′ k7		d m7 s7	d m7	d′ n7	d′ n7	i7 s7
=3fp	i8,i′ s8	j8	j8 k8	k8		m8 s8	m8	n8	n8	i8 s8
=2p,1p	i9–11	j9–11	j9–11 k9–11	k,11		m9–11	m9–11	n9–11	n9–11	i9–11

(16Aiii) TL imperative

sub=	=ms	=fs	=mp	=fp
obj				
=∅	o	o	q1	q1
=3ms			e′23 / q2	q2
=3fs			e′23 / q3	q3
=1s			q6	q6
=3mp	d / p		d / q7	d / q7
=3fp	p		q8	q8
=2mp			q9	
=2fp				q10
=1p			q11	q11

a. int pf 3ms^2ms <nŝqyK> and sim pf 1s^2ms <Pr9TyK> reflecting the 2fs shape [-Ǐx], though both Yem and Ash trad prons maintain the (nonsyncretic) 2ms shape: y[næššǝq̥ā̊x] (Mor 298), a[pǝra9tǝ̥̊x] represented by Margolis with silent (unpointed) <y> (Mar 58, 153*). If genuine, these instances of syn— special cases of formal gender merger (fgm), §16.1—are unusual by virtue of merging in the direction unmarked-to-marked, m > f, though the converse is the rule (as in the otherwise similar **l**, below).[5]

a′. 3fs > 3ms in the intransitive pf, a manifestation of fgm in the unmarked direction f > m. Morag reports that some of his Yemeni informants follow the lead of the spelling in realizing the syncretism in trad pron, while others restore the nonsyncretic 3fs; e.g., <wnPl mnrTˀ> 'vĕnafla hamĕnora' performed either as y[ůnfǽl mǝnār3̥θǻ] (3ms form of the verb 'fell' despite fs gender of the postposed subject 'the lamp') or as y[wǝnǽflǻ mǝnār3̥θǻ] (with 3fs, duly agreeing with the subject). See Mor 124 (with n. (b) for relevant literature).

b. pf <nqtn> 'he seized me', <ˀŝB9n> 'he adjured us' (Mar 58), interpretable as [næqtǽn], [ˀæšbǝ9ǽn], where number neutralization in [-ǽn], 1s or 1p, results as a byproduct of lap (§17.9) < *-ánī (1s) or < *-ánā (1p). This syncretism is usually avoided in TL by the tendential regularity that plural object suffixes occur mediated via bridge -n(n)- while homoparadigmatic singulars do not (§7.4.3). Thus, though [næqtǽn] is unmarked, [ˀæšbǝ9ǽn] would usually appear as c[ˀæšbǝ9innǽn].

c. cau pf 3ms^3fp <ˀPrŝnhw> though performed nonsyncretically as y[ˀæfrǝšinnǝhí̥] (Mor 326); int pf 3ms^3fp y[sæmminnǝhů́] (Mor 326 ith n. 70).

d. pf a[ššǝðǐn(ǯ)hő́] 'he cast them' (Mar 169*), a[davrinhő́] 'he led them' (Mar 101*), a[ˀayθǐnhő́] 'I brought them' (Mar 92*), a[ˀayθǐn(ǯ)hő́] 'they brought them' (lc)—homonymous with 'I brought them', just adduced—

a[kə̆raxĭnə̆ăhő] 'they wrapped them' (Mar 126*), a[šə̆qalinhő] ~ [šaqlinhő] 'we took them' (Mar 175*), a[šannĭnə̆hő] 'we changed them' (Mar 174*).[6] This four-point syncretism may be attributed to the (coincidental? teleologic?) synergy of several independent change nexuses, to be illustrated sketchwise on the basis of the sim strong *QaSaM* though other binyanim and gĕzarot are at times involved in the actual examples (as prominently the defective gizra above). (*) 3ms^3mp, the (relative) null case: *Qə̆SáM* + *ʔin(nə̆)hő* (i-pat, §17.15.1) > [Qə̆SaMinhő]; (*) 1s^3mp: *Qə̆SáMiθ* + *ʔin(nə̆)hő* mtr (§17.12) > *Qə̆SáMī* + *ʔin(nə̆)hő* > [Qə̆SaMinhő]; (*) 3mp^3mp: *Qə̆SaMu* + *ʔin(nə̆)hő* pin (§17.17) > *Qə̆SaMī(n)* + *ʔin(nə̆)hő* > [Qə̆SaMĭnhő];[7] (*) 1p^3mp: *Qə̆SáMn* + *ʔin(nə̆)hő* > [Qə̆SaMinhő] (with dissimilatory loss of 1p *n* ?).[8] As just seen, these four nexuses make for full-blown syncretism, with the possible reservation of vowel length, [. . .ī. . .] / [. . .i. . .], an unresolved issue (§17.4) that also arises in all four nexuses in the defective verb, which otherwise falls out the same as the strong verb with but minor adjustments. Syncretism (d) also makes a strong showing in the imp system, where together with the simi-lar (d') (next) it affects most subject persons; see §17.15.1 TL (17.15B).

d'. Imperfective manifestation of (d) on stems with subject *T*-; see §17.15.1 TL (17.15B).

e. e.g., pf a[zammentéh] 'she invited him (Mar 109*), a[gə̆reðtéh] 'you scratched him' (Mar 100*), a[ʔazmentéh] 'I invited him' (Mar 109*); y[tə̆væ9tinnə̆hí] 'hi hizhira ʔotan', y[fə̆tærtinnűn] 'ʔataַ patarta ʔotan' (Mor 292) ([-innűn] 3fp via (f'), below; for [-innə̆hV̆] ~ [-innV̆n] in 3p object pronouns, §7.4.2)—a multi-point syncretism whereby the suffix complexes 3fs^obj, 2ms^obj, 2fs^obj (cf. (f) below), 1s^obj, and 2pl^3mp (for this, see §17.15.1 TL (17.15B)) all preferentially assume the same shape. (For some variable failures of syn (e) in Ash trad pron, see §15.3.1.3 n. 29b.)

e'. pf a[tə̆fastúah] (~ [tafsī̆θúah] by pin, §17.17) 'you seized him', a[tə̆nē̄θúah] 'you recited it(f)' (Mar 178*f.) ([-úah] ← -ű̄h by ptg, §17.16); y[sækkentűn] 'ʔatem sikkantem' (Mor 147), y[qæbbeltűn] 'ʔatem qibbaltem ʔoti' (Mor 299). Such cases turn on apocope of differential -*V̄* by lap (§17.9): 2mp^3ms *-tű̄hị vs. 2mp^3fs *-tű̄hā (cf. the -lap Yem variant, y[tæfsī̄θúhā], Mor 194); intr 2mp *-tű̄n vs. tr 2mp^1s *-tűnị. Similarly, in the impa: mp^3ms a[tafsúah] 'seize him!', mp^3fs a[tifsúah] 'seize her!' (Mar 179*) (for 1ʃa ~ 1ʃi, sip §176.25) < lap *-ű̄hū, *-ű̄hā. (Morag reports -lap variants for mp^3mp, y[tæfsú̱hū]~ [tifsú̱hū], Mor 298).[9]

f. intr pf, a[šə̆váqt] 'you(ms or fs) left' (Mar 168*), apocopating neutral-ization by sap/lap (§17.22/§17.9) < *šabáqtă̱, *šabáqtị̱; in the tr, such as a[ʔazmentéh], y[fə̆ṭærṭinnún] ((e) above) being systematically ambiguous as to subject gender, 2ms or 2fs. It is possible that the transitive manifestation of (f) originated as part and parcel of (e), but it is equally possible that tr (f) represents a realignment, which in turn may have contributed to the development of (e). More on this below, under S̲R̲.

f′. pf 2ms^3fp y[fə̆ṭærtinnū́n] 'ʾata patarta ʾotan' (Mor 292), masculine-in-form (genderwise unmarked) *-innū́n* serving for feminine-in-form (marked) *-innī́n*.

g. Similar to (a) (cf. also n. 5), int pf 1s^2m̲s̲ <ḥsrTy̲K≫, <ś̲Drty̲K> but in trad pron y[ḥæssertā̲x], y[šæddærtā̲x] (Mor 299).

g′. Hypothesized extension of pf 3mp^obj forms to serve as 3fp^obj.

h. Similar to (g′), hypothesized extension of pf 2mp^obj forms to duty as 2fp^obj.

h′. See M̲.

i. The E phenomenon of neutralizing the 3ms ≠ 1p distinction in the light impf by using as prefix either *n-* or, rarely, *l-*. In TL, this syncretism is statistically resisted by the distributional bias that *n-* usually signals 1p (as in common Semitic) while *l-* almost always marks 3m. See prp for full details (§17.19).

i′. impf 3ms^3mp – 3ms^3fp neutralization, the former (unmarked) serving for the latter (marked); cau y[læšhĭnnə̆h̲ū̲́] (Mor 329 with n. 80).

j. The syncretism of impf 3fs and 2ms, both being signaled by *T-*, is of ancient vintage within Semitic, possibly dating from Afroasiatic.

k. In the intransitive, impf 2ms ≠ 2fs is usually maintained distinct by suffixation of 2fs with *-ī́(n)* (loss of *-n* by TL-favored mtr, §17.12), also in the def verb, note, e.g., y[(dī)θihwə̆yī́n (dī)θiṣbə̆yī́n] '(še)tihyi (še)tirci' (Mor 256) where the group *-iyī̆*, as frequently, fails to undergo e-cnd (§8.1.1); however, in de facto syncretic sim impf y[tistæfī́] 'tifḥĕdi' (Mor 264) *-iyī́* has apparently undergone e-cnd, which then after mtr leads to neutralization with the masculine: [-ī́] < 2ms *-íyi (cf. [tistæxī́] 'tĕcape', lc) either by e-cnd or failing that sap (§17.22) to the tune of dme (§8.1.1), <2fs *-iyī́na by e-cnd^sap^mtr.[10] In the transitive, impf 2ms ≠ 2fs is taken to be systemically neutralized by 2ms^obj formally sitting in for 2fs^obj; cf. (g′), (h).

l. impf 1s^3f̲s̲ <ʾśqly̲h> appearing to reflect the 3ms shape [-ḗh] though at least Yem trad pron maintains the (nonsyncretic) 3fs shape [-ǽh], y[ʾæšqə̆lǽh] (Mor 295). Similar to (a) and (g) except for the direction of the possible syncretism, marked there (f formally replacing m), unmarked here (m replacing f). (Note that in the present case, even if bridge *-ay-* (n. 5) was involved, homonymy with 3ms might well still have resulted: [-ḗh] < *-áyh by coa (§11.1), < *-íh by mid^l-anc (§17.11, §2.3.1).)

m. Another instance of marked > unmarked gender neutralization: sim rmp impf 3fp y[lištə̆rū̲́] 'hen tutarna' (Mor 264).

n. Like (m) for the 2nd person: sim impf 2f̲p̲ y[tištō̲n] ~ t[tištū̲́n] (Mor 256 with n. 45)(for *ō* ~ *ū*, see §15.3.2).

o. Marked > unmarked qua f > m in the cau impa: f̱s y[ʔætlī́] 'hadliki' (Mor 273) (for auslaut -ī as characteristic of the ms def impa, see §8.1.3; the corresponding fs is characteristically -*Ay*, also attested—y[ʔætlǽy], lc).

p. int impa ms^3mp sitting in for ms^3fp: y[šæppə̥şinnə̊hū̱] (Mor 298).

q. In the intr impa, cau fp y[ʔæḥwū̱], though spelled <ʔhwy̱> (and if this should reflect [ʔahwī́] < lap *ʔaḥwíya, syncretism is in turn incurred with suffixless ms, ≤ *ʔaḥwī́). In the tr impa, systemic fp^obj > mp^obj neutralization is assumed; cf. (g', h, k).

r, r'. See M̱.

s. sim pf a[ṭə̊9eminnū́n] 'he tasted them', a[qə̊ṭalī̊nnū́n] 'they killed them' (Mar 118*, 159*); y[kæθvinnə̊hū̱] 'hu katav ʔotam', y[šæqlī̊nnə̊hū̱] 'hem lakḥu ʔotam' (Mor 291, 294)—replacement of 3mp finite -ū̊- (cf. unreplaced y[qæṭlū̊nnə̊hū̱] 'hem hargu ʔotam', Mor 293) by participial -ī̊ via pin (§17.17) leading to structural homonymy of 3mp^3mp with subject-suffixless 3ms^3mp, full homonymy with only the reservation of possible vowel length difference dependent on application or not of css (§17.4); cf. syncretism (d) above.[11] A similar situation is found in the impf.

t–z'. See M̱, S̱Ṟ, ṮṞ, S̱M̱.

A summary classification of TL syncretism along the parameters catalogued in §16.1 is plotted in (16B). With reference to this as well as the individual syncretisms charted in (16A) and discussed immediately above, various conclusions may be drawn about TL's syncretic behavior:

(α) TL is the most syncretically active of the five dialects treated.

(β) The majority of TL syncretisms key on *gender*—fgm (§16.1)—almost always in the marked > unmarked direction, f > m, (a', c, f', g', h, I', k, l, m, n, o, p, q), the two cases in the opposite direction both being questionable (a, g); and one is ambiguous as to direction (f).

(γ) Gender neutralization of the subject is more thorough in transitives than in intransitives. Observe, for instance, on (16Aii, iii) that in (k, m, q) subject neutralization is categorical in the transitive but variable in the intransitive. Note, moreover, that in (k) intransitive neutralization is arguably phonetic (in such as [tištæxī́], [-ī́] ambiguously ⇐ /-i 3√y/ (2ms) or ⇐ /-i 3√y – īn/ (2fs)), while transitive neutralization is phonological (i.e., the underlying representations for 2ms^obj and 2fs^obj are identical in intrinsic phonetic structure); see further (ε) below.[12]

(δ) The majority of TL syncretisms are primary-conflative, all of these cases in turn constituting gender neutralizations.

(ε) Most TL syncretisms are phonological, whether primarily so (e.g., notably, gender neutralizations—fgm—realized by replacing an f affix with a corresponding m affix unmediated by a phonological rule) or secondarily (e.g., (b), where restructuring of the suffix morphemes for object 1s and 1p as com-

monly /n/ is diachronically triggered—hence secondary—by lap, §17.9, of *nī
and *nā, whose differential vowels were irretrievably lost to the synchronic
system). There seem to be no fully phonetic syncretisms in TL, there always
being some phonological componency (classified in (16B) as "mixed"). Thus,
in (e′) though the neutralizations in [-úah] are phonetic, synchronically deriving from either ^ms /-ūhū-/ or ^fs /-ūhā-/ (cf. the Yem variants for the living
alternations), [-Tū́n] derives from /-tūn/ whether intr or tr^1s, the fact that in
the latter value < *=tū́nī being wholly a matter of diachronics (cf. discussion
of (b) just above).

(ζ) Syncretism in TL appears to be especially concentrated in 3p, whether
subject or object.

(16B) TL

type	primary/ secondary	pure/ conflative	phonological/ phonetic	categorical/ variable
a	primary	conflative	phonological	variable
a′	primary	conflative	phonological	variable
b	secondary	conflative	phonological	variable
c	primary	conflative	phonological	variable
d	unclear[13]	pure	probably mixed[13]	variable
d′	unclear[13]	pure	probably mixed[13]	variable
e	primary	pure	phonological	virtually categorical[14]
e′	secondary	mixed	mixed	categorical
f	secondary	conflative	phonological	categorical
f′	primary	conflative	phonological	variable
g	primary	conflative	phonological	variable
g′	primary	conflative	phonological	categorical
h	primary	conflative	phonological	categorical
h′				
i	unclear	pure	phonological	almost categorical[15]
i′	primary	conflative	phonological	variable
j	primary	pure	phonological	categorical
k	mixed	conflative	mixed	categorical in transitive, variable in intransitive
l	primary	conflative	phonological	variable

(16B) TL

type	primary/ secondary	pure/ conflative	phonological/ phonetic	categorical/ variable
m	primary	conflative	phonological	categorical in transitive, variable in intransitive
n	primary	conflative	phonological	categorical
o	primary	conflative	phonological	variable
p	primary	conflative	phonological	variable
q	primary	conflative	phonological	categorical in transitive, variable in intransitive
r				
r′				
s	unclear	mixed	phonological	variable
t				
t′				
u				
v				
w				
x				
x′				
y				
z				
z′				

M (16Ci)　　　　　　M perfective

sub=	=3ms	=3fs	=2ms	=2fs	=1s	=3mp	=3fp	=2mp	=2fp	=1p
obj										
=Ø	*g′1*		*f1*	*f1*		*g′1*	*g′1*	*h1*	*h1*	
=3ms			*f2* *r′*	*f2* *r′*	*r′*	*g′2* *h′*	*g′2*	*h2*	*h2*	
=3fs			*f3*	*f3*		*g′3* *h′*	*g′3*	*h3*	*h3*	
=2ms			*f4*	*f4*		*g′4*	*g′4*	*h4*	*h4*	
=2fs			*f5*	*f5*		*g′5*	*g′5*	*h5*	*h5*	
=1s			*f6*	*f6*		*g′6*	*g′6*	*h6*	*h6*	
=3mp			*f7*	*f7*		*g′7*	*g′7*	*h7*	*h7*	
=3fp			*f8*	*f8*		*g′8*	*g′8*	*h8*	*h8*	
=2mp	r		*f9*	*f9*		*g′9*	*g′9*	*h9*	*h9*	
=2fp	r		*f10*	*f10*		*g′10*	*g′10*	*h10*	*h10*	
=1p			*f11*	*f11*		*g′11*	*g′11*	*h11*	*h11*	

M (16Cii)   M imperfective

sub= obj	=3ms	=3fs	=2ms	=2fs	=1s	=3mp	=3fp	=2mp	=2fp	=1p
=∅	i1	j1 k1	j1 k1	k1				*n1*	*n1*	i1
=3ms,fs	i2,3	j2,3	j2,3 *k2,3*	*k2,3*		*m2,3*	*m2,3*	*n2,3*	*n2,3*	i2,3
=2ms,fs	i4,5	j4,5	j4,5 *k4,5*	*k4,5*		*m4,5*	*m4,5*	*n4,5*	*n4,5*	i4,5
=1s	i6	j6	j6 *k6*	*k6*		*m6*	*m6*	*n6*	*n6*	i6
=3mp	i7 s7	j7	j7 *k7*	*k7*		*m7* s7	*m7*	*n7*	*n7*	i7 s7
=3fp	i8	j8	j8 *k8*	*k8*		*m8*	*m8*	*n8*	*n8*	i8
=2m,fp	i9,10 s9,10	j9,10	j9,10 *k9,10*	*k9,10*		*m9,10* s9,10 t	*m9,10*	*n9,10*	*n9,10*	i9,10
=1p	i11	j11	j11 *k11*	*k11*		*m11*	*m11*	*n11*	*n11*	i11

(16Ciii)   M imperative

sub= obj	=ms	=fs	=mp	=fp
=∅	t′	t′	t′	t′
=3ms			*q2*	*q2*
=3fs			*q3*	*q3*
=1s			*q6*	*q6*
=3mp			*q7*	*q7*
=3fp			*q8*	*q8*
=2mp			*q9*	
=2fp				*q10*
=1p			*q11*	*q11*

M syncretisms not evidenced by TL:

h′. sim pf 3mp^3f̱s [afkǘy̱] (~ nonsyncretic [afkǘ]) (Nm 279, where Nöldeke explicitly recogniozes the neutralization: "Die Endung <uia> {spelling [-ūy]} enthält oft ein Suffix, das weiblich sein sollte")—[-ǘy] < e-cnd *-ǘhī, [-ǘ] < *-ǘhẚ by sap/lap^mtr.

r. cau pf 3ms^2f̱p [asqenxǫ́n] (~ nonsyncretic [asqenxé̱n]) (Nm 280) (√slq; [-sq-] < sim -ssə̌q- < -slə̌q-, §17.21.2).

r′. The 1s subject suffix in such as pf def 1s^3ms (with pp object , §17.15.2) <šritibH> [šə̌rīθīB́í] 'ich wohnte darin' is assumed to be derived by mitosis of restructured /īt/ (V-length by l-anc, §2.3.1) to /ītīt/, which is then subjected to various rules (s-e-cnd, s-spr, s-m-pat) to surface as indicated; for details, see §13, §17.15.2, and the earlier but detailed treatment in Malone 1998a (differing from this book in a few points). However, structurally homonymous 2s forms like <rbi̱ti̱bH> [rə̄βī̱θī̱Bí] 'du wohntest darin' (Malone 1998a: 13) enjoy no such phonologically motivated derivation. The hypothesis to be adopted here is that they represent *copycat formations*, whereby a pattern original to 1s is extended, outside the normal channel of rules, to 2s—an instance of primary syncretism.

t. sim impf 3mp^2fp [nīhešBonxón] (~ nonsyncretic [nehšəβĬnnắxḛn]) (Nm 281) (the variation in miškal shape, -*hešB*- ~ -*hšəβ*-, via ±auf, §4.4; if the bridge vowel is -*ă*-, -*nx*- ~ -*nnăx*- is via ±sim, §17.26; if -*ā*-, via +anc, §2.3.1—the spelling <a> allows either interpretation; 3mp *o* ~ *Ĭ* via pin, §17.17 hedging on css, §17.4—; +pin may likewise trigger syncretism (s) here, [nehšəβĬnnắxḛn] being also construable as 3ms^2fp).

t'. In the nondefective impa, uncompensated across-the-board subject neutralization is the most frequent disposition for the intransitive verb: e.g., sim [QŏSóM] < **QŏSúM, *QŏSúMī, *QŏSúMū, *QŏSúMā* via lap, §17.9.

Some observations about syncretism in M, both per se and in comparison with TL:

(α) M is generally less syncretic than TL, with one exception: M is more syncretic than TL in *intransitive subject neutralization* (save apparently impf 3p, where the m ≠ f distinction is maintained—contrast TL (m1)). Thus, as we have just seen under (t'), subjects are preferentially neutralized across the board in the nondefective impa for M,[16] while in TL they are *either* maintained (by -lap of at least fs *-*ī* and mp *-*ū*) *or* restored (by hii, §7.2(δ), most clearly in fp but possibly also in fs, mp followed by mtr, §17.12, making for homography with -lap—<-y>, <-w>) *or* occasionally continued in mutated form (by i-lap, e.g., sim rmp mp <ʾyṯwr> ~ -lap or +lap^hii^mtr <ʾytrw̱>, Mar 42). The pf is similar (whereas in TL differentiation is the rule, in 3mp primarily by i-lap, in 3fp by hii). In the impf, syncretism is virtually categorical, the lone exception being explicitly 2fs [tīmettéy], explicit via -*ey* (§17.2) (the miškal is hol > gem, §6.2.2.1, on *√mWt 'die').

(β) In the transitive, both dialects show more wide-ranging syn of the subject than of the object— although object syn is notably more robust in TL than in M (TL: a, b, c, e', f', g, g', h, i', l, p; M: h, h', r, t).

(γ) Though the s^obj cells have been left blank in (16Ciii) out of uncertainty as to whether syncretism is the rule for M in the tr impa with singular subject, in the defective verb, there are at least occasional cases of distinct ms^obj ≠ fs^obj when the object is plural: contrast, e.g., ms^3mp [qŏri̱nnón] 'call(ms) them!' vs. fs^3mp [mŏleynnón] 'fill(fs) them!' (Mal 645, 648). This pattern stems from the distinct def fs intransitive auslaut -*ey* (§8.1.3) getting caught in

inlaut upon suffixation of the originally independent3p object pronouns (i-pat,
§17.15.1)—a pattern in M then extended to all plural objects (note for instance
[ašmeynnán] 'make(fs) us hear!' (Mal 663), root originally *√sm9 but restructured to /√šmy/ in the wake of dgt, as frequently; §9.2.3.2).

(δ) No analog of TL (e) has been entered in the pf 3fs^obj, 2s^obj, 1s^obj
cells of (16Ci) because M spelling renders <t> ambiguous between [t] and
[θ], and possible differential vowel length distinctions are not orthographically
indicated either. Despite these uncertainties, however, the general disposition
of the orthography makes it likely that M does in fact sport syncretism (e):
thus, for instance, <-tH> spells any of 3fs^3ms, 2s^3ms, 1s^3ms; <-tak> either
3fs^2ms or 1s^2ms; <-tan> either 3fs^1s or 2s^1s (contrat SR (especially) and
TR below).

(16D)   M

type	primary/ secondary	pure/ conflative	phonological/ phonetic	categorical/ variable
a–e′				
f	primary	conflative	phonological	categorical
f′–g				
g′	mixed	conflative	mixed	categorical in transitive, variable in intransitive
h	primary	conflative	phonological	categorical in transitive, variable in intransitive
h′	primary	conflative	phonological	variable
i	unclear	pure	phonological	categorical
i′				
j	primary	pure	phonological	categorical
k	primary	conflative	phonological	virtually categorical[17]
l				
m	primary	conflative	phonological	categorical
n	primary	conflative	phonological	categorical
o [18]				
p				
q	primary	conflative	phonological	categorical
r	primary	conflative	phonological	variable
r′	primary	pure?	phonological	variable
s	unclear	mixed	phonological	variable
t	primary	conflative	phonological	variable
t′–z′				

SR (16Ei)   SR perfective

sub=	=3ms	=3fs	=2ms	=2fs	=1s	=3mp	=3fp	=2mp	=2fp	=1p
obj										
=∅	g′1		f	f		g′1	g′1			
=3ms										
=3fs	g′3		e3		e3		g′3			
=2ms	g′4					e′6	g′4			
=2fs	g′5?					e′6	g′5?			
=1s	b1	b2	b3	b4		b6	b7	b8	b9	
=3mp										
=3fp										
=2mp	g′9					g′9	g′9			
=2fp	g′10						g′10			
=1p	b1	b2	b3	b4		b6	b7	b8	b9	

SR (16Eii)   SR imperfective

sub=	=3ms	=3fs	=2ms	=2fs	=1s	=3mp	=3fp	=2mp	=2fp	=1p
obj										
=∅	i1	j1	j1							i1
=3ms	i2	j2	j2							i2
=3fs	i3	j3	j3							j3
=2ms	i4	j4	j4							i4
=2fs	i5	j5	j5							i5
=1s	i6	j6	j6							i6
	b1	b2	b3	b4		b6	b7	b8	b9	
=3mp	i7	j7	j7							i7
=3fp	i8	j8	j8							i8
=2mp	i9	j9	j9							i9
=2fp	i10	j10	j10							i10
=1p	i11	j11	j11							i11
	b1	b2	b3	b4		b6	b7	b8	b9	

(16Eiii)   SR imperative

sub=	=ms	=fs	=mp	=fp
obj				
=∅	t′	t′	t′	t′
=3ms				
=3fs				
=1s	b1	b2	b3	b4
=3mp				
=3fp				
=2mp				
=2fp				
=1p	b1	b2	b3	b4

SR is the syncreticaly most conservative dialect of the five chosen for the survey. But although all SR syncretisms are shared by either TL or M, there are some unique points of disposition or distribution:

(α) SR shows no across-the-board manifestations of the m > f gender neutralizations of transitive subject as manifested by TL and M (f, g′, h, k, m, n, q). Note, for instance, pf 2mp^3ms [QšSaMtunnə́y] ≠ 4fp^3ms [QšSaMtɛnnə́y], impf 2ms^3fs [tɛQSə́Mî́h] ≠ 2fs^3fs [tɛQSə́Mînî́h], impa mp^1s [QuSMū̃nə̃́n] ≠ fp^1p [QšSoMē̃nə̃́n].

(β) Relatedly, while in TL (and plausibly in M, (δ)) above syn (e) neutralizes any potential alternations that might justify positing underlying phonological distinctions between intransitive pf 2ms and 2fs, SR having only weakly realized syn (e) (as 2ms^3fs = 1s^3fs) shows such alternations pervasively, with the consequence that the opposition 2ms ≠ 2fs is motivatedly coded phonologically in the intransitive as well. Thus, although in both dialects 2ms [QšSáMt] < d-lap *QaSáMtā and homonymous (syncretic) 2fs [QšSáMt] < d-lap *QaSáMtī, in TL equally homonymous 2ms^1s= 2fs^1s [QšSaMtán] offers no phonetic differences which might justify positing some 2ms ≠ 2fs distinction at the phonological level; whereas in SR 2ms^1s [QšSaMtə̃́n] ≠ 2fs^1s [QšSaMtî́n] *does* provide such phonetic differences—so that one may posit not only 2ms^1s [QšSaMtə̃́n] ⇐ /QaSaMtā-n/ vs. 2fs^1s [QšSaMtî́n] ⇐ /QaSaMtī-n/, but accordingly also intransitive 2ms [QšSáMt] ⇐ s-lap /QaSaMtā/ and 2fs [QšSáMt] ⇐ s-lap /QaSaMtī/. Thus, whereas in TL syn (f) was classified as phonological (16B), in SR it will be classified as phonetic (16F)—leading to the conclusion that syn (f) is more thoroughly grounded in TL than in SR.[19]

(γ) Though SR does field disambiguating renovations in the nondefective intransitive of the whole impa and 3p of the pf in response to lap, it is more like M than like TL in allowing the original, lap-triggered syncretisms (g′, t′) to coexist as variants. Thus syncretic [QšSV̂M] (< lap *QVSV̂Mū, *QVSV̂Mā) alongside hii-rendered (§7.2(δ)) [QšSV̂Mṹn], [QšSV̂Mḗn] (for fp [-ēn], §7 n. 15).

(δ) Unlike TL and M, which regularly disambiguate first person objective *-an* by using (1p) or omitting (1s) bridge *-Inn-*, SR allows its ambiguous reflex (< lap 1s *-anī, 1p *-anā) to remain, making for pervasive conflative syncretism (b) throughout the system, *-an* ambiguously signaling 'me' or 'us'.[20]

(ε) While both M and SR manifest intransitive syncretism in the pf across 3ms, 3mp, and 3fp traceable to neutralization by lap (g′), SR alone shows a noteworthy transitive deployment, with 3ms^obj and 3fp^obj being identical when obj = 3fs, 2ms, perhaps 2fs, 3mp, 2fp: note, e.g., Brockelmann's sketch paradigms (B 144f.), 3fs [QaSMə̃́h], 2ms [QaSMə̃́x], 2fs [QaSMέx] (tagged with a postpositive asterisk asa unattested), 2mp [QšSaMxə̃́n]. Since in the balance of object persons, the 3ms^obj ≠ 3fp^obj opposition is clearly maintained to the tune of 3fp *-a-*, e.g., 3ms^1s [QaSMán] ≠ 3fp^1s [QaSMə́n], it would seem that at least the syncretisms 3ms^3fs = 3fp^3fs and 3ms^2ms = 3fp^2ms follow from the coincidence that, postconsonantally, SR deploys ancipitally long bridge *ā* in both 2ms and 3fs objects, while postvocalically a bridge is dispensed with, and that the vowel making the latter environment postvocalic is 3fp *ā*, homonymous with the bridge; hence, e.g., [QaSMə́x] qua 3ms^2ms < *QaSaM-ā́ka*, with bridge *ā*, while qua 3fp^2ms < bridgeless *QaSaMā́-ka*, with subject suffix *ā*. Against this backdrop, replacement of the remaining 3fp^2 forms by corresponding 3ms^2 shapes would succeed in generalizing the syncretism from 3fp^2ms = 3ms^2ms to 3fp^2 = 3ms^2.[21] However, if this syncretism should be cognate to that discussed in TR under (β) below, the rationale just presented becomes less plausible. Also problematic are instances, albeit rare, of 3mp^2mp participation; e.g., [alaṣxṓn] (B 101, Ns 132). Might a unifying diachronic factor be spotty erstwhile ancipitally *short* medial tokens of 3p subject 3mp *-u-*, 3fp *-a-*, subsequently deleted by reduction (cf. n. 21b)?

(16F)

			SR	
type	*primary/* *secondary*	*pure/* *conflative*	*phonological/* *phonetic*	*categorical/* *variable*
a–a′				
b	secondary	conflative	phonological	categorical
c–e				
f	secondary	conflative	phonetic	categorical
f′–g				
g′	primary in transitive, secondary in intransitive	mixed	phonological in transitive, phonetic in intransitive	categorical in transitive variable in intransitive
h–h′				
i	unclear	pure	phonological	categorical
i′				
j	primary	pure	phonological	categorical
k–t				
t′	primary	conflative	phonetic	variable
u–z′				

TR (16Gi)   TR perfective

sub= obj	=3ms	=3fs	=2ms	=2fs	=1s	=3mp	=3fp	=2mp	=2fp	=1p
=∅			f	f						
=3ms		e2			e2			h2	h2	
=3fs	g′3	e3	e3		e3 u?		g′3	h3	h3	
=2ms		e4			e4	e′45		h4	h4	
=2fs						e′45		h5	h5	
=1s	g′6						g′6	h6	h6	
=3mp				e7	e7 u?			h7	h7	
=3fp								h8	h8	
=2mp								h9	h9	
=2fp								h10	h10	
=1p	g′11	e11	e11		e11		g′11	h11	h11	

SR (16Gii)   TR imperfective

sub= obj	=3ms	=3fs	=2ms	=2fs	=1s	=3mp	=3fp	=2mp	=2fp	=1p
=∅		j1	j1							
=3ms		j2	j2							
=3fs		j3 s3	j3 s3	s3				s3	s3	
=2ms	s4	j4	j4			m4 s4	m4			
=2fs		j5	j5							
=1s	s6	j6	j6			m6 s6	m6			
=3mp		j7	j7 v							
=3fp		j8	j8 v							
=2mp		j9	j9							
=2fp		j10	j10							
=1p		j11	j11							

(16Giii)   TR imperative

sub=	=ms	=fs	=mp	=fp
obj				
=∅			q	q
=3ms				
=3fs				
=1s				
=3mp	s		s	
=3fp				
=2mp				
=2fp				
=1p				

TR is conservative in syncretism, though not as much so as SR. It sports two syncretisms unique unto itself:

u. pf 1s^3fs sb[yŏhævittắh] (Da 366), 2fs^3mp tb[wīhāvittinnū́n] (Da 365). The syncretic nature of this overlap is by no means foregone. If syncretism is indeed afoot, it presumably involves 2fs copycatting 1s *itt*, the latter on its own turf representing generalization of allomorph *IT* from auslaut to inlaut (to the tune of repair-strategic gemination of $T \rightarrow tt$); for details, §15.2.2.2, §17.6, and cf. M syn (r′). Note that (u), if it should be genuinely syncretic, instantiates *partial* syncretism, inasmuch as *-iitắh ≠ -ittinū́n*.

v. Marked > unmarked gender replacement in impf 2ms^3fp sb[tiflāḥinnū́n] (~ nonsyncretic bb&tb[tiflॕ̌ḥinnín]) (Da 372) (for 2ʃ[ā] ~ [ॕ̌], §17.15.1 T̲R̲ (ι)); variant [ā] has also been repair-strategically lengthened).

Some other points:

(α) In the pf, syn (e) is spottier than in TL, though considerably more developed than in SR. For instance while [-tǽh] is syncretic across 3fs^3fs, 2ms^3fs, and 1s^3fs, [-téh] spans 3fs^3ms and 1s^3ms with 3fs^3ms standing apart as [-tॕ̌hī]; and 2fs is syncretic as subject only in [-tinnū́n] as 2fs^3mp = 1s^3mp. Syncretism (f) is manifested in TR in two ways: secondarily via 2ms = 2fs [-t] < sap (§17.22) *-ta, *-ti*; or in primary fashion via the variable use of basically masculine allosffix [-tā] as feminine; e.g., [9ॕ̌vǽðtā] 'du(f) tatest' (Da 261). The disposition of syn (f) as phonological or phonetic depends on how one treats intr [-tā] ~ [-t] synchronically (the diachronic situation is clearly < *-tā (lap does not occur in TR) ~ < sap *-ta/*-ti*). The most plausible resolution is probably mixed: [-tā] ~ [-t] phonologically, the long-vowel option being lexically marked as such; but 2ms vs. 2fs [-t] phonetically, ⇐ /-ta/ and /-ti/, respectively—for reasons similar to but stronger than those posited for SR under (β) above.[22]

(β) In reference to pf syncretism (g′): (*) Dalman states without demonstration that 3mp^obj at times substitutes for 3fp^obj (Da 361). (*) He also states that 3fp ā shortens to æ /__^3fs, ^1s, ^1p, e.g., int [ʔāršɁ9ǽnī] 'sie(fp) stiessen mir zu' (1c) (← ʔarr by mls, §9.3.1); contrast cau [ʔæθqšnā̱hī] 'sie(fp) bereiteten ihn'. The resulting 3fp^obj = 3ms^obj syncretism bears comparison with that discussed for SR above under (ε).

(γ) Like TL and M (d, s), TR shows syncretism keying on pin (§17.17) in interaction with nasal-bearing suffixation (§7.1.2, §7.1.4), and with some nice twists at that. Thus in impf, 2fp^3fs [tšqæyyšmi̊nnǽh] 'ihr(f) stellet sie(fs) auf' (Da 373), reflecting pin-replacement of m̲p̲ u̇ by i̊ with the fp value being given by primary syn f > m, contracts possible syncretism with 2fs̲^3fs (cf. in sketch defective cau impf 2fs^3ms [tæQSi̊nnéh] ← taQSiyinníh via e-cnd, §8.1), and possible syncretism again with 2ms̲^3fs with [-inn-] as bridge (exenergic, §7.1)—in which case 3fs̲^3fs is immediately implicated via syn (j).

(16H)			TR	
type	primary/ secondary	pure/ conflative	phonological/ phonetic	categorical/ variable
a–d'				
e	primary	pure	phonological	categorical
e'	secondary	conflative	phonetic	categorical
f	mixed	conflative	phonetic	variable
f'–g				
g'	primary	pure	phonological	categorical
h	primary	conflative	phonological	categorical
h'–i'				
j	primary	pure	phonological	categorical
k–l				
m	primary	conflative	phonological	variable
n–p				
q	primary	conflative	phonological	variable
r–r'				
s	at least partially primary	mixed	phonological	variable
t–t'				
u	primary	pure?[23]	phonological	variable
v	primary	conflative	phonological	variable
w–z'				

SM (16Ii)   SM perfective

sub=	=3ms	=3fs	=2ms	=2fs	=1s	=3mp	=3fp	=2mp	=2fp	=1p
obj										
=∅		e1?	f1	f1	e1?	g'1	g'1			
=3ms	w	e2? w	f2	f2	e2?	g'2	g'2	h2	h2	
=3fs			f3	f3		g'3	g'3	h3	h3	
=2ms		e4?	f4	f4	e4?	g'4	g'4	h4	h4	
=2fs			f5	f5		g'5	g'5	h5	h5	
=1s			f6	f6		g'6	g'6	h6	h6	
=3mp	d78?	d78? y2?	f7	f7		g'7	g'7	h7	h7	
=3fp	d78?	d78? y2?	f8	f8		g'8 y6?	g'8	h8	h8	
=2mp			f9	f9		g'9	g'9	h9	h9	
=2fp			f10	f10		g'10	g'10	h10	h10	
=1p	d11?		f11 d11?	f11		g'11	g'11	h11	h11	

SM (16Iii)   SM imperfective

sub=	=3ms	=3fs	=2ms	=2fs	=1s	=3mp	=3fp	=2mp	=2fp	=1p
obj										
=∅	z	j1 z	j1			m1	m1 z'		z'	
=3m–fs		j2–3	j2–3 k2–3	k2–3		m2–3	m2–3		n2–3	n2–3
=2m–fs		j4–5	j4–5 k4–5	k4–5		m4–5	m4–5		n4–5	n4–5
=1s		j6	j6 k6	k6		m6	m6		n6	n6
=3mp		j7	j7 k7	k7		m7	m7		n7	n7
=3fp		j8	j8 k8	k8		m8	m8		n8	n8
=2mp		j9	j9 k9	k9		m9	m9		n9	n9
=2fp		j10	j10 k10	k10		m10	m10		n10	n10
=1p		j11	j11 l11	k11		m11	m11		n11	n11

(16Iiii)   SM imperative

sub=	=ms	=fs	=mp	=fp
obj				
=∅		x16	x17	x111
=3ms			*q2*	*q2*
=3fs			*q3*	*q3*
=1s	x16		*q6*	*q6*
=3mp	x17		*q7*	*q7*
=3fp			*q8*	*q8*
=2mp			*q9*	
=2fp				*q10*
=1p	x111		*q11*	*q11*

SM has several syncretisms particular unto itself:

w. Cf. <Br(ʾ)Th> t[bā̆rā́te] 'er hat ihn geschaffen', <ʾnDyTh> t[ændiyyā́te] 'sie brachte ihn' (Macs 233). This syncretism is dually secondary, depending as it does on: (*) the coincidence that *T* is included in both the reflex of 3fs **at* and the original accusative preposition, which various later dialects incorporated as an object marker (tom, §17.30); (*) late lengthening of the vowel in **at* by the smc (§22.1 (22B)) in t[ændiyyā́te] vis-à-vis early lengthening of **2ʃa* as part of e-cnd (§8.1) in t[bā̆rā́te]. (While this nexus does constitute syncretism, its crucial dependence as such on trad pron leaves us chronologically uncertain as to what phase of the genuine SM dialect trad pron represents. Given the guidelines tentatively adopted in this book for the reconstruction of SM pronunciation in the classical period (§24.1), the specific nexus under consideration here falls short of full syncretism; see §24.2 SM *√brʾ, *√nðy.

y. On the surface of it, straightforward cases of 3mp object suffix <-(n)wn> being extended to 3fp function, where they alternate with nonsyncretic <-(n)yn>: <šB(ʾ)Twn> ~ <šwTyn> 'sie legte sie {die Götzen}' (Macs 233) (for <B> ~ <w> representing [β] < **w*, see §21.1 (21D, E)); <ṭrD(w)nwn> t[ṭā̆rā̆dúnnon] ~ <ṭrDwnyn> t[ṭā̆rā̆dúnnen] 'sie vertrieben sie(fp)' (Macs 227). But the catch is that in both cases there is at least some contextual evidence that the masculine forms might be justified in their own right. With regard to <šB(ʾ)Twn> ~ <šwTyn>, the direct object in the Samaritan Targum (Gen 31:34) in agreement with the object suffix is <TrPyh>, a lexeme that is (usually) masculine in both Aramaic and Hebrew ([tǝrɔfîm]); so unless gender neutralization in the marked direction m > f is at play (a possibility, as per TL (a, g)), <-wn> is out-and-out masculine, in agreement with a heteroclitic noun, <TrPyh>. In the case of <ṭrD(w)nwn> ~ <ṭrDwnyn>, the m option may be calquing the Hebrew [wayyɔ̆rɔšǔ̈m], which is formally m-suffixed despite the femininity of the object ('daughters') (Exod 2:17).

x. Syncretism in the impa between certain subject-suffixal allomorphs and certain object-suffixal allomorphs, specifically: <-y> t[-ī] as either fs (< *-ī) or (ms^)1s (< ndr *-nī, §17.13); <-wn> t[-on] as either mp (< *-Ůn imported from impf by hii, §7.2(δ)) or (ms^)3mp (possibly a reflex of suffixed *hům^EL, §7.4); <-n> t[-ɑn] as either fp (< *-ǎn from impf by hii) or (ms^)1p (possibly < sap *-ana, §2.3.4.4 1p). Observe how at least the latter two syns may depend upon trad pron.

z. A few apparent cases of y-prefixed light impfs, hence formally 3ms, being used in lieu of expected 3fs t-prefixed items: <yšry> 'sie soll wohnen' (~ expected <Tšry>) (Macs 208); and from the copular verb √hwy, <yy> (~ expected <T(h)wy> ~ <Tyy>) (Macs 218) (for missing 1√h and 2√w, see §9.2.2, §17.32).

z′. In at least one form, impf 3fp prefixed by *T-*, which in the plural is normal for Aramaic at large solely in 2fp: <wTwhy(ʔ)n> t[wtuwwíyɑn] 'und sie(f) liessen leben' (Macs 221). (Note 1√w (§6.1.2 (6C) with n. 12), which shows that this is not simply a knee-jerk fitting out of the original Hebrew form, <wThyyn> [wattɔ̌hayyḗnɔ] Exod 1:17, with Aramaic phonetics). This syn will be called *feminine t generalization* (ftg).[24]

Some other points:

(α) Though for the most part SM is like SR in abstaining from pf syncretism (e) in favor of differentiation (not, however, necessarily overlapping with SR in specific devices of differentiation), it is possible but by no means foregone that the variational pair *AT ~ IT* occasionally functions indiscriminately as either 3fs or 1s subject suffixes; note, e.g., <ʔTryhyT> 'sie ist zufrieden' (Macs 196), <wʔynqʔTh> ~ <wnqyTh> 'und sie saugte ihn', <ʔGrʔTK> (~ <ʔGrT(y)K>) 'ich habe dich gemietet' (Macs 171, 182, 227). If so, the usage would probably have arisen as a case of pure syncretism from the canonical similarity of 3fs *AT* and 1s *IT* as intransitive suffixes, then generalized for use transitively as well (cf. §15.2.2). However, there are some grounds for balking: (*) *IT* seems not otherwise to occur in SM as an inlaut subject suffix shape; (*) neither 3fs *IT* for 1s *AT* appear to be supported in trad pron, e.g., <šmšʔTK> 'ich habe dich gedient' may be pronounced t[šæmmíštɑk] (though possibly this trad pron is intended to couple exclusively with the variant <šmšTK>) (Macs 227); (*) there are other apparent uses of <ʔ> for expected *I* not readily explainable as representing *A*, e.g., in <yshnʔnh> 'er soll es vertreten' (~ <yshn(n)h>) (Macs 228) where <ʔn> presumably spells the bridge *Inn*, in SM (and likely Aramaic at large), always realized with a palatal vowel (cf., e.g., t[sāmɑktínne] 'ich habe ihn versehen', Macs 227). There may rather be some arcane ml strategy afoot here; the (apparent) vagaries of SM mls, particularly as concerns the guttural letters, are extraordinary (Macs 3ff.).

(β) Variants of pf 3fs^obj and 2ms^obj lacking the expected subject-suffixal *T* and so, other processes being equal, incurring possible syncretism (d) with corresponding 3ms^obj: e.g., (d11) int <ḥyynn> ~ cau <ʾwḥnn> 'hast uns am Leben erhalten' (Macs 220) (1√w by m-cis, §6.1.2), cf. <ʾḥzynn> 'er zeigte uns' (Macs 233); <ʾšBynwn> as a third variant with <šB(ʾ)Twn> ~ <šwTyn> cited under (y) above (and so justifying the 4-cell distribution of (d78) on (16Ii), 3ms^3fp and 3fs^3fp in addition to 3ms^3mp and 3fs^3mp), cf. <w(ʾ)mṭnwn> 'und er kam zu ihnen' (Macs 233). Since auslaut truncation of 2ms *T* is un-attested in Aramaic at large and that of 3fs *T* is rare or nonexistent in SM (mtr, §17.12), it will not be plausible to field the same account of this pattern (d) for SM as was done in the case of TL. It will rather be assumed that the loss of *T* here represents part of a primary syncretic process.

(γ) SM shows at least one possible instance of primary pf 2ms > 2fs syncre-tism (f1) on (16Ii))—note the marked direction of the gender replacement—in <šqrTy By> 'du hast mich betrogen'; see §13 SM (δ) for discussion.

(16J) SM

type	primary/ secondary	pure/ conflative	phonological/ phonetic	categorical/ variable
a–c				
d	primary	mixed	phonological	variable
d′				
e	primary	pure	phonological	variable
e′				
f	primary in transitive, mixed in intranstivie	conflative	unclear	categorical in transitive, variable in intransitive
f′–g				
g′	primary	conflative	phonological	categorical in transitive, variable in intransitive
h–i′				
j	primary	pure	phonological	categorical
k	primary	conflative	phonological	categorical
l				
m	primary	pure	phonological	categorical in transitive, variable in intransitive
n–v				
w	secondary	conflative	phonetic	variable
x	secondary	pure	phonetic	variable
y	primary	conflative	phonological	variable
z	primary	conflative	phonological	variable
z′	primary	conflative	phonological	variable

16.3. Summary and General Overview

A highpoint profile of syncretism in Aramaic is displayed in (16K), where the left column lists (groups of) syncretisms subject to two qualifications: shared but less than pan-Aramaic status (i.e., syns particular to one dialect are omitted, but so is pan-Aramaic (j)); and either primary or mixed status (i.e., syns arising purely as a consequence of other changes, typically phonetic changes, are omitted). Extrapolated syncretisms have been separated out, tagged as such by a postpositive asterisk. **g″** represents a specific subpattern of **g′**; **r′** and **u** are treated as aspects of the same ultimate syncretic pattern. All this will be discussed in the sequel.

The dialects are listed in descending order of syncretic robustness (with fudging on M and SM, which are in this respect roughly equal).

Each dialect is scored at the foot of its column, in terms of of the overall number of syns undergone (unparenthesized) in addition to a shared + particular breakdown (parenthesized).

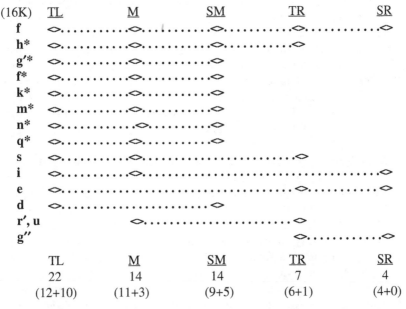

(16K)	TL	M	SM	TR	SR
f					
h*					
g′*					
f*					
k*					
m*					
n*					
q*					
s					
i					
e					
d					
r′, u					
g″					
	TL	M	SM	TR	SR
	22	14	14	7	4
	(12+10)	(11+3)	(9+5)	(6+1)	(4+0)

(α) <u>The fgm complex</u> (f, h, g′, k, m, n, q). Overwhelmingly, formal gender merger is the most active and pervasive ingredient in Aramaic syncretism. It is shared by all five dialects surveyed in (f), whereby in one fashion or the other—more on this directly—the gender distinction is suspended between 2ms and 2fs of the pf. It assumes the strong, "extrapolated" form throughout most subsystems of TL, M, and SM (f*, k*, m*, n*, q*) and makes at least modest inroads in TR as well (h*)—all cases where subject gender in transitive complexes is neutralized in the unmarked direction—that is, f^obj > m^obj. Then, too, it makes a heavy showing among dialect-specific syns (8/10 in TL, 3/4 in M, 2/5 in SM, 1/2 in TR)—especially in object pronouns (there are but two cases of dialect-specific fgm subject syn, TL (o) and SM (z)). Returning to non-extrapolated (f), a predisposition toward pf 2ms-2fs syncretism may have been stimulated here by virtue of intr [-t] < sap (§17.22) *-ta, *-ti, common to all five dialects; and though the opposition continued at half-mast in TR and SM, where alternant *-tā, *-tī were not neutralized by lap (§17.9), variant *primary* fgm managed to make at least some inroads into these dialects despite partial continuation of the opposition (TR 2fs [9ˀvǽðt̠ā], SM 2ms <šqrT̠y>; see TR (β), SM (γ)). Might this perhaps adumbrate something of a long-term teleology in fgm for Aramaic, part of the family's drift, a proclivity to neutralize 2f–2m gender (at least within certain limits) either opportunistically via sound change (secondary syncretism) or, failing that, directly by morpheme replacement (primary syncretism)?

(β) <u>The In(n) complex</u> (s, d). Either or both of two nexuses are involved, one relatively simple (i) and the other requiring appeal to a syncretic "leap"—at least provisionally, given limitations on the corpus culled to date (ii):

(i) Replacement of the vowel in (ex)energic mp $\overset{\circ}{u}n(n)$ by participial $\overset{\circ}{i}$ (pin, §17.17), resulting in $\overset{\circ}{i}n(n)$, induces possible neutralization with either of two other formatives: nonplural exenergic subsequently bridge morpheme in(n), or in(n) functioning as lead-off constituent in a 3p object pronoun; §7.1, §7.4. A largely open issue is the length of the $\overset{\circ}{i}$ involved (due to uncertainty about css, §17.4). Examples of the 3p object variety, TL (s); of the bridge-object variety, TR (γ).

(ii) Perhaps in the wake of a threshold number of preliminary processes, *In(n)* emerges as a sort of generalized subject-bridge portmanteau in the pf, though no dialect appears to have reached a stage where all possible subjects (or /__objects for that matter) are conveyable. An especially clear case is that of TL (d) in the pf, for 3ms^3p – 1s^3p – 3mp^3p – 1p^3p, "preliminary processes" being notably pin (immediately involving 3ms^3p – 3mp^3p, exactly as in (i) above) and mtr (adding 1s^3p), the syncretic "leap" then possibly adding 1p^3p. A more questionable manifestation is that of SM, discussed under (β) of that rubric, a pattern rendered questionable by the apparent absence of preliminary processes, SM giving no evidence of either pin or (at least in this area of the morphophonology) mtr. And this uncertainty is magnified by the database accident that all instances culled up to this point are purely orthographic, unaccompanied by possibly revealing trad pron. Nonetheless, the surface similarity of the SM cases to those of TL is striking—in which vein note that most of the relevant TL forms (d) and all of those of SM are defective verbs.

(γ) The 3ms – 1p complex (i). E-characteristic prefix replacement (prp, §17.19) triggering system-wide syncretism in impf between 3ms and 1p—though with a statistical bias in TL, which dialect also sporadically fields a structural disambiguation (n. 15).

(δ) The T^object complex (e). A syncretic nexus in the pf whereby *T*-containing singular subjects appear in homogeneous form—actually or apparently reflecting vowelless *t* irrespective of φ-role—and are followed by sequel strings homogeneous per φ-role of the object; that is to say, in the nondefective verb a *t*(-bridge)-object string is differential in shape only per (-bridge)-object though functionally any of 3fs^obj, 2ms^obj, 2fs^obj, or 1s^obj may be conveyed. Thoroughness of this syncretism per dialect is correlative to general robustness of syncretism at large, TL ≫ TR ≫ SR—a correlativity which bids fair to be maintained, at least in monotonic form, if M should be determined to participate (M (δ)): TL ≥≥ M ≫ TR ≫ SR. Diachronically, it is unclear whether (e) represents retention or innovation within Aramaic (n. 19b)—though the correlation just considered, TL (≥≥ M) ≫ TR ≫ SR, may make trhe innovation hypothesis appear a bit more likely. (Note also that the *T*^object complex even subsumes a *plural* subject in the case of TL 2p^3mp; see §16.2 TL (e) above, as well as §17.15.1 TL (17.15B).)

(ε) The 2s – 1s complex (r′, u). What these processes have in common is "copycat" extension into 2s of 1s morphology in the pf—the 1s itself having been markedly extended, by mit in M (*C* → *CV*) and by trp in TR (*C* → *VC*).

(ζ) The 3ms – 3fp complex (g″). In the pf transitive of TR and SR, certain 3ms^obj and 3fp^obj slots are neutralized: when obj = 1 in TR = 2 (though uncertainly for 2fs) in SR, and = 3fs in both dialects (albeit in somewhat different form; ancipitally short [-æh] in TR, long [-ōh] in SR). Though a trp-based account of (g″) might be mounted for SR (§16.2 SR (ε)), such a tack won't work for TR (§16.2 TR (β)). It is possible that, while the apparent trp-effect in SR may at least in part reflect some dialect-internal spread of the phenomenon, the basic syncretism itself stemmed from an ancient ancipiality of the pf 3fp suffix, *ā* or *a*, which would render the latter variant homonymous with 3ms *a* and so make for the syncretic effect; but that *ā* subsequently gained ascendancy in Aramaic at large, traces of the old *ā* ~ *a* lingering only in TR and SR. (SR might even show traces of an ancient mp *ū* ~ *u*; §16.2 SR (ε).)[25]

Notes to §16

[1] "*n* . . . coded by *p*"; because even in a totally nonsyncretic system *n* and *p* are rarely equal, notably due to markedness factors where one or more categories are signaled by the absence of formal marks—*privative* organization. A system where *n* = *p* is *equipollent*. For more on markedness, see §15.2.1.1 n. 3 and, in specific association with syncretism, passim below.

[2] A nontrivial question for linguistic theory is why such an odd beast as pure syncretism should exist in the first place. It might be suspected to arise at the behest of some sort of *economy principle*, whereby the number of formal signals in an inflectional system shrinks downward even in the face of functional malaise. It might moreover be suspected that a combination of primary and secondary syncretism may first prepare the ground for the emergence of pure syncretism by reducing the number of formal categories to some critical number—critical in the sense that the teleology of "save-a-signal" economy emerges as a force on its own account, with pure syncretism collapsing signals with little regard any more to functional rhyme or reason.

[3] Earlier dialects almost certainly show less syncretism, though determination of the matter is hard put—save in the case of B—because of the unrevealing orthography. All Aramaic dialects, of course, evidence the pan-Semitic neutralization of 3fs and 2ms impf (syncretism (j)). In addition, at least P, N, CP, and G manifest some later syncretic inroads; see §16.3.

[4] These charts are quite informal, and one must accordingly be cautious about drawing overly firm conclusions on the basis of cursory inspection. For one thing, more-or-less comparable syncretisms may be disparately represented; e.g., in (16Ai), the pair

(a) and (g) differ only in subject person, as likewise do (c) and (f′). Then there are "extrapolated" syncretisms, set in italic; e.g., *(g′)* and *(h)* in (16Ai), witnessed not by positive attestation but rather by silence of the secondary sources in the matter of alternative encoding in such a way as to lead the examiner strongly to suspect that the dialect in question does in fact consistently show the pertinent syncretism. Such plottings may be contrasted with similar but less-filled-out plottings of various other syncretisms, whose spotty distribution may often signal no more than spotty representation in an adventitious sample; e.g., again in (16Ai), (e). Some syncretisms are plotted to the tune of numerical tags indicating commonality across various φ-slots; e.g., in (16Ai), (e2) indicates that essentially the same syncretism is found for 3fs^3ms, 2ms^3ms, 2fs^3ms, and 1s^3ms as is found in (e3) for 3fs^3fs, 2ms^3fs, 2fs^3fs, and 1s^3fs. Throughout, syncretisms identifiable, or at least comparable, across dialects will be signaled by use of the same letter; e.g., (f) in the pf of all five dialects, whether in tense plottings (16Ai, 16Ci, 16Ei, 16Gi, 16Ii), value tabulations (16B, 16D, 16F, 16H, 16J), or in-text discussion. (Note in this latter vein that initial discussion of a given syncretism under one dialect often tacitly carries over to dialects treated in the sequel; thus, coverage of (f) as expressed under TL is germane enough to hold for M, SR, TR, and SM as well.)

[5] Alternatively, it might be possible <y> originally represented the bridge **ay*, otherwise clearly attested only in SR (§2.3.2.4 n 14b)—but if so, what has led to its apparent replacement in the traditions by the usual 2ms bridge [Ā]?

[6] (a) Accurate interpretation of Ash trad pron of sub^3ms with respect to *V* length and presence/absence of [ə] is a slippery matter indeed, and the following criteria have been gingerly adopted: (*) [i̥] when the input *V* is taken as long (the short [i] eventuality arising from the possible action of css (§17.4) /__nn prior to (p-)smp (§17.26 with n. 136)); (*) [ə] when Margolis marks the preceding <i(y)> with the diacritic meteg (§17.15.1 n 65); (*) [ə] when Margolis fails to mark the preceding <i(y)> with meteg and yet that <i(y)> is interpretable as [i̥]; (*) [i] and no [ə] when the input *V* is taken as short.

(b) In the Yemeni tradition, cf. [šəqælinnəhū̃] ~ [šæqlinnəhū̃] 'lakaḥti ʔotam' (Mor 293 with n. 13), [šæqli̥nnəhū̃] 'lakḥu ʔotam' and 'lakaḥnu ʔotam' (Mor 294); also [ḥəzi̥nnəhū̃] 'raʔa ʔotam' (Mor 322), [ʔæ9əli̥nnəhū̃] 'hixnisu ʔotam' (Mor 321) ([. . .9ə. . .] ← ...99ə. . . by p-smp, §17.26 with n. 136).

[7] Note the absence of i-lap, which with pin would lead either to @[QəSūMinhó] or to @[QəSīMinhó] depending on whether i-lap^pin or pin^i-lap. Are pin and i-lap perhaps mutually exclusive?

[8] See n. 13 below.

[9] The variants are spelled 3√<s> ~ 3√<ś>, best interpreted as residual historical spelling: <ś> [s] < <ś> *[ś]; see snm, §17.27.

[10] Why has 1ʃ[æ] escaped reduction to ə?

[11] Observe the difference in stem shape between a[QəSaM-] and y[QæSM-], perhaps reflecting more thorough morphophonological integration of 3p object suffixation in the Yemeni tradition than in the Ashkenazic; cf. §7.4, §15.2.1.2, §17.15.1. On the other hand, the matter may actually not be so simple, Yem trad pron systematically showing [QəSeM-] with *2ʃi cases at least with 3ms^3mp; e.g., y[šəʔelinnəhū̃] 'hu šaʔal ʔotam', Mor 291. This canonical preference may just smack of reading pronunciation, by providing a rationale (or rationalization) for ml <y> in such as <ŝʔylynhw>; cf. the similar suspicion for TR, §17.15.1 TR (ζ). On the other hand, the issue cannot be smugly closed on that note either, Yem trad pron liberally allowing discrepancies from the received spelling, as noted at various spots in this work (e.g., §17.25 TL) and amply via footnotes throughout Morag's book; note most clearly here y[qætļu̥nnəhū̃], just cited in the text, being spelled <qtlynhw>, Mor 293 n. 15—see also discussion of syns (a, q, l, q).

[12] (a) "identical intrinsic phonetic structure: i.e., the possibility is left open that, relative to one's specific theory of phonology, the gender distinction is phonologically coded, perhaps by diacritic features.

(b) It is possible that some universal regularity is afoot in the tr-intr difference treated under this point (γ)—say, a tendency toward a sort of *markedness economy*—keeping marked structures within certain limits—by more stringent replacement of marked by unmarked (f by m) within overarching marked categories (tr) than within corresponding unmarked categories.

[13] Since various of the effects involved in these syncretisms are specific to immediate pronoun attachment, i-pat (§17.15.1), and i-pat totally invests these syncretisms, it is impossible to fully assess the primary/secondary and phonological/phonetic parameters. For instance, in the case of *QšSáMn-ʔin(nǎ)hő* → [QšSaMinhő], since the conditions for the possible dissimilatory elision of the first (1p) *n* – *n*-haplology, §17.15.1 (δ)—appear not to be attested elsewhere than in this frame (a frame also including the f counterpart /__ʔinhé), we cannot rightly say whether the loss of 1p *n* is secondary—attributable, say, to a dissimilatory matrix of coincidentally extremely narrow scope—or primary—i.e., an operation specifically geared to creating the syncretism itself. Whatever the overall disposition of (d, d′) might turn out to be, however, there do seem to be at least some aspects characterizable as secondary and phonetic: e.g., *QšSaMiθ-ʔin(nǎ)hő* → [QšSaMĭn(š)hő], involving as it does s-mtr (§17.12) (s-mtr being motivated by alternations such as [QšSáMiθ] ~ [QěSáMīθ]).

[14] "virtually" in consideration of the few Ash 3fs forms in [Cθ] cited in §15 n. 29b.

[15] Except for Standard Literary Babylonian; see §17.19 n. 101. There is also sporadic restoration of the 3ms ≠ 1p by tacking on –(n)an to clich the 1p value; §15 n 21.

[16] (a) For the defective verb, see §8.1.3.

(b) The M penchant for intransitive subject syn perhaps even occasionally takes the form of *un*doing a *restored* contrast. Thus sim pf 3fp [něfaqyő̃n] 'sie kamen aus' (Nm 223), where the syncretic form c[něfáq] (< lap *napáqā*) may have had its contrastive power renewed, as occasionally in the pf and impa, by -y V̊n (§7.2 (δ) n. 18)—but by the *masculine* form -yōn, despite the feminine function. (The hedges—"perhaps", "may"—on "*un*doing a *restored* contrast," inasmuch as such restoration-cum-undoing presupposes a chain along the lines of *napáqā* . . . (c) > *něfáq* (d) > *něfaqyán* (e) > *něfaqyő̃n*, where (d) restores and (e) undoes, this being a chain that is functionally an accordion in that *něfáq* and *něfaqyő̃n* are syncretic (secondarily and primarily, respectively) while intervening *něfaqyán* in nonsyncretic. If rather a shorter chain should be assumed, such as *napáqā* . . . (c) > *něfáq* (e) > *něfaqyő̃n*, might we not conclude that renewal by -yōn at least sometimes serves some function other than either restoration of lost contrasts or syncretism?)

[17] See (α) in the text ([tīmettéy]).

[18] See (γ) in the text.

[19] (a) This synchronic solution is not uniquely determined for SR (few such solutions ever are). For instance, one might take it that the differential [š] ≠ [ī] are functionally synchronically as *bridge vowels* (§2.3.2) that accordingly would not appear in the intransitive, so that we would be left with transitive /QaSaMt-ā-n/ ≠ /QaSaMt-ī-n/, over against intransitive syncretic /QaSaMt/, just like TL. Adoption of such an analysis would undermine the presumed

status difference proposed in the text for SR vs. TL vis-à-vis intransitive pf 2s under syn (f), rendering both classifiable as phonological.

(b) Diachronically, it might appear that the 2s^obj shapes of SR represent the original pA structures more faithfully than the corresponding TL shapes, these latter having been leveled by syn (e). However, the opposite development seems equally plausible; so that, e.g., original (after sap and bridge formation) *QaSáMtā, *QaSáMtī; *QaSaMtánī is, via less-marked-stem-based transparentation (§15.2.2), replaced by QaSáMtā, QaSáMtī; QaSaMtắnī, QaSaMtī́nī, the less-marked intransitive stems (QaSaMtā, QaSaMtī) substituting for the more marked transitive shape (QaSaMt).

[20] Orthographically, however, the forms are disambiguated by historical spelling of 1s with silent <-y>: <-any> 'me', <-an> 'us'.

[21] (a) Since this syncretism involves replacement of a marked shape (3fp) by an unmarked (3ms), it could pass muster as transparentation (§15) if it were not for the fact that an *anti*transparent effect is achieved, setting up ambiguity (between 3fp^obj and 3ms^obj) rather than disambiguity. But are such effects always devoid of overlap? An explicit, articulated theory of transparentation and syncretism is a desideratum.

(b) Whatever its precise diachronic rationale, what is the synchronic disposition of this syncretism? Taking off from the observation that nondefective intransitive pf 3ms and 3fp are systematically homonymous phonetically, e.g., both sim [QǒSáM], it might be possible to posit (*) restructuring of 3fp as /QV̊SaM/ (suffixless, or with an empty suffix (zero morpheme)) and (*) repartition of the reflexes of original 3fp suffix *-ā- as ancipitally long bridges in alternation with reflexes of ancipitally short *-a- —so that, e.g., 3fp^2ms [QaSMə́x] ⇐ /QV̊SaM-ặk/, 3fp^2mp [QǒSaMxə́n] ⇐ /QV̊SaM-ặkōn/, bridges underscored. (See also next in the text, concerning 3mp^2mp.)

[22] The evidence from inlaut vowel distribution in the transitive is actually sharper in the case of TR: (a) 2ms^obj shows inlaut [-ā-] ~ [-æ-] ([-tāhī], [-tānūn]; [-tæh], [-tænī], [-tænā]) and auslaut [-ā] ~ [-∅] ([-tā] ~ [-t]); (b) 2fs^obj shows inlaut [-i-] ([-tini], [-tinnūn]) and auslaut [-∅] ([-t]); (c) if 2ms inlaut and auslaut [ā] are cross-identified, as Occam's Razor suggests they should be, the option of considering the inlaut vowels to represent bridges without auslaut counterparts, an option considered for TL (n. 19a), is precluded; (d) calibrating inlaut and auslaut distribution with an eye to pattern congruity, we arrive at 2ms /tā/ ~ /ta/ (free choice in intransitives, lexical choice in transitives—e.g., / tā/ /__hī, /ta/ /__nī), 2fs /ti/, and a rule s-sap dictating $\mathring{V} \Rightarrow \emptyset$ /__#.

[23] However the possibility exists that 1st person – 2nd person merger makes for a *natural* category, sometimes called "interlocutive." Evidence for an interlocutive category having been organic in proto-Semitic, or pre-Semitic, may be witnessed in the independent personal pronouns where *ʔan- is com-

mon to 1 and 2 excluding 3—a pattern still describable in B (modulo only *a >
[ă] by red): 1s [ʔắnɔ̌], 2ms [ʔánt], 1p [ʔắnáhnɔ̌], 2mp [ʔantűn].

[24] "normal in Aramaic *at large*": however, at least P (perhaps categorically) and G ("zuweilen" in √hwy) show 3fp *t-* ; note P <TBrKn> 'they(f)
will bless', <Thwyn> 'they(f) will be' (HC 350, 359), and G <Thwwn> (Da
352). M shows at least one similar form, int rmp [t̲estakrắ] (~ usual [n̲estakrắ])
'sie(f) werden geschlossen' (Nm 228)—which, however, is not syncretic since
in M the value with which it would be ambiguous, 2fp, is itself always neutralized > 2mp by syn (n).

[25] In addition to the five dialects chosen for special attention in this chapter, inroads of syncretism (pan-Semitic (j) apart) are manifested in at least
P, N, CP, and G. All of these but N witness some secondary merger, if only
sporadically, induced by lap (§17.9); cf. syns (f, g′, t′, q). Then P and G show
impf 3fp – 2fp syncretism, as just discussed in the preceding note ([24]). Both
N (questionably) and G (certainly) occasionally exhibit primary fgm—N
<9BD̲w> 'elles firent' (Cg 79), G <PTh̲w̲n> 'öffnet(f)!' (Da 275); syns (g′, q).
And CP manifests secondary impf 3ms – 1s syncretism, redolent of the E 3ms
– 1p complex ((γ) above); §15 n. 23.

17. Other Processes

17.1. Å-Replacement (arp)

M, CP, and P show palatal vocalism in their 1p subject suffixes. At least in M and CP, this appears in alternation with the low vocalism normal for Aramaic at large, as well as with vowelless -*n* < lap *-nā*—alternation being at least to some degree chronologically conditioned in CP ("<-n> [-n], <-n(y)h> [-nē], <-nn> [-nan], später [-nen]"—Sg 62) but structurally conditioned in M ([-na] or [-nā] /__pp, if the former then ← -*nan* with adconsonantal assimilation of auslaut -*n* to pp-anlaut *b*, *l*, §17.15.2; [-n] categorically /__(bridge) obj or variably / ī__#—that is, in the defective verb with 2√i; [-nīn] /__# elsewhere—that is, as the unmarked intransitive shape of the suffix; cf. Macm 262, 269, 335). CP but not also M shows the phenomenon in its 1p object suffix: "<-(ʔ)n> [-an], sp{ät} [-en]; <-nn> [-nan], sp{ät} <-nyn>; <-nh>, sp{ät} auch <-nyh> [-nē]; nach Vokal [-n], [-nan] {und so weiter}, [-nē]"—Sg 33. (For <h> as palatal ml in CP, Sg 9.) For P, note <qrynn̲y̲> 'we called' (HC 407).

Schulthess interprets the palatal vocalism in CP as [ē] in auslaut, [e] in inlaut; M, where it appears only in inlaut, has [ī] to judge by both trad pron (Mal 282) and the Modern language (Macm 262). In default of knowing how Schulthess determined his phonetic values, CP will be cautiously interpreted as [-nĪ] ~ [-nI̊n].

Nomenclaturally, the phenomenon under discussion will be tagged as *Å-replacement* (arp), inasmuch as the Aramaic-at-large *ā* (of *-nā*) or *a* (of nasal-added -*nan*, §7.2 (δ) n. 11) de facto appear to be replaced by *I*. And while, literally, such replacement may lie behind the pattern, there are other possibilities as well. Noting that pA sports both *-nā* and (rarely) *-nū* (§2.3.4.3), it may be that the complementary possibility *-nī* was available, too, captured only in P, CP, and M. Another hypothesis turns on the fact that at least CP and M show the palatal effects likewise in their 1p independent pronouns: CP "<ʔnn>, sp{ät} <ʔnyn>, {gospel codex} A <ʔnyn>. . . ; <ʔnh>, sp{ät} auch <ʔnyh>" (Sg 32); M <anin> ~ <anen> t[ánīn], m[ánī(n)] ~ [ēnī] (Macm 154). Schulthess suggests that the (CP) palatal 1p pronouns may be (the result of) ablaut formations vis-à-vis 1s (Sg 32). Plausible idea; 1s *ʔanā́ vs. 1p *ʔanī́ may well have existed as an option in pA, then spread to the homologous suffixes, at least locally, traces surviving in the three dialects considered here.[1]

17.2. *ay* Development (ayd)

According to Margolis's Ashkenazic tradition, TL fields a novel suffix allomorph for 3fs and 1s pf, [-ay], an innovation to be called *ay development* (ayd)—a phenomenon not attested in the Yemeni tradition as documented by Morag. Margolis presents two examples for each φ-slot: 3fs sim rmp <ˀyKn9ˀy̱> a[ˀikkan9áy̱] 'she humbled herself', int rmp <ˀynG9ˀy̱> a[ˀinnagá9ay̱] 'she became leprous'; 1s sim <ˀzlˀy̱> a[ˀazláy̱] 'I went', sim <ḥ ŝ ˀy̱> a[ḥaššáy̱] 'I cared' (Mar 41, 124*; 45, 134*; 37 n. **XX**, 85*; 49, 116*).

The hypothesis to be adopted in this book is that ayd represents an extension (and reinterpretation) from the defective verb, in a way to be explained below. The relevant defective string is the 2ʃ -3√y – suffix auslaut string -*Ay*, in both 3fs and 1s ← mtr (§17.12) -*a 3√y* – *T*, with homonymous suffix *T* (§2.3.4.3); cf. 3fs <sgˀy̱> a[sǝ̆γáy̱] y[sǝ̆γǽy̱] 'hifliga' (Mar 52, 140*; Mor 252); 1s <B9ˀy̱> ~ <B9yy̱> a[bǝ̆9áy̱] y[bǝ̆9ǽy̱] 'hayiti carix' (Mar 52, 95*; Mor 253).[2] It will be assumed that the transmutation of defective portmanteau -*Ay* to strong suffix -*Ay* was via metanalysis to the tune of the theory of *quasi-inert strings* developed in §15.3.2. In particular, the fact that defective verbs have at least the option for their major plerematic divide to fall after 2√, rather than after 3√ as in nondefectives, allowed -*Ay* of (say) def 3fs/1s *QǝSÁy* to be metanalyzed as suffixal. (The metanalysis would be similar to that of 3mp -*ō*, cf. (§15 (15N), except that the latter then underwent transparentive reshaping to -*ū* while -*Ay* stayed put.)

(ayd might also explain the hapax impf 2fs ending in M <timitai̱> 'you(fs) will die' (Macm 257, 316, 431), [tímettéy̱] (on √mtt < √mWt by hollow-geminate merger, §6; for the stem shape excluding the suffix, §6.2.2.1). However, the very fact that this is the only instance of an impf verb form explicitly suffixed for 2fs in the dialect, which otherwise evinces pervasive 2fs > 2ms neutralization by fgm (§16.1), weakens the evidence for ayd as origin of this token of <-ai> [-ey]. This is because model forms like [teQSéy̱] < mtr *tIQSáyn* < e-cnd *tIQSay+ín* are, due to fgm, unattested, forcing us to assume that the new suffix was created by q.i.s.-guided metanalysis—as above—before the model was lost by fgm. The consequence of this is that the evidence needed to make the case is largely or totally speculative. And this shaky position is rendered all the more precarious by the fact that M, unlike G (§17.12.2 **G** (β)), gives no independent evidence for the crucial step [-éy̱] < -*áyn*. If it did, we should expect, e.g., to find sim mp participles ending in <-ai>; whereas what we actually find is -mtr <-in> (suggesting [-ḗn] or [-ín] < (hei <) coa -*ayn*), or occasionally +mtr <-ia> (suggesting [-ḗ] or [-í]; for <-ia> as the usual spelling of auslaut [-Í], §21.8 (21M), §11.2 n. 17)—cf. <atiṉ>, <baniṉ>, <hawiṉ> ~ <hawia̱> (DM 42, 66, 133).)

17.3. *Bring* Blending (brb)

Variable fielding of a root √yty in the causative in the broad sense of 'bring', called *bring blending* (brb) on the assumption (following Schulthess Sg 66) that it involves at least partial melding of √yty (< car √ʾty, §9.2.1.2) and √mty, sim sense of both 'come', cau sense 'bring', though following a tacit suggestion of Jastrow (1903: 506) √nty might also be involved (sim sense 'bend', cau sense 'incline (toward)'). In any event, cau √yty is attested in CP and G (llcc; Jastrow's examples are from G sources: <ʾyyty ly KwlB?> 'hand me a pair of tongs', <yyty lyh mh. . .> 'shall bring for himself something. . .').

Root blending of this sort might possibly instantiate partial transparentation on the base (qua replacing part) of a *radical*, in which case brb would complement the example of *schematic* trp adduced in §15.5.2—though it is not clear whether blending makes for an intuitively more transparent relation between form and function.

Informally, √A X √B . . . X √C → √D; here √yty X √mty X √nty → √yty.[3]

7.4. Closed-Syllabic Shortening (css)

Closed-syllabic shortening (css) is taken to be a persistent or reprise process, of long standing within Aramaic, whereby a long vowel is shortened in a closed syllable—presumably to alleviate the tension induced by the conflicting articulatory space interests of the vowel's expanded length requirements and the structural cramping attendant upon syllable closure. Closed-syllabic shortening is frequently differentially sensitive to type of syllable closure, pressure for css being proportional to the number of consonants in the coda—so that, to cite a commonplace situation, a dialect may shorten $\bar{V}$ in $\bar{V}CC\#$ (a classic doubly closed syllable configuration) but leave it be in $\bar{V}C\#$. Moreover, there seem at times to be factors bearing on css above and beyond the strictly syllabic. To mention but two: (α) *CC* appears sometimes to have special css-triggering power, even when only the first *C* is codal; that is, $\bar{V}$ in $\bar{V}CCV$ may sometimes shorten just like $\bar{V}$ in $\bar{V}CC\#$, even when (as almost always) syllabification is $\bar{V}C \mid CV$ and *V* in $\bar{V}C\#$ fails to shorten.[4] (β) Geminate clusters appear at times to induce css more strongly than heterophonous clusters. Since geminates rarely occur in word-final position, this property normally intersects with (α): thus, $\bar{V}C'C'V$ may sometimes shorten to $\overset{\circ}{V}C'C'V$ while $\bar{V}C'C''V$ (*C'C''* = heterophonous) fails to. (In the jargon of traditional Semitics, the syllable in *VC'C'* is said to be "verschärft.")

Returning specifically to Aramaic, the effects of css are at times quite palpable but at other times quite elusive. As an example of the first type, note B palatal passive pf 2ms [tĕqéltɔ] (BL 104f) < *θaqīltā (*t* < *θ* by occ, §17.14), where css is presupposed by midding (§17.11), which applies only to short vowels. css also lies behind the $\overset{\circ}{V}$ ~ $\bar{V}$ alternation in the pA hollow causative, which may have contributed to the rapprochement, and ultimately partial merger, of the hollow and geminate gĕzarot (§6.1.1.1). Even as css in B [tɔ̆qélt5] is cued by <e>, <α> ~ <æ> signals variation of css in Sabbionetan TR fp energic [-ānn-] ~ [-ænn-] (for examples, see Da 373). Often, however, orthography leaves us in the lurch as to whether css has applied or not; thus, there is an alternant to B [tɔ̆qélt5] spelled with <i> (lc), which might be interpreted as either-css [tɔ̆qíltɔ̄] or as +css [tɔ̆qíltɔ̄] (B conditions for mid permitting as they do the [éCC] ~ [íCC] variation). Presence ~ absence of ml <W> (= <w,y>) may sometimes be indicative of -css ~ +css respectively; e.g., B <y:šam̃:šuwn̈eh> ~ <y:šam̃:šun̈eh>, BL 124, perhaps qua [yɔ̆šammɔ̆šūnnéh] ~ [yɔ̆šammɔ̆šunnéh], respectively. However, ideally such judgments should be based on antecedent comprehensive analysis of <W> distribution in the relevant dialects.

In any event, uncertainty as to css occurrence will be indicated as V̊.[4']

17.5. Causative *y/w*-Spread (cys)

In the wake of wpl (§17.34), changing *1√w to 1√y in all binyanim but the causative, the following gross distribution obtained:

(17.5A)

	causative	**other binyanim**
*1√w	w	y
*1√y	y	y

The imbalance in (17.5A) might be ironed out in any of four a priori plausible ways, three of which converge on the same result:

(α) cau 1√w > 1√y like noncau 1√y; or

(β) noncau (* 1/w >) 1√y > 1√w like cau 1√w (an accordion process); or

(γ) cau 1√w > 1√y like cau 1√y ≤ *1√y (abutting upon the same de facto pattern as (α)); or

(δ) cau (*1√y ≥) 1√y > 1√w like cau 1√w.

Of the three resulting configurations, two are attested:[5]

(17.5B) (α, γ)

	cau	**noncau**
*1√w	(y)	y
*1√y	y	y

TR   *√wmʔ ≥ √wmy ~ √ymy; *√wdy ≥ √wdy ~ √ydy

G   *√wtr ≥ √wtr ~ √ytr

CP   *√wθb ≥ √wtb ~ √ytb (rmp ~ plain respectively)

(δ)   **cau**   **noncau**

	cau	noncau
*1√w	w	y
*1√y	(w)	y

(I *√ynq > √wnq (in the infinitive))

TR *√ynq > √wnq

G *√ynq ≥ √ynq ~ √wnq

SR *√ybs > √wbs; *√ynq ≥ √ynq ~ √wnq

(TL *√ynq > √wnq (in the infinitive))

M *√ynq > √wnq; *√yl > √wl

 (Observe that *√ynq > √wnq is attested to one

 degree or another in all pertinent dialects)

(β)   **cau**   **noncau** (apparently not attested)

	cau	noncau
*1√w	w	(w)
*1√y	y	y

17.6. Epenthesis (epn)

17.6.1. Description

∅ → V̆ prm (§14.1) → V̊/C__C#—i.e., a reduced vowel is inserted between the members of an auslaut consonant cluster and, being thus in a closed syllable, immediately undergoes mandatory promotion to full-vowel status—a hook-up of processes to be dubbed *epenthesis* (epn). While it would be possible to assume epenthesis directly to full vowel without going through a reduced-vowel stage, certain details of vowel coloring in B (§4.1.2 n. 6b) will be facilitated by the reduced-vowel assumption—which in any event seems developmentally more plausible (and has been classically proposed at least once, Spitaler 1968).

In turn, at least in SR and M the resulting epenthetic V̊ undergoes late ancipital lengthening (§2.3.1) to V̄; while in TR, TL, and M the epenthetic V occasionally analogically spreads to positions where it is not phonologically justified (§15.2.2.2).

In verb morphology, systematic epn is limited to Ct# in the perfective, t a subject suffix, which moreover in all dialects but B always has the value 1s.[6]

In accordance with the assumptions of §4.1, pA stress comes in two patterns, in the pf sensitive to whether 3fs *-at# is extrametrical or not: -extrametrical -át#, the oxytone pattern (o-str); or +extrametrical -ăt#, the barytone pattern (b-str). Since whenever the conditions for epn are met, Ct#, the mechanism generating o-str and b-str reacts identically in either event, the immediately resulting string will always be barytone V́CV̊t#—a string, however, then variably modifiable to VCV́t# via r-o-str, presumably to bring the results of epn into line with the generally prevailing morphophonology, which allows for o-str ~ b-str; cf. (17.6A):

(17.6A)	**before epn**	>	**epn**	>	**after epn**
3fs	(b-str) -V́Cat		(b-str) -V́Cat		(b-str) -V́Cat
	~ (o-str) -VCát		~(o-str) -VCát		~(o-str) -VCát
1s	-V́Ct (b-str)		-V́Cit (b-str)		-V́Cit
					~(o-str) -VCít

In all dialects but B, the epenthetic vowel is invariably colored ĭ by sco (§17.23), which then promotes to *i* -subject (per dialect) to subsequent processes, notably mid (§17.11) and l-anc (§2.3.1). Since, moreover, *t* is spirantizable (§5.1) by the epenthetic vowel, and the *Ct#* resulting from *Cta#, Cti#* by sap (§17.22) is exempt from epn, the following general order of patterns and processes may be assumed, where r-o-str, spr, and sap need not (so far) be ordered among themselves though each must follow epn (which in turn must follow str):[7]

(17.6B) str^epn^(r-o-str), spr, sap

However, as preluded in §15.3.1.3 along with (15L), Tiberian B variably manifests an alternative to (17.6B), whereby the subchain epn^(r-o-str) is bypassed in favor of a *subsequent* run of epn—call it r-epn—with rather different properties from primary epenthesis. That is, for Tiberian B, (17.6B) is replaced by (17.6C) where epn is variable (= may be bypassed), along with r-o-str, which it feeds. This will be further developed immediately below in §17.6.2.

(17.6C) str^(epn^(r-o-str)^)r-epn^spr, sap

17.6.2. The Individual Dialects

O̱, I̱. Evidence for epn in these dialects is subtly indirect, through spellings like O <mTT>, I <myTT> 'I died' attesting to 1s suffixal [-IT]. This evidence is qualified as indirect in that the shape [-IT] may be assumed to have arisen in 3√t verbs like these not as the result of primary epenthesis, but rather via analogically motivated copy-cat epenthesis; see §15.3.1.2 for discussion. Patently, however, copy-cat epn as response can hardly have arisen in the absence of primary epn as stimulus.

Ḇ. As intimated above, the Tiberian register of B shows various special subdevelopments. Consider first the display in (17.6D). In (i) we see oxytone cases, accountable in terms of (17.6C)—specifically, str^epn^r-o-str^spr—with the qualification that sco, in addition to providing the unmarked option of ĭ (prm > *i* mid > *e*) as in Aramaic at large, likewise provides the marked option ă (prm > *a*) as per [hɔθqšnáθ]—and though ă is clearly marked in relation to epn, it may be noted that ĭ ~ ă typifies A verb sco at large; e.g., as part of Aufsprengung (§4.4.1). However, the register also shows barytone instances of epn—not only 1s (ii), but 3fs as well (iii)—and when it does, a different pattern of sco is employed: exactly that, in fact, which holds for Tiberian Hebrew

(THP 93), dictating assimilation to a nonlabial glide 3√ (i.e., *ă/H__*, *ĭ/y__*) and neutral reduced vowel articulation elsewhere (i.e., open fronted mid ɛ̆; §17.23, §21).[8] These complications may be captured if we assume: (*) that primary epn was variable and limited to 1s; (*) that subsequent to r-o-str but prior to spr and sap, epenthesis recurred, r-epn, categorical now for 1s as well as for 3fs; and (*) that r-epn was characterized by Tiberian-Hebrew-like schwa coloring—call it sco'—rather than by the run-of-the-mill Aramaic schwa coloring—sco—accompanying primary epen. Comnprehensively, elaborating on (17.6C): str^(epn[sco]^(r-o-str)^)r-epn[sco']^spr, sap.

(17.6D) **1s**   (i) [9avðéθ]   (ii) [haqémɛθ]
                       [hɔθqə̆náθ]   [hiškáhaθ]
        3fs   (iii) [haddéqɛθ]
                                          [hištə̆xáhaθ]
                                          [hēθáyiθ]

But there is one more complication implicated with B epenthesis. B also shows an epenthesis-like process in the environment */H__t#*, *t* = 2s, a reprise necessarily following sap (because otherwise 2s *t* would not occur in auslaut: *t#* < sap *ta#* / *ti#*); call it r'-epn. And r'-epn makes for barytone structures, with sco', where moreover *t* fails to spirantize; [hištə̆xáhat] in §15.3.1.3 (15L). Thus, building onto what has already been proposed:[9]

(17.6E) str^(epn[sco]^(r-o-str)^)r-epn[sco']^spr, sap^r'-epn[sco']

The developmental chain in (17.6E) may appear elaborate, but with one possible exception is diachronically quite natural, involving as it does the interweaving and partial overlap (imbrication) of various processes; see (77.6F), where X___Y = X^Y:

(17.6F) str_____r-o-str
              epn_____r-epn_____r'-epn
              sco_____ sco'_____

Moreover, str____r-o-str and epn____r-epn____r'-epn involve diachronically commonplace sorts of development: recapitulation of a process (str____r-o-str) after an intervening event (epn) has created new structures capable of feeding that process; and gradual spread of a process across different categories of targets (epn____r-epn, starting variable on 1s, becoming categorical on 1s and picking up 3fs) and finally reasserting itself under especially favorable phonetic conditions when yet another candidate category becomes available (r-epn____r'-epn, 2s /H__#; for the propensity for gutturals to involve vowel-creating processes, see §9.3.1).[10]

Harking back to the "one possible exception" anent diachronic naturalness, it is not at first blush clear how sco___sco' might involve evolution of *ĭ* ~ *ă* to *ă/H__* ~ *ĭ/y__* ~ *ɛ́*. In §4.1.2 a *wave-theoretic* account is proposed, whereby the two realizations of sco are not directly and unilinearly related, so that it would be a false premise to take sco' as evolving from sco.[11]

TR. All relevant intransitive forms cited by Dalman end in <iyT>, interpretable as [-iθ]; e.g., [9švǽðiθ], [(ů̃)sGéðiθ], sb[tǎxóliθ], cau [ʾǽškǽḥiθ] (note epenthetic *i* (sco) vs. B *a* in (17.6D) (sco')) (Da 261). For transitive forms with transparentized medial *IT*, see §15.2.2.2.[12]

CP. [-IT] cued by <-CyT>, <-ÇT>, or <-CyT>: <ʾmryT> 'ich sagte' (Sg 8), <o̥lyT̂> 'ich trat ein', <ḥ̥šT̂> 'ich litt' (Sg 68). Note also the transparentized, copy-cat case of [-TIT] via <-ṬT> or <-TT>: <ṅḥṬT>, <ʾḥTT>; §15.3.1.2, cf. also under Q, I above. (For spr-hedging [-IT] rather than [-Iθ], see §12.2 n. 12.)

SM. [-iθ] in verbs with strong 3√, like <ʾDBqT̲> t[iddā̃béqət] 'ich halte mich fest'; [-ḗθ] auslaut in degutturalized 3√H verbs, like <ʾšTB9T̲> ~<ʾšT9BT̲> ~ <hšTB9T̲> t[ištǽbét̲] 'ich habe geschworen' (Macs 154). (For relation of trad pron, smc in §22.1 (22B).)

G. <-yT> ~ (occasionally) <-T>, hence [-Iθ]: <šBqyT> 'ich verliess', <DḥlyT> 'ich fürchtete', <šm9(y)T> 'ich hörte', <šlhyT> 'ich sandte', <ʾšKhyT> 'ich fand' (Da 261). (Note again the difference in epenthetic color between the latter form and B [hiskáhạθ], (17.6D).)

SR. [-ḗθ], with late-ancipital length, §2.3.1; e.g., [yɛð9ḗθ] 'weiss ich' (Ns 194).[13]

TL. <-(y)T> [-iθ], usually truncated (mtr, §17.12) to <-y> [-ī]: <ʾmrT> 'I said', <šm9yT> 'I heard' a[šǎmá9iθ] (Mar 37, 172*) ~ truncated [sǎmá9ī] (Mar 172*); y[9ǎvǽðiθ] ~ [9ævðí̃]. For forms with transparentized medial *IT*, §15.2.2.2.

M. [-īθ], witnessed by both trad pron and Modern cognates as [-īt], *i* mid > *e* l-anc > *ē* hei > *ī*. In view of the regular length, transparentized medial allomorphs—spelled <it>—are interpreted as [īT]; §15.2.2.2.

17.7. First Radical Filling (frf)

To the extent that the *1√w gizra of pA lacked overt (phonetic) expression of 1√ in the simple imp system, *first radical filling* (frf) is the mechanism, or set of mechanisms, whereby the later dialects filled in this deficiency in the impf—presumably to bring the gizra into better canonical accord with the verb system at large.[14] Since defective orthography largely masks any occurrence in most of the older dialects, attention will be focused on B, TR, CP, SM, SR, and TL; G and M will also be briefly discussed, though neither is especially revealing. The two central, alternative tools of frf are: (α) insertion of 1√y, which might be part of out-and-out lexical metaplasm from 1√w to 1√y, rapprochement between the two gĕzarot having possibly already been stimulated by wpl (§17.34);[15] and (β) gemination of 2√ , making for a surface effect like that of geminate verbs (gmf-4u, §3.2 (3M)) or of 1√n (rna, §17.21). To the extent that frf may have been a later change, the simplest assumption is that it operated—or came to operate—on the phonological level, inasmuch as after its occurrence there is no real trace of processes having applied which otherwise the absence of 1√[w] would have invited to apply. Notably, with the exception of the two variant B readings to be adduced in n. 18 below, there is no trace of reduction of the impf prefix vowel having occurred before patch-up by gemination or 1√y-insertion. That is, for instance, pA 3ms *yaSúMi of root *√wSM will surface via frf in later dialects exactly as if it derived from (α) *yaySúMi or (β) *yaSSúMi rather than from *yəySÚM or *yəSSÚM—though the hedged wording ("the simplest assumption," "no real trace") is intended to admit the possibility that prm (§14.1) plus other processes might have been subsequently brought to bear, lending the appearance that red had never applied.[16] There seems also to have been at least one alternative to frf proper designed to bring 1√w *-V̊SV̊M into line with prevailing morphophonological and syllabic canons: (γ) metaplasm to hollow -V̊QV̄M with 2√ (S) metanalyzed as 1√ (Q)—a strategy which bypasses the deficiency of -V̊SV̄Ms having a light initial syllable (V̊ rather than heavy strong V̊1√C) and addresses the form's overall lightness by upping the weight of the final string from CV̊M to CV̄M. It should also be noted that (δ) frf is preempted in those cases, relatively few but not merely residual, where 1√w surfaced in pA and was inherited as such into at least some dialects.[17]

An alternative conception of (α, β, γ, δ) will be spelled out under B below, but the disposition just proposed here will be the one at least nominally adopted.

B (BL 142). Likely only gemination (β) and preservation of *1√w (δ):[18] *√wθb 'sit' (also occ, §17.14) [yittív], *√wkl 'be able' [yikkúl] ~ [yūxál] (note the (β) ~ (δ) alternation for the same lexeme, and also the ablaut difference, *yakūli ~ *yiwkāli suggesting a 1√w retention pattern similar to that of Classical Arabic mentioned in n. 17; *iw > uw = ū by din, dme). There is a possible instance of y-insertion (α) in [yēṭáv] 'be good', but there is no evidence for *1√w origin of this root (√yṭb), which is apparently a metaplastic variant of √ṭWb also found in O, I, TR, and SM; cf. also n. 5 above.

*1√w-provenience of geminating (β) [tindá9] 'know' ([nd] < dd by gds, §17.8) is possible but not foregone, the strongest A-internal evidence to that effect being CP's variable showing of <w> where *1√w would have been; see below. Brockelmann relates the A root to South Semitic √yd9 (1928: 296), while Drower and Macuch connect it with Arabic √wd9 (DM 188). If the etymology should be *1√y, perhaps V 1√y 2√C' > VC'C' is a minority option to 1√y being preserved. In fact, this possibility suggests an alternative to looking at gemination as compensatory replacement for 1√w-lessness. Comprehensively, perhaps things fall out for A as in (17.7A). According to this conception, *1√w and *1√y work out largely in parallel except for *1√w's unstable nonrealization option (ii), *V 2√C' V̊) which is compensated by metaplasm to hollow ((γ), > VC'V̄). This aside, *1√w (i) and *1√y (iii) change along parallel lines, though they differ in the frequency with which a given option is followed. Specifically: they may remain unaltered (γ, γ'), a minority option for *1√w (i) but likely the majority option for *1√y (iii); they may switch values of 1√ semivowel (α, α'), possibly the majority option for *1√w (i) under the bellwether of wic (§17.33) but a rare option for *1√y (iii) stimulated *either* by the general similarity (hence confoundability) of the two gĕzarot *or* by the specific precedent of cys, should cys has occurred first (§17.5, (17.5B)); or 1√ may be totally assimilated to 2√ (β, β'), another minority option for both gĕzarot. (SM may provide a bit of evidence for at least (β); see below.)

(17.7A) p̲A (i)   *V 1√w 2√C' V̊   ~ (ii) *V 2√C' V̊

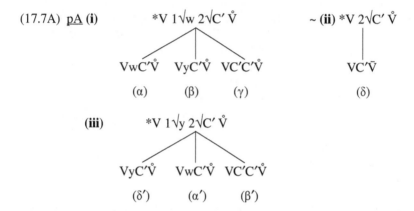

TR (Da 309f.).   (α) *√wrθ 'inherit' [yērǽθ] (observe the accordion 3√[θ] <spr *t* < occ *θ), *√wkl [nēxól] (~ (β)); (β) *√wkl [yikkól] (~ (ā)), *√wθb 'sit' [yittév]; (γ) *√wld 'be born' [tŏlĩð], *√wzp 'borrow' [tŏzĩf].[18']

CP (Sl 79–89). Especially noteworthy for preservation of a reflex of *√w (δ), (plausibly coalesced with the prefix vowel, §11.2): *√wld <Twl(y)D>, *√wzp <yw̱zP> ~ <ywzyP>, *√wqd 'burn'<ywqD>, *√wqr 'be heavy' <ywqrwn> ~ <ywq̊r̊wn>.[19] Pattern (α) is probably reflected in <y°m°̊> 'iurat', plausibly [ēmḗ] (for <y°̊> [ē], §14.2 CP (β)), *√wm? (Brockelmann 1928: 308). Pattern (β) in such as <yTB> (*√wθb) and <yqrwn> (*√wqr) where absence of ml for 2ʃ makes (γ) unlikely. Spellings like <TyKwl> (*√wkl) are ambiguous between (α) ([tēxÚl]), (γ) ([tēxúl]), as well as (β) [tIkkÚl].

SM (Macs 180f.). (α) *√wrθ <yyrT> t[yĩrat], *√wld <T(y)lD> t[tĩḷad]; (γ) *√whb 'give' <wyhB> t[w(ŏ)yắʾəb] ← reconstructed living SM [wŏyăhĩβ] < *wa=yahĩbi (for the warping sound changes of trad pron, §22.1 (22B)); (δ) *√wkl <y(w)Kl> t[yúkɑl]; (β) no unambiguous evidence under the auspices of frf proper, but there appear to be at least a few instances of *1√wC' > C'C'* in the *causative* of *√wθb—<w²TBh> t[wættḗbe] 'und setzte ihn', <²TB> t[ǽttəb] 'setz hin!' (Macs 183)—forms that may lend some support to the approach to frf sketched in (17.7A), 1√w here being clearly *replaced* rather than a void of 1√w being *filled*. (Observe, with Macuch (Macs 184), that cau rmp of this root does not undergo *wC′ > C′C′*: <yT<u>w</u>TB> t[yittútɑb] 'siedlet sich an'.)[20]

<u>G</u> (Da 309f.). No evidence for (δ), but, beyond that, all we can conclude with any confidence is the appearance of at least two of (α, β, γ): e.g., on *√whb <TyhB> ~ <ThyB>; while the first variant might be either (α) ([tēhéβ]) or (β) ([tIhhéβ]), the second invites interpretation as either (β) or (γ) ([tǎhíβ]).[21]

<u>SR</u> (Payne Smith 1903: 191–98). (α) *√wld [nēláð], *√wzp [nēzáp], *√wrθ [nēráθ]; (β) *√wθb [nɛttéw].

<u>TL</u> (Mor 201f., Mar 122*). (α) *√wrθ y[lērúθ] a[tēróθ], *√wzp y[nēzéf] ~ [nēzúf]; (β) *√wθb y&a[littév]; (γ) *√wld y[tǎlíð].

<u>M</u> (Macm 309). In default of relevant instances of trad pron or Modern cognates (and the Modern language lacks the impf category altogether), the orthography leaves us with pervasive ambiguity between (α) and (β): *√wθb <nitib>, either as (α) [nīθéβ] or as (β) [nittéβ], from the same root also <nit-bun>; *√wqr <niqar>; *√wqd <niqad> ~ <niqud>; *√whb <nihba>. There is no evidence for (δ); and while (γ) lacks any direct attestation, the matter is complicated by the fact that M undergoes pervasive hollow > geminate neutralization in the sim impf (§6.2.2.1), so that any (γ)-resolutions might have mutated to appear like (β).

A few final remarks on frf:

• The distribution of the various ref resolutions do not obviously pattern in a genetically revealing way.

• Though some roots show invariance of frf resolution across dialects—most clearly *√wθb, always (β) in unambiguous cases—others decidedly do not: thus *√wld shows (α) (SM, SR), (γ) (TR, TL), or (δ) (CP); while *√wkl evinces (α) (TR), (β) (B, TR—note α ~ β within TR), or (δ) (B—note β ~ δ within B).

• Muraoka and Porten observe that, in all cases rendered unambiguous by vocalization and pointing, the geminate resolution only affects spirantizable (§5.1) 2√—that is, *p, t, k, b, d, g* (MP 122 n. 564). If this restriction should turn out to be generally true across the dialects, a few of the (β)-instances hypothesized above would have to be revisited (e.g., for G, M). MP rightly wonder what might have led to this correlation (should it turn out to be genuine).

• There may be confusion, if only analytic confusion, between frf and ips (§15.3.1.1). For instance, might frf bleed (preempt) ips, or conversely? Or might ips and frf, in particular frf of type (α), constitute one and the same phenomenon within the bailiwick of *1√w sim impf? Or might type (γ) frf feed ips? All this remains to be worked out.

17.8. Geminate Dissimilation (gds)

Geminate dissimilation (gds) is a sporadic process whereby a geminate cluster is decomposed into nasal + singleton. The nasal is homorganic to the consonantism making up the geminate when homorganicity is articulatorily possible, and otherwise emerges as dentoalveolar [n], the dntalv comprising the least-marked position of articulation for nasals (and possibly all orders of consonants except glides). Thus, e.g., *bb* → [mb], *dd* → [nd], *gg* → [ŋg] (to be represented as [ng] in view of the "phonemic bias" investing the broad-phonetic transcription employed in this book, §20.1); *99* → [n9].

In the finite verb, gds appears to be limited to three or perhaps four dialects—I, B, SM (perhaps), M—though, beyond the verb, traces show up in one or two other dialects as well (e.g., TR [ḥingín] 'Festspiele', Da 102; cf. SR [ḥaggṓ]).

In all its manifestations, gds appears to be lexically conditioned, being limited to one or a few specific lexemes, while failing to manifest in other lexemes, the majority, of similar structure.

In I̲ and B̲, gds is confined to simple √yd9 'know' and causative √9l 'enter' (cau 'bring (in)'). I <yn̲D9> (~ -gds <y̲D9>), Kutscher 1970: 71, where [nd] ← *dd* ← *1*√*yd* (or *1*√*wd*) as per §17.7; <yn9l>, L 66, <hn9lT>, L 18, where [Vn9Vl] ← *V99Vl* with 1√9 → *99* by gmf-4u (§3, (3M)). B [ʾindá9], [tindá9], [yin̲d̲9ū̃n]; pf [han̲9él], but impa [ha9(9)élnī] ~ [h5̲9̲élnī] (BL 168), where *a99* when not subject to gds may be subject to mls (§9.3.1) with or without compensatory lengthening of the prefixal vowel, respectively → [5̲9] or → [a9] (unless mls fails to apply in the latter variant, [a99] however being spelled <a9> due to a Tiberian spelling rule disallowing <9> to be marked with the grapheme dages, i.e., @<9̯>).

SM. Perhaps cau <ʾnDh> t[ǽnda] 'brachte' and all other homoparadigmatic forms if, as Macuch believes (Macs §19), *nd* < *dd* < §9.2.3.1 *1*√*9d*, this specific form < **ha9díʾa* or **ha9díya* through the filter of d-adn (§9.1.4), <-h> t[-a] representing [-ā] ⇐ |-I 3√ʾ| a marked option in lieu of unmarked [-ī] ⇐ |- I 3√y| via s-adn. (For [-ā] ~ [-ī] as an option in SM, Macs 214; for the competing etymologies of this root in Aramaic, Brockelmann 1928: 511.)[22]

M. Causative [han̲séq] 'he made ascend' (DM 332) < *hassíq* < las (§17.21.2) **haslíqa*, ~ -gds [asséq] (lc), prefixal *a-* < adl (§9.3.2) *ʾa-* < i-hlc (§9.1.2) ha-; int rmp [eθhambál] 'he was ruined' (Macm 267) < **hithabbála* (*h* > Ø by hlr, §9.2.2; *ḥ* > *h* by dpr, §9.3.2), [neθnangár] 'he shall be flogged' (DM 289) < **yitnaggári* (*y-* > *n-* by prp, §17.19), [ū=eθnangál] 'and they projected' (lc) < **wa=hitnaggálū* (*wa=* > *ū* by lco, §12.2 M (δ); *-ū* > Ø by lap, §17.9); int (plain) [nīrand̲ṓ̃ón] 'they'll rouse' (Macm 128) < **yiraddidū̃nna* (the full and lengthened prefix vowel [ī] replacing reduced ṓ (< *i*) by ips, §15.3.1.1).

Of these M cases of gds, the former two involve variation/alternation with alloroots (the first three-way, involving las in addition to gds: √slq ~ √ssq ~

√nsq, see DM 332 for examples of all three; the second two-way across binyanim, √hmbl in the intensive (plain or rmp) ~ √hbl in the simple (plain or rmp),
e.g., [hǯβál] 'was convulsed', [eθhǯβél] 'was perverted', DM 129). The latter
three, on the other hand, are invariantly quadriradical, being restructured by
gds to √ /nngr/, √ /nngl/, √ /rndd/; (cf. n. 22).

Apart from the unsurprising similarity of I and B, some hint of transdialecti-
cal cohesiveness in gds between B (with I) and M have been seen in the facts
that M shows gds in a few nonverb verbs of √yd9 (see Nm §150 for the particulars) and that B forms its cau infinitive of √slq with gds ([hanₛ5qɔ̄́]; contrast
-gds forms, pf active and passive [hasₛíqū] and [husₛáq]).

Kutscher (1970: 71f., 88) offers an ingenious solution to a potential diachronic anomaly. On the assumption that I is (approximately) a unilinear
descendant of O, he observes that it is anomalous for *regressive nasal assimilation* (rna, $nC' > C'C'$) to apply categorically in O but only variably in
I. For if I is a diachronic development of O, this would imply that I partially
undid the assimilation that O had thoroughly accomplished—a presumably unusual if not impossible situation. This explication of Kutscher's is laid out in
(17.8A), where the allegedly anomalous unfolding of rna (i) is contrasted with
the straightforward behavior of gds (ii). However, Kutscher goes on, if rna is
rather instead taken to be a categorical process withi no qualification for dialect, and if the order rna^gds is assumed, we obtain the coherent (and simpler)
nexus laid out in (17.8B). Here, the partial undoing of rna in I is a legitimate
consequence of the independent action of gds, not a diachronically discrepant
counteraction of rna itself. (Y has been added to the diagrams because it reacts
to rna similarly to O; see §17.21. Kutscher does not mention Y one way or the
other in this connection.)

(17.8A)   Y,O   I

    (i)   *nC'   +rna > C'C'   ±rna > nC' ~ C'C'

    (ii)   *C'C'   -gds ≥ C'C'   ±gds > nC' ~ C'C'

(17.8B)   Y,O   I

         *nC'   +rna >

                          }   C'C'   +gds > nC' ~ C'C'

         *C'C'   ≥

However, the hypothesis in (17.8B) is disquieted by the fact that most later
A dialects manifests nC' ~ $C'C'$ where $n < *1$√n but no trace of anything that
might be taken as gds otherwise. This statistical bias suggests that something

separate from gds lies behind at least some of the $*1\sqrt{n} > nC' \sim C'C'$ cases—something that we might continue to dub "rna." One way of capturing this separateness of the processes involves taking Y and O to be (largely) developmentally independent from the rest of Aramaic, as in (17.8C) where I inherits variable rna from pA while Y and O strengthen into categorical and gds develops later, roughly at the time of I. More support for this approach, and notably for the idea of Y and O being on a (largely) separate track from the rest of A, will be adduced in §17.15 (in particular with n. 23) and §17.21.[23] (No position will be taken on a possible linear relation between Y and O.)

(17.8C)   pA ±rna $(nC' > nC' \sim C'C)$

+rna $(nC' > C'C)$ <u>Y,O</u>   I ±gds $(C'C' > C'C' \sim N'C')$

17.9. Long Apocope (lap); Infixing Long Apocope (i-lap)
17.9.1. Description

Long apocope (lap) dictates that long, unstressed auslaut vowels be dropped; in symbols, $\overset{\acute{}}{V} \to \emptyset \, / \_\#$. In the verb system, lap when uncompensated plays special havoc in the intransitive impa, where all four subject oppositions are funneled into one neutralization: e.g., sim ms $*Q\breve{a}S\acute{u}M$, fs $*Q\breve{a}S\acute{u}M\bar{\imath}$, mp $*Q\breve{a}S\acute{u}M\bar{u}$, fp $*Q\breve{a}S\acute{u}M\bar{a} \to Q\breve{\vartheta}S\acute{U}M$. Similarly, three-way neutralization supervenes in the pf: e.g., sim 3ms $*QaS\acute{a}Ma$ (where -*a* is priorly lost by sap, §17.22), 3mp $*QaS\acute{a}M\bar{u}$, 3fp $*QaS\acute{a}M\bar{a} \to Q\breve{\vartheta}S\acute{a}M$. Long apocope is especially robust in two of the three E dialects, SR and M. It is less active but palpable in the third E dialect, TL, as well as in P (possibly), CP, and G. Mention was made of the havoc played by lap "when uncompensated." And indeed, all of the dialects manifesting lap likewise manifest at least some de facto compensation for lap-lost signals by hii (§7.2 (δ)), whereby allomorphs of the lost suffixes from elsewhere in the verb system are attached to the neutralized stem: e.g., SR $Q\breve{\vartheta}S\acute{a}M$ in its value of impa mp or pf 3mp comes to alternate with $Q\breve{\vartheta}SaM\acute{u}n$, with -*ūn* imported from the impf.

Infixing long apocope (i-lap) is a special case of lap, applying exclusively to stems affixed with (3)mp -*ū*, whether impa, pf, or even impf, whereby -*ū* is effectively infixed into the stem, replacing 2ʃ; thus, sim pf $*QaS\acute{a}M\bar{u} \to Q\breve{\vartheta}S\acute{u}M$. As concerns its origins, i-lap may have begun as a vowel harmony process (cf. mvh, §2.3.2.1 with n. 5) with the resulting, normally short labialized 2ʃ subsequently lengthened in analogical solidarity with variant forms not undergoing i-lap and still retaining suffixed -*ū*. Such a possible origin of i-lap is sketched for int pf 3mp in (17.9A):[24]

(17.9A) $*QaSS\acute{\imath}M\bar{u}$ mvh $> QaSS\overset{\acute{}}{U}M\bar{u}$ lap $> QaSS\overset{\acute{}}{U}M > QaSS\acute{u}M$

Infixing long apocope is fully developed only in TL; it makes a sporadic appearance in G (subject to the reservations expressed in n. 26 below) and, perhaps, M.

17.9.2. The Individual Dialects

P. Of the 23 tokens of nondefective pf 3mp verbs listed in Hillers and Cussini's glossary (HC 333–421), 10 are spelled with <3√> as the last letter, suggesting the operation of lap, vs. 13 ending in <w>, suggesting [-ū] unaffected by lap. While some verbs might on this basis be adjudged +lap (e.g., <ḥPr> 'they excavated', HC 367) and others -lap (e.g., <ŝPrw> 'they did good', HC 417), yet others are variably +lap (e.g., <qrB> ~ <qrBw> 'they offered', HC 407).

However, such spellings do not unambiguously bespeak the operation of lap, because P gives evidence of a (somewhat surprising) orthographic quirk whereby auslaut (long) vowels are at times left unrepresented, even when stressed: e.g., <yḥw> 'he'll show' (HC 363) [yŏḥawwḗ], <9n> 'he answered' (HC 398) [9ŏnā́], <qr> (~ <qrˀ> ~ <qrh>) 'he called' (HC 407) [qŏrā́].

CP. There is clear orthographic evidence for (variable) lap only in the case of (3)mp *-u, e.g., pf <msr> (~ <msrw>) 'sie uberlieferten', impa <9Br> (~ <9Brw>) 'gehet hin!' (Sg 17); less certainly (but probably) for *-a in pf 1p <-n> if < *-na (Sg 62). (Expected reflexes of *-a in (3)fp have been prompted by palatal endings, pfr, §7.2 ( ); expected impa 2fs *-i is apparently always represented by <-y>, Sg 62.)[25]

G. For (3)mp *-ū, the hierarchy of options seems to be +hii (far and away the option of choice) -Ǔn ≫ unchanged -ū or +i-lap -ū- (unclear if these can be mutually ranked) ≫ +lap -∅; e.g., (pf examples) <slq̱wn> ≫ <yhBw>, <nPwl> ≫ <ˀmr> (Da 254f., 262). For *-ā, only pf <-n> (a minority option, Da 95) < *-nā (also possibly as obj—though ancipitally short *-na may be responsible; <ˀylPṉ>, §24.2 under *√ˀlp), (3)fp *-ā regularly giving way to +hii -ằn or -Ǐn when not replaced by -Ǔn (Da 255, 275) via fgm (§16.1). Impa 2fs *-ī regularly either remains (<ŝqyly̱> 'nimm!', Da 277) or gives way to +hii -īn (<zwBny̱n> 'kaufe!', Da 276), while minoritry-option endingless forms like <zByn> 'kaufe!' (Da 275) might either reflect +lap (< *zŭbínī) or formally masculine counterparts (< *zŭbín) pressed into gender-neutralizing service by fgm.[26]

SR. Categorical lap, no trace of i-lap. Nondefective intransitive pf and impa forms may remain unrepresented, though plurals may regain distinctivity via hii. On the sketch of the unmarked simple verb: impa [QŏSóM] < ms *QŭSúM, fs *QŭSúMī, mp *QŭSúMū, fp *QŭSúMā; pf [QŏSáM] < 3ms *QaSáMa (apocope by sap), 3mp *QaSáMū, 3fp *QŭSáMā— +hii variants mp [QŏSoMún], fp [QŏSoMén], 3mp [QŏSaMún], 3fp [QŏSaMén]. Observe how the hii-imported suffixes are attached to the *phonetic* stem shape—phonetic shy of stress adjustment (sta)—while in G the *phonological* stem was the target; contrast (b) in n. 27, where the SR fp impa is illustrated, with (a) in n. 26 for G.

TL. While i-lap is robust, evidence for lap is scanty at best. There is never any lap of *-$\bar{u}$, which is solely (variably) subject to i-lap (see below). Though there are instances of suffixless fs impa suggesting $\emptyset$ < *-$\bar{\imath}$ (again variably, -$\bar{\imath}$ usually being retained)—e.g., <qwm> 'rise(fs)!' a&y[qū́m] (Mar 51, 158*; Mor 131), y[nə̆ṭéf] 'harimi!' (Mor 131)—gender neutralization to ms via fgm (§16.1) might rather be responsible. (Note that fgm unambiguously occurs in the fp: e.g., y[ṭə̆vílū̲] 'tevolna!', vs. –fgm y[qə̆ṭulî́n] 'harogna!', Mor 131.) As concerns *-$\bar{u}$, direct evidence for loss by lap is rare—e.g., y[zǽl] 'hayu zolot' (Mor 127) < *zállā (lap^deg, §3.1 (3Fvii))—as are cases of its maintenance just so—e.g., y[yə̆qǽrā̲] 'hayu yĕkarot' (Mor 127); usually, a hii-imported suffix appears in its stead: [-Ān] in the pf (3fp) ([-Ån] in the Halaxot Pĕsukot), [-īn] in the impa (fp) (§7.2 (δ) TL with n. 17)—suggesting but falling short of clinching that hii is moving into the space voided by lap (*chaîne de traction*, Martinet 1964: §2.28–§2.29), thus providing indirect evidence for lap having taken place.[28]

i-lap: Margolis's tables reveal +i-lap forms varying with –i-lap forms (these latter tagged with "†" as conservative/archaic/archaizing) in the following +/– ratios: 3mp pf sim (Mar 37, 49, 51) 5/10, sim rmp (Mar 41) 1/4, int (Mar 43) 1/2, int rmp (Mar 45) 2/1, cau (Mar 46, 49, 51) 2/6, cau rmp (Mar 47) 0/1— comprehensively, 11/24. 3mp impf sim (Mar 38f., 49, 51; items tagged with "†" are not only -i-lap forms, but likewise those failing to undergo mtr (§17.12) and prp (§17.19), which failures, be it noted, may cooccur with -i-lap as marks of conservatism: e.g., +i-lap +prp <lyhDw̲r>, -i-lap + mtr +prp <l(y)Grsw̲>, but -i-lap -mtr -prp <y̲sPDw̲n>, Mar 38) 2/17, sim rmp (Mar 41) $\emptyset$/1, int (Mar 43) $\emptyset$/4, int rmp (Mar 45) $\emptyset$/6, cau (Mar 46, 49, 51) $\emptyset$/4, cau rmp (Mar 47) $\emptyset$/2— comprehensively 2/34, where be it observed i-lap is confined to the simple verb. Verbs inflected mp impa sim (Mar 38f., 49, 51) $\emptyset$/11, sim rmp (Mar 42)) 1/1, int (Mar 43) $\emptyset$/3, int rmp (Mar 45) $\emptyset$/$\emptyset$ (no instances provided one way or the other), cau (Mar 46, 49, 51) $\emptyset$/3, cau rmp (Mar 47) $\emptyset$/$\emptyset$ (no instances provided)—comprehensively 1/18, where it will be noted the sole +i-lap case is sim rmp. All in all, the profile suggested for i-lap by Margolis's tables is 16%, or 14 applications out of a sample of 90 forms listed. It also appears that, overall, i-lap is most robust in the pf of the tenses and in the sim of the binyanim—which, should the pf be adjudged the least marked of the tenses at large, suggests a commonly found linguistic distributional bias: *the less marked the category, the more complexity* (here reckoned via amount of process occurrence) *internal to the category*.[29] Some examples: 3mp pf sim y+a[šə̆lúq] (Mor 126, Mar 142*), sim rmp a[ʔippə̆ṭū́r] (Mar 150*) y[ʔiš̌š̌ə̆ðúf] (Mor 141) (*T 1√ → 1√ 1√* by rrf, §10), int rmp a[ʔištabbús] (Mar 168*) y[ʔištæqqū́r] (Mor

154) (*T 1/š* → *št* by rmt, §10), cau a[ʔaškúaḥ] (Mar 171*) (*ūḥ* → *uaḥ* by ptg, §17.16) y[ʔæhdŭr] (Mor 157); 3mp impf sim a[lɛhdŭr] (Mar 105*) y[nizbŭn] (Mor 130); note also hollow 3mp sim pf y+a[ṣŭð] (Mor 212, Mar 155*), where lengthening of the harmonically labialized schematics is vacuous—i.e., the fourth step of (17.9A) is unnecessary: **ṣắdū* vha, spr > *ṣŭðū* lap > [ṣŭð].

It might finally be mentioned here that Wajsberg (2005) considers the (apparent) retention of long unstressed auslaut vowels against the grain of lap largely to reflect Palestinian importation.

<u>M</u>. An interesting facet of M lap is that while in strict auslaut (/__#) it is categorical—[pə̆ráš] 'they understood' (Mal 348) < **parášū*—preceding an enclitic (/__=) it is variable (usually failing to apply)—[aβaðū̆βáx] 'sie thaten dir' (Nm 355) < **9abádū=bắka*, but [qāmbî] 'sie standen darin' (lc) < **qắmū=bíhi* (for the special behavior in M of pp-enclitics like [-βāx], [-bī], see §17.5.2; for dgt and prm of *9ă-* (< red **9a-*) to [a-], §9.3.1; [-î] < hei, hap *-éh* <l-anc *-éh* < mid *-íh* < sap **-íhi*—§11.1, §9.2.2, §2.3.1, §17.11, §17.22). Unlike SR, M usually fails to compensate for lap in intr pf and impa, though it occasionally does so via the M-specific suffixes (3)mp [-yỏn], (3)fp [-yẳn] ([amár] ~ [amaryỏn] 'they said', Mal 348), and very rarely via hii (note [peršón]) as variant to [pə̆ráš] 'they understood', cited above, Mal 350)—though hii regularly applies in the (3)mp defective verb, where it would appear to be functionally otiose, given preservation of distinctivity by e-cnd; e.g., [qə̆rỏn] 'they called', 'call(mp)!' (Macm 333, 336). (For all these secondary suffixes in M, see §7.2 (δ) with n. 19, §15.2.1.3, §15.6 with n. 43, §17.12.2 n. 57.)

In M, i-lap is sporadic at best; all that has come to light is <hṣub> (~ <hṣab>) 'they shrank' (DM 151)—unless this represents not +i-lap [hə̆ṣŭβ], but rather [hə̆ṣóβ] with 2ʃ either labialized /__{B, P, m}, as occasionally (Macm 116), or original **u* (Macm 261).

17.10. Lowering (low)

V̊ → *A* /__*3√L*, i.e., a short 2 lowers by anticipatory assimilation to an immediately following low 3√ , i.e., *H* (*ʔ, h, 9, ḥ*) or *r*.

Low is attested at least as early as I (cf. cuneiform <áš-ka-ḫi-i> 'find(f)!' in the Erech inscription (Gordon 1937–39: 11), [ʔaškáḥī] < **haškíḥī*). It is a variable process (cf. again the Erech participle <a-si-ir> 'one who ties' (ibid. 116), [ʔắsir]), perhaps tending to stall more frequently with focal *U* than *I* and also more before conditioning *r* than before the gutturals (cf. again I <9zwr> 'hilf!', if the reading is correct (L §32a)). (Kutscher 1970: 23 adduces the Akkadian transcription <bir adad> of the O personal name <Br hDD> in support of his claim that low had not yet occurred in O, <bir> plausibly spelling [bir] (< ***bin*) not yet become [bar].)

Is there a correlation, in the later dialects, between waning of low and waning of gutturals (§9.3.2)? Offhand, this seems to be most natural, but a look at the specifics prompts various further questions: (α) When waning of gutturals falls short of deletion, whether by laxing or depharyngealization, does waning of low follow suit? Only concrete distributional analysis will reveal the answer. (β) When certain laryngeals are apparently spared the waning, does waning of low nevertheless occur in their environment? For instance, given the fact that guttural waning in SR is (apparently) limited to loss of ʔ, might the failure of low in the case of an impf like [nɛðbóh] (B 36) or an impa like [dǝwoḥūnɔ́y] (§15.2.1.3) be causally affected though ḥ itself has seemingly remained unscathed? Again, distributional studies are probably needed: if in a given dialect (or register or even text) a statistically significant correlation should result between low failure with respect to (a) segment(s) X and guttural weakening of (a) segment(s) Y, it might be that weakening anywhere within the guttural segment class at large is accompanied by a general debilitation of the class as a whole qua conditioner. But in default of uncovering such correlations, it will be prudent to search around for possible answers elsewhere—in the case of SR [nɛðbóh], [dǝwoḥūnɔ́y], *either* general variability of low, antedating ʔ-loss, throughout the dialects (in particular, recall from above, as concerns focal *U*) *and/or* the possibility of transparentive spread of [o] from the strong verb in the wake of low losing its phonetic grounding independently of ʔ-loss (see also §15.2.1.3 n. 8).

The morphophonological condition on low, that the [+low]-spreading *C* be *3*√, is motivated to account for such contrasts as, e.g., M [ūaškaḥtennón] 'and I found them' (Macm 542) with /__3√h vs. [nεhtí] 'he will injure' (DM 140) with /__1√h, and [bεhrí] 'he chose him' (DM 53) with /__2√h.

(Since both low and attenuation (att) are variable, it might be possible to replace the *3*√-requirement by clever manipulations of the conditions of these processes, especially since there are forms on the surface instantiating the mirror image of the dispositions just sampled: e.g., [šabbiḥtí] 'I praised him' (DM 447) with /__3√h and [aḥkíθ] 'I laughed' (DM 9) with /__2√h. However, while [ūaškaḥtennón] ~ [šabbiḥtí] apparently attest to the variability of low, tout court, 1ʃ[a] in [aḥkíθ] is forthcoming only //1√y__ or //1√∅ (< *ʔ, *9)__ (§9.3.2), and it is uncertain that ±low, ±att manipulation would produce anything simpler than the *3*√ condition (which essentially follows the approach codified for Hebrew in THP 67f.).)

17.11. Midding (mid); Adguttural Midding (a-mid); Atonic Opening (aop)

17.11.1. Midding

As of B at the latest, the Aramaic dialects show a tendency to drop the high vowels *i and *u to e and o, a process to be called *midding* (mid). Looking at the dialects where this phenomenon can be tracked with any confidence (B, TR, SR, TL, M),[30] a plausible account is that the process began with the midding of *i* and *u* in stressed closed syllables—*either* with midding as a transient change chronologically posterior to sap (§17.22) *or* as a persistent change extending from earlier than epn (§17.6) until after sap, the choice depending on how forms like pf 1s [QǎSé̱Miθ] are interpreted. Midding will be persistent if *i > e* in such forms is in fact due to midding qua intrinsically phonetic process; but if it is rather due to transparentive mimicking of 3ms [QǎSé̱M] (§15.2.1.1), a transient construal can be defended. In the former eventuality,. we would have derivations like those in (17.11A); in the latter case, persistence of mid could be replaced by transience as in (17.11B):[31]

(17.11A)		*QaSíMa	*QaSíMt
persistent	*mid*		QaśéMt
	epn		QaSéMit
	sap	QaSíM	
	mid	QaSéM	
	(other changes)	[QǎSéM]	[QǎSéMiθ]

(17.11B)		*QaSíMa	*QaSíMt
transient	*epn*		QaSiMit
	sap	QaSíM	
	mid	QaSéM	
	trp (r-mid)		QaSéMit
	(other changes)	[QǎSéM]	[QǎSéMiθ]

Abstracting away from subsequent developments in specific dialects, it seems that 3fs *QaSíMat* underwent early transparentive r-mid *2ʃ í > é* while homoparadigmatic 3mp, 3fp *QaSíMū, *QaSíMā* failed to. If the development in (17.11A) is assumed, this suggests that the immediately analogical model for 3fs was 1s *QǎSéMiθ* (whether or not red/spr had yet occurred, as long as mid had), sharing with 3fs as it does the tonosyllabic-segmental scaffolding *QǎSV̊MV̊θ*. And though this explanation for early *QǎSéMaθ* is unavailable if the development in (17.11B) is assumed, another is readily plausible: that *both* 1s and 3fs underwent early transparentive r-mid (on the model of homoparadigmatic *QǎSéM, QǎSéMt(ā), QǎSéMt(í), QǎSéMnā*) while 3p *QǎSíMū, QǎSíMā* failed to because /__CV̄ was an inhibiting factor—an explanation suggested (retrospectively) by the propensity of TR and TL mid to stall in this environment (§17.11.3). Later yet, however, this anticonditioning resistance was to be overcome in some dialects, which do eventually show (some) midding /__CV. Indeed, mid was ultimately in certain dialects to spread to other positions likewise outside the pale of the original conditions, notably to unstressed vowels (2p *QǎSe̱Mtū́n, QǎSe̱Mtī́n*) even when also open-syllabic (3fs *QǎSe̱Máθ*). In its most advanced form, midding of *i* to *e* spreads to a point just short of categorical; this is most clearly the case for SR, though also eventually generalized *i > e to the near hilt if only in a stage of the dialect subsequent to the Classical (= M) focused on in this book.

The situation with *u > o seems more volatile and capricious than that of *i > e, sometimes appearing to lag behind, at other times to encroach upon unstressed positions in dialects where *i > e has not.

Robusntess of midding for the dialects to be principally considered in this subchapter is roughly as in (17.11C):

$$(17.11C) \quad SR \quad \gg \quad M \quad \gg \quad \begin{Bmatrix} TR \\ TL \end{Bmatrix} \quad \gg \quad B$$

17.11.2. Adguttural Midding and Atonic Opening

While midding, at any rate in its initial stages, is essentially a *tonosyllabic* process, driven by factors of stress and syllabification, at least two dialects give evidence of a superficially similar high > mid mechanism which is *assimilatory* in nature. Specifically, in Tib B and Ash TL i > e variably /H, i.e., in adjacency to a guttural. This process, to be called *adguttural midding* (a-mid), is assimilatory by virtue of the fact that gutturals (ʔ, h, 9, $ḥ$) are articulatorily low while mid vowels (as e) are lower than high vowels (as i)—so that, strictly speaking, we are dealing with partial lowering (while the typologically similar process low (§17.10) instantiates total lowering).

Adguttural midding appears to be intimately tied up with another process, *atonic opening* (aop), whereby close mid vowels (e, o) drop one notch to open (ɛ, ɔ) when in an unstressed closed syllable.[32] The intimate connection between the two processes is specifically that a-mid always feeds aop—that is, every e produced by a-mid in Tib B or Ash TL is realized as [ɛ] by virtue of aop.

A corollary of this relation is that a-mid only applies in unstressed closed syllables. However, when a-mid is regressive ($iHC \rightarrow eHC$) the closed syllable may then following aop ($iHC \rightarrow eHC \rightarrow \varepsilon HC$) be variably opened by the action of *excrescence* (exc), §4.3, ($iHC \rightarrow eHC \rightarrow \varepsilon HC \rightarrow \varepsilon Hə̆C$), whereupon the excrescent schwa assimilates by sco, §17.23, through the porous guttural to the color of the preceding vowel ($iHC \rightarrow eHC \rightarrow \varepsilon HC \rightarrow \varepsilon Hə̆C \rightarrow \varepsilon HĕC$). All this predicts that a-mid always occurs as part of one of three chains:[33]

(17.11D) i. $HiCC(\ldots)\acute{V}$ a-mid $\rightarrow HeCC(\ldots)\acute{V}$ aop $\rightarrow H\varepsilon CC(\ldots)\acute{V}$
       ii. $CiHC(\ldots)\acute{V}$ a-mid $\rightarrow CeHC(\ldots)\acute{V}$ aop $\rightarrow C\varepsilon HC(\ldots)\acute{V}$
      iii. $CiHC(\ldots)\acute{V}$ a-mid $\rightarrow CeHC(\ldots)\acute{V}$ aop $\rightarrow C\varepsilon HC(\ldots)\acute{V}$
            exc $\rightarrow C\varepsilon Hə̆C(\ldots)\acute{V}$ sco $\rightarrow C\varepsilon HĕC(\ldots)\acute{V}$

Though a-mid entails aop in both dialects, the reverse implication holds only for Ash TL, where the two processes appear to be coterminous.[34] In Tib B, on the other hand, there are occasional instances of unstressed closed-syllabic *e* from sources other than a-mid—and while most of these undergo aop to [ ], at least one fails to. Examples follow in §17.11.3.[35]

17.11.3. The Individual Dialects

B̲. The stressed closed-syllabic 2ʃ of sim pf 3ms [qə̆rέv] and the epenthetic suffixal vowel of 1s [qirvέθ];[36] contrast the unstressed 1ʃ of the latter ([qirvέθ]) and the suffixal vowel of 1s bb[9ǽvǽði̯θ]. For midding induced in a closed syllable subsequently opened by epn, cf. cau pf 3fs [haddέqɛθ] (< *haddíqt, miškal formed on √dq by gmf-4u, §3 (3M); Tiberian-shape epn to the tune of sco', §17.6.2 B).

Scrutiny of the incidence of *i > e in connection with the orthographic system of accents (tĕ9amim, §21.6) reveals a variability in B midding, hinting that it is still in the developmental stage. In 9 out of 10 cases of mid failing to occur, the <i> representing the [í] in question is marked by a conjunctive ta9am (§21.6 (21K)); e.g., <taᵈiq> (Dan 2:40), spelling [taddíq], is marked by merxa (<‿>). A likely interpretation of this imbalance is that in B: (α) mid was variably sensitive to *degree* of stress, such that a certain threshold amount favored the process; (β) degree of stress in turn was sensitive to prosodo-syntactic conditions, whereby given constituents (e.g., words) *X Y* in intimate prosodo-syntactic connection, it was regular for *X* to be subordinate to *Y* and accordingly to manifest reduced stress—e.g., in this example, [taddíq wə̆θērŏa9] 'shall break and crush'; and (γ) lower degrees of stress were characteristically marked by conjunctive tĕ9amim.[37]

The Babylonian register of B shows a much more robust profile of *i > e*, which at least in the verb is categorical (BL §6b′); e.g., in the preceding example, bb[tæddέq].[38] This greater robustness carries over to *u > o*, which in the Tiberian register is perhaps in the verb limited to one form, while in the Babylonian register it is considerably more active; e.g., 'you write' at Dan 6:9, tb[tiršúm], bb[tiršóm].[39]

Transparentive extension of midding in B is incipient at best, showing up only in sim pf 3fs [bə̆ṭeláθ])%15.2.1.1) and possibly a few variants accepted by C. D. Ginsburg, e.g., [hizdə̆mẹntún] 'ihr habt verabredet' (Dan 2:9), ~ normal [hizdə̆mintún] (BL §35k). These forms will be discussed in n. 40 below. There is also one case of possible nontransparentive extension of *i > e* to an affix: the reflex of the exenergic object suffix bridge *inn §7.1) in [yišʔə̆lẹnxón], assuming attendant application of aop and smp (§17.26) (usually the reflex of this bridge retains [i], e.g., [yə̆sēzə̆vịnxón] (BL 177)); similarly, -trp extension to a schematic in sim pf 3fs [nɛfqáθ], subsumed under p-att in §12.1.[40]

B prefix-triggered a-mid(^aop) occurs in 2 of 3 forms /1s__CC ([ˀɛv9é̃],
[ˀɛqré̃], but [ˀindá9], BL 171), where it might be possible to subsume the
change under p-att (§12.1); and in 6 of 22 or so forms (variants tallied in)
/rmp ˀ__CC ([ˀɛštanní̃] (~ -a-mid [ˀištanní̃]), [ˀɛštōmám], [ˀɛθkə̌riyyáθ] (~
[ˀiθkə̌riyyáθ]), [ˀɛštannṍ] ~ [ˀɛštanníw] (~ -a-mid [ˀištannṹ]), [ˀɛθ9ăqárṍ] (~ -a-
mid [ˀiθ9ăqárṍ]), BL 173–75). Observe that a-mid never occurs in the frame /
rmp h__CC (always like [hi̱štə̌xáḥat], BL 173); for ˀ ~ h in rmp and cau prefixes, §9.1.2, §2.2.2. As concerns radical-triggered a-mid(^aop), 8 of 8 defective sim impfs show the effect /__ 1√H, e.g., [lɛhwé̃] ~ [lɛhě̌wé̃] (exc^sco),
[tɛ9dé̃], [lɛhɛwyṍn] (auf, §4.4.1); on the other hand, 2 of 2 nondefective 1√Hs
show non-attenuated prefixal [a] ([ta̱9bə̌ðṹn] ~ aufgesprengt [ta̱9avðdṹn],
[ya̱ḥlə̌fṹn] (but bb[yi̱ḥlə̌fṹn])). This distribution plausibly favors the hypothesis, expressed in §12.2 B, that the vocalism in def sim imp *2ʃa 3√y either
antedates development of the ablaut pattern *i. . .a* or that this ablaut pattern was
early extended to sim imp verbs with *2ʃa 3√y. The reason for this favoritism
emerges from a comparison of the (simplified) derivations in (17.11E) and
(17.11F).

(17.11E), assuming ablaut pattern *i. . .a* for √hwy (and other 1√H defectives), provides a straightforward accounting of the resulting difference in
prefixal vocalism between the 1√H defectives (prefixal [ɛ]) and nondefectives
sporting other ablaut patterns, like *a. . .u* (prefixal [a]). On the other hand
(17.11F) would on the same assumptions—notably including failure of attenuation (including p-att) /__ 1√H—counterfactually predict retention of prefixal
[a] inherited unchanged from ablaut pattern *a. . .u* or *a. . .I.[41]

(17.11E)		*lihwáyi	*yaḥlupú̃na
sap (§17.22), c-cnd (§11.1)	lihwé̃	yaḥlupú̃n
spr (§5.1), red (§4.2)	—	yaḥlə̌fú̃n
-p-att (§12.1), +a-mid^aop	[lɛhwé̃]	[yaḥlə̌fú̃n]

(17.11F)		*lahwúyi *or* *lahwíyi
din (§8.1.1 n. 1)	lahwáyi	—
sap, c-cnd	lahwé̃	lahwí̃
-p-att	@[lahwé̃]	@[lahwí̃]

TR. With the same purport as the canonical *i > e* examples initially cited
for B, [rə̌hé̱m] 'er liebte' (Da 258), [(dī)rhé̱miθ] '(dass) ich liebte' (Da 261).
Unlike the situation with B, there is no trace of variability, under tonosyllabic-
syntactic conditions or otherwise.[42]

Concerning *u > o*, midding in the cardinal stressed closed-syllabic environment is preferred but, as Dalman puts it (albeit for slightly different reasons)
"wird. . .ohne feste Regel angewandt" (Da 267): usually like [tæ9só̱q] 'be-

drückst' but at times (especially in the Sabbionetan register) like sb[ti9ǐsuɪ̯q] (Da 270) (reference here to 2ʃ only; for the difference in prefixal color, att (§12); for the supernumerary [ǐ] apud Sabbioneta, §4.5).

Transparentive extension of 2ʃe to positions unjustified by the original phonetic conditions is widespread, though systematic pockets of resistance remain: [dǝlę́qæθ] 'sie verbrannte' (Da 260), [sārᴇvtűn] 'ihr waret widerspensting' (Da 263), [dīlᴇðǽθnī] 'dass sie mich gebar' (Da 364). Pockets of resistance notably include stems whose auslaut is a suffix of shape -$\bar{V}$, i.e., pf 3p, impa p and fs: [zǎ9íqū] 'sie(m) schrieen', [ů̥rkívā] 'und sie(f) ritten' (Da 262f), [ʔæθqífī] 'ergreife(fs)!' (Da 277). (Resistance overcome: [ʔōtę́vā] 'tatet(f) Gutes' (~ resistant sb[ʔētívā]) (Da 312; for cau [ʔō̲-] ~ [ʔē̲-] ← ʔa 1√w- ~ ʔa 1√y-, cys, §17.5).) TR also shows *u > o in originally closed syllables opened by epn: sb[tǎxǫ́liθ] 'ich wurde Kinderlos' (Da 261); and there is transparentive extension of u > o: [šǎðǫ́xæθ] 'sie wurde rühig' (Da 260), sb[tirgǫminnűn] 'du wirst sie(p) steinigen' (Da 371).

TL. Deployment of mid i > e in TL shows agreement between Yem and Ash traditions under all conditions but /__ ´CV. Agreement includes categorical application (α) under the stressed, closed-syllabic condition (y&a[šǎxę́v], Mor 125, Mar 174*) even when the final syllable is subsequently opened by epn (y&a[šǎfę́liθ], llcc), as well as (β) under other tonosyllabic conditions except /__ ´CV subject to availability of a homoparadigmatic model, specifically 2ʃ [e] (as in least-marked pf 3ms [QǎSéM])—e.g. y&a[sAkkᴇntűn], Mor 147, Mar 142*;[43] y[šǎʔᴇlinnǎhǘ], Mor 291, a[tǎ9ᴇminnűn], Mar 118*. The traditions likewise agree on i > e failing in default of the stressed, closed-syllabic condition if no transparentive model is available—e.g., sim rmp pf y[ʔi99ǎnǽš], a[ʔibbǎlá9], Mor 140, Mar 99*.

Coming now to the condition /__ ´CV, disposition of the Yem tradition is easily stated: transparentive r-mid i > e takes place under all subconditions (e.g., pf 3fs y[yǎlę́ðæθ], Mor 124) *except* /__ ´C$\bar{V}$#, where it never takes place whether the environing $\bar{V}$# is original (e.g., pf 3mp y[šǎxívū]) or derived by mtr (§17.12) < VC# (e.g., sim pf 1s Y[nǎsívī], int pf 3fs y[zæbbínā], Mor 146). The Ash tradition agrees with respect to the original /__ ´CV# subcondition, where i > e uniformly stalls (e.g., pf 3mp a[šǎxívū], Mar 171*) but differs concerning /__ ´CVC#: here, i > e varies in pf 1s (a[šǎfélī], but a[šǎθíqī]; Mar 174*, 176*) while it stalls in pf 3fs (a[yǎlíðaθ], Mar 121*).

This overall distribution suggests that mid i > e started out as proposed in §17.11.1, with the Ash realizations of the 1s forms ([QǎSę́Miθ] ~ [QǎSę́Mī] ~ [QǎSíMī]) giving the edge to the hypothesis of (17.11A) whereby mid would have commenced primarily in 1s and thence spread secondarily to 3fs. Thereafter, r-mid would have spread to other positions, encountering resistance only /__ ´CV.

Moreover, resistance in the frame /__ ´CV̄# developed new energy, in that when mtr transformed -*iθ* to -*ī*, the new cases of V̄# thus engendered also sufficed to thwart mid, categorically pursuant to the Yem tradition (y[nə̆sívī]), variably pursuant to the Ashkenazic (a[šə̆fɛ́lī], a[šēθíqī]).[44] All in all, the sweepingness of the joint effect of *i* > *e*, both primary mid and r-mid (trp), on 2ʃ suggests [e] as the unmarked value of 2ʃ |I| in TL, perhaps of |I| generally, at least in the finite verb—and if so, the correct conclusion may be that of *rule reversal* qua replacement sounded in n. 44, likely even to the tune of restructuring, so that the original palatal mid would have metamorphosed into /e/ ⇒ |i| /Y, where /Y approaches being /__CV̄#.[45]

The distribution of *u* > *o* in TL is only partially parallel to that of *i* > *e*. While Ash shows invariant [ó] in closed stressed syllables, Yem vacillates [ó] ~ [ú], at times with seemingly whimsical morphological bias: e.g., in sim impf intr regularly [u] in 3ms, but [ó] ~ [ú] in other -slots—3ms y[liṭ9úm] but 3fs y[tišqól] ~ [tišqúl] (Mor 129f.); Ash invariantly as a[liṭ9ǫ́m], a[tiqṭǫ́l] (Mar 118*, 159*).

In cases like sim impa fs y&a[šə̆qúlī] (Mor 131, Mar 175*), with original *-ī*, failure of mid may be attributed to default of the closed-syllabic condition with nonoccurrence of transparentation which was further stalled by the /__ ´CV̄# factor. On the other hand, in surface type-homonymous sim pf 1s y&a[šə̆θúqī], with [-ī] < *-*iθ* by mtr, either both factors or the /__ ´CV̄# factor alone may be involved—cf. the account of [šə̆fɛ́lī], [nə̆sívī], etc. above.

While no instances have emerged of closed-syllabic transparentation involving *u* > *o*, Yem shows [o] ~ [u] in open-syllabic cases: sim impf 3ms^3mp y[lišqolinnə̆hű], Y[nigrusinnə̆hű] (Mor 295), sim impa fp y[qǒṭulín] (Mor 131. Though in the sim impf Ash shows either no transparentation (a[lišqǒlinhő], Mar 175*) or at best halfway-house ḥaṭaf transparentation (3ms^1p a[lifrǒqinnán], Mar 153*),[46] in the sim impa we find fp a[qǒṭulőn] (Mar 159*).

Deployment of a-mid(^aop) in Ash TL is similar to that of Tib B but has encroached onto one area where it was absent in B. In /1sˀ__CC, a-mid/p-att applies unexceptionally (a[ˀɛɣlé] Mar 156*, a[ˀɛttén] Mar 139* (√ntn, rna, §17.21), a[ˀɛšqól] Mar 175*, etc.); in /rmp ˀ__CC, only 1 of 8 forms shows the effect (1s int rmp a[ˀɛšṭa9(9)ár] Mar 156*), the balance like 1s sim rmp a[ˀimmə̆léx] Mar 131*, 3fs sim pf a[ˀiθnasváθ] ~ [ˀinnasvő] Mar 137* (-rrf, -mtr ~ +rrf, +mtr; §10.1, §17.12), etc.[47] Ash TL √HSy sim impfs uniformly show miškal *-*iHSay-* and subsequent a-mid^aop, as was the case with B, (e.g., a[lɛḥɛ̆wế] Mar 106*, a[tɛḥɛ̆ṭế] Mar 112*, a[tɛḥɛwín] Mar 106*, perhaps a[ˀɛḥɛ̆mĭnnéh] Mar 114*); and likewise so behave the two nondefective √HSMs with lexically specified *2 ʃa, i.e., they also show miškal -*iHSaM-*: a[lɛḥráv], a[tɛḥɛ̆ṣáθ], Mar 115*. However, B and Ash TL part ways concerning their reaction to nondefective √HSMs of miškalim *-*aHSuM-* and *-*aHSiM-*. While B failed to attenuate these, allowing the prefix to survive as [a], Ash

TL uniformly applies p-att to the 5 or 6 lexemes built on *-aHSuM- (√ḥlṭ, √ḥrb, √ḥrq, √ḥšb, √9rq, and perhaps √hdr (< dgt and occ (§9.2.2, §17.14) *√hðr);[48], e.g., a[lɛḥɛ̆lót] Mar 113*), and shows ±p-att alternation with the two lexemes built on *-aHSiM- (√9bd, √ḥlp; e.g., a[ʔɛ9béð], but a[na9béð] Mar 145*, a[lɛḥléf] ~ a[laḥléf] lc).

SR. In SR, mid *i* > *E* (= Nes ɛ, Jac *e*) has become an unconditional change with but one hitch: in at least the Jacobite register, and according to Nöldeke and Brockelmann, Nestorian as well (Ns §47, B §49), there are a few cases of *i*-retention in certain favoring environments (the palatal glide, sibilants)—but as Nöldeke puts it, the difference is "für die Grammatik ohne jede Bedeutung"—that is, in modern terms, presumably subphonemic and in any event no verb examples are adduced.[49]

When it comes to *u > o, Nestorian patterns pretty much like TR, as may be illustrated with frame examples from the sim impa: [ó] in stressed closed syllables (ms [QŏSóM, and following lap, §17.9, the remaining φ-slots as well, which, when not disambiguated by transparentive hii, §17.9.2, are all homonymous with ms, e.g., mp < *QăSúMū);[50] [u] other than 2ʃ in closed, unstressed syllables (mp^1s [QuSMún]); [o] again by transparentive spread when 2ʃ ends up in unstressed open syllables (hii-disambiguated mp [QŏSoMún]). In Jacobite *u > o is inoperative in the verb,[51] possibly by accordion from an earlier *o* derived under conditions similar to those of Nestorian (i.e., **u > *o > u); thus jc [QŏSúM], jc[QuSMún], jc[QŏSuMún].

M. The principal clue to the M disposition of mid resides in the traditional pronunciation when, as normally but not invariantly, this is congruent with the Classical orthography; i.e., when t[i,e] are reading <i,e> (but not necessarily in that order, <e> being no more than a mnemonic transcription of a M letter, etymologically *9, serving primarily a general palatal function; §21.8) and when <u,o> are reading <(e)u> (in this case <e> merely indicating anlaut). Unfortunately, the available trad pron corpus is limited, and so results have been partly extrapolated (a risky but necessary procedure). On this basis, then, we may say that M mid, in parallel for both *i and *u, shows (α) generally [é], [ó] in stressed closed syllables (representative are [zabbén] 'he sold', [šŏmattón] 'you(pl) heard', <zabin>, <šmatun> t[šŏmátton], Mal 282f.—[tt] in the second case < *9t, §9.2.3.1; recall that in M trad pron stress is normally penultimate, §22.3) though occasionally [ó] ~ [ú] ([nimrón] ~ [nimrún] 'they'll say', <nímrun> t[nímron] ~ t[nímrun], Mal 284); (β) [e] ~ [i], [o] ~ [u] in unstressed closed syllables ([nɛγtól] ~ [niγtól] 'will kill', <nigtul> t[nɛ́γtol] ~ t[níγtol], Mal 283—note √gtl < √qtl by emphatic dissimilation, §9.1.3 n. 9; [(a)martollí] 'you(mp) said to him', [(a)marullí] 'they(mp) said to him', <(a)martulH>, <(a)marulH> t[(a)martóllí], t[(a)marúllí], Mal 282—for anlaut [a ~ Ø], §17.33; for 3ms object [-í], §11.1); and (γ) [e] (no available data for the labial) in unstressed open syllables ([eháβ] 'he gave', <ehab> t[éhaβ], Mal 280 < yŏháβ by ymn, §14.1). Developmentally, unstressed closed-syllabic [e] ~ [i], [o] ~ [u] is best interpreted as spread of mid in progress. (In the Modern language, [e,o] have become well nigh unconditional reflexes of *i, *u).

17.12. Morpholexical Truncation (mtr)

17.12.1. Description

Loss of auslaut consonantism, with compensatory lengthening of the nucleus if short; there are three conditions: (α) -*T* of the light subject suffixes of shape -*VT* (3fs, 1s); (β) -*n* (and possibly –*nn*)[52] of the heavy suffixes; (γ) 3√ of various roots. The process in any of its manifestations will be called *morpholexical truncation* (mtr).

Mtr is attested in SM ((β) and some (α), though the latter not above suspicion of being based on Hebrew), G (some (α), restricted (β)), TL ((α) and (β) highly developed, the only dialect to show (γ)), and M (restricted (β) only).

When (β) involves heavy subject suffixes, as it usually does (only TL shows extension to object suffixes), it is sometimes difficult or impossible to distinguish mtr from the null case of unchanged inheritance of suffixes never equipped with auslaut consonantism to begin with. This ambiguity is directly possible in the case of the impf, where, e.g., a reflex of the mp long-imperfective or energic-imperfective, *-*ūna* or *-*ů̄nna*, respectively, might, after sap(§17.22)^(deg)^mtr, be indistinguishable from the reflex of original short-imperfective *-*ū*. A prized clue to the actual origin in some such cases is weakening reduction of 2ʃ bespeaking oxytone stress (e.g., 2mp [tiQSₐ̊Mű]) vs. the absence of such weakening when the stress is (or was) barytone ([tiQSÚMū])—the oxytone case reflecting original long or energic impf (*taQSuMúna or *taQSuMů̄nna) while the barytone reveals an original short impf (*taQSúMū). However, the attested forms are not always so clear—especially not in SM—and there are instances which are, due to morphophonological happenstance, systematically ambiguous in default of explicit indication of the accent (e.g., reflexes of hollow taQūMúna/taQūMů̄nna vs. taQűMū). Indirectly, such ambiguities may also arise in the impa and pf systems, due to -*n(n)*-bearing suffixes that have spread from the impf and so compete with original vowel-auslaut desinences (hii, §7.2 (δ)).

The situation just described sometimes constitutes an accordion nexus, specifically when a pf or impa verb undergoing a chain of *two* mutations , hii^mtr, is confused with a verb which has actually undergone *no* mutations—and the occasion for false judgment may turn in either direction, one whereby the investigator misclassifies a conservative form (no mutations) for a changeling one (two mutations); and vice versa. For instance, SM <9lw> t[9ǽllu] 'tretet herein!' (Macs 199) might reflect *either* pA *9állū, with no change in desinence (except for quantity) in trad pron, *or* reflexes of the same stem with two changes in desinence (in addition to quantity), *-*ū* hii (plus stress adjustment)

> -*Ǔn* mtr > **-ú́*. (Note that the stress of SM trad pron is not evidential for earlier stages of the dialect; in this case, the corresponding form in living SM is interpretable as [9allū], hedging on stress; §24.1.)[53]

It might also be surmised that the very existence of -equivalent suffixes (especially) of shape -*V̄′* and -*V̄′n* (< **-V̄′na*) at an early period, most particularly after weakening or loss of the long–short impf opposition had brought them into (or near to) asemantic alternation -*V̄′* ~ -*V̄′n*, provided a stimulus for the emergence of mtr.

17.12.2. The Individual Dialects

SM. (α) <w9BD<u>h</u>> t[wæbǽd̠a̠] ~ <w9BD<u>T</u>> t[wæbǽd̠a̠t] 'und sie machte' (Macs 145), where however Macuch plausibly cautions that the former variant might bear a desinence borrowed from Hebrew. (In fact, he reports (Macs 146) a correlation between the revival of Hebrew among the Samaritans and an increase in the use of Hebrew grammatical shapes.)

(β) <ṭrw> t[ṭ͏̆éru] 'haltet!' vs. <ṭr> t[ṭár] 'halte!' (Macs 186), where this specific discrepancy in 2ʃ suggests earlier *ə̆* vs. *a*, respectively, which in turn suggests oxytone **ṭə̆rǔ́* maintained after mtr had truncated hii-derived ***ṭərǓn*; contrast <Pwqw> t[fǔ́qu] 'kommt heraus!' and <Pwq> t[fóq] 'komm heraus!' (Macs 139), where the discrepancy derives totally from smc (§22.1), and continuance is probable from mtr-less **pÚqū*, **pÚq*. (These are 1√n impas, plausibly lacking phonetic manifestation of 1√n *ə̆* since pA (and beyond); §1.6 with n. 17.)

G. (α) <slyqˀ> [sə̆lÍqā̠] 'sie stieg auf', and two other similar forms at Da 254.[54]

(β) Perhaps <T<u>h</u>tyy> 'you(fs) will sin' (Kutscher 1976: 46f.), if interpreted as [tIḥtáy], with [-áy] < mtr -*áyn* < e-cnd (§8.1), sap long impf **-ayína*. Though the evidence for mtr solely on G's statistical penchant for generalizing (reflexes of the) long impf would be weak (n. 53), likelihood of this being a bona fide instance of mtr is bolstered by G's independent proclivity to truncate auslaut *n* from the sequence -*ayn* irrespective of morphological origin (Kutscher 1976: 43–51).

TL. (α) Typified by <zB<u>n</u>y> 'I bought' vs. †<ˀmr<u>T</u>> 'I said'; <ŝKyB<u>ˀ</u>> 'she lay down', <ŝql<u>h</u>> ~ †<sql<u>T</u>> 'she took' (Mar 37)—where Margolis notes the dominance of mtr by marking -mtr forms with "†" as conservative.

(β) Similarly, <n(y)Grs<u>w</u>> ~ <l(y)Grs<u>w</u>> 'they'll study' vs. †<ysPD<u>wn</u>> 'they'll wail' (Mar 38), where the "†"-marked form is also conservative by dint of retaining prefixal <u>y</u>- (§17.19).[55] Likewise, other φ-slots in the impf: <TzBn<u>w</u>> ~ †<TzBn<u>wn</u>> 'you(mp) will buy', <T9BD<u>y</u>> 'you(fs) will do' vs. †<T(y)D<u>h</u>l<u>yn</u>> 'you(fs) will fear' (lc). (That such *n*-less shapes are the product of mtr rather than retentions of the original short impf, at least generally, follows not only from trad pron—e.g., <l(y)Grsw> a[liɣə̆sú̃] (Mar 100*), y[ligə̆sú̃]

(Mor 130)—but also from the orthographic fact that homoparadigmatic forms with clearly nonreduced 2ʃ[U] or 2ʃ[I] are (almost) always spelled with <w>, <y>: e.g., <lyzBy̱n> 'he'll buy' (Mar 38) [lizbén] as homoparadigmatic to <Tz-Bnw>, better taken as [tizbə̆nű] (< mtr *tizbə̆nún*) than as residual short impf @[tizbínū], which would be spelled (@)<TzBynw>.)[56] The only form types from outside the impf system that give clear evidence of mtr are a subset of sim pf 3mp's according to Yemeni trad pron, e.g., y[pæsṭű] 'pastu' (Mor 126) < mtr *paštún*. In Margolis's Ashkenazic trad pron this slot is uniformly treated as barytone, hence -mtr, [Qə̆SáMū], e.g., the current example a[pə̆šáṭū] (which Margolis also prefaces with "†" (Mar 154*) to mark it as conservative by virtue of maintaining auslaut [-ū] contra i-lap (Morag also lists several tokens of [Qə̆SǽMū] for Yem trad pron (Mor 126)).[57] Mtr of object pronouns is attested in the 3p and 2p: y[kæθvinnə̆hű] (Mor 291f), a[kaθvinhő] (Mar 126*), both ← *kaθvinnə̆hÚn*, Ash trad pron showing smp and mtr, Yem trad pron mtr alone. The discrepancy in vowel height might be due *either* to Ash showing mid^mtr (§17.11.3), while Yem shows mtr alone, *or* to Yem subjecting the mtr-lengthened *V̄* to hei (§11.1), while Ash fails to. The hei hypothesis is a tad more likely in that, under the alternative account, both traditions should be expected to show [ē] for the feminine counterpart vowel (cf. again §17.11.3, on the differing conditions for TL mid between *i* and *u*), while actual results follow parallel suit to the masculine: y[ʔæmrinnə̆hí̱] 'hu ʔamar ʔotan' (Mor 291f), a[ʔanhǎrinhḗ̱] 'he caused them(f) to shine' (Mar 135*).

(γ) Auslaut 3√ may be dropped in the sim impf and cau impa of √qWm (a[tēqű] y[tīqű] 'it(f)(= the question) stands (= remains unanswered)', for the discrepancy in pefixal vocalism, see §15.3.1.1 n. 22b; a[ʔōqḗ] 'raise!', Mar 158*f.), as well as in the sim pf 3ms of variouis roots (√ʔzl a[ʔǎzɔ́] 'went', √nšb a[nǎšɔ́] 'blew', √sgr a[sǎɣɔ́] 'locked', Mar 85*, 139*f.). √ʔmr 'say' perhaps also manifests 3√ loss by mtr, but an alternative—or cooccurrent—possibility is blending with √ymy; see §11.2 n. 13b).

M̲. (β) As a matter of course only in the fp suffix: 3fp [nə̆βaṭyán] ~ [nə̆βaṭyá̱] 'kamen hervor' (Nm 223f) (for the anlaut [y] of 3p suffixes like [-yā(n)], see §7.2 (δ) n. 18); impf [nīremzán] ~ [nīremzá̱] 'winken' (Nm 228); note how the occurrence of auf clinches the oxytone interpretation of forms like the latter; had it been a barytone relic of the short impf rather than a mtr-derived form, we should expect something like @[nermáza̱] (for 2ʃ[a], see DM 436).[58]

17.13. n-drop (ndr)

Deployment of the 1s object suffix in shape -*ī* in lieu of inherited shape -*nī*, a phenomenon mnemonically to be called *n-drop* (ndr) though the novel shape need not literally have been formed from the older by dropping the *n*. It seems likeliest that the use of -*ī* spread to the verb system from the nominal and prepositional systems (perhaps especially the latter, as will become clear), where *-ī* is the normal inherited shape of the 1s suffix. Above and beyond the fact that both formatives are 1s in value, and phonetically similar to boot, there are two general reasons and one specific reason for the plausibility of a nominal-prepositional orgin for verb obj 1s *-ī*: Generally (α) the morphosyntactic-semantic relations between noun/preposition and *-ī* are quite similar to those obtaining between verb and *nī*; especially, the relation preposition-*ī* falls out quite similarly to verb-*nī*, inasmuch as both morphosyntactically instantiate head-complement and, though elusively of precise characterization, both semantically invest similar roles in the complement to the head (e.g., patient, theme, goal). Then (β) in Aramaic at large, the shape of a given pronominal cluster (person-number-gender combination) is identical (modulo phonological conditions) whether functioning as complement to a noun/preposition or to a verb—with the sole exception of 1s, which rather shows *-ī* and *-nī*, respectively. So, a priori there would have existed pattern-pressure to iron out this one discrepancy. Finally, a specific enabling condition for encroachment of *-ī* onto the verb paradigm is that (γ) 1s obj already *was* signaled by *-ī* whenever a dialect availed itself of the periphrastic expression of pronominal object—that is, conveyance of the object relation by means of a special accusative preposition, e.g., [yɔ̄θ-] in B; note an early instance in construction with *-ī* itself, O <y{T}y> (De 59). Moreover, of most direct relevance, three dialects came to incorporate such prepositions morphologically into the verb as suffixes (tom, §17.30), in the process dragging along their 1s prepositional object markers of shape *-ī* (e.g., CP <DwywT̲y> 'machten mich elend' Sg 78, SM <wP̲ṣT̲y> 'und er hat mich gerettet' Macs 233, √pṣy)—*and these three dialects are exactly those that manifest ndr*: CP, SM, and G.

One additional possible disposing factor for the development of ndr involves transitive 1s obj verb forms ending in *-X-nī*, where the morphophonology at large allows the homoparadigmatic intransitive form to be parsed *-X ~ -Xn* (for any of the multitude of reasons detailed in §7). The idea is that if the transitive 1s obj form should then be apprehended on the model of the intransitive *-Xn* alternant, metanalysis of the 1s obj to shape *-ī* is forced; that is, *-X-nī* is reparsed as *-Xn-ī*. Sample types where such a nexus might arise are when $X = (3)$mp *u* so that intransitive *-ū ~ -ūn* (e.g., short impf ~ long impf, §7.2 (γ), or correspondingly in pf/impa courtesy of hii, §7.2 (δ), or in any tense when *-ū* variably ← *-ūn* by mtr, §17.12 (β)) enables transitive *-ūnī* to be correspondingly parsed *-ū-nī ~ -ūn-ī*; for example, SM intransitive impa <9l̲w> t[9ǽllu̲] 'kommt herein!' (Macs 199) but <ByT̲wn> t[bíton] 'übernachtet!' (Macs 192), hence <šGrwn̲y> t[šæggārū́ni] 'sendet mich!' segmentable as either *šæggārū-nī* or *šæggārūn-i* (the t[u] ~ [o] ~ [ū] alternation in these forms does not detract from the analysis suggested, all deriving as they do ← *ū* by smc, §22.1). The *-X ~ -Xn* nexus, to the extent that it is (was) actually operative, seems likeliest to be a *reinforcing* factor to ndr already present, at least inchoatively, in a dialect; because in the total absence of any inkling of a verb-objective -*ī*, -*Xnī* might well resist meta-analysis as -*Xn-ī* even in the face of homoparadigmatic intransitive -*X* ~ -*Xn*.

Now to the three dialects manifesting ndr: pf/impa forms lacking overt subject suffixes will be adduced first dialect by dialect; and following that, impf forms for the various dialects.

C̲P̲. It is impossible to get a bead on how strong a role ndr may play in CP, given the paucity of candidate forms listed in Sg. In fact, the only unambiguous instance cited is <Prq̲y̲> 'er rettete mich' (Sg 78).

S̲M̲. ndr appears unambiguously in about 50% of pf 3ms^1s and impa ms^1s forms sampled from Macs, to wit: <šlḥy> t[šællǽʔi] 'hat mich gesandt' (~ -ndr <šlḥny> T[šællǽni]), Macs 226, <w(ʔ)Pṣʔy> 'und hat mich gerettet' (~ +tom <w(ʔ)PṣTy>), Macs 233 (defective verb—in trad pron would likely be c[wfāsǽʔi] ~ c[wifsǽʔi], ±pro, §17.18); <Prqy ... wDBqy> t[fērǽqi ... wdēbǽqi] 'errette mich ... und erlöse mich', Macs 29.

G̲. To judge by Dalman's listings, ndr is categorical in pf 3ms^1s and variable in impa ms^1s—thus, from the nondefective verb: pf <nŝq̲y̲>, <ʔsBry>, <ʔrKBy>, <ʔ⁹ly> (Da 362)[59]; impa <ŝBqy> but <ʔlPn̲y̲>, <ŝyzBy> ~ <ŝyzBny> (Da 375).

Partially due to happenstance of available data and partially to structural factors, it has been relatively easy to detect the operation of ndr on the otherwise suffixless stems of pf and impa, 3ms^1s and ms^1s, respectively. However, less felicitous happenstance of corpus and other structural factors make the balance of the verb system less tractable to clear ndr detection. The one pervasive problem stems from the morphophonological lability of *n(n)*, detailed in §7 (and an aspect of which informs the -*Xnī* factor discussed above). In the impf, the three dialects manifesting ndr are likewise among those preferentially linking stem to object suffix via a nasal-bearing bridge (§7.1). To cite a concrete example of the bearing of this fact on uncertainty about ndr, take CP <yqtwln̲y̲> 'tötet mich' (Sg 78). Assuming <w> as ml for [Ŭ], should the interpretation be [IqṭŬl-énn-ī], with nasal-bearing bridge [enn] and ndr-derived obj [ī], or rather [IqṭUl-á-nī], lacking a nasal-bearing bridge (with vocalic [a] instead, §2.3.4.4) and original obj [nī]? At least two additional possibilities exist, both less likely but not implausible: [IqṭŬl-nī], -ndr and bridgeless (less likely in that total bridgelessness of transitives is rare in Aramaic except in the impa, §2.3.3 (β)); and [IqṭŬl-énn-ī] ← *IqṭUl-énn-nī* containing both bridge *enn* and original *nī* with the virtual *nnn* being automatically realized as geminate [nn] due to A's absolute intolerance of overlong consonants (less likely in that dialects clearly sporting *Inn+nī* separate the two by bridge *A*, e.g., B [wīðaḥăl-inn-á-nī] (BL 177), TR [yirḥŏm-inn-ǽ-ni] (Da 370). On balance, any interpretation of CP <yqtwlny> must fall back onto the essentially statistical factor that in the impf transitive a greater number of clear forms tend to use nasal bridges than not; hence <yqṭwlny> is at least somewhat more likely to realize +ndr [IqṭŬl-énn-ī] than -ndr [IqṭŬl-á-nī] (while both *IqṭŬlnī* and *IqṭŬl-énn-nī* are less likely yet).[60] The situation is similar in SM and G, except that more ample attestation of impf transitives heightens the likelihood that the 1s obj forms with singleton <n> do indeed represent +ndr nasal bridge-ī. The most probable conclusion is that ndr applies in the impf of all three dialects: with an unknown degree of robustness in CP (paucity of attested forms); perhaps categorically in SM, at least in forms with light subject (e.g., <yqṭlny> Macs 228 qua +ndr [yiqṭŏl-énn-ī], likewise <TBrKny> lc—less certainty about ndr in heavy-subject forms like <wyšBqwny> Macs 148, <wTšGrwny> Macs 227, since other φ-cells are themselves ambiguous in a way parallel to +ndr *-Ŭnn-ī* or -ndr *-ū-nī*, e.g., <ṮhwGwnh> 'ihr sollt es feiern', Macs 229); G appears to be variable (e.g., +ndr <TTyByny> but -ndr <Ṭqṭl(y)nny>, Da 371).

17.14. Occlusion (occ)

Of the four coronal slit fricatives inherited into Aramaic from proto-Semitic, three, *θ, *ð, and *θ̣, were shifted by *occlusion* (occ) to the corresponding stops, *t, d,* and *ṭ*. The fourth member of this series, voiced emphatic *ð̣, was preempted from occlusion by spirant-hopping backward to the uvular position and thus becoming *R* (§9.1.3, §17.24).

While occ had apparently not yet arisen in Y or O, it makes itself felt as of I—fully, according to some (e.g., L 9, Kutscher 1970: 9f.)—and has clearly reached the state of an unconditional change, or virtually so, in at least B, TR, CP, SM, SR, and TL.

The qualifications "fully, according to some" and "at least" are prompted by less than full certainty as to whether prima facie orthographic representation of [θ], [ð], and [θ̣] in I, P, N, and M bespeaks *synchronic* spelling, in which case presumably occ was variable, or rather *historical* spelling, in which case occ may well have operated unconditionally.[61] In the two dialects where such orthographic representation is most heavily represented, I and M, plausible evidence exists that we are in fact dealing with historical spelling. For I, see Kutscher 1970: 69f. For M, evidence takes the form of a consistent pattern among three data types: Classical orthography, traditional pronunciation thereof, and phonetic reflexes in Modern M. Whenever spellings are found in the first of these three modes suggesting failure of occ to apply, trad pron always follows suit, while the Modern language always shows reflexes suggesting that occ had in fact applied. Given the primacy at large in scientific linguistic research of attested as opposed to reconstructed language structures, this M pattern will be interpreted to the effect that the dialect had in fact undergone occ unconditionally—and that the accord of trad pron with orthography vindicates Macuch's judgment that trad pron is largely "ābāgādical" in nature, i.e., *reading pronunciation* (Macm 60, 641).[62] Though there are plenty of verb examples attesting to +occ, none simultaneously suggesting -occ and coupled with trad pron and/or Modern M reflexes have come to light. A representative noun example is the reflex of pA *$\underline{d}ahab\bar{a}$ 'gold' (emphatic state): <zahba> t[záhβa] m[dáhβa] (Macm 66, 504).

A few examples of occ from various dialects:

*θ — B [yə̄θ́ív] 'er sass' (BL 173) (note the accordion effect, θ occ > *t* spr > θ); P <ḥDṮ> 'he restored' (HC 363).

*ð — N <ḎKrT> 'elle s'est souvenue' Cl 82) (but the passive participle still shows <z> for (original) ð, <ẕKyr> ~ <ḎKyr> (lc)); M <aḫaḏtinun> 'I shut them' (Mal 345).

*θ — B [niṯréθ] 'ich bewahrte' (BL 25); SM <r9ṯT> 'sie rannte' (with <9> functioning as ml (Macs 5); this spelling varies with <rṣT>, with <ṣ> for (original) θ, a form that Macuch considers to be "hebraisierend" (Macs 190).

17.15. Pronoun Attachment (pat)

At stake are two historically distinct processes, each involving postpositive attachment of a pronominal constituent to a verb: *immediate pronoun attachment* (i-pat), %17.15.1; and *mediate pronoun attachment* (m-pat), §17.15.2. (A third process, typologically similar but not involving pronoun attachment per se, is treated in §17.3 n. 3c.)

17.15.1. Immediate Pronoun Attachment (i-pat)

I and B express the 3p pronoun object relation *periphrastically*—by means of what at cursory judgment of the texts might appear to be independent words but probably should be taken to be enclitics.[63] In contradistinction to this, the object relation of other φ-roles is expressed *morphologically*, by suffixes. Later dialects, with the notable exception of SR (and variably TL, Mar 57), are then found to extend morphological expression of the object relation to 3p pronouns as well. And while this discrepancy between I and B on the one side and most of the remaning dialects on the other might at first pass be interpreted as an isoglottic difference possibly reaching back to pA, there is evidence internal to at least TR, TL, and M (via explicit orthography or traditional pronunciation) that the 3p object suffixes are (often) more loosely attached to their verb hosts than are (most) other object suffixes—"loosely" in the more precise sense that the host (especially this) and the object tend to undergo rules better bespeaking two independent units than they would one fully, mutually amalgamated constituent. This looseness of attachment in turn suggests that the 3p object markers in the post-I and B dialects got suffixed to their hosts relatively recently, as cued by the rules applying to stem and object as if they were independent units. And a plausible explanation of this state of affairs is that I and B reflect a pA quirk—periphrastic encoding of the stem-object relation for 3p pronominal objects—and that this quirk was subsequently ironed out in most later dialects (at times but incompletely, as witness the selfsame loose stem-3p organization in TR, TL, M). This latterday suffixation of the 3p object markers will be called *immediate pronoun attachment* (i-pat) ("immediate" differentiating it from the brand of pat to be considered in §17.15.2, where attachment is mediated by a preposition).

Periphrastic expression of the 3p pronoun object in I and B: <nPlG hmw . . .> 'wir wollen sie . . . teilen', <(ṣByT) ʾhnsl hm> '(wünsche) ich sie wegzunehmen' (De 51); [ůnś̌ő himmốn] 'and it carried them away' (Dan 2:35), [wš̌hōθév himmő̃] 'and he made them to dwell' (Ezr 4:10).

For +i-pat dialects (at least P, TR, CP, SM, G, TL, M), see §7.4.1 (with n. 26), §15.2.1.2. For loose attachment resulting from i-pat, cf. TL y[š̌ə̌ʾelinnə̌hű] 'šaʾal ʾotam' (with staminal *š̌ə̌ʾel-* preserving segmental aspects of free y[š̌ə̌ʾél] 'šaʾal', Mor 384, sacrificing only the accent to stress adjustment)—contrast tightly attached y[hænqinnű̃n] 'ḥanak ʾotam', where staminal *hænq-* ⇐ s-red |ḥanaq-| reflects run-of-the-mill word-internal disposition as in y[pǽθqéh] 'kivno', Mor 291 (the tight organization of such as [hænqinnű̃n] is probably secondary, as a first step reflecting analogical reshaping of *hə̌naq-* to *hanq-* on the model of the usual stem+obj organization for V-initial object pronouns, and then as a follow-up step full integration into the prevailing morphophonology via synchronic rule manipulation; cf. §17.9.2 nn. 26, 27.[64]

Apart from the issue of loose or tight attachment, i-pat entails certain other adjustments of the resulting stem+suffix word:

(α) First and pervasively, stress adjustment dictates that the staminal accent be deleted (or at least demoted to secondary), the new word being marked off with the accent of the object marker—which is tantamount to saying that the new stem+suffix unit is resubmitted to the prevailing A stress rule, which in either manifestation (oxytone or barytone) is end-oriented, dictating that either the ultima (oxytone) or penult (barytone) be accented (§4.1).[65]

(β) As assumed in n. 64, an initial ʾ- of the 3p object formative is dropped upon suffixation to a stem ending in *C*, whether a minimal stem ending in 3√ (TL [š̌ə̌ʾelinnə̌hű] ← . . .*n*ʾ. . .) or an expanded stem ending in a subject-suffixal consonant (TL strong sim pf 2s^3mp y[fə̌tærṭinnű̃n], Mor 292, ← . . .*t*ʾ. . ., def sim pf 3fs^3mp y[š̌ə̌ðēθinnə̌hű], Mor 322). When the stem ends in *V*, normally initial ʾ*i-* of the 3p formative is elided (TR minimal stem def sim pf 3ms^3mp [hə̌zān(n)ű̃n], Da 385, < . . . +ʾ*i*. . . , the hedge on *n(n)* depending on whether degemination (deg, §3.1 (3Fvii)) of *nn* occurs /V__ (the supralinear vocalization leaves us in the lurch here, the disambiguating grapheme dageš being rarely used, <hə̌zanuwn>); expanded stem strong int pf 2ms^3ms [qǽyyemṭā̃nű̃n], Da 365, ← . . .*ā̃*+ʾ*i*. . . (a bit more confidence here that deg has applied since the word is spelled with a dageš marking the suffixal *C*, as well as the int-characteristic 2√, <qaᵛẙeymṭanuwn> (in the transliteration adopted in this book, <t>

= <T̊> for nongeminate *t*, §21.1 (21F)), suggesting that the absence of dageš in the medial <n> bespeaks [n] ← *nn*). The commonest manifestation of i-pat elision, $V' + ?i → V'$, involves $V' =$ mp *ū*, most clearly in the pf and impa: with a TR example, pf int 3mp^3mp [tārixŭn̥(n)ún], Da 367, ← . . . *ū* + *?innún*. In the impf, the amalgamation turns out the same—e.g., TR [yə̆šæmmə̆šŭn̥(n)ún], Da 373—but with considerable ambiguity of derivation, since the pre-pat verb may be the short impf (§2.2.1.2), in which case amalgamation proceeds in the same manner as for the pf/impa (here *yə̆šæmmə̆šŭ̥ + ?innún*) but may alternatively be the long or exenergic impf, in which case presumably some sort of haplological loss of *n* is involved (*yə̆šæmmə̆šŭn + ?innún*)—redolent perhaps of a possible original pA (or earlier) process that amalgamated long-impf **ūna, **īna, **āna with energic **inn to yield *ŭnna, *ĭnna, *ånna (§2.2.1.2), and in fact reflexes of that ancient amalgamation may have provided something of a model for the later i-pat melding of -*Ŭn-?innún*.[66]

(γ) While the patterns of amalgamation treated under (β) are essentially *progressive*, involving suppression of the 3p object-pronominal anlaut *?I* by preceding staminal or suffixal vocalism, it is possible that some resulting amalgamation patterns may rather betray *regressive* suppression of the staminal or subject vocalism by the *I* of the object pronoun (though not also by the object's *?*, which is lost in either event). The problem is: each such case allows one or more alternative interpretations, so we cannot say for sure that a regressive-amalgamating mechanism exists. Thus TL a[kə̆raxĭnə̆hő] 'they wrapped them' (§16.2 TL (d)) might derive from *kə̆ráxū + ?inə̆hő* by regressive eclipsis of *ū* by *i*, but it might alternatively derive from *kə̆ráxī + ?inə̆hó*, where participial -*ī* has replaced -*ū* by pin (§17.17) and the amalgamational direction of [-inə̆hő] ← -*ī + ?inə̆hő* is undeterminable. Or M <ḥzinun> 'he saw them' (Macm 368), which might be [ḥə̆zennón] qua reflex of *ḥə̆zá̆ + ?ennón* by regressive amalgamation, but then again the pre-amalgamational parts might be *ḥə̆zí + ?ennón*, with a stem built on **2ʃi*. (Such are admittedly rare in the intransitive verb, but M appears to have a penchant for deploying marked constituent types in pat-affected stems—including the selfsame **2ʃi* in the sim pf; see §17.15.2 and Macm 333.)[67] As a final example, when G intr forms like <msrTh> 'du übergabst' (Da 260) are compared with 3mp-object transitives like <TB-9Tynwn> 'du hast sie gesucht' (Da 365), it at first blush looks like the *ā* of *tā* ([mə̆sártā] has been regressively eclipsed by the *I* of -*?InnŬn* ([tə̆va9tInnŬn]). However, <-Th> [-tā] ≤ long-ancipital *-*tā* (§2.3.1) is actually the minority preference for the 2ms intr of in G, the usual encoding being <-T> [-t] < sap (§17.22) short-ancipital *-*ta*; se Da 260, where forms in [-t] outnumber those in [-tā] 5 to 3 in the strong verb (with comparable, perhaps even higher, ratios holding in the marked gĕzarot as well, as per inspection of appropriate sections Da 292–358). And, accordingly, it seems even more likely that <-Tynwn> in

<Tb9Tynwn> and other similar forms reflects *-TInnV̊n* ← *-t+ʔInnV́n* with no vowel amalgamation at all.

(δ) TL and M show haplological loss of 1p *n* upon i-pat suffixation of the *n(n)*-bearing 3mp formative—*n haplology* (nhp). The amount of material deleted differs in the two dialects, loss being limited to 1p *n* itself in TL while in M the anlaut *(ʔ)I* of the 3mp string goes along for the ride. Moreover, while the process is variable in TL, it appears to be categorical in M—though the scarcity of attested forms makes it difficult to be sure.

Examples of TL: contrast *n*-retaining y[šə̆xæẖninnə̆hű] a[šə̆xaḥnin(ə̆)hő] 'we forgot them' (Mor 294, Mar 171*) with haplological y[šə̆ʔelinnə̆hű] 'šaʔalnu ʔotam' a[šə̆qalin(ə̆)hő] 'we took them' (Mor 294, Mar 175*). Both traditions may also show phonological integration of the i-pat-formed verb word: note as variant to the last example, a[šaqlin(ə̆)hő] y[šæqlinnə̆hű] (Mor 175*, Mor 294).[68] With the defective verb, loss of *n* appears to precede and feed the progressive elision process discussed under (β): *šannī-n-ʔinə̆hő* → *šannī-ʔinə̆hő* → a[šannīnə̆hő] 'we changed them(m)' (Mar 174*), *tə̆nā-n-ʔin(ə̆)hḗ* → *tə̆nā-ʔin(ə̆)hḗ* → a[tə̆nān(ə̆)hḗ] 'we recited them(f)' (Mar 178*), similarly a[ḥăzān(ə̆)hő] 'we saw them(m)' (Mar 112*) (observe also *n*-retaining (via allosuffix [-nə̄]) a[ḥazēnə̄nə̆hḗ], lc, undergoing only (β)-elision ← *ḥăzē-nə̄-ʔinə̆hḗ*).[69]

Returning now to something intimated at the outset, M's haplological loss of 1p *n* differs from TL's in at least one respect and quite likely two. The certain difference is that loss of the 1p elements pulls along with it the anlaut *(ʔ)I-* of the 3p string (the fudge on the presence of *ʔ* in recognition of M's ultimate unconditional loss of this guttural, §9.3.2) so that all that remains of this string is the auslaut *-C(C)VC*: [pə̆θahnón] 'we opened them(m)', [pə̆θahnén] ~ [efTahnén] 'we opened them(f)' (cf. <ptahnun> t[pə̆táhnun], Macm 86, <ptahnin> t[eftáhnen], Macm 163), [ballïnhón] 'wir nützen sie ab' (cf. <balinhun>, Nm 291). Illustrative derivations follow, simplified to the highlights; input 1p allomorph *n* is assumed, but this will be further discussed immediately below: *pə̆θah-n-(ʔ)ennén* → *pə̆θah-∅-(∅)∅nnén* deg (§3.1 (3Fvii)) → *pə̆θah-nén*; *ballï-n-(ʔ)enhón* → *balli-∅-(∅)∅nhón* ccs? (§17.4) → *ballï-nhón*. (For the *nn ~ nh* alternation in M 3p pronominal elements, §7.4.2.) In addition to this difference in the size of the deleted string, M may part ways with TL in the shape of the 1p formative involved. This is because though both dialects sport 1p allomorph *n* (< lap, §17.9, *nā*), in anlaut—where it must be at the very first stage of i-pat—it is unrestricted only in TL, M limiting it to defective verbs while at large (including variably in defectives) fielding the innovative *nīn* (§17.1). The long and the short of this fact is that M i-pat in nondefective verbs might actually have involved *double n*-drop, to boot feeding (β)-style elision: *pə̆θah-nīn-(ʔ)ennén* → *pə̆θah-∅ī∅-(ʔ)ennén* → *pə̆θah-∅∅∅-(∅)∅nnén* → *pə̆θah-nén*. (And the possibilities do not stop here, since i-pat may just have occurred early enough diachronically to capture general E 1p allomorph *nan* or even general A *na*; §17.15.2.)

(ε) Most other mutations on the novel stem+suffix combination engendered by i-pat are probably best considered of the same ilk as the *QŏSAM-* → *QASM-* miškal modifications discussed above for TL—that is, integrations into the morphophonology by harmonizing the results of i-pat with the rest of the transitive paradigm. Noteworthy in this regard is phonologization of the light suffixes 3fs *-Aθ* and 1s *-Iθ*, which under i-pat for the most part emerge as vowelless *T*, in its stop value *t* postconsonantally. Though alternative paths for this result may be envisaged, even diametrical paths, the upshot is that the subject component (*T*) in these reshaped forms emerges in the same shape as it would had the 3p object *always* been suffixal, as is the case with the object markers of other φ-values; that is, the newly attached 3p suffixes are subject to the same synchronic rules, in the same order, as are object suffixes at large. (For various perspectives on the 3fs and 1s subject suffixes in transitivers, see §2.3.4.3, §15.2.2.3, §16.3 (δ).) Consider by way of illustration, on 1s^3mp: TR [šællæḥtinnū́n] (Da 366), rather than the like of @[šællæḥiθinnū́n] (with epenthesized and spirantized subject suffix, as in intr [9ættǽriθ̱], Da 261); CP <ṭlmThwn> (Sg 78)(contrast intr <ʔmryT>, Sg 8); G <ḥsrThwn> (Da 366) (vs. intr <šBqyT>, Da 261);[70] TL y[ššqæltinnŏhū́] (Mor 293) (vs. y[ššmǽ9iθ̱], Mor 125); M <nsabṭinun> (Nm 282) (vs. <nipqiṯ>, Nm 223). (For TL variants where such phonological integration fails to take place, see §15.2.2.3.)

(ζ) Looking back over these paragraphs dealing with i-pat-induced impact on the unit so amalgamated, it is noteworthy how the *ʔ* presumably initial to the 3p string disappears without a trace; and in this vein note especially how in deletion processes like those treated in (β) and (γ), if it were not for the *ʔ* we would be dealing with classical instances of vowel contact elision, whereby a vowel cluster—a universally unstable combination—is dispelled by loss of either the first member (regressive elision, cf. (γ)) or the second (progressive, cf. (β)). All this hints that there may have been no *ʔ* anlaut on the 3p word to begin with, as gingerly speculated—and gingerly rejected—in note 64.

For additional vantages on the matter of (α–ζ), see §17.26 n. 136.

Now some i-pat specifics in individual dialects:

TR. In subject-suffixless forms undergoing i-pat—that is, pf 3ms^3p, impf 3ms^3p and other light forms, impa ms^3ms—phonological integration is a minority option. However, the variation that does exist must be qualified in various ways, of which three will be considered here:

(η) Dalman tells us (Da 361, 369) that, in the earliest mss, phonological integration—specifically, application of r-red to 2ʃ which then surfaces as [š]—is absent. Unsurprisingly, since phonological integration is likely to take several generations to run full course.

(θ) Phonological integration of the sim pf 3ms^3p is absent, though it does take place (variably) in the canonically similar sim impa ms^3p: thus pf [dǎværinnũn] (Da 363), never the like of @[dævrinnũn]; yet in the impa unintegrated sb[ˀissārinnũn] ~ integrated tb[ˀæsrinnũn] (Da 376).[71] Why this pf – impa lopsidedness?

(ι) Dalman mentions (lc), and his copious examples confirm, that what in this book is taken to be phonological integration via r-red of 2ʃ is heavily biased to *A*, whether reflecting original **a* (by ablaut, §1.1.1 n. 6)—e.g., [yilbǎšinnũn] (Da 371) < *yilbáši*—or assimilated by low (§17.10)—e.g., cau [tišmǎ9innũn] (Da 372) (with marked prefixal attenuation, §12) < **tašmḭ9i*; contrast [yǎθǎrexinnũn], sb[tirgominnũn] (Da 371). Such a distribution smacks as a little peculiar, since low vowels (*A*) are inherently more sonorant than mids (*e, o*) and accordingly less prone to undergo reduction processes (Malone 1972b). If anything, we might expect the bias to run in the opposite direction, with *A* tending to *avoid* r-red and *e, o* leaning toward it. A clue to a partial answer for this puzzle may be afforded by the observation that *all* the cases of *e, o* r-red-escape documented by Dalman show the 2ʃ indicated orthographically by ml—e.g., the two examples just cited are spelled <yǎTɑreᴡKiᴡuwn>, <Tir:goᴡmiyᴡuwn>—while *none* of the few cases of *e, o* r-red application do: thus [tixtǎvinnũn] <TiKTǎBiynuwn>, contrasted with its variant [tixtovinnũn] <TiKtowBinuwn> (lc). Moreover, *A*-cases are likewise never indicated by ml, whether undergoing r-red—the examples from above are spelled <yilBǎšinuwn>, <Tišmǎ9inuwn>—or escaping it (as frequently in the Sabbionetan register, where also normally repair-strategic 2ʃ lengthening supervenes: variants to the latter, sb[yilbāšinnũn] <yil:bašiyᴡuwn>, sb[tašmā9innũn] <Taš:ma9iyᴡuwn>). This phonetic-orthographic correlation suggests that the vocalizers, excepting at least the Sabbionetan, interpreted the lack of ml in haṣer manuscripts as *organic vowellessness* and routinely vocalized 2ʃ in all such cases with perfunctory bb<ǎ>, tb<:>. Perhaps the Sabbionetan register, devoid of such tinkering, affords a truer picture of the real disposition of post-i-pat 2ʃ r-red in TR. Short of actually tallying up all of Dalman's examples, it would seem that in any event there is no sharp ±r-red bias between *A* and *e, o*, to judge by the Sabbionetan cases. (See also §6.2 n. 11 for TL.)

Possibly symptomatic of i-pat's relatively recent impact on TR is a rather notable amount of "turbulence" in certain 3p-object φ-slots, notably pf 3fs^3mp and impf mp^3mp, turbulence in the form of a dramatic number of alternative encodings, perhaps bespeaking uncertainty as to how best to patriate the novel object suffix. In 3fs^3mp, amalgamation of the new suffix complex usually assumes the form *-Aθnũn*, quite likely (segmentally) aping 3fs^1s and 3fs^1p, *-Áθnī, -Áθnā*, involving the combinatory behavior of these two other homoparadigmatic object suffixes containing inlaut *n* (§2.4.3). Moreover, like these, the new combination proceeds via transparentation with less marked stem base

(§15.2.2); e.g., [nə̆sevæθnũn] (Da 364), cf. intr [nə̆sévæθ] (Da 292).The Sabbionetan register complicates matters by *mitosing* (mit, §13) the 3fs suffix, and
following that up with various other operations along the lines of (17.15A)
(rps = repair strategy). In mp^3mp primary amalgamation is via type-(β) elision (pf 3mp^3mp [ˀællefů̃-n(n)ũn], Da 367; impf 3mp^3mp [yə̆šæmmə̆šů̃-n(n)
ũn] or [yə̆šæmmə̆šů̃n-n(n)un], Da 373) with variation propagated by mit, as
with 3fs above, (pf [ˀællefů̃n(n)ů̃n(n)ũn], alternant of [ˀællefů̃n(n)uń] above;
impf [yištə̆hů̃n(n)ů̃n(n)ũn], Da 373) or mit plus pin, §17.17 (tb[yiqtə̆lĩnů̃nnũn],
lc).[72]

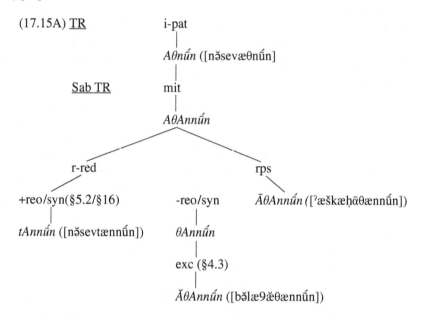

(17.15A) <u>TR</u>   i-pat
         |
       Aθnũn ([nə̆sevæθnũn]
         |
 <u>Sab TR</u>   mit
         |
       AθAnnũn

  r-red   rps

+reo/syn(§5.2/§16) -reo/syn *ĀθAnnũn* ([ˀæškæhā̆θænnũn])
  | |
tAnnũn ([nə̆sevtænnũn]) *θAnnũn*
         |
       exc (§4.3)
         |
     Ă̆θAnnũn ([bə̆læ9æ̆θænnũn])

  <u>CP, G</u>. These dialects show a 3mp object suffix of shape <-hwn>, CP consistently, G sporadically: CP <B9w̥Thẘn> 'er sandte sie' (Sg 60) ([bə̆9UThŮn],
2ʃ[U] generalized from the imp system, §12.2 n. 11, §15.6); G <nsBhwn> 'er
nahm̥sie' (Da 363). Since both dialects sport a free 3mp pronoun of shape
hInnŮn, if i-pat lies behind the suffixed forms, then *either* a special sort of
"internal" elision is involved, whereby -*Inn*- is dropped while *h*. . .*Ůn* is
maintained—contrast (β, γ) above—*or* the free pronoun was still of shape
*hInnə̆hŮn or the like (§7.4.2) when i-pat applied. Alternatively, i-pat is not
involved at all, and the dialects share an isogloss with O—G partially, CP
perhaps wholly—whereby 3p object suffixation was inherited from pA; cf. the
derivational tree in n. 64a, which should in that case be accordingly adjusted.
Also, in some or even most CP cases, neither i-pat nor pA suffixation might be
involved but rather suffixal <-hwn> may have come in as part and parcel of tom

(§17.30), whereby an original independent pp like *yāt*-object was suffixed to the verb. This seems possible for CP, since with one exception all the verbs with 3mp obj cited in Sg show <T> immediately preceding <hwn>, and such a <T> could represent a portmanteau of tom-introduced *T* with another *T* realizing either 3√T (<B9wThẘn>) or a subject suffix (<ṭlmThwn> 'ich schädigte sie' (Sg 78) (for possible bimorphemic allegiance of single <C> letters, cf. §15.3.1.2 n. 26). (The one exception alluded to above is impf <yDBrynhwn> 'er leitet sie', Sg 79, where the string <-ynhwn> might be understood *either* as exenergic bridge *-In(nə̆)-* + 3p *-hŮn*—CP preferentially fields exenergic stems in the tr impf (§7.1, §7.4.3)—*or* as thoroughly 3mp *–In(nə̆)hŮn, in which case* < *hInnə̆hŮn* as speculated above.) Note finally that <-hwn> is a minority option in G, which usually shows varying degrees of "external" elision of the types described in (β, γ) above: <-ynwn>; <-nwn>; <-wn> (e.g., with examples from pf: 2ms <TB9Tynwn> Da 365, 3mp <ʔŝKhynwn> Da 367 if elision is regressive (γ); 3mp <ṭ9nwnwn>, <ʔŝKhynwn> if <y> may alternatively be accounted for by pin (§17.17) lc; 2ms <BrKThwn> Da 365; 2ms <ḥnqTwn> lc, 3ms <Bz9wn> Da 363. And as with CP, in the cases where the 3p string is preceded by <T>, tom may be involved rather than i-pat).

SM. Even as TR, TL, and M bear witness to the reality of i-pat by showing 3p-suffixed stems in (segmentally) intransitive shape, so SM testifies to i-pat by showing some 3ms^3mp def pf stems with a trace of the 3ms independent pronoun *hū* between stem and obj suffix; e.g., <wm9wnwn> 'und er schlug sie' (Macs 233). This is evidential for i-pat in that, forms like <wm9wnwn> aside, the SM-specific phenomenon of hū-suffixation is limited to def pf 3ms *intransitive* forms; thus <wm9wnwn> must have been formed by tacking <-nwn> onto intransitive <wm9w> (for details on such forms, see §2.3.2.4 n. 14c). Observe that traces of such a *hū* appear in no other φ-slots, solely in 3ms^3mp.

TL. Both traditions break about even in phonological integration via 2ʃ reduction, though in the simple verb they partially differ as to where they show such integration. In the derived binyanim, the overwhelming tendency is to integrate—e.g., int impf 3mp^3mp Yem [līræhqĭnnə̆hű] (Mor 301) ← smp, §17.26 *-ḥḥə̆q-* ← r-red *-ḥḥIq-*, Ash [nə̆zabbə̆nĭnə̆hő](Mar 108*) (for y[lī-], a[nə̆-], §15.3.1.1, §17.19; for y[-ĭnnə̆hű], a[-ĭnə̆hő], §17.12.2 (β))—with holdouts in stray pockets such as cau impa mp^3mp y[ʔōzịfŭnnə̆hű] (Mor 314). In the sim verb, the traditions also agree on integrating the impa (y[šævqinnə̆hű] Mor 296, a[šavqin(ə̆)hő] Mar 168*) but show differences in the other tenses: in the impf, Ash always integrates ([ʔεqṭə̆lin(ə̆)hő] ~ [ʔεqṭə̆linnűn], Mar 159*) but though Yem favors integration as well, it shows variability at least for 3mp^3mp ([lišqə̆linnə̆hű] ~ [lišqọlinnə̆hű], Mor 295); and while Ash fails to integrate in the pf ([qə̆talinnűn] Mar 159*, [ṭə̆9eminnűn] Mar 118*), Yem integrates 2ʃ *a ([kæθvinnə̆hű], Mor 291) but fails to integrate 2ʃ *i ([šə̆ʔelinnə̆hű], lc)—a suspicious distribution to the extent that such 2ʃ *i forms are spelled with <y> while 2ʃ *a forms are always devoid of ml; cf. <u>TR</u> (ι) above.

The most striking byproduct of i-pat in TL, whether organically or merely incidentally induced, is the spread of 3p-object syncretism. Much of this can be read off the display in (17.15B), synthesized from the lisings in Mor 291–327 and where necessary (pf 1p^3mp) supplemented with Ashkenazic patterns from Mar 112*, 171*, 174f*.[73] This display especially highlights what might be taken as the progress of two syncretic waves, the *first* propagating -*Tĭnnə̆hű* as convergent suffixal manifestation of sub^3mp for *T*-bearing subjects (pf 3fs, 2s, 1s, 2p) and -*ĭnnə̆hű* for other sub^3mp slots (pf 3ms, 3p, 1p; virtually the entirety of the impa system), and the *second* wave generalizing -*ĭnnə̆hű* toward *any* sub^3mp role (in (17.15B) shown making inroads into pf 3fs and 1s, only 2s and 2p remaining resistant). Moreover, the ascendancy of -*ĭnnə̆hű* is overlaying the defective verb as well, qua generalized portmanteau of the post-2√ string in many sub^3mp -slots.[74] Observe that aspects of -*ĭnnə̆hű* may lay claim to a congeries of (overlapping) historical origins, as will probably frequently be found to hold of syncretic strings. Involved in this convergence are: pronominal **inn* (§7.4, e.g., strong pf 3ms^3mp), 2ʃ *i (n. 67, e.g., defective pf 3ms^3mp), formal gender merger (§16.1, strong pf 3fs^3mp), epenthesized 1s *IT* (§17.6, strong pf 1s^3mp), participial intrusion (§17.17, e.g., 3mp^3mp), haplological loss ((δ) above, pf 1p^3mp).

(17.15B)			**strong**	**defective**
pf	*3ms^3mp*	(2ʃ *a)	QæSMinnə̆hű	Qŏ̥Sĭnnə̆hű
		(2ʃ *i)	Qŏ̥SeMinnə̆hű	
	3fs^3mp		Qŏ̥SV̊Mtinnə̆hű,	Qŏ̥Sē̄θinnə̆hű
			Qŏ̥SVMæθnű̊n	
		(int)	QæSSə̆Minnə̆hű	
	2s^3mp		Qŏ̥SV̊Mtinnə̆hű	Qŏ̥Sē̄θinnə̆hű,
				QæSθinnə̆hű
	1s^3mp		Qŏ̥SV̊Mtinnə̆hű,	Qŏ̥Sē̄θinnə̆hű
			Qŏ̥SVMĭnnə̆hű	
	3mp^3mp		QæSMŭnnə̆hű,	Qŏ̥Sŭnnə̆hű,
			Qŏ̥SMĭnnə̆hű	Qŏ̥Sĭnnə̆hű
	2p^3mp		Qŏ̥SæMtĭnnə̆hű	
	1p^3mp (Ash)		Qŏ̥SaMnĭn(ə̆)hő,	Qŏ̥Sān(ə̆)hő,
			Qŏ̥SaMĭn(ə̆)hő	(int) QaSSĭn(ə̆)hő
impf	*light^3mp*		-Qŏ̥Sə̆Minnə̆hű,	-QSĭnnə̆hű
			-QSUMinnə̆hű	
	heavy^3mp		-iQSə̆Mĭnnə̆hű	-iQSĭnnə̆hű
impa	*ms^3mp*		Qə̆æSMinnə̆hű	
	mp^3mp	(cau)	ʔæQSiMŭnnə̆hű	(int) QæSSĭnnə̆hű

M. Though there is some variation, by and large, M presents a clearcut pattern of 2ʃ-reductive i-pat integration specific unto itself: (κ) Integration is the rule in the derived binyanim where the 3p object suffixes (m *-ennon, -enhon*; f *-ennen, -enhen*) normally trigger the rules expected in view of their phonological shape; thus, e.g., cau pf 3ms^3mp *naQSəMennón* with reduced 2ʃ no differently from 3ms^1s *naSQəMán*. Similarly in the int, though 2ʃ red is a bit disguised by the action of smp (§17.26); *nīQaSMennón* like *nīQASMán* (← *nīQaSSəMennón, nīQaSSəMán*). (λ) In the simple pf and impa, 2ʃ fails to reduce when the 1ʃ would be itself reduced, i-pat aside; e.g., pf 3ms^3mp *QəSaMennón*, impa ms^3mp *QəSoMennón*. (μ) Though in the simple impf, 2ʃ reduction does go through—e.g., 3ms^3mp *neQSəMennón*—such reduction normally contrasts with Aufsprennung in the case of object suffixes not involved in i-pat, so that, e.g., 3ms^2ms preferentially shows *nīQeSMáx* rather than *neQSəMáx*; and in §15 n. 43 the view is defended that M has here developed a secondary opposition, red vs. auf, corresponding to -red vs. +red in the other dialects. Hence, whether forms like *neQSəMennón* are as integrated into the phonology as the ilk of *nīQeSMáx* is a question that cannot receive a simple "yes"/"no" answer. (ν) Finally, M generalizes the i-pat-induced pattern for 3p object suffixes to *all* plural object suffixes, making for such as 3ms^2fp *QəSaMenxén*, impf 2s^1p *teQSəMennán* (§15.2.1.2, §15.5.1).

17.15.2. Mediate Pronoun Attachment (m-pat)

In Aramaic, as in many other languages with impoverished case systems, grammatical functions borne by arguments of the verb may be encoded through prepositions. Frequent in this role are *lV̊-* for dative ('to') and *bV̊-* for locative ('in') or instrumental ('by'); and whenever these—or other prepositions, for that matter—construct with personal pronouns as complement, the resulting constituent will be referred to as a *prepositional pronoun* (pp). In turn, pps—especially those encoding grammatical functions like dative, locative, instrumental, etc.—tend prosodically to combine with their governing verbs as enclitics. Indeed, this state is rendered explicit a few times in B by the grapheme *makef*, marking that the group *V-pp* has been united as one macroword under the stress of the pp, while the stress of the verb has been reduced to secondary ([hùsǎfaθ=lí] 'sie wurde mir hinzugetan', Dan 4:33) or altogether lost (([ʾǎmar=léh]) 'er sagte ihm' (Dan 2:24).[75] Clitic-group behavior of *V-pp* might also be witnessed: by CP <DyzlBˀ> 'dass ich auf ihm gehe' (Sg §5), analytically <D-yzl-bˀ> 'that-V-pp', [dĪzel=bĪ́], (for <y> [Ī], sar §9.2.1.2; [bĪ́] ← *bĪh*, mtr §17.12) though possibly m-pat has applied to render fully suffixal [dĪzelbĪ́] (see below); by SM <lˀ TGzy ln> 'belohne uns (nicht)' to judge by Macuch's transcription into trad pron as [(ḷā) tigzī-ḷan] (Macs 208) on the assumption that his hyphenization may be a way of conveying the present book's [. . . tigzí=ḷɑn], penultimate stress by smc bespeaking *ḷan* as the tail-end of a clitic group rather than a full-blown word sui generis (in which case the rules of smc would lead us to expect something like @[. . . tígzi ļǽn] (or @[. . . tígzi ļǽn], Macs 322);[76] by G <ˀzlh> 'he went', an ethical dative form interpretable as [ˀɜzIllḛ́h]/[azIllḛ́h] (cf. Modern Hebrew *halax lo*) (Kutscher 1976: 33 with n. 78); and perhaps by Yem TL sim pf 3mp-pp forms that Morag represents as [QæSMū pp], e.g., [pǽštūlǽh], [ˀǽmrūlḛ́h], [bǽṣrūlɜ̌hú] (Mor 126). These are likely to be clitic along the lines of [pǽštū=lǽh], [ˀǽmrū=lḛ́h], [bǽṣrū=lɜ̌hú], the verb having sacrificed its accent under enclisis, whereupon 2ʃ is syncopated by (a rerun of) reduction: *pašáṭū lǽh* enclisis → *pašaṭū=láh* (r-)red → [pǽštū=lǽh]. (The hedge on the primary or rerun status of reduction is prompted by the fact that 1ʃ emerges as [æ]. If the input to enclisis were *Qɜ̌SáMū pp* simpliciter, the reemergence of consistent *a*-color of the earlier reduced 1ʃ would have to be explained. So either *Qɜ̌SáMū pp* is encliticized on the phonological level, /QaSaMū pp/ or encliticization took place before **QaSáMū* reduced to *Qɜ̌SáMū*. In the former case, we would be dealing with r-red; in the latter case, with primary red.)[77]

Given this pretooling of *V-pp* as a clitic group, at least M pushes things a step further, and whenever pp is headed by *lV̊-* or *bV̊-* attaches the pp to the verb as suffix—a development to be called *mediate pronoun attachment* (m-pat). The mechanics of m-pat may be followed with the help of the examples in (17.15C).

The most straightforward cases merely involve attachment of the pp (underscored) to the tune of stress adjustment de facto consisting in loss of accent from the verb (but see n. 75c); (17.15(ci)), e.g., *pɜ̌láy lǽx* → [pɜ̌laɣlǽx]. Observe that the 2s suffix *-t* apparently fails to trigger *CCC*-dispelling repair strategies like exc (§4.3), auf (§4.4), or epn (§17.6), rather leaving groups like *rtb*, *xtl* intact ("apparently" because there is no orthographic trace of any disruptive vowel; and though exc to the like of [dartɜ̌Bí̊] is not out of the question, <∅> being an option for [ɜ̌]-representation, medial *CCɜ̌C* of other origins (notably ← red *CCV̊C /__V*) is normally spelled <CCC> ~ <CCiC> (§21.8)—but no variants like (@) <dartibH> have yet come to light.

However, other subject-suffixal consonants, in particular 3fs or 1s *T* and 3p or 2p *n*, when postvocalic normally undergo assimilation /__pp: regressively from dative *l* (*VCl* → *Vll*), progressively from the environing vowel when locative/instrumental *b* follows (*VCb* → *V̄B*). Examples are provided in (17.15C(ii)), including rare instances of failure to assimilate in the case of *T* (no failures of *n*-assimilation have come to light): thus [amartollí̊] ← *amarton+lí̊*; [arhū̄Bí̊] ← *arhŪn+bí̊*;[78] [qɜ̌rı̊llí̊] ← *qɜ̌rı̊θ+lí̊* but no assimilation in similarly structured [eθı̊θlí̊], and in parallel for assimilated 3fs [hɜ̌nå̊llí̊] but unassimilated [aθå̊θlón]; [qɜ̌rı̄Bí̊]. Unlike 3fs and 1s *T*, 2s *T* is resistant (though not totally immune) to assimilation, an issue to which we shall briefly return.

As discussed in §15.2.1.1, light-suffixed sim pf forms undergoing m-pat assume barytone as opposed to oxytone accentuation—this latter otherwise the norm for M—presumably to avoid stress clash; thus in (ii) of (17.15C) [amarı̊llı́] ← *amárīθ-lī́* rather than @[amrı̊llı́] ← *amrīθ-lī́*. And, in fact, m-pat tends to "catch" archaic or otherwise special verb forms generally. Some of the most prominent cases are sampled in (iii): [tə̆raṣnallón] and [nə̆faqnāBı́] show composition with older 1p *-nā* (§2.3.4.3) or *-nān* (§7.2 (δ) n. 11) rather than with otherwise usual *-nīn* (as in [nə̆faqnı́n], §7.1); [yă̆haβlán] fails to show ymn (§14.2) (though [e̦haβallı́] does); [tebbă̆ðollá̊] shows failure of smp (§17.26), normal for free forms of similar structure (note [te̦bDón]); [eṣṭə̆βá̊Tbı́] shows lowering (§17.10) of 2ʃ i /__9 followed by degutturalization, *i9 → a9 → ă̊*, in this originally 3√H verb (√ṣb9) while free [eṣṭə̆βé̦T] shows metanalysis to 3√y; [hə̆βā̲lán] ~ [ahBā̲lán] show the unusual impa suffix *-ā* (§2.3.4.1), while free forms ([háβ]) never do; and [ne̦šbe̦qlón], [ı̊mı̲lı́] (= [ı̊miylı́]) show palatal 2ʃ, in contrast to the free form [te̦šbó̦q] and the variant [ı̊mā̲lı́].

To this list of m-pat stem peculiarities might be added inflection for 3mp pf (and mp impa) in the nondefective verb by *-Un*, as seen in (ii) (e.g., [amaru̲llı́]), inasmuch as importation of *-Un* from impf to pf/impa (hii, §7.2 (δ)) is commonplace for the free M verb only in the defective gizra.[79]

A final peculiarity to be treated here is the propensity, especially strong in the def verb, to undergo *mitosis* (§13) of pf 3fs *-aT* and 1s *-ĪT*—and by rare extension, sometimes of 2s *-T*. Though questions remain about this process, it has the net effect of producing a postpositive copy of the suffix (which in the case of 2s *-T* parasitically apes the vowel of 1s *-ĪT*). Thus, strong [afre̦štIlxon] may be taken to derive from |apreš-e̦te̦t-lakón|, which undergoes s-spr^s-red(^s-l-anc) to yield |afreš-θĪθ-lə̆xón|, s-reo and s-assimilation to |afre̦štIllə̆xón|, and finally s-smp to [afre̦štI̊lxón]. Derivation of def forms is complicated by the role of s-e-cnd in melding 2ʃ 3√y with the suffix vowel; see §8.1 and Malone 1998a for details. Examples from (iv) with the copied vowel underscored are 3fs [hə̆nå̆θallı́], 2s [hə̆we̦TĪBı́], 1s [hə̆zīθillı́]. (The hedge on vowel length of *-Ĭ-* in the 1s cases, and derivatively perhaps in 2s cases as well, is due to uncertainty as to exactly how *late anticipality*, l-anc (§2.3.1), interacts with mitosis. While it is clear that l-anc normally applies to 1s in the absence of m-pat (and mit)—thus [afrə̆šı́θ] 'I explained', <apri̦šit> (DM 381)—it seems equally clear that if it applied to m-pat forms *before* mit, we would counterfactually derive forms like @[afrə̆ši̦θĪlxón] ⇐ |apreš-ītīt-lakón|, rather than correct [afre̦štI̊lxón].)

It is unclear, even somewhat puzzling, why m-pat should correlate with these staminal peculiarities. Likely enough, there is more than one factor at work. Thus, the tendency toward 2ʃ i vocalism might reflect extension to m-pat forms of the preference for 2ʃ i in transitives (§12.2 <u>M</u> (γ3)), a factor also making itself felt in i-pat (n. 67); alternatively or additionally, M generalization of attenuation (§12) may be involved in the case of strong verbs like [nešbȩqlón] (iii). Then there are archaic formations trapped by m-pat, or at least formations which have elsewhere in the language at large gone out of general coinage, *either* in that a form used with m-pat has been replaced ([nə̆faqnā̱Bí́]) *or* dropped out without replacement ([hə̆β̱ālán]), *or* by virtue of a linguistic change exempting the m-pat string (-ymn [yă̆haβlán], -smp [tebbə̆ðollā́], unmetanalyzed [eṣṭə̆β̱å̆Tbí́]). It is also conceivable that there is a subtle length or weight factor at work, whereby longer/heavier formations tend to be used in m-pat, a position taken in Malone 1998a with respect to mit but likewise arguable vis-à-vis various other m-pat preferences:[80] impa -*ā* vs. its absence, -smp *C′C′ə̆* vs. +smp *C′*, +hii -*Un*- vs. -hii -∅- (< lap).[81]

(17.15C)

(i) [pə̆laɣlā́x] 'he allotted to thee' <plaglak> (Mal 314)

[aðrextlén] 'thou settest them(f)' <adriktlin> (DM 114)

[då̆rtbí́] 'thou didst dwell therein' <dartbH> (Mal 335)

[nehwīlā̆́x] 'may thou have' (an. 'may (there) be to thee')
  t[nahwǐlax] (Mal 284)

[nehwi̊lxón] 'may ye have' (an. 'may (there) be to ye'
  t[nehwǐlxon] (Mal 284)

[arhā̱Bí́] 'smelleth at it' t[arhā́bī] (Macm 484)

(ii) [qə̆rīBí́] 'I called in it' t[aqrǐbi] (mal 282)

[amarullí́] 'they said to him' t[(a)marúllī] <amarulH> (Mal 282)

[amarullí́] 'they said to me' t[amarólle] <amarulia> (Mal 282)

[amartollí́] 'ye said to him' t[(a)martóllī] (Mal 282)

[afrə̆si̊lxón] (~ [afrešti̊lxón] under (iv)) 'I explained to ye'
  (Malone 1998a: 13)

[hə̆nå̆llí́] 'it(f) pleased me' <hnalia> (Malone 1998a: 12)

[qə̆rii̊llí́] (~ [qə̆rīθi̊llí́] under (iv)) 'I called him' (Malone 1998a: 12)

[aθå̆lón] (~ [aθå̆θallón] under (iv)) 'she came to them' (Mal 328)

[amari̊llí́] 'I said to him' t[amaríllī] (Mal 341)

[eθi̊θlí́] 'I came to him' (Mal 343)

[arhūBí́] 'they smelled at it' y[arhū́bī] (Mal 484)

(iii) [i̊malí́] ~ [i̊milí́] 'he swore to me' <emalia> ~ <emilia> (Mal 314)

[nə̆faqnāBí́] 'we went out in it' (Macm 269)

  (vs. [nə̆faqnín] 'we went out' (DM 304))

[tə̆raṣnallón] 'we raised for them' <traṣnalon> (Macm 269)

[yă̆haβlán] 'gab uns' (Nm 245)

  (vs. [ehaβallí́] 'she gave to him' t[ehaβállí́] (Mal 326, Macm 97))

[eṣṭə̆β̱å̆TBí́] 'bist darin getauft' (Nm 234f)

  (vs. [eṣṭə̆β̱é̆T] 'bist getauft' (lc))

[hə̆β̱ālán] ~ [ahBālán] 'gib uns!' (Nm 246)

  (vs. [hā́β] 'give!' (DM 189))

[nešbeqlón] 'may he remit (to) them' (DM 447)
    (vs. [tešbóq] 'you'll remit' (lc))
[tebbădðollắ] 'ye will do to her' <tibidulH> (DM 2)
    (vs. tebDón] 'ye will do' (lc))
(iv) [hăzīθĬllí] 'I saw him' t[hăzītíllī] (Mal 282)
    [afreštĬlxón] (~[afrăšĬlxón] under (ii)) 'I explained to ye'
        (Mal 1998a: 13) (cf. m[bădaqtéllax] 'I put thee' (Macm 270))
    [hăweTiBí] ~ [hăwēTbí] 'thou werst in it' (Malone 1998a: 13)
    [hănåθallí] 'it(f) pleased him' <hnatalH> (Malone 1998a: 12)
    [qărīθĬllí] (~ [qărĬllí] under (ii)) 'I called him' (Malone 1998a: 12)
    [aθåθallón] (~ [aθåθlón] under (ii)) 'she came to them' (Mal 328)
(v) [eθkarraxbí] ~ [eθkarkūBí] 'they surrounded him'
    (an. 'they were circled at (around) him') (Mal 501)

17.16. Pataḥ Gĕnuva (pgn)

A process akin to lowering (§17.10), perhaps even a special case thereof, *pataḥ gĕnuva* (pgn)—"furtive" pataḥ—consists in regressively low-assimilating the second half (mora) of a close ([+high]) long vowel to a guttural coda in auslaut position. This is formulated casually in (17.16A(i)); and a bit more rigorously—autosegmentally (§23.4)—in (17.16A(ii)), where the feature [+low] of H ([-sto]) "rubs off," technically spreads (dotted line), onto the adjacent mora (μ) of the nucleic (N) vowel, in the process cutting off (pair of strokes across the association line) that mora from its sister—effectively making for a [+high] [+low] vowel cluster.

(17.16A) (i) $V'V' H \# \rightarrow V'a H \#$, where V' = close (i.e., *i, e, u, o*).

    (ii)

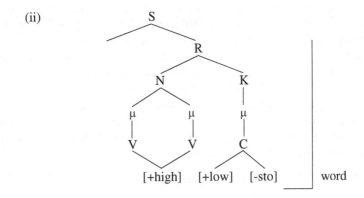

    →

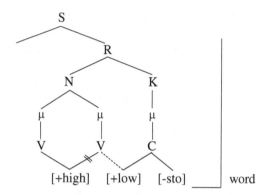

Of the dialects with sufficiently expressive orthography or trad pron to provide testimony, pgn may be found in B (Tiberian register only), TR, and TL
(apparently variable in the Yemeni register). Examples:

B. [šǝlíaḥ] 'er wurde ausgestreckt' (BL 39)—contrast [kǝθív] (= kǝθíiv)
failing the H condition, or [pǝθíḥū] failing the # condition—[tēróa9] 'sie wird
zertrümmern' (lc, in this book, see §9.3.1 n. 40)—contrast Babylonian register
[tēró̱9].

TR. [wīsúæ9] 'und er wird tünchen'—contrast [yǝmǖθ] 'er wird sterben'
(Da 320), cau pf and impa [ʾǝɣíæh] 'erregte' and 'errege!' (Da 324).

TL. 3mp pf forms with "infixed" -ū- by i-lap (§17.9), a[ʾaškúah] 'they
found' (Mar 171*), a[pǝrúah] 'they fled' (Mar 152*); pf 3mp^3ms ← -ú-h
only Ash: a[qaṭlúah] (Mar 159*), but -pgn y[šæqlúh] (Mor 293); impa mp^3ms
← -ú-h: both traditions—a[tafsúah] (Mar 179*), y[šævqúæh] (Mor 297). For ī,
cau pf 3ms y[ʾæθlíæ9] (Mor 157) ← 2ʃ ī lengthened by ssl (§17.28). (Margolis provides no evidence one way or the other for Ash ī-pgn in the finite verb
but does attest to same in the passive participle, as does Morag for Yem: e.g.,
a[yǝðía9], y[yǝðíæ9] 'yadua9', Mar 120*, Mor 365.)

It is striking that the 3ms object suffix -éh fails to succumb—e.g., B [saθréh]
'er zerstörte ihn' (BL 39) ≠ @[saθréah], and similarly in TR, TL—a failure
rightly noted as puzzling by Bauer and Leander (lc) and other traditional luminaries; cf. §2.3.4.4 n. 32, §11.2 n. 14.[82]

17.17. Participial Intrusion (pin)

17.17.1. Description

Five dialects (TR, SM, G, TL, M) give evidence of variable importation
of plural participial subject endings into the finite tenses, a phenomenon to be
called *participial intrusion* (pin).

At least for the intransitive verb, the clearest way of describing the upshot of pin in the commonest cases is phonological replacement (*restructuring*) of a formally mp subject suffix by the corresponding participial complex. For instance: TR int rmp pf 2mp /ʔit-QaSSiM-tūn/ by /ʔit-QaSSiM-ittūn/, e.g., -pin tb[ʔizdæbbentū́n] (√zbn: metathesis of rmp /t/ and 1√ /z/ by rmt, §10; marked att, type (γ), 2ʃ *a* → [e], §12) vs. +pin [ʔiθrā9ǰmittū́n], Da 263, compare full nonfinite participial sim [yā́ðǰittū́n], Da 284f.; and TL int impf 3mp, Ash plain [lǰxannǰfī́] (Mar 124*) like participial [yǰðǰ9ī́] (Mar 119*), but Yem rmp [likkænnǰfḗ] (Mor 154) like participial [nā́fǰqḗ] or, with deletional reduction of 2ʃ and css (§17.4), [9ævðḗ] (Mor 133).

When it comes to the transitive verb, a parallel statement like "replace the subject-object complex by the corresponding participial complex" would at times yield the wrong results, most clearly in TR. What rather seems to be called for is something like *"replace the finite subject string by the corresponding intransitive participial subject string and leave the finite object string in place."* Thus, TR sim impf 3mp^2ms <yiDBǰqiynɑK> would be interpreted either as [yiðbǰqīnā́x] with participial -*īn*- substituting for finite -*ŭnn*- or as [yiðbǰqi̊nnā́x] if the -*nn*- of finite -*ŭnn*- is interpreted as exenergic bridge (§7.1) rather than as part of the φ-suffix per se, in which case participial -*in+nn*- → [-ı̊nn-] in that, pan-Aramaically, any long segment normally weighs in at 2 morae (μμ) no matter how many singletons are contributed by the morphology (§23.5, cf. §17.15.1 (β)), and the value of [ī] depends on whether css (§17.4) applies or not. If, on the other hand, the finite subject-object complex were simply to be replaced by a corresponding participial complex, the resulting shape of the 3mp subject component might counterfactually be predicted to be -*ay*- (cf tb[sānǰʔa̠yxón]) or various coalescences (§11) thereof (close -*ē*- as in tb[rā́ðǰfȩ̄xón], open -*ǣ*- as in bb[sānǰʔǣ̠nā]), reflexes of *-*ay*- being the A encodation at large of participial mp /__object.[83]

Though there might be some scattered evidence of feminine participial suffixes being used in pin (see §17.17.2 <u>SM</u>), the usual importee appears to be mp /-ī(n)/, either as the sole constituent, qua subject, or qua component of more complex elements (e.g., in TR [ʔiθrā9ǰmı̣ttū́n] cited above). This being the case, pin-insertion is, apart from a few disguised surfacings in the defective verb (see §17.17.2 <u>TL</u>) or the (infrequent) appearance of -*ē* in intransitive auslaut (as in TL y[likkænnǰfḗ] above), primarily manifested by a straightforward reflex of /ī(n)/ containing a common denominator of shape [Ĭ], in transitives occurring between stem and (the remainder of) a pronominal suffix complex[84]—a manifestation that might lend itself to reinterpretation as a species of *bridge* (§2.3.2).[85] And against this backdrop, the process might conceivably join forces with the trp-driven spread of 1s allomorph -*ĬT*- to medial position (§15.2.2.2), whereupon -*Ĭ*- /stem__suffix would have lost its character as a mark of *plural* subject and have become (or be becoming) a mark of subject irrespective of number. And against *this* backdrop might be understood stray cases in at least TL, where -*Ĭ*- cooccurs with 2s subject, otherwise historically unjustified. See §17.17.2 <u>TL</u> for details (as well as a caveat).

The course of these developments is laid out in a simplified manner in (17.17A), where X = stem and Y = suffixal material, whether subjectival, objectival, or both concurrently. At stage I, some suffix complexes with mp subject commence in *Ŭ* (e.g., pf 3mp^obj) while others lack this vocalism (at least in anlaut position, e.g., pf 2mp^∅ or 2mp^obj); 1s^obj and 2(m)s^obj are largely syncretically homonymous (e.g., via syn (e) §16.2). At stage II, pin inserts *Ĭ* as anlaut in mp complexes (de facto replacing any anlaut *Ŭ*) and trp-instigated r-epn inserts *Ĭ* as anlaut to medial 1s.[86] At stage III, these *Ĭ*s metanalyze as bridges, as suggested by the grouping stem-bridge-suffix.[87] Finally, at stage IV, 2(m)s is drawn into the set of neobridgeful encodations. (The developments sketched in (17.17A) are by no means equable. While pin affects TR, SM, TL, and M, r-epn shows up only in TR and TL; and extension of bridge marking to 2(m)s affects TL alone, inchoatively at best.)[88]

(17.17A)	mp	1s	2(m)s
stage I	X-(Ŭ)Y	X-TY	X-TY
stage II	X-ĬY	X-ĬTY	X-TY
stage III	X-Ĭ-Y	X-Ĭ-TY	X-TY
stage IV	X-Ĭ-Y	X-Ĭ-TY	X-Ĭ-TY

17.17.2. The Individual Dialects; Synopsis

<u>TR</u>. pf 2mp [ʾiθrā9šmittū́n] (§17.17.1); impf 3mp^2ms [yiðbǎqinǽx], 3mp^1s [yiqtǎlīnǽnī] (Da 372), 3mp^3mp tb[wīsōðīnū́nnū́n], tb[yiqtǎlīnū́nnū́n] (Da 373) (note mitosed obj suffixes, [-ū́nnū́n], §13 <u>TR</u> (γ)).

<u>SM</u>. Clearly pin-derived are pf sim rmp 1p <ʾTrhs<u>nn</u>> t[itrēṣṣínnɑn] 'wir hoffen' (Macs 154) (t[...ēṣṣ...] ← smc(§22.1)...*Iḥṣ*... ← att (§12.2 <u>SM</u> (γ)) ...*aḥṣ*...) and impf sim 2mp^3mp <Tšw<u>y</u>nwn> ~ <TšB<u>y</u>nwn> 'ihr werdet sie anziehen' (Macs 234, 410) (for <yn> as intr participial mp, Macs 209; for <w> ~ <B> reflecting *w > b* in trad pron, §21.1 (21D)). Less certain are <Dʾnṣyr<u>y</u>n> t[dɑnṣírɑn] 'die sich untergeworfen haben' (Macs 145) as sim passive pf 3mp, and <ḥzy<u>ʾn</u>> ~ <ḥzy<u>ʾTh</u>> t[ā́zyɑn] ~ [āzyā́tɑ] 'sie(f) sahen' as sim active pf 3fp, since they may alternatively be genuine participles syntactically deployed in a fashion similar to perfectives (a possibility explicitly acknowledged by Macuch for the feminine forms, Macs 209). Should they be genuine instantiations of pin, however, the feminine forms are unique in showing importation of fp suffixes (note also absolute <-ʾn> t[-ɑn] ~ determined <-ʾTh> t[-ā́tɑ]).

<u>G</u>. cau pf 2mp <ʾrym<u>yTw</u>n> (Da 255) (hollow √rWm), 3mp^3mp <ʾšKh<u>yn</u>wn> (Da 367); cau impf 2mp^3mp <Tq(y)m<u>yn</u>wn> (Da 373). G is apparently the sole dialect to show extension of pin into the impa: sim mp

<ʔymwryn̲> (Da 301) (note likely promotion of *1√ʔə̆-* to [(ʔ)Ǐ-], §9.2.1.2, §9.3.1; and failure of *2 ʃU* to lower, §17.10)—hence [(ʔ)ǏmUrín̲], cau mp^3mp <ʔyyTy̲nwn> (Da 392). G may also show some extension of 1s participial <-nʔ> into pf, as demonstrated below for TL ((β) with n. 92); cf. Wajsberg 2006: 37f. with nn. 27, 28.

T̲L̲. TL shows the most robust incidence of pin, both in frequency of the garden variety (i.e., mp) (α) and in fielding novel extensions (β).

(α) pf int rmp 2mp y[ʔit̲t̲ællə̆līθ̲ǘ] (n. 84) a[ʔit̲t̲allə̆līθ̲ǘn̲] (Mar 117*), sim 1p <9Bry̲nn̲> a[9avrinán̲] (Mar 37 note β, 146*), int 1p y[9æyyə̆ninnǽn̲] (Mor 221), sim 2mp^3ms <TPs(y̲)Tw̲h̲> a[tafsīθ̲úah] (Mar 59, 179*) ([-úah] via pgn, §17.16), sim 1p^3ms <BDqy̲ny̲h̲> (Mar 59), sim 3mp^1s <ŝBqy̲n> a[šavqín̲] (Mar 58, 168*), sim 3mp^3mp y[kə̆ræxi̲nnð̆hú] (Mor 294) a[kə̆raxīnð̆hó] (Mar 126*), defective sim 3mp^3mp and 1p^3mp (by syncretism, §16.2 (d)) <ḥzn̲hw> a[ḥăzān̲(ə̆)hó] (Mar 59, 112*)[89] ← open coa n(§11.2) . . .*ayn* ← e-cnd (§8) . . .*a 3√y-īn*, sim 1p^3mp y[šæqli̲nnə̆hú](Mor 294) a[šaqli̲nð̆hó] (Mar 175*), sim 3mp^3fp <ḥzy̲nhy> (Mar 59) plausibly interpretable as c-a[ḥăzay̲n̲(ə̆)hé] (note that intransitive def mp participles in Ash trad pron may end in -mtr, -coa, +epn [-ayin] ~ -mtr, +coa [-ān] ~ +mtr, -coa [-ay] in addition to finite-imported ±mtr [-ō(n)], Mar 94*, 95*, 140*);[90] impf int plain 3mp a[lə̆xannə̆fí̲], int rmp 3mp y[likkænnə̆fé̲] (§17.17.1), int (plain) 3mp^3mp y[līræḥqi̲nnə̆hú] (Mor 301) a[nə̆zabbə̆nī̲nð̆hó] (Mar 108*), sim 3mp^3fp <nyKly̲nhy> (Mar 61) (√ʔkl; sar, §9.2.1.2).

(β) As intimated above (§17.17.1), TL shows a form or two that might be interpreted as witnessing inchoative extension of pin—*-Ǐ-* semantically bleached and metanalyzed as a bridge—to the singular: pf sim 2s^3fs <ʔmry̲Th> (Mar 59).[91] And the rudiments of a different sort of pin extension may be seen in pf int 1s y[pæyyésn̲ā̲], where the *singular* participial suffix *-n* appears on a finite stem.[92] Finally, the possibility that TL was beginning (?) to extend pin-propogataed *ĭ(n)* to a novel position is suggested by pf int 2mp^1s <sKnTy̲n> (Mar 58), presumably [sakkentí̲n],[93] which Margolis then proposes (Mar 142*) correcting to [sakkentű̲n] (*sakken-tű̲-n* 'endanger-2mp-1s').[94]

M̲. M is the dialect with the least showing of pin, only one form to date having come to light: impf sim 3mp^2mp <nihšabinakun> (~ -pin <nihišbu̲nkun>) (Nm 281), interpretable as [nehšăβi̲nă̲xón] or [nehšăβenn̲ă̲xón] (~ [nīhešBonxón]) (the variants also differ in -auf (unmarkedly /__plural object suffix) ~ +auf, §17.15.1, and in the presence in the first variant of a bridge vowel [ă] or [ā] which is lost in the second by smp, §17.26, [. . .onxón] ← . . .*onnă̆xón*).

The incidence for pin (exclusive of 1s *-nā*) over the five dialects is synoptized in (17.17B), where uppercase letters indicate occurrence in pf, plain lower case in impf, and primed lower case in impa.

To judge by the number of marks entered, TL shows the most robust profile of pin, and M the weakest—conclusions supported by the discussion above in the text. It is difficult to rank the remaining three dialects, short of noting them as intermediate:

TL ≫ TR, SM, G ≫ M.

Unsurprisingly, all but one attribution (and that questionable) occupy the right-hand side of the display, the side plotting plural subjects—and pin operates prototypically on mp.

Observe that the three heaviest-filled cells, 2mp^∅, 3mp^3mp, and 2mp^3mp, all have in common a *palatal-labial vowel sequencing* (e.g., TR [ˀiθrā9ӟmi̯ttṵ́n], TL [kӟræxi̱nnӟhṵ́], SM <Tšwy̲nw̲n>, G <ˀyyТy̲nw̲n>). At least in the transitive slots, this (possible) pattern might be abetted by a tendency to dissimilate . . . $\overset{\circ}{U}$ . . . $\overset{\circ}{U}$ . . . → . . . $\overset{\circ}{I}$ . . . $\overset{\circ}{U}$ . . .).

(17.17B)

sub=	3ms	3fs	2ms	2fs	1s	3mp	3fp	2mp	2fp	1p
obj: ∅						SM? tl	SM?	TR G TL g′		SM TL
3ms								TL		TL
3fs			TL?							
2ms						tr				
2fs										
1s						TL tr		TL?		
3mp						G TL tr tl		sm g g′		TL
3fp						TL tl				
2mp						m				
2fp										
1p										

17.18. Prothesis (pro)

17.18.1. Description and Illustration

Occasionally, in most or all dialects (at least O (noun only), B, TR, CP, SM, G, SR, TL, M), an initial group #CV̆C is transformed to #(ˀ)V̆CC, where V̆ will be said to be inserted by *prothesis* (pro). (For ˀ, see below.)

Since the process is critically conditioned by V̆, before the rise of reduction (§4.1) prothesis in the verb was essentially limited to the sim impa, by hypothesis of this book of original shape *QV̆SV̆M (§1.1.1 with n. 7). But perhaps due to deficiency of available textual material, we find no prothetical impas in the earliest dialects—though O does show a trace of pro in the nominal form <ʔŝm> 'Name' (De 42), one of a handful of biradical nouns often suspected of reflecting the unusual (and unstable) proto-Semitic canon **$Q\breve{V}M$ (or even vowelless **QM).[95] In any event, if <ʔŝm> should reflect O-vintage pro, it is likely to have been pronounced [ʔíŝmu] (in alternation with pro-free <sm> (lc), which plausibly spells [šúmu] or [šímu], where prm (§14.1) has applied as an alternative to pro in resolving the A-anomalous canon $Q\breve{V}M$). The pro-resolution <ʔŝm> moreover provides a bellwether for the (virtually) A-wide practice of spelling the prothesis with <ʔ>, a usage likely at least in the earlier period to represent a true phonetic [ʔ] ancillary to pro, thereby providing a canonically required onset—much, in fact, like the Arabic so-called *hamzatu 'l-waṣl*; cf. [ʔismu], fully cognate to O [ʔíŝmu], as reconstructed here ([s] is the regular Arabic reflex of pSemitic **ŝ). However, in the later dialects, after <ʔ> had become conventional for spelling prothesis, it may be questioned whether phonetic [ʔ] continued to be realized as a concomitant to pro, especially as dialects began to give evidence of ʔ-loss in other environments (§9.2.1, §9.3.2). Clearly, in a dialect like SR, where ʔ is traditionally assumed to have totally vanished as a phonetic reality, the use of <ʔ> in representing prothesis has become purely stylized historical spelling. The policy in this book will accordingly be to interpret pro phonetically in any of three ways, depending on assessment of ʔ-loss in the pertinent dialect: [#ʔV̊] (e.g., O), [#(ʔ)V̊] (e.g., G), [#V̊] (e.g., SR)—and of this group of transcriptions the default will be [#(ʔ)V̊], bespeaking uncertainty as to whether pro-induced <ʔ> has actual phonetic substance.

The prothetic $\breve{V}$ is to some extent in all dialects, indeed perhaps exclusively in most dialects, realized as palatal [I]—though at least SM and perhaps TL also variably show prothetic [A]. The fact that these two vowels, in the order [I] ≫ [A], coincide with the pattern seen in various promotions of $\breve{V}$, e.g., as part of Aufsprengung (§4.4.1), suggests that prothesis itself may have taken the primary form of reduced vowel insertion, the results then being secondarily promoted to full vowel status: i.e., $\#C\breve{V}C \rightarrow \#(\?)\breve{V}CC$ prm $\rightarrow \#(\?)\mathring{V}CC$.

Examples of pro from the dialects:

B. [ʔištíw] 'sie tranken' (BL 155) ← *šəθíw* < e-cnd (§8.1.1) *šatíyū (note the accordion effect, *t* spr > θ reo > *t*; §5.2 B (α)).

TR. Though Dalman adduces no instances of pro for TR, Macuch (Macs 207) cites (tb)[ʔištíθī] 'I drank' from the Onkelos Targum. (The form is tentatively prefaced here with "tb" since Macuch presents it in Tiberian orthography, but he may simply be using such as a vehicle of transcription.)

CP. As in B and TR (as well as all other dialects with the apparent exception of M), instances from √šty 'drink': sim pf 3fs and 3mp, <ʔŝTT>, <ʔŝTw>;

sim impa mp <ʾyšTw> (Sg 72f). The modus operandi of ymn in CP (§14.2) strongly suggests that pro-correlative <ʾ> is purely graphological.

<u>SM</u>. With prothetic [I]: e.g., <ʾmṭy> t[ímṭi] 'ist nahegekommen' (Macs 214), hence [(ʾ)imṭî]; similarly <ʾrTy> t[írti] 'erbarme dich!', <ʾrmy> t[érmi] 'wirf!' (Macs 215)—and the plural corresponding to the latter t[írmu] 'werfet!', spelled <hrmw> (Macs 209) (with ml <h>, unusual in A at large for marking prothesis but not unusual in SM where weakening and ultimate loss of the gutturals (§9.3.2) has led to widespread (apparently) free variation among guttural letters in ml function); <ʾTqP> t[étqəf] 'wurde stark' (~ nonprothetic <TqyP> t[téqɑf]) (Macs 144).

With prothetic [A]: e.g., t[ǽrti], t[ǽrmi], t[ǽtqɑf] as variants to forms just cited; also <ʾšTT> t[ǽstɑt] 'sie trank' (Macs 206), <ʾrKn> t[ǽrkɑn] 'demütigte sich' (Macs 144).

Macuch (lc) considers several t[æ]-prothetic forms to be cases of "formalen Wandel zum Afel." But while this may de facto be so given the de facto merger of t[æ-] by pro and by inheritance from cau *ʾa- (and/or < ha-, §9.1.2), before concurring with him we would have to examine other factors—e.g., whether lexically t[ɑ] < 2ʃ i is justified in the corresponding sim forms, as it is structurally in the cau. (It would also be nice to run across conclusive evidence of formal merger with cau, e.g., participial t[m-].) But if it should turn out that *all* presumed cases of prothetic t[æ-] actually do constitute change of formal allegiance to cau, we might have to reassess the claim that any such a thing as [A]-prothesis exists at all in the Aramaic verb. (Cf. also <u>TL</u> below.)

<u>G</u>. <ʾyšTy> ~ <ʾyšTh> 'er trank' (Da 337), [(ʾ)IšTî] ~ [(ʾ)IšTǽ]; for ml <-h> [-ā]. In lieu of more frequent <-ʾ>, cf. equally prothetic sim pf 3ms <ʾyB9h> ~ nonprothetic <B9ʾ> (lc); <ʾyzmr> 'schnitt' (Da 94).[96]

<u>SR</u>. Only √šty, e.g., sim pf 3ms [ɛštî], sim impa ms [ɛštáy] (Malone 1974a: 5).

<u>TL</u>. From √šty, e.g.: <ʾ(y)šTw> (~ -pro <šTw>) 'trinket!' (Mar 54), a[ʾištēθéh] 'I drank it' (Mar 176*), y[ʾišθî] 'šata' (Mor 251 with n. 7)—there is also a variant reading [ʾæštî], which Morag (lc) interprets as a shift to cau but might rather instantiate [A]-prothesis (cf. above). A few (orthographic) examples from other roots: <ʾyšTyq> (~ <šTyq>) 'he was silent' (Mar 31), <ʾynṭr> (~ <nṭr>) 'guard!', <ʾymṣy> 'he could' (Mar 52).

<u>M</u>. <eptalH> [ePTālî], <eptulia> [ePTollî], respectively, 'they opened for him, for me' (Mal 356) (*√pth after *ḥ > Ø (§9.3.2), both forms probably subsequently metanalyzed to as 3√ /y/ (§9.2.4), though derivation without this recourse is likewise possible; observe also the variation in the pp-suffixed signal of 3mp subject, unambiguously encoded in the case of [ePTollî], de facto

syncretic with 3ms in the case of [ePTā̆lī́] (see §17.15 n. 79); and note the homonymy of the pp shape [-lī́], either ≤ 1s *-lī́ or < 3ms *-lī́h. Observe too that
the trad pron of <šma> ~ <šuma> (sco, §17.23) 'he heard' is prothetic t[éšmā]
despite the absence of orthographic cue (Macm 124).

17.18.2. Theoretical Issues

Aramaic prothesis implies a few ramifications of interest and, maybe,
puzzles for linguistic theory.

First of all, if the examples culled from the various dialects are pooled,
they fall into two major groups and one minor residual group. One of the major groups comprises roots wuth sibilant 1√, predominantly 1√š (√šty (first
and foremost), √štq, √šry, √šm9, √šty, √zmr). A subset of this group, those
roots with 1√Σ 2√Ŧ (sibilant-dentoalveolar stop) are susceptible to a theory
developed in Malone 1999 for similar but not identical phenomena in M morphophonology, a theory in particular attempting to answer the question of why
there may be a special proclivity for Σ and Ŧ to cluster. Adapted to the issue at
hand, an account of 1√Σ 2√Ŧ prothesis would run as follows, based on a sketch
example of the sim pf 3ms por sim impa ms. Substituting 1√Σ and 2√Ŧ into
QSM, a form *#ΣV̆ŦV̊M#* will contain a quasi cluster of Σ and Ŧ. But the mutual
bonding power between Σ and Ŧ (as measured in terms of shared features and
modeled by plotting a given shared feature only *once*, and linking it to each
manifesting segment by association lines) is so strong that a mere weak reduced vowel (an inert element, in the sense of Malone 1995) cannot withstand
the bonding pressure squeezing it between Σ and Ŧ (a pressure modeled by
increasing the number of "wedged" association lines), with the consequence
that it, V̆, is extruded (deleted), which leads to the creation of a true cluster at
the beginning of *#ΣŦV̊M#*.[97] However, since Aramaic syllabic canons disal-
low anlaut clusters, pro applies as a repair strategy effecting resyllabification
as in (17.18A):

(17.18A)

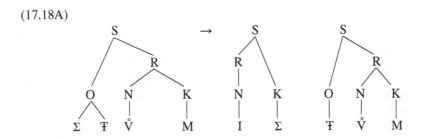

Whereas this technique may work unadulterated for roots like √šty, √štq,
and √šty, it would have to be modified to accommodate the like of √šry, √šm9,
and √zmr, since otherwise 2√ would contain too few features in common with

$1\sqrt{}$ to effect sufficient "wedging" to extrude $\ensuremath{\breve{V}}$. While some recent soundings in the phonological literature touching on special clustering properties for sibilants (e.g., Hall 2002) lend hope to success for such modification, the second— and larger—group of pro-attested roots is quite different indeed. This sample, $\sqrt{}$nsm, $\sqrt{}$ngb, $\sqrt{}$nbq, $\sqrt{}$nsr, $\sqrt{}$ntr, $\sqrt{}$mty, $\sqrt{}$msy, $\sqrt{}$rkn, and $\sqrt{}$rmy, will be argued to comprise onset clusters that violate the so-called *Sonorancy Hierarchy* for syllabic well-formedness, according to which sequencing outward from the syllabic nucleus, whether progressively through the coda or, as here, regressively through the onset, consonants must monotonically decrease in sonority. That the roots just listed fail this requirement may be read off the version of the Sonorancy Hierarchy given in (17.18B), arranged specifically for onsets:[98]

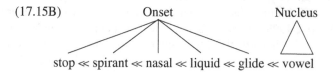

(17.15B)   Onset   Nucleus

stop ≪ spirant ≪ nasal ≪ liquid ≪ glide ≪ vowel

In terms of (17.18B), four of the ten roots flaunt the hierarchy because a less sonorant stop intervenes between the nucleus and a more sonorant nasal ($\sqrt{}$ngb, $\sqrt{}$nbq, $\sqrt{}$ntr, $\sqrt{}$mty—e.g., for the moment ignoring the ∂, in *mə̆ṭî́* 'approached', where nucleic *î* is adjacent to the stop *ṭ*, which is less sonorant than the nasal *n*), while in the case of three roots a nasal is separated from the nucleus by a spirant ($\sqrt{}$nšm, $\sqrt{}$nṣr, $\sqrt{}$mṣy); in two, the infringement is of stop ≪ liquid ($\sqrt{}$rkn, $\sqrt{}$rty), while in the last case, the violation is of spirant ≪ nasal ($\sqrt{}$mṣy).[99]

Of course, all this discussion of $1\sqrt{}$ $2\sqrt{}$ clusters violating the Sonorancy Hierarchy must reconcile with the fact that in our focal frame, $Q\ensuremath{\breve{V}}S\ensuremath{\breve{V}}M$, $1\sqrt{}$ and $2\sqrt{}$ do not officially form a cluster, being separated by $\ensuremath{\breve{V}}$. However, the hypothesis to be gingerly launched here is that even as $\ensuremath{\breve{V}}$ in the case of $1\sqrt{}\Sigma$ $\ensuremath{\breve{V}}$ $2\sqrt{}T$ groups is too weak to preventthe natural attraction of the flanking radicals from bonding (in "wedges"), so here $\ensuremath{\breve{V}}$ *is too weak to forestall a clustering violation of the Sonorancy Hierarchy*. That is, in languages with a certain typology of reduced vowels, as Aramaic, a group $C\ensuremath{\breve{V}}C$ will constitute what may be called a *semicluster*, and semi-clusters may react like full clusters with respect to some, though probably not all, syllabic constraints.

In reaction, then, to the violation of the Sonorancy Hierarchy so incurred, the offending $Q\ensuremath{\breve{V}}S$ semi-cluster is dispelled by prothetically aided resyllabification to $(\ensuremath{{}^{\ensuremath{\text{?}}}})\ensuremath{\breve{V}}QS$, where Q now functions as coda to the prothetic $\ensuremath{\breve{V}}$ and S remains the sole (hence nonviolative) segment of the original onset.[100]

Finally, the "minor residual group" of prothetic forms sampled for the corpus involves a handful of roots whose $1\sqrt{}$ $2\sqrt{}$, $1\sqrt{}$ being other than a sibilant, either plot the same on the Sonorancy Hierarchy (waiving spr, n. 99) ($\sqrt{}$tqp, $\sqrt{}$ptʔ), or plot differently but in conformity ($\sqrt{}$dlq, $\sqrt{}$b9y). No specific rationale will be proffered here for forms built on these roots undergoing pro; perhaps with the sibilant and sonorancy factors as bellwethers, pro began to shed its specific role as a repair strategy and became a sound change sui generis.

17.19. Prefix Replacement (prp)

17.19.1. Jussive-Precative prp (j-prp); Nasalizing prp (n-prp)

In addition to or in lieu of phonetic reflexes of proto-Semitic *y- as third personal impf preformative (always masculine in the singular, usually epicene in the plural), some Aramaic dialects show *l*- and/or *n*-. Moreover, when *l*- alternates with *n*- in this function, there is sporadic extension of the alternation into the first person plural, a syncretism evidently motivated by the homonymy between the newfangled third person *n*- with the *n*- inherited from pSemitic as preformative for the first person plural. The general process will be referred to as *prefix replacement* (prp), the specific manifestations as *jussive-precative prp* (j-prp; see below for justification of the label) and *nasalizing prp* (n-prp). One tack on the overall development is laid out in flowchart (17.19A):

(17.19A)   **I**   >   **II**   >   **III**   >   **IV**

3:   y-   l-   l- ~ n- ⎫

                                    ⎬   l- ~ n-

1p: n-   n-   -n ⎭

Note how II > III implies that *l*- is earlier than *n*- in third person value and allows the further possibility that *n*- somehow developed from *l*-. It is in fact customary to assume that *n*- did develop from *l*-, though there is no consensus on the specific mechanism involved. As concerns antecedent *y*- > *l*-, on the other hand, it is widely and probably correctly assumed that this change started as a pattern generalization from an ancient jussive-precative conjugation where the third person (short) impf was prefixed by *l- either preceding or replacing *y- (both patterns are in fact attested, e.g., in Arabic and Akkadian, respectively). In any event, such jussive-precative force—or more generally nonveridical force—is still strongly evident in G, where it never wanes (e.g., jussive <ḻym²> 'er sage' vs. indicative <γym²>; Da 264, 300) and appears as far back as Y (<PḺKTŝh> 'und er soll ihn . . . zerschmettern', DR I 214:31). On the other hand, there seems to be no trace of the presumed original nonveridical force in the other dialects where *l*- appears: B, only in the copular verb √hwy ([lɛhɛ̆wḗ], [lɛhɛ̆wṓn], [lɛhɛwyṓn]); TL, as the statistically favored choice over frequent *n*- and residual *y*- (e.g., <ḻyzyl> ~ <n̲yzyl> ~ <γyzyl> 'he'll go', Mar 38);[101] and M, as an occasional alternative to the predominant *n*- (e.g., [ḻešlóm] 'ist vollendet', Nm 216).

As stated, the dialects showing *l-* ~ *n-* for third person **y-* also show sporadic extension of *l-* ~ *n-* into the 1p slot: e.g., TL a[lǎqaddém] ~ [nǎqaddém] 'we'll anticipate' (Mar 158*), M [līyaðkár] 'wir wollen nennen' (Nm 216).[102]

It is also likely that the trajectory sketched in (17.19A) had one more stage, V, where the syncretic (3, 1p) alternation *l-* ~ *n-* is ironed out in favor of *n-*; see (17.19B). Though M comes near to achieving this result, the only dialect to fully generalize *n-* as the prefix for both 3 and 1p is (Classical) SR: e.g., [nɛddá9] (B 93) on √yd9 'know' (for the geminate [dd], see §17.7).[103]

(17.19B)   **I**   >   **II**   >   **III**   >   **IV**   >   **V**

  3:   y-   l-   l- ~ n- ⎫

                 ⎬   l- ~ n-   -n

  1p: n-   n-   -n ⎭

17.20. *put* Causativization (ptc)

Minimally, two and as many as four dialects show at least some development of their reflexes of **√śWm* 'put' as formal causatives under semantic-syntactic conditions where other dialects use the simple conjugation.

TR. Uncertain. While Jastrow (1903: 1535) lists only simple forms (for the Targum Onkelos), Dalman (1938: 286) lists in addition to explicit simple (tb) [tǎsúm] (Lev 19:14) "*Aph.* Vorlegen" unexemplified and without reference to text or (as follows) dialect/register.

CP. With the tell-tale causative prefix <ʔ->, cf. <ʔsym> 'er legte', <ʔsymT> 'ich legte' (Sg 69f.).

SM. Macuch plausibly lists <ʔšym> t[ã̌šəm] 'ich werde legen > vermehren' as a causative (Macs 196), but the possibility cannot be excluded that is is actually a simple form, < **ʔaśīmi*, trapped out in the ablaut pattern **a. . .i (ī)* (§1.1.1 n. 6) with the color of **a* post-reductionally maintained through sco by inheritance (§17.23.3). (Unfortunately, Macuch cites no examples of hollow impf simples with **2ʃī* from other roots. He does cite <ʔmwT> t[ḗmot], where the palatality of the prefix vowel reflects *either* **a-* > red not subject to sco and emerging from the smc (§22.1) as [ē-], *or* **a-* > *i-* by generalized (open-syllabic) attenuation (cf. §12.2 SM (α)). But whatever the true account of the prefixal coloring here might be, this is a **2ʃ ū* verb, and we just can't be sure that the SM ablaut patterns developed for these in the same way as for **2ʃ ī* lexemes.)

M. Drower and Macuch list a medley of simples and causatives (DM 321); note, e.g., simple <samilH> 'I put on him' ([samellī̌]), causative <asimit> 'I put' (either [assǎmī̌θ] or [asīmī̌θ], §6.2.1.1).[104]

17.21. Regressive *n*-Assimilation (rna); *l*-Assimilation (las)

17.21.1. Regressive *n*-Assimilation (rna)

The primary manifestation of rna is total contact assimilation of 1√n to 2√: B sim impf 3ms [yippél] (Dan 3:6) < **yanpíli*; TR cau rmp impf 3ms [yittæppǽq] (Da 297) < **yithanpíqi*; SM cau <ˀPq> t[ǽbbəq] 'bring heraus!' (Macs 98) <*hanpíq; SR [ɛppóq] 'ich werde ausgehen' (ns 110); TL <ˀṮn> 'I'll give' y[ˀættén] a[ˀɛttén] (Mor §8.12; Mar 39, 139*); M <apiq> 'bring out!' [appéq], cf. Modern [áffeq] (Macm 294f).

There is evidence for rna in just about all A dialects (N may be an exception, Cg 81), where, moreover, with two apparent exceptions, it is variable. The apparent exceptions are Y and O, where the process seems to be categorical;[105] and while it is not impossible for a linguistic process to weaken from categorical to variable, the normal direction is the other way around, so that taking Y and O as linearly ancestral to the remaining dialects would commit us to accepting—without supporting evidence—an unusual developmental nexus.[106] But since, on the basis of considerations distinct from rna, Y and O have already been taken to be developmentally independent from the rest of A (§17.8 especially (17.8C); §17.15 especially n. 64a), the uncomfortable conclusion of a categorical > variable chain will be obviated by adopting the trajectory in (17.21A):[107]

(17.21A)   pA *variable rna*

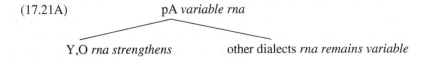

Y,O *rna strengthens*   other dialects *rna remains variable*

The question has frequently arisen in the literature as to whether *1*√*n* is capable of being assimilated by 2√ under rna, the issue presumably being that glides (Γ) may be articulatorily too weak, or have too impoverished a position of articulation, to spread to an immediately preceding consonant. Of course, not all linguistic changes with ostensible phonetic content are phonetic processes sensu stricto. They are frequently *copy-cat* changes, analogically motivated, such that, typically, a primary phonetic change *X > Y/Z* is imitated—or even continued—by a successor analogical change *X > Y/Z**, where *Z** represents a widening or generalization of original condition *Z*—special cases of reprise changes ("imitated") or (the second half of) persistent changes ("continued"), respectively. In the present case, instances of *1*√*n > Γ'/__Γ'* would, so interpreted, constitute widening of the original conditions, say /__*F'* where *F'* = a full-blown (true) consonant—that is, one with a strongly contoured oral position of articulation, now generalized to include glides, which lack this property. Using features, the generalization would be from /__[-syllabic, + consonantal] to /__[-syllabic,{+consonantal, -consonantal}] which factors to /__[-syllabic].

So the possibility of $1\sqrt{n} > \Gamma'/\_\_\Gamma'$ can by no means be ruled out a priori by appeal to phonetic factors, no matter how cogent such factors might be when considered in strictly phonetic space. And in any event, there is already at least one well-documented case of total regressive assimilation by gutturals (= non-oral glides)—namely, eclipsis of the rmp prefix *T* by $1\sqrt{H}$, at least variably, in most late dialects (rrf, §10).

Turning now specifically to rna, once an interfering factor has been side-tracked, only very few clear cases of $1\sqrt{n} > \mathit{T}/\_\_\Gamma'$ remain, cases like SR [nɛh(h)ów] 'ist mager', [nɛh(h)áz] 'stosst' (contrast -rna [nɛnhám] 'brullt') (B 89, Ns 21). The interfering factor is the apparent widespread (and early) occurrence of rna is the root √nht 'descend': e.g, I <yh̬Twn> 'sie steigen hinab' (L 57), B cau impf 2ms [tah(h)éθ] (Ezra 6:5), TR cau rmp pf 3ms [ʾittæh(h)ǽθ] (Da 297), CP <yh̬wT> 'steigt hinab' (Sg 61), SM <yyʕT> t[yiyyǽt] 'er steigt herab' (Macs 186) (for *ḥ > <9> t[∅], §9.3.2), G sim impf 3ms <yyh̬wT> (Da 292), SR [nɛh(h)óθ] (B 84), TL cau impf 1p y[næh̬éθ] a[nah(h)éθ] (Mor §8.14, Mar 136*), M [neh(h)óθ] 'he goes down' (<nih̬ut> t[néh̬oθ]) (Macm 50).

However, not all verb forms presumed to be built on √nht fit so easily into this scheme of things. Notably, the B cau impa ms [ʾăh̬éθ] (Ezra 5:15) and the TR cau pf 3ms [ʾǎh̬éθ] (Da 295) could only derive from *hanḥît(a) if a chain rna^mls (§9.3.1), making for nḥ > ḥḥ > ḥ, fed (r-)red and so justified prefixal a → [V̆]. But, by the testimony of the forms we have just seen in the preceding paragraph (and others like them), this is improbable. A more likely explanation is that forms like B [ʾǎh̬éθ], TR [ʾǎh̬éθ] derive not from √nht but from a doublet root √ht—cf. Arabic ḥatta 'fall (of leaves)' (Brockelmann 1928: 424, DM 292)—caught in the sway of the geminate-hollow metaplasm so common in the causative (§6). In that case, froms like [ʾăh̬éθ], [ʾǎh̬éθ] would derive immediately by r-red from ʾaḥÍT, where the singleton ḥ stems not from the phonetic process mls but from a metaplastic (restructuring) operation with the teleology of narrowing the gap between cau geminates (canonical -AQQIM-after gmf-4u, §3.2 (3M)) and hollows (canonical -AQÍM-). This hypothesis has the advantage of independent motivation, in that both dialects show other symptoms of geminate-hollow metaplasm in the causative.[108]

17.21.2. *l*-assimilation (las)

Two seemingly maverick root assimilations, both widespread in A, have been related to rna in an interesting way by Kutscher (1970: 21). Both cases involve total contact assimilation of √l, regressive in one instance (√lqh 'take', -V*lq*V*ḥ*- → -V*qq*V*ḥ*-), progressive in the other (√slq 'ascend', -V*sl*V*q*- → -V*ss*V*q*-); both will be subsumed here under the rubric *l-assimilation* (las). Kutscher proposes that las copies rna on a semantic basis, in that 'take' and 'ascend' are antonyms to 'give' (+rna √ntn) and 'descend' (+rna √nht), respectively; and that out of lexical-semantic solidarity las followed the lead of rna in bringing it about that both lexical pairs be characterized by pf–impf alternation of shape *QVSVM – VQQVM / VSSVM.* (But since both model verbs, √ntn and √nḥt, undergo rna in the same direction, why does only √lqḥ follow suit while √slq reverses direction to *-VssVq-* rather than rendering @-*VllVq-* as might be expected? And is the idea tarnished at all by the fact that SR shows evidence of las-like *zl* → *zz* in the case of *lˁzl* 'go', e.g., sim impf 3mp [nēzzū́n] (B 18), despite absence of the semantic underpinning enjoyed by ostensibly similar albeit reverse *sl* → *ss* in the case of √slq? Observe also that the presumed model verb √ntn is not attested in O—though Kutscher proposes that its absence from extant texts may be merely accidental; 1970: 48.)

Behavior of the individual dialects vis-à-vis las is summarized in (17.21B) (blank = (relevant forms of) root not attested; + = only *VQQVM / VSSVM* attested; ± = *VQQVM / VSSVM* ~ *VQSVM*).

(17.21B)	√**slq**	√**lqḥ**
Y		+
O	+	±
I		±
B	+ [109]	
P	+ [110]	
N		
TR	+	
CP	±	
SM	+	
G	+	
SR	+	
TL	±	
M	+ [109]	

17.22. Short Apocope (sap)

Short apocope (sap) refers to the dropping of short unstressed auslaut vowels, in the verb system specifically of desinential **-i* (notably: per se indicative suffix of the light long impf; component of ancipitally short 2fs pf **-ti*) or **-a* (in impf perhaps limited to componency in heavy suffixes **-înna,* **-ŭnna, *-ånna*; in pf per se as 3ms subject marker, and otherwise component in such as ancipitally short 3ms **-ta,* 2fp **-tinna*). As detailed in §2.3.2, sap is by hypothesis critical in the metanalysis of word-internal alternants of such instances of **i, *a* to the status of *bridges* (bridge formation, brf), the basic idea being—most clearly in the case of morpheme-coterminous impf indicative **i* and pf 3ms **a*—that loss of auslaut manifestation (by sap) increased beyond a critical threshold uncertainty as to the function of the remaining inlaut tokens and so led to their being definitively reinterpreted from full suffixal elements on morphological-semantic par with other suffix components, to quasi-suffixal characteristically asemantic markers mediating (bridging) between stem and suffix complex proper or between constituents of the suffix complex proper; see (17.22A), where S = stem, D = desinence (auslaut suffix), $V = i$ or a before brf, B = (reflexes of) i or a after brf, and X = (beginning of) inlaut suffix:[111]

(17.22A)	I	sap >	II	brf >	III
intr	S-(X)V#		S-(X)#		S-(X)#
tr	S-(X)VD#		S-(X)VD#		S-(X-)B-D#

sap also plays a central role in the development, or more properly *non*development, of epenthesis (§17,6), a process that effectively mutates encodation of the pf 2s ≠ 1s opposition from one of differential suffixation of the former (*-ta, *-ti ≠ *-t) to differential canonization (quasi-infixational) of the latter (-T ≠ -IT; in some dialects subsequently enhanced by late-ancipital lengthening, §2.3.1: -T ≠ -ĪT); see the illustration in (17.22B):[112]

(17.22B)		**2ms**	**2fs**	**1s**
		QaSáMta	QaSáMti	QaSáMt
epn		—	—	QaSáMit
+r-o-str		—	—	QaSaMít ~ QaSáMit
sap		QaSáMt	QaSáMt —	
(other changes)				

examples: B [9ăváðt] TR [9ŏvǽðt] B bb[9æνðéθ]~[9ắvǽðiθ]

17.23. Schwa Coloring (sco)

Aramaic reduced vowels (V̌), or schwas in the broad sense, may come in a variety of colors, as for instance represented by (but not necessarilty limited to) the so- called *ḥataf vowel* graphemes (§21.5); e.g., Tiberian < ĕ, ă, ɔ̆ > signal schwas with open mid palatal, low, and open mid labial coloring, respectively. The family of patterns and processes making for such coloration will be generically called *schwa coloring* (sco).[113]

sco comes in three varieties: sco *by inheritance* (the schwa has such-and-such color from the start or maintains the color of a full vowel upon reduction); sco *by assimilation* (spreading) from an environing segment; and sco *by default* (the dialect provides a "designated" color).

Before further discussing the ins and outs of sco, it will be useful to set forth two excursuses in §17.23.1.

17.23.1. Two Excursuses

17.23.1.1. The Identity of ɔ̆

There are basically two polar traditional positions on the nature of ɔ̆, the vowel represented, inter alia, by the supralinear slant stroke grapheme of the

Babylonian pointing system, in this book transcribed <ə̆>, and by the grapheme known as *šĕva na9* 'mobile schwa' in the Tiberian tradition, in this book transcribed < : > and assigned phonetic value (vs. < : > qua *šĕva naḥ* 'quiescent schwa'). The two positions, not always explicitly articulated, are that (α) ə̆ represents a unitary phoneme (or phone), likely to be identified as a mid central unrounded vowel, or alternatively that (β) ə̆ is an umbrella symbol for a family of sounds determinable by phonetic environment (and presumably immediately available to the native or at least competent speaker/reader without conscious calculation). The view tentatively adopted in this book combines aspects of both these positions. Compositely over the dialects, ə̆ will be taken to represent a balance between two norms, one *palatal* and the other *low*, the palatal manifestation being along the lines of a slightly centralized unrounded open mid front vowel—representable as [ɛ̆] (cf. Tiberian hataf segol <ɛ̆>) or [ĕ], the choice depending on the cardinality of the hosting vowel system, §20.2 (20H, I, J)—while the low realization was probably central (perhaps a tad farther back than the vowel signaled by Tiberian hataf pataḥ, <ă>, the color being pretty much that of IPA [ɐ]). Though there may well be dialect differences, most types of Aramaic likely sport both these norms, most again in accord with the ranking [ɛ̆] ≫ [ă]. At the same time, however, allophony deviating from ɛ̆ ~ ă seems here and there to be in evidence along the lines of position (β); e.g., high [ĭ] may appear in various palatal environments.

An unresolved issue concerns the relation of the presumed phoneme ə̆, along with its palatal/low norms and family of allophones, to the vowels represented by the *hataf* graphemes, most notably Tiberian <ɛ̆, ă, ə̆>. Do the hatafim represent *V̆*-realizations *internally* (phonetically) distinct from those of various allophones of implicitly subsumed under graphemes like <ə̆>, < : >? Or are the hatafim only *externally* different, i.e., in distribution? This issue, not to be resolved in this book, is quite similar to that posed for Tiberian Hebrew in regard to its reduced vowel system; cf. THP 88–90. Throughout, the general policy will be to treat ə̆ as an irreducible, appealing (indirectly) to its internal structure only under special circumstances, as when discussing the color of full vowels promoted from reduced (§14.1).[114] On the other hand, hataf-correlative reduced vowels like ɛ̆, ă, ə̆ will be explicitly treated in terms of their overt color.

17.23.1.2. The Specter of *Schematisierung*

To judge by the orthographic representations, two registers across distinct dialects exhibit suspiciously close patterns of sco resolution—a situation all the more suspicious in that the *trans*-dialectal registers showing the similarity are more similar in their sco behavior mutually than they are to their fellow *intra*-dialectal registers. This nexus is sketched in the diagram of (17.23A), where the Tiberian register of B deploys a form of sco (call it sco2) quite similar to that of Ashkenazic TL, while the forms of sco found in Babylonian B and Yemeni TL stand apart (sco1, sco3).

(17.23A)

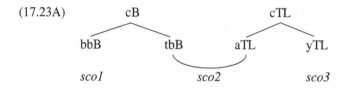

It is plausible that the apparent developmental anomalies of (17.23A) betray genuine linguistic correspondences being warped by *orthographic Schematisierung* (cf. also §11.1 n. 1). No concerted effort will be made to isolate specific effects, but it will be wise to keep this possibility of Schematisierung in mind while the ins and outs of sco for the dialects are considered; especially in §17.23.3. But first some more general detail on the three modes of sco—inheritance, assimilation, and default.

17.23.2. Description

The pattern sco by *inheritance* is a null case, in that $\check{V}$ in this circumstance does not gain or change color but rather maintains whatever color it already has, whether this color is inherent (lexical) or has been imparted by some process other than sco itself; e.g., Tib B sim impa [ʾắxúlī], [ʾɛ̆már] where [ắ], [ɛ̆] manifest the first terms of the *low*-labial and *palatal*-low ablaut sequences characteristic of the (original) sim impa system (§1.1.1 n. 6), or SM sim pf t[Qɑ̆̄SɑM] promoted from *Qɑ̆́SáM* by smc (§22.1) where the color of reduced 1ʃ ă reflects *1ʃ a characteristic of the pf (all binyanim).

In sco by *assimilation* (spreading) from an environing segment, the segment imparting its color may be an adjacent consonant, occasionally /__C (labial in the case of M [šŬmắ] 'he heard', DM 469, palatal in B bb[lihwĭyắn] 'seien sie(f)', BL 161) but more frequently /C__ where C = guttural—and where moreover sco is usually ambiguous between inheritance and assimilation (e.g., B sim pf 3ms [9ă̆váð] < *1ʃ a or impf 3ms^2mp [yiš̌ʾắlɛnxṍn] < *2ʃ a, BL 173, 177) but not always (e.g., B sim impa mp [hă̆wṍ] ~ inheritance-derived [hɛ̆wṍ], BL 161). When not adconsonantally driven, sco by assimilation is vowel-driven in /$\check{V}$H__, that is, the preceding short vowel assimilates $\check{V}$ right through the (porous, transparent) guttural, e.g., B sim impf 3fs [tɛhɛ̆wɛ̄̆]. (Note that *vowel*-driven sco /$\check{V}$H__ takes precedence over *consonant*-driven sco /H__. While this could be captured by tightening the environment of the latter to /{$\bar{V}$,C,#}H__, simpler /H__ can be maintained by appealing to the so-called *Elsewhere Condition*, Kenstowicz 1993: 217, 220, whereby of two rule conditions in an inclusion relation, the syntagmatically *including* condition—here /$\check{V}$H__—takes precedence over the *included* condition—here /H__.)[115]

The pattern sco *by default* occurs in lieu of an inherited or assimilated value when a dialect chooses, so to speak, what is sometimes called a "designated" color for the job. The designated color may, in turn, be idiosyncratic or system-wide. A possible example of idiosyncratic default sco is *a* as value of reduced 2ʃ in B sim pf [tiqăfáθ]'sie wurde übermütig' (Dan 5:20).[116] System-wide default sco in probably all A dialects is ŏ. This might be (but need not be, §17.23.1.1) the same thing as saying that sco fails to apply; and if only for the sake of expository ease, it will be the general policy in this book not to mention sco in the derivation of [ŏ]—i.e., to take the view that sco by system-wide default is the same thing as sco failing to apply.

Some high points of sco in the various dialects and traditions will now be presented in §17.23.3.

17.23.3. The Individual Dialects

Tiberian: Tib B, Ash TL. The similarity between these two systems prompts at least some suspicion of orthography-based Schematisierung, as discussed in §17.23.1.2. However, when one resists the temptation toward beguilement by the superficial gestalt of the common Tiberian writing system and its conventional "spelling rules," the actual similarity is seen to be concentrated in a few shared major patterns. And yet the perception of the similarity, whether attributable to Schematisierung (as seems likely) or to genuinely shared linguistic developments, is considerably enhanced by the differences that each of these registers/traditions manifests from its genetic sister register/tradition. That is, the perception of a special bond of some sort between Tiberian B and Ashkenazic TL is magnified by the differences between Tiberian B and Babylonian B; and the same perception is enhanced again by the differences between Ashkenazic and Yemeni TL.

The focal similarity between Tib B and Ash TL appears to reside in the sharing of two quite general rules of progressive-assimilatory sco, as well as certain crucial processes feeding one of these sco rules fore and fed by it aft. The two rules are *advocalic* assimilation (through a porous guttural) of $\check{V}$ to $\check{V}'$ /$\check{V}'H$__ and *adconsonantal* assimilation of $\check{V}$ to ă /$\{\bar{V},C,\#\}H$__. Stated comprehensively, these two processes boil down to saying that a schwa ($\check{V}$) immediately following a guttural (H) will pick up the color of any short vowel immediately preceding the guttural (V'), or in the absence of such a vowel—that is, when the guttural is immediately preceded by a long vowel, consonant, or the front edge of the word ($\bar{V}$, C, $\#$)—will pick up the (low) color of the guttural itself. Thus: tbB *lɛhăwṓn* → [lɛhŭwṓn] (BL 161), aTL *tɛhăwḗ* → [tɛhŭwḗ], where ŏ absorbs the color of ɛ through the transparent guttural *h*; *dɔ̄hă̆lī́n* → [dɔ̄hă̆lī́n] in both registers/traditions (BL 176, Mar 102*), ŏ where lowers to [ă] following the guttural *h*, which, though preceded by a vowel, is preceded by a *long* vowel rather than by the requisite short; tbB [ʾiθ9ă̆qárɔ̄]and aTL [liθ9ă̆véð] (BL 134, Mar 145*) display the assimilans guttural (9) preceded by a consonant (θ); and in tbB [ʾă̆zál], [hă̆qém], [hă̆zɔ̄́] (BL 175), aTL [ʾă̆zál], [hă̆ðár], [hă̆zɔ̄́] (Mar 85*, 105*, 112*), the guttural effecting the assimilation is in word-initial position.

The shared sco subprocess $\overset{\circ}{V}'H\overset{\circ}{V} \rightarrow \overset{\circ}{V}'H\overset{\circ}{V}'$ is enabled by another shared process crucially feeding it: *excrescence* (§4.3) of the assimilandum $\overset{\circ}{V}$; with tbB [lɛhg̱wő̃n] and aTL [tɛhg̱wé̃] contrast bbB[lihwő̃n] (BL 161) and yTL[tihwé̃] (Mor 360), where excrescence is absent. And the shared nexus of processes fed by sco (or more properly by exc^sco) is *Aufsprengung* (§4.4.1); note, for instance, aufgesprengt tbB [ta9av̌ðű̃n] (BL 129) ← auf *ta9ăv̌ðű̃n* ← exc^sco *ta9b̌ðű̃n* (itself an attested variant, lc), and aTL [ʔah̲arvéh] (Mar 116*) ← *ʔah̲ăřɔvéh* ← *ʔah̲řɔvéh*. Aufsprengung is alien to both Bab B and Yem TL (note the Yem TL correspondent of the latter form, [ʔæh̲řɔvéh], Mor 363).

That sco in Tib B and Ash TL thus agrees in the major general patterns is not to say there are no differences between the two registers/traditions concerning this process. For instance, while Tib B shows sco by inheritance of the old ablaut pattern in the sim intr impa, as we saw in §17.23.2, [ʔăxúlī], [ʔ̌ɛmár], but with some inroads of the generalized palatal 1ʃ impa (sco by default) characteristic of later A, [ʔe̱zél] ~ [ʔ̌ɛzɛl] (BL 139) (with promoted 1ʃ, at least in the second variant favored by stress retraction, §17.15.2 n. 75), Ash TL regularly shows palatal 1ʃ: [ʔ̌ɛxól], [ʔ̌ɛmár], [ʔ̌ɛzílī] (Mar 85*, 87*).[117]

When it comes to the vowel color subsystem involved in sco for the two registers, the face-value deployment in the transcription for both registers/traditions of the traditional Tiberian set < ɛ̌, ă, ɔ̌ > may lull into an unwarranted sense of relationship. Several points involve this judgment: (α) Most of the other A systems also sport palatal-low-labial triads of reduced vowels, so that the difference between these and the Tiberian might boil down to mere norm of phonetic realization—e.g., Tib [ɛ̌] vs. Bab [ĭ] in the case of the palatal—leaving the major phonological architecture of the systems quite similar.[118] (β) It is in fact not foregone that Ash TL fields ɛ̌, ă, ɔ̌ after all; see Margolis's statements at Mar 13 where < ɔ̌ > is said to be used "dem {Rechtschreibens}system zuliebe" in lieu of Margolis-surmised [ŭ] ("man wird aber wohl {solches} gesprochen haben"), and the form [tɛ9éróq] is tacitly taken to have perhaps been [ti9íróq] (Margolis's *ti̭ɛ̌ro̭q*). This all suggests that Ash TL might actually deploy ĭ, ă, ŭ rather than ɛ̌, ă, ɔ̌.[119] (γ) An observation on the labial $\overset{\circ}{V}$, whether ɔ̌ or ŭ: deployment of this sco coloring differs between Tib B and Ash TL, the former register using it in association with the labial passive (§1.1.3)— e.g.. aufgesprengt [hɔh̲o̱rváθ] (BL 174) ← *hɔh̲řɔváθ* ← *hɔh̲rɔváθ*, the latter tradition using it in a couple of cases of transparentively motivated (§15.5.2) sco by inheritance, e.g., [ninqɔ̌ṭű̃] (or [ninqǔ̱ṭű̃]) (Mar 13, 139*) rather than normally expected -sco c[ninqɔ̌ṭű̃].

(For an additional type of schwa coloring characteristic of Tib B, sco′, see §17.6.2.)

<u>Tiberian: Tib TR (including Sab TR), Yem TL</u>. The situation in Yemeni TL may be made short shrift of: sco never applies—or equivalently, it always

applies in the system-wide default mode (§17.23.2). Thus, compare with Ash-kenazic [ˀăxálī], [tiðhˑǎlī́n], [lɛhˑɛ̆wḗ], [ˀɛ̆márī] (Mar 87*, 102*, 106*, 88*) Yem [ˀɔ̆xǽlī], [tiðhˑɔ̆lī́n], [lihwḗ], [ˀɔ̆mǽrī] (Mor 353, 359, 360, 166); and when (variable) promotion follows up in sim impa /#ˀ__, the inherent palatal norm of ə becomes manifest: [ˀīzél], [ˀexól] (Mor 165); contrast Ash [ˀɛ̆zílī], [ˀɛ̆xól] (Mar 85*, 87*), which undergo idiosyncratic default sco but fail to promote.[120] On the other hand, the Tiberian register of TR, including the Sabbionetan subregister, does manifest sco, most clearly (α) rendering colors ī̊, ă (β) by vowel-driven assimilation in the frame /V̌H__ where the results usually but not always promote to V̌: sb[tæ9æbDū́n], sb[tɔ̆9ibrū́n] (Da 273) (aufgesprengt cases, §4.5), sb[ˀæ9æbǽr] ~ tb[ˀæ9æ̆vǽr] (Da 259), sb[yi9i̊róq] (Da 269) (ī̊ be-traying uncertainty concerning the quantity of <iy> in <yi9iyroq>, there being no special diacritic for "ḥataf ḥirik," §21.5).

Though the evidence is sparse, Tib TR, unlike Tib B, seems not to un-dergo adconsonantal assimilatory sco /H__ (as opposed to vocalic assimilation /V̌H__) but rather *either* to forego sco so that ɔ̆ emerges or to undergo sco by inheritance. In available forms, sim impa ms of *√hwy, both patterns would converge on the same result: *hĭwáy > [hɔ̆wǽy] = [hɛ̆wǽy], cf. attested spell-ings tb<h:wæy>, sb<hɛ̆wæˀy>, Da 354. (Both these spellings are noteworthy, the former for violation of the Tiberian "spelling rule" against @<H:>, the latter for being a rare, perhaps unique, instance of the vowel point ḥataf segol in Sabbioneta; see §20.2.) With promotion: sim impa ms [ˀexúl] ← ˀɔ̆xúl (Da 300), sim impf 1s [ˀehḗ] (√hwy, +wdr: §9.3.1, §17.32); with repair-strategic syllable closure, sim impa ms^3mp sb[ˀissārinnū́n] ← ˀess. . . (by rule reversal of mid, *i* ⇒ *e* /stressed (closed syllable_)* reversed to *e* ⇒ *i* /unstressed (closed syllable))* ← prm ˀɔ̆ss. . . ← rps ˀɔ̆s. . . (for discussion of other aspects of this form, see §17.15.1 TR (θ) with n. 71).

Tib TR also shows occasional instances of sonorant Aufsprengung (§4.4.2), e.g., sb[yizirqū́n], cf. excrescent-aufgesprength sb[tɔ̆9ibrū́n] cited above. Both types of Aufsprengung are alien to Yem TL.

<u>Babylonian: Bab B, Bab TR.</u> Despite the shared orthography, these sys-tems show rather discrepant forms of sco: (α) Bab B manifests all three sco col-ors ([ĭ], [ă], [ŭ]—this latter rarely, e.g., by inheritance in labial passive [gŭlī́], BL 67), while Bab TR sco is limited to palatal ([ĭ]). (β) Bab B sco occurs, variably, in more environments than Bab TR and under partially discrepant conditions. Some high points are synoptized in (17.23B) and (17.23C), now to be discussed, starting with (17.23B) for Bab B.

Following a laryngeal (ˀ, *h*) in initial position (environment (i)), the hypoth-esis very gingerly adopted is that V̌ (whether original or < *V̌ by red) splits into two sets vis-à-vis sco based on color: while a palatal vowel fails to undergo sco but undergoes promotion (ĭ → ɔ̆ → e), a labial or low vowel does undergo sco—without promotion—either to *ă* or *ĭ* under conditions remaining to be precisely determined: descriptively, to *ă* in the active pf, to *ĭ* in the impa or in the passive pf. (Much uncertainty here; for one thing, the original sim impa may have had *1ʃ*ĭ* rather than *1ʃ*ă*; cf. §1 n. 6—and note that one Tib B variant of bb[hĭqīmǽθ] at Dan 7:5 also shows palatal sco, [hĕqīmáθ], suggesting the possibility of original palatal vocalism in the cau passive as well, though probably in alternation with labial, *i ~ *u.

The voiced pharyngeal *9* initially or postconsonantally (environment (ii)) triggers sco to [ǽ] alone (only < *a attested). (Voiceless pharyngeal *ḥ* seems not to trigger sco, but this may merely be the appearance of things from a limited corpus; examples, BL 161.)

Gutturals immediately after *V̊* (iii) are best interpreted as assimilatorily inert, the schwa following the guttural rather picking up the color of the *V̊* through the guttural.[121]

Regressive assimilation may occur in the environment /__{H,y} (=/__Γ, i.e., immediately preceding a glide) (iv).

Sonorant Aufsprengung (v) yields [ī] promoted from palatal default sco *i*: ← *ĭ*Λ ← *ə̆*Λ ← Λ̥ ← Λə̆ (§4.4.2).[122]

Coming now to Bab TR (17.23C), we find /#ʔ__ either +sco to *i*, or −sco to the tune of variable promotion (environment (i′)).

The /*V̊H*__ condition (iii) is restricted to palatal *iH*, and the assimilated *ĭ* may promote with excrescent Aufsprengung ([ti9ibrū́n]) or without it ([tə̆9iróq]) (for details on formations like these, §4.5).

Aufsprengung condition (v) seems identical to that of Bab B, but analogs of conditions (ii, iv) are wanting.[124]

(17.23B)   Babylonian B

		+sco	-sco
(i) /#{ʔ,h}__	**ă (sim pf)*	[ʔǽmǽr](BL 139)	~ -prm [ʔə̆mǽr](BL 140)
	**ă (sim pf)*	[hǽwǽyθā̆]	-prm [hə̆wḗθ](BL 161)
	**ă (active cau pf)*	[hǽqémtā̆] ~ (perhaps)	-prm [hə̆qémtā̱](BL 149)
	**ă (sim impa)*	[ʔĭxúlī](BL 139)	
	**ŭ (passive cau pf)*[hĭqīmǽθ](BL 149)		
	**ĭ (sim impa)*		+prm [ʔemǽr](BL 139)
	**ĭ (int impf 1s)*		+prm [ʔeḥæwwḗ](BL 152)
	**ĭ (cau impf 1s)*		+prm [ʔeḥōŏǽ9innḗh](BL 67)
(ii) /{#,C}9__		[9ǽvæǽðiθ](BL 129)	[9ə̱vǽðtā̆](BL 128)
		[yiṭ9ǽmū́n](BL 8)	
(iii) /VH__		[yə̆ṭæ9ǽmǔnnḗh]	[yə̆vǽhə̆lǔnnḗh](B130)
(iv)	/__Γ	[ʔehōŏǽ9innḗh](BL 67)	[yə̆hōŏə̱9ū́n](BL 143)
		[lihwĭyā́n](BL 153)	[mə̆šænnə̱yā́](BL 164)
(v)	/__Λ	+prm [yiθirmḗ]	[tiθrə̆mṓn](BL 164)
		+prm [hæšiḷṭǽx](BL 45)	[yiḥlə̆fū́n](BL 30)

(17.23C)   **Babylonian TR**

		+sco	-sco
(i′) /#ʔ__	*ă sim impa*	[ʔ<u>ĭ</u>zél]	-prm [ʔ<u>ǝ</u>xúlū](Da 300f.)
			+prm [ʔ<u>e</u>lǽmū], [ʔ<u>e</u>hóð](Da 300f.)
	ĭ int impf 1s		-prm [ʔ<u>ǝ</u>xǽppǽr](Da 272)
			+prm [ʔ<u>e</u>šællém](Da 272)
(iii) /VH__		±prm [yi9<u>ĭ</u>roq] ~	[yi9róq](Da 269)
		+prm [ti9<u>ĭ</u>brū́n] ~	[ti9bǝrū́n](Da 273)
		+prm [tǝ9<u>ĭ</u>róq](Da 270)	
(v)	/__Λ	+prm [yisimqū́n]	[yišmǝ9ū́n](Da 272)

<u>CP</u>. [Ŭ] (or promoted [U]) appears to be an option, by default sco, in sim impa /H__, <9wBDw> 'facite!' (Sl 140) (~ <9BDw>, plausibly -sco [ǝ]); while [Ĭ] seems to be a variable option /š__ irrespective of tense, sco by assimilation: sim impa <šTwm> 'verstumme!', interpreted by Schulthess (Sg 62) as [šĭθóm] (retranscribed), also sim pf <šyDyT> 'warf' (Sg 67) (~ -sco <šDʔ>, <šDw>, etc.; Sl 201).

<u>SM</u>. sco by inheritance is the norm in various categories, notably sim pf where the original low color of *1ʃ *a* is retained; e.g., reconstructed living SM*păqáð > t[fắkɑd] <PqD> 'befahl' (Macs 145) (see §22.1 for smc and other processes leading to trad pron). -sco (t[ē]) is the unmarked situation in sim impa whatever the color of 2ʃ, whether neutralized as usual by ssn to t [ɑ], §12.2 <u>SM</u> (α), (t[dḗbɑq] <DBq>, Macs 148) or rare -ssn reflexes of *ĭ, *ŭ (t[kḗfɘl] <KPl>, <Krwz>—no trad pron provided for the latter, but Macuch tells us its 1ʃ is pronounced with t[ē], Macs 149). 2√H forms evince *1ʃ Ā – 2ʃ ɘ* vocalism in trad pron (<Dhl> t[dǽʔɘl] 'fürchte!', <ʔhB> t[ắʔɘb] 'gib!' Macs 74), which makes it possible that they are residual continuations of the ancient ablaut pattern *QăSiM, hence sco by inheritance; but in the case of <ʔhB> it is more likely that its etymon sported original *2ʃ *a* and that 1ʃ t[Ā] derives from regressive adconsonantal assimilation /__2√H (cf. Bab B, (17.23B (iv)), the ultimate end result 2ʃ t[ɘ] reflecting SM-specific dissimilation of low-low vowel clusters to low-palatal (§22.1 (22B (vi (β))): hence, in the smc *ʔăháβ . . . → (ʔ)ĀAβ → (ʔ)ĀIβ . . . → [ắʔɘb] (earliest etymon *hab, ʔă- courtesy of wic, §17.33). Finally, there appear to be a few reflexes of 1ʃ Ŭ, by whatever subtype of sco (cf. CP, M); e.g., <swBr> 'verzeihe!' (Macs 149).

<u>G</u>. [Ĭ] (or promoted [I]) is a variable option /{ʔ, 9}__ in the sim impa; e.g., <ʔyz(y)l>, <9yBD>, §9.3.1.

<u>SR</u>. A medley of sco by inheritance, assimilation, and default—all demonstrable on the *1√ʔ verb where the color of 1ʃ V̆ becomes visible by promotion to V̊ (to the tune of 1√ʔ > Ø, §9.3.1). Inheritance sco dictates preservation of the ancient ablaut *ĭ . . . *a*, *ă . . . *u* in sim impa, as in Tib B (§17.23.2): [ɛmár], [ɑxól]. Default sco dictates, inter alia, Ĕ̊ as the unmarked color of reduced

1ʃ in the simple pf, which is basically the whole story in the Jacobite register: [eθ̱ál], [e̱θó̌], [e̱fó], [e̱rá9]. In Nestorian, however, low color is dictated
as a special case for defective *1√ʔ verbs ([ap̱ɔ̌]), with the exception of *√ʔty
'come', which, if Brockelmann is correct (B 90), maintains or restores palatal
color on the analogy of antonymic *√ʔzl 'go' ([ɛθó̌] like [ɛzál]), an instance of
default sco through lexical idiosyncracy; and sco by assimilation makes for
low rather than palatal color /__r ([ará9]); B 153*, 165*, 192*. (For labial V̆
in SR, see sip, §17.25.)

M̲. M is like SR in showing deletion of ʔ to the tune of prm, *#ʔV̆ > #V̊,
but differs from SR in extending the process to 9, *#9V̆ → #V̊ (§9.3.1). The
M story of sco /*#{ʔ,9}__ then becomes somewhat complex, what with the
Classical orthography and Modern pronunciation giving conflicting testimony;
with sco working differently in the sim pf and the sim impa; and with the testimony of Modern pron being partially discrepant in the sim pf between *1√ʔ
and *1√9. The particulars are displayed in (17.23D) (data from Macm 296,
298, 302, 306).

(17.23D)   *1√ʔ   *1√9

	Classical orthography	**Modern pronunciation**	**Classical orthography**	**Modern pronunciation**
sim pf		[é̱mar]		[é̱βad]
	<a̱mar>	[áxal]	<a̱bad>	
sim impa	<e̱zil>		<e̱bid>	
	<e̱zal>		<e̱bad>	
	<e̱kul>		<e̱bud>	
	<a̱zil>		<a̱bid>	
	<a̱mar>			
	<a̱mur>		<a̱bud>	
		[ó̱xol]	<e̱ubud>	[ó̱βod]

Perhaps the following picture can be reconstructed for Classical M: (*) sco
by inheritance in at least the *1√ʔ sim pf, [amár] < ʔămár, perhaps also for *1√9
though these may have been assimilated to the pattern later, upon the phonetic
demise of 9 (§9,2.3), [aβáð]; (*) in the case of sim impa, a medley of all three
types of sco—inheritance (of the old ablaut pattern, [amór] and [aβóð], [azél]
and [aβéð], [ezál] and [eβáð]), assimilation (vowel harmony, [ezél] and [eβéð],
[amár], [oβóð]),[125] and default (with Ĭ as unmarked, [exól] and [eβóð]);
(*) of these varieties, asimilation was generalized into the Modern language
([óxol] and [óβod]), while in the pf default was extended ([émar] and [éβad]),
though not to total displacement of the old inheritance pattern ([áxal]).

M orthography occasionally represents [V̆] (via <V̆>) /#[H]__ (which in M
boils down to /#[h]__), e.g., [hă̱ðaryó̌n] <ha̱dariun> 'they turned back' (DM

131), as also /#[y]__ ([yăhaβlán] <yahablan> 'he gave us'—it is the pp [-lán], which catalyzes retention of [ă] here (§17.15.2), #yǎ normally resolving to [ī] or [e] (§14.2), cf. <ehab> m[éhaβ] 'he gave (Macm 34) [eháβ]). It may also be recalled from §17.23.2 that M at times shows regressive-assimilatory sco /#C__C, [šŬmắ].

17.24. Spirant Hopping (shp)

Though the proto-Semitic voiced emphatic interdental spirant *ɖ̣ ultimately merges with *9* in Aramaic (ufb, §9.1.3),[126] in the pristine era (Y, O) its reflex is consistently spelled <q>—a spelling that sporadically lingers even after the change to *9*, not only in the earlier days of the change (I, B) but here and there in the later period as well (at least M). Examples: Y <yrqy> 'es wird ihm gefallen' (DR I 214: 20), O <rqh> 'besänftigen' (De 77), both < *√rɖ̣y; I and B <ʾrqʾ> (~ ufb-derived <ʾr9ʾ>) 'Erde' (L 10, BL 26) < *ʾarɖ̣ắ; M <arqa> 'earth'.

This prima facie unexpected spelling of the reflex of a coronal spirant with a letter designed to represent a uvular stop has prompted various hypotheses over the years, and that proffered in this book is a version of one of the most prominent of these ideas. To wit, it will be taken that *ɖ̣ underwent *spirant hopping* (shp) from coronal to uvular position, hereby becoming a voiced uvular spirant [R], subsequently spelled <q> because this was the sole uvular letter in the prevailing alphabet(s).[127]

Though there is no direct testimony to the pronunciation of <q> in its presumed role of representing [R],[128] this phonetic identification makes sense of various dissimilatory processes that otherwise would appear more mystyerious; see §9.1.3.

17.25. Simple Imperative Promotion (sip)

When 2ʃ V̆ is lost from (a reflex of) sim impa *QV̆SV̆M- by deletional reduction making for shape QV̆SM-, now closed-syllabic 1ʃ V̆ promotes to full vowel status. If all else were equal, the results of this promotion should be given by the intersection of schwa coloring (§17.23) and promotion (§14.1), perhaps modified by attenuation (§10). However, study of the table in (17.25A) will reveal that such a result is not forthcoming. If it were, there would either be no discrepancies in color distribution between columns 1 and 2, or should there be any, they should be exclusively attributable to the action of attenuation in column 1 following promotion. But while a similar expectation is in fact met for columns 3 and 4, where all color discrepancies result from the differential action of att (possibly) (3) and sco (4), in the case of columns 1 and 2, differential action of att and sco will at best account for CP.[129] The striking divergence of the remaining six dialects suggests the possibility of some supervenient factor explicitly targeting one or both of columns 1, 2. And in fact, it will be the work of this subchapter to develop such a hypothesis: that closed-syllabic 1ʃ in the sim impa (column 1) is subject to a special type of prm crucially involving color manipulation, a process to be called *simple imperative promotion* (sip); and that the unaccounted-for discrepancies in chroma between columns 1 and 2 follow from this special process.

(17.25A) **Sketch tabulation of 1ʃ reduced vowel color** under four conditions with (columns 1, 3) or without (columns 2, 4) closed-syllabic promotion. Vowel color is displayed in the fixed (strictly expository) order *I* (palatal), *A* (low), *U* (labial), length indication omitted for simplicity of exposition, e.g., *I* may = reduced *Ĭ* (-prm) or *I̊*, *Ī* (+short prm, +long prm) ; see text for details on column 1, §17.23 for columns 2 and 4, §12 for column 3. Entries in columns 2 and 4 are limited to explicitly chromatic vowels, so that initial ~*I(. . .)* or ~*A(. . .)* is short for *ə̆~I(. . .)*, *ə̆~A(. . .)* and a blank cell implicitly contains *ə̆*.

	1 *sim impa *1ʃV̆ > V̊* *(/closed syllable)*	2 *sim impa *1ʃV̆* *(/open syllable)*	3 *sim pf *1ʃa* *(/closed syllable)*	4 *sim pf *1ʃa > V̆* *(/open syllable)*
TR	I~A	~I	I~A	
CP	U	~I~U	A	~I
SM	A?	~I~A~U	A	~A
G	I~A?~U	~I	A?	
SR	U	~I~A	I~A	~I~A
TL	I~A~U?	~I	A	~A?
M	I~U	~I~A~U	I~A	~A~U

The hypothesis informing sip depends on the idea, seen earlier (§1.3 n. 13), that an Aramaic scheme with multiple schematics often contains a *dominant* schematic, which characteristically bears the semantic weight of the scheme. In the sim impa subsystem, the dominant is 2ʃ, whose color at least originally witnessed to the dynamic/neuter value of the lexeme, while the color of 1ʃ was determined by ablaut (§1.1.1). According to sip, when 2ʃ was lost by reduction, its color was initially (α) transferred to 1ʃ (usurping the color invested in this schematic by sco ±att) and later, at least in some dialects, (β) generalized to other sim impas.

In sketch, allowing *X́* = stressed vocalic-anlaut suffix and *V̆* = 1ʃ with color determined by ablaut or sco, *QV̆SV̊′MX́* red > *QV̆SMX́* sip > *QV̊′SMX́*.[130]

The usual color value imparted by sip is *labial*, *QUSMX́*—exclusively so in CP and SR, almost exclusively so in M, well represented in G, and enjoying at least some representation in the Ashkenazic tradition of TL. A plausible reason for this ascendancy of ʃU is that **u* is the mark par excellence of the dynamic simple verb in the imp system; transitive verbs are prototypically dynamic, and by far the commonest type of suffix triggering the red^sip chain—*X́* in the sketch derivation above—is an *object* suffix, always part of a transitive verb.

Since a palatal value of sip, *QISMX́*, would coincide with the unmarked palatal value imparted by sco, what remains to be accounted for is the impressive showing by *low* sip coloration, *QASMX́*, which appears variably in TR and TL, possibly in G as well, and may be the exclusive color of sip in SM. The fact that both pertinent forms cited by Dalman for TR are 3√r verbs, as is the sole relevant SM form cited by Macuch (see below), and that 1√r verbs obtain 2∫A by low (§17.10), hints that at least originally low sip coloration derived by transference from 2∫ in the general manner proposed. But if so, it became fully generalized in at least the Yemeni trad pron of TL without apparent regard to homoparadigmatic 2∫ coloration.[131]

Examples from the dialects:

<u>TR</u>. mp^3fs tb[ʔ<u>i</u>xlûhū]; mp^3mp [ʔæ̃srinnű́n], tb[tæ̃vrinnű́n] (Da 376).

<u>CP</u>. ₅qw<u>t</u>9h> 'hau sie ab!' (Sg 80), <šw<u>m</u>9̊wn> 'höret!' (Sg 62) qua [šU̲m9Ůn] (pace Schulthess's disagreement with such an analysis; note that in this case red—more precisely, r-red—is triggered not by an object suffix but by a subject suffix imported from the impf (hii, §7.2 (δ)).

<u>SM</u>. Solely on the basis of <wʔmrw> t[wæ̃mru] 'und saget!' if derived by smc (§22.1) from something like sip-colored *wə̃ʔamrű́* (possibly ultimately < *waʔ<u>î</u>marű́* with marked oxytone stress, §4.1, though unmarked barytone *waʔ<u>î</u>máru̅* is alternatively conceivable if *-ú̃* < mtr, §17.12, *-Ůn* imparted from the impf by hii). On the other hand, the [æ] of [wǽmru] might have nothing to do with sip and rather derive from the unreduced proclitic **wa=*, though the precise details of such a would-be derivation are unclear. (For reduced or unreduced proclitics in A at large, see §14.2 n. 11.)

<u>G</u>. Assuming ml-less <∅> [a], the choices appear to be ranked *U ≫ A* in the intransitive, while all three colors alternate without clear preference in the transitive: e.g., imtr <zw̲Bnyn> 'kaufe(fs)!', <KBŝyn> 'unterdrucke(fs)!' qua [ka̲ßšĭn], <Pw̲Thwn> 'offnet!', <lBŝwn> 'legt an!' (Da 276f); tr <ŝy̲Bqyh> 'verlasse ihn!' <ŝBqy> 'verlasse mich!' (<-y> for [-ī] ny ndr, §17.13), <ŝw̲Bqyn> 'verlasse sie(fp)!' (Da 375f).[132]

<u>SR</u>. [qu̲wrūnɔ́̃n] 'begrabt mich!' (Ns 136). (See n. 132.)

<u>TL</u>. The evidence is mixed. The orthography and the Ash trad pron attest to variants in *I∫ i* (e.g., <ŝy̲Bqn> (~ <ŝBqn> 'leave me!' (Mar 60), a[t<u>i</u>fsɛ́h] 'seize him!' (Mar 179*)), while Yem trad pron shows consistent [æ] even when the relevant text shows spelling with ml <y> (e.g., <ty̲rPan> y[tæ̃rfǽn] 'tĕfos (ʔet rĕxuši) bĕ xoaḥ!' (Mor 296 with n. 28). Also, Margolis interprets at least some ml-less forms of <ŝBq> as containing 1∫ [ɔ], e.g., the variant <ŝBqn> adduced above is rendered as a[šɔvqán] (M 168*); others are performed with 1∫ [a], e.g., fs^3ms <ŝBqyh> a[šavqíah] (Mar 61, 168*). Though not without a

bit of uneasiness about Margolis's interpretation of 1ʃ [ɔ], the gingerly conclusion is that TL is like G in showing all three colors of *1ʃ V but ranked dialect-
specifically as (provisionally) A ≫ I ≫ U.

<u>M</u>. Overwhelmingly <(e)u> [o], with <e> [e] limited to /#__ of mp^3ms
where it varies with the labial version at that; e.g., <eubruia> ~ <ebruia> 'geht
daruber!' (Nm 278), [oβrúy] ~ [eβrúy].[133]

17.26. Simplification (smp)

Simplification (smp) of the group C'C'V̆ to C'. In the dialects where this phenomenon might lend itself to detection, it is absent in Yem TL;[134] inconclusive
(for the verb) in SR;[135] in B and Ash TL apparently limited to the sequence
*-inn-ə̆-, -exenergic-bridge- (e.g., B impf 3ms^2mp [yə̆šēzə̆vi̱ṉxṍn]—con-
trast 3ms^2ms [yə̆šēzə̆vin̲n̲ṍx] (BL 143)—; Ash TL pf 1s^2mp [baddarti̱ṉxṍ],
Mar 93*—contrast Yem TL [bæddærti̱n̲n̲ə̱̆xū́], Mor 355);[136] sporadic in
TR and SM (in the former affecting, occasionally, only W'W'—int pf 3ms^1s
bb[šæwyǽnī], Da 69, sbor int impf 3ms^3fs sb[diyqæymǽh], Da 330—contrast -smp 1s^2fs tb[ʔǽqæyyə̱̆minnı́x], Da 372; in SM cau pf 3mp <ʔsqw>
t[ǽsqu], Macs 188, with [s] ← ssə̌ ← §17.21 slə̌ —contrast cau impa <ʔPqw>
t[æb̲b̲ḗqu], lc, with bbē ← smc, §22.1 ppə̌ ← §17.21 npə̌); lastly, smp is robust
only in M, where it has become the unmarked response to C'C'V̆.[137]

17.27. *Sin* Merger (snm)

The process *sin merger* (snm) refers to the merger in Aramaic of the mysterious proto-Semitic voiceless coronal sibilant conventionally transcribed as
"ś," whether the merger was to the dentoalveolar s (*frontwards sin merger*,
f-snm) or to the palatal š (*backwards sin merger*, b-snm). Tracking the progress of snm through the dialects will be discussed with the aid of (17.27A)
(p. 383).[138]

In an overall way, the distribution of "◊" in the columns headed by <ŝ> and
<s> suggests that *ś > s was absent in older Aramaic but robust in the later dia-
lects. Note next that the distribution of the other descriptors, "a few cases" and
"sometimes," pattern in roughly a cat's-cradle manner with "◊," suggesting
thay *ś > s started out as a minority option (I?—see L 10f., Kraehling 1953:
242, Kutscher 1970: 70; B) which, possibly following an interlude of rough
balance (P), ends up as the majority option in those dialects where it has not
become fully categorical (SM, G, M?).

But although snm may perhaps have actually run its course this way, as a
long-lived stabilizing shift of marked ś to unmarked dentoalveolar s, there is
the hint at the existence of an alternative stabilization, to palatal š. This hint
is provided by the trad pron of SM and M, most clearly the former, where instances of [š] as a reflex of *ś can be ascertained by the comparative method:
e.g., SM <ṣ̌B9> t[šǽbæ] 'wurde satt' (Macs 175), M √šWḥ if cognate to Arabic

(17.27A) **Aramaic reflexes of *ś**

	orthographic representation				trad pron
	<ŝ>	<ś>	<š>	<s>	
Y	◊				
O	◊				
I	◊			a few cases?	
B		◊		a few cases	
P	sometimes			sometimes	
N	◊				
TR				◊	
CP				◊	
SM		a few cases?		◊	<š>[š], <s>[s]
G	a few cases			◊	
SR				◊	
TL	a few cases			◊	<ŝ> and <s> (both [s])
M			a few cases?	◊	<š>[š], <s>[s]

√šWḥ (DM 453)[139]— for M trad pron, cf. the passive participle lexicalized as 'greedy', <ših> t[šʹí] (Macm 87).

However, there are so few relevant trad pron forms available in either dialect that the possibility cannot be excluded that we are rather dealing with sporadic root variants reflecting *š—especially in M, where the etymological connection to roots with *ś is shaky to begin with. And in the case of SM, there is another possible alternative to the hypothesis of *ś > š: that readings like t[šǽbæ] represent a sort of interlingual reading pronunciation on the basis of Arabic, where š is the normal reflex of *ś (n. 139), cf. in this specific example šabi9a; observe in this connection that Arabic is normally the first language among modern Samaritans.

The uncertainty investing all this hinges largely on the fact that the letter <ŝ> in most Northwest Semitic alphabets is, in unpointed texts, ambiguously representative of either š or (some other reflex of) ś (n. 138); and that being the case we cannot, in default of independent evidence like trad pron, rule out an even wider role for *ś > š as competitor to *ś > s than that just sketched. In particular, it could imaginably be the case that *any* instance of <ŝ> < *ś in *any* dialect might represent palatally resolved [š] rather than unresolved [ś]. However, this unsettling possibility cannot be posited without careful qualification for any early dialect that we want to take as unilinearly ancestral to a later dialect showing *š > s*. For to do so might paint us into the absurd corner of *merger reversal* (Hoenigswald 1960: 117) in entailing that, first, **š and **š̃ merge to *š and, then, all and only those tokens of *š derived from **š remerge with *š to *s*, while the balance of *š-tokens—those ≤ **š̃—remain as š̃. That is, the impossible nexus in (17.27B) must not be incurred, where the three distinct trajectory lines (wavy, solid, dashed) each track a distinct protosegment:

(17.27B)   **I**   **>**   **II**   **>**   **III**

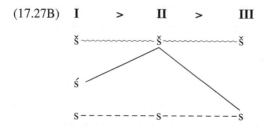

For example, if one were *both* to interpret O <ŝ> as invariantly [š] *and* to assume O as a unilinear ancestor of CP, then one could not take O √<ŝB9> 'be full', qua √[šb9], as an etymon of CP √<sB9>, qua √[sb9], without explaining why O √<ŝm9> 'hear' corresponds to CP √<šm9> rather than to a nonexistent CP @√<sm9>.[140]

(Given the overall uncertainty about *š > š̃ over against the certainty and generality of *š > s*, whenever the context permits, the simple designation "sin merger" (snm) will be used for the latter, although more narrowly it denotes a generic over both processes. However, when the context requires it, the specific labels introduced at the outset will be employed: f-snm for *š > s*, b-snm for *š > š̃.)

17.28. Second Schematic Lengthening (ssl): rmp ssl, cau(sative) ssl

Starting sporadically in I and settling in at least in SM, TL, and M, 2ʃ *I* variably → *ī* , a phenomenon to be called *second schematic lengthening* (ssl). Apart from I, where there is possible evidence of at least one instance of ssl in cau rmp, the process crystallizes in either sim rmp (TL, M) or plain cau (SM, TL)—species of ssl to be tagged *rmp ssl* and *cau(sative) ssl*, respectively.[141] Though TL gives evidence of both manifestations, neither showing is as robust as that of SM for cau ssl or as M's with rmp ssl. Though ssl appears to be limited to the four dialects cited, it is not out of the question that the process may actually be more widespread but obscured by orthographic underdetermination—notably in dialects where <y> may function as ml for either [i̊] or [ī] (e.g., CP), or where despite vocalization midding (§17.11) applies variably and both 2ʃ [i̊] and 2ʃ [ī] are homographically <i> (e.g., B) if ml <y> fails to disambiguate.

In rmp ssl, lengthening may plausibly be attributed to the analogical stimulus of the 2ʃ *ī* characteristic of the homoparadigmatic palatal passive (given the semantic affinity between passive and rmp, which ultimately facilitated replacement in the later dialects of the former by the latter); and though no such stimulus is readily apparent for cau ssl, the fact that Hebrew regularly shows 2ʃ *ī* in its causative may turn out to be significant on the wider genealogical horizon.

I. Possibly <ˀšTmy9> 'nišma9' (Kutscher 1970: 70, L §34e) as a reflex of *ˀištamī9a* with rmp-ssl-lengthened 2ʃ [ī] spelled <y>; note too the failure of lowering (§17.10) /__3√9, suggesting bleeding by ssl.[142] Also, from the I-vintage Aśoka inscription, perhaps cau rmp <ˀThḥsynn> 'they were made strong' (§9.2.2)—though it is unsettling that <y> at the same time bespeaks palatal *ī as 2ʃ in the cau rmp, rather than expected *a (§1.1.3).

SM. There is evidence for variable cau ssl from both orthography and trad pron. Of the former type are spellings of 2ʃ *I* with ml <y> despite /__3√L (as with I above), e.g., <hmtyr> 'liess regnen', as well as appearance of <y> despite expected reduction to [V̆], e.g., <TqryBwn> 'werdet darbringen'. Of the latter type is primarily the appearance of t[î́] < *ī in lieu of generally expected t[ḗ] < *ī (despite subsequent lengthening and stressing of either reflex by smc, §22.1), e.g., <TwrKwn> t[tūrī́kon] 'werdet verlängern' (Macs 178). There are also numerous cases of both types of evidence converging: e.g., <hlByšT> (~ <hlBšT> ~ <ˀlBšT>) t[ælbī́šæt] 'sie bekleidete', and t[tæqrī́bon] spelling <TqryBwn> (above). (All unsourced examples are from Macs 159–61).

TL. rmp ssl: a[ˀibbə̄lī̄9ɔ̄] 'she was swallowed' (~ -ssl a[ˀibbal9ɔ̄́]) (Mar 94*). (Note that Morag cites only -ssl y[ˀibbæl9ɑ̄́] (§5.211). cau ssl: y[ˀæθlī́æ9] 'hitlia9' (Mor 157), with [í̄æ] ← pgn (§17.16) *ī*.

M. rmp ssl <etibhirt> [īθeBhī́rt] 'thou wert chosen' (~ -ssl with expected +low <etibhart> [īθeBhɑ́rt] (Mal 462). Note also the like of <etimniit> 'I was appointed' interpretable as [īθemnīyī́θ] rather than expected c<etiminit> c[īθemnī́θ] (cf. <etiqrit> [īθeqrī́θ] 'I was called forth') (Mal 464). Without the interference of ssl, defective sim rmp pf 1s verbs normally end in <-it> [-ī́θ] < *-í 3√yt = *-ī́t, whereby epn (§17.6) fails to take place. With the advent of ssl, however, the (new) length of 2ʃ *I* was by hypothesis safeguarded from neutralization by transparentive deployment of the strong suffixal allomorph -ī́θ.[143] (Note in all these forms, by the way, the [e] between the rmp prefix of 1√, hallmark of the M-robust process Aufsprengung, §4.4.1; rmp-prefixal *ī*θ—rather than @eθ—by repair-strategical lengthening, §15.3.1.1.)

It will have been noted from all four dialects that ssl appears to bleed lowering; e.g., TL y[ˀæθlī́æ9] ← *ˀaθlī̄9 . . . ← *hatlī9(a), whereas if low had applied first we should expect @[ˀæθlɑ̄9] (← ssl *ˀaθlɑ̄9 ← low . . . *hatlī9(a).) The cross-dialectal homogeneity of this distribution suggests that, historically, ssl arose earlier than (and hence could bleed) low, d-ssl^low rather than d-low^ssl. And while it cannot be excluded that d-low^ssl mutated into s-ssl^low, presumably for reasons of phonological pattern optimization, unmutated d-ssl^low feels to constitute a more plausible (and simpler) account.

17.29. Tonic Lengthening (tln); Tonic Opening (top)

At least Tiberian B and TR irrespective of register give evidence of a variable process of *tonic lengthening* (tln), whereby stressed vowels are rendered long. Tonic lengthening especially affects stressed vowels occurring in intonationally prominent positions—vowels traditionally said to be "in pause" (hefsex), and in the Tiberian Bible marked with major disjunctive tĕ9amim, notably siluk (at the end of a verse) or atnaḥ (in mid-verse); §21.6. (In this book, vowels in pause are marked "V̆"—in contradistinction to nonpausal (primary) stress ("in context," hekšer) "V́," or secondary stress "V̀"—even when occurring in texts unscored by tĕ9amim; §20.3.)

Tonic lengthening at times extends to nonpausal primary-stressed vowels, $V́ \rightarrow V́$, either unconditionally or under circumstances that remain to be determined. Unlike the cognate process in Hebrew (THP 95–7), tln in Aramaic precedes and bleeds midding (§17.11), so that with chromatic vowels we get ï, *í* → ï̈, *í̈* and ü, *ú* → ü̈, *ú̈* (in Hebrew the opposite ordering returns such as *ē̈*, *ō̈*). The low low vowel gives ä, *á* → ɔ̈, *ɔ́* (Tib B), ä̊, *á̊* (TR).

A complication in recognizing tln, at least for Tib B, is that an apparent instance of +tln [í̈] might in actuality be a case of -mid [í], the orthography normally representing either via <i(y)>. The ambiguity arises due to the convergence of both processes being variable, so that the failure of a palatal vowel to mid might be due either to preemption by tln ([í̈]) or to the permissible option of mid not to apply ([í]). A similar uncertainty attends interpretation of labial <u(w)> in both dialects: +tln [ú̈] vs -mid [ú], the pattern of labial midding being extremely paltry in B and in TR involving apparent widespread free alternation (§17.11). (Use of the term "apparent" here is crucial and in fact tacitly extends to all manifestations of variability in mid and tln. Nothing short of a thorough carding of representative texts in both dialects will facilitate anything approaching firm judgments of given tokens as affected by either process. With this caution in mind, a synopsis of distributions is presented in (17.29A) bare of any commitments to relative frequency. The squiggle following each pair of forms indicates tln alternation for a given vowel-accent pairing, normally but not always as variae lectiones in different editions for the same book, chapter, and verse; e.g., +tln [ʔĕmɔ̈r] and -tln [ʔĕmä̆r] as reflexes of *ä in the sim impa ms 'say!' at Dan 4:6. Note also that book, chapter, and verse, as well as scholarly source, are explicitly indicated only for the first of paired tln entries; e.g., again, both [ʔĕmɔ̈r] and [ʔĕmä̆r] occur at Dan 4:6 and are adduced by Bauer and Leander at BL 139.)[144]

(17.29A) Tib B	TR
*ă	
+*tln* [ʔɛ̆mɔ̆r]~ (Dan 4:6; BL 139)	[pæqqeðtănī] (Deut 26:14; Da 365)
-*tln* [ʔɛ̆măr]~	[qæyyemtắnā] (Exod 47:25)
*á	
+*tln* [baqqɔ̆rū]~ (Ezra 4:1; BL 134)	sb[ʔæsseqtắnā](Exod 17:3; Da 365)
-*tln* [baqqárū]~	[šɔ̆væqtǽnī]
*ï	
+*tln* [sɔ̆yï̆ð](Dan 2:46; BL 102)	sb[yɔ̆šællï̆m]~ (Exod 21:19; Da 61 n. 2)
[yiθ9ăvï̆ð]~ (Ezra 6:12; BL 129)	
-*tln* [yiθ9ăvɛ̆ð]~	[yɔ̆šællɛ̆m]~
*í	
+*tln* [qabbḯl]~ (Dan 6:1; BL 111)	[šɔ̆lḯm] (Gen 47:15; Da 257)
-*tln* [qabbél]~	[sɔ̆léq] (Gen 19:28; Da 258)
*ü	
+*tln* [yisgü̆ð] (Dan 3:6; BL 98)	[tifrü̆q]~ (Exod 13:13; Da 267)
-*tln*	[tifröq]~ (Sperber 2004: 111)
*ú	
+*tln* [yēxū́l] (Dan 4:30; BL 31)	sb[yiškū́v] (Lev 15:4; Da 55)
-*tln* [góddū](Dan 4:20; BL 167)	sb[tiškóv] (Lev 15:20)

Finally, B shows variable incidence of *open k-coa* ($11.2) in pause, as opposed to (and varying with) unmarked close k-coa in the defective impf: [nɔ̆hawwɛ̄̆] (~ close [nɔ̆hawwɛ̄̆]), [nɔ̆haḥăwɛ̄̆] (~ [nɔ̆haḥăwɛ̄̆], [ʔăhawwɛ̄̆] (~ [ʔăhawwɛ̄̆]), [yɔ̆haḥăwɛ̄̆] (~[yɔ̆haḥăwɛ̄̆]). Since [ɛ] is lower than [ē], and pausally lengthened vowels bid fair to have enhanced sonorancy, this pattern will be taken to reflect the natural compatibility between articulatory lowness and acoustic sonorancy (Malone 1972b); the process will be called *tonic opening* (top).[145]

17.30. *T* Object Marking (tom)

In CP, SM, and G, a residue of the proto-Aramaic accusative preposition **yāt* (Brockelmann 1908: 314) is variably incorporated into the verb as as suffix, a pattern to be called *T object marking* (tom).

The tag "*T*" hedges on the exact shape(s) assumed by the marker upon incorporation. Orthographic evidence fromm all three dialects as well as SM trad pron suggest postvocalic *T* (cf. S < <ḥzTh> t[āzắt̪a] 'er sah sie(fs)', Macs 233, <šlḥwTy> T[šællǽʔū́t̪i] 'lasst mich gehen!', Macs 230); and postconsonantally *īT* (SM <w²nyq(y)Th> t[wīnīqī́te] 'und ich werde ihn saugen', Macs 183; CP <ṣDyThwn> 'er erfasste sie(mp)', Sg 79 (√ṣWd); G <TPŝyTwn> 'er ergriff sie(mp)', Da 360) or alternatively under some conditions perhaps *T* alone (G <²GyBwnTh> 'sie(mp) antworteten ihr(fs)', Da 367).[146]

The latter form suggests a relatively late date for tom, following incorporation into the pf of 3mp *Ůn* from the impf, hii, §7.2 (δ) (hii > *ʾɔγī́v(ū)* + *Ůn* → *ʾɔγīvŮn* tom > *ʾɔγīvŮn* + *Tắh* → [*ʾɔγīvŪntắh*])—though the possibility cannot be excluded that the *T* was later inserted into *ʾɔγīvŮnnắh* after the prefabricated sub-obj complex -*Ůnnắh* had been imported into pf by hti, §7.2 (ζ). A similar but somewhat stronger case for the lateness of tom can be made vis-à-vis the SM-specific suffixation of *hū* 'he' onto 3ms defective pfs, §2 n. 8c: <wm9wTwn> 'und er schlug sie(mp)', Macs 233, *ůmḥắ* (or likely already *ům9ắ*, §9.3.2) + *hú* > *ům9ắ(h)ū* tom > *ům9ắ(h)ū* + *TŮn* probably r-cnd^r-coa → [*ům9ŪTŮn*]. The case for late tom may be stronger here in that we apparently find no cases of such a medial <w> in transitive sim pf 3ms forms which are *T*-less; e.g., while /__3mp <nwn> we find <mṭnwn> 'er kam zu ihnen' (Macs 233), we find nothing like @<mṭwnwn>. (Of course, Macuch's relevant corpus is extremely small.)[147]

Of the three dialects manifesting tom, both SM and G have a hearty showing of the process, while it is more modest in CP (where it is limited to pf). A few examples in addition to those already adduced: SM <GlTyn> t[gālắtan] 'er hat sie(fp) offenbart', <²ršTyn> t[æršắtən] 'er hat uns befohlen' (Macs 233)—note the homopgraphic and trad-pron-homonymous 3fp and 1p object suffixes, <-yn> t[-ən], <²PqDTK> 'ich verordne dich' (Macs 228); CP <KsyTn> 'er deckte uns zu' (Sg 78), <DwywTy> 'sie machten mich elend' (lc); G <ys²BTyh> 'er erklärt ihn zu unrein' (Da 370), <ŝwBqTy> ~ <ŝBqwTyh> 'lasse(fs) ihn!' (Da 376)—for other aspects of these variants, see n. 147 and §17.25 (sip).

Restriction of tom to CP, SM, and G plausibly follows from its being a relatively late process not shared by SR, TL, or M due to the scarcity of the preposition *yāt* in the Eastern dialects.[148]

17.31. *u* Apocope (uap)

If one accepts the classical view whereby the pA pf 1s suffix was of shape -*tu* and the impf declarative suffix of shape *-u*, then *u apocope* (uap) names the process dropping the *u* in auslaut earlier than epenthesis (§17.6) and hence feeding the latter's break-up of word-final clusters. Relevant events are sketched in (17.31A) (i) on the basis of the sim intransitive pf; contrast (ii), a homoparadigmatic transitive (1s^2ms) where uap and hence epn are thwarted by failure of the auslaut condition, and (iii) where the thwarting vowel (*a* of 2ms *-ta*) is then lost by short apocope (§17.22)—essentially a subsequent generalization of uap extending the apocope to the nonlabial short vowels, *i* and *a*.[149]

(17.31A) (i) *QaSáMtu (ii) *QaSaMtúkā (iii) *QaSáMta
uap QaSáMt — —
epn QaSáMit — —
sap — — QaSáMt

In this book, for reasons enumerated in other sections (§2.3.4.1, §2.3.4.3, §7,2), uap is omitted as A-internally unmotivated at least in the verb system, the pA 1s suffix being taken to have been vowelless *-t and the declarative suffix *i.[150] (Formulation of uap is nevertheless provided here in view of widespread acceptance of *-tu, *-u as correct for pA. In any event, modification of the book's position in accommodation of *-tu, *-u and uap would be minimal.)

17.32. *w* Drop (wdr)

Minimally, eight dialects (P, TR, CP, SM, G, SR, TL, M) show at least some instances of the sim impf of √hwy abbreviated by loss of 2√w—a pattern to be called *w drop* (wdr). Moreover, to judge by vocalized spellings (TR, SR) and some trad pron (TL), the process is either ancient enough to have preceded reduction (§4.2) or was followed up by a reprise of reduction. This is so in that the result of wdr affecting, say, 3ms *yIhwÍ* is [yə̆hÍ], with prefixal *I* weakened to [ə̆] in a pretonic open syllable, rather than @[yIhÍ] as might be expected had the moment for (reprise) reduction passed by the time wdr took place: *yIhwÍ* (r-)red ≥ *yIhwÍ* wdr > @[yIhÍ].[151]

A bit of evidence for assuming wdr^r-red rather than wdr^(primary) red may be gathered from a plausible interpretation of a bias in the distribution of wdr categories, set forth in (17.32A). As may be seen here, while all eight dialects show evidence of wdr under condition (i) —/__-Í <k-coa (§11) *-áyi or coa/sap (§11, §17.22) *-íyi- and condition (ii) —/__Ǔ(n) <e- coa +mtr (§11, §17.12) -áwn < e-cnd (§8.1) -ayǓn < sap(+ deg) (§17.22, §3.1 (3Fvii)) -ayúna/-ayŭnna—, only three show wdr under condition (iii) —/__Ӑ(n) < e-cnd+mtr -ayӑn < sap(+deg) -ayӑna/-ayӑnna.[152] This lopsided distribution seems more plausible if the reason for the majority of dialects failing to show wdr /__Ӑ(n) (α) has nothing to do with /__Ӑ(n) being less conducive to wdr than /__Ǔ(n) or /__Í, but rather (β) bespeaks the relative infrequency of the frame /__Ӑ(n) due to the relative scarcity of e-cnd of *-ayā (§8.1), and invites the conclusion that (γ) the immediate operative factor for wdr's failure here was inhibition of the process /__ə̆.[153] In summary: (δ) wdr applies /__V̆ unrestrictedly, thus under conditions (i) and (ii) without constraint and under condition (iii) modulo the relative infrequency of this frame due to an independent restriction on e-cnd (which indirectly feeds wdr); but (ε) wdr fails to apply /__ə̆, specifically in the string -ə̆yӑ(n) < r-red -ayӑ(n), (ζ) not < primary red -ayӑ(n) for the reason stated at the outset: if r-red were to be excluded from consideration, the order red^wdr would predict results like @[yIhI] rather than actually attested [yɜ̱hÍ].

Finally, it is possible but not foregone that at least CP shows some extension of wdr beyond the root √hwy (condition (iv)). The reason this extension is less than conclusive is that a spelling like <yrw̯n> need not spell [yɜrŮn], but might rather haplographically represent [yIrw̯Ůn], with 2√[w] intact, <w> concurrently spelling both [w] and adjacent [Ů].[154]

(17.32A)

	P	TR	CP	SM
(i)	3ms <yh²> (~<yhw²>)	3ms [yɜhɛ́] ~[yɜhǽ] 1s sb[²ehɛ́] (~ sb[²ehwɛ́] ~bb[²æhwɛ́])	1s <yhy> 2ms <thy> ~<th²> (~<thw²>?)	3ms <yhy> t[yã́²i] ~<yy> t[yı̃́] ~<hy> t[ı̃́] (~<yhyy> t[yɛ́yyi]) 1s <²hy> t[ã́²i] <why> (~<w²wy> t[wɛ́bi])
(ii)	3mp <yh(w)n>	3mp [yɜhón]	3mp <yhwn> 2mp <Thwn> (~<Thwwn>²)	3mp <yhwn(w)> t[yṹn(u)]
(iii)		2fs [ũθ(ɜ)hǽn]	3fp<yhn> ~<yhyn>	3fp <yhn> t[yɛ́n] (~<²hyyn>)
(iv)?			3mp <yrwn> (~<yrwwn>)	

	G	SR	TL	M
(i)	3ms <yh²> ~<yy²> ~<yy> (~<lhwy>)	3ms [nɜhɛ́] (~[nɛhwɛ́])	3ms a&y[yɜhɛ́] (~ a[yɛhɜ̆wɛ́] ~y[yihwɛ́]) a[nɜhɛ́] (~ y[nihwɛ́])	3ms <lihia> ~ <nihia> ~ <lehuia> ~ <nihiua>)
(ii)	3mp <yhwn> ~<yywn> (~<yhwwn>)	3mp [nɜhón] (~c[nɛhwón])	3mp <nyhw> a[nɜhó]	3mp <nihu(n)> ~<nehu>

17.33. Weak Imperative Change (wic)

Primarily by inheritance from pSemitic, a large number of triradical verbs in early Aramaic systematically appeared in the sim impa bereft of one radical. This is notably so in all *√w verbs and many *√n verbs, which show up minus their first radical (cf. for *√wθb, O <ŝBw> 'wohnt!' (De 74) with <ŝ> [θ] (§17.14), I <TB> 'weile!' (L 59f.) after *t < θ* by occ (§17.14); for *√wd9, B [dá9] 'wisse!' (BL 142); for *√nḥt, I <ḥT> 'komm herab!' (L 57); for *√npq, B [púqū] 'kommt heraus!' (BL 136). A similar abridgement held of *√slq, which in the sim impa showed up minus $2\sqrt{}$l (cf. TR [sǽq] 'steig herauf!' (Da 294)).[155]

Largely overlapping this early period of stable triradical ~ biradical distribution, the sim impa's of $*1\sqrt{}^{\,?}$ verbs remain thoroughly triradical. But then, following the period of TR, such forms themselves begin to alternate between the full *?SM* shape and truncated *SM*: e.g., on $*\sqrt{}^{\,?}$kl 'eat', CP <?Kwl> ~ <Kwl> (Sl 5), TL y[? xol] (Mor 165) a[?ɔ̌xól] ~ [kól] (Mar 87*)—a variation especially pervasive on the antonymous pair of motion verbs $*\sqrt{}^{\,?}$zl 'go' and $*\sqrt{}^{\,?}$ty 'come': e.g., SM (fs) <?zly> t[ēzáli] (ms) <zl> t[zǽl] (Macs 103, 177), G (ms) <?yz(y)l> (mp) <zylw> (Da 301f) and (ms) <?yT?> ~ <T?> (DA 357), SR (ms) [zél] and [tɔ̌] (B 91).

Overlapping this development, in turn, or perhaps slightly later, the reflexes of the truncated $*1\sqrt{}$w imperatives inherited down the pike from pSemitic begin to alternative with innovatory full, triradical forms—i.e., forms having in anlaut either [yV-] (< *wV- pan-Aramaically by wpl, §17.34) or [(?)Ĭ-] (< yV- by ymn, §14.1):[156] e.g., on $*\sqrt{}$wθb > $\sqrt{}$ytb, CP <yTB̦> ~ <TB̦> (Sl 88), TL (mp) <?yTyBw> ~ <TyBw> (Mar 39), M <etib> ~ <tib̦> (Macm 310); on $*\sqrt{}$whb > $\sqrt{}$yhb 'give', SM (fs) <yhBy> ~ <hBy> ~ <hwy> (Macs 181) with <w> by inverse spelling (§21.1 (21E)) (see also forms discussed in §17.23.3), G (mp) <y(h)Bwn> ~ <hBw(n)> (Da 310) with <hB> ~ <B> in the first variant [hB] ~ [bb], §9.2.2). Similarly the number of phonetically $1\sqrt{}$n-bearing variants <ḥT> 'komm herab!' and <ṭr> 'bewahre!' (L 57), contrast SM $1\sqrt{}$n-bearing <nhT> ~ <n9T> t[nǽt] (Macs 186f.), G <ḥwT> ~ <nḥwT> (Da 294), TL $1\sqrt{}$n-bearing (ms) y[nɔ̌héθ] a[nɔ̌hóθ] but $1\sqrt{}$n-less a&y[ḥúθū] (Mar 136*, Mor 185f.), M $1\sqrt{}$n-bearing <nṭar> ~ <nṭur> (Macm 293f.).

Though there are both qualitative and quantitative differences among the dialects with respect to their participation in all this, the fundamental trend may be one of cross-paradigmatic (and cross-lexical) leveling whereby a morphophonological alternation *generalizes* rather than, as frequently, resolving itself itself in favor of one of the alternants. Concretely, we may speculate along lines like the following: (α) To begin with, there was some variation in the $*1\sqrt{}$n verbs inherited from pSemitic, in the sim impa ms *nV̌SV̌M* (for some roots/stem types) ~ *SV̌M* (for others); (β) then $1\sqrt{}^{\,?}$ verbs begin to follow suit, apheresis of *?V̌-* being likely facilitated by the general lability of ? (§9.2.1), the tendency to truncate probably situationally enhanced in the case of the high-frequency verbs of motion /?ty 'come' and /?zl 'go', all the more so in abruptness-friendly imperatives 'come (here)!', 'go (away)!'; (γ) now that a sizeable pattern of long~short variation has been established in the sim impa, the remaning short singletons—$\sqrt{}$slq and the $1\sqrt{}$y (< $*1\sqrt{}$w) verbs—begin to develop long impa variants.[157]

This overall developmental hypothesis—*weak imperative change* (wic)—is diagrammed in (17.33A). Participation of the dialects is sketched in (17.3B).[158]

(17.33A)
markedness
status of the
sim impa
shape types

in A at large	**I** >	**II** >	**III**
unmarked	long	long~short	long~short
marked	long~short (1√n)	long~short (1√n, 1√?)	long~short (1√n, 1√?, 1√y, √slq)
marked	short (1√y, √slq)	short (1√y, /slq)	

(17.33B)	1√n	1√?	1√y (< *1√w)	1√slq
Y,O,I,B,(P),(N),TR	long~short	long	short	short
CP	long~short	long~short	short	short
SR, TL	long~short	long~short	long~short	short
SM, G	long~short	long~short	long~short	short
— — — — — — —	— — — —	— — — —	— — — —	— — —
M	long~short	long	long~short	long~short

Observe that the overall developmental progression portrayed in (17.33B), displayed above the dotted line, is not necessarily fully in phase with the chronological progression of the dialects (to the extent that this can be determined, §19). That is, some older dialects may be more advanced with respect to the trend than some younger dialects.

In this general vein, observe that M is isolated (beneath the dotted line) as possibly falling outside the main trend. The crucial maverick aspect of M in this regard is its failure to field short 1√? forms, a datum that might be interprested in either of two diametrical ways: (*) M never developed any short 1√? forms to begin with, in which case it would devolve wholly upon the 1√n verbs (and perhaps the **1√y verbs, n. 157) to trigger long~short variation in the 1√y (< *1√w) and √slq categories; (*) M did once in fact evince long~short variation in 1√?, but ended up reverting to invariant (unmarked) long behavior—perhaps as part of a dialect-specific trend to fully generalize long. (This latter hypothesis receives support from the fact that in Modern M both 1√n and 1√y imperatives have lost the old short variants completely; Macm 294f., 314).[159]

17.34. *w* Palatalization (wpl)

w palatalization (wpl) is the name to be given the manifestation in the Aramaic verb of the general Northwest Semitic change of onset *1√w to *y*: Y <y̧ŠBT> 'ich habe gesessen' (DR I 214:8), [yaθíbt]; O <yD9> 'wissend' (De

46) assuming with DM 188 cognation of the root with Arabic √wd9 (contra Brockelmann 1928: 296);[160] I <yhBT> 'ich gab', <yTy̱{D9}> 'es wird bekannt gemacht' (L 60)—note for A at large that formulation of wpl as applying to *onset* *1√w as opposed to the same segment in *anlaut*, as traditionally assumed, correctly predicts the change to apply to *r̊mp* forms of sim and int (below), while the same segment as *coda* is exempted in the cau, plain or rmp, I <hw̱D9>'machte bekannt' (lc) (though secondarily codal *1√w occasionally > *y* for reasons of paradigmatic homogenization as discussed in §17.5); B sim plain [yə̆hav=] (Dan 2:37) (procliticized form, §20.3, §21.7), rmp [yiθyə̆hív] (Dan 4:13), int rmp [ʔiθyə̄9átū] (Dan 6:8) ([. . . ǝ9. . .] < *a99* by mls, §9.3.1) (all forms cited BL 142f); P sim pf 3ms <yD9>, <yhB>, <yTB> (HC 369, 371); N sim plain <yhBw> 'ils donnèrent', sim rmp <yTylD> 'il naîtra' (Cl 103); TR <yD9>, <yhB>, <ylD> (Dalman 1938: 180, 183); CP <yr(w)T> 'er erbte', <yqyDT> 'sie brannte' (Sg 60, 62, 75); SM sim plain <yTB> t[yắtɑb], int rmp <ʔTyqrT> 'sie wurde schwer' (Macs 144, 183); G <yTB>, <yhB>, <yrT>, <yD9> (Da 308f.); SR sim plain pf [īðá9], sim rmp impf [nɛθīðá9] (Ns 115) (for anlaut and inlaut [ī] ← ymn yə̆, §14.2): TL sim plain <(y)hBw> (for the *y*-less variant, §17.33 n. 159a), sim rmp <ʔ(y)TyhyBT>, int rmp <ʔyyqr> (Mar 37, 41, 45) (the last form a[ʔiyyaqqár] Mar 121*, y[ʔiyyæqqǽr] (Mor 367,[. . .iyy. . .] < ...*iTy*. . .by rrf, §10);[161] M reflexes of *√wld 'bear' (note the M-specific peculiarity of 2√1–3√d metathesis in this root) sim plain [yeðláθ] ~ [yaðláθ] (±att), <iidlat> ~ <iadlat> Macm 13, 111, m[yédlat] Macm 445), int rmp [eθyaddál] (<etiadal> t[etyáddal] Macm 95).

The occasional exceptions to wpl cluster in the intensive: TR [yə̆wæddḗ] (Da 311); CP, Schulthess provides no specific examples, but states that "{e} inige Verba schwanken im . . . Etpa. {int rmp} zwischen *Ii̯* und *u̯* {1√y and 1√w}" (Sg 75); G pf 3fp <ʔyTwD9yn> (for 3fp <-yn>, §7.2 ( ) with n. 13), impf 3mp <yyTwwTrwn> (Da 314); SR [wa9(9)ɛð], [ɛθwa9(9)að] 'bestellen' (Ns 114). N <wqP> 'il consacra', a possible sim exception, may as Cantieau hints be borrowed from Arabic *waqafa*—but in any event he brands the form as "très douteux" (Cl 90).[162]

Notes to §17

[1] It is conceivable that in the case of CP at least part of what is being taken here as arp derives from (overlap with) the CP proclivity toward palatalization in various environments, notably *a* → *I* in stressed closed syllables (§12 n. 11).

[2] (a) A somewhat uneasy aspect of the mtr analysis of defective -*Ay* is the apparent absence of pf def 3fs or 1s forms spelled <-ʔyT> or <-yyT>, which would betray -mtr variants ending in [-AyT], though ±mtr alternants for strong 3√ forms are commonplace (3fs -mtr <-T> [-Aθ] +mtr <-ʔ> [-Ā], 1s +mtr <-y> [-ī] -mtr <-yT> [-iθ]). (b) For [-Ay] as opposed to coalesced [-ē], see §11 n. 1. (c) Does auslaut 3fs/1s [-Ay] of the defective verb show up in any other dialect than TL? G shows one prima facie instance, <B9ʔy̱> 'ich brauchte' (Da 343); but G never shows mtr of 1s <-yT> [-IT] in verbs with strong

3√, so perhaps we must be wary of assuming that <B9ʔy> represents a pure G form. Might it be an intrusion from TL? (Cf. §17.9 n. 26.)

[3] With few exceptions—e.g., brb, ptc (§17.20)—lexically based changes will not be systematically treated in this book, though partial or informal observations will occasionally be made, as in the sequel of this note. (a) Root blendings, like brb, are distinct from but often related to various other phenomena, a few of which will be mentioned here (b, c). Another root blending is TL √ntn X √yhb → √ntb 'give'; e.g. impf 3ms y&a[nittév] (Mor 366, Mar 120*), with [tt] ← 1√n t by rna (§17.21). Some blendings, as this one, have a definite directionality; in this case, √ntn → √ntb (as opposed to √yhb → √ntb), cued not only be relative simplicity (single 3√n → 3√b rather than double 1√y → 1√n and 2√h → 2√t) but even more cogently by the fact (cf. (b) below) that, the blend √ntb aside, the impf of the sim 'give' lexeme in TL has an exponent √ntn with 2ʃe (e.g., 1s y[ʔættén], a[ʔɛttén]—Mor 374, Mar 139*) while the exponent of the pf is solely √yhb (the impa may be expressed by either root). So interpreting [nittév] as a result of √ntn → √ntb requires only replacing 3√n by 3√b while √yhb → √ntb would in addition to double √yh → √nt require the root being replaced to occur in trappings, the impf, from which it is normally restricted. (Notationally for such directional cases, perhaps the root to be replaced might be bold-faced: **√ntn** X √yhb → √ntb.) (b) Root blendings of the sort just discussed are *syntagmatic*, in that the roots involved in the blend are cooccurrently realized, albeit in truncated form. Thus, √ntn is realized in √ntb by 1√ 2√, while √yhb manifests through 3√. Distinct from but sometimes antecedent to such syntagmatic blending is a sort of *paradigmatic* mixing, whereby two or more roots are "blended" into the verb system via assignment to designated slots while retaining their word-wise indepdendence. Thus, as we have seen in TL, putting the syntagmatic blend √ntb aside, the root √ntn occurs in the impf, √yhb in the pf, and both in the impa—but distributed paradigmatically as alternative choices, not cooccurrently as blends proper (e.g., ms 'give!' may be either [tén] or [hÁv] (1√n missing since pSemitic, §1.6 with n. 7, 1√y apherized by wic, §17.33). CP and SR are similar, differing in that impa shows only √yhb—as well as in one additional regard to be discussed under (c) below; SM shows √ntn ~ √yhb in pf/impa. Paradigmatic "blending" of this sort is customarily labeded *suppletion*—the term to be used for it in the sequel, syntagmatic blending normally to be referred to as *blending* tout court. (c) Though the results of root blends are syntagmatically organized—thus, parts of √ntn and √yhb cooccur in √ntb—paradigmatic factors are involved in their origins—thus √ntn and √yhb conspire to create a blend by dint of being synonymous but alternative resources within the same overarching system, not by dint of literally cooccurring in one and the same linguistic string. However, Aramaic at times shows *hybrid blends* where linguistic material from outside a root gets incorporated as a radical into the root exactly by dint of systematically cooccurring with the root in one and the same linguistic string. Thus, at least CP and SR show √ntl 'give', where 3√l represents lexicalization of a regressive assimilation 3√n l > 3√l l induced by the commonplace collocation of this prototypically datival verb with an immediately following prepositional phrase headed by the dative preposition *l(V)- '*to'. In CP, the lexicalization is variable (√ntl ~ √ntn in the impf, √yhb in pf/impa), while in SR it has gone to completion (√ntl in impf, √yhb in pf/impa)—Sl 79, 129; B 87, Payne Smith 1903: 188, 354. SM shows a few additional roots whose 3√l may have a similar origin: <ħgl> ~ <9gl> 'sehen', <Psql> 'schwören'; and at least one with 3√b which may

have originated from assimilation to locative *b(V)-*, <šqlB> 'zerstören'—Macs 99f., 166, 168.

[4] Intervocalic heterosyllabic consonantism is sometimes called *interlude*—and interludes are frequently found to have special properties not fully reducible to syllabic theory (narrowly construed); see, e.g., Jensen 2000.

[4'] The diachronic illustration of css offered here is simplified for the sake of exposition, the actual situation being possibly more complex. Specifically, as discussed at various spots in §6, at least some manifestations of css bid fair to have been registered phonetically in proto-Aramaic itself, though plausibly *synchronically* geared to the operation of a phonological rule, call it s-css. If so, and assuming B [tǎqéltɔ] to be a case in point, the example in the text would technically have to be corrected along the lines of (a), where the action of css is not diachronic but synchronic (irrelevant processes suppressed):

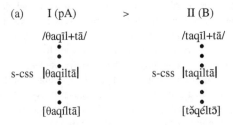

(a)   I (pA)   >   II (B)

           /θaqīl+tā/   /taqīl+tā/

    s-css |θaqiltā| s-css |taqiltā|

           [θaqíltā]   [tǎqéltɔ]

Complicating the matter even more, the status of css-linked [V̄ ~ V̊] may then further have been perturbed, under a variety of conditions, by the development of a pair of antithetical processes ironing out the alternation in favor of either [V̄] (*long schematic generalization*, lsg) or [V̊] (*short schematic generalization*, ssg). Details in §6.

[5] (a) "gross distribution"; there are some instances of *w* in one cranny or other binyanim for some dialects—namely, simple plain impf of *1√w and, just possibly, even of *1√y (perhaps only one root in one dialect; see frf, §17.7, and wpl, §17.34, for details). While the *1√w instances of sim plain impf *w* date from pA, any possible instances of *1√y > w in the same morphological niche are secondary, and whether their appearance postdates or predates cys is unclear. (A desideratum yet to be achieved is clear exposition of the chronological and interative relations among cys, frf, wic (§17.33), and wpl.)

(b) Sources are L 59; Da 307, 312, 346f.; Sg 76, Sl 89; B 94; Mor 208; Nm 244. Other, incidental radical changes include adn (TR, §9.1.4) and occ (CP; §17.14). The sample, based on these secondary sources and checked against etymologies, for the most part provided in Brockelmann 1928 or DM, may well be underrepresentative both of the dialects cited and within these.

(c) There are also items unclear of etymology; e.g., is the verb root which is lexically related to nominal *√ṭWb 'good' *√yṭb or *√wṭb?—in the cau, O shows √y (<hyṭBTh>, De 80, Kutscher 1970: 48, MP 123), I and TL show √w (<hwṭBTm>, L 60; participial <mwtyB>, Sokoloff 2002: 495), while TR shows √y ~ √w (<ʔytyB> ~ <ʔwtyB>, Jastrow 1903: 576). (Beyer (1986: 15) considers the 1√w-resolution to be Eastern, but neither SR nor M appear to have any reflexes of cau √Wṭb one way or the other.)

[6] "systematic epn"; for the qualification, see §17.6.2 <u>TR</u>.

[7] Things would work out more simply if *i* in 1s *-it* were not epenthetic but dated from pA as does the *a* of 3fs *at*, because in that event (17.6A) could be replaced by (a) below and this chapter could self-destruct. However, assumption of pA 1s *-it* leaves at least three phenomena unexplained: (*) the alternation of *i* in 1s *-it* with various other vowels under conditions accountable (ultimately) as epenthetic—see especially §17.6.2 **B** below; (*) the role of midded 2ʃ e in pf 1s forms as analogical bellwether for the copycat midding in pf 3fs forms, a role that could only exist if the 2ʃ e in the 1s once occurred in a syllable closed by 1s *-t* but hardly by *-it*—see discussion of (17.11B) in §17.11; (*) similarly, the pattern of closed-syllabic shortening in (original) hollow causatives (§6.1.1.1).

(a) **3fs**   (*b-str*) -V́Cat   ~   (*o-str*) -VCát
    1s   (*b-str*) -V́Cit   ~   (*o-str*) -VCít

[8] Some observations about entries in (17.6D): (a) [hɔθqǒnáθ] 'ich wurde wieder eingestetzt' (Dan 4:33) varies with unmarked *i*-epenthetic [hɔθqǒnɛ́θ]. Bauer and Leander take [hɔθqǒnáθ] to be a 3fs form stemming from a (reconstructed) text variant with slightly different wording (BL 116). It also varies with [hɔθqǒnɔ̄́θ], the long [ɔ̄́] of which might instantiate *either* (manqué) ancipital lengthening of the 1s suffix nucleus, as is regular for SR and M (below and §2.3.4.3) *or* tonic lengthening (§17.29)—note that the <ɔ> is marked with the taʕam *zakef* (§21.6), a sometime trigger to pause-induced tln at least in Tiberian Hebrew (THP 31). (b) [hăqémɛθ], [haddéqɛθ]. Observe how assumption of an initial, reduced-vowel stage in epn provides a plausible explanation for the color of [ɛ] as the ultimate product of an epenthetic process within a vowel system like that of Aramaic, figuring as the neutral reduced color. Were it not for this assumption, one would be at pains to account for the midness of unstressed [ɛ] in a system whose unstressed chromatic vowels are normally high, [i], [u], unless adguttural; see §17.11. (c) [hăqémɛθ]. 2ʃ [é] rather than [í] via css and ssg; §6.1.1.1.

[9] Alternatively, failure of 2 *t* to spirantize may be transparentive in origin or residual manifestation of a pA quirk to retain suffixal 2 *t* as occlusive; see §15.3.1.3. Adoption of this tack would not appreciably affect the complexity of (17.6E), removing only spr from the chain. (Recall that this process has a persistent span in B; §5.2 **B** (α).)

[10] The identification of the focal process as r'-epn has been hedged upon (introduced vaguely as "an epenthetic-like process in the environment /H__t# . . .") in view of the fact that a quite similar TR process discussed in §8.1.3 with n. 14 was identified as *excrescence*. However, the B process could not be taken as excrescence with no further ado, because exc in B *feeds* spirantization (§5.2 **B** (α)), so that 2ms [hištǒxáhat] would incorrectly be reshaped to homonymy with 3fs [hištǒxáhaθ]. In TR, on the other hand, exc only *variably* feeds spr (§5.2 **TR** (α)), so that the requisite account of exc-processed [ʔǽ9ǽd] (≠ @[ʔǽ9ǽð]) in §8.1.3 is enabled. When all is said and done, however, the discrepancy may well be no more than terminological. The processes excrescence and epenthesis are a priori functionally and formally quite similar and might even ultimately be mutually identifiable. In such an event, "excrescence"—or more narrowly "excrescence^promotion"—in §8.1.3 with n. 14 might be replaced by a rerun of "epenthesis"; or similar but reverse adjustments might be made in the present context.

[11] The Babylonian register, whose attestation is admittedly fragmentary and less informative than the Tiberian (e.g., stress is not indicated), gives no evidence for sco'.

Thus, corresponding to 3fs tb[haddéqεθ] (17.6D (iii)), we find bb[hæddeqæθ], where [-æθ] might simply reflect *-at—though sco'-generated -εθ might just as plausibly be afoot, since [æ] in a 6-color vowel system like that of Bab B may correspond to [ε] in a 7-color system like that of Tib B; §20.2 (γ). (Other Bab correspondences to Tib forms in (17.6D), both under (i): [9ævðéθ] ~ [9ævǽðiθ]—note the barytone option in the latter variant—(Dan 3:15, BL 129); [huθqǒnǽθ] (Dan 4:33, BL 116).)

[12] TR also shows at least one apparent instance of staminal epn, <yiysæK> (Da 345), seemingly a defective sim (short) impf 3ms built on √sky (< *√śky) with truncation of -*ē*# ← *2ʃ a 3√y* # in imitation of the Based-Truncated (THP 44f.) Hebrew form [yíʂεf] 'let him look' at Gen 31:45. If so, the <æ> is epenthetic, like Hebrew [ε]; the whole form being interpretable as [yísæx], [yǐsǽx], or even [ísæx], [īsǽx] (§14.2 TR). Furtrher evidence that <æ> is epenthetic is given by the unepenthesized Sabbionetan variant <yɔs:K:> (with a seemingly anomalous prefix vowel).

[13] In the Jacobite, register the epenthetic vowel is spelled with length-ambiguous <e> (rǒvōʂō, §21.4 (21H)) interpretable *either* as +l-anc [ē] without the usual, register-specific heightening to [ī] (§11.2) *or* as -l-anc [e].

[14] For the complementary mechanism in the impa, see wic (§17.33).

[15] Unless wpl was later than frf, see n. 17b below. In either eventuality, overall rapprochement between the 1√y and 1√w gězarot is also contributed to by cyl (§17.5).

[16] For concrete illustration of this issue, consider TL [tēróθ] and TR [yikkól] (cf. below in the text), taking as 1√w-less proto-forms *tarúθi* and *yakúli*. What if frf applies late, specifically after red (in association with other processes) has changed these forms to tǎróθ and yǎxól? The resulting tǎróθ and yǎxxól would needs then undergo various retoolings in order to abut upon the actually attested forms—not all such retoolings being necessarily assumable without (significant) further ado. Specifically,while yǎxxól might plausibly end up as [yikkól] assuming base-line resolution of ǎ by prm (§14.1) as *E* (with raising to *i* as appropriate to a closed-syllabic unstressed vowel) and reo (§5.2 **B**) of *xx* to *kk*, on the basis of purely parallel considerations we might expect tǎróθ to emerge as @[tīróθ]. On the other hand, if frf is assumed *either* to be a phonetic-level process (= classical sound change) occurring prior to reduction (and other early processes) *or* to be a phonological-level process even if occurring subsequent to reduction (and other processes), everything works out pretty straightforwardly. Specifically, *either* *tarúθi* frf > tayrúθi d-sap, d-e-coa, d-mid > [tēróθ], *yakúli* frf > yakkúli d-sap, d-att > [yikkól]; *or* assuming post-reductional [tǎrÚθ], [yǎxÚl] are phonologically represented as, plausibly, /tirut/ and /yikul/, frf as a phonological-level change (or as manifested through restructuring) rendering |tiyrut| and |yikkul| will guarantee [tēróθ] and [yikkól] if appeal is made to motivated synchronic continuation of relevant diachronic processes (d-changes > s-rules) plus |iy| s-din (§8.1.1 n 1) ⇒ |ay| s-coa ⇒ [ē] to bring to results into accord with independently prevailing |V 1√y| behavior. (In the foregoing demonstration the accordion *θ occ (§17.14) > *t* spr > θ has been omitted with an eye to disemburdening the exposition a bit.)

[17] (a) In the traditional literature, the plausibility has sometimes been overlooked of pA's at least variable tolerance of overt 1√w on the simple impf, as well as straightforward reflexes of such 1√w's lasting into several descendant dialects; see below. (Note incidentally that Classical Arabic likewise shows variable 1√[w] ~ [Ø] in the sim impf, 1√[w] regularly appearing in the ablaut frame 1ʃ a–2ʃ a; e.g. *yaw̱hamu* 'feels ap-

petite'.) (b) Even though filling by *y*-insertion (type (α)) is possibly the most frequent manifestation of frf in A at large, as clearly it is in SR, and wpl^frf can provide an explanation for that, the very fact that frf and associated patterns—(α, β, γ, δ)—assume so many forms might rather suggest frf^wpl. In either event, the matter cannot be fully adjudicated without considering the disposition of cys (§17.5).

[18] However, mention should be made of one variant reading explainable as instantiating pattern (γ)—[yɔ̄θív], BL 143—as well as two other variant readings suggesting full escape from frf: [yɔ̄θív], [yɔ̄ðá9] (lc).

[18′] In default of revelatory extra-Aramaic cognates, etymology as *√w is assumed via convergence of A-internal patterns in TR (γ) and CP (δ)—though the evidential value of (δ) might be less than airtight (cf. discussion under B of (α′) in (17.7A)).

[19] Consider also 'know' <ywD9>, whether < *√wd9 or *√yd9; cf. discussion under B above.

[20] A few additional roots may show cau 1√w C′ > C′C′ as well: *√wqd as per <wʔqDnh> (note the absence of <w> between prefixal <ʔ> and 2√<q>), *√wsp 'add, do again' <wʔsP>. However, the latter form shows coalescence rather than gemination of 1√w in trad pron (t[wǔ̠sɔ̄f]), while a homoparadigmatic form evinces the expected orthographic-trad pron pairing <w> t[ū]: <TwsP> t[tǔ̠sɔf]; and the former shows a pf alternant where <w> t[ū] likewise prevails: <wʔwqDT yTh> t[wū̠qḗðǎt yǎ́ta] 'und ich habe es verbrannt' (Macs 183). So we may be simply dealing with ḥaser (ml-less) writing of t[ū], perhaps specifically in the frame /<wʔ>___ (<w> = the conjunctive proclitic, <ʔ> = the 1s prefix).

[21] These interpretations ignore the possibility of mls (§9.3.1), which, if it should apply, would neutralize the difference between (α) and (β), changing *Ihh* to *ēh*. A form void of this factor is <TyTBwn> (*√wθb), representing either [tēθ(ɔ̄)BǓn] via (α) or [tɪttɔ̄βǓn] via (β)—the latter likely, since in clear cases throughout A *√wθb appears to choose gemination; see end of this subchapter (§17.7) below.

[22] (a) Since in SM only the causative of *√9dʔ/y is attested, and all instances of 1√ and 2√ are hence contiguous, there are no forms of this verb where gds fails to apply. Hence, the root has been lexically metanalyzed (restructured) to √/ndX/, where *X* represents whatever value *3√ʔ / *3√y has (via adn) evolved into synchronically. Contrast with this state of affairs the situation in I and B where the gds-created alloroots continue to alternate synchronically with alloroots escaping gds either by dint of failing to meet the conditions of gds (e.g., B sim pf [9ál], BL 167, where [9] realizes singleton |9|) or because gds is variable (e.g., B [hɔ̄9élnī] cited in the text, where s-gds fails to apply despite |99|, which then degeminates via s-mls, §9.3.1).

(b) It is also possible that t[ǽndα] is built not on * /9dʔ/y, but rather on *√nðy (for the etymology, Brockelmann 1928: 415), hence *hanðáya with ultimate [nd] deriving from *nð to the tune of occlusion (> nd) followed by failure to geminate. In fact, this *√9dʔ/y / *√nðy ambiguity extends to *all* SM causative forms; see §24.2 SM under the respective roots.

[23] (a) "on a (largely) separate track": the qualification being prompted by the possibility of various sorts of wave-developmental leakage; see §18, and specifically for the matter of Y and O, §17.21 with n. 107. (b) Partially in line with (a), the apparent patness of (17.8C) is belied by the fact that subsequent dialects by no means present a

uniform trajectory for gds, and notably M is particularly active. The impact of gds has often been attributed to an Akkadian substratum; see e.g. Kaufman (1974: 120f.).

[24] (a) The value [ū] is likely, as being the most straightforward interpretation of both Yemeni and Ashkenazic TL trad pron. (Both Morag and Margolis convey this by <uw>, per se ambiguous between [ū] and [u], but other factors in trad pron converge to make [ū] more likely than [u] for the infix; notably, both traditions agree on +mid, §17.11, [o] in sim impa ms [Qə̆Só̱M], and the tonosyllabic similarity of this frame to that of i-lap-affected forms suggests that if i-lap left a short vowel it would be realized in trad pron as [o]—which in fact may be bespoken in the vocalized Codex Halberstamm, <ʔɔm<u>owr</u>>; Da 254 n 4.)

(b) A point against the developmental hypothesis of (17.9A) might be the dearth of attested forms congruent with stage *QaSSÚmū*, though conservative analogs corresponding to *QaSSÍMū* abound, as also do fully +i-lap forms like *QaSSű̱M*. Note, however, TL cau impa y[ʔæ̱ḥz<u>ū̱</u>qu] 'haḥaziku' (Mor 159) (though conceivably the 2ʃ in this form transparentively mimics that of the simple verb, cf. §15.5.2—a change instigated by the fact that in TL√ḥzq may be a "causativum tantum" with a semantic function more akin to that of a simple verb; cf. Malone 1974a).

(c) Though 2ʃ of verbs targeted by i-lap usually starts out as short, this is not inevitably the case. Notably, 2ʃ of hollow verbs starts out as long (see under <u>TL</u> below).

[25] (a) Pace Schulthess's interpretation of such <y>s—and the mp <w>s likewise—as "stumm." (b) The first variant of def <šry> ~ <šryw> 'sie begannen' (Sg 17) bears pondering in the event the second variant represents +e-cnd (§8.1) [šarríw], inasmuch as lap would not per se apply to -*iw*. Two possibilities come to mind: s-lap has become phonologized in CP so that s-lap^s-e-cnd (via rule reordering from d-e-cnd^d-lap) resulting in the representation effected not being *šarríw* but /šarriyū/ (or some similar, intermediate derivative); alternatively <šry> represents a +pin (§17.17) form whose suffix has been (partially) reshaped by the mp participial ending, perhaps [šarrḗ] < pin *šarrő* <e-cnd *šarráyū (for *-2ʃ a 3√y in lieu of or alternating with *-2ʃ i 3√y, see din §8.1.1 with n. 1 and note specifically the attested alternant <šrw>, Sg 72).

[26] (a) Note that Kutscher challenges the presence of i-lap in G, considering it a TL intrusion (1976: 15). (b) Observe the contrasting deployment of schematic mls in <ŝqyly>, <zwBnyn>, interepretable as [šə̆qÍlī], [zUβnín], the latter form giving evidence that hii has become phonologized in G, -*in* being added not to the *phonetic* stem (à la LP, synchronically introduced into the derivation at a later lexical stratum) as are hii-originated suffixes notably in SR (n. 27 below), but rather to the *phonological* stem (introduced before the first stratum = at the phonological/lexical level) so that /zə̆bIn – īn/ s-str, s-spr, s-red ⇒ |zə̆βnín| s-sip ⇒ [zUβnín]. Diachronically, it may be speculated that such cases of phonologization undergo an antecedent stage where assimilation to the canons of the grammar is, so to speak, more touch-and-go, achieved not yet through structural accommodation to the phonology—lexical-level introduction, etc.—but by a species of analogical reshaping attendant upon attachment of the imported suffix, the reshaping reflecting speakers' (largely unconscious) efforts to bring the new stem+suffix combinations into better sync with the overarching system than would result from merely allowing the new combines to fall out as they may. In this case, the analogical reshaping would plausibly take as model preexisting stem+suffix combinations precedently structurally similar in certain regards, notably transitive stem+object syntheses

like [šUlqä́h] (ms^3fs), [9UrBán] (ms^1s), [šUβqín] (ms^3fp) (Da 375f.). Following this preliminary stage, likely as part and parcel of the language acquisition of a later generation (or generations) not party to the original suffix importation, full structural integration of the processes would at last be achieved. A sketch of such a developmental chain appears in (c) (on a reflex of *QšSúM* for more direct comparability with SR in n. 27); see §23.3 for nuts-and-bolts of the LP conventions investing such displays. wrb = word building, str = strsss (§4.1), ars = analogical reshaping, sta = stress adjustment—these latter two being subprocesses of hii = heavy intransitive importation—, rst = restructuring, red = reduction (§4.2), sip = simple imperative promotion (§17.25). Observe that preliminary hii, at stage III, manifests the run-of-the-mill behavior of a change-become-rule in being last ordered in the phonology, while at post-integrational stage IV it has migrated deep into the phonology—as deep as possible, in fact, manifesting as restructuring by replacing suffix /ī/ with imported /īn/. Transition from III to IV instantiates a special case of *rule reordering*. (Some accessory speculation on preliminary instances of phonologization like hii at stage III: it may well be that the form assumed by such analogical reshapings often differs in subtle ways, or even not so subtle ways, from the form finally settling in after integration, here IV. No such differences have, to my knowledge, yet come to light. See Malone 1992a.)

(c)   **I**   *d-lap >*   **II**
                 /QšSUM, ī/   /QšSUM, ī/
    stratum 1: *s-wrb* |QšSUMī| **stratum 1:** *s-wrb* |QšSUMī|
                    s-str |QšSÚMī| *s-str* |QšSÚMī|
                                                           s-lap |QšSÚM|

                              [QšSÚMī]   [QšSÚM]

                 d-hii >   **III**   *d-rst >*   **IV**
                 [+d-ars]
                 [+d-sta]   /QšSUM, ī/   *s-hii*   /QšSUM, īn/
    stratum 1: *s-wrb* |QšSUMī| **stratum 1:** *s-wrb* |QšSUMín|
                    s-str |QšSÚMī| *s-str* |QšSUMín|
                    s-lap |QšSÚM| *s-red* |QšSMín|
                    s-hii   *s-sip* |QUSMín|
                 [+s-ars]
                 [+s-sta] |QUSMín |
                              [QUSMín]   [QUSMín]

[27] Mechanically, G and SR differ in that SR hii lacks concomitant analogical reshaping (ars), so that addition of the imported suffixes involves simple tacking onto the phonetic stem without modification other than stress adjustment (sta); see (a) at stage III. Subsequently, the effects of this nexus are synchronically integrated by deferring addition of the new suffixes until after the rules have applied which would otherwise have resulted in suffixation-attendant reshaping of the type (at least roughly) diachronically achievable by ars. In Lexical Phonology, such a synchronic organization is readily available by relegating suffixation to a lexical stratum posterior to that housing the rules to be avoided (*counterbled*)—stratum 2 at stage IV in (a). Had a standard Generative Phonological model been employed, like that codified in Chomsky and Halle 1968,

for instance, such a result would have been difficult or impossible to achieve, since it is a normal tenet of standard phonologies that all morphological operations—here suffixation via wrb—precede en bloc all phonological operations. Consequently, in a standard GP model the synchronic effects of SR-style hii would needs be achieved indirectly—e.g., by immunizing 2ʃ from synchronic reduction (s-red) in coconstruction with certain suffixes—namely, those supplied by d-hii, the immunization being implemented by calibrated diacritic features built into the formulation of s-red and lexically supplied to the suffixes in question (for one approach to this, see THP 32, <u>Syntactic Features</u>).

(a)

		I	*d-lap >*				**II**
		/QšSoM, ā/					/QšSoM, ā/
stratum 1:	*s-wrb*	|QšSoMā|		**stratum 1:**	*s-wrb*	|QšSoMā|
	s-str	|QšSóMā|			*s-str*	|QšSóMā|
						s-lap	|QšSóM|
		[QšSóMā]					[QšSóM]

	d-hii >	**III**	*d-rst >*				**IV**
	[+d-sta]	/QšSoM, ā/					/QšSoM/
stratum 1:	*s-wrb*	|QšSoMā|		**stratum 1:**	*s-wrb*	|QšSoM|
	s-str	|QšSóMā|			*s-str*	|QšSóM|
	s-lap	|QšSóM|					
	s-hii						
	[+s-sta]	|QšSoMḗn|		**stratum 2:**	*s-hii*	|QšSóM , ēn|
					s-wrb	|QšSóMēn|
					s-sta	|QšSoMḗn|
		[QšSoMḗn]					[QšSoMḗn]

[28] (a) Though all dialects showing evidence of lap also show evidence of hii, the opposite does not hold; note especially SM, but also TR and perhaps even I (§7.2 (δ)). On the other hand, there is often at least a de facto functional relation between them, hii providing wherewithal for lap-affected dialects to express φ-oppositions that might otherwise be lost. Note also in TL that though hii applies to (3)fp, it fails to apply to (3)mp in the nondefective verb (see n. 29)—exactly the turf of i-lap (next in the text). (b) Observe that in the Yem tradition [-ān] is hii-attached to the phonological stem but [-īn] to the phonetic stem; cf. nn. 26 and 27. The Ash tradition, on the other hand, shows exclusively phonetic stem attachment (§7.2 (δ) <u>TL</u>).

[29] Omitted from the Margolian tables surveyed are those of the defective verb (Mar 52–55), inasmuch as *condensation* (§8.1) may well preempt i-lap, whether in the form of e-cnd (*-a 3√y ū → -aw, *-i 3√yū → -iw) or p-cnd (*-i 3√y ū → -i(ʔ)ū), cnd preserving as it does the (3)mp plural signal (albeit in altered form) and hence depriving i-lap of any functional effect. Alternatively, i-lap might go through despite being functioning otiose, in which case, however, it would converge with affix-based transparentation of the type discussed in §15.3.2, e.g., y[pænnū̠́] = *pænnū́w* ← i-lap *pannáw/ panníw* ← e-cnd *pannáyū/*panníyū.

[30] Though SM trad pron shows a clear [i, e, u, o] distribution, its patterns are in large part determined by SM-specific developments having nothing directly to do with the process(es) called "midding" in this book; see smc (§22.1 (22B)).

[31] Though type examples in the initial presentation are limited to sim pf, midding itself is not so limited, as will emerge from ensuing consideration of actual forms (§17.11.2).

[32] aop is plausibly a *laxing* process, open mid vowels often being systematically lax in various languages (e.g., English); cf. also the discussion in §17.23.

[33] Since excrescence may apply to gutturalless clusters, *CC*, a fourth chain is predicted to be (a), where assimilatory sco would be frustrated by the absence of a guttural in the proper spot. However, no such strings have been found in Tib B or Ash TL.

(a) $HiCC(\ldots)\acute{V}$ a-mid $\rightarrow HeCC(\ldots)\acute{V}$ aop $\rightarrow H\varepsilon CC(\ldots)\acute{V}$ exc $\rightarrow H\varepsilon C\breve{\vartheta}C(\ldots)\acute{V}$

[34] With the qualification that partial attenuation (p-att, $a \rightarrow \varepsilon$) be decomposed into att^a-mid^aop ($a \rightarrow i \rightarrow e \rightarrow \varepsilon$); see §12 n 1 for discussion.

[35] (a) For more on a-mid and related matters, see §11 n. 1 and §12 n. 4. (b) It is possible that a-mid (*without* aop) occasionally shows up at least in the Sabbionetan register of TR; note 1s impf <ʔe̲hwey> (§17.32, Da 354), plausibly interpretable as [ʔe̲hwḛ̃]. Possibly a-mid is variably catalyzed by the flanking gutturals, though in other similarly flanked items *either* a-mid fails to apply (sb[ʔi̲9ɪ̃bǽr]) *or* is preempted by the failure of attenuation (§12) to apply (sb[ʔæ̲9æ̆béð]). Forms from Da 272.

[36] For epenthesis√*stem___suffix* acquiring suffixal rather than staminal affiliation, §15 n. 29a.

[37] Subordination of the type under discussion here often takes the form of *proclisis* of *X* to *Y*, in Tiberian orthography represented by the grapheme *makef* and transcribed in this book "=" (§21.7), *X=Y*. In light of this, consider the groups in (a):

(a) (i) [yinte̲n=lḗh] 'may give to him' (Dan 2:16)
    (ii) [yinti̲n=lḗh] variant of (i), BL 136

At issue here is the underscored alternation, respectively suggesting (i) +mid^+aop ([ε]) and (ii) -mid^-aop ([i]). How might this be explicated, on the assumption that proclisis (here, of the verb to the pp) characteristically involves less stress on the proclitic than on a full-blown word but more than, say, on a bound pretonic morpheme like a prefix? One possibility is sketched in (b, c), where a system of four stresses (b) interacts with two rules where stress plays a critical role in the structural description (c), whether positively (mid) or negatively (aop). Two rather natural assumptions are involved: that proclitics (as well as various other prosodo-syntatically subordinate constituents) are assigned rank-3 stress; and that the rules discussed here are coded for sensitivity to stress rank—specifically, mid requiring *stronger* stress and aop requiring *weaker* stress. Moreover, rank-3 behaves as borderline, eliciting variable rule reaction, whereupon the reaction of aop follows suit. This in turn explains the variation in (a) as resulting from satisfaction of two of the three possible rule-reaction combinations in response to focal rank-3 strsss: (i) ±mid^ ±aop and (ii) ±mid^ ±aop. The forms of (a) may now be fleshed out more fully as in (d).

(b) **s t r e s s   l e v e l s**

stress rank	description	domain	symbol
1	strongest	prosodically most prominent constituent ("pause")	V̈
2	second strongest	prosodically unmarked constituent ("context")	V́
3	second weakest	proclitic or other subordinate constituent	V̀
4	weakest	pretonic position within a word	V *or* V̌

(c) **s t r e s s   t h r e s h o l d s   f o r   r u l e s**

stress rank	rule	reaction
1	+mid	-aop
2	+mid	-aop
3	±mid	±aop
4	-mid	-aop

(d) (i) [yintèn=léh]

   (ii) [yintùn=léh]

As stated, two of three possible rule combinations have been illustrated, +mid +aop [ɛ̀] and -mid -aop [ì]. The third possibility, +mid -aop [è], will be discussed and illustrated in n. 40. (A fourth *logical* possibility, -mid +aop, is impossible in actuality, since +aop requires its input to be +mid.)

Note also in passing that +mid -aop as stress rank 1 in the Tiberian register is de facto rare, for the reason—irrelevant in the present connection—that in Tib mid is normally bled by tonic lengthening (tln, §17.19), which preempts mid. And note finally that a similar account of similar patterns is given in §17.15.2 n. 75.

[38] Indeed, the Bab register shows <e> even in pausal forms, where Tib shows <i>; see tln (§17.19) for discussion.

[39] The sole Tib verb form showing **u* > [o] may be the gem sim impa [gǫ́ddū] 'haut um!', which Bauer and Leander consider to be a Hebraism exactly because of the [o] (BL 168).

[40] In Malone 1988 (theoretically updating Malone 1972a), it was proposed that transparentized verbs of various sorts lend themselves to integration within the prevailing synchronic morphophonology (of TR, in that case) via Lexical Phonology (LP, §23.3), the idea being that transparentized *bases* (items taken as analogical models) should be subject to word-building operations (wrb) on a later LP stratum than corresponding constituents (usually stems) of nontransparentized verbs. As it turns out, this idea provides a simple account of transparentized variants like Ginsburg's *hizdămẹntū́n*, cited above in the text, assuming their legitimacy as bona fide variants of nontransparentized forms like *hizdắmintū́n*. Moreover, the results lend themselves to synthesis with the proposals made in n. 37 concerning stress and midding. Consider first a cross-section of an LP synchronic derivation of the nontransparentized variant [hizdắmintū́n], in (a). Let us assume for simplicity that the underlying representation of the miškal,

/hitzamin/, has already undergone autosegmental operations of association and tier conflation (§23.4). The first thing that happens, on stratum 1, is word building, whereby stem and suffix are amalgamated; and then various rules apply seriatim (for these, see §4.1/§14 n. 17, §10, §4.2) abutting upon *hizdə̆mintū́n*. This in turn serves as input to stratum 2, devoid only of wrb but otherwise showing the same rules and ordering as stratum 1. However, in the case of this form the rules all apply vacuously, with the consequence that the form surfaces unchanged as [hizdə̆mintū́n]. The corresponding derivation of transparentized *hizdə̆mentū́n* is given in (b), whereby the only difference is that word building is deferred until stratum 2, with the net consequence of bringing to the surface [hizdə̆mè̜ntū́n], where the secondary stress on 2ʃ [è̜] is retrospectively responsible both for -mid and for -aop, a legitimate combination for stress rank 3 in terms of n. 37c, as may be seen. So [hizdə̆mè̜ntū́n]—assuming its bona fides (it is after all a variant reading proposed/accepted by only one scholar)—may join [yintè̜n] and [yintṳn] of n. 37d in manifesting three of the four logical combinations of ±mid ±aop implicit in n. 37c for stress rank 3—the fourth possibility, -mid +aop, being ruled out as impossible.

(a)	**stratum 1**	/hitzamin, tūn/	(b)		/hitzamin, tūn/
	wrb	|hitzamintūn|			
	str/sta	|hitzamintū́n|	*str/sta*		|hitzamín, tū́n|
	rmt	|hizdamintū́n|	*rmt*		|hizdamín, tū́n|
	red	|hizdə̆mintū́n|	*red*		|hizdə̆mín, tū́n|
	mid	—	*mid*		|hizdə̆mén, tū́n|
(a)	**stratum 2**	|hizdə̆mintū́n|	(b)		|hizdə̆mén, tū́n|
			wrb		|hizdə̆méntū́n|
	str/sta	—	*strsta*		|hizdə̆mè̜ntū́n|
	rmt	—	*rmt*		—
	red	—	*red*		—
	mid	—	*mid*		—
		[hizdə̆mintū́n]	~		[hizdə̆mè̜ntū́n]

[41] Notice also the failure of p-att /1√H__ in the light-suffixed sim pf intransitives: [9a̲vðéθ], [ʾa̲mréθ]; contrast attenuated [qi̲rvéθ], [ši̲m9éθ], etc. (BL 173).

[42] The fact that in pause [ḯ] often appears while [é] appears in context, especially in the Sabbionetan register (Malone 1974b), does not strictly speaking reflect variability of md but rather variability of tln bleeding mid; see §17.29 for details.

[43] The Yem tradition shows a variant [sǽkkæ̜ntū́n]; cf. §2 n. 22.

[44] "to thwart mid"; since the original run of mid had already resulted in y&a *Qə̆SéMiθ*, it was too late for the new mtr-created *Qə̆SéMī́* (and analogs in other binyanim) to be affected by a static constraint against mid√__CV̄#. Hence, the constraint had to *reprise*, a dynamism that might settle in synchronically in one of two ways: either by *rule reordering*, whereby earlier order s-mid^s-mtr (reflecting the diachronic chronology of changes) mutated to s-mtr^s-mid; or by *rule reversal*, whereby something along the lines of |i| ⇒ |e| /X is replaced by or joined by |e| ⇒ |i| /Y, where conditions Y are (fully or partially) complementary to conditions X. (In the event |i| ⇒ |e| is synchronically *joined* by |e| ⇒ |i|, we are faced with a *flip-flop* nexus, which sometimes lends itself

to amalgamation of both rules as a unitary variably-stated process; see Malone 1970, 1972b.)

[45] (a) Clearly, the brunt of palatal mid in the finite verb is on 2ʃ I as focus. This aside, the only finite verb targets are two object suffixes: 3ms -*éh* (long vowel by l-anc, §2.3.1) and 2fs in the Ash tradition, -*éx* (Yem shows e-anc-lengthened -*íx*). (b) To judge by examples presented in Morag (1967–68: 78), the scope of palatal mid in the TL register of Halaxot Pĕsukot is considerably narrower than that for TL at large as presented here, though precise conditions remain to be worked out (note, surprisingly, that mid *fails* in sim pf 3ms, [QŏSíM] rather than [QŏSéM).

[46] Recall the caveats on this form in §15.5.2.

[47] (a) The informal frame for this a-mid subcondition, "/*rmp* ʔ__*CC*," imputes [+rmp] for descriptive handiness to the string at large with no commitment to specific structural locus; but observe that given the assumptions of this book, while such a locus might be the *C* immediately following the dash, whether straightforwardly rmp *T* itself or a rrf-engendered embodiment of 1√, the locus in the impf forms could *not* be ʔ, which by hypothesis (§1, §9.2.2) can only be the 1s subject prefix.

(b) The mid color of [ē] in the forms sim rmp pf 2s [ʔē̆9ăsáqt] (~ [ʔiθ9ăsáqt]), Mar 149*, and int rmp impf 1s [ʔē̆9akkáv], Mar 147*, is attributable to mls (§12 n. 4; cf. n. 35 of this subchapter).

[48] The hedge is that though√hdr on the surface manifests 2ʃ [a] (a[lɛhdár], Mar 105*), this may be due to low (§17.10), the root originally perhaps having selected *2ʃ u (cf. the SR cognates under √hdr in Payne Smith 1903: 128); and what is crucial to know, but not known, is whether forms like a[lɛhdár] should be classified along with such as [lɛhráv] (a-mid^aop) or alternatively along with such as [lɛh̆ɛlót] (p-att).

(b) It may have been observed that √hrb is doubly classified, lexically selecting either *2ʃ a (a[lɛhráv]) or *2ʃ u (a[lɛhróv]).

[49] (a) "according to Nöldeke and Brockelmann(,) Nestorian as well." The qualification on Nestorian is prompted by the fact that this register uses the same vowel point (rŏvōṣō karyō, §21.4) for both the midded ([ɛ]) and the retained ([i]) short palatal vowel, while Jacobite employs distinct vowel points (hăvōṣō for [i], rŏvōṣō for [e]).

(b) Note that while in Jacobite the phoneme-to-allophone relation in question is realized as /e/ [e, i] (conditions omitted), in Nestorian it rather takes the form /ɛ/ [ɛ, i]. Since the Nestorian system also contains a *close* mid [e] (abstracting away from length), closer to [i] along the dimension of tongue height than is *open* mid [ɛ], we might rightfully ask what accounts for the nonadjacent spacing in the allophonic set [ɛ, i]. A plausible answer is that Nestorian [ɛ, i] were *lax* vowels, while [e] was *tense*, and that the tense-lax opposition lay along the high-low track in *checkered* distribution, much as in the case of American English (but having fewer oppositions and realized without the aid of diphthongization): note, e.g., the series <beat> [biyt] ≫ <bit> [bɪt] ≫ <bait> [beyt] ≫ <bet> [bɛt], where "≫" = "high than" and where [iy, ey] = tense, [I], [ɛ] = lax. Nestorian [i] ≫ [e] ≫ [ɛ] would then be comparable to English [ɪ] ≫ [ey] ≫ [ɛ] as concerns their places in high-low/tense-lack space (though dissimilar in phonemic alignment). For more on [ɛ] as a lax vowel in Aramaic, see n. 32 above in this subchapter.

[50] This result automatically follows only if d-lap^d-mid. If rather d-mid^d-lap, we end up in the first instance with ms QŏSóM, fs mp fp @QŏSúM, so that mid would have to reprise with the accordion d-mid^d-lap^d-r-mid. Should this be the case, a follow-up

with rule reordering would be likely: d-mid^d-lap^d-r-mid > s-lap^s-mid, whereby mid and r-mid amalgamate in the ordering position of the latter.

[51] "in the verb"; and in fact pervasively, but with the possible variable exception of reflexes of the quantifier *kull* 'all' when spelled <kol> (Ns §48)—a quirk likely to be widespread in A; see, e.g., Da 122 on TR <kɑl>, BL §6k′, §25g on B <kɔl>.

[52] Alternatively, solely -*n*, which however may have shrunk from *nn* by degemination (§3.1 (3Fvii)).

[53] Statistically, all the dialects subject to mtr favor (reflexes of) the long or energic impf over (those of) the short impf (§7.2 (γ)), which provides a weak kind of circumstantial evidence that a random *n(n)*-less impf will be derivationally an instance of +mtr rather than a retention of the original short impf. Caveat indagator, however; statistical evidence is easily abused (Malone 1970b).

[54] Dalman interprets these forms as due to Babylonian influence. He cites no evidence for this conclusion, but the cumulative picture emerging throughout the present book rather clearly points to some sort of close relationship between G and TL. It must be left to the philologists to determine the exact nature of this relationship, which will provisionally be assumed to constitute a *straddle* between the two dialects (§18.2). (E. Y. Kutscher also considers various apparent G patterns to be Babylonian imports; see, e.g., §17.9.2 n. 22a, §19 n. 12a. Other possible instances of TL influence on G may be seen in §17.13 n. 59.)

[55] For extremely common infixed forms like <lyhD<u>w</u>r> 'they'll return' (lc), see i-lap, §17.9.2. (In the impf, original short impfs are the most likely candidates for i-lap, directly threatened as they were by apocopatory loss of the distinctive φ-signal *-*u*.)

[56] The argument from orthography is statistical rather than absolute, given the fluidity of TL spelling canons.

[57] (a) Müller-Kessler and Kwasman (2000: 159f.) claim dialect variation for mtr within TL.

(b) The TL verb pronounced [pæšṭű] in Yem trad pron bears comparison with M [peršón] (§17.9.2), since both in the wake of d-hii bespeak the embedding of corresponding s-hii more deeply into the phonology, deeply enough to make for feeding of the rules that normally apply to a stem suffixed with a *V*-initial formative. Had this not occurred (as, e.g., it fails in SR), the resulting forms would have been @[pɘšæṭő], @[pɘrašű]. (Note that while [pe̱ršón] has also undergone attenuation, §12, as characteristically triggered in M by the oxytone pf subject suffixes that surface as 3fs [-áθ] and 1s [-íθ], TL y[pǽšṭű] fails to attenuate—unsurprisingly, since the corresponding 3fs and 1s suffixes are stressless in TL, so that att of forms bearing them is forestalled.)

[58] "Only as a matter of course in the fp": Nöldeke (Nm 267) reports two 3mp instances in the sim impf of √hwy 'be'—<nihu> ~ <nehu>, both interpretable as [nīhű] (since wdr(§17.32)^(r-)red is assumed, impf-prefixal [ī] is taken to be restored by ips (§15.3.1.1); φ-prefixal [n] by prp (§17.19)). These forms alternate with expected <nihun> [nīhón].

[59] Dalman also adduces int <qPḫ²y> 'schlug mich', adding the comment "{mit} babylonischem Suffix" (lc n. 1) in reference to <-²y>. This provides food for thought on several fronts: (a) If <-²y> = [-ay] with the (pre-ndr) value nominal/prepositional sg^1s, it does indeed bid fair to be a Babylonian borrowing, assuming the correctness of the traditional view that TL pressed originally *pl*^1s -*ay* into double duty as *sg*^1s

when unstressed sg^1s -*i* was lost by lap (§17.9), a development shared by M for the same reason. However, G sg^1s -*i* did *not* fall victim to lap, so that pl^1s > sg^1s -*ay* would not (for that reason) have developed in G. Therefore, any such sg^1s -*ay* in G must have been borrowed (a conclusion to which Dalman assents without stating his reasons: "Vereinzelte babyl. aramäischen {sg^1s nominal forms—*JLM*} finden sich in den galil. Texten . . . {zum Beispiel} <ḥylm²y> . . .", Da 203). (b) However, TL did not undergo ndr, so the entirety of the form <qPḥ²y> must not be a borrowing, but solely the suffix <-²y> (another conclusion that Dalman appears to concur with, again without adducing his reasoning). (c) If (a, b) are well taken, why would G have borrowed a suffix of dissimilar function between recipient and donor (TL)? (d) Assuming a borrowing-justificatory answer to (c) can be found, observe that borrowed [-ay] qua ndr-fulfilling instantiation of 1s obj provides support for the idea, adopted above, that the origin of ndr-engendered [-ī] is nominal/prepositional. (e) Finally, however, there is a fully G-internal possibility to be considered in explanation of <-²y> qua objective 1s: that this spelling represents suffix [-ay] or perhaps [-a(²)ī] directly derived by ndr from -*anī*, i.e., -*nī* along with its associated bridge *a* (§2.3.2). Hitherto, it has been tacitly assumed that bridges were *omitted* under metanalysis by ndr, but this assumption may have to be reviewed.

[60] In all these interpretations, [I] < *yI*- by ymn (§14.2).

[61] (a) The spellings in question, appearing first in Y and O, are [θ] by <ŝ> (but by <s> in the Tell Fakhariyah register of O; Woodhouse 2003: 276), [ð] by <z>, and [θ̣] by <ṣ>, whereby plausibly the Aramean borrowers of the originally Canaanite orthography (perhaps Phoenician) assigned Canaanite letters to non-Canaanite consonants on the basis of correspondences deduced from frequent cognates—a procedure enabled by the close genetic bonds of the two languages; thus, they spelled A *ḏahabu* 'gold' <zhB> because they (correctly) felt the kinship of this word, and hence of its component sounds, to Canaanite *zahabu*, etc. See De 32–37 for excellent discussion.

(b) This same example may be used to elucidate the sense in which synchronic and diachronic interpretations of variable spelling most plausibly correlate with incomplete and complete sound change, respectively. Suppose that <z, D> may spell [ð, d], respectively; and that is involved in changing to *d* but we are not sure how far the process may have (yet) gone toward completion. Then, continuing the supposition, we are presented with a text where the word for 'gold' is spelled <zhB> ~ <DhB>. Why should this be so? In one contingency, the spelling system may be attuned to the language as it is at the time the text is set down—it is a *synchronic* spelling system—and hence 'gold' is spelled this way because it is *pronounced* this way, which evidently implies that the change ð > z has not (yet) gone to completion; rather, pronunciation of *ð-bearing words (like 'gold') are wavering between the old fashion ([ð], spelled <z>) and the new ([d], spelled <D>). In another contingency, however, older spellings may not necessarily have been adjusted to subsequent changes but rather cooccur with newer spellings in one and the same text—we are dealing with (partial) *historical* spelling—and hence 'gold' is spelled with <z> because it *used* to be pronounced with [ð], while cooccurrent renditions with <D> bespeak synchronic updating. (These possibilities by no means exhaust the issue at large of sound change and its possible impact on orthography. A sampling of possibilities is laid out in (c) for the general type of situation we are dealing with here, where [x] = [ð], [y] = [d], and <x> = <z>, <y> = <D>. The synchronic interpretation of <z ~ D> discussed above corresponds to contingency (1α) in (c), while the alternative historical-synchronic medley interpretation answers to (1βi, iii).)

(c) Premises: At stage I, [x] and [y] are independent units of the consonant system, spelled <x> and <y>, respectively;

At stage II, [x] > [x] ~ [y], i.e., [x] begins to change variably to [y] (= [x] and [y] begin to merge in favor of [y]);

There may be a stage III where [x] > [y], i.e., [x] has categorically changed to [y] (= [x] and [y] have unconditionally merged in favor of [y]).

post-stage-I spelling   plausible interpretations

(1) <x ~ y>   (α) stage II: *synchronic spelling*

(β) stage III: the completed merger has made available two spellings for one segment. Their distribution may be dictated by any number of factors, some quite whimsical. In instances **(i)** where <x> spells [y] < stage I [x], we have *historical spelling*; **(ii)** where <x> spells [y] ≤ stage I [y], we have *inverse spelling*; **(iii)** where <y> spells [y] < stage I [x], we have synchronic spelling, as under (α) above; **(iv)** where <y> spells [y] ≤ stage I [y], we have indifferently both synchronic and (trivially) historical spelling.

(2) <y>   stage III: if only one of the two available letters is to survive as spelling of [y], <y> seems the likelier choice—at least if the issue is determined by a generation of scribes (or others) old enough to have experienced variable stage II where the reality of the process [x] > [y] was still perceived.

(3) <x>   stage III: a sort of generalized inverse spelling—improbable except as a later-generation resolution of <x ~ y> ((1β) above) when ignorance of the original [x] > [y] might allow any number of fanciful criteria to dictate the final choice of <x> over <y>.

Consider finally that the uncovering of *inverse spelling* (1βii; 3) is frequently taken as evidential for a sound change having gone to completion, as, e.g., Kutscher proposed for *ð > d in I (1970: 70). Kutscher's case may be taken as representative of this suggested interpretation of inverse spelling. Armed with the knowledge that occlusion of *ð to d has impacted I, but not knowing whether it should be taken as still variable (*ð > ~ d) or rather as unconditional (konsequent durchgeführt; *ð > d), and faced with textual evidence that reflexes of *ð are variably represented (<z> ~ <D>—for <z> representing [ð], see above in this note, below in the text, and §21.1), the two prima facie interpretations are: (*) <z> [ð] ~ <D> [d]—occlusion is still variable; and (*)<z> [d] ~~ <D> [d]—occlusion has become unconditional, and <z> [d] represents historical spelling. Then Kutscher uncovers an instance of [dīn] 'judicial ruling', whose etymology is uncontroversially *dīnu, spelled <zyn>, and concludes on that basis that I <z> ~ <D> is to be interpreted as wholly [d], the second of the prima facie interpretations offered above. How might inverse spelling furnish such disambiguation?

Compare the displays in (d, e), constituting mock-ups of the case before us; for the sake of balance, the (constructed noun) [dūv] 'flow' has been added, etymologically *ðūbu—in contrast to [dīn] whose initial was always d (*dīnu). In both competing nexuses, the inverse spelling has been bold-faced (lower righthand side), and in both instances is identical: [d] spelled anti-etymologically <z>, as per [dīn] spelled <zyn>. What might motivate or at least enable spellings of this sort? In the case of the uncon-ditional occlusion hypothesis, (e), there is a straightforward answer: the unqualified merger of *ð* and *d* to [d] has left the system with *two* possible ways of spelling [d], <d> or <z>. The fact that <z> is anti-etymological in cases like <zyn> (as opposed to such as <zwB>) is purely irrelevant to the synchronic status of things—and is more-over beyond the ken of the normal speaker (writer, scribe) to begin with. So inverse (anti-etymological) spelling is perfectly compatible with an interpretation of graphemic alternations such as <z> ~ <d> as representing a constant value, here [d], with one of the two letters (here <z>) in non-inverse cases (as here in representation of [dūv]) constitut-ing historical spelling.

On the other hand, the situation with the variable occlusion hypothesis, (d) is quite different. Interpreting deployment of alternate letters (here <z> ~ <d>) in representation of distinct sounds (here [ð] ~ [d]) does not, at least on the surface of it, provide the sys-tem with alternate ways of spelling the same sound. So, again at least on the surface of it, inverse spellings (as here [dīn] <zyn>) would in such cases remain a puzzle.

(d) I.   [ð] <z> , [ðūb] <zwB> ; [d] <D> , [dīn] <Dyn>
   II. *variable occlusion*: [ð] > [ð] ~ [d] ; [d] ≥ [d]
   III. [ð] <z> ~ [d] <D> , [ðūv] <zwB> ~ [dūv] <DwB> ; [d] <D> , [dīn] <Dyn>
        ~ [d] <z> , [dīn] <zyn>
(e) I.   [ð] <z> , [ðūb] <zwB> ; [d] <D> , [dīn] <Dyn>
   II. *unconditional occlusion*: [ð] > [d] ; [d] ≥ [d]
   III. [d] <z> ~ [d] <D> , [dūv] <zwB> ~ [dūv] <DwB> ; [d] <D> , [dīn]
        <Dyn> **~ [d] <z> , [dīn] <zyn>**

Finally, to return briefly to the hedged wording above, "at least on the surface of it." It seems possible that at least some times, be it ever so infrequently, the very co-existence of alternatives within the system represented with distinct graphemes—as here (d), [ð] <z> ~ [d] <D> in spelling [ðūv] <zwB> ~ [dūv] <DwB>—might seduce some writers/scribes into overgeneralizing the spelling pattern by extending it to pairs where it is not etymologically justified (and where in fact the phonetic disposition is discrepant)—as here (d), [d] <z> ~ <D> in spelling such as [dīn] <zyn> ~ <Dyn>. So though the matter may not remain fully open, it remains at least entrouvert.

[62] Without prejudice to the fact that M trad pron can at times provide us with important clues as to the original state of affairs. This potential is most clearly realized with aspects of the orthography that lend themselves to more than one representative function, so that the discharge of one particular function in trad pron cannot be readily explained as an unambiguous, automatic reaction, as it may be in the case of abagadical reading. Actual examples include the ambiguity of <V'> , <C'> as to length ([V̆'] vs. [V̊'] vs. [V̄'], [C'] vs. [C'C']), §6.2.2.1, and the ambiguity of palatal and labial letters (like <i>, <u>) as to height (like [i] vs. [e], [u] vs. [o]), §17.11.3.

[63] In this connection, it might be remarked that in B 9 of 11 cases of the 3mp pronoun functioning as direct object show the immediately preceding verb marked with a *conjunctive ta9am* (Dan 2:35, 3:22 ; Ezra 4:10, 4:23, 5:5, 5:11, 5:14, 5:15, 7:17)—cer-tainly not conclusive evidence of a host-enclitic relation between verb and pronoun, but

likely compatible with such a relation since marking of *X* with a conjunctive ta9am in a string *XY* normally expresses a close prosodic relation between *X* and *Y* (§21.6)—and the host-enclitic relation a very close prosodic bond indeed. In that vein, however, it is striking that no token of 3p object pronoun in B is linked to its verb host by *makef*, a grapheme expressing an especially close form of enclisis (§21.7); for this in m-pat, see §17.15.2 below. (For completeness, here are the two tokens of objective 3mp whose verbs are marked by *disjunctive* tĕ9amim: [rɔ̆mố²innū̆n] 'they threw them', ta9am = zakef, Dan 6:25; [wɔ̆haddéqεθ himmố̆n] 'and broke them in pieces', ta9am = tifḥa, Dan 2:34. What accounts for these exceptions?)

[64] "*V*-initial object pronouns"; but since most dialects undergoing i-pat show independent 3p pronouns with initial *hIn-* or *²In-* (§7.4.1), what happens to the *h*/*²* upon attachment? The prevailing A tendency at large would be adconsonantal assimilation of *-3√C ²-* and either that or no change for *-3√C h-* (§9.2.1.1, §9.2.2), so that, e.g., TL a[ʈɔ̆9eminnū̆n] 'he tasted them' (Mar 118*) should more likely be @[ʈɔ̆9e**mm**innū̆n]. The actual outcome of i-pat might be interpreted as support for the influential vintage hypothesis (e.g., BL §38s) that pronoun attachment was anteceded historically by a process of pronoun *de*tachment (pdt), whereby 3p object pronouns would originally have been *suffixal*, the prima facie evidence for this suggestion being O, which indeed does appear to encode the 3p pronominal object relation suffixally: e.g., <thŝB<u>hm</u>> 'du wirst sie zurückführen', <²rq<u>hm</u>> 'ich werde sie besänftigen' (De 80). ((*) Y presents no relevant evidence with respect to i-pat one way or the other. (*) There appears to be vacillation between suffixal and periphrastic encodation in the mid-7th century B.C.E. Ashur letter (O? Y?); see MP 143 n. 670. Elsewhere, the same authors present a clear and concise statement on the tenure of early 3p object suffixation: "a lingering feature attested, albeit admittedly only weakly, right from the OA period (Sefire) through the Ashur letter and the Hermepolis papyri and down to the Ahiqar proverbs"; MP 171 n. 711.) If in fact there was such an event in the history of A as pronoun detachment, we could take it that the etyma of suffixes like that in TL [ʈɔ̆9eminnū̆n] had *always* begun with a vowel, specifically **i,* and maintained this property even during the period—attested to us in B—when these formatives were fullfledged words (or at least half-words qua enclitics) thanks to pdt; in which event the <²> of pronouns like TL <²ynwn> (Mar 16) would *either* be a purely orthographic element ([innū̆n]) *or* represent *hamzatu 'l-waṣl,* spelling [²] inserted by a synchronically low level ("phonetic") rule at the behest of a phonotactic requirement that all words and enclitics commence with a consonant ([²innū̆n] ⇐/innun/) so that, when i-pat came along, the formative would be attached either just so ([ʈɔ̆9ém + [innū̆n] plus stress adjustment) or at a shallow level preceding the application of purely phonetic (as opposed to phonological) rules ([ʈɔ̆9ém| + |innū̆n| plus sta). Militating against the hypothesis of pdt is that this view entails acceptance of a rather peculiar accordion: First, A starts off with suffixal 3p object pronouns (stage of O), next it excorporates the same pronouns as words/enclitics (stage of I, B), and finally it reincorporates these words/enclitics as suffixes again (post-B stage). True, accordion chains have been adopted at various junctures in this book (see references in §25 under "accordion"). But this specific chain strikes as typologically implausible; first, a burst toward analytic syntax (pdt), and then, a few centuries later, an implosion back toward synthetic (pdt). At the very least, it would be desirable to seek independent coeval symptoms of these peculiarities. Observe also that a second rather

suspicious accordion partially overlaps that of pdt-pat: while *regressive nasal assimilation* (rna, §17.21) applies robustly in Y and especially in O (which does *not* show pdt), it makes a weak showing in I (which *does* show pdt) and then begins to bound back again subsequently (which is to say, overlapping the i-pat dialects with the exception of B fore and SR aft, both lacking i-pat despite strong showing with rna). A more plausible account of these patterns would have it that *Y and O are not linearly ancestral to subsequent forms of A*, and hence that suffixation of 3p objects and the strict form of rna in both dialects are irrelevant to the polar dispositions of I (and partially polar state of B)—a stance that chimes with various other aspects of especially Y over against other types of A (e.g., §7.1 with n. 1, §7.2 (α), §9.1.2, §11.2, §17.8 with (17.8C) and n. 23, §17.21). Hence, in this book a developmental pattern will tentatively be adopted closer to that of (a) than to that of (b)—and the like of TL [ṭɜ̌ɂeminnűn] ≠ @[ṭɜ̌ɂemminnűn] will be attributed to the marked option $VC''V \rightarrow VC'V$ (§9.2.1.1) (see, however, (ζ) and <u>SM</u> below). (Y is hypothesized to act like O with respect to 3p object expression, though no relevant forms happen to be attested; but no commitment is made to a linear relationship between the two dialects.)

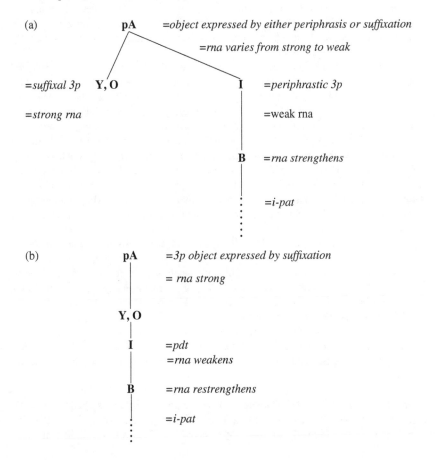

(a)   pA   =object expressed by either periphrasis or suffixation

=rna varies from strong to weak

=suffixal 3p   Y, O   I   =periphrastic 3p

=strong rna   =weak rna

B   =rna strengthens

=i-pat

(b)   pA   =3p object expressed by suffixation

= rna strong

Y, O

I   =pdt
     =rna weakens

B   =rna restrengthens

=i-pat

[65] (a) "or at least demoted to secondary." Secondary accentuation might in fact be captured by Margolis's use of the diacritic *meteg* in his representation of TL Ash trad pron, e.g., what was interpreted as [ṭə̆9eminnǘn] in n. 64 is spelled by him <ṭ:9ęmiňuwn> (Mar 118*) which then more narrowly might be taken as [ṭə̆9èminnǘn]. However, Margolis fields meteg in various other roles not as likely to represent secondary stress—e.g., in the homorizous noun <ṭạ9ămɔʾ> (lc); and the most plausible summary conclusion is that he is in almost all cases using the meteg to indicate *open syllabicity*, especially *either* when this occurs under marked circumstances (notably, when the nucleus so marked is *short*, as in <ṭ:9ęmiňuwn>, but also when the syllable so marked is open by virtue of a phonological rule, e.g., <gɔraš:tex> 'I divorced you(fs)', Mar 101*, [gɔ̄raštéx] ⇐ mls, §9.3.1, |garraštéx|) *or* when the next following vowel point is <:> (because specific morphophonological knowledge aside, this grapheme might in the absence of meteg be interpreted as [Ø] (šěva naḥ), e.g., <bɔr:xuwn> 'they blessed me', Mar 96*, might without meteg be interpreted as @[bɔrxún] rather than correctly as [bɔ̄rə̆xún]) or, derivatively, a ḥataf, <ă, ĕ, ɔ̆> (e.g., <ṭɔ̆ḥăniy> 'grinding(mp)', Mar 117*, [ṭɔ̆ḥănî] though <ă> qua [ă] necessarily marks the syllable as open)—this latter case being perhaps the only circumstance where open-syllabic meteg marking has sacrificed its functional role to become a mere spelling rule: "use meteg to indicate an open syllable opened by a reduced vowel (whether than reduced vowel is ambiguously indcated (šěva) or not (ḥataf)."

(b) It was mentioned that Margolis uses meteg "in almost all cases" to indicated open syllabicity. However, at least in the case of <sakẹn:tɔx> and <sakẹn:tuwn> (Mar 142*), interpretable as [sakkentɔ́x], [sakkentún] where [e] is *closed*-syllabic, Margolis appears to be using meteg in the function codified by Gesenius as indicating "that the vowel should not be hastily passed over in pronunciation" (Kautsch and Cowley 1910: 64)—meaning, specifically in this case, that the rule atonic opening (§17.11.2) should not apply to lax the *e* to ε. However, in view of the *transparentive* rationale licensing such instances of [e] in TL, §15.5.1, it seems altogether likely that such closed-syllabic instances of meteg in TL could be explicated as representing *secondary stress* along the lines suggested for similar B cases in n. 40 above. And if so, all Margolian usage of meteg might indeed be reduced to either or both of secondary stress or open syllabicity, as hinted at the outset of this note.

[66] For some dialects, notably CP, SM, and G, the question of i-pat -Ŭn-ʾInnūn amalgamation also arises in pf/impa, due to possible prior action of hii (§7.2( )).

[67] TL likewise shows *I* at the stem-suffix seam in the defective sim transitive pf with 3p object, categorically according to Morag's Yemeni listing (y[ḥə̆zĭnnə̆hǘ] plus four additional instances, Mor 322), variably in Margolis's Ashkenazic reporting (e.g. a[šə̆ðĭnə̆hő] ~ [šə̆ðɔ̆nə̆hő], Mar 169*).

[68] In the Ash forms, the interpretation [-in(ɔ̆)hő], hedging on whether simplification (§17.26) of -innə̆hő is complete or partial, reflects Margolis's failure to use the grapheme meteg (see n. 65), <-in:how>, while conversely [-inə̆hő] reflects meteg-bearing <-ịn:how>.

[69] For the status of [ā] in Ash TL, see §11 n. 1; for its specific appearance in def sim pf 1p of an independent (intransitive) verb, cf. a[bə̆9ắn] 'we required' (Mar 95*); [ē] in a[ḥăzēnɔnə̆hḗ] reflects the regularity of intransitive allos like a[bə̆9ḗnɔ̄] (specifically this) and a[bə̆9ēnán] (lc); for [-nɔ̄] ~ [-nan], see §7.2 (ð) n. 11. Similar distribu-

tion in Yemeni (Mor 255), the a[ā] (y[æ]) ~ [ē] difference in 1p pf being conditioned by√__*C#* ~√__*CV* respectively; §11.2 TL.

[70] The evidence for CP and G is statistical, in that interpretation of such as <ḥsrṮhwn> qua [hassarṮInnÛn] rather than epenthesized [hassVrIθInnÛn] depends upon the tendential regularity that most but not all clear instances of [Iθ] in CP and G orthography are spelled <yT>, though a minority are in fact written without ml as <T>. Nothing has been cited from SM because in this dialect the ml for [Iθ] appears much less frequently than in CP and G (and, unfortunately, trad pron provides no testimony for the sole 1s^3mp provided by Macuch, <šm9Twn> 'ich habe sie gehört', Macs 227).

[71] The Sabbionetan variant is unintegrated in the narrow sense used here, but it is *doubly* subjected to repair strategies to forefend against unstressed open-syllabic short vowels: 2√s is geminated to render 1∫ i closed-syllabic, and 2∫ a is lengthened, i.e., *ʔisarinnún → ʔissārinnún.* (For *ʔi.* . . ← *ʔɔ.* . . , see §17.23.3.)

[72] mp^3mp variants are spread pretty evenly, except that +mit -pin *-ŭn(n)ŭn(n)ún* is clearly the most frequent choice in the impf. In regard to the mechanics of mit on mp^3mp, the fact that all clear cases of this process target *subject* formatives—including that of 3fs^3mp just surveyed—suggests that *-ŭn(n)ŭn(n)ún* should be interpreted as *-ūnŭn(n)ún* analyzable as *-ūnŭ-n(n)ún* where *-ūnŭ-* represents mitosis of subjectival *-ūn.* However, while this works fine for the impf, with *-ūn* as reflex of intransitive long **-ūna* (apocope of **a* by sap, §17.22), it is uncomfortable for the pf where the normal 3mp sub suffix is *n*-less *ū,* incapable of mitosis, and importation of *-ūn* by hii is a rarity (§7 n. 12). Various escape hatches from this discomfort can be imagined, the most promising being to permit mit to operate across formatives, by "borrowing" the anlaut consonantism of objectival *-n(n)ún: -ŭ̄-n(n)ún* mit → *ŭ̄-n(n)-ŭ̄-n(n)-ún.*

[73] While the display is for the most part presented in terms of sketch forms from the simple verb, its distributions largely hold for derived verbs as well (notably int, cau).

[74] Recall the hypothesis of q.i.s.s developed in §15.3.2, wherein 2√ in defective verbs marks the major plerematic divide. And in this vein, note the variant def pf 2s^3mp formation *Qɔ̌Sθinnɔ̌hú* (on√mhy, y[mæḥθinnɔ̌hú] 'hiketa ʔotam', Mor 322 n. 54).

[75] (a) The secondary stress of the former example corresponds to the primary in the variant [hŭ̌šǎfaθ lí̌] (BL 24). That verb and pp in this variant are intimately bonded prosodically is cued both by the fact that [hŭ̌šǎfaθ] is marked by the conjunctive ta9am *merxa* (§21.6) and, especially, by the fact that [hŭ̌šǎfaθ] has undergone *stress retraction* (srt) from suffixal *-áθ* to prefixal (prefixal-radical portmanteau) *hū-* to alleviate the *stress clash* registerd in *hŭšǎfáθ lí̌,* where two primary-stressed syllables are uncomfortably adjacent across too weak a prosodo-syntactic boundary to function as an effective buffer (more on stress retraction below, under (b))—boundary weakness being symptomatic of intimate prosodic bonding. But while intimate prosdic bonding is a hallmark of clitic grouping, it is unsettled in the general linguistic literature how tight such bonding must be to ensure fullblown clisis. One possibility is that both [hŭ̌šǎfaθ lí̌] and [hŭ̌šǎfaθ =lí̌] are indeed clitic groups, each falling within the range of permissible bonding variation; but another possibility would have it that only [hŭ̌šǎfaθ =lí̌] is truly clitic, [hŭ̌šǎfaθ lí̌] bespeaking intimate bonding, but not intimate enough to constitute clitic organization—in which case, the permissible variation would be one of enabling either +clisis or -clisis in encoding this particular instance of the V-pp relation. The

matter will not be settled in this book, where commitment will be limited to assuming that clisis (here enclisis) falls somewhere between affixation (here suffixation) and independent-word organization with respect to degree of bonding. See also the similar account of similar patterns proffered in §17.11 n. 37.

(b) Other cases from B of verb-targeting stress retraction are [wǒyĕmar lếh] 'und er sagte zu ihm' (Dan 4:32), [yǒhîvaθ lǒhốn] 'sie würde ihnen gegeben' (Dan 7:12), [mếnnī šǒfǝṭî́n] 'verordne Richter!' (Ezra 7:25). Note how in the second example the schwa in lǒhốn fails to provide a sufficiently strong buffer between -hốn and -váθ to preempt the retraction; cf. the case of M [amarellǒxón] in §15 n. 5 for the role of bufferless though not for that of stress retraction per se, and see THP 94f. for stress retraction (Stress Adjustment) in Tiberian Hebrew.

(c) The Aramaic V-pp clitic groups examined here and throughout are taken to involve *en*clisis of the pp to the verb as host and, correspondingly, upon m-pat *suf*fixation of the same pp onto the verb as host. However, the use of the terminology is unsettled in the field at large, especially with reference to clisis, so that some would take it that in an Aramaic V-pp clitic group it is rather the *verb* that is being *pro*cliticized to the pp, presumably because it is the verb that ends up sacrificing its stress while that of the pp is maintained. In this book, however, the view taken is that the pp, qua more grammatical item than the (more) lexical verb, is the member of the duo being subordinated; and that the fact the resulting group assumes the stress of the pp is but an accidental byproduct of the actual accentual mechanism: the constituents V and pp *both* subordinate (usually sacrifice) their original stress trappings upon amalgamation by clisis, whereupon the new unit is *restressed* in accordance with the pattern obtaining for the language. And this pattern, being end-oriented (§4.1), de facto restresses the pp.

[76] [Note intentionally omitted.]

[77] As Morag illustrates (1c), though *QæSMū* is generally fielded$\sqrt{\_\_}$pp, there are exceptions in both directions: on the one hand, such as [šǒlæḥū lǒhū] (which if encliticized it perhaps best interpreted as [šǒlæ̀ḥū=lǒhū́]), on the other hand such as [ʔæmrū ræbbānæn]—and also the fact that at least $\sqrt{\text{ʔ}}$zl 'lalexet' has apparently lexicalized *QæSMū* as its 3mp pf. (Food for thought: how were such non-cliticized instances of *QæSMū* stressed?)

[78] cau *arhŮn* presumably ←r-e-coa *arháwn* (§11.1) ←r-e-cnd (§8.1) $a\sqrt{r}\sqrt{ha}\sqrt{y}Ún$ ← *ʔa*$\sqrt{r}\sqrt{ha}\sqrt{h}Ún$ by metanalysis from 3√H to 3√y upon degutturalization (§9.2.3.2), and even earlier metanalysis to geminate√rḥ from hollow√rWḥ (§6.2, DM 425). This analysis is not without its problems, however—not merely for this form, but for the general assumption that the lexeme in question is cau $\sqrt{rḥy}$ ←$\sqrt{rḥ}$ ←$\sqrt{rWḥ}$. For one thing, an antecedent geminate form of this structure would not normally appear in the marked shape *ʔarḥaḥUn* (by gmf-4m (3N)) but rather in the unmarked shape *ʔarraḥUn* (by gmf-4u (3M)), which would metanalyze to *@arrŮn*, not *arhŮn*. The matter will be left unresolved. (There is also some hedging on the precise color of the second vowel in *arhŮn*. We should normally expect (r-)e-coa in structures like this to yield [ō], which in turn should render [arhōBî]. Perhaps the cue here by the traditional pronunciation is misleading, since trad pron often enough appears to go its own puzzling way. Or perhaps transparentation of *ō* to *ū* has applied (§15.3.2). There are too few similar forms to be sure one way or the other.

[79] This conclusion would not be materially affected if the suffix in question were taken not to be *-Un* but original *n*-less pf/impa *-ū*—not impossible since the unexceptionality of *n*-assimilation hypothesized above reflects the fact that the *n* never surfaces in m-pat forms. The reason for assuming *-Un* to be involved in m-pat is primarily that *-Un* is much more frequent in its bailiwick, the defective verb, than is *-ū*; see §7.2 (δ). But in either event, the commonest encodation of 3mp pf and mp impa in the M intransitive is suffixless, via uncompensated lap (§17.9). In fact, suffixless forms may also occur under m-pat, sometimes alternating with suffixed variants (as illustrated in (17.15Cv).

[80] A number of these m-pat specializations pose interesting questions of origin. For instance, is the use of older 1p *-nā*/*-nan* evidence that m-pat preceded the general replacement of these shapes by *-nīn* (§17.1)? Or does m-pat date from a time when *-nin* had in fact made its entry but still alternated with the older shape(s), which got generalized in the new construction (m-pat) while falling out of coinage elsewhere? Historical linguists appear to have often taken note of developments like this latter in other languages.

[81] While M is all hands down the only A turf where m-pat has taken root and flourished, it is not out of the question that it might have been witnessed at least inchoatively elsewhere as well. Thus CP <lʔ KPl lḥ> 'es kümmert ihn nicht' (Sg §18.1), if [lā=x(ǝ̄)PallĬh] < *lā=x(ǝ̄)Páθlĭh* 'not=concerns to+him'. (For a cognate construction in TL, see §12.2 n. 17.)

[82] (a) A process cognate, possibly identical, to Aramaic ptg in Tiberian Hebrew is codified in THP 67f., where in fact it is treated as a special case of the Hebrew counterpart of low (Assimilatory Lowering). Since the Aramaic and Hebrew ptg processes are nearly the same, justification for the properties here attributed to the A manifestation—including the claim that ptg splits a long vowel into two shorts ($\bar{V}'a$) rather than adding a short to the unchanged long as per the traditional view ($\bar{V}'a$)—can be tracked in the literature cited op cit. (p. 66, under <u>References</u>).

(b) Since the Hebrew analog of ptg also holds for the Babylonian register of that language, though under somewhat different conditions from those of the Tiberian register (Bauer and Leander 1922: §18k), it is striking that there is no trace of the process in the Bab register of B—perhaps all the more so given the fact that, as per examples cited, the Bab register of TR *does* evidence ptg.

(c) The "close" condition (featurally captured with [+hi], see §20.2 (20E)) prevents results like hollow pf 3ms @[QóaH] ← *QǒH*—an effect perhaps alternatively capturable by ordering the systemic vowel shift $\bar{a} \rightarrow \delta$ (§20.2 (ζ)) to follow ptg, since a result like [QáaH] should be expected to be equivalent to [QắH] and instantiate ptg vacuously at best. (Note, however, that Bab Hebrew apparently does evidence the like of [QáæH]—and even [QǽæH] (lc): perhaps unsettling food for thought vis-à-vis the $\bar{V}$- splitting hypothesis of ptg adopted in this book.)

(d) Though Ash TL not infrequently incurs suspicion of Schematisierung induced by the Tiberian orthography in which Margolis couches his interpretation (e.g., §17.23.1.2), such a charge against ptg may be defused by the fact that Yem TL also bears witness to this process—and though Morag likewise uses Tiberian orthography to convey his informants' pronunciation, he is more liberal in flying in the face of generally accepted

Tiberian "spelling rules" in other areas; note, e.g., that he gives <H:> (for [Hə̆]) where Margolis sticks to prescribed <Hă> ([Hă]).

[83] A complicating factor is that pin appears to be but one reciprocal half of a larger change complex whose other half might be labeled "fin," *finite intrusion*, whereby aspects of finite verb structure and inflection are rubbing off onto the participle—including, of direct relevance here, object-suffix shapes originating in the verb system. Thus, TR and G sport a number of transitive participles whose object pronouns are attached via (ex)energic *(I)nn*, as TR ms^2ms <mPyšynK> and mp^3ms <mqyymynyh> (Da 381f., unfortunately neither vocalized), G ms^1s <Dmŝmŝyny> and mp^2ms <mḥŝDwnk> (Da 394)—the latter, moreover, bearing finite (3)mp *Ūnn* (<wn>) in lieu of participial *in*. fin is especially advanced in TL (which, as will be picked up below, also shows the most robust profile for pin), to the extreme, in fact, that in Yem trad pron a number of paradigmatic slots have totally merged with isofunctional pf slots. This holds with special sweepingness in the simple defective participle, where several intransitive forms are indistinguishable from pf equivalents: e.g., 2ms [qə̆Sḗθ], 1(m)p [Qə̆Sēnæn], mp [Qə̆Sû] (though there are less than fully merged alternants, like [QæSû], as well as non-merged -fin shapes, like [Qū̆S(y)ḗ]), 2mp [Qə̆Sēθû] (~ partially merged [Qə̆Sīθû]); see Mor 257–61. The most immediate relevance of this note is that the reciprocal impact of finite and participial forms makes it difficult to fully isolate the conditions of either.

[84] (a) Note in this regard that there is no evidence for the shape *ē* other than in auslaut in Yem trad pron. Indeed, the few relevant forms cited by Morag in the same register for *in*laut position all agree on showing $\mathring{\imath}$: int rmp pf 2mp [ʔiṭṭællə̆lị̊θû] (Mor 264), sim pf3mp^3mp [kærxị̊nnə̆hû] (Mor 294), sim pf 1p^3mp [šæqlị̊nnə̆hû] (lc) (though admittedly the $\mathring{\imath}$ of the latter two forms may rather reflect the 3mp object, §17.15.1 (γ)).

(b) "a common denominator of shape [Ĩ]": as per *-ī(n)* = *-īn* ~ *-ī* (*-ī* arising in the first place by mtr, §17.12), whose *n* might moreover possibly be subject to contact assimilation√__C and the *ī* subject to css, §17.4 (if, e.g., TL 2mp [-ittũn] ← *-īn-tũn*).

[85] Albeit as a pregnant bridge when appearing as sole subject exponent, (3)mp. However, it is not unusual for morphemes in languages to share semantic and asemantic functions—as in fact is already true of other A bridges; e.g., *-ā-* in 2ms *-áx* vs. *-ī-* in 2fs *-íx* (§2.3.4.4).

[86] pin and r-epn are displayed at the same stage as an expository simplification; in reality, one very likely occurred earlier than the other.

[87] Another expository simplification, even distortion, since bridges are perhaps best taken as suffixal constituents (§2.3.2)—but in any event of a different character than φ-suffixal (as $\mathring{I}$ was at stage II).

[88] TL may be characterized by two additional inchoative pin-derived phenomena: insertion of participial *ī within* 2mp *-tūn* rather than *before* it, making for *-tīn*; and importation to pf of 1s *-nā* (as possibly also G). See §17.17.2.

[89] Margolis lists the interpretation a[ḥăzān(ə̆)hố] explicitly only for 1p^3mp (Mar 112*), though he adduces the spelling <ḥznhw> for both (Mar 59).

[90] For the Yemeni tradition, the forms reported by Morag might be aligned with these Ashkenazic renditions as follows: [-yā̆n] ~ [-æn] ~ [-yē] ~ [-ū] (Mor 257–61).

[91] Three remarks on this form: (a) Its genuineness might be called into question, inasmuch as Margolis lists it in his (interpreted) vocabulary as 1s^3fs, a[ʔamrīθáh] (Mar 88*), as likewise does Morag Yemeni y[ʔæmrīθǽh] <ʔmryTʔ> (Mor 293 with n. 10).

(b) Assuming its bona fides, the intercalated *-ī-* may be challenged as an extension of pin: because the only other dialect to date showing a similar form, CP—cau <ʔKryTh> 'erkanntest ihn' (Sg 78)—itself shows no evidence for orthodox (= mp) pin. (c) Meta-analysis of *-Ǐ-* from φ-element to bridge also shows up in the participial system per se, to judge by forms such as a[9ɔ̄vɔ̄ð̣ín̰ɔ̄] 'I do' (Mar 145*).

[92] A Martinesque *chaîne*-development may conceivably be involved (Martinet 1964: §2.28, §2.29), to the extent that the original 1p̲ pf suffix *-nā* may have been re-placed by innovative *-n* (< *-nā* by lap, §17.9) or *-næn* (§7.2 (δ) n. 11) or the pin-derived counterpart of this latter, *-innæn*—a development along the lines of (a), where *-nā* (*-nĀ*) changes allegiance from 1p (stage I) to 1s (stage IV) without incurring ambiguity at any step along the way.

(a)	1s	1p̲
stage I	-iθ	-nā
stage II	-iθ ~ -ī (*mtr*)	-nĀ ~ -n ~ -nAn ~ -innAn
stage III	-iθ ~ -ī	-n ~ -nAn ~ -innAn
stage IV	-iθ ~ -ī ~ -nĀ (*r-pin*)	-n ~ -nAn ~ -nnAn

A problem for the *chaîne* in (a) is the possibility that 1p *-nĀ* never completely vanished from the dialect. Both Morag and Margolis list all four 1p suffix shapes (Mor 127, Mar 137); and though Margolis flags 1p *-nɔ̆* with "†" as archaic/archaizing, he flags innova-tive *-nan* in the same way. But while possible overlap of original 1p and innovative 1s *-nĀ* would discomfit the *chaîne* of (a) in the sense proffered, no anomalous development would be entailed; cooccurrence of the two *-nĀ*s would simply bespeak an instance of *conflative syncretism* (§16.1), *-nĀ* having effectively generalized its function from "first person plural" to "first person," irrespective of number.

[93] However, even assuming [sakkentín] to be a genuine form need not commit one to the view that pin is responsible. Alternatively, we might be witnessing encroach-ment of the unusual (but A-attested) ancipitally long 1s allomorph *-īn* (< lap *-īnī*)and concomitant elision of 2mp *ū*: [sakkentín] < *sakkentū́-īn*.

[94] As a final observation on unusual pin deployments in TL, note int rmp pf 3mp <ʔynB w̲y̲> (Mor 270). Though Morag's informants pronounce this [ʔinnæbbū́], the su-pernumerary <-y> just might represent a reflex of participial *-ī* (or, in Yem trad pron, perhaps *-ē* ; §17.17.1), in which case the pin-imported suffix would not be *replacing* finite *-ū* but be *added to it*. Slim chance, maybe, but this might just be a residual form revealing something of the mechanics of pin in its earliest stages.

[95] There is, however, internal-reconstructive evidence that prothesis of sim impa forms subject to *retraction with bobbing* in TR, SR, and TL emerged in an early pre-reduction period, before these dialects arose per se. See §8.1.3 n. 14, where this early manifestation of prothesis is labeled *e-pro*.

[96] In the sim pf, pro in G seems especially frequent in forms with 2 I; cf. the list-ings in Da 258.

[97] Pictorially, (a) extrudes *V̆* to become (b). *1, 2, . . . n* represent shared features that, being represented only once apiece, through their association lines wedge over the segments they invest. The greater the phonetic/phonological similarity of the segments, the larger the number of features wedged over them; and the greater the number of wedges, the stronger the pressure to extrude any intervening element, here *V̆*. We may

also assume that intervening elements may vary in strength and that the weaker the element, the less counterpressure it is capable of exerting against the extrusion. (This sort of account lends itself to service elsewhere in A phonology as well; e.g., in explicating the frequent absence of $2\int \mathring{V}$ between the final two identical radicals of geminate verbs (§3.2 (3G)) while $2\int \bar{V}$, with a stronger long vowel, remains unextruded.)

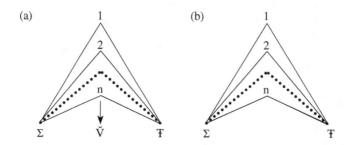

[98] For some good discussion of this, see Kenstowicz 1994: 254f. (Kenstowicz uses the term "Sonorancy Sequencing Principle.")

[99] This rough-and-ready account glosses over the possible impact of spirantization (§5.1) of $2\sqrt{}$, but nothing of substance is changed because none of the roots here involve stop « spirant.

[100] (a) One at least slightly disquieting aspect of this account is the deletion of $\check{V}$. Would not $\#Q\check{V}S\check{V}M\text{-} \to \#(^{\textit{ʔ}})\mathring{V}Q\check{V}S\check{V}M\text{-}$, with $\check{V}$ retained, be enough to assuage the violation?

(b) Another perspective on the group of roots under discussion here capitalizes on the fact that *all begin with sonorant 1√* and so assimilates their prothetic behavior to that of *sonorant Aufsprengung* (§4.4.2). Under this view, the $\mathring{ə}$ would "implode" into the sonorant (Λ), rendering it vocalic ($\underset{\circ}{\Lambda}$), a segment that then would unpack into a $\mathring{V}C$ sequence ($\mathring{V}\Lambda$): $\#\Lambda\mathring{ə}S\ldots \to \#\underset{\circ}{\Lambda}S\ldots \to \#(^{\textit{ʔ}})\mathring{V}\Lambda S\ldots$. It might in fact be possible, ultimately, to subsume other forms of prothesis under *excrescent Aufsprengung* (§4.4.1) and so unify both processes (prothesis and Aufsprengung) by collapsing $\#C\mathring{ə}C\ldots$ (prothesis) and $CC\mathring{ə}C\ldots$ (Aufsprengung) through generalization of the first term of the structural description ($\{\#, C\}$) as "non-vowel." Ideas such as this have in fact been suggested on and off over the past hundred years or so, whether for Aramaic or for other Semitic languages; but of course there are several issues remaining to be addressed and worked out before anything like an adequate theory could be developed.

[101] According to Müller-Kessler and Kwasman (2000: 160), *y-* is retained in the Standard Literary Babylonian register. Margolis also reports a number of *y-* retentions in what is presumably TL at large, marking such forms with "†" as conservative/archaic/archaizing; see, e.g., the sampling adduced at Mar 38f., 43, 45f., 51f.

[102] G shows a few instances of 3 *n-*, one of which Dalman plausibly characterizes as "babylonischer Einschlug" (Da 265)—plausible in that when the instance is examined in context, <Dlʔ n̂ww lhw> 'damit man sie nicht erkläre', the excerpt is seen to contain an additional symptom of TL morphophonology, the absence of suffixal <-n> (by mtr, §17.12) on <n̂ww> and <lhw>. (As regards the verb, contrast Margolis's

tables (Mar 52f.) and the forms listed by Dalman (Da 345f.).) An additional case of 3 *n-* in G is adduced by Kutscher (1976: 15), who likewise considers it a TL intrusion.

[103] The qualification "Classical" in view of the fact that Old Syriac still shows traces of *y*-: e.g., <yšTKḥwn> 'they'll be found' (Drijvers 1972: 112). (For specifics on the distribution of *y*- in Old SR, see Drijvers 1972: xii.)

[104] (a) For reflexes of *š, §17.27. (b) It is unclear what motivated the transfer of *√šYm from sim to cau. (For an (uncompleted) change in the opposite direction, *√škḥ 'find' in SR, Malone 1974a.)

[105] However, the presumed status of Y as an rna-categorical dialect is less than foregone considering the meagerness of the extant corpus, exactly three pertinent forms: <yT{n}w> 'sie geben' and two tokens of <yTh> 'er wird geben' (DR I 214:4, 23).

[106] A way out of interpreting at least O as having categorical rna is suggested by Degen, who proffers that <C> may ambiguously represent [C] ~ [nC] (De 40f.). At first blush, the existence of such a spelling convention for an Aramaic dialect seems quite implausible, but it is noteworthy that six out of seven instances of Palmyrene proper names reported by Hillers and Cussini as coappearing in Greek or Latin transcription and there containing *nC*, show that *nC* is represented in P by <C> alone (HC 430, 437): e.g., <ʾlKsḎrs> Greek <Alexandrou>, <ʾtny²> Greek "Antonia" (thus cited in HC)—and perhaps most cogently Semitic(²) <mTBwl> Greek <Mant(a)bōleiēn>, since here it is easier to dismiss the escape-hatch possibility that the inferred pronunciation [nt] might simply reflect a foreign (Greek/Latin) canon. The sole instance of <nC> [nC] is furnished by the masculine counterpart of <ʾtny²>: <ʾntwnys> Greek <Antōniō> Latin <Antonio>. (As concerns the orthographic representation of native P verbs culled from Hillers and Cussini's glossary, four out of five show 2√<C> where historically we expect 1√*n* 2√C, the one possible exception being the variant doublet <y{nT}n> (~ <yTh>) (HC 391), where, however, as indicated by the curly braces <nT> has been restored to the original transcription.) From all this we may conclude that the hypothesis now to be proffered should be taken with due caution.

[107] Since the book's theoretical underpinning is essentially wave-theoretical, with appeal to tree-theoretical genealogies for the most part as simplifying expository devices in cases where the relevant isoglosses are distributed in a(n asymptotically) discrete fashion (§18), it will be useful to be clear about how tree-theoretic notions like "linearly ancestral" and "developmentally independent" are to be interpreted. For purposes of illustration, tree (a) and equivalent wave display (b) have been enriched from the tree labeled (a) in n. 64 (§17.15). In brief, a developmental relationship is taken to be linear (and hence in a strong sense dependent) if dialect Z is later than dialect W, and Z is circumscribed by all (rarely) or most (usually, for some explicit threshold setting) of the isoglosses that circumscribe W. Thus M in (b) is taken to be linearly ancestral from B (by dint of isoglosses *1 2 5 6 7 8*) which is in turn linearly ancestral from I (*1 2 5 6 7*) and I from pA (*1 2*); but none of M, B, I are linear from Y, O by virtue of failing to be circumscribed by *3 4*, while Y, O on the other hand are linear from pA by virtue of *1, 2*.

"Developmental independence," in a limiting case, (usually a simplifying one), would obtain between X and Y if neither is circumscribed by isoglosses other than those commonly circumscribing both; thus Y, O are independent of I because *5 6 7* are not shared by I, even as I is independent from Y, O by virtue of a similar disposition for

3 4. (Again, in most nonidealized actual cases, we will want to talk about "few/most isoglosses" rather than "no/all isoglosses," adopting some explicit threshold value for "few/most".)

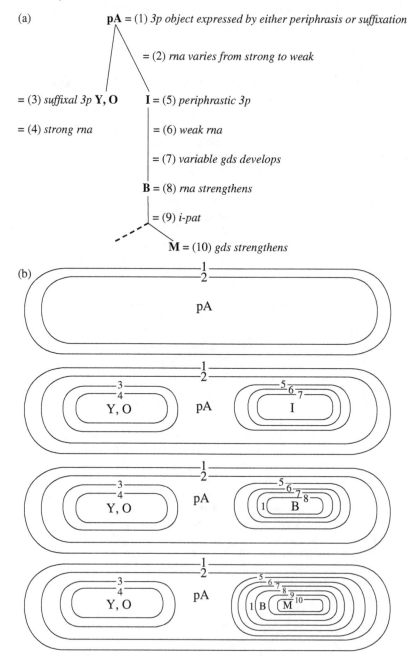

(a)   **pA** = (1) *3p object expressed by either periphrasis or suffixation*

= (2) *rna varies from strong to weak*

= (3) *suffixal 3p* **Y, O**   **I** = (5) *periphrastic 3p*

= (4) *strong rna*   = (6) *weak rna*

= (7) *variable gds develops*

B = (8) *rna strengthens*

= (9) *i-pat*

M = (10) *gds strengthens*

(b)

[108] And though the preferred direction for such metaplasm runs hollow > geminate rather than geminate > hollow, as here (*-AQQIM-* > *-AQIM-*), rapprochements in either direction are attested; §6.1.

[109] M shows one form <ha<u>n</u>siq> 'he made ascend' (DM 332) [hanséq] where las (*ha<u>s</u>lî́q* → *ha<u>ss</u>î́q*) feds gds, §17.8 (*ha<u>ss</u>î́q* → [hanséq]). A similar account holds for the B cau infinitive [lŏma<u>ns</u>ŏqŏ́] (Brown 1979: 1104).

[110] No relevant finite verb forms are attested in P, but the cau passive participle shows las, <m<u>s</u>q> (HC 392).

[111] The chart in (17.22A) simplifies out a few complications detailed in §2.3.2, notably the role of vowel harmony in the development of brf. Another simplification involves the one-dimensional deployment of the hyphen in (17.22A), meant to suggest the demarcative function of the bridge with no prejudice to the more complex, two-dimensional (hierarchical) organization actually imputed. The representations in (17.22A) are mapped onto hierarchical counterparts in (a). Notice that while brf in the intransitive is vacuous (there is no bridge), in the transitive it is manifested by a switch in bracketing—from left-allegiance (e.g., *{{SV}D}*) to right-allegiance (*{S{BD}}*).

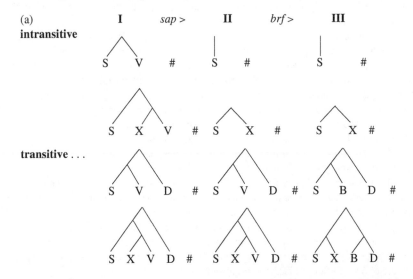

[112] (a) Observe the role of recurring oxytone stressing in this. As spelled out in §4.1, the Aramaic stress pattern is taken to be enforced by a persistent surface-oriented process which (re)applies, in most or all dialects, immediately in the wake of most changes, demanding resatisfaction of its (str's) structural description—here in the wake of epn, which adds a new vowel capable of being stressed. Conversely sap, applying next, does nothing to prompt a rerun of str.

(b) At the outset, the vowels targeted by sap were said to be "specifically in the verb system . . . *-i* . . . or *-a*". *-u* is omitted by virtue of the decision taken in this book (§2.3.4.3) to reconstruct the pA pf 1s suffix as *-t* rather than *-tu* as traditionally. If, however, *-tu* is taken to be the correct shape, the change *u apocope* must be called upon to lose the *u* earlier than the action of epn, upon which the balance of the derivation works out identically to (17.22B); see §17.31 for details. (In the *nominal* system, *-u* might still be required to explicate the development of A segolate formations like **QáSMu > QŏSÁM / QŏSÍM* (Malone 1971a), though once again **QáSM* might be posited on the view that nominative singular case was unmarked (zero) in pA; for more, §17.31.)

[113] "reduced vowels . . . schwas in the broad sense": since the term "schwa" tout court most frequently refers to the segment *ŏ* as a special (limiting) case of reduced vowel, it might be more straightforward to call the construct in question "reduced vowel coloring" or the like. The term actually adopted is out of solidarity with the similar Hebrew phenomenon dubbed "Schwa Coloring" in THP 88–90.

[114] Promotion in fact supplies a significant portion of the evidence that Aramaic *ŏ* is decomposable into [ɛ̆] ~ [ă]. Another source of evidence is the M practice of representing *ŏ* as <i ~ a> (in addition to <∅>); §21.8.

[115] (a) Observe that, strikingly, *V̄H* groups with *CH* and *#H* rather than with *V̊H*; e.g., B participial [dōḥǎl̥ín] ≠ @[dōḥŏ̰l̥ín] (verb examples are rare). This is peculiar inasmuch as a priori one would expect long vowels to be more virulent active assimilators than short vowels. (b) A mixed case of sco both by inheritance and by assimilation is represented by pA *1ʃV̊ of the sim geminate impa picking up the color of extruded *2ʃ V̊; see §3.2 (3I).

[116] Observe that the lexeme √tqp selects *2ʃi ([tŏqi̥f], Dan 4:8, 4:17—lengthening by tln, §17.29; [tŏqḛ́ft], Dan 4:19), so that sco by inheritance is ruled out.

[117] (a) Two of these lexemes show some sim impa variants with *1√ʔV̊ lost by wic (§17.33): [kól]; [zél], [zílī] (Mar 85*, 87*). (b) "generalized palatal 1ʃ impa (sco by default)": perhaps equivalently, generalized palatal 1ʃ impa following as a consequence of sco failing to apply and the unmarked palatal color of *ŏ* hence surfacing; cf. §17.23.1.1, §17.23.2. "sco by *default*": in what follows, some unsettled and/or arbitrary analytic decisions will be made with respect to this in various dialects.

[118] To pinpoint the difference in terms of rules, one might say that Tiberian deploys a-mid^aop (§17.11.2) while Babylonian does not.

[119] "suggests," but is far from clinching—because Margolis's statements leave us in the dark as to whether he is *reporting* on his own usage and that of his teachers or *reconstructing*, by his lights, the usage of his Gaonic forebears.

[120] (a) Admittedly an uncomfortable distinction, in that promotion of presumed indiosyncratic-colored *ɛ̆* and of system-wide colored *ŏ* might both converge onto [ī] (long prm), [e] (short prm). This is a manifestation of the uncertainty concerning the nature of *ŏ* set forth in §17.23.1.1; cf. also n. 117b.

(b) Another uncomfortable aspect of *ŏ*-evaluation in Yem TL is that, although Morag appears to neutralize all schwa manifestations in the Tiberian point <:>, he provides rules for its realization (Mor 91f.) that dictate regressive assimilation to *V̊* in the frame /__ΓV (Γ = a guttural or ẙ)—e.g., (his phonetic transcriptions provided here in phonetic brackets [ ]) <l:ʔɔriyseh> [lo̯ʔoːriseh]—and low color elsewhere—e.g., <d:qaʔ> [dᵃga]. If these rules should reflect the original TL state of matters, or one of several such genuine states, observe that the frame /__Γ V is *regressive* whereas that shown in Ash TL (as well as some other dialects) is *progressive* (/V̊H__), and that unmarked low realization of schwa represents one of the two norms assumed for A *ŏ* realization in §17.23.1.1. Observe also that this norm *conflicts* with the palatal norm manifested by promoted sim impa 1ʃ *ŏ* as treated in the text ([ʔīzél], [ʔɛxól])—which takes us smack dab back to the uncomfortable issue set forth in part (a) of this note. And it is with commensurate uncomfortableness that the color conflict between such as [dᵃga] and [ʔīzél], [ʔe̱xól] leads to the tentative conclusion that the <:>-realization rules described by Morag date from developments in TL trad pron postdating the living dialect. (To add to the uncertainty: Morag reports without comment that the trad pron norm for 1ʃ ȝ in the sim rmp is not low [a] (his [ᵃ]) but palatal [e] (his [ᵉ]); Mor 140.)

[121] (a) In satisfaction of the frame /V̊H__, H = 9, h of the examples should be taken as shortened ← geminate 2√HH = 99, hh of intensive original/underlying forms by mls (§9.3.1).

(b) Since the putatively inert H of the examples is low like the putatively assimilating V̊ = æ, and there are no extant cases of V̊ ≠ æ, environment (iii) might technically be scotched in favor of a generalized (ii) along the lines of /{#,C,V̊}H__; but /V̊H__ is more likely in view of the organicity of /V̊H__ with V ≠ A in other dialects (including Tib B; see (c) next).

(c) In Bab B, V̊ in the frame /V̊H__ is never excrescent; contrast Tib B [lɛh̬wõn] with Bab B unexcresced [lihwõn], and aufgesprengt hence promoted Tib B [lɛh̬ɛwyõn] with Bab B [lihĭwã́n] (BL 153). (Some cases of V̊H = V̊9 apparently capable of excrescing to V̊9V̊ in Tib B rather (variably) *amalgamate* to pharyngealized [V̱] in Bab B; unamalgamated [ti9dḗ] ~ amalgamated [ti̱ðḗ] (~ [tæ̱ðḗ] ← tæ9dḗ), BL 161.)

[122] Observe that no cases have come to light deciding conflicts between environments (iv, v) and (i, ii, iii), Bauer and Leander documenting no Bab B forms in frames such as /V̊H__ (iii+v).

[124] A few comparative sco-related observations on Tib TR and Bab TR might be useful, illustrated with a sim impf 2ms sketch frame on √HSM: (a) in both registers, *iHȝ* obligatorily undergoes sco to *iHĭ*, thus such as @[tiH̬S̬óM] never occurs while the like of [tAH̬S̬óM] may (in Bab TR); (b) the low counterpart *AHȝ always*_undergoes sco → *AH̬Ă* in Tib TR but *never* in Bab TR, thus the like of [tAH̬S̬óM] is restricted to Bab TR while Tib TR always shows +sco [TaH̬ăS̬óM] (-prm) or [taHaS̬óM] (+prm); (c) *A* failures to r-reduce in either register—thus while both registers may sport such as [t̬HiS̬óM], neither will show the like of @[t̬HAS̬óM]. (Perhaps this failure of *A* to r-reduce is connected to the inherently greater sonority of low vowels; Malone 1972b.)

[125] Vowel harmony at large in the phonology has increased from Classical to Modern M (Malone 1997).

[126] Various other claims have been launched about this segment, e.g., that it contained a lateral component (Moscati et al. 1964: 127).

[127] Since Northwest Semitic "emphasis" is arguably uvularization (Malone 1976a), the spirant hopping in this case may actually be a species of deletion, specifically involving loss of the coronal component of ̣ð as a consequence of which the uvular component emerges unrivaled. But be that as it may, pure cases of spirant hopping are quite common in the world's languages, Semitic included. In the latter vein, one of the best known cases, though not under that rubric, is proto-Semitic $*θ > š$ in Akkadian and Hebrew. It may also be suspected that the peculiar development of 2√x in various forms of the Modern M root for 'die' (e.g., §15.3.1.2 n. 25) is the product of $θ$ hopping to x. However, elaboration on this would take us a bit too far afield.

[128] The only evidence from trad pron on this < q > is from M, where <arqa> is consistently pronounced t[ára] (Macm 77)—a realization probably reflecting ufb-

derived *ʔar9ā́ after the loss of 9 (§9.2.3.1), in which case the appearance of <q> in <arqa> would constitute historical spelling, as in fact is being implicitly assumed for all instances of <q> spelling *R in at least the later dialects.

[129] "perhaps modified by attenuation . . . the differential action of att (possibly)": the hedged wording in view of the fact that the impact of attenuation on 1ʃ of the sim impa may well be rendered vacuous, inasmuch as the unmarked manifestation of schwa coloring on this schematic leads to the same result in any event. That is, while attenuation effects 1ʃ A → 1ʃ I , even apart from this, we normally have 1ʃ ӟ (sco → 1ʃ Ĭ) prm → 1ʃ I; i.e., whether sco is taken actively to palatalize 1ʃ ӟ to 1ʃ Ĭ first, which then promotes to 1ʃ I , or sco is taken to lie fallow while prm brings out the inherent palatality of ӟ (on this uncertainty, see §17.23.1.1), the result is still 1ʃ I , exactly the same as would be given by attenuation.

[130] sip is a *transderivational* process, inasmuch as once 2ʃ has been lost by red, its color is phonetically gone from the string *syntagmatically*. Therefore, it can only be retrieved *paradigmatically*, by lifting it from homoparadigmatic forms that have not been subject to red—notably corresponding intransitive forms where 2ʃ characteristically bore the stress and hence was immune to red: ms QV̆SV̆M; fs, mp, fp QV̆SV̆MV̄. However, should sip live on as a synchronic rule, it lends itself to autosegmental modeling *syntagmatically*, as portrayed in (a). Prior to red, we will assume a level where the melodic tiers (root (√), scheme (ʃ)) have been associated to the skeleton (C, V) but tier conflation has not yet taken place. Then, let us assume that red applies in such a way as to delete the second schematic qua skeletal position (V), not qua melody (2ʃ) which it preserves as an unassociated *floater* (note the "snips" in the association line, ≠, indicating disassociation). Finally, by sip, 2ʃ reassociates leftward (dotted line) to the skeletal position corresponding to the first schematic, whereupon the 1ʃ melody is disassociated (≠).

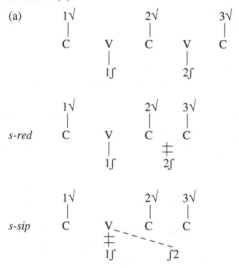

[131] Possibly low-coloring sip gains some favor by virtue of the fact that, in the dialects where it is manifested, unattenuated 1ʃ A also prevails in much of the sim tran-

sitive *pf*. If so, we would be dealing with an instance of inter-tense *syncretism* (§16); e.g., *QASMX́* would then encode both 3ms^X in the pf and ms^X in the impa (in each case, be it noted, the least-marked slot in the respective transitive paradigm). (However, on the side of reservation, note that while both of the TR instances of sip (below), ms^3mp, are of shape *QASMX́*, all Dalman's examples of pf 3ms^3mp are rather of shape *Qə̆SAMX́*; Da 363 (for the shape difference in its own terms, see §17.15.1).)

[132] G and SR show some spread of 1ʃ U from the sim plain impa into the sim rmp impa: G <ʾyT9wrqyn> 'werde(fs) ausgerissen|' (Da 277), SR [εθkurkúy] (§15.5.2). While evidently transparentive extensions from sip, these applications differ from sip proper in that the 1ʃ being colored was not originally a reduced vowel, though it may have become one (by red) in the case of <ʾyT9wrqyn> assuming a pre-hii shape along the lines of *ʾlθ9ə̆rΊqī* (< *hit9arΊqī*). It is not clear whether this technical difference between the original sip process and its extension to rmp has any more than terminological import.

[133] Note that the same variation is found in the ms^3ms reflex of *√whb 'give', whose sim impa was originally, qua *1√w, bereft of phonetic realization of 1√ 1ʃ (§1.5 with n. 16); thus <euhbuia> ~ <ehbuia> 'gebt ihm|' (lc) [ohBúy] ~ [ehBúy]. The first-blush impression is that this originally foreshortened impa form was *initially* provided with a phonetically manifested 1√ 1ʃ by weak imperative change (wic, §17.33) and only *subsequently* did sip manipulate the coloring of the new 1ʃ. However, though simplicity might thus dictate s-wic^s-sip should these processes have lived on *synchronically* (which seems doubtful), *diachronically*, sip might just as plausibly have *preceded* wic, this latter then proceeding with its task of 1√ 1ʃ-addition in such a way as to imitate the sip-induced properties of the forms used as models. The point being made here is a general one. Processes may often arise of a sort we might notate as *X(y)*, a change with essential content *X* in some sense modified by the results of an antecedent process *Y*. Thus the actual events in history will have been *Y^X(y)*. However, investigation of the bare contents of the processes will suggest that matters can be simplified by factoring out the "*y* coefficient" of *X(y)*, and positing instead *X^Y*, where *X* is a version of *X(y)* purged of its *y*-content. Synchronically, all else being equal, *X^Y* may be fine; but diachronically, it may be spurious. The summary moral might be phrased in any number of ways. Here's one:

(a) Inasmuch as synchronic viability may often inform internal reconstruction, s-X^s-Y may suggest d-X^d-Y.

(b) However, for certain kinds of processes, the actual events may be d-Y^d-X(y). Cf. also §4.2 n. 18.

[134] Morag lists [ʾænšǽy] 'saxahti' as a variant reading of -smp rmp [ʾinnə̆šǽy] (Mor §12.21), with nn ← Tn (rrf, §10); but [ʾænšǽy] appears rather to be a causative (Mor §12.51), where gemination would never have arisen in the first place.

[135] The phenomenon does arise, under whatever conditions, outside the verb system, as per spellings like <rεkθɔʾ> for expected <rεgθɔʾ> 'Begierde' (B 42, Ns §21B) bespeaking regressive voice assimilation from θ, which would be only likely in the wake of smp: [rεkθɔ́] ← rεgθɔ́ ← rεggə̆θɔ́ (root√rg (√rgg)). Pending documentation of similar cases in the verb, the question of smp for SR in the purview of the book remains in abeyance.

[136] When under special circumstances the vowel immediately preceding exenergic *nn* is long, in the Ash tradition the *nn* appears as [n] but [ə̆] is preserved/restored immediately following it: illustrating with pf examples √__3mp object suffix (by far the majority for the phenomenon in any event), def int 3ms^3mp [dallīnə̆hṓ] (Mar 103*)—contrast straightforwardly +smp strong [zabbə̆ninhṓ] (Mar 108*)—, def sim 3ms^3mp [ḥǎzṓnə̆hṓ], 3mp^3mp [ḥǎzōnə̆hṓ] (Mar 112*), strong [šǎvaqūnə̆hṓ] (Mar 168*). It is unclear whether these results bespeak what might be called *partial simplification* (p-smp), whereby *C'C'ə̆* → *C'ə̆* (the analog of smp in Tiberian Hebrew also shows such a special case, THP 82f. (Medial Shortening)), or rather regular smp followed by excrescence (§4.3)—in either event the function of the retained (p-smp) / restored (exc) schwa being therapeutic, to preclude a super-heavy syllable of shape *V̄CC*. However, though superficially the complementary patterns look airtight—p-smp or exc when the nearest preceding *V* is long, smp if it is short—when one looks beneath the surface at derivations, a few forms evince behavior that can only be guessed at. Thus, take the near minimal pairs int pf 3ms^3mp [dallīnə̆hṓ] (p-smp/exc) and int pf 1s^3mp [šawwinhṓ] (smp), Mar 103*, 169*. Since the former is taken to be derived from *dallī'innə̆hṓ* by i-pat (§17.15.1) and the latter from *šawwī-T 'innə̆hṓ* by mtr (§17.12) ^i-pat, mtr-loss of the 1s suffix *T* prior to i-pat should predict that both forms will be homonymous save for root differences (√dly vs. √šwy). A purely technical response might have it that during i-pat the former resolves the group . . . *ī* - *'i*. . . by *progressive V*-elision (§17.15.1 (β)) to . . . *i* - *∅∅*. . . while the latter rather selects *regressive V*-elision (§17.15.1 (γ)) to . . . *∅* - *∅i*. . . . But this is mere guesswork—as would be extension of the mechanism to another difficult form, sim impf 3ms^3mp [lišdinhṓ] (Mar 169*) from *lišdḗ 'innə̆hṓ*, so that it likewise undergoes regressive *V*-elision to *lišd∅* - *∅innə̆hṓ* before smp proceeds to derive the surface form. What factor might there be that would select progressive elision for one form but regressive elision for the other two?

[137] (a) smp in M is disfavored under an apparent hodgepodge of marked circumstances; for instance, in approximate descending order of strength of smp-disfavoring in three token (vs. root)-counted samples: (71%) heavy-suffixed sim forms of verbs wherein gemination is effected by contact assimilation of 1√ and 2√ (e.g., <tikirinin> 'thou wilt hold them(f) back' (DM 17) qua [tekkə̆rennén] (*√9kr, §9.2.3); (60%) sim verbs, whether heavy- or light-suffixed, wherein gemination is effected by gmf, §3 (i.e., "true" geminate verbs, as traditionally understood, in addition to those merged from hollow, §6.2.2.1), in which case -smp may be implemented via preemption by Aufsprengung rather than via failure of smp tout court, e.g., <tilitH> 'thou cursest him' (DM 233) qua either +auf [tīleṭṭī́] or -smp [tellə̆ṭī́]; (41%) light-suffixed cau forms of "true" or hollow-merged geminate verbs, e.g., <nanidH> 'erschüttert ihn' (Nm 276) qua [nannə̆ðī́]. It is anybody's guess whether there is any principled patterning here or whether we are merely faced with the statistical vagaries of a small corpus complicated by philological (notably orthographic) uncertainty. And the picture becomes even stranger when it is seen that in the complementary areas of the last nexus cited—heavy-suffixed "true"/hollow-merged geminate causatives, light- or heavy-suffixed contact-assimilated geminate causatives—the incidence of -smp plummets to 0%—i.e., soars to 100% +smp in the samples taken (asymptotically complete from Nöldeke's (Nm) sections on the strong verb). Finally, there may be some relation to the systematic ex-

ceptions to Aufsprengung (§4 n. 24), but if so, the overarching gestalt remains to be revealed.

(b) To judge by the Modern language, there is a chance that smp in M involved compensatory *V*-lengthening, perhaps subject to morphological conditioning. Note, e.g., that in the Modern paradigms for cau pf √npq and √slq (Macm 295), 3ms [a√C′√C′e 3√C] alternates with +smp 3fs [ā√C′ 3√C] (e.g., [áffeq] 'he brought out', [áfqat] 'she brought out'), though canonically similar 1s fails to show the effect ([áfqīt] 'I brought out'). Alternatively, we may be dealing with some sort of [V̄CCV̊] – [V̊CCV̄] balance developed within the Modern language (Malone 1997).

[138] (a) In (17.27A), "√" indicates the totality or majority of occurrences.

(b) The symbol <ŝ>, in (17.27A) and throughout the book as a whole, refers to a letter distinct from <s>, spelling reflexes of both *ś and *š, and not further per se disambiguable as to pronunciation. That is, <ŝ> is used for cases where (the descendant of) 𝓦 per se (i.e., out of context) represents or may represent two or more distinct segments. Specifically:

    <ŝ> is used—
- in Y, O, I, P, N ([ś] or [š]?);
- in G ([ś] or [š] or [s]?);
- in TL ([š] or [s]?).

    <ŝ> is *not* used—
- in B (disambiguated diacritically as [ś] or [š]—"sin sĕmolit" vs. "šin yĕminit"—hence <ś> and <š> are used, respectively);
- in SM and M (where trad pron clinches that the unadorned letter always represents [š], whether < *š or sporadically < *ś—hence, <š> is used);
- in TR, CP, *Classical* SR (where all instances of *ś > [s] spelled <s>; hence <š> may be safely used for [š] < *š).

However—
- <ŝ> is used in *Old* SR, for the same reason as in Y, O, I, P, N above (Drijvers 1972: 114, 116).

[139] Arabic š is the regular reflex from proto-Semitic of either *ś or *θ (the latter irrelevant here, except to note that it may instantiate spirant hopping, §17.24).

[140] This example of unilinearity is merely hypothetical, but of course if the earlier dialect (II) is taken *not* to be unilinearly related to the latter (III), the caveat on the irreversibility of merger will be unnecessary—and we will be dealing with trajectories like those in (a) rather than (17.26B). (Recall apropos that O has on other bases been called into question as unilinearly related to later A; §17.21.1 with n. 107.)

(a)   **I**   >   **II**   >   **III**

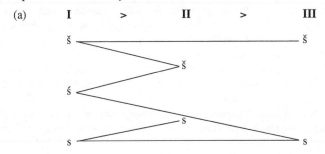

[141] No one-letter abbreviations will be provided for "causative-" and "rmp-" tagging subspecies of ssl, since the most straightforward candidates, "c-" and "r-," are preempted for other usages (§26.1).

[142] While Leander supports the ssl interpretation and adduces the *QaSīM* hypothesis proffered above, Kutscher rather interprets <y9> as representing depharyngealized [ī] (cf. §9.2.3.1).

[143] The general tendency is probably widespread enough to merit codification (a):

(a) A linguistic change that in a given environment would be neutralized (apply vacuously) will frequently enlist an ancillary change precluding/undoing such neutralization.

In this case, ssl√__*3*√*y* + *T#*, *T* = 1s, would all else being equal apply vacuously, because both +ssl *īyT#* and -ssl *iyT#* would surface as [īθ#] (dme, §8.1.1, plus the two-μ weight limit on homogeneous segmentism, cf. §17.17.1). So trp (§15) is enlisted to replace -T by making for +ssl *īyīθ#* vs. -ssl -*iyT#*, the former surfacing as [-īyīθ#] ([īθemnīyī́θ]), the latter as [-īθ#] ([īθeqrī́θ]).

[144] tln seems to be alien to the Babylonian register of B. Thus, corresponding to Tiberian [sə̆γī́ð], [tištə̆vī́q], [yə̆hašpī́l], [zə̆9ī́q], [mallī́l]—as well as questionably extended +tln [bōrī́x] and [hēmī́n] (the latter being scored by a conjunctive ta9am, merxa, is especially prone to be -mid [hēmī́n], §17.11)—Bab B uniformly presents correspondents with <e>; BL 102, 107, 113, 131, 140, 167. (It is uncertain whether the Bab forms answering to Tib items in [ī] should be interpreted as containing -tln but pausal [ĕ], or rather -tln [é] with the phenomenon of pausality itself absent from the register, at least as a phonological reality.)

[145] (a) The Babylonian register, again, shows no analog of top: [ʔeħæwwĕ̈], [{yə̆}hæħwĕ̈], [{nə̆}hæħwĕ̈] (BL 158, 164). (b) The pausal [ɛ] – contextual [ē] relation bespoken by top has at least typological affinity with facets of [ɛ̄] – [ē] distribution in Hebrew, notably in the nominal absolute–construct states, respectively, the construct state being marked by subordinate stress hence lesser sonorancy; note also the Hebrew process of Tonic Lowering (THP 95–97). (c) Observe that top is limited to √ħwy 'declare'.

[146] The shape *īT* may follow from *yə̆T* by ymn (§14.2), *yə̆T* being generalized from frequency of construction with vocalic-anlaut object suffixes and derived by r-red from *yaT* if shortening from *yāT* can be assumed (cf. the later A subordinator *də̆* < *ðī*). *T* in turn facilely reflects left elision (§17.15.1 (γ)), at least postvocalically. The value of *T*, [t] or [θ], is given by dialect-specific conditions on spr.

[147] Superficially similar to the SM phenomenon, G shows evidence of a dialect-specific labial bridge vowel in the transitive sim impa (§2.3.2.4 n. 14): ms^3ms <ŝBqwTh> (with tom-inserted *T*), <PThwnh> (in construction with bridge *(I)nn*); fs^3msalso <ŝBqwTh> (syncretic with ms^3ms via fgm, §16.1).

[148] While *yāt* is sometimes used in older TL, in the later dialect (and in the E dialects generally) it is functionally replaced by (originally datival) *lV̊* (Mar 84f., B 115, Nm 390 n. 2).

[149] Deferment of at least the apocope of -*a* is unsurprising, given the universal high sonority—and commensurate resistance to loss—of low vowels; Malone 1972b.

On the other hand it is unclear whether *-i* , the patner of *-a* in sap, should be expected to be inherently more resistant to loss than *-u*.

[150] "unmotivated at least in the verb system": largely of one cloth with the postulation of **-u* as declarative suffix in the verb system is hypothesis of the same vowel as nominative suffix in the nominal system. Offhand, that view likewise seems unsupported by A-internal evidence.

[151] However, M shows full-vocalic prefixes due to the later action of transparentive impf prefix strengthening (§15.3.1.1), wdr^ips; see the forms in (17.32A) below.

[152] Data in (17.32A) from HC 359, Da 354, Sg §51.2, Sl 49, Macs 218, B 98, Mar 52, 106*, Mor 36, Nm 268 n. 1, 267f. Some points on the examples aside from wdr: TR [ē] ~ [æ], close ~ open k-coa (§11.2); CP 1s <y->, ymn (§14.2); SM for most facets of trad pron, §22.1, for absence of *h* in spelling and/or trad pron, dgt (§9.2.2, §9.3.2, §21.2 (ζ)), [ắ] in t[yắ²i] and t[ắ²i] < prefixal *ă* promoted, stressed, and lengthened by smc (§22.1), <hy> in 3ms <hy> and 1s (copulative) <why> as inverse spelling for [ī] since <hy> [hǏ] dgt > <hy> [Ǐ] effectively left <h> interpretable as a silent letter in spelling [Ǐ] whether etymologically justified or not (cf. <gh> in English <delight>) and probably reinforced in the present case lingering etymologically justified <h> in (some) homorizous forms, auslaut <-w> t[-u] in <yhwnw> t[yứnu] probably representing pleonastic suffixal *-ū* shoring up a canonically threatened form in the wake of wdr; G <yy(²)>, <yywn> *h*-less by dgt (§9.2.2). At least the latter G form and a few SM forms appear to show reflexes of 2√y, like Hebrew, rather than normal A 2√w: 3fp <²hyyn> and 3ms <yhyy> t[yẽyyi] (alternatively <hy> as inverse spelling for [Ǐ] is excluded, at least in the case of the latter, because the length of [ē] in t[yẽyyi] betrays ← *Ih* (c-pra(γ)^c-dgt (β), §22.1 (22F)), with true linguistic rather than mere orthographic *h*. The fp palatal factor (§7.2 (δ) with n. 13) is betrayed in CP <yhyn> and perhaps in SM <²hyyn> just cited.

[153] The likeliest reason for (almost) exclusive confinement of wdr to √hwy (for the qualification "almost", see discussion of condition (iv) below in the text) is the high natural text frequency of copulative verbs (as √hwy), and the ensuing tendency in speech toward contraction and simplification. This granted, if wdr were to apply √_ə̆, . . .*Vhwə̆yÅ*. . . would → . . .*Vhə̆yÅ*. . . . But the selfsame tendency toward contraction and simplification driving wdr would then bid fair to elide the inherently weak schwa (r-red), and the resulting . . .*VhyÅ*. . . would by virtue of its *hy* undercut the declustering function borne by wdr in the first place. (Cf. the hypothesis suggested in §17.28 n. 143a.)

[154] (a) The questioned CP forms along with a few additional 2√<w>-bearing items are marked by Schulthess as bowdlerized on the authority of (presumably) Paul Lagarde ("in solo cod. A occurrentes correct{a}ri debentur, teste Lagardio", Sl 49).

(b) Some orthographic forms of √hy(y) 'live' give the specious impression of having undergone wdr (or "ydr")—specfically, forms apparently lacking representation of 2√y, e.g., <yhy>. But on the evidence of vocalized forms, such would not represent @[yə̆hǏ] but rather [yIhhǏ] or +mls (§9.3.1) [yǏhǏ] (e.g., TR [yēhẽ], Da 354) betraying √hy(y) qua geminate (see §8.1.1 n. 7).

[155] At least in earlier A, *1√w verbs stand apart from *1√n verbs and *√slq in one regard that might ultimately have some bearing on a proper understanding of the mechanics of the change(s) discussed in this subchapter: while most *1√w verbs apparently lacked a phonetic reflex of 1√ not only in sim impa, but in sim impf as well, *1√n

verbs and *√slq seem to have shown gemination of the radical adjacent to *1√n, *2√l in the sim impf (and in the entire cau system also); i.e., /1√nC′/ ⇒ [C′C′], /s 2√l/ ⇒ [ss]. For these latter assimilations, see §17.21; for various teleologically similar processes in the case of *1√w, see §17.7.

[156] The fact that the effects of ymn are registered in only a subset of the dialects undergoing wic does not necessarily imply d-wic^d-ymn, as a naive internal reconstruction might suggest. Since wic in any event is a *phonological* as opposed to phonetic change, inasmuch as it crucially involves impacting one area of a verb's paradigm (that where some phonetic realization of 1√y < *1√w is maintained) on another (that where there is no such realization), wic construed in Generative Phonological terms will virtually automatically be interpretable as: *either* a *rule deletion*, whereby a rule apherizing just such a 1√y coupled with the immediately following 1ʃ is expunged from the phonology, with the consequence that some phonetic realization of this string will then be allowed; *or* as a *restructuring*, whereby some value of 1√ 1ʃ is added to the underlying representation—let us simply call it /yV-/. This being the general scaffolding of things, /yV-/ will emerge as [yV-] in dialects lacking ymn (narrower specification of [V] depending on processes like trp and sco, §15, §17.23) and as [(ʔ)Ǐ-] in dialects undergoing (having undergone) ymn (§14.2). And such +ymn results can be achieved whether d-wic^d-ymn (derivations in (a) below) or d-ymn^d-wic ((b) below); under either ordering, (i) = sim impa, (ii) = elsewhere. Since a similar point has already been demonstrated in §14.2 n. 18 on the rule deletion model (where the rule apherizing /yV-/ was called "s-kwatz"), here the restructuring model will be explicated. In both (a)(i) and (b)(i), the restructuring impact of d-wic assumes the form of inserting /yV-/ into the phonological representation qua exponent of 1√C 1ʃ V on the homoparadigmatic analogy of forms which already enjoyed such exponency—such as the homorizous sim pf, supplying the lexical identity of 1√C as /y/ and the class of heterorizous sim impas, supplying the morphological identity of 1ʃ V (plausibly as /ʒ/, but for simplicity here /V/, not further specified). The major workings of the homoparadigmatic forms are laid out in (a)(ii) and (b)(ii). Observe that derivations are *transderivational* (global) in that ingredients of those in (i) are fed by ingredients of those in (ii). Specifically, the appearance of /yV-/ in (i) (as of stage II in (a), stage III in (b)) despite absence of phonetic reflexes since pSemitic—thus /∅-/ at stage I—is enabled by its continued homoparadigmatic realization as [yV-] or [(ʔ)Ǐ-] in (ii).

(a)	**I**	*d-wic >*	**II**	*d-ymn*	**III**
(i)	/∅-/		/yV-/		/yV-/
					s-ymn
	[∅-]		[yV-]		[(ʔ)Ǐ-]
(ii)	**I**	*d-wic ≥*	**II**	*d-ymn >*	**III**
	/yV-/		/yV-/		/yV-/
					s-ymn
	[yV-]		[yV-]		[(ʔ)Ǐ-]

(b)	I	*d-ymn* ≥	II	*d-wic* >	III
(i)	/Ø-/		/Ø-/		/yV-/
					s-ymn
	[Ø-]		[Ø-]		[(ʔ)Ĭ̊-]
(ii)	I	*d-ymn* >	II	*d-wic* ≥	III
	/yV-/		/yV-/		/yV-/
			s-ymn		*s-ymn*
	[yV-]		[(ʔ)Ĭ̊-]		[(ʔ)Ĭ̊-]

[157] Development of long variants, specifically but not exclusively in 1√y < *1√w verbs, is likely also to have been enhanced by the original long canon of 1√y ≤ *√y lexemes. However, the paucity of clearly attested sim impas in this gizra renders it impossible to solidly document this influence.

[158] Values under the various headings of (17.33B) are partially extrapolated, attestation from several of the dialects being insufficient. Note in particular that extant inscriptions and texts show no impas for either P or N.

[159] (a) There is some evidence of incipient wic-encroachment into the canonically similar sim pf—what might be called incipient "wpc"—especially in the case of √slq: **SM** <sq> 'stieg herauf', <sqw> t[sắqu] 'sie kamen hinauf' (Macs 98, 185), <TB> t[tắb] 'wohnte' (Macs 139f) (there is also extension of wpc to some 1√n roots: <SB> 'nahm', <Pq> 'kam heraus', <Pl> 'ist gefallen', <ʔ9T> t[ắɛt] 'kam herunter'— ~ -wpc <n9T> t[nắɛt], lc (for <ʔ>, <9> in lieu/spite of *2√ḥ, §9.3.2, §21.2 (ζ)); **TL** <hBw>'they gave' (§17.34), hapax <sqw> 'they ascended' (Mar 37 n. δ —a form that Margolis then tentatively guesses to be metanalytic geminate a[sáqqū], Mar 143*); **M** <saq> 'he ascended', <ṣub> 'they shrank' (§9.2.4, DM 314—note the Modern reflex of the former, [sắq], Modern M having fully metaplasticized this lexeme to hollow; lc). Also, is it suspicious that M shows long > short in wpc, while in wic M is the only dialect to show consistent short > long?) (Apheresis of initial *a* in forms of √ʔmr, like <(a)martulH>, may also involve wpc, though distance of the apheretic syllable from the stress might point to a separate etiology; for forms, see §24.2; **G** *1√ʔ procliticized sim pf forms like <wBD>, <wmr>, <Dmr> (Da 299) are perhaps better considered to have undergone Ø < ʔ (§9.3.2 n. 42) than wpc, preservation of <ʔ> in anlaut of nonprocliticized forms (<ʔBD>, <ʔmr>, etc., lc) bespeaking an orthographic prop for the initial vowel as in SR and M, §21.3.

(b) For the possibility of wic-like extension (of ʔV̆- → Ø-) beyond the sim verb, see §12.2 CP (γ).

[160] (a) Degen cites no finite cases of wpl on √wd9. (b) Observe that requiring the changeling segment to be radical might account for the universal failure of wpl to palatalize conjunctive *wa-*.

[161] The form a[wīháv] = [wiyháv] 'and he gave' (Mar 120*) is instructive, deriving as it does < att *wa=yháv* < red *wa=yaháv* < spr, sap *wa=yahába* < wpl *wa=wahába*. If wpl had occurred late enough to follow reduction, it would have been bled by 1√w

ending up in codal position, *wa=wháv* syllabified as *wa=w|háv*, predicting an outcome like @[wōháv].

[162] It is a matter of speculation whether the retrenchment of 1√w in Aramaic (and more generally in Northwest Semitic) by wpl may be linked to the even more drastic retrenchment of 3√w, especially in the verb, in both cases by merger with *y*. Appearance of 3√w in the A verb is extremely rare; e.g., √thw in TL, y[kī́ hēxī́ də̆θæhhə̆wū́ . . . nə̆θæhhə̆wū́ . . .] 'kĕšem šetamhu . . . yitmə̆hu . . .' (Mor 267).

Part Two

Genealogy and Dialectology

18. Family Tree Theory, Wave Theory, and Reconstruction

18.1. Family Tree Theory [1]

In accordance with the *family tree theory* (Stammbaumtheorie), assiduously developed in the 19th century on the model of Darwinian biological speciation, a language (say, *L* in (18A)) may over time break up into *daughter* languages (or dialects—from the strictly linguistic point of view the terms "language" and "dialect" are interchangeable) characterized by certain changes (in sound pattern, morphosyntactic structure, lexicon, etc.) gradually setting them apart from their own linguistic progenitor(s) (thus *M* is differentiated from *L* by virtue of having undergone change(s) ζ). Since any language (dialect) has the inherent propensity to change, the process of differentiation may be repeated; thus *M* in turn may in time develop into dialect *Q* (characterized by change(s) θ) and dialect *R* (characterized by ι). *Q* and *R* are each *daughter* dialects with respect to *M* as their *mother*, and *sisters* with respect to one another. (In the same vein, *Q* and *R* may be considered "granddaughters" of *L* as their "grandmother," but such terminology is not normally used). Dialects may be reckoned as (relatively) conservative or (relatively) innovative on the basis of the quantity and quality of changes they undergo. Abstracting away from the question of quality in the simplified demonstration undertaken here, *S* is more conservative than *Q* or *R*; because while *S* is differentiated from *L* by one (set of) changes η, *Q* and *R* are each differentiated by two: *Q* by ζ and θ, *R* by ζ and ι. In basic family trees, time and space are normally displayed in a relative and stylized fashion, such that, e.g., in (18A) the length of the branches and the degree of aperture of the angles formed at the branches are irrelevant. Occasionally in this book, however, the vertical dimension may be modified by manipulating the length of the branches to suggest (approximate) coevality of daughters. Interpreted this way, (18A) would convey that *S* is (roughly) contemporary with *Q* and *R*, while (18B) would mark *S* as coeval with *M*, and *R* as earlier than *Q*. Similar manipulations will at times be effected with the spatial dimension, specifically the horizontal in using graphic adjacency to suggest geographical adjacency. Read this way, (18A) would convey that *R* is spoken on a territory flanked by those where *Q* and *S* are spoken.

(18A) *earlier*

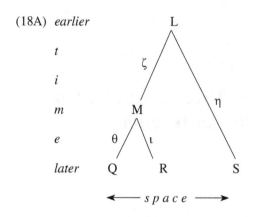

t

i

m

e

later

← *s p a c e* →

(18B)

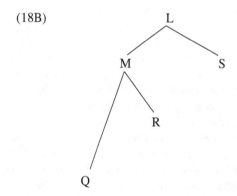

The tree in (18A) indicates that examination of the dialects portrayed has revealed the following incidence of linguistic changes:

(18Ci) L : none
     M : ζ
     S : η
     Q : ζ, θ
     R : ζ, ι

What if, in addition to this, *R* and *S* are discovered to have undergone κ, so that (18Ci) is replaced by (18Cii)?

(18Cii) L : none
     M : ζ
     S : η, κ
     Q : ζ, θ
     R : ζ, ι, κ

In unadulterated family tree theory, a developmental nexus like that of (18Cii) defies plotting unless it is assumed that κ constitutes two independent changes (more on this later), as in (18Di). But if the assumption is that κ represents a single, unitary change (or a single complex of changes), family tree theory rules out the like of (18Dii)—whereby dialect *R* would have double ancestry—or (18Diii)—whereby dialects *R* and *S* would do so to, say, cross-pollinate.

(18D) (i)   (ii)

(iii)

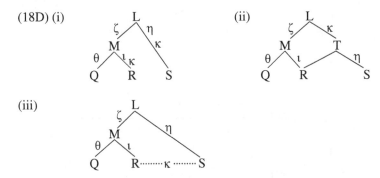

Ultimately, the reason for tree-theoretic strictures against the like of (18Dii, iii) is likely to be inertial baggage from Darwinian biological theory, inasmuch as normal biological organisms do not have multiple sets of blood parents (18Dii), and once separate species are formed they can for the most part no longer interbreed (18Diii).[2] But is such a model fully appropriate for *linguistic*, as opposed to biological, organisms? In a word, *no*. As concerns multiple ancestry, (18Dii), one of the most tried and true exemplars of such a phenomenon are so-called *pidgin* languages, and hence also the frequent progeny of pidgins, the *creoles*.[3] And as concerns "cross-pollination," (18Diii), we have one of the commonest and most pervasive of all change type, *interdialectal borrowing*, sometimes called *diffusion*. It is certainly impossible for any investigator to undertake an in-depth study of any language group without uncovering multiple incidence of diffusional change—and Aramaic is no exception.

18.2. Wave Theory: The Basics [4]

Partially in response to their growing awareness of the limitations of family tree theory, in the late 19th century, scholars developed an alternative model, the so-called *wave theory* (Wellentheorie). Essentially based on codification and systematization of dialect geography, wave theory depends crucially on the notion of *isogloss*, an imaginary line bounding a speech region within which a linguistic change has spread. Over time, isoglosses may themselves change, expanding, contracting, moving from one area of a speech region to another, or even disappearing.[5] Also, new isoglosses may appear within older ones, or overlap them.

Wave theory is capable of expressing almost any pattern that tree theory can. Thus, (18A) is expressible along the lines of (18E), where each of the three levels in the tree (= each horizontal array of dialect symbols: *L*, *M*, *QRS*) corresponds to a distinct stage (I, II, III) of isoglottic patterns—none at I; ζ at II, defining the new dialect *M* as a differentiation / breakaway from *L*; and the three most recent dialects at III, *Q*, *R*, and *S* defined respectively by ζ and θ (note importantly how the defining power of the older ζ lingers on), by ζ and ι, and by η.[6]

(18E) **I**

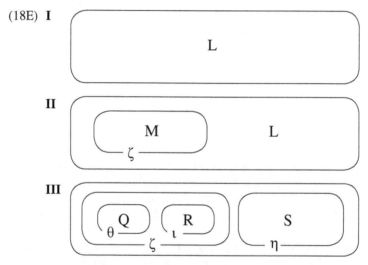

If chronological phasing is as per (18B), IIa – Iib in (18F) replace II in (18E) (stages I and III remain the same):

(18F) **IIa**

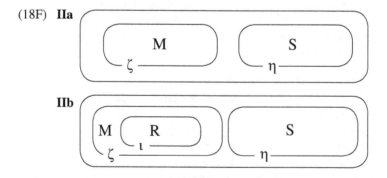

Importantly now, the diffusional pattern defying the expressive power of tree theory, involving change κ being shared by dialects *R* and *S* despite a genealogical disposition otherwise as in (18A), is portrayable as in (18G) (replacing (18E) at stage III). This is interpretable as the result of change κ spreading between *R* and *S* (either direction) after the formation of dialect boundaries. We will have occasion to refer to diffusional changes as *straddles*. Thus, in (18G), change κ constitutes a straddle between dialects *R* and *S*; equivalently, κ straddles *R* and *S*.

(18G)

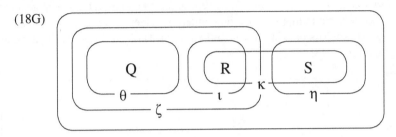

Though pure-state tree theory is unable to capture diffusional patterns like that of κ expressed in (18G), it will be convenient at various junctures of the book to avail ourselves of notationally simpler tree representations in lieu of cumbersome, sprawling wave diagrams. This is merely an expository convenience, and the representations so employed are still intended to be essentially wave-theoretic. In this vein, straddles, as (18G), will be represented by a dashed horizontal branch, as in (18Diii).[7]

While diffusion can account for two or more dialects' sharing a change developed *after* differentiation of the dialects in question, it sometimes happens that two or more dialects share a similarly patterned change which actually developed *before* the dialects separated. Consider again the distribution of in κ (18D). As portrayed in (18G) (or conveniently as in (18Diii)), such a κ developed after *R* and *S* had separated. But what if there should be evidence that κ had an *early* origin, say even as early as *L*? Scrutiny of the configuration of (18A) will show that such a development defies representation in pure-state tree theory—unless certain interlocking events are specially assumed, notably later disappearance of κ—called it "anti-κ," or "-κ"—from *Q*, the sister of *R*, as displayed in (18H):

(18H)

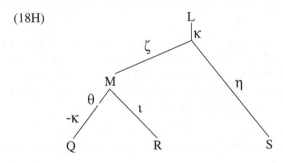

However, though traces of changes do at times die out, it is undesirable in default of evidence to posit negative changes like -κ simply as di ex machina to enable coherent accounting of skewed patterns like early κ (*L*) ending up in select descendant dialects (*R*, *S*) while showing no trace in others (*Q*). Wave theory provides a possible recourse in terms of the notion of *dialect pocket* (or *isogloss pocket*): a change-bounding region that remains static across generations while surrounding regions may undergo dialect-forming, isoglottic clustering. As isogloss pocket for κ is laid out in (18I) (superposed on the general scaffolding of (18E)).

(18I) **I**

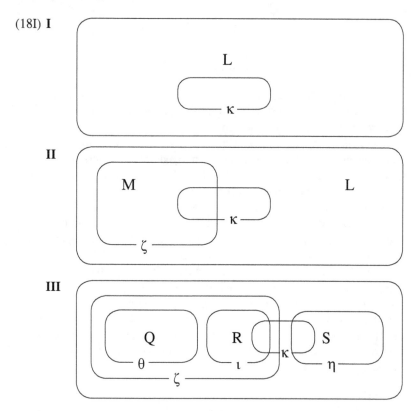

For expository convenience, isogloss pocketing will at times be displayed tree-fashion (cf. the ilk of (18Diii) for straddling) in terms of what will be called *shafts*. Shafts will assume the form of dashed branches plotted to some extent athwart the prevailing genealogical branching of the tree. Shafting for κ is portrayed in (18J), a convenience-equivalent of (18I):

(18J)

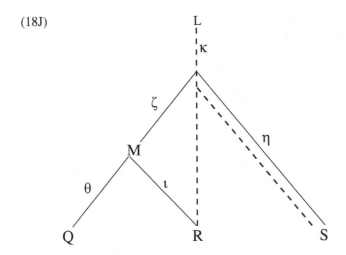

18.3. Wave Theory: Modalities of Isogloss

Isoglosses may be fielded in a number of interesting modes, two pairs of which are *synchronic-diachronic* and *phonetic-phonological*. In the *synchronic* mode, only processes are marked off that are *currently* affecting the speech area; in the *diachronic* mode, on the other hand, processes are marked off if they have *ever* affected the speech area, even if their synchronic effect has long since been neutralized. In the *phonetic* mode, only processes directly affecting articulation are marked off; while in the *phonological* mode a process will be marked off as long as it has the status of a rule—even if its direct phonetic impact has long since been muted.

In this book, isoglosses will normally be fielded in the diachronic mode, with the phonetic-phonological dimension available for exploitation either way, as the task at hand may dictate. Consider a situation where a change, call it α, has over time lost territory on a given speech area; that is, the geographical distribution of the speakers impacted by the change has shrunk. Assuming the synchronic and phonetic modes, this nexus might be portrayed as in (18K), where the area affected by α has successively diminished over three stages. In the *diachronic* mode, however, the situation would be portrayed as in (18L), where the successively narrower regions are simultaneously represented.

The diagrams in (18L) incidentally capture one possible distribution of a *persistent* change, a change whose impact continues over a significantly long period of time (rather than impacting abruptly and then ceasing to exist as a phonetic force, as is characteristic of more run-of-the-mill *transient* changes). Thus, at stage III of (18L), in the innermost region change α has persisted from stage I (α_1) through II (α_2) to III (α_3).

One may ask whether a persistent change need correlate, as in this illustration, with diminution of the region affected. The answer is no. Persistent *expansion* is a possible too, and may be represented as in (18M). Likewise, persistence without size alteration may occur, as in (18N).[8]

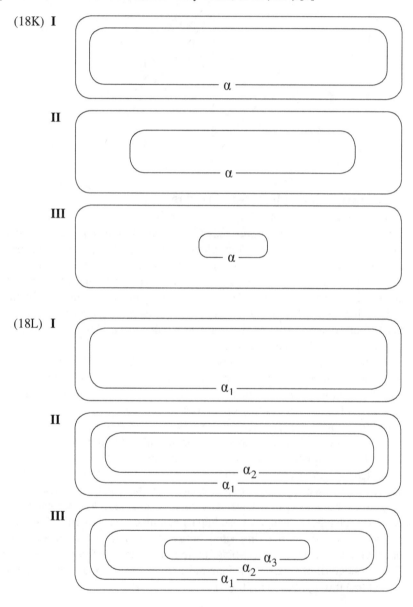

(18M)

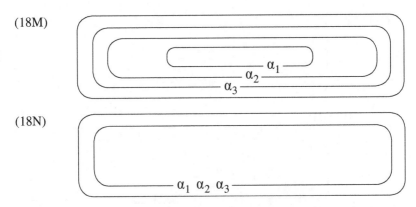

(18N)

Sometimes a change will disappear for a time and then return, rather than persisting uninterruptedly. Such *reprise* changes are isoglottically indistinguishable from persistent changes at the stage they come into effect but will be cued by the presence of a preceding fallow stage, whereas an otherwise similar persistent rule would be explicitly represented. Continuing the red-auf-red illustration from n. 8, if we understand the second application of red to be one reprise rather than persistence, we might have the like of (18O). If rather persistence is assumed, we would have (18P).

(18O) **I**

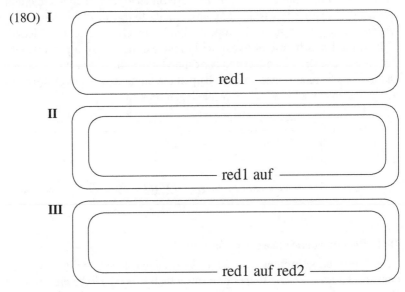

II

III

(18P) **I**

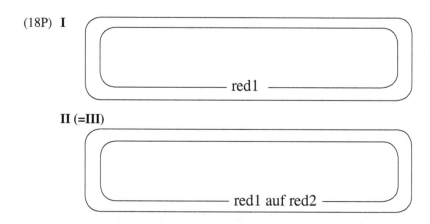

red1

II (=III)

red1 auf red2

It often happens that a follow-up change, whether persistent or reprise (*re-run* will be used as a noncommittal generic) develops differences over time from the way it started out. Commonly, a change will *generalize* its scope of application—though narrowing of scope is likewise a possibility. In either event, prime ticks may be used to suggest the mutation of content in changes: $\alpha1$ $\alpha2$ ... $\alpha n = \alpha$ as a rerun change (persistent or reprise) without substantial change of content; $\alpha1$ $\alpha'2$ ... $\alpha''n$ = a rerun change with contentual mutation (say, $\alpha1$ applies to auslaut long vowels, $\alpha'2$ to open-syllabic long vowels whether or not in auslaut, $\alpha''3$ to open-syllabic vowels irrespective of length).

It will at times be useful to explicitly indicate the loss of a process, rather than simply ceasing to portray the corresponding isogloss. For this, a *negative change* may be represented with the help of the minus sign. Thus (18Q) explicitly indicates that after a spell of rerunning, α dies out.

(18Q)

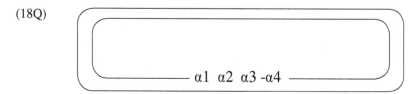

$\alpha1$ $\alpha2$ $\alpha3$ -$\alpha4$

18.4. Reconstruction: Description

Reconstruction to infer earlier forms of languages stardardly proceeds by comparing the *cenematic* shapes of forms which are taken to be *plerematically* similar within a narrowly circumscribed range. Cenematic loci of variation so uncovered, normally but not necessarily *segments* (consonants and vowels including any suprasegmental properties like tone, stress, length), are then mutually evaluated on the assumption that the items containing the loci were once cenematically identical, any variation among them being attributable to linguistic change. The array of such loci are said to be (mutual) *correspondences*.

While any number of criteria may be brought to bear in evaluating an array of correspondences and inferring the original shape thereof, one of the commonest is a rule of thumb that might be called "Majority Rules." In this light, consider the array of sketch correspondences in (18R) (i), and assume for the nonce that these correspondences pertain to forms on the same genealogical level (an issue to which we will shortly return). Following the guideline of Majority Rules, the array of correspondences in (18R) (i) would be "solved" as in (ii), interpretable to the effect that α β α α γ arose from α (the asterisk indicating the inferential status of this surmise; *α is *reconstructed* rather than attested) by α changing (>) to β in *W* and to γ in *Z*—while remaining unchanged in *V, X,* and *Y,* the Majority in this case.

(18R) (i) **V**   **W**   **X**   **Y**   **Z**
            α   β   α   α   γ

      (ii) **U**   **V**   **W**   **X**   **Y**   **Z**
            *α > α   β   α   α   γ

Reconstruction comes in two principal modalities, *internal* and *external*, where external reconstruction is commonly known as the *comparative method*. In external reconstruction, the forms subsuming the correspondences belong to separate (but by hypothesis related) languages (or dialects); thus, *V, W, X, Y,* and *Z* in (18R) might be, say, B, TR, SM, SR, and M, in which case *U* would be proto-Aramaic (pA). In internal reconstruction, on the other hand, the forms hosting the correspondences all belong to the same language (dialect) and are differentiated by language-internal (dialect-internal) categorization. In such a case, *V, W, X, Y, Z* might represent distinct slots in a paradigm, their commonality being identity of lexical item.[9]

Though reconstruction is a diachronic tool, internal reconstruction tendentially bears an important synchronic correlation. Namely, the solution to the correspondences—e.g., *α > α β α α γ in (18R) (ii)—is frequently isomorphic to a synchronic phonological relation—in this case, α ⇒ α β α α γ. This holds presumably because sound changes are the commonest progenitors of phonological rules; when a change like α > α β α α γ affects a family of morphologically related forms, as required in internal reconstruction, then for at least a certain amount of time a sort of equivalence relation will be established among α, β, and γ, an equivalence relation native speakers will internalize roughly along lines like these: "α occurring in (forms like) *F* under paradigmatic conditions *V, X, Y* is equivalent to β in (forms like) *F* under conditions *W* and to γ in (forms like) *F* under conditions *Z*." But this is exactly the sort of relation that phonological rules are designed to capture.[10]

However, while the frequent isomorphism thus obtaining between sound changes and phonological rules undeniably provides a useful tool—and analytic shortcut—to the internal reconstructor, the tool is fraught with danger. This is because, as detailed in §23.2, phonological rules often undergo *mutations* that throw them out of kilter with their own historical origins. One of the most baneful of these mutations for the historical investigator is *rule reordering*, sketchwise portrayed in (18S) whereby a pair of rules, α and β, switch their derivational order from α^β to β^α. The bane for the historical investigator is this. Applying the isomorphism rule-of-thumb, the investigator may have reached the conclusion that the synchronic nexus $F\,\beta \Rightarrow G'\,\alpha \Rightarrow H'$ bespeaks diachronic $F\,\beta > G'\,\alpha > H'$; whence also might be concluded that change β is older than change α. But in reality, the opposite is true; α is older than β—the appearance to the contrary being due to the fact that α and β, qua rules, have mutated their synchronic order of application from α^β to β^α.[11]

(18S)   **I**   >   **II**
　　　　/F/　　　　　/F/
　　　　α|G|　　　　β|G'|
　　　　β[H]　　　　α[H']

While the "mutation" of *rule addition* is internal-reconstructively straightforward, the remaining two types of rule mutation treated in §23.2 (catalogued in (23J) and touched upon in n. 10 of the present chapter), *deletion* and *modification*, can also discomfit internal reconstruction. Two particularly bothersome subtypes will be sketched here, *accordioning* (deletion) and *rule inversion* or *reversal* (modification).[12]

In accordioning, sketched in (18T), a change (β) impacts the phonology with the effect of undoing the work of a prior change (α), with the consequence that the internal reconstructor sees *no* changes where in effect there were actually *two* (α and β). Uncorrected, accordioning lends the false impression than an innovative dialect (innovative by virtue of having undergone two changes) is conservative (having undergone no changes at all). (Note in this illustration that the sound change triggering the accordioning is $G\ d\text{-}\beta > F$, and that the ensuing rule deletion is double: both $s\text{-}\alpha$ and $s\text{-}\beta$ are lost, α being undone by β and β self-destructing in the process).

(18T)   **I**   α>   **II**   β>   **III**   >   **IV**
　　　　/F/　　　　　/F/　　　　　/F/　　　　　/F/
　　　　　　　　　　　　　　　　　α|G|
　　　　[F]　　　　　α[G]　　　　β[F]　　　　　[F]

In *rule inversion*, we are essentially dealing with a structural change resulting from a shift in distributional weight between two competing allophones, *a* ~ *b*. Suppose possible distribution for these allophones is exhaustively statable under five conditions, C, D, E, F, and G; and suppose that at first (stage I) a is the clearly unmarked allophone, occurring under all conditions but C, which hosts b. Given the complementary distribution obtaining between a and b, a situation of this sort clearly justifies setting up a as the phoneme and hypothesizing a rule whereby /a/ ⇒ [b] under C rather than an alternative /b/ ⇒ [a] under D, E, F, G. Suppose then, however, a series of *rule generalizations* (the most frequent sort of rule modification, §23.2), whereby /a/ ⇒ [b] begins successively extending from C alone to the other conditions. Once a critical number of conditions have joined C in hosting [b], the distributional balance will have shifted from [a] as unmarked allophone to [b], and at that point /b/ will replace /a/ as the phoneme—an instance of *restructuring* (§23.2 with (23G))—and the rule will correspondingly have mutated from /a/ ⇒ [b] to /b/ ⇒ [a]. This is *rule inversion*. The illustration just presented is sketched in (18U) (i), with the phoneme-allophone distribution displayed in (18U) (ii).

The pitfall for the internal reconstructor is clearly stated. In default of adequate evidence for the development of the rule inversion itself, naïve internal reconstruction will lead to the false conclusion that the original segment was *b, while in fact it was *a.[13]

(18U) (i)	**I**	a ⇒ b /C	(*but* a = a /D, E, F, G) >
	II	a ⇒ b /C, D	(*but* a = a /E, F, G) >
	III	a ⇒ b /C, D, E	(*but* a = a /F, G) <u>rule inversion</u> >
	IV	b ⇒ a /F, G	(*but* b = b /C, D, E)

(ii)		C	D	E	F	G
	I	/a/ [b]	/a/ [a]	/a/ [a]	/a/ [a/	/a/ [a]
	II	/a/ [b]	/a/ [b]	/a/ [a]	/a/ [a/	/a/ [a/
	III	/a/ [b]	/a/ [b]	/a/ [b]	/a/ [a]	/a/ [a]
	IV	/b/ [b]	/b/ [b]	/b/ [b]	/b/ [a]	/b/ [a]

18.5. Limitations of Reconstruction

The joint frequency of *rerun changes* on the one hand, §18.3, and of *rule mutations* on the other, §18.4, unfortunately impacts negatively on the historical investigator in seriously diminishing the reliability of even the most time-cherished analytic helpmates for *determining a change's relative chronology*. In the case of rule mutations, this effect was clearly indicated case type by case type above. In rerun changes, the effect comes about from the difficulty of distinguishing the primary change (α) from its follow-up (α'), whether persistent manifestation or reprise.[14] And the resulting analytic purblindness is often aggravated by a kind of masking effect, whereby the later α' hides the effects of the earlier α.

True, the investigator may luck out by coming across various ancillary facts or events helping to anchor the chronology, facts or events either of a linguistic or an extralinguistic nature. Examples of the latter sort include independently datable orthographic transcriptions—whether in the object language itself, or graphemic inserts within a foreign text. Prime among the linguistic sorts of helpmate is intervention of another change, β, between α and α', which either *feeds* α' in a way which obviously it could not have fed α (because it, β, didn't exist yet); or alternatively *bleeds* α' (and, of course, not α). In the feeding scenario, forms impacted by α' may be marked in a way—called it "β-marked"—distinguishing them from earlier analogs touched only by α. And in the bleeding nexus, a structurally determinable set of forms may be exempted from the action of α'—exactly those targeted by β—while no such exemption would have affected earlier α-susceptible analogs.

However, helpmates of the sorts just envisaged do not arise as frequently as might be desired and, most often, the analyst must just stumble on to the tune of a fragmentary chronology of changes at best. This in fact is the case with the panoply of changes set forth in this book (exceptions duly noted in appropriate spots).

Notes to §18

[1] There are numerous excellent sources on family tree and wave theory. For splendid classical accounts, see Sturtevant 1931 and Bloomfield 1933. For an overall consideration of these theories and historical linguistics at large, see Lehmann 1992. A recent technical application to Indo-European genealogy but with much general theoretical relevance is Nakhleh, Ringe, and Warnow 2005.

[2] "for the most part": the qualification accommodates unusual exceptions like the mule (sterile offspring of a male ass and female horse (mare)).

[3] See Holm 1988.

[4] For references at large, see n. 1 above.

[5] However, important qualifications on these modes of isoglottic change will be discussed in §18.3.

[6] By convention, isoglosses will be plotted to leave elbow room for easy reading. Thus in (18E) (III), the space between isoglosses θ, ι, and ζ is devoid of any but expository significance.

[7] In the sketches heretofore employed, capital Roman letters have been used for dialect variables and lowercase Greek letters as variables for isoglosses. In the interests of simple exposition, these usages have tacitly omitted mention of certain real-world aspects of isoglosses and language nomenclature. First of all, real dialect areas are normally set off by *bundles* of isoglosses rather than by individual tokens—though nothing airtight can be said about the number of individual isoglosses required to constitute such a bundle or about qualitative prerequisites of changes involved. Relative to this,

ζ, η, θ . . . may in appropriate sketches be interpreted as bundles, though in the right context singleton interpretations may be in order (e.g., κ in (18G)). Then to *L, M, Q,* . . . as nomenclatural variables, it should be kept in mind that while in most sketches in §18 they are freely used to identify random dialects in turn defined by random isogloss bundles, yet in the real world: (*) not all isogloss bundles define actual dialect areas, though the more prominent the bundle, quantitatively and qualitatively, the more likely real dialect differentiation becomes; (*) conditions for actual dialect formation are characteristically geographical, political, and ethnic in addition to linguistic (isoglottic) in the narrow sense, though extralinguistic differences (geographical, etc.) tend to promote isogloss formation; (*) discrepancies are commonplace among different perspectives on dialect definition—so that, e.g., scholars may recognize distinct dialects, or fail to, where speakers of the speech forms in question do the opposite; or the names used (if any) may vary between scholars and natives, as they may between synchronic and diachronic vantage (notably, labels such as "proto-Aramaic" (pA) and "proto-Semitic" were never used by the ancient peoples to whom these speech forms were native).

[8] (a) Persistent changes were said to impact over a *significantly* long period of time. One type of significance is imparted by the emergence of a second change during the course of the persistence such that this supervenient change feeds the persistent process. A candidate for an actual case from Aramaic may be seen in §4.5 where in some dialects reduction persists around Aufsprengung (red^auf^red), while in others it transiently precedes Aufsprengung (red^auf). Thus starting from a sim impf 2mp like *tIQSUMŭn*, we might have in the transient case *tIQSUMŭn* red > *tIQSə́Mŭn* auf > *tIQISMŭn*, but in the persistent instance *tIQSUMŭn* red > *tIQSə́Mŭn* auf > *tIQISMŭn* red> *təQISMŭn*.

(b) Transient changes were said to impact *abruptly*. This too should be understood in a relatve sense—for instance, as a way of conveying that the process in question fails to apply, qua rule, at more than one phonological level. For instance, continuing the illustration just provided under (a) above, reduction applies transiently in deriving *tIQISMŭn*, inasmuch as red effects *2 ʃU > ə́* but then fails to extend to prefixal *I* after auf has opened its syllable and, in so doing, has made it technically possible for red to apply again.

[9] The hedge on applicability of Majority Rules vis-à-vis "forms on the same genealogical level" anticipates the eventuality that in studying an array of correspondences like α β α α γ under the comparative method, the majority status of α might be specious due to the fact that the manifesting dialects are found to be genealogically subgrouped to the exclusion of the dialects manifesting β and γ. That is, while Majority Rule is (usually) effective in positing proto-values for correspondences in the case of dialects that turn out to be related in the manner of (a) below—here, the three αs are indeed on the same genealogical level—yet, the rule of thumb fails if the genealogical relations should turn out to be along the lines of (b). The reason for this may be seen in scrutiny of the competing solutions presented in (c, d): whereas (a) truly lends itself to an *α-solution like (ci)—only two changes need be posited, α > β and α > γ, while competing (cii) and (ciii) would require four each—yet (b) does not pari passu lend itself to solution (di) over against (dii, diii). As may be seen, each of (di), (dii), and (diii) requires two changes. Here, Occam's Razor leaves us in the lurch.

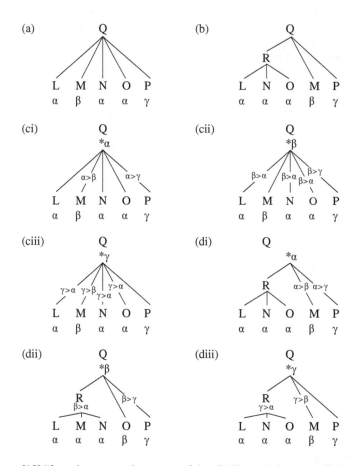

[10] "for at least a certain amount of time." *All* sound changes will almost certainly live on as synchronic rules for at least a generation or so, even changes of unconditional loss of grammatical signals which, by virtue of being lost without a trace, are thenceforth irretrievable by the speakers. However, at least during the first generation, there will be conservative speakers—usually older ones—who will not participate actively in the change, and by whose speech accordingly innovative speakers subject to the change will continue to be aware of the linguistic function of the signals now missing in their own usage. For a certain spell, therefore, the change will live on by virtue of a sort of transpersonal grammar; and will not be fully lost to the community, qua rule, until the conservative generation has died out. The following generation will then have undergone the phonological mutation known as *rule loss* or *rule deletion* (§23.2 (23J)).

[11] (a) A nonpareil demonstration of chronologically layered internal reconstruction may be seen in Chafe 1959.

(b) Mutations of rule ordering, as strikingly bizarre and mathematicoid as they might at first blush appear, are rather common in languages at large. Indeed, they lose much of their impression of bizarreness when it is recognized that they are often diachronically mediated by linguistic changes of an ordinary, even common-sense sort, which just happen to impact upon the structures they affect *as if* two preexisting rules reversed their applicational order. The reason the mediating change metamorphoses into rule reordering is that the generation hosting the change gives way to a new generation not party to the original change or its motivation, a generation which—like every generation of speakers of any language—must induce its own grammar anew from the interplay of forms and meanings (expression and content) to which it is exposed; and rule reordering often turns out to be the computationally most facile way of achieving the goal (granted the conventions that linguists have adopted for explicating such matters, in this case the trappings of Generative Phonology; §23). An Aramaic case in point is elaborated in Malone 1971a, where the mediating change is teleologically *analogic*, the goal being to change segolate stems from shape $Q\mathring{V}S\mathring{V}M$ (like Hebrew) to shape $Q\mathring{\partial}S\mathring{V}M$ for the sake of better paradigmatic homogeneity. (In Malone 1969, mediating changes of this sort are called "A-rules"). In upshot, the nexus in (18S) is missing a stage, that of the mediating change, call it "γ," as portrayed in (c) below. At stsage II, γ survives as a last-ordered synchronic rule. But the way it interacts with β and α is *as if* β and α switched their order, and nothing above and beyond that. And so that is exactly the way the new generation comes to "understand" things, at stage III.

(c)	**I**	γ >	**II**	>	**III**
	/F/		/F/		/F/
	α|G|		α|G|		β|G'|
			β|H|		
	β[H]		γ[H']		α[H']

[12] The phenomenon of accordioning may actually be broader than the rule-mutating sort presented here.

[13] A ripe field for rule inversion in Aramaic involves alternations between *i* and *e*, especially in the Eastern dialects (SR, TL, M)where /i/ has plausibly given way to /e/ (as assumed for the cognate case of Tiberian Hebrew in THP, where rules are revamped from traditional **i > e* to /e/ ⇒ [i]); see especially the discussion for TL in §17.11.3 with n. 44. Here and there intimations also crop up of an accordion *i > e > i,* with the last step (*e > i*) instantiating the inversion;, e.g., §17.23.3 Tib TR. (In the text, inversion was cast in terms of /a/ ⇒ [b] being replaced by /b/ ⇒ [a]. But at least some of these cases of *i > e > i* may actually synchronically manifest the accordion /i/ ⇒ \|e\| ⇒ [i], an unstable nexus to be sure but one wherein \|e\| → [i] would no less qualify as a genuine instance of inversion than would /e/ ⇒ [e]. And although this specific surmise concerning Aramaic *i, e* could only be vindicated by thorough synchronic analysis, a task beyond the pale of this book, the general hypothesis remains: a nexus combining accordioning and inversion may at times be synchronically manifested in the chain /x/ ⇒ \|y\| ⇒ [x], an accordion by virtue of /x/ = [x] and involving inversion by dint of the coexistence (in the same phonology) of /x/ ⇒ \|y\| and \|y\| ⇒ [x].

[14] An interesting distinction is drawn by Blevins (2004: 48–51) between two sorts of reruns—more narrowly, reprises—those instantiating what she calls *parallel evolution* and those manifesting *convergent evolution*. While parallel evolution involves changes similar in structural/functional etiology no less than in de facto content, convergent changes typically agree in de facto content only, while possibly differing widely

in the congeries of factors that led to their coming about. Offhand, the majority of explicitly recognized (or stipulated) reruns treated in this book are of the parallel type. Nakhleh et al. field the term "parallel development" to refer to similar developments within the same overall genealogical complex *other* than those linearly related—i.e., other than those in this book dubbed reruns. At the same time, their definition of what they call *backmutations* is virtually identical to this book's *reprises* (2005: 383 n. 5).

19. Aramaic Dialect Relations

In (19A) appears a comprehensive listing, alphabetized by three-letter abbreviations, of the majority of the processes and patterns hypothesized in this book. For many of these, a profile is given of the individual dialects, ranked in accordance with either (or both) of two general systems or, alternatively, in terms of various special systems explained case by case in the notes provided.

The two general systems:

(α) + ≫ v ≫ i ≫ -. +: a process applies (or a pattern holds) (almost) categorically; v: variable application (with no commitment to relative frequency of (non)application , but see (α′), next); i : infrequent/rare application (with no commitment to whether the process/pattern might be incipient, moribund, or neither); - : (virtual) nonapplication.

(α′) +|- ≫ -|+. A more fine-tuned statement of variability, occasionally provided data allowing: +|- = application more frequent/robust than nonapplication; -|+ = nonapplication more frequent/robust than application.

(β) I ≪ II ≪ III ≪ . . . . Hypothesized developmental stages for a process/ pattern, I being the least developed, the highest Roman numeral indicating the most developed. (While there is a tendency for developmental vigor to correlate positively with chronological progression, this is at best a tendency. Some cases to the contrary will merit special discussion; e.g., spr and coa under (δ) toward the end of the chapter.)

Blank cells indicate either uncertainty of assignment, or irrelevance of providing a profile from the vantage of differentiating between dialects (for instance, if all dialects would score identically).

The cells corresponding to processes/patterns limited to only one or to all A dialects are left blank, but the dialect(s) affected are noted in parentheses; e.g., ayd is specific to TL, while epn is likely to be Common Aramaic.

The charts in (19B–D) are similar in purpose and organization to (19A) but deal with subcases of processes rather than with whole processes. Similarly (19E), which, however, deals with processes not granted a three-letter label.

(19A)	Y	O	I	B	P	N	TR	CP	SM	G	SR	TL	M
aap (§9.1.4) alef apocope													
adn (§9.1.4) alef-defective neutralization	i?	–	v	+	+	+	+	+	+	+	+	+	+
adr (§9.2.1.1, §9.3.2 n. 42) alef drop	–	–	–	–	–	–	–	+	+	+?	+	–	+
ads (§9.1.1)[1] alef dissimilation	+	+	+				–	–	–	–	–	–	–
aga (§9.2.1.1 n. 14b) advocalic guttural assimilation													
a-mid (§17.11.2) adguttural midding													
anc (§2.3.1) ancipitality													
aop (§17.11.2) atonic opening													
apl (§9.2.1.2) alef palatization	–	–	–	–	–	–	–	v	+	+	–	+	+
arp (§17.1) A replacement	–	–	–	–	+?	–	–	v	–	–	–	–	v
ars (§17.9.2 n. 26) analogical reshaping													
att (§12) attenuation							I					I	II
auf (§4.4)[2] Aufsprengung			v				v	v	v		v	v(a)	v
ayd (§17.2) *ay* development					(TL)								
b-phd (§1.3) backwards pharyngeal dissimilation							v	v	v?	v	v		v
brb (§17.3) *bring* blending	–	–	–	–	–	–	–	v	–	v	–	–	–
brf (§2.3.2) bridge formation													

(19A)	Y	O	I	B	P	N	TR	CP	SM	G	SR	TL	M
b-snm (§17.27) backwards sin merger													
b-str (§4.1) barytone stress	(see **str**)												
car (§9.2.1.2) causative alef replacement	–	–	v	+	+	+	+	v	+	+	+	+|–	+|–
c-dgt (§22.1 (22B)) Samaritan Circuit degutturalization	(SM)												
cis (§6.1.2) causative initial strengthening	(see **g-cis, i-cis, m-cis**)												
cnd (§8) condensation													
coa (§11.1) coalescence			v	v (II?)	v		v (II?)	v	v	v (I?)	v (I?)	v (I?)	v (I?)
c-pen (§22.1 (22B)) Samaritan Circuit penultimation	(SM)												
c-pra (§22.1 (22B)) Samaritan Circuit prosodic adjustment	(SM)												
c-prm (§22.1 (22B)) Samaritan Circuit promotion	(SM)												
c-sad (§22.1 (22B)) Samaritan Circuit schwa-alef drop	(SM)												
css (§17.4) closed syllable shortening													
cta (§7.4.2) categorical assimilation				+	+		+	+	+	+	+	–	–
c-ult (§22.1 (22B)) Samaritan Circuit ultimation	(SM)												
c-vcr (§22.1 (22B)) Samaritan Circuit vowel cluster reduction	(SM)												

(19A)	Y	O	I	B	P	N	TR	CP	SM	G	SR	TL	M
cys (§17.5)[3] causative *y/w* spread			(δ)v				(α, γ)v (δ)v	(α, γ)v		(α, γ)v (δ)v	(δ)v	(δ)v	(δ)v
dca (§10 n. 3b) dentoalveolar contact assimilation													
deg (§3.1 (3Fvii)) degemination													
dgt (§9.1.3 n. 6) degutturalization													
dia (§15.3.1.1 n. 21) disambiguative impf attachment													
din (§8.1.1 n. 1) dipthong interchange													
dme (§8.1.1) dipthong- monophthong equivalence													
dpr (§9.3.2) depharyngeali- zation	−	−	−	−	−	−	−	−	v	−	−	v	+
e-anc (§2.3.1) early ancipitality													
eas (§9.1.3 n. 8) emphatic assimilation													
e-cnd (§8.1) early condensation													
e-dgt (§9.2.2 n. 25) early degutturalization					(SM)								
eds (§9.1.3 n. 8) emphatic dissimilation													
epn (§17.8) epenthesis					(plausibly cA)								
e-pro (§8.1.3 n. 14) early prothesis													

(19A)	Y	O	I	B	P	N	TR	CP	SM	G	SR	TL	M
exc (§4.3) excrescence													
f-cnd (§8) full condensation													
fgm (§16.1)[4] formal gender merger							I		II		I	IV	III
fin (§17.17.1 n. 83) finite intrusion													
fma (§2.3.4.3 2p) final *m* assimilation	–	–	v	+	+	+	+	+	+	+	+	+	+
f-phd (§9.1.3) forwards pharyngeal dissimilation	–	–	–	–	–	–	–	v	v	v	v	v	v
f-red (§4.2.1) full reduction					(see **red**)								
frf (§17.7)[5] first radical filling				β δ			α β γ	α β? γ? δ	α γ δ	α? β? γ? δ	α β γ	α β γ	α? β? γ?
f-snm (§17.27) forwards sin merger	–	–	–|+ ?	–|+ ?	v	–	+	+	+|– ?	+?	+	+?	+|– ?
ftg (§16.2 <u>SM</u>) z′ with n. 24 feminine *t* generalization					+				i	v			i
g-cis (§6.1.20[6]) geminate causative initial strengthening			v				–		–		v	v	v (/+?)
gds (§17.8) geminate dissimilation			II	II					I?				III
ghr (§6.3)[7] geminate-hollow rmp nexus			I	I?			II	I	I	I	I	II′	II/ III
gmf (§3.2)[8] geminate formation	4u	4u 5	1u 2u 4u~m 5	1u~m 2u 4u 5	4u 5	5?	1u 2u 3u 4u 5	1u 2u 3u 4u~m 5	1u~m 2u~m 4u~m 5	1u~m 2u~m 4u~m	1u 2u 4u 5	1u~m 2u 4u~m 5	1u 2u 3u~m 4u 5

(19A)	Y	O	I	B	P	N	TR	CP	SM	G	SR	TL	M
gsr (§4.5 (4G) n. 25) geminate spirant reocclusion													
gta (§9.3.2) guttural assimilation													
gtl (9.2.1) guttural laxing	−	−	−	−	−	−	−	v	+	v	−	−	−
hap (§9.2.2) *h* apocope	−	−	−	i?	i	−	i	i	v	i	−	v	+
hei (§11.1)[9] heightening											v (>i) (*Jac*)		v (>i)
hgn (§6.1)[10] hollow-geminate neutralization				v			v		v	−	v	v	v
hgr (§6.1) hollow-geminate rapprochement				v			v		v		v	v	v
hii (§7.2 (δ)) heavy intransitive importation	−	−	i	−	−	−	i	v	v	v	v	v	v
hlr (§9.2.2) *h*-less rmp	−	−	v	−	+		+	+	+	+	+	+	+
hrb (§6.3)[11] hollow rmp blur				1	+?		1a	1?	2	1	1i	1	1i
hrm (§6.3 SM) hollow rmp metaplasm						(SM)							
hti (§7.2 (ζ)) heavy transitive importation		−	−	−			v	−	v	v	v	v	v
i-cis (§6.1.2) increasing causative initial strengthening		⸱		v			v				−	−	−
i-hlc (§9.1.2) initial *h*-less causative	−	−|+	v	v	+	+|−	+	+	+|−	+	+	+	+
i-lap (§17.9)[12] infixing long apocope	−	−	−	−	−	−	−	−	−	v/−	−	v	i?

(19A)	Y	O	I	B	P	N	TR	CP	SM	G	SR	TL	M
i-pat (§17.15.1)[13] immediate pronoun attachment	−	−	−	−	+		+	+	+	+	−	v	+
ips (§15.3.1.1) impf prefix strengthening								II			I	II	III
itl (§8.1.3) imperative tonic lengthening				−				i			+	−	
j-prp (§17.9) jussive-precative prefix replacement	(see **prp, n-prp**)												
k-coa (§11.1) condensatory coalescence	(probably cA)												
l-anc (§2.3.1) late ancipitality	(see (19B))												
lap (§17.9) long apocope	−	−	−	−	v?	−	−	v	−	v	+	v	+
las (§17.21.2)[14] *l*-assimilation		α+		α+	α+		α+	αv	α+	α+	α+	αv	α+
	β+	βv	βv										
l-cnd (§8.2) late condensation	−	−	−	−	−	−	−	−	−	−	+	v	+
lco (§12.2 B (δ) with n. 8)[15] labial coalescence				+ (Tib)			v				+		+
low (§17.10) lowering													
l-pro (§8.1.3 n. 14) late prothesis	(see **pro**)												
lsg (§6.1.1.1) long schematic generalization				v							+	v?	+
m-cis (§6.1.2) metathetic causative initial strengthening									v?	v		v	
m-hlc (§9.1.2) medial *h*-less causative	+?	−|+	−|+	−|+	+	+	+	+	+	+	+	+	+

(19A)	Y	O	I	B	P	N	TR	CP	SM	G	SR	TL	M
mid (§17.11)[16] midding				I (Tib)			II				IV	II	III
mit (§13) mitosis	(see **vco**)												
mls (§9.3.1) medial low shortening				+			+				v	v	v
m-pat (§17.15.2) mediate pronoun attachment	(M)												
m-sis (§6.1.1.2) metathetic simple initial strengthening	(SM)												
mtr (§17.12)[17] morphological truncation									α? β	α β		α β	β
mvh (§2.3.2.1) with n. 5 minor vowel harmony													
nae (§7.2 (δ) n. 9) *nā* extension	–	–	–	–	–	–	–	v	v	v	v	v	v?
ndr (§17.13) *n* drop	–	–	–	–	–	–	–	v	v	v	–	–	–
nhp (§17.15.1 (δ)) *n* haplology												v	+
n-prp (§17.19)[18] nasalizing prefix replacement	–	–	–	–	–	–	–	–	–	–	III	I	II
oba (§22.1) obstruent adjustment	(SM)												
occ (§17.14) occlusion	–	–	+ *prob.*	+	+/v	+/v	+	+	+	+ *prob.*	+	+	+ *prob.*
o-str (§4.1) oxytone stress	(see **str**)												
pat (§17.15) pronoun attachment	(see **i-pat, m-pat**)												
p-att (§12.1) partial attenuation													

(19A)	Y	O	I	B	P	N	TR	CP	SM	G	SR	TL	M
p-cnd (§8.1) partial condensation													
p-coa (§11.1) partial coalescence													
pdt (§17.15.1 n. 64) pronoun detachment													
pfr (§7.2 (δ) with n. 13 palatal factor	–	–	–	–	–	–	–	v	v	v	v	v	v
pga (§9.2.1.1 n. 14b) progressive guttural assimilation													
phd (§9.1.3) pharyngeal dissimilation													
pin (§17.17) participial intrusion								v	v		v		v
p-red (§4.2.1) partial reduction	(see **red**)												
prf (§10)[19] progressive rmp fusion	–	–	–	–	–	–	v I	v I′	–	v I	–|+ I′	v II	v II
prm (§14.1) promotion													
pro (§17.18) prothesis	–	–	–	i	–	–	i	i	v	v	i	v	v
prp (§17.19)[20] prefix replacement	–	–	–	I	–	–	–	–	–	I?	IV	II	III
p-smp (§17.26 n. 136) partial simplification													
ptc (§17.20) *put* causativization	–	–	–	–	–	–	i?	v	i?	–	–	–	v
ptg (§17.16)[21] pataḥ gĕnuva				+ *(Tib)* – *(Bab)*			+					+ *(Ash)* v *(Yem)*	

(19A)	Y	O	I	B	P	N	TR	CP	SM	G	SR	TL	M
rca (§9.2.2) rmp-causative assimilation							+	+	+	+	+	+	+
rdm (§9.2.1.1 n.14a) radical metathesis						(M)							
red (§4.2)[22] reduction				+	+	+	+	+	+	+	+	+	+
				ζ:p			ζ:p	ζ:p?	ζ:p~f?		ζ:f	ζ:p	ζ:f
reo (§5.2)[23] reocclusion				2√C_			√C_				√C_		
rga (§9.2.1.1 n. 14b) regressive guttural assimilation													
rmt (§10) rmp metathesis			+	+|−	v?	v	+	v	+|−	+	+	+|−	+
rna (§17.21) regressive nssal assimilation	+	+	v	v	v		v	v	v	v	v	v	v
rps (§17.15.1 (17.15A)) repair strategy													
rrf (§10)[24] regressove rmp fusion		−	−	i I	v II	−	v II	v I	v II	v III	v I	v IV	v IV
rst (§23.2) restructuring													
rwb (§8.1.3) retraction with bobbing		−	−	−			v	−	−	−	v	i	−
sad (§9.2.1.2) schwa-alef drop	−	−	−	−	−	−	v	v	v	−?	+	v	+
sap (§17.22) short apocope				+	+	+	+	+	+	+	+	+	+
sar (§9.2.1.2) simple alef replacement	−	−	−	+	−	−	+	v	v	+	+	+	−
scc (§3.1 (3Fvi)) special color copy													
sco (§17.23) schwa coloring													
scr (§7.2 (γ), §12.2 n. 11) stressed closed-syllabic raising						(CP)							

(19A)	Y	O	I	B	P	N	TR	CP	SM	G	SR	TL	M
shp (§17.24) spirant hopping	(pA)												
sip (§17.25) simple impa promotion							I/A	U	A?	I/A?/U	U	I/A/U?	I/U
smc (§22.1 (22B)) Samaritan Circuit	(SM)												
smp (§17.26) simplification													
snm (§17.27) sin merger	(see **f-snm**)												
snp (§10) snap	(M)												
spr (§5.1)[25] spirantization				+ /{v/w}_	+	+	+ /{v/w}_	+	+	+	+ /V_	+	+
srt (§4.1.2 <u>B</u>, §17.5.2 n. 75) stress retraction													
ssg (§6.1.1) short schematic generalization													
ssl (§17.28)[26] second schematic lengthening			i (*rmp*)							v (*cau*)		v (*rmp*)	v (*rmp*)
ssn (§12.2 <u>SM</u> (α)) second schematic neutralization	(SM)												
sta (§14.2 <u>G</u> n. 17) stress adjustment													
str (§4.1)[27] stress				o|b (*Tib*) b|o (*Bab*)			b|o	b~o	b|o	b|o	o	b~o (*Yem*) b|o (*Ash*)	o|b
svs (§20.2 (γ, ζ)) systematic vowel shift													
swh (§4.4.1) schwa haplology													
syn (§16)[28] syncretism							I		III		I	IV	III

(19A)	Y	O	I	B	P	N	TR	CP	SM	G	SR	TL	M
tln (§17.29) tonic lengthening				v			v						
tom (§17.30) *T* object marking								v	v	v			
top (§17.29) tonic opening	(B)												
trp (§15) transparentation	(see **ips** and (19C))												
uap (§17.31) *u* apocope													
ufb (§9.1.3) uvular fricative backing	(pA)												
umr (§20.2 (γ)) unconditional merger													
vco (§13)[29] vowel copy							α β γ		α β γ(i)? δ(i)?			α	α β δ(i)
vdc (§14.2 <u>CP</u> n. 11) vowel declustering													
vha (§13) vowel harmony	(see **vco**)												
vlg (§15.2.2.2 n. 20) vowel lengthening													
vpg (§9.2.4) voiceless pharyngeal glottalization	−	−	−	−	−	−	−	−	−	−	−	i	+
vpl (§9.2.4) voiceless pharyngeal laxing	−	−	−	−	−	−	−	i	+	v	−	−	−
wdr (§17.32) *w* drop					v		v	v?	+	v	v	v	v
wic (§17.33)[30] weak imperative change								s	sl	sl	sl	sl	l
wpc (§17.33 n. 159a)[30] weak perfective change								s	s			s	s

(19A)	Y	O	I	B	P	N	TR	CP	SM	G	SR	TL	M
wpl (§17.34) w palatization						(pA)							
wrb (§23.3) word building													
ymn (§14.1)[31] y monoph- thongization			I				III	IV	IV	I	III	I	II

(19B)	Y	O	I	B	P	N	TR	CP	SM	G	SR	TL	M
l-anc (§2.3.1)[32] late ancipitality													
number-gender: mp				−			−				−	−	+
subject: 1s				−			−				+	−?	+
3mp				−			−				−	−	+
2mp				v			−				+	−	−
2fp							−				+		−
object: 3ms				+			+				+	+	+
3mp				v *(-pat)*			−				+ *(-pat)*	− *(Yem)* + *(Ash)*	−
3fp				− *(-pat)*			−				+ *(-pat)*	− *(Yem)* + *(Ash)*	−
2mp				+			+				+	− *(Yem)* + *(Ash)*	−
2fp											+	− *(Yem)*	−

(19C)	Y	O	I	B	P	N	TR	CP	SM	G	SR	TL	M
trp (§15)[33]													
_nonreduced 2ʃV̌ (§15.2.1.1 §15.2.1.2, §15.2.1.3; §15.5.1)				I			IIIa				IIIb	IIa	IIb

(19C)	Y	O	I	B	P	N	TR	CP	SM	G	SR	TL	M
_sim pf hol [QĀM] (§15.2.1.4)				i							+ (Ash) / − (Yem)	+	+
_pf 1s medial [-ĬT-] (§15.1.2.2)							v					v	v
_[-ū-(-)] as realization of -A 3√y + mp(-) in the defective verb (§15.3.2)				i			i				i		
1ʃ[U] in sim rmp impa (§15.5.2)										v	v		

(19D)	Y	O	I	B	P	N	TR	CP	SM	G	SR	TL	M
syn (§16)[34]													
_the In(n) complex							v		v			v	v
the 3ms–1p complex											+	+	+
the T^object complex							II				I	IV	III or IV
the 2s–1s complex							i?						i
the 3ms–3fp complex							v				v		

(19E)	Y	O	I	B	P	N	TR	CP	SM	G	SR	TL	M
§17.3 n. 3													
√ntn ~ √yhb suppletion								+	v		+	+	
√ntl								v			+		

Thirty-three of the processes in (19A), or subprocesses thereof, are selected as being especially unlikely to emerge independently in two or more dialects. These may be called *primary* isoglosses and appear in (19A) with their labels boxed. On the assumption that dialects sharing in common one or more such isoglosses do so by virtue of descending from a common ancestor dialect where the isogloss(es) originated, 24 of the 33 primaries conspire to justify all but two branchings in the genealogical tree of (19F). Specifically, the branchings numbered from (2) through (8) are justified, relevant primaries being noted on each branch.

If the primary isoglosses are then supplemented by *secondaries*, selected from (19A–E) on the basis of gross compatibility with the distribution of the primaries, the result is the complete tree of (19F), with addition of branchings (1) and (9). Forty-one secondaries conspire to produce this effect. These are listed in column (ii) of (19G), as are the primaries in column (i).[35] (Columns (iii–iv) will be discussed presently.)

All in all, the genealogy of (19F) is consonant with the characterization of the dialects proffered in §0.1 of the introductory chapter. The genealogy implies that Y and O (branch 1) broke off from Aramaic at large, which later subsequently developed into I (branch 2). B then developed from I (3); P, N, and TR from B (4, 5); and a split formed between W and E (6, 7, 8). Finally, E diverged into an upper (northern) and lower (L, southern) branch (9).

(If misunderstood, these genealogical claims might be quite disturbing to traditional conceptions of Aramaic dialect relations. But for one thing, "X developed from Y" does *not* mean that Y has its roots in the *historically attested instantiation* of X—so, for instance, the claim is not being made that the Palmyrene dialect is descended from exactly the Aramaic of the books of Daniel and Ezra. The sense rather is that Palmyrene by and large represents a development of/from the *general kind* of language represented in Biblical Aramaic. Also, the genealogy is not meant to be exhaustive; it hardly could be, given the premise that that the thirteen dialects studied in this book represent but a sample (§0.1). So an ideally complete tree would contain a significant number of additional branches at every level—and indeed probably additional levels as well.)

Returning to (19G), columns (iii) and (iv) fill out and complement the genealogical functions of (19F) in various ways. The *interpolated* isoglosses of (iii) are changes surmised to pertain to branches 2 and 3 in the overall panorama of Aramaic development, but changes which—given orthographic limitations of the extant corpora—remain per se unverified. Column (iv) provides some likely *chronological orderings* of the processes for the given branch. (It is of course likely that the actual chronological profile was both richer and more complex; but cogent chronological ordering of linguistic changes is notoriously elusive of reconstruction, as has been pointed out at various spots in the book, e.g., §18.5. Recall also from the discussion of §5.3 that "spr◊red" indicates a *loop* relation (cf. §23.3), i.e., spirantization and reduction *overlapped* chronologically, so that at some times/places spr preceded red, and at others red preceded spr.)

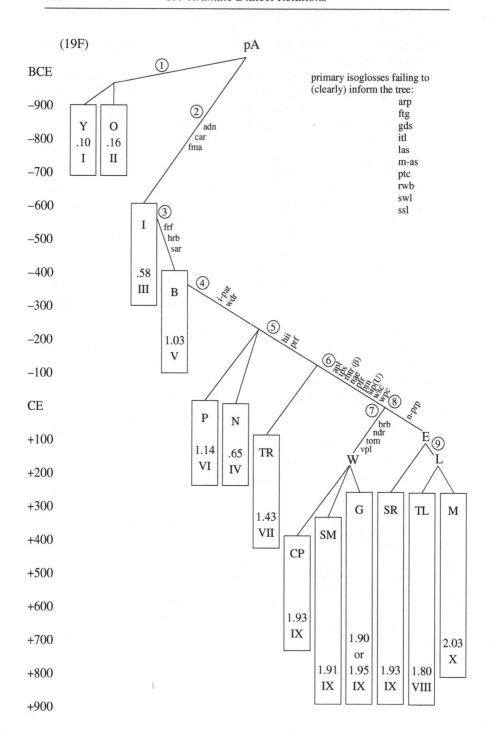

(19F)

pA

BCE

primary isoglosses failing to
(clearly) inform the tree:
arp
ftg
gds
itl
las
m-as
ptc
rwb
swl
ssl

(19G)	(i)	(ii)	(iii)	(iv)
	primary	**secondary**	**interpolated**	
branch	**isoglosses**	**isoglosses**	**isoglosses**	**ordering**
(1)		suffixal 3p obj		
		rna (categorical)		
(2)	adn	coa	gds	
	car	f-snm?		
	fma	gmf (1u,2u)		
		hlr		
		occ		
		rmt		
		rna(variable)		
		periphrastic 3p obj		
(3)	hrb	auf red	mid	spr◊red
	frf	cta rrf		auf, cta?, ghr, hrb, pro?, ymn?
	sar	ghr sap		
		hap spr		
		pro ymn		
(4)	i-pat	i-hlc(strong)		wdr^r-red
	wdr	lap		
		m-hlc(strong)		
(5)	hii	fgm		
	prf	f-snm(strong)?		
		hti		
		rca		
		sad		
		syn		
(6)	apl	adr?		
	ips	√ntn ~ √yhb		
	mtr(β)			
	nae			
	pfr			
	pin			
	sip(U)			
	wic			
	wpc			
(7)	brb	gmf(2m)		
	ndr	gtl		
	tom			
	vpl			
(8)	n-prp	f-phd		n-prp^syn(3ms–1p)
		l-cnd		
		prp(strong)		
		syn(3ms–1p)		
(9)		l-anc(1s)		
		nhp		
		trp(QĀM)		
		vpg		

Given the number and nature of the processes and patterns catalogued in (19A–E, G), it should be possible to devise at least a tentative *developmental ranking* for the thirteen dialects. This is indicated in (19F), with the figures entered beneath the dialect label: a decimal value ranking *.10* (least developed) ≪ *2.03* (most developed), corresponding to a Roman numeral *I* ≪ . . . ≪ *X*. By and large, these rankings are congruent with the (approximate) chronology, older dialects being less developed (= more conservative) than later dialects (increasingly less conservative, more "changeling"). A pair of deviations from this correlation are B and N, N profiling as more conservative than B. And the significant degree of chronological overlap of the later dialects, in particular the West – East dialects, renders it difficult to say which if any might be out of developmental sequence—though it is striking that the two L dialects are mutually so discrepant, relatively conservative TL (rank VIII) over against changeling M (rank X). Observe that, more in consonance with the chronology, all the other West – East dialects score at rank IX.[36]

Many of the processes and patterns in (19A-E) do not lend themselves to facile tree-genealogical plotting. There are several possible reasons for this: philological lacunation leading to spotty, incomplete distribution; inadequacy of a given process/pattern to forming a viable isogloss for internal-linguistic reasons; flotsam and jetsam of bona fide isoglosses eroded with the passage of time. And yet some apparently intractable isoglosses will turn out to be perfectly well behaved if looked at as representing *straddles*, i.e., (horizontal) *wave changes* rather than (vertical) tree changes; see the general discussion of straddles in §18.2. Some good candidates for straddling involve isoglosses crossing the West – East frontier: for instance, i-lap and m-cis between Western G and Eastern TL (m-cis perhaps also involving Western SM); the 1ʃU sim rmp impa case of trp straddling G and SR (see (19C)); and dpr linking SM in the West with TL and M in the East. All this is portrayed by the the three horizontal dashed lines in the lower right of the tree in (19H).

Plausible instances of other sorts of wave configuration may be uncovered as well. For example, g-cis and lsg way well have emerged in a *dialect pocket* of B, where they then remained in more or less stationary form until the much later development of the E dialects including the area circumscribed by the relevant isoglosses. This situation is portrayed as a *shaft* in (19H), specifically by the dashed line slanting down from B to E ("outside" of the solid tree-genealogical line connecting the same dialects). The shaft is also explicitly wave-theoretically plotted in the five chronological-successive diagrams of (19I).

Certain properties tend to characterize, or at least occur more frequently with, various sorts of isoglottic patterns. Thus, shafting tends to run down along well-behaved tree-genealogical paths, betraying itself by leaving no apparent trace between an earlier origin (B in the case of the shaft portrayed in

(19H)) and a later terminal (E in the same case). Had the behavior of g-cis and lsg been purely tree-genealogical, we should rather expect these changes to have left traces in at least most of the dialects along the diachronic path from B to E (that in, in P, N, TR, and the W dialects).[37]

When an otherwise shaft-like pattern grossly violates the expectation of tree-path manifestation, it is incumbent upon the investigator to search for an alternative explanation. Thus the disjoint distribution of ftg—P, SM, G, M—seems to defy plotting along any clear tree-trajectory, suggesting that something else is going on. Since ftg plausibly instantiates an unstable morphological pattern within Aramaic, it seems to lend itself to *independent loss across A dialects at large*; and if so, we are actually dealing with a *negative change*, independently adopted as a resolution of morphological instability in various dialects, specifically B, N, TR, CP, SR, and TL. This is portrayed by the six plottings of "-ftg" in (19H). In sum, ftg is being interpreted as an ancient Aramaic pattern which at some time along the developmental trajectory of the family became unstable and was accordingly expunged in 6 of 10 later dialects, not by virtue of common origin of the expungement but rather by dint of typological convergence on the same solution.

(19H)

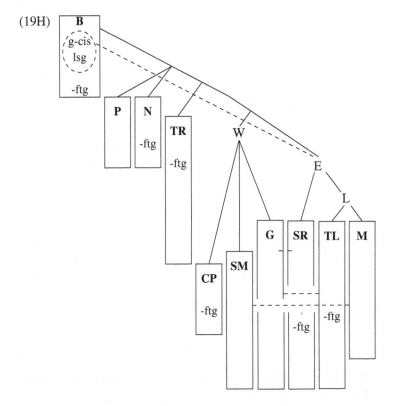

(19I)

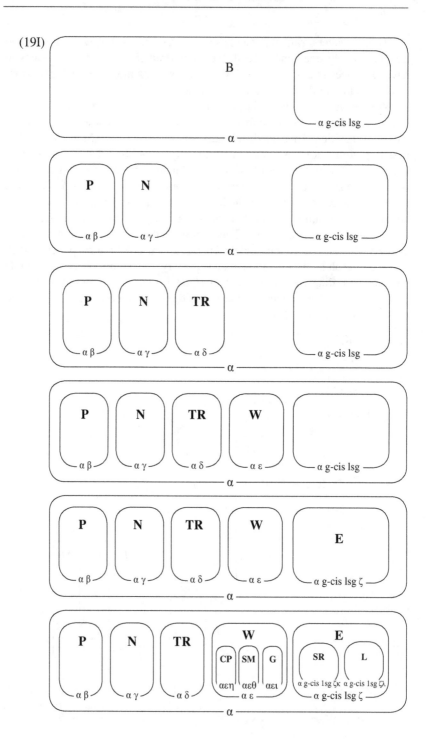

Finally, as alluded to in §0.1, in the significant work of Beyer 1986, various claims are made that potentially challenge the genealogical profile offered in (19F). These claims are inextricably tied up with Beyer's considering various dialects to be what in the terminology of the present work will be called *anachronic dialects*, i.e., forms of language whose parts manifest discrepant chronological origins; for instance the vowels (as revealed, say, by pointing) representing a later stratum than the consonants.[38] Three important cases are considered here under rubrics (γ, δ, ε):

(γ) What is called TR in this book is Beyer's extreme exemplar of an anachronic dialect, being "a mixture of Hasmonaean . . . in which the original Targum was composed . . . and Jewish Old Babylonian," one moreover whose "pointing . . . established in the 10th cent. [CE], is based on the pronunciation of south-eastern Middle Aramaic [that is, essentially on the pronunciation of the dialect treated in this book as TL—*JLM*]" (Beyer 1986: 22 with n. 15). Since Hasmonaean is "the written language of Jerusalem and Judaea under the Hasmonaeans (142–37 B.C.)" and Jewish Old Babylonian dates from the 7th century CE (ibid 20, 33), the trajectory down to TL imparts to TL a compositional span of more than eleven centuries.

At least when the focus is kept on the verb, the diachronic profile elaborated for TR in the present book shows few if any telltale signs in support of the dialect's presumed anachronic status. Most starkly, none of the isoglosses tabulated in (19A–E) as setting off the E dialects, or under them the L dialects of which TL is one, hold for TR. Thus, absent from TR is any trace of n-prp, the primary isogloss characterizing E; nor does TR show evidence for any of the secondary changes marking E (f-phd, l-cnd, strong prp, 3ms-1s syn listed under (8) in (19G)), nor for those marking off L (nhp, vpg, 1s l-anc, [QĀM] trp under (9)).[39]

Since Beyer specifically mentions the (orthographic) *vocalization* of TR as being based on the pronunciation of TL, we might expect to find some reflection of such a transfer in the sound changes targeting *vowels*. In particular, we might hope to find cases where TR and TL mutually show more similar profiles of some vocalic isogloss than might at large be expected. Though most candidate isoglosses appear to leave us in the lurch in this regard, one does turn out to be suggestive in the direction proffered by Beyer. The workings of *mid* are quite similar in TR and TL. Note in (19A) that both these dialects, and only these, are categorized at developmental stage II; see §17.11 for details.[40]

(δ) From the vantage of time-span, Beyer takes B to be an anachronic dialect even more protracted than TR, its "texts . . . originally produced in Achaemenid Imperial Aramaic," hence 5th–3rd century BCE, "first definitively established along with the canon in the 1st cent. A.D.," and with its vocalization "finalized in the 10th cent. A.D."

Beyer allows, however, that the 1st-century CE canonization introduced at least some "later orthographic conventions and grammatical forms," and that the 10th-century vocalization "preserved older elements" (ibid 15, 19 with n. 12). The net effect of these two episodes of adjustment—updating in the 1st century CE, preserving earlier features in the 10th century CE—appear to be that B's anachronic status is "foreshortened," the dialect as reflected in extant texts settling in approximately as portrayed in (19F): a dialect on balance less conservative than I (with a developmental profile of 1.03, stage V, compared to I's .58 at stage III) but more conservative than any of the later dialects (with the possible exception of N, as mentioned earlier).

At the same time, there may be a few telltale symptoms of B's anachronic status among the isogloss patterns of (19A). Thus, both spr and coa appear to show B at a more advanced developmental stage than chronologically later dialects, which might just point to the late date of B's vocalization.

(ε) The hypothesis that the pointing of TL stands behind the pointing of B and Bab TR (Beyer 1986: 45f.) may receive some support from at least a few isogloss profiles: for example mid, whose robustness for Bab B contrasts with its rather weak showing in Tib B (see especially the discussion in §17.11 under <u>B, TR, TL</u>); and sip (irrelevant in B, but for TR and TL note in particular (17.25A) in §17.25). On the other hand, findings for sco (§17.23.3) show significant discrepancies between Bab B and Bab TR (see (17.23B) and (17.23C)), though these are a few points of similarity between Bab TR and Yem TL (notably /1√__ in the sim impa).

Notes to §19

[1] ads in TR through M is bled (preempted) by sar or rga; so the minus marks should not be interpreted to the effect that ads started out robustly (in Y, O, I) and over time simply petered out.

[2] "v(a)" under TL indicates variability in the Ashkenazic tradition; auf appears not to occur in the Yemeni tradition.

[3] I.e., type (δ) cys occurs in I, SR, TL, and M, variably; types (α, γ, δ) occur in TR and G, variably; while types (δ, γ) alone occur in CP, variably. (For the definition of the types, see §17.5.)

[4] Only the five dialects treated in §16 are listed; see especially §16.3 (α).

[5] α, β, γ, δ refer to subtypes of frf; see §17.7 and compare n. 3 above.

[6] g-cis constitutes part of hgn in the causative; hence the distributions of the two isoglosses are not independent.

[7] For the ranking, see (6R) in §6.3.

[8] For all entries, see (3G–M, P) in §3.2.

[9] Only palatal hei considered (*e > i*), variable in both SR and M, but limited to the Jacobite register of the former.

[10] These two changes are not independent, hgn being a limiting case of hgr.

[11] For the types 1, 1a, 1i, 2 see §6.3 n. 44. (Importantly, these notations do not iconically encode developmental stages, though a progressive developmental factor may well be involved.)

[12] The alternative scoring for G, "-," reflects Kutscher's view that apparent i-lap forms in G are TL intrusions; §17.9.2 n. 26a.

[13] For O, see §17.15 n 64.

[14] α refers to √slq, β to √lqh.

[15] lco in B is limited to the Tiberian register, where it is categorical.

[16] Palatal midding only $(i > E)$; in the case of B, stage I for the Tiberian register only (for the Babylonian register, see (ε) below, at the end of the chapter).

[17] For mtr types α and β, see §17.12.

[18] Note that the stage numbering employed here is not identical to that appearing for prp below, nor for that used in (17.19A, B).

[19] Stage I subsumes variable fusion of $ʔ$ $(Tʔ > tt$); stage I′ subsumes variable fusion of both $ʔ$ and dentoalveolars $(Tʔ, TⱦF > tt$); stage II subsumes categorical fusion of $ʔ$ ("subsumes," so there is no conflict with the overall assignments of "v" in TL and M, inasmuch as the process remains variable under other subconditions).

[20] Stage numbering not identical to that of (17.19A, B); cf. n. 18 above.

[21] Note the differences in registerial distribution for B and TL.

[22] The sense is that red at large is categorical from B at the earliest onward, but under subcondition (ζ) differs as indicated (p = partial, i.e., $V̄CV̊CV > V̄CV̆CV$; f = full, $V̄CV̊CV > V̄CCV$).

[23] For the stated conditions, see §5.3 (β).

[24] Developmental stages refer to increasingly wider admissibility of fused consonants: I, dentoalveolars; II, dntlalvs plus stomatics; III, dntlalvs plus stomatics plus gutturals; IV, dntalvs plus stomatics plus gutturals plus consonants at large (which boils down to consonants at large, tout court).

[25] That is, spr is categorical from B onward under the conditions indicated (precise conditions for P, N, CP, SM, G, TL, M uncertain); see §5.3 (β), as well as (δ) below toward the end of the present chapter.

[26] ssl apparently occurs in the four dialects indicated under the parenthesized morphological conditions.

[27] I.e., stress follows the oxytone (ultimate) or barytone (penultimate) pattern as indicated (and for B and and TL, in the register/tradition as indicated).

[28] See also fgm above, as well as (19D) below.

[29] α, β, γ, δ are subconditions of vco.

[30] short and long manifestations of wic, wpc.

[31] Developmental stages based on the first column of (14B) in §14.1.

[32] That is, l-anc occurs under the subtypes indicated. "(-pat)" means that pronoun attachment (§17.15) does not occur in B and SR, so that l-anc affects the independent 3p pronouns (qua verb objects). Note the qualifications for tradition under TL.

[33] Select subtypes of trp; note the stipulations for TL tradition concerning [QĀM].

[34] (a) Listing limited to the five dialects treated in §16. For the types of syncretism plotted, see §16.3 (β–ζ). (Another syncretic complex is listed under fgm in (19A).) (b) See the qualification given in §16.3 (γ).

[35] Various restrictions on the isoglosses in (19G) appear in parentheses following the isogloss label. For instance, "sip(U)" means that the type of sip listed here is that where $V̆ > U$ (see §17.25 (17.25A)); the specification "(strong)" means that the process in question favors application (+ or +|–) or occurs at an advanced developmental stage.

[36] The input scores of the isoglosses used in arriving at these profiles—scores for a selection of the isoglosses listed in (19A–E)—are provided in tabulation (a) below. The input scores were derived for the ranking systems (α, α', β, special) introduced at the beginning of the chapter as follows: (*) for (α), -, i , v, + = 0, 1, 2, 3; (*) for (α'), -|+ = 1.5, +|- = 2.5; for (β), I = 1, II = 2, etc.; for special systems with multiple categories of application, 1 is assigned for fewest categories, 2 for the number of categories next up, etc. (e.g., mtr, where a single category (α) ranks 1, two categories (α, β) ranks 2); (*) in the case of mixed systems, .5 for II coassigned with i , -|+, v, +|-, +; 1 for III under the same coassignment conditions; 1.5 for IV, etc.; (*) for all systems, ? assignments are omitted from the input. Finally, the input scores for a given dialect combine with the total number of assignments to that dialect as follows: (*) sum value of all input scores divided by the number of scores evaluated (e.g., for Y—twenty-six 0s plus 3 plus four 0s *divided by* thirty-one = 3/31 = .10).

Ten ranks of conservatism are obtained from this algorithm, I = most conservative, X = least conservative; numerical scores differing by 1 or 2 are conflated—thus SC, SM, G, and SR all place at IX.

However, rankings are provisional at best, two factors in particular making for possible shakiness of results: (*) the informality and looseness of many basic assignments (e.g., in default of explicit criteria for deciding whether an assignment should be "v" or "+"); and, relatedly, (*) the lack of firm criteria for deciding when an assignment should be "-" (a pattern/process does not hold/apply) or rather "∅" (blank cell; holding/ application of a pattern/process is undeterminable or irrelevant). This latter difficulty immediately leads to the possibility of unwarranted rank inflation/deflation, in that assignment of "∅" in lieu of what should in fact be "-" renders the final score commensurately higher than it should be (or lower in case of the reverse assignment). In view of these uncertainties—probably irremediable in light of extant corpus conditions—the summary conservatrism rankings proffered in (19F) should be taken with a grain of salt. Observe, finally, that the alternative scoring for G depends on whether i-lap is reckoned as a bona fide process for the dialect, 1.95 if it is, 1.90 if it is not; cf. n. 12.

But in either event, G places at developmental level IX, as an essentially changeling dialect. (However, G would rank as less changeling—more conservative—if the form <qbylynhw> were assumed to be genuine rather than as a Talmudic intrusion (cf. Kutscher's judgment in §7.4.1), inasmuch as the dialect's score on cta would then be demoted from 3 toward or to 0 (if to 0, the profile ranking score would fall at 1.83, whereby G would approach developmental level VIII, where TL is reckoned).)

(a)

ranking systems α, α', special, or mixed

from (19A)	Y	O	I	B	P	N	TR	CP	SM	G	SR	TL	M
adn		-(0)	v(2)	+(3)	+(3)	+(3)	+(3)	+(3)	+(3)	+(3)	+(3)	+(3)	+(3)
adr	-(0)	-(0)	-(0)	-(0)	-(0)	-(0)	-(0)	+(3)	+(3)		+(3)	-(0)	+(3)
apl	-(0)	-(0)	-(0)	-(0)	-(0)	-(0)	-(0)	v(2)	+(3)	+(3)	-(0)	+(3)	+(3)
arp	-(0)	-(0)	-(0)	-(0)		-(0)	-(0)	v(2)	-(0)	-(0)	-(0)	-(0)	v(2)
brb	-(0)	-(0)	-(0)	-(0)	-(0)	-(0)	-(0)	v(2)	-(0)	v(2)	-(0)	-(0)	-(0)
car	-(0)	-(0)	v(2)	+(3)	+(3)	+(3)	+(3)	v(2)	+(3)	+(3)	+(3)	+|-(2.5)	+|-(2.5)

from (19A)	Y	O	I	B	P	N	TR	CP	SM	G	SR	TL	M
cta				+(3)	+(3)		+(3)	+(3)	+(3)	+(3)	+(3)	-(0)	-(0)
dpr	-(0)	-(0)	-(0)	-(0)	-(0)	-(0)	-(0)	-(0)	v(2)	-(0)	-(0)	v(2)	+(3)
fma	-(0)	-(0)	v(2)	+(3)	+(3)	+(3)	+(3)	+(3)	+(3)	+(3)	+(3)	+(3)	+(3)
f-phd	-(0)	-(0)	-(0)	-(0)	-(0)	-(0)	-(0)	v(2)	v(2)	v(2)	v(2)	v(2)	v(2)
f-snm	-(0)	-(0)			v(2)	-(0)	+(3)	+(3)			+(3)		
ftg					+(3)				i(1)	v(2)			
g-cis				v(2)			-(0)		-(0)		v(2)	v(2)	
gtl	-(0)	-(0)	-(0)	-(0)	-(0)	-(0)	-(0)	v(2)	+(3)	v(2)	-(0)	-(0)	-(0)
hap	-(0)	-(0)	-(0)		i(1)	-(0)	i(1)	i(1)	v(2)	i(1)	-(0)	v(2)	+(3)
hgn				v(2)			v(2)		v(2)		-(0)	v(2)	v(2)
hii	-(0)	-(0)	i(1)	-(0)	-(0)	-(0)	i(1)	v(2)	v(2)	v(2)	v(2)	v(2)	v(2)
hlr	-(0)	-(0)	v(2)	-(0)	+(3)		+(3)	+(3)	+(3)	+(3)	+(3)	+(3)	+(3)
hti		-(0)	-(0)	-(0)			v(2)	-(0)	v(2)	v(2)	v(2)	v(2)	v(2)
i-cis				v(2)			v(2)				-(0)	-(0)	-(0)
i-hlc	-(0)	-|+(1.5)	v(2)	v(2)	+(3)	+|-(2.5)	+(3)	+(3)	+|-(2.5)	+(3)	+(3)	+(3)	+(3)
i-lap	-(0)	-(0)	-(0)	-(0)	-(0)	-(0)	-(0)	-(0)	-(0)	v(2) or -(0)	-(0)	v(2)	
i-pat	-(0)	-(0)	-(0)	-(0)	+(3)		+(3)	+(3)	+(3)	+(3)	-(0)	v(2)	+(3)
itl				-(0)			i(1)				+(3)	-(0)	
lap	-(0)	-(0)	-(0)	-(0)		-(0)	-(0)	v(2)	-(0)	v(2)	+(3)	v(2)	+(3)
l-cnd	-(0)	-(0)	-(0)	-(0)	-(0)	-(0)	-(0)	-(0)	-(0)	-(0)	+(3)	v(2)	+(3)
lco				+(3)			v(2)					+(3)	+(3)
lsg				v(2)							+(3)		+(3)
m-hlc	-|+(1.5)	-|+(1.5)	-|+(1.5)	+(3)	+(3)	+(3)	+(3)		+(3)	+(3)	+(3)	+(3)	+(3)
mls				+(3)			+(3)				v(2)	v(2)	v(2)
mtr										α β (2)		α β (2)	β(1)
nae	-(0)	-(0)	-(0)	-(0)	-(0)	-(0)	-(0)	v(2)	v(2)	v(2)	v(2)	v(2)	
ndr	-(0)	-(0)	-(0)	-(0)	-(0)	-(0)	-(0)	v(2)	v(2)	v(2)	-(0)	-(0)	-(0)
nhp												v(2)	+(3)
n-prp	-(0)	-(0)	-(0)	-(0)	-(0)	-(0)	-(0)	-(0)	-(0)	-(0)	III(3)	I(1)	II(2)
occ	-(0)	-(0)	+(3)	+(3)	+/v(2.5)	+/v(2.5)	+(3)	+(3)	+(3)	+(3)	+(3)	+(3)	+(3)
pfr	-(0)	-(0)	-(0)	-(0)	-(0)		-(0)	v(2)	v(2)	v(2)	v(2)	v(2)	v(2)
prf		-(0)	-(0)	-(0)	-(0)	-(0)	v(2) I	v(2) I'	-(0)	v(2) I	-|+(1.5) I'	v(2.5) II	v(2.5) II
pro	-(0)	-(0)	-(0)	i(1)	-(0)	-(0)	i(1)	i(1)	v(2)	v(2)	i(1)	v(2)	v(2)
prp	-(0)	-(0)	-(0)	I(1)	-(0)	-(0)	-(0)	-(0)	-(0)	-(0)	IV(4)	II(2)	III(3)
ptc	-(0)	-(0)	-(0)	-(0)	-(0)	-(0)		v(2)		-(0)	-(0)	-(0)	v(2)
ptg				+tb(1.5) -bb			+(3)					+a(1.5) vy	
reo				I(1)			II(2)				II(2)		
rmt	+(3)			+|-(2.5)		v(2)	+(3)	v(2)	+|-(2.5)	+(3)	+(3)	+|-(2.5)	+(3)
rna	+(3)	+(3)	v(2)	v(2)	v(2)		v(2)	v(2)	v(2)	v(2)	v(2)	v(2)	v(2)
rrf		-(0)	-(0)	i(1) I	v(2.5) II	-(0)	v(2.5) II	v(2) I	v(2.5) II	v(3) III	v(2) I	v(3.5) IV	v(3.5) IV

from (19A)	Y	O	I	B	P	N	TR	CP	SM	G	SR	TL	M
rwb		-(0)	-(0)	-(0)			v(2)	-(0)	-(0)	-(0)	v(2)	i(1)	-(0)
sad	-(0)	-(0)	-(0)	-(0)	-(0)	-(0)	v(2)	v(2)	v(2)		+(3)	v(2)	+(3)
sar	-(0)	-(0)	-(0)	+(3)	-(0)	-(0)	+(3)	v(2)	v(2)	+(3)	+(3)	+(3)	-(0)
spr				+(4) III	+(3)	+(3)	+(3.5) II	+(3)	+(3)	+(3)	+(3) I	+(3)	+(3)
vco							α β(3) γ		α β(3) γ(i)? δ(i)?			(1)	α β(2) δ(i)
vpg	-(0)	-(0)	-(0)	-(0)	-(0)	-(0)	-(0)	-(0)	-(0)		-(0)	i(1)	+(3)
vpl	-(0)	-(0)	-(0)	-(0)	-(0)	-(0)	-(0)	i(1)	+(3)	v(2)	-(0)	-(0)	-(0)
wdr				v(2)			v(2)		+(3)	v(2)	v(2)	v(2)	v(2)
wic								s(1)	s(2) 1	s(2) 1	s(2) 1	s(2) 1	l(1)

from (19B)

l-anc	Y	O	I	B	P	N	TR	CP	SM	G	SR	TL	M
number-gender: mp				-(0)			-(0)				-(0)	-(0)	v(2)
subject: 1s				-(0)			-(0)				+(3)		+(3)
3mp				-(0)			-(0)				-(0)	-(0)	+(3)
2mp				v(2)			-(0)				+(3)	-(0)	-(0)
2fp							-(0)				+(3)		-(0)
object: 3mp				v(2)			-(0)				+(3)	-y(1.5) +a	-(0)
3fp				-(0)			-(0)				+(3)	-y(1.5) +a	-(0)
2mp				+(3)			+(3)				+(3)	-y(1.5) +a	-(0)
2fp											+(3)		

from (19C)

from 19A	Y	O	I	B	P	N	TR	CP	SM	G	SR	TL	M
trp *QĀM*				i(1)							+(3)	-y(1.5) +a	+(3)

from (19E)

	Y	O	I	B	P	N	TR	CP	SM	G	SR	TL	M
suppletion √*ntl*								v(2)			+(3)		

ranking system β

from (19A)	Y	O	I	B	P	N	TR	CP	SM	G	SR	TL	M
att							I				I		I
fgm							I		II		I	IV	III
ghr			I				II	I	I	I	I	II′	II/III
ips								II			I	II	III
mid				I(*tb*)			II				I	II	III
syn							I		III		I	IV	III
ymn			I				III	IV	IV	I	III	I	II

from (19C)	Y	O	I	B	P	N	TR	CP	SM	G	SR	TL	M
trp *non-reduced 2ʃV̂*				I			IIIa				IIIb	IIa	IIb

from (19D)	Y	O	I	B	P	N	TR	CP	SM	G	SR	TL	M
syn *T^obj*							II				I	IV	III/IV

ranking score	Y	O	I	B	P	N	TR	CP	SM	G	SR	TL	M
fraction	$\frac{3}{31}$	$\frac{6}{37}$	$\frac{22}{38}$	$\frac{60}{58}$	$\frac{42}{37}$	$\frac{22}{34}$	$\frac{93}{65}$	$\frac{85}{44}$	$\frac{91.5}{48}$	$\frac{82 \, or \, 80}{42}$	$\frac{133.5}{69}$	$\frac{118.5}{66}$	$\frac{134}{66}$
decimal	.10	.16	.58	1.03	1.14	.65	1.43	1.93	1.91	1.95 *or* 1.90	1.93	1.80	2.03

[37] Another tendential property of shafting might be proposed: that the change in question should be *variable* in the earlier dialects of the shaft—because if it were categorical, it is unclear how the claim could be maintained that it was isolated in a dialect pocket. And indeed, this prediction appears to be borne out in the case of g-cis and lsg, which are, respectively, variable (v) and infrequent (i) in B; see (19A). (In contrast, the distributional status of shafted changes seems unconstrained in later dialects, where they may well have spread with impunity.)

[38] Although this example is at least in part paralinguistic (philological), involving as it does orthography, more or less purely linguistic cases of anachronicity not only exist, but abound and are well attested. The incidence of French morphological "doublets" is a case in point, whereby genealogically well-behaved reflexes of Latin coexist with "learned" (re)formations (re)borrowed directly from Latin; in fact, the verb corresponding to *doublet* provides an instance: fully genealogical *doubler*, reborrowed *dupliquer*. (One symptom of doublets, and hence of other sorts of anachronic patterning, would be, in the (re)borrowed formations, *absence of traces of (some) otherwise expected linguistic changes*.)

[39] Similarly, Kutscher's claim that TR "was . . . vocalized . . . in Babylonia" and that "{i}ts vocalization apparently reflects some Eastern Aramaic dialect" as per the fact that the sim pf 3fs is *QəSVMAθ* "as apparently in the Aramaic of the Babylonian Talmud" rather than *QiSMAθ* "as, e.g., in Biblical Aramaic" (1972: 267). The primary difficulty with this view is that the canon *QəSVMAθ* is *not* an Eastern trait. It is absent altogether from SR (which shows exclusively *QɛSMAθ*); and is present in M only in pp

formations, while otherwise *QeSMaβ* rules the roost. Furthermore,*QəˇSVMAθ* is prominent in the Western dialects CP, CM, and G (the latter *pace* Kutscher 1972: 272; cf.
the sample of forms adduced §4.1.2 G̲). In these cases, moreover, it is often rendered
palpable independently of vocalization or trad pron by the orthographic presence of
ml <y>, <w> in the case of *2ʃi, *2ʃu respectively:, e.g., CP <yqyDT> 'sie brannte',
G <ŝqw̲9T> 'sie versank'. See §4.1.2. And in this connection, TR a̅lso typically shows
ml <y>, <w> for *2ʃ in its pf 3fs items—e.g., <DəˇleyqæT> 'verbrannte', <ḥə̌šow̲KæT>
'wurde finster' (Da 260)—an unexpected feature if a new *QəˇSVMAθ* pointing were
merely superposed on an original *QiSMAθ* consonantal text.

[40] The superficially similar disposition of ghr is best judged illusory in light of the
explication in §6.3; see especially the diagrams in (6H, M, P).

Part Three

Appendixes and Supplemental Matters

20. Phonetic Systems

20.1. Consonants

A composite phonetic chart of the consonants assumed for the Aramaic dialects appears in (20A), where the double asterisk marks proto-Aramaic (or pre-Aramaic) segments assumed to have disappeared (by merger, §9.1.3) prior to the formation of Y and O; while a single asterisk marks the subset of segments posited to have obtained in pA and either remained or redeveloped into Y and O. Parentheses signal consonants susceptible to double characterization—e.g., the gutturals taken either as obstruents (upper right region of the chart) or as glides (lower right). Pairs of such segments represented by distinct symbols are marked as going together by double or triple parenthesization—e.g., the voiced (vd) labial spirant either as labiodental $(((v)))$, the value usually assumed for A, or as bilabial $(((\beta)))$, the value reported by Macuch (Macm) for M and assumed in the present book to have been the norm in SM and G (in addition to M).[1] In a similar vein, note that the voiceless (vl) coronal fricative s is alternatively classified as an apicoalveolar (the classical understanding, cf. Brockelmann 1908) or as a lateralized dentoalveolar (cf. Steiner 1977). In this book, normally one of such double analyses is implicitly or explicitly assumed—e.g., the voiced coronal emphatic obstruent as fricative $\eth$ rather than as stop d—though motivated simultaneous appeal to both cannot be ruled out. Observe that several subclasses of manner of articulation (plotted by rows, vertically) are binarily subdivided: vl/vd = voiceless/voiced, lt/md = lateral(lambdic)/medial(rhotic), tn/lx = tense/lax. It might be noted that most of the consonants that entered Aramaic subsequent to the period of pA—those not marked by the asterisk, primarily the slit fricatives $\varphi = f$, x, γ, $\beta = v$—did so by the agency of one process, *spirantization* (§4.1).[2] On the other hand, a number of asterisked segments disappeared either from all A dialects as of B at the latest ($d = \eth$, θ, R) or from several later dialects (especially gutturals)—most of this is documented in §9; for $\theta > t$, see §17.14.

A few general points:

(*) The consonants tabulated in (20A) are *phonetic* in nature, although most also incidentally (would) appear as units at deeper levels of the phonology as well. For the most part, moreover, the phonetic nature investing the consonants is *broad* (as opposed to *narrow*), conveying as frugal an amount of articulatory/acoustic detail as compatible with (or deriving from) the reconstructive/phonological-analytic enterprise of the book.

Furthermore, broad-phonetic representation as deployed here may at times betray what might be called a "phonemic bias," decisions on capturing/omitting phonetic detail being decided by (implicit) reference to phonology. Thus no velar nasal (ŋ) is tabulated despite the likely realization of dentoalveolar *n* as such in environments like /__*k, g* (cf. §7.8); for this missing   , *n* is employed.

(*) Consonants may at times be classified elsewhere in the book via dimensions athwart those fixing the array in (20A); e.g., a partition of fricatives into *sibilants* (*s, ṣ, ś, š, z*) vs. *spirants* (all others).

(*) (20A) is a *composite* system, implicitly serving in a joint manner in the representation of the individual dialects as well as of their reconstructed ancestors back to (or a bit beyond) proto-Aramaic. Phonetic specifics for the individual dialects emerge first and foremost process by process in the work of Part One (chapters §1–§17), and—more holistically—invest the phonetic forms reconstructed for the specific dialects in the comprehensive index of forms (§24).

(20A)

			labial		coronal						dorsal		guttural	
			bilabial	labiodental	interdental	uvularized (emphatic) interdental	dentralveolar	uvularized (emphatic) dentralveolar	apico-alveolar or lateralized dentroveolar	palatal	velar	uvular (uvularized (emphatic) velar)	pharyngeal	laryngeal
obstruent	stop	vl	*P, π				*t	*ṭ			*k	*q		(*ʔ)
		rd	*b				*d	((**ḍ)			*g			
	fricative	vl	((((φ))))	((((f))))	*θ	*θ̣	*s	*ṣ	*ś	*š	x	**X	(*ḥ)	(*h)
		vd	(((β)))	(((v)))	*ð	((ð̣))	*z				γ	*R	(*ʕ)	
sonorant	nasal		*m				*n							
	liquid	lt					*l	*ḷ						
		md					*r							
	glide	tn											(*ḥ)	(*h)
		lx	*w							*y			(*ʕ)	(*ʔ)

Feature assignments to the consonants of (20A) are displayed in (20B) and (20C), assignments which largely follow those developed for Tiberian Hebrew in THP 28–30 supplemented by a few features pressed into sevice for specific Aramaic applications elsewhere in the book. (Since feature analysis is but modestly broached in the present work, the reader is referred to THP for discussion, which for the most part holds for Aramaic as well. In addition, features are explained in this work case by case, as need dictates.)

(20B) **obstruents**

	p	π	t	ṭ	k	q	b	d	d̠	g	φ	f	θ	θ̠	s	ṣ	ś	ś̠	š	x	X	β	v	ð	ð̠	z	γ	R
segmental	+	+	+	+	+	+	+	+	+	+	+	+	+	+	+	+	+	+	+	+	+	+	+	+	+	+	+	+
syllabic	-	-	-	-	-	-	-	-	-	-	-	-	-	-	-	-	-	-	-	-	-	-	-	-	-	-	-	-
sonorant	-	-	-	-	-	-	-	-	-	-	-	-	-	-	-	-	-	-	-	-	-	-	-	-	-	-	-	-
consonantal	+	+	+	+	+	+	+	+	+	+	+	+	+	+	+	+	+	+	+	+	+	+	+	+	+	+	+	+
stomatic	+	+	+	+	+	+	+	+	+	+	+	+	+	+	+	+	+	+	+	+	+	+	+	+	+	+	+	+
coronal	-	-	+	+	-	-	-	+	+	-	-	-	+	+	+	+	+	+	-	-	-	-	-	+	+	+	-	-
high	-	-	-	-	+	-	-	-	-	+	-	-	-	-	-	-	-	+	+	-	-	-	-	-	-	-	+	-
low	-	-	-	-	-	-	-	-	-	-	-	-	-	-	-	-	-	-	-	-	-	-	-	-	-	-	-	-
back	-	-	-	+	+	+	-	-	+	+	-	-	-	-	-	+	-	+	+	-	-	-	-	-	+	-	+	+
labial	+	+	-	-	-	-	+	-	-	-	+	+	-	-	-	-	-	-	-	-	-	+	+	-	-	-	-	-
distributed	+	+	-	+	+	-	+	-	+	+	+	-	-	+	+	+	-	+	-	+	-	-	+	+	+	+	-	-
rilled	-	-	-	-	-	-	-	-	-	-	-	-	-	+	+	+	+	+	-	-	-	-	-	-	-	-	+	-
nasal	-	-	-	-	-	-	-	-	-	-	-	-	-	-	-	-	-	-	-	-	-	-	-	-	-	-	-	-
lateral	-	-	-	-	-	-	-	-	-	-	-	-	-	-	-	-	-	+	-	-	-	-	-	-	-	-	-	-
continuant	-	-	-	-	-	-	-	-	-	-	+	+	+	+	+	+	+	+	+	+	+	+	+	+	+	+	+	+
tense	+	-	+	-	+	-	-	-	-	-	-	+	+	+	+	+	+	+	+	+	+	-	-	-	-	-	-	-
voiced	-	-	-	-	-	-	+	+	+	+	-	-	-	-	-	-	-	-	-	-	-	-	+	+	+	+	+	+
RTR	-	-	-	+	-	+	-	-	+	-	-	-	-	-	+	-	+	-	-	-	-	-	+	-	-	-	+	+

(20B) **sonorants**

	m	n	r	l	l̥	w	y	ḥ	9	h	?
segmental	+	+	+	+	+	+	+	+	+	+	+
syllabic	-	-	-	-	-	-	-	-	-	-	-
sonorant	+	+	+	+	+	+	+	+	+	+	+
consonantal	+	+	+	+	+	-	-	-	-	-	-
stomatic	+	+	+	+	+	+	+	-	-	-	-
coronal	-	+	+	+	+	-	-	-	-	-	-
high	-	-	-	-	-	+	+	-	-	-	-
low	-	-	+	-	-	-	-	+	+	+	+
back	-	-	-	-	+	+	-	+	+	-	-
labial	+	-	-	-	-	+	-	-	-	-	-
distributed	+	-	-	-	+	-	-	-	-	-	-
rilled	-	-	-	-	-	-	-	-	-	-	-
nasal	+	+	-	-	-	-	-	-	-	-	-
lateral	-	-	-	+	+	-	-	-	-	-	-
continuant	-	-	+	+	+	+	+	+	+	+	-
tense	-	-	-	-	-	-	-	+	-	+	-
voiced	+	+	+	+	+	+	+	-	+	-	-
RTR	-	-	-	-	+	-	-	+	+	-	-

(α) Consonant archiphonemes:

C	*consonantal*	[-syllabic]
Σ	*sibilant*	{s, ś, z, ṣ, š} [-syllabic, +rilled]
P; T; K; B; D; G		{p, f (φ); t, θ; k, x; b, v (β); d, ð; g, γ}
		[-syllabic, -sonorant, -rilled, +high/-back]
Ŧ	*dentoalveolar stop*	{t, ṭ, d, ḍ} [-syllabic, -sonorant, +coronal,
		-continuant]
H	*guttural*	{ʔ, h, 9, ḥ} [-syllabic, -stomatic]
L	*low consonant*	{guttural, r} [-syllabic, +low]
W	*semivowel*	{w, y} [-syllabic, -consonantal, +stomatic]
Γ	*glide*	{guttural, semivowel} [-syllabic, -consonantal]
Λ	*resonant*	{nasal (= m, n), liquid (= r, l, ḷ), semivowel
		(= w, y)} [-syllabic, +sonorant, +stomatic]

(β) As a matter of systemic (paradigmatic fact), an Aramaic consonant may be single(ton) (short) *C′* or geminate (long) *C′C′*, though low consonants often resist gemination, expected instances tending to shorten with or without compensatory lengthening of an immediately preceding vowel ($\mathring{V}L'L' \to \mathring{V}L'$); mls, §9.3.1. Phonotactically (syntagmatically), however, the distribution of geminates tends to be restricted in a way similar to other consonant clusters (*CC*). (For additional remarks on the phonotactics of Aramaic consonants, see §23.5.)

20.2. Vowels

A composite display of Aramaic vowels appears in (20D), an asterisk once again tagging segments assumed for pA as well as early dialects like Y and O. All vowels are represented in abstraction of length, which throughout the history of Aramaic, at least in the Classical period, was distributed in three grades: long ($\bar{V}$), short ($\mathring{V}$), and reduced ($\breve{V}$). In pA and most descendant dialects, the long–short opposition is largely independent of a vowel's color (some exceptions will be adduced in the excursus at the end of this section), while the reduced vowel is either unmarkedly fixed at mid central or, if possessed of other colors, subject to various constraints; see §17.23 (and for the special case of SM, see again the excursus below). Prior to the emergence of reduction (§4.2) and excrescence (§4.3), the major sources of $\breve{V}$ in the later dialects, the reduced vowel was (by hypothesis of this book) also morphophonologically restricted, in the verb limited to 1ʃ of the simple imperative, and perhaps repair-strategically enlisted to break up morphologically engendered superheavy groups like *CCC* (→ [CCŏC]); cf. §2.3.2.1 (α). All length grades are subject to phonotactic restrictions, and though details vary from dialect to dialect, certain tendencies are widespread. Only the short vowel is fully free in closed syllables; in fact, the other two grades tend to neutralize quantitatively to $\mathring{V}$ when closed-syllabic, $\bar{V}$ by css (§17.4), $\check{V}$ by prm or sip (§14, §17.25).

Note in (20D) the inclusion of a few archiphonemes, *I* (nonlow palatal vowel), *E* (mid palatal vowel in abstraction of openness), *U* (nonlow back vowel), *A* (low vowel or mid back vowel). These archiphonemes prove useful in discussing certain regularities in abstraction of register or tradition of pronunciation (e.g., ɛ in Nes SR largely corresponds to *e* in Jac SR, so its common distribution can be stated in terms of *E*; similarly, ɔ in Tib B vis-à-vis ā in Bab B, hence *Ā*). Archiphonemes also make it possible to provide (partial) phonetic representations in the face of uncertainty as to whether given processes have applied or not (e.g., [I] for [i]/[e] when it is unclear whether midding, §17.11, has applied).

Observe finally the cospecificaton of Aramaic front vowels as flat and back vowels as rounded, with reference to the contouring of the lips during articulation. Such coarticulation is identifiable with palatalization/labialization, respectively, an effect manifested phonologically in various rules where front vowels show an affinity with palatal consonants like *y*, *š*, and back vowels in parallel fashion with labial *C*s like *w*, *m* (e.g., §17.11.3 <u>SR</u>, §12.2 n. 11, (δ) below in this section). Articulatorily, the degree of flattening/rounding increases from low to high tongue position, so that, e.g., *i* is the flat or palatal vowel par excellence, and *æ/a* the weakest.[3]

(20D)

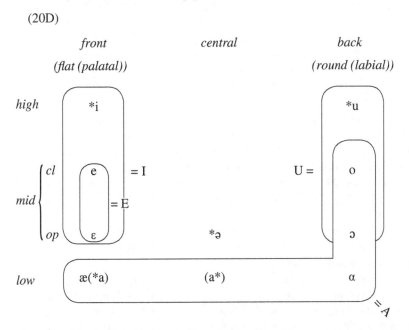

V	*vowel*

V̄	*long vowel*
V̊	*short vowel*
V̌	*reduced vowel (schwa)*

V̈	*pausal stress (hefsek)*	⎫
V́	*primary stress ("contextual," hekšer)*	⎬ see §20.3 below
V̀	*secondary stress*	⎭

Vowel features are given in (20E), once again following THP except for the feature [+front/[-front] which replaces THP's [-back]/[+back]. (Note that the double feature assignment for the vowel A reflects the disjunctive disposition of this quasi-archiphoneme discussed in n. 3.)

(20E)

	i	e	ε	æ	a	u	o	ɔ	α	ə	I	E	U	A *or* A	
segmental	+	+	+	+	+	+	+	+	+	+	+	+	+	+	+
syllabic	+	+	+	+	+	+	+	+	+	+	+	+	+	+	+
sonorant	+	+	+	+	+	+	+	+	+	+	+	+	+	+	+
consonantal	-	-	-	-	-	-	-	-	-	-	-	-	-	-	-
stomatic	+	+	+	+	+	+	+	+	+	+	+	+	+	+	+
high	+	+	-	-	-	+	+	-	-	-					
mid	-	+	+	-	-	-	+	+	-	+		+		-	+
low	-	-	-	+	+	-	-	-	+	-	-	-	-	+	-
front	+	+	+	+			-	-	-	-	+	+	-		-
labial	-	-	-	-		+	+	+	+	-	-	-	+		+
tense	+	+	+	+	+	+	+	+	+	-	+	+	+	+	+

Vowel systems, abstractive of length, are displayed in (20G, H, I) for those dialects/registers/traditional pronunciations for which sufficient evidence exists. Though being an integral constituent in all these systems, schwa is omitted from the charts due to uncertainties as to its realization(s) (§17.23).

In displays (20J, K) two vowel systems are presented for dialects other than those covered by (20G, H, I). For these, see point (ι) below.

A number of observations are in order:

(α) The alternative plotting of [a] in the 7- and 5-color systems as low front or low central reflects the fact that this vowel at times evinces palatal behavior; see (δ) below and n. 3 above.

(β) Though certain orthographies come close to uniquely assigning a given grapheme (point) to a given phone(me), charts (20G, H, I) plot phonetic segments, not orthographic symbols. Thus, e.g., either [a] (20G) or [æ] (20H) may be spelled with the Tiberian point pataḥ, depending on what register or traditional pronunciation is being served (in the case of trad pron, by decision of the authors to use the Tiberian system as mode of representation—Morag for Yem TL, Margolis for Ash TL).

(γ) In the case of registers of the same dialect with vowel systems differing in size, diachronic development is assumed from the larger to the smaller:[4]

	Tib B		Bab B	
	ε̊, å	>	æ̊	(*unconditional merger* (umr))
possibly	ε̄, ē	>	ē	(umr)
	ɔ̄	>	ā	(*systemic vowel shift* (svs))
	i̊, e̊, ů, o̊	>	i̊, e̊, ů, o̊	(*vacuous systemic shift*)

	Nes SR		Jac SR	
	ū, ō	>	ū	(umr, §11.2)
	ɔ̄	>	ō	(svs)
	ī, ē	>	ī, ē	(*vacuous systemic shift*)
	ε̊	>	e̊	(svs)
	i̊, ů, å	>	i̊, ů, å	(*vacuous systemic shift*)

(δ) While low front vowels are normally short (å, æ̊) and low back vowels are normally long (ɔ̄, ā)—cf. n. 3 above—there are circumstances where the opposite correlation holds:

ā, ǣ. **TR** and **TL** occasionally in lieu of [ē] by open coa and open k-coa (§11)[5] (and possibly *a²#* > *ā#* by r-adn too late for the systemic > *ɔ̄#* in the wake of primary adn; §9.1.4 n. 12); **Nes SR** *āy* occasionally by assimilation (mvh) ← *ɔ̄y*, but **Jac SR** by dissimilation in sandhi *malkā́w* ← *malkɔ́-(h)ū* 'er ist König' (Ns §49B);[6] for **SM** trad pron [æ], see §22.1.

ɔ̄, å. **Tib B** and **Ash TL** [ɔ̄] by aop of *o* (§17.11) or prm/sip of ɔ̄ (§14, §17.25); for **SM** trad pron [å], §22.1; **Nes SR** [ɔ̄w], [ɔ̄(ʾ)ū] commonly assimilated from *åw, å(ʾ)ū* by mvh (Ns §49B);[7] and at least the Halaxot Pәsukot register of **TL** likewise variably shows [ɔ̄w] (~ [æw]) (Morag 1967–68: 85 n. 75).

(ε) The equivocation in assigning the Tiberian register of TR a 7-color system (20G) or a 6-color system (20H) stems from the fact that Dalman seems to adduce only one [ε]-containing form for the register, the participle [mәnah(h)ε̊mxón] 'euer Tröster' (Da 382). In default of discovering more instances of [ε] in other sources, Tib TR will be provisionally treated as a 6-color system. (Relatedly, only one instance of reduced <ε̆>—hataf segol—is provided, gingerly interpreted as [ɔ̄] ([ɔ̆]); see §17.23.3 for discussion.)

(ζ) Since the choice of phonetic vowel symbols in this book is partially geared with an eye to betraying membership in systems of a given cardinality irrespective of whether specific sound changes are (ultimately) responsible for those systems, terminal phonetic vowels in derivations (whether diachronic or synchronic) will often be tacitly introduced. This will notably but not exclusively be true of *low vowels*, so that, for instance, a terminal derivational step involving a nonhigh non-mid back long low vowel will without special comment assume the form $\bar{a} \rightarrow$ [ɔ] in a 7-color system (20G) but $\bar{a} \rightarrow$ [ɑ̄] in a 6-color system (20H). When it is deemed necessary to be explicit about such a step, the term *systemic vowel shift* (svs) will be used.

(η) Though the four traditional pronunciations employed as ancillary in reconstruction (SM, Yem TL, Ash TL, M) are accommodated in (20G, H, I), only the 6-color vowel system of Yem TL trad pron (cf. §12.2 n. 16) and the 5-color system of M trad pron are likewise assumed for the actual TL and M dialects as reconstructed. For reconstructed SM, see (ι) below. (Note also that equivocation on whether M trad pron should be interpreted as 5-color (provisionally adopted in this book) or as 6-color stems from an issue similar to that discussed for Tib TR under (ε) above: Macuch (Macm) seemingly adduces only one form with t[æ], elsewhere consistently deploying t[a]; see §14.2 n. 20a.)

(θ) The systematic omission of schwa from (20G, H, I) for the reasons adduced in the prefatory remarks to these comments (α–ι) may not fully hold for the schwa of SM traditional pronunciation (20H), concerning which the authorities consulted (Macs, Ben-Ḥayyim 1961–77, Vikser 1981) fail to make clear whether a reduced or full (short) vowel is involved. The provisional interpretation of this book is that the schwa of SM trad pron is—against the grain of Classical Aramaic at large—*unmarkedly full(short)-vocalic*, hence transcribed "[ə]" without the breve diacritic—but systematically *reduced-vocalic* when part of the conjunctive proclitic, where it is accordingly transcribed with the breve, t[wə̆-]; see §22.1.

(ι) While the displays in (20G, H, I) are geared to dialects/registers/trad prons of sufficiently rich interpretability, the displays in (20J, K) are offered for dialects lacking such immediacy of interpretation—including at least one case, SM, where trad pron is in upshot adjudged to have undergone significant development *posterior* to the dialect's actual stage of florescence (see §22.1). (However, though florescent SM is reconstructed here (in (20J)) as having a 5-color system, the possibility must be entertained that it actually sported a 6-color system, to judge by the earlier of its two pointing systems ((21Ji) in §21.4). On the other hand, the points corresponding to *æ* and in that system do not appear to distribute as representing short and long *V*s respectively, a datum that leads to the possibility that they were largely free variants in spoken SM. Thus SM will be reconstructed as having *one* low vowel irrespective of length, $\overset{\circ}{\bar{a}}$. Hence (20J).)

For criteria gingerly adopted in assigning (20J, K) to a given dialect, see §24.1. It might be mentioned that the primary events hypothesized to lead from earlier system (20K) to later system (20J) are the emergence of *coalescence* (§11), ushering in the changes *ay* > *ē*, *aw* > *ō*, and *midding* (§17.11), ushering in *i* > *e*, *u* > *o*. (And note finally that although systems (20I) and (20J) are substantively identical, (20J) lacks the associated processes often figuring in the dynamics of (20I). For instance, while *ā* > *ō* in Jac SR (20I), for the dialects assumed in (20J) *ā* ≥ *ā*.)

(20G) <u>7-color systems</u> (Tiberian-i (Tib B, Ash TL, *possibly* Tib TR); Nes SR)

i	(Tib *ḥirik*;	**u**	(Tib *šuruk/kubuc*;
	Nes *ḥə̆wɔ̄ṣɔ̄*)		Nes *9ə̆ṣɔ̄ṣɔ̄ alīṣɔ̄*)
e	(Tib *cerey;*	**o**	(Tib *ḥolam;*
	Nes *rə̆wɔ̄ṣɔ̄ arrīxɔ̄*)		Nes *9ə̆ṣɔ̄ṣɔ̄ rə̆wīḥɔ̄*)
ε	(Tib *segol;*		(Tib *kamac;*
	Nes *rə̆wɔ̄ṣɔ̄ karyɔ̄*)		Nes *zə̆qɔ̄pɔ̄*)
(a)		**(a)** (Tib *pataḥ;*	
		Nes *pə̆θɔ̄ḥɔ̄*)	

(20H) <u>6-color systems</u> (Tiberian-ii (Yem TL, *likely* Tib TR);
Babylonian (Bab B, Bab TR);
SM trad pron; *possibly* M trad pron)

i	(Tib *ḥirik*)	**u**	(Tib *šuruk/kubuc*)
e	(Tib *cerey*)	**o**	(Tib *ḥolam*)
æ	(Tib *pataḥ*)	**α**	(Tib *kamac*)

(20I) <u>5-color systems</u> (Jac SR; M, *likely including* trad pron)

i	(Jac *ḥə̆vōṣō*)	**u**	(Jac *9ə̆ṣōṣō*)
e	(Jac *rə̆vōṣō*)	**o**	(Jac *zə̆qōfō*)
(a)		**(a)** (Jac *pə̆θōḥō*)	

(20J) <u>5-color reconstructed systems</u> (*for* I, P, N, CP, SM, G)

i		**u**
e		**o**
(a)	**(a)**	

(20K) <u>3-color reconstructed systems</u> (*for* pA, Y, O)

i		**u**
(a)	**(a)**	

20.3. Stress and Boundaries

Three degrees of stress are assumed, from strongest to weakest: *pausal* (V̋), *primary (contextual)* (V́), and *secondary* (V̀). Stressless vowels are usually left unindicated (V) but at certain spots are explicitly marked as such by a superposed "x".

Primary stress is assigned by rule (§4.1), and the the word hosting a stress so assigned without subsequent change is traditionally said to occur "in context" (*běhekšer*).

However, at least in B, primary strength may be strengthened to pausal when the host word occurs "in pause" (*běhefsek*)—that is, in the prosodically most salient position of a phonological phrase or perhaps other high-level prosodic group (for these matters, see §23.5). In the other direction, again at least in B, primary stress may under certain conditions be moved backward to the nearest full vowel in the same word (so-called *stress retraction*, srt, §17.15.2 n. 75) or demoted to secondary, or even deleted. In fact, sometimes stress retraction and demotion to secondary may coincide. These possibilities are sketched in (20L):[8]

$$(20\text{L}) \ldots \mathring{V}(C_1^2\check{V})C_1^2\mathring{V} \ldots \rightarrow$$

(i) $\ldots\acute{V}(C_1^2\check{V})C_1^2\mathring{V}\ldots$ *stress retraction*

(ii) $\ldots\mathring{V}(C_1^2\check{V})C_1^2\mathring{V}\ldots$ *demotion to secondary*

(iii) $\ldots\mathring{V}(C_1^2\check{V})C_1^2\mathring{V}\ldots$ *stress deletion*

(iv) $\ldots\mathring{V}(C_1^2\check{V})C_1^2\mathring{V}\ldots$ *(i) and (ii) combined*

As concerns boundaries, important for their role as domain-indicators for phonological processes, three may be assumed, again presented from the strongest to the weakest: *major* (‖), *(disjunctive) word* (#), *(conjunctive) word* (#), *clitic* (=), *morpheme* (+). Absence of a boundary is negatively represented by close-quarter juxtaposition of phonetic-phonological symbols (i.e., lack of spacing). This mode of representation is also often tacitly extended to morpheme boundaries, which are thus usually not indicated—because it is characteristic of simple morpheme boundaries in languages at large, including Aramaic, to be phonologically inert under most circumstances. The parenthesization appearing above in the word boundaries signals that the distinction between disjunctive and conjunctive will normally be foregone in this book, both being symbolized by "#" alone.[9] There tends to be an inclusion relation among the boundaries in a sense illustrable on the basis of the string sketched in (20M), letting capital letters stand for arbitrary phonetic-phonological substrings: (α) Suppose *n* processes may be contracted between (operate across) *F* and *G* subject only to satisfaction of their structural descriptions. Then *n-p* may operate across *EFGH*, where most frequently $p = \emptyset$; *n-p-q* across *DEFGHI*; *n-p-q-r* across *CDEFGHIJ*; *n-p-q-r-s* across *BCDEFGHIJK*; *n-p-q-r-s-t* across *ABCDEFGHIJKL*. That is, the stronger the boundary on the hierarchy in (20N), the more processes it provides a delimitative domain for (i.e., the fewer the processes that may apply across it). But we do not expect to find processes that apply across a stronger boundary and yet fail to apply across a weaker. And this relation of (non)application is fully transitive. Thus, take spirantizaton (§5.1). At least in Biblical Aramaic, this process is bounded by #, so that if

B is a vowel and *C* one of *p, t, k, b, d, g*, spirantization may *not* apply /*B*__#*C*^(d) nor a fortiori /*A*__||*B*; but it *may* apply in any of /*C*__#*D*, /*D*__=*E*, /*E*__+*F*, or /*F*__*G*. (β) At the same time, there may be processes whose application is conditioned *within* (not across) a stronger boundary to the exclusion of a weaker. This holds at least for the most salient (and clearest) cases of tonic lengthening (tln) in Biblical Aramaic (§17.29), where the word hosting the stressed vowel to be lengthened must occur /__||. On the other hand, tln will not normally be triggered in any of /__#, /__#, /__=, or /__+.[10]

(20M) A || B #́ C #́ D = E + F G + H = I #́ J #́ K || L

(20N) || ≫ #́ ≫ #́ ≫ = ≫ +

For specifics on stress and/or boundaries in action, see inter alia §4, §5, §17.11 (especially n. 37), §17.15 (especially n. 75), §17.29.

Notes to §20

[1] The question of [v] vs. [β] in Aramaic at large is by no means settled, despite the commoner fielding of [v], a practice also adopted in this book. It is moreover possible that both realizations may appear in one and the same dialect, whether as conditioned variants or freely. (It might also be noted that one or the other manifestation could be favored under specific circumstances; e.g., *β* is more likely than *v* to have merged with [w], as in Nestorian SR; §5.2.)

[2] Absent from this listing of spr-generated fricatives are θ, ð, dating as they do from pA independently of spirantization. Interestingly, the original θ, ð occluded to *t, d* pan-Aramaically (§17.14) prior to the emergence of spr, so that when this latter process came about it triggered an accordion θ, ð occ > *t, d* spr > θ, ð.

[3] A bit of explication is in order on various points:

(a) Strictly speaking, *A* is not an archiphoneme, because given the category and feature assumptions adopted in this book there is no way of defining the grouping {æ, a, α, ɔ, o} without appealing to disjunction ("low vowel *or* mid back vowel").

(b) The result in (a) stems from the fact that traditional vowel charts, including those used in this book, are excessively (and unrealistically) stylized. In these, rectangular or chevron organization is customary, though natural contouring of vowel space would reveal asymmetries such as horizontal space decreasing from high through mid to low as well as vertical space from front through central to back. Likewise and more directly apposite to the result in (a), there are no angular seams in the trajectory high front^low front^low back^high back; rather, the progression is smooth along a lopsided arc—and as a consequence the sequencing æ/a^α^ɔ^o does not actually encounter a discrete angular turn upward from α to ɔ. These observations are portrayed in (d), replacing the traditional configuration in (e).

(c) Against this background, the dynamic/diachronic basis for *A* = {æ, a, α, ɔ, o} is easy to state: given the relatively cramped spacing allotted to low vowels, the phonological opposition low front vowel ≠ low back vowel will be facilitated, both articulatorily and perceptually, by enhancing either the palatal coarticulation of the front vowel and/or the labial coarticulation of the back vowel. But since the force of such coarticulations

increases from low to high, the natural tendency is to enhance the front vowel by raising *æ/a* > ε and the back vowel in parallel fashion—the point being made here—α > ɔ.
(The apparently more drastic shift *a* > *o* is proper to a 5-vowel system, with only one
mid back vowel; see (20I) below.) Relatedly, languages frequently implement these
enhancements at the service of sharpening the long/short opposition borne by a single
low long vowel, so that, e.g., labialization will be systemically either increased in the
case of the *short* low vowel (as in Hungarian) or in the case of the *long* low vowel—as
in the case of Tiberian traditions of Aramaic (and Hebrew), where flat low short [a] is
pitted against rounded long [ɔ̄], though the latter is "officially" not low but open mid.

(d)

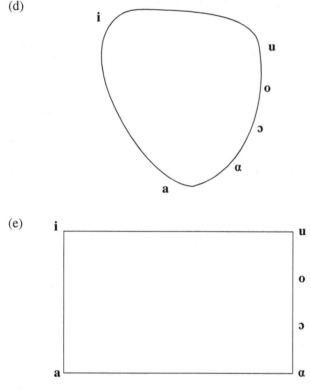

(e)

[4] (a) Because these correspondences are meant to convey system-to-system comparison maintaining segment-to-segment similarity to the extent possible, conditional
mergers are omitted even when prominent in the development of the register in question; e.g., Nes SR *ī, ē* > Jac SR *ī* (§11.2) is left out because there are also conditions
under which *ī, ē* ≥ *ī, ē*, and this latter better shows up the similarity of the two systems.
Also, identity correspondences are omitted if originating by distinct processes in either
register; e.g., *ā* in Nes SR and Jac SR (see (δ)) below in the text)—in which connection note also that *ā* does not occur in Tib B. Though ɔ̄ does occur in Tib B, it strictly
speaking has no reflexes in Bab B; because in Tib B it exclusively originates < *ů* via
mid^aop (§17.11) whereas under the same circumstances in Bab B *ů* ≥ *ů*. Similarly *o*

in Nes SR, which exclusively arises < *ŭ* by mid while in Jac SR *ŭ* ≥ *ŭ*; and Nes SR *ɔ̆*
exclusively < *ă* by a labialization process ((δ) below) alien to Jac SR. Finally, Nes SR
has neither *ĕ* nor *ɛ̆*.

(b) A similar relation might hold between traditional pronunciations for TL >
YemTL, but the likelihood is marred by the suspicion of Schematisierung on the side of
what passes for Ash TL as reported by Margolis (in Mar) (cf., e.g., §17.23.1.2.)

[5] While other Tiberian subregisters of TR show [æ], the Sabbionetan shows [ā].
This may be interpreted to the effect that Sab TR has come to enforce strict *æ̈* ≠ *ā*, so
that *ǣ* shunted to *ā*; i.e., *ay(i)*(k-)coa > *ǣ* > *ā*. If so, synchronically open (k-)coa in Sabbionetan may well have metamorphosed from the status of a coalescent process strictly
speaking (where *a* and *y(i)* pool their features), to deletion plus compensatory lengthening along the lines of (a) below, where upon deletion of *y(i)* the now empty mora (μ) is
filled by spreading from *a*.

(a)   μ   μ   μ   μ   μ   μ
       a   y   (i)   ⇒   a   ∅   ⇒   a   a

[6] Admittedly a suspicious analysis, polar processes being taken to motivate one and the same vowel movement in similar environments in two closely
related registers. An explanation is suggested by the fact that the phonologic
space of Jac SR contains only one vowel (*o*) where Nes SR shows two (*o, ɔ*). If
the norm for the Jacobite segment was indeed *close* mid, it may be that a condensation like *malkṓw* would have entailed a diphthong with nucleus and glide
uncomfortably close in articulation (cf. §14.2 <u>SM</u>); so dissimilation to the res-
cue, > *malkā̆w*. (Certainly diphthongs like [ow] are not universally spurned—
standard American and British English host them, for example—but languages
at large tend to field diphthongs with more generous nucleus-glide spacing.)

[7] (a) Observe however in a Nes SR trad pron recorded by Hoberman (1997: 264) a
rendition as [a:w] (his transcription, [V:] being equivalent to [V̄] of this book) of what
here would be predicted to be [ɔ̆w]. (b) Does the Nes SR assimilation *ăw* → [ɔ̆w] also
apply when *w* ← *b* by spirantization (§5.2)? Since vowel assimilation of this type bids
fair to be a last-level "phonetic" process, the answer is likely to be affirmative; but in
default of a decisive answer, in this book the hedge notation *"Aw"* will be employed
whenever *w* ← *b*; e.g., §15.3.1.2 n. 26.

[8] The qualification "at least in B" signals that most aspects of stress and boundary
patterning in the Classical Aramaic dialects are readily inferable from the rich Tib B
graphemic system (vowel pointing, tĕ9amim, makef, etc.; §21.6, 7), but weakly if at all
reflected in the other sources employed in this book. Caution must thus be exercised in
extrapolating from B to the other dialects, though certain key patterns—most especially
primary stress—may be internal-reconstructed with the help of even modest vowel
pointing and matres lectionis deployment alone.

[9] In fact, in contexts where boundary behavior is not an issue, even more drastic
symbological liberties will often be taken, spacing alone standing in for and boundary
stronger than clitical (so that *X Y* may be *X#Y*, *X#Y*, or (rarely) even *X‖Y*); and close-
quarter writing may stand in for any boundary weaker than conjunctive word (so that
XY may be *X=Y, X+Y,* or of course boundaryless *XY*).

[10] Boundaries are appealed to with an eye to a balance among descriptive adequacy, projected familiarity on the part of the reader, and expository simplicity. A more thorough treatment, beyond the pale of this book, should aim to capture the patterns in terms of domain-edges of prosodic and/or syntactic categories. (Some work in this area for Tiberian Hebrew may be seen in Aronoff 1985, Malone 1989c, and Dresher 1994.)

21. Orthography [1]

21.1 Letters Representing Consonants

The basic graphemic-phonetic correlations of unsupplemented Aramaic consonantal orthography are presented in (21A)—"consonantal" in omitting the use of letters in conveyance of vowel information (qua so-called *matres lectionis* (ml), for which see §21.2) and "unsupplemented" in omitting diacritic accretions-providing vowels (so-called *points*, §21.4), cantillational scoring incidentally furnishing information on accentuation (so-called *tĕ9amim*, "accents," §21.6), and various other intercalated marks giving a potpourri of morphophonologically relevant properties (§21.7). Supplemental markings giving directly consonantal information will be discussed in the present section, immediately following (21A).

The one-to-many cases of spelling-to-pronunciation between the second and third columns of (21A) are subject to four sorts of interlocking explanation, all connected to the vintage hypothesis that the Arameans borrowed their orthography from some Canaanite group, probably the Phoenicians, in conjunction with the assumption that some characteristic Aramaic sound changes preceded the date of borrowing while others followed.

(*) The diachronic correlates of spelling with <9> are a bit complex. <9> is the sole spelling of [9] as *either* reflex of pA *9, *or* reflex of pA *R in the wake of uvular fricative backing (ufb, §9.1.3). The interpretation of this correlation is that ufb preceded the borrowing of Phoenician orthography and that at the time the borrowing took place Aramaic had a segment [9] < *9, *R which was straightforwardly spelled with Phoenician <9>.

(*) However, after pA *R had merged with 9 by ufb, [R] was *reintroduced* into Aramaic by spirant hopping (shp, §17.24) < pA *ð, subsequent to the adoption of Phoenician spelling, and later merged with [9] by a *reprise* of ufb. Reintroduced [R], which is assumed to have been a phonetic reality in the earlier dialects, is consistently spelled <q>, by hypothesis because <q> was the sole uvular letter provided by the Phoenician alphabet. Moreover, even after reintroduced [R] in later Aramaic merged with [9] by r-ufb, <q> continued in some dialects to be used for [9] (< R) by historical spelling—though competed by <9> which ultimately became the preferred or even unique letter for the job.

(*) <z> spelling [ð], <ŝ> spelling [θ], and <ṣ> spelling [θ] in the early dialects before these segments occluded (occ, §17.14) to *d, t, ṭ* is taken to reflect the facts: that Phoenician had merged *ð, *θ, *θ̣ into [z, š, ṣ], which accordingly were spelled <z, š, ṣ> taken into Aramaic as <z, š, ṣ> (for the symbol "<ŝ>," see §17.27); that a large number of transparent Phoenician-Aramaic cognates facilitated the correlation of Aramaic [ð, θ, θ̣] with Phoenician [z, š, ṣ], respectively; and that the licensing power of this correlation was reinforced by a palpable amount of perceived phonetic similarity between [ð] and [z], [θ] and [š], and [θ̣] and [ṣ]. (Indeed, it is plausibly a deficit of phonetic similarity between Aramaic [R] and Phoenician [ṣ] (< *θ̣) which disfavored <ṣ> as a spelling for Aramaic [R] (< *θ̣) and adoption of nonetymological <q> instead, as discussed in the preceding point.)

(*) The spelling <ŝ> [ś] in the earlier dialects is accounted for in a way similar to <ŝ> [θ], differing mainly in the fact that sin merger (snm, §17.27) is later involved, rather than occlusion.

For more on most of this, see §9.1.3.[2]

(21A)

Hebrew equivalent	Transliteration	Y & O phonetic values (unchanged from pA except for R <shp *ð>)	Other phonetic values in various other dialects (and reference to the processes responsible
א	<ʾ>	[ʾ]	[∅] (adr)
ב	<B>	[b]	[v, β, w] (spr)
ג	<G>	[g]	[ɣ] (spr)
ד	<D>	[d]	[ð] (spr)
ה	<h>	[h]	[∅] (dgt, hap)
ו	<w>	[w]	[β, b] (*see below under* SM *and* §5.3 n. 13c)
ז	<z>	[z, ð]	
ח	<ḥ>	[ḥ]	[ḫ] (dpr), [9] (gtl), [∅] (dgt)
ט	<ṭ>	[ṭ]	
י	<y>	[y]	
כ, ך ,ך	<K>	[k]	[x] (spr)
ל	<l>	[l]	[ḷ] (*see* §22.1)
מ, ם	<m>	[m]	
נ, ן	<n>	[n]	
ס	<s>	[s]	
ע	<9>	[9, R]	[∅] (dgt)
פ, ף	<P>	[p]	[f, φ] (spr)
צ, ץ	<ṣ>	[ṣ, θ̣]	
ק	<q>	[q, R]	
ר	<r>	[r]	
ש	<ŝ>	[š, ś, θ]	
ת	<T>	[t]	[θ] (spr)

Some dialects/registers/texts are scored by ancillary diacritic systems providing phonetic information supplementary to that conveyed by the basic letter-based orthography. While most of these diacritic usages relevant to this book will be treated in §§21.3, 21.4, 21.5, a few instances directly pertinent to consonants are briefly discussed here.

(α) The important change *spirantization* (spr, §5.1) triggered alternations between the nonemphatic singleton stops *p, t, k, b, d, g* and their slit fricative (spirant) counterparts *f/φ, θ, x, v/β, ð, γ*. Moreover, various factors soon led to the phonemicization of these alternations, most notably the action of *reduction* (red, §4.2), in its full (deletional) form. This process often counterbled spirantization by removing a vowel that prior to being deleted had changed an immediately following stop to fricative, with the consequence that the resulting consonant-fricative cluster ended up contrasting with a priorly existing consonant-stop cluster. The mechanism is illustrated with the pair of TR nouns in (21B), where post-reductionally the spirantal status of [v] in [dæhvá̃] can no longer be predicted on the basis of the phonetic string alone, surface-contrasting as it does with the stop status pof [p] in [kæspá̃] (examples taken from Da 136, 146).[3]

(21B) *dahabá̃ spr > dahavá̃ red > [dæhvá̃] 'das Gold'
       *kaspá̃   ≥ [kæspá̃] 'das Silber'

The resulting contrast is diacritically marked in a number of systems, three of which have been appealed to in partially determining the phonetic interpretation of forms in this book.

Tiberian/Babylonian dageš.   This diacritic (in Tiberian usage in the form of a dot normally placed within a letter and in Babylonian pointing often represented by a tiny superposed <G>) generically conveys *fortition*, which in turn may assume any one (or two concurrently) of three manifestations: *occlusive* (stopped) value of *P, T, K, B, D, G*, i.e., [p, t, k, b, d, g] as opposed to fricative [f/φ, θ, x, v/β, ð, γ]; *geminate* value of any (geminable) consonant in the environment /V__V as opposed to singleton; *per se pronounced* value of <h> as opposed to the use of this letter as a mater lectionis—dageš in this latter function normally being called *mapik*. The first and second of these functions of dageš may, moreover, cooccur, in fact *must* cooccur, in the frame /V__V (the subject of Malone 1975). These four situations are illustrated with the (Tiberian) B forms in (21C) (cf. BL 171–77):[4]

(21C) (i)   [tɛ9dé̠], 2ms [hišt̠ə̆xáħat]
             (*contrast* [θ̠šhōð̠ə̆9ůnnání], [yū̠xál], 3fs [hišt̠ə̆xáħaθ])
       (ii) [yə̆maḏ̠él]
             (*contrast* [yə̆maḏ̠él])
       (iii) [bə̆nayθə̆h̠] *whose last letter is* <h> *with dageš (mapik)*
             (*contrast* [mə̆t̠ɔ́] *whose last letter is* <h> *without dageš (mapik)*)
       (iv) [yə̆maggár]

In the major sources used for this book, dageš is a prominent feature of B and TR.[5]

Syriac.   The SR system is like the full, dageš-rafe system in deploying paired diacritics antithetical in function, a superposed dot indicating the stop value of P, T, K, B, D, G (referred to as *quššɔyɔ* 'hard') and an infraposed dot indicating the spirantal value (*rukkɔxɔ* 'soft'). However, unlike dageš, the quššɔyɔ diacritic is per se limited to conveying the occlusive value of P, T, K, B, D, G, i.e., function (i) of (21C)—though the analog of function (21C) (iv) follows by implication inasmuch as intervocalic *t, k, b, d, g* in SR, as in all Classical A dialects, are necessarily geminate (for the exemption of *p* in Nestorian, §5.2). Per se, gemination is unmarked. And the issue of pronouncing or failing to pronounce <h> does not arise, this letter not being used as a mater lectionis (§21.2) in the dialect; *all* <h>s in SR are pronounced [h].[6]

Samaritan.   SM indicates the stop value of <w> or <P> by a superposed stroke, a stop value that in trad pron is manifested as voiced bilabial, whether singleton [b] or geminate [bb] (Macs 46–48). To get a bead on this bizarrely restricted diacritic usage, let us start with a bird's eye view over the panoply of nonnasal labial consonants with their reflexes in SM spelling and trad pron. In view of aspects of these reflexes, it seems plausible that in early (or pre-) SM spr of **p, **b produced bilabial rather than labiodental fricatives, *φ, *β. The panoply is given in (21D).[7]

(21D)   *p   > t[b]   <P̄>, <P>   ~ t[f]   <P>
        *pp   > t[bb]   <P̄>, <P>   ~ t[ff]   <P>
        *φ   > t[b]   <P̄>, <B>   ~ t[f]   <P>
        *b   > t[b]   <B>
        *bb   > t[bb]   <B>
        *β   > t[b]   <w>, <B>
        *w   > t[b]   <w>, <w̄>, <B>
        *ww   > t[bb]   <w>, <w̄>, <B>

A plausible way of understanding (21D)—and hence the function of the diacritic in <w>, <P>—is laid out in (21E). Armed with the outset assumption that the norm for the early SM / pre-SM labial spirants was bilabial (φ, β) rather than labiodental, we first assume that SM underwent a change of *obstruentization* whereby the voiced bilabial semivowel *w* merged with the spirant β (I > II). Next we assume that all nonnasal labials collapsed into either *b* or *f* (II > III), presumably under the influence of Arabic (and while Arabic also has *w*, we may guess that whatever factors led SM to priorly lose its own *w* still prevailed). This pair of changes proceeded along the path of least resistance, following the hierarchy of this violable guideline: *preserve voice where possible*. Thus the voiced items (*b*, β) merge to *b* , eschewing *f*, while the voiceless items (*p*, φ) are free to, so > *b* ~ *f*. Coming now to spelling, a medley of types were employed (i, ii, iii, iv, v), not as disparate as at first they may seem. Thus all segments might be spelled either historically (i, iii, iv) or synchronically, i.e., as straightforwardly representing the new phonetic shape—or the indifferently old/new shape if the change was vacuous (ii, iii, iv). This leaves only inverse spelling (v), whereby after $w > \beta > $ [b] left the dialect de facto with three ways of spelling [b], <w> or <B> or <w̄>, at least two of them were pressed into service in spelling $\beta > $ [b], <B> along historical and/or synchronic lines, or <w> inversely.

Against this backdrop, there emerges a plausible function for the superposed diacritic stroke: *it signals that the historical spelling so marked (<w̄>, <P̄>) is now pronounced* [b].[8]

SM also has a seldom used diacritic for gemination, in the shape of a supralinear wedge pointed rightward, <Č> (Macs 49), in its rare appearance in this book to be transliterated with Arabic *šadda* (<Č>), as generally for all Aramaic gemination devices—discussion to follow after (21E).

(21E)

I *obstruentization*	II *reocclusion, voicing, labio-dentalization*		III (i) *historical spelling*	III (ii) *updated (synchronic) spelling*	III (iii) *both of the preceding concurrently*	III (iv) *historical spelling not necessarily updated*	
w	> β	> t[b]	<w> or	<B> or	<w̄>		
ww	> ββ	> t[bb]	<w> or	<B> or	<w̄>		
p	> p	> t[b]	<P>		or <P̄>	~ t[f] <P>	
pp	> pp	> t[bb]	<P>		or <P̄>	~ t[ff] <P>	
φ	> φ	> t[b]		<B>	or <P̄>	~ t[f] <P>	(v)
b	> b	>				t[b] <B>	*inverse*
bb	> bb	>				t[bb] <B>	*spelling*
β	> β	>				t[b] <B>	or <w>

In this book, transliteration of consonants will from one angle be homogeneous and yet from another heterogeneous. It will be homogeneous in using one system of symbols for all dialects (except Mandaic, which will be treated separately; §21.8) despite differences in letters/diacritics, or in the shape or distributional pattern of the same. Thus singleton occlusives *P, T, K, B, D, G* will be rendered as <p, t, k, b, d, g> no matter how occlusion is specifically indicated in the pertinent dialects. Similarly, singleton spirantal *P, T, K, B, D, G* as <f, θ, x, v, ð, γ > even though—and this is part of the heterogeneity— *all* dialects, with only minor exceptions, write corresponding stops and spirants with the same letter short of diacritics.[9]

Special notation is also required in view of the fact that all dialects show at least a statistical implication between occlusive status and gemination of *P*, *T*, *K*, *B*, *D*, *G*, as mentioned earlier: letting *B*, *b* stand for the entire series, geminate *BB* is virtually always occlusive [bb], restricted to intervocalic position, while conversely an occurrence of intervocalic occlusive *b* is (with the exception of Nes SR *p*, above) always geminate [bb].[10] This being the case, at least the Tiberian Masoretes used one symbol, dageš, for both functions (Malone 1975). In this book, however, for the sake of clarity and computational ease, the two functions will be transliterated distinctly: <b> for occlusion, and an adaptation of the Arabic diacritic *šadda* for gemination—so that unadorned <b> renders *singleton* <B> + dageš, while <b̆> renders *geminate* <B> + dageš.

This use of šadda also makes it possible more generally to represent differently instances of *any* geminate/long consonant, qua <C̆′>, on the one hand and occurrences of two adjacent tokens of the same letter, qua <C′C′>, on the other.

All this is summarized in (21F), where also non-*PTKBDG* consonants are represented by *m* (except for the special case of *mapik* in (ix)). And be it finally observed that in Tiberian/Babylonian texts where dageš is deployed consistently enough for occlusion without the benefit of a paired rafe symbol for spirantization, the bare letter may be interpreted (at some risk, it's true) as spirantal; see line (iv).

(21F)	*Tiberian rendering*		*transliteration*	*phonetic value*
(i)	ב		<B>	[B] (= {[b], [v]}
(ii)	בּ	/V__V	<b̆>	[bb] (= [b:])
(iii)	בּ	/elsewhere	<b>	[b]
(iv)	בֿ = ב		<v>	[v]
(v)	בב		<BB>	[B(V)B]
(vi)	מ		<m>	[m]
(vii)	מּ		<m̆>	[mm] (= [m:])
(viii)	ממ		<mm>	[m(V)m]
(ix)	ה	/__#	<h̆>	[h]

*   *   *

(β) CP and SR sport a special manipulation of the letter-cum-diacritic combination <p>, representing the standard Aramaic voiceless bilabial stop [p], to convey the value of Greek <π>—a sound conventionally taken to differ from Aramaic [p] in lacking aspiration (cf. the feature table in (20B), where this distinction is captured by declaring the Aramaic [p] to be [+tense] but Greek [π] to be [-tense]).

<π> impinges on the work of this book both by the fact that it appears in a few verbs adapted from Greek—notably <πεῖσαι> 'persuade' reworked in both

dialects as a hollow causative, [απῑs] (Payne Smith 1903: 444, Sl 156) and by the fact that, at least in CP, it may replace Aramaic *b* in at least √πlm 'stupere' (Sl 158).

For more on <π>, see Ns §§15, 25, Sl 5f.

(It might be noted that TL is like SR and CP in adapting Greek <πεῖσαι> into its verb system, but differs in deploying the unadorned <P>-grapheme to represent the alien π; see §24.2 T̲L̲ under √pys.)

*   *   *

(γ) The Tiberian and Babylonian Masoretes use a pair of diacritics to disambiguate the voiceless coronal rilled fricative 𝚠, per se transliterated <ŝ> in this book, as either 𝚠́—so-called "šin (yĕminit)," representing the palatal [š], to be transliterated <š>—or 𝚠—"sin (sĕmolit)," probably representing in the earlier period the sibilant conventionally transcribed by Semitists as [ś], whatever its precise value (for this, see §20.1), and in the later period merging with the dentoalveolar [s], and in either case transliterated <ŝ> in this book. The use of <ŝ> as a transliteration of nondisambiguated carries over into phonetic interpretation, where [ŝ] is used in parallel fashion. For details and more discussion, see §17.27.

*   *   *

(δ) In later SM texts, a small Arabic <9> superposed on a word-initial letter, usually <ḥ> but occasionally other guttural letters including <9> itself, indicates that the consonant so marked is pronounced [9] (Macs 51f.). This diacritic is noteworthy in attesting to either of two SM pharyngealization processes: the systemic laxing of *ḥ* to [9] (§9.3.2); or in certain lexemes (never verbs?) pharyngeal spread (Macs 52).

21.2. Letters Representing Vowels (Matres Lectionis)

The table in (21G) displays in condensed form the major deployments for all dialects but Mandaic (§21.8) of *matres lectionis* (mls, Lesemütter, ʾimot kĕriya), i.e., the use of originally consonantal letters to convey vocalic information.

For all columns, vowels and semivowels are focal while consonants and boundaries are environmental: i.e., $\mathring{I}C = \mathring{I} / \_\_C$, $\bar{I}\# = \bar{I} / \_\_\#$, etc.

For monophthongs (first nine columns (= first three column groups)), mls are with one exception presented irrespective of how the vowel in question arose; e.g., $\mathring{I}$ might be original or via attenuation, $\mathring{A}$ original or via lowering, $\bar{A}$ original of via early condensation. The one exception is that the vowel in question *not* have arisen from a diphthong or the auslaut triphthong **ayi#*, for which the last five columns (three column groups) are specialized.

The diphthongs (fourth and fifth column groups) may be original or derived (e.g., *ay* < e-cnd **ayī*) and subsume the possible application of later coalescent processes; e.g., in the case of *ay*, whether realized as [Ay] (-coa) or [Ē] / [Ā] (+coa).[11]

For the last column, *ayi#* = *a 3√y* + indicative/declarative suffix *i* in word-final position subject to k-coa where applicable; so that as of B at the latest the focal vowel will normally be [Ē] / [Ā] (< k-coa *ayi*).

It is assumed that the reflexes of *ayC*, *ay#*, and *ayi#* converged after breakdown of the long–short opposition in the impf, i.e., commencing with I and completed by B.

(21G)

	(1) ĬC	(2) ŬC	(3) ĂC	(4) ĪC	(5) ŪC	(6) ĀC	(7) Ī#	(8) Ū#	(9) Ā#	
Y	<∅>	<∅>	<∅>		<w>	<∅>	<y>	<w>		...
O	<∅>	<∅>	<∅>		<∅~w>	<∅>	<y>	<w>		...
I	<∅>	<∅>	<∅>	<y~∅>	<w~∅>	<∅>	<y>	<w>	<h>	...
B	<∅>	<∅>	<∅>	<y~∅>	<w~∅>	<∅>	<y>	<w>	<h~ʔ>	...
P	<∅>	<∅>	<∅>	<y>	<w~∅>	<ʔ~∅>	<y~∅>	<w~∅>	<ʔ~∅>	...
N	<∅>	<∅>	<∅>	<y>	<w>	<∅>	<y>	<w>	<h~ʔ>	...
TR	<y~∅>	<w~∅>	<∅>	<y>	<w>	<∅>	<y>	<w>	<ʔ>	...
CP	<y~∅>	<w>	<∅~ʔ>	<y~∅~ʔ>	<w>	<∅~ʔ>	<y>	<w>	<ʔ>	...
SM	<∅>	<w>	<∅~ʔ>	<y~9>	<w>	<∅~9~ʔ~h>	<y>	<w>	<ʔ~h>	...
G	<y~∅>	<w~∅>	<∅>	<y>	<w>	<∅>	<y>	<w>	<ʔ~h>	...
SR	<∅>	<w>	<∅>	<y>	<w>	<∅>	<y>	<w>	<ʔ>	...
TL	<y~∅>	<w>	<∅>	<y>	<w>	<∅>	<y>	<w>	<ʔ~h>	...

	(10) *ayC	(11) *awC	(12) *ay#	(13) *aw#	(14) *ayiC
Y	<y>	<w>	<y>		<y>
O	<y>	<w>	<y>	<w>	<h>
I	<y~∅>	<w>	<y~h>	<w>	<h>
B	<y>	<w>	<h~ʔ>	<w>	<h~ʔ>
P	<y>	<w>	<h~ʔ>	<w>	<h~ʔ>
N	<y>	<w>	<ʔ~h>	<w>	<ʔ~h>
TR	<y>	<w>	<y>	<w>	<y>
CP	<y~ʔ>	<w>	<ʔ~ʔy~y~ ~h~yh>	<w>	<ʔ~y>
SM	<y>	<w>	<y~h~ʔ>	<w>	<y~h~ʔ>
G	<y>	<w>	<y~ʔ~yy>	<w>	<y~ʔ>
SR	<y>	<w>	<y>	<w>	<ʔ~y>
TL	<y>	<w>	<y~ʔy>	<w>	<y>

Various observations on (21G):

(α) It is traditionally assumed that mls arose in West Semitic writing via incremental generalization of historical spelling vis-à-vis changes that created long vowels; thus, e.g., after *ay* > *ē* by coalescence, if the original spelling <y> was maintained it would thenceforth de facto spell [ē]. Though there remain some loose ends to this traditional view, it seems in general sound. Witness to this that ml's are always (symbols for) *glides*, the most labile consonants of the Aramaic repertory. Those specific glides, moreover, which are known to have undergone changes resulting in long vowels—e.g.: coalescence in the case of semivowels (stomatic/oral glides) *y, w*; alef drop, *h* apocope, and degutturalization in the case of the gutturals (in which vein observe that SM, with its massive loss of these, is most lavish in fielding guttural mls; note <9>, <ʾ>, and <h> for [ā] /__C).

(β) Though the correlation is imperfect, there is a general tendency for mls to extend their distribution (and hence function) along the temporal axis from older to later dialects. This is most striking in the generalization of the ml function from long to short vowels (columns 1–3); thus, short medial labial vowels ([Ů]) go unrepresented till TR, at which stage <w> appears variably as a ml and subsequently becomes categorical in this role in all dialects but G.

(γ) Though B normally signals long [ī] with <y>, an [ī] derived by tonic lengthening (§17.29) from short *i* typically remains unrepresented by ml.

(δ) Notice that P shows the quirk of leaving final long vowels variably unrepresented. (While at first blush this might be taken not to reflect an orthographic quirk at all, but rather P's having undergone variable *long (vowel) apocope* and hence leaving ∅# < V̄# unrepresented, such a view is shown in §17.9.2 to be untenable.)[12]

(ε) Concerning the several spellings for (reflexes of) CP *ay# (column 12): <ʾ> plausibly renders [ē], a pairing that also appears under ĪC (column 4) (<Tʾ9wl> 'trittst ein' [tē9Úl], prefix vowel transparentively promoted, §15.3.1.1), *ayC (column 10), and *ayi# (column 14); <ʾy> probably spells uncoalesced [ay]; <h ~ yh> appear to be limited to the palatalized (§7.2 (δ) with n. 13) 3fp pf, e.g., <9lh> 'sie traten ein', <qmyh> 'sie standen auf', whatever the precise phonetics (likey [9allḗ], [qāmḗ]). (Examples from Sg 7–9.)

(ζ) SM's use of guttural letters as mls, in the wake of the massive degutturalization (§9.3.2, §22.1) characteristic of this dialect, shades off into a larger tableau where these letters appear to be added—or omitted—virtually at the whim of the scribe. See Macs 3–39 for ample details and documentation.

(η) The digraphs <yy> (G) and <ʾy> (TL) under *ay# (column 12) are used unambiguously for uncoalesced [Ay] (as in CP, (ε) above), while <y> is probably best taken as ambiguous between -coa [Ay] and +coa [Ē].

(θ) Various later dialects, e.g., TR, CP, G, TL, may at times represent reduced vowels with mls, in this using the same patterns as evinced for ĪC, ŮC,

ÅC. It is, however, possible that at least some such presumed instances of <Γ>
[V̆] are actually cases of <Γ̊> [V̊], the reduced V̆ having promoted to full V̊
status. Cf. discussion in §17.23.3.

21.3. Letters Representing Empty (Ghost) Consonants

We have seen that historically spelled consonants may live on as matres lectionis (§21.2) or as graphemic morphophonemes (n. 12).[13] At least one other
type of function is suggested in the event the historical consonants distribute
in a linguistically patterned manner still in evidence though the phonetic units
themselves have vanished. A case in point for minimally those dialects undergoing alef drop or other significant degutturalization (§9), SM and SR as well
as likely CP and G (M too, but irrelevantly under this specific heading; see
§21.8) is <C> *representing a synchronically empty (diachronically vanished)
consonant*—of the type called "featurally unspecified melodic unit" in Malone
1991, *ghost consonant* for short. Thus in SR, <ʔ> continues to mark vanished
1√ʔ In verbs like [alléṣ] 'bedrängen' spelled <ʔaleṣ> (B 135). Even though it
is dubious that /ʔ/ can per se be justified any longer as continuing synchronic
exponency of the radical function, it is equally clear or clearer that the overall
warp and woof of SR morphophonology demands that *some* radical be recognized here, whatever its precise featural content. And this radical is orthographically represented by <ʔ>.

Ghost-representative <ʔ> may possibly also be deployed in non-etymologi-
cal slots, notably to mark the empty onset of a prothetic syllable (§17.18), like
SR [ɛští] 'drink' spelled <ʔɛštiy>, or of what is possibly the second vowel-initial syllable in hiatus in hollow active participles like [qɔ́ɛ́m] spelled <qɔʔɛm>.
However, in both these cases the <ʔ> may be etymological after all. This may
be so in participles by virtue of a process common to several dialects whereby
y → ʔ intervocalically (the mirror image of apl, §9.2.1.2)—cf. the homoparadigmatic feminine [qɔ́ymɔ́], where the change is frustrated by dint of the *y* occurring postreductionally /V__C rather than /V__V. And in the prothetic case,
it is likely enough that the original form was [ʔĪští], with [ʔ] inserted in fulfill-
ment of a canonical requirement banning vowel-initial words (or syllables)—
an interpretation rendered all the more plausible by the fact that conservative
dialects which have not otherwise undergone alef drop, like B, also show <ʔ> in
prothetic forms: thus <ʔiš:tiyw> 'sie tranken' (BL 44) more probably spelling
[ʔištíw] than onsetless [ištíw].[14]

Though ghost consonants are usually represented etymologically, i.e., by
straightforward historical spelling, even in SM despite its extensive degutturalization—thus *1√ʔ* t[ắbɑd] spelled <ʔBD>, *1√h* t[ắbɑ] <ḥwh>, *1√h* t[ắzɑ]
<ḥzh> (Macs 170)—yet this dialect often shows nonetymological spelling in-
tervocalically, or what would be intervocalic were it not for the insertion (in
trad pron) of anti-hiatic [ʔ] (§22.1 (22B) (vi) (ɛ)); for instance, the hollow par-

ticiple t[sǽˀəd], etymologically *śåḫid, spelled <s9D> (~ etymological <sḫD>) (Macs 174).[15]

21.4. Vowel Points

The values of the main pointing systems used as evidential in this book are set forth in (21H). A given point transcribed as <V′> correlates with corresponding [V̊′] in tables (20G, H, I) of chapter 20. Apropos, two things should be borne in mind: (α) the choice of transcribing symbol is *not* constant for a given pointing system but varies across phonologies in accordance with the number of color contrasts utilized in the pertinent system—thus, the Tiberian point *pataḥ* is transliterated either <a> for a 7-color system (first column) or <æ> in the case of a 6-color system (second column); (β) a given point is quantity-wise neutral between long (V̄) and short (V̊), a distinction which in a given dialect/register/text may either be conveyed by presence/absence of ml (e.g., <ey> for [ē]) or remain unsignaled. Observe also that the cross-system correspondences given by horizontal lines in (21H) are meant to be no more than general and approximate; in particular, they abstract away from process differences which often affect cognates—for instance, Nestorian SR <e> (first column) may in an actual form correspond to Jacobite <i> when reflexes of *ē̆ are being represented, and hence -hei [ē] in Nestorian but +hei [ī] in Jacobite (§11.2).

(21H)	7-color systems [Tiberian-i (Tib B, Ash TL trad pron), Nes SR]	6-color systems [Tiberian-ii (Tib TR, Yem TL trad pron), Babylonian (Bab B, Bab TR), SM]	5-color systems [Jac SR, M (§21.8)]
	<i>	**<i>**	**<i>**
	(Tib *ḥirik*, Nes ḥə̆wɔ̄sɔ̄)	(Tib *ḥirik*)	(Jac ḥə̆vōṣō)
	<e>	**<e>**	
	(Tib *cerey*, Nes rə̆wɔ̄ṣɔ̄ arrīxɔ̄)	(Tib *cerey*)	**<e>** (Jac rə̆vōṣō)
	<ɛ>		
	(Tib *segol*, Nes rə̆wɔ̄ṣɔ̄ karyɔ̄)		
	<a>	**<æ>**	**<a>**
	(Tib *pataḥ*, Nes pə̆θɔ̄ḥɔ̄)	(Tib *pataḥ*)	(Jab pə̆θōhō)
	<ɔ>	**<ɑ>**	**<o>**
	(Tib *kamac*, Nes zə̆qɔ̄pɔ̄)	(Tib *kamac*)	(Jac zə̆qōfō)
	<o>	**<o>**	
	(Tib *holam*, Nes 9ə̆ṣɔ̄ṣɔ̄ rə̆wīḥɔ̄)	(Tib *holam*)	
	<u>	**<u>**	**<u>**
	(Tib *šuruk/kubuc*, Nes 9ə̆ṣɔ̄sɔ̄ alīṣɔ̄)	(Tib *šuruk, kubuc*)	(Jac 9ə̆ṣōṣō)

Two additional pointing systems will be briefly mentioned here—systems that due to their ambiguous nature are employed gingerly, if at all, in the interpretational work of this book. When letters scored by points of these systems appear in cited forms, the points are replicated by a(n approximate) copy of the original mark, rather than being alphabetically transcribed as is the practice with the major pointing systems (table (21H)).

CP (Sg 9–11). An upper/lower point gingerly correlates with the values in (21I) (—"gingerly": as Schulthess remarks, "Im gegenwärtigen Chaos aber ist gar vieles falsch; das Richtige ist nur aus der phonetischen Schreibung und Dialektvergleichung zu erkennen"). Though in well-behaved manuscripts, <w̥> represents a high rounded vowel and <ẘ> a mid rounded vowel, generally positioning of the point seems not to be consistently calibrated with the high–mid distinction; and Schulthess is very suspicious of the genuineness of ml-less <C̥>, <C̊> for labial vowels (thus the question marks).

Observe, finally, that in "alten (mit gelber Tinte geschriebenen) Hss." the *superposed* dot on <ʾ>, i.e., <ʾ̇>, according to Schulthess requires a *palatal* rather than low reading—though some of his attributions of palatality would require defense (e.g., <ḥmʾ̇> 'sah' which he takes to be palatalized *hᵉmā̊*). On balance, phonetic interpretation based on CP points must proceed with circumspection.[16]

$$(21I) \quad \text{<C\underset{\circ}{y}>} \quad \text{[C\overset{\circ}{I}]} \qquad\qquad \text{<C\underset{\circ}{w}>}\,(\,\text{<C̥>}\,?\,) \quad \text{[C\overset{\circ}{u}]}$$

$$\text{<C̥>} \begin{cases} \text{[C\overset{\circ}{I}]} \ \textit{generally,} \\ \text{[\overset{\circ}{I}C]} \ \textit{when C is codal} \end{cases} \qquad\qquad\qquad\qquad\qquad \Big\} \text{[C\overset{\circ}{U}]}$$

$$\text{<(C)\overset{?}{̊}>} \quad \text{[(C)\overset{\circ}{e}]} \ \textit{in old mss} \quad \text{<C\overset{\circ}{w}>}\,(\,\text{<C̊>}\,?\,) \quad \text{[C\overset{\circ}{o}]}$$

$$\text{<C̊>}\ \text{[C\overset{\circ}{a}]}$$

SM (Macs 49–51). At the outset of his discussion of SM pointing, Macuch cautions us that "{a}bsolute Konsequenz war von den Samaritanern bei ihrer Vokalisation genau so wenig zu erwarten wie bei ihrer konsonantischen Schrift. . ." and reminds us again toward the end of his treatment of "dem inkonsequenten und uneinheitlichen Gebrauch der sam. Vokalzeichen." Against this backdrop, the two systems of SM pointing are set forth in (21J), (i) portraying the native system and (ii) that adapted from Arabic. Presumably under the symmetricizing pressure of system (i), which is fully supralinear, the Arabic palatal point *kasra* of system (ii) was often superposed (<C̄>), leading immediately to confoundment with conventionally superposed *fatḥa*, signaling a low vowel. As a consequence of this, in manuscripts so affected <C̄> excludes only [CŮ]. Adding to the ambiguity, the two systems could apparently be intermingled; and Macuch tells us of a manuscript where [CĪ̊] is spelled either <C̄> or <Č>. He tells us of several other intricacies as well, not to be detailed here. In default of carefully assessing manuscripts one by one for their idiosyncracies in deploying points, great caution is recommended in using these diacritics toward the phonetic interpretation of SM.

(21J) (i)   <C̀>   [CĬ]   <Ĉ> [CŮ]

      <Č>   [Ce̊]

      <C̄>   [Cæ̊]   <Ċ> [Cå̧]

   (ii)   <C̣>, <C̣̄> [CĬ]   <C̣> [CŮ]

        kasra   *ḍamma*

                 <C̄> [CÅ̊]

                 fatḥa

                 <(C)ˀ̃> [(C)Ā]

                 madda

                 <Ċ> [CĀ], *or* [CÅ̊] *with prothetic* [Å̊](§17.18)

21.5. The Representation of Reduced Vowels

In TR, CP, G, and TL, matres lectionis may have been occasionally used to signal reduced vowels just as they were used to signal short vowels—except that shorts were probably so represented more frequently. That is, for these dialects the first three columns in (21G) might be perhaps more accurately labeled *ĬC, ŬC, ĂC*.[17] Similarly, the pointing systems used for Bab B, TR (both registers), and CP may also have been extended to signal explicitly colored reduced vowels, i.e., the so-called *ḥatafim*—see §17.23 for these; for the vowel points, see (21H) (column 2) and (21I). The hedged wording in the attribution of *V̆*-representation—"may have been . . . used," "might be . . . labeled"—alludes to the possibility, discussed in §17.23, that reduced vowels symbolized in the manners just discussed may actually be short vowels promoted from reduced.

For SM and TL, the question of *V̆*-representation is intricately tied up in various ways with the traditional pronunciations used as vehicles for providing these dialects with a phonetic interpretation. As discussed in the following chapter (§22), the trad prons of at least SM and Yem TL *may* reflect bona fide later stages of the dialects—the Yem TL trad pron provisionally subject to a few prosodic modifications, as suggested in §22.2. With these qualifications in mind, SM, to take its trad pron at face value, has: (α) by the Samaritan Circuit (smc) (§22.1 (22B) (ii)) promoted its equivalents of *V̆* in the other dialects to *V̊*, orthographically represented in the ways appropriate for *V̊* treated earlier above ((21G), (21J)); (β) by the same smc (re)introduced [ə], not necessarily reduced, as a reflex of posttonic closed-syllabic *Ĭ*, and hence spelled as appropriately for *Ĭ* (again (21G) and (21J)). We now turn to (further) discussion of TL, along with B, TR, and SR. (M is treated separately, in §21.8.)

For the remaining systems to be discussed (B, SR, TL, SR), a distinction must be drawn between reduced vowels of implicit and explicit chroma (color), traditionally referred to as *schwa* and *ḥataf*, respectively. As discussed in §17.23, the actual phonetic distinction that should be attributed to schwa vs. ḥataf remains an unsettled matter. At least this is so on the side of schwa, because, while it is rather clear that ḥatafim should be understood as chromatic vowels of the normal sort (specifiable in terms of height, tongue advancement, lip contouring) but with reduced energy (notably, extra short with diminished articulatory space), it is largely unclear whether schwa should be understood as a reduced vowel with coloring sui generis—likely mid central-to-front unrounded—or rather as a family of reduced phones with precise coloring determinable by the phonetic environment in a way so automatic to native/competent users of the language that the Masoretes (or analogous language scholars in other traditions) felt that one orthographically undifferentiated symbol would suffice.

Whatever the ultimate disposition of the distinction, in the various systems to be considered, schwa is represented with *one* symbol (when represented at all) while the ḥatafim are represented with *several* symbols (when represented at all).

In <u>Tiberian systems</u> (with the exception of the way Morag deploys his version to convey Yem trad pron of TL, to which we shall return), no distinction in *symbol* is made between representing true schwa—so-called *šĕva na9*, "mobile schwa"—[ə], and absence of any sound under certain syllabic conditions (after the first member of a consonant cluster, and in auslaut after the second member as well)—so-called *šĕva naḥ*, "quiescent schwa". Both are symbolized by an infraposed pairs of dots arranged vertically, in this book transcribed <C:>.[18]

In <u>Babylonian systems</u>, on the other hand, only true schwa (šĕva na9) is represented, by a supraposed horizontal stroke slightly tilted down to the right, in this book transcribed <Cə̆>.

Some examples: Tib B [bə̆nás] 'er zürnte' spelled <b:nas> (ta9am, §21.7, here and in other examples in this section omitted) Bab B[bə̆nés] spelled <bə̆nes> (BL 102), Tib B [tištə̆víq] 'sie wird überlassen' <tiš:t:viq> Bab B [tištə̆véq] <tistə̆veq> (BL 107); Sab TR (The Sabbionetan register is couched in Tiberian, §0.1) [yə̆9ibǽr] 'geht vorüber' <y:9iybær> Bab TR [yə̆9ibǽr] <yə̆9iyBær> (Da 269), Sab TR [tiḥbót] 'schlägst ab' <tiḥ:Bowṭ> Bab TR [tæḥbót] <tæḥBowṭ> (Da 270f.), Tib B [9ăváðt] 'du hast gedient' <9ăvaðt:> (BL 129) Bab TR [9ə̆vǽðṭ] <9ə̆væðṭ> (Da 260).

Although both Margolis and Morag use the Tiberian system in representing their respective trad prons of TL, Margolis deploys the notation strictly in accordance with the conventional rules, including the matter of schwa, while Morag leaves the first member of a consonant cluster unadorned. Thus, Ash TL [qə̆tált] 'you killed' <q:talt:> (Mar 159*) Yem TL [qə̆tǽlt] <q:tælt:> (Mor 381), Ash TL [tiqtól] 'you'll kill' <tiq:tol> (Mar 159*) Yem TL [tiqtúl] <tiqtuwl> (Mor 381). This decision of Morag's on consonant clusters makes possible an unambiguous interpretation of two adjacent <C> letters—cluster or noncluster?—in a way beyond the powers of standard Tiberian (as Margolis's) without appeal to ancillary symbols (like *meteg*, §21.7); e.g., the quasi-minimal pair of the fs sim participle, one with long 1ʃ (-css, §17.4), the other with short 1ʃ (+css)—[qāṭŏlā́] spelled <qaṭ:laʔ> vs. [qæṭlā́] spelled <qæṭlaʔ> (Mor 132).

SR usually leaves [ŏ] unsymbolized, but occasionally in poetry marks it with an infraposed horizontal stroke in which event, and only in which event, the transcription <Cŏ> will be employed. Thus, from The Life of Saint Ephrem (prose), Jac SR [lŏtáš] 'schärfte' <lṭaš>, but from a poem by this saint, Jac SR [rŏðáw] 'sie lebten' <rŏðaw> (B 25*, 45*).

Chromatic reduced vowels, the so-called ḥatafim, are represented in Tiberian B as amalgams of the relevant vowel point (segol, pataḥ, kamac) with the schwa diacritic, and are transcribed in this book <ĕ, ă, ŏ>; e.g., Tib B [ʔămár] 'sagte' <ʔamar>, [ʔăxúlī] 'iss (fs)!' <ʔăxuliy>, [ʔĕmár] 'sage (ms)!' <ʔĕmar> (BL 139). In Babylonian B, ḥatafim (assuming they exist, which is the provisional interpretation of this book, §17.23.3) are transcribed with the same vowel point as the corresponding full (short) vowel, thus answering to the first two Tiberian forms just cited, Bab B [ʔǽmǽr] <ʔæmær>, [ʔíxúlī] <ʔixuliy> (lc).[19]

While Bab TR works out like Bab B, Tib TR (including Sab TR) differs from Tib B in representing some ḥataf vowels with the corresponding full-vowel point. This at least holds of ḥatafim for which the Tiberian system provides no special symbols, notably [ĭ]: thus, Sab [yi9ĭróq] <yi9iyroq> (§17.23.3)—though, once again, the possibility cannot be excluded that at least some such vowels are actually promoted, full vowels. On the other hand, where the Tiberian system does provide a conventional symbol, that may be used— e.g., tb[ʔæ9ǽvǽr] <ʔæ9ǽvær>; but the possibility cannot be excluded, in the reverse direction to that suggested for [ĭ] <i(y)>, that Tib/Sab TR may sometimes employ <æ> for [ǽ] despite the availability of a symbol for ḥataf pataḥ; thus answering to <ʔæ9ǽvær> just cited, the Sabbionetan subregister shows <ʔæ9æbær> (lc)—for more on all this, see §9.3.1. (Since Dalman adduces only one instance of Sabbionetan <ĕ>, this graphie is interpreted as [ŏ]—admittedly an uncomfortable decision; see §17.23.3 for discussion.)

While Ash TL treats ḥatafim, both in phonetic realization and graphemic representation, in the same way as Tib B does, Yem TL shows no ḥatafim at all—though Morag records schwa (spelled < : >, above) as being realized by a family of context-sensitive allophones (§22.2).

SR likewise shows no ḥatafim.

21.6. Accentual Diacritics (*tĕ9amim*)

The books of the Tiberian Bible—including the Biblical Aramaic books of Daniel and Ezra—are scored by a system of primarily musicological diacritics called *tĕ9amim*, "accents" (singular *ta9am*). Tĕ9amim incidentally provide a good deal of important linguistic information, primarily as concerns stress and boundaries.

Viewed from the vantage of their bearing on linguistic phenomena in B, tĕ9amim may be ranked into three or perhaps four degrees of strength, as portrayed in (21K).

In a largely regular but not altogether exceptionless way, the distribution of accents calibrates with the distribution of various B linguistic properties: (α) most tĕ9amim graphically modify the syllable bearing the primary stress (being supra/infraposed to the syllable's graphemic nucleus);[20] (β) $<\overset{p}{\underset{p}{V}}>$ marks vowels bearing pausal stress, $[\overset{''}{V}]$, as often does $<\overset{p/d}{V}>$; (γ) $<\underset{p}{V}>$ marks the word ending a major prosodic domain, i.e., one bounded by ‖; (δ) similarly, $<\overset{d}{V}>$ marks the word ending a disjunctive prosodic domain, bounded by #; (ε) the domain-marking function of $<\overset{p/d}{V}>$ varies between that of $<\underset{p}{V}>$ and that of $<\overset{d}{V}>$; (ζ) $<\overset{c}{V}>$ marks the word ending either a conjunctive prosodic domain (bounded by $\overset{c}{V}$) or a clitic prosodic domain (bounded by =). (For ‖, $\overset{d}{\#}$, $\overset{c}{\#}$, =, see §20.3.)

In turn, the stresses/boundaries so (indirectly) signaled by the tĕ9amim correlate in various ways with linguistic processes, usually as triggers (e.g., $[\overset{''}{V}]$ as trigger for tln) or enablers/inhibitors (e.g., spr fails to apply across ‖ or $\overset{d}{\#}$); see again §20.3.

(21K) rank	label	transcription	tĕ9amim (*rarely occurring items omitted*)
I (*strongest*)	pausal	$<\overset{p}{V}>$	atnaḥ, siluk
IIa	pausal/ disjunctive	$<\overset{p/d}{V}>$	zakef
IIb	disjunctive*	$<\overset{d}{V}>$	tifḥa, rĕvia9, zarka, pašta, yĕtiv, tĕvir, gereš, pazer, tĕliša gĕdola, lĕgarmeh
III (*weakest*)		$<\overset{c}{V}>$	munaḥ, mĕhupax,
	conjunctive*		merxa, darga, ʾazla, tĕliša kĕtana

*Generically, *contextual*.

A few examples:
$<hi\theta{:}y{:}h\overset{p}{\underset{\sim}{i}}v>$, marked by siluk, (Ezra 6:4) spelling [hiθyŏšhĭ̈v] 'shall be given' with tln (§17.29) induced by pausal stress on 2ʃ, the pausal stress in turn induced by the fact that the word so marked ends a major prosodic domain (bounded by ‖).[21] Contrast this with $<yi\theta{:}9\check{a}v\overset{d}{\underset{\sim}{e}}\eth>$, marked by tifḥa (Ezra 6:11) spelling [yiθ9ăvéð] 'it shall be made' where tln fails to apply because the contextual accent ([é]) is not prominent enough to trigger vowel lengthening.

(Observe also a chain reaction in this pair of cases: the length induced by $\overset{"}{V}$ in the former case inhibits mid (§17.11), so that the stressed vowel surfaces as [ī] rather than @[e̊]; while conversely in the second case, $\acute{V}$ fails to induce lengthening so that mid successfully applies with the consequence that *í* → [é].)

<ʔăz̪ăluw viv:hiylw>, ʔazla (and mĕhupax), (Ezra 4:23) [ʔăz̪ălū # vi=vhīlū̆] 'went û̆ in=haste', where the conjunctive accent ʔazla marking *ʔăzálū* indirectly signals a conjunctive boundary (#) between *ʔăzálū* and the immediately following word, and # is weak enough for the power of spirantization (§5.1) to go right through it with the consequence that *ū* can change the *b*-anlaut of the following word to the spirant [v-].[22]

21.7. Other Graphemic Devices

B. If only *one* function should be borne by the grapheme *meteg*, to be transcribed <Ṿ>, it would be *secondary stress*, *whether* induced on a pretonic syllable separated from the primary stress by at least one stressless syllable (<y:hǫwv:ðuwnᵈ> [yə̆hǫ̆və̆ðun] 'they shall ask mercy', Dan 2:18; <yiš:tax:l:lûwn> [yĭštaxlə̆lū̆n] 'they will be repaired', Ezra 4:13, 16) *or* demoted from a primary stress on a proclitic constituent (<lẹ̆h=hі̂y?> [lệh=hі̂] 'it (fs) is his', Dan 2:19)[23] *or* with both of these conditions obtaining simultaneously, the demoted stress *either* remaining in situ ([wə̆lḁ̪=lɛhĕ̆wốn] 'but they shall not be', Dan 2:43) *or* giving evidence of stress retraction (cf. (20J) (iv) in §20.3) ([lèhĕ̆wē=vằh] 'shall be in it', Dan 2:41). Interestingly, there are also a few cases of secondary-stressed *schwa*; <t:ḥaḥăwŏ̃n> [tə̆ḥaḥawốn] 'you shall tell', Dan 2:6; [bə̆nē=ʔănɔ̄šɔ́] 'the children of men', Dan 2:28.[24]

When *X* is procliticized to *Y*, this is normally signaled orthographically by placing a raised horizontal stroke between the two constituents, a stroke known as *makef* and transcribed in this book with the equal sign, a symbol that is also used for the corresponding clitic boundary (§20.3): <X=Y> spelling [X=Y]. Some examples are given in the preceding paragraph.

The end of a Biblical verse is made explicit by the grapheme *sof pasuk*, a vertical alignment of two diamonds following the verse's last word. In this book, sof pasuk will be transcribed <‖>, likewise used for the major boundary (§20.3), appropriately since a Biblical verse (virtually) always coincides with the final edge of a major prosodic domain. Thus ending the first Aramaic verse in the Book of Daniel (2:6): <. . .wufir:šḗh ḥaḥawŏniy‖> [. . .ûfiršḗh # ḥaḥăwŏnī‖].

CP. SR. Two diacritics originating in SR are occasionally used: (α) a single supraposed dot (in SR called *sə̆yɔ̄mɔ̄*, "setting") indicating a 3fs reading of <-h> (rather than 3ms), to be transcribed <-ḣ>, in CP interpretable as [-å̆h] (as opposed to 3ms [-Íh]), e.g., <qwṭ9ḣ> 'hau sie ab!'; and in SR as [-Āh] (vs. 3ms [-ēh]), e.g., <qṭlTḣ> 'du hast sie getödtet'; (β) a pair of supraposed dots (*sə̆yɔ̄mē*, "settings") indicating plurality, to be transcribed <C̈>, in CP usable with plural-subject verbs at large (e.g., <nTB̊l9> 'wir werden verschlungen') but in SR stylized in the verb as a mark of fp subject (e.g., <q̊ṭaly > 'sie töteten', <nεṭlɔn > 'sie werden töten'). See Sg 6, 80; Ns 7, B 11.

Other SR diacritics include *linea occultans,* indicating nonpronunciation (silent letter): §8.1.4, §8.2.1, §9.2.2, §21. n. 6, §25. (And in this connection, note that another way of indicating silence of a letter in SR is to leave it unvocalized within an otherwise vocalized word; e.g., <ṭaly> [qǒṭál], cited immediately above. There is some evidence, moreover, that silent <y> in SR developed a more or less purely morpheme-representing function, denoting femininity; see §7.2 n. 13.)

TL. Of the Tiberian devices treated above for B, Margolis avails himself only of *meteg* in his conveyance of Ashkenazic trad pron. However, his conditions for use of this diacritic are a bit different; see the discussion in §17.15.1 n. 65.[25]

21.8. Mandaic Orthography

Mandaic is renowned as the sole Classical Aramaic dialect to have gained a full-blown alphabetic system by generalizing matres lectionis to vowel letters on formal and functional par with consonant letters. All other systems that developed full alphabetic potential did so by supplementing the vowel function of matres lectionis with ancillary pointing systems.[26]

A chart summarizing the fundaments of M writing and its transcription appears in (21L).

Observe that upon depharyngealization of *ḥ* to *h* (§9.3.2), the old letter for *ḥ* became morphologically specialized for spelling suffixal -*h* of 3ms -*Íh* and 3fs -*ắh*, desinences which subsequently > [-ī], [-ā] by hap (§9.2.2), a morphemic spelling which Macuch in his (co)publications renders as <ẖ> and the present author as <H> in his. All other instances of M [h], whether < *ḥ* or ≤ *h*, are synchronically spelled <h>, with the M reflex of the original Aramaic letter for *ḥ:*, e.g., <hauitak> 'I showed thee' (DM 134), [hawwīθắx] < *ḥawwītắk(a)*; <huit> 'I was' (DM 133), [hǒwíθ] < *hawít*.

Another instance of morphemic spelling is the special form of <d> molded to represent the subordinating proclitic [d(ǎ)=] < *ðī* , Macuch-transcribed as <ḏ> and Malone-transcribed as <Δ> in this book (but as <D> in earlier publications).

The chart in (21M) displays the usual spellings of long and short vowels in anlaut, inlaut, and auslaut. The digraphs represent conventional spelling freezes upon the demise of *ʾ, *9 (adl, dgt). Auslaut <-ia> for [-Ī] (all auslaut vowels are long in M, as in most other A dialects) has at times been taken, probably correctly, to have originated in historical spelling of determinate masculine plural -*ē* < *-ayyā, <-ʾy> (for the enabling morphophonological change, see Brockelmann 1908: 454). In anlaut, <eu> is by far more common than <au>.[27]

Though <e> is the usual spelling of anlaut [Ĭ], this grapheme at times appears in inlaut and auslaut as well (e.g., in forms of √hwy 'be'; impf 3ms [lehwî] spelled <lihuia> ~ <lehuia>, impa ms [hŏwî] spelled <huia> ~ <hue>—DM 133). Though such use of <e> is rare in most contexts, it is rather frequent in spelling [Ĭ] adjacent to [y] (which latter is always spelled <i>); e.g., [nĭyafrŏšán] 'instructeth me' <neiaprišan>, DM 381. (This use of <e> for a palatal vowel adjacent to [y] also extends to reduced Ĭ; see below.)[28]

(21L) Hebrew t r a n s l i t e r a t i o n   phonetic/morphological values

equivalent	Nm	DM, Macm	this book	(when not in digraphs)
א	א	a	<a>	[å̊]
ב	ב	b	<b>	[b, β]
ג	ג	g	<g>	[g, γ]
ד	ד	d	<d>	[d, ð]
		ḏ	<Δ>	*proclitic* [d(ŏ)=]
ה	ה	h	<h>	[h] ̥
ו	ו	u	<u>	[w, Ů]
ז	ז	z	<z>	[z]
ח	ח̄	ḥ	<H>	*suffixal 3ms* [-ī], *3fs* [-ā]
ט	ט	ṭ	<ṭ>	[ṭ] ̥
י	י	i	<i>	[y, Ĭ]
כ,ך ,ך̄	ך ,כ	k	<k>	[k, x]
ל	ל	l	<l>	[l]
מ, ם	מ ,ם	m	<m>	[m]
נ, ן	נ ,ן	n	<n>	[n]
ס	ס	s	<s>	[ṣ]
ע	ע	ꜥ	<e>	[Ĭ]
פ, ך	פ ,ך	p	<p>	[p, f]
צ, ץ	צ ,ץ	s	<s>	[ṣ]
ק	ק	q	<q>	[q]
ר	ר	r	<r>	[r]
ש	ש	s	<š>	[š]
ת	ת	t	<t>	[t, θ]

(21M)	/#__	/-__-	/-__#
Ĭ	<e>	<i, e>	<ia, e>
Ů	<eu, au>		<u>
å̊		<a>	

Mandaic representation of reduced vowels is via the hierarchy

<∅>, <i>(~<e>/y) ≫ <a> ≫ <u>,

i.e., most frequently [V̆] either goes unrepresented (<∅>) or is spelled with palatal <i> [29] (for <e>, see below), less frequently with low <a>, and rarely with labial <u>—the letters so used probably but not necessarily capturing the actual chroma of the reduced vowel token in question; see §17.23. When the choice is palatal, <e> at times appears instead of / in alternation with <i> when adjacent to [y] (cf. above for the analogous spelling of [Ï̊]); e.g., [bĭyún] 'they sought me' <beiun> (~ <biun>, where [Ĭ] goes unrepresented)—and for <i> in this function, [bĭyúx] 'they sought thee' <biiuk> ~ <biuk>: DM 44.)

For "abagadical pronunciation" (reading pronunciation), see §22.3 n. 8 and references there cited.

Notes to §21

[1] Mandaic is excluded from consideration until §21.8, where it is granted special treatment.

[2] For demurrals on the account here proffered of the rationale for the Aramaic one-to-many spellings, see Degen's discussion in De 32–35. Note, however, that he offers a different interpretation of the Aramaic reflex of *ð, a difference that renders his arguments less applicable to the overall account adopted here.

[3] *dahabā́ < **ðahabā́ by occlusion (§17.14), the spirant-stop relation mediated by occ having nothing directly to do with the stop-spirant nexus triggered by spr under discussion here.

[4] [θə̆hōōð9ŭnnánī] instantiates spr across a weak (clitic-like) boundary, [hén lɔ̄́#
θə̆hōōð9ŭnnánī] 'unless you tell me' (Dan 2:5), where [lɔ̄́] is accentually scored with a conjunctive accent, mĕhupax; see §20.3 and §21.6 below. For the minimal pair 2ms [hištə̆xáḥat] – 3fs [hištə̆xáḥaθ], see §15.3.1.3.

[5] (a) Dageš is also a feature of Margolis's and Morag's TL transcriptions (Mar, Mor), but their use of Tiberian orthography is in the spirit of a modern scholarly convenience rather than as a naïve orthographic framework for texts presumed to be original by the scribes or editors. (b) In some texts, dageš is paired with *rafe*, an antithetical diacritic marking *P T K B D G* as [f θ x v ð γ]. However, rafe does not appear in the sources consulted for this book.

[6] (a) However, SR does have a device for indicating nonpronunciation of a letter, a supraposed or infraposed horizontal stroke, *linea occultans* (in the former case also called *marhăṭ̄nɔ̄*); B11. It might be noted that nonpronunciation refers to the failure to realize the phonetic content unmarkedly conveyed by the letter in question, though the phonological/historical presence of that content may continue to make itself felt. Thus in the word [mə̆ðĭ̊ṭṭɔ̄́] 'town' ⇐ /mV̊dīntā/ (< *madīnṭā́) the geminate [tt], assimilated from *nt* by rna (§17.21), is spelled <n̄T > though the <n> is not precisely unpronounced, realized as it is by/as the first mora of [tt]. (Observe that synchronic postulation of /n/ is justified by homoparadigmatic continuation of the absolute-state form of this noun, [mə̆ðīṇɔ̄́]; Payne Smith 1903: 252.)

(b) CP has a stop-spirant marking system nominally similar to that of SR—yet its use is apparently so chaotic and helterskelter (Sg 5) that it will not be appealed to at the service of phonetic interpretation in this book. (For the special case of *T*, see §12.2 n. 12.)

[7] Omitted from (21D) are the variable gemination of *b* in trad pron /9V__V (§22 n. 2a, (22B) (ι, κ)), and the regular manifestation of **w* as t[w] or t[wŏ] in the reflexes of the conjunctive proclitic **wa=* (§22.1).

[8] The change "reocclusion" mediating stages II and III applies vacuously in the case of *p* > t[b] and *pp* > t[bb]; see §5.3 n. 13, where the overarching change is demonstrated to affect nonlabials as well.

[9] "minor exceptions": for instance, the occasional use of <w(w)> rather than <B> for [v/β] (e.g., in G, Da 104f.).

[10] "statistical implication," "virtually always": in principle, the interplay of spirantization and reduction makes it possible to get geminate fricatives, like [vv] from *bV̊b* when *V̊* is deleted. A Hebrew example is [ů̄vēra x̠x̠ɔ́] 'and He will bless thee' (Deut 7:13); see THP 167. To date, no compelling Aramaic instances have come to light; but the mechanism of processes adopted predicts that they could.

[11] The use of <y> in rendering noncoalesced reflexes like [Ay] is strictly speaking consonantal spelling (§21.1); but such will be included here anyway because it is frequently impossible to be sure whether coalescence (or some other monophthongizing process) has occurred.

[12] While generally the dialects that have truly undergone lap update their orthography in failing to represent the apocopated vowel, *[-V̄] <-Γ> > [-∅] <-∅>, SR stands alone in showing historical spelling for this nexus in the case of the chromatic vowels: *[-ī] <-y> > [-∅] <-y>, *[-ū] <-w> > [-∅] <-w>. Since, moreover, lap in these cases lives on as a rule (d-lap > s-lap) because of alternation between auslaut [-∅] and homoparadigmatic inlaut positions where [-ī-], [-ū-] are maintained, hence /ī, ū/ ⇒ [∅] /__#, we are eo ipso facto dealing with *morphophonemic spelling*—the silent letters continue to convey (parts of) living morphemes still pronounced in other environments. Another case of morphophonemic spelling in SR was considered in n. 6 where <n̄T > spelling [tt] in the determinate form of the lexeme 'town', [mŏðī t̠t̠ɔ́], correlates with /nt/ by virtue of the *n* living on elsewhere in the paradigm, e.g., absolute [mŏðī n̠ɔ́]. (The cause-and-effect relation between historical and morphophonemic spelling is somewhat similar to that between sound changes and synchronic rules: while in each pair some instances of the former live on as instances of the latter, not all do. Thus, although the cluster [bb] in the SR lexeme [gabbɔ̄r] 'mighty' is spelled <n̠B>, unlike the case of 'town' the **nb* has no living manifestation anywhere in the synchronic paradigm, where [bb] is constant—even in the related int verb; see Payne Smith 1903: 74.)

[13] Or both, whether concurrently or in tandem. For the former case, consider instances of a ml simultaneously spelling not only, say, a long vowel qua long vowel, but at the same time a living consonantal morphophoneme that fails to surface phonetically; thus 1√y in the B causative verb 'bring', which in the labial passive pf 3fs coalesces (undergoes s-coa) in [hē̠θáyiθ], spelled <ey>, though it fails to in the active pf 3ms [ha y̠θī], spelled <ay>—the <y> in both instances spelling 1√|y| (historically < *1√ʔ by car, §9.2.1.2, irrelevantly here). For the second case type, in tandem involvement of both ml and morphophonemic spelling, consider SR <w> spelling the mp suffix /ū/ in auslaut where it is no longer pronounced, hence [∅], though it continues to be realized phonetically in inlaut—this is the morphophonemic function. However, in the earlier period when the auslat <w> was pronounced (i.e., preceding lap, §17.9), it served as a ml for [ū] without ever having seved as a true consonant letter (having rather acquired

the ml function through generalization, in the way discussed in §21.2). Thus, in temporal tandem, <w> qua ml ∧ <w> qua morphophoneme.

[14] Similar here is the Arabic usage of so-called *hamzatu 'l-waṣl*, a <ʾ> marking the onset of prothetic syllables and realized as [ʾ] in sentence-initial position. If the preceding word ends in a vowel, the <ʾ> remains silent and the vowel of its syllable is elided; i.e., <. . .V'#ʾVC. . .> is pronounced [. . .V'C. . .] and <. . . C'#ʾVC. . .> is pronounced [. . . . C'VC. . .]. (This contrasts with *hamzatu 'l-qaṭ9*, a <ʾ> whose realization is [ʾ] in all contexts, notably manifesting √ʾ.)

[15] It must be cautioned that the distribution of silent <Γ>, in any dialect, for the most part simply mimics the distribution of *Γ lost to the ravages of sound change, without necessarily giving any information on the presence of the abstract linguistic entities called ghost consonants. On the other hand, if we assume that ghost consonants actually exist (a position argued for in Malone 1991), silent <Γ> constituites a priori a likely gauge for their presence, if only imperfectly. It will be especially useful to be on the lookout for *deviations* of silent <Γ> patterning from that dictated by historical spelling tout court. All this said, one plausible function for ghost consonants is that of providing *default onsets*, on the assumption that at least some structural requirements for syllables can be filled by phonetically null elements. Consider in this light SR plain sim pf [ɛxál] <ʾɛxal> 'hat gegessen' and rmp sim pf [ɛθɛxél] <ʾɛθʾɛxél>. For most languages, a string [. . .VCV. . .] will syllabify [. . .V|CV. . .], grouping the intervocalic C rightward to become onset of the second syllable (rather than leftward to become coda of the first); and if this regularity holds for SR, syllabification will render [ɛ|xál], [ɛ|θɛ|xél]—graphemically <ʾɛ|xal>, <ʾɛ|θʾɛ|xɛl>, where the anlaut <ʾ>s straightforwardly distribute as ghost onsets, but not <ʾ> in <θʾɛ>, inasmuch as the actual onset is [θ]. We might of course conclude that the <ʾ> in <θʾɛ> is not meant to signal a ghost consonant to begin with, being no more than an instance of historical spelling. However, there is at least one writing system that functions just this way and where historical spelling is ruled out. This is Korean *hankul*, where empty onsets are systematically spelled with a silent <ŋ>; and where, moreover, morphological grouping preempts phonological syllabification in determining the distribution of silent <ŋ> (for some discussion of this, see Martin and Lee 1986: xxii–xxix, §§ IV and VIII). The SR spellings follow suit, <ʾɛ|xal> being dictated wholly by phonological syllabification with no conflict from morphology, but the rmp form being rather <ʾɛθ|ʾɛ|xal>, where the morphological unity of the prefix is orthographically reflected as a graphemic priority, thereby stranding the second <ɛ> as a graphemic syllable and so completing its spelling with <ʾ> for the onset. In systems of this type, the orthographic module shows morphological dictates overriding the phonological (specifically phonetic) module. Only further exploration can determine whether this possible homology between Korean and Syriac is real or coincidental.

[16] (a) Though CP points in manuscripts assume the shape of dots, in this book they are transcribed with small circles so as to forfend against confuson with the (infraposed) dot transcribing emphasis/pharyngeality. Thus, e.g., <ṭrq> 'certavit' (Sl 77) is interpreted as [ṭĭráq] (or [ṭĭréq], §12.2 n. 11) where the infraposed "o" renders the vowel point, and "." the emphasis (uvularization) of the anlaut coronal stop. (b) For <Ç> [ĬC], note <9ĮTwn> [9ə̆lĮltŬn], §3.3.

[17] Observe that in earlier dialects mls are never used to represent V̊ (and thus a fortiori not V̊ either).

[18] (a) Consequently, in such systems, <C:> is per se ambiguous between [Cə̆] and [C], though other factors may—in fact, usually do—lead to disambiguation. One factor is phonological context, so that, e.g., <#C:> will invariably represent [#Cə̆] given the general Aramaic prohibition against word-initial consonant clusters (the possible scattered exceptions to this prohibition are absent from Tiberian-served dialects). Another factor is ancillary orthographic symbols, of which two will receive attention in this chapter: cooccurrence (as a complex symbol) with a vowel point, making for a ḥataf vowel—see directly below; and cooccurrence with a so-called *meteg* under the vowel signaling the nucleus of the immediately preceding symbol—see §17.15.1 n. 15 and §21.7.

(b) Note that the pair of vertically arranged dots constantly investing unpointed word-final Tiberian <K> (see (21A)) are in this book *not* taken as instantiating schwa but as merely homographic with it. However, when independently of this the rules of Tiberian pointing call for schwa <:> in an auslaut <C>, specifically as the final <C> in an orthographic cluster, by haplograhy only one set of points appear in <K#>; e.g., Sab <yɔs:K:>, not @<y s:K::> —§17.6.2 n. 12.

[19] For the difference in vowel coloring between Tib B [ă] and Bab B [ĭ], see §17.23.3 (17.23B), where there is also discussion of the fact that the Bab B counterpart of Tib B [ʔə̆már] is [ʔemár], with promoted 1ʔ.

[20] Exceptions are so-called *postpositive* or *prepositive* tĕ9amim, which graphemically modify a word at its end or beginning, repetively. In their rare appearance in this book, such tĕ9amim will be transcribed with a small raised "d" or "c" at the appropriate edge of the word.

[21] In the Tiberian graphemic system, ‖ is sometimes—as here—symbolized by a pair of vertically arranged diamonds called *sof pasuk*, signaling the end of a Biblical verse. See §21.7.

[22] (a) The rather slight treatment of B tĕ9amim presented in this section is largely based on the framework employed in THP for Hebrew and further informed by Joüon 1923: §15. (b) The assumption of "prosodic boundaries" corresponding to classes of tĕ9amim in an almost one-to-one fashion ("disjunctive prosodic domain," etc.) is largely makeshift in default of a full-blown study of Aramaic prosodology in its own right; for suggestive relevant work on Hebrew, see Aronoff 1985, Malone 1989d, Dresher 1994. (c) Though the system of tĕ9amim employed for B is likely the most thorough and developed of extant systems (being part and parcel of that devised by the Tiberian Masoretes for the Bible at large), there are a few other ta9am systems for other sorts of A dialect, unfortunately beyond the pale of this book.

[23] [lĕh=hī̆], illustrating secondary and stronger stresses adjacent over the clitic boundary, is cited in default of verb-containing instances in the corpus scanned for purposes of §21.7 (the Aramaic portions of Daniel 2 and Ezra 4 as presented in Kittel 1937).

[24] Assuming identification of secondary stress as the function of meteg is largely correct, this should be construed as a necessary but not also sufficient condition for the appearance of this diacritic, at least for the texts as presented in Kittel 1937: e.g., with [tə̆haḥăwṓn], contrast [tə̆haḥăwunnắnī] (Dan 2:9); with [wə̆lɔ̃=lɛhĕwṓn], contrast [lɔ̃=hištə̆xáḥ] (Dan 2:35).

[25] Discussion of "other graphemic devices" in this section is quite limited, being essentially restricted to devices attested in forms appearing in this book. For fuller treatment of devices at large, see pertinent grammars of the dialects. (Note especially Macuch's detailed consideration of SM, Macs 40–48.)

[26] (a) "fullblown alphabetic system," though lexically frozen traces of the old ḥaser (solely consonantal) orthography remain; e.g., <rba> 'great' [rabbā́] (cf. t&m[rábbā]; Macm 13, 504). For unmarked spelling of the same miškal-gizra (geminate segolate), cf. <sada> 'barrier' [saddā́] (t[sáddā́]); Macm 171.

(b) The major expressive advantage from generalizing mls to vowel letters consists in providing representation for short vowels (and to a lesser degree reduced vowels, as will be picked up later in the text). However, there was also some *loss* of expressive power, to the extent that with the older ml way of doing things the opposition [V̄′] ≠ [V̊′] was at least *statistically* conveyed by <W′> ≠ <∅>, a graphemic opposition neutralized once <W′> was extended to become the normal way of spelling [V′] long *or* short. At least on paper, this backlash may appear potentially noxious, especially when coupled with the fact that M possesses no device for indicating consonantal gemination. Thus, <QaSiM> may spell any of several miškalim: [QaSeM] (e.g., [šaméš] 'sun' . . . for the unreduced 1ʃ, see Malone 1969); [QaSSeM], [QāSeM], or [QaSSīM] (a three-way opposition illustrable on one and the same root, √bsm—int pf c[bassém] 'burned incense', sim participle c[bāsém] 'delighting (in something)', c[bassī́m] 'fragrant'; DM 48, 67).

[27] Indication of the anlaut as "#__" vs. auslaut as "-__#" accommodates the fact that [ō] 'or' < *ʔaw is spelled <eu>, not <u>.

[28] It is perhaps worth pondering that development of a letter originally representing the voiced pharyngeal *9, here <e>, to represent a palatal vowel (see (21L)) is also a hallmark of Punic and Yiddish.

[29] The choice <∅> ~ <i> seems to have pronounced morphological biases, e.g., <∅> being the prime choice for 1ʃ (notably for [Q̊SVM] of the sim pf/impa) while <i> may be more frequent than <∅> for 2ʃ. For more on the <∅> ~ <i> representation of [š], see §6.2.2.1.

22. Traditions of Pronunciation

22.1. Samaritan

The core hallmark of SM traditional pronunciation[1] will be taken to be the *Samaritan Circuit* (smc), a set of seven processes operative late enough in the history of the dialect not to have left much orthographic impact. Some facets of smc are reprises of earlier SM changes; this is notably true of *degutturalization* (dgt) and allied processes, precedent manifestations of which are treated in §9.

The smc is laid out in (22B), with sample derivations in (22C).

The section ends with consideration of a few trad pron issues outside smc.

Thumbnail *C* and *V* inventories for SM trad pron appear in (22A), length omitted; cf. §20 (20A, D , H).

(22A)

		t	ṭ		k	q
	b		d		g	
		f	s	ṣ	š	
			z			
	m		n			
			r			
			l	ļ		
	w		y		9	ʔ
		i	u			
		e	ə	o		
		æ	α			

(22B) (i) <u>The Samaritan Circuit</u> (smc) consists in a chain of at least seven late processes (spelled out in (ii–viii)) characterizing trad pron (for the possibility of a c-change between c-prm and c-pen, see §9.2.3.1 n. 28):

c-prm^c-pen^c-pra^c-dgt^c-vcr^c-ult^r-c-pra

(ii) *circuit promotion* (c-prm)

$\breve{V} \rightarrow \mathring{V}$, i.e., reduced vowels promote to short. (*Assumed exception:* the vowel of the conjunctive proclitic t[wə̆-] (see below, at the end of this section.)

(iii) *circuit penultimation* (c-pen)

Stress recedes to the penult.

(iv) *circuit prosodic adjustment* (c-pra)
    (α) Open unreduced syllables which are tonic or pretonic lengthen,

whereby short palatal vowels become $\bar{e}$ and short labial vowels become $\bar{u}$.

(α′) Especially when the syllable begins with 9, the next following *C* may lengthen instead of the nuclear vowel.[2]

(β) Open unreduced syllables which are posttonic shorten, whereby long palatal vowels or palatal-offgliding diphthongs become *i* (*lexical exception*: the 3ms suffix $\bar{e}$ retains mid coloring) and long labial vowels or labial-offgliding diphthongs become *u*.

(γ) Closed syllables shorten (low-vocalic syllables variably), whereby:

$$\acute{\overset{\circ}{I}}C\# \to \acute{e}C\#,\ \overset{\circ}{\check{I}}C\# \to \check{o}C\# \qquad \overset{\circ}{\acute{U}}C\# \to oC\#$$
$$\overset{\circ}{\check{I}}CC \to iCC \sim eCC \qquad\qquad \overset{\circ}{\check{U}}CC \to uCC$$
$$(\text{and } \overset{\circ}{\check{I}}ww \to iww \sim uww)$$

(v) *circuit degutturalization* (c-dgt)[3]

(α) $VH\# \to \bar{V}\#$

(β) $VHC'C \to \bar{V}C'C'V$, or occasionally $\bar{V}'CV$

(γ) $VC'HV \to VC'\bar{V}$

(δ) $VH'H'V'' \to \bar{V}\bar{V}'' \sim \bar{V}V''$

(ε) $\overset{\circ}{V}H'V'' \to \overset{\circ}{V}\bar{V}'' \sim \overset{\circ}{V}V''$

(ε) $\check{V}H'V'' \to V'' (\sim \bar{V}''?)$ (equivalent to c-sad, §9.2.1.2)

(ζ) in each of (α–ε), when $\check{V} \to \bar{V}$ /H and $\check{V} = I$ or U, $\bar{V} = \bar{e}$ or $\bar{u}$, respectively.

(22B) (vi) *circuit vowel cluster reduction* (c-vcr)

When a vowel group in hiatus is formed, $VV(')$, by the action of c-dgt (δ, ε), any of four outcome types are possible, choices among the four and details of specific resolutions governed by at best partially understood conditions:

(α) <u>nonresolution</u>: $VV' \to VV'$

(input strings found— *AI, AU*)

(β) <u>dissimilation</u> (<u>palatalization</u>): $VV \to VV'$

(input strings found— *AA*)

(γ) <u>gliding</u>: $VV(') \to V''W'W'V'''$

(input strings found— *AI, IA, UA, UU*)

(δ) <u>amalgamation</u>: $VV(') \to V''$

(input strings found— *AA, AI, IA, IU*)

(ε) whenever c-vcr leaves two vocalic nuclei in contact (α, β), hiatus is dispelled by ʔ.

(vii) *circuit ultimation* (c-ult)

A closed-syllabic long-vocalic ultima attracts the stress.

(viii) *reprise circuit prosodic adjustment* (r-c-pra)

(α) and (β) of c-pra (iv) ((γ) fails to reprise)

(22C) smc illustrations:[4]

(α) nið9ál   (β) wš̆=yiγ9Ű́n

	(α)	(β)
c-prm		
c-pen	níð9al	wš̆=yiγ9Ű́n
c-pra		wš̆=yéγ9on / wš̆=yíγ9on
c-dgt	níðāl	wš̆=yéγūn / wš̆= yíγūn
c-vcr		
c-ult	níðā́l	wš̆=yeγű́n / wš̆=yiγű́n
r-c-pra	néðā́l	wš̆=yēγű́n
	t[nēdā́l]	t[w yēgű́n]
	<nDḥl>	<wyGḥwn>
	'wir fürchten'	'und sie mögen kämpfen'
	(Macs 123)	(Macs 123)

(γ) ye9kămŰ̥́n (δ) ya9kemŰ̥́n (ε) iθămár

	(γ)	(δ)	(ε)
c-prm	ye9kamŰ̥n	ya9kemŰ̥n	iθamár
c-pen	ye9kámŰ̥n	ya9kémŰ̥n	iθámar
c-pra	ye9kā́mon	ya9kḗmon	ēθā́mar
c-dgt	yēkkā́mon	yākkḗmon	
	t[yēkkā́mon]	t[yākkḗmon]	t[ētā́mɑr]
	<yḥKmwn>	<yḥKmwn>	<ʔTʔmr>
	'sie wissen'	'sie (be)lehren'	'wurde gesagt'
	(Macs 172)	(Macs 172)	(Macs 172)

(ζ) yĕháβ (η) iθra99ám (θ) tĕ9abbár

	(ζ)	(η)	(θ)
c-prm	yeháβ		te9abbár
c-pen	yéhaβ	iθrá99am	te9ábbar
c-pra	yḗhaβ		tē9ábbar
c-dgt	yḗāβ	iθrā́ām	tēábbar
c-vcr	yḗβ	iθrā́m	tébbar
	t[yéb]	t[itrā́m]	t[tébbɑr]
	<yhB>	<ʔTrḥm>	<T9Br>
	'gab'	'erbarme dich!'	'du wirst überführen'
	(Macs 173)	(Macs 123)	(Macs 173)

(ι) tĕ9aβár   (κ) wš̆=9ăβárŰ̥́n / wš̆=9ăβárŰ̥́n

	(ι)	(κ)
c-prm	te9aβár	wš̆=9ăβárŰ̥n / wš̆=9ăβárŰ̥n
c-pen	te9áβar	wš̆=9aβárŰ̥n
c-pra	tē9áββar	wš̆=9aββā́ron
c-dgt	tēáββar	w=aββā́ron
c-vcr	tébβar	
	t[tébbɑr]	t[wɑbbā́ron]
	<T9Br>	<w9Brn>
	'du wirst übergehen'	'und sie kamen durch'
	(Macs 173)	(Macs 156)

(λ) ye99áθ (μ) yĕra99ém
c-prm yera99ém
c-pen yá99aθ yerá99em
c-pra yerá99ăm
c-dgt yḗāθ yērä́əm
c-vcr yíyyāθ yērä́ʾəm
c-ult yiyyä́θ
t[yiyyä́t] t[yērä́ʾəm]
\<yy9T>~\<y9T>~\<yʾ9T> \<yrḥm>
'wird herabsteigen' 'wird lieben'
(Macs 186) (Macs 174)

(ν) taṣlī́9 ~ taṣlá9 (ξ) w=appĕqéh
c-prm w=appeqéh
c-pen táṣlī9   táṣla9 w=appéqēh
c-pra táṣlə9 w=appḗqəh
c-dgt táṣlē   táṣlā w=appḗqē
c-vcr
c-ult
r-c-pra táṣli   táṣla w=appḗqe
t[táṣli] ~ [táṣlæ] t[wæbbéqe]
\<Tṣlyḥ> ~ \<Tṣlḥ> \<wʾPqh>
'es wird gelingen' (Macs 176) 'und brachte ihn heraus' (Macs 72)

(ο) mī́θ (π) mīθáθ
c-prm
c-pen mī́θaθ
c-pra méθ
t[mét] t[mī́tɑt]
\<myT> \<myTT>
'er starb' (Macs 190) 'sie starb' (Macs 190)

(ρ) gă9ázū (σ) yi9zä́
c-prm ga9ázū
c-pen yí9zē
c-pra gā9ä́zu yí9zi
c-dgt gāä́zu yézzi ~ yézi
c-vcr gāʾēzu
c-ult
t[gāʾézu] t[yézzi] ~ [yézi]
\<G9zw> \<yḥzy>
'sie haben überquert' 'sieht'
(Macs 144) (Macs 207)

Samaritan trad pron bears the mark of several other processes not strictly part of the Circuit, lacking as they do the applicational dependency defining the Circuit. These processes will be assumed, with little evidence, to applying following the Circuit, so that their effects show up in the trad prons provided in (22C) above:

(*) By what may be called *obstruent adjustment* (oba), all nonlabial spirants (slit fricatives) occlude (become homorganic stops), while labials become $b \sim f$ in accordance with the conditions detailed in §21.1 with (21D, E).

(*) Schwa aside (see below), the five-color system of later general Aramaic ($\overset{\circ}{\imath}, \overset{\circ}{e}, \overset{\circ}{a}, \overset{\circ}{o}, \overset{\circ}{u}$; §20.2 (20J)) maps onto the six-color system of SM trad pron (§20.2 (20H)) in an iconic, one-to-one fashion except for the split $\overset{\circ}{a} \to [\overset{\circ}{æ} \sim \overset{\circ}{\alpha}]$, by a group of processes generically falling to the bailiwick of *systemic vowel shift* (svs); §20.2 (γ). With the exception of the observations in §9.2.3.1, no thorough attempt will be made in this book to sort out the few conditioning factors largely submerged in apparent free variation; much useful discussion is provided in Macs 80–83.

(*) It is possible SM trad pron has two schwas quantitatively, a reduced-vocalic [ə̆] realized exclusively in proclitic [wə̆-] (invariantly transcribed vowelless by Macuch, as *w-*) and a full(short)-vocalic [ə] elsewhere, specifically as given by circuit prosodic adjustment (22B (iv) (γ)) (transcribed by Macuch as ẹ). If on the other hand SM trad pron schwa should be quantitatively unitary, it is probably reduced. Whatever the quantity, SM trad pron schwa should be taken qualitatively to be *either* out-and-out flat (unrounded) mid front—less likely—*or* flat mid central lying close to [ê] in phonetic space—more likely.

(*) Corresponding to *l* in the later Aramaic dialects at large, SM trad pron evinces a light [l] and a dark [ḷ], classified in this book as, respectively, (plain) dentoalveolar and uvularized (emphatic) dentoalveolar (§20 (20A)). Consolidating from Macuch's discussion (Macs 73f.), [ḷ] is for the most part evoked by regressive assimilation from: *either* low back , in which case the assimilatory power can move through an intervening consonant or (presumably conjunctive) word boundary (and hence a fortiori through a clitic boundary as well, §20.3); *or* from an emphatic consonant. Macuch does not tell us whether in this latter case, which appears to be the weaker of the two, a word boundary may intervene. Assuming it may, a rough-and-ready descriptive formulation would be:

(22D) l → ḷ /__(#̊, =) (C) {å̊, ṭ, ṣ, q}

22.2. Talmudic

While traditional pronunciations of SM and M were presented by the source scholar (in both cases, Rudolf Macuch) in versions of standardized Romanized phonetic transcription, the source scholars of TL (Shlomo Morag and Max Margolis) chose rather to avail themselves of Tiberian orthography—orthodox in Margolis's case, slightly modified in the case of Morag. As a consequence of the fact that this Tiberian orthography is not in the first place designed as a vehicle for unbiased phonetic notation, more interpretive conjecture was required in retranscribing both trad prons of TL into the symbolistic system adopted for this book than was needed for doing the same with SM or M trad pron. This requirement especially holds for Yemeni; see immediately below for specific interpretive liberties taken witrh transcriptions of both sorts of TL trad pron.

Yemeni TL. Morag's decision to transcribe his informants' performance of Yem trad pron into Tiberian orthography in the specific manner he did poses certain difficulties for retranscription into the system used in this book; in particular, concerning (α) schwa on the one hand, and (β) stress and vowel length on the other. These retranscriptional difficulties are aggravated by certain facets of of Yem trad pron itself, which neutralize some cardinal phonetic features of original spoken TL.

(α) Morag eschews ḥataf symbols, confining himself to < : > which, though usually or always unambiguous as bearing the value of šĕva na9, ɜ (§21.5), yet in actual trad pron reflects a family of colors depending (largely) on phonetic environment. The decision in this book is to follow Morag's (apparent) interpretation and transcribe any reduced vowel in Yem trad pron as [ɜ].

(β) Stress in actual Yem trad pron is seemingly variable, though tendentially dependent on number of syllables (2, 3) coupled with structural disposition thereof (open, closed). It is unclear whether true accentual minimal pairs are possible, or just more favored – less favored accentuations of given string types. Vowel length, in turn, is predictable in terms of stress, the accented syllable being the long one. The slippery nature of these structural assignments prompts the somewhat incautious decision in this book to impose stress and vowel length on Yem trad pron from diachronic extrapolation—as long as the level of confidence is high (and in default of this, appropriate hedges will be adopted, e.g., [V̥] in the case of a nonreduced vowel of uncertain length status, or leaving an uncertainly stressed word unadorned by "ʹ."[5]

A thumbnail sketch of Yem trad pron *C*s and *V*s appears in (22E), length omitted (cf. §20 (20A, D, H)).

Note the absence of a uvular position of articulation, *q* having been replaced by [g] (Mor 91) (though in this book retranscribed with *q* in cases where < *q* seems beyond doubt).

(22E)

p			t	ṭ		k		
b			d			g		
	f	θ	s	ṣ	š	x	h	h
	v	ð	z			γ		
m			n					
			r					
			l					
w				y		9	ʔ	

i		u
e	ə	o
æ		α

Ashkenazic TL. To judge prima facie, Margolis's Ash trad pron (as codified in Mar) would be quite similar to the pronunciation assumed for Biblical A, differing only by a few discrepancies in inventory (e.g., lacking *ś* (> *s* by snm, §17.27), perhaps showing *ĭ*, *ŭ* instead of *ĕ*, *ŏ*, §17.23.3) or in distribution (e.g., tolerating closed-syllabic unstressed *e* where B normally shows *ɛ* (by aop, §17.11.3)).[6] However, despite its preservation of certain plausibly original traits (Malone 1998b), the suspicion arises in a number of areas that Margolis's representation of TL pronunciation has been unduly schematized on the basis of standard Tiberian systems (notably Tib B) and to some extent reconstructed rather than transmitted (see, e.g., §17.23.1.2).[7]

While it is possible to glean a good deal about vowel length and stress from Margolis's (essentially traditional) deployment of vowel pointing and the diacritic *meteg* (see especially §17.15.1 n. 65), a certain amount of conjecture has proved unavoidably necessary. In the event a case was simply undecidable, uncertain (long/short) vowel length has been transcribed [V̥], while uncertainty as to a word's stressed syllable has led to simple omission of "ˊ" anywhere in the word.

At any rate, inventory sketches follow in (22F) (quantity abstracted out for consonants and full vowels, indicated only for reduced vowels) (cf. §20 (20A, D, G)).

(22F)

p			t	ṭ		k	q		
b			d			g			
	f	θ	s	ṣ	š	x		ḥ	h
	v	ð	z			γ			
m			n						
			r						
			l						
w				y		9	ʔ		

```
        i       u
        e       o
        ε       ɔ
            a
        ĭ       ŭ
            ă
```

22.3. Mandaic

The inventory of (Classical) M and its traditional pronunciation (by *tarmīdī*, Mandean priests, reading the sacred scriptures) are identical (22G)—subject to the nontrivial qualification that the interpretation of the Classical dialect itself is reconstructed.

Despite its conservative appearance in most respects save its loss of all gutturals but *h* (§9.3.2), the inventory itself is moot on distributional differences from earlier Aramaic (including, by hypothesis, M itself)—most notably the distribution of *f, θ, x, β, ð, γ*, which with a few salient exceptions pattern like the Modern dialect (Malone 1997) rather than like the Classical.[8]

The vowel inventory differs from that of Classical M in containing the opposition æ ≠ α, while Classical M reconstructs to *a* alone. (Yet trad pron *æ* is quite rare in the verb system; one example is <iahbat> t[yæhβαt] 'she gave', Macm 97.)

Noteworthy suprasegmentally in trad pron are: (α) penultimate stress as the default pattern (except that *ə̆* is unstressable) where Classical M is reconstructed as showing default accent on the ultima; and (β) freer distribution of both *V̊* and *V̄*, including frequent promotion of medial *ə̆* to *V̊*. Both these properties, (α) and (β), largely follow Modern M (Malone 1997).

As with the TL inventories in §22.2, length is abstracted out except for *V̄*. Cf. §20 (20A, D, H).

(22G)

p			t	ṭ		k	q	
b			d			g		
	f	θ	s	ṣ	š	x		h
β		ð	z			γ		
m			n					
			r					
			l					
w					y			

```
        i       u
        e   ə̆   o
        æ       α
```

Notes to §22

[1] For SM traditional pronunciation at large, see Macs *passim*, but in particular starting with Macuch's copious discussion in chapter 14 (pp. 57–69).

[2] (a) This process (α, α') is redolent of the two Hebrew processes *Major (Length-ening) Tonic Change* and *Pretonic Lengthening* conflated (THP 85–87, 95f.). Though there are differences between the two languages' versions of the processes, the similarity holds even down to the quirk of marked *C*-lenthening showing a penchant for guttural involvement. Specifically, Hebrew has a marked form of Pretonic Lengthening whereby $\overset{\circ}{V}C'V \rightarrow \overset{\circ}{V}C'C'V$ (so-called *min PL*), perhaps most prominently when C' = $\hbar$, instead of unmarked $\rightarrow \bar{V}C'V$ (= *maj PL*); and SM shows a consonantal form of lengthening rendering $\overset{\circ}{V}C'V \rightarrow \overset{\circ}{V}C'C'V$, especially /9__ whether $\leq$ *9 or < *$\hbar$ by laxing (§9.3.2)—e.g., t[9ábbɑr] 'übergehen' <9Br> (*9), t[9ázzɑr] 'zurückkehren' <ḥzr> ~ <9zr> (*$\hbar$) (Macs §52a). As Macuch correctly remarks, in forms like these, the simple binyan de facto merges with the intensive (though he does not qualify that the merger will only be complete with 3√L ints, triggering 2ʃI → [A] by low, §17.10, coinciding with 2ʃA original to sims; e.g., int t[šǽggɑr] <šGr> could just as well be a c-pra-derived simple—which would *not* in parallel hold for an int with a non-*L* 3√ like t[qǽbbəl], Macs 156). Further examples of (α') will be seen in (22B) (ι, κ)).

(b) Prima facie exceptional to the mid coloring expected from c-pra lengthening of *Í* is the fs sim imp of √⁷hk 'go' (~ /hlk), t[líki] <lKy> (Macs 177), rather than @[léki] (loss of 1√⁷ 1ʃ by wic, §17.33). However, t[líki] will be expected if we should be dealing with metaplastic √lyk, a possibility hinted at by the entry *<lwk> in Macuch's Philologisches Register (Macs 166, under the entry <hlk>).

[3] While (α) and the second options of (β, δ, ε) are unremarkable—loss of a syllabic coda (*H*) with compensatory lengthening of the nucleus ($\bar{V}$)—the remaining cases pack a couple of surprises from the point of view of general expectations in phonology at large: namely, (a) compensatory lengthening of a nucleus upon loss of an *onset* (γ, first options of δ and ε); and (b) *double* compensation upon the loss of a coda simultaneously functioning as lead-off member of a medial cluster (first option of β), lengthening *both* of the immediately preceding nucleus (*VH*. . . → $\bar{V}$. . .) *and* of the immediately follow-ing coda leading off the medial cluster (. . .*HC'* → . . .*C'C'*). Despite a good deal of futile tinkering and casting about for an escape-hatch from these conclusions, the evidence intractably remains to the effect that (a) and (b) are indeed genuine facets of SM trad pron (examples will be forthcoming in (22C))). On the other hand, quirk (b) has been argued for in a related dialect (Malone 1989c); and (a) seems to violate no foundational principles of Autosegmental Phonology (specifically, no basic principles of spreading theory). Prosodic trees showing the mechanics of the deletions-cum-compensation as-sumed are presented in (c) (S = syllable, R = rime; onsets are consonants immediately left-dominated by S, while codae are *C*s immediately right-dominated by R, while nu-clei are *V*s immediately dominated by R; vertical lines lead downward from segments *(V, H, C,* . . .) to feature geometries (unportrayed); $\neq$ = pruning (deletion), dashed lines = spreading (downward, leading to feature-sharing below the point of convergence with the solid line).) Generalizing over (c), deleted gutturals always trigger spreading to an adjacent *V*, whether leftward (α, β), rightward (γ, ε), or both (δ), while spreading to an adjacent *C* may only take place rightward (thus β but not also γ). Observe that gutturals which remain unassimilated (second options of δ and ε) are simply deleted. An alterna-tive hypothesis for the (b)-cases is developed in §4.3.

(c) [for α]

[for β]

or occasionally

[for γ]

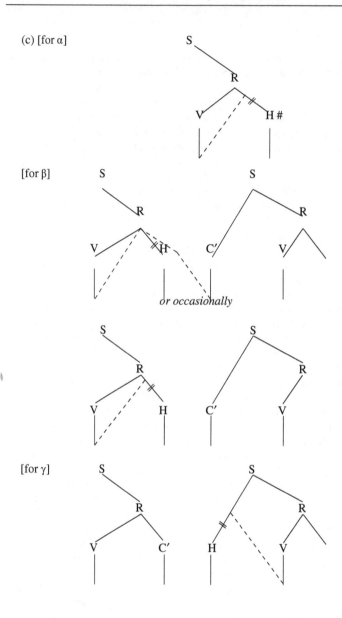

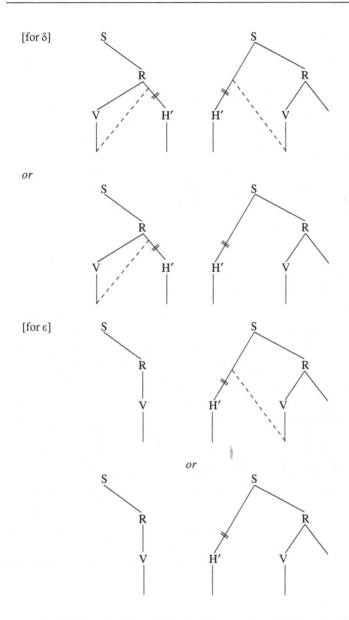

[4] (a) The inputs to these derivations betray prior operation of various processes, whether shared widely with other dialects (e.g., att, red, cnd, exc, hii, rna, mid, ssl, low, r-anc, k-coa) or more narrowly characteristic of SM (notably vpl, §9.2.4, and uncompensated adr, §9.2.1.1, §9.3.2 n. 42). Circuit outputs also differ from trad prons (given in t[   ] = square brackets prefixed by t) in that the latter undergo various SM-specific processes listed following (22C).

(b) The decision to interpret the root underlying t[wə̆yēgū́n] (β) as deriving from *√g9y rests on inferences from the etymologies offered in DM (p. 72, under √GAA), Brockelmann 1928 (p. 129, under √g9ˀ), and Cohen et al. 1993–99 (III: 164, under √Gℇ/W/Y).

[5] In re (α), the schwa coloring rules reported by Morag for Yem trad pron are redolent of those codified by Ben Asher in *Dikdukey haTĕ9amim* for Tiberian Hebrew: regressive assimilation onto V̆ through a guttural or y from V in the next syllable. However, while Ben Asher fields [Ĕ] as default color (THP 89), Morag claims [Ă] for Yem trad pron (though [Ĕ] appears without comment for 1ʃ of the sim rmp) (Mor 91f., 140). In re (β), synthesizing and abstracting from Morag's statements (Mor 117–19), a *tendential* formulation of unmarked stress assignment for Yem trad pron might be: *in words of two or more syllables, accent the earliest open syllable.*

[6] This discrepancy may not be absolute, B showing a few instances of *e* / _˘CC in *variae lectiones* (§17.11.3 n. 40).

[7] Skepticism on the full genuineness of Margolis's representations bids fair to be strengthened by comparisons with other Ashkenazic channels of transmission. Thus, while Margolis presents the action of spr (§5.1) on *p, *t, *k, *b, *d, *g as fully spirantized [f, θ̠, x, v, ð̠, ɣ], the same as B, the Aramaic portions of Yiddish uniformly show [f, s̠, x, v, d̠, g] (discrepancies underscored).

[8] (a) One of these exceptions is [ð], which in trad pron is forthcoming only in one formative, t[kǽð] 'when', reading Classical <KΔ> (note the spelling, unusual both in being purely consonantal (ḥaser) and in employing the morphogram <Δ>, §21.8), reconstructed in the Classical dialect as [káð] while the Modern dialect shows [kéθ].

However [ð] does exist in the Modern dialect, where it is used in Arabic borrowings. Replicating the same sound in the donor language, and spelled with special diacritics as <d̠> (Macm 12). More generally, several other members of the slit fricative series likewise evince widened distribution in Modern M due to borrowings from Arabic (or Persian), under which circumstance they are also spelled with the diacritic <˳> (lc).

(b) In general, the investigator must be alert for instances of *ābāgādical pronunciation,* Macuch's term for reading pronunciation (Macm 641), specifically the tendency for the *tarmīdī* to guide their oral performance of the holy scriptures in terms of spellings deployed even when they may be merely historical. See §6.2.2.1 with n. 26, §9.2.2 n. 21, §17.14 with n. 62.

23. The Generative-Phonological Perspective

23.1. Classical Generative Phonology (GP) [1]

Among other goals, Generative Phonology aims to explicate speakers' implicit knowledge of what might be called the code whereby morphosyntactic configurations of lexical items are expressed through phonetic structures (strings of segments—vowels; consonants—hierarchized in syllables and other prosodic configurations; the whole modulated by accentuation—stress; and tones—intonation).

In classical GP, itself following the lead of the most explicit work in *morphophonemics* from the antecedent so-called Structural period, the central part of the explication takes the form of *derivations*, whereby abstract phonetic strings—so-called *phonological* representations—are successively deformed by phonological *rules* until they are realized as relatively concrete *phonetic* representations.

Phonological representations, sometimes called *underlying*, are built up from lexical items, or *lexemes*—usually but not always consisting of strings of (abstract) vowels and consonants plus possible *accentual* properties (stresses, tones)—the lexemes in turn being organized into superstrings hierarchized by *prosodic* and/or *morphosyntactic* principles (the issue remains unsettled; prosody, to the extent it represents a linguistic linguistic module, is typically considered to be at least in part a deformation of morphosyntactic organization as "prepped" in the direction of phonetic manifestation).

Morphosyntactic/prosodic relations contracted by adjacent lexemes (or longer units consisting of lexemes, or indeed smaller units contained within lexemes, the smallest being *morphemes*) are often reified in terms of *boundaries* taken to exist between constituents.

With this much framework built up, a sketch derivation is supplied in (23A), where *A, B, . . . I* stand for segments (vowels, consonants), and the diamonds represent boundaries—say, word boundaries (where *word* is taken to be a lexeme plus possible inflectional *affixes*: e.g., prefixes, suffixes). First, *replacement* rule **R1** replaces underlying segment /C/ with *intermediate* segment |J|. (Typically, replacement rules modify segments into similar segments rather than out-and-out substituting them with wholly new segments.) Next, *deletion* rule **R2** drops |B|, after which *insertion* rule **R3** adds |K|; and *reordering* rule **R4** interchanges (*metathesizes*) |G| and |H|. Finally, *incorporation* rule **R5** demotes |AJ| from word status to that of a prefix on |DKE| (or conversely, suffixes |DKE| to |AJ|); and *excorporation* rule **R6** splits |FHGI| into two words, |FHG| and |I|. The rules exhausted, we end up with the phonetic string [. . .AJKE(<>)FHG(<>)I. . .], where the parentheses hint at the unsettled ussue of whether (and how) boundaries survive into phonetic structure.

(23A)   /. . .ABC<>DE<>FGHI. . ./
R1 |. . .ABJ<>DE<>FGHI. . .|
R2 |. . .AJ<>DE<>FGHI. . .|
R3 |. . .AJ<>DKE<>FGHI. . .|
R4 |. . .AJ<>DKE<>FHGI. . .|
R5 |. . .AJDKE<>FHGI. . .|
R6 |. . .AJDKE<>FHG<>I. . .|
          [. . .AJDKE(<>)FHG(<>)I. . .]

Segments are decomposable into bundles (or *matrices*) of *features*, or in more recent work into complexes of features called *feature geometries*. A feature may be either *monolithic* or *binary*. If monolithic, a segment not characterized by the property the feature is designed to express simply lacks that feature in its matrix/geometry; thus, while the matrix in (23B) (i) represents a segment codefined by the property *F*, via the monolithic feature [F], the matrix in (23) (ii) models a segment similar in other properties but lacking *F*. Binary features, on the other hand, model presence/absence of properties with the aid of *coefficients*, "plus" indicating presence of the property, "minus" indicating its absence; see the matrices in (23) (iii) and (iv) respectively.[2]

(23B) (i) $\begin{bmatrix} F \\ G \\ H \end{bmatrix}$ (ii) $\begin{bmatrix} G \\ H \end{bmatrix}$ (iii) $\begin{bmatrix} +F \\ +G \\ +H \end{bmatrix}$ (iv) $\begin{bmatrix} -F \\ +G \\ +H \end{bmatrix}$

Feature geometries, in this book used for the most part in name only, consist of two or more matrices, typically including singleton matrices, organized into *trees*. In such geometries, monolithic features often (but not always) occur as monoliths in the upper reaches (where they *classiufy* lower dependencies), while binary matrices tend to appear in the lower reaches (in *classified* position) where, moreover, they frequently contain more than one feature. An example is given in (23C).

(23C)

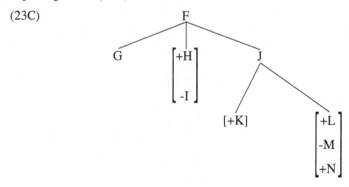

For concrete GP applications to Aramaic nexuses, see §6.1.2 n. 7, §11.2 n. 11, §13 n. 2, §14.2 nn. 11 and 17, §16.2 <u>SR</u> (β) n. 19.

23.2. Synchronic-Diachronic Relations

Generative Phonology is, au fond, a *synchronic* conception. In early work on extending the conception into the diachronic sphere—and indeed in much current work as well—the view was (is) taken that language change should be modeled wholly as a relation between successive synchronic states.[3] To see how this works, let us hark back to (23A) and assume that at one chronological stage the language contained no rules, so that the sketch-word /ABC/ at that stage was isomorphically pronounced [ABC]. At the *following* chronological stage, however, let us assume that the selfsame word /ABC/ came to be pronounced [ABJ]. The whole picture might then be represented as in (23D), concerning which we could say that the system operative at stage I has mutated by a change-type called *rule addition*. In particular, rule **R1** has been added to the phonology with the consequence that /ABC/ is now pronounced [ABJ].

(23D)	I	>		II
	/ABC/			/ABC/
			R1	|ABJ|
	[ABC]			[ABJ]

Next, suppose that **R2** is added to the phonology, under the condition $B \Rightarrow \emptyset / \_\_J$, i.e., B is dropped when immediately followed by J. This would give us the result in (23E).

(23E)	I	>	II	>	III
	/ABC/		/ABC/		/ABC/
		R1	|ABJ|	**R1**	|ABJ|
				R2	|AJ|
	[ABC]		[ABJ]		[AJ]

Continuing the procedure in this fashion, we will finally end up with (23A) at stage VII, by which time all six rules will have been added to the phonology. This somewhat ideal sketch case answers to the rule-of-thumb formulated in (23F).

> (23F) In simple situations, the traditional notion of "sound change" may be explicated as a phonological rule added at the end of the derivational order .[4]

This sort of outcome was advisedly called "somewhat ideal," because in actuality phonological systems rarely stay for very long in just the predicted disposition. Take the case of the phonological representation /ABC/ in (23E). What does it mean to say that /ABC/ continues to exist at stage III although the corresponding pronunciation is now [AJ]? This will only be possible as

long as the interplay of the morphosyntax / lexicon and phonetics continue
to justify coding [J] as /BC/, a justification normally licensed because in one
or more paradigms [J] in one slot (or set of slots) corresponds to [BC] in another (set). But we know that it is commonplace for sound changes to strike a
language and within a generation or so disappear without leaving traces in the
form of living alternations like the *J ~ BC* for the sake of argument assumed
here. So what if, instead of indefinitely living on as a rule in (23E) (III), **R2**
finally dropped out of the synchronic life of the language? Let's assume that
this does in fact happen, subsequent to stage III, at stage IV. The normal result
is portrayed in (23G).

(23G)	III	>	IV
	/ABC/		/AC/
	R1 |ABJ|		**R1** |AJ|
	R2 |AJ|		
	[AJ]		[AJ]

This represents a very common nexus: *rule loss* or *rule deletion* (**R2** disappears from the synchronic phonology) to the tune of *restructuring*, rst, (the
underlying representation is restructured, in a manner of speaking, to reflect the
impact of the rule that has been lost—in this case, since **R2** was a deletion rule
the underlying representation registers deletion of the ssegment(s) that used to
be deleted by the rule.

Less frequently, rule loss may take place without concomitant restructuring,
in which case we would have a result like (23H).

(23H)	III	>	IV′
	/ABC/		/ABC/
	R1 |ABJ|		**R1** |ABJ|
	R2 |AJ|		
	[AJ]		[ABJ]

In such a situation, it is as if the rule, and corresponding sound change, had
never existed; a result that leaves the historical analyst a victim of the baneful
phenomenon of *accordioning* (§18.4 with (18T)):

(23I)	II	>	III	>	IV′ *(indistinguishable from II)*
	/ABC/		/ABC/		/ABC/
	R1 |ABJ|		**R1** |ABJ|		**R1** |ABJ|
			R2 |AJ|		
	[ABJ]		[AJ]		[ABJ]

It turns out that several types of mutation wreaked synchronically by rules
upon segments (or other phonological units) are answered by corresponding
mutations wreaked diachronically upon rules themselves:

(23J) replacement rule   *corresponding to*   rule modification
      deletion rule   rule deletion
      insertion rule   rule addition
      reordering rule   rule reordering

The rule types (first column of (23J)) were each illustrated in sketch form in (23A), while of the rule mutations (second column) addition was illustrated of **R1**, **R2** in (23D, E), and deletion of **R2** in (23G, H, I). Rule modification occurs when a rule alters its operation—most commonly but by no means exclusively through generalizing (extending) its pale of operation, (23K), where **R2** generalizes from deleting medial B to deleting both medial and final B— while rule reordering interchanges the applicational order of two rules, usually adjacently, (23L), where **R7** replaces L by O immediately preceding M and **R8** replaces M by P immediately following O:

(23K)   /ABCB/   >   /ABCB/
     R1 |ABJB| **R1** |ABJB|
     R2 |AJB| **R2′** |AJ|
           [AJB]   [AJ]

(23L)   /LMOM/   >   /LMOM/
     R7 |OMOM| **R8** |LMOP|
     R8 |OPOP| **R7** |OMOP|
           [OPOP]   [OMOP]

Questions of rationale might arise concerning rule mutations. Granted rule addition as a straightforward mechanism for capturing sound change (23D), rule deletion as a way of registering the demise of a process as a living force (23G), and rule modification as a manner of expressing a process's change in scope (23K), what might motivate a bizarre-seeming phenomenon like rule reordering? Though none of the mutation types has been found, in languages at large, to be restricted to one function, rule reordering at times captures *analogical reshaping*, in particular the generalization throughout a paradigm of one allomorphic shape (typically the majority shape) at the expense of another (typically a minority shape). One reason reordering can serve this function is that switching the applicational order of two rules may bring it about, for instance, that the *new* first-applying rule—e.g., **R8** in (23L)—fails to effect a change which would detract from the unity of the paradigm, in that the condition prerequisite to effecting that change must be supplied by the partner rule—**R7** in (23L)—which, however, is now ordered too late to apply. Thus, in the wake of the rule reordering in (23L), **R8** cannot change the first M to P because this M follows L, rather than O as required; and **R7**, being relegated to subordinate applicational order, cannot effect $L \Rightarrow O$ in order to help **R8**. To complete the picture, we must see how $M \Rightarrow P$ (in the case of the first M)

might detract from paradigmatic unity, and accordingly how frustration of this change could serve that unity. A mockup is supplied in (23M), where second-positioned *M ~ P* may represent some morpheme in its own right or perhaps function as a component of some larger morpheme (say, *MOP ~ POP*); and we may assume that first-positioned *Q, R, O, S* are, say, inflectional prefixes. Observe how reordering to **R8^R7**, as discussed above, reinstates paradigmatic unity by abrogating *M ~ P* in favor of *M* alone.[5]

(23M)   [QMOP]
        [RMOP]
        [OPOP]   **R8^R7** >   [OMOP]
        [SMOP]

While linguists may in general hold that abstractness should not per se be held to be a flaw of analysis, one may with equal right wonder whether naïve speakers of a language desirous of ironing out *M ~ P* to *M* might not do so less arcanely than by rule reordering as just sketched—even granted that the impulse to iron out the paradigm may be below the level of (collective) consciousness. That is, more straightforward than (23L) would seem something like (23N), where **R9**—an instance of analogy-triggered rule addition—specifies the like of *"replace* P *by* M *whenever* M *alternates with* P (M ~ P), *and the alternant* M *occurs in more paradigmatic slots than the alternant* P."

(23N)   /LMOM/   >   /LMOM/
        R7 |OMOM| **R7** |OMOM|
        R8 |OPOP| **R8** |OPOP|
                                    R9 |OMOP|
             [OPOP]   [OMOP]

In fact, I submit that, in principle, the like of (23L) and (23N) may *both* be realistic approximations of what actually transpires under circumstances like those stated, but that the models are allottable to different generations. For the first generation of speakers, those for whom the (nascent) analogical reshaping is a living phenomenon, (23N) is appropriate, with its special analogy-inspired rule addition **R9**—an "A-rule" in the seminal terminology of Malone 1969. However, for subsequent generations of speakers, those who are not party to the live-wire analogical reshaping but rather mere heirs to the inherited patterns devoid of a priori, special function—for these speakers, who must induce the structure of the received phonology anew, at mother's knee, (23L) represents a tighter, more efficient organization than does (23N). Thus, comprehensively, we have:

(23P)	I	>	II	>	III
	/LMOM/		/LMOM/		/LMOM/
R7	|OMOM|	**R7**	|OMOM|	**R8**	|LMOP|
R8	|OPOP|	**R8**	|OPOP|	**R7**	|OMOP|
		R9	|OMOP|		
	[OPOP]		[OMOP]		[OMOP]

It seems possible that other types of rule mutation as well, not reorderings alone, may likewise be heralded—diachronically preceded as first step—by special rule additions along the lines of **R9**.[6]

As was expressed at the outset of this section, it has traditionally been and continues in large part to be a basic assumption of historical GP that diachrony be modeled as a relation between successive synchronic states. The suspicion lingers, however, that there may be more to diachrony than just that; in particular, that there may be ontology sui generis to diachronic phenomena above and beyond mediating between successive synchronic states. Though in the prevailing state of the art, this area is conceptually murky, in this book at least its existence is acknowledged by frequently giving a label to the diachronic ">" —if only a label shared by the corresponding synchronic process. Thus, harking back to (23D), nexuses like this will often be replaced with the ilk of (23Q) ("**d–x**" = diachronic **x**, "**s–x**" = synchronic **x**; §0.2):

(23Q)	I	**d-1**	>	II
	/ABC/			/ABC/
			s-1	|ABJ|
	[ABC]			[ABJ]

For concrete GP applications in diachrony, see §3.2 n. 6, §6.2 n. 15, §7.2 (δ) n. 8, §8.1.2 (α), §8.1.2 with n. 11, §14.2 n. 18, §15.2.2.2 n. 20, §15.6, §17.7 n. 16, §17.9.2 nn. 26 and 27, §17.33 n. 156.

23.3. Lexical Phonology (LP)

In the original conception of Generative Phonology assumed in §23.1 and §23.2, a phonological derivation consists of a series of ordered rules—or ordered blocs of rules—fed by an underlying representation. The underlying representation, in turn, is usually taken to consist of a string of lexical items organized by the morphosyntax or by prosodic rules in part formed as a function of the morphosyntax.

Over the years, however, scholars have taken note of a variety of language data not readily tractable to a format like this. In particular, the assumption has been questioned that the lexicon antecede the phonology in whole cloth. Perhaps, rather, the lexicon might interface with the phonology at points other than initial. Paul Kiparsky is widely credited with being the first to respond to this challenge integrally, with the development of a full-blown theory known as *Lexical Phonology* (LP) (Kiparsky 1982). The followimg sketch is partial, simplified, and selective, being tacitly relativized to the several applications offered throughout the book where LP seems especially suitable for the explications of patterns in the Aramaic verb.

In lieu of a phonology commencing with a unitary, lexicon-cum-morpho-syntax-informed level of underlying representations, LP envisages a sequence of several phonological *strata*—the number probably language-specific—each stratum containing an initial level housing a *word-building* function (wrb) and feeding a sequence of phonological rules, some stratum-specific and others *iterative* across all (or most) strata.

A hypothetical three-stratum illustration is provided in (23R), where iterative rules are prefixed with "**i**" and stratum-specific rules appear unprefixed. While there is no full consensus on specific regularities informing LP structure and operation, those assumed for this mockup are of the type frequently proposed: (α) in a given stratum, wrb applies first; (β) some stratum-specific rules apply *before* the iterative rules, others *after;* (γ) as indicated by flanking bows (( )) two rules may be *looped*, meaning they may apply in either order; (δ) with the partial exception of the first stratum, whose initial level is given by the lexicon, and of the last stratum, whose output level is relayed to the syntax (and ultimately interpreted phonetically), the output level of an immediately preceding stratum becomes the input level to its successor stratum.

In stratum I, the lexicon provides four morphemes, not yet composed; and of these, it falls to stratum I to compose two: /ABC/ and /DE/ wrb ⇒ |ABCDE|. Then this new unit and the two morphemes remaining uncomposed are run through the rules, which on this stratum consist exclusively of iteratives: **i1** replaces E with I, **i2** effects $A \Rightarrow J$ in anlaut and $\Rightarrow K$ elsewhere, while **i3** remains inactive.

In II, |F|, perhaps a suffix, is added to |JBCDI| (⇐ /ABC, /DE/), whereupon pre-iterative II-specific **4** epenthesizes A / $I\_\_F$. **i1** has nothing to do, but **i2** changes **4**-epenthesized A to K, and **i3**—whose job it is to apocopate the last segment in overlong (> 7) constituents—whittles *JBCDIKF* to *JBCDIK*.

Lastly, in III, word-building accomplishes the final synthesis: pre-iterative III-specific **5** and **6** apherize J and change auslaut K *to* E respectively; **i1** and **i3** respond with $E \Rightarrow I$ and $I\# \Rightarrow O\#$, respectively; then the post-iterative *looped* pair **7** and **8** change C to I (the job of **7**) and modify each immediately post-I segment from X to X' (the work of **8**). It may be seen that the order **7^8** returns the final result *BID'. . .* , because prior $C \Rightarrow I$ by **7** provides an I to effect the change $D \Rightarrow D'$; but **8^7** makes for a final result *BID. . .* , in that *ID* was still *CD* at the time **8** changed *IK* and *IH* to *IK'* and *IH'*.

(23R) I   /ABC/ , /DE/ , /F/ , /GEHA/
      wrb |ABCDE| , — , —
      i1 |ABCDI| , — , |GIHA|
      i2 |JBCDI| , — , |GIHK|
      i3 —   , — , —

    II |JBCDI| , |F| , |GIHK|
      wrb |JBCDIF| , —
      4 |JBCDIAF| , —
      i1   —   , —
      i2 |JBCDIKF| , —
      i3 |JBCDIK| , —

    III |JBCDIK| , |GIHK|
      wrb |JBCDIKGIHK|
      5 |BCDIKGIHK|
      6 |BCDIKGIHE|
      i1 |BCDIKGIHI|
      i2   —
      i3 |BCDIKGIH|
      (**7**) |BIDIKGIH| ~ |BCDIK'GIH'|
      (**8**) |BID'IK'GIH'| ~ |BIDIK'GIH'|

For concrete LP applications to Aramaic, see §5.2 n. 10, §11.2 <u>SR</u>, §14.2 nn. 11 and 17, §15.2.1.1 nn. 4 and 6, §15.2.1.3 nn. 9 and 10, §15.6 n. 43, §17.9.2 nn. 26 and 27, §17.11.3 n. 40.

23.4. Autosegmental Phonology (AP)

The original impetus for Autosegmental theory derived from the observation that in certain tonal languages strings of tones frequently failed to align in the a priori expected way with the strings of syllables they were, in classical GP, presumed to modify. Specifically, while the notion that tones should be modeled as features (or other one-to-one associates) of vowels proved unproblematic when the number of tones and vowels was the same—*HL* (high-low) when composed with *CVCV* might be represented as $C\overset{H}{V}C\overset{L}{V}$—unexpected results were often forthcoming when the number was discrepant. Thus when *HL* was associated with a monosyllable, the resulting configuration might be a falling (contour) tone, representable as $C\overset{HL}{V}$, with both tones occupying what was presumed to be one space; or when association was to a polysyllable, results like $C\overset{H}{V}C\overset{L}{V}C\overset{L}{V}C\overset{L}{V}$ were typical—in lieu of expected $C\overset{H}{V}C\overset{L}{V}CVCV$, where the supernumerary syllables would remain toneless.

Such patterns led to the conception that tones on the one hand and vowels/consonants on the other might start out their phonological existence on *distinct* *tiers—as autosegments—*only subsequently to be wedded into an integrated representation.[7]

The fundamental idea is illustrated in (23S), where representations start out as unassociated ordered pairs of {tones, segments} as in (i), (iii), (v), and are subsequently amalgamated by *rules of association* that provide instructions like *"associate each item on the tonal tier with a vowel on the segmental tier, moving left to right and returning one-to-one tone-to-vowel attachments* (ii) *unless forced by many-to-one attachment in default of a sufficient number of vowels* (iv) *or to one-to-many attachment in default of a sufficient number of tones* (vi)."[8]

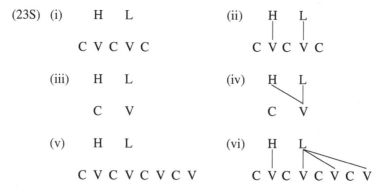

(23S) (i)   H   L   (ii)   H   L

               C V C V C   C V C V C

       (iii)   H   L   (iv)   H   L

                 C   V   C   V

       (v)   H   L   (vi)   H   L

               C V C V C V C   C V C V C V C V

Over the years since its inauguration, Autosegmental theory has been extended far beyond its tone-vowel crucible. Of greatest moment for the work of this book, and Semitic linguistics more generally, is John McCarthy's proposed explication of *internal-flective morphology.* This extension of autosegmentalism proposed the interaction of *three* tiers, which in the terminology of this book will be called *radical* (accommodating the morphological root), *schematic* (for the morphological scheme, or vowel pattern), and *skeletal* (providing a template, or canon, for mutual radical-schematic construction).[9] (Generically radical and schematic tiers are referred to as *melodic,* special cases of vowel-consonant (segmental) tiers at large. And a segment in such an AP role is called a *melody.* See further below.)

The basic workings of this extension are displayed in (23T, U), for the simple perfective and simple imperfective, respectively—the latter on the view that the traditional "prefix" vowel of the sim impf is actually 1ʃ (§1 n. 4) and adopting the simplifying assumption that ablaut has already been registered (§1 n. 5). The basic morphemes (radical, skeletal, schematic) are first taken from the lexicon as an ordered triplet (i), then associated (ii), and finally subjected to an operation known as *tier conflation* (iii) (McCarthy 1986, Malone 1989a).[10]

(23T) (i) *radical tier*   Q   S   M

       skeletal tier   C   V   C   V   C

       schematic tier   a

(ii)

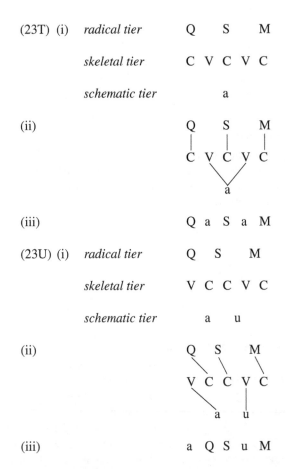

(iii)   Q   a   S   a   M

(23U) (i) *radical tier*   Q   S   M

       skeletal tier   V   C   C   V   C

       schematic tier   a   u

(ii)

(iii)   a   Q   S   u   M

Though the skeletal tier plays an especially vital role in the explication of specifically Semitic morphophonology, it came in work of post-McCarthian vintage to be employed quite generally in autosegmental models in that for instance noninterdigitational morphemes , such as prefixes or suffixes, are represented in a way similar to that of (23T, U), with the difference that one, unified *melodic* tier would correspond to the radical-schematic duo posited for internal-flective systems; e.g., (23V) for the rmp prefix **hit-*. [11]

(23V) (i) *melodic tier*   h   i   t   (ii) h   i   t   (iii) h   i   t

       skeletal tier   C   V   C   C   V   C

Additional AP mechanisms are explained and utilized at various spots throughout the book: notably *spreading* (plus accessory notions) in explication of assimilation, sketchwise treated in the following section of this chapter (§23.5 with (23Y)(ii) and n. 13), and doing actual work with Aramaic in §3 (passim), §10 with n. 12, §20.2 n. 5, §22.1 n. 3, §9.2.1.2 n. 20, §17.25 n. 130. Other AP applications include *Geminate Integrity* (§5.1 n. 1, §15.3.1.2 with n. 24), the *Obligatory Contour Principle* (§6.2.2.1 n. 27), the nature of the skeleton (§9.1.3 n. 7), the nature of association (§11.1 n. 3), *antiwedging* (§17.18.2 with n. 97).

23.5. Syllabic and Prosodic Structure

In languages at large, a *syllable* (*S*) consists obligatiorily of a *nucleus* (*N*) and optionally of an *onset* (*O*) and/or a *coda* (*K*). While nucleus and coda are considered to be intimately attached as immediate constituents of a *rime* (*R*), the onset is taken to stand apart; (23W):

(23W)

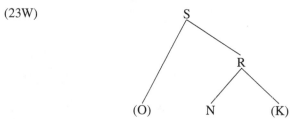

Prototypical exponents of onset and coda are consonants, the number permissible in clusters descending in frequency across languages from nearly universal one (*C*) through frequent two (*CC*) and occasional three (*CCC*) to rarely occurring higher numbers. From proto-Aramaic through must of the Classical period, the value of *O* was set at exactly one (*C*), the default being [ʔ] (e.g., in the wake of prothesis, §17.16); though in later dialects that underwent adr (§9.2.1.1), e.g., SR, M, vowel-initial words became canonically legitimate. The coda, on the other hand, has always been optional in Aramaic, and when present could not exceed singleton status until the emergence of sap (§17.22), while earlier any such codal *CC* that might have been inherited (notably in the case of 3√ clustering with 1s pf *-t) or arisen (notably via uap, §17.31, in nominals) was repair-strategically resyllabified by excrescence in inlaut (§2.3.2.1 (α)) or epenthesis in auslaut (§17.8).[12]

The prototypical exponent of a nucleus in languages at large is a vowel, as it is in Aramaic. In A, long or short vowels ($\bar{V}$, V respectively) are permitted, subject to phonotactic restrictions (e.g., long vowels in closed syllables are frequently shortened, §17.4). (The status of reduced vowels ($\ddot{V}$) is not as clear-cut. Heavily restricted in earlier A (e.g., in encodation of the simple imperative, §1.1.1 with n. 7, or repair-strategically inserted by exc, §2.3.2.1 (α)), they achieve wider distribution in later A thanks principally to reduction, §4.2; but their possible status as "inert elements," n. 14 below, §3.2 n. 6, §15.2.1.1 n. 5, raises unsettled questions about their viability to serve as full-blown nuclei.)

The status of glides (Γ), especially the stomatic glides or *semivowels* (*w*, *y*), tends to be ambivalent in languages, and Aramaic is no exception. In some cases, the evidence may be that Γ is functioning equivalently to *C* as (a member of) *O* or *K*. In other instances, overall patterning seems to betray *V*-like behavior as a member of a nucleus, in which case it may be referred to as (nucleic) *satellite*. Thus if a glide is determined to be functioning as a satellite in *V*Γ, it is commonly called an *offglide* (of/to the nuclear *V*); and similarly the satellite role of Γ in Γ*V* merits the label *onglide* (of/to *V*).

Comprehensively in (23X), strings like Γ*V* and *V*Γ tend to be ambiguous between (i) and (ii), as well as between (iii) and (iv). In Classical Aramaic, there is probably a split, the favorite assignments being (i) and (iv); that is, ongliding is disfavored (or absent) (ii), while offgliding is commonplace (iv).

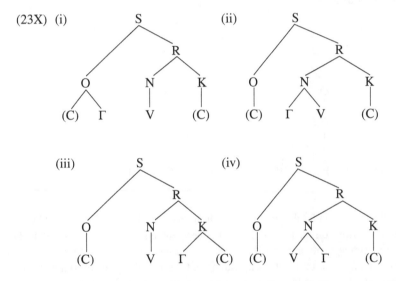

The consonantism found at the juncture where two syllables meet within a word is sometimes called *interlude*. A valuable rule-of-thumb for the syllabification of interludes is: (α) apportion the interlude to coda fore and onset aft pursuant to the language's coda and onset allowances at auslaut and anlaut, respectively, higher-valued (less-marked) allowances taking precedence over lesser-valued; (β) in case of a tie on (α), maximize the onset. Taking the Aramaic of a -adr +sap dialect (see above) in illustration, . . . *VCC′V″*. . . (containing the interlude *CC′*) would syllabify . . . *VC|C′V″*. . . because . . . *VC#* contains a permissible coda and *#C′V″*. . . a permissible onset, and because @. . . *VCC′|V″*. . . is ruled out in that @#*V″*. . . is ruled out, and because @. . . *V|CC′V″*. . . is ruled out in that @#*CC′V″*. . . is ruled out. In a +adr +lap dialect . . . *VC|C′V″*. . . would likewise win despite the permissibility of ...$VCC'|V''$... because though $\#V''$... is fine yet ...$VCC'\#$ is lesser valued than ...$VC\#$. In all Aramaic dialects ...VCV''... would syllabify as ...$V|CV''$... on the basis of (β).

The syllable is not a unit hermetic unto itself but rather an intermediate structure with attachments below and above.

Below, a syllable attaches to the skeletal tier, whose positions in turn dominate feature geometries. This is sketched in (23Y) (i) (F = feature geometry). One geometric portrayal of *spreading* is given in (ii), the process whereby the phonetic contents of a deleted constituent (the coda; "≠" = the branch is pruned with all its dependencies) are rerouted to an adjacent constituent (the nucleus; spreading via the slanting dashed line downward). This sketch example illustrates the common process of compensatory lengthening of a vowel nucleus upon loss of the homosyllabic coda.[13]

(23Y) (i)   (ii)

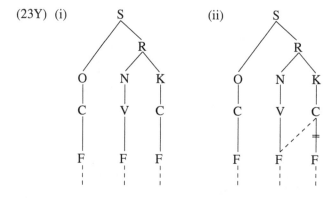

While the skeletal tier captures phonological *length*, CVC in (23Y) expressing three units, the partially independent issue of phonological *weight* is sometimes explicated by the *mora* (μ), an element associated with skeletal positions as a function of their attachment to specific types of syllabic terminals. Attachment or lack of it proceeds by conventions like the following: (γ) an onset never bears weight; (δ) nucleic positions bear one mora apiece; (ε) codae may or may not bear weight, on a parametric (language-specific) basis—in Aramaic, codae usually do bear weight, either one mora per the entire coda or, perhaps in some dialects, one mora per codal position; (ζ) there may be upper (or lower) limits on weight—in Aramaic, upper nucleic weight may (usually) be set at two (μμ), though under certain circumstances three may be countenanced (μμμ—so-called "superheavy syllables"). An illustrative representation appears in (23Z), which μ-scores (23Y):[14]

(23Z)

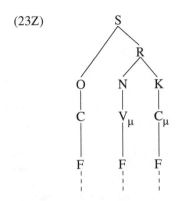

Above the syllable, there is what is commonly called *prosodic structure*, an organizational halfway-house between morphosyntax and phonology. In most general theories of *prosody* (or less ambiguously, *prosodology* following Malone 1989d, the shorter term being confoundable with a distinct sense in poetics), at least six suprasyllabic layers of structure are recognized. These are laid out in (23Z′), for the most part following Nespor and Vogel 1982 and calibrated with rough-and-ready equivalents used in this book.

(23Z′)   layers of prosodic structure above the syllable

general-linguistic label at large	rough equivalent in this book (§20.3, §21.6, §21.7)
utterance	—
intonational phrase	major/pausal string (*in B, externally bounded by pausal tĕ9amim*)
phonological phrase	disjunctive string (*in B, often externally marked by disjunctive tĕ9amim and internally by conjunctive tĕ9amim*)
clitic group	clitic group (*in B, often internally marked by makef*)
phonological/prosodic word	prosodic word (*typically orthographically represented without internal spacing*)
foot	foot (*hosts iambic/trochaic stress feet within so-called Metrical Stress Theory, §4.1.1 n. 2*)

Notes to §23

[1] Coverage is eclectic, largely geared to applications elsewhere in the book (most of them cross-referenced throughout the chapter). Coverage is also unabashedly heterodoxical, though formulations and modes of analysis are developed within legitimate

channels of Generative Phonology at large. Several topics are simply mentioned in the course of the chapter, being developed elsewhere in the book (references provided). An excellent introduction to most of the topics treated here—and many more—is Kenstowicz 1994.

[2] Expressing the presence/absence of a feature via monolithic or binary modeling constitutes a special case of *privative* vs. *equipollent* representation, respectively—though here with more reference to the metalanguage (the symbolic language used by the analyst) than to the object language (the language being studied). See §15 n. 3.

[3] A preeminent example is King 1969.

[4] It is this sort of nexus, unraveled backward (from phonetic level back toward the phonological), which enables the important historic-linguistic tool of *internal reconstruction* (§18.4). Such unraveling is especially facilitated when a rule at derivational level *L* <u>feeds</u> a successive rule at level *L+1*, as here **R1** feeds **R2** (because the *J* conditioning the loss of *B* by **R2** was introduced by **R1**). This is so in that the feeding relation typically allows the analyst to determine the relative chronology of the changes corresponding to the rules.

[5] Other applicational relations between the two rules may lead to a comparable result; for instance, the new first-ordered rule may come to *feed* its partner in such a way as to bring about paradigmatic homogeneity that would not otherwise obtain (that in fact did not obtain prior to the reordering). Thus, in Malone 1971a, a case is made for Aramaic segolate formations (**QV̊SM*) being originally like their Hebrew cognates in manifesting absolute/construct allostems with stress *preceding* 2√ ([QV̊SV̊M]), while in all other paradigmatic slots stress *followed* 3√, and hence also 2√ ([QV̊SMX́], [-X́] suffixal). However, a reordering from str^epn (cf. §4.1, §17.6) to epn^str, in consonance with other rules (like reduction) could reshape the absolute/construct to [Qə̆SV̊M]), whereupon *all* members of the paradigm would show post-2√ accentuation.

[6] This position is argued for in Malone 1992a.

[7] Seminal works for AP are Williams 1976 and Goldsmith 1976.

[8] "instructions *like* 'associate. . .'": Mode of attachment is actually a rather unsettled issue, and numerous proposals have been made since the promulgation of AP in the attempt to find a unitary algorithm. The left-to-right procedure suggested here would at the very least require qualification; see also n. 10 below, as well as §3 (3F) (i) with n. 2.

[9] The seminal work is McCarthy 1979[1985]. As sketched in §0.2.1, *internal-flective morphology*, sometimes called "interdigitational," refers to the typically Semitic mode of morphological organization whereby consonants (with normally lexical value) are interwoven with vowels (normally bearing grammatical information) to form basic stems, of the type called *miškalim* in this book; see Malone 1979, whence also derives much of the specific terminology used in association with internal flexion in this book (e.g., "scheme, schematic").

[10] As intimated in n. 8, simple left-to-right association will not be sufficient for all AP purposes. In internal flexion, for instance, it works out nicely for the simple verb in cases like (23T, U), however would give the wrong results for the usual form (but see n. 8) of the intensive with its characteristically geminate 2√; see (a) below. Various solutions have been proposed for this snag in the literature. McCarthy's original idea was to use a special rule ((18) in McCarthy 1979: 256); in this book, the job will be done by prespecifying the 2√ slots for identical realization, symbolized in (b) below by

$C'C'$ (§0.2) (similar to the "linkage" device used in Mal, a work technically pre-AP in vintage but de facto employing a good deal of autosegmental modeling).

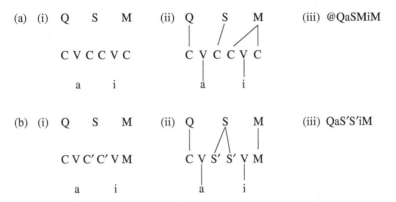

(a) (i) Q S M   (ii) Q S M   (iii) @QaSMiM

C V C C V C   C V C C V C

a   i   a   i

(b) (i) Q S M   (ii) Q S M   (iii) QaS′S′iM

C V C′ C′ V M   C V S′ S′ V M

a   i   a   i

[11] An alternative conception of the skeletal tier—not merely in internal-flective systems, but in languages at large—was proposed by Levin 1985. In accordance with this view, the skeleton (skeletal tier) is purely positional, devoid of any prefabricated commitment to vowel or consonant content, so that the skeletons for both sim pf and impf would be identical, $X\,X\,X\,X\,X$; association of radical and schematic elements is then guided by the *syllabic values* preattached to the per se skeletal slot—see §23.5, next. Despite the merits of such an analysis, the C, V model will with few exceptions (e.g., §9 n. 7) be employed in this work for its greater perspicuity. (The X, X model is employed for Aramaic in Malone 1989c, 1991.)

[12] In addition to *quantitative* restrictions on consonantism in syllabic roles, notably the number of Cs permissible in onset/coda clusters, there are also restrictions of a *qualitative* order. Most notable of these are the sequencing requirements imposed by the *Sonorancy Hierarchy*; see §17.18.2.

[13] Conventions will be required to adapt the branching and labeling of the syllabic tree to the results of spreading; e.g., (ii) will be transformed into (a) below. Adoption of an X, X model (note 11) obviates some but by no means all such adaptation, though judicious manipulation of the order of operations can also be brought to bear—e.g., building the syllabic tree *after* spreading. For some Aramaic applications (with the X, X model), see Malone 1989c, 1991.

(a)

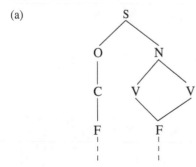

[14] Moraic patterning in Aramaic is treated in Malone 1989c, 1991, 1995. In the latter work it is also proposed that reduced vowels are systematic exceptions to convention (δ), lacking weight qua "inert elements" (see also §15.2.1.1 n. 5).

Part Four

Indexes

24. Aramaic Verb Forms

24.1. Introduction

Most Aramaic forms treated in the book are listed in §24.2, whose organization is discussed in the present section. Listing in §24.2 is limited to fully specified verb items (originally) contextualized in some primary source (notably as opposed to sketch items adduced solely in a secondary source, e.g., a root devoid of further grammatical complementation).

Entries are listed in the first instance by dialect (in the order Y, O, I, B, P, N, TR, CP, <u>SM</u>, G, SR, <u>TL</u>, M), secondarily by reconstructed pA *√root (sequenced in accordance with a derivative of one common North Semitic alphabetic order, ʾ, b, g, d, ð, h, w, W, z, ḥ, ṭ, y, k, l, m, n, s, 9, R, p, π, ṣ, θ, q, r, ś, š, t, θ), and tertially by morphological classification of form (inter alia: sim (rmp), int (rmp), cau (rmp); pf, impf, impa; 3, 2, 1; m, f; s, p; sub, sub^obj).

An individual entry typically *starts with* a <transliterated form> (§21) (occasionally absent, notably in the case of most of Margolis's (Mar) Ash <u>TL</u> forms, in default of firm criteria for determining the text-original orthographic representation) accompanied by a t[traditional pronunciation] (§2.2) when available (and/or—in the case of M—a m[modern pronunciation] when available) *followed by* a morphological classification *followed by* a [phonetic interpretation] *followed by* the *reconstructed pA etymon <u>followed by</u>* indication of the (§relevant passage(s) in the body of the book) and *ends with* a reference to the primary or secondary source whence the form has found its way into the book. Notes, remarks, or notations occasionally appear at appropriate spots within an entry, often in {curly braces}.

• In reconstruction, whether to pA (*__) or to phonetic interpretation for the specific dialects ([ ]) various simplifying and streamlining guidelines have been adopted, as will be detailed here as well as at various spots in the sequel. Concerning reconstruction to pA, for instance, linguistic changes determinable on the basis of the comparative method (§18.4) to have occurred in (the formation of) cA are assumed to have predated (hence informed) pA when they apply unconditionally but to have have postdated pA when they result in variation or alternation. Thus, ufb (§9.1.3) *precedes* pA (hence pA *√hṭʾ 'sin' < pre-A **√Xṭʾ) while wpl (§17.34) *follows* pA (hence pa *√wθb 'sit', not @*√yθb) inasmuch as 1√w remains unchanged in codal position, so that subsequent to wpl we have alternating 1√y ~ 1√w rather than unconditional 1√y.

Anachronism may at times creep into reconstructed pA forms by virtue of what are actually later changes being counterfactually treated as if they were pre-A. Thus, while the alloroot √ʔpk is in the case of three dialects (CP, S̲M̲, M) assumed to date back to pA as a choice over (antecedent) rival √hpk, chances are good that the change √ʔpk < √hpk actually postdated pA by many centuries.

In the case of presumed root metaplasms, pA reconstruction is routinely given in terms of the innovative root shape though the possibility, often even likelihood, cannot be excluded that pA knew only the original root form; e.g., under M *√wdl (< **√wld), *wadálat in lieu of *waládat.

Four-radical roots historically derivative of fossilized causatives (notably with ex-prefix **š-, **h-) are primarily listed under the guise of quadriradicals (quad); e.g., under I, *√šyzb (< **š+√yzb). Similarly, four-radical roots suppleting triradicals in various miškalim are listed primarily as quadriradicals; e.g., under B, *√rWmm (< **√rWm). (However, formations with reflexes of **š-, **h-, etc. retaining the *synchronic* function of homoparadigmatic causatives are listed under the pertinent triradical; e.g., SR jc[eštawdš9úy] under *√wd9.)

Roots taken to be homonymous (as opposed to polysemous) are list-differentiated by glosses (while otherwise root glosses are routinely omitted); e.g., under T̲L̲, *√škh 'find' vs. *√škh 'forget'.

• Either of two diametrical procedures are followed when the orthographic form in the secondary source consulted does or may deviate from that of the unconsulted primary source: *either* it is normalized (the usual procedure in the case of SR, revamped into full Nestorian (transliterated) from the hybrid Jacobite-Nestorian or pure Jacobite transcription of most sources employed (e.g., B (= Brockelmann 1965, §27), Ns, Du); *or* it is omitted in favor of an interpreted phonetic form (as in the case of most of Margolis's Tiberian renditions of Ash T̲L̲ (see above), and in the case of forms, notably TR, couched homogeneously in Tiberian orthography by Dalman 1938—e.g., *√bḥn under TR).

Occasionally, phonetic interpretations are not essayed, in which case tacit reference is invited to the book passage cited where the form is discussed; e.g., S̲M̲ <wʔPqwTy> under *√npq.

Normally, information concerning tĕ9amim (§21.6) is provided for Tiberian B orthographic transcriptions only to the extent that an accentual variable is placed on the penultimate syllable of barytone forms—mostly "t" for accent (ṭa9am) at large, with no further specification—and in default of this indication, ultimate (oxytone) accentuation is implied. Occasionally, however, more information is provided, via "p," "c," "c" (pausal, disjunctive, conjunctive), not necessarily limited to the penult, and sometimes, too, identification of the specific accent is given in curly braces immediately following the transcribed form. Forms taken to be proclitic normally end in "=" (makef), in which case absence of an accentual mark implies stresslessness rather than ultimate stress. (Examples of most of these situations may be seen under *√ʔmr for B.) Occasionally *derivative* accentual information is provided for TR, in particular for certain forms from the Onkelos Targum as calibrated to corresponding passages in the Hebrew Pentateuch; see, e.g., under *√pqd.

Untagged orthographic transcriptions and phonetic interpretations are understood in the case of B to be Tiberian (as opposed to Babylonian), in the case of TR to be Babylonian (as opposed to Tiberian, special case Sabbionetan), and in the case of SR to be Nestorian (as opposed to Jacobite).

As a rule, cliticized forms, whether proclitic or enclitic, have been reconstructed into pA as full-word forms separated from their hosts by a conjunctive word boundary (#̥; see §20.3). Notable exceptions are the proclitic particles normally written at close quarters with their hosts, in the verb system primarily the conjuntive markers *wa= 'and', *pa= 'and then'.

If an indicated ta9am is prepositive or postpositive (i.e., graphemically positioned in the nontransliterated text at the right (anlaut) or left (auslaut) edge of the word rather than beneath/above the accented syllable), transcription follows suit, only reversing the orientation; e.g., under B *√hwy, <wahăwowᵈ> indicating a postpositive disjunctive (pašta), in the transliteration positioned at the right (auslaut) edge.

Ash T̲L̲ forms prefixed by "†" are in Margolis's estimation conservative/ archaic/archaizing; e.g., †<ʔmryT> under *√ʔmr, [yɛhɛ̆wɛ̃] under *√hwy.

• Although in grammatically glossing imperfective forms, the short conjugation ("short impf") is as a rule explicitly cited only for those earlier dialects where (something of) the semantic force of the long–short opposition is maintained (§7.2), yet occasionally "(short) impf" is indicated for later dialects when licensed by the nonveridical (e.g., jussive) sense of the contextualized form being cited; e.g., M <nihuilak> under *√hwy.

• A number of tidying decisions have been provisionally made concerning occurrence or nonoccurrence of changes in the face of orthographic mootness (for the rationale of these points, refer especially to genealogy (19F) in §19 concerning the presumed proximity of the dialects in question): Y and O are assumed to be unchanged from pA in default of evidence to the contrary; I and, to a lesser extent, P and N are taken to be much like B (thus, *i* in an unstressed closed syllable when not adjacent to a guttural is assumed not to undergo (generalized) midding to *e* (§17.11), while no commitment is made to the midding or not of *i* in a *stressed* closed syllable; in counterpoint, the W dialects CP and G are taken to be similar to TR in the disposition of various changes (so that, for instance, stressed closed-syllabic *i is* assumed to mid to *e*, while no position is taken on whether mid may have generalized into closed unstressed position, where for that reason its reflexes are transcribed with noncommittal [I]); to the

extent unclued by trad pron, the phonetic interpretation of S̲M̲ is by and large
assumed to reflect a stage closely preceding the emergence of the Samaritan
Circuit (§22.1)—" by and large" because, for a congeries of reasons, it has
proved difficult to apply this criterion with rigor.

Though variants and alternant interpretations/reconstructions *are* for the
most part adduced, listings are not necessarily exhaustive; see cited passages
in the body of the book for additional possibilities from case to case.

• Reconstructions to pA are subject to a certain amount of stereotyping, primarily at the behest of expository simplicity. Thus, later 3ms object suffixes of
ultimate shape [-I̊h] (e.g., B, TR, SR [-ēh]) are stereotypically reconstructed to
(pre-bridge, §2.2.1.4) alloshape *-*hi*, while in reality antecedents of alloshape
*-*hu* (§2.3.4.4) would likewise end up as [-I̊h].

In the case of formal gender merger (fgm, §16.1), pA reconstruction is
guided by form rather than function; e.g., T̲L̲ under *√ṭbl, *ṭăbílū rather than
*ṭăbílā.

*   *   *   *   *   *

Section §24.3 consists of a comprehensive root index calibrated to §24.2.

24.2. Index of Forms by Dialect

Ya'udic

*√hwy   \<hwT> sim pf 3fs [hawā́t] < *hawayát or *hawáyat (§8.1.1 with n. 6) DR I
#215:2.

*√wθb   \<yŝBT> sim pf 1s [yaθíbt] < *waθíbt (§17.34) DR I #214:8.

*√hq   \<Thq> sim impf 2ms [taḥḥúq] < *(same) (§3.3) DR I #214:34.

*√ktš   \<PlKTšh> conj sim impf 3ms^3ms [pa=laktkúšhi] < *(same) (§17.19) DR I
#214:31.

*√l9y   \<wTl9y> conj sim impf 3fs [wa=til9áy] or [wa=tal9í̂] < *(same) (§9.2.3.1
n. 30) DR I #214:32.

*√ntn   \<yTh> sim impf 3ms [yattín] < *yantín (§17.21.1 n. 105) DR I 214:23.
\<yT{n}w> sim impf 3mp [yattínū] < *yantínū (§17.21.1 n. 105) DR I#214:4.

*√pWš   \<wPŝŝ> conj int pf 3ms [wa=pāšíša] < *(same) (§6.2.1 n. 16) DR I #215:8. {*in
all likelihood an incorrect interpretation; more likely as given under *√pš,
next entry, concerning which see also DR II:227*}

*√pš   \<wPŝŝ> conj int or sim pf 3ms [wa=paššíša] or [wa=pašáša] < *(same) (§3.3)
DR I #215:8 {*see also under* *√pWš, *preceding entry*}

*√qr'   \<qrny> sim pf 3ms^1s [qarā́ni] < *qara'ā́nī (§9.1.4) DR I #214:13.

*√rRy (< **√rðy)   \<yrqy> sim impf 3ms [yirRáy] < *(same) (§11.2 (11A), §17.24)
DR I #214:18, 22.

*mWt   \<mTT> sim pf 1s [mítit]/[mītít] or [mắtit]/[mātít] (or possibly [mítǝt]/[mắtǝt]
< *mít(ǝ̆)t / *mắt(ǝ̆)t) (§15.3.1.2) DR I #226.4.

Old Aramaic

*√ʔbd   <ʔhʔBD> ~ <ʔhBD> cau impf 1s [ʔihaʔbídi] ~ [ʔihabbídi] < *ʔihaʔbídi (§9.2.1.1 with n. 13) De 71f with n. 64.

*√hwy   <{h}wT> sim pf 3fs [hawā̆t] < *hawayát or *hawáyat (§8.1.1 with n. 6) De 76
        <yhwh> sim impf 3ms [yihwḗ] < *yihwáyi (§11.2 (11A)) De 76.
        <Thwy> sim short impf 3fs [tihwáy] < *(same) (§11.2 (11A)) De 77.
        <hwy> simp impa ms [hă̆wī́] < *(same) (§8.1.3) De 77.

*√wθb   <ŝBw> sim impa mp [θíbu] < *(same) (§17.33) De 74.

*√Wṭb   <hyṭBTh> cau pf 1s^3ms [hayṭíbtǝhi] < *(same) (§17.5 with n. 5) De 80; MP 123.

*√mḥ̣   <wymḥ̣ʔhy> conj sim impf 3ms^3ms [wa=yimḥạʔíhī] < *(same) (§9.1.4 n. 11) Steiner 2000–2001: 240.

*√ml   <ymll> int impf 3ms [yimallíli] < *(same) (§3.3) De 73.

*√sb   <ysB> sim impf 3ms [yassúbi] < *(same) (§3.3) De 72.

*√9br   <y9Brnh> sim impf 3ms^3ms [ya9burinníhi] < *(same) (§7.1) De 109.

*√rRy (<**√rð̣y)   <ʔrqhm> int impf 1s^3mp [ʔiraRRēhúm] < *ʔiraRRay(i)húm (§17.15.1 n. 64) De 80.

*√šly   <ŝlw> sim impa mp [šĭláw] < *šĭ́láyū (§8.1.1) De 77.

*√šm9   <yTŝm9> sim rmp or cau rmp short impf 3ms [yitšamí9] or [yittašmá9] < *yitšamí9 or *yithašmá9 (§10) De 42.

*√šry   <Tŝryh> sim short impf 2ms^3ms [tišráyhi] or [tašrī́hi] < *(same) (§7.1) De 114.

*√θWb   <ThŝBhm> cau impf 2ms^3mp [tihaθībihím] < *(same) (§17.15.1 n. 64) De 80.

Imperial Aramaic

*√ʔmr   <yʔmr> sim impf 3ms [yIʔmár] < *yaʔmúri (§9.2.1.1 with n. 13) L 21; MP 124.
        <n̄m{r}> sim impf 1p [nimmár] < *naʔmúri (§9.2.1.1 with n. 13) L21.

*√ʔty   <ʔTh> simp impa ms [ʔθθá̆] < *ʔítáy or perhaps *ʔitáʔ (§8.1.3 n. 15) L 67; MP 142.
        <ʔTyh> cau impa fs^3ms [ʔattī́h]/[ʔēθī́h] < *haʔtiyī́hi (§8.1.1) MP 148.
        <hyTy> cau pf 3ms [hayTī́]/[hēθī́] < *haʔtíya (§9.2.1.1) MP 142.
        <yhyTh> cau impf 3ms [yǝhayTḗ]/[yǝhēθḗ] < yihaʔtáyi (§11.2) L 67; MP 142.
        <yhTw> ~ <yTw> ~ <yhyTw>   cau short impf 3mp [yǝhattáw]/[yǝhattṓ]
        /[yǝhāθáw]/[yǝhāθṓ] ~ [yattáw]/[yattṓ]
        /[yāθáw]/[yāθṓ] ~ [yǝhayTáw]
        /[yǝhayTṓ]/[yǝhēθáw]/[yǝhēθṓ]
        < *y(ih)aʔtáyū (§9.2.1.1) MP 142.

*√bny   <yBnwn> sim impf 3mp [yivnṓn] < *yibnayū̆na (§8.1.1) L §40f.

*√b9y (< **√bRy)   <TB9h> sim short impf 2ms [tiv9ḗ] < *tib9áyi (§11.2) L 63.

*√brk   <BrKTKy> int pf 1s^2fs [barrixtíxī]/[bārixtíxī] < *barríktǝkī (§2.3.4.4) Kutscher 1970: 170; MP 144.

*√gz   <Gzh> sim impa ms^3fs [guzzā̆h] < *gúzha (§3.3) L 66; MP 133, 147.

*√gly   <TGly> sim short impf 2ms [tiɣláy] < *tigláy* (§11.2) L 63.

*√gš   <hGŝŝ> cau pf 3msa [haɣšĺš] < *hagšíša* (§3.3) L 67; MP 133f.

*√hwy   <hwT> sim pf 3fs [hə̆wæ̃θ] < *hawayát* or *hawáyat* (§8.1.1 with n. 6) L 64;
           MP 135.

           <ʾhwh> sim impf 1s [ʾIhwḗ] < *ʾihwáyi* (§11.2) L 63; MP 137.

*√wd9   <yD9> ~ <ynD9> sim impf 3ms [yiddá9] ~ [yindá9] < *yidá9i* (§17.8) Kut-
           scher 1970: 71.

           <TD9n> sim short impf 2fp [tiddə̆9ã́n] < *tida9án* (§2.3.4.2) MP 105.

           <yTy{D9}> sim rmp impf 3ms [yiθyə̆ðá9] < *yitwadí9i* (§17.34) L 60.

           <hwD9> cau pf 3ms [hawDá9]/[hōðá9] < *hawdí9a* (§17.34) L 60; MP 59.

*√whb   <yhBT> sim pf 1s [yahBĺθ]/[yə̆hávịθ] < *wahábt* (§17.34) L 60.

*√wld   <ylDTy> ~ <ylTy> sim pf 2fs [yə̆lĺðtī] ~ [yə̆lĺttī] < *walídtī* (§10 n. 3) Kraeh-
           ling 1953: 180; Kutscher 1970: 72.

*√Wṭb   <hwṭBTm> cau pf 2mp [hawṭivtǗm]/[hōṭivtǗm] < *hawṭibtúm* (§17.5 n. 5) L
           60; MP 98, 123.

*√wθb   <TB> sim impa ms [tĺv] < *θíb* (§17.33) L 59f.

*√zhr   <ʾzDhrw> int rmp impa mp [ʾizdah(h)árū] < *hitzahhárū* (§10) L 20; MP 17,
           116.

*√ḥsn   <ʾThḥsynn> cau rmp pf 3mp [ʾiθhaḥsīnún] < *hithaḥsínū* {*questionable; note
           *2ʃi in lieu of expected *a, and the unexpected importation of impf* -ūn (*hii*)}
           (§9.2.2, §17.28) Coxon 1977: 297.

*√mWt   <myTT> ~ <mʾTT> sim pf 1s [mĺθiθ]/[mīθĺθ] ~ [mǽθiθ]/[māθĺθ] < *mĺt(ə̆)t* ~
           mǽt(ə̆)t (§15.3.1.2, §17.6.2) MP 131.

*√mr   <Tmr> sim short impf 2ms [timmár] < *(same)* (§3.3) L 66.

*√nḥt (or possibly *√ḥt)   <yḥTwn> sim impf 3mp [yV̌ḥ(ḥ)ə̆θún] < *yanḥutúna* or
                            possibly *yaḥḥutúna* (§17.2.1.1) L 57.

           <ḥT> sim impa ms [ḥǗθ] < *ḥút* (§17.33) L 57.

*√nθr   <ṭr> sim impa ms [ṭar] < *θar* or *θúr* (§17.33) L 57; MP 12 n. 54, 126.

*√nśʾ   <ś ʾ> sim impa ms [śã́] < *śáʾ* (§8.1.3) L §42a; MP 126, 128.

*√sbl   <ʾsBlnK> int impf 1s^2ms [ʾə̆sabbə̆linnã́x] < *ʾisabbilinníka* (§7.1) L 51; MP
           145.

*√9ðr   <9ə̆zwr> sim impa ms [9ə̆zǗr] < *9ə̆ðúr* (§17.10) L §32a.

*√9l (< **√Rl)   <9l> sim pf 3ms [9ál] < *9álla* (§3.3 with nn. 6 and 7) L 66.

           <9lT> sim pf 1s [9álliθ]/9allĺθ] < *9ált* (§3.3 with nn. 6 and 7) L 66;
           MP 133.

           <9lw> sim pf 3mp [9állū] < *(same)* (§3.3 with nn. 6 and 7) L 66.

           <hn9lT> cau pf 1s [han9ə̆lĺθ]/[han9ĺliθ] < *ha99ílt* (§3.3, §17.18)
           L 66.

           <yn9l> cau impf 3ms [yan9ĺl] < *y(ih)a99íli* (§17.8) L 66.

*√9r   <9w̄wry> sim impa fs [9 úrī] < *9úrrī*{?} (§6.2.2 n. 19) L 28.

*√9št   <9ŝTT> sim pf 1s [9IšTĺθ]/[9ašTĺθ] or [9ŝšã́θiθ] < *9ašát(ə̆)t* (§15.3.1.2)
           Kutscher 1970: 79.

*√plg   <nPlG> int short impf 1p [nə̆fallĺɣ] < *nipallíg* (§17.15.1) L 51.

*√ṣby   <ṣByT> sim pf 1s [ṣə̆vḗθ] or [ṣə̆vĺθ] < *ṣabáyt* or *ṣabít* (§17.15.1) L 51.

*√qWm   <qmw> sim impa mp [qúmū] or possibly [qǗmmū] < *qúmū* (§6.2.2.1 n. 19)
           L 61; MP 131.

*√rg   <TrGG> int short impf 2ms [tăraggíɣ] < *tiraggíg (§3.3) L 66; MP 134.

*√rhR (< **√rhð̠)   <ʾrh9h> sim short impf 1s^3ms [ʾV̆rh̬9ĕh] < *ʾV̆rh̬V̆Rhi (§7.1, §9.1.3 n. 6) Kutscher 1970:82; MP 9, 104, 146.

*√rty   <rTʾ> int impa ms [rattḗ] < *rattáy (§8.1.3) L §40d, o.

*√šbq   <šBqwhy> sim impa mp^3ms [šV̆vqǘhī] < *šăbuqǘhī (§8.2.2) L 52.

*√šyzb (< **š+ √yzb)   <šzBK> quad pf 3ms^2ms [šēzə̆vǽx] < *šayzibáka (§11.2) L 61.

*√škh̬ ('find')   <ʾšTKh̬w> sim rmp pf 3mp [ʾĬštə̆xáh̬u] < *hitšakíh̬ū (§10) L 20; MP 59, 118.

     <áš-ka-h̬i-i> {cuneiform} cau impa fs [ʾaškáh̬ī] < *haškíh̬ī (§17.10) Gordon 1937–39: 11.

*√šm9   <ʾšTmy9> sim rmp pf 3ms [ʾĬštə̆mí9]/[ʾĬštə̆mía9] < *hitšamí9a (§17.28 with n. 142) Kutscher 1970: 70.

Biblical Aramaic

*√ʾbd tb<t:howveð>   cau short impf 2ms tb[tə̆hōvéð] bb<tə̆hōvǽð> < *tihaʾbíd ~ perhaps *tihaʾbád {with *2ʃa < pre-Aramaic **2ʃi by Philippi's Law, scantily traceable in A, whereby stressed i lowers to a in a closed syllable} (§9.2.1.2) BL 140; Dan 2:24.

*√ʾzl tb<ʾăzal>   sim pf 3ms tb[ʾăzál] bb[ʾæzǽl] ~ [ʾæzél] < *ʾazála ~ *ʾazíla (§9.3.1 with n. 34, §17.23.3) BL 139; Dan 2:17.

     <ʾézɛl=> ~ <ʾezêl> sim impa ms [ʾézɛl=] ~ [ʾezel] < *ʾăzíl(#̬) (§9.3.1, §17.23.3) BL §18p, §44k–l; Ezra 5:15.

*√ʾkl tb<yeʾxul>   sim impf 3ms tb[yēxǘl] bb[yōxǘl] < *yaʾkúli (§9.2.1.2, §11.2, §17.29 (17.29A)) BL 139; Dan 4:30.

     <teʾxul> sim impf 3fs [tēxǘl] < *taʾkúli (§12.2) BL 139; Dan 5:16.

     tb<ʾăxûliy> sim impa fs tb[ʾăxúlī] bb[ʾĭxúlī] < *ʾăkúlī (§17.23.2, §17.23.3 with (17.23B) and n. 123) BL 139; Dan 7:5.

*√ʾmr tb<ʾamar=>   sim pf 3ms tb[ʾămar=] {stressless} bb[ʾæ̆mær] ~ [ʾə̆mær]{whatever the stress} < ʾamára #̬ (§17.5.2, §17.23.3 (17.23B)) BL 139f.; Dan 2:12.

     <ʾam:reθ> sim pf 1s [ʾamréθ] < *ʾamárt (§12.2, §17.11.3 n. 41) BL 139; 4:5.

     tb<w:yĕʾmar> {merxa} conj sim impf 3ms tb[wə̆yĕ̆mar] bb[wə̆yōmær] {whatever the stress} < *wa=yaʾmúri #̬ (§17.15.2 n. 75) BL 139; Dan 4:12.

     <neʾmar> sim impf 1p [nēmár] < *naʾmúri (§9.2.1.1) BL 139; Dan 2:36.

     tb<ʾĕmar> sim impa ms tb[ʾĕmár] bb[ʾemǽr] < ʾĭmár (§11.11 n. 1, §17.23.2, §17,23.3 with (17.23B)) BL 139; Dan 4:6.

     <ʾĕmǎr> ~ <ʾĕmǒr> {siluk} sim impa ms [ʾĕmǎr] ~ [ʾĕmǒr] < ʾĭmǎr (§17.29 with (17.29A)) BL 139; Dan 4:6.

*√ʾty   <hay:θiy> cau pf 3ms [hayθí] < *haʾtíya (§11.2) BL 169; Dan 5:13.

     <heyθåyiθ> ~ <he(y)θə̆yiθ> ~ <heyθíyaθ> cau pas pf 3fs [hēθáyiθ] ~ [hēθə̆yiθ] ~ [hēθíyaθ] < *huʾtáyt ~ *huʾtíyat {why the unexpected occurrence

of tln on at least the second variant?} (§4.1.2, §11.2 with n. 7,
§17.6.2 with (17.6D)) BL 169; Dan 6:18.

tb<heyθɔ̇yuw> {tifḥa} cau pas pf 3mp tb[hēθɔ́yū] bb[hæyθɑ́yū] ~ [hēθɑ́yū]
< *huʾtáyu {forms offbeat because of failure of e-cnd, @[-θō], as
well as unexpected tln, @[-θÁyū]} (§11.1, §11.2) BL 169; Dan
3:13.

*√bhl   <y:vạhalɔx> int short impf 3ms^2ms [yɔ̆vah(h)ălɔ́x] < *yibahhilíka (§7.1) BL
131; Dan 4:16.

    <y:vạhăluwx> int short impf 3mp^2ms [yɔ̆vah(h)ălū́x] < *yibahhilúka (§7.1)
BL 131; Dan 5:10.

    tb<y:vạhaluwn̊e̊h> int impf 3mp^3ms tb[yɔ̆vah(h)ălů̊nnḗh]
bb[yɔ̆væh(h)ɔ̆lů̊nnḗh] < *yibahhilů̊nnáhi (§17.23.3 (17.23B)) BL
131; Dan 5:6.

    <y:vạhăluṅ̊ɑ̊niy> int impf 3mp^1s [yɔ̆vah(h)ălunnánī] < *yibahhilunnánī
(§9.3.1) BL 59, 131; Dan 4:2.

*√bṭl   <b:ṭe(y)laθ > ~ <b:ṭilaθ > sim pf 3fs [bɔ̆ṭelɑ́θ] ~ [bɔ̆ṭ̊ilɑ́θ] < *baṭilát (§4.2.1
with n. 12, §5.2.1.1) BL 102f.; Ezra 4:24.

*√bny   <b:nɔ̇hiy> sim pf 3ms^3ms [bɔ̆nɔ̇hī] < *banayáhī (§2.3.4.4) BL 161; Ezra
5:11.

    <b:now> sim pf 3mp [bɔ̆nṓ] < *banáyū (§11.2) BL 161; Ezra 6:14.

*√b9y (**√bRy)   <b:9ɔ́ʾ> {munaḥ} sim pf 3ms [bɔ̆9ɔ́] < *ba9áya (§8.1.1) BL 161;
Dan 2:49.

    tb<wuv:9ɔ̇h> {munaḥ} conj sim pf 3ms tb[ů̊v9ɔ́] bb[wiv9ɑ̊́] < *wa=ba9áya
(§12.2 with n. 8) BL 161; Dan 2:16.

    <ʾɛv:9ę̇ʾ=> ~ <ʾɛv9ė̇ʾ> sim impf 1s [ʾɛv9ė̀=] ~ [ʾɛv9ė́] < *ʾib9áyi(#̇) (§12.2,
§17.11.3, BL 161; 164; Dan7:16.

*√bqr   <baqᵂɑ̊ruw> ~ <baqᵂɔ̊ruw> int pf 3mp [baqqárū] ~ [baqqɔ́rū] (§17.29 (17.29A))
BL 134; Ezra 4:19.

*√brk   tb<b:borᵖɑ̊x> int pf 3ms tb[bɔ̆rî́x] bb[bū̊rė̊́x] < *barríka (§9.3.1, §17.29 n. 144)
BL 58, 131; Dan 2:19.

*√gd   <gȯ̊duw> sim impa mp [góddū] < *gúddū (§3.3, §17.11.3 n. 39, §17.29
(17.29A)) BL 167; Dan 4:11, 20.

*√gzr   tb<hiθ:g:zɛ́rɛθ> ~ <ʾiθ:g:zɛ́rɛθ> sim rmp 3fs tb[hiθgɔ̆zɛ́rɛθ] ~ [ʾiθgɔ̆zɛ́rɛθ]
bb[hiθgɔ̆zɔ̆ɛ́ræθ] ~ [ʾiθgɔ̆zɛ́ræθ] < *hitgazírt (possibly ~ *hitgazírat)
(§2.3.4.3, §4.1.2 n. 6) BL 134; Dan 2:34, 45.

*√gly   tb<găliy> ~ <gɔ̆liy> sim pas pf 3ms tb[gălî́] ~ [gɛ̆lî́] bb[gŭlî́] < *galíya ~
*gulíya (§17.23.3) BL 67, 164; Dan 2:19, 30.

*√dWr   <t:ðuw> sim impf 2ms [tɔ̆ðů̊r] < *tadúri (§6.2.2) BL 148; Dan 4:18.

*√dq   <dɔ̇quw> sim pf 3mp [dɔ́qū] < *dáqqū (§6.2.2) BL 148; Da 330 n. 2; Dan
2:25.

    tb<hadȧ̇qɛθ> ~ <hadȧ̇qɛθ> cau pf 3fs tb[haddɛ́qɛθ] ~ [haddéqɛθ] bb[hæddéqæθ]
< *haddáqt {ʃa possibly a trace of Phillipi's Law; cf. above under
*√ʾbd} (§4.1.2, §17.6.2 with (17.6D) and nn. 8 and 11, §17.11.3)
BL 168; Dan 2:34, 45.

    <hadȧ̇quw> cau pf 3mp [haddíqū] < *(same) (§3.3) BL 168; Dan 6:25.

tb<tadíq> {*merxa*} cau impf 3fs tb[taddíq] bb[tæddéq] < **t(ih)addíqi*
(§17.11.3 with n. 38) BL 168; Dan 2:40, 44.

*√ðḥl   <wiyðaḥălin̈ániy> conj int impf 3ms^1s [wīðaḥ(ḥ)ǎlinnánī] <
*wa=yiðaḥḥilinníni (§17.13) BL 131; Dan 4:2.

*√hwy   tb<hăweyθ> sim pf 1s tb[hǎwḗθ] bb[hǎwḗθ] < **hawáyt* (§11.2) BL 161; Dan
4:1, 7:2.

tb<wahăwowᵈ> {*pašta*} conj sim pf 3mp tb[wahǎwṓ] bb[wæhwṓ] <
*wa=hawáyū (§12.2 with n. 8) BL 263; Dan 2:35.

tb<lɛhĕwę²=>, <lɛhĕweh> ~ <lɛhwe²> sim impf 3ms tb[lɛhĕwè=], [lɛhĕwḗ] ~
[lɛhwḗ] bb[lihwḗ] < **yihwáyi(#̊)* or *lihwáyi(#̊)* (§17.11.3, §17.19)
BL 161, 164; Dan 2:20, Ezra 4:12.

tb<tɛhĕwe²> ~ <tɛhĕweh> sim impf 3fs tb[tɛhĕwḗ] bb[tihwḗ] < **tihwáyi*
(§11.1 n. 1, §11.2, §12.2) BL 161; Dan 2:40, 41.

tb<tɛhĕwe²> sim impf 2ms tb[tɛhĕwḗ] bb[tihwḗ] < **tihwáyi* (§17.23.3) BL
161; Dan 2:40.

tb<lɛhĕwon> sim impf 3mp tb[lɛhĕwṓn] bb[lihwṓn] < **yihwayúna* or
*lihwayúna (§4.3, §4.4.1, §17.19, §17.23.3 with n. 121) BL 161;
Dan 2:43, 6:29; Ezra 6:10.

tb<lɛhɛw:yɔn> sim impf 3fp tb[lɛhɛwyǎ́n] bb[lihwĭyǎ́n] (§4.4.1, §4.4.2,
§17.11.3, §17.19, §17.23.2, §17.23.3 n. 121 and (17.23B)) BL 161;
Dan 5:17.

<hăwow> ~ <hĕwow> sim impa mp [hǎwṓ] ~ [hĕwṓ] < **hĭwáyū* (§17.23.2)
BL 161; Ezra 6:6, 4:22.

*√hWk   <y:hɔx> sim short impf 3ms[yǎhɔ́x] < **yihák* (§6.1.1.2 with n. 6) BL 148;
Ezra 5:5, 7:13

<wiyhax> ~ <wiyhɔx> conj sim short impf 3ms [wīháx] ~ [wīhɔ́x] <
*wa=yihák (§6.1.1.2 with n. 6, §6.2.2, §12.2 with n. 8) BL 148f.;
Ezra 6:5.

*√hymn   (plausibly < **h+ √²mn) tb<heymin> {*merxa*} quad pf 3ms tb[hēmín]
bb[hēmén] < **haymína* (§9.2.1.2 with n. 16, §17.29 n. 144) BL 140; Dan
6:24.

*√wd9   tb<y:ða9> sim pf 3ms tb[yǎðá9] bb[(²)īðǽ9] < **wadá9a* (§14.2) BL 142; Dan
5:21.

<yið:9eθ> sim pf 1s [yið9éθ] < **wadá9t* (§4.1.1) BL 142; Dan 4:6.

<y:ða9> sim impf 3ms [yǎðá9] < **yidá9i* {*doubtful; variant reading of con-
ventionally accepted participial* [yɔ̄ðá9]} (§17.7) BL 143; Ezra
7:25.

<tin:da9> sim impf 2ms [tindá9] <**tidá9i* (§17.7, §17.8) BL 142; Dan 2:30.

<²in:da9> sim impf 1s [²indá9] < **²idá9i* (§12.2, §17.8, §17.11.3) BL 142;
Dan 2:9.

<yin:d:9uwn> sim impf 3mp [yindǎ9ú̃n] < **yida9úna* (§17.8) BL 142; Dan
4:14.

<da9> sim impa ms [dá9] < **(same)* (§17.33) BL 142; Dan 6:16.

tb<howða9:t̂ɛnɔ²> ~ <howða9:tân ²> ~ possibly <howða9:tɔ̂nɔ²> cau pf
2ms^1p tb[hōða9ténɔ̄] ~ [hōða9tánɔ̄] ~ possibly [hōða9tɔ̂nɔ̄]
bb[hōð9ætǽnā] < **hawdi9tánā* (§2.3.4.4 n. 39) BL 143; Dan 2:23.

tb<ʔăhọwð:9iñeͮh> cau impf 1sˆ3ms tb[ʔăhōðə̆9innéͤh] bb[ʔehōðəæ̈9innéͤh] <
*ʔihawdi9inníhi (§17.23.3 (17.23B)) BL 67, 143; Dan 5:17.

*√whb   tb<y:hav= > sim pf 3ms tb[yə̆hav=] bb[(ʔ)īhæv] {whatever the stress} <
*wahába # (§14.2, §17.34) BL 142; Dan 2:37.

<wịyhiyvå̊θ>, <y:hiyvå̊θ>, <y:hịyva l:hown> (conj) sim pas pf 3fs [wīhīvåθ],
[yə̆hīvåθ], [yə̆hívaθ # lə̆hón] < (wa=)wahibát, *wa=wahībát #
lahúm (§4.1.2, §17.15.1 n. 75) BL 142; Dan 5:28, 7:11, 12, 27.

<yiθ:y:hi(y)v> ~ <yiθ:y:hev> sim rmp impf 3ms [yiθyə̆hív] ~ [yiθyə̆hév] <
*yitwahíbi (§14.2, §17.34) BL 143; Dan 4:13.

*√wkl   <yiküͮl> ~ <yuwxal> sim impf 3ms [yikkúl] ~ [yūxál] < *yakúli ~ *yiwkáli
(§17.7) BL 142; Dan 3:29.

*√wsp   tb<hụwsăfaθ=> ~ <hůwsafaθ> {merxa} cau pas pf 3fs tb[hụ̀săfaθ=] ~ [hůsăfaθ]
bb[hūsə̆fæθ] {whatever the stress} < *huwsipát # (§17.15.2 with n. 75) BL
24, 143; Dan 4:33.

*√w9θ   <ʔiθ:yɔ9å̇ṭuw> int rmp pf 3mp [ʔiθyɔ9áṭū] < *hitwa99áθū (§17.34) BL 143;
Dan 6:8.

*√wθb   <y:θiv> sim pf 3ms [yə̆θív] < *waθíba (§17.14) BL 143; Dan 7:9.

<yiͮti(y)v> ~ <yθiyv> sim impf 3ms [yittív] ~ [yə̆θíͤv] or possibly [yə̆θív] <
*yaθíbi (§17.7) BL 142f; Dan 7:26.

<w:howθev> conj cau pf 3ms [wə̆hōθév] < wa=hawθíba (§17.15.1) BL 143;
Ezra 4:10.

*√Wṭb   <yeyṭav> sim impf 3ms [yēṭáv] < *yiṭábi or *yayṭábi (§17.7) BL 142; Ezra
7:18.

*√zmn kə̆tiv   <hiž̆:min:tuwn > ~ kĕrey <hiz:d:min:tuwn > {pašta} ~ <hiz:d:mentuwn>
sim rmp pf 2mp [hizzə̆mintún] ~ <hizdə̆mintún> ~ <hizdə̆mèntún] <
*hitzamintúm (§10, §15.5.1, §17.11.3 with n. 40) BL 109, 111; Dan 2:9.

*√z9q   tb<z:9ịq> sim pf 3ms tb[zə̆9íq] bb[zə̆9ḛ̈q] < *za9íqa (§17.29 n. 144) BL 131;
Dan 6:21.

*√ḥbl (< **√Xbl)   <ḥab̆:lůwhiy> int impa mpˆ3ms [ḥabbə̆lúͤhī] < *ḥabbilúͤhī (§2.3.4.4,
§8.2.2) Brown 1979: 1116; Dan 5:6.

*√ḥzy   tb<ḥăzɔh> sim pf 3ms tb[ḥázɔ̈] bb[ḥə̆zɔ̈̈] < *ḥazáya (§17.23.3) BL 161; Dan
4:20, 7:1.

tb<ḥazàyθɔh> sim pf 2ms tb[ḥăzáyθɔ̈] bb[ḥə̆zǽyθɔ̈] < *ḥazáytā (§11.1) BL
161; Dan 2:41.

tb<ḥăzeyθuwn> sim pf 2mp tb[ḥăzēθúͤn] bb[ḥə̆zēθón] < *ḥazaytúm (§2.3.4.3,
§7.7, §8.1 n. 1, §11.2) BL 161; Dan 2:8.

*√ḥwy   tb<y:haḥăwḛͤh> ~ <y:haḥăwḛͤh> {siluk} cau impf 3ms tb[yə̆haḥăwḛ̈] ~
{yə̆haḥăwḛ̈} bb[{yə̆}hæḥwḛ̈] < *yihaḥwǎyi (§4.3, §17.29 with n. 145) BL
165; Dan 5:12.

tb<n:haḥăwḛͤh> ~ <n:haḥăwḛ̈ʔ> ~ <n:haḥăwḛͤh> {siluk} cau impf 1p
tb[nə̆haḥăwḛ̈] ~ [nə̆haḥăwḛ̈] bb[nə̆hæḥwḛ̈] < nihaḥwǎyi (§17.29
with n. 145) BL 165; Dan 2:7.

<y:haẘiñániy> int impf 3msˆ1s [yə̆ḥawwiͤnnánī] < *yiḥawwiy(i)nnínī (§11.1)
BL 164; Dan 5:7.

tb<ʾăḥawê̌ʾ> ~ <ʾăḥawê̌ʰh> ~ <ʾăḥawê̌h> {siluk} int short impf 1s tb[ʾăḥawwê̌]
~ [ʾăḥawwê̌] bb[ʾeḥæwwê̌] < *ʾiḥawwăy (§11.2 with nn. 5 and 6,
§17.23.3 (17.23B), §17.29 with n. 145) BL 164f.; Dan 2:24.

tb<n:ḥawê̌ʾ> ~ <n:ḥawê̌ʰh> ~ <n:ḥawê̌ʰh> {siluk} int impf 1p tb[nǎḥawwê̌] ~
[nǎḥawwê̌] bb[nǎḥæwwê̌] < *niḥawwăyi (§17.29 with n. 145) BL
164f.; Dan 2:4.

*√ḥWṭ (< **√XWṭ)   <yaḥiytuw> ~ <yoḥiytuw> cau short impf 3mp [yaḥīṭū] ~
[yǒḥīṭū] < *yaḥīṭū (§6.1.2 with (6C) and n. 9, §6.2) BL 151;
Ezra 4:12.

*√ḥy(y)   <ḥĕyiy> sim impa ms [ḥĕyī] < *ḥăyī (§8.1.3) BL 170; Dan 2:4.

*√ḥlp (< **√Xlp)   tb<yaḥ:l:fuwn> sim impf 3mp tb[yaḥlǒfún] bb[yiḥlǒfún] <
*yaḥlupúna (§12.2, §17.11.3, §17.23.3 (17.23B)) BL 30, 128f.;
Dan 4:13.

*√ḥrb (< **√Xrb)   <ḥoḥor:vaθ> cau pas pf 3fs [hoḥorváθ] < *huḥribát (§17.23.3)
BL 130; Ezra 4:15.

*√ḥtm (< **√Xtm)   <ḥaθ:máh> ~ <ḥaθ:moh> sim pf 3ms^3fs tb[ḥaθmáh] ~ [ḥaθmǒ́h]
bb[ḥæθmǽh] < *ḥatamáha (§2.3.4.4, §12.2) BL 129; Dan 6:18.

*√ṭ9m   tb<y:ṭa9ămuwňeh> int impf 3mp^3ms tb[yǒṭa9(9)ǎmǔnnéh]
bb[yǒṭǽ9(9)æmǔnnéh] < *yiṭa99imǔnnáhi (§17.23.3 (17.23B)) BL 131 with
n. 1; Dan 5:21.

*√kry   <ʾiθ:k:riy̌aθ> ~ <ʾεθ:k:riy̌aθ> sim rmp pf 3fs [ʾiθkǒriyyáθ] ~ [ʾεθkǒriyyáθ] <
*hitkariyát (§15.2.1.1 with n. 4) BL 164; Dan 7:15.

*√kl   <yiš:tax:l:luwn> cau rmp impf 3mp [yištaxlǒlún] < *yitšaklalúna (§6.3, §10
n. 1) BL 168, Brown 1979: 1197; Ezra 4:13, 16.

*√ktb   <k:θav> sim plain pf 3ms [kǒθáv] < *katába (§4.2.2) BL 102; Dan 6:26, 7:1.
<k:θiyv> sim pas pf 3ms [kǒθív] < *katíba BL 104; Ezra 5:7, 6:2.

*√lbš   <til:baš> sim impf 2ms [tilbáš] < *tilbáši (§12.2) BL 142; Dan 2:9.

*√mṭy   <m:ṭɔθ> ~ <m:ṭaθ> ~ <m:ṭɔyaθ> sim pf 3fs [mǒṭɔ́θ] ~ [mǒṭáθ] ~ [mǒṭɔyáθ] <
*maṭayát (§15.2.1.5, §15.4) BL 161, 164; Dan 4:19, 21.

*√ml   tb<malil̆> int pf 3ms [tb[mallíl] bb[mællê̌l] < *mallíla (§17.29 n. 144) BL
167; Dan 6:22.
<y:malil̆> int impf 3ms [yǒmallíl] < *yimallíli (§3.3) BL 167; Dan 7:25.

*√mny   <mĕňiy> int impa ms [ménī] < *mannī́ (§8.1.3 with n. 18, §17.15.1 n. 75) BL
164; Ezra 7:25.

*√nWd   <t:nuð> sim impf 2ms [tǒnúð] or [tǒnúð] < *tanúdi (§6.2.2) BL 148; Dan
4:11.

*√nḥt (~ *√ḥt)   <taḥeθ> cau impf 2ms [taḥ(ḥ)éθ] < *tanḥíti or *taḥḥíti (§17.21.1)
BL 137; Ezra 6:5.
<ʾaḥeθ> ~ <ʾǎḥeθ> cau impa ms [ʾaḥ(ḥ)éθ] ~ [ʾǎḥéθ] < *haḥḥít
(§17.21.1) BL 137; Ezra 5:15.

*√nṭl   tb<niṭ:leθ> sim pf 1s tb[niṭléθ] bb[næṭléθ] < *naṭált (§12.2) BL 136; Dan 4:31.

*√npl   <yiṗel> sim impf 3ms [yippél] < *yanpíli (§17.21.1) BL 136; Dan 3:6.

*√npq   tb<nεf:qaθ> sim pf 3fs tb[nεfqáθ] bb[nǒfǽqæθ] < *napaqát ~ *napáqat (§12.1
n. 1) BL 136; Dan 2:13.
<pù(w)quw> sim impa mp [púqū] < *(same) (§17.33) BL 136; Dan 3:26.

*√nθr   <niṭ:réθ> sim pf 1s [niṭréθ] < *naθárt (§17.14) BL 136; Dan 7:28.

*√nšʾ   <wun:šɔʾ> conj sim pf 3ms [ůnšɔ̃] < *wa=naśáʾa (§17.15.1) BL 168; Dan
2:35.

<šeʾ> sim impa ms [šé] < *šáʾ (§8.1.3) BL 168; Ezra 5:15.

*√ntn   <yin:tin= > ~ <yin:tɛn= > sim impf 3ms [yintìn=] or [yintin=] ~ [yintèn=] or
[yintɛn=] <*yantíni # (§17.11.3 n. 37) BL 136; Dan 2:16.

<tin:ten> sim impf 2ms [tintén] < *tantíni (§12.2) BL 136; Ezra 7:20.

*√sgd   tb<s:γǐ̊ð> sim pf 3ms tb[sǎγǐð] bb[sǎγě̊ð] < *sagída (§17.29 (17.29A)) BL
102; Dan 2:46.

<yis:gǔ̊ð> sim impf 3ms [yisgǔ̊ð] < *yasgǔdi (§17.29 (17.29A)) BL 98; Dan
3:6.

*√sWp   <tɔsef> cau impf 3fs [tɔ̄séf] < *t(ih)asípi (§6.1.2) BL 151; Dan 2:44.

*√sgr   <wṣǎγar> conj sim pf 3ms [ůsǎγár] < *wa=sagára (§12.2 with n. 8) BL 40,
134; Dan 6:23.

*√slq   <sil:qaθ> ~ <sil:qɔθ> sim pf 3fs [silqáθ] ~ [silqɔ̃θ] < *saliqát ~ *saliqā̆t {rare
ancipital lengthening; §2.3.4.3} (§2.3.4.3, §4.2.2) BL 137; Dan 7:20, 8.

*√str   <saθ:reh> sim pf 3ms^3ms [saθréh] < *satará̆hi (§12.2, §17.16) BL 134; Ezra
5:12.

*√9bd   <9ǎvað> sim pf 3ms [9ǎvað] < *9abáda (§17.32.2) BL 129; Dan 3:1.

tb<9ǎvaðt:> sim pf 2ms tb[9ǎváðt] bb[9ǎvǽðtā] < *9abádta ~ *9abádtā
(§17.22 (17.22B), §17.23 (17.23B)) BL 129; Dan 4:32.

tb<9av:ðeθ> sim pf 1s tb[9avðéθ] bb[9ǽvðéθ] ~ [9ǽvǽðiθ] < *9abádt
(§4.1.1, §4.1.2 n. 5, §5.2, §12.2, §17.6.2 with (17.6D) and n. 11,
§17.11.3 with n. 41, §17.22 (17.22B), §17.23.3 (17.23B)) BL
129; Dan 3:15, 6:23.

<ta9:b:ðuwn> ~ <tɑ̇9av:ðuwn> sim impf 2mp [ta9bǎðǔn] ~ [ta9avðǔn] <
*ta9budǔna (§5.2, §12.2, §17.11.3, §17.23.3) BL 129; Ezra 6:8,
7:18.

<yiθ:9ǎvǐ̊ð> ~ <yiθ:9ǎvě̊ð> sim rmp impf 3ms [yiθ9ǎvǐð] ~ [yiθ9ǎvě̊ð] <
*yit9abídi (§17.29 (17.29A)) BL 129; Ezra 6:12.

*√9dy   tb<tɛ9:deʾ> sim impf 3fs tb[tɛ9dé] bb[ti9Dé] ~ [tịðé] ~ [tɛ̰ðé] < *ta9dáyi
(§4.2.1, §11.1 n. 1, §17.11.3, §17.23.3 n. 121) BL 161; Dan 6:9, 13.

*√9l (< **√Rl)   <9al> sim pf 3ms [9ál] < *9álla (§15.3.1.2) BL 167; Dan 2:16.
kĕtiv <9VlVlaθ> ~ kĕrey <9aĩaθ> sim pf 3fs [9ǎlǎlaθ] or perhaps [9ǎlalá̊θ]/
[9ǎlálaθ] ~ [9allá̊θ] < *9alalát/*9alálat ~ *9allát (§3.3) BL 167;
Dan 5:10.

<han:9el> cau plain pf 3ms [han9él] < *ha99íla (§3.3, §17.8) BL 167; Dan
2:25, 6:19.

<hu9ǎ̊luw> cau pas pf 3mp {difficult form} (§3.2 n. 5) BL 168; Dan 5:15.

<ha9èl:niy> ~ <hɔ9èl:niy> cau impa ms^1s [ha9(9)élni] ~ [hɔ̄9élni] <
*ha99ílni (§17.8) BL 168; Dan 2:34.

*√9qr   kĕtiv <ʾiθ:9ǎqáruw> {fgm} ~ kĕrey <ʾi(y)θ:9ǎqàrɔh> ~ <ʾɛθ:9ǎqàrɔh> sim
rmp pf 3fp [ʾiθ9ǎqárū] ~ [ʾiθ9ǎqárɔ̃] ~ [ʾɛθ9ǎqárɔ̃] < *hit9aqírū ~ *hit9aqárā
(§17.11.3) BL 134; Dan 6:24.

*√ptḥ   <p:θiyḥuw> sim pas pf 3mp [pǎθíḥī] < *patíḥū (§17.16) BL 134; Dan 7:10.

*√ṣb9 (< **√ṣbR)   tb<yiṣ:ṭaba̅9>   int {*but* sim *in the Bab register*} rmp impf 3ms
tb[yiṣṭabbá9] bb[yiṣṭă̄vǽ9] < **yitṣabbá9i* ~ **yitṣabí̄9i* (§10) BL 135; Dan
4:12, 5:21.

*√θl   <taṭ:lel> cau impf 3fs [taṭlél] < **t(ih)aθlí̄li* (§3.3) BL 168; Dan 4:19.

*√qbl   <qabé̄l> ~ <qabí̄l> int pf 3ms [qabbél] ~ [qabbí̄l] < **qabbí̄la* (§17.29 (17.29A))
BL 111; Dan 6:1.

*√qWm   tb<hăqiym> ~ <hăqeym> cau pf 3ms tb[hăqí̄m] ~ [hăqém] bb[hæ̆qí̄m] <
*haqí̄ma (§17.23.3) BL 149; Dan 6:2, 3:2.

tb<hăqêym:tɔ> cau pf 2ms tb[hăqémtā] bb[hæ̆qémtā] ~ perhaps [hɔ̆qémtā]
{*the latter in a passage where the standard reading is 1s, not 2ms*}
< **haqímta* (§17.23.3 (17.23B)) BL 149; Dan 3:23 (, 3:14?)

tb<hăqêymɛθ> cau pf 1s tb[hăqémɛθ] bb[hæ̆qémiθ] ~ [hæ̆qemǽθ] or
[hæ̆qémæθ] < **haqímt* (§4.1.1, §4.1.2 with n. 6, §6.1.1.1, §17.6.2
with (17.6D) and n. 8) BL 149; Dan 3:14.

<hăqiymuw> cau pf 3mp [hăqí̄mū] < **haqí̄mū* (§6.1.1.1) BL 149; Ezra 6:18.

tb<hɔ̆qi(y)maθ> ~ <hĕqimaθ> ~ <hăqimaθ> cau pas pf 3fs tb[hɔ̆qī̄máθ] ~
[hĕqī̄máθ] ~ [hăqī̄máθ] bb[hĭqī̄mǽθ] < **huqī̄mát* (§1.3 n. 13,
§6.1.1.1, §17.23.3 with (17.23B) and n. 123) BL 149; Dan 7:4,5.

tb<y:qiym> ~ <y:hɔqe(y)m>   cau impf 3ms tb&bb[yɔ̆qí̄m] ~ tb[yɔ̆hɔqém]
bb[yɔ̆hāqém] ~ [yɔ̆hāqí̄m] < **y(ih)aqí̄mi* (§6.1.1.1 with n. 4, §14.2)
BL 151; Dan 2:44, 5:21, 6:16.

*√qn?   <tiq:ne?> sim short impf 2ms [tiqné̄] < **tiqná?* (§11.2) BL 161; Ezra 7:17.

*√qr?   tb<?ɛq:re?> sim impf 1s tb[?ɛqré̄] bb[?iqré̄] < **?iqrá?i* (§11.1 n. 1, §12.2,
§17.11.3) BL 161; Dan 5:17.

*√qrb   <q:rev> sim pf 3ms [qɔ̆rév] < **qaríba* (§17.11.3) BL 131; Dan 3:26.

<qir:veθ> sim pf 1s [qirvéθ] < **qaríbt* (§5.2, §17.11.3 n. 41)) BL 131; Dan
7:16.

*√rby   *kĕtiv* <r:váyθɔ> ~ <r:vêyθɔ> ~ *kĕrey* <r:vaθ> sim pf 2ms [rɔ̆váyθɔ̄] ~ [rɔ̆véθ] ~
? [rɔ̆váθ] < **rabáytā* {*the kĕrey variant* [rɔ̆váθ] *defies derivation on the basis
of the assumptions adopted in this book*} (§15.3.1.3 n. 28) BL 161; Dan 4:19.

*√rWmm (< **√rWm)   <hiθ:rowmâm:tɔ> int rmp pf 2ms [hiθrōmámtɔ̄] < *hitrawmámta*
{*miškal-suppleting for* *hitrawwámtā} (§6.2.1 n. 16) BL 149; Dan 5:23.

*√rmy   <r:mow> sim pf 3mp [rɔ̆mó̄] < **ramáyū* (§8.1.1) BL 164; Dan 6:17, 25.

tb<r:miyw> (conj) sim pas pf 3mp tb[r miw] bb[wirmí̄yū] < **(wa=)ramí̄yū*
(§8.1.1 with n. 2) BL 164; Dan 3:21, 7:9.

tb<yiθ:r:me?> sim rmp impf 3ms tb[yiθrɔ̆mé̄] bb[yiθirmé̄] < **yitramáyi*
(§4.4.2, §17.23.3 (17.23B)) BL 164; Dan 3:6, 6:8, 13.

tb<tiθ:r:muwn> ~ <tiθ:r:mown> sim rmp impf 2mp tb[tiθrɔ̆mún] ~
tb&bb[tiθrɔ̆mó̄n] < **titramayú̄na* (§15.3.2, §17.23.3 (17.23B)) BL
164; Dan 3:15.

*√rR (< **√rθ)   tb<w:θerŏ9a> {*siluk*} conj sim impf 3fs tb[wɔ̆θē̄rŏ̄a9] bb[Tē̄rŏ̄9] <
*wa=taRRŭ9i (§1.2 n. 9, §9.3.1 n. 40, §17.11.3 with n. 17, §17.16) BL 167;
Dan 2:40.

*√ršm   tb<tir:šum> sim impf 2ms tb[tiršúm] b[tiršóm] < **taršúmi* (§9.3.1 n. 40,
§12.2 with n. 4, §17.11.3) BL 98; Dan 6:9.

*√śWm   \<śɔ̄m:t > ~ \<śâm:t > ~ \<śam:t:> sim pf 2ms [śɔ́mtɔ̄] ~ [śámtɔ̄] ~ [śámt] < **śǽmta* ~ **śámtā* ~ **śámta* (§2.3.4.3, §6.2.2, §15.2.4 with n. 11, §15.4) BL 148f.; Dan 3:10.

   \<śɔ̄mεθ> sim pf 1s [śɔ́mεθ] < **śǽmt* (§4.1.1) BL 148; Ezra 6:12.

   \<śiym> sim pas pf 3ms [śîm] < **śîma* (§1.3 n. 13) BL 149; Dan 3:29, Ezra 4:19.

   tb\<śumaθ> śim paś pf 3fś tb[śūmáθ] bb[śōmǽθ] < **śūmát* {*/śuyam+at/ ?} ~ **śawmát* {*/śayum+at/ ?} (§1.3 n. 14) BL 149; Dan 6:18.

   \<yiẗ:śɔm> ~ \<yiẗ:śem> ~ \<yiẗ:śim> sim rmp impf 3ms [yittǒśɔ́m ~ [yittǒśém] ~ [yittǒśím]/[yittǒśîm] < **yitśími* (§6.3) BL 145f, 149; Ezra 4:2.

*√š²l   \<yiš:²äl n:xown> sim impf 3ms^2mp [yiš²älεnxɔ́n] < **yiš²alinnikúm* (§17.11.3, §17.23.2) BL 131; Ezra 7:21.

*√šbḥ   \<saḃ:heθ> int pf 1s [šabbǒḥéθ] < **šabbíḥt* (§4.1.1, §4.2.2) BL 134; Dan 4:31.

   tb\<sabạ̊ḥuw> int impa mp tb[šabbáḥū] bb[šæbbíḥū] < **sabbíḥu* (§15.5.1) BL 134; Dan 5:23.

*√šbq   tb\<tiš:t:vîq> sim rmp impf 3fs tb[tištǒvîq] bb[tištǒvê̊q] < **titšabìqi* (§17.29 n. 144) BL 107; Dan 6:21.

*√šwy   \<saẅiyw> int pf 3mp [šawwíw] < **šawwíyū* (§8.1.1) BL 164; Dan 5:21.

   \<yiš:taẅeh> int rmp impf 3ms [yištawwế] < **yitšawwáyi* (§10) BL 165; Dan 5:12.

*√šWmm (< *√šm)   \<²εš:towmam> int rmp pf 3ms [²εštōmám] < **hitsawmama* {*miškal-suppleting for* *hitšammáma} (§6.2.1 n. 16, §17.11.3) BL 167; Dan 4:16.

*√šyzb (< **š+ √yzb)   \<y:šeyz:viñox> quad impf 3ms^2ms [yǒšēzǒvinnɔ́x] < **yišayzibinníka* (§4.2.1, §4.2.2, §7.1, §17.26) BL 143; Dan 6:17.

   \<y:še(y)z:vin:xown> quad impf 3ms^2mp [yǒšēzǒvinxɔ́n] < **yišayzibinníkum* (§2.3.4.4, §5.2 with n. 4, §17.11.3, §17.26) BL 143; Dan 3:15.

*√škḥ ('find')   \<haš:kåḥaθ> cau pf 1s [haškáḥaθ] < **haškíḥt* (§4.1.2, §15.3.1.3, §17.6.2 with (17.6D)) BL 135; Dan 2:25.

   tb\<hiš:t:xåḥaθ> cau rmp pf 3fs tb[hištǒxáḥaθ] bb[hištǒxǽḥæθ] < **hitšakíḥt* (§4.1.2, §15.3.1.3, §17.6.2 with (17.6D)) BL 134; Dan 5:11.

   \<hiš:t:xåḥat> sim rmp pf 2ms [hištǒxáḥat] < **hitšakíḥta* (§5.2, §15.3.1.3 (15L), §17.6.2 with nn. 9 and 10, §17.11.3) BL 134; Dan 5:27.

   \<t:haš:kåḥ> cau impf 2ms [tǒhaškáḥ] < **t(ih)aškíḥi* (§12.2) BL 135; Ezra 4:15, 7:16.

*√škn   \<sakin> int pf 3ms [šakkín] < **šakkína* (§15.5.1) BL 111; Ezra 6:12.

*√šlḥ   \<š:liḥa> sim pas pf 3ms [šǒlíaḥ] < **šalíḥa* (§17.16) BL 134; Dan 5:24.

*√šlṭ   tb\<haš:l:ṭox> cau pf 3ms^2ms tb[hašlǒṭɔ́x] bb[hæšilṭɔ́x] < **hašliṭáka* (§4.4.2, §17.23.3 (17.23B)) BL 126; Dan 2:38.

*√šm9   \<šim:9eθ> sim pf 1s [šim9éθ] < **šamí9t* (§4.1.1, §17.11.3 n. 4) BL 134; Dan 5:14, 16.

*√šmš   \<y:šaṁ:šu(w)ñeh> int impf 3mp^3ms [yǒšammǒšûnnếh] < **yišammišûnníhi* (§17.5) BL 124; Dan 7:10.

*√šny   \<š:nòwhiy> sim pf 3mp^3ms [šǒnɔ́hī] < **šanayûhī* (§8.2.2) Brown 1979: 1116; Dan 5:6.

tb<šañiyw> int pf 3mp tb[šanníw] bb[šænníyū] < *šanníyu (§8.1.1 with n. 2)
BL 164; Dan 3:28.

kătiv <ʾiš:tañiy> ~ *kătiv* <ʾɛš:tañiy>, *kărey* <ʾis:tañiw> ~ *kărey* <ʾis:tañuw>
~ *kărey* <ʾɛš:tañow> int rmp pf 3ms, 3mp [ʾistannī́] ~ [ʾɛštannī́],
[ʾištanníw] ~ [ʾištannū́] ~ [ʾɛštannṓ] < *hitšanníya, *hitšanníyū ~
*hitšannáyū (§17.11.3) BL 165; Dan 3:19.

*√špl tb<y:haš:pī́l> cau impf 3ms [yăhašpī́l] bb[yăhæšpḗl] < *y(ih)ašpili (§17.29
n. 144) BL 113; Dan 7:24.

*√šry <šəriyw> int pf 3mp [šə̆ríw] < *šarríyū (§8.1.1) BL 164; Ezra 5:2.

*√šty <ʾiš:tiyw> sim pf 3mp [ʾištíw] < *šatíyū (§5.2, §17.18.1) BL 164; Dan 5:3, 4.

*√štr <šaθ:reh> sim pf 3ms^3ms [šaθrḗh] < *šataráhi (§2.3.4.4) BL 134; Ezra 5:12.

*√tqn tb<hɔθ:q:naθ> ~ <hɔθ:q:nɔθ> ~ <hɔθ:q:neθ> {zakef} cau pas pf 1s tb[hɔθqă̆náθ]
~ [hɔθqă̆nɔ́θ] ~ [hɔθqă̆nɛ́θ] < *hutqínt (§17.6.2 with (17.6D) and nn. 8, 11) BL
115f.; Dan 4:23.

*√tqp tb<tįq:faθ> ~ <tiqă̆faθ> sim pf 3fs tb[tiqă̆fáθ] ~ [tiqă̆fáθ] bb[tiqă̆fǽθ] < *taqi-
pát (§4.2.1, §4.3, §12.2 with n. 5) BL 46, 102; Dan 5:20.

*√θql <t:qil:tɔ(ʾ)> ~ <t:qèl:tɔʾ> sim pas pf 2ms [tă̆qī́ltɔ] ~ [tă̆qéltɔ] < *θaqī́ltā (§17.4)
BL 104f.; Dan 5:27.

Palmyrene

*√ʾḥð (< **√ʾXð) <yḥDnh> sim impf 3ms^3ms [yaḥ(ḥ)ă̆ðinnḗh] < *yaʾḥuðinníhi
(§9.2.1.1 with n. 13) HC 336.

*√ʾmr <yʾmr> sim impf 3ms [yV̆ʾmár] < *yaʾmúri (§9.2.1.1 with n. 13) HC 340.
<yʾmrwn> sim impf 3mp [yV̆ʾmărŪn] < *yaʾmurū́n(n)a (§7.2 (γ)) HC 340.

*√ʾty <ʾyTy> ~ <ʾTy> cau pf 3ms [ʾayTī́] ~ [ʾēθī́] (or [ʾāθī́]/[ʾattī́]) < *haʾtíya (§9.2,
§11.2) HC 344.

*√bny <Bnw> sim pf 3mp [bă̆náw] or bă̆nṓ] < *banáyū (§8.1.1) HC 347.

*√b9y (< **√bRy) <Dy yB9h> sbor sim plain impf 3ms [dī̆ # yiv9ḗ] < *ðī̆ # yib9áyi
(§11.2) HC 248.
<Dy yTB9ʾ> sbor sim rmp impf 3ms [dī̆ # yiθbă̆9ḗ] < *ðī̆ # yitba9áyi (§11.2)
HC 348.

*√br <ʾBrh> cau pf 3ms^3ms [ʾabbă̆rḗh] < *habbiráhi (§3.3) HC 350.

*√brk <TBrKn> int impf 3fp [tă̆varră̆xắn]/[tă̆vārră̆xắn] < *yibarrikắn(n)a or perhaps
*tibarrikắn(n)a (§7.2 (γ), §16.2 n. 24, §16.3 n. 25) HC 350.

*√hwy <hwT> sim pf 3fs [hă̆wắθ] < *hawáyat (§8.1.1) HC 359.
<yhwʾ> ~ <yhʾ> sim impf 3ms [yIhwḗ] ~ [yă̆hḗ] < *yihwáyi (§17.32 with
(17.23A)) HC 359.
<yhwn> ~ <yhn> sim impf 3mp [yIhwṓn] (or [yă̆hṓn]) ~ [yă̆hṓn] <
*yihwayū́n(n)a (§11.2, §17.32 with (17.32A)) HC 359.
<Thwyn> sim impf 3fp [TV̆hwă̆yắn] < *tahwiyắn(n)a (§16.2 n. 24, §16.3
n. 25) HC 359.

*√wd9 <yD9> sim pf 3ms [yă̆ðá9] < *wadá9a (§17.34) HC 369.

*√whb <yhB> sim pf 3ms [yă̆háv] < *wahába (§17.34) HC 369.

*√wθb <yTB> sim pf 3ms [yă̆θháv] < *waθába (§17.34) HC 371.

*√zbn <yzBn> int rmp impf 3ms [yizzabbán] < *yitzabbáni (§10) HC 362.

*√ḥdθ <hDT> int pf 3ms [ḥaddÍ̆θ] < *ḥaddíθa (§17.14) HC 363.

*√ḥwy   <yḥw> int impf 3ms [yǝḥawwḗ] < *yiḥawwáyi (§17.9.2) HC 363.

*√ḥpr   <ḥPr> sim pf 3mp [ḥǝfárū] < *ḥapárū (§17.9.2) HC 367.

*√ntn   <yTn> ~ <y{nT}n> sim impf 3ms [yittín] ~ possibly [yintín] < *yantíni
          (§17.21.1 n. 106) HC 391.

*√9ðr   <9Drn(w)n> sim pf 3ms^3mp [9ǝðarinnŮn] or [9aðrinnŮn] < *9aðára #
          h/ʾin(nv̊)húm (§7.4.1) HC 395.

*√9l (< **√Rl)   <yTʾy9l> ~ <{y}Tʾ9l> cau rmp impf 3ms possibly [yiθʾI99ál] ~
          [yiθʾa99ál] (§6.3 SM n. 41) HC 396.

*√9ny   <9n> sim pf 3ms [9ǝnä́] < *9anáya (§17.9.2) HC 398.

          <9nh> ~ <9ynh> ~ <9{ny}hy> ~ <9ny> sim pf 3ms^3ms [9ǝnä́h(ī)] ~ [9ĭnä́h(ī)]
          ~ perhaps [9ǝnáyhī]/[9ǝnḗhī] ~ perhaps [9ǝnḗ] < *9anayáhĭ ~
          *9anayáhī ~ perhaps *9anáyhī ~ perhaps *9anáyhi (§9.2.2) HC
          398.

*√ptḥ   <yPTḥyhy> ~ <yPTḥh> sim impf 3ms^3ms [yiftǝḥíhī] ~ [yiftǝḥḗh] <
          *yiptaḥíhī ~ *yiptaḥíhi (§2.3.4.4) HC 402.

*√θl   <ṭll> int pf 3ms [ṭallíl] < *θallíla (§3.3) HC 368.

*√qrʾ   <qrʾ> ~ <qrh> ~ <qr> sim pf 3ms [qǝrä́] < *qaráʾa (§17.9.2) HC 407.

*√qrb   <qrB(w)> int impf 3mp [qarrívū]/[qārívū] < *qarríbū (§17.9.2) HC 407.

*√śWm   <ʾTŝm> sim rmp pf 3ms either [ʾittǝśv̊m] (or possibly [ʾittǝśv̊m]) or [ʾiθśím]
          (or possibly) [ʾiθśím]) < *hitśíma (§6.3) HC 415.

*√špr   <ŝPrw> sim pf 3mp [šǝfárū] < *sapárū (§17.9.2) HC 417.

Nabatean

*√bny   <Bnʾ> ~ <Bnh> sim pf 3ms [bǝnä́] < *banáya (§8.1.1) Cg 83.

*√ðkr   <DKrT> sim pf 3fs [dǝxáraθ] or [daxráθ]/[dixráθ] < *ðakárat or *ðakarát
          (§17.14) Cl 82.

*√ḥwy   <yhwʾ> sim impf 3ms [yIhwḗ] < *yihwáyi (§11.2) Cg 84, 108.

*√whb   <yhBw> sim pf 3mp [yǝhávū] < *wahábū (§17.34) Cl 103.

*√wld   <yTylD> sim rmp impf 3ms [yiθyǝlíð] < *yitwalídi (§17.34) Cl 103.

*√wqp   <wqP> sim pf 3ms [wǝqáf] ⟸ √waqap/ {may be borrowed from Arabic; "très
          douteux"} (§17.34) Cl 90.

*√zbn   <yTzBn> int rmp impf 3ms [yitzabbán] < *yitzabbáni (§10) Cg 73.

*√zry   <yzTry> sim rmp impf 3ms [yiztǝrí] or [yiztǝrḗ] < *yitzaríyi or *yitzaráyi
          (§10) Cl 92.

*√9bd   <9BDw> sim pf 3fp {fgm} [9ǝváðū] < *9abádū (§16.3 n. 25) Cg 79.

*√pṣ   perhaps <yTpṣ>, <yTpṣṣ> sim, int rmp 3ms [yiθpíṣ], [yiθpaṣṣáṣ] < *yitpíṣṣi,
          *yitpaṣṣáṣi (§3.3) Cg 81.

*√qbr   <yqBrwn> sim impf 3mp [yiqbǝrŮn] < *yaqburǚn(n)a (§7.2 (γ)) Cl 141.

*√qrʾ   <qry> {questionable} sim impa ms [qǝrí] < *qǐráʾ (§8.1.3) Cl 144.

Targumic

*√ʾbl   <ʾiTʾæBæl> int rmp pf 3ms [ʾiθʾæbbǽl] < *hitʾabbála (§9.2.1.1 with n. 13,
          §10) Da 303.

*√ʾzl   <ʾiyzeyl> sim impa ms [ʾizél] < *ʾǎzíl (§17.23.3 with (17.23C) and n. 123) Da
          300.

*√ʔḥð (< **√ʔXð)   bb<ʔə̆ḥæDæT̄huwn> sb<ʔæḥæDTæ̃n̆uwn> sim pf 3fs^3mp
bb[ʔə̆ḥæðæθnű̆n] sb[ʔə̆̆ḥæðTænnű̆n] < *ʔaḥáðat # h/ʔin(nV̊)hám (§17.15.1
(17.15A)) Da 364.

tb<ʔæḥ̆æDiyñ̆αK> sim impf 1s^2ms [ʔæḥ(ḥ)æ̆ðinnᾰx] < ʔaʔḥuðinníka (§9.2.1.2
n. 17) Da 372.

<ʔeyḥowD> sim impa ms [ʔeḥóð] < *ʔᾰḥúð (§17.23.3 with (17.23C) and
n. 123) Da 300.

<ʔiTæḥæD> int rmp pf 3ms [ʔittæḥ(ḥ)æ̆ð] < *hitʔaḥḥáða (§9.2.1.1 with n. 13)
Da 303.

*√ʔkl   bb<ʔə̆Kowl> sb<ʔeyKuwl> sim impa ms bb[ʔə̆xól] sb[ʔexúl] < *ʔᾰkúl (§17.23.3)
Da 300.

<ʔə̆Kuwluw> sim impa mp [ʔə̆xúlū] < *ʔᾰkúlū (§17.23.3 (17.23C)) Da 301.

tb<ʔiK:luwhα> sim impa mp^3fs [ʔixlű̆hā] < *ʔᾰkulű̆hā (§17.25) Da 376.

*√ʔlm   <ʔeylæmuw> sim impa mp [ʔelæ̆mū] < *ʔĭlámū (§17.23.3 (17.23C)) Da 301.

*√ʔlp   <ʔælePuwnuwnuwn> ~ <ʔælePuwnuwn> int pf 3mp^3mp [ʔællefű̆n(n)ű̆n(n)un]
~ [ʔællefű̆n(n)un] < *ʔallípū # h/ʔin(nV̊)hám (§7.6, §13 with nn. 5 and 6,
§17.15.1 with n. 72) Da 367.

*√ʔsy   tb<yæ̃šiyñ̆ænα> int impf 3ms^1p tb[yæssĭnnǽnā] < *yiʔassiy(i)nnínā (§7.7
n. 33) Da 389.

<ʔæsiyniy> int impa ms^1s [ʔæssĭ̆nī] < *ʔassĭnī (§§2.3.3 n. 15) Da 391.

*√ʔsr   bb<ʔæsrinuwn>   tb[ʔæs:rinuwn]   sb[ʔiyš̆αriyñ̆uwn]   sim   impa   ms^3mp
bb&tb[ʔĭsrinnű̆n] tb[ʔissārinnű̆n] < ʔĭsár # h/ʔin(nV̊)hám (§17.15.1 with n. 71,
§17.23.3, §17.25) Da 376.

*√ʔty   bb<ʔeyTæ̆> sb<ʔiyTᾰ> sim impa ms bb[ʔeθǽ] bb[ʔiθᾱ̆] < *ʔĭtáy or perhaps
*ʔitᾱ̆ʔ (§8.1.3 with nn. 15 and 16) Da 357 with n. 2.

bb<ʔeyTæ̆> tb[ʔeyTᾰ> sb[ʔiyTᾰ> sim impa fs bb[ʔeθǽ] tb[ʔēθᾱ̆] sb[ʔiθᾱ̆] <
*ʔĭtáyī (§8.1.3 n. 16) Da 357.

<ʔæy(y)Tiy> ~ <ʔeyTiy> cau pf 3ms [ʔæyTĭ̄] ~ [ʔēθĭ̄] < *haʔtíya (§11.2 with
n. 10) Da 358 with n. 2.

sb<yæy:Teyñ̆αh> cau impf 3ms^3fs sb[yæyTĕ̆nnᾰ̆h] < *y(ih)aʔtay(i)nníha
(§7.7 n. 33) Da 389.

sb<ʔæyTeyneyh̆> cau impf 1s^3ms sb[ʔæyTēnĕ̆h] < *ʔ(ih)aʔtay(i)nníhi (§7.7
n. 33) Da 389.

bb<ʔeyTæ̆> sb<ʔiyTᾰ> cau impa ms bb[ʔēθǽ] sb[ʔĭ̄θᾱ̆] < *haʔtáy or perhaps
*haʔtĭʔ (§8.1.3 n. 16) Da 358.

*√bdr   bb<BæDŏrinuwn> ~ sb<Bædᾰriynuwn> int pf 3ms^3mp bb[bæddŏrinnű̆n]
sb[bæddārinnű̆n] < *baddíra # h/ʔin(nV̊)hám (§7.4.1) Da 363.

*√bhθ   <bŏheyT̄hα> sim pf 1p [bŏhéθnā] < *bahíθnā (§2.3.4.3) Da 263.

tb<tibæh:tiyn> sim rmp impf 2fs [tibbæhtĭ̄n] < *titbahiθína (§5.2, §10) Da
253, 271.

<yibæhTuwn> sim rmp impf 3mp [yibbæhtű̆n] < *yitbahiθű̆na (§10) Da 253.

*√bWt   <BαTuw> sim pf 3mp [bᾰ̆θū] < *bā́tū (§6.2.2) Da 319.

*√bz   <bæzuw> sim pf 3mp [bǽzzu] < *bázzū (§6.2.2 with n. 18) Da 330.

<bæznα> sim pf 1p [bǽznā] < *báznā (§6.2.2) Da 330.

<tiybowz> sim impf 2ms [tibbóz] < *tabbúzi (§3.3) Da 330.

<ʔiTBŏzeyz> sim rmp pf 3ms [ʔiθbŏzéz] < *hitbazíza (§6.3) Da 334.

*√bḥn   [bǒḥæntä́hī] sim pf 2ms^3ms [same] < **baḥantä́hī* (§8.2.2) Dalman 1938: 51.

*√bl9   bb<Bǒlæ9æTⁿuwn> sb<b:læ9ǽTæ̃ⁿuwn> sim pf 3fs^3mp bb[bǒlæ9æθnű́n]
         sb[bǒlæ9æθænnű́n]   < *balá9at ⸗ h/*ʾin(nV̊)húm* (§13 with nn. 3 and 6,
         §17.15.1 (17.15A)) Da 364.

         <wuBlæ9ɑʾ> conj sim pf 3fp [ů̃v(ǒ)læ9ā̃] < **wa=balá9ā* (§2.3.4.3) Da 263.

*√bny   <bǒney> ~ <bǒniy> sim impa ms [bǒnḗ] ~ [bǒnī́] < *bǐnáy ~ **bắnī́* (§8.1.3) Da
         348.

*√b9y (< **√bRy)   <TiB9æn> sim impf 2fs [tiv9ǽn] < **tib9ayī́na* (§8.1.1, §11.2
         with n. 11) Da 246.

*√brk   <bɑreyK> int pf 3ms [bāréx] < *barríka (§9.3.1) Da 92.

*√gWḥ (< **√gWX)   <ʾǒGiyḥæ> cau pf 3ms [ʾǒɣíæḥ] < *hagíḥa (§6.1.1.1, §17.16)
         Da 323.

*√gly   <ʾiTgǒliy> sim rmp impa ms [ʾiθgǒlī́] < **hitgalī́* (§8.1.3) Da 348.

*√gnb   <yiGnowB> sim impf 3ms [yiɣnóv] < *yagnúbi (§12.2) Da 269.

*√gndr <gændær> quad pf 3ms [gændǽr] < *gandíra (§1.1.2 n. 8) Da 252.

*√gry   <TiTgɑrown> int rmp impf 2mp [tiθgārṓn] < **titgarrayū́na* (§8.1.1 n. 1) Da
         347.

*√dbq   <yiDBǒqiynɑK> sim impf 3mp^2ms [yiðbǒqīnä́x] or [yiðbǒq̊innä́x] <
         **yadbuqű̃nnáka* (§17.17.1, §17.17.2) Da 372.

         sb<yæD:b:qɑ̃ⁿɑK> cau impf 3fp^2ms sb[yæðbǒqānnä́x] < **y(ih)adbiqānnáka*
         (§7.7 n. 33) Da 373.

*√dbr   tb<D:Bæriⁿuwn> sim pf 3ms^3mp [dǒværinnű́n] < *dabára ⸗ h/*ʾin(nV̊)húm*
         (§7.4.1, §17.15.1) Da 363.

*√dlq   <Dǒleyqæ̊T> sim pf 3fs [dǒléqæ̊θ] < *dalíqat (§17.11.3) Da 260.

*√ðWb   sb<yidowB> sim impf 3ms sb[yiddóv] < **yaðű̊bi* (§6.2.2) Da 320.

*√ðḥl   sb<tiydæ̊ḥæluwn> sim impf 2mp sb[tiddæḥæ̊lű́n] < **tiðḥalű̃na* (§4.5 (4G)
         with n. 25) Da 241, 273.

*√ðkr   <ʾiDǒKær> sim rmp pf 3ms [ʾiddǒxǽr] < *hitðakíra (§10) Da 259.

*√hwy   bb<lihwey> ~ bb<yǒhey> ~ bb<yǒhæʾ> ~ sb<y:heʾ> sim impf 3ms bb[lihwḗ]
         ~ bb&sb[yǒhḗ] ~ bb[yǒhǽ] < *lihwáy {*perhaps*} ~ *yihwáyi (§17.32 with
         (17.32A) and n. 152) Da 354.

         bb<ʾæhwey> ~ bb<ʾeyhey> ~ sb<ʾehwey> sim impf 1s bb[ʾæhwḗ] ~ bb[ʾehḗ]
         ~ sb[ʾehwḗ] < *ʾihwáyi* (§9.3.1, §17.11.2 n. 35, §17.23.3, §17.32
         with (17.32A) and n. 152) Da 354.

         <yǒhown> sim impf 3mp [yǒhṓn] < **yihwayū́na* (§17.32 with (17.32A) and
         n. 152) Da 354.

         <wuThæn> conj sim impf 2fp [ů̃θhǽn] < **wa=tihwayána* (§17.32 with
         (17.32A) and n. 152) Da 354.

         <wuhwiy> conj sim impa ms [ů̃hwī́] < **wǎ=hawī́* (§12.2) Da 240.

         bb<hiwæʾy> ~ sb<hě̃waʾy> {*see §17.23.3*} ~ tb<h:wæʾy> {*sic*} ~ bb<hiwæʾ>
         sim impa fs bb[hǐwǽy] ~ sb&tb[hǒwithǽy] ~ bb[hǐwǽ] < *hǐwáyī
         (§8.1.3 n. 16, §17.23.3) Da 354.

*√wdy   <yǒwæDey> int impf 3ms [yǒwæddḗ] < *yiwaddáyi (§17.34) Da 311.

*√wd9   bb<yǒDæ9> sb<yi(y)Dæ9> sim pf 3ms bb[yǒðǽ9] ~ sb[īðǽ9] < *wadá9a
         (§14.2 with n. 8) Da 309 with n. 1.

*√whb   bb\<yŏhæB> ~ sb\<yihæB> sim pf 3ms bb[yŏhǽv] ~ sb[īhǽv] < *wahába
(§14.2 with n. 8) Da 309 with n. 1.
tb\<wiyh Biyt̯iyň̯uwn> conj sim pf 2fs^3mp tb[wīhāvittinnū́n] < *wa=wahábtì̊
h/ʾin(nV̊)húm (§13 n. 6, §15.2.2.2 n. 18, §15.6 (β), §16.2 TR (u))
Da 365.
\<yŏhæBiyT> sim pf 1s [yŏhǽviθ] < *wahábt (§15.2.2.2) Da 309.
bb\<yŏhæBTæh> sb\<y:hæBiyt̯ah> sim pf 1s^3fs bb[yŏhævtǽh] sb[yŏhævittā́h]
< *wahábtə̆ha (§15.2.2.2 with nn. 18 and 19, §15.2.2.3 with (15D),
§15. 6 (β), §16.2 TR (y)) Da 366.
tb\<hæBiň̯aʾ> impa ms^3fs tb[hævinnā́] < *hábha (§7.1) Da 374.

*√wzp   \<TŏziyP> sim impf 2ms [tŏzíf] < *tazípi (§17.7) Da 310.

*√wkl   \<yiKowl> sim impf 3ms [yikkól] < *yakúli (§17.7 with n. 16) Da 309.
\<niKowl> ~ \<neyKowl> sim impf 1p [nikkól] ~ [nēxól] < *nakúli (§17.7) Da
310.

*√wld   \<DiyleyDæThiy> sbor sim pf 3fs^1s [dīlēðǽnī] < *ðì̊ # walidátnī (§15.5.1,
§17.11.3) Da 364.
\<TŏliyD> sim impf 3fs [tŏlī́ð] < *talídi (§17.7) Da 310.
bb\<ʾiTyŏleyD> bb&sb[ʾiyTiyliyD> sim rmp pf 3ms bb[ʾiθyŏléð] bb&sb[ʾiθīlíð]
< *hitwalída (§14.2 with n. 8) Da 313.

*√wrθ   \<yeyræT> sim impf 3ms [yērǽθ] < *yiráθi (§7.7, §11.2) Da 309.

*√wθb   tb\<ʾowTeyBiň̯aK> cau impf 1s^2ms [ʾōθevinnā́x] < *ʾ(ih)awθibinníka
(§15.5.1) Da 372.

*√Why   bb\<ʾowhæʾ> ~ \<ʾowhæʾiy> sb\<ʾowhaʾy> cau impa fs bb[ʾōhǽ] ~ [ʾōhǽ(ʾ)ī]
sb[ʾōhǽy] < *hawháyī (§8.1.1 with n. 3, §8.1.3) Da 348.

*√Wtb   bb\<yiytæB> sb\<yeytæB> sim impf 3ms bb[yītǽv] sb[yētǽv] < *yitábi ~
*yaytábi (§11.2) Da 309.
\<ʾytyB> ~ \<ʾwtyB> cau pf 3ms [ʾētév] ~ [ʾōtév] < *haWtíba (§17.5 n. 5) Jastrow 1903: 576.
bb\<ʾowteBaʾ> ~ sb\<ʾeytiyBaʾ> cau pf 3fp bb[ʾōtévā] ~ [ʾētívā] < *haWtíbā
(§17.11.3) Da 312.

*√zbn   \<ʾizDæBæn> int rmp pf 3ms [ʾizdæbbǽn] < *hitzabbána (§10) Da 259.
tb\<ʾiz:dabeyn:tuwn> int rmp pf 2mp [ʾizdæbbentū́n] < *hitzabbantū́m (§12.2,
§17.17.1) Da 363.

*√z9q   \<zŏ9iyquw> sim pf 3mp [zŏ9íqū] < *za9íqū (§17.11.3) Da 262.

*√zrq   \<yiyziyrquwn> sim impf 3mp [yĭzirqū́n] < *yazruqū́na (§4.4.2, §4.5 n. 27,
§17.23.3) Da 94.

*√hwy   \<hæwiyʾæT> int pf 3fs [hæwwî̊(ʾ)æθ] < *hawwíyat (§15.2.2.1 with (15A) and
n. 15) Da 342.

*√hWb   \<hæBiyT> sim pf 1s [hǽbbiθ] < *hā́bt (§6.2.2 with n. 18) Da 319.
bb\<yŏhuwB> sb\<yihuwB> sim impf 3ms bb[yŏhū́v] sb[īhū́v] < *yahū́bi
(§14.2 with n. 8) Da 320.

*√hWs   \<hæsTaʾ> sim pf 2ms [hǽstā] < *hā́stā (§6.2.2) Da 319.

*√hWr   \<DiThæwær> sbor int impf 2ms [diThæwwǽr] < *ðì̊ # tihawwíri (§11.1) Da
318.

*√hzy   \<wæhzaʾ> conj sim pf 3ms [wæhzā́] < *wa=hazáya (§12.2) Da 240.

    <ħæzɑʔæh> sim pf 3ms^3fs [ħə̆zɑ̄ʔǽh] < *ħazayáha (§15.2.1.5 with n. 14, §15.6 (β) with n. 44) Da 385.

    <ħə̆zɑnuwn> sim pf 3ms^3mp [ħə̆zɑ̄n(n)ǔn] < *ħazáya # h/ʔin(nV̊)húm (§17.15.1) Da 385.

    <ħə̆zeyTiy> sim pf 1s [ħə̆zḗθī] < *ħazáyt (§13 with n. 2) Da 343.

    <wuħziy> conj sim impa ms [ůħzī́] < *wa=ħắzī́ (§12.2) Da 240.

    <wæħziy> sim impa fs [wæħzī́] < *wa=ħắzíyí (§8.1.1) Da 348.

    <ʔæħzə̆yæna>̓ cau pf 3ms^1p [ʔæħzə̆yǽnɑ̄] < *haħziyánɑ̄

    <yiħzeynæniy> cau impf 3ms^1s [yiħzě̆n(n)ǽnī] < *y(iħ)aħzay(i)nníni (§12.2) Da 388.

*√ħy(y) <Teyħey> sim impf 2ms [tēħḗ] < *tiħħáyi (§17.32 n. 154) Da 354.

*√ħl (< **√Xl) <ħæ̇leliyT> int pf 1s [ħælléliθ] < *ħallílt (§3.3) Da 332.

    <ʔiytæħæl> cau rmp pf 3ms [ʔittæħ(ħ)ǽl] < *hithaħħála (§6.3, §9.3.1) Da 334.

*√ħnk <yəæħnə̆Key> sim impf 3ms^3ms [yæħnə̆xḗh] < *yaħnukíhi (§7.1) Da 268.

*√ħsn <yæħsə̆niyneh> sim impf 3ms^3ms [yæħsə̆ninnḗh] < *yaħsuninníhi (§7.1) Da 270.

*√ħpy (< **√Xpy) <ħə̆fɑhiy> sim pf 3ms^3ms [ħə̆fǽhī] < *ħapayáhi (§8.2.2) Da 385.

*√ynq bb<ʔowniyqiyhuw> sb<ʔowneqiyhuy> cau impa fs^3ms bb[ʔōniqī́hū] sb[ʔōneqī́hī] < *hawniqī́hū ~ *hawniqī́hī (§4.5 n. 26, §8.2.2, §15.5.1 n. 35) Da 376.

*√kbš <KæBšuwhɑ>̓ sim pf 3mp^3fs [kævšű̆hɑ̄] < *kabašű̆hɑ̄ (§2.3.4.4) Da 367.

*√khy <Kə̆hɑT> sim pf 3fs [kə̆hắ̆θ] < *kaháyat (§15.2.1.5) Da 342.

    sb<K:hɑyɑ>̓ tb<K:hæẙɑ>̓ sim pf 3fp sb[kə̆hắ̆yɑ̄] tb[kə̆hǽyyɑ̄] < *kaháyɑ̄ (§8.1.1 with n. 5, §15.2.15, §15.4) Da 344.

*√ksy <yiTKæsæ>̓ int rmp impf 3ms [yiθkæssǽ] < *yitkassáyi (§11.2 with n. 9) Da 91.

*√kpr <ʔə̆KæPær> int impf 1s [ʔə̆xæppǽr] < *ʔikappíri (§17.23.3 (17.23C)) Da 272

*√ktb <TiKTə̆Biynuwn> ~ <TiKTowBinuwn> sim impf 2ms^3mp [tixtə̆vinnűn] ~ [tixtovinnűn] < *taktúbi #̊ h/ʔin(nV̊)húm (§17.15.1) Da 371.

*√lbš bb<yilBə̆šinuwn> sb<yil:bašiynuwn> sim impf 3ms^3mp bb[yilbə̆šinnűn] ~ [sb[yilbɑ̄šinnűn] < *yilbáši #̊ h/ʔin(nV̊)húm (§17.15.1) Da 371.

*√mWt <meyTæT> sim pf 3fs [méttæθ] < *mítat (§6.2.2 with n. 18) Da 314.

    <yə̆muwT> sim impf 3ms [yə̆mű̆θ] < *yamúti (§17.16) Da 320.

*√mħ̓ <wumħownuwn> ~ <wumħuwnuwn> conj sim pf 3mp^3mp [ůmħōnűn] ~ [ůmħūnűn] < wa=maħá̓ū #̊ h/ʔin(nV̊)húm (§11.2, §15.3.2) Da 387.

    <mə̆ħeyniy> sim impa ms^1s [mə̆ħḗnī] < *mĭ̄há̓nī (§11.2 with n. 11) Da 391.

*√ml̓ tb<mil̊eyTiy> int pf 1s tb[millḗθī] < *mallí̓t (§8.1.1 n. 1, §12.2) Da 343.

*√mny <mæn̊ey> int impa ms [mænnḗ] < *mannáy (§8.1.3, §11.2 with n. 11) Da 348.

*√mn9 <mæn9æniy> sim pf 3ms^1s [mæn9ǽnī] < *manni9ání (§4.2.2) Da 362.

*√nb̓ <ʔiTnæb̊iy> int rmp impa ms [ʔiθnæbbí̓] < *hitnabbí̓ (§8.1.3) Da 348.

*√nWħ (< **√nWX) <ʔanæħ> cau impa ms [ʔānǽħ] < *haníħ (§6.1.2 with (6C)) Da 316.

*√nħt (~ possibly *√ħt) <ʔə̆heyT> cau pf 3ms [ʔə̆hé̆θ] < * haħħíta (§17.21.1) Da 295.

    tb<ʔæ̆heyTTeyh> bb<ʔə̆hæTTeyh> cau pf 3fs^3ms tb[ʔæ̆heθtḗh] bb[ʔə̆hæθtḗh] < *haħħitáhi (~ *haħħatáhi?) (§15.3.1.2, §15.3.2 n. 30) Da 364.

<ʔiTæḥæT> cau rmp pf 3ms [ʔittæḥ(ḥ)ǽθ] < *hithanḥáta* (or perhaps *hithaḥḥáta*) (§17.21.1) Da 297.

*√nṭl   <yiTnæṭæl> int rmp impf 3ms [yiθnæṭṭǽl] < *yitnaṭṭáli* (§10) Da 297.

bb<Tinæṭæl> sb<Tiynæṭæl> tb<tinæ̃ṭæl> int rmp 3fs/2ms [tinnæṭṭǽl] < *titnaṭṭáli* (§10) Da 297.

*√ns   <ʔiTnŏseys> sim rmp pf 3ms [ʔiθnŏsés] < *hitnasísa* (§3.3) Da 333.

*√nsb   <nŏseyBæT> sim pf 3fs [nŏšévæθ] < *nasíbat* (§17.15.1) Da 292.

bb<nŏseyBæTnuwn> sb<n:seyBtæ̃uwn> sim pf 3fs^3mp bb[nŏsevæθnũn] sb[nŏsevtænnũn] < *nasíbat # h/ʔin(nV̊)húm* (§2.3.3 n. 15, §17.15.1) Da 364.

<næsBuwhiy> sim pf 3mp^3ms [næsbũhī] < *nasibũhī* (§5.2, §8.2.2) Da 367.

*√nsy   <næsiy> int pf 3ms [næssî] < *nassíya* (§15.2.2.1 with (15A)) Da 341.

<nisiyTiy> int pf 1s [nissîθi] < *nassît* (§12.2) Da 343.

*√npq   <yiTæPæq> cau rmp impf 3ms [yittæppǽq] < *yithanpáqi* (§17.21.1) Da 297.

*√sʔb   <ʔisTaʔæBæT> int rmp pf 3fs [ʔistā̊ʔǽvæθ] < *hitsaʔʔábat* (§10) Da 307.

*√sgd   <wusGeyDiyT> conj sim pf 1s [ůsgéðiθ] < *wa=sagídt* (§17.6.2) Da 261.

*√sWb   <seyBiyT> sim pf 1s [sébbiθ] < *så̊bt* (§6.2.2 with n. 18) Da 319.

*√slq   <sŏlêyq> {pašta} sim pf 3ms [sŏléq] < *salíqa* (§17.29 (17.29A)) Da 258; Gen 19:28.

<sæq> sim impa ms [sǽq] < *sĭláq* (§17.33) Da 294.

bb<ʔæseyqTæ̃nʔ> sb<ʔæseyq:Tα̃naʔ> {munaḥ} cau pf 2ms^1p bb<ʔæsseqtǽna] sb[ʔæsseqtǻnā] < *hasliqtánā ~ *hasliqtǻnā* (§17.29 (17.29A)) Da 365; Exod 17:3.

*√smk   <TismowK> sim impf 2ms [tismóx] < *tasmúki* (§12.2) Da 270.

*√smq   <yiysiymquwn> sim impf 3mp [yĭsimqũn] < *yismaqúna* (§4.4.2, §17.23.3 (17.23C)) Da 272.

*√srb   <sαreyBTuwn> int pf 2mp [sārevtũn] < *sarribtúm* (§17.11.3) Da 263.

*√9bd   <9ŏBæDT> ~ <9ŏBæDTaʔ> sim pf 2fs {fgm} [9ŏvǽðt] ~ [9ŏvǽðtā] < *9abádti ~ *9abádtā* (§16.2 <u>TR</u> (α), §16.3 (α)) Da 261.

<9ŏBæDiyT> sim pf 1s [9ŏvǽðiθ] < *9abádt* (§17.6.2) Da 261.

bb<yæ9ŏBeyD> sb<yæ9əæbeyD> sim impf 3ms bb[yæ9ŏBéð] sb[yæ9æbéð] < *ya9bídi* (§4.3, §4.5 (4G), §12.2) Da 269.

bb<Tæ9BŏDiyn> sb<Tæ9æb:Diyn> sim impf 2fs bb[tæ9bŏðín] sb[tæ9æb(ŏ)Dín] < *ta9bidína* (§4.5 (4G), §7.2 (γ)) Da 271.

sb<ʔæ9æbeyD> sim impf 1s sb[ʔæ9æbéð] < *ʔa9bídi* (§4.5, §17.11.3 n. 35) Da 272.

sb<yæ9æb:Duwn> sim impf 3mp sb[yæ9æb(ŏ)Dũn] < *ya9biduna* (§4.4.1, §4.4.3 (β), §4.5) Da 272.

bb<yæ9BŏDαn> sb<yæ9æb:Dαn> sim impf 3fp bb[yæ9bŏðǻn] sb[yæ9æb(ŏ)Dǻn] < *ya9bidǻna* (§7.2 (γ)) Da 273.

bb<Tæ9BŏDuwn> sb<Tæ9æb:Duwn> sim impf 2mp bb[tæ9bŏðũn] sb<t 9 b( )Dun] < *ta9bidúna* (§17.23.3) Da 273

sb<9iyBeD> sim impa ms sb[9ĭvéð] < *9ăbíd* (§9.3.1) Da 93.

*√9br   sb<y:9iybær> sim impf 3ms sb[yŏ9ibǽr] < *ya9búri* (§4.5 (4G)) Da 269.

bb<ʔiy9iyBær> ~ <ʔæ9Bær> ~ <ʔæ9æBær> sb<ʔiy9iybær> sim impf 1s
    bb[ʔi9i̊Bǽr] ~ [ʔæ9bǽr] ~ [ʔæ9æ̊Bǽr] sb[ʔi9ɾbǽr] < *ʔa9búri (§4.5
    (4G), §17.11.3 with n. 35) Da 272.

<yi9Bə̆ruwn> ~ <yiy9iyBruwn> sim impf 3mp [yi9bə̆rŭ́n] ~ [yi9iBrŭ́n] <
    *ya9burŭ́na (§4.5 (4G)) Da 272.

bb<Ti9Bə̆ruwn> ~ <Ti9iBruwn> ~ <Ti9iBə̆ruwn> ~ <Tæ9bə̆ruwn>
    sb<Tiy9:b:ruwn> ~ <ti9ib:ruwn> ~ <t:9ib:ruwn> sim impf 2mp
    bb[ti9bə̆rŭ́n] ~ [ti9iBrŭ́n] ~ [ti9iBə̆rŭ́n] ~ [tæ9bə̆rŭ́n] sb[ti9bə̆rŭ́n]
    ~ [ti9ib(ə̆)rŭ́n] ~ [tə̆9ib(ə̆)rŭ́n] < *ta9burŭ́na (§4.5 (4G), §7.2 (γ),
    §15.3.1.1, §17.23.3 with (17.23C)) Da 268, 273.

tb<ʔæ9:bær> ~ <ʔæ9æ̆vær> sb<ʔæ9æbær> cau pf 3ms tb[ʔæ9bǽr] ~ [ʔæ9æ̆vǽr]
    sb[ʔæ9æbǽr] < *ha9bíra (§9.3.1 n. 35, §17.23.3) Da 259.

<tæ9ə̆Bær> cau impf 2ms [tæ9ə̆Bǽr] < *t(ih)a9bíri (§4.5 (4G), §8.1.3 n. 14)
    Da 271.

*√9dy   <9ə̆Dɑʔ> sim pf 3ms [9ə̆ðɑ̃́] < *9adáya (§8.1.1) Da 341.

bb<yi9Dey> ~ <yə̆9iDey> sb<yiy9iDyDey> sim impf 3ms bb[yi9dé̃] ~
    [yə̆9iDé̃] sb[yi9i̊Dé̃] < *yi9dáyi (§11.2) Da 345.

tb<9ædiyʔæTXown> int pf 3fs^2mp [9æddi̊(ʔ)æθxṍn] < *9addiyatkúm (§5.2,
    §8.1.1, §8.1.2 n. 8) Da 364.

sb<ʔæ9æDiy> cau pf 3ms sb[ʔæ9æðĩ́] < *ha9díya (§4.5 (4G)) Da 257.

<Ti9Down> cau impf 2mp [ti9dṍn] < *t(ih)a9dayŭ́na (§12.2) Da 347.

bb<ʔæ9D> sb<ʔæ9æd> cau impa ms bb[ʔæ̊9d] sb[ʔæ̊9æd] < *ha9dĩ́ or *ha9dáy
    (§8.1.3 with n. 14, §17.6.2 n. 10) Da 348.

*√9Wr (< **√RWr)   <ʔiTə̆9ær> sim rmp pf 3ms [ʔittə̆9ǽr] < *hit9íra (§6.3) Da 324.

*√9l (< **√Rl)   <9ɑl> sim pf 3ms [9ɑ́l] < *9álla (§6.2.2) Da 330.

    <9ælæT> sim pf 3fs [9æll̊ǽθ] < *9allát (§6.2.2 with n. 18) Da 330.

    <9æliyT> sim pf 1s [9ǽlli̊θ] < *ált (§3.3, §6.2.2 with n. 18) Da 330.

    <9ɑluw> sim pf 3mp [9ɑ́lū] < *9állū (§6.2.2) Da 330.

    <9ælɑʔ> sim pf 3fp [9ǽllɑ̄] < *9állā (§6.2.2 with n. 18) Da 330.

    <yey9owl> sim impf 3ms [yē9ól] < *ya99úli (§9.3.1 n. 40) Da 328, 330.

    <9uwl> ~ <9owl> sim impa ms [9ŭ́l] ~ [9ól] < *9úl (§3.3, §6.2.2) Da 314f.,
    331.

    <ʔiTɑ9æl> cau rmp pf 3ms [ʔittɑ̄9ǽl] < *hitha99ála (§6.3) Da 334.

*√9ny   <9æniyTæh> int pf 3fs^3fs [9ænnĩ́θæ̆h] < *9annĩ́tha (§15.2.2.1 with (15A))
    Da 386.

*√9rR (< **√rð)   <ʔɑrə̆9æniy> int pf 3fp^1s [ʔɑrə̆9ǽnī] < *9arriRánī (§9.1.3 (α),
    §16.2 TR (β)) Da 261.

*√9rq   bb<yi9rowq> bb&sb<yi(y)9iyrowq> sim impf 3ms bb[yi9róq]
        bb&sb[yi9i̊róq] < *ya9rúqi (§4.5 (4G), §9.3.1 n. 40, §12.2,
        §17.23.3 with (17.23C)) Da 269.

    <Tə̆9iyrowq> sim impf 2ms [tə̆9iróq] < *ta9rúqi (§4.5 (4G), §17.23.3 with
    (17.23C)) Da 270.

*√9šq   bb<Tæ9šowq> sb<Tiy9iyšuwq> sim impf 2ms bb[tæ9šóq] sb[ti9i̊šúq] <
    *ta9šúqi (§17.11.3) Da 270.

*√9θr   <9æTæriyT> int pf 1s [9ættǽriθ] < *9aθθírt (§17.15.1) Da 261.

*√plḥ bb<TiPlə̆ḥiň̃iyn> tb<TiP:l:ḥiň̃iyn> sb<TiP:lɑhiyň̃uwn> sim impf 2ms^3mp
{*fgm*} bb&tb[tiflǻḥinín] sb[tiflāḥinnūn] < *tipláḥi ⫟ h/ʔin(nV̊)hín ~ *tipláḥi ⫟
h/ʔin(nV̊)húm (§16.2 TR (v)) Da 272.

*√pqd <Pæqɔ̆DɑK> int pf 3ms^2ms [pæqqɔ̆ð̆ǽx] < *paqqidáka (§4.2.2) Da 362.
<PæqeyDTǻniy> {*9atnaḥ*} int pf 2ms^1s [pæqqeð̆tǻni] < *paqqidtǻnī (§17.29
(17.29A)) Da 365; Deu 26:14.
<PæqeyDTɑK> int pf 1s^2ms [pæqeð̆tǽx] < *paqqídtə̆ka (§15.5.1) Da 366.

*√prq <TiPrǔ̊wq> ~ <TiPrŏ̊wq> {*siluk*} [tifrǔq] ~ [tifrŏq] < *taprǔqi (§17.29
(17.29A)) Da 267, Sperber 2004: 111; Exod 13:13.
bb<ʔæProwq> sb<ʔiyP:ruwq> sim impf 1s bb[ʔæfróq] sb[ʔifrúq] < *ʔaprúqi
(§12.2 with n. 15) Da 272.
tb<yiP:r:quwň̃ænɑʔ> sim impf 3mp^1p tb[yifrɔ̆qǔ̊nnǽnā] < *yapruqǔ̊nnánā
(§7.2 (ɛ)) Da 373.
bb<Pɔ̆rowqniy> tb<P:rowqiň̃iy> sim impa ms^1s bb[pɔ̆róqnī] tb[pɔ̆roqínnī] <
*pǎrúqnī (§2.3.4.4) Da 375.

*√prš sb<TɑPiyr:šuwn> cau impf 2mp [tāfiršǔn] < *t(ih)aprišǔna (§4.5 (4G) with
n. 26) Da 273.

*√ṣWd tb<wiṣowDiynuwň̃uwn> conj sim impf 3mp^3mp [wīṣōðīnǔ̊nnǔn] { [ō] ← ū
by din, §8.1.1 n. 1?} < *wa=yaṣūdǔ̊na ⫟ h/ʔin(nV̊)húm (§17.17.2) Da 273.

*√ṣWt <ʔæ̈ṣ̈eyT> cau pf 3ms [ʔæ̈ṣ̈éθ] < *haṣīta (§6.2) Da 316.

*√ṣlb <ʔiṣ̆tɔ̆liyB> sim rmp pf 3ms [ʔiṣ̆tɔ̆lǐv] < *hitṣalíba (§10) Da 307.

*√ṣly <ṣæliy> int impa ms [ṣællǐ] < *ṣallī (§8.1.3) Da 348.

*√qbl <qæBiyluw> int pf 3mp [qæbbílū] < *qabbílū (§13) Da 262.

*√qWm <qɑm> sim pf 3ms [qǻm] < *qǻma (§6.2.2) Da 319.
<qæmæT> sim pf 3fs [qǽmmæθ] < *qǻmat (§6.2.2 with n. 18) Da 319.
<qæmɑʔ> sim pf 3fp [qǽmmā] < *qǻmā (§6.2.2 with n. 18) Da 319.
<quwm> sim impa ms [qǔm] < *qǔm or perhaps *qúm (§6.2.2) Da 320.
<qæ̈yeymtɑnuwn> int pf 2ms^3mp [qæyyemtānǔn] < *qayyímtā ⫟
h/ʔin(nV̊)húm (§17.15.1) Da 365.
<qæyeymtǽnɑʔ> int pf 2ms^1p [qæyyemtǽnā] < *qayyimtánā (§17.29
(17.29A)) Da 365; Exod 47:25.
bb<Diyqæy̆ɔ̆ymæh> sb<diy:qæy:mæ̈h> sbor int impf 3ms^3fs
bb[dīqæyy̆ɔ̆mæ̈h] sb[dīqæymæ̈h] < *ð̆ǐ ⫟ yiqayyimíha (§15.3.1.s
n. 26, §17.26) Da 370.
tb<ʔæqæ̈y̆:miň̃iyK> int impf 1s^2fs tb[ʔæ̈qæyy̆ɔ̆minníx] < *ʔiqayyiminníki
(§17.26) Da 372.
sb<T:qæy:mæň̃ɑ̈h> tb[t:qæy:ymuwň̃æ̈h] bb<tɔ̆qæyy̆ɔ̆muwň̃æ̈h> ~
<Tɔ̆qæy̆ɔ̆yminæh> int impf 2fp^3fs {*fgm*} sb[tɔ̆qæyy̆ɔ̆mænnǻh]
(or [tɔ̆qæymænnǻh]) tb&bb[tɔ̆qæyy̆ɔ̆mǔ̊nnǽh]
bb[tɔ̆qæyy̆ɔ̆mǐ̊nnǽh] < *tiqayyimannáha ~ *tiqayyimǔ̊nnáha
(§16.2 TR (γ)) Da 373.
<ʔɔ̆qeym> cau pf 3ms [ʔɔ̆qém] < *haqīma (§6.1.1.1) Da 323.
<ʔiTɑqæm> cau rmp pf 3ms [ʔittāqǽm] < *hithǻqama (§6.3) Da 326.

*√qWṣ <qæsuw> sim pf 3mp [qǽṣṣū] < *qǻṣū (§6.2.2 with n. 18) Da 319.

*√ql <qæliyT> sim pf 1s [qǽlliθ] < *qált (§12.2) Da 330.

*√qnʔ   sb<ʔæq:niynuwn> cau impf 1s^3mp sb[ʔæqnīnū́n] < *ʔ(ih)aqníʔi ̥̊ #
h/ʔin(nV̊)húm (§17.7 n. 33) Da 390.

*√qrʔ   <qə̆row> sim pf 3mp [qə̆rṓ] < *qaráʔu (§8.1.1) Da 348.
<qə̆rowhɑʔ> ~ <qə̆ruwhɑʔ> sim pf 3mp^3fs [qə̆rṓhā] ~ [qə̆rū́hā] < *qaraʔū́hā
(§8.1.1 n. 1) Da 387.
<wuqræʔɑʔ> conj sim pf 3fp [ůqrǽʔā] < *wa=qaráʔā (§8.1.1) Da 344.
tb<q:rɑhɑʔ> sim impa ms^3fs tb[qə̆rů́hā] < *qĭráʔhā (§9.1.4 n. 10) Da 39.
<qə̆ræn> sim impa fp [qə̆rǽn] < *qĭráʔā (§7.2 (δ) n. 10) Da 349.

*√qtl   <qə̆ṭælTiyK> sim pf 1s^2fs [qə̆ṭæltī́x] < *qatáltə̆ki (§ 2.3.1, §2.3.4.4) Da 366.
<yiqṭə̆luwnæniy> ~ <yiqṭə̆linæniy> sim impf 3mp^1s [yiqṭə̆lů́nnæ̆ni] ~
[yiqṭə̆lī́n(n)æ̆nī] < *yaqtulů́nnánī (§17.17.2) Da 372.
bb<yiqṭə̆luwnuwnuwn> tb<yiq:t:linuwn̊uwn> sim impf 3mp^3mp
bb[yiqṭə̆lununnun] ~ tb[yiqṭə̆līnů́n(n)ů́n] < *yaqtúlū (or
yaqtulů́n(n)a) # h/ʔin(nV̊)húm (§7.6, §13 with nn. 5 and 6,
§17.15.1 with n. 72, §17.17.2) Da 373.
bb<ʔæTq̊ə̆ṭiyl> sb<ʔiyTq̊:ṭiyl> sim rmp impf 1s bb[ʔæθq̊ə̆ṭī́l] sb[ʔiθq̊ə̆ṭī́l] <
*ʔitqatíli (§12.2 n. 15) Da 272.

*√rgz   <rə̆Geyz> sim pf 3ms [rə̆γéz] < *ragíza (§4.2.2) Da 258.

*√rgm   bb<Tirgə̆minuwn> sb<Tir:gowmiyn̊uwn> sim impf 2ms^3mp
bb[tirgə̆minnū́n] ~ sb[tirgominnū́n] < *targúmi # h/ʔin(nV̊)húm (§17.11.3,
§17.15.1) Da 371.

*√rdy   <ʔiTrə̆Dɑʔ> ~ <ʔiTræ̆dɑʔ> sim ~ int impa fs [ʔiθrə̆ðɑ́̆] ~ [ʔiθræddɑ́̆] < *hitradáyī
~ *hitraddáyī (§8.1.3 n. 16) Da 348.

*√rdp   <ræDPuwK> sim pf 3mp^2ms [ræðpúx] < *radapúka (§5.2) Da 366.
*√rWm   <ʔə̆reymiyT> cau pf 1s [ʔə̆rémiθ] < *harímt (§6.1.1.1) Da 323.
*√rḥm   <rə̆ḥeym> sim pf 3ms [rə̆ḥém] < *raḥíma (§17.11.3) Da 258.
<riyḥə̆mæh> sim (or possibly int) pf 3ms^3fs [riḥə̆mǽh] (or possibly
[riḥḥə̆mǽh]) <*raḥimáha (or possibly *raḥḥimáha) (§12.2 with
nn. 9 and10) Da 363.
<Dirḥeymiy T> sbor sim pf 1s [dirḥémiθ] < *ðī́ # raḥímt (§17.11.3) Da 261.
<yirḥə̆min̊æniy> sim impf 3ms^1s [yirḥə̆minnǽnī] < *yirḥaminníni (§17.13)
Da 370.

*√rṭs   <ræṭšænɑʔ> sim pf 3ms^1p [ræṭšǽnā] < *raṭašánā (§2.3.4.4) Da 363.
*√rkb   <wurkiyBɑʔ> conj sim pf 3fp [ůrkávā] < *wa=rakíbā (§5.2, §12.2, §17.11.3)
Da 240, 263.

*√rmy   bb<rə̆mowhiy> ~ <rə̆meyhiy> sb[r:miyhiy] sim impa ms^3ms bb[rə̆mṓhī] ~
[rə̆mḗhī] sb[rə̆mī́hī] < *rĭmáyhū ~ *rīmáyhī ~ *rămī́hī (§8.1.1 n. 1, §8.1.4) Da
391.
<wurmæʔ> conj sim impa fs [ůrmǽ] < *wa=rĭmáyī (§8.1.1, §11.2 with n. 11)
Da 348.

*√r9m (< **√rRm)   <ʔiTrɑ9ə̆miTuwn> int rmp pf 2mp [ʔiθrɑ9ə̆mittů́n] <
*hitra99amtúm (§17.17.1, §17.17.2) Da 263.
*√rRy (< **√rðy)   <ʔiTrə̆9iyTiy> sim rmp pf 1s [ʔiθrə̆9í̆θī] < *hitraRī́t (§13 with n. 2)
Da 343.
*√rq   <yirowq> sim impf 3ms [yĭr(r)óq] < *yarrúqi (§9.3.1 n. 40) Da 328.

*√śgʾ bb<ʾæsGiyT> tb<ʾæs:GiyTiy> cau [pf 1s bb[ʾæsgíθ] tb[ʾæsgíθī] < *haśgíʾt (§13 with n. 2) Da 343.

*√śky <yiysæK> sim (short) impf 3ms [yísæx]/[yĭsǽx] or [ísæx]/[īsǽx] < *yiśkáy (§17.6.2 n. 12) Da 345.

*√śWm [tə̆súm] sim impf 2ms [same] < *táśúmi (§17.20) Dalman 1938: 286.

*√šʾr <ʾištə̆ʾær> sim rmp pf 3ms [ʾištə̆ʾér] < *hitšaʾíra (§10) Da 306.

*√šbḥ <yə̆šæBə̆ḥuwnuwnuwn> int impf 3mp^3mp [yə̆šæbbə̆ḥū̆n(n)ū̆n(n)ū̆n] < *yišabbíḥū (or yišabbiḥū̆n(n)a) ⅋ h/ʾin(nV̊)húm (§7.6) Da 367.

sb<y:šæ̆b:ḥæ̊næniy> int impf 3fp^1s sb[yə̆šæbbə̆ḥænnǽnī] < *yišabbiḥannánī (§7.7 n. 33) Da 373.

*√šbq <šə̆BæqTǽniy > {zaqef} sim pf 2ms^1s [šə̆væqtǽnī] < *šabaqtánī (§17.29 (17.29A)) Da 365; Gen 31:28.

*√šdk <šə̆DowKæT> sim pf 3fs [šə̆ðóxæθ] < *šadúkat (§17.11.3) Da 260.

*√šwy <šæwyæniy> int pf 3ms^1s [šæwyǽnī] < *šawwiyánī (§§11.1 n. 4, §17.26) Da 69.

<šæwiyTiy> int pf 1s [šæwwíθī] < *šawwít (§8.1.1 n. 1, §13 with n. 2) Da 343.

<šæw> int impa ms [šǽw] < *šawwí (§8.1.3 with n. 14) Da 348.

bb<šæwyə̆hɑʾ>, sb<šæ̊wiyhɑh> int impa ms^3fs bb[šæwyə̆hā] {apparently}, sb[šæwwíhā] < *šawwīhá {possibly}, *šawwíhā (§2.3.3 n. 15) Da 391.

*√šW9 <wiyšuw9æ> conj sim impf 3ms [wīšúæ9] < *wa=yašúwi (§17.16) Da 320.

<ʾiTšša9> sim rmp pf 3ms [ʾittə̆šá9] < *hitší9a (§6.3) Da 324.

*√šḥl <šə̆ḥælTeyh> sim pf 1s^3ms [šə̆ḥælté̆h] < *šaḥáltə̆hi (§2.3.1) Da 366.

*√šṭḥ <yištə̆ḥuwnuwnuwn> sim impf 3mp^3mp [yištə̆ḥū̆n(n)ū̆n(n)un] < *yišṭáḥū (or yišṭaḥū̆n(n)a) ⅋ h/ʾin(nV̊)húm (§17.15.1 with n. 72) Da 373.

*√šyzb (< **š+ √yzb) <ʾæšteyzæB> quad rmp impf 1s [ʾæštēzǽv] < *ʾitšayzábi (§12.2 n. 15) Da 272.

*√šyṣy (perhaps < **š+ √yṣy) <šeyṣə̆yuwhiy> quad pf 3mp^3ms [šēṣə̆yúhī] < *šayṣiyúhī ((§4.2.2) Da 387.

<yišteyṣey> quad rmp impf 3ms [yištēṣé̆] < *yitšayṣáyi (§8.1.1 n. 1) Da 346.

*√škb sb<yiš:KuwB> {merxa} sim impf 3ms [yiškū̆v] < *yaškúbi (§17.29 (17.29A)) Da 55; Lev 15:4.

sb<Tiš:kowB> {merxa} sim impf 2ms [tiškóv] < *taškúbi ((§17.29 (17.29A)) Da 55; Lev 15:20.

*√škḥ ('find') bb<ʾešKæhæThuwn> sb<ʾæs:KæhæTɑ̊ñuwn> cau pf 3fs^3mp bb[ʾæškæhæθnū̆n] sb[ʾæškæhāθæ̊ñnū̆n] < *haškíḥat ⅋ h/ʾin(nV̊)húm (§17.15.1 (17.15A)) Da 364.

sb<ʾæš:Kæhtɑnɑʾ> cau pf 3fs^1p [ʾæškæhtǽnā] < *haškiḥátnā (§5.2 n. 6) Da 364.

<ʾešKæhiyT> cau pf 1s [ʾæškǽhiθ] < *haškíht (§4.1.2, §17.6.2) Da 261.

bb<næšKæh> sb<niš:Kæh> cau impf 1p bb[næškǽh] sb[niškǽh] < *n(ih)aškíhi (§12.2) Da 274.

*√šlhy (perhaps < **š+ √lhy) <yišTælhiy> quad rmp impf 3ms [yištælhí] < *yitšalhíyi (§8.1.1 n. 1) Da 346.

*√šlḥ <šælḥæniy> sim pf 3ms^1s [šælhǽnī] < *šalaḥánī (§12.2) Da 362.

<šǽlæḥtiyn̈uwn> int pf 1s^3mp [šællæḥtinnū́n] < *šallī́ḥt ̊# h/ˀin(nV̊)hum
(§17.5.1) Da 366.

<wiyšælæḥ> conj int impf 3ms [wīšællǽḥi] < *wa=yišallī́ḥi (§12.2) Da 269.

tb<y:šælæḥiyn̈uwn> ~ <y:šæl:ḥiyn̈uwn> int impf 3ms^3mp tb[yǝ̌šællæḥinnū́n]
~ [yǝ̌šællǝ̌ḥinnū́n] < *yišallī́ḥi ̊# h/ˀin(nV̊)hum (§4.2.1) Da 371.

*√šlm   <šǝ̌līmy> {*merxa*} sim pf 3ms [šǝ̌līm] < *šalī́ma (§17.29 (17.29A)) Da 258;
Gen 19:28.

bb<yǝ̌šælê̌ym> sb<y:šællḯym> int impf 3ms bb[yǝ̌šællêm] sb[yǝ̌šællïm] <
*yišallïmi (§17.29 (17.29A)) Da 267; Exod 21:19.

<ˀeyšæleym> int impf 1s [ˀešællém] < *ˀišallími (§17.23.3 (17.23C)) Da 272.

*√šm9   tb<šim:9eT> sim pf 1s [šim9éθ] < *šamí9t (§12.2) Da 78.

<wušmǽ9uw> conj sim pf 3mp [ǔšmǽ9ū] < *wa=šamí9ū (§2.3.4.3) Da 262.

<yišmǝ̌9uwn> sim impf 3mp [yišmǝ̌9ū́n] < *yišma9ū́na (§17.23.3 (17.23C))
Da 272.

bb<Tišmǝ̌9inuwn> sb<Tæš:mɑ9iyn̈uwn> cau impf 2ms^3mp bb[tišmǝ̌9innū́n]
sb[tæšmɑ̄9innū́n] < *t(ih)ašmí9i ̊# h/ˀin(nV̊)hum (§17.15.1) Da
372.

*√šmš   <yǝ̌šæmǝ̌šuwnuwn> int impf 3mp^3mp [yǝ̌šæmmǝ̌šǔn(n)ǔn] < *yišammī́šu
(or yišammišǔn(n)a) ̊# h/ˀin(nV̊)hum (§17.15.1 with n. 72) Da 373.

*√šny   [ˀištænnǽyū] int rmp pf 3mp [same] < *hitšannáyū (§11.1, §15.4 (15S)) Dal-
man 1938: 429.

*√š9y   <yištæ9uwn> int rmp impf 3mp [yištæ9(9)ǔn] < *yitša99ayū́na (§8.1.1 n. 1,
§15.3.2) Da 347.

*√šqy   bb<ˀæšqæniy> sb<ˀæš:qæniy> cau impa ms^1s bb&sb[ˀæškǽnī] < *hašqáyni
(§11.2 with n. 1) Da 391.

*√šty   [ˀištḯθī] sim pf 1s [same] < *šatī́t (§17.18.1) Macs 207.

bb<wušTiyuw> ~ <wušTiyˀuw> sb[wuš:Tiyuw] conj sim pf 3mp bb[ǔštíyū] ~
[ǔští(ˀ)ū] sb[ǔštíyū] < *wa=šatíyū (§8.1.1) Da 343.

<ˀešT> sim impa ms [ˀéšt] < *šǎtī́ / *šïtáy (§8.1.3 with n. 14) Da 348.

*√tly   sb<ˀiT:liyw> sim rmp pf 3mp [ˀittǝ̌líw] < *hittalíyū (§8.1.1) Da 344.

*√tqn   <ˀæTqǝ̌nɑhiy> cau pf 3fp^3ms [ˀæθqǝ̌nɑ̌hī] < *hatqinɑ̌hī (§8.2.2, §16.2 <u>TR</u>
(β)) Da 361.

*√tqp   <yiTqæP> sim impf 3ms [yiθqǽf] < *yitqápi (§12.2) Da 269.

<TæqeyPhiy> int impa ms^3ms [tæqqéfhī] < *taqqíphī (§2.3.4.4) Da 375.

<ˀæTqiyPiy> cau impa fs [ˀæθqífī] < *hatqípī (§17.11.3) Da 277.

*√trk   <TɑriyKuwnuwn> int pf 3mp^3mp [tūrixǔn(n)ǔn < *tarrī́kū ̊# h/ˀin(nV̊)hum
(§17.15.1) Da 367.

<yǝ̌TɑreyKin̈uwn> int impf 3ms^3mp [yǝ̌θθɑ̄rexinnū́n] < *yitarrī́ki ̊#
h/ˀin(nV̊)hum (§17.15.1) Da 367.

*√θbr   tb<TæB:riynuwn> sim impa ms^3mp [tævrinnū́n] < *θǎbur ̊# h/ˀin(nV̊)hum
(§17.25) Da 376.

*√θWb   <TæBT> sim pf 2fs [tǽvt] < *θǎ́bti (§6.2.2) Da 319.

<TæBTuwn> sim pf 2mp [tævtǔn] < *θǎbtū́m (§6.2.2) Da 320.

<TæBnɑˀ> sim pf 1p [tǽvnɑ] < *θǎ́bnɑ (§6.2.2) Da 320.

<ˀǝ̌TeyBæT> cau pf 3fs [ˀǝ̌θévæθ] < *haθíbat (§6.1.1.1) Da 323.

<ˀǝ̌TiyBuw> cau pf 3mp [ˀǝ̌θívθ] < *haθíbū (§6.1.1.1) Da 323.

<ʔʒTeyBnαʔ> cau pf 1p [ʔʒθévnā] < *haθíbnā (§6.1.1.1) Da 323.

<ʔʒTeyBnαhiy> cau pf 1p^3ms [ʔʒθévnắhī] < *haθibnắhī (§2.3.3 n. 15, §2.3.4.3) Da 368

<yαTiyB> cau impf 3ms [yāθív] < *y(ih)aθíbi (§6.1.2) Da 317.

* √θkl   bb<TʒKeyliyT> sb<t:KowliyT> sim pf 1s bb[tʒxéliθ] sb[tʒxóliθ] < *θakílt ~ * θakúlt (§4.1.2, §15.2.1.1, §17.6.2, §17.11.3) Da 261.

* √θny   <wuTtæn̈eynuwn> conj int impf 2ms^3mp [ǔttænnĕn(n)ǔn] < *wa=tiθannáyi # h/ʔin(nV̊)húm (§15.3.1.2 n. 26) Da 389.

Christian Palestinian

* √ʔbd   <ʔwBD> cau pf 3ms [ōvéð] < *haʔbída (§9.2.3.2) Sl 1.

     <ʔBDT> cau pf 3fs [IbbǯðáT] < *haʔbidát (§12.2) Sg 66.

* √ʔzl   <DyzlBʔ> sbor sim (short) impf 1s^pp(3ms) [dēzel(=)bḗ] < *ðí̆ # ʔaʔzíl(i) # bíhi (§17.15.2) Sg §5.

* √ʔkl   <y(ʔ)Kwl> sim impf 1s [ēxÚl] < *ʔaʔkúli (§14.2) Sg 65.

     <ʔKwl> ~ <Kwl> sim impa ms [V̊xÚl] ~ [KÚl] < *ʔăkúl (§17.33) Sl 5.

* √ʔkp   <lʔ KPL lḫ> negative sim pf 3fs^pp(3ms) perhaps [lā=KǯPallḗh] < *lấ # ʔakV̊pát # líhi (§17.15.2 n. 81) Sg 13.

* √ʔmr   <ʔmryT> sim pf 1s [amréT] or [V̊márIT] < *ʔamárt (§17.6.2, §17.15.1) Sg 8.

     <ʔTʔmr> ~ <ʔTmr> sim rmp pf 3ms [ITǯmar] (or perhaps [ITV̊már]) ~ [Ittǯmár] < *hitʔamíra (§9.2.1.1 with n. 13) Sg 65.

* √ʔsy   <ysʔ> int impf 1s [Issḗ] < *ʔiʔassáyi (§12.2) Sg §34.1, §53.2a2.

* √ʔpk (< **√hpk)   <ʔPKT> cau pf 3fs [appÍxaT] or [appǯxáT] < *haʔpíkat or *haʔpikát (§9.2.2 n. 24) Sl 52.

* √ʔrs (or *√9rs)   <ʔTʔrsT> ~ <ʔTrsT> sim rmp 3fs [ITarsáT] ~ [IttarsáT] < *hitʔarisát (or *hit9arisát) (§9.2.3.1, §10) Sg 65.

* √ʔty   <ʔT̆ʔ> sim pf 3ms [ITắ] < *ʔatáya (§8.1.1) Sg 9.

     <ʔTw> sim pf 3mp [ITŏ̆] < *ʔatáyū (§11.2) Sg 72.

     <yʔTy> ~ <yyTʔ> ~ <yʔ̆Tʔ> sim impf 3ms perhaps uniformly [ēTḗ] (though other possibilities exist such as [ēTí] ~ [yayTḗ] ~ [ēTḗ] respectively; see §14.2} < *yiʔtáyi (~ *yaʔtíyi) (§11.2) Sg 73.

     <ʔyTh> ~ <ʔ̆ʔTʔ> sim impa ms possibly [ITắ] ~ [ITḗ] < *ʔitáy or perhaps < *ʔʔitáʔ ~ *ʔʔitáy (§8.1.3 n. 15) Sg 65, 73.

     <ʔT̆ʔy> sim impa fs [IT̆ăy] < *ʔʔitáyī (§8.1.3) Sg 73.

     <ʔ̆ʔTw> sim impa mp [ITắ] < *ʔitáyū (§8.1.1) Sl 20.

     <ʔ̆ÿTy> ~ <ʔT̆y> cau pf 3ms [ēTí] ~[attí]/[āTí] < *haʔtíya (§9.2.1.1) Sl 20.

* √bz   <ʔTBzz> sim rmp pf 3ms [ITbǯzéz] < *hitbazíza (§3.3, §6.3) Sg 69.

* √bly   <yBylʔ> sim impf 3ms [IvĬlḗ] < *yibláyi (§4.3) Sg 29.

* √b9y (< **√bRy)   <yBw9wn> sim impf 3mp [IvŬ9Ǔn] < *yib9ayǔn(n)a (§4.3) Sg 29.

* √b9θ   <B9w̯ThW̌n> sim pf 3ms^3mp [bǯ9UThÚn] < *ba9áθa # húm or perhaps *ba9aθahúm (§12.2 n. 11, §17.15.1) Sg 29, 60.

* √gWb   <ʔTGBwn> sim rmp pf 3mp [Ittǯya̯vǓn] < *hitgíbū (§6.3) Sg 24.

* √dbq   <yDByqT> sim rmp pf 3fs [IddǯvÍqaT] or [IddǯvíqaT] or [IddǯvīqáT] < *hitdabíqat or *hitdabiqát (§4.1.2 with n. 7) Sg 62.

*√dbr <yDBrynhwn> sim impf 3ms^3mp [Iðbӗr̃InhŪ̃n] or [IðbarInhŪ̃n] < *yidbári
       # húm or *yidbarihúm or conceivably *yidbári # h/ʔin(nV̌)húm (§7.4.2 n. 27,
       §17.15.1) Sg 79.
*√dwy <DwywTy> int pf 3mp^1s perhaps [dawwӗyūTĨ́]/[dawwӗyū́Tĩ] or
       [dawwӗyUttĨ́] / [dawwӗyÚttĩ] < *dawwíyū # yátí (§17.13, §17.30) Sg 78.
*√dmk <DffKӧ̃n> sim impa mp [dӗmUxŪ̃n] < *dӑmúkū (§7.2 (δ)) Sl 73.
*√ðkr <TDKrwn> ~ <TTKrwn> sim rmp impf 2mp [tIddaxrŪ̃n] ~ [tIIttaxrŪ̃n] <
       *titðakirū̃n(n)a (§10 with n. 9) Sg 21.
*√hwy <Thʔ> ~ <Thy> (~ <Thwʔ>ʔ) sim impf 2ms [tӗhḗ] / [tēhḗ] possibly ~ [tӗhĨ́] /
       [tēhĨ́] (~ [tIhwḗ]ʔ) < *tihwáyi (possibly ~ *tahwáyi) (§17.32 with (17.32A))
       Sg §51.2.
       <yhy> ~ <yhynʔ> sim impf 1s [ēhḗ] / [ēhĨ́] ~ [ēhēnã́] / [ēhīnã́] < *ʔihwáyi /
       **ʔahwíyu ~ *ʔihwáyi # ʔanã́ / *ʔahwíyi # ʔanã̆ (§15.3.1.1 with n. 21,
       §17.32 with (17.32A) and n. 152) Sg §16 Anmerkung 1, §15.2.
       <yhwn> sim impf 3mp [ēhṍn] or [Ihwṍn] < *yihwayū̃n(n)a (§17.32 with
       (17.32A)) Sg §51.2.
       <yhn> ~ <yhyn> sim impf 3fp [ēhã́n] ~ [ēhĨ́n] < *yihwayã́n(n)a (§17.32 with
       (17.32A) and n. 152) Sg §51.2.
       <Thwn> (~ <Thwwn>ʔ) sim impf 2mp [tӗhṍn]/[tēhṍn] or [tIhwṍn] <
       *tihwayū̃n(n)a (§17.32 with (17.32A)) Sg 51.2.
*√wd9 <ẙD9T̂ > sim pf 1s [yað9éT] < *wadá9t (§12.2) Sg 76.
       <yTD9T> sim rmp pf 2ms [ITIðá9t] or [ITIðé9t] < *hitwadí9ta (§14.2) Sl 79.
       <ywD9> sim impf 3ms [yŪðá9] or [yŪðé9] < *yidá9i (§17.7) Sl 79.
*√whb <yhB̊wy> sim pf 3mp^3ms [yahBŭ̃y] < *wahabū́hī (§7.2 (ζ)) Sg 79.
*√wzp <ywzP> ~ <yẘzyP> sim impf 3ms [yŪzéf] < *yazípi (§17.7) Sl 82.
*√wkl <yKl> ~ <yʔKl> ~ <ẙKyl> sim pf 3ms [yӗxél] ~ [yӑxél] < *wakíla (§14.2) Sg
       24, 76.
       <TyKwl> sim impf 2ms [tēxÚl] or [tIkkÚl] or [tӗxúl] < *takúli (§17.7) Sl 83.
*√wld <Twl(y)D> sim impf 3fs [tŪléð] < *talídi (§17.7) Sl 83.
       <ʔTlyD> sim rmp pf 3ms [ITIléð] < *hitwalída (§14.2) Sg 76.
*√wmʔ < yʔm̊ʔ> sim impf 3ms [ēmḗ] < *yimáʔi (§17.7) Sl 84.
*√wsp <ʔTwsP̊> cau rmp pf 3ms [Ittōséf] < *hithawsápa (§12.2 n. 11) Sg 60.
*√wqd <yqyDT> sim pf 3fs [yӗqĨ́ðaT] < *waqídat (§4.1.2, §17.34) Sg 75.
       <ywqD> sim impf 3ms [yŪqÚð] < *yaqúdi (§17.7) Sl 86.
*√wqr <ywqrwn> ~ <ywq̊rwn> ~ <yqrwn> sim impf 3mp [yŪq(ӗ)rŪ̃n] ~ [ēq(ӗ)rŪ̃n]
       or [IqqӗrÚn] < *yiqarū̃n(n)a (§17.7) Sl 86.
*√wrθ <yrT> ~ <yrwT> sim pf 3ms [yӗráT]/[yӗréT] ~ [yӗrÚT] < *waráθa (§17.34)
       Sg 60, 62.
       <yʔrwT> sim impf 3ms [ērÚT] < *yarúθi (§14.2) Sg 75.
*√wθb <wTB> conj sim pf 3ms [wITév] < *wa=waθíba (§14.2 n. 11) Sg 76.
       <yTB> sim impf 3ms [ēTév] or [Ittév] < *yaθíbi (§17.7) Sl 88.
       <TB> ~ <yTB̊> sim impa ms [tӗ́v] ~ [yӗTév] < *θíb (§17.33) Sl 88.
*√zbn <yzBnyn> sim impf 3fp [Izbӗp̃Ĩ́n] < *yazbunã́n(n)a (§7.2 (γ, δ)) Sg 62.
       <zBnyn> sim impa fp [zӗvUnĨ́n] < *zӑbúnā (§7.2 ( )) Sg 62.
*√zlp <ʔzDlP> sim rmp pf 3ms [Izdӗléf] < *hitzalípa (§10) Sg §54.1.
*√hkm <yʔḥKmn> cau impf 3fp [yaḥkӗmã́n] < *y(ih)aḥkimã́n(n)a (§7.2 (δ)) Sg 63.

*√ḥmy   \<yḥm̥ˀ> sim impf 3ms [Iḥmḗ] < *yiḥmáyi (§12.2) Sl 65.

*√ḥrm   \<yṮhrmwn> cau rmp impf 3mp [yIttaḥrə̆mŪn] or possibly [yIttå̆ḥIrmŪn] <
        *yithaḥramū̆n(n)a (§4.4.1, §7.2 (γ)) Sg 21, 70.

*√ḥs   \<ḥš̌Ṭ > sim pf 1s [ḥaš̌š̌éT]/[ḥáš̌š̌IT] < *ḥást (§17.6.2) Sg 68.

*√ṭmr   \<ˀṭmr> sim rmp pf 3ms [Iṭṭə̆már]/[Iṭṭə̆mér] < *hiṭṭamíra (§10) Sg 22.

*√ksy   \<KsyT̄h> int pf 3msˆ1p [kassīTán] < *kassíya ǂ yātána (§17.30) Sg 78.

*√ml   \<ml(y)l> int pf 3ms [mallél] < *mallíla (§3.3) Sl 111.

*√mlˀ   < ˀ̥Ṯmlẉ > sim rmp pf 3mp [ITmə̆lú̆]/[ITmə̆ló̆] < *hitmalíˀū (§11.2) Sl 111.
        \<ˀṮmlˀyn> sim rmp pf 3fp [ITmalĪn] < *hitmalíˀā (§7.2 (δ)) Sl 73.

*√mny   \<ˀṮm̊ṅwn> sim rmp pf 3mp [ITmə̆nón̆] < *hitmanáyū (§7.2 (δ)) Sl 72.

*√msr   \<msrw> ~ \<msr> sim pf 3mp [mə̆sárū] ~ [mə̆sár]/[mə̆sér] < *masárū (§17.9.2)
        Sg 17.

*√nḥt (possibly ~ *√ḥt)   < n̥ḥṬṪ > sim pf 1s [naḥTéT] < *naḥát(ə̆)t (§15.3.1.2,
        §17.6.2) Sl 122.
        \<ˀ̥ḥṬṪ> cau pf 1s [aḥ(ḥ)ə̆TéT] < *hanḥít(ə̆)t (§12.3.1.2, §15.3.1.2, §17.6.2) Sl
        122.

*√ntn   \<ˀ̥Tl > sim impf 3ms [Ittél] < *yantíni ǂ lV̆. . . (§14.2 with n. 9) Sg 29.

*√slq   \<š̌lqT > sim pf 1s [salqéT] < *salíqt (§4.1.2) Sg 2.

*√9bd   \<9B̊yD> sim pf 3ms [9š̌véð] < *9abáda (§12.2 n. 11) Sg 60.
        \<y9BD> sim impf 3ms [I9béð] < *ya9bídi (§14.2) Sg 61.
        \<y9BDˀnˀ> sim impf 1s [I9beð̆š̌ná̆] < *ˀa9bídi ǂ ˀaná̆ (§15.3.1.1 n. 21) Sg §16
        Anmerkung 1.
        \<9ByD> ~ \<9BD̥> sim impa ms [9š̌véð] < *9ă̆bíd (§12.2 n. 11) Sg 60.
        \<9BDw> ~ \<9wBDw> sim impa mp [9š̌vÍð̆ū] ~ [9Ŭvĺð̆ū] {though lack of ml
        2ʃ\<y> rather suggests [9UvDú̆], at least for the second variant} <
        *9ă̆bídū {or *9ă̆bidū̆?} (§17.23.3) Sl 140.

*√9br   \<9Brw> ~ \<9Br> sim impa mp [9š̌várū] ~ [9š̌vár]/[9š̌vér] < *9ă̆búrū (§17.9.2)
        Sg 17.

*√9l (< **√Rl)   \<9yl> sim pf 3ms [9él] < *9álla (§12.2 n. 11) Sg 68.
        \<9̥lyT> sim pf 1s [9alléT]/[9állIT] < *9ált (§12.2, §17.2) Sg 68.
        \<9lṮwṇ> ~ \<9lļTwn> ~ \<9llTwn> sim pf 2mp [9altŪn] ~ [9š̌laltŪn] ~
        [9š̌lIltŪn] < *altú̆m ~ *9alaltú̆m (§3.3) Sg 68.
        \<9wlw> sim impa mp [9Úllū] < *9úllū (§3.3) Sg 69.

*√9rs   See *√ˀrs

*√9rR (< **√9rð)   \<ˀwr9> cau pf 3ms [ōrá9]/[ōré9] < *ha9ríRa (§9.1.2 (α), §9.2.3.2)
        Sl 19.

*√prq   \<Prqy> sim pf 3msˆ1s [pə̆ráqī] < *parqqánī (§17.13) Sg 78.

*√ṣWd   \<ṣDyThwn> sim pf 3msˆ3mp [ṣā̆ðĪThŪn] < *ṣă̆da ǂ yātahúm (§17.30) Sg 79.
        \<ˀTṣyD> sim rmp pf 3ms [Ittə̆ṣĪð] < *hitṣída (§6.3) Sg 70.

*√ṣlb   \<ˀṣtlB> sim rmp pf 3ms [Iṣṭə̆lév] < *hitṣalíba (§10) Sg §54.1.
        \<ˀṣlBw> sim rmp pf 3mp [Iṣṣə̆lÍvū] < *hitṣalíbū (§10) Sg 22.

*√θl   \<ˀθl> ~ \<ˀθll> cau pf 3ms [aṭṭél] ~ [aṭlél] < *haθθíla ~ *haθlíla (§3.3) Sl 73.

*√θlm   \<θlmThwn> int pf 1sˆ3mp [ṭallImtš̌hŪn] < *θallímt ǂ húm (§17.15.1 with
        n. 70) Sg 78.

*√qWm   \<yˀqwm> sim impf 3ms [ēqú̆m] < *yaqú̆mi (§14.2) Sg 25, 70.

*√qṭ9   \<qwṭ9h> sim impa msˆ3fs [qUṭ9ā̆h] < *qĭṭá9ha (§17.25) Sg 80.

*√qṣ   <Tqwṣ> sim impf 2ms [tIqqÚṣ] < *taqqúṣi (§3.3) Sg 69.

*√qtl   <yqṭwlny> sim impf 3ms [IqṭÚlénnī] or [IqṭÚlánī] < *yaqtulínnī or *yaqtulínī
          (§17.13) Sg 78.

*√rwy   <yrwwn> ~ <yrwn> sim impf 3mp [Irwṓn] possibly ~ [ērṓn] < *yirwayū̌n(n)a
          (§17.32 (17.32A)) Sg §51.2.

*√rmy   <rmẙ> sim impa ms [rə̆mḗ] < *rĭmáy (§8.1.3) Sg 73.

*√śWm   <ʾsym> cau pf 3ms [ʾə̆sī́m] < haśī́ma (§17.20) Sg 69.

          <ʾsymT> cau pf 1s [ʾə̆sī́mIT]/[ʾə̆sī́mḗT] < *haśímt (§17.20) Sg 70.

*√šʾl   <yʾšwl> sim impf 1s [ēšÚl] < *ʾašʾúli (§14.2 CP (β)) Sg 66.

*√šbḥ   <šB9> sim pf 3ms [šə̆vá9]/[šə̆vé9] < *šabī́ḥa (§9.2.4) Sg 19, Sl 199.

*√šbq   <šBqT > sim pf 3fs [šavqáT] < *šabaqát (§4.1.2, §12.2) Sg 62.

          <ʾšTBq> sim rmp pf 3ms [ʾIštə̆véq] < *hitšabíqa (§10) Sg 54.1.

*√šdy   <šyDyT> sim pf 2s or 1s [šÍðḗT] < *šadáyta or *šadáyt (§4.2.2 with n. 17,
          §17.23.3) Sg 27.

*√škḥ ('find')   <ʾšKyḥT> cau pf 2ms [aškéḥt] < *haškíḥta (§12.2 n. 1) Sg 62.

          <yšKḥnh> ~ <yšKḥh> cau impf 3ms^3ms [Iškə̆hInnḗh] ~ [Iškə̆hḗh] <
          *y(ih)aškihinníhi ~ *y(ih)aškihíhi (§7.1) Sg 78f.

*√šm9   <šmw9> sim pf 3ms [šə̆mÚ9] < *šamí9a (§12.2 n. 11, §15.6 (β)) Sg 60.

          <yšmw9 > sim impf 3ms [IšmÚ9] < *yišmá9i (§12.2 n. 11, §15.6 (β)) Sg 210.

          <šwm̊9wn> sim impa mp [šUm9Ũn] < *šĭmá9ū (§17.25) Sg 62.

*√šry   <šrẘ> ~ <šryw> ~ <šry> int pf 3mp [šarrṓ]/[šarṓ] ~ [šarríw]/[šaríw] ~ perhaps
          [šarrḗ]/[šarḗ] < *šarráyū ~ *šárriyū (§17.9.2 n. 25) Sg 17, 72.

*√šty   <ʾšTT> sim pf 3fs [IštåT] < *šatáyat/*šatayát (§17.18.1) Sg 72.

          <ʾšTw> sim pf 3mp [Ištṓ] < *šatáyū (§17.18.1) Sg 72.

          <ʾyšTw> sim impa mp [Ištṓ] < *šitáyū (§17.18.1) Sg 73.

*√štm   <šTẘm > sim impa ms [šÍTÚm] < *šătúm (§17.23.3) Sg 62.

*√tmh   <ʾTmẖ> sim rmp pf 3ms [Ittə̆méh] < *hittamíha (§15.3.1.2 n. 26) Sl 221.

*√θbr   <ʾTBrT> int rmp pf 3fs [Ittabbə̆ráT] or [IttabbáraT] < *hitθabbarát or
          *hitθabbárat (§10) Sg 22.

Samaritan

*√ʾbd   <yʾBD> t[yíbɑd] sim impf 3ms [yīβáð] < *yiʾbádi (§9.2.3.2 with n. 32) Macs
          176.

          <yʾBDwnK> ~ <ʾBDwTK> int {?} impf 3mp^2ms perhaps
          [y(ɜ̆ʾ)abbə̆ðŨn(n)ắx] or [ī̆ʾabbə̆ðŨn(n)ắx]/[iyyabbə̆ðŨn(n)ắx] ~
          [ī̆ibbə̆ðū̄θắx]/[ī̆bbə̆ðŨttắx] {though interpretation of the second
          orthographic variant is especially shaky} < *yiʾabbidŭn(n)áka
          (§14.2) Macs 229.

*√ʾgr   <ʾGrTK> ~ <ʾGRTyK> ~ <ʾGRʾTK> sim pf 1s^2ms [ʾáɣartắx]/[aɣartắx] ~
          [ắɣartĬ̆x]/[aɣartĬ̆x] {fgmʾ} ~ [ắɣarắθắx]/[aɣarắθắx] {?} < *ʾagártə̆ka ~ pos-
          sibly ʾagártə̆ki (§16.2 SM (α)) Macs 171, 227.

*√ʾzl   <zl> t[zắl] sim impa ms [zál] < *ʾĭzal or *ʾăzíl (§17.33) Macs 103.

          <ʾzly> t[ēzắli] sim impa fs [ʾə̆záli] < *ʾĭzálī or *ʾăzílī (§17.33) Macs 177.

*√ʾkl   <yyKl> t[yíkɑl] cau impf 3ms [yīxál] < *y(ih)aʾkíli (§9.2.3.2) Macs 178.

*√ʾmr   <ʾmr> t[ắmɑr] sim pf 3ms [ắmár]/[amár] < *ʾamára (§9.2.3.1) Macs 11, 171.

<ʔmrT> ~ <ʔmrTy> sim pf 1s [ʔamáriθ]/[amáriθ] ~ [ʔamárTī]/[amárTī] or [ʔam(ă)rÍθī]/[am(ă)rÍθī] < *ʔamárt (§13) Macs 146.

<ʔmrw> ~ <ʔmrwn> sim pf 3mp [ʔămárū]/[amárū] ~ [ʔămarŮn]/[amarŮn] < *ʔămárū (§7.2 (δ)) Macs 99.

<yymr> t[yÍmær] sim impf 3ms [yīmár] < *yaʔmúri (§11.2) Macs 113, 176.

<wʔmrw> t[wǽmru] conj sim impa mp [w(ɔʔ)amrŮ] < *wa=ʔămúrū or *wa=ʔămurŮ (§17.25) Macs 148.

<(w)ʔT(ʔ)mr> t[(w)ētắmar] (conj) sim rmp pf 3ms [(w(ɔʔ))iθămár] < *(wa=)hitʔamíra (§9.2.1.1 n. 13, §9.2.3.1) Macs 90, 153.

*√ʔpk (< **√hpk)   <TyPK> t[tÍfɑk] sim impf 2ms/3fs <*taʔpúki (§9.2.2 n. 24) Macs 12, 367.

*√ʔrk   <TwrKwn> t[tūrÍkon] cau impf 2mp [tūrīxŮn] < *t(ih)aʔrikŭn(n)a (§17.28) Macs 159–61.

*√ʔty   <ʔTʔ> ~ <ʔTh> t[ắtɑ] sim pf 3ms [ʔăθắ]/[aθắ] < *ʔatáya (§8.1.1) Macs 341.

<ʔTyTy> ~ <ʔTyT> t[ātÍti] ~ [ắtɔt] sim pf 2fs [ʔăθÍθī]/[aθÍθī] ~ [ʔăθÍθ]/[aθÍθ] < *ʔatÍtī ~ *ʔatÍti (or *ʔatáytī ~ *ʔatáyti) (§2.3.4.3, §11.2) Macs 206.

<ʔTw> t[ắtu] sim pf 3mp [ʔăθÚ]/[aθÚ] < *ʔatáyū (§8.1.1) Macs 207.

<ʔTy> t[ắti] sim pf 3fp [ʔăθÍ]/[aθÍ] < *ʔatíyā (§11.2) Macs 206.

<ʔTY> t[ếti] ~ <ʔTh> sim impa ms [ʔɔθÍ]/[IθÍ] possibly ~ [ʔăθắ]/[Iθắ] < *ʔitáy possibly ~ *ʔÍtáʔ (§8.1.3 n. 15) Macs 209.

*√bWš (< **√bʔš)   <hBʔšT> ~ <hB9šT> ~ <ʔB9šT> ~ <B9šT> t[ūbÍšɔt] cau {~ sim ?} pf 1s [ʔăβÍšiθ]/[aβÍšiθ] < *habíʔšt { ~ *bÍšt?} (§6.1.1.1, §6.1.1.2 (6C) n. 11) Macs 95f.

*√bṭn   <BṭnT> t[bāṭắnāt] sim pf 3fs [băṭánaθ] < *baṭánat or *baṭínat (§4.1.2 with n. 8) Macs 145.

*√bky   <BKT> t[bắkɑt] sim pf 3fs [băxắθ] or [băxáθ] < *bakáyat (§13) Macs 205.

*√bny   <yBny> ~ <yBnh> t[yÍbni] sim impf 3ms [yiβnÍ] < *yibnáyi (§12.2) Macs 207.

*√brʔ   <Br(ʔ)Th> t[būrắte] sim pf 3ms^3ms [bărāθÉh] < *baraʔáhi (§16.2 SM (w)) Macs 233.

*√brk   <BrK> t[bǽrrɑk] int pf 3ms [barréx] < *barríka (§9.3.1) Macs 156.

<TBrKny> int impf 2ms^1s [tɔβarrɔxénnī] < *tibarrikinníni (§17.13) Macs 228.

*√gd   <GD> t[gǽd] sim impa ms [gáð] < *gúd (§6.2.2) Macs 198.

*√gzy   <TGzy ln> t[tigzÍ|ɑn] sim sim (short) impf 2ms^pp(1p) [tiɣzÍ=lan] < *tigzáy # lána (§17.15.2 with n. 76) Macs 322.

*√ghn   <GhnT> ~ <G9nT> sim pf 3fs [gă9Ínaθ] < *gahínat (§9.2.4) Macs 173.

*√gly   <GlTyn> t[gā|ắtən] sim pf 3ms^3fp [gălāθÍn]/[gălắttÍn] < *galáya # yātahín (§17.30) Macs 233.

*√gml   <wʔᵛG'm'lT<> int rmp pf 2m{?}s {if m, via fgm} [w(ɔʔ)iggammálti] < *wa=hitgammáltī (§13) Macs 90.

*√gnb   <yGnB> t[yÍgnæb] sim impf 3ms [yiɣnáβ] < *yagnúḥi (§12.2) Macs 147.

*√g9y   <wyGhwn>t[w(ɔ)yēgŭn] conj sim impf 3mp [wɔyiɣ9Ůn] < *wa=yig9ayŭn(n)a (§22.1 (22C) (β)) Macs 123.

*√gš   <Gšš> t[gǽššɔš] int pf 3ms [gaššéš] < *gaššíša (§3.3) Macs 200.

*√dbq   <DBq> t[dḗbɑq] sim impa ms [dɔβáq] < *dăbúq (§17.23.3) Macs 148.

<wDBqy> t[w(ŏ)dēbắqī] conj sim impa ms^1s [wŏDŏβáqī] < *wa=dăbúqni* (§17.13) Macs 29.

<DBqn> t[dēbắqɑn] sim impa fp [dŏβaqą̆n] < *dăbúqā* (§7.2 (δ)) Vilsker 1981: 62.

<ʔDBqT> t[iddābế́qət] sim rmp pf 1s [(ʔ)iddăβéqiθ] < *hitdabíqt*

*√dWr   <D9(y)r> ~ <Dr> t[dǽr] ~ [dǽr] ~ [dór] sim impa ms [dắr] ~ [dár] ~ [dÚr] < *dắr* ~ *dúr* (§6.2.2) Macs 191.

*√ðḥl   <nDḥl> t[nēdắl] sim impf 1p [niŏ9ál] < *niðḥáli* (§4.3) Macs 123.

<Dḥl> t[dæ̃́ʔəl] sim impa ms [dă9él] < *ðăḥíl* (§17.23.3) Macs 74.

*√ðkr   <DKrThy> t[dākɑrtắni] sim pf 2ms^1s [dăxartą̆ni] < *ðakartắnī* (§7.5 with n. 31) Macs 227.

<TTDKrwn> t[tētidkắron] sim rmp impf 2mp [tIθiðkárUn] {?} < *titðakirún(n)a* (§10 with n. 6) Macs 154.

*√hwy ~ *√hyy   <hwyTwn> t[ŏbĩ́ton]sim pf 2mp [hăβīθÚn]/[aβīθÚn] < *hawaytúm* or *hawītúm* (§9.2.3.2) Macs 209.

<yhyy> t[yẽ́yyi] ~ <yhy> t[yᾱ́ʔi] ~ <yy> t[yĩ́] ~ <hy> t[ĩ́] sim impf 3ms [yehyĩ́] ~ [yăhĩ́] ~ [yĩ́] ~ [ĩ́] < *yihyáyi* ~ *yahyíyi* (§17.32 with (17.32A) and n. 152) Macs 218.

<Thwy> ~ <Tyy> ~ <yy> sim impf 3fs {*fgm*} [tehwĩ́] ~ [tŏyĩ́] ~ [(y)ĩ́] < *tihwáyi* ~ *yihwáyi* (§16.2 SM (z)) Macs 218.

<ʔhy> t[ᾱ́ʔi] sim impf 1s [ʔăhĩ́]/[ahĩ́] < *ʔahwíyi* (§17.32 with (17.32A) and n. 152) Macs 218.

<wʔwy> t[wẽ́bi] ~ <why> conj sim impf 1s [w(ŏʔ)ŏβĩ́] ~ [w(ŏʔ)ĩ́] < *wa=ʔihwáyi* (§17.32 with (17.32A) and n. 152) Macs 218.

<yhwn> ~ <yhwnw> t[yú̃n] ~ t[yú̃nu] sim impf 3mp [yŏhú̃n]/[yú̃n] ~ [yŏhú̃nū]/ [yú̃nū] {*the* [h]-*less realizations are more likely*} < *yihwayú̃n(n)a* (§17.32 with (17.32A) and n. 152) Macs 218.

<yhn> t[yắn] ~ ⸲ʔhyyn⸲ sim impf 3fp [yŏhắn] ~ possibly [īhyắn]/[ĩyyắn] or [īhyІn]/[ĩyyІn] < *yihwayắn(n)a* ~ *yahwiyắn(n)a* (§17.32 with (17.32A) and n. 152) Macs 218.

*√hymn (plausibly < ** h+ √ʔmn)   <yhymnwn> ~ <yymnwn> t[yīmȩ̂́non] ~ <ʔymnwn> t[īmȩ̂́non] quad impf 3mp perhaps [yŏhīmᾰ̧nÚn] ~ [yīmᾰ̧nÚn]~ īmᾰ̧nÚn] < *yihayminú̃n(n)a* (§11.2, §14.2) Macs 176f.

*√hlk   <yhlK> ~ <ylK> sim impf 3ms [yehláx] ~ [yelláx] < *yihláki* (§9.2.2) Macs 366.

*√wdy   <wyTwDy> t[w(ŏ)yittudi] conj cau rmp impf 3ms [wŏyittōŏ́i] < *wa=yithawdiyi* or *wa=yithawdayi* (§9.2.2 n. 22) Macs 216.

*√whb   <ʔB> t[ǽb] ~ <ʔhB> t[ᾱ́ʔab] sim impa ms [(ʔ)áβ] ~ [ʔăháβ]/[aháβ] < *háb* (§14.2 n. 16, §17.23.3) Macs 74, 182.

<hBy> ~ <hwy> ~<ʔyhBy> sim impa fs [háβī] ~ [īháβī] < *hábī* (§17.33) Macs 181.

<hBw> t[ế́bu] ~ [ǽbu] ~ <ʔBw> t[ế́bu] ~ [ǽbu] ~ <ʔhBw> t[ᾱ́ʔébu] sim impa mp [héβū]/[éβū] ~ [háβū]/[áβū] ~ [ʔahéβū]/[ahéβū]/[aʔéβū] < *híbū* ~ *hábū* (§14.2 n. 16) Macs 11, 98, 174, 181.

<yyB> perhaps sim rmp impf 3ms [yiyyéβ] < *yitwahíbi* (§10) Macs 180.

*√wkl   \<y(w)Kl> t[yŭkɑl] sim impf 3ms [yūxál] (possibly ~ [yikkál]) < *yV̊wkáli* (possibly ~ **yikáli*) (§17.7) Macs 180.

*√wld   \<T(y)lD> t[tī̆lɑd] sim impf 3fs [tīláθ] < **tiládi* (§17.7) Macs 180.

\<TlDy> t[tī́ldi] ~ [tī̆ā̆di] sim impf 2fs [tīlDī́] ~ [tīlă̆ðī́] (or perhaps [tīláðī]) < **tiladī́ / *tiladī̆n(n)a* (perhaps ~ **tiládī*) (§4.2.2 with n. 16) Macs 180.

\<ʾylD> t[ī̆lɑd] sim impf 1s [(ʾ)īláθ] < **ʾiládi* (§4.2.2 n. 16) Macs 180f.

\<wyylDn> t[w(ʒ̆)yī̆ā̆dən] conj sim impf 3fp [wʒ̆yīlă̆ðĬn] < **wa=yiladắn(n)a* (§4.2.2 n. 16, §7.2 (γ)) Macs 181.

\<ʾTylD> t[ētī́lǝd] sim rmp pf 3ms [ʾʒ̆θīléθ]/[eθīléθ] < **hitwalída* (§14.2) Macs 182.

*√wsp   \<wʾsP> t[wŭ̄sǝf] conj cau impf 1s [w(ʒ̆ʾ)ūséf] < **wa=ʾ(ih)awsípi* (§17.7 n. 20) Macs 183.

*√wqd   \<wʾwqDT> t[wūqédɑt] conj cau pf 1s [w(ʒ̆ʾ)ūqédiθ] < **wa=hawqídt* (§17.7 n. 20) Macs 183.

\<wʾqDnh> conj cau impf 1s^3fs [w(ʒ̆ʾ)aqqʒ̆ðinnắh] < **wa=ʾ(ih)awqidinníha* (§17.7 n. 20) Macs 182.

*√wqr   \<ʾTyqrT> sim rmp pf 3fs [(ʾ)Iθīqáraθ] < **hitwaqírat* (§17.34) Macs 183.

\<DʾwqrTnn> t[dūqɑrtắnɑn] sbor cau pf 2ms^1p [d(ʒ̆ʾ)ōqartānán] < **ðī́ # hawqirtắna* (§7.5) Macs 227.

*√wrθ   \<yyrT> t[yī́rɑt] sim impf 3ms [yīráθi] < **yiráθi* (§17.7) Macs 181.

\<wyyrTwn> t[w(ʒ̆)yīrắton] conj sim impf 3mp [wʒ̆yīrăθŬn] < **wa=yiraθŭ̄n(n)a* (§4.2.2 n. 16) Macs 181.

*√wθb   \<yTB> ~ \<TB> t[yắtɑb] ~ [táb] sim pf 3ms [yă̆θáβ] ~ [táβ] < **waθába* (§17.33 n. 159, §17.34) Macs 139f., 144.

\<wʾTBh> t[wættḗbe] conj cau pf 3ms^3ms [w(ʒ̆ʾ)attʒ̆βéh] < **wa=hawθibáhi* (§17.7) Macs 183.

*√z9q   \<z9q> t[zắeq] sim pfd 3ms [ză̆9áq] < **za9áqa* (§9.2.3.1) Macs 173.

\<ʾzD9q> t[izdḗq] sim rmp pf 3ms [(ʾ)izdă̆9éq] < **hitza9íqa* (§10) Macs 153f.

*√ḥwy   \<yḥBwn> ~ \<yhBwn> t[iyyắbbon] int impf 3mp [iyyaaββŬn] < **yihawwayŭ̄n(n)a* (§14.2 with nn. 14 and 15) Macs 212.

\<ḥwy> t[ắbbi] int impa fs [9aββī́] < **ḥawwíyi or *ḥawwáyi* (§8.1.1, §8.1.3) Macs 12.

*√ḥWg   \<TḥwGwny> sim impf 2mp^1s [tʒ̆9ūyŭ̄n(n)ī] < **taḥūgū́nī* (§17.13) Macs 229.

*√ḥzy   \<ḥzTh> t[ā̆zắtɑ] sim pf 3ms^3fs [9ăzā̆θắh] < **ḥazáya # yátáha* (§17.30) Macs 233.

\<ḥz(y)T> ~ \<ḥzʾTy> sim pf 1s [9ăzī́θī] ~ [9ăzī́θī] < **ḥazáyt or *ḥazī́t* (§13) Macs 206.

\<ḥzyʾn> ~ \<ḥzyʾTh> t[ắzyɑn] ~ [ā̆zyắtɑ] sim pf 3fp [9azyắn] ~ [9azyā̆θắ] < **ḥazáyā {alternatively these forms might be true participles, as Macuch notes}* (§17.17.2) Macs 209.

\<yTḥzy> t[yētắzi] cau or sim rmp impf 3ms [yiθa9zī́] or [yi9θ9ăzī́] < **yithaḥzíyi / *yithaḥzáyi or *yitḥazíyi / *yitḥazáyi* (§9.2.2 n. 22) Macs 216.

\<ʾḥzynn> cau pf 3ms^1p [(ʾ)aḥzīnán] < **haḥziyắnā* (§16.2 <u>SM</u> (β)) Macs 233.

*√ḥy(y) (~ *√ḥwy?) <wḥ(y)w> t[wǣyu] conj sim pf 3mp perhaps [wa9yū́] < *wa=ḥayáyū (§11.1 n. 4) Macs 219.

<ḥyynn> int pf 2ms^1p [9ayyî̄nán] {?} < *ḥayyītánā (§16.2 SM (β)) Macs 220.

<ʔwḥnn> cau pf 2ms^1p [(ʔ)ū9ĭnnán] {?} < *haḥyītánā or possibly *hahwitana (§16.2 SM ( )) Macs 220.

<wTwḥy(ʔ)n> t[w(ŏ)tuwwíyɑn] conj cau impf 3fp [wŏTū9ŏyǎ̂n] < wa=t(ih)aḥyiyǎ̂n(n)a or possibly *wa=t(ih)aḥwiyǎ̂n(n)a (§16.2 SM (zʹ) with n. 24) Macs 221.

<w(y)Twḥy> t[w(ŏ)yittúwwi] ~ [wittúwwi] conj cau rmp impf 3ms [wŏyittū9î́] < *wa=yithaḥyíyi / *wa=yithaḥyáyi or possibly *wa=yithaḥwíyi / *wa=yithaḥwáyi (§6.1.2 with (6C) and n. 12, §14.2 with n. 14) Macs 184.

*√ḥkm <yḥKm> t[yḗkkæm] sim impf 3ms [ye9kám] < *yiḥkámi (§12.2) Macs 172.

<yḥKmwn> t[yēkkǎ̂mon] sim impf 3mp [ye9kămǓn] < *yiḥkamǔ̂n(n)a (§9.2.4, §22.1 (22C) (γ)) Macs 172.

<yḥKm> ~ <y9Km> t[yǎ̆kkəm] cau impf 3ms [ya9kém] < *y(ih)aḥkími (§9.2.3.2 with n. 31) Macs 173.

*√ḥmy <ḥmh> ~ <9mh> t[9ǎ̆mɑ] sim pf 3ms [9ămǎ́] < *ḥamáya (§9.2.4) Macs 171.

<Dy9mwnn> t[ædyēmmǔ̂ne] sbor sim impf 3mp^3ms [(ʔ)aðye9mūnḗh] < *ðî́ # yiḥmayūnáhi (§7.2 (ε)) Macs 229.

<wʔ9mynnh> conj cau pf 3ms^3ms [w(ŏʔ)a9mĭnnḗh] < *wa=haḥmíyihi (§7.1) Macs 233.

*√ḥrb (< **√Xrb) <wḥrBw> ~ <w9rBw> conj sim pf 3mp [wŏʔaráβū] or [wa9(ă)ráβū] < *wa=ḥarábū (§9.2.4) Macs 146.

*√ḥśk <ḥsK> t[9ǎ̆sɑk] sim pf 3ms [9ăśax] < *ḥaśáka (§9.2.4) Macs 171.

*√ḥšb <ḥšBh> t[9ūšǎ̆bɑ] sim pf 3ms^3fs [9ašǎ̆βǎ̂h] < *ḥašabáha (§4.2.2 n. 16) Macs 226.

*√ṭmr <Dṭmrw> t[diṭṭāmǎ̄ru] sbor sim pf rmp 3mp [d(ŏʔ)iṭṭămárū] < *ðî́ # hiṭṭamírū (§10) Macs 154.

*√ṭrd <ṭrD(w)nwn> ~ <ṭrDwnyn> t[ṭārādúnnon] ~ [ṭārādúnnen] sim pf 3mp^3mp~3fp {? gender value of the object uncertain} [ṭăraðUnnǓn] ~ [ṭăraðUnnî̄n] < *ṭarádū # h/ʔin(nV̌)húm ~ *ṭarádū # h/ʔin(nV̌)hín (§16.2 SM (y)) Macs 233.

*√kWnn (< **√kWn) <Kwnnh> t[kūnénnē] int impa ms^3ms [kūn(ŏn)innḗh] < *kawnínhi {miškal-suppletion for *kawwínhi?} (§7.1 with n. 6) Macs 194.

*√kpl <KPl> t[kĕ́fəl] sim impa ms [kŏfél] < *kăpíl (§17.23.3) Macs 149.

*√krz (< Greek kēruss-) <Krwz> sim impa ms [kŏrÚz] as if < @ *kărúz (§17.23.3) Macs 149.

*√lbš <ylBšnh> ~ <ylBšh> sim impf 3ms^3ms [yilbŏ̆šinnḗh] ~ [yilbŏ̆šḗh] < *yilbašinníhi ~ *yilbašíhi (§7.1) Macs 228.

<hlByšT> ~ <ʔlByšT> t[ælbî́šæt] cau pf 3fs [(ʔ)albî́šaθ] < *halbíšat (§17.28) Macs 159–61.

*√mWt <ʔmwT> t[ḗmot] sim impf 1s [ʔŏmǔ́]/[emǔ́θ] < *ʔamǔ́ti (§17.20) Macs 191.

*√mḥʔ <mḥw> ~ <m9w> t[mǣʔu] sim pf 3ms [mă9Ǔ] < mahắʔa # hú (§2.3.2.4 n. 14c) Macs 203.

<m9wnwn> ~ <m9wTwn> sim pf 3ms^3mp [mă9Ŭn(n)Ŭ̊n] ~ [mă9Ū̊θŬ̊n] < *maḥáʾa # hū̊ # h/ʾin(nV̊)húm ~ *maḥáʾa # hū̊ # yātahúm (§2.3.2.4 n. 14c, §13, §17.15.1, §17.30) Macs 234.

<ym9y> t[yæmǽʾi] sim impf 3ms [yamă9í̊] < *yamḥV̊ʾi (§4.3, §12.2) Macs 207.

*√mty　<ʾmty> t[ímti] sim pf 3ms [(ʾ)imtí̊] < *matíya (§17.18.1) Macs 214.

<wmṭnwn> ~ <wˀmṭnwn> conj sim pf 3ms^3mp [wŏmăṭắn(n)Ŭ̊n] or [wam(ŏ̆) ṭắn(n)Ŭ̊n] ~ [w(ŏ̆ʾ)imṭắn(n)Ŭ̊n] < *wa=maṭáya # h/ʾin(nV̊)húm (§7.4.1, §16.2 <u>SM</u> (β)) Macs 233.

*√mṭr　<hmṭyr> cau pf 3ms [(h)amṭír] < *hamṭíra (§17.28) Macs 159–61.

*√ml　<wˀmllh 9mK> conj int (short) impf 1s # pp(2ms) [wa(ŏ̆ʾ)mallŏ̆lắ # 9immắx] or [w(ŏ̆ʾ)ŏ̆mallŏ̆lắ # 9immắx] < *wa=ʾimallilá # 9ímmŏ̆ka (§2.3.4.1) Macs 116.

<wˀmll lwTK> conj int (short) impf 1s # pp(2ms) [wa(ʾŏ̆)mallę́l # lŏ̆wā̊θáx] or [w(ŏ̆ʾ)ŏ̆mallel # lŏ̆wā̊θáx] < *wa=ʾimallíl # lV̊wātV̊ka (§2.3.4.1) Macs 116.

*√nŏy (or possibly *√9dy)　<ʾnDh> t[ǽndɑ] cau pf 3ms [(ʾ)andắ] < *hanŏáya (or possibly *ha9dáya) (§17.8 with n. 22) Macs 93.

<ʾnDyTh> t[ændiyyǽte] cau pf 3fs^3ms [(ʾ)andiyắθéh] {*with transparentive preservation of* 2ʃi—*quite uncertain*} < *hanŏiyáthi (or possibly *ha9diyáthi) (§16.2 <u>SM</u> (w)) Macs 233.

<yThDy> t[yittǽndi] cau rmp impf 3ms [yiitandí̊] < *yithandíyi / *yithandáyi (or possibly *yitha9díyi / *yitha9dáyi) (§9.2.2 n. 22) Macs 216.

*√nḥt (possibly ~ *√ht)　<n9T> ~ <ʾ9T> t[nǽt] ~ [ǽt] sim pf 3ms [nă9á̊θ] ~ [9á̊θ] < *naḥáta ~ *ḥátta (§17.33 with n. 159) Macs 139f.

<nḥTT> ~ <n9TT> t[nǽttɑt] sim pf 3fs [na9Tá̊θ] < *naḥitát (§4.1.2, §4.2.2, §12.2) Macs 174.

<yy9T> sim impf 3ms [yī9á̊θ] < *yinḥáti or possibly *yiḥḥáti (§17.2.1.1) Macs 186.

<nḥT> ~ <n9T> t[nǽt] sim impa ms [nŏ̆9á̊θ] < *ḥát (§17.33) Macs 186f.

<wTḥTwn> ~ <wT9Twn> ~ <wTy9Twn> conj cau impf 2mp [wŏ̆Ta99ŏ̆θŬ̊n]/ [wŏ̆Ta9TŬ̊n] ~ [wŏ̆Te99ŏ̆θŬ̊n]/[wŏ̆Te9TŬ̊n] < *wa=t(ih)anḥitū̊n(n)a or possibly *wa=t(ih)aḥḥitū̊n(n)a (§12.2) Macs 188.

<hy9Twnh> cau impa mp^3ms [he99ŏ̆θūnéh] < *hanḥitū̊hi or possibly *haḥḥitū̊hi (§7.2 (ζ) with n. 22) Macs 230.

*√nyq (< **√ynq)　<wˀnyq(y)Th> t[wīnīqíte] conj sim impf 1s^3ms [w(ŏ̆ʾ)ŏ̆nīqīθéh] or [w(ŏ̆ʾ)enīqīθéh] < *wa=ʾaníqi # yātáhi {*smc as formulated predicts* (@)t[wēnīqí̊te]} (§16.2 <u>SM</u> (α), §17.30) Macs 183.

*√nsb　<sB> sim pf 3ms [sáβ] < *nasába (§17.33 n. 159) Macs 139f.

<nsBTy> t[nāsǽbti] ~ <nsBTyT> sim pf 2fs [năsáβtī] ~ possibly [năsáβtiθ] or [năsaβtí̊θ] < *nasábtī (§13 n. 7) Macs 146.

<wˀTnsBT> t[wētænsébɑt] conj sim rmp pf 3fs [w(ŏ̆ʾ)iθansÍβaθ] < *wa=hitnasíbat (§4.4.2) Macs 154.

*√npl　<Pl> sim pf 3ms [pál] < *napála (§17.33 n. 159) Macs 139f.

*√npq　<Pq> sim pf 3ms [páq] < *napáqa (§17.33 n. 159) Macs 139f

<Pwq> t[fóq] sim impa ms [póq] < *púq (§17.12.2) Macs 139.

<Pwqw> t[fū́qu] sim impa mp [pÚqū̃] < *puqu* (§17.12.2) Macs 139.

<ʔPqT> t[æbbḗqət] cau pf 1s [(ʔ)appéqiθ] < *hanpíqt* (§2.3.2.4 n. 14) Macs 188.

<wʔPqwTy> conj cau pf 1s < *wa=hanpíqt* (§2.3.2.4 n. 14c) Macs 188.

<ʔPq> t[ǽbbəq] cau impa ms [(ʔ)appéq] < *hanpíq* (§17.21.1) Macs 98.

<ʔPqw> t[æbbḗqu] cau impa mp [(ʔ)appÍqū̃] < *hanpíqū* (§17.26) Macs 188.

<hPqwh> cau impa mp^3ms [(h)appə̆qū́h] < *hanpiqū́hi* (§7.2 (ζ) with n. 23) Macs 230.

*√nṣr   <Dʔnṣyryn> t[dɑnṣī́rən] sbor sim pas pf 3mp {*unless the form is participial*} [danṣīrī́n] < *ðī̊́ # naṣīrū* (§1.1.1 n. 3, §17.17.2) Macs 145, 151.

*√nθr   <tr> t[ṭɑ́r] {*whence the vowel length?*} sim impa ms [ṭar] < *θúr* (§17.12.2) Macs 186.

<ṭrw> t[ṭḗru] sim impa mp [ṭə̆rū́] < *θúrū* or *θurū́* (§17.12.2) Macs 186.

*√sḥn   <ysḥnh> ~ <ysḥnnh> ~ <ysḥnʔnh> sim impf 3ms^3ms [yishə̆nḗh] ~ yishə̆ninnḗh] < *yishaníhi ~ *yishaninnī́hi* (§16.2 SM (α)) Macs 228.

*√skm   <ʔTsKmw> t[ētæskḗmu] sim rmp pf 3mp perhaps [(ʔ)iθaskÍmū] < *hitsakímū* (§10 with n. 6) Macs 154.

*√slq   <sq> sim pf 3ms [sɑ́q] < *salíqa* (§17.33 n. 159) Macs 98.

<sqw> t[sɑ̃́qu] sim pf 3mp [sɑ́qū̃] < *salíqū* (§17.33 n. 159) Macs 185.

<ʔsTlq> t[istɑ̃́ləq] sim rmp pf 3ms [(ʔ)istaléq] < *hitsalíqa* (§10) Macs 153f.

<ʔsqw> t[ǽsqu] cau pf 3mp [(ʔ)asqū̃́] < *haslíqū* or *haslíqū̃* (§17.26) Macs 188.

*√smk   <smKThh> ~ <smKTh> t[sɑ̃mɑktínne] ~ [sɑ̃mɑ́kte] sim pf 1s^3ms [sə̆maxtinnḗh] ~ [sə̆maxtḗh] < *samáktə̆hi* (§7.1, §16.2 SM (α)) Macs 227.

*√9bd   <9BDh> t[9ɑ̃b(b)ɑ́de] sim pf 3ms^3ms [9aβɑ̆ðḗh] < *9abadáhi* (§4.1.2 n. 8, §12.2 with n. 13) Macs 226.

<w9BDT> ~ <w9BDh> t[wæbɑ̃́dɑt] ~ [wæbɑ̃́dɑ] conj sim pf 3fs [wə̆9ɑ̆βɑ́ðaθ]/[wa9(ɑ̆)Bɑ́ðaθ] ~ [wə̆9ɑ̆βɑ́ðɑ]/[wa9(ɑ̆)Bɑ́ðɑ] < *wa=9abádat* (§17.12.2) Macs 145.

<9BDThh> t[9ɑ̃bɑdtɑ̃́ne] sim pf 2ms^3ms [9ɑ̆βaðtɑnḗh] < *9abadtā́hi* (§7.5) Macs 227.

<9BDThwn> t[9ɑ̃bɑdtɑ̃́non] sim pf 2ms^3mp [9ɑ̆βaðtɑnŪ̃n] < *9abádtā # h/ʔin(nV̂)húm* (§7.5) Macs 227.

<y9BD> t[yḗbbəd] ~ [yḗbbɑd] sim impf 3ms [ye9bḗð] ~ [ye9bɑ́ð] < *ya9bídi* (§9.2.3.2 with n. 32) Macs 172.

<ʔT9BD> t[ētǽb(b)əd] ~ [ētǽb(b)ɑd] sim rmp pf 3ms [(ʔ)iθ9ɑ̆βéð] ~ [(ʔ)iθ9ɑ̆βɑ́ð] < *hit9abída* (§9.2.3.1 with n. 29) Macs 90.

*√9br   <9Br> t[9ɑ̃́bɑr] ~ [9ɑ́bbɑr] sim pf 3ms [9ɑ̆βɑ́r] < *9abára* (§9.2.3.1 n. 28) Macs 155, 171.

<w9Brn> t[wɑbbɑ̃́ron] conj sim pf 3mp [wə̆9ɑ̆βarŪ̃n] or [wa9(ɑ̆)BarŪ̃n] < *wa=9abárū* (§7.2 (δ), §9.2.3.1 n. 28, §22.1 (22C) (κ)) Macs 156.

*√9dy   {*see* *√nðy, *with which in cau* *√9dy *may have become neutralized:* *. . .a9dV. . . rga > . . .addV. . . < rna . . .andV. . . < occ *. . .anðV. . .; *and* *. . .a9dV. . . rga > . . .addV. . . gds > . . .andV. . . < occ *. . .anðV. . .*}

*√9l (< **√Rl)   <9(ʔ)l> t[9ɑ́l] ~ <9ll> t[ɑ̃́lɑl] sim pf 3ms [9ɑ́l] ~ [9ă̆lɑ́l] < *9álla ~ *9alála* (§3.3) Macs 197.

<9lw> ~ <9llw> t[9ǽllu] ~ [9ēḷā́lu] sim impa mp [9állū] ~ [9ɔ̌lálū] < *9úllū ~
*9ǎlúlū or perhaps *9állū ~ (9ĭlálū (§3.3, §17.12.1) Macs 199.

<ʔT9l> ~ <ʔT9yl> t[ittíyyæl] cau rmp pf 3ms perhaps [(ʔ)ittiyyál] < *hitha99ála
(§6.3 with n. 41) Macs 202.

*√9rR (< **√9rð)   <D9r9> ~ <D9rh> ~ <Dhr9> t[dǽræ] sborn sim pf 3ms [dɔ̌9ǎrá̄]/
[da9(ǎ)rá̄] ~ [dǎrá̄] < *ðĭ́ # 9aráRa (§9.1.3 (α), §9.2.3.1) Macs 12.

*√9rq   <9rq> ~ <ʔrq> t[ā́ɾaq] sim pf 3ms [9ǎráq] ~ [aráq] < *9aráqa (§9.2.3.1) Macs
11, 171.

*√pṣy   <w(ʔ)PṣTY> ~ <w(ʔ)Pṣʔy> conj sim pf 3ms^1s perhaps [wɔ̌Pǎṣā́θĭ́]/
[wɔ̌Pǎṣá̄θĭ] ~ [w(ɔ̌ʔ)aPṣā́θĭ́]/[w(ɔ̌ʔ)aPṣá̄θĭ] or [waf(ǎ)ṣā́θĭ́]/[waf(ǎ)ṣá̄θĭ]
~ [wɔ̌Pǎṣā́ʔθĭ́]/[wɔ̌Pǎṣá̄ʔθĭ] ~ [w(ɔ̌ʔ)aPṣā́ʔĭ́]/[w(ɔ̌ʔ)aPṣá̄ʔĭ] or [waf(ǎ)ṣā́ʔĭ́]/
[waf(ǎ)ṣá̄ʔĭ] <*wa=paṣáya # yātĭ́ ~ *wa=paṣayánĭ §17.13) Macs 233.

*√pqd   <PqD> t[fáqɑd] sim pf 3ms [pǎqáð] < *paqáda (§17.23.3) Macs 145.

<ʔPqDTK> sim impf 1s^2ms perhaps [(ʔ)ifqɔ̌ðĭ́θǽx] or [(ʔ)ifqaðtǽx] < *ʔapqúdi
yātáka (§17.30) Macs 228.

*√prq   <Prqy> t[fēɾǎ́qi] sim impa ms^1s [pɔ̌ráqĭ] < *pǎrúqnĭ (§17.13) Macs 29.

<ʔTPrq> ~ <ʔPrq> t[itfǎ́ɾaq] ~ [iffǎ́ɾaq] sim rmp pf 3ms [(ʔ)Iθpǎráq] ~
[(ʔ)ippǎráq] < *hitparíqa (§10) Macs 152.

*√ṣdy   <TṣtDy> t[tiṣtǽdi] sim rmp impf 2ms [tiṣṭaðĭ́] < *titṣadíyi or *titṣadáyi (§10)
Macs 153f.

*√qdš   <TTqDšwn> t[titqaddǎ́šon] int rmp impf 2mp [tiθqaddǎšÚ̌n] <
*titqaddašǔ̄n(n)a (§4.2.2) Macs 158.

<htqDšw> ~ <htqDšwn> t[itqaddǎ́σu] ~ [itqaddǎ́šon] int rmp impa mp
[(h)iθqaddášū]/[(h)iθqaddǎ́ššŭ̄] ~ [(h)iθqaddǎšÚ̌n] < *hitqaddášū
(§7.2 ( )) Macs 151.

*√qWm   <qwmh> t[qŭ́mɑ] ~ <qwm> sim impa ms [qūmǎ́] ~ [qŭ́m] < *(same) (§2.3.4.1)
Macs 116.

<hw'q'm> ~ <ʔwqm> t[iwwǎ́qɑm] ~ [uwwǎ́qɑm] sim rmp pf 3ms [(ʔ)
iwwǎqám] < *hitqĭ́ma (*/hitqawim+a/) (§6.3) Macs 192f.

<wqyʔmn> t[w(ɔ̌)qiyyǎ́mɑn] conj int {?} pf 3ms^1p [wɔ̌qiyyǎmán] {or possi-
bly [wɔ̌qiyyāmán]} < *wa=qayyimána {or possibly, following Macuch, built on qiyyām expropriated as a quasi-intensive miskal}
(§12.2) Macs 193.

<ʔqymh> t[āqĭ́me] cau pf 3ms^3ms [ʔǎqīmĕ́h]/[aqīmĕ́h] < *haqīmáhi
(§6.1.1.1) Macs 195.

<hqmT> t[āqĕ́mət] cau pf 1s [ʔǎqÍmiθ]/[aqÍmiθ] < *haqímt (§6.1.1.1, §6.1.2
(6C) n. 11) Macs 196.

<yqymnh> t[yūqīmínne] cau impf 3ms^3ms [yǎqīminnĕ́h] < *y(ih)aqīminníhi
(§7.1) Macs 196.

<ʔqmnh> cau impa ms^3ms [ʔǎqīminnĕ́h]/[aqīminnĕ́h] < haqímhi (§7.1) Macs
196.

*√qṣ   <Tqṣ> t[tíqqɑṣ] sim impf 2ms [tiqqáṣ] < *tiqqáṣi/*taqqúṣi (§3.3, §12.2) Macs
198.

*√qrʔ   <qrʔ> t[qǎ́ɾɑ] sim pf 3ms [qǎrá̄] < *qará̄ʔa (§9.2.3.1) Macs 175, 205.

*√qrb	<yqrBwn> ~ <yqrBw> t[yæqrî́bon] ~ [yæqrî́bu] cau impf 3mp [yaqrīβÚn] ~
[yaqrīβú]/[yaqrī́βū] < *y(ih)aqribŭ́n(n)a (possibly ~ *y(ih)aqrî́bū) (§7.2 (γ))
Macs 161.
<TqryBwn> t[tæqrî́bon] cau impf 2mp [taqrīβÚn] < *t(ih)aqribŭ́n(n)a
(§17.28) Macs 159–61.

*√qry	<qrˀTˀ> sim pf 3fs [qărắθa] < *qaráyat (§13) Macs 206.

*√qtl	<yqtlny> sim impf 3ms^1s [yiqtǝlénnī] < *yiqtulinnínī (or perhaps *yiqtulínnī)
(§17.13) Macs 228.

*√rby	<rˈB < y Ṭ́> {*what is the function of the* "o" *over the* "T" ?} sim pf 2m{?}s
[răβî́T] < *rabáyta or *rabî́ta (§13) Macs 90.

*√rWḥ	<ˀTryhT> ~ <ˀTryhyT> sim rmp pf 3fs [(ˀ)iθrî́ḥaθ] {~ *possibly suffix-supple-
tive* [(ˀ)iθrî́ḥiθ} < *hitrî́ḥat (§§6.3 with n. 38, §16.2 SM (α)) Macs 38.

*√rWm	<ˀTrˀm> t[itrắm] sim rmp pf 3ms [(ˀ)iθrắm] < *hitrî́ma (§6.3 with n. 39) Macs
196.
<wDˀTrm> t[w(ǯ)dittắrɑm] conj sbor sim rmp pf 3ms [wǝD(ǯ)ittărắm] <
*wa= ðî́ # hitrî́ma (§6.3 with n. 39) Macs 196.

*√rWmm (V *√rWm)	<ˀTrwmm> t[itrúmǝm] int rmp pf 3ms [(ˀ)iθrūmém] < *hitraw-
míma {*miškal-suppletive for* *hitrawwáma} (§6.3) Macs 192.

*√rWθ	<r9ṭT> ~ <rṣT> {*spelling with* <ṣ> "hebraisierend," <*Macs 190*} sim pf 1s
[rắṭiθ] < *rắθt (§17.4) Macs 5.

*√rḥṣ	<ˀTrḥṣnn> t[itrēṣṣínnɑn] sim rmp pf 1p [(ˀ)iθre9ṣinnán] < *hitraḥíṣnā (§12.2,
§17.17.2) Macs 154.

*√rkb	<w(ˀ)rKByn> ~ <w(ˀ)rKBy> t[wærkắbən] ~ [wærkắbi] conj sim pf 3fp [w(ǯ)
arKaβÍn] ~ [w(ǯ)arKaβí]/[w(ǯ)arKáβī] < *wa=rakaba (§7.2 (γ)) Macs 146.

*√rkn	<ˀrKn> t[ắrkən] sim pf 3ms possibly [(ˀ)arKén] < *rakína (§17.18.1) Macs
144.

*√rmy	<ˀrmy> t[ắrmi] ~ [ǽrmi] sim impa ms [(ˀ)ermî́] ~ possibly [(ˀ)armî́] <
*rămî́/*rĭmáy (§17.18.1) Macs 206, 215.
<hrmw> t[írmu] sim impa mp [(ˀ)irmű́] < *rĭmáyū (§17.18.1) Macs 209.

*√ršy	<ˀršTyn> t[æršắtən] cau pf 3ms^1s [(ˀ)aršāθÍn]/[(ˀ)aršắttÍn] < *haršáya #
yātánī (§17.30) Macs 233.

*√rt	<yrTT> t[yírtɑt] sim impf 3ms [yirtáθ] < *yartúti (§3.3) Macs 197.

*√rty	<ˀrTy> t[írti] ~ [ǽrti] sim impa ms [(ˀ)irTî́] ~ possibly [(ˀ)arTî́] < *rătî́/*rĭtáy
(§17.18.1) Macs 206, 215.

*√śˀb (< *√śWb)	<sˀB> t[sắb] sim pf 3ms [sắˀáβ] < *śaˀíba (§9.2.3.1) Macs 173.

*√śb9	<šB9> t[šắbæ] sim pf 3ms [šắβá9] {?} < *śabí9a (§17.27) Macs 175.

*√śgˀ	<ysGyˀn> t[yæsgiyyắn] sim impf 3fp [yasgǝyắn] {*or less likely* [yasgǝ́ˀắn]} <
*yaśgiˀắn(n)a (§7.2 (γ)) Macs 215.

*√śhd (or *√śWd < **√śhd)	<ˀs(y)D> t[ắsəd] cau impf 3ms [ˀăséð]/[aséð] or [ˀăsî́ð]/
[asî́ð] < *hashída or *hasî́da (§9.2.2 n. 25) Macs 174f.

*√śWm	<ˀšym> t[ắšəm] sim or cau impf 1s [ˀăšî́m]/[ašî́m] < *ˀasî́mi or *ˀ(ih)asî́mi
(§17.20) Macs 196.

*√śˀr (or *√śWr < **√śˀr)	<ˀšyrw> t[ắšîru] cau pf 3mp [ˀăšî́rū]/[ašî́rū] < *hašˀíru
or *hašî́rū (§9.2.2 n. 25) Macs 174f.

*√šb9	<ˀšTB9T> ~ <ˀšT9BT> t[ištæβ́t] sim rmp pf 1s [(ˀ)ištăBéθ] < *hitšabí9t
(§17.6.2) Macs 154.

*√šbq <wyšBqwny> conj sim impf 3mp^1s [wăyišbăqÚn(n)ī] < *yašbuqǘn(n)ánī or
*wa=yašbuqǘnī (§17.13) Macs 148.

*√šgr <šGrwny> t[šæggārǘni] int pf 3mp^1s [šaggarūnī] < *šaggirǘni (§17.13)
Macs 226.
<wTšgrwny> conj int impf 2mp^1s [wăTăššaggărÚn(n)ī] or [waθ(ă)
šaggărÚn(n)ī] < *wa=tišaggirǘn(n)ánī or *wa=tišaggirǘnī
(§17.13) Macs 227.

*√šwy <nšwy> t[nǽšbi] sim (short) impf 1p [našβī́] < *našwíy(i) (§12.2) Macs 208f.
<šẃyTh> ~ <šB(ʔ)Ṭwn> int pf 3fs^3fp~3mp {? *gender value of the object
uncertain*} [šaββāθÍn]/[šaββăθÍnn] ~ [šaββāθÚn]/[šaββăθÚn] < *šawwáyat #
h/ʔin(nV̆h)ín ~ *šawwáyat # h/ʔin(nV̌)húm (§16.2 SM (y)) Macs 233.
<Tšwynwn> int impf 2mp^3mp [tăšaββínnÚn]/[tăšaββĕnnÚn] <
*tišawwiyǘn(n)a / *tišawwayǘn(n)a # h/ʔin(nV̌)húm (§17.17.2) Macs 234.
<ʔšBynwn> cau pf 3fs^3mp [(ʔ)ašβăyannÚn] {?} < *hašwíyat # h/ʔin(nV̌)húm
(§16.2 SM (β)) Macs 233.

*√škḥ ('find') <nšKḥ> t[níškæ] cau impf 1p [niškắ9] < *n(ih)aškíḥi (§12.2) Macs
175.

*√šlḥ <šlḥny> ~ <šlḥy> t[šællǽni] ~ [šællǽʔi] int pf 3ms^1s [šallă9ánī] ~ [šallṣ9í]/
[šallá9ī] < *šallaḥánī (§17.13) Macs 109, 226.
<šlḥwTy> t[šællǽʔúti] int impa mp^1s [šallă9ūθí]/[šallă9ū́θí] < *šalláḥu #
yātí (§17.30) Macs 230.

*√šm9 <šm9> t[šǽmæ] sim pf 3ms [šămá9] < *šamá9a (§9.2.3) Macs 175, 205.
<šm9tWn> t[šæmǽtton] sim pf 2mp [šăma9tÚn] < *šami9túm (§9.2.3.2)
Macs 175.
<nšm9> t[níšmæ] sim impf 1p [nišmá9] < nišmá9i (§2.3.4.1 with n. 16) Macs
175.
<nšm9h> t[nišmǽ] sim short impf 1p [nišmă9ắ] < *nišma9ắ (§2.3.4.1 with
n. 16) Macs 175.
<šmqny> {*sic*} t[šămǽʔínni] sim impa ms^1s [šăma9énnī] < *šĭmá9nī
(§2.3.4.4) Macs 229.
<ʔštm9> ~ <ʔšm9> t[ištǽmæ] ~ [iššǽmæ] sim rmp pf 3ms [(ʔ)ištămá9] ~
[(ʔ)iššămá9] < *hitšamí9a (§10) Macs 153f.

*√šmš <šmšTK> ~ <šmšʔTK> t[šæmmíštɑk] int pf 1s^2ms [šammištắx] <
*šammíštăka (§16.2 SM (α)) Macs 227.

*√šqr <šqrT> ~ <šqrTy> sim pf 2ms {*fgm*} [šăqárt] ~ possibly [šăqártī] < *šaqárta
~ *šaqártī (§13, §16.3 (α)) Macs 146.

*√šry <Tšry> ~ <yšry> sim impf 3fs {*fgm*} [tíšri] ~ [yíšri] < *tišráyi/*tašríyi ~
*yišráyi/*yašríyi (§16.2 SM (z)) Macs 208.
<šry> t[íšri] sim impa ms [(ʔ)išrí] perhaps ~ [šắrí] < *šắrí/*šĭráy (§8.1.3)
Macs 209.

*√šty <ʔšTT> t[ǽštɑt] sim pf 3fs [(ʔ)aštă̄θ] < *šatáyat (§17.18.1) Macs 206.

*√tqp <TqyP> ~ <ʔTqP> t[tékăf] ~ [étkăf] ~ [ǽtkăf] sim pf 3ms [tăqéf] ~ [(ʔ)iTkéf]
~ possibly [(ʔ)aTkéf] < *taqípa (§17.18.1) Macs 144.

Galilean

*√ˀbd   <ˀBD> sim pf 3ms [ˀə̆βáð]/[aβáð] < *ˀabáda (§17.33 n. 159) Da 299.

*√ˀzl   <ˀzlh> sim pf 3ms^pp(3ms) [ˀə̆zIlléh]/[azIlléh] < *ˀazíla ǁ̊ líhi (§17.15.2) Kutscher 1976: 33 with n. 78.

         <ˀ(y)zyl> sim impa ms [ˀĬzél]/[Izél] < *ˀăzíl (§9.3.1, §17.33) Da 276–78.

         <zylw> sim impa mp [zÍlū] < *ˀăzílū (§17.33) Da 301.

*√ˀkl   <TyKwl> sim impf 2ms [tēxÚl] < *taˀkúli (§11.2) Da 300.

         <ˀyyKl> cau pf 3ms [(ˀ)ayKél] < *haˀkíli (§11.2) Da 302.

*√ˀlp   <ˀylPn> int pf 3ms^1p [(ˀ)Illə̆fán] < *ˀallipána/*ˀallipánā (§17.9.2) Da 363.

         <ˀlPny> int impa ms^1s [(ˀ)alléfnī] < *ˀallípnī (§17.13) Da 375.

*√ˀmr   <ˀmr> sim pf 3ms [ˀə̆már]/[amár] < *ˀamára (§17.9.2, §17.33 n. 159) Da 255, 299.

         <wmr> conj sim pf 3ms [wə̆már]/[wamár] < *wa=ˀamára (§17.33 n. 159) Da 299.

         <Dmr> sbor sim pf 3ms [də̆mar]/[damár] < *ðí̊ ǁ̊ ˀamára (§17.33 n. 159) Da 299.

         <ˀmwr> sim impa ms [ˀĬmÚr]/[ImÚr] < ˀămúr (§9.3.1) Da 276–78.

         <ˀymwryn> sim impa mp [ˀĬmUrín]/[ImUrín] < *ˀămúrū (§17.17..2) Da 301.

         <ˀTˀmr> ~ <ˀTmr> sim rmp pf 3ms [(ˀ)Iθˀə̆már] ~ [(ˀ)Ittə̆már] < *hitˀamíra (§9.2.1.1 with n. 13) Da 303.

*√ˀrs (or */9rs)   <ˀrsTh> sim pf 2ms^3fs [ˀə̆rastá̊h]/[arastá̊h] < *ˀarastá̊ha (or *9arastá̊ha) (§9.2.3.1) Kutscher 1976: 81.

*√ˀšl   (see *√šˀl)

*√ˀty   <ˀTy> ~ <ˀyTˀ> ~ <Tˀ> sim impa ms [ˀĬθéˊ]/[Iθéˊ] ~ [ˀĬθáˊ]/[Iθáˊ] ~ [táˊ] < *ˀítáy perhaps ~ *ˀítáˀ (§8.1.3 n. 15) Da 357.

         <ˀyyTynwn> cau impa mp^3mp [(ˀ)ayTīnÚ̊n] < *haˀtíya ǁ̊ h/ˀin(nV̊)húm (§17.17.2) Da 392.

*√bz9   <Bz9wn> sim pf 3ms^3mp [bə̆za9Ú̊n]/[baz9Ú̊n] < *bazá9a ǁ̊ h/ˀin(nV̊)húm (§17.15.1) Da 363.

*√bl9   <ˀyTBl9> sim rmp pf 3ms [(ˀ)Iθbə̆lá9] < *ḥitbalí9a (§10) Da 259.

*√bl9s   <ˀTBl9swn> quad pf 3mp [(ˀ)Iθbal9ə̆sÚ̊n]/[(ˀ)Iθbal9asÚ̊n] < *ḥitbal9ásū (§1.1.2 n. 8) Da 252.

*√b9y (<**√bRy)   <B9ˀ> ~ <ˀyB9h> sim pf 3ms [bə̆9áˊ] ~ [(ˀ)IB9áˊ] < *ba9áya(§17.18.1) Da 337.

         <B9ˀy> sim pf 1s [bə̆9áy] {*perhaps not a genuine G form*} < *ba9áyt (§17.2 n. 2) Da 343.

         <B9ˀ> sim impa ms [bə̆9éˊ] < *bi9ay (§8.1.3) Da 348.

*√brˀ   <yTBry> sim rmp impf 3ms [yIθbə̆réˊ]/[yIθbə̆ríˊ] < *yitbaráyi/*yitbaríyi (§11.2) Da 345.

*√brk   <BrKThwn> int pf 2ms^3mp [barrIxtånnÚ̊n]/[bārIxtånnÚ̊n] < *barríktá̊ ǁ̊ h/ˀin(nV̊)húm (§17.15.1) Da 365.

*√gWb   <ˀGyBwnh> ~ <ˀGyBwnTh> cau pf 3mp^3fs [ˀə̆γīβÚ̊n(n)á̊h]/[aγīβÚ̊n(n)á̊h] ~ [ˀə̆γīβÚ̊nTá̊h]/[aγīβÚ̊nTá̊h] < hagībú̊ha (§17.30) Da 367.

*√gly   <nyGlynwn> cau impf 1p^3mp [nIγlě̊n(n)Ú̊n]/[nIγlî̊n(n)Ú̊n] < *n(ih)agláyi ǁ̊ h/ˀin(nV̊)húm / *n(ih)aglíyi ǁ̊ h/ˀin(nV̊)húm (§12.2) Da 390.

*√dḥk   <nD9wK> [nĪð9Úx] < *nadḥúki (§9.2.4) Kutscher 1976: 73.

*√ðḥl   <DḥlyT> sim pf 1s [dV̌ḥléθ]/dǝ̆ḥĺlθ] < *ðaḥílt (§17.6.2) Da 261.

*√hwy (possibly ~ *√hyy)   <hw(w)T> sim pf 3fs [hǝ̆wǟθ] < *hawáyat/*hawayát (§8.1.1 with n. 6) Da 353.

  <hwyyT> ~ <hwyT> sim pf 2ms [hǝ̆wáyT] ~ [hǝ̆wḗT] (or [hǝ̆wî́T]) < *hawáyta possibly ~ *hawî́ta (§11.2) Da 354.

  <hww> sim pf 3mp [hǝ̆wố] < *hawáyū (§11.2) Da 354.

  <lhwy> ~ <yhʾ> ~ <yyʾ> ~ <yy> sim impf 3ms [lIhwḗ]/[lIhwî́] ~ [yǝ̆hé] ~ [yǝ̆yḗ]/[yiyyḗ] ~ {?} [yḗ]/ [yî́] < *lihwáyi/*lahwíyi possibly ~ *yihyáyi (possibly ~ *yahyíyi) (§17.32 with (17.32A) and n. 152) Da 354.

  <yhwwn> ~ <yhwn> ~ <yywn> sim impf 3mp [yIhwố n] possibly ~ [yǝ̆hố n] ~ [yǝ̆yố n]/[yiyyố n] < *yihwayŭ́n(n)a (possibly ~ *yihyayŭ́n(n)a) (§17.32 (17.32A) and n. 152) Da 354.

  <Thwwn> sim impf 3fp [tIhwǟn] < *tihwayǟn(n)a (§16.2 n. 24, §16.3 n. 25) Da 352f.

*√wd9   <yD9> sim pf 3ms [yǝ̆ðá9] < *wadá9a (§17.34) Da 309.

  <ʾyTwD9yn> int rmp pf 3fp [(ʾ)Iθwaddǝ̆9ǐn] < *hitwaddá9ā (§17.34) Da 314.

*√whb   <yhB> sim pf 3ms [yǝ̆háβ] < *wahába (§17.34) Da 308.

  <whB> conj sim pf 3ms [wIháβ] <*wa=wahába (§14.2) Kutscher 1976: 17.

  <DhB> sbor sim pf 3ms [dIháβ] < *ðî́ # wahába (§14.2) Kutscher 1976: 17.

  <yhBw> sim pf 3mp [yǝ̆háβū] < *wahábū (§17.9.2) Da 254.

  <DhBwn> sbor sim pf 3mp [dIhaβŬn] < *ðî́ # wahábū (§14.2 with n. 17) Kutscher 1976: 17).

  <TyhB> ~ <ThyB> sim impf 2ms possibly [tēhéβ] ~ [tIhhéβ] < *tahî́bi (§17.7 with n. 21) Da 309f.

  <hBw> ~ <hBẉn> ~ <yhBẉn> ~ <yBẉn> sim impa mp [hǝ̆βú] ~ [hǝ̆βŬn]/ [haβŬn] ~ [yIhBŬn] ~ [yIbbŬn] < *habu (§9.2.2, §17.33) Da 309.

*√wld   <ʾTylD> sim rmp pf 3ms [(ʾ)Iθyǝ̆léð] < *hitwalída (§12.2) Da 313.

  <TTyylD> sim rmp impf 3fs [tIθyǝ̆léð] < *titwalídi (§14.2) Da 313.

*√wmʾ (perhaps X *√ʾmr)   <yymʾ> sim impf 3ms [yēmǟ] < *yimáʾi (§17.19) Da 300.

  <lymʾ> sim short impf 3ms [lēmǟ] < *limáʾ (§17.19) Da 364.

*√wrθ   <yrT> sim pf 3ms [yǝ̆ráθ] < *waráθa (§17.34) Da 308.

*√wtr   <yyTwwTrwn> int rmp impf 3mp [yIθwattǝ̆rŬn] < *yitwattarǔ́n(n)a (§17.34) Da 314.

*√wθb   <yTB> sim pf 3ms [yǝ̆θáβ] < *waθába (§17.34) Da 308.

  <TyTBwn> sim impf 2mp [tēθ(ǝ̆)BŬn]/[tIttǝ̆βŬn] < *taθibǔ́n(n)a (§17.7 n. 21) Da 309f.

  <ʾwTBynyh> cau pf 3ms^3ms [(ʾ)ōθ(ǝ̆)BInnéh] < *hawθibáhi (§7.1) Da 363.

*√zbn   <zwBnyn> ~ <zByn> sim impa fs {fgm} [zUβnǐn] ~ [zǝ̆βén] < *zăbúnī ~ *zăbún (§7.2 (δ) n. 12, §17.9.2 with n. 28, §17.25) Da 276.

*√zmr   <ʾyzmr> sim pf 3ms [(ʾ)Izmár] < *zamára (§17.18.1) Da 337.

*√z9r   <z9yrT> sim pf 3fs [zǝ̆9Íraθ] < *za9írat (§4.1.2) Da 260f.

*√zr9   <ʾyzDr9wn> sim rmp pf 3mp [(ʾ)Izdǝ̆ra9Ŭn]/[(ʾ)Izdar9Ŭn] < *hitzarí9ū (§10) Da 262.

*√ḫṭʾ (< **√Xṭʾ)   <Tḫṭyy> sim impf 2fs [tIḫṭáy] < *tiḫtáʾín(n)a (§17.12.2) Kutscher 1976: 46f.

*√ḫṭl   <yḫṭlwn> sim impf 3mp [yIḫṭɔ́lŪ̆n] < *yiḫtalǔ̄n(n)a (§7.2 (γ)) Da 272.

*√ḥmy   <yḥmy> cau impf 3ms [yaḥmḗ]/[yaḥmî̄] < *y(ih)yaḥmáyi/*y(ih)aḥmíyi (§11.2) Da 345.

*√ḥmR (< **√ḥmð)   <yḥm9wn> sim impf 3mp [yVḥmɔ́9Ū̆n] < *yaḥmuRǔ̄n(n)a (§7.2 (γ)) Da 345.

*√ḥnq (< **√Xnq)   <ḥnqTwn> sim pf 2ms^3mp [ḥɔ̆naqtŪ̆n] < *ḥanáqta #̟ h/ʾin(nV̇)húm (§17.15.1) Da 365.

*√ḥsl   <ḥsylyT> sim pf 1s [ḥɔ̆sÍllθ] < *ḥasílt (§4.1.2) Da 260f.

*√ḥsr (< **√Xsr)   <ḥsrThwn> int pf 1s^3mp [ḥassartInnŪ̆n] < *ḥassírt #̟ h/ʾin(nV̇)húm (§17.15.1 with n. 70) Da 366.

*√ḥrb (< **√Xrb)   <ḥryB> sim impa ms [ḥĬréβ] < *ḥăríb (§9.3.1) Da 276–78.

*√ṭ9y   <ʾṭ9wnwnwn> cau impa mp^3mp [(ʾ)aṭ9Ū̆n(n)Ū̆n(n)Ū̆n] < *haṭ9áyū #̟ h/ʾin(nV̇)húm (§7.6, §17.15.1) Da 367.

*√yṭy (< *V̇ʾṭy X *√mṭy)   <yyṭy> cau impf 3ms [yayṭî̄]/[yayṭḗ] < *y(ih)aʾṭíyi / *y(ih)aʾṭáyi X *y(ih)amṭíyi /̟ *y(ih)amṭáyi (§17.3) Jastrow 1903: 576.

*√kbš   <KBŝyn> sim impa fs [kaβšĬn] < *kăbúšī (§17.25) Da 276.

*√kḫš   <ʾKḫŝyn> cau pf 3fp [(ʾ)axḫIsĬn] / [(ʾ)axḫɔ̆šĬn]̟ < *hakḫíšā (§7.2 (δ)) Da 263.

*√lʾy (or *√l9y)   <ʾyl9wn> sim rmp pf 3mp [(ʾ)Ill(ɔ̆)Ū̆n] or [(ʾ)Illɔ̆9Ū̆n] < *hitlaʾúyū or *hitla9áyū (§§9.2.3.1 with n. 30) Kutscher 1976: 81.

*√lbš   <lBŝwn> sim impa mp [laβšŪ̆n] < *lăbúšū (§17.25) Da 375.

*√lqy   <ylqy> sim impf 3ms [yIlqḗ]/[yIlqî̄] < *yilqáyi / *yalqíyi (§11.2) Da 345.

*√mWt   <ymwT> sim impf 3ms [yɔ̆mû̄θ] < *yamúti (§14.2) Da 320.

*√mṭy   <mṭwn> sim pf 3mp [mɔ̆ṭő̄n] < *maṭáyū (§8.1.1) Da 343.

*√msr   <msrTh> sim pf 2ms [mɔ̆sártā] < *masártā (§17.15.1) Da 260.

*√nḫt (~ possibly *√ḫt)   <yyḥwT> sim impf 3ms [yɔ̆hÚ̇θ] < *yanḥúti or possibly *yaḥḥúti (§17.21.1) Da 292.

<ḥwT> ~ <nḥwT> sim impa ms [ḥÚ̇θ] ~ [nɔ̆ḥÚ̇θ] < *hut (§17.33) Da 294.

*√nsb   <nsBhwn> sim pf 3ms^3mp [nɔ̆saβhŪ̆n] < *nasába #̟ h/ʾin(nV̇)húm (§17.15.1) Da 363.

*√npl   <nPwl> sim pf 3mp [nɔ̆fū́l] < *napálū (§17.9.2) Da 354.

*√npq   <ʾPqwh> cau impa mp^3ms [(ʾ)appɔ̆qǔ̄h] < *hanpiqǔ̄hi (§7.2 (ζ)) Da 376.

*√nšq   <nŝqy> sim pf 3ms^1s [nɔ̆šáqī] < *našaqánī (§17.13) Da 362.

*√sʾb   <ysʾBTyh> int impf 3ms^3ms [yɔ̆saʾʾIβTéh] / [yɔ̆sāʾIβTéh] < *yisaʾʾíbi #̟ yātáhi (§7.1 n. 4) Da 370.

*√sbr   <ʾsBry> cau pf 3ms^1s [(ʾ)asbárī] < *hasbiránī (§17.13) Da 362.

*√slq   <slyqʾ> sim pf 2fs [sɔ̆lÍqā] < ̟*salíqat (§17.12.2 with n. 54) Da 254.

<slqwn> sim pf 3mp [sɔ̆laqŪ̆n] / [salqŪ̆n] < *saláqū (§7.2 (δ), §17.9.2) Da 262.

*√9bd   <9BDTyn> sim pf 2fs [9ɔ̆βaðtĬn] < *9abádtī̆ (§7.2 ( ) n. 12) Da 261.

<y9BDynyh> sim impf 3ms^3ms [yV̇9bɔ̆ðInnéh] < *ya9bidinníhi (§7.1) Da 370.

<9B(y)D> sim impa ms [9Ĭβéð] < *9ăbíd (§9.3.1) Da 276–78.

<ʾyT9ByD> ~ <ʾy9ByD> sim rmp pf 3ms [(ʾ)Iθ9ɔ̆βéð] ~ [(ʾ)I99ɔ̆βéð] / [(ʾ) e9(ɔ̆)βéð] < *hit9abída (§10) Da 359.

*√9l (< **√Rl) <9lyT> ~ <9llyT> sim pf 1s [9állІθ]/[9alléθ] ~ [9šlálІθ] < *9ált ~ *9alált (§3.3) Da 330.

<ʔy9ll> sim rmp pf 3ms [(ʔ)I99šlél] / [(ʔ)ē9(š)lél] < *hit9alíla (§6.3) Da 333.

<ʔ9ly> cau pf 3msˆ1s [ʔa99Ílī] / [ʔā9Ílī] < *ḥa99iláni (§17.13) Da 362.

*√9qr <ʔyT9wqryn> sim rmp impa fs [(ʔ)Iθ9Uqrİn] < *hit9aqírī (§15.5.2, §17.25) Da 277.

*√9rs (See *√ʔrs)

*√9θr <ʔy9Tr> sim rmp pf 3ms [(ʔ)I99šθár] / [(ʔ)ē9(š)Tár] < *hit9aθíra (§10) Da 259.

*√pny <yTPny> int rmp impf 3ms [yIθpanné̃]/[yIθpannī́] < *yitpannáyi / *yitpanníyi (§11.2) Da 345.

*√psq <ʔyPsyq> sim rmp pf 3ms [(ʔ)Ippšséq] < *hitpasíqa (§10) Da 259.

*√prsm <ʔyPrsn> quad rmp pf 3ms [(ʔ)Ipparsán] < *hitparsáma (§2.3.4.3 n. 28) Kutscher 1976: 59.

*√ptḥ <PTḥwnh> sim impa msˆ3ms possibly [pšθaḥUnné̃h] or [paθḥUnné̃h] < *pǐtáḥhi (§2.3.4.3 n. 28, §17.30 ṇ. 147) Da 375f.

<PwTḥwn> sim impa mp [pUθḥŪn] ≲ *pǐtáḥū (§7.2 ( ), §17.25) Da 277.

<PTḥwn> sim impa fp {fgm} [pšθaḥŪn] < *pǐtáḥū (§16.3 n. 25) Da 275.

*√ṣWd <ʔyTṣD> sim rmp pf 3ms [(ʔ)Ittšṣá̊δ] < *ḥiṭṣída (§6.3) Da 325.

<ʔyTṣyDwn> sim rmp pf 3mp [(ʔ)IttšṣİδŪn] / [(ʔ)IttšṣīδŪn] < *hitṣídū (§6.3) Da 325.

*√ṣly <yṣly> int impf 3ms [yšṣallé̃] / [yšṣallī́] < *yiṣalláyi / *yiṣallíyi (§11.2) Da 345.

*√ṣn <Tṣnn> sim impf 3fs [tIṣnán] < *tiṣnáni (§3.3) Da 330.

*√ṣrk <ʔyṣtrKT> sim rmp pf 3fs [(ʔ)IṣtarKá̊θ] / [(ʔ)Iṣtšrİxaθ] < hitṣarikát / *hitṣaríkat (§10) Da 260.

*√θ9n <ṭ9wnwn> sim pf 3mpˆ3mp [ṭš9anŪn(n)Ūn] < *θa9ánū # h/ʔin(nV̊)húm (§176.15.1) Da 367.

*√qbl <qBylynwn> ~ <qBylynhw> int pf 3msˆ3mp [qabbIlInnŪ́n] ~ [qabbIlInhŪ́] < *qabbílū # h/ʔin(nV̊)húm (§7.4.1) Kutscher 1976: 14 {who questions the bona fides of the second variant}

*√qWm <Tqymynwn> ~ ,<Tqmynwn> cau impf 2mpˆ3mp [tšqīmİnnŪ́n] ~ possibly [tIqqšmİnnŪn] < *t(ih)aqīmū́n(n)a # h/ʔin(nV̊)húm or *t(ih)aqímu # h/ʔin(nV̊)húm (§17.17.2) Da 373.

<ʔyTwqm> cau rmp pf 3ms [(ʔ)Ittōqám] < *hithaqā́ma (§6.1.2 with (6C)) Da 326.

*√ql <qlyl> int pf 3ms [qallél] < *qallíla (§3.3) Da 332.

*√qpḥ (< **√qpX) <qPḥʔy> sim pf 3msˆ1s possibly [qafḥáy] < qapaḥánī (§17.13 n. 59) Da 362.

<qPḥnyh> sim impa msˆ3ms [qšfaḥInné̃h] < *qǐpáḥhi (§7.1) Da 375.

*√qtl <Tqtl(y)nny> sim impf 2msˆ1s [tIqtšlInnánī] < *taqtulinníni (§17.13) Da 371.

*√rWm <ʔrymyTwn> cau pf 2mp [ʔšrīmIttŪ́n] / [arimIttŪ́n] or [ʔšrīmī̊θŪ́n] / [arīmī̊θŪ́n] < *harimtǔm (§17.17.2) Da 255.

*√rkb <ʔrKBy> cau pf 3msˆ1s [(ʔ)arKÍβī] < *harkibáni (§17.13) Da 362.

*√s²b   <ys²BTyh> int impf 3ms^3ms perhaps [yɔ̌saᵐɔ̌βīθéh]/[yɔ̌sā²(ɔ̌)Biθéh] or
           [yɔ̌saᵐIβTéh]/[yɔ̌sā²IβTéh] < *yisaᵐíbi ǂ yātáhi (§17.30) Da 370.

*√š²l ~ *√²šl (< **√š²l)   <²yšT²lT> ~ <²yTšlT> sim rmp pf 3fs [(²)šta²láθ]/[(²)Ištɔ̌²Ílaθ]
           ~ [(²)Ittašláθ]/[(²)Ittɔ̌šÍlaθ] < *hitša²ilát / *hitša²ílat (§10 with n. 7) Da 306.

*√šbq   <šBqyT> sim pf 1s [šIβqéθ]/[šaβqéθ] or [šɔ̌βáqIθ] < *šabáqt (§17.6.2) Da
          261.

          <šBqyh> sim impa ms^3ms [šIβqéh] < *šăbúqhi (§17.25) Da 375.

          <šwBqTyh> ~ <šBqwTyh> sim impa ms/fs^3ms {fgm ²} possibly [sUβqɔ̌θéh]
          ~ [šaβqUttéh]/[šaβqūθéh] < *šăbúqhi (§2.3.2.4 n. 14, §17.30 with
          n. 147) Da 375f.

          <šBqy> sim impa ms^1s perhaps [šɔ̌βÚqī] but the lack of ml 2ʃ<w> suggests
          oxytone [šaβqī́] < *šăbúqnī (§17.13, §17.25) Da 375.

          <šwBqyn> sim impa ms^3fp [šUβqĪn] < *šăbúq ǂh/²in(nV̊)hín (§17.9.2 with
          n. 26, §17.25) Da 376.

          <šBqwnyh> sim mp^3ms [šɔ̌βaqŮnnéh] / [šaβqŮnnéh] < *šăbuqűhi (§7.2 (ζ))
          Da 376.

*√šwy   <nšww> int short impf 3mp [nɔ̌šawwṓ] < *lišawwáyū {? form plausibly
          Babylonian} (§17.19 n. 102) Da 265.

*√šyzb (< **š+ √yzb)   <šyzBny> ~ <šyzBy> quad impa ms^1s [šēzéβnī] ~ [šēzÍβī] <
          *šayzíbnī (§17.13) Da 375.

*√škḥ ('find')   <²šKḥwn> cau pf 3ms^3mp [(²)škɔ̌ḥŮn] < *haškíḥa ǂ h/²in(nV̊)húm
          (§7.4.1) Da 363.

          <²šKḥyT> cau pf 1s [(²)aškɔ̌ḥéθ] / [(²)aškáḥIθ] < *haškíḥt (§17.6.2) Da 261.

          <²šKḥynwn> cau pf 3mp^3mp [(²)aškɔ̌ḥĪnnŮn] < *haškíḥū ǂ h/²in(nV̊)húm
          (§17.15.1, §17.17.2) Da 367.

          <nyšKḥ> cau impf 1p [nIškáḥ] < *n(ih)aškíḥi (§12.2) Da 274.

*√šlq   <šwlqh> sim impa ms^3fs [šUlqáh] < *šălúqha (§17.9.2 with n. 26) Da 375.

*√šm9   <šm9yT> ~ <šm9T> sim pf 1s perhaps [šam9éθ] ~ [šɔ̌má9Iθ] < *šamí9t
          (§17.6.2) Da 261.

*√šql   <šqyly> sim impa fs [šɔ̌qÍlī] < *šăqílī (§17.9.2 with n. 26) Da 277.

*√šq9   <šqw9T> sim pf 3fs [šɔ̌qÚ9aθ] < *šaqú9at (§4.1.2) Da 260f.

*√šty   <²šTy> ~ <²šTh> sim pf 3ms [(²)IšTí] ~ [(²)IšTǎ] < *šatíya ~ *šatáya (§17.18.1)
          Da 337.

*√tb9   <TB9Tynwn> sim pf 2ms^3mp [tɔ̌βa9tInnŮn] < *tabá9ta ǂ h/²in(nV̊)húm
          (§17.15.1) Da 365.

*√tpś   <TPšyṬwn> sim pf 3ms^3mp [tɔ̌fasĬttŮn] / [tɔ̌fasīθŮn] or [tafsĬttŮn] /
          [tafsīθŮn] < *tapáśa ǂ yātahúm (§17.30) Da 360.

*√tqn   <yṬqn> int impf 3ms [yɔ̌θaqqén] < *yitaqqíni (§14.2) Da 269.

*√θWb   <TTyByny> cau impf 3ms^1s [tɔ̌θīβénnī] < *t(ih)aθībinnínī (§17.13) Da 371.

Syriac

*√²zl   ns<²εzal> jc<²ezal> sim pf 3ms ns[εzál] jc[ezál] < *²azíla (§17.23.3) B 90.
          <nez̄luwn> sim impf 3mp [nēz(z)ű́n] < *ya²zilű́na (§17.21.2) B 18.
          <zεl> sim impa ms [zél] < *²ăzíl (§17.33) B 91.

*√²ḥð (< **√²Xð)   <²εTtḥεD> sim rmp pf 3ms [εttεḥéð] < *hit²aḥíða (§10) B 90.

√ʔkl ns<neʔxowl> jc<neʔxuwl> sim impf 3ms ns[nēxól] jc[nēxúl] < *yaʔkúli* (§5.2 n. 7, §9.2.1.2 with n. 9) B 90.

<ʔaxowl> sim impa ms [axól] < *ʔăkúl* (§17.23.3) B 90.

√ʔlṣ <ʔalaṣxown> sim f 3ms^2mp [alaṣxõn] < *ʔalaṣakúm* {?} (§16.2 SR (ε)) Ns 132, B 101.

√ʔmr ns<neʔmar> jc<niʔmar> sim impf 3ms ns[nēmár] jc[nīmár] < *yiʔmári* (§9.2.1.2 with n. 19, §11.2) Ns 112, B 90.

<ʔεmar> sim impa ms [εmár] < *ʔĭmár* (§17.23.3) B 90.

<ʔεTεʔmár> sim rmp pf 3ms [εθεmár] < *hitʔamíra* (§10) B 90.

√ʔpy ns<ʔaPɔʔ> jc<ʔePoʔ> sim pf 3ms ns[apɔ́] jc[efɔ́] < *ʔapáya* (§17.23.3) B 90.

√ʔty ns<ʔεθɔʔ> jc<ʔεθɔʔ> sim pf 3ms ns[εθɔ́] jc[eθɔ́] < *ʔatáya* (§17.23.3) B 90.

<tɔʔ> sim impa ms [tɔ́] < *ʔĭtáy* or perhaps *ʔĭtáʔ* (§8.1.3 with n. 15, §17.33) B 96.

<ʔaytiy> cau pf 3ms [aytī́] < *haʔtíya* (§11.2) Ns 113.

√bhl BεhlaT> sim plain pf 3fs [bεlláθ] < *bahilát* (§9.2.2) Du 101.

<ʔεTBahlaT> sim rmp pf 3fs [εθballáθ] < *hitabahilát* (§9.2.2) Du 101.

√bhθ <ʔAvhεtt> cau pf 2ms [Awhét] < *habhíθtắ* (§15.3.1.2 n. 26) Ns 20.

<ʔAvhεttɔn> cau pf 2ms^1p [Awhεttɔ́n] < *habhiθtánā* (§15.3.1.2 n. 26) Ns 20.

√bz <Bεzaθ> sim pf 3fs [bεzzáθ] < *bazzát* (§12.2 n. 14) Ns 123.

<bowz> sim impa ms [bóz] < *búz* (§3.3) Ns 123.

<bowzeyn> sim impa fp [bozén] < *búzzā* (§15.2.1.3 n. 9) Ns 123.

<ʔεθbzε z> sim rmp pf 3ms [εθbɔ̆zéz] < *hitbazíza* (§3.3) Ns 123.

<ʔabᵂεzeyn> cau impa fp [abbεzén] < *habbízā* (§15.2.1.3) Ns 123.

<ʔεtᵂaᵂbaz> cau rmp pf 3ms [εttabbáz] < *hithabbáza* (§6.3) Ns 123.

√bṭn <Bεṭnaθxown> ~ <Bṭεnθxown> sim pf 3fs^2mp [bεṭnaθxṍn] ~ [bɔ̆ṭεnθɔ̆xṍn] < *baṭinatkúm* perhaps ~ *baṭintɔ̆kúm* (§15.3.2 n. 30) Ns 132.

√byʔ <bayaʔ> int pf 3ms possibly [bayyắ] < *bayyíʔa* (§9.1.4 with n. 12) Ns 109.

<bayaʔθ> int pf 3fs [bayyáθ] < *bayyiʔát* (§9.1.4 with n. 12) Ns 109.

jc<bayaʔw> int pf 3mp jc[bayyáw] < *bayyíʔū* (§9.1.4 with n. 12) Ns 109.

√brk <ʔεθbarx> int rmp impa ms [εθbárrɔ̆x] < *hitbarrák* (§8.1.3 n. 14) Ns 103.

√dḥy <nTThʔ> sim rmp impf 3ms [nεttɔ̆ḥɛ́] < *yitdaḥáyi* (§10 with n. 9) Du 106, Nm 212f. n. 3.

√dḥq <nTTḥq> sim rmp impf 3ms [nεttɔ̆ḥéq] < *yitdaḥíqi* (§10 with n. 9) Du 106, Nm 212f. n. 3.

√dny <ʔεTDniy> sim rmp pf 3ms [εθdɔ̆nī́] ~ [εddɔ̆nī́] < *hitdaníya* (§10) Du 105 with n. 1.

√ðbḥ <nεDBowḥ> sim impf 3ms [nεðbóḥ] < *yaðbúḥi* (§17.10) Payne Smith 1903: 81, B 36.

<DBaḥ> ~ <DBowḥ> sim impa ms [dɔ̆wáḥ] ~ [dɔ̆wóḥ] < *ðăbúḥ* (§15.2.1.3) Payne Smith 1903: 81.

<dvowḥuwnɔyhy> sim impa mp^3ms [dɔ̆woḥūnɔ́y] < *ðabuḥúhī* (§7.2 (ζ), §15.2.1.3 with n. 8, §17.10) Ns 136.

√ðḥl <tεðaḥliyn> sim impf 2fs [tεðaḥlī́n] < *tiðḥalína* (§4.4.1) Ns 37.

√ðkr <nTTKr> sim rmp impf 3ms [nεttɔ̆xár] < *yitðakíri* (§10 with n. 9) Du 106, Nm 212f. n. 3.

*√hwy   <ẖwɔˀ> sim pf 3ms [=wɔ̄́] or [=wɔ̄] < *#̥ *hawáya* (§9.2.2 n. 26) Du 318.

<nɛhweˀ> ~ <nheˀ> sim impf 3ms [nɛhwḗ] ~ [nə̆hḗ] < *yihwáyi (§17.32 with (17.32A)) B 98.

<nhown> sim impf 3mp [nə̆hṓn] < *yihwayúna (§17.32 with (17.32A)) B 98.

*√hymn (<*h+ √ˀmn)   <haymɛn> quad pf 3ms [haymɛ́n] < *haymína (§11.2) Ns 113.

*√wd9   <yiDa9> sim pf 3ms [īð́a9] < *wadá9a (§17.34) Ns 115.

{*Old SR*} <ˀyD9T> sim pf 3fs [(ˀ)Ið9áθ] < *wadá9at (§14.2) Ns 115 n. 1, Sg 76.

<yɛD9eT> sim pf 1s [yɛð9ḗθ] < *wadá9t (§12.2 with n. 14, §17.6.2 with n. 13) Ns 194.

<nɛTiyDa9> sim rmp impf 3ms [nɛθīð́a9] < *yitwadí9i (§14.2, §17.34) Ns 115.

jc<eštawD9uwh̄y> cau rmp pf 3mp^3ms jc[eštawð́ə9úy] < *hitšawda9úhī (§8.2.1) Ns 141.

*√whb   <yẖB> sim pf 3ms [yÁw] < *wahába (§9.2.2 n. 26) Du 101.

<yahbɔh> sim pf 3ms^3fs [yahbɔ̄́h] < *wahabáha (§4.2.2, §12.2) Ns 132.

*√wzp   <neˀzaP> sim impf 3ms [nēzáp] < *yizápi (§17.7) Payne Smith 1903: 191.

<teˀzpiyn> sim impf 2fs [tēzpī́n] < *tizapína (§4.2.1 with n. 14, §4.2.2) B 137.

<tɛθyazpiyn> sim rmp impf 2fs [tɛθyazpī́n] < titwazipína (§5.2) B 137.

*√wld   <neˀlaD> sim impf 3ms [nēláð] < *yiládi (§17.7) Payne Smith 1903: 191.

*√wmˀ   <yimay> ~ <yimiy> sim impa ms [imáy] ~ [imī́] < *máˀ (*/wĭmaˀ/) (§8.1.3) B 95.

*√wrθ   <yirɛθw> ~ <ˀyrTw> sim pf 3mp [īréθ] < *waríθū (§14.2) Ns 115.

<neˀraT> sim impf 3ms [nēráθ] < *yiráθi (§17.7) Payne Smith 1903: 197.

*√wtr   {*Old SR*} <ˀyTrT> sim pf 1s [(ˀ)Iθrḗθ] < *watárt (§14.2) Ns 115 n. 1, Sg 76.

*√wθb   <nɛTɛB> sim impf 3ms [nɛttéw] < *yiθábi (§17.7) Payne Smith 1903: 198.

*√zbn   <nɛzɛbnuwn> sim impf 3mp [nɛzɛbnū́n] < *yazbinúna (§4.4.1, §5.2) Ns 37.

*√zky   <ˀɛzdak̊iy> int rmp pf 3ms [ɛzdakkī́] < *hitzakkíya (§10) B 16.

*√ḥdy (< **√Xdy)   <ḥðiy> sim impa ms [ḥə̆ðī́] < *hadíya (§8.1.3) B 95.

*√ṭWb   <ˀɛTṭayAB> int rmp pf 3ms [ɛṭṭayyÁw] ~ [ɛθṭayyÁw] < *hiṭṭayyába (§10) Du 105f. with n. 1.

*√ṭšy   <waṭṭašeˀ> conj int impf 2ms [waṭṭaššḗ] < *wa=tiṭaššáyi (§10) Ns 20.

*√kˀb   <kɛˀbaθ> ~ <keˀvaθ> sim pf 3fs [kɛbbáθ] ~ [kēwáθ] < *kaˀibát (§5.2 with (5A) and n. 7) Ns 108.

*√kWl   <ˀak̊iyl> cau pf 3ms [akkī́l] < *hakíla (§6.1.2 with (6C) and n. 13) Ns 121.

*√kWn   <ˀak̊iyn> cau pf 3ms [akkī́n] < *hakína (§6.1.2) Ns 121.

*√kns   <ˀɛkanšɛxy> int impf 1s^1fs [ɛkkannə̆šéx] < *ˀikannišíki (§15.3.1.1) Ns 134.

*√krk   <ˀɛTKarKuwhy> ~ <ˀɛTKuwrKuwhy> sim rmp impa mp^3ms [ɛθkarkúy] ~ [ɛθkurkúy] < *hitkarikúhī (§15.5.2, §17.25 n. 132) Ns 142.

*√ktb   <kaθbeh> sim pf 3ms^3ms [kaθbḗh] < *katabáhi (§5.2) Du 115.

<kɛθbaθ> sim pf 3fs [kɛθbáθ] < *katabát (§5.2) Du 115.

<tɛKTowBiyn> sim impf 2fs [tɛxtowī́n] < *taktubína (§12.2 with n. 14) Du 173.

<ˀɛKTowB> sim impf 1s [ɛxtów] < *ˀaktúbi (§12.2 with n. 14) Ns 198.

<ˀɛθkaθ̄b> sim rmp impa ms [ɛθkáθb] < *hitkatíb (§8.1.3 n. 14) Ns 103.

*√mWt   <miyθ> sim pf 3ms [mī́θ] < *mī́ta (§15.3.1.2 n. 25) B 141.

<miyTt> sim pf 2ms [mī́θt] or [mī́t] < *mī́ttắ (§15.3.1.2 n. 26) Ns 121.

<miyθeθ> sim pf 1s [mιθḗθ] < *mī́t(ə̃)t (§15.3.1.2 with n. 25, §15.4) B 141.

*√ml   <malɛl> int pf 3ms [mallél] < *mallíla (§3.3) Payne Smith 1903: 273.

*√nhz   <nɛhaz> sim impf 3ms [nɛh(h)áz] < *yinházi (§17.21.1) Ns 21.

*√nhm   <nɛnham> sim impf 3ms [nɛnhám] < *yinhámi (§17.21.1) Ns 21.

*√nḥb (< **√nXb)   <nɛḥowv> sim impf 3ms [nɛḥ(ḥ)ów] < *yanḥúbi (§17.21.1) B 89.

*√nḥṭ (~ possibly *√ḥṭ)   <nɛḥowθ> sim impf 3ms [nɛḥ(ḥ)óθ] < *yanḥúti or possibly *yaḥḥúti (§17.21.1) B 84.

*√npq   <ʔɛṕowq> sim impf 1s [ɛppóq] < *ʔanpúqi (§17.21.1) Ns 110.

   <napquwnɔxown> cau impf 3mp^2mp [nappə̆xunɔ̄xón] < y(ih)anpiqūnakúm (§2.3.4.4) Ns 134.

*√smk   <ʔɛstmɛx> sim rmp pf 3ms [ɛstɛméx] < *hitsamíka (§10) B 24.

*√9bd   <ʔɛ9BɛD> sim impf 1s [ɛ9béð] < *ʔa9bídi (§12.2 with n. 14) Ns 201.

√9bdd (<√9bd)   <9Avdɛð> quad pf 3ms [9Awdéð] < *9abdída (§1.1 n. 1, §1.1.2 n. 8) Ns 125f.

*√9hd   jc<9ehað> sim pf 3ms [eháð] < *9aháda (§9.1.3 n. 6) B 23.

*√9rR (<**√9rð)   ns<ʔara9> jc<ʔera9> sim pf 3ms ns[ará9] jc[erá9] < *9aráRa (§17.23.3) B 35.

*√Rḥk (<**√ðḥk)   <gḥɛx> sim pf 3ms [gə̆ḥéx] < *Rahíka (§9.1.3 (β)) Brockelmann 1928: 113.

*√R9ṭ (<**√ð9ṭ) <g9áṭ> sim pf 3ms [gə̆9áṭ] < *Ra9áṭa (§9.1.3 (β)) Brockelmann 1928: 127.

*√pk   <pax> sim pf 3ms [páx] < *pákka (§5.2 with nn. 9 and 10, §15.3.1.2) Ns 123.

   <pɛḱeθ> sim pf 1s [pɛkkḗθ] < *pákt (§3.3, §5.2 with nn. 9 and 10) Ns 123.

   <paxuwn> sim pf 3mp [paxű̄n] < *pákkū (§5.2 with nn. 9 and 10) Ns 123.

   <paxeyn> sim pf 3fp [paxḗn] < *pákkā (§5.2 with nn. 9 and 10) Ns 123.

*√πys (< Greek *peis-*)   <ʔɛ́πiys> sim rmp pf 3ms [ɛttə̆πī́s] as if < @ *hitπī́sa (§6.3) Ns 120.

*√ṣdq   <tzadqiyniywh̄y> int impf 2fs^3ms [tə̆zaddə̆qīnī́w] < *tiṣaddiqīnáhū (§2.3.4.4) Ns 133.

*√ṣlb   <ʔɛsṭlɛv> sim rmp pf 3ms [ɛsṭə̆léw] < *hitṣalíba (§10) B 24.

*√qbl   <qaḃlan> int pf 3ms^1p [qabbə̆lán] < *qabbílanā (§2.3.4.4) Ns 132.

   <qaḃleθ> int pf 1s [qabbə̆lḗθ] < *qabbílt (§4.2.2) Ns 193.

*√qWm   <qɔmt> sim pf 2ms [qə̆́mt] < *qắmtắ (§15.2.1.4) B 141.

*√qṣ   <ʔɛθqṣɛṣ> sim rmp pf 3ms [ɛθqə̆́ṣéṣ] < *hitqaṣíṣa (§6.3) Ns 123.

*√qrʔ   <Tɛqreynɔny> ~ <Tɛqreyniyny> sim impf 2fs^3ms [tɛqrēnə̆́n] ~ [tɛqrēnín] < *tiqraʔīnánī (§15.5.1 n. 38) Du 203.

*√rḥm   <raḥɛmeyh> int impa ms^3fs [raḥ(ḥ)ə̆méḥ] < *raḥḥímha (§15.5.1) Ns 134.

*√šʔl   <nɛšɛʔluwn> sim impf 3mp [nɛšɛlű̄n] < *yišʔalűna (§10) B 87.

*√šbḥ   <nšabḥuwneh> ~ <nšabḥuwnɔyh̄y> int impf 3mp^3ms [nə̆šabbə̆ḥūnéḥ] ~ [nə̆šabbə̆ḥūnɔ́y] < *yišabbiḥūnáhī ~ **yišabbiḥunáhī (§2.3.4.2, §7.2 (ɛ)) Ns 134.

*√šby   <wašBɔw> conj sim pf 3mp [wašbɔ́w] < *wa=šabáyū (§12.2) Du 375.

*√šbq   <tɛšabquwn> sim impf 2mp [tɛšabqű̄n] < *tašbuqűna (§4.4.1 with n. 23) Ns 37.

*√škḥ ('find')　<ʔɛškaḥ> cau pf 3ms [ɛškaḥ] < *haškíḥa (§12.2 with n. 14) Brockelmann 1928: 775.

　　{Old SR} <yšTKḥwn> sim rmp impf 3mp perhaps [yIštaxəḥū́n] < *yitšakiḥū́na (§17.19 n. 103) Drijvers 1972: 112.

*√šlm　<ʔašlɛməyhy> cau impa ms^3ms [ašlɛmə́y] < *hašlímhī (§15.5.1) Ns 135.

*√šm9　<šma9ayny> sim impa ms^1s [šə́ma9áyn] < *šĭmá9nī (§15.5.1) Ns 134.

*√šrgrg　<šraɣrɛɣ> quinquiradical pf 3ms [šə́raɣrɛ́ɣ] ⇐ √š(ə̆)ragreg/ {denominal from a Persian-borrowed noun, Brockelmann 1928: 806} (§1.1.2 n. 8) Ns 126.

*√šry　<(lə²) Tɛšreyəyhy> sim impf 2fṣ^3ms [(lə̄=) Tɛšrēyə́y] < *(lắ ᵒ#) tišrayíhī (§15.5.1 n. 38) Du 203.

*√šty　<ʔɛštiy> sim pf 3ms [ɛštī́] < *šatíya (§17.18.1) B 38, Malone 1974a: 5.

　　<ʔɛštay> sim impa ms [ɛštáy] < *šitáy (§8.1.3) B 95, Malone 1974a: 5.

　　<ʔɛštəy> sim impa fs [ɛšt y] < *šitáyī (§8.1.3) B 96.

*√štq　<šθɛq> sim pf 3ms [šə́θɛq] < *šatíqa (§4.2.2) Ns 103.

*√twy　<ʔɛTtwɔ²> sim rmp pf 3ms [ɛttəwɔ́] < *hittawáya (§8.1.3) B 96.

*√tmh　<ʔaθmhɔn> cau pf 3fp^1p [aθmə̆hɔ́n] < *hatmihā́nā (§2.3.4.3) Ns 139.

*√θbr　<ʔɛTTaBar> ~ <ʔɛttaBar> int rmp pf 3ms [ɛθtabbár] ~ [ɛttabbár] < *hitθabbára (§10) Du 105 with n. 1.

Talmudic

*√ʔzl　a[ʔăzál] ~ [ʔăzɔ̄́] sim pf 3ms [ʔə̆zǽl] ~ [ʔə̆zā̃] < *ʔazála (§17.12.2, §17.23.3) Mar 85*.

　　<ʔzlʔy> a[ʔazláy] sim pf 1s [ʔæzlǽy] < *ʔazált (§17.2) Mar 37 n. α, 85*.

　　{Standard Literary Babylonian} <wyʔzlwn> conj sim impf 3mp [wə̆yIʔzə̆lū́n] < *wa=yaʔzilū́na (§9.2.1.2 n. 18) Müller-Kessler and Kwasman 2000: 162f.

　　<ʔyzyl> y[ʔīzél] ~ <zyl> a[zél] sim impa ms [same] < *ʔăzíl (§17.23.3 with n. 117) Mor 165; Mar 38, 85*.

　　a[ʔɛ̆zílī] ~ [zílī] sim impa fs [ʔə̆zílī] ~ [zílī] < *ʔăzílī (§17.23.3 with nn. 117 and 120) Mar 85*.

*√ḥð (< **√Xð)　<ʔyTḥyD> y[ʔittə̆ḥī́ð] a[ʔittə̆ḥéð] sim rmp pf 3ms [same] < *hitʔaḥíða (§10) Mor 352; Mar 41, 86*.

*√ʔkl　<ʔKlyT> y[ʔə̆xæliθ] ~ <ʔKly> y[ʔə̆xǽlī] a[ʔăxálī] sim pf 1s [ʔə̆xǽliū] ~ [ʔə̆xǽlī] < *ʔakált (§17.23.3) Mor 353, Mar 87*.

　　<TyKwl> sim impf 2ms [tēxÚl] < *taʔkúli (§9.2.3.2) Mar 38.

　　<DTyʔKwl> sbor sim impf 2ms [də̆TIʔKÚl] < *ði ⸗# taʔkúli (§9.2.1.2 n. 18) Müller-Kessler and Kwasman 2000: 162f.

　　<nyKlynhy> sim impf 3mp^3fp [nēxə̆lī̃n((n)ə̆)hī̃] < *yaʔkulū́na ⸗# h/ʔin(nV̆)hín (§17.17.2) Mar 61.

　　<TyKlwn> y&a[tēxə̆lū́n] sim impf 2mp [same] < *taʔkulū́na (§4.2.2) Mor 165, Mar 87*.

　　<ʔ(y)Kwl> y[ʔexól] a[ʔɛ̆xól] ~ <Kwl> a[kól] sim impa ms [ʔexól] ~ [ʔə̆xól] ~ [kól] < *ʔăkúl (§17.23.3 with nn. 117 and 120, §17.33) Mor 165; Mar 38, 87*.

*√ʔmy (< *√wmy (< **√wm²) X *√ʔmr)　<ʔm²> y[ʔə̆mā̃] sim pf 3ms [same] < *ʔamáya (§11.2 n. 13) Mor 353.

a[lēmṓ] sim impf 3ms [lēmḗ] < *ya²máyi {?} (§11.2 n. 13) Mar 88*.

<Tym²> y[tēmḗ]sim impf 2ms [*same*] < *ta²máyi (§11.2 n. 13) Mor 353.

<²ym²> y[²emḗ] a[²ĕmṓ] sim impa ms [²emḗ] ~ [²ŏmḗ] < *²ĭmáy (§11.2 n. 13) Mor 353, Mar 88*.

*√²mr (see also *√²my)   <²mryTh> sim pf 2ms^3fs {?} [²æmrīθǽh] < ²amartā́ha (§17.17.2 with n. 91) Mar 59.

t<²mryT> ~ a[²ămárī] sim pf 1s [²ŏmǽriθ] ~ [²ŏmǽrī] < *²amárt (§2.3.4.3, §17.6.2, §17.12.2) Mar 37, 88*.

a[²ămrīθáh] <²mryT²> y[²æmrīθǽh] sim pf 1s^3fs [²æmrī́θǽh] ~ [²æmrīθā́] < *²amártāha (§15.2.2.2, §17.17.2) Mar 88*, Mor 293 with n. 100.

<²mrw> y [²æmrū́] sim pf 3mp [*same*] < *²amárū (§17.15.2 with n. 77) Mor 126.

<²mrynhy> y[²æmrĭ̂nnŏhī́] ~ <²mrynhw> y[²æmrĭ̂nnŏhū́] sim pf 3mp^3fp {*fgm*} [²æmrĭ̂nnŏhĪ́] ~ [²æmrĭ̂nnŏhŪ́] < *²amárū # h/²in(nV̌)hín ~ h/²in(nV̌)húm (§17.12.2) Mor 292.

a[²ămárn] sim pf 1p [²ŏmǽrn] < *²amárnā (§2.3..4.3) Mar 88*.

<²Tmr> sim rmp pf 3ms [²ittŏmár] < *hit²amíra (§9.2.1.1 with n. 13) Mar 41.

*√²šl (< *√š²l)   <²yTŝyl> sim rmp pf 3ms [²ittŏšél] / [²ittŏšíl] < *hit²ašíla (§10 n. 7) Mar 41.

<²yTŝly> sim rmp pf 1s [²ittŏšílī] < *hit²ašílt (§10 n. 7) Mar 41.

<²wŝlh> a[²ŏšílŏ] cau pf 3fs [²ŏšílā́] < *ha²šílat (§10 n. 7) Mar 46, 168*.

*√²ty   <²Twn> a[²ăθṓn] sim pf 3mp [²ŏθṓn] < *²atáyū (§7.2 (δ), §8.1.1) Mar 52, 91*.

<²Th> y[²ŏtā́n] sim pf 3fp [²ŏθā́n] < *²atáya (§8.1.1 with n. 6) Mor 276.

<T²> y[tǽ] a[tṓ] sim impa ms [tǽ] ~ [tā́] < *²ĭtáy or perhaps *²ĭtá² (§8.1.3 n. 15) Mor 277, Mar 91*.

<T²y> y[tǽy] a[táy] sim impa fs [tǽy] < *²ĭtáyī (§8.1.3, §11.2 with nn. 12 and 13) Mor 277, Mar 91*.

<²Tw> y[²ŏtū́] a[²ē̌θṓ] sim impa mp perhaps [²ŏθū́] ~ [²ŏθṓ] < *²ĭtáyū (§11.1 n. 1) Mor 354, Mar 91*.

<²TyK> a[²ŏθŏyṓx] cau pf 3ms^2ms [²ā̌θŏyā́x] < *ha²tiyáka (§9.2.1.1 with n. 13) Mar 41, 92*.

{*Halaxot Pĕsukot*} <²æTæy> cau pf 3fs [²ættǽy] < *ha²táyt (§9.2.1.1 with n. 13) Mor 116 n. 121.

a[²ayθīθah] cau pf 2ms^3fs [²æyTīθǽh] < *ha²tītáha (§9.2.1.1 with n. 13) Mar 92*.

<²yT²y> a[²ayθay] ~ [²ē̌θáy] cau pf 1s [²æyTǽy] ~ [²ē̌θǽy] < *ha²táyt (§11.2 with nn. 12 and 13) Mar 53, 92*.

a[²ayθĭ̂n(ŏ)hṓ] cau pf 1s^3mp [²æyTĭ̂n(ŏ)hŪ́] < *ha²tī́t # h/²in(nV̌)húm (§16.2 TL (α)) Mar 92*.

a[²ayθí(²)ū] ~ [²ayθíw] cau pf 3mp [²æyTí(²)ū] ~ [²æyTíw] < *ha²tíyū (§8.1.1) Mar 92*.

<²yyTy> y[²æytĭ̂] a[²ayθĭ̂] cau impa ms [²æyTĭ̂] < *ha²tĭ̂ (§8.1.3 n. 17) Mor 280, Mar 92*.

a[²ē̌θṓ] ~ <²yyTy> y[²æytĭ̂] cau impa fs [²ē̌θā́] ~ [²æyTĭ̂] < *ha²táyī {?} ~ *ha²tíyī (§8.1.3 n. 17) Mar 92*, Mor 280.

*√bdq   <BDqynyh> sim pf 1p^3ms [bə̆ðqīnḗh] / [bæðqīnḗh] < *badaqnā̆hi* (§17.17.2) Mar 59.

*√bdr   <BDrTynkw> y[bæddærtinnə̆xū̆] a[baddartinxố] int pf 1s^2mp [bæddærtin(nə̆)XŪ̆] < *baddirtə̆kúm* (§17.26) Mor 355, Mar 93*.

*√bWt   <BT> y[bắθ] sim pf 3ms [*same*] < *bắta* (§6.2.2) Mor 355.

*√bky   <BKw> y[bə̆xū̆] sim pf 3mp [*same*] < *bakáyū* (§8.1.1 n. 1) Mor 253.

*√bl9   a[ʾibbə̆lá9] sim rmp pf 3ms [ʾibbə̆lǽ9] < *hitbalí9a* (§17.11.3) Mar 99*.
     a[ʾibbal9ɔ̄́] ~ [ʾibbə̆lī9ɔ̄́] <ʾBl9h> y[ʾibbæl9ɑ̄́] sim rmp pf 3fs [ʾibbæl9ɑ̄́]
     ~ [ʾibbə̆lī9ɑ̄] / [ʾibbə̆lī9ɑ̄́] < *hitbali9át* possibly ~ *hitbalí9at* (§17.28) Mar 94*, Mor §5.211.

*√b9y (< **√bRy)   <B9ʾy> y[bə̆9ǽy] a[bə̆9áy] sim pf 1s [bə̆9ǽy] < *ba9áyt* (§17.2 with n. 2) Mor 253; Mar 52, 95*.
     <B9w> y[bə̆9ū̆] a[bə̆9ố] sim pf 3mp [*same*] < *ba9áyū* (§11.2) Mor 253f., Mar 95*.
     <B9n> y[bə̆9ǽn] a[bə̆9ǽn] sim pf 1p [bə̆9ǽn] < *ba9áynā* (§11.2 with n. 13) Mor 255, Mar 95*.
     <nB9y> y&a[niv9ḗ] sim impf 1p [*same*] < *nib9áyi* (§11.2 with n. 13) Mor 356, Mar 95*.
     <B9y> y&a[bə̆9í] sim impa ms [*same*] < *bă̆9í* (§8.1.3) Mor 257, Mar 95*.

*√bṣr   <Bṣrw> y[bæṣrū̆] sim pf 3mp [*same*] < *baṣárū* (§17.15.2 with n. 77) Mor 126.

*√brk   a[bə̆rə̆xū̆n] int pf 3mp^1s [bā̆rə̆xū̆n] < *barrikúnī* (§17.15.1 n. 65) Mar 96*.

*√bšl   <Bšlynn> y[bæššelinnǽn] int pf 1p [*same*] < *baššílnā* (§15.5.1 with n. 39) Mor 147.
     a[baššéli] int impa fs [baššéli] < *baššíli* (§15.5.1) Mar 96*.

*√gz   <lGzw> ~ <lGwzw> ~ <lGzzw> sim impf 3mp [liggə̆zū̆] ~ [liggŪzū̆] / [liggŪzū] ~ [liɣzə̆zū̆] < *yagguzū́na* (possibly ~ *yaggúzū*) ~ *yagzuzū́na* (§3.3) Mar 49.

*√gly   a[ʾɛɣlḗ] sim impf 1s [ʾiɣlḗ] or perhaps [ʾæɣlḗ] < *ʾigláyi* (§17.11.3) Mar 99*.
     <TGly> y[tə̆ɣællī́] int impf 2fs [*same*] < *tigallíyina* (§8.1.1) Mor 268.

*√gmr   a[ʾaɣmī́rū] cau impa mp [ʾæɣmīrū] < *hagmírū* (§15.5.1) Mar 99*.

*√gnb   <gnBʾ> y[gænvɑ̄́] sim pf 3ms^3fs [gænBɑ̄́] < *ganabáha* (§4.2.2) Mor 124.

*√gr   a[gə̆rár] sim pf 3ms [gə̆rǽr] < *garára* (§15.4 with (15V)) Mar 101*.

*√grd   a[gə̆reðtḗh] int pf 2ms^3ms [gā̆reðtḗh] < *garridtáhi* (§16.2 TL (e)) Mar 109*.

*√grs   <nGrwsynhw> y[nigrusinnə̆hū̆] sim impf 3ms^3mp [niɣrusinnə̆hŪ̆] < *yagrúsi* # h/ʾin(nV̊)húm (§17.11.3) Mor 295.
     <l(y)Grsw> y[ligrə̆sū̆] a[liɣrə̆sū̆] ~ <n(y)Grsw> a[niɣrə̆sū̆] sim impf 3mp [liɣrə̆sū̆] ~ [niɣrə̆sū̆] < *yagrusū́na* (§7.2 (γ) with n. 8, §17.9.2, §17.12.2) Mor 130; Mar 38, 100*.

*√grš   a[gə̄raštéx] int pf 1s^2fs [gā̆ræštéx] < *garráštə̆ki* (§2.3.4.4, §17.15.1 n. 65) Mar 101*.
     <nGršh> y[nīɣā̆rə̆šéh] int impf 3ms^3fs [*same*] < *yigarrišíha* (§15.3.1.1) Mor 300.

*√dbr   a[də̆varinhố] sim pf 3ms^3mp [də̆værinhŪ̆] < *dabára* # h/ʾin(nV̊)húm (§7.4.1, §16.2 TL (d)) Mar 101*.

*√dWṣ / *√dṣy   a[dɔ̄ṣɔ̆yéh] {?} sim pf 3ms^3ms (§3.4 n. 8) Mar 102*.

*√dly   <Dly> y[dɔ̆lí] ~ <Dl> y[dǽl] a[dál] sim (possibly ~ int) impa ms [dɔ̆lí] ~ [dǽl] < *dǎlí (possibly ~ *dallí) (§8.1.3 n. 17) Mor 257, Mar 103*.
a[dallīnɔ̆hő̄] int pf 3ms^3mp [dællīnɔ̆hŰ] < *dallíya # h/ʔin(nV̊)húm (§17.26 n. 136) Mor 103*.

*√drs   <ʔiyDriysæn> sim rmp pf 3fp [ʔiddɔ̆rīsǽn] < *hitdarísā (§7.2 (δ) n. 16) Morag 1967–68: 74.

*√ḏḥl   <T(y)Dḥly(n)> y[tiḏḥɔ̆lí(n)] a[tiḏḥắli(n)] sim impf 2fs [tiḏḥɔ̆lí(n)] < *tiḏḥalína (§17.12.2, §17.23.3) Mor 359; Mar 38, 102*.

*√ḏkr   <yDKrynK> sim impf 2ms^2ms [yiḏkɔ̆rinnắx] < *yiḏkarinníka (§7.1) Mar 60.

*√ḏq   a[ʔizdaq(ɔ̆)qīnán] sim rmp pf 1p [ʔizdæq(ɔ̆)qīnǽn] < *hitḏaqíqnā (§6.3) Mar 110*.

*√hwy   <hwh> sim pf 3ms [hɔ̆wắ] < *hawáya (§8.1.1) Mar 52.
a[hăwáyɔ̄] sim pf 3fs [hɔ̆wǽyā] < *hawáyat (§15.4 with (15S)) Mar 106*.
a[hăwayɔ́n] sim pf 3fp [hɔ̆wæyắn] < *hawáyā (§11.1, §15.4 with (15S) and n. 33) Mar 106*.
a [hăwḗnɔ̄] ~<hwyyn> a[hăwáyin] sim pf 1p [hɔ̆wḗnā] ~ [hɔ̆wǽyn] < *hawáynā (§11.2 with n. 13) Mar 52, 106*.
<yhwy> y[yihwḗ] a[yɛhɔ̆wḗ] ~ <lyhwy> y[lihwḗ] a[lɛhɔ̆wḗ] ~ <nhwy> y[nihwḗ] ~ <yhʔ> ~ <yhy> y[yɔ̆hḗ] a≠[yɔ̆hḗ] ~ a[nɔ̆hḗ] sim impf 3ms [yih(ī)wḗ] ~ [lih(ī)wḗ] ~ [nihwḗ] ~ [yɔ̆hḗ] ~ [nɔ̆hḗ] < *yihwáyi / *lihwáyi (§17.11.3, §17.23.3, §17.32 with (17.32A)) Mor §12.12, Mar 106*.
<Thwy> y[tihwḗ] a[tɛhɔ̆wḗ] sim impf 2ms [tih(ī)wḗ] < *tihwáyi (§11.1 n. 1, §17.23.3) Mor 360, Mar 106*.
<Thwyyn> y[tihwɔ̆yín] a[tɛhɛwyín] sim impf 2fs [tihwɔ̆yín] ~ [tihiwyín] < *tahwinyína (§11.1 n. 1, §16.2 TL (k)) (Mor 256, 360; Mar 106*.
<nyhw> a[nɔ̆hő̄] sim impf 3mp [*same*] < *yihwayűna (§17.32 with (17.32A)) Mar 52, 106*.
<Thww> a[tɛhɔ̆wő̄] sim impf 2mp [tihĭwő̄] < *tihwayűna (§11.1 n. 1) Mar 52, 106*.

*√wd9   <hwD9T> y[hōḏǽ9t] a[hōḏá9at] cau pf 2ms [hōḏæ9(æ)t] < *hawdí9tǎ (§5.3 n. 13, §15.3.1.3) Mor 308, Mar 120*.

*√whb   (see also *√ntb)   a[wīháv] conj sim pf 3ms [wīhǽv] < *wa=wahába (§17.34 n. 161) Mar 120*.
<yhBK> y[yæhbắx] sim pf 3ms^2ms [yæhBắx] < *wahabáka (§5.3 n. 13).
<yhBT> ~ <yhBʔ> y[yɔ̆hǽvæθ] ~ [yæhbắ] sim pf 3fs [yɔ̆hǽvæθ] ~ [yæhBắ] < *wahábat ~ *wahabát (§5.3 n. 13) Mor 202f.
†<yhBw> ~ <hBw> sim pf 3mp [yɔ̆hǽvū] ~ [hǽvū] < *wahábū (§17.33 n. 159, §17.34) Mar 37.
<hB> y[hǽv] a[háv] sim impa mss [hǽv] < *háb (§17.3 n. 3) Mor 365, Mar 120*.
†<ʔ(y)TyhyBT> sim rmp pf 3fs [ʔiθyɔ̆hÍvæθ] / [ʔiθyɔ̆hÍvæθ] < hitwahíbat (§17.34) Mar 45.

*√wzp   <nyzyP> y[nēzéf] ~ [nēzúf] sim impf 3ms [*same*] < *yazípi ~ *yazúpi (§17.7) Mor 201.

<ʾwzyPynhw> y[ʾōzifŭnnŏhŭ̃] cau impa mp^3mp [ʾōzifŭnnŏhŨ̃] < *hawzípu ǂ h/ʾin(nV̊)húm (§17.15.1) Mor 314.

*√wld   <ylDT> y[yŏléðæθ] a[yŏlíðaθ] sim pf 3fs [yŏlí̃ðæθ] < *walídat (§12.2, §17.11.3) Mor 124, Mar 121*.

<T(y)lyD> y[tŏlí̃ð] sim impf 3fs [*same*] (or possibly [tēléð]/[tilléð]) < *talídi (§17.7) Mor 201 with n. 19.

<ʾTylyDʾ> y[ʾiθyŏlí̃ðā] a[ʾiθyŏlí̃ðŏ] sim rmp pf 3fs [ʾiθyŏlí̃ðā] < *hitwalídat (§14.2) Mor 205, Mar 121*.

*√wmʾ   (see *√ʾmy)

*√wqr   <yqrʾ> y[yŏqærā] sim pf 3fp [yŏqærā] / [yŏqærā̃] < *waqárā (§7.2 (δ) with n. 15, §17.9.2) Mor 127.

<ʾyyqr> y[ʾiyyæqqǽr] a[ʾiyyaqqár] int rmp pf 3ms [ʾiyyæqqǽr] < *hitwaqqára (§17.34) Mor 367; Mar 45, 121*.

*√wrθ   <lyrwT> y[lerúθ] sim impf 3ms [*same*] < *yarúθi (§17.7) Mor 201.

<TyrwT> y[terúθ] a[terōθ] sim impf 2ms [*same*] < *tarúθi (§17.7 n. 16) Mor 201, Mar 122*.

*√wθb   <yTyB> ~ <ʾyTyB> sim pf 3ms [yŏθév] ~ [(ʾ)īθév] < *waθíba (§14.2 with n. 18) Mar 37.

<wʾyTyB> y[wīθév] conj sim pf 3ms [*same*] < *wa=waθíba (§14.2 with n. 19) Mor 200.

<yTyBT> a[yŏθévt] ~ <ʾyTyBT> sim pf 2ms [yŏθévt] ~ [(ʾ)īθévt] < *waθíbtā̊ (§14.2 with n. 18) Mar 37, 122*.

<lyTB> y&a[littév] sim impf 3ms [*same*] < *yaθíbi (§17.7) Mor 201, Mar 122*.

<TyBw> ~ <ʾyTyBw> a[(ʾ)īθívū] sim impa mp [tívū] ~ [(ʾ)īθívū] < *θíbu (§14.2 with n. 18, §17.33) Mar 39, 122*.

<ʾwTyB> y&a[ʾōθév] cau pf 3ms [*same*] < *hawθíba (§11.2) Mor 267, Mar 122*.

a[ʾōθevnḗh] cau pf 1p^3ms [*same*] < *hawθíbnŏhi (§2.3.4.3) Mar 86*.

*√zbn   <zBny> sim pf 1s [zŏvǽnī] possibly ~ [zævnī] < *zabánt (§17.12.2) Mar 37.

<lyzByn> sim impf 3ms [lizbén] < *yazbíni / *lazbíni (§17.12.2) Mar 38.

<ʾyzBwn> y[ʾæzbún] sim impf 1s [ʾæzbún] perhaps ~ [ʾizbún] < *ʾazbúni (§12.2 with nn. 15 and 16) Mar 129 with n. 32.

<nzBwn> y[nizbŭ̃n] sim impf 3mp [*same*] < *nazbúnū (§17.9.2) Mor 130.

t<TzBnwn> ~ <TzBnw> sim impf 2mp [tizbŏnŭ̃n] ~ [tizbŏnŭ̃] < *tazbunúna / *tazbinúna (§17.12.2) Mar 38.

a[zabbŏninhṍ] int pf 3ms^3mp [zæbbŏninhŨ̃] < *zabbína ǂ h/ʾin(nV̊)húm (§17.26 n. 136) Mar 108*.

<zBynh> y[zæbbínā] int pf 3fs [*same*] < *zabbínat (§17.11.3) Mor 146.

a[nŏzabbŏnĭnnŏhṍ] int impf 3mp^3mp [nŏzæbbŏnĭnnŏhŨ̃] < *yizabbinúna ǂ h/ʾin(nV̊)húm (§17.15.1, §17.17.2) Mar 108*.

<ʾyzDBn> y[ʾizdæbbǽn] a[ʾizdabbán] int rmp pf 3ms [ʾizdæbbǽn] < *hitzab-bána (§10) Mor 360, Mar 108*.

*√zl   <zl> y[zǽl] sim pf 3fp [*same*] < *zálla (§17.9.2) Mor 127.

*√zmn   a[zammentéh] int pf 3fs^3ms [zæmmentéh] < *zammináthi* / **zammíntə̆hi* (§16.2 TL (e)) Mar 109*.

a[ˀazmentéh] cau pf 1s^3ms [ˀæzmentéh] < **hazmint hi* (§16.2 TL (e, f)) Mar 109*.

*√zrq   <ˀyzDryq> a[ˀizdə̆réq] ~ <ˀyzryq> y[ˀizzə̆ríq] a[ˀizzə̆réq] sim rmp pf 3ms [*same*] < **hitzaríqa* (§10) Mor 142, Mar 110*, Sokoloff 2002: 422.

*√ḥd   <ḥDD> int impa ms [ḥæddéð] < **haddíd* (§3.3) Mar 48.

*√ḥðr   a[ḥă̆ðár] sim pf 3ms [ḥŏ̆ðǽr] < **haðára* (§17.23.3) Mar 105*.

a[lɛhdár] sim impf 3ms [lihdǽr] / [læhdǽr] < **yaḥðúri* / **laḥðúri* (§17.11.3 n. 47) Mar 105*.

<lyhDwr> a[lɛhdű̆r] sim impf 3mp [lihdű̆r] / [læhdű̆r] < **yaḥðúrū* / **laḥðúrū* (§7.2 (γ) n. 8., §17.9.2) Mar 38, 105*.

<ˀhDwr> y[ˀæhdű̆r] cau pf 3mp [*same*] < **haḥðírū* (§17.9.2) Mor 157.

<nhDr> y[nihdǽr] ~ [næhdǽr] a[nɛhdár] cau impf 3ms [nihdǽr] / [næhdǽr] < **y(ih)aḥðíri* (§12.2) Mor 102f. with n. 53, Mar 106*.

cau impf 1p [nihdǽr] / [næhdǽr] < **n(ih)aḥðíri* (§9.2.4) Mar 106*.

*√ḥwy   <ˀḥwy> y[ˀæhwű̆] cau impa fp {*fgm*} [ˀæhwű̆] ~ [ˀæhwî] < **haḥwáyū* ~ **haḥwíyā* (§16.2 TL (q)) Mor 273 with n. 151.

*√ḥWk   <ˀḥyKT> y[ˀæhéxt] a[ˀahíxt] cau pf 2ms [ˀæhéxt] / [ˀæhíxt] < **haḥíktå̊* (§6.1.1.1, §6.1.2 with (6C) and n. 9, §6.2) Mor §10.51, Mar 111*.

<ˀḥyKw> y[ˀæhíxū] cau pf 3mp [*same*] < **haḥíkū* (§6.1.1.1) Mor §10.51.

*√ḥzy   a[ḥăzố] sim pf 3ms [ḥŏ̆zắ] < **hazáya* (§17.23.3) Mar 112*.

a[ḥazɔ̄nə̆hố] ~ <ḥzynhw> y[ḥŏ̆zĭnnə̆hű̆] sim pf 3ms^3mp [ḥŏ̆zānnə̆hŰ̆] ~ [ḥŏ̆zĭnnə̆hŰ̆] < **hazáya* ~ *haziya* ⧧ *h/ˀin(nV̆)húm* (§16.2 TL (δ) n. 6, §17.15.1 n. 37, §17.26 n. 136) Mar 112*, Mor 321f.

<ḥzyT> y[ḥŏ̆zḗθ] sim pf 2ms [ḥŏ̆zḗT] < *hazáytå̊* (§3.4) Mor 253.

t<ḥzyT> a[ḥăzḗθ] ~ <ḥzyTy> y[ḥŏ̆zḗθī] a[ḥăzḗθī] ~ <ḥzˀy> y[ḥŏ̆zǽy] a[ḥăzáy] sim pf 1s [ḥŏ̆zḗθ] ~ [ḥŏ̆zḗθī] ~ [ḥŏ̆zǽy] < **hazáyt* (§11.2 with nn. 12 and 13, §13) Mar 52, 112*; Mor 253.

a[ḥăzɔ̄nə̆hố] ~ [ḥăzān(ə̆)hố] sim pf 3mp^3mp [ḥŏ̆zɔ̄nə̆hŰ̆] ~ [ḥŏ̆zæn(ə̆)hŰ̆] < **hazáyu* ⧧ *h/ˀin(nV̆)húm* (§17.15.1 with nn. 68 and 69, §17.17 with n. 89, §17.26 n. 136) Mar 112*.

a[ḥăzān(ə̆)hố] sim pf 1p^3mp [ḥŏ̆zæn(ə̆)hŰ̆] < **hazáynā* ⧧ *h/ˀin(nV̆)húm* (§17.15.1 with nn. 68 § 69, §17.17.2 with n. 89) Mar 112*.

<ḥzynhy> ~ a[ḥăzēnɔ̄nə̆hế] sim pf 1p^3fp [ḥŏ̆zæynə̆hÎ] ~ [ḥŏ̆zēnānə̆hÎ] < **hazáynā* ⧧ *h/ˀin(nV̆)hín* (§17.15.1, §17.17.2) Mar 59, 112*.

*√ḥzq   <ˀḥzwqw> y[ˀæhzű̆qū] cau impa mp [*same*] < **haḥzíqū* (§17.9.1 n. 24) Mor 159.

*√ḥṭ (< **√Xṭ)   <ḥṭṭ> y[ḥāṭét] possibly int pf 3ms [*same*] < **hāṭíṭa* {*miškal-suppleting for* @*ḥaṭṭíṭa} (§6.2.1 n. 16) Mor 243.

*√ḥṭˀ (< **√Xṭˀ)   a[tɛhĕ̆ṭế] sim impf 2ms [tiḥĭ̆ṭế] < **tiḥṭáˀi* (§17.11.3) Mar 112.

*√ḥkr   a[ḥăxarnóah] sim pf 1p^3fs [ḥŏ̆xærnúæh] < **hakarnű̆hå̊* (§2.3.4.3 n. 30) Mar 113*.

*√ḥl (< **√Xl)   <nyḥl> y[nēhél] sim impf 3ms [*same*] < **yaḥḥíli* (§9.3.1 n. 40) Mor 362.

a[nittɔ̌ħál] ~ [littɔ̌ħál] ~ [littɔ̌ħíl] ~ <nyTħyl> y[nittɔ̌ħíl] cau rmp impf 3ms [nittɔ̌ħǽl] ~ [littɔ̌ħǽl] ~ [littɔ̌ħíl] ~ [nittɔ̌ħíl] < *yithaħħáli ~ perhaps *lithaħħáli (§6.3) Mar 113*, Mor 241.

*√ħlṭ (< **√Xlṭ)	a[lɛħĕlót] sim impf 3ms [liħílóṭ] < *yaħlúṭi / *laħlúṭi (§17.11.3 n. 47) Mar 105*.

*√ħlp (< **√Xlp)	a[lɛħlóf] ~ [laħléf] ~ <lħlyP> y[liħléf] sim impf 3ms [liħlóf] ~ [lǽħléf] ~ [liħléf] < *yaħlúpi / *laħlúpi ~ *yaħlípi / *laħlípi (§9.3.1 n. 40, §17.11.3) Mar 113*, Mor 363.

*√ħmy	a[ʔɛħɛmǐnnéħ] <ʔyħmynyh> y[ʔæħmēnéħ] sim impf 1s^3ms [ʔiħǐmǐnnéħ] ~ [ʔæħmēnéħ] ~ perhaps [ʔiħmēnéħ] < *ʔaħmiy(i)nníhi ~ *ʔiħmay(i)nníhi (§7.7 n. 33, §17.11.3) Mar 114*, Mor 324 with n. 63.

*√ħnq (< **√Xnq)	<ħnqynwn> y[ħænqinnűn] sim pf 3ms^3mp [same] < **ḥanáqa ̞ # h/ʔin(nV̊)húm (§7.4.1, §17.15.1 with n. 64) Mor 291.

*√ħsr (< **√Xsr) <ħsrTK> y[ħæssertǽx] int pf 1s^2ms [same] < *ḥassírtɔ̌ka (§15.5.1) Mor §15.21.

<ħsrTyK> y[ħæssertǽx] int pf 1s^2ms {fgm} [ħæssertíx] ~ [ħæssertǽx] < *ḥassírtɔ̌ki ~ *ḥassírtɔ̌ka (§16.2 TL (g)) Mor 299.

*√ħṣ	<Tyħwṣ> y[tēħűṣ] sim impf 2ms [same] < *taħħúsi (§6.2.2 with n. 20) Mor 235.

*√ħṣd	a[tɛħĕṣáð] sim impf 2ms [tiħíṣáð] < *tiħṣádi (§17.11.3) Mar 115*.

*√ħrb (< **√Xrb)	a[lɛħróv] ~ [lɛħráv] sim impf 3ms [liħróv] ~ [liħráv] < *yaħrúbi / *laħrúbi ~ *yaħríbi / *laħríbi (§17.11.3 with n. 48) Mar 118*.

<ʔħrByh> y[ʔæħrɔ̌véħ] a[ʔaħarvéħ] cau pf 3ms^3ms [ʔæħrɔ̌véħ] ~ [ʔæħærBéħ] < *haħribáhi (§4.4.1, §5.3 n. 13, §17.23.3) Mor §15.31, Mar 115*.

*√ħš	<ħšʔy> a[ħaššáy] sim pf 1s [ħæššǽy] < *ħást (§17.2) Mar 49, 116*.

*√ħšb	<lyħšB> y[liħšǽv] ~ <lyħšwB> a[lɛħšóv] sim impf 3ms [liħšǽv] ~ [liħšóv] < *yiħšábi / *liħšábi ~ *yaħšúbi / *laħšúbi (§11.1 n. 1) Mor 363, Mar 116*, Sokoloff 2002: 486.

*√ṭbl	<ṭBylw> y[ṭɔ̌vílū] sim impa fp {fgm} [same] < *ṭăbílū (§17.9.2) Mor 131.

*√ṭs	<ʔyṭws> y[ʔiṭṭűs] ~ [ʔetus] sim rmp pf 3ms [same] {?} < *hiṭṭíssa {derivation of the second variant is difficult, even assuming hollow-geminate rapprochement, §6.1} (§6.3 n. 43) Mor 241 with n. 40.

*√ṭ9m	<ṭ9ymynwn> a[ṭɔ̌9eminnűn] sim pf 3ms^3mp [same] < *ṭa9íma ̞ # h/ʔin(nV̊)húm (§7.4.1, §15.2.1.2, §16.2 TL (s), §17.11.3, §17.15.1 with nn. 64 and 65) Mar 59, 118*.

<lṭ9wm> y[liṭ9úm] a[liṭ9óm] sim impf 3ms [same] < *yaṭ9úmi / *laṭ9úmi (§12.2, §17.11.3) Mor 129, Mar 118*.

*√ṭrp	<ṭyrPn> y[ṭærfǽn] sim impa ms^1s [tærPǽn] ~ [ṭirPǽn] < *ṭărúpnī (§17.25) Mor 296 with n. 28.

*√ylp (< **√ʔlp)	<lylPn> y[lēlɔ̌fǽn] a[lēlæfɔ̌n] sim impf 3ms [lēlɔ̌fǽn] < *yaylapána (§7.2 (γ)) Mor 366; Mar 38, 87*.

*√kʔb	<wyK9wB> conj sim impf 3ms [wɔ̌yixʔóv] / [wɔ̌yikkóv] < *wa=yaʔkúbi (§9.2.3.1) Müller-Kessler and Kwasman 2000: 163.

*√kWn	<ʔyTKn> y[ʔittɔ̌xǽn] sim rmp pf 3ms [same] < hitkína (§6.3) Mor 219. a[kawwén] int pf 3ms [kæwwén] < *kawwína (§11.1) Mar 123*.

*√kl <	ʔKll> y[ʔikkɔ̌lǽl] sim rmp pf 3ms [same] < hitkalíla (§6.3 n. 42) Mor 240.

*√kn9   <ʔKn9ʔy> a[ʔikkan9áy] sim rmp pf 3fs [ʔikkæn9ǽy] < *hitkani9át (§17.2) Mar
41, 124*.

*√knp   <lKnPy> a[lɔ̆xannɔ̆fí] int plain impf 3mp [læxænnɔ̆fí] < *yikannipū́na /
likannipū́na (§17.17.1, §17.17.2) Mar 124.

<lKnPy> y[likkænnɔ̆fḗ] int rmp impf 3mp [same] < *yitkannapū́na /
*litkannapū́na (§17.17.1, §17.17.2) Mor 154.

*√krk   a[kɔ̆raxi̊nɔ̆hő́] <KrKynhw> y[kærxi̊nnɔ̆hű́] sim pf 3mp^3mp [kɔ̆ræxi̊nɔ̆hÚ̊] ~
[kærxi̊nnɔ̆hÚ̊] < *karákū # h/ʔin(nV̊)húm (§§16.2 TL (α), §17.15.1, §17.17.1
n. 64, §17.17.2) Mar 126*, Mar 294.

*√ktb   a[kaθvinhő́] <KTBynhw> y[kæθvinnɔ̆hű́] sim pf 3ms^3mp [kæθvin(nɔ̆)hÚ̊] <
katába # h/ʔin(nV̊)húm (§16.2 TL (s), §17.12.2, §17.15.1) Mar 196, Mor
291f.

*√lwy   <ylwwnyh> a[yɔ̆lawwōnḗh] int impf 3mp^3ms [yɔ̆læwwōnḗh] <
yilawwayūnáhi (§7.2 ( ) n. 21) Mar 61, 127.

*√lWṭ   a[lɔ̆ṭɔ̆θḗh] sim pf 1s^3ms perhaps [lū̆ṭɔ̆θḗh] < *lắṭṭɔ̆hi (§15.2.1.4 n. 12) Mar
127*.

*√lqṭ (see also *√nqṭ)   <lqṭnhw> y[liqqɔ̆ṭinnɔ̆hű́] int pf 3ms^3mp [same] < *laqqíṭa #
h/ʔin(nV̊)húm (§12.2) Mor 298, 369.

*√mWr   <ʔmyr> y[ʔɔ̆mér] cau pf 3ms [same] < *hamíra (§6.1.1.1) Mor 227.

*√mWt   at[yɔ̆mūθű́n] ~ at[yɔ̆mūθű́] ~ a [limmɔ̆θű́n] ~ <lymwTw> y&a[lēmūθű̄]
sim impf 3mp [yɔ̆mūθű́n] ~ [yɔ̆mūθű́]/[yɔ̆mű́θū] ~ [limmɔ̆θű́n] ~ [lēmūθű́]/
[lēmű́θū] < *yamūtū́na / *lamūtū́na perhaps ~ *yamū́tu / *lamū́tu (§6.2.2
with n. 20, §15.3.1.1) Mar 129*, Mor 214.

*√mḥʔ   <mḥTynhw> y[mæḥθinnɔ̆hű́] sim pf 2ms^3mp [mæḥTinnɔ̆hÚ̊] < *maḥáʔta #
h/ʔin(nV̊)húm (§17.15.1 n. 74) Mor 322 n. 54.

<ʔmḥynyh> y[ʔæmḥi̊nnḗh] sim impf 1s^3ms [same] < *ʔimḥáʔinníhi (§7.7
n. 33) Mor 324 n. 61.

*√mṭy   <lmṭyn> y[limṭɔ̆yǽn] ~ [limṭɔ̆yín] sim impf 3ms^1p [same] < *yamṭiyínā /
*lamṭiyínā (§2.3.4.4) Mor 323.

<ʔmṭwhw> ~ <ʔmṭwy> y[ʔæmṭő́y] cau impa mp^3ms [ʔæmṭő́hū] ~ [ʔæmṭő́y] <
*hamṭayű́hū ~ *hamṭayű́hī (§7.2 (ζ), §8.2.1, §8.2.2) Mar 61, Mor
238 n. 76.

*√mlʔ   <lymly> y[līmællḗ] ~ [līmællí̊] int impf 3ms [same] < *yimallíʔi / *limallíʔi
(§8.1.1 n. 1) Mor 267 with n. 117.

*√mlk   <ʔymlyK> y[ʔæmmɔ̆lí̊x] a[ʔimmɔ̆léx] sim rmp impf 1s [ʔæmmɔ̆lí̊x] ~
[ʔimmɔ̆lí̊x] ~ [ʔimmɔ̆léx] < *ʔitmalíki (§12.2 n. 15, §17.11.3) Mor 143 with
n. 108, Mar 131*.

*√mny   <mnw> y[mɔ̆nő́] ~ [mɔ̆nű́] sim impa mp [same] < *mı̆náyū (§8.1.1 n. 1) Mor
257.

*√msr   a[liθmɔ̆sér] sim rmp impf 3ms [same] < *yitmasíri / *litmasíri (§15.4 with
(15V)) Mar 132*.

*√mṣ   a[maṣṣḗθ] <mṣyT> y[mǽṣt] ~ [mɔ̆ṣḗθ] sim pf 2ms [mæṣṣḗT] ~ [mǽṣt] ~
[mɔ̆ṣḗT] < *mắṣtā ~ *maṣáytā̊ {with quasi-radical y} (§3.4 with n. 8, §6.2.2,
§15.3.2 n. 30) Mar 132*; Mor 234, 253.

*√mṣʔ   <ymṣy> sim pf 3ms [(ʔ)imṣí̊] < *maṣíʔa (§17.18.1) Mar 52.

*√nbʔ   <ʔynBwy> y[ʔinnæbbū́] int rmp pf 3mp [ʔinnæbū́y] {?} < *hitnabbáʔū
(§127.17.2 n. 94) Mor 270.

*√ng9   <ʔnG9ʔy> a[ʔinnaggá9ay] int rmp pf 3fs [ʔinnæggǽ9æy] < *hitnaggá9at
(§17.2) Mar 45, 134*.

*√ndḥ   <ʔDḥwhy> a[ʔaddǝḥū́hī] cau pf 3mpˆ3ms [ʔæddǝḥū́hī] < *handihū́hī (§8.2.2)
Mar 59, 135*.

*√nhr   a[ʔanhǎrinhḗ] cau pf 3msˆ3fp [ʔænhǒrinhĪ̃] < *hanhíra #h/ʔin(nV̊)hín
(§17.12.2) Mar 135*.

*√nWm   <nym> y[nwyém] sim pf 3ms [same] < *nắma (*/nayim+a/) (§6.2.2) Mor
371.

        <lynym> y[lēnī́m] ~ [lēnū́m] sim impf 3ms [same] < yanī́mi / *lanī́mi ~
*yanū́mi / *lanū́mi (§15.3.1.1) Mor 213 with n. 9.

        a[nēnū́m] sim impf 1p [same] < *nanū́mi (§15.3.1.1) Mar 136*.

*√nWp   <lynPPyh> y[līnāfǝfḗh] int impf 3msˆ3ms [same] < *yināpipíhi {miškal-
suppleting for *yinawwipíhi } (§6.2.1 n. 16) Mor 222.

*√nḥt (possibly ~ *√ḥt)   a[nǝḥóθ] ~ <nḥyT> y[nǝḥéθ] sim impa ms [same] < *nǎḥút
       ~ *nǎḥít (§17.33) Mar 136*, Mor 185.

        <ḥwTw> y&a[ḥúθū] sim impa mp [same] < *ḥútū (§17.33) Mor 186, Mar
136*.

        <nḥyT> y[næḥéθ] a[naḥ(ḥ)éθ] cau impf 1p [næḥ(ḥ)éθ] < *n(ih)anhíti or pos-
sibly *n(ih)aḥḥíti (§17.21.1) Mor §8.14, Mar 136*.

*√nṭp   <nṭP> y[nǎṭéf] sim impa fs [same] < *nǎṭípī or perhaps *nǎṭíp {fgm} (§17.9.2)
Mor 131.

*√nsb   <nsyBy> ~ <nsBy> y[nǝsívī] ~ [næsvī́] sim pf 1s [nǝsívī] ~ [næsBī́] < *nasíbt
(§17.11.3) Mor 372.

        a[ʔinnasváθ] ~ [ʔinnasvṓ] sim rmp pf 3fs [ʔinnæsBǽθ] ~ [ʔinnæsBā] < *hitna-
sibát (§17.11.3) Mar 137*.

*√npl   <wnPl> y[ů̃nfǽl] ~ [wǒnæflā́] conj sim pf 3fs {fgm} [same] < *wa=napála ~
*wa=napalát (§16.2 TL (aʹ)) Mor 124 with n. 6.

*√npq   a[ʔappeqθḗh] cau pf 3fsˆ3ms [ʔæppeqθḗh] < *hanpiqáthi (§15.3.2 n. 30) Mar
138*.

*√nqṭ (possibly < *√lqṭ)   <nqṭn> a[naqtán] sim pf 3msˆ1s [næqtǽn] < *naqaṭánī
(§4.2.2, §16.2 TL (b)) Mar 58, 138*.

        <nynqwtw> a[ninqǒṭū́] sim impf 3mp [ninqǔṭū́] < *yanquṭū́na (§17.23.3)
Mar 13.

*√nšb   a[nǝšṓ] sim pf 3ms [nǝšā́] < *našába (§17.12.2) Mar 139.

*√nšy   <ʔnšʔy> y[ʔinnǒšǽy] sim rmp pf 1s [same] < *hitnašáyt (§17.26) Mor §12.21.
        y[ʔænšǽy] possibly cau pf 1s [same] < *hanšáyt (§17.26) Mor §12.21.

*√nšq   <nšq(y)K> a[našqṓx] sim pf 3msˆ2ms {possibly fgm} [næšqǽx] possibly ~
[næšqĪ̃x] < *našaqáka possibly ~ *našaqáki (§2.3.4.4, §16.2 TL (a) with n. 5)
Mar 58, 139*.

        <nŝqyK> y[næššǝqáx] int pf 3msˆ2ms {possibly fgm} [næššǝqǽx] possibly
~ [næššǝqĪ̃x] < *naššiqáka possibly ~ *naššiqáki (§2.3.4.4, §16.2
TL (a) with n. 5) Mor §15.21 with n. 38.

*√ntb (< *√ntn X *√whb)   a[nittév] ~ <lyTB> y[littév] sim impf 3ms [same] < *yantíni
X *yihábi possibly *lantíni X *lihábi (§17.3 n. 3) Mar 120*, Mor 366.

*√ntn (see also *√ntb)   <ʔTn> y[ʔættén] a[ʔɛttén] sim impf 1s [ʔættén] possibly ~ [ʔittén]
    < *ʔantíni (§17.3 n. 3, §17.11.3, §17.21.1) Mor 185, Mar 139*.
    a[tén] sim impa ms [*same*] < *tín (§17.3 n. 3) Mar 139*.

*√nθr   <nTrn> y[næθrä́n] a[nǎ̆θarä́n] sim pf 3fp [næθrä́n] ~ [nǎ̆θærä́n] < *naθárā
    (§7.2 (δ) with n. 15, §15.2.13) Mor 127, Mar 139*.

*√nθr   <nṭr> ~ <ʔynṭr> sim impa ms [nǎ̆ṭǽr] ~ [(ʔ)inṭǽr] < *nǎ̆θúr (§17.18.1) Mar 39.

*√sbr   <sBrnʔ> a[sǎ̆várnä́] sim pf 1p [sǎ̆várnä] < *sabárnā (§7.2 (δ) n. 9) Mar 37,
    140*.

*√sgr   a[sǎ̆γä́] sim pf 3ms [sǎ̆γä́] < *sagára (§17.12.2) Mar 140*.

*√skn   <sKntyK> y[sækkæntíx] int pf 1s^2fs [*same*] < *sakkántǎ̆ki (§2.3.4.4 with
    n. 34, §16.2 TL (e′), §17.15.1 n. 65) Mor 147 n. 124.

    <sKnTwn> y[sækkæntű̆n] a[sakkentű̆n] int pf 2mp [sækkæntű̆n] ~
        [sækkentű̆n] < *sakkantű̆m ~ *sakkintű̆m (§2.3.4.4 n. 34, §17.11.3
        with n. 43, §17.15.1 n. 65) Mor 147 n. 124, Mar 142*.

    <sKnTyn> int pf 2mp^1s [sækkentín] < *sakkintű̆nī (§17.17.2 with n. 93) Mar
    58.

*√slq   <slwq> y&a[sǎ̆lű̆q] ~ <sqw> sim pf 3mp [sǎ̆lű̆q] ~ [sǽqū] < *saláqū (§17.9.2,
    §17.33 n. 159) Mor 126; Mar 37 n. δ, 142*.

*√smy   <smynhw> y[sæmminnǎ̆hű̆] int pf 3ms^3fp [sæmminnǎ̆hŰ̊] < *sammíya # h/
    ʔin(nV̊)húm (§16.2 TL (c)) Mor 326 with n. 70.

*√spd   t<ysPDwn> sim impf 3mp [yispǎ̆dű̆n] < *yaspudű̆na (§7.2 (γ), §17.9.2,
    §17.12.2) Mar 38.

*√spy   <TysTPy> y[tistǎ̆fí] sim rmp impf 2fs [*same*] < titsapiyína (§16.2 TL (k)) Mor
    264 with n. 102.

*√9bd   <9BDyT> ~ <9BDy> y[9ǎ̆vǽðiθ] ~ [9ævǒ̆í] sim pf 1s [9ǎ̆vǽðiθ] ~ [9ævǒ̆í] <
    *9abádt (§4.1.2, §17.6.2) Mor 125.

    <T9BDy> sim impf 2fs [ti9bǎ̆ǒ̆í] / [tæ9bǎ̆ǒ̆í] < *ta9bidű̆na (§§17.12.2) Mar
    38.

    <ʔy9ByD> a[ʔɛ9béð] sim impf 1s [ʔi9béð] / possibly [ʔæ9béð] < *ʔa9bídi
        (§12.2 with nn. 15 and 16, §17.11.3) Mar 129, 145*.

    <l9BDw> y[li9bǎ̆ǒ̆ű̆] a[lɛ9bǎ̆ǒ̆ű̆] sim impf 3mp [li9bǎ̆ǒ̆ű̆] < *ya9bidű̆na /
        la9bidű̆na (§12.2 with nn. 15 and 16) Mor 130, Mar 145.

    <n9ByD> y[ni9véð] a[na9béð] sim impf 1p [ni9béð] ~ [næ9béð] < *na9bídi
        (§12.2 with nn. 15 and 16, §17.11.3) Mor 130, Mar 145*.

    <9yByD> y[9ǎ̆véð] a[9ǎvéð] sim impa ms [9ǎvéð] possibly ~ [9evéð] /
        [9ívéð] < *9ǎ̆bíd (§9.3.1) Mar 38f, 54, 145*; Mor 131 with n. 44.
    a[liθ9ǎvéð] sim rmp impf 3ms [liθ9ǎ̆véð] < *yit9abídi / *lit9abídi (§17.23.3)
    Mar 145*.

*√9br   <9Brynn> a[9avrīnán] sim pf 1p [9ævrīnǽn] < *9abárnā (§17.17.2) Mar 37
    n. β, 146*.

    <ny9Br> y[ni9bǽr] sim impf 3ms [*same*] < *yi9bári (§9.3.1 n. 40) Mar 363.

*√9dy   <9Dw> y[9ǎ̆ǒ̆í] sim pf 3mp [*same*] < *9adáyū (§8.1.1 n. 1, §11.2) Mor 254.

*√9Wt   <9Wt> y[9æwwéθ] int pf 3ms [*same*] < *9awwíta (§11.1) Mor 221.

*√9yn   <9ynynn> y[9æyyǎ̆ninnǽn] int pf 1p [*same*] < *9ayyínnā (§17.17.2) Mor
    221.

<ly9ynn> y[lī9æyyenǽn] a[lə̆9ayyennán] int impf 1p [lī9æyyenǽn] ~
[lə̆9æyyen(n)ǽn] < *ni9ayyíni (§15.3.1.1 with n. 21) Mor 222, Mar
146*.

*√9kb <ʾy9KB> y[ʾæ99ækkǽv] a[ʾē9akkáv] int rmp 1s [ʾæ99ækkǽv] ~ [ʾē9ækkǽv]
< *ʾit9akkábi (§12. 2 n. 15, §17.11.3 n. 47) Mor 154 with n. 163, Mar 147*.

*√9l (< **√Rl) <9yyl> y[9ə̆yél] sim pf 3ms [*same*] < *9álla or more likely *9alíla
{*probably at first phonologically* */9alil+a/ *but subsequently reshaped to*
*/9ayil+a/} (§1.3 n. 12, §6.2.2) Mor 376.

    <9ylʾ> y[9æylā̆́] sim pf 3fs [*same*] < *9allát or more likely *9alilát {*prob-
ably at first phonologically* */9alil+at/ *but subsequently reshaped
to* */9ayil+at/} (§1.3 n. 12, §6.2.2) Mor 376.

    <ly9wl> y[lē9úl] sim impf 3ms [*same*] < *ya99úli / *la99úli (§9.3.1 n. 40)
Mor 376.

    <9wl> y&a[9ól] ~ y[9úl] sim impa ms [*same*] < *9úl (§6.2.2) Mor 215, 257;
Mar 129*.

    <9yl> y[9æyyél] a[9ayyél] int pf 3ms [9æyyél] < *9allíla (§6.2.1, §11.1) Mor
243, Mar 147*.

    <ʾ9lynhw> y[ʾæ9ə̆lĭnnə̆hū́] cau pf 3mpˆ3mp [ʾæ9ə̆lĭnnə̆hŪ] < *ha99ílū #
h/ʾin(nV̊)húm (§16.2 TL (d) n. 6) Mor 321.

*√9md (< **√Rmd) a[lēmoð] sim impf 3ms [*same*] < *ya9múdi / *la9múdi (§9.2.3.2)
Mar 88*.

*√9nš <ʾy9nš̂> y[ʾi99ə̆nǽš] sim rmp pf 3ms [*same*] < *hit9anáša (§17.11.3) Mor
140.

*√9ṣb <ʾy9ṣyBw> y[ʾi99ə̆ṣĭ̂vū] a[ʾi9ăṣĭ̂vū] sim rmp pf 3mp [ʾi9(9)ə̆ṣĭ̂vū] < *hit9aṣíbū
(§9.3.1) Mor 376, Mar 149*.

*√9qr <ʾy9qwr> y[ʾi99ə̆qū́r] ~ t<ʾyT9qrw> ~ t<ʾy9qrw> sim rmp pf 3mp [ʾi99ə̆qū́r]
~ [ʾi9ə̆qū́r] ~ [ʾi9(9)æqǽrū] < *hit9aqírū (§10) Mor 141, Mar 41.

*√9rq <Ty9yrwq> ~ <Ty9rwq> a[tɛ9ĕróq] ~ [tɛ9róq] sim impf 3fs [ti9ĭ̆róq] ~ [ti9róq]
< *ta9rúqi (§4.3, §17.23.3) Mar 38, 135*.

*√9śq a[ʾiθ9ăsáqt] ~ [ʾē9ăsáqt] sim rmp pf 2ms [ʾiθ9ə̆sǽqt] ~ [ʾē9ə̆sǽqt] < *hit9aśáqtā̆
(§17.11.3 n. 47) Mar 149*.

*√9θr <ʾy9Try> y[ʾi99ættǽrī] a[ʾi9attárī] int rmp pf 1s [ʾi9(9)ættǽrī] < *hit9aθθárt
(§9.3.1 n. 40) Mor 377, Mar 150*.

*√pd9 <PD9wh> ~ <PDywh> int pf 3mpˆ3ms [pæddə̆9úh] ~ [pæddə̆yúh] <
paddi9úhi (§9.2.3.2) Mar 150.

*√pys (< Greek *peys-*) <Pysnʾ> y[pæyyésnā] int pf 1s [*same*] as if < *payyíst (§7.2 (δ)
n. 9, §17.17.2 with n. 92) Mor 221.

*√pṭr <PṭrTynwn> y[fə̆ṭærtinnū́n] sim pf 2msˆ3fp {*fgm*} [pə̆ṭærtinnū́n] < *paṭártā̆
h/ʾin(nV̊)húm (§16.2 TL (e, f, f′), §17.15.1) Mor 292.

    a[ʾippə̆ṭū́r] sim rmp pf 3mp [*same*] < *hitpaṭírū (§17.9.2) Mar 150*.

*√plg <ʾyPlyGw> y&a[ʾippə̆lī́γū] sim rmp pf 3mp [*same*] < *hitpalígū (§10) Mor
141, Mar 151*.

*√pny <Pnw> y[pænnū́] int pf 3mp [*same*] < *pannáyū (§15.3.2, §17.9.2 n. 29) Mor
268.

*√prḥ a[pə̆rúaḥ] sim pf 3mp [pə̆rúæḥ] < *paráḥu (§17.16) Mar 152*.

*√prR (< **√prð)   <Pr9yn> y[pær9ín] ~ [pær9ǽn] ~ <Pr9n> sim impa ms^1s [*same*]
< *pắrúRnī (§2.3.4.4) Mor 296 with n. 35, Sokoloff 2002: 936.

*√prq   <lyPrwqynn> y[lifroqinnǽn] a[lifrǒqinnán] sim impf 3ms^1p [lifroqinnǽn] ~
[lifrŭqinnǽn] < *yapruqinnínā / *lapruqinnínā (§2.3.4.4, §15.5.1 with n. 40,
§15.2.2, §17.11.3) Mor 295; Mar 13, 153*.

*√prš   <ʾPrŝnhw> y[ʾæfrǎšinnǎhí] cau pf sms^3fp {*fgm*} [ʾæfrǎšinnǝhÚ] ~
[ʾæfrǝsinnǝhÍ] < *hapríša # h/ʾin(nV̆)húm ~h/ʾin(nV̆)hín (§16.2 TL (c))
Mor 302.

*√pśl   <lyPslwhw> sim impf 3mp^3ms [lifsǝlúhū] < *yapsulúhū / *lapsulúhū (§7.2
(ε)) Mor 295.

*√pšṭ   <Pŝṭw> y[pæašṭú] a[pǝšáṭū] sim pf 3mp [pæšṭú] ~ [pǝšǽṭū] < *pašáṭū
(§17.12.2) Mor 126, Mar 154*.

*√ptq   <PTqyh> y[pæθqéh] sim pf 3ms^3ms [*same*] < *pataqáhi (§17.15.1) Mor
291.

*√ṣby   <DyTyṣByyn> y[dīθiṣbǝyín] sbor sim impf 2fs [*same*] < *ðī́ # taṣbiyína
(§16.2 TL (κ)) Mor 256 with n. 37.

*√ṣWd   <ṣwD> y&s[ṣū́ð] sim pf 3mp [*same*] < *ṣắdū (§17.9.2) Mor 213, Mar 155*.

*√ṣWt   <syyT> y[ṣǝyéθ] sim pf 3ms [*same*] < *ṣắθa */ṣayit+a/ (§1.3 n. 12, §6.2.2)
Mor 211.

*√ṣ9r   <nṣṭ9r> y[niṣṭæ9ǽr] a[niṣṭa9(9)ár] int rmp impf 3ms and 1p [niṣṭæ9(9)ǽr] <
*yitṣa99ári and *nitṣa99ári (§9.3.1, §10) Mor 154, 380; Mar 156*.
a[ʾɛṣṭa9(9)ár] int impf 1s [ʾiṣṭæ9(9)ǽr] / [ʾæṣṭæ9(9)ǽr] < *ʾitṣa99ári
(§17.11.3) Mar 137*.

*√θl   a[ʾiṭṭallǝlīθū́n] <ʾyṭllyTw> y[ʾiṭṭællǝlīθū́] int rmp pf 2mp [ʾiṭṭællǝlīθū́(n)] <
hitθallaltū́m (§17.17.1 n. 84) Mar 117, Mor 364.

√θl9   a[ʾaṭlá9] ~ [ʾiṭlá9] cau pf 3ms [ʾæṭlǽ9] ~ [ʾiṭlé9] < haθlí9a (§12.2) Mar 118.

*√qbl   <qBylTwn> y[qæbbeltū́n] int pf 2mp^1s [*same*] < *qabbiltū́nī (§16.2 TL (eʹ))
Mor 299.
<nqBlyh> y[nīqǎbbǝléh] int impf 1p^3ms [*same*] < *niqabbilíhi (§15.3.1.1)
Mor 301.

*√qbr   <yqBrwnyh> a[yiqbǝrunnéh] sim impf 3mp^3ms [*same*] < yaqburunnáhi
(§7.2 (ε)) Mar 61, 157*.

*√qdm   <qDmwK> a[qaddǝmúx] int pf 3mp^2ms [qæddǝmúx] < *qaddimúka
(§2.3.4.3) Mar 58, 158*.
a[nǒqaddém] ~ [lǒqaddém] int impf 1p [nǒqæddém] ~ [lǒqæddém] < *niqad-
dími (§17.19) Mar 158*.
<lqDmw> y&a[liqdǝmú] cau impf 3mp [*same*] < *y(ih)aqdimúna ~
l(ih)aqdimúna (§12.2) Mor 380, Mar 158.

*√qWm   <qmT> y[qǽmt] a[qǒmt] sim pf 2ms [qǽmt] ~ [qǒmt] < *qámtå perhaps ~
qắmtå (§6.2.2, §15.2.1.4 n. 12) Mor 211, Mar 158.
<Tyqw> y[tīqú] ~ y&a[tēqú] sim impf 3fs [*same*] < *taqúmi (§15.3.1.1 n. 15,
§17.12.2) Mor 213 with n. 12, Mar 158*.
a[liqqǒmú] ~ [lēqūmū] sim impf 3mp [liqqǒmú] ~ [lēqūmú] / [lēqúmū] <
*yaqūmúna / *laqūmúna perhaps~ *yaqúmū / *laqúmū (§6.2.2
with n. 20) Mar 158*.

<qwm> y&a[qū́m] sim impa ms [*same*] < *qū́m* (§6.2.2) Mor 215, 25; Mar 147*.

    sim impa fs [*same*] < *qū́mī* or perhaps *qū́m* {*fgm*} (§17.9.2) Mor 131; Mar 51, 158*.

<ʾwqym> y&a[ʾōqém] cau pf 3ms [*same*] < *haqī́ma* (*/haqwim+a/) (§6.1.2) Mor 227, Mar 159*.

*√qly   <qlTh> y[qǝ̄lā̄θǽh] ~ [qæltǽh] sim pf 3fs^3fs [*same*] < *qalayátha* (§15.3.2) Mor 322 with n. 52.

*√qnʾ   a[qǝ̆nḗθ] sim pf 2ms [qǝ̆nḗT] < *qanáʾtā̊* (§5.3 n. 13) Mar 160*.

*√qṣ   <qṣ> y[qā́ṣ] sim pf 3ms [*same*] < *qáṣṣa* (§6.2.2) Mor 233.

    <ʾyTqṣṣw> y[ʾiθqǝ̆ṣǽṣū] sim rmp pf 3mp [*same*] < *hitqaṣáṣū* (§3.6 with n. 42) Mor 382.

*√qθr   <Tqtryh> y[tiqtǝ̆rḗh] sim impf 2ms^3ms [*same*] < *tiqθaríhi* (§2.3.4.4 n. 32) Mor 381.

*√qrʾ   <ʾqrynwhw> y[ʾæqrīnū́hū] cau pf 1p^3ms [*same*] < *haqriʾnuhu* (§2.3.4.3) Mor 328.

*√qrb   <qryByT> y[qāréviθ] a[qǝ̄réviθ] int pf 1s [qāréviθ] < *qarríbt* (§9.3.1) Mor 118, Mar 161*.

*√qr9   <Tqr9wnyh> y[tiqrǝ̆9unnḗh] sim impf 2mp^3ms [*same*] < *tiqra9unnáhi* (§7.2 (ε) with n. 22) Mor 296.

*√qš   a[qǝ̆šéšn] ~ [qaššēnán] sim pf 1p [qǝ̆šéšn] ~ [qæššēnǽn] < *qašíšnā* perhaps ~ *qášnā* (or possibly *qašáynā*) (§15.4 with (15U) and n. 32) Mar 163*.

*√qtl   a[qatlḗh] sim pf 3ms^3ms [qætlḗh] < *qataláhi* (§2.3.4.4 n. 32) Mar 159*.

    a[qǝ̆talinnū́n] sim pf 3ms^3mp [qǝ̆tælinnū́n] < *qatála* # *h/ʾin(nV̊)húm* (§17.15.1) Mar 159*.

    a[qǝ̆taltḗh] sim pf 1s^3ms [qǝ̆tæltḗh] < *qatáltǝ̆hi* (§15.2.1.4 n. 12) Mar 159*.

    a[qatlúah] ~ <qtlwhw> y[qætlū́hū] sim pf 3mp^3ms [qætlúæh] ~ [qætlū́hū] < *qatalū́hi* ~ *qatalū́hū* (§8.2.1, §8.2.2, §17.16) Mar 159*, Mor 293.

    a[qǝ̆talī̊nnū́n] ~ <qtlwnhw> y[qætlī̊nnǝ̆hŪ̊] sim pf 3mp^3mp [qǝ̆tælī̊nnū́n] ~ [qætlū̊nnǝ̆hŪ̊] < *qatálū* # *h/ʾin(nV̊)húm* (§16.2 TL̲ (s)) Mar 158*, Mor 293.

    a[tiqtól] sim impf 2ms [*same*] < *taqtúli* (§17.11.3) Mar 159*.

    a[ʾεqtǝlī̊n(ǝ̆)hő̊] ~ t[ʾεqtǝlinnū́n] sim impf 1s^3mp [ʾiqtǝlĪ̊n(ǝ̆)hŪ̊] ~ [ʾiqtǝlinnū́n] or perhaps [ʾæqtǝlī̊n(ǝ̆)hŪ̊] ~ [ʾæqtǝlinnū́n] < *ʾaqtúli* # *h/ʾin(nV̊)húm* (§17.15.1) Mar 159*.

    <qtwlyn> y[qǝ̆tulī́n] ~ <qtwln> a[qǝ̆tulṓn] sim impa fp [qǝ̆tulī́n] ~ [qǝ̆tulǽn] < *qǎtúlā* (§4.1.2 n. 10, §7.2 (δ) with n. 15, §15.2.1.3, §17.9.2, §17.11.3) Mor 131; Mar 8, 159*.

*√rgš   a[ʾargéšiθ] cau pf 1s [ʾærgéšiθ] < *hargíšt* (§15.2.2.2) Mar 164*.

*√rhq   <lyrhqynhw> y[līræhqī̊nnǝ̆hū́] int impf 3mp^3mp [*same*] < *yiraḥḥiqū́na* # *h/ʾin(nV̊)húm* (§17.15.1, §17.17.2) Mor 301.

*√rks   <ʾrKs> y[ʾirrǝ̆xǽs] a[ʾērǝ̆xás] sim rmp pf 3ms [ʾirrǝ̆xǽs] ~ [ʾērǝ̆xǽs] < *hitrakása* (§9.3.1 n. 40, §12.2 n. 4) Mor 383, Mar 165*.

*√rmy   <nyrmy> y[nirmḗ] sim impf 3ms [*same*] < *yirmáyi* (§9.3.1 n. 40) Mor 383.

*√rR (< **√rð)   <ʾyTr9> y[ʾittǝ̆rǽ9] a[ʾittǝ̆rá9] cau rmp pf 3ms [ʾittǝ̆rǽ9] ~ [ʾittūrǽ9] < *hitharráRa* (§63) Mor §11.21, Mar 166*.

*√rq   \<rqh> ~ \<rqqh> sim pf 3fs [ræqqą̄́] ~ [rə̆qǽqū] < *raqqát ~ *raqáqat (§3.3) Mar 49.

\<Tyrwq> y[tirróq] sim impf 2ms [*same*] < *tarrúqi (§9.3.1 n. 40) Mor 384.

*√śgʾ   \<sGʾy> y[sə̆ɣǽy] a[sə̆ɣáy] sim pf 1s [sə̆ɣǽy] < *śagíʾt (§17.2 with n. 2) Mor 252; Mar 52, 140*.

*√śky   \<TysTKy> y[tistæxī́] sim rmp impf 2ms [*same*] < titśakíyi (§16.2 TL (κ)) Mor 264 with n. 102.

*√šʾl (see also *√ʾšl)   \<šʾyl> y[šă̆ʾél] sim pf 3ms [*same*] < *šaʾíla (§17.15.1) Mor 384.

\<šʾylynhw> y[šə̆ʾelinnə̆hū́] sim pf 3ms^3mp [šə̆ʾelinnə̆hU̇́] < *šaʾíla ǂ h/ʾin(nV̇)húm (§7.4.1, §15.2.1.2, §16. 2 TL n. 11, §17.11.3, §17.15.1 with n. 64) Mor 291.

*√šb9   \<ʾšB9n> cau pf 3ms^1p [ʾæšbə̆9ǽn] < *hašbi9ánā (§16.2 TL (b)) Mar 58.

*√šbq   \<šBqny> y[šævqǽnī] sim pf 3ms^1s [*same*] < *šabaqánī (§12.2) Mor §15.11.

a[šə̆váqt] sim pf 2ms/2fs [šə̆vǽqt] < *šabáqtā̊ / *šabáqtī̊ (§16.2 TL (f)) Mar 168*.

\<šBqyn> a[šavqī́n] sim pf 3mp^1s [šævqī́n] < *šabaqū́nī (§17.17.2) Mar 58, 168*.

a[šə̆vaqūnə̆hő̆] sim pf 3mp^3mp [šə̆vaqūnə̆U̇́] < *šabáqū ǂ h/ʾin(nV̇)húm (§17.26 n. 136) Mar 168*.

\<šBqn> a[šə̆vqán] ~ \<šyBqn> sim impa ms^1s [šuvqǽn] ~ [šivqǽn] < *šăbúqnī (§17.25) Mar 60, 168*.

a[šavqīn(ə̆)hő̆] ~ \<šBqynhw> y[šævqinnə̆hű̆] sim impa ms^3mp [šævqī́n((n)ə̆)hU̇́] < šăbúq ǂ h/ʾin(nV̇)húm (§17.15.1) Mar 168*, Mor 296.

a[šavqúah] ~ \<šBqwhw> y[sqvqű̆hu] ~ \<šyBqwh> y[šævqű̆h] sim impa mp^3ms [šævqúæh] ~ [šævqű̆hū] ~ [šivqű̆h] ~ [šævqű̆h] < *šăbuqű̆hi ~ *šăbuqű̆hū (§8.1.3 n. 17, §17.16) Mar 168*, Mor 296f. with n. 3.

\<šBqyh> a[šavqíah] sim impa fs^3ms [šævqíæh] < *šăbuqī́hi (§17.25) Mar 61, 168*.

*√šbš   a[ʾištabbű̆š] int rmp pf 3mp [ʾištæbbű̆š] < *hitšabbášū (§17.9.2) Mar 168*.

*√šdy   a[šə̆ði̊nə̆hő̆] ~ [šə̆ðə̄nə̆hő̆] sim pf 3ms^3mp [šə̆ði̊nə̆hU̇́] ~ [šə̆ðānə̆hU̇́] < *šadíya ǂ h/ʾin(nV̇)húm ~ *šadáya ǂ h/ʾin(nV̇)húm (§16.2 TL (d), §17.15.1 n. 67) Mar 169*.

\<šDyTynhw> y[šə̆ðē̄θinnə̆hű̆] sim pf 3fs^3mp [šə̆ðē̄θinnə̆hU̇́] < *šadáyt ǂ h/ʾin(nV̇)húm (§17.15.1) Mor 322.

a[lišdinhő̆] sim impf 3ms^3mp [lišdinhU̇́] < *yišdáyi/lišdáyi ǂ h/ʾin(nV̇)húm (§17.26 n. 136) Mar 169*.

*√šdp   \<ʾyšDwP> y[ʾiššə̆ðű̆f] sim rmp pf 3mp [*same*] < *hitšadípū (§17.9.2) Mor 141.

*√šdr   \<šDrTyK> y[šæddærtǽx] int pf 1s^2ms {fgm ʾ} [šæddærtĪ̊́x] {ʾ} ~ [šæddærtǽx] < *šaddírtə̆ki {ʾ} ~ *šaddírtə̆ka (§2.3.2.4 n. 14, §16.2 TL (g)) Mor 299 with n. 47.

*√šhy   \<lšhynhw> y[læšhì̆nnə̆hű̆] cau impf 3ms^3fp {fgm} [læšhì̆nnə̆huU̇́] < *y(ih)ašhíyi / l(ih)ašhíyi ǂ h/ʾin(nV̇)húm (§16.2 TL (Iʾ)) Mor 329 with n. 80.

*√šwy   a[šawwinhṓ] int pf 1s^3mp [šæwwinhŰ] < **šawwī́t* ⁺ *h/ʔin(nV̊)húm* (§17.26
n. 136) Mor 169*.

<lyŝwyyK> int impf 3ms^2ms [līšæwwŏyǽx] < *yišawwiyíka / *lisawwiyíka
(§7.1) Mar 60.

*√škb   <ŝKyB> y&a[ŝŏxév] sim pf 3ms [*same*] < *šakíba (§4.2.2, §17.11.3) Mor
123, Mar 171*.

<ŝKyBʔ> y[šæxbǻ] sim pf 3fs [ŝŏxívā] ~ [šæxBǻ] < *šakíbat ~ *šakíbat
(§4.1.2, §12.2, §17.12.2) Mar 37, Mor 124 with n. 3.

<ŝKyBw> y&a[ŝŏxívū] sim pf 3mp [*same*] < *šakíbū (§17.11.3) Mor 126,
Mar 171*.

*√škḥ ('find')   <ʔŝKḥyh> a[ʔaškŏḥḗh] cau pf 3ms^3ms [ʔæškŏḥḗh] < *haškiḥáhi
(§4.2.2) Mar 171*.

<ʔŝKḥTyh> y[ʔæškæḥtḗh] cau pf 1s^3ms [*same*] < *haškíḥtŏhi (§15.2.2.3)
Mor §15.31.

<ʔŝKḥyTh> y[ʔæškŏḥḭθǽh] cau pf 1s^3fs [*same*] < *haškíḥtŏha (§15.2.2.2
with n. 20) Mor 303 with n. 67.

a[ʔaškaḥtinhṓ] ~ [ʔaškŏḥḭθinhṓ] cau pf 1s^3mp [ʔæškæḥtinhŰ] ~ [ʔæškŏḥḭθinhŰ]
< *haškíḥt ⁺ *h/ʔin(nV̊)húm* (§15.2.2.2 n. 20, §15.2.2.3 with (15D))
Mar 171*.

a[ʔaškúah] cau pf 3mp [ʔæškúaeh] < *haškíḥū)§17.9.2, §17.16) Mar 171*.

*√škḫ ('forget')   <ŝKhnynhw> y[ŝŏxæḥninnŏhű] a[ŝŏxaḥnin(ŏ)hṓ] sim pf 1p^3mp
[ŝŏxæḥnin((n)ŏ)hŰ] < *šakáḥnā ⁺ *h/ʔin(nV̊)húm* (§17.15.1 with n. 68) Mor
294, Mar 171*.

*√šlḥ   <slḥw> y[ŝŏlǽhű] sim pf 3mp [*same*] < *šaláḥu (§17.15.2 n. 77) Mor 126.

*√šly   <ʔŝTlyn> y[ʔištŏlǽyn] ~ [ʔištŏlī́n] sim rmp pf 1p [*same*] < *hitšaláynā ~
*hitšalínā (§8.1 n. 1) Mor 264 with n. 100.

*√šmwd9   (< **š+ √mwd9)   a[ʔištŏmōðæ9nŏhī] quinquiradical rmp 1p^3ms
[ʔištŏmōðæ9núhī] as if < *hitšamawda9núhī {*fossilized cau rmp denominal
from* mōða9} (§2.3.4.3 n. 30) Mar 120*.

*√šmṭ   a[ʔištŏmeṭθán] sim rmp 3fs^1s [ʔištŏmeṭTæn] < *hitšamiṭátnī (§15.3.2 n. 30)
Mar 173*.

*√šm9   <ŝm9yT> ~ [ŝŏmá9ī] sim pf 1s [ŝŏmǽ9iθ] ~ [ŝŏmǽ9ī] < *šamí9t (§17.6.2,
§17.15.1) Mar 37, 88*.

<lyŝTm9n> y[lištæm9ǽn] a[lištam9ŏ́n] simrmp impf 3fp [lištæm9æn] ~
[lištæm9ǽn] < *yitšami9ánna ~ *yitšami9ǽna / *litšami9ánna ~ *litšami9ǽna
(§10) Mor 386, Mar 173*.

*√šny   a[šannīnŏhṓ] int pf 1p^3mp [šænnīnēhŰ] < **šannī́nā* ⁺ *h/ʔin(nV̊)húm* (§16.2
T͟L (d), §17.15.1) Mar 174*.

*√špl   <ŝPylyT> y&a[ŝŏféliθ] sim pf 1s [*same*] < **šapī́lt* (§4.1.2, §15.2.1.1, §17.11.3)
Mor 125, Mar 174*.

*√špṣ   <ŝPṣynhw> y[šæppŏ́sinnŏhű] int pf 3ms^3fp {*fgm*} [*same*] < *šappíṣa ⁺
h/ʔin(nV̊)húm (§16.2 T͟L (p)) Mor 298 with n. 42.

*√šql   a[šaqlḗh] sim pf 3ms^3ms [šæqlḗh] < *šaqaláhi (§12.2) Mar 175*.

<ŝqlT> ~ <ŝqlh> sim pf 3fs [ŝŏqǽlæθ] ~ [ŝŏqǽlā] / possibly [šæqlǻ] < *šaqálat
possibly ~ *šaqalát (§17.12.2) Mar 37.

<šqlT'> y[šɔ̆qæltḗh] sim pf 3fs^3ms [šɔ̆qǽltḗ] ~ [šɔ̆qǽltḗh] *šaqaláthi
(§15.3.2 n. 30) Mor 292 with n. 5.

a[šɔ̆qáliθ] ~ [šɔ̆qálī] sim pf 1s [šɔ̆qǽliθ] ~ [šɔ̆qǽlī] < *šaqált (§12.2) Mar
175*.

<šqlTynhw> y[šɔ̆qæltinnɔ̆hǘ] ~ <šqlynhw> y[šɔ̆qælinnɔ̆hǘ] ~ [šæqlinnɔ̆hǘ]
sim pf 1s^3mp [šɔ̆qæltinnɔ̆hǗ] ~ [šɔ̆qælinnɔ̆hǗ] ~ [šæqlinnɔ̆hǗ] <
*šaqált # h/'in(nV̊)húm (§16.2 TL (d) n. 6 and (s)) Mor 2903 with
n. 13.

<šqlwh> y[šæqlǘh] sim pf 3mp^3ms [same] < *šaqalǘhi (§17.16) Mor 293.

<šqlynhw> y[šæqlĭnnɔ̆hǘ] sim pf 3mp^3mp [šæqlĭnnɔ̆hǗ] < *šaqálu #
h/'in(nV̊)húm (§16.2 TL (d) n. 6 and (s)) Mor 294.

a[šɔ̆qalinhő] ~ [šaqlinhő] <šqlynhw> y[šæqlinnɔ̆hǘ] sim pf 1p^3mp
[šɔ̆qælinhǗ] ~ [šæqlin(nɔ̆)hǗ] < *šaqálnā # h/'in(nV̊)húm (§16.2
TL (d) with n. 6, §17.15.1 with n. 68, §17.17.1 n. 84, §17.17.2) Mar
175*, Mor 294.

<lšqwlynhw> y[lišqolinnɔ̆hǘ] <lšqlynhw> y[lišqɔ̆linnɔ̆hǘ] a[lišqɔ̆linhő] sim
impf 3ms^3mp [lišqolinnɔ̆hǗ] ~ [lišqɔ̆lin(nɔ̆)hǗ] < *yašqúli /
lašqúli # h/'in(nV̊)húm (§17.11.3, §17.15.1) Mor 295, Mar 175*.

<Tšqwl> y[tišqól] ~ [tišqúl] sim impf 3fs [same] <*tašqúli (§17.11.3) Mor
130.

<'šqwl> y['æšqól] <'(y)šqwl> a['ᵉšqól] sim impf 1s ['æšqól] ~ ['išqól] <
*'ašqúli (§11.1 n. 1, §12.2 with n. 15 and 16, §17.11.3) Mor 121;
Mar 38, 175*.

<'šqlyh> y['æšqɔ̆lḗh] sim impf 1s^3fs {fgm} ['æšqɔ̆lḗh] ~ ['æšqɔ̆lǽh] <
*'ašqulíhi ~ *'ašqulíha (§16.2 TL (l)) Mor 295.

<šqwly> y&a[šɔ̆qúlī] sim impa fs [same] < *šắqúlī (§17.11.3) Mor 131, Mar
175*.

*√šqr <'yŝTqwr> y['ištæqqǘr] int rmp pf 3mp [same] < *hitšaqqárū (§17.9.2) Mor
154.

*√šry <šryTwh> y[šɔ̆rē̆θǘhā] ~ [šɔ̆rī̆θǘhā] sim pf 2mp^3fs [same] < *šaraytǘhā ~
*šarītǘhā (§8.1.1 n. 1) Mor 323 with n. 55.

<lyŝTrw> y[lištɔ̆rǘ] sim rmp impf 3fp {fgm} [same] < *yitšarayǘna /
*litšarayǘna (§16.2 TL (m)) Mor 294.

*√šty <yŝTy> y['išθî́] ~ ['æštî́] sim pf 3ms [(')išTî́] ~ [(')æšTî́] < *šatíya (§17.18.1)
Mor 251 with n. 7.

a['ištē̆θḗh] sim pf 1s^3ms [(')išTē̆θḗh] < *šatáytɔ̆hi (§17.18.1) Mar 176*.

<TŝTwn> y[tištû́n] ~ [tištő́n] sim impf 3fp {fgm} [same] < *tištayǘna (§8.1.1
n. 1) Mor 251 with n. 45.

*√štq <ŝTw> ~ <'yŝTw> sim impa mp [šɔ̆θő́] ~ [(')išTő́] < *šitáyū (§17.18.1) Mar 54.

<ŝTyq> ~ <'yŝTyq> sim pf 3ms [šɔ̆θéq] ~ [(')išTéq] < *šatíqa (§17.18.1) Mar
31.

<ŝTyqy> y&a[šɔ̆θíqī] ~ <ŝTwqy> y&a[šɔ̆θúqī] sim pf 1s [same] < *šatíqt ~ *
šatúqt (§17.11.3) Mor 125 with n. 11, 388; Mar 176*.

*√tb9 <TB9Tynhy> y[tɔ̆væ9tinnɔ̆hî́] sim pf 3fs^3fp [tɔ̆væ9tinnɔ̆hî́] < *tabá9at #
h/'in(nV̊)hín (§16.2 TL (e)) Mor 292.

*√thw   \<DThww> y[dǧθæhhǯwǘ] sbor int pf 3mp [*same*] < *ðī́ # tahhiwǘ* (§17.34 n. 162) Mor 267.

        \<nThww> y[nǧθæhhǯwǘ] int impf 3mp [*same*] < *yitahhiwǘna* (§17.34 n. 162) Mor 267.

*√tly   \<ʾyTly> y[ʾætlǽy] ~[ʾætlī́] {*fgm*} cau impa fs [ʾiθlǽy] ~ [ʾiθlī́] ~ [ʾæθlǽy] ~ [ʾæθlī́] < *hatláyī ~ *hatlī́* (§16.2 <u>TL</u> (o)) Mor 273 with n. 150.

*√tl9   \<ʾTly9> y[ʾæθlíæ9] cau pf 3ms [*same*] < *hatlī́9a* (§17.16, §17.28) Mor 157.

*√tpś   a[tafsúah] sim pf 3mp^3ms [tæfsúæh] < *tapaśúhi* (§17.16) Mar 179*.

        \<TPsyTwh> a[tasfsīθúah] ~ \<TPsTwh> sim pf 2mp^3ms [tæfsīθúæh] ~ [tǧfæstúæh] < *tapaśtúhi* (§16.2 <u>TL</u> (e′), §17.17.2) Mar 59, 179*.

        y[tæfsīθúhā] sim pf 2mp^3fs [*same*] < *tapaśtúhā* (§16.2 <u>TL</u> (e′)) Mor 194.

        a[tifsḗh] sim impa ms^3ms [*same*] < *tǎpúshi* (§17.25) Mar 179*.

        \<TPśwhw> y[tifsúhū] ~ \<TPswhw> y[tæfsúhū] sim impa mp^3ms [*same*] < *tǎpusúhū* (§16.2 <u>TL</u> (e′) with n. 9) Mor 296.

*√tqn   \<lyTqnw> y[līθæqqǧnǘ] int impf 3mp [*same*] < *yitaqqinǘna / *litaqqinǘna* (§15.3.1.1) Mor 148.

*√θbr   \<TBrʾ> y[tæbbǧrǘ] int pf 3fs [*same*] < *θabbirát* (§4.2.2) Mor 146.

*√θWb   \<ʾyTwTB> y[ʾittōθǽv] a[ʾittōθǽv] cau rmp pf 3ms [ʾittōθǽv] < *hithaθǽba* (*/hit+ha+θwab+a/) (§6.1.2 with (6C), §6.3) Mor 219, Mar 177*.

*√θny   \<Tnw> y[tǧnǘ] sim pf 3mp [*same*] < *θanáyū* (§8.1.1) Mor 254.

        ta[tǧnáynǘ] sim pf 1p [tǧnǽynā] < *θanáynā* (§11.2 with n. 13) Mar 178*.

        a[tǧnān(ǧ)hḗ] sim pf 1p^3fp [tǧnæn(ǧ)hī́] < *θanáynā #h/ʾin(nV̊)hín* (§17.15.1 with nn. 68 and 69) Mar 178*.

*√θql   \<ʾTqyl> y[ʾittǧqī́l] sim rmp pf 3ms [*same*] < *hitθaqíla* (§10) Mor 142.

        a[ʾittǧqī̊lā] sim rmp pf 3fs [ʾittǧqī̊lā] < *hitθaqílat* (§10) Mar 179*.

Mandaic

*√ʾzl   \<azil> ~ \<ezil> ~ \<ezal> sim impa ms [ezál] ~ [ezál] ~ [ezál] < *ʾǎzíl ~ *ʾízál* (§17.23.3 (17.23D)) DM 12.

*√ʾḥð (< **√ʾXð)   \<ahadtinun> sim pf 1s^3mp [ahaðtennón] < *ʾaḥáðt # h/ʾin(nV̊)húm* (§7.14) Mal 345.

*√ʾkl   \<akaliun> sim pf 3mp [axalyṓn] < *ʾakálū* (§2.3.4.3) Macm 263.

        \<nikul> t[níxxol] sim impf 3ms [nikkól] < *yaʾkúli* (§9.2.1.2) Mal 284.

        \<ekul> sim impf 1s [ekkól] < *ʾaʾkúli* (§12.2) Macm 297.

        \<akul> ~ \<ekul> sim impa ms [axól] ~ [exól] < *ʾǎkúl* (§17.23.3 (17.23D)) DM 17.

        \<etkil> sim rmp pf 3ms [etKél] < *hitʾakíla* (§10 with n. 10) Macm 301.

        \<aukil> cau pf 3ms [okkél] < *haʾkíla* (§9.2.3.2) Macm 299.

*√ʾmr   \<amar> m[émar] sim pf 3ms [amár] < *ʾamára* (§9.2.3.2, §17.23.3 (17.23D)) Macm 296, 500.

        \<amarilH> t[amaríllī] sim pf 1s^pp(3ms) [amarı̊llī́] < *ʾamárt # líhi* (§17.15.2 with (17.15C)) Mal 341.

        \<amarilkun> sim pf 1s^pp(2mp) [amarellǧxón] < *ʾamárt # lakúm* (§15.2.1.1 n. 5, §17.15.1 n. 75) DM 23, Nm 241.

        \<amar> ~ \<amariun> sim pf 3mp [amár] ~ [amaryṓn] < *ʾamárū* (§17.9.2) Mal 348.

<(a)marulH> t[(a)marúllī] sim pf 3mp^pp(3ms) [(a)marullî] < *ʔamárū ̊# líhi (§17.11.3, §17.15.2 with (17.15C)) Mal 282.

<amarulia> t[amarólle] sim pf 3mp^pp(1s) [amarollî] < *ʔamárū ̊# lî (§17.15.2 with (17.15C) and n. 79) Mal 282.

<(a)martulH> t[(a)martóllī] sim pf 2mp^pp(3ms) [(a)martollî] < ʔamartúnna ̊# líhi (§17.11.3, §17.15.2 with (17.15C)) Mal 282.

<nimar> t[nímmar] sim impf 3ms [nimmár] < *yaʔmúri (§9.2.1.1 with n. 13, §9.2.1.2, §9.2.3.2) Macm 91, 113.

<amur> ~ <amar> sim impa ms [amór] ~ [amár] < *ʔămúr (§17.23.3 (17.23D)) DM 23.

<etmar> t[etmar] sim rmp pf 3ms [etmár] < *hitʔamíra (§9.2.3.1 with n. 29) Macm 90.

*√ʔsr <asarinhan> sim pf 3ms^1p [asarenhán] < ʔasaránā (§7.4.2 n. 29) Nm 279.

<estar> t[éstar] sim rmp pf 3ms [esTár] < *hitʔasíra (§10 with n. 12) DM 30.

*√ʔp <apun> sim pf 3mp [appón] < *ʔáppū (§7.2 ( )) Mal 350.

*√ʔpk (< **√hpk) <apku> ~ <apkuia> sim pf 3mp^3fs {fgm} [afKū́] ~ [afKū́y] < *ʔapakū́hā ~ *ʔapakū́hī (§16.2 M (h')) Nm 279.

*√ʔšd <eštid> t[éšted] sim rmp pf 3ms [ešTéð] < *hitʔašída (§10 with n. 12) DM 40, Macm 90.

*√ʔty <atatlun> ~ <atatalun> sim pf 3fs^pp(3mp) [aθā̊θlón] ~ [aθā̊θallón] < *ʔatáyat ̊# lahúm (§17.15.2 with (17.15C)) Mal 328.

<etilH> sim pf 1s^pp(3ms) [eθíllî] < *ʔatít ̊# líhi (§17.15.2 with (17.15C)) Mal 343.

<ata> sim impa ms [aθá̊] < ʔítáy or perhaps *ʔítáʔ (§8.1.3 n. 15) Macm 33.

<atian> sim impa fp [aθyā̊n] < *ʔatíyā (§7.2 (δ)) Mal 656.

<atia> int/cau pf 3ms [attî] < *ʔattíya / *haʔtíya (§5.1 n. 1, §9.2.1.1 n. 15) DM 42.

<aitia> t[éyθī] cau pf 3ms [eyTî] < *haʔtíya (§11.2) Mal 282.

<aitiun> ~ <atiun> cau~ int/cau pf 3mp^1s [eyTyū́n] ~ [atyū́n] < *ʔattiyū́nī ~ **haʔtiyū́nī (§9.2.1.1 with n. 15) DM 42.

*√bhθ <abhittinun> cau pf 1s^3mp [aβheθtennón] < *habhíθt ̊# h/ʔin(nV̊)húm (§15.3.1.2, §15.3.2 n. 30) Macm 294.

*√bhr <bihrH> sim pf 3ms^3ms [behrî] < *baharáhi (§17.10) DM 53.

<bhur> sim impa ms [bŏhór] < *băḥúr (§15.4 with (15V)) DM 53.

<bhurinun> sim impa ms^3mp [bŏhorennón] < *băḥúr ̊# h/ʔin(nV̊)húm (§15.4 with (15U)) Nm 269.

<etibhart> ~ <etibhirt> sim rmp pf 2ms [īθeBhárt] ~ [īθeBhírt] < *hitbahírta (§17.28) Mal 462.

*√bṭl <nibaṭil> t[nībáṭṭel] ~ [nibbáṭṭel] int impf 3ms [nīβaṭṭél] ~ [nibbaṭṭél] < *yibaṭṭíli (§15.3.1.1, §15.4) Macm 128.

*√bly <balinhun> int pf 1p^3mp [ballî̊nhón] < *ballî̊nā ̊# h/ʔin(nV̊)húm (§17.15.1) Nm 291.

*√brk <birku> sim pf 3mp [berKū́] < *barákū or perhaps *barakū́ (§4.1.2) Mal 345f.

<brakinkun> sim pf 3ms^2mp [bŏraxenxón] < *barrikakúm (§15.5.1) Nm 269.

<nibrikinan> ~ <nibrakinan> ~ <nibirkinan> sim impf 3ms^1p [neβbrăxennán]
~ [nīβerKennán] < *yabrukínā (§15.5.1 n. 41) Nm 279.

<barik> t[bárrex] int pf 3ms [barréx] < *barríka (§9.3.1) Macm 264.

*√bšqr   <bašqartH> ~ <bašqirtH> quad pf 1s^3ms [bašqartî̆] ~ [bašqertî̆] < *bašqírtăhi (§15.4 with (15U)) DM 71.

*√gb   <egababH> sim impf 1s^3ms [ī̆γaBăβî̆] < *ʔigbabíhi (§6.2.2.1 n. 27) DM 79.

<etigbib> sim rmp pf 3ms [ī̆θeGBéβ] < *hitgabíba (§4.4.1 with n. 23, §6.3) Macm 322, Mal 454.

<etgibat> sim rmp pf 3fs [eθgebbáθ] < *hitgabibát (§6.3) Macm 322.

*√gbl   <etgiblat> sim rmp pf 3fs [eθgeβláθ] < *hitgabilát (§12.2) Macs 266.

*√gWr   <tigirun> t[tī̆gérron] sim impf 2mp [tī̆yerrón] < *tagūrúnna (§6.2.2.1 with (6D)) Nm 249, Mal 545f.

*√dgr   <edgar> t[édgar] sim rmp pf 3mp [edGár] < *hitdagírū (§10) Macm 267.

*√dWr   <dartbH> sim pf 2ms^pp(3ms) [dart(ă)Bî̆] < *dárta ⸗ *bíhi* (§17.15.2 with (17.15C)) Mal 335.

*√dḥy   <dhunan> sim pf 3mp^1p [dăhonnán] < **daḥayú̆na* (§7.2 (ζ)) Macm 370.

*√drk   <adriktlin> cau pf 2ms^pp(3fp) [aðrext(ă)lén] < *hadríktă ⸗ *lahín* (§17.15.2 (17.15C)) DM 114.

*√ðkr   <leiadkar> cau impf 1p [liy(y)aðkár] < **n(ih)aðkíri* (§17.19) Nm 216.

*√hwy   <hua> t[hówā̆] ~ [éhwā̆] sim pf 3ms [hăwā̆] < *hawáya (§8.1.1 n. 6) Mal 310.

<huitbH> ~ <huitibH> sim pf 2ms^pp(3ms) [hăwĕ̆Tbî̆] ~ [hăwēTī̆Bî̆] < *hawáytă ⸗ *bíhi* (§17.15.2 with (17.15C)) Malone 1998a: 13.

<huen> ~ <he(n)> sim pf 3fp [hăwî̆n] ~ [hî̆(n)] < *hawíyā (§7.2 (δ) n. 21) Nm 267.

<huaitun> sim pf 2mp [hăweyTón] < **hawaytú̆m* (§9.2.3.2) Macm 335.

<huinin> ~ <huainin> sim pf 1p [hăwī̆nî̆n] ~ [hăweynî̆n] < **hawî̆nā* ~ *hawáynā (§8.1.1 n. 1) Nm 264.

<lehuia> ~ <nihuia> ~ <lihia>~ <nihia> sim impf 3ms [lehwî̆] ~ [nehwî̆] ~ [lī̆hî̆] ~ [nī̆hî̆] < *yihwáyi / *lihwáyi and/or *yahwíyi / *lahwíyi (§17.32 with (17.32A)) Nm 267, 268 with n. 1.

<nihuilak> t[nahwî̆lax] sim (short) impf 3ms^pp(2ms) [nehwī̆lắx] < **yahwíy(i)* ⸗ *láka* / **yihwáy(i)* ⸗ *láka* (§17.15.2 (17.15C)) Mal 284.

<nihuilkun> t[nehwî̆lxon] sim (short) impf 3ms^pp(2mp) [nehwī̆lxón] < **yahwíy(i)* ⸗ *lakúm* / **yihwáy(i)* ⸗ *lakúm* (§17.15.2 (17.15C)) Mal 284.

<ehuia> sim impf 1s [ehwî̆] < *ʔahwíyi / *ʔihwáyi (§12.2) DM 133.

<nihun> ~ <nihu> ~ <nehu> sim impf 3mp [nī̆hő̆n] (or possibly [nehwő̆n]) ~ [nī̆hő̆] < *yihwayúnna (§17.12.2) Nm 228.

*√hWq   (plausibly < **√9Wq, cf. Malone 1985: 113)

<tihqun> ~ <tihiqun> sim impf 2ms [tehqón]/the(h)ăqón] ~ [teh(h)ăqón]/ [tī̆heqqón] < *tahūqúnna (§6.2.2.1 with (6D)) DM 137.

*√hnʔ   <hnatalH> sim pf 3fs^pp(3ms) [hănă̊θallî̆] < **haná̓at* ⸗ *líhi* (§13, §17.15.2 with (17.15C)) Malone 1998a: 12

<hnalia> sim pf 3fs^pp(is) [hănă̊llî̆] < **haná̓at* ⸗ *lî̆* (§17.15.2 with (17.15C)) Malone 1998a: 12.

*√wdy <audibun> cau pf 3fp^pp(3mp) [oddīBón] < *hawdíyā ̊# bahúm (§7.2 (δ)
n. 20) Nm 261.

*√wdl (< **√wld) <iidlat> m[yédlat] ~ <iadlat> sim pf 3fs [yeðláθ] ~ [yaðláθ] <
*wadalát (§11.2 n. 17, §14.2 n. 20, §17.34) Macm 13, 131, 445.

<etiadal> t[etyáddal] int rmp pf 3ms [eθyaddál] < *hitwaddála (§17.34)
Macm 95.

*√wd9 <eda> t[ī́ða] sim pf 3ms [īðá̊] < *wadá9a (§14.2) Mal 310.

<edun> t[íddun] sim pf 3mp perhaps [īðón] but possibly [iddón] (§14.2 n. 20)
Macm 135.

<edanin> t[īdánnīn] sim pf 1p [īðannī́n] < *wadá9nā (§14.2) Mal 370.

*√whb <ehab> t[éhaβ] sim pf 3ms [eháβ] < *wahába (§14.2, §17.11.3, §17.23.3) Mal
280.

<iahablan> sim pf 3ms^pp(1p) [yŏhaβlán] < *wahába ̊# lánā (§17.15.2 with
(17.15C), §17.23.3) Nm 245.

<iahbat> t[yǽhβat] sim pf 3fs [yahBáθ] < *wahabát (§14.2 n. 20, §22.3)
Macm 97.

<ehabalH> t[ehaβállī] sim pf 3fs^pp(3ms) [ehaβallī́] < *wahábat ̊# líhi
(§17.15.2 with (17.15C)) Macm 97, Mal 326.

<iahbit> t[yéhβīt] ~ [éhbīt] sim pf 1s [yahBī́θ] (/[yehBī́θ]ʔ) ~ [ehBī́θ] <
*wahábt (§12.2, §14.2 n. 20) DM 189, Macm 97.

<ehabilH> t [ehaβillī] sim pf 1s^pp(3ms) [ehaβillī́] < *wahábt ̊# líhi (§14.2)
Mal 341.

<nihba> sim impf 3fp [nĭhBá̊] / [nehBá̊] < *yihabánna (§17.7) Macm 309.

<hab> sim impa mss [háβ] < *háb (§17.15.2 with (17.15C)) DM 189.

<(a)hbalia> sim impa ms^pp(1s) [hə̆βālī́] ~ [ahBālī́] < *habá̊ # lī́ (§2.3.4.1
with n. 17) Nm 246.

<(a)hbalan> sim impa ms^pp(1p) [hə̆βālán] ~ [ahBālén] < *habá̊ ̊# lánā
(§17.15.2 with (17.15C)) DM 189.

<euhbuia> ~ <ehbuia> sim impa mp^3ms [ohBŭ́y] ~ [ehBŭ́y] < *habŭ́hī
(§17.25 n. 133) Nm 278.

<ethib> t[étheβ] sim rmp pf 3ms [ethéβ] < *hitwahíba (§14.2 n. 20) Mal 97.

*√wmʔ <ema> ~ <iama> sim pf 3ms [emá̊]/[īmá̊] ~ [yămá̊] < *wamáʔa (§14.2 n. 20)
DM 192.

<emalia> ~ <emilia> sim pf 3ms^pp(1s) [emālī́]/[īmālī́] ~ [emīlī́]/[īmīlī́] <
*wamáʔa ̊# lī́ (§17.15.2 with (17.15C)) Mal 314.

*√wqd <niqad> ~ <niqud> sim impf 3ms [nīqáð]/[neqqáð] ~ [nīqóð]/[neqqóð] <
*yiqádi ~ *yaqúdi (§17.7) Macm 309.

*√wqr <niqar> sim impf 3ms [nīqár]/[neqqár] < *yiqári (§17.7) Macm 309.

*√wθb <etib> t[ī́teβ] ~ [íteb] sim pf 3ms [īθéβ] < *waθíba (§14.2) Mal 308.

<iatbat> t[yétβat] sim pf fs [yaθBáθ](/[yeθBáθ]ʔ) < *waθíbat (§14.2 n. 20)
Macm 97.

<etbit> t[étβīt] ~ [ítβīt] sim pf 1s [eθBī́θ] ~ [īθBī́θ] < *waθíbt (§14.2) Mal 339.

<nitib> sim impf 3ms [nīθéβ]/[nettéβ] < *yaθíbi (§17.7) Macm 309.

<nitbun> sim impf 3mp [nīθBón]/[netBón] < *yaθibúnna (§17.7) Macm 309.

<tib> ~ <etib> sim impa ms [téβ] ~ [īθéβ]/[eθéβ] < *θíb (§17.33) Macm 310.

<autib> t[ótteβ] cau pf 3ms [ottéβ] < *hawθíba (§11.2 with n. 17) DM 194, Mal 282.

<autban> ~ <eutban> t[ótban] cau pf 3ms^1s [otBán] < *hawθibánī (§11.2 with n. 17) DM 194, Mal 282.

<autibuia> ~ <autbuia> t[ottébūy] ~ [ótbūy] cau pf 3mp^3ms [ottə̆βűy] ~ [otBűy] < *hawθibűhī (§11.2 with n. 17) DM 194, Mal 283.

*√zbn <zabin> t[zábben] int pf 3ms [zabbén] < *zabbína (§17.11.3) Mal 282f.

*√zky <nizkia> sim impf 3ms [nezkî́] < *yazkíyi (§6.2.2.1 n. 28) DM 168.

<ulanizikiun> conj negative sim impf 3mp [ūlānīzeKyón] < *wā=lắ ⫰ yazkiyúnna (§6.2.2.1 n. 28) DM 168.

*√zmr <latizmrun> ~ <latizimrun> negative sim impf 2mp [lāTezmə̆rón] ~ [lāTīzemrón] < *lắ ⫰ tazmurúnna (§6.2.2.1 (6D) with n. 29) DM 169.

*√zqr <ezdaqar> int rmp pf 3ms [ezdaqqár] < *hitzakkára (§10) Malone 1999: 251.

*√zrmby <nizdrambia> quinquiradical impf 3ms [nezdə̆rambî́] < *yitz(ə̆)rambíyi / *yitz(ə̆)rambáyi (§1.1.2 n. 8) DM 171, Macm 251.

*√ḥbl (< **√Xbl)   <hbal> sim pf 3ms [ḥə̆βál] < *ḥabála (§17.8) DM 129.

<hiblat> sim pf 3fs [heβláθ] < *ḥabalát (§12.2) DM 129.

<hamblat> int pf 3fs [hambə̆láθ] < *ḥabbilát (§4.4.1 n. 23) DM 129.

<ethambal> int rmp pf 3ms [eθhambál] < *hitḥabbála (§17.8) DM 129.

*√ḥð̣r <hadariun> sim pf 3mp [ḥă̆ðaryő̃n] < *ḥaðárū (§17.2.3.3) DM 131.

<ehdar> sim pf 1s [ehdár] < *ʾaḥð̣úri / *ʾiḥð̣ári (§12.2) 131.

*√ḥzy <hza> m[hézẵ] sim pf 3ms [ḥə̆zẵ] < *ḥazáya (§9.2.4) Macm 87, 571.

<hzinun> sim pf 3ms^3mp [hæzennón]/[ḥə̆žĭnnón] < *ḥazáya ⫰ h/ʾin(nV̊)húm or possibly *ḥazíya ⫰ h/ʾin(nV̊)húm (§17.15.1) Macm 368.

<hzit> m[hézet] t[ézhet] ~ <hzait> sim pf 2ms [ḥə̆zḗT] ~ [ehzḗT] ~ [ḥə̆zéyT] < *ḥazáytẵ (§11.2 with n. 16) DM 138; Macm 119, 350; Mal 281.

<hzitilH> t[ḥə̆zītíllî] sim pf 1s^pp(3ms) [ḥə̆zīθíllî] < *ḥazít ⫰ líhi (§17.15.2 with (17.15C)) Mal 282.

<hzun> m[hézōn] sim pf 3mp [ḥə̆zṍn] < *ḥazáyū (§11.2 with n. 16) Macm 334, 350.

<ehzia> t[éhzī] sim pf 3fp [ehzî́] < *ḥazíyā (§7.2 (δ) with n. 21) Mal 362.

<hzia> m[hézī] sim impa ms [ḥə̆zî́] < *ḥăzî́ (§8.1.3) Macm 336, 352.

<hzai> m[héze] sim impa fs [ḥə̆zḗ] < *ḥăzáyī (§8.1.3, §11.2) DM 138; Macm 336, 352.

<hzunin> sim impa mp^3fp [ḥə̆zŏ̃nnén] < *ḥĭzáyū ⫰ h/ʾin(nV̊)hín (§8.1.1) Macm 374.

*√ḥWl <ehaial> int rmp pf 3ms [eh(h)ayyál] / [īhayyál] < *hitḥayyála (§10) Macm 267.

*√ḥṭʾ (< **√Xṭʾ) <nihṭia> sim impf 3ms [nehṭî́] < *yiḥṭáʾi (§17.10) DM 140.

*√ḥy(y) <hia> sim pf 3ms [ḥə̆yắ] < *ḥayáya (§11.2 n. 16) DM 140.

<nihiia> t[néhyī] sim impf 3ms [nehyî́] < *yiḥyáyi (§11.2) DM 141, Mal 284.

*√ḥml <lahamlat> negative sim pf 3fs [lāhamláθ] < *lắ ⫰ ḥamalát (§12.2) DM 149.

*√ḥp <hup> sim impa ms [hóf] < *ḥúp (§3.3) Macm 318.

*√ḥṣb <hṣab> ~ <hṣub> ~ <ṣub> sim pf 3mp [ḥə̆ṣáβ] ~ [ḥə̆ṣű́β] ~ [ṣű́β] < *ḥaṣábū (§9.2, §17.9.2, §17.33 n. 159) DM 151.

Mandaic 621

*√ḥrb (< **√Xrb) <ahribiun> cau impa mp [ahreβyṓn] < *haḥríbū (§2.3.4.2 with n. 18) Macm 275.

*√ḥšb <nihšabinakun> ~ <hihišbunkun> sim impf 3mp^2mp [nehsə̆βīnăxón] ~ [nīhešBonxón] < *yaḥsubunnákum (§16.2 M (t)) Nm 281.

<ethašab> int rmp pf 3ms [eθhaššáβ] < *hitḥaššába (§10) Macm 266.

*√ṭm <aṭmun> cau pf 3mp^1s [aṭmū́n] / [aṭṭə̆mū́n] < *haṭṭimū́nī (§6.2.2.1 (6D) with n. 32) DM 180.

*√ṭrš <niṭarsun> sim rmp impf 3mp [neṭṭaršón] < *yiṭṭarišúnna (§10) DM 183.

*√kWn <akin> cau pf 3ms [akkén] < *hakī́na (§6.1.2) DM 208.

*√ksy <kasitinkun> ~ <kasaitinkun> int pf 1s^2mp [kassīθenxón] ~ [kasseyTenxón] < *kassītkúm ~ *kassaytkúm (§8.1 n. 1) Nm 288.

*√krk <etkarkubH> ~ <etkarakbH> int rmp pf 3mp^pp(3ms) [eθkarKūBī́] ~ [eθkarraxbī́] < *hitkarrákū ⦙̊ bíhi (§17.15.2 (17.15C)) Mal 501.

*√lbš <albišak> cau pf 3ms^2ms [albə̆šáx] < *halbišáka (§4.4.1 n. 23) Mal 329.

<nalb(i)šak> cau impf 3ms^2ms [nalbə̆šáx] < *y(ih)albišíka (§9.1.3 n. 3) Nm 273.

*√lṭ (< **√lWṭ) <tiliṭH> sim impf 2ms^3ms [tīleṭṭī́] / [tellə̆ṭī́] < *talluṭíhi (§17.26 n. 137) DM 233.

*√lqṭ <lgaṭ> sim pf 3ms [lə̆γáṭ] < *laqáṭa (§4.2.2) Macm 263.

<ligṭan> sim pf 3ms^1s [leγṭán] < *laqaṭánī (§12.2) DM 230.

<lgaṭin(h)un> sim pf 3ms^3mp [lə̆γaṭenhón] ~ [lə̆γaṭennón] < *laqáṭa ⦙̊ h/ʔin(nV̊)húm (§7.4.1, §15.5.1 n. 41) Macm 356.

<ligṭat> sim pf 3fs [leγṭáθ] < *laqaṭát (§4.2.2, §12.2) Macm 263.

<ligṭuiH> t[léγṭūy] sim pf 3mp^3ms [leγṭū́y] < *laqaṭū́hī (§7.2 (δ), §8.2.1) Macm 163.

<ligṭu> t[léγṭū] sim pf 3mp^3fp [leγṭū́] < *laqatuha (§11.2 n. 16) Mal 282.

<eligṭak> sim impf 1s^2ms [īleγṭáx] < *ʔalquṭíka (§15.5.1 n. 41) Nm 280.

<elgiṭinkun> sim impf 1s^2mp [elgə̆ṭenxón] < *ʔalquṭinnikúm (§15.5.1 n. 41) Nm 280.

<niligṭun> t[nīláγṭon] sim impf 3mp [nileGṭón] possibly ~ [nilaGṭón] < *yalquṭúnna (§7.2 (γ), §15.3.1.1) Macm 125.

<uetilgiṭ> conj sim rmp pf 3mp [ūīθelGéṭ] < *wa=hitlaqíṭū (§4.4.2) DM 231.

*√mWt <mitt> sim pf 2ms [méθt] < *mī́ttå̄ (§5.2 n. 8, §15.3.1.2 with n. 26) Macm 12, 325.

<mittun> t[méθton] sim pf 2mp [meθtón] < *mīttúm (§15.3.1.2, §15.4) Macm 12.

<nimut> sim impf 3ms [nemmóθ] < *yamū́ti (§6.2.2.1 n. 28) DM 263.

<timitai> sim impf 2fs [tīmettéy] < *tamūtī́na / *tamū́tī (§16.2 M (α) (16D) n. 17, §17.2) Macm 257, 316, 431.

<nimitiun> sim impf 3mp [nīmeθyón] < *yamūtúnna (§6.2.2.1 n. 28) Nm 249.

*√mk <nimuk> sim impf 3ms [nemmóx] < *yammúki (§3.3) Macm 316.

*√ml <malil> int pf 3ms [mallél] < *mallíla (§3.3) Macm 461.

*√mlʔ <mlainun> sim impa fs^3mp [mə̆leynnón] < *mĭlá̄ʔī ⦙̊ h/ʔin(nV̊)húm (§6.2 M (γ)) Mal 645, 648.

*√mny   <etimniit> sim rmp pf 1s [iθemnīyîθ] < *hitmanît (§17.28 with n. 143) Mal
        464.

*√mšḥ   <mišit> sim pf 1s [messîθ] < *mašáḥt (§9.2.2 n. 24) Malone 1985: 97.

*√nbṭ   <nbaṭia(n)> sim pf 3fp [nǝβaṭyắ(n)] < *nabáṭā (§17.12.2) Nm 223f.

*√ngd   <ninigduia> sim impf 3mp^3ms [nīneGDúy] < *yangudúhī (§7.2 (ε)) Mal
        540f.

*√ngl   <uetnangal> conj int rmp pf 3mp [ūeθnangál] < *wa=hitnaggálū (§17.18
        with n. 22) DM 289.

*√ngr   <nitnangar> int rmp impf 3ms [neθnangár] < *yitnaggári (§17.8 with n. 22)
        DM 289.

*√nWd   <anidH> ~ <andH> cau pf 3ms^3fs [annǝðắ] or perhaps [anīðắ] perhaps ~
        [anDắ] < *hanīdahá (§6.2.2.1) Nm 275.

        <nanidH> ~ <nandH> cau impf 3ms^3ms [nannǝðî] perhaps ~ [nanDî] <
        *y(ih)anīdíhi (§17.26 n. 137) Nm 276.

*√nhr   <anhirat> ~ <anhrat> ~ <anharat> ~ <anhurat> cau pf 3fs [anhǝráθ] < *hanhirát
        (§6.2.2.1 (6D) with n. 31) Mal 385

        <anhiritilun> cau pf 1s^pp(3mp) [anhǝrīθellón] < *hanhírt ꝑ lahúm (§15.2.2.2
        n. 20) Nm 226.

*√nz   <ninzun> sim impf 3mp [nenzón] < *yinnazúnna (§6.2.2.1 (6D) with n. 30)
        Nm 249.

*√nḥ (< *√nWX)   <etnihat> sim rmp pf 3fs [eθneh(h)áθ] < *hitnaḥḥát (§12.2) Macm
        322.

*√nḥt (possibly ~ *√ḥt)   <nihut> t[néhoθ] sim impf 3ms [neh(h)óθ] < *yanḥúti /
        *yaḥḥúti (§9.3.1, §17.21.1) Macm 106.

        <ahit> t[áhheθ] cau pf 3ms [ahhéθ] < *hanḥíta / *haḥḥíta (§9.3.1) Macm 106.

        <anh(i)tit> cau pf 1s [anhǝθîθ] < *hanḥít(ǝ́)t (§15.3.1.2 with n. 25) Nm 294.

*√nsb   <nsabtinun> sim pf 1s^3mp [nǝsaβtennón] < *nasábt ꝑ h/ʔin(nV̊)húm
        (§17.15.1) Nm 282.

        <ninisbunH> sim impf 3mp^3ms [nīnesBonnî] < yinsabunnáhi (§7.2) Mal
        540f.

        <etinsib> t[ītánseβ] sim rmp pf 3ms [īθenséβ] < *hitnasíba (§15.3.1.1) Macm
        125.

*√npl   <npalalH> sim pf 3fs^pp(3fs) [nǝfalallắ] < *napálat ꝑ láha (§13, §15.2.1.1)
        DM 303, Malone 1998a.

        <ninpulbun> sim impf 3ms^pp(3mp) [nenpolbón] < *yanpúli ꝑ bahúm (§15.4
        with (15U)) DM 303.

*√npq   <nipqit> sim pf 1s [nefqîθ] < *napáqt (§17.15.1) Nm 223.

        <npaqiun> sim pf 3fp {fgm} [nǝfaqyǒn] < *napáqū (§16.2 M̲ (α) n. 16) Nm
        223.

        <npaqnin> sim pf 1p [nǝfaqnîn] < *napáqnā (§17.15.2 with (17.15C)) DM
        304.

        <npaqnabH> sim pf 1p^pp(3ms) [nǝfaqnāBî] < *napáqnā ꝑ bíhi (§17.15.2
        with (17.15C)) Mal 269.

        <apiq> m[áffeq] cau impa ms [appéq] < *hanpíq (§17.21.1) Macm 294f.

*√npš   <ninpuš> sim impf 3ms [nenpóš] < *yanpúši (§15.4 with (15V)) DM 304.

*√nθr   <nṭur> ~ <nṭar> sim impa ms [nǝṭór] ~ [nǝṭár] < *θur (§17.33) Macm 293f.

*√sbr <neiasbrak> cau impf 1p^3ms [niy(y)asbǝrắx] < *n(ih)asbiríka (§9.1.2 n. 3) Nm 273.

*√sgd <nisigda> sim impf 3fp [nīseGDắ] < *yasgudánna (§4.4.1) Mal 543.

*√sdr <estadar> int rmp pf 3ms [estaddár] < *hitšaddára (§10) Malone 1999: 251.

*√sḥp <esthip> sim rmp pf 3ms [estǝhéf] < *hitsaḥípa (§10) Malone 1999: 251.

   <nisihpun> sim rmp impf 3mp [nessehPón] < *yitsaḥipúnna (§10) Malone 1999: 251.

*√slq <saq> m[sắq] sim pf 3ms [sáq] < *saláqa (§17.33 n. 159) DM 314.

   <hansiq> ~ <asiq> cau pf 3ms [hanséq] ~ [asséq] < *haslíqa (§17.8, §17.21.2 n. 109) DM 332.

   <asqinkin> ~ <asqinkun> cau pf 3ms^3fp {fgm} [asqenxén] ~ [asqenxón] < *hasliqakín ~ *hasliqakúm (§16.2 M (r)) Nm 280.

*√9bd <abad> m[éβad] sim pf 3ms [aβáð] < *9abáda (§9.2.3.1) Macm 296, 518.

   <abdat> ~ <ebdat> sim pf 3fs [aβDáð] ~ [eβDáθ] < *9abadát (§12.2) DM 2.

   <abadubak> sim pf 3mp^pp(2ms) [aβaðūBắx] < *9abádu ‡ báka (§17.9.2) Nm 355.

   <nibad> t[níββad] sim impf 3ms [nibbáð] < *yi9bádi (§9.2.3.2) Macm 91.

   <ebad> ~ <ebid> sim impf 1s [ebbáð] ~ [ebbéð] < *ʔi9bádi ~ *ʔa9bídi (§12.2) DM 2.

   <tibdun> sim impf 2mp [tebDón] < *ti9badúnna (§17.15.2 with (17.15C)) DM 2.

   <tibidulH> sim impf 2mp^pp(3fs) [tebbǝðollắ] < *ti9badúnna ‡ láha (§17.15.2 with (17.15C)) DM 2.

   <ebid> ~ <abid> ~ <ebud> ~ <abud> ~ <eubud> m[óβod] ~ <ebad> sim impa ms [eβéð] ~ [aβéð] ~ [eβóð] ~ [aβóð] ~ [oβóð] ~ [eβáð] (§17.23.3 (17.23D)) DM 2, Macm 306.

   <etbid> t[étβed] sim rmp pf 3ms [etBéð] < *hit9abída (§9.2.3.1 with n. 29, §10 with n. 10) Macm 90, 301.

*√9br <eubruia> ~ <ebruia> sim impa mp^3ms [oβrűy] ~ [eβrűy] < *9ibarűhī (§17.25) Nm 278.

   <abirtunH> cau pf 2mp^3fs [abbertonnắ] < *ha9birtűha (§12.2) DM 4.

*√9dy <adia> cau pf 3ms [addĩ́] < *ha9díya (§9.2.3.2) Macm 299.

*√9kr <tikirinin> sim impf 2ms^3fp [tekkǝrennén] < *ta9kúri ‡ h/ʔin(nV̌)hín (§17.26 n. 137) DM 17.

*√9l (< **√Rl) <aiil> int pf 3ms [ayyél] < *9allíla (§6.2.1) Macm 320.

*√Rḥk (< **√ḏḥk) <ehkat> sim pf 3fs [ehKáθ] < *Raḥikát (§9.1.3 (α)) DM 9.

   <ehkit> ~ <ahkit> sim pf 1s [ehKĩ́θ] ~ [ahKĩ́θ] < *Raḥíkt (§9.1.3 (α), §17.10) DM 9.

   <ehikibun> sim pf 1s^pp(3mp) [īhexīBón] / [ehexīBón] < *Raḥíkt ‡ bahúm (§9.1.3 (α)) DM 9.

   <tigihkun> sim impf 2mp [tīγehKón] < *tiRḥakúnna (§9.2.4) DM 81.

*√plg <plaglak> sim pf 3ms^pp(2ms) [pǝlaγlắx] < *palága ‡ láka (§17.15.2 with (17.15C)) Mal 314.

*√plḥ <plah> t[pǝlắ] sim pf 3ms [pǝlắ] < *paláḥa (§9.2.4) Macm 87.

*√ps <pasH> sim pf 3ms^3ms [passĩ́] < *passáhi (§12.2) DM 375.

   <pasat> sim pf 3fs [passáθ] < *passát (§3.3, §12.2) Macm 145.

<past> m[pást] sim pf 2ms [pást] < *pástā̊ (§6.2.2.1) Macm 145.

<etipsis> ~ <etpsis> ~ <etpis> sim rmp pf 3ms [īθePsés] ~ [eθpə̆sés] ~ [eθpés]
    < *hitpasísa ~ *hitpíssa (§3.3) Macm 149.

*√psq   <psaqinan> sim pf 3ms^1p [pə̆saqennán] < *pasaqánā (§15.5.1) Nm 279.

*√prq   <etparaqt> int rmp pf 2ms [eθparráqt] < *hitparráqtā̊ (§10) Macm 266.

    <eparqit> int rmp pf 1s [epparqíθ] < *hitparráqt (§10) Macm 267.

*√prš   <praš> ~ <piršun> sim pf 3mp [pə̆ráš] ~ [peršón] < *parášū (§§7.2 (δ),
    §15.2.1.3 n. 10, §15.6 with n. 43, §17.9.2, §17.12.2 n. 57) Mal 348, 350.

    <prašian> sim pf 3fp [pə̆rašyǎ̆n] < *parášā (§7.2 (δ) with n. 19) Mal 363.

    <aprišilkun> ~ <aprištilkun> cau pf 1s^pp(2mp) [afrə̆šelxón] / [afrə̆šilxón]
    ~ [afreštelxón] / [afreštiilxón] < *hapríšt # lakúm (§17.15.2 with
    (17.15C)) Malone 1998a: 13.

    <leiaprišinkun> cau impf 3ms^2mp [liy(y)afrə̆šenxón] < *y(ih)aprišikúm /
    *l(ih)aprišikúm (§15.3.1.1) Nm 280.

    <eiapriš> cau impf 1s [iy(y)afréš] < *ʔ(ih)apríši (§15.3.1.1) Nm 227.

*√ptḥ   <eptalH> sim pf 3ms^pp(3ms) [ePTalí] < *patáḥa # lihí (§17.18.1) Mal 356.

    <eptalia> sim pf 3ms^pp(1s) [ePTalí] < *patáḥa # lí (§17.18.1) Mal 356.

    <ptahnin> t[pə̆táhnīn] sim pf 1p [pə̆θahnín] < *patáḥnā (§9.2.4) Macm 86.

    <ptanH> t[pə̆tánnī] sim pf 1p^3ms [pə̆θanní] < *patáḥnə̆hi (§9.2.4) Macm 86.

    <ptahnun> t[pə̆táhnun] sim pf 1p^3mp [pə̆θahnón] < *patáḥnā # h/ʔin(nV̌)húm
    (§9.2.4) Macm 86.

    <ptahnen> t[eftáhnen] sim pf 1p^3fp [pə̆θahnén] ~ [ePTahnén] < *patáḥnā #
    h/ʔin(nV̌)hín (§17.15.1) Macm 163.

*√ṣb9 (< **√ṣbR)   <ṣbun> m[ṣóβon] ~ <ṣbu> sim pf 3mp [ṣə̆βṓn] ~ [ṣə̆βū́] < *ṣabá9ū
    (§7.2 (δ) with n. 20) Mal 351.

    <eṣṭbit> sim rmp pf 2ms [eṣṭə̆βḗT] < *hitṣabí9tā̊ (§17.15.2 with (17.15C))
    Macm 286.

    <eṣṭbatbH> sim rmp pf 2ms^pp(3ms) [eṣṭə̆βā̊Tbí] < *hitṣabí9tā̊ # bíhi
    (§17.15.2 with (17.15C)) Nm 235.

*√ṣWt   <tiṣitun> sim impf 2mp [tīṣettón] or [teṣṣə̆θón] < *taṣūtúnna (§6.2.2.1) Macm
    317.

*√ṣmr   <eṣṭamar> int rmp pf 3ms [eṣṭammár] < *hitṣammára (§10) Malone 1999:
    252.

*√θ9n   <tan> sim pf 3ms [ṭán] < *θa9ána (§9.2.3.1) Macm 329.

*√qWm   <qambH> sim pf 3mp^pp(3ms) [qambí] < *qā́mū # bíhi (§17.9.2, §17.15.2)
    DM 407.

    <niqum> t[níqum] ~ [níqqom] sim impf 3ms [nīqū́m] ~ [niqqóm] < *yaqū́mi
    (§15.3.1.1) Macm 324.

    <niqmun> t[néqmon] sim impf 3mp [neqmón] < *yaqūmúnna (§6.2.2.1) Nm
    247, Mal 537.

    <qum> m[qóm] sim impa ms [qóm] < *qū́m (§6.2.2.1) DM 407, Macm 326.

    <aqim> m[á̆qqem] cau pf 3ms [aqqém] < *haqī́ma (§6.2 with n. 15) DM 407,
    Macm 328.

    <aqmat> m[á̆qmat] cau pf 3fs [aqmáθ] < *haqīmát (§6.2 with n. 15, §6.2.2.1)
    Macm 320, 328.

*√qWṣ   \<uetqis> conj sim rmp pf 3ms [ueθqés] / [ueθqī́s] < *wa=hitqī́ṣa (§6.3) DM 408.

*√qnʔ   \<(e)qnia> t[éqnī] sim pf 3fp [qə̆nī́] ~ [eqnī́] < *qanáʔā (§7.2 (δ) with n. 21) Mal 362.

*√qrʔ   \<qra> sim pf 3ms [qə̆rā́] < *qaráʔa (§9.2.3.1) Macm 333, 618.

\<qrit> sim pf 2ms [qə̆réT] < *qaráʔtā̊ (§11.2) Macm 334.

sim pf 1s [qə̆rī́θ] < *qaráʔt (§11.2) Macm 334.

\<qribH> t[aqrī́bī] sim pf 1s^pp(3ms) [qə̆rīBī́] < *qaráʔt ﹟ bíhi (§17.15.2 with (17.15C)) Mal 282.

\<qrilH> ~ \<qritilH> sim pf 1s^pp(3ms) [qə̆rī̆llī́] ~ [qə̆rīθī̆llī́] < *qaráʔt ﹟ líhi (§13, §17.15.2 with (17.15C)) Malone 1998a: 12.

\<qraitun> sim pf 2mp [qə̆reyTón] < *qaraʔtū́m (§9.2.3.2, §11.2) DM 414, Macm 335.

\<qrinun> sim impa ms^3mp [qə̆rī̆nnón] < *qĭráʔ ﹟ h/ʔin(nV̊)húm (§16.2 M (γ)) Mal 645, 648.

\<qrun> sim impa mp [qə̆rṓn] < *qĭráʔū (§17.9.2) Macm 333, 396.

\<etiqrit> sim rmp pf 1s [ī̆θeqrī́θ] < *hitqarī́ʔt (§17.28) Mal 464.

*√qtl   \<gṭaliun> m[gə̆ṭályṓn] sim pf 3mp [gə̆ṭalyṓn] < *qatálū (§7.2 (δ) with n. 15) Mal 352.

\<nigṭul> t[néγṭol] ~ [nī́γṭol] sim impf 3ms [neγṭól] ~ [niγṭól] < *yaqtúli (§17.11.3) Mal 283.

\<nigiṭlH> sim impf 1p^3ms [nī̆γeṭlī́] < *naqtulíhi (§7.1) Mac 516.

*√qθr   \<gṭaribH> sim pf 1s^pp(3ms) [gə̆ṭarīBī́] < *qaθárt ﹟ bíhi (§13) DM 88, Malone 1998a.

*√rby   \<rbitiH> sim pf 1s^pp(3ms) [rə̆βī̆θī̆Bī́] < *rabī́t ﹟ bíhi (§16.2 M (r′)) Malone 1998a: 13.

*√rg   \<tirigun> t[tī̆reggón] sim impf 2mp [tī̆reggón] < *tirragúnna (§6.2.2.1 with (6D)) Nm 249, Mal 546.

*√rgz   \<rgazian> sim pf 3fp [rə̆γazyā̆́n] < *ragázā (§2.3.4.3) Macm 263.

\<šargzun> cau pf 3mp^1s [šargə̆zū́n] < *šargizū́nī (§6.2.2.1 (6D) with n. 33) Mal 405.

*√rgl   \<etirgil> sim rmp pf 3ms [ī̆θerGél] < *hitragíla (§4.4.2) DM 231.

*√rd   \<nirandidun> int impf 3mp [nī̆randə̆δón] < *yiraddidúnna (§17.8 with n. 22) Macm 128.

*√rdp   \<radpunan> ~ \<rudpunan> int pf 3mp^1p {*if genuine*} [radPonnán] ~ [rod-Ponnán] < *raddipū́nā (§12.2 n. 14) Nm 280.

*√rWm   \<arimat> t[arī́mat] cau pf 3fs [arrə̆máθ] / [arīmáθ] < *harīmát (§6.2.2.1 with (6D)) Nm 251, Maqcm 321.

\<etaram> cau rmp pf 3ms [ettarrám] < *hitharā́ma (§6.3) Macm 323.

*√rhy (< **√rWḥ)   \<arhabH> t[arhā́bī] cau p 3ms^pp(3ms) [arhāBī́] < *harḥáya ﹟ bíhi (§17.15.2 (17.15C)) Macm 284.

\<arhubH> cau pf 3mp^pp(3ms) [arhūBī́] < *harḥáyū ﹟ bíhi (§11.2 n. 16, §17.15.2 with n. 78) Macm 383f.

*√rmz   \<nirimza(n)> sim impf 3fp [nī̆remzán] ~ [nī̆remzā̆́] < *yirmazánna (§7.2 (γ) with n. 8, §17.22.2) Mal 543.

*√rmy   \<rmu> sim pf 3mp [rə̆mū̆́] < *ramáyū (§11.2) Macm 334.

*√šb9 <sbaian> sim pf 3fp [sə̆βāyắn] < *šabí9ā (§7.2 (δ) with n. 19) Mal 363.

*√šWm <samilH> sim pf 1s^pp(3ms) [sāmellî] <*šắmt ǂ lîhi (§17.20) DM 321.

<asimit> cau pf 1s [assə̆mîθ] / [asīmîθ] < *hašímt (§17.20)) DM 321.

<etasimat> cau rmp pf 3fs [ettassə̆máθ] < *hithašāmát (§6.3) Macm 323.

*√šṭy <nasṭunan> cau impf 3mp^1p [nasṭonnán] < *y(ih)asṭayunnánā (§7.2 (ζ)) Macm 373.

*√šʔl <šal> sim pf 3ms [šál] < *šaʔála (§9.2.3.1) Macm 329.

<nišul> sim impf 3ms [neššól] < *yašʔúli (§9.1.3 n. 7) Macm 329.

<nišilunH> sim impf 3mp^3ms [neššə̆lonñ] / [nīsellonñ] < *yašʔulunnáhi (§9.1.3 n. 7) Macm 329.

<šul> sim impa ms [šól] < *šă̆ʔúl (§9.1.3 n. 7) Macm 330.

<šaiil> int pf 3ms [šeyyél] < *šaⁿʔíla (§9.1.3 n. 7) Macm 330.

<šailat> ~ <šiilat> t[šéylat] int pf 3fs [šeyláθ] < *šaⁿʔilát (§11.1 n. 4) Macm 17.

<nišailunakin> ~ <nišailunkin> int impf 3mp^2fp [nīšeylonnắxén] ~ [nīšeylonxén] < *yišaⁿʔilunnakín (§2.3.4.2) Mal 59.

*√šbḥ <šabihtH> int pf 1s^3ms [šabbehtî] < *šabbíḥtə̆hi (§12.2, §17.10) DM 447.

*√šbq <nišbiqlun> sim impf 3ms^pp(3mp) [nešbeqlón] < *yašbúqi ǂ lahúm < (§17.15.2 with (17.15C)) DM 447.

<tišbuq> sim impf 2ms [tešbóq] < *tašbúqi (§17.15.2 with (17.15C)) DM 447.

<tišibqan> ~ <tišbqan> sim impf 2ms^1s [tīšeBqán] ~ [tešbə̆qán] < *tašbuqínī (§4.4.1, §15.5.1 n. 41) Nm 271, Mal 526.

<ešbiqinkun> sim impf 1s^2mp [ešbə̆qenxón] < *ʔašbuqinnikúm (§4.4.1 n. 23) DM 447.

<šubqan> ~ <šubqin> sim impa ms^1s [šoβqán] ~ [šoβqén] < *šabúqnī (§2.3.4.4) Mal 643.

<eštbiq> sim rmp pf 3ms [eštə̆βéq] < *hitšabíqa (§4.4.1 n. 23) DM 448.

*√šdr <šadartH> ~ <šadirtH> int pf 2ms^3ms [šaddartî] ~ [šaddertî] < *šaddírtə̆hi (§12.2, §15.5.1) DM 450.

*√šWṭ <ašiṭṭinun> ~ <ašiṭinun> cau pf 1s^3mp [aššeṭṭennón] ~ [aššeṭṭennón] < *hašiṭṭ ǂ h/ʔin(nV̊)húm (§10 n. 3, §15.3.1.2 n. 26) DM 454.

*√škḥ ('find') <uaškahtinun> conj cau pf 1s^3mp [ūaškahtennón] < *wa=haškíḥt ǂ h/ʔin(nV̊)húm (§17.10) Macm 542.

<aškanin> ~ <aškinin> cau pf 1p [aškannín] ~ [aškennín]/[aškīnín] < *haškíḥna (§12.2) DM 465.

<liška> cau impf 3ms [leškắ] < *y(ih)aškíḥi / *l(ih)aškíḥi (§12.2) DM 464.

<laniška> negative cau impf 3ms [lāneškắ] < *lắ ǂ y(ih)aškíḥi (§12.2) DM 464.

*√šlḥ <ašlhan> t[ášlə̆han] ~ <ašlan> t[ášlan] cau pf 3ms^1s [ašlə̆hán] ~ [ašlán] < *hašliḥánī (§9.2.4) Macm 83.

*√šlm <lišlum> sim impf 3ms [lešlóm] < *yašlúmi / *lašlúmi (§17.19) Nm 216.

*√šm9 <š(u)ma> t[éšmā] sim pf 3ms [šŬmắ] / [šə̆mắ] possibly ~ [ešmắ] < *šamí9a (§9.2.3.1, §17.18.1, §17.23.2, §17.23.3) Macm 124, 333, 618.

<šimat> t[šímat] sim pf 3fs [šīmáθ] < *šami9át (§9.1.3 n. 7, §9.2.1.1 n. 14) Macm 92.

<šmatinan> ~ <šmitinan> sim pf 2ms^1p [šə̆mattennán] ~ [šə̆mettennán] /
[šə̆mīTennán] <*šami9tā̊nā (§12.2) DM 469.

<šumaiun> sim pf 3mp [šŬmāyŏ̃n] / [šə̆māyŏ̃n] < *šamí9ū (§7.2 (δ) with
n. 19) Mal 353.

<šmatun> t[šə̆mátton] ~ <šmaitun> sim pf 2mp [šə̆mattón] ~ [šə̆meyTón] <
§9.2.3.2, §17.11.3) Macm 286, Mal 282f.

<šmanin> t[šə̆mánnīn] sim pf 1p [šə̆mannín] < *šamí9nā (§9.1.3 n. 7) Macm
92.

<ašmainan> cau impa fs^1p [ašmeynnán] < *hašmi9ī́nā (§16.2 M̲ (γ)) Mal
663.

*√špl   <tišiplun> t[tīšáflon] sim impf 2mp [tīšeflón] perhaps ~ [tīšaflón] < *tašpilúnna
(§6.2.2.1 with n. 25 and (6D)) Mal 546.

*√šql   <eštqil> sim rmp pf 3ms [eštə̆qél] < *hitšaqíla (§10) Malone 1999: 254.

*√šry   <šritibH> sim pf 1s^pp(3ms) [šə̆rīθīBí̃] < *sarí́t # bíhi (§16.2 M̲ (r′)) Malone
1998a: 13.

*√tqn   <taqinH> int pf 1p^3ms [taqqenní̃] < *taqqínnə̆hi (§15.3.1.2 n. 26) Nm 277.

*√trṣ   <traṣnalun> sim pf 1p^pp(3mp) [tə̆raṣnallón] < *tarā́ṣnā # lahúm (§7.2 (δ)
n. 9, §17.15.2 with (17.15C)) Macm 269.

<etriṣ> t[étreṣ] sim rmp pf 3ms [etréṣ] < *hittaríṣa (§10) Macm 267.

<etriṣt> sim rmp pf 2ms [etréṣt] < *hittaríṣtā̊ (§15.3.1.2 n. 26) Nm 223.

24.3. Cross-Dialectal Distribution of the Roots in the Index

	Y	O	I	B	P	N	TR	CP	SM	G	SR	TL	M
√ʔbd		•		•				•	•	•			
√ʔbl					•								
√ʔgr									•				
√ʔzl			•			•	•	•	•	•	•	•	•
√ʔḥð (< √ʔXð)				•		•				•	•	•	
√ʔkl			•		•	•	•	•	•	•	•	•	•
√ʔkp								•					
√ʔlm					•								
√ʔlp (*see also* √ylp)					•			•					
√ʔlṣ									•				
√ʔmy (< √wmʔ X√ʔmr)											•		
√ʔmr (*see also* √ʔmy, √wmʔ)	•	•	•					•		•	•	•	•
√ʔsy						•	•						
√ʔsr						•							•
√ʔp						•							•
√ʔpy										•			
√ʔpk (< √hpk)							•	•					•
√ʔrk							•						
√ʔrs							•		•				

	Y	O	I	B	P	N	TR	CP	SM	G	SR	TL	M
√ʔśd													•
√ʔšl (< √šʔl)								•			•		
√ʔty			•	•	•		•	•	•	•	•	•	•
√bdq												•	
√bdr							•					•	
√bhl				•							•		
√bhθ							•				•		•
√bWš									•				
√bWt							•				•		
√bz							•	•			•		
√bz9										•			
√bḥn							•						
√bḥr													•
√bṭl				•									•
√bṭn									•		•		
√byʔ											•		
√bky									•			•	
√bly								•					•
√bl9							•			•		•	
√bl9s										•			
√bny			•	•	•		•			•			
√b9y (< √bRy)			•	•	•		•	•		•		•	
√b9θ									•				
√bṣr												•	
√bqr				•									
√br					•								
√brʔ									•	•			
√brk			•	•	•		•		•	•	•	•	•
√bšl												•	
√bšqr													•
√gb													•
√gbl													•
√gd				•					•				
√gWb								•		•			
√gWḥ (< √gWX))							•						
√gWr													•
√gz		•										•	

	Y	O	I	B	P	N	TR	CP	SM	G	SR	TL	M
√gzy									•				
√gzr			•										
√gḥn									•				
√gly			•	•			•		•	•		•	
√gml									•				
√gmr												•	
√gnb							•		•			•	
√gndr							•						
√g9y									•				
√gr												•	
√grd												•	
√gry							•						
√grs												•	
√grš												•	
√gš			•						•				
√dbq							•	•	•				
√dbr							•	•				•	
√dgr													•
√dwy								•					
√dWṣ / √dṣy												•	
√dWr				•					•				•
√dḥy										•			•
√dḥk										•			
√dḥq										•			
√dly												•	
√dlq							•						
√dmk								•					
√dny										•			
√dq				•									
√drk													•
√drs												•	
√ðbḥ										•			
√ðWb							•						
√ðḥl				•			•		•	•	•	•	
√ðkr					•		•	•	•		•	•	•
√ðq												•	
√hwy	•	•	•	•	•	•	•	•	•	•	•	•	•

	Y	O	I	B	P	N	TR	CP	SM	G	SR	TL	M
√hWk				•									
√hWq (*plausibly* < √9Wq)													•
√hyy (*see* √hwy)									•	•			
√hymn					•				•		•		
√hlk									•				
√hn?													•
√wdy							•		•				•
√wdl (< √wld)													•
√wd9			•	•	•		•	•		•	•	•	•
√whb (*see also* √ntb)			•	•	•	•	•	•	•	•	•	•	•
√wzp							•	•			•	•	
√wkl				•			•	•	•				
√wld			•			•	•	•	•	•	•	•	√wld
√wm?									•	•	•	√?my	•
√wsp				•				•	•				
√w9θ				•									
√wqd								•	•				•
√wqp					•								
√wqr								•	•		•		•
√wrθ							•	•	•	•	•	•	
√wtr										•	•		
√wθb	•	•	•	•	•		•	•	•	•	•	•	•
√Wḥy							•						
√Wṭb		•	•	•			•						
√zbn					•	•	•	•		•	•	•	•
√zhr			•										
√zky											•		•
√zl												•	
√zlp								•					
√zmn				•								•	
√zmr										•			•
√z9q				•			•		•				
√z9r										•			
√zqr													•
√zry					•								
√zrmby													•
√zr9										•			

	Y	O	I	B	P	N	TR	CP	SM	G	SR	TL	M
√zrq							•					•	
√ḥbl				•									•
√ḥd												•	
√ḥdy (< √Xdy)										•			
√ḥdθ					•								
√ḥðr												•	•
√ḥwy				•	•		•		•			•	
√ḥWb (< √XWb)							•						
√ḥWg									•				
√ḥWṭ (< √XWṭ)				•									
√ḥWk												•	
√ḥWl													•
√ḥWs							•						
√ḥWr							•						
√ḥzy				•			•		•			•	•
√ḥzq												•	
√ḥṭ (< √Xṭ)												•	
√ḥṭʔ (< √Xṭʔ)									•			•	•
√ḥṭl										•			
√ḥy(y)				•			•		•				•
√ḥkm								•	•				
√ḥkr												•	
√ḥl (< √Xl)							•					•	
√ḥlṭ (< √Xlṭ)												•	
√ḥlp (< √Xlp)				•								•	
√ḥmy								•	•	•		•	
√ḥml													•
√ḥmR (< √ḥmð̣)										•			
√ḥnk (< √Xnk)							•						
√ḥnq (< √Xnq)										•		•	
√ḥsl										•			
√ḥsn			•				•						
√ḥsr (< √Xsr)										•		•	
√ḥp													•
√ḥpy								•					
√ḥpr						•							
√ḥṣ												•	
√ḥṣb													•

	Y	O	I	B	P	N	TR	CP	SM	G	SR	TL	M
√ḥṣd												•	
√ḥq	•												
√ḥrb (< √Xrb)				•					•	•		•	•
√ḥrm								•					
√ḥśk									•				
√ḥš								•				•	
√ḥšb												•	•
√ḥt (see √nḥt)													
√ḥtm (< √Xtm)				•									
√ṭbl												•	
√ṭWb											•		
√ṭm													•
√ṭmr								•	•				
√ṭš												•	
√ṭ9y										•			
√ṭ9m				•								•	
√ṭrd									•				
√ṭrp												•	
√ṭrš													•
√ṭšy											•		
√yṭy										•			
√ylp (< √ʔlp)									•				
√ynq (see also √nyq)						•							
√kʔb											•	•	
√kbš							•			•			
√khy							•						
√kWl											•		
√kWn (see also √kWnn)											•	•	•
√kWnn (< √kWn)									•				
√kḥš										•			
√kl				•								•	
√kn9												•	
√knp												•	
√knš											•		
√ksy							•	•					•
√kpl									•				
√kpr							•						

	Y	O	I	B	P	N	TR	CP	SM	G	SR	TL	M
√krz (< *Greek* kēruss-)									•				
√kry				•									
√krk											•	•	•
√ktb				•			•				•	•	
√ktš	•												
√l'y										•			
√lbš				•			•		•	•			•
√lwy											•		
√lWṭ (*see also* √lṭ)											•		
√lṭ (< √lWṭ)													•
√l9y	•									√l'y			
√lqṭ (*see also* √nqṭ)											•	•	
√lqy										•			
√mWr											•		
√mWt		•	•				•		•	•	•	•	•
√mḥ'		•					•		•		•		
√mṭy				•					•	•	•		
√mṭr									•				
√mk													•
√ml		•		•				•	•		•		•
√ml'							•	•			•	•	
√mlk											•		
√mny				•			•	•			•		•
√mn9							•						
√msr								•		•	•		
√mṣ											•		
√mr			•										
√mšḥ													•
√nb'							•				•		
√nbṭ													•
√ngd													•
√ngl													•
√ng9												•	
√ngr													•
√ndḥ											•		
√nðy									•				
√nhz											•		

	Y	O	I	B	P	N	TR	CP	SM	G	SR	TL	M
√nhm											•		
√nhr												•	•
√nWd				•									•
√nWḥ (< √nWX; see also √nḥ)							•						
√nWm												•	
√nWp												•	
√nz													•
√nḥ (< √nWḥ < √nWX)													•
√nḥb											•		
√nḥt (see also √ḥt)			•	•			•	•	•	•	•	•	•
√nṭl				•			•						
√ntp												•	
√nyq (< √ynq)									•				
√ns							•						
√nsb							•		•	•		•	•
√nsy							•						
√npl				•					•	•		•	•
√npq				•			•		•	•	•	•	•
√npš													•
√nṣr									•				
√nqṭ (possibly < √lqṭ)												•	
√nś?			•	•									
√nšb												•	
√nšy												•	
√nšq										•		•	
√ntb (< √ntn X √whb)												•	
√ntn (see also √ntb)	•			•	•			•				•	
√nθr												•	
√nθr			•	•					•		•	•	
√s?b							•			•			
√sb		•											
√sbl			•										
√sbr										•		•	•
√sgd				•			•						•
√sgr				•									
√sdr													•
√sWb							•						

	Y	O	I	B	P	N	TR	CP	SM	G	SR	TL	M
√sWp				•									
√sḥn									•				
√sḥp													•
√skm									•				
√skn												•	
√slq				•			•	•	•	•		•	•
√smy												•	
√smk							•		•		•		
√smq							•						
√spd												•	
√spy												•	
√srb							•						
√str				•									
√9bd				•		•	•	•	•	•	•	•	•
√9bdd (< √9bd)											•		
√9br		•					•	•	•			•	•
√9dy				•			•		•			•	•
√9ðr			•		•								
√9hd	•										•		
√9Wr (< √RWr)							•						
√9Wt												•	
√9yn												•	
√9kb												•	
√9kr													•
√9l (< √Rl)			•	•	•		•	•	•	•		•	•
√9md (< √Rmd)													•
√9ny					•		•						
√9nš												•	
√9ṣb												•	
√9qr			•							•		•	
√9r			•										
√9rs (see √ʾrs)													
√9rq							•		•			•	
√9rR (< √9rð)							•	•	•		•		
√9śq												•	
√9šq							•						
√9št			•										
√9θr							•			•		•	

	Y	O	I	B	P	N	TR	CP	SM	G	SR	TL	M
√Rḥk (< √ðḥk)											•		•
√R9ṭ (< √ð9ṭ)											•		
√pd9												•	
√pWš (see also √pš)	•												
√pṭr												•	
√pys (from Greek peis-; see also √πys)												•	
√pk											•		
√plg			•									•	•
√plḥ						•							•
√pny										•		•	
√ps													•
√psq										•			•
√pṣ					•								
√pṣy									•				
√pqd						•			•				
√prḥ												•	
√prsm										•			
√prR (< √prð)												•	
√prq							•	•	•			•	•
√prš							•					•	•
√pśl												•	
√pš (see also √pWš)	•												
√pšṭ												•	
√ptḥ				•	•					•			•
√ptq												•	
√πys (from Greek peis-; see also √pys)											•		
√ṣby			•										
√ṣb9 (< √ṣbR)				•									•
√ṣdy									•				
√ṣdq											•		
√ṣḥy							•						
√ṣWd							•	•		•		•	
√ṣWt							•					•	•
√ṣlb							•	•			•		
√ṣly							•			•			

	Y	O	I	B	P	N	TR	CP	SM	G	SR	TL	M
√ṣmr													•
√ṣn										•			
√ṣ9r												•	
√ṣrk										•			
√θl				•	•			•				•	
√θlm								•					
√θl9												•	
√θ9n										•			•
√qbl				•			•			•	•	•	
√qbr						•						•	
√qdm												•	
√qdš									•				
√qWm			•	•			•	•	•	•	•	•	•
√qWṣ							•						•
√qt9									•				
√ql							•			•			
√qly												•	
√qnʾ				•			•					•	•
√qpḥ (< √qpX)										•			
√qṣ								•	•		•	•	
√qrʾ	•			•	•	•	•		•		•	•	•
√qrb				•	•				•			•	
√qry									•				
√qr9												•	
√qš												•	
√qtl							•	•	•	•		•	•
√qθr												•	•
√rby				•					•				•
√rg			•										•
√rgz								•					•
√rgl													•
√rgm								•					
√rgš												•	
√rd													•
√rdy								•					
√rdp								•					•
√rwy									•				

	Y	O	I	B	P	N	TR	CP	SM	G	SR	TL	M
√rWḥ (*see also* √rḥy)									•				
√rWm (*see also* √rWmm)							•		•	•			•
√rWmm (< √rWm)				•					•				
√rWθ									•				•
√rḥy (< √rWḥ)													•
√rḥm							•				•		
√rḥR			•										
√rḥṣ									•				
√rḥq												•	
√rṭš							•						
√rkb							•		•	•			
√rkn									•				
√rks											•		
√rmz													•
√rmy				•			•	•	•			•	•
√r9m							•						
√rR (< √rð)				•									•
√rRy (< √rðy)	•	•					•						
√rq							•				•		
√ršy									•				
√ršm				•									
√rt									•				
√rty			•						•				
√ś'b									•	•			
√šb9									•				•
√śg'							•		•		•		
√śhd									•				
√śWm				•	•		•	•	•				•
√śty													•
√śky											•		
√š'l				•						•	•	•	•
√š'r							•		•				
√šbh					•		•	•			•		•
√šby											•		
√šb9									•		•		
√šbq			•	•			•	•	•	•	•	•	•
√šbš												•	

	Y	O	I	B	P	N	TR	CP	SM	G	SR	TL	M
√šgr									•				
√šdy								•				•	
√šdk							•						
√šdp												•	
√šdr												•	•
√šhy												•	
√šwy				•			•		•	•		•	
√šWṭ													•
√šWmm (< √šm)				•									
√šW9							•						
√šḥl							•						
√šṭḥ							•						
√šyzb (< š+√yzb)			•	•			•			•			
√šyṣy (*perhaps* < š+√yṣy)							•						
√škb							•					•	
√škḥ ('find')			•	•			•	•	•	•	•	•	•
√škḥ ('forget')												•	
√škn				•									
√šlhy							•						
√šlḥ				•			•		•			•	•
√šlṭ				•									
√šly		•											
√šlm							•				•		•
√šlq										•			
√šm (*see* √šWmm)													
√šmwd9 (<š+√mwd9)												•	
√šmṭ												•	
√šm9		•	•	•			•	•	•	•	•	•	•
√šmš				•			•		•				
√šny				•			•					•	
√š9y							•						
√špl				•								•	•
√špṣ												•	
√špr					•								
√šqy							•						
√šql										•		•	•
√šq9										•			
√šqr								•				•	

	Y	O	I	B	P	N	TR	CP	SM	G	SR	TL	M
√šrgrg											•		
√šry		•		•				•	•		•	•	•
√šty				•			•	•	•	•	•	•	
√štm								•					
√štq											•	•	
√štr				•									
√tb9										•		•	
√thw												•	
√twy	•										•		
√tly								•				•	
√tl9												•	
√tmh								•			•		
√tpś										•		•	
√tqn				•			•			•		•	•
√tqp				•			•		•				
√trk							•						
√trṣ													•
√θbr							•	•			•	•	
√θWb		•					•			•		•	
√θkl							•						
√θny							•					•	
√θql				•								•	

25. Technical Terms

[Defined here for the most part are terms appearing multiple times throughout the book; terms confined to one specific section are frequently omitted, as are those whose technical senses are deemed close enough in accord with the commonly accepted senses at large (lay senses). In alphabetizing phonetically (or similarly) transcribed terms, most symbols are assimilated to their nearest Romanized equivalent (e.g., <ḥ> is ordered qua <h>) though three (<ʔ>, <9>, <š>) are simply discounted (e.g., <sšyɔmē> is ordered as if it were <syame>). The number of cross-references, if any, provided per entry to relevant passages in the body of the book depends upon assumed usefulness]

*　　*　　*

ābāgādical pronunciation Mandaic reading pronunciation. *§22.3 n. 8, §17.14.*

ablaut *[German]* Lexically dictated vowel covariation; e.g., in this book between 2ʃ of the sim imp and sim pf (*§1.1.1 n. 2*), or between 2ʃ and 1ʃ / prefix *V* of the sim impa (*§1.1.1 n. 6*); ablaut is often called "apophony."

accordion A development, typically but not necessarily a sound change, *X > Y > X*, which frequently sets up the analytic illusion of <u>no</u> change (as if *X ≥ X*) while in fact <u>two</u> changes have intervened (*X > Y* and its (apparent) mirror, *Y > X*). *§23.2 with (23I), §2.3.4.3 <u>3fs</u> and <u>3p</u> n. 26 and <u>1p,</u> §4.2.1 n. 14, §4.3 <u>B</u>, §5.2 with nn. 5 and 8 and 9, §8.1.2 n. 9, §12.1 n. 1, §12.2 n. 5 and (δ), §12.2 <u>B</u> (δ) with n. 7, §12.2 CP n. 11, §13 nn. 3 and 36, §12.2 <u>M</u> (γ3), §15.5.1 n. 36, §15.5.2, §16.2 <u>M</u> n. 16, §17.5, §17.7 with nn. 16 and 18a, §17.11.3 with n. 50, §17.12.1, §17.14, §17.15.1 n. 64,§17.18.1, §18.4 with (18T) and n. 13, §20 n. 2.*

affix Generic term for *prefixes, suffixes, infixes* (morphemes, often with a grammatical function, coforming a word with a stem).

anlaut *[German]* (In) word-initial position.

antigemination *See* **Obligatory Contour Principle**.

antiprocess implementation Accomplishment of a transparentive goal (analogical reshaping) by omission of (part of) a process routinely employed in shaping the corresponding untransparentized forms. *§15.4.*

antiwedging In autosegmental theory, a hypothetical tension induced by one-to-many association whereby a resulting "wedge" structure is relieved either by *extrusion to* or by *meiosis to*

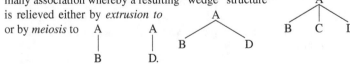

§3.1 with (3F), §3.2, §17.18.2 with n. 97.

archimorpheme   A (possibly abstract) generic morpheme, or more loosely (possibly abstract) generative formative, specifically one lending itself to being taken as common denominator formative to the set of formatives for which it serves as archimorpheme; for example, given the set of pf subject suffixes characterizable as {3mp, 3fp, 2mp, 2fp, 1p}, the corresponding archimorpheme is {p} (= pf subject suffix which is *plural* irrespective of person or gender). *§7.*

archiphoneme   A (possibly abstract) generic phoneme, or more loosely (possibly abstract) generic segment, specifically one lending itself to being taken as common denominator to the set of segments for which it serves as archiphoneme. In feature terms, if a set of segments is compositionally $\begin{bmatrix} A \\ B \end{bmatrix}$ $\begin{bmatrix} A \\ C \end{bmatrix}$ $\begin{bmatrix} A \\ D \end{bmatrix}$, their archiphoneme will be compositionally [A]. *§7, §20.1 (α), §20.2 with (20D).*

assimilandum   *See* **dissimilandum**.

assimilans   *See* **dissimilandum**.

association *(autosegmental)*   Connection of *melodic tiers* (notably root and scheme) to the *skeleton*. *§23.4, §3.1, §3.2, §17.11.3 n. 40, §17.25 n. 130.*

auslaut *[German]*   (In) word-final position.

Autosegmental Phonology *(AP)*   A theory of morphophonological organization whereby linguistic forms are analytically dispersed into quasi-independent levels, or *tiers*, ultimately composed / brought together by an operation called *tier conflation*. *§23.4, §1.3 n. 14, §3, §5.1 n. 1, §6.2.2.1 n. 27, §9.1.3 n. 7, §9.2.1.2 n. 20, §10 with n. 12, §11.1 n. 3, §15.3.1.2 with n. 24, §17.16, §17.18.2 with n. 97, §17.25 n. 130, §20.2 n. 5, §22.1 n. 3.*

barytone   Stress(ed) on the penult (second-last syllable); antonym: oxytone. *§4.1.*

binyan *(plural:* **binyanim***) [Hebrew]*   Any of six conventionally recognized lexical-derivational conjugations: simple *(sim, G, peal);* intensive *(int, D, pael);* causative *(cau, C, afel)*—plus their respective reflexive mediopassive *(rmp, t)* counterparts: sim rmp *(Gt, ethpeel);* int rmp *(Dt, ethpael);* cau rmp *(Ct, ettafal).*

bleed   A process *X* is said to *bleed* a process *Y* if *X* precedes *Y* and wreaks a change that directly or indirectly prevents *Y* from applying; antonym: feed. *§23.1, §4.5, §5.3, §10 M, §17.7, §17.11 nn. 37 and 42, §17.28, §17.29, §18.5 with n. 14, §19. (19A) n1.*

blend   A lexeme is a *blend* when it is constituted by two (or more) other lexemes pooling their pleherematic resources; the term "blend" in this book refers specifically to *root* lexemes built of *radicals* contributed by two other roots, all three lexemes being (asymptotically) synonymous. (Distinguish portmanteau, q.v., which refers to a formative simultaneously expressing functions which elsewhere in the system are conveyed by independent formatives, typically without any sharing of formal structure.) *§17.3 n. 3.*

bridge   A suffix-like formative, typically semantically vacuous, mediating between stem and object. *§23.2.*

cenematic   Relating to the *expression* side of language, as opposed to the *content* side; antonym: plerematic. *§15.3.1.1, §15.5.2 n. 42, §18.4.*

chain   In this book, an ordered series of processes; distinguish from chaîne, where in addition to the order, there is a cause-effect relation. *§9.1.3 with nn. 5 and 7, §9.2.3.1, §9.2.3.2, §12.2 M (γ2), §16.2 M n. 16, §17.6.1, §17.6.2 with n. 9, §17.9.2 n. 26, §17.15.1 n. 64, §17.21.1, §17.25, §18.4 n. 13.*

chaîne *[French]*   A pair of tandem changes standing in a cause-effect relation; distinguish from chain, where the members of a tandem pair are not necessarily causally related. *§6.3 n. 35, §6.3 M, §7.2 n. 9, §9.1.3, §15.5.1 n. 41, §17.9.2 TL, §17.17.2 n. 92.*

change *(linguistic)*   Mutation in the form or function of a linguistic item or system; changes, especially phonetic changes, often live on as synchronic *rules.*

chromatic   With respect to vowels, *palatal (front)—i, e, ε, æ*—or *labial(rounded)/ velar—u, o, ɔ—*; antonym: achromatic / dull *(low unrounded)*—prototypically *a*. Chroma (often referred to as *color*) tends to increase with tongue height, so that, e.g., a high front vowel (*i*) has more chroma than a low front vowel (*æ*).

clitic   Generic term for *proclitic, enclitic*—morphemes, typically with a grammatical function, combining with a word in a degree of morphophonological cohesion higher than that between two fully independent words but lower than that between an affix and a stem. *§23.5, §14.2 n. 11, §17.15.2 with n. 75.*

clitic group   A prosodic unit consisting of a phonological / prosodic word joined to a clitic. *§23.5 with (23Z′), §17.15.2 n. 75.*

coda *(K)*   Any consonantism (a single consonant or a cluster) ending a syllable. *§23.5.*

coefficient   In *feature* theory, an operation on or specification of a *core* feature; prototypical coefficients are "+, -" (+*F* = the presence of *F*, -*F* = the absence of *F*), though often other possibilities exist as well (e.g.: α*F* = the set {+*F*, -*F*} = "*F* of whatever value"—often conventionally employed to indicate "a given, arbitrary feature constituency"—; u*F* / m*F* = "*F* of unmarked / marked value"). *§15.2.2.1 n. 17.*

color   *See* **chroma.**

Common Aramaic *(cA)*   A Common Aramaic process or pattern is one affecting all Aramaic dialects, irrespective of choronological stage; it follows that proto-Aramaic (pA) was a species of Common Aramaic, but not conversely.

comparative method   A prime tool of historical linguistic reconstruction whereby the original shapes (and functions) of proto-items (segments, stems, words, etc.) are inferred from study of their reflexes in descendant languages / dialects. Synonym: external reconstruction. *§18.4.*

conjunctive   (*) A species of cotextual (q.v.).
             (*) An Aramaic proclitic having largely conjunctive or sequential semantic force, notably *wa= 'and', *pa= 'and then' (as well as reflexes of these).

contextual   In the first instance, a Tiberian accentual grapheme (*ta9am*) of weaker rank than pausal (q.v.); and, derivatively, a linguistic *stress* of commensurate strength represented by that ta9am; and derivatively again, a *prosodic domain* hosting / enabling that stress. Thus in sketch, <V̬> or <V̬> represents [V́] hosted in a domain right-bounded by # or # respectively: {...[V́]...V̬} or {...[V́]...#}. Contextual phenomena in turn break down into *disjunctive* and *conjunctive* sub-types. *§21.6* (ta9am), *§20.3* (stress), *§23.5* (prosodic domain)*; §17.11.3* <u>B</u> *with n. 37, §17.15.1 n. 63, §17.15.2 n. 75, §17.29, §20.2 (20D(ii)), §21.1 n. 4.*

copy-cat process   A novel process *X* historically mimicking a preexisting process *Y* because of some perceived similarity between a configuration of units (e.g., sequence of vowels and consonants) *Y′* constituting the focus-cum-conditions of *Y* and another configuration *X′* now itself interpreted as a focus-cum-conditions configuration; the changes wreaked by both rules will be identical or nearly so. *§13, §16.2* <u>M</u> *(r′), §16.3(ε), §17.6.2 O, I,* <u>CP</u>, *§17.21.1.*

counterbleed   A process *X* counterbleeds a process *Y* if (*) in the order *X^Y* application of *X* would prevent application of *Y*, but in fact (*) the actual order is *Y^X*. *§21.1 (α), §17.9.2 n. 27.*

counterfeed   A process *X* counterfeeds a process *Y* if (*) in the order *X^Y* application of *X* would trigger application of *Y*, but in fact (*) the actual order is *Y^X*.

dageš *[Hebrew]*   A Masoretic diacritic grapheme indicating gemination of a consonant (in this book symbolized < C >) and/or the occlusive (stop) value of *B, G, D, K, P, T* (in this book symbolized <b, d, g, k, p, t> for the simplices and <b̭, g̭, ḓ, k̭, p̭, ṱ> for the geminates). *§21.1 with (21F), §17.15.1 ( ).*

defective *(def)*   *See* **gizra.**

derivation   The operation of deriving one form (shape) from another by synchronic rule(s) (less frequently in usage, by diachronic change(s)); or an instance / presentation of such an operation.

derived   (*) *See* **derivation.**
        (*) Any of the *binyanim* except the simple plain (or except the simple plain / simple rmp—usage varies a bit).

diachronic   Characterizing a linguistic system as it changes through time; synonym: historical; antonym: synchronic.

diacritic   (*) An orthographic mark, usually associated with a specific letter but at times with an entire word, directly or indirectly providing linguistic information (normally cenematic but sometimes plearematic); vowel points are technically diacritics, but rarely so called.
        (*) Diacritic *feature* = a feature providing information other than the intrinsically phonetic (e.g., number, gender).

dialect   Designation stereotyped to refer to any of the thirteen Aramaic language types taken as prime focus of this book, or kindred linguistic groupings; not to be understood strictly in the conventional dialectological sense. *§0.1.*

dialect pocket   A hypothetical subregion of an overarching linguistic-geographical space out of which or into which specified changes fail to spread (perhaps over a specified time span)—although changes at large may move out of / into the pocket. Changes originating within a dialect pocket, and specified in the way just indicated, later manifest *local* as opposed to the *global* distribution normally expected; typically, a pocket-engendered change will end up confined to only one or two of several descendant dialects. The trajectory of a pocket change from its originating space through time into the later dialect(s) affected by it is called a *shaft.* *§18.2 with (18I, J), §19 with (19H), §6.3 with n. 44, §7.2 n. 11, §7.4.2 with (7B, C), §8.1.3 n. 14, §9.1.3 n. 37, §9.2.3.2, §11.2 n. 12.*

disjunctive *See* **contextual.**

dissimilandum A segment whose feature componency is modified to make the segment *less* similar to some other specified cooccurrent segment (the *dissimilans*); in $X \rightarrow Y / Z$, where Y is less similar to Z than X is, X = dissimilandum, Z = dissimilans. (A parallel definition holds for **assimilandum** and **assimilans**, changing only "less similar" to "more similar.") *§9.1.3 with n. 9, §9.2.1.1 n. 15.*

dissimilans *See* **dissimilandum.**

dynamic *(verb)* A verb lexeme prototypically denoting volitional physical action on the part of the entity denoted by the subject; antonym: neuter. *§0.2.1, §1.1.1 n. 2, §17.25.*

Elsewhere Condition A convention dictating that some conditions (environments) of a process take applicational precedence over others; in particular, more *specific* conditions take precedence over more *general* conditions—so if D and E are both conditions triggering a complex process $A \rightarrow B / D$, $A \rightarrow C / E$ but E is more specific than D, the subprocess $A \rightarrow C / E$ will take applicational precedence over the subprocess $A \rightarrow B / D$. *§17.23.2.*

ʾem keriya *(plural:* **ʾimot keriya***) [Hebrew]* *Same as* **mater lectionis**. *§21.2.*

empty segment. *Same as* **zero segment.**

enclitic Postpositive *clitic*, following the word it constructs with.

energic Originally a partition of the imperfective conjugation characterized by suffixation in **(V)nn*, but in this book normally used for reflexes of the suffix **(V)nn* itself in its role as a *bridge* morpheme; sometimes called exenergic. *§2.3.2, §7.1.*

equipollent A mode of organization whereby a system of entities (or properties, etc.) is indicated in positive terms for all members. Suppose for instance the system deals with forms $(a, b, c, \ldots)$ conveying meanings $(A, B, C, \ldots)$; then an equipollent representation of meaning-form couplings for A, B, C, D might be Aa, Bb, Cc, Dd. Antonym of equipollent: privative. *§23.3 n. 2, §15.2.1.1 with n. 3, §15.2.2.1 with n. 7, §16.1 n. 1.*

exeneregic In this book, a synomyn of **energic** for the bridge-like reflexes of the originally energic suffix **(V)nn.*

extrametrical An extrametrical syllable is one which does not count (is inorganic) in computing a constituent's stress pattern; in Aramaic, as in many languages, only *auslaut* syllables may be extrametrical. *§4.1 with n. 2, §17.6.1.*

extrusion *See* **antiwedging.**

fake geminate A geminate cluster $C'C'$ whose members are (partial) representations of distinct morphemes, e.g., stem + suffix. *§5.1 n. 1, §5.2 n. 8, §9.2.2 n. 23, §10 SR with n. 8, §15.3.1.2.*

family tree theory   A theory of linguistic genealogical development characterized by disallowing changes from (geographically) crossing dialect lines, and rather confining them strictly to movement within dialectally homogeneous space. *§7.4.2 with (7B), §8.1, §9.2.3.2.*

feature   Hypostasis of a property as a component of the element attributed with that property, symbolized within square brackets; a feature may be *binary* or *monolithic*, in which respective cases presence / absence of a feature F is indicated [+F] / [-F] on the one hand or [F] / [   ] on the other (i.e., "[   ]" *privatively* denotes the absence of F). *§23.1, §15.2.2.1 with n. 7, §15.6.*

feature geometry   A model of feature organization whereby features are structured hierarchically, in tree-like fashion (rather than being organized in simple "matrices," as once held). *§23.3 with (23C), §23.5 with (23Y).*

feed   A process X is said to feed a process Y if X precedes Y and wreaks a change which directly or indirectly enables Y to apply; antonym: <u>bleed</u>. *§18.3 n. 8, §18.5 with n. 14, §23.2 nn. 4 and 5 §5.2, §8.1.1 n. 4, §9.1.4 n. 12, §9.2.3.2, §11.2 n. 17, §12.1, §15.6, §17.6.2 B with n. 10, §17.7, §17.11.2, §17.12.2 n. 57, §17.15.1 ( ), §17.21.1, §17.21.2 n. 109, §17.23.3, §17.31, §17.32.*

floater   In autosegmental theory, a melody dissociated from (or possibly never associated to) a skeletal position. *§17.25 n. 130.*

focus   The part in a rule that is changed / replaced; e.g., in $X \Rightarrow Y / Z$, X is the focus (equivalently in the so-called "transformational format": sd X Z, sc Y 2.
$$1\quad 2$$
§6.1.2 n. 7, §14.1.

foot   The lowest (least inclusive) prosodic constituent, taken by many to dominate the nonprosodic (phonological) constituent *syllable*. In Metrical Stress Theory, feet play a central role in generating stress patterns, an *iambic* foot being stress-final ($S\acute{S}$, S a syllable), a *trochaic* foot stress-initial ($\acute{S}S$). *§23.5 with (23Z'), §4.1.1 n. 2.*

formative   A morphological constituent, typically one tightly organized and of relatively simple structure (limiting case, minimal; "morph"). *§15.3.1.1, §15.5.2, §15.4 with (15W), §15.6, §17.13.*

fractional merger   A merger or neutralization whereby two or more forms become phonologically (more) similar or even indistinguishable, but the merger falls short of affecting the entire paradigm; contrast full, integral, partial merger. *§6.2 n. 15.*

fricative   In this book, generic for *sibilant* (rilled fricative) and *spirant* (slit fricative), qq.vv. *§20.1, §5.1.*

full merger   A merger or neutralization whereby two or more forms become cenematically indistinguishable phonetically (though not necessarily also phonologically); contrast fractional, integral, partial merger. *§6.2 n. 15.*

fusion   (*) *See* **Obligatry Contour Principle**.
   (*) Total consonantal assimilation resulting in a geminate (cf. the changes prf and rrf in §10).

geminate   (*) A cluster of two identical consonants; a long consonant. Symbolization: *C'C'*.

(*) *See* **gizra**.

Geminate Integrity   A principle immunizing geminate clusters from various sorts of changes. *§5.1 n. 1, §9.2.2 n. 23, §10 SR, §11.1 with n. 4, §15.3.1.2 with n. 24.*

Generative Phonology *(GP)*   Successor to Structural Phonemics, Generative Phonology holds to the primacy of *morphophonemic* relations dynamically modeled by derivations mediating between abstract cenematic representations structured as a partial function of morphosyntax and broad-phonetic strings; the classical (structural) phoneme is viewed as epiphenomenal at best, and as a pseudo-entity at worst. *§23, §3.2 n. 6, §6.1.1.2, §6.1.2 n. 7, §6.2 n. 15, §6.3 SM, §7.2 (δ) n. 18, §7.2 (η), §8.1.2 (α) with n. 11, §11.2 n. 11, §13 n. 2, §14.2 nn. 11 and 17 and 18, §15.2.2.2 n. 20, §15.6, §16.2 SR (β) with n. 19, §17.7 n. 16, §17.9.2 nn. 26 and 27, §17.33 n. 156.*

ghost segment   A "zero" or "empty" segment, one devoid of all features (or properties) except for the definitional [+segmental] (*§20 (20B, C, E)*). Ghost segments normally reflect diachronic deletion of of actual substantive segments which for various reasons retain at least a *positional* synchronic reality. Ghost segments will be informally symbolized with "∅" (∅, [∅], |∅|, /∅/), although the same symbol may also be used more broadly and loosely to convey other sorts of empty entities or positions—e.g., in *§9.1.3 n. 7*, where ∅ marks a segmental position devoid of even the feature [+segmental], as in (i) below; contrast (ii). In both, the outcome may be represented as *a* ∅ *c* as long as the technical difference is not a matter of concern in the context.

(i) melodic tier   *a*   *b*   *c*   →   *a*   *c*
                         | | | | |
    skeletal tier   *X*   *X*   *X*   *X*   *X*   *X*

(In (i), as in §9.1.3 n. 7, *O* may stand for the melodic "space" between *a* and *c*)

(ii) melodic tier   *a*   *b*   *c*   →   *a [+segmenal] c*
                         | | | | | |
                        X   *X*   *X*   *X*   *X*   *X*

(In (ii) *[+segmental]* = ghost segment)

gizra *(plural:* **gĕzarot***) [Hebrew]*   Any of a varying number of morphophonemic classes (in this book, always of the verb), e.g.: *geminate* (gem), characterized by having two rather than three underlying radicals, one of which often surfaces as a geminate cluster; *hollow* (hol), characterized by usually showing a long vowel and no consonantal radical between the first and third radicals (though a semivocalic second radical surfaces under certain circumstances); *defective* (def, *nāqiṣ*), characterized by a phonologically labile glide as third radical (usually *y*) with a propensity to condense / coalesce with adjacent vocalism.

glide   *See under "Γ" in §26.2.*

global rule   A species of rule having the power to access other loci of a derivation (or even of the linguistic system) than that where it is functioning (e.g., at a given derivational level). Various sorts of global rules have been posited (though by no means always generally accepted):, e.g., *transderivational rule*, having the power to access (parallel derivations of) homoparadigmatic forms; *peeking rule*, having the power to access the (potential) output of the derivation in which it itself is functioning. *§6.2.2.1 n. 28, §11.2 SR, §15.4, §17.25 n. 130, §17.33 n. 156.*

hamzatu 'l-qaṭ9 *[Arabic]*   *See* **hamzatu 'l-waṣl.**

hamzatu 'l-waṣl *[Arabic]*   [ʔ] inserted by rule in repair-strategic removal of various canonical violations; in at least some Aramaic dialects, notably to provide a syllabically required onset in the wake of such operations as partial condensation (antihiatic *?*) or prothesis—contrast hamzatu 'l-qaṭ9 = [ʔ] derived from a positive segment, whether /ʔ/ (the null case) or some other segment by replacement (e.g., [ʔ] ← *y* by dissimilation). *§21.3 n. 14, §8.1.1, §9.1.2, §12.2 B (γ), §14.2 nn. 7 and 8, §14.2 CP (α), §14.2 TL n. 19, §14.3, §15.2.1.5, §17.15.1 n. 64, §17.18.1.*

ḥaser *[Hebrew]*   Orthographic representation unabetted by vowel points or matres lectionis; purely consonantal spelling. *§21.8 n. 26, §22.3 n. 8, §0.2.2, §14.2 SR, §17.7 n. 20.*

ḥataf *(plural:* ḥatafim*) [Hebrew]*   Normally, a vowel point representing a chromatic schwa (e.g., Tiberian <ĕ>, <ă>, <ŏ>); more generally, a chromatic schwa whether orthographic or cenematic. *§21.5, §17.15.1 n. 65, §17.23.*

ḥatuf *[Hebrew]*   Adjective form of **ḥataf.**

heavy *(-suffixed)*   In the imp system, forms containing either the number-gender suffixes *(§2.2.1.2)* or non-null reflexes of such suffixes, or the mood suffix **-ā (§2.2.1.2)* or a non-null reflex thereof; in the pf system, forms or reflexes of forms containing either a 2p subject suffix *(§2.2.1.3)* or a non-null reflex thereof, or an *n*-bearing 3p subject suffix (courtesy of hii, hti *(§7.2 (δ, ζ))*. Antonym: light(-suffixed). *§2.2 n. 1b, §7, §17.12.1, §17.26 n. 137.*

heavy syllable   *See* **light syllable.**

hefsek *[Hebrew]*   Pause (in the prosodic sense); see **pausal.**

hekšer *[Hebrew]*   Context (in the prosodic sense); see **contextual.**

historical spelling   Etymological spelling, whereby (*) an original [x] <x>, [y] <y> (*) is disrupted by a sound change [x] > [y] / Z and followed by a "lagged" spelling [x] <x>, [y] <x> (~ <y>), whereby new tokens of [y] (those < [x]) continue to be spelled <x>; contrast inverse spelling. *§21.1 with (α) and SM with (21D), §21.2 (α, δ) with n. 12, §21.8, §2.3.4.3 n. 21, §9.1.3 n. 6, §9.1.4 n. 12, §9.2.1.1, §9.2.2 with n. 21, §9.2.3.1, §9.3.1 n. 36, §11.2 I and P, §16.2 nn. 9 and 20, §17.14 with n. 61, §17.18.1, §17.24 n. 128.*

hollow *(hol)*   *See* **gizra.**

iambic   *See* **foot.**

imperfective (impf)   That Common Aramaic conjugation, typified by being concurrently prefixal (primarily for distinctions of person, *§2.1*) and suffixal (for mood, number, and gender, *§2.2*), originally partitioned into three subconjugations—the *long* impf, primarily an aspectual imperfective/incompletive; the *short* impf, serving various nonveridical functions (e.g., subjunctive, jussive); the *energic*, functionally like the long impf but conveying various nuances of force / emphasis / focus)—and later trading in the aspectual function for one of future tense; sometimes called "prefix conjugation," or "9atid" [Hebrew].

inert vowel   A reduced vowel ($\breve{V}$, $\bar{\partial}$) as hypothesized (in Malone 1994, 1995) to lack *moraic weight (§23.5)* and/or other characteristic syllabic-vocalic properties. *§3.2 n. 6, §15.2.1.1 n. 5.*

infix   An affix interrupting (occurring within) the stem it composes with.

inlaut *[German]*   (In) word-medial position.

integral merger   A merger or neutralization whereby two or more entire paradigms become (more) similar or even indistinguishable. The changes driving integral merger characteristically trigger *restructuring* (lexico-phonological mutation). Contrast fractional, full, partial merger. *§6.2 n. 15.*

interdigitation   The morphophonological operation whereby a *root* and *scheme* are composed together to form an *internal-flective stem (miškal). §0.2.1.*

interlude   An intervocalic consonant cluster. *§23.5, §17.4 n. 4.*

intermediate *(level)*   A form X' at the intermediate level ($|X'|$) occurs anywhere in synchronic space anywhere within the phonology between its counterpart on the *phonological* (lexical, underlying) level (/X/) and its counterpart on the *phonetic* level ([X'']); different levels are mediated by different rules, whose special application may be taken to transform a given level to its successor level.

internal flexion   Semitic-characteristic system of stem building whereby largely lexical (*root*) consonants interdigitate with largely grammatical (*scheme*) vowels. *§23.4, §0.2.1.*

intonational phrase   High unit of prosodic organization, beneath the *utterance* and above the *phonological phrase*; in this book equivalent to "pausal string." *§23.5 with (23Z').*

intransitive (intr)   In this book, refers to a verb form lacking an object suffix even when the verb itself may be syntactically transitive; antonym: transitive.

inverse spelling   Anti-etymological spelling, whereby (*) an original [x] <x>, [y] <y> (*) is disrupted by a sound change [x] > [y] / Z and followed by a realignment in spelling such that (*) [x] <x>, [y] <x> (~ <y>). That is, though [y] never changed, it comes to be spelled (sometimes) <x>—presumably because the sound change [x] > [y] has made available *two* possible spellings of [y], <x> and <y>, and speakers (writers / scribes) no longer know how to select between them. Inverse spelling is often called "hypercorrect spelling." The uncovering of inverse spelling can provide a useful tool in tracking and dating sound change. *§21.1 (α) SM with (21D), §9.2.2, §9.2.3.1, §14.2 CP (α), §17.14 n. 61, §17.32 n. 152.*

iterative *(process)*   An iterative process, normally a (synchronic) rule, is one which keeps applying until *all* instances of its conditions have been satisfied. (Iterativity differs from persistence in the locus of the multiple instances of conditions: on the _same_ level of application (and usually in the same form) for iterativity, on _distinct_ levels (and often in distinct forms) for persistence. _§23.3, §4.2.2 with n. 12, §8.1.1 n. 7._

kĕrey _[Aramaic]_ A Biblical Aramaic form as it is traditionally pronounced (as conveyed by Tiberian vocalization), when this pronunciation is incompatible with the corresponding written form; antonym: kĕtiv.

kĕtiv _[Aramaic]_ A Biblical Aramaic form as it is written / spelled consonantally, when this graphie is incompatible with the traditional pronunciation; antonym: kĕrey.

Lesemutter _[German]_   _Same as_ **mater lectionis.**

lexical Characterizing the systematic inventory of a language's basic (nonderived) items (e.g., morphemes) in abstraction of any phonological processes that may apply to them for the purpose of investing them with pronunciation; the term "lexical level" is often used synonymously with "underlying level" (or "phonological level").

lexicalization A linguistic property becomes lexicalized when its distribution / disposition is no longer predictable by rule, but rather must be stipulated as part and parcel of some lexical item, or class of lexical items.

Lexical Phonology _(LP)_ A generative-phonological theory characterized by an intermingling of phonological and morpholexical operations, organized into an ordered series of _strata_ partially differing among themselves on which operations they house. _§23.3, §5.2 n. 10, §11.2 SR, §14.2 nn. 11 and 17, §15.2.1.1 nn. 4 and 6, §15.2.1.3 nn. 9 and 10, §15.6 n. 43, §17.9.2 nn. 26 and 27, §17.11.3 n. 40._

light _(-suffixed)_ In the imp system, forms or reflexes of forms other than those containing either the number-gender suffixes _(§2.2.1.2)_ or non-null reflxes of such suffixes, or the mood suffix *-_ā_ _(§2.2.1.2)_ or a non-null reflex thereof; in the pf system, intransitive forms ending in suffixes of canon -$\check{V}C$, notably 3fs -_AT_ or 1s -_IT_ (derived by epn, _§17.6_, from *-_t_). Antonym: heavy(-suffixed). _§2.2. n. 1b, §7, §9.2.2, §12. 1 (β), §12.2 CP (β), §15.2.1.1, §15.5.1 n. 41, §17.13, §17.15.1 (ε) and TR, §17.26 n. 137._

light syllable A syllable bearing one unit of weight (one _mora_, μ), while a heavy syllable bears more than one mora. _§23.5, §4.1.1 n. 2._

linea occultans _[Latin]_ A SR graphemic diacritic indicating nonpronunciation (silent letter(s)), normally in the form of a supralinear or sublinear horizontal stroke signaling muteness of the letter(s) so marked, hence <X$\overline{Y}$Z> / <X$\underline{Y}$Z> = [XZ]. (Occasionally in word final position, <X$\overline{Y}$Z> = [X], as if the power of the linea occultans extended to <Z>; but actually <Z> in such cases is silent for reasons sui generis; see _§21.7_). _§21.1 n. 6, §8.1.4, §8.2.1, §9.2.2._

loop A phonological nexus, especially but not exclusively in Lexical Phonology, where two rules at adjacent applicational levels variably apply in _either_ order; in symbols for rules X and Y, $X \overset{\frown}{\underset{\smile}{}} Y$. _§23.3._

makef *(=)*   Tiberian diacritic marking that one constituent, normally a potential word (*X*), is prosodically subordinmated to another constituent, normally also a potential word (*Y*): *X=Y.* The type of prosodic subordination involved is normally *proclisis* (wherein *X* functions as the proclitic, *§23.5*), though other modes of subordination may also occasionally be found. *§21.7,§15.2.1.2 n. 7, §17.11.3 n. 37, §17.15.1 n. 63, §17.15.2.*

marked   The antonym of **unmarked** (q.v.). In simple cases, all but one member of a system—the unmarked member—will be marked, while in more subtle cases members may vary in degree of markedness. Let there be a system *A, B, C*, where *C* is unmarked; then *A* and *B* may be marked; but then again, *A* may be more marked (most marked) and *B* less marked. *§15, §16.*

mater lectionis *(ml) (plural:* **matres lectionis***) [Latin]*   A(n originally) consonantal letter, typically a glide and notably <w, y, ʾ, h>, spelling a vowel; also referred to as "ʾem kěriya" [Hebrew], "Lesemutter" [German].

meiosis   *See* **antiwedging.**

melody   In autosegmental theory, any of the elements on a *segmental* (vocalic, consonantal) tier (as opposed to, e.g., the *skeletal* tier, or tiers housing such *prosodic* elements as tones). In Semitic morphophonology, there are two central melodic tiers: that hosting the consonantal *root* (whose melodies are *radicals*), and that hosting the vocalic *scheme* (where the melodies are *schematics*). *§23.4, §3.1, §11.1 n. 3, §15.3.1.2 with n. 24.*

merger reversal   A presumed case of two (or more) sounds first merging *unconditionally* to one sound *(x > z, y > z)* and then sorting themselves out again *(z > a, z > b,* where *x > z > a* and *y > z > b*). Merger reversal is standardly, and correctly, viewed as impossible. *§17.27*

metanalysis   A species of **restructuring** (q.v.) where the primary change is relational rather than substantive; for instance, an item may be reclassified grammatically, or shift its allegiance in morphosyntactic bracketing (as, e.g., in bridge formation, *§2.3.2*).

metaplasm   *See* **restructuring.**

meteg *[Hebrew]*   A Tiberian sublinear graphemic diacritic (< Ṿ >) whose generic function has been aptly characterized by Gesenius as indicating "that the vowel should not be hastily passed over in pronunciation" (Kautsch and Cowley 1910: 64), and whose primary specific roles are as a mark of *open syllabicity* or *secondary stress. §21.7, §17.15.1 n. 65.*

Metrical Stress Theory   A generative phonological theory of stress assignment crucially dependent upon the prosodic concept of *foot. §23.5 with (23Z′), §4.1.1 n. 2.*

mini-pattern   A typically subtle, local, sporadic "design" factor arising from what might be called *poetic whim* as opposed to intrinsically phonetic or semantic dynamism. *§13 n. 6.*

miškal *(plural:* **miškalim***) [Hebrew]*   Internal-flective stem.

mora *(μ)*   Minimal unit of prosodic / syllabic weight; usually fielded as a paraconstitu-
ent to the syllable. *§20.2 n. 5, §21.1 n. 6, §23.5 ,§8.1.1 n. 4, §11.1 with n. 3, §13
n. 8,§14.1 n. 6,§17.16, §17.17.1.*

morphophonemic   *Same as* **morphophonologic(al).**

morphophonemic spelling   Orthographic representation which at least de facto
captures deeper-than-surface facets of the phonology; e.g., SR <n̄t> spelling /nt/
although the pronunciation is [tt]. Most but not all instances of morphophonemic spelling are byproducts of **historical spelling** (q.v.). *§21.1 n. 6, §21.2 n. 12,
§2.3.4.3 n. 21.*

morphophonologic(al)   Largely synonymous with *phonologic(al)*, except that a form
at the phonological (lexical, underlying) level is not normally said to be at the
"morphophonological level." (The term "morphophonologic(al)" tends to be used
rather than "phonologic(al)" when there is special focus on the relation between
morphology and phonology.)

nāqiṣ *[Arabic]*   Defective (gizra). *§15.3.2 n. 30.*

neuter *(verb)*   A verb lexeme prototypically denoting involuntary nonaction on the
part of the entity denoted by the subject; antonym: dynamic. *§0.2.1, §1.1.1 n. 2,
§17.25.*

nikud *[Hebrew]*   *Same as* **pointing** (q.v.).

nucleus *(N)*   The core of a syllable; though nuclei are protypically vocalic, sonorants
(§20.1) frequently figure as nucleic constituents as well—in Aramaic, a role limited to the semivowels *(y, w)*. *§23.5.*

Obligatory Contour Principle *(OCP)*   An autosegmental principle (or guideline)
disallowing adjacent elements on a *melodic tier;* i.e., using m = melodic element,
X = skeletal position: (a) melodic tier @ m' m' . Among correctives that have

skeletal tier X X

been proposed for OCP violations are *fusion* (b) and *antigemination* (c):

(b)   (a) → m' (c)   (a) → m' V m'

                X X X X X

§6.2.2.1 n. 27, §15.3.1.2.

obstruent   *See* **sonorant.**

onset *(O)*   Any consonantism (one consonant or consonant cluster) beginning a syllable. *§23.5.*

oxytone   Stress(ed) on the *ultima* (final syllable); antonym: barytone. *§4.1*

paradigm   *See* **paradigmatic.**

paradigmatic X and Y are in a paradigmatic relation if they stand in a mutual disjunctive relation, "(either) X or Y"; linguistic items (constructions, words, morphemes)
are paradigmatically related whenever they in some sense represent *alternatives*
as opposed to *cooccurrences*; a systematic display of items so related, normally
but not exclusively inflectional affixes, is called a *paradigm*; antonym of "paradigmatic": syntagmatic. *§20.1 (β), §15.2.1.1 n. 3, §15.2.1.3, §17.3 n. 3, §17.25 n. 130.*

parameter   A dialect-specific "setting" value for the application of a rule or presence of a pattern, often expressed in binary terms; e.g., given a rule *R*, dialect *D* may evince application of *R* (parameter setting +*R*), *E* may fail to show *R* (setting -*R*), while *F* may show variable application (±*R*). *§3.4, §4.1.2 n. 6, §4.5, §5.2 <u>TR</u>.*

partial merger   A merger or neutralization whereby two or more forms become cenematically (more) similar phonetically (though not necessarily also phonologically); contrast <u>fractional, full, integral merger</u>. *§6.2 n. 15.*

pausal   In the first instance, a Tiberian accentual grapheme (*ta9am*) of the strongest rank; and derivatively a linguistic stress of commensurate stress represented by that ta9am; and derivatively again, a high-ranking prosodic domain hosting / enabling that stress. Thus in sketch, <V̊> represents [V̊] hosted in / enabled by a domain right-bounded by //: {...[V̊]...//}. With "pausal," contrast contextual. *§20.2 (20Dii), §20.3 (stress), §21.6 (ta9am), §23.5 (prosodic domain), §11.2 n. 6, §17.6.2 n. 8, §17.11.3 n. 37, §17.29.*

peeking rule   *See* **global rule.**

perfective *(pf)*   That Common Aramaic verb conjugation, typified by being purely suffixal *(§2.21.3)*, originally functioning aspectually as perfective / completive and later temporally as preterite; sometimes called "suffix conjugation" or "9avar" [Hebrew].

persistent *(process)*   A change / rule that over a certain time span / across a certain number of phonological levels occurs / applies whenever its conditions are met; some persistent processes may be totally unconstrained as to time span / number of phonological levels (more likely in the case of a persistent rule than in the case of a persistent change). *§18.3 with n. 8, §18.5 with n. 4, §3.3 n. 7, §4.1.2 n. 6, §4.2.1, §5.1 n. 3, §5.2 with nn. 8 and 9, §5.3, §6.1.1.1, §17.11.1, §17.21.1, §17.22 n. 112.*

φ-features ("phi"-features)   Verb-inflectional grammatical features (notably features of tense, person, gender, number, grammatical function (subject, object)).

phonologic(al)   Characterizing the system of patterns and processes relating morphosyntactic structure to phonetic (pronounced) realization; a form in phonologic(al) representation *loosely* refers to a form presented at any level of abstraction anywhere between the morphosyntactic and phonetic , or *strictly* to such a form at the maximally abstract level (the *lexical* level, the *underlying* level).

phonologization   A diachronic change whereby a phonetic or intermediate-level segment in a given context (at times the null context) is "upgraded" to phonological / underlying status; in symbols, either (a) or (b):

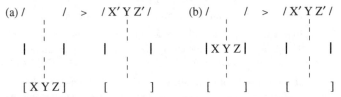

(in these displays, *Y* is the phonologized segment, and *X__Z* or *X'__Z'* is context; *X, Z* may or may not = *X', Z'*)

phonotactics   The totality of constraints governing a dialect's permissible sound combinations, especially those relating to syllable structure.

plain   Any *non-rmp binyan,* designation omitted context allowing; e.g., the plain *simple* binyan is normally referred to as "simple (sim)" rather than as "plain simple (plain sim)."

plerematic   Relating to the *content* side of language, as opposed to the *expression* side; *semantic / morphosyntactic.* Antonym: cenematic. *§18.4, §15.3.2, §15.5.2 n. 42.*

pointing *(nikud [Hebrew])*   Any of a number of orthographic diacritic systems primarily conveying vocalic information, but occasionally other sorts of linguistic information as well. *§21.4.*

portmanteau   A morphological formative (morph) simultaneously serving two or more morphological functions, or simultaneously representing two or more morphemes, especially when those functions are normally served by singleton morphemes elsewhere in the system; in sketch, allowing *M, N* to be morphemes with features [+m], [+n] respectively, a portmanteau might be a morph *P* containing features $\begin{bmatrix} +m \\ +n \end{bmatrix}$. *§2.3.4.4 3ms, §12.2 n. 15, §15.3.1.1, §15.3.2.*

prefix   Prepositive *affix,* preceding the stem it composes with.

pregnant   When a formative which is normally asemantic appears in a context where it conveys meaning, it is called "pregnant." *§17.17.1 n. 85.*

prepositional pronoun *(pp)*   (Reflexes of) either of the proclitic prepositions $*b\overset{\circ}{V}=$ 'in, by' (locative, instrumental) / $*l\overset{\circ}{V}=$ 'to' (dative) taking a pronominal suffix as complement, especially when the whole then encliticizes to a verb (string so formed: *verb=pp*). *§17.15.2.*

privative   A mode of organization whereby a system of entities (or properties, etc.) is indicated in positive terms for all members but one, and the presence / occurrence / force of this one is indicated *negatively,* by the absence of any specification. Suppose the system deals with forms $(a, b, c, \ldots)$ conveying meanings $(A, B, C, \ldots)$; then a privative representation of meaning-form couplings for A, B, C, D might be *Aa, Bb, Cc, D*—equivalent symbologically to *Aa, Bb, Cc, D*∅, where ∅ = zero. In such a case, *D* is said to be the *unmarked member* of the meaning set. Antonym of "privative": equipollent. *§23.1 n. 2,§9.2.3.1 n. 27, §15.2.1.1 with n. 3, §15.2.2.1 with n. 17, §15.6, §16.1 n. 1.*

process   Generic term for "change" (diachronic) and "rule" (synchronic).

proclitic   Prepositive *clitic,* preceding the word it constructs with. *§17.11.3 n. 37.*

proportional deployment   Implementation of an analogical *(transparentive)* change $D > E$ in $A : B = C : D > E$, where the change $D > E$ would appear unmotivated in absence of the enabling proportion $A : B = C : D$. *§15.5.1 n. 41, §17.15.1 M (µ).*

prosodic organization, prosodology, prosody   In the narrow sense, a sphere of linguistic organization considered by many to mediate between syntax and phonology. Though there are many unsettled questions (including the very existence of prosody), the lower (phonology-abutting) level of prosodic structure may be taken as that of the *foot*, itself organzing phonological *syllables*. Prosodic structure then builds successively (and exhaustively) upward toward the syntax, to culminate in the (prosodic) *utterance*. *§23.5 with (23Z').*

prosodic word   A prosodic unit typically constituted by a *stem* plus its *affixes*, but in Aramaic plausibly including certain tightly bound *clitics*—notably *proclitics* conventionally written at close quarters with their host word (e.g., <w> 'and', <l> 'to'). *§23.5 with (23Z').*

proto-Aramaic *(pA)*   The type of Aramaic hypothesized to be ancestral to all descendant forms of the language.

quadriradical *(quad)*   Roots with four radicals instead of the usual three. *§1.1.2 n. 8.*

quasi-inert string *(q.i.s.)*   A phonological string (of segments—vowels and/or consonants) failing to manifest full-blown contrastive / phonemic force, and so lending itself to various "empty"—asemantic—functions at the behest of the morphophonology at large; e.g., as "filler" of empty skeletal positions. *§15.3.2, §3.4, §17.2.*

radical   Any of the (consonantal) building blocks of a *root* morpheme. Symbology: $\sqrt{}$ (generic), $1\sqrt{}$ or Q (first [initial] radical), $2\sqrt{}$ or S (second [medial] radical), $3\sqrt{}$ or M (third [final] radical). *§0.2.1.*

register   Roughly, "subdialect" of the "dialects" studied in this book, or kindred subgroupings; not to be strictly identified with "register" in the technical sociolinguistic sense. *§0.1 with n. 2.*

repair strategy   A phonetic / phonological operation prompted by incurrence of a violation of some canonical pattern in the prevailing phonological system. No hard-and-fast criteria distinguish repair strategies from run-of-the-mill phonetic / phonological processes, though it might be noted that repair strategies tend to be *persistent*. In this book, some repair strategies have been defined as full-blown processes, while others have simply been appealed to ex tempore and left unnamed (an undesirable looseness in analysis, if truth be told). *§20.2, §1.1.2 n. 8b, §2.3.3 (γ), §2.3.4.3 n. 22, §3.2 n. 6, §4.1.1 n. 3, §4.4.1, §4.5 with nn. 24 and 25, §7.2 n. 18, §7.4.1 n. 24, §9.1.2, §9.1.3 n. 9, §13 n. 3, §13 TL (α) with n. 8, §14.2 n. 20c, §15.2.1.3, §15.2.2.2 with nn. 18 and 20, §15.2.2.3, §15.3.1.1, §15.5.2, §15.6 (β), §16.2 TR (u, v), §17.15.1 (κ, ι) with n. 71, §17.15.2, §17.18.2, §17.23.3, §17.26 n. 136, §17.28 M.*

reprise *(change)*   A change that for typological or analogical (transparentive) reasons recurs some time (or times) subsequent to its original (primary) occurrence. *§18.3, §18.5 with n. 14, §21.1, §4.1.2 n. 6, §9.2.3.2, §9.3.1 n. 37, §12.2 SM (γ), §17.4, §17.11.3 nn. 44 and 50, §17.21.1.*

rerun   Generic term for "persistent" and "reprise." *§18.5 with n. 14, §3.3 n. 7, §4.1.2 n. 6, §4.2.1, §4.5, §5.2, §6.1.1.1, §17.15.2.*

resolved foot   A heavy syllable serving as point of prosodic neutralization between *trochaic* and *iambic* feet. *§4.1.1 n. 2.*

restructuring   Replacement of phonological encoding (usually partial, e.g., one or two phonemes) at the underlying level or within the lexicon; when a root is restructured, especially by transfer from one weak gizra to another, the traditional term is "metaplasm." *§18.4, §23.2 with (23G), §3.2 n. 6, §6.2 n. 15, §6.4, §15.2.2.2 n. 20, §15.6,§16.2 n. 21, §17.7 n. 16, §17.8 n. 22 and M, §17.9.2 n. 26, §17.11.3 with n. 44, §17.17.1, §17.33 n. 156.*

rime *(R)*   Syllabic constituent consisting of the *nucleus (N)* and the *coda (K)* (if there is one). *§23.5.*

root *(√)*   *Internal-flective* morpheme consisting of a lexically specified sequence of consonants *(radicals). §0.2.1.*

rule   A synchronic process viewed as transforming a form from one shape to another; synchronic analog (and often descendant) of diachronic *change*, though genetically related rules and changes need not be fully isomorphic.

rule addition   A mutation in the synchronic phonology whereby a new rule is added, normally on the last derivational level. Last-level rule addition is the normal way that a sound change first gets into the phonology as a synchronic process, though later this may be obscured by subsequent mutations. *§18.4, §23.2, §6.2 n. 15, §17.9.2 n. 26.*

rule conspiracy   A nexus whereby two or (typically) several independent rules manifest convergent outputs, especially when the outputs then appear to serve some common synchronic function not directly predictable from the corresponding rules. (There is no consensus in the literature as to the status of rule conspiracies, some claiming that the relevant nexuses arise from mere coincidence, or are even scholarly contrivances.) *§15.3.1.1.*

rule deletion   A mutation in the synchronic phonology whereby a rule is dropped. There are three general cases (putting aside rarer nexuses or special complications): (*) The rule is deleted, but its content shows up on the phonological level (by *restructuring)*—case (a) below; (*) two rules are deleted, one (the later) so to speak undoing the other (the earlier)—case (b); (*) the rule is deleted without compensation, whereby a more abstract form surfaces (is pronounced)—case (c). Especially cases (b) and (c) are often prompted by *analogical* considerations *(transparentaztion)*, whereby the new forms are in some way more homogeneous paradigmatically.

(a)	I	>	II	(b)	I	>	II	>	III	(c)	I	>	II
	/A/		/B/		/A/		/A/		/A/		/A/		/A/
	r |B|				*r* |B|		*r* |B|				*r* |B|		
	[B]		[B]				*r'* |C|				[B]		[A]
					[B]		[A]		[A]				

(Observe that case (c) is like case (b) with the intermediate stage dropped. When more is known, it might turn out that all apparent cases of (c) are actually cases of (b).) *§18.4 n. 10 and (18T), §23.2 with (23G), §3.2 n. 6, §6.4, §14.2 n. 18, §15.2.2.2 n. 20, §17.33 n. 156.*

rule inversion   *Same as* **rule reversal** (q.v.).

rule loss   *Same as* **rule deletion** (q.v.).

rule modification A species of mutation whereby a rule changes in content from one diachronic stage to another. *§18.4, §23.2 with (23K), §14.1 n. 4.*

rule reordering A mutation of the synchronic order of two rules, normally applying at adjacent derivational levels, such that the rules switch levels: I   >   II

$$\text{rule } R \qquad \text{rule } S$$
$$\text{rule } S \qquad \text{rule } R.$$

§18.4 with (18S) and n. 11 , §23.2 (23J), §3.2 n. 6, §5.2 n. 9, §11.2 n. 12, §15.4 n. 34, §17.9.2 nn. 25 and 26, §17.11.3 nn. 44 and 50.

rule reversal A mutation in a rule whereby the *focus* becomes the *change* (and vice versa), and the *conditions* become (a subset of) their own complement:

$$(x \Rightarrow y / z) > (y \Rightarrow x / -z).$$

§18.4 with (18U) and n. 13, §7.7 n. 33, §15.5.1 n. 35, §17.11.3 n. 44, §17.23.3.

šadda *[Arabic]* Orthographic diacritic for gemination: < $\overset{w}{C}'$ > represents [C′C′] (or /C′C′/, |C′C′|). *§21.1 (α).*

schematic Any of the (vocalic) building blocks of a *scheme* morpheme. Symbology: ʃ (generic), 1ʃ (first schematic), 2ʃ (second schematic). Traditional synonym: (first, second) stem vowel. *§0.2.1.*

Schematisierung *[German]* Artificial warping or skewing of the linguistic structure of a text in the direction of some presumed correct or ideal linguistic model. *§20.2 n. 4, §22.2, §0.1 TL, §3.2 n. 5, §4.5 n. 24, §5.3 n. 13, §7.4.1 n. 24, §8.1.1 n. 5, §9.3.1 n. 38, §11.1 n. 1, §15.2.2.2 with n. 18, §15.3.1.3 n. 29, §17.16 n. 82, §17.23.1.2, §17.23.1.3.*

scheme (ʃ) Internal-flective morpheme consisting of a lexically specified sequence of vowels (*schematics*); in the general Semitistic literature often called vowel pattern. *§0.2.1.*

schwa (ə) A reduced vowel ($\breve{V}$), either in its generic role (= any of the whole family of reduced vowels in a given dialect) or in its specific role as the unmarked manifestation of reduced vowel in a given dialect, whether in a particular context or at large. Contrast ẖataf, a reduced vowel whose chroma is explicitly indicated. "schwa" may refer to either phonetic / phonological space ([ə], /ə/, |ə|) or to its orthographic representation (<ə>, < : >). *§21.5, §17.23.*

schwa (šěva) na9, naḥ *[Hebrew]* The Tiberian schwa grapheme (< : >), respectively when pronounced (*na9* "mobile," [ə]) or when silent (*naḥ* "quiescent," [∅]). *§21.5, §4.5, §17.15.1 n. 65.*

segment Generic for "vowel" and "consonant."

segolate A *miškal* of original shape *$Q\overset{\circ}{V}SM$, or any reflex thereof. *§23.2 n. 5, §12.2 G.*

shaft Trajectory of a change originating in a **dialect pocket** (q.v.). *§18.2 with (18I, J), §6.3 n. 44, §9.2.3.2, §19 with (19H, I) and n. 37.*

sibilant Rilled fricative (*s, ś, z, ṣ, š*) as opposed to slit fricative (in this book called "spirant"; *f (φ), θ x, v (β), ð, γ). *§20.1, §5.1.*

skeleton In autosegmental representations, a level of organization whereby, specifically in internal-flective stem building, consonantal *radicals* are duly interweaved with vocalic *schemes*; a skeleton will at times be represented as a sequence of bare (featureless) consonants and vowels (e.g., *C V C C V C*), and at times as a sequence of abstract segmental positions devoid of inherent consonantal / vocalic properties (e.g., *X X X X X X*). *§23.4,§3.1, §9.1.3 n. 7, §11 n. 3, §15.3.12 with n. 24.*

Sonorancy Hierarchy   A ranking of consonants in accordance with the relative pho-netic sonorancy of their manners of articulation, associated with the proposal that the structuring of consonant clusters tendentially reflects the ranking. *§23.5 n. 12, §17.18.2.*

sonorant   The most vowel-like class of consonants, in Aramaic consisting of *nasals* ≫ *liquids* ≫ *glides* (ranked from most to least ideally consonantal); antonym: <u>ob-struent</u> (the least vowel-like class of consonants, in Aramaic consisting of *stops* ≫ *fricatives*, again ranked from more to less ideally consonantal). *§20.1.*

spirant   In this book, <u>slit fricative</u> (notably *f(φ)*, *θ*, *x*, *v(β)*, *δ*, *γ*) as opposed to <u>rilled fricative</u> (or <u>sibilant</u>: *s, ś, z, ṣ, š*), though in the linguistic literature at large "spirant" and "fricative" tend to be used interchangeably. *§20.1, §5.1.*

staminal   Adjective form of "stem."

straddle   A manifestation of relationship between two dialects by dint of *diffusional spread* of one or more changes from one of the dialects to the other (as opposed to *genealogical inheritance* from a common ancestral dialect). *§18.2, §17.12 n. 54, §19 with (19H).*

spreading   Autosegmental explication of *assimilation*, the idea being that (parts of) adjacent *feature geometries* might reassociate to neighboring segments. Letting *X*, *Y* = *skeletal positions* and *F*, *G* = segments qua feature geometries associated to skeletal positions, diagram (a) below represents *total regressive assimilation*: the feature content of *X* (= *F*) is snipped off (≠) and *X* reassociates to the feature con-tent of *Y* (= *G*)—*G* has *spread* to *F* (by replacing it), the result being (b). *Progres-sive assimilation* works out the same in reverse (≠ on *Y*, ⁄ from *Y* drawn down to *F*).

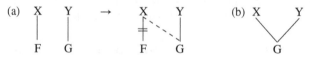

§20.2 n. 5, §22.1 n. 3, §23.5 with (23Yii) and n. 13, §9.2.1.2 n. 20, §10 with n. 12, §17.16, §17.25 n. 130.

stratum   In Lexical Phonology, one of a variable number of mutually ordered levels of representation, each typically housing one or more *word-building* operations and sequences of phonological *rules*. *§23.3, §5.2 n. 10.*

stress clash   The adjacency, over a sufficiently weak (or nonexistent) morphosyntac-tic / prosodic boundary, of two *(primary-)stressed* syllables, a configuration often relieved either by weakening one of the stresses (limiting case, deleting it) or by moving one of the stresses out of offending adjacency (in Aramaic, the work of *stress retraction*, srt, *§4.1.2 B, §17.15.2 n. 75*). *§15.2.1.1.*

stretch   In the *diachronic* mode, a period of time during which a change is active or across which a *chain* of changes has occurred; in the *synchronic* sense, a homologous cross-section of a derivation (wherein a rule or sequence of rules applies). *§11.2 SR.*

strong *(gizra)*   A verb (class) manifesting no morphophonemically special behavior, at least as conceived of traditionally or relative to the matter under focus (e.g., verbs with *spirantizable* (spr) radicals—*p, t, k, b, d, g*—are normally construed as strong); antonym: weak.

structural change *(sc)*   The mutation or replacement effected by a rule; e.g., in $X \Rightarrow Y \mathbin{/} Z$, the structural change is Y (equivalently in the so-called "transformational format+ — sd: X   Z

$$\quad 1\qquad 2$$

$$sc:\quad Y\quad 2).\qquad \S 6.1.2\ n.\ 7.$$

structural description *(sd)*   Combined statement of a rule's *focus* and *conditions* in the so-called "transformational format"—a formulation frequently adopted for phonological rules of *metathesis*; e.g., sd: X   Y   Z

$$\quad 1\qquad 2\qquad 3$$

$$sc:\quad 2\qquad 1\qquad 3$$

which says "metathesize $X\,Y$ to $Y\,X$ when /___Z". *§6.1.2 n. 7, §9.1.1 n. 2, §11.1 n. 4.*

suffix   Postpositive *affix*, following the stem it composes with.

suprasegmental   Phonetic / phonological properties in addition to those defining the *segment,* i.e., in addition to the dimensions / features informing charts (20A, B, C) for consonants (*§20.1*) and (20Di, E) for vowels (*§20.2*)—in particular for Aramaic, properties of *vowel length* and *stress* (*§20.2 (20Dii), §20.3*); though *gemination* of consonants may be considered suprasegmental as well (*§20.1 (β)*). *§18.4.*

sǝyɔ̄mē *[Syriac]*   A SR (and CP) diacritic grapheme consisting of a row of dots usually signifying that the word so marked is *plural* (in any of a variety of ways); sǝyɔ̄mē is normally suprapositive, and in this book is transcribed "Ẍ" (X = the host word). *§21.7, §7.2 n. 13, §8.1.3 n. 14.*

synchronic   Characterizing a linguistic system as to its function and structure at any given moment independently of its history; antonym: diachronic.

synchronic spelling   Orthographic representation where the letters are geared (and perhaps redeployed) to reflect the prevailing linguistic (usually phonetic / phonologic) state of the language; contrast historical spelling, where letters are deployed in such a way as to reflect an earlier stage of the system: while *[x] <x> > [y] <x> sketches historical spelling, *[x] <x> > [y] <y> sketches corresponding synchronic spelling. *§17.14 n. 61.*

syntagmatic X and Y are in a syntagmatic relation if they stand in a mutual conjunctive relation, "(both) X and Y"; linguistic items are syntagmatically related whenever they cooccur in a text (in the broad sense, including utterances, sentences, etc.) in any way, such as one providing an environment for another (under a rule), or one agreeing with another grammatically, etc.; antonym: paradigmatic. *§20.1 (β), §15.2.1.3, §17.3 n. 3, §17.25 n. 130.*

ta9am *(plural:* **tĕ9amim***) [Hebrew]*   Any member of a system of graphemic diacritics, notably the Tiberian system, in the first instance probably designed to provide a musicological (cantillational) scoring of the text, but as a byproduct providing valuable information on *tonosyllabic* and *prosodic* structure; in English frequently called "accent (accents)." *§21.6, §17.15.1 n. 63, §17.15.2 n. 75, §17.6.2 n. 8, §17.11.3 B with n. 37.*

tense   At large, a semantic opposition of *time* (as opposed to *aspect*), but in this book used as a convenient generic for *perfective, imperfective,* and *imperative.*

therapeutic strategy   Same as **repair strategy** (q.v.), but usually targeting a state of affairs with the potential to impair communication (e.g., an instance of what is sometimes called *pernicious homonymy*) rather than violative of per se cenematic canons. *§7.2 n. 9, §17.26 n. 136.*

tier   Level of autosegmental representation connected to other such levels by *association*, the resulting complex constituting a complete morphophonologic representation of a form. *§23.4.*

tier conflation   An operation whereby the *associated tiers* of an autosegmental representation are collapsed together into one *linearly organized string. §23.4, §3.1 with n. 1, §6.2.2.1 n. 27, §15.2.1.1 n. 4, §17.11.3 n. 40, §17.25 n. 130.*

tonosyllabic   That portion of a phonological string consisting of *syllabic* structure interacting with *stress (tonic)* properties. (In the linguistic literature at large, this facet of phonological activity is often referred to as "prosodic," a usage usually avoided in this book out of uncertainty as to whether stress phenomena are indeed prosodic, rather than appertaining to an interacting but independent module. *See §20.3, §23.5.) §17.11.3 TL.*

transderivational rule   *See* **global rule.**

transient process   A process whose occurrence / application is confined to a given point in time *(change)* or to a given derivational level *(rule)*; antonym: <u>persistent process</u>. *§18.3 with n. 8, §17.11.1 with (17.11A, B).*

transitive *(tr)*   In this book, refers to a verb form ending in an object suffix; antonym: <u>intransitive</u>.

transparizand   A form having undergone, or subject to undergoing, *transparentive (analogical) reshaping. §15.3.1.1, §15.6.*

trochaic   *See* **foot.**

underlying representation   In the phonologic sense, the most abstract level of representation; sometimes called <u>phonological</u> representation (par excellence); largely synonymous with <u>lexical</u> representation.

unmarked   A member of a system is said to be *unmarked*—or the *unmarked member*—under any of a variety of circumstances, sometimes rigorously formulated, sometimes rather loosely and impressionistically. A common rigorous exploitation is to dub the **privative** (q.v.) member unmarked. A common loose explotation is to reckon the unmarked member as the one occurring *most frequently* (in some specified mode) vis-→-vis other members. Antonym: marked. *§15, §16.*

verschärft *[German]* *Geminate* (consonsant cluster). *§17.4.*

wave theory A theory of genealogical development characterized by changes (geographically) crossing dialect lines (as well as moving *within* a given dialect area); contrast family tree theory. *§18.2, §18.3,§4.1.2 nn. 6 and 11, §7.2 n. 11,§7.4.2 with (7C), §8.2, §9.2.3.2, §9.3.2 n. 43, §17.21.1 with n. 107, §19.*

weak *(gizra)* *See* **strong.**

yā'u 'l-waṣl *[Arabic]* Repair-strategic insertion of [y], primarily in palatal contexts, to restore violated syllabic canons; see **hamzatu 'l-waṣl.** *§9.1.2 n. 3, §9.2.1.2 n. 20, §15.2.1.5.*

zero segment *(∅)* The space vacated by a phonetic / phonologic process, normally when the vacancy continues to play some sort of synchronic role; see **ghost segment** (itself a special case of zero segment). Synonym: empty segment. *§21.3, §15.3.1.2 n. 26.*

26. Abbreviations and Symbols

[Alphabetic items precede in §26.1, analphabetic items follow in §26.2. Mixed alphabetic-analphabetic items, or those which are in one fashion or another ambiguous of classification, are for the most part listed in §26.2. This includes but is not limited to (*) Greek letters and (*) Roman letters modified/accompanied by analphabetic marks/symbols (except that hyphenated lower-case prefixes to processes appear in §26.1—see [i] below).

Three sorts of items, though otherwise appropriate for §26, are indexed elsewhere in the book:

[i] three-letter abbreviations of patterns or processes, which are listed in §19 (19A–D), though §26.1 does include general abbreviations modifying pattern/process designations (e.g., e- "early");

[ii] most phonetic symbols for specific consonants and vowels, which are listed in §20 (especially §20.1 (20A) for the former, §20.2 (20D) for the latter), though archiphonemic symbols (e.g., D = {d, ð}) as well as various special/unusual cases are additionally listed in §26;

[iii] abbreviations for bibliographic references, which are listed in §27, as also are symbols/abbreviations exclusively used in such references, e.g., AOS = "(meeting of the) American Oriental Society"]

26.1. Alphabetic

a	Ashkenazic (traditional pronounciation of TL)
A	Aramaic; archiphoneme for reflexes of *a ((§20, (20D)))
Anm	Anmerkung ("note")
Ash	Ashkenazic (traditional pronunciation of TL)
B	Biblical (Aramaic); archiphoneme for {b, v/β} ((§20.1))
Bab	Babylonian (register)
bb	Babylonian (register)
BCE	Before the Common (Christian) Era (= BC)
c-	process in the Samaritan Circuit ((§22.1, (22B)))
C	consonant
cA	Common Aramaic
cau	causative
CE	(during the) Common (Christian) Era (= AD)
conj	conjunctive
cX	*See §26.2*

d- diachronic (mode of a process)
D archiphoneme for {d, ð} ((§20.1))
Dan (biblical book of) Daniel
def defective (gizra)
Deut (biblical book of) Deuteronomy
dntalv dentoalveolar
e- early (manifestation of a process, as opposed to *late*) ((§3.3 n. 7)
E Eastern (Aramaic) = {SR, TL, M};
archiphoneme for front mid vowel ((§20, (20D)))
Exod (biblical book of) Exodus
Ezra (biblical book of) Ezra
f feminine (gender)
F feature (complex)
G Galilean (Aramaic); archiphoneme for {g, γ} ((§20.1)))
gem geminate (gizra)
Gen (biblical book of) Genesis
H Archiphoneme for guttural = {ʔ, h, 9, ḥ} ((§20.1));
Mandaic morphogram spelling for 3ms -ī, 3fs -ā ((§21.8))
hol hollow (gizra)
I Imperial (Aramaic);
archiphoneme for nonlow front vowel ((§20, (20D)))
imp imperfective-imperative subsystem
impa imperative
impf imperfective
int intensive
IPA International Phonetic Alphabet
Jac Jacobite (Western register of Syriac)
jc Jacobite (Western register of Syriac)
Jer (biblical book of) Jeremiah
K archiphoneme for {k, x} ((§20.1));
(syllabic) coda
l- late (manifestation of a process (as opposed to early)—special case of
reprise) ((§3.3 n. 7))
L Lower (branch of Eastern Aramaic = {TL, M});
archiphoneme for [+low] consonants (= {r; H} = {r; ʔ, h, 9, ḥ}) ((§20.1)))
lc (in) loco citato = (at) the passage most recently cited (of the work most
recently referenced
Lev (biblical book of) Leviticus
llcc (in) locis citatis (plural of *lc*)
LP Lexical Phonology ((§23.3))
lt lateral ((§20.1, (20A)))
lx lax ((§20.1, (20A)))
m marked;
Modern (Mandaic pronunciation)
M third radical (= 3√); Mandaic (Aramaic)
md medial ((§20.1, (20A)))

mod pron   modern pronunciation (notably of Mandaic)
n   (end)note, (foot)note
N   Nabatean (Aramaic); (syllabic) nucleus; nasal
Nes   Nestorian (Eastern register of Syriac)
nn   (end)notes, (foot)notes (plural of *n*)
ns   Nestorian (Eastern register of Syriac)
O   Old (Aramaic); (syllabic) onset obj object
obj.   object
OBL   Obligatory Contour Principle ((§6.2.2.1 n. 27))
p   proto- (e.g., *pA*, *pSem*); plural (number)
p-   partial (version of a process)
P   Palymrene (Aramaic); archiphoneme for {p, f/φ} ((§20.1, (20A)))
pas   passive
pf   perfective
p.o.a.   position of articulation
pp   prepositional pronoun ((§17.15.2))
Q   first radical (= 1√)
q.i.s.   quasi-inert string ((§15.3.2))
qq.v.   quae vide ("which(pl) see" = plural of *q.v.*)
quad   quadriradical
q.v.   quod vide ("which(sg) see": *X q.v.* is an instruction to seek out *X* in some systematic array (such as an index))
r-   reprise (rerun or persistence of a process) ((§3.3 n. 7))
R   voiced uvular fricative ((§20.2, (20A)))
rmp   reflexive-mediopassive
RTR   retracted tongue root (cenematic feature) ((§20.1, (20B, C)))
s   singular (number)
s-   synchronic (mode of a process)
S   second radical (= 2√); syllable
Sab   Sabbionetan (subregister of Tiberian TR)
sb   Sabbionetan (subregister of Tiberian TR)
sc   structural change ((§6.1.2 n. 7))
sd   structural description ((§6.1.2 n. 7))
sim   simple (binyan)
SM   Samaritan (Aramaic)
SR   Syriac (Aramaic)
sub   subject
t   (in) traditional pronunciation
T   archiphoneme for {t, θ} ((§20.1))
tb   Tiberian (register)
Tib   Tiberian (register)
TL   Talmudic (Aramaic) (= the dialect of the Babylonian Talmud and related language forms)
tn   tense ((§20.1, (20A)))
tr   transitive ((§2.3.2.1 (β)))
TR   Targumic (Aramaic) (= the dialect of the Onkelos and Jonathan Targums)

trad pron	traditional pronunciation
u	unmarked
U	archiphoneme for reflexes of *u ((§20, (20D)))
V	vowel (irrespective of color, length, or stress); unstressed vowel (in contexts where this sense is clear) (*for* V *with diacritics, see §26.2*)
vd	voiced ((§20.1, (20A)))
vl	voiceless ((§20.1, (20A)))
w	with
W	Western (Aramaic); archiphoneme for {w, y} ((§20.1))
X	voiceless uvular spirant ((§20.1, §9.1.3)); commonly used as a general variable (as multiply in §26.2), sometimes with Y, Z as cooccurrent variables with possibly different values. (A special case of the variable use is to mark skeletal positions devoid of consonantal/vocalic commitment, e.g., §9.1.3 n. 7)
y	Yemeni (traditional pronunciation of TL)
Y	Ya²udic/Samalian (Aramaic); general variable (see X)
Yem	Yemeni (traditional pronunciation of TL)
Z	general variable (see X)

26.2. Analphabetic

[1] *X — X is *reconstructed* (as opposed to *attested*); i.e., its shape is cobbled together by inference based on the comparative method/internal reconstruction.

[2] **X — X is reconstructed (see [1]) as being earlier than some equally reconstructed descendant/reflex, say Y; hence **X > *Y.

[3] @X — X fails to occur (because ungrammatical or otherwise incomptabile with the prevailing system).

[4] cX — X is *constructed* (as opposed to *attested*); i.e., its existence is extrapolated on the analogy of homoparadigmatic attested forms.

[5] †X — X is an archaic/archaizing/conservative form (notation used by Margolis 1910 (Mar)).

[6] X' — X of a given content/identity; e.g., $C'C'$ = a geminate cluster, whereas CC', $C'C$, or CC may be heterophonous. (By extension, a string like $X'Y'$ = a string whose constituents maximally agree (in features); e.g., $C'T'$ = a cluster whose first member is a consonant agreeing in all permissible features with the second member, a dentoalveolar stop (§10, and [65] below.)

[7] $X,''$ X''' — Used like X' in contexts requiring two or three possible distinct Xs.

[8] X_n^m — A string of minimally n Xs and maximally m; e.g., X_3^5 is the set {XXX, XXXX, XXXXX}.

[9] $X̣$ — X is (phonetically/phonologically) emphatic/pharyngeal(ized)/uvularized.

[10] $X̥$ — (*) X is vocalic (e.g., [l̥] = vocalic [l]).
(*) X orthographically has a sublinear dot (CP, §21.4 n. 16).

[11] $X̊$, $V̈$ — (*) X orthographically has (a) supralinear dot(s) (CP, SR).
(*) $V̊$ signals a *short* vowel, as opposed to *long* ($V̄$) or *reduced* ($V̆$).

[12] [X]   (*) *X* is a phonetic representation, or pronunciation.
                  (*) *X* is a feature (bundle).
                  (*) *X* is a subprocess (see [44]).
[13] /X/   *X* is a phonological representation.
[14] |X| *X* is a (phonologically) intermediate representation.
[15] <X>   *X* is an orthographic representation, or transliteration.
[16] {X}   (*) *X* is a *set*, e.g., {*A, B, C*} (or) $\begin{pmatrix} A \\ B \\ C \end{pmatrix}$) = the set of elements *A, B, C*

                  (= often equivalently, the *paradigm* of *A, B, C)*. Relatedly, *A, B,* and
                  C are systematically available choices in some context: "either *A* or *B*
                  or *C*. . ."
                  (*) *X* is *morphological/syntactic* (rather than *phonological*); used
                  inter alia to capture morphological structure (just) prior to/as input to
                  the phonology.
                  (*) *X* is morphologically (or otherwise) organized/bracketed; e.g.
                  {*A*{*BC*}} = first comes *A* and then *BC* as a unit (dendrologically
                  equivalent =

). Singleton {*A*} conveys that *A* is a simple
                  formative,

                  A   B   C
                  usually morpheme.
                  (*) In transcriptions from primary sources, *X* is *restored* (inasmuch as
                  the original evinces at that spot either a lacuna or a smudged/
                  damaged/ jumbled graphie).
                  (*) *X* is a comment/supplement/gloss intercalated within a
                  direct quotation from some source.
[17] *(italicized) X*   In addition to standard usages (emphasis, contrast, highlighting,
                  etc.), an *italicized* linguistic form (or part thereof) presents that
                  form with no commitment as to its linguistic level/status (e.g.,
                  phonological, phonetic, intermediate).
[18] X > Y, Y < X   *X* changes into *Y* (*diachronic* relation).
[19] X ⇒ Y, Y ⇐ X   *X* is transformed into/corresponds on the next level toward the
                  phonetic to *Y* (*synchronic* relation).
[20] X → Y, Y ← X   Generic for >, < and ⇒ , ⇐ ([18], [19]) (mutation with no
                  further commitment to diachronic/synchronic relation).
[21] X ≻ Y, Y ≺ X   *X* changes to *Y* for *analogical* reasons (§9.2.3.2).
[22] X ≥ Y, Y ≤ X   *X* changes to *Y* in the sense that the *system or dialect* housing *X*
                  changes to the system/dialect housing *Y*, although from the point of
                  view of *substance X = Y*.
[23] X ≫ Y, Y ≪ X   *X* ranks higher than *Y* on some scale.
[24] X^Y   (*) (process) *X* precedes (process) *Y*.
                  (*) *X* is subject to *Y* as object.
[25] X⌣Y   *X* and *Y*, processes, are in a *loop*; i.e., they may apply in either order,
                  X^*Y* or *Y*^*X* (§23.3).

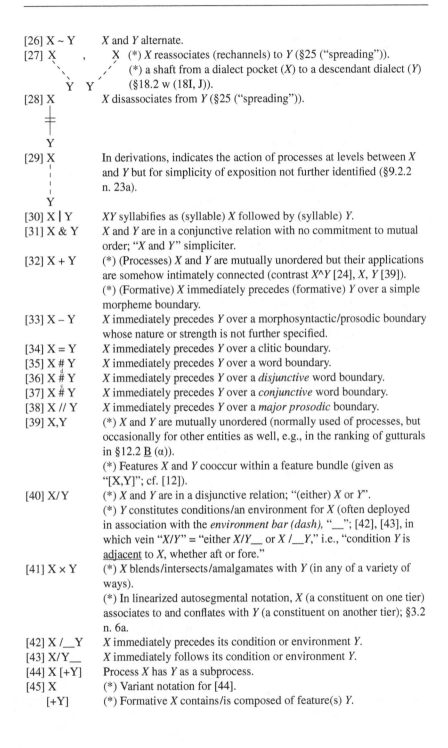

[26] X ~ Y   *X* and *Y* alternate.

[27] X   ,   X   (*) *X* reassociates (rechannels) to *Y* (§25 ("spreading")).

                     (*) a shaft from a dialect pocket (*X*) to a descendant dialect (*Y*)

      Y   Y   (§18.2 w (18I, J)).

[28] X   *X* disassociates from *Y* (§25 ("spreading")).

    Y

[29] X   In derivations, indicates the action of processes at levels between *X*

                and *Y* but for simplicity of exposition not further identified (§9.2.2

                n. 23a).

    Y

[30] X | Y   *XY* syllabifies as (syllable) *X* followed by (syllable) *Y*.

[31] X & Y   *X* and *Y* are in a conjunctive relation with no commitment to mutual order; "*X* and *Y*" simpliciter.

[32] X + Y   (*) (Processes) *X* and *Y* are mutually unordered but their applications are somehow intimately connected (contrast *X^Y* [24], *X*, *Y* [39]).

                (*) (Formative) *X* immediately precedes (formative) *Y* over a simple morpheme boundary.

[33] X – Y   *X* immediately precedes *Y* over a morphosyntactic/prosodic boundary whose nature or strength is not further specified.

[34] X = Y   *X* immediately precedes *Y* over a clitic boundary.

[35] X # Y   *X* immediately precedes *Y* over a word boundary.

[36] X #̣ Y   *X* immediately precedes *Y* over a *disjunctive* word boundary.

[37] X #̣ Y   *X* immediately precedes *Y* over a *conjunctive* word boundary.

[38] X // Y   *X* immediately precedes *Y* over a *major prosodic* boundary.

[39] X,Y   (*) *X* and *Y* are mutually unordered (normally used of processes, but occasionally for other entities as well, e.g., in the ranking of gutturals in §12.2 <u>B</u> (α)).

                (*) Features *X* and *Y* cooccur within a feature bundle (given as "[X,Y]"; cf. [12]).

[40] X/ Y   (*) *X* and *Y* are in a disjunctive relation; "(either) *X* or *Y*".

                (*) *Y* constitutes conditions/an environment for *X* (often deployed in association with the *environment bar (dash)*, "__"; [42], [43], in which vein "*X/Y*" = "either *X/Y__* or *X /__Y*," i.e., "condition *Y* is <u>adjacent</u> to *X*, whether aft or fore."

[41] X × Y   (*) *X* blends/intersects/amalgamates with *Y* (in any of a variety of ways).

                (*) In linearized autosegmental notation, *X* (a constituent on one tier) associates to and conflates with *Y* (a constituent on another tier); §3.2 n. 6a.

[42] X /__Y   *X* immediately precedes its condition or environment *Y*.

[43] X/Y__   *X* immediately follows its condition or environment *Y*.

[44] X [+Y]   Process *X* has *Y* as a subprocess.

[45] X   (*) Variant notation for [44].

    [+Y]   (*) Formative *X* contains/is composed of feature(s) *Y*.

[46] < Č^w >	Orthographic convention (via Arabic *šadda*) for geminate (long) *C* (= *C'C'*).
[47] C:	Geminate (long) *C*; in this book normally transcribed as *C'C'*.
[48] V̄	Long vowel.
[49] V̊	Short vowel.
[50] V̆	Reduced vowel.
[51] V́	Vowel with primary stress.
[52] V̀	Vowel with secondary stress.
[53] V̎	Vowel with pausal stress.
[54] V̌	Unstressed vowel; context allowing, alternatively symbolized by unadorned *V* (§26.1).
[55] V̇	Vowel subject to early ancipitality (§2.3.1).
[56] Ṿ	Vowel subject to late ancipitality (§2.3.1).
[57] ∅	Zero (empty) segment, ghost segment; occasionally used for other sorts of absence as well.
[58] 1, 2, 3	First, second, third person.
[59] √	Root, radical.
[60] ∫	Scheme, schematic.
[61] μ	Mora (unit of weight).
[62] Γ	Glide: broadly, archiphoneme for {semivowel; guttural} = {w,y; ?, h, 9, h}; narrowly, quasi-archiphoneme for {semivowel; laryngeal guttural} = {w, y; ?, ḥ} (In Aramaic morphophonology, it is usually this smaller set that plays a role).
[63] Λ	Archiphoneme for resonant consonants {nasal; liquid; semivowel} = {m, n; r, l, ḷ; w, y} (§20.1).
[64] Σ	Sibilant; archiphoneme for {s, ś, z, ṣ, š}.
[65] Ŧ	Dentoalveolar stop; archiphoneme for {t, ṭ, d, ḍ}.

27. Bibliographical References

[The listing includes abbreviations of heavily referenced sources as well as of frequently occurring components of listings at large, e.g., *NACAL* (North American Conference on Afroasiatic Linguistics)]

AOS = (meeting of the) American Oriental Society

Aronoff, Mark. 1985. Orthography and Linguistic Theory: The Syntactic Basis of Masoretic Hebrew Punctuation. *Language* 61: 28–72.

B = Brockelmann 1965

Barth, Jacob. 1894[1967]. *Die Nominalbildung in den Semitischen Sprachen.* Hildesheim: Georg Olms.

Bat-El, Outi. 1989. Phonology and Word Structure in Modern Hebrew. PhD dissertation, University of California at Los Angeles.

Bauer, Hans, and Pontus Leander. 1922[1962b]. *Historische Grammatik der hebräischen Sprache des Alten Testamentes.* Hildesheim: Georg Olms.

——— . 1927[1962a]. *Grammatik des Biblisch-aramäischen.* Hildesheim: Georg Olms.

Ben-Asher, M. 1970. Dikduk hapo9al haʔarami ba 'Halaxot Pĕsukot'. *Lĕšonénu* 34: 278–86.

Ben-Ḥayyim, Z. 1961–77. *9Ivrit vĕ-ʔAramit, nosaḥ Šomron,* I–IV. Jerusalem: Academy of the Hebrew Language.

Beyer, Klaus. 1986. *The Aramaic language.* Translated from German by John F. Healey. Gättingen: Vandenhoeck & Ruprecht.

——— . 1987. Die neuesten aramäischen Inschriften aus Taima. *ZDMG* 137: 285–96.

BL = Bauer and Leander 1927[1962a]

Blevins, Juliette. 2004. *Evolutionary Phonology.* Cambridge: Cambridge University Press.

Blevins, Juliette, and A. Garrett. 1998. The Origins of Consonant-Vowel Metathesis. *Language* 74: 508–56.

Bloomfield, Leonard. 1933. *Language.* New York: Holt, Rinehart, & Winston.

Bohas, Georges. 1993. OCP et la persistence des représentations sous-jacentes. *LOAPL* 4: 35–40.

Bolozky, Shmuel. 1977. Fast Speech as a Function of Tempo in Natural Generative Phonology. *Journal of Linguistics* 13: 217–38.

Breuer, Yochanan. 2003. Šem ha9ecem baʔaramit šel haTalmud haBavli lĕfi mĕsorat Teyman, *Lĕšonénu* 65: 121–41.

Brockelmann, Carl. 1908[1961]. *Grundriss der vergleichenden Grammatik der semitischen Sprachen, I: Laut- und Formenlehre.* Hildesheim: Georg Olms.

——— . 1928. *Lexicon syriacum.* Halle: Max Niemeyer.

————. 1965. *Syrische Grammatik.* Leipzig: VEB Verlag Enzyklopadie.

Brown, Francis. 1979. *The New Brown-Driver-Briggs Gesenius Hebrew and English Lexicon, with an Appendix Containing the Biblical Aramaic.* Reprinted, Lafayette, IN: Associated Publishers & Authors.

Cantineau, J. 1932a. *Le nabatéen, I: notions générales—écriture, grammaire.* Paris: Ernest Leroux.

————. 1932b. *Le nabatéen, II: choix de texts—lexique.* Paris: Ernest Leroux.

Cg = Cantineau 1932a

Chafe, Wallace L. 1959. Internal Reconstruction in Seneca. *Language* 35: 477–95.

Chomsky, Noam, and Morris Halle. 1968. *The Sound Pattern of English.* New York: Harper & Row.

Cl = Cantineau 1932b

CLS *n* = Papers from the *n*th Regional Meeting of the Chicago Linguistic Society

Cohen, David, François Bron, and Antoine Lonnet. 1993–99. *Dictionnaire des racines sémitiques ou attestées dans les langues sémitiques,* fascicules I–VIII. Leuven: Peeters.

Cowley, A. 1923[1967]. *Aramaic Papyri of the Fifth century B.C.* Reprinted, Osnabruck: Otto Zeller.

Coxon, Peter. 1977. The Nunation Variant in the Perfect of the Aramaic Verb. *JNES* 36: 297–98.

Da = Dalman 1905, 1927[1960]

Dalman, Gustaf. 1905, 1927[1960]. *Grammatik des jüdisch-palästinischen Aramäisch.* Reprinted, Darmstadt: Wissenschaftliche Buchgesellschaft.

————. 1938[1967]. *Aramäische-neuhebräisches Handwörterbuch zu Targum, Talmud und Midrasch.* Reprinted, Hildesheim: Georg Olms.

De = Degen 1969

Degen, Rainer. 1969. *Altaramäische Grammatik.* Wiesbaden: Franz Steiner.

DM = Drower and Macuch 1963

Donner, H., and W. Röllig. 1966–69. *Kanaanäische und aramäische Inschiften,* I, II, III (mit einem Beitrag von O. Rössler). Otto Harrassowitz, Wiesbaden.

DR I, II, III = Donner and Röllig 1966–69, I, II, III

Dresher, B. Elan. 1994. The Prosodic Basis of the Tiberian System of Accents. *Language* 70: 1–52.

Drijvers, H. J. W. 1972. *Old-Syriac (Edessean) Inscriptions.* Leiden: Brill.

Drower, E. S., and R. Macuch. 1963. *A Mandaic Dictionary.* Oxford: Clarendon.

Du = Duval 1881[1969]

Duval, Rubens. 1881[1969]. *Traité de grammaire syriaque.* Reprinted, Amsterdam: Philo.

Fassberg, Steven E. 2000–2001. Hilufey habinyanim *ʔetpǝ9el/ʔetpa9al* bĕSurit, *Lĕšonénu* 63: 247–78.

Fitzmeyer, Joseph A. 1971. *The Genesis Apocryphon of Qumran Cave 1.* Rome: Biblical Institute Press.

Garbell, Irene. 1965. *The Jewish Neo-Aramaic Dialect of Persian Azerbaijan.* The Hague: Mouton.

Garbini, Giovanni. 1960. *Il semitico di nord-ovest.* Quaderni della Sezione Linguistica degli Annali. Naples: Istituto Orientale di Napoli.

Garr, W. Randall. 1985[2004]. *Dialect Geography of Syria–Palestine, 1000–586 BCE.* Reprinted, Winona Lake, IN: Eisenbrauns.

————. 1987. Pretonic Vowels in Hebrew. *Vetus Testamentum* 37: 129–53.

————. 1991. **ay > a* in Targum Onkelos. *JAOS* 111: 712–19.

GL = General Linguistics

Goldsmith, John. 1976[1979]. *Autosegmental Phonology.* New York: Garland [*originally an MIT dissertation*].

Gordon, Cyrus H. 1937–39. The Aramaic Incantation in Cuneiform. *Archiv für Orientforschung* 12: 105–17.

————. 1940. The Cuneiform Aramaic Incantation. *Orientalia* 9: 29–38.

Greenberg, Joseph H. 1950. The Patterning of Root Morphemes in Semitic. *Word* 6: 162–81.

Hall, Nancy. 2006. Cross-Linguistic Patterns of Vowel Intrusion. *Phonology* 23: 387–429.

Hall, T. A. 2002. Against Extrasyllabic Consonants in German and English. *Phonology* 19: 33–75.

Harris, Zellig S. 1939. *Development of the Canaanite Dialects.* New Haven, CT: American Oriental Society.

HC = Hillers and Cussini 1996

Hillers, Delbert R., and Eleonra Cussini. 1996. *Palmyrene Aramaic Texts.* Baltimore: Johns Hopkins University Press.

Hoberman, R. 1991. ʾAramait ḥadaša vĕšitat hašiḥzur hahašvaʾati. *Mĕsorot* 5–6: 51–76.

————. 1997. The Modern Chaldean Pronunciation of Classical Syriac. Pages 253–65 in A. Afsaruddin and A. H. M. Zahniser, eds., *Humanism, Culture, and Language in the Near East.* Winona Lake, IN: Eisenbrauns.

Hoenigswald, Henry M. 1960. *Language Change and Linguistic Reconstruction.* Chicago: University of Chicago Press.

Holm, John. 1988. *Pidgins and Creoles, I, II.* Cambridge: Cambridge University Press.

JAOS = Journal of the American Oriental Society

Jastrow, Marcus. 1903[2004]. *Dictionary of Talmud Babli, Yerushalmi, Midrashic Literature and Targumim.* Reprinted, New York: Judaica Treasury.

Jensen, John T. 2000. Against Ambisyllabicity. *Phonology* 17: 187–235.

JNES = Journal of Near Eastern Studies

Joüon, Paul, SJ. 1923. *Grammaire de l'hébreu biblique.* Rome: Pontifical Biblical Institute.

Kahle, Paul. 1913[1966]. *Masoreten des Ostens.* Hildesheim: Georg Olms.

Kaufman, Stephen A. 1974. *The Akkadian Influences on Aramaic.* Chicago: University of Chicago Press.

————. 1984. On Vowel Reduction in Aramaic. *JAOS* 104: 87–95.

Kautsch, E., and A. E. Cowley. 1910. *Gesenius' Hebrew Grammar.* 2nd English edition. Oxford: Clarendon.

Kenstowicz, Michael. 1994. *Phonology in Generative Grammar.* Cambridge, MA: Blackwell.

King, Robert D. 1969. *Historical Linguistics and Generative Grammar.* Englewood Cliffs, NJ: Prentice-Hall.

Kiparsky, Paul. 1982. Lexical Phonology and Morphology. Pages 3–91 in I. S. Yang, ed., *Linguistics in the Morning Calm*. Seoul: Hanshing.

Kittel, Rudolf, ed. 1937. *Biblia Hebraica*. Stuttgart: Württembergische Bibelanstalt.

Klar, Kathryn A., and Terry L. Jones. 2005. Linguistic Evidence for a Prehistoric Polynesia-Southern California Contact Event. *Anthropological Linguistics* 47: 369–400.

Kraeling, Emil G. 1953. *The Brooklyn Museum Aramaic Papyri*. New Haven: Yale University Press.

Kuryłowicz, Jerzy. 1945[1966]. La nature des procès dits "analogiques." Pages 158–74 in Eric P. Hamp, Fred W. Householder, and Robert Austerlitz, eds., *Readings in Linguistics II*. Chicago: University of Chicago Press.

——— . 1962. *L'apophonie en sémitique*. 'S-Gravenhage: Mouton.

——— . 1972. *Studies in Semitic Grammar and Metrics*. Wrocław: Polska Akademia Nauk.

Kutscher, E. Y. 1970. *Toldot haʔAramit, I. Histadrut haStudentim*. Jerusalem: Hebrew University.

——— . 1972. Aramaic. Pages 259–89 in vol. III of *Encyclopedia Judaica*. Jerusalem: Keter.

——— . 1976. *Studies in Galilean Aramaic* (translated from Hebrew and annotated with additional notes from the author's handcopy by Michael Sokoloff). Ramat-Gan: Bar-Ilan University Pressss.

L = Leander 1928[1966]

Leander, Pontus. 1928[1966]. *Laut- und Formenlehre des Ägyptisch-Aramäischen*. Hildesheim: Georg Olms.

Lehmann, Winfred P. 1992. *Historical Linguistics*. 3rd edition. London: Routledge.

Levin, Juliette. 1985. A Metrical Theory of Syllabicity. PhD dissertation, Massachusetts Institute of Technology.

Lipinski, Edward. 1997. *Semitic Languages: Outline of a Comparative Grammar*. Leuven: Peeters.

LOAPL = Langues Orientales Anciennes, Philologie et Linguistique

Lowenstamm, Jean, and Jean-François Prunet. 1987. *Le tigrinya et le principe du contour obligatoire*. Manuscript. Université de Québec à Montreal.

Macm = Macuch 1965

Macs = Macuch 1982

Macuch, Rudolf. 1965. *Handbook of Classical and Modern Mandaic*. Berlin: de Gruyter.

——— . 1982. *Grammatik des samaritanischen Aramäisch*. Berlin: de Gruyter.

——— . 1989. *Neumandäische Chrestomasthie mit grammatischer Skizze, kommentierter Übersetzung und Glossar (unter Mitwirkung von Klaus Boekels)*. Wiesbaden: Harrassowitz.

Mal = Malone 1967

Malone, Joseph L. 1967. A Morphologic Grammar of the Classical Mandaic Verb. PhD dissertation, University of California at Berkeley.

——— . 1969. Rules of Synchronic Analogy: A Proposal Based on Evidence from Three Semitic Languages. *Foundations of Language* 5: 534–59.

————. 1970a. Two Hypotheses on the Origin of an Aramaic Apocope-Paragoge Process. *Glossa* 4: 206–11.

————. 1970b. In Defense of Non-Uniqueness of Phonological Representations. *Language* 46: 328–35.

————. 1971a. Wave Theory, Rule Ordering, and Hebrew-Aramaic Segolation. *JAOS* 91: 44–66.

————. 1971b. Systematic Metathesis in Mandaic. *Language* 47: 394–415.

————. 1972a. Juncture in the Aramaic verb of the Onkelos and Jonathan Targums. *JNES* 31: 156–66.

————. 1972b. A Hebrew Flip-Flop Rule and Its Historical Origins. *Lingua* 20: 422–48.

————. 1972c. The Mandaic Syllable-Adjustment Circuit and Its Historical Origins. *CLS* 8: 473–81.

————. 1974a. The Development of the Anomalous Syriac Verb *eškaḥ* 'to find': A Case of Convergent Factors in Linguistic Change. *Afroasiatic Linguistics* 1.2: 1–10.

————. 1974b. The Isolation of "Schematisierung": A Service of Linguistics to Philology. *JAOS* 94: 395–400.

————. 1975. Systematic vs. Autonomous Phonemics and the Hebrew Grapheme *dagesh*. *Afroasiatic Linguistics* 2.7: 113–29.

————. 1976a. Messrs Sampson, Chomsky and Halle, and Hebrew Phonology. *Foundations of Language* 14: 251–56.

————. 1976b. Phonological Evidence for Syntactic Bracketing: A Surprise from Tiberian Hebrew. *CLS* 12: 486–94.

————. 1979. Semitic "Internal Flexion" and Morphophonological Theory. *CUNY Forum* 7–8 = pp. 88–102 in Ed Battistella, ed., *Proceedings of NELS* 9, part 2.

————. 1985. Classical Mandaic Radical Metathesis, Radical Assimilation, and the Devil's Advocate. *GL* 25: 92–122.

————. 1988. Lexical Phonology and the Aramaic Verb of the Onkelos and Jonathan Targums. AOS 198 / NACAL 16, Chicago.

————. 1989a. Geminates, the Obligatory Contour Principle, and Tier Conflation: The Case of Tiberian Hebrew. *GL* 29: 111–30.

————. 1989b. Phonological Uniqueness? Maybe, After All! The Case of [qə̃na:] 'to nest' Reopened. AOS 199 / NACAL 17, New Orleans.

————. 1989c. Mandaic Compensatory Lengthening: A Problem for Moraic Phonology. Manuscript, Barnard College Linguistics Department.

————. 1989d. Prosodic Domains for Tiberian Hebrew Phonology. NACAL 17, New Orleans.

————. 1991. Underspecification and Phonological Assignment of Phonetic Strings: The Case of Classical Mandaic [qen:a:] 'nest'. Pp 130–33 in *Actes du XIIème Congrès International des Sciences Phonétiques*. Aix-en-Provence.

————. 1992a. Diachronic-Synchronic Dystony: A Case from Classical Mandaic. *GL* 32: 36–57.

————. 1992b. Poetic vs. Cybernetic Factors in Ma9lula Aramaic Prosody. Colloquium presented at the State University of New York. February 21.

————. 1993. *Tiberian Hebrew Phonology*. Winona Lake, IN: Eisenbrauns.

———— . 1994. More on Prosodic Circumscription in Classical Mandaic: The Derived Verb. Second Colloque sur les Langues Chamito-sémitiques, Sophia Antipolis.

———— . 1995. La circonscription prosodique en mandéen classique. *LOAPL* 5–6: 233–57.

———— . 1997. Modern and Classical Mandaic Phonology. Pages 141–59 (= chapter 10) in volume 1 of Alan S. Kaye, ed., *Phonologies of Asia and Africa.* Winona Lake, IN: Eisenbrauns.

———— . 1998a. Suffix Metastasis and Phonological Change in Classical Mandaic. *GL* 36: 1–16.

———— . 1998b. The Reconstruction of Babylonian Aramaic and the Problem of Tiberian-Based Schematisierung. AOS 208, New Orleans.

———— . 1998c. Analogy and Morphophonological Change in the Babylonian Aramaic verb. NACAL 26, New Orleans.

———— . 1999. Metathesis and Antiwedging in Classical Mandaic. *GL* 36: 227–55.

———— . 2004. Morphophonological Variation in the Aramaic Verb of the Onkelos and Jonathan Targums. AOS 214 / NACAL 32, San Diego.

Mar = Margolis 1910

Margolis, Max L. 1910. *Lehrbuch der aramäischen Sprache des Babylonischen Talmuds.* Munich: Beck.

Martin, Samuel E., and Young-Sook C. Lee. 1986. *Beginning Korean.* Rutland, VT: Charles E. Tuttle.

Martinet, Andre. 1964. Économies des changements phonétiques. 2nd edition. Berne: A. Francke.

McCarthy, John J. 1979[1985]. *Formal Problems in Semitic Phonology and Morphology.* New York: Garland (*originally an MIT Ph.D. dissertation*).

———— . 1986. OCP Effects: Gemination and Antigemination. *Linguistic Inquiry* 17: 207–63.

Mor = Morag 1988

Morag, Shelomo. 1964. Biblical Aramaic in Geonic Babylonia. Pages 111–31 in *Studies in Egyptology and Linguistics in Honor of H. J. Polotsky.* Jerusalem: Israel Exploration Society.

———— . 1967–68. Lĕtorat hahege haʾAramit haBavlit. *Lĕšonénu* 31: 67–88.

———— . 1972. Ἐφραθά (Mark VII.34): Certainly Hebrew, Not Aramaic? *Journal of Semitic Studies* 17: 198–202.

———— . 1972–73. Meḥeker haʾAramit haBavlit vĕxitvey hayad šel haGĕniza. *Tarbiẓ* 42: 60–78.

———— . 1988. ʾAramit bimsorat Teyman: Lĕšon haTalmud haBavli. Jerusalem: Ben Zvi Institute, Yad Izhak Ben Zvi, and the Hebrew University of Jerusalem.

Moscati, Sabatino et al. 1964. *An Introduction to the Comparative Grammar of the Semitic languages.* Wiesbaden: Harrassowitz.

MP = Muraoka and Porten 2003

Müller-Kessler, Christa. 1999. Aramäische Beschwörungen und astronomische Omina in nachbabylonischer Zeit, das Fortleben mesopotamischer Kultur im Vorderen Orient. Pages 427–43 in Johannes Renger, ed., *Babylon.* Saarbrucken: SDV Saarbrucker Druckerei und Verlag.

————. 2003. Aramaic '*k*', *lyk*' and Iraqi Arabic ^c*aku, māku*: The Mesopotamian Particles of Existence. *JAOS* 123: 641–46.

Müller-Kessler, Christa, and Theodore Kwasman. 2000. A Unique Talmudic Aramaic Incantation Bowl. *JAOS* 120: 159–65.

Muraoka, T., and B. Porten. 2003. *A Grammar of Egyptian Aramaic*. 2nd revised edition. Leiden: Brill.

NACAL = (meeting of the) North American Conference on Afroasiatic Linguistics

Nakhleh, L., D. Ringe, and T. Warnow. 2005. Perfect Phylogenetic Networks: A New Methodology for Reconstructing the Evolutionary History of Natural Languages. *Language* 81: 382–420.

Nespor, Marina, and Irene Vogel. 1982. Prosodic Domains of External Sandhi Rules. Pages 225–55 in Harry van der Hulst and Norval Smith, eds., *The structure of phonological representations*, part I. Dordrecht: Foris Publications.

Nm = Nöldeke 1875[1964]

Nöldeke, Theodore. 1875[1964]. *Mandäische Grammatik*. Reprinted, Darmstadt: Wissenschaftliche Buchgesellschaft.

————. 1898[1966]. *Kurzgefasste syrische Grammatik*. Reprinted, Darmstadt: Wissenschaftliche Buchgesellschaft.

Ns = Nöldeke 1898[1966]

Odden, David. 2006. Minimality and Onsetless Syllables in Zinza. *Phonology* 23: 431–41.

Payne Smith, R. 1903[1998]. *A compendious Syriac Dictionary*. Reprinted, Winona Lake, IN: Eisenbrauns.

Pearce, Mary. 2006. The Interaction between Metrical Structure and Tone in Kera. *Phonology* 23: 259–86.

Pedersen, Holger. 1931[1962]. *The Discovery of Language: Linguistic Science in the 19th Century*. Translated from Danish by J. W. Spargo. Bloomington, IN: Indiana University Press.

Petermann, J. H. 1873. *Brevis linguae Samaritanae grammatica, liiteratura, chrestomathia cum glossario*. Carolsruhae et Lipsiae.

PS = Payne Smith 1903[1998]

Rosén, Haiim B. 1962. *A Textbook of Israeli Hebrew*. Chicago: University of Chicago Press.

Rosenthal, Franz. 1967. *An Aramaic Handbook*. 2 volumes in 2 parts each. Wiesbaden: Harrassowitz.

Schulthess, Fridericus [Friedrich]. 1903. *Lexicon Syropalaestinum*. Berlin: Georg Reimer.

————. 1924[1965]. *Grammatik des christlich-palästinischen Aramäisch*. Hildesheim: Georg Olms.

Sg = Schulthess 1924[1965]

Sl = Schulthess 1903

Sobin, Nicholas. 1997. Agreement, Default Rules, and Grammatical Viruses. *Linguistic Inquiry* 28: 318–43.

Sokoloff, Michael. 2002a. *A Dictionary of Jewish Babylonian Aramaic*. Ramat Gan: Bar Ilan University Press / Baltimore: John Hopkins University Press.

————. 2002b. *A Dictionary of Jewish Palestinian Aramaic.* Ramat Gan: Bar Ilan University Press / Baltimore: John Hopkins University Press.

Sperber, Alexander, ed. 2004. *The Bible in Aramaic.* Leiden: Brill.

Spitaler, Anton. 1938. *Grammatik des neuaramäischen Dialekts von Maʿlūla (Antilibanon).* Leipzig: Deutsche Morgenländische Gesellschaft.

————. 1968. Zum Problem der Segolisierung im Aramäischen. Pages 193–99 in Studia Orientalia in Memoriam Caroli Brockelmann. Halle: Martin-Luther Universität Halle-Wittenberg.

Steiner, Richard C, 1977. *The Case for Fricative Laterals in Proto-Semitic.* New Haven, CT: American Oriental Society.

————. 2000–2001. Šělošet kělalot nimracot mitox hakĕtovet haʾAramit miBukan. *Lěšonénu* 63: 237–46.

THP = Malone 1993

Vilsker, L. H. 1981. *Manuel d'araméen samaritain.* Translated from Russian by Jean Margain. Paris: Centre National de la Recherche Scientifique.

Wajsberg, Eljakim. 2004–2006. Halašon haʾAramait šel hayĕcira haʾErec-Yisrěʾelit baTalmud haBavli. *Lěšonénu* 66 (2004) 243–82; 67 (2005) 301–26; 68 (2006) 31–61.

Waltke, B. K., and M. O'Connor. 1990. *An Introduction to Biblical Hebrew Syntax.* Winona Lake, IN: Eisenbrauns.

Watkins, Calvert. 1962. *Indo-European Origins of the Celtic Verb, I: The Sigmatic Aorist.* Dublin: Dublin Institute of Advanced Studies.

Williams, Edwin. 1976. Underlying Tone in Margi and Igbo. *Linguistic Inquiry* 7: 463–83.

Woodhouse, Robert. 2003. The Biblical Shibboleth Story in the Light of Late Egyptian Perceptions of Semitic Sibilants: Reconciling Divergent Views. *JAOS* 123: 271–89.

ZDMG = Zeitschrift der Deutschen Morgenlandischen Gesellschaft

Zoll, Cheryl. 2003. Optimal Tone Mapping. *Linguistic Inquiry* 34: 225–68.

CPSIA information can be obtained
at www.ICGtesting.com
Printed in the USA
BVHW072313031019
560175BV00003B/7/P